AUSTRALIA IN THE WAR OF 1939-1945

SERIES ONE
ARMY

VOLUME V
*SOUTH-WEST PACIFIC
AREA—FIRST YEAR*

Kokoda to Wau

AUSTRALIA IN THE WAR OF 1939-1945

SERIES I (ARMY)

I. To Benghazi. *By Gavin Long.**
II. Greece, Crete and Syria. *By Gavin Long.**
III. Tobruk and El Alamein. *By Barton Maughan.*
IV. The Japanese Thrust. *By Lionel Wigmore.**
V. South-West Pacific Area—First Year. *By Dudley McCarthy.**
VI. The New Guinea Offensives. *By David Dexter.*
VII. The Final Campaigns. *By Gavin Long.*

SERIES 2 (NAVY)

I. Royal Australian Navy, 1939-42. *By G. Hermon Gill.**
II. Royal Australian Navy, 1942-45. *By G. Hermon Gill.*

SERIES 3 (AIR)

I. Royal Australian Air Force, 1939-42. *By Douglas Gillison.*
II. Air War Against Japan, 1943-45. *By George Odgers.**
III. Air War Against Germany and Italy, 1939-43. *By John Herington.**
IV. Air Power Over Europe, 1944-45. *By John Herington.*

SERIES 4 (CIVIL)

I. The Government and the People, 1939-41. *By Paul Hasluck.**
II. The Government and the People, 1942-45. *By Paul Hasluck.*
III. War Economy, 1939-42. *By S. J. Butlin.**
IV. War Economy, 1942-45. *By S. J. Butlin.*
V. The Role of Science and Industry. *By D. P. Mellor.**

SERIES 5 (MEDICAL)

I. Clinical Problems of War. *By Allan S. Walker.**
II. Middle East and Far East. *By Allan S. Walker.**
III. The Island Campaigns. *By Allan S. Walker.**
IV. Medical Services of R.A.N. and R.A.A.F. *By Allan S. Walker.*

* Published.

The writers of these volumes have been given full access to official documents, but they and the general editor are alone responsible for the statements and opinions which the volumes contain.

Published by
The Naval & Military Press Ltd
5 Riverside, Brambleside, Bellbrook
Industrial Estate, Uckfield, East Sussex,
TN22 1QQ England
Tel: +44 (0) 1825 749494
Fax: +44 (0) 1825 765701
www.naval-military-press.com
www.military-genealogy.com

In reprinting in facsimile from the original, any imperfections are inevitably reproduced and the quality may fall short of modern type and cartographic standards.

SOUTH-WEST PACIFIC AREA—FIRST YEAR
Kokoda to Wau

by

DUDLEY McCARTHY

The Naval & Military Press Ltd

CONTENTS

		Page
Preface		xi
List of Events		xiii

Chapter

1	REINFORCEMENT OF AUSTRALIA	1
2	THE ISLAND BARRIER	34
3	KANGA FORCE	84
4	THE JAPANESE ADVANCE TO KOKODA	108
5	MILNE BAY	147
6	WITHDRAWAL TO IORIBAIWA	193
7	IORIBAIWA: AND A COMMAND CRISIS	229
8	TO TEMPLETON'S CROSSING	254
9	EORA CREEK	280
10	OIVI-GORARI	311
11	THE BUILD-UP BEFORE BUNA	336
12	THE AMERICANS AT BUNA	356
13	ON THE SANANANDA TRACK	384
14	GONA	418
15	THE AUSTRALIANS AT BUNA	459
16	BUNA GOVERNMENT STATION TAKEN	484
17	THE END OF THE ROAD	497
18	WAU	534

APPENDIXES:

1	After Alola	592
2	Timor	597
3	Brisbane, November 1942	625
4	Abbreviations	628

INDEX 631

ILLUSTRATIONS

	Page
The bombing of Darwin, 19th February 1942	66
Major-General B. M. Morris and some of his staff	66
Port Moresby	66
Bombs falling on the Port Moresby waterfront	67
An anti-aircraft position at Port Moresby	67
Salamaua	67
Kudjeru	67
A group of New Guinea Volunteer Rifles	130
Brigadier S. H. W. C. Porter with 30th Brigade officers and O.C. Kanga Force	130
Gona Mission	130
Native stretcher bearers in the Owen Stanleys	131
A wounded infantryman at a staging post in the Owen Stanleys	131
"D" Company, 39th Battalion on the way to the base area	146
A parade of the 39th Battalion at Menari	146
Major-General C A. Clowes	147
Lieut-General S. F. Rowell	147
Milne Bay	147
Abandoned Japanese tanks at Milne Bay	178
M.v. *Anshun* at Milne Bay	178
Kit inspection of American troops in Australia	179
General Grant tanks of the 1st Armoured Division	179
The track from Owers' Corner	194
Native carriers on the Kokoda Track	194
Kokoda village and airfield	194
A native carrier line at Eora Creek village	195
A 25-pounder field gun of the 14th Field Regiment	195
Loading supplies for air dropping	210
Dropping supplies from a transport plane near Nauro	210
Brigadier A. W. Potts and some of his staff	211
The Owen Stanleys, looking north from a high point near Nauro	211
The "Golden Stairs", rising towards Imita Ridge	242
Major-General A. S. Allen and Brigadier K. W. Eather	243
The 2/33rd Battalion crossing the Brown River	243
Survivors of the 2/27th Battalion at Itiki	274
The march of the 16th Brigade through Sydney	274
The 16th Brigade on the Kokoda Track	275
Mr F. M. Forde, General Douglas MacArthur and General Sir Thomas Blamey	306
Raising the flag at Kokoda after its recapture on 2nd November	307
A group of American and Australian officers at Wanigela	307
The Kokoda-Wairopi track, near Oivi	322

	Page
Wounded Australians at the M.D.S. Kokoda	322
The destruction of the Wairopi bridge	322
Lieut-General Robert L. Eichelberger	323
Brigadier J. E. Lloyd	323
Crossing the Kumusi River at Wairopi	323
Bombing and strafing Japanese positions at Gona	323
An aid post on the track to Gona	418
Corporal F. R. Smith and Private W. A. Musgrove of the 2/33rd Battalion	418
Buna Government Station	418
Australian and Japanese casualties at Gona	419
Major-General G. A. Vasey; Brigadiers J. R. Broadbent and G. F. Wootten; and Lieut-General E. F. Herring	450
The 2/9th Battalion at Cape Endaiadere	450
Last moments of a Japanese bid for freedom	450
Infantry-tank cooperation in the Buna area	451
Australian Bren gunners at Giropa Point	451
A mortar crew and a General Stuart tank in action at Giropa Point	451
A Vickers gun in action in the Buna area	466
A smashed Japanese pill-box at Giropa Point	466
Clearing the tree-tops of snipers at Buna	467
A gun emplacement and observation post of the 2/5th Field Regiment at Buna	498
Three infantrymen during a lull in the fighting at Gona	499
A Papuan boy guiding a wounded Australian at Buna	499
Australians moving forward to take up the fight at Sanananda	514
Sanananda	514
Conditions at Sanananda	515
The beaches at Buna, after the fighting	530
Tending graves at Gona	530
Wau airfield	531
The arrival of the 17th Brigade at Wau	531
A section of the Wau-Bulldog road	562
On the move forward from Wau	562
A line-up of native boys in Portuguese Timor	563
An Australian patrol in Portuguese Timor	563

MAPS

	Page
The Pacific Theatre	19
Territories of Papua and New Guinea	34
Western Pacific and Indian Ocean areas	37
The Kokoda Track	114
Milne Bay	156
The withdrawal from Isurava, 30th August to 5th September 1942	216
The approach to Oivi-Gorari, 31st October to 8th November	313
Allied advance on Buna-Gona area, 16th to 21st November	370
Kanga Force dispositions, 17th April 1943	585

SKETCH MAPS

Australia: Military Districts, Commands and defended ports	7
Philippine Islands	35
Wau-Lakekamu River mouth area	51
Wau-Salamaua-Lae area	52
Observation posts, Komiatum-Salamaua area	60
Bay of Bengal	78
Coral Sea Battle	81
Lower Markham Valley	87
The raid on Salamaua	93
Kokoda-Buna area	123
Kokoda-Alola area	128
Solomon Islands	148
Guadalcanal	149
Milne Bay, 6 p.m. 25th August 1942	160
Milne Bay, 6 p.m. 28th August	173
Milne Bay, 6 p.m. 31st August	179
Isurava-Alola, 26th August	199
Isurava-Alola, afternoon 29th August	205
Isurava-Alola, 3 p.m. 30th August	210
The Japanese advance to Menari, 5th-8th September	220
Ioribaiwa, noon 15th September	230
Imita Ridge, 20th September	233
Imita Ridge, noon 23rd September	246
The 2/27th Battalion's withdrawal from Menari	250
Templeton's Crossing, 6 p.m. 12th October	270
Templeton's Crossing, 6 p.m. 16th October	273
Templeton's Crossing, 6 p.m. 20th October	285
Eora Creek, 22nd-23rd October	288
Eora Creek, 27th-28th October	301

Oivi-Gorari, nightfall 9th November	324
Gorari, 10th-11th November	326
D'Entrecasteaux Islands	346
Allied advance across Owen Stanley Range towards Buna, 26th September-15th November	353
Routes of Allied advance on Buna-Gona area from mid-November	357
Situation before Buna, evening 30th November	370
The Australian advance on Sanananda and Gona	385
Sanananda Track, 20th November	387
Sanananda Track, evening 21st November	389
Sanananda-Killerton Tracks, 21st-30th November	396
The Japanese defences at Gona	420
Gona area, 27th November	423
Gona area, 6 p.m. 29th November	428
Gona area, 6 p.m. 4th December	436
Haddy's village, nightfall 15th December	444
Cape Endaiadere-Strip Point area, 18th to 23rd December	455
The clearing of Old Strip, 23rd to 29th December	467
Giropa Point, 1st-2nd January 1943	481
American operations before Buna to 17th December	486
American operations before Buna, 18th December to 2nd January	495
Allied dispositions on Sanananda Track prior to 19th December	502
Sanananda Track, 24th December	506
Sanananda Track, 8 a.m. 12th January	514
Final operations along Sanananda Track, 15th-22nd January	518
The Buisaval and Black Cat Tracks	535
Routes of advance on Mubo, 11th January 1943	541
Wau-Mubo area, dawn 28th January	549
Wau-Mubo area, dawn 30th January	552
The Japanese attack on Wau, dawn 30th January	553
Wau-Crystal Creek area, dawn 31st January	556
Wau-Crystal Creek area, nightfall 3rd February	559
Wau-Crystal Creek area, dawn 6th February	564
Wau-Mubo area, nightfall 9th February	569
Wau-Bulldog road	579
Routes of main 21st Brigade escape groups after Alola	593
Portuguese Timor	599
Timor-northern Australia area	612

PREFACE

THIS volume is concerned mainly with the operations of the Australian army in Papua and New Guinea (except those in New Britain and New Ireland, which were dealt with in the preceding volume of this series) from the beginning of the war with Japan up to the end of April 1943. It records also (though naturally in lesser detail) the operations of the American ground forces in that area, and during that period, from the time of their first entry into action in November 1942; and the American operations on and around Guadalcanal which, in certain vital respects, were the key to developments in Papua and New Guinea from August 1942 until the end of that year. While these Australian and American operations were taking place, a small Australian guerilla force was fighting in Timor, and the story of that fighting is carried forward from March 1942 where the author of the preceding volume left it.

Principally, however, this is the story of the fighting along the Kokoda Track, at Milne Bay, in the coastal swamps of the Buna-Sanananda-Gona area, and around Wau—and of the events which led immediately up to that fighting. In it there is none of the wild, heart-thrilling drama of great bodies of men meeting on wide battlefields in the shocks of massed encounter. Instead, for the most part, it is the story of small groups of men, infinitesimally small against the mountains in which they fought, who killed one another in stealthy and isolated encounters beside the tracks which were life to all of them; of warfare in which men first conquered the country and then allied themselves with it and then killed or died in the midst of a great loneliness.

Fundamentally this story is concerned with the Australian infantryman whom I first knew when in the ranks myself (and later as an officer) in the 2/17th Battalion, A.I.F., and whose qualities of courage, endurance, comradeship and skill-at-arms, from personal experience first roused my love and admiration in the deserts of North Africa and in Tobruk. I had then no inkling that it would fall to my lot in these later years to chronicle the doings of such men in other battalions of the Australian Army in the vastly different setting represented by New Guinea—a setting in which, from my own earlier experiences as a young New Guinea Patrol Officer, I would have said it was quite impossible even for these great men to perform the deeds which they made their commonplace daily occasions. And so, first from my own experiences among them, and later from years of steeping myself in the records of their deeds to such an extent that I could truly say that the contemplation of them indeed changed the whole basis of my own approach to the problems of living and dying, I offer whatever of merit and personal sacrifice this book might represent as a tribute to these men and with the hope that others may be inspired as I have been by the stories of their lives and deaths.

Because the story is primarily that of the infantry soldier, I have feared that less than justice might have been done to many other brave and devoted men—gunners, sappers, signallers, staff officers, and the many thousands in the various services which kept the infantryman in the field. I take comfort, however, from the certainty that these men will agree that the emphasis is as properly placed as it can be within the covers of one book. Similarly the story has in it comparatively little of generals and generalship; for it belongs most of all to the private soldier, the infantry N.C.O. and the battalion officer. Nor have I forgotten that the campaigns could not have been fought at all without the air forces and the magnificent application of their skill and courage at critical times, and without the naval forces whose operations were vital to the success of the operations ashore; but it is the purpose of other volumes to record the exploits of these in detail.

It would be a poor tribute to the Australian soldiers who defeated them, and poor history, not to recognise the outstanding martial attributes of the Japanese. Their record is marred by deeds of barbarism and wanton cruelty of a kind quite beyond our own understanding. But despite this they were superb in their acceptance of death as a soldier's obligation, and they were worthy of any soldier's steel in the way they themselves fought and died.

The stuff from which this story is made is to be found primarily in the war diaries of all the units which were engaged. But round that strong thread have been woven details gathered from many other sources: from various published works; from letters and other personal papers; from conversations and discussions and personal accounts; from the many most valuable interviews recorded by Gavin Long while the war was still in progress; from War Cabinet papers. I would like to pay a personal tribute to the work of my old friend, Lieut-Colonel A. G. Fenton, who wrote the first narrative of the earlier part of the Kanga Force operations before his death in the last stages of the war in one of the many aircraft which set out across New Guinea and never returned. I am also deeply indebted to Samuel Milner, American war historian and good friend of Australia, whose *Victory in Papua* provided the broad basis for the story of American operations in Papua and much of the material for "the Japanese story". I am grateful also for the help of those many former officers and men of the Australian Army who have read and criticised and added to this narrative, and given their time for discussion and patient explanation.

Throughout the years of work which this book has represented I have been unfailingly sustained and guided by the wisdom, scholarship, patience, faith, and friendship of the General Editor, Gavin Long, and by the quiet and humorous comradeship, ever-ready aid and great skill of Bill (A. J.) Sweeting of Mr Long's staff.

D.McC.

Canberra,
12th June 1958.

LIST OF EVENTS

FROM AUGUST 1941 TO APRIL 1943

Events described in this volume are printed in italics

1941	5 Aug	*Lieut-General Sir Iven Mackay appointed G.O.C. Home Forces*
	25 Aug	British and Russian troops enter Iran
	7 Oct	Mr Curtin becomes Prime Minister of Australia
	19 Oct	State of siege proclaimed in Moscow
	7-8 Dec	Japanese attack Malaya and Pearl Harbour
1942	23 Jan	Japanese capture Rabaul
	3 Feb	*First Japanese air raid on Port Moresby*
	14 Feb	*Cessation of Civil Government in Papua*
	19-20 Feb	Japanese forces land on Timor
	28 Feb-1 Mar	Japanese invade Java
	8 Mar	Japanese troops enter Rangoon *Japanese forces occupy Lae and Salamaua*
	9 Mar	*Leading brigade of 7th Division A.I.F. arrives Adelaide*
	17 Mar	General MacArthur arrives in Australia
	26 Mar	*General Blamey becomes Commander-in-Chief, Australian Military Forces*
	5 Apr	*Japanese carrier-borne aircraft attack Colombo*
	6 Apr	*41st U.S. Division arrives in Australia*
	18 Apr	*G.H.Q., S.W.P.A. established at Melbourne*
	5-8 May	*Battle of the Coral Sea*
	6 May	*Corregidor surrenders*
	26 May	German offensive in Western Desert begins
	31 May-1 June	Japanese midget submarines attack Sydney Harbour
	4-6 June	*Battle of Midway Island*
	7 June	Japanese land in Aleutian Islands
	21 July	*Japanese land Gona area, Papua*
	7 Aug	*Americans land in Solomons*
	19 Aug	Dieppe raid
	25-26 Aug	*Japanese land at Milne Bay*

1942	17 Sept	*Japanese drive over Owen Stanleys halted at Imita Ridge*
	23-24 Oct	Battle of El Alamein begins
	2 Nov	*Kokoda recaptured*
	7-8 Nov	Allied landings in French North Africa
	12 Nov	British Eighth Army captures Tobruk
	12-15 Nov	*Naval battle of Guadalcanal*
	22 Nov	Russians announce launching of counter-offensive at Stalingrad
	9 Dec	*Australians capture Gona*
	21 Dec	British and Indian troops cross Burma frontier and advance in direction of Akyab
1943	2 Jan	*Buna Government Station captured*
	23 Jan	*Organised Japanese resistance in Papua ends*
	29 Jan	British Eighth Army enters Tripoli *Japanese attack Wau airfield*
	18 Feb	9th Australian Division arrives Fremantle
	2-4 Mar	Battle of Bismarck Sea
	20-21 Mar	Eighth Army moves against Mareth Line
	23 Apr	*Headquarters 3rd Australian Division established at Bulolo*

CHAPTER 1

REINFORCEMENT OF AUSTRALIA

BY early March 1942, the Japanese thrust had struck deep into the Pacific to the south and wide to the south-west. Along its southern axis the Filipino and American forces in the Philippines were isolated and wasting fast; after the fall of Rabaul on 23rd January the Japanese were on the move through the Australian Mandated Territory of New Guinea; Port Moresby was under aerial bombardment from 3rd February onwards; Japanese aircraft were questing southward over the Solomon Islands. Along the south-west axis the British had surrendered Singapore on 15th February and, by 7th March, had begun the retreat from Rangoon which was to carry them right out of Burma; a threat to India was developing; the Netherlands East Indies were rapidly being overrun; on the Australian mainland Darwin, Broome and Wyndham had been heavily raided from the air.

The Japanese armies thus controlled the area within an arc which embraced the Western Pacific, passed through the Solomons and New Guinea and south of the Indies to Burma. This arc pressed down almost upon Australia whose nearest friendly neighbours on either side were now disadvantageously placed: the United States, separated by some 3,000 miles of ocean, was weaker than Japan on sea, on land and in the air; India, which had sent its best formations to the Middle East and Iraq, had lost some in Malaya, and had others fighting in Burma, was now garrisoned mainly by raw divisions.

In Australia itself some military leaders had long foreseen this very situation. But now, of four experienced divisions of volunteers of the Australian Imperial Force (A.I.F.), one had been lost in Malaya and in the islands north of Australia and the other three, which had been serving in the Middle East, were still overseas. The absence of these *élite* troops at a critical time in Australia had also been foreseen and the "calculated risk" accepted, because it was by no means certain when they went abroad that, if Australia itself were threatened with invasion, the situation in other theatres would permit of their recall. Even if it would, the return of such an army could not be accomplished for some months after the necessity first became apparent. Consequently preparations for the local defence of Australia had had to be based substantially on plans for the use of the home army.

By the end of June 1940 (when, with France falling, enlistments in the A.I.F. vastly increased) the militia, a force comparable with the British Territorial Army or the American National Guard, had dwindled in numbers to 60,500, although its authorised strength was 75,000 to 80,000—a decline in which the greatest single factor had been enlistments for oversea service. The Government then decided to increase the militia's strength by calling up more men as defined in Class 1 of the *Defence Act*—unmarried men and widowers without children, between the ages of 18 and 35. By July 1941, virtually all men in Class 1 had become liable for service and by the end of August the militia numbered 173,000. Of these, however, only 45,000 were serving full time. As the call-ups continued it became clear that, apart from voluntary enlistment for oversea service, the two most important factors reducing the numbers available to the militia were the system of exempting men engaged in "essential" industry or giving them seasonal leave (which affected nearly 30 per cent of all men liable for service in Class 1), and medical unfitness, either temporary or permanent, which debarred nearly 14 per cent of the class from service.

But lack of continuity in the training of such forces as could be gathered together was also a handicap. When war with Germany began, first one month's, then three months' additional training had been ordered. Later the 1940-41 policy provided that serving and potential officers and non-commissioned officers should be intensively trained for 18 to 24 days as a preliminary to a camp period of 70 days, that militiamen (other than these) who had completed 90 days' training in 1939-40 should undergo 12 days' special collective training, and that the rest of the militia should carry out 70 days' training. A further complication was added in July 1941, when "trained soldiers" (those who had already undergone 90 days' training) and recruits became liable for three months' and six months' training respectively in each year. The fragmentary nature of the training was thus an important factor in preventing a high general standard of efficiency being achieved. Each unit, however, had a nucleus of key men serving full time and, when the War Cabinet approved the six months' recruit training system, it also approved proposals for the enlargement and more intensive training of these groups—that officers, warrant and non-commissioned officers, specialists and essential administrative personnel, not exceeding 25 per cent of the strength of each unit, should form a training and administrative cadre and, when the unit itself was not in camp, should undergo special training.

There were other impediments to efficiency. The most energetic and capable of the younger officers had gone to the A.I.F. The senior appointments were filled by officers who had seen hard service in the war of 1914-18 and there were many such veterans in the middle ranks. These strove to maintain efficiency and keenness, but suffered many handicaps, including a serious shortage of equipment of all kinds—even rifles, of which large numbers had been sent to England in 1940.

While it was the largest and most important part of the army in Australia, the militia did not, however, constitute the whole of it. At the end of August 1941, the Permanent Military Forces in Australia numbered 5,025; there were 12,915 in garrison battalions, and 43,720 in the Volunteer Defence Corps (V.D.C.). The formation of an Australian Women's Army Service (A.W.A.S.) had been approved on 13th August.

The garrison battalions, filled mostly by old soldiers of the previous war, had their origin in the "War Book"[1] plans for mobilisation, which had

---
[1] See G. Long, *To Benghazi* (1952), p. 34, in this series.

provided for the raising of battalions for the local protection of the coast defences—"ten garrison battalions to relieve ten battalions of the field army allotted to the local protection of the forts". A further impulse toward this end had come from the Returned Soldiers' League through a resolution passed at its Twenty-Second Annual Congress at Hobart in November 1937. It stated that "Congress deems it necessary that a national volunteer force be raised from ex-servicemen and others between the ages of 41 and 60 years for local defence and to relieve existing forces from certain necessary duties in the event of a national emergency".[2]

During the crisis in France the Federal Executive of the League, on 31st May 1940, followed this resolution with a declaration "that a Commonwealth-wide organisation of ex-servicemen for home defence purposes be established and that a scheme with that object be framed forthwith".[3] The Government agreed and decided to form an Australian Army Reserve on the general lines which the League had envisaged. Class "A" was to include volunteers up to 48 years of age, medically "fit for active service" and not in reserved occupations, who would be prepared to be posted to militia units and undergo the normal training prescribed for those units. Class "B" was to include volunteers not eligible for Class "A" and to be divided into two groups—Garrison Battalions' Reserve and the R.S.L. Volunteer Defence Corps. The garrison reserve would enlist for the duration of the war while the V.D.C. was "to be organised by the R.S.S. & A.I.L.A. on flexible establishments approved by Army Headquarters and should carry out such voluntary training as can be mutually arranged between G.O.Cs and State branches of the League in association with the existing area organisation".[4] So the formation of the V.D.C. began on 15th July 1940.[5]

But at first the V.D.C. had little more to sustain it than the enthusiasm of its own members since the army was preoccupied with training and equipping the A.I.F. and the militia, and little material could be spared for the new corps. By the end of 1940 the V.D.C. numbered 13,120 and two considerations were becoming obvious: first that the Government would have to revise in some measure its stated intention of not accepting any financial responsibility for this voluntary, part-time, unpaid organisation (except that involved in arming, and later, clothing it); and second that it must be brought more directly under the control of the army. In February 1941, therefore, the War Cabinet approved the expenditure of £157,000 on uniforms for the corps, following that in May with a vote of a further £25,000 for general administrative expenses. In May also the Military Board assumed control, foreseeing that roles of the V.D.C. would

---

[2] *On Guard with the Volunteer Defence Corps* (1944), pp. 70-73.
[3] *On Guard*, p. 74.
[4] *On Guard*, p. 79.
[5] Distinguished soldiers of the 1914-18 War, most of them too old to receive appointments in the AIF or militia, became the VDC leaders in the various States, under General Sir Harry Chauvel as Inspector-in-Chief. In Queensland the Corps Commander was Brig-Gen L. C. Wilson; in New South Wales Maj-Gen H. Gordon Bennett; in Victoria Maj-Gen Sir John Gellibrand; in South Australia Brig-Gen R. L. Leane; in Western Australia Brig-Gen A. J. Bessell-Browne; and in Tasmania Lt-Col L. M. Mullen.

be to act as a guerilla force, to engage in local defence, and to give timely warning to mobile formations of the approach of enemy forces.

Both the V.D.C. and the A.W.A.S. were symbols of a growing urgency in the war situation—the former through the spontaneity of its growth; the latter through the emphasis it placed on the increasing shortage of manpower.[6] The formation of an Australian Women's Army Service would release men from certain military duties for employment with fighting units. No members of the Women's Service were to be sent overseas without the approval of the War Cabinet. It was to be some months, however, before recruitment was under way, even on a limited scale, and before plans for the training of the A.W.A.S. began to be systematised.

It was to weld together this partly-equipped (by the standards of modern war) and partly-trained force, that, in August 1941, Major-General Sir Iven Mackay[7] had been recalled from command of the 6th Division in the Middle East to become General Officer Commanding-in-Chief, Home Forces. As far back as 1937 Major-General J. D. Lavarack, then Chief of the General Staff, had proposed that, in the event of a crisis, a Commander-in-Chief should be appointed. At the Imperial Conference that year, however, the War Office and the Air Ministry had expressed the view that Service Boards should continue to function in an emergency provided that sole responsibility for the direction of operations was vested in a Chief of Staff. These views had been recalled by the War Cabinet in its discussions in May 1941 of a proposal by the Minister for the Army, Mr Spender, to appoint Lieut-General V. A. H. Sturdee as Commander-in-Chief with Major-General J. Northcott as Chief of the General Staff. Convinced, apparently, by the argument that the Military Board system was necessary to coordinate the control and administration of the A.I.F. in the Middle East, the Far East and Australia, and the militia and kindred organisations at home, Spender at length modified his recommendations and proposed the appointment of a G.O.C.-in-Chief of the Field Army in Australia. This the War Cabinet had approved in principle. In June the Minister for the Army had further explained that he considered such an appointment necessary because the weight of administrative work prevented the Chief of the General Staff from adequately controlling training and preparation for war. He urged the appointment of an officer concerned only with preparations of the army for war to ensure the single control and direction of military operations, as being psychologically more satisfactory to the people of Australia. Discussion revolved round the points that, if the Military Board was to continue to function under a G.O.C.-in-Chief, with considerable delegations, the situation would virtually revert to the one then existing; if matters had necessarily to be referred to the G.O.C.-in-Chief, with the Military Board still in existence, it would make

---

[6] The formation of a Women's Auxiliary Air Force had been approved six months previously.

[7] Lt-Gen Sir Iven Mackay, KBE, CMG, DSO, VD, NX363. (1st AIF: CO 4 Bn 1916-18, 1 MG Bn 1918; Comd 1 Inf Bde 1918-19.) GOC 6 Div 1940-41; GOC-in-C Home Forces 1941-42, Second Army 1942-44. High Commnr for Aust in India 1944-48. University lecturer and schoolmaster; of Sydney; b. Grafton, NSW, 7 Apr 1882.

for centralisation and congestion. A final decision had again been deferred to allow the Minister for the Army to consider these points. On 11th July, however, the War Cabinet directed that a G.O.C.-in-Chief, Home Forces, should be appointed; he would be superior to the General Officers Commanding in the regional Commands for the direction of operations, equal in rank to the Chief of the General Staff, but subordinate to the Military Board which would remain the body to advise the Minister for the Army and, through him, the War Cabinet. The question of the authority to be delegated to the Home Forces commander by the Military Board was left to be decided later. The appointment of General Mackay was then confirmed on 5th August 1941.

If Mackay had been in any way deceived by the grandiloquence of his new title his illusions were soon dissipated when he assumed command on 1st September. Initially there was reluctance to grant him the substantive promotion he had been promised. He found, too, that his authority did not extend over the forward areas of New Guinea and the Northern Territory; nor was he to be responsible for "the defence of Australia" as such, as this responsibility remained with General Sturdee, the Chief of the General Staff. In short his command was far more circumscribed than he might have expected, with the added disadvantage of calling for a political finesse to the possession of which he laid few claims. He was a gallant and successful soldier, with a long record of distinguished service to his country, and a man of instinctive and unassuming courtesy. But neither his qualities of character and temperament nor the academic seclusion of his life between the wars fitted him well for the role of a senior military adviser to a Cabinet inexperienced in military affairs.

If the terms of Mackay's appointment were unsatisfactory to himself they were equally so to General Sturdee who, while he agreed in principle with the appointment, disagreed with the way in which the principle had been carried out. Mackay was junior to him in the Army List and, in fact, if not in the terms of his appointment, Sturdee's subordinate. But Mackay had the right of direct access to the Minister. It was only because of the forbearance of the two generals that the arrangement worked as well as it did.

From the beginning, therefore, the appointment of the General Officer Commanding-in-Chief, Home Forces, was an unsatisfactory compromise which pleased none of those most immediately concerned and, if only for that reason, could not produce the best results. That it did little to provide the psychological balm which Mr Spender had hoped for was suggested in a blunt statement by *The Sydney Morning Herald*:

> The Government has appointed a Commander-in-Chief in Australia, but that is not sufficient unless he has the authority proper to that position. It may be that his functions and those of the Chief of Staff at Army Headquarters have been precisely and correctly defined and can lead to no conflict between them; but if so the public is not aware of it.[8]

---

[8] *The Sydney Morning Herald*, 18 Dec 1941.

It was in these circumstances that Mackay turned to his task. In his planning he was bound to accept the existing doctrine that there were certain areas vital to the continuance of the economic life of Australia which must be held and to be guided by the arrangements designed to give effect to that doctrine. Military thinking had long been based on the premises that "an invading force . . . will endeavour to bring our main forces to battle and defeat them. The most certain way to do this will be to attack us at a point which we must defend. The objective of an invading force therefore will probably be some locality in which our interests are such that the enemy will feel sure that we shall be particularly sensitive to attack. Thus the geographical objective of land invasion would be some compact, vulnerable area, the resources of which are necessary to the economic life of Australia."[9] So the problems of the defence of the Newcastle-Sydney-Port Kembla area to which the above conditions plainly applied, became the paramount ones in Australian defence thinking. That area contained almost a quarter of the Australian population, the chief commercial ports, the only naval repair establishments in the country, and the largest industrial plants; these were dependent upon the large coal deposits which the area contained.

Accordingly the Army staff had then decided that "the plan for the concentration of Australian land forces to resist invasion must therefore provide first of all for the initial defence of these vital areas and for the concentration of the main force to deal with the enemy's main attack as quickly as possible after its direction becomes definitely known. The plan must then provide for the security of other important areas which might, if entirely denuded of mobile land forces, be attacked by minor enemy forces with far-reaching effect."[1] In broad outline the following were seen to be the requirements of the plan of concentration for the land defence of Australia:

(a) Provision for the initial defence of the Sydney-Newcastle areas.
(b) Provision for the concentration as quickly as possible of the main army to deal with the enemy's main attack.
(c) Provision for the defence of other areas regarded as sufficiently important.

No part of this planning meant that there would be a rush to concentrate in the areas likely to sustain the main enemy attack (i.e. the Sydney-Newcastle-Port Kembla areas) as soon as mobilisation began. This was simply the basic planning. The decision to undertake or defer concentration would be taken in the first weeks of the war in accordance with the movements and apparent intentions of the enemy. Planning, therefore, provided that "in the case in which a decision to defer concentration is taken, training will take place either at places of mobilisation or at places of preliminary concentration, or at both. . . . If the order to move to the main area of concentration is deferred for a longer period than six weeks

---
[9] Military Operations Appreciation (undated)—The Concentration of the Australian Land Forces in Time of War.
[1] Military Operations Appreciation—The Concentration of the Australian Land Forces in Time of War.

after the completion of mobilisation, the assembly of formations for manoeuvre training in places of preliminary concentration should be undertaken."[2]

In accordance with this general outline Mackay was required to think in terms of the defence of his vital areas plus provision for the defence of Brisbane, Melbourne, Hobart, Adelaide, Fremantle and Albany. Nor,

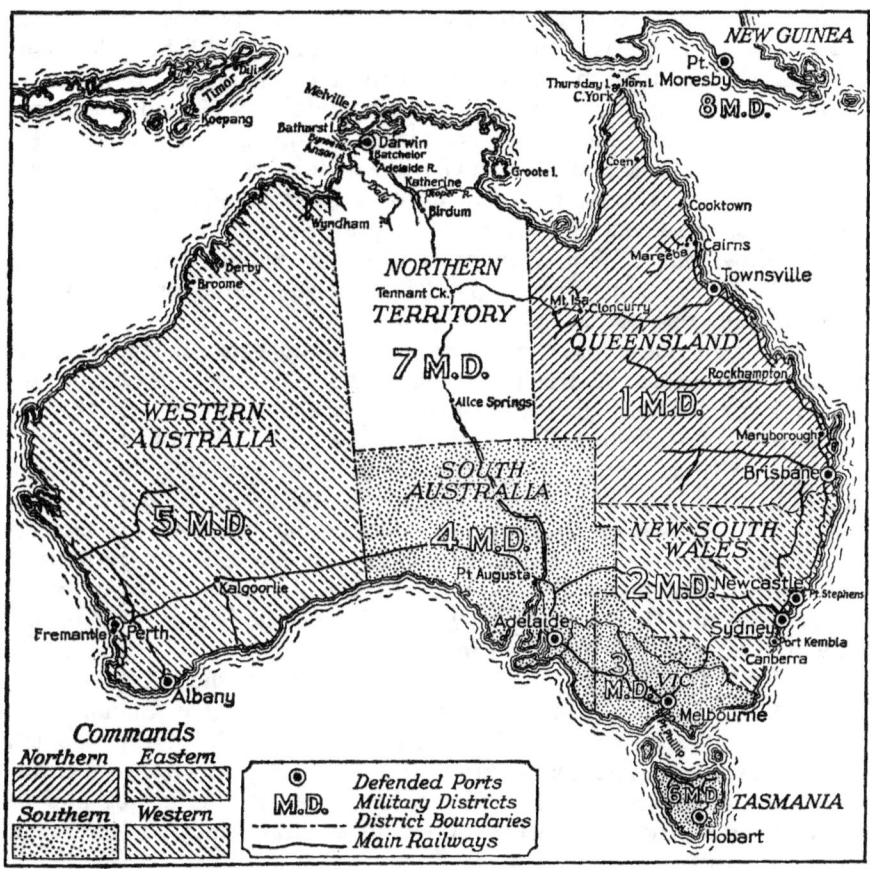

although they were outside the areas for which he was responsible, could his planning eliminate the needs of the Northern Territory and Papua-New Guinea, since any increase of strength there would reduce the force available to him. This force would consist basically of the 1st and 2nd Cavalry Divisions, the 1st, 2nd, 3rd and 4th (Infantry) Divisions, with the components of a fifth division and corps troops. In addition fixed defences were provided at Thursday Island, Townsville, Brisbane, Newcastle, Sydney, Port Kembla, Port Phillip, Adelaide, Hobart, Fremantle,

[2] Military Operations Appreciation—The Concentration of the Australian Land Forces in Time of War.

Albany and Darwin, with coast guns which ranged from 4-inch to 9.2-inch in calibre. The major part of six divisions was marked for ultimate concentration in the Sydney-Newcastle-Port Kembla areas, but Mackay had to combat a feeling in the country at large that forces raised in an area were designed particularly for the defence of that area.

On 4th February 1942 Mackay produced and Sturdee "generally concurred in" a memorandum stating the principles mentioned above but extending the area of concentration to embrace Melbourne, and Brisbane where newly-arrived American detachments had established themselves.

Mackay wrote that the Melbourne-Brisbane region, 1,000 miles from north to south, had scarcely five divisions to defend it. He did not propose, therefore, while the main areas remained equally threatened, to attempt to defend either Tasmania or Townsville with more troops than were in those areas then. The troops then in north Queensland—a few battalions —should remain there for reasons of "morale and psychology". He asked that the Government should either confirm his proposal not to reinforce Townsville or Tasmania or else give "some further direction regarding the degree of such defence".

On paper the home forces of February 1942 appeared fairly formidable; in reality deficiencies in strength, training and particularly equipment were likely for some months to make them less powerful in the field than perhaps three well-trained, well-equipped divisions. In addition Mackay was well aware that he could not defend his main areas simply by clustering his forces round the immediate vicinity of those areas. Fully alive to the intrinsic importance of Brisbane and Melbourne he none the less considered them chiefly important as defining the flanks, or perhaps the front and rear, of his most vital areas so that, in effect, to carry out the task of protecting Newcastle-Sydney-Port Kembla, he had to think in terms of the vast area Brisbane-Melbourne.

Mr F. M. Forde, the Minister for the Army in the recently elected Labour Government, whose electorate was in north Queensland, recommended that the Cabinet decide to defend "the whole of the populated area of Australia". This discussion was still in progress later in February when knowledge that the 6th and 7th Divisions were returning and that an American division had been allotted to Australia radically altered the situation.

The machinery for command and planning in Australia at this time had been strengthened. Mackay's headquarters was established in Melbourne and provision had been made for movement into the field of the necessary sections if the "Strategic Concentration" planned were ordered. Throughout the country the system of area commands was still operating and it was planned that the General Officer Commanding, Eastern Command, would assume coordinating control in the main concentration area pending movement into the field of Army Headquarters. He would thus have the status of a corps commander and, as the basic planning provided for the creation of an army of two corps to replace Eastern Command in the main areas when concentration was ordered, he would be the commander designate of the corps to be deployed in the Sydney-Port Kembla area.

In February 1941, War Cabinet had approved the establishment of certain important Intelligence and planning organisations. These were the Central War Room, to facilitate control of operations on the highest military plane through direct meetings between the Chiefs of Staff or their deputies; the Combined Operations Intelligence Centre with the function of making Intelligence appreciations on strategical questions for the Chiefs of Staff and collecting and assessing urgent Intelligence for distribution to the Services, to the Central War Room, to New Zealand and Singapore; Area Combined Headquarters located at Townsville, Melbourne, Fremantle and Darwin, to facilitate the cooperation of the navy and air force in trade defence in the focal areas; and Combined Defence Headquarters to coordinate the operations of the naval, military and air forces allotted for the defence of the areas which included a defended port. In addition certain purely planning organisations had been approved in September. Of these the most important, the Chiefs of Staffs Committee, was to be concerned with planning on the highest military level for the defence of Australia, and initial planning for that body was to be carried out by a Joint Planning Committee.

General Mackay, busy with constant travelling, inspecting and advising, did not at first add to this list by setting up a separate Home Defence Headquarters, but functioned through and from Army Headquarters. Unceasingly he attempted to drive home lessons that his experience in the Middle East had confirmed. Of the most important of these the first concerned the spirit which made an army, so he preached a doctrine of alertness, intensity in training, sacrifice and service. The second was that modern war demanded a high degree of physical efficiency and so he drove his forces to hard training. The third concerned mobility; he urged that the war in Australia would be one of swift movement; that attack might come from any direction, therefore defence should not be based only on strongpoints looking out to sea and the hope that the invaders would land at the required spot so that they could be mown down; that the army should be prepared to move at short notice and fight in any direction.

But Mackay could do little more than had been done before his arrival—and not least because of the inherent defects of the militia system itself. This system, however, should be judged against the background of the voluntary system on which it was superimposed; up to the beginning of December 1941, this had yielded 187,500 men to the A.I.F., and 59,700 men to the R.A.A.F., while 20,900 men were serving in the Navy. These were volunteers for a war which was still remote from their own country and already they represented almost 4 per cent of the Australian population. In addition many volunteers were serving in the militia—men who had become suspicious of European quarrels, were unwilling to volunteer for unrestricted service, but ready to fight in defence of their homes.

Meanwhile, equipment which might have given militia training greater effectiveness had been going overseas. Thus, in February 1941, the War Cabinet ruled that, in view of the deficiency of 39,588 serviceable rifles for the army and requirements of 40,000 and 4,500 respectively for the Volunteer Defence Corps and the air force, no more deliveries of rifles should be made for the present to the United Kingdom or other Empire countries (except New Zealand) or to the Netherlands East Indies. On the other hand, at the end of April 1941, the Chief of the General Staff, in view of the fact that Australia was not immediately threatened, told the War Cabinet that though the provision of an additional 1,179 Vickers machine-guns was necessary to complete the initial equipping and war wastage reserve of the Australian Military Forces, this was not of immediate urgency. The War Cabinet thereupon approved the dispatch of 25 guns a month to the Netherlands Indies and the equal division of the remaining guns coming from the factory (175 monthly) between air force and Indian orders with the proviso that 50 should go to the Free French forces in New Caledonia as soon as possible. On 11th June, it was pointed out that 53 field guns had already been sent to the Middle East and Malaya since the war began; Australia was below initial requirements and had no reserves. It was then decided that no additional field artillery should be permitted to leave Australia until 25-pounders were well into production, and no anti-tank guns beyond an allotment to the United Kingdom of 25 a month from July onwards should be spared.

The year 1941 saw a quickening of preparations for war. At the beginning of the year the Cabinet approved the formation of an armoured corps and the army began to raise and train the 1st Armoured Division, as a fifth division of the A.I.F. Although orders had been placed in the United States for 400 light tanks for initial training and equipment, Australia was pressing ahead with her own tank production program, hoping to have a first tank produced in November and 340 by August 1942. The anti-aircraft defences were being equipped by the Australian ordnance factories, forty-four 3.7-inch guns having been made available by the end of April, with a promised rate of production on army orders of eight a month. There was a generally increasing rate in the production of weapons and equipment of many different kinds. Orders were issued for the continuous manning of coastal and anti-aircraft defences. Additional troops were sent to Port Moresby and Darwin and a battalion group was sent to Rabaul. Australian-American cooperation in the construction of airfields in north-east and north-west Australia developed. A program of tactical road building was being pushed ahead: from Tennant Creek to Mount Isa; an all-weather road from Darwin to Adelaide River; a Port Augusta-Kalgoorlie road. Telephone communications with isolated areas were improved.

On 7th-8th December 1941 Japan attacked. The Army's first official news of this came through the Combined Operations Intelligence Centre at 7 a.m. on 8th December with reports of the landings at Kota Bharu in Malaya. Cancellation of all leave followed, final preparations for mobilisation were made. At a War Cabinet meeting the same day General

Sturdee (who, about one week earlier, had asked the Prime Minister, Mr Curtin, for an additional 100,000 men) proposed that divisions in cadre forms be called up for training on a basis which included the actual fighting organisation but excluded the rearward services. No immediate action was taken on those proposals and Sturdee was asked to provide fuller information. This he did next day saying that, excluding reinforcements and certain maintenance units, the strength that he proposed for the militia at this stage was 246,000 men, of whom 132,000 were already on full-time duty. To allow time for further consideration, however, the War Cabinet decided immediately to recall to service only 25,000 militiamen and approved the recruitment of 1,600 more women for the Australian Women's Army Service. On the 11th, it approved revised proposals by Sturdee that, as it had been found that only 132,000 men were on full-time duty, the Army would require immediately a further 114,000. This entailed calling up Classes 2 and 3—married men, or widowers, without children, between the ages of 35 and 45, and married men, or widowers with children, between the ages of 18 and 35. The Ministers noted that a further 53,000 would be required to complete the full scale of mobilisation including first reinforcements; and approved that 5,000 of the Volunteer Defence Corps should be called up for full-time duty on aerodrome defence and coastwatching—a curious development considering the essential nature of that corps.

The Chiefs of Staff had advised the War Cabinet on 8th December that the most probable Japanese actions were, in order of probability, attacks on the outlying island bases, which would take the form of attempts to occupy Rabaul, Port Moresby and New Caledonia on the scale, at each place, of one division assisted by strong naval and air forces; raids on or attempts to occupy Darwin—a strong possibility in the event of the capture of Singapore and the Netherlands East Indies; and naval and air attacks on the vital areas of the Australian mainland. They concluded that the defeat of the Allied naval forces, or the occupation of Singapore and the Netherlands Indies with a consequential establishment of bases to the north-west of Australia, "would enable the Japanese to invade Australia". Sturdee said that, to counter these probable moves, he would require forces of a minimum strength of a brigade group in each of the three areas Rabaul, Port Moresby and New Caledonia, and the better part of a division at Darwin.

Soon afterwards the War Cabinet considered the dispositions and strengths of the militia then actually in camp or on full-time duty. In Queensland 1,563 men were manning the fixed defences at Thursday Island, Townsville and Brisbane; the field army was 15,071 strong with the nucleus of one brigade in the Cairns-Townsville area, of one brigade in the Rockhampton-Maryborough area and, in the Brisbane area, of one cavalry brigade group and one infantry brigade group as a command reserve, and one battalion for local defence. One garrison battalion was on coast defence duties and two on internal security duties. The total "full-time and in camp" strength was 16,400.

In New South Wales, there were 3,900 on fortress duty at Port Stephens, Newcastle, Sydney and Port Kembla. The field army, including base and lines of communication units, numbered 34,600, with the 1st Cavalry Division (except for a brigade group on the coast south of Port Kembla) on the coast north of Port Stephens, the bulk of the 1st Division covering the Sydney-Port Kembla area, one brigade group of four battalions in the Newcastle area and the 2nd Division in the Sydney area as Command reserve. Garrison battalions, very much below strength, numbered 1,777 men. All of these, with various training and similar units, totalled 43,807.

In Victoria 46,500 men were in camp or on full-time duty: 2,120 were manning the fixed defences and 38,600 (including base troops) were in the field army, of which the 3rd Division was held as Army reserve; the 2nd Cavalry Division (containing only one brigade group of four regiments) and the 4th Division (of two brigades each of four battalions) were disposed as the Melbourne Covering Force together with certain non-divisional units which included some armoured and other A.I.F. units. Two garrison battalions were on coast defence duty and one on internal security duties.

There were 10,810 troops in South Australia and 4,380 in Tasmania.

In remote Western Australia were 1,900 in its coastal forts, and one brigade group of four battalions, one light horse regiment and a machine-gun regiment in the field army which, with base troops, totalled 8,180. Four garrison battalions had a total of 1,150.

In the Northern Territory, excluding the 2/21st and 2/40th Battalion groups which had been ordered to the Netherlands East Indies immediately on the outbreak of war, were the 19th Battalion, and two A.I.F. battalions—the 2/4th Machine Gun and the 2/4th Pioneer. Two militia battalions and an A.I.F. Independent Company were moving north from South Australia. With base units the force totalled 6,670.

In the Mandated Territory of New Guinea, the Solomon Islands and the New Hebrides, with the main strength (2/22nd Battalion group) in the Rabaul area, there were 2,158 troops including approximately 1,138 A.I.F. At Port Moresby, in the Territory of Papua, 1,088 men were stationed including some Papuans and some 30 A.I.F.

In addition to the troops thus deployed throughout Australia and the islands there were on the mainland on 8th December 31,900 of the A.I.F. including about 2,800 men destined for employment in Ambon and Timor.

After the formal declaration of war on 9th December, the army moved swiftly to battle stations and the work of preparing defences. A tangled undergrowth of barbed wire sprang up over beaches many of which, until then, had been city playgrounds. Fields of fire were cleared. Guns were emplaced. Training was intensified. And the strength of the army increased daily. Proclamations calling up the later classes defined in the *Defence Act* began to take marked effect. From actual registration there were no exemptions. Enlistments in the A.I.F. rose steeply as they had always done when the need and the opportunity to serve could be seen more clearly. The monthly figure, which had fallen to 4,016 in October and 4,702 in November rose to 10,669 in December and 12,543 in January. These figures were by no means as spectacular as those of June of 1940 when over 48,000 men enlisted, one main cause being a War Cabinet decision that prevented members of the militia from enlisting in the A.I.F. or R.A.A.F. Women also offered in daily increasing numbers and the first recruits in New South Wales for the A.W.A.S were interviewed on 26th December by female officers who had already been trained. On 1st January 1942 the first twenty-eight female recruits were formally enlisted. By 5th February enlistments in the A.I.F. since its formation in 1939 totalled 211,706, and 222,459 were in the militia and other forces.

Before and soon after the outbreak of war with Japan a group of senior officers who had distinguished themselves in the Middle East were recalled to lead militia formations or fill important staff posts. On the day when General Mackay became G.O.C.-in-Chief, Home Forces, Brigadier S. F. Rowell, formerly General Blamey's chief of staff, became Deputy Chief of the General Staff with the rank of major-general. On 12th December Major-General H. D. Wynter, who had been invalided home from Egypt, was appointed to Eastern Command, which embraced the vital east coast areas. Ten days later General Mackay established his own headquarters and to him, soon afterwards, went Major-General Vasey[3] as his chief of staff. At the same time Brigadiers Clowes,[4] Robertson,[5] Plant,[6] Murray[7] and Savige[8] were promoted and given Home Army commands: Clowes, an expert artilleryman, 50 years of age, who had commanded the Anzac Corps artillery in Greece, took over the 1st Division; Robertson, 47, the 1st Cavalry Division; Plant, 51, Western Command; Savige, 51, the 3rd Division; and Murray, 49, the Newcastle Covering Force.

In the period from December 1941 to March 1942, while these experienced and energetic leaders were rapidly building the Home Army to a new peak of strength and efficiency, American reinforcements were arriving and battle-hardened veterans of the A.I.F. were on their way back from the Middle East.

---

[3] Maj-Gen G. A. Vasey, CB, CBE, DSO, VX9. (1st AIF: 2 Div Arty and BM 11 Inf Bde.) AA&QMG 6 Div 1939-41; GSO 1 6 Div 1941; Comd 19 Bde 1941; GOC 6 Div 1942, 7 Div 1942-44. Regular soldier; of Melbourne; b. Malvern, Vic, 29 Mar 1895. Killed in aeroplane crash 5 Mar 1945.

[4] Lt-Gen C. A. Clowes, CBE, DSO, MC, TX2050. (1st AIF: 2 Bty and 2 Div Arty.) CRA I Corps 1940-41; GOC 1 Div 1942, NG Force and Milne Force 1942, 11 Div 1942-43; Comd Vic L of C Area 1943-45. Regular soldier; of Warwick, Qld; b. Warwick, 11 Mar 1892.

[5] Lt-Gen Sir Horace Robertson, KBE, DSO, VX20321. (1st AIF: 10th LH Regt; GSO 3 Yeo Mtd Div.) Comd 19 Inf Bde 1940-41, AIF Rfct Depot 1941; GOC 1 Cav Div 1942, 1 Armd Div 1942-43, Western Comd 1944-45, 5 Div and 6 Div 1945. Regular soldier; of Melbourne; b. Warrnambool, Vic, 29 Oct 1894.

[6] Maj-Gen E. C. P. Plant, CB, DSO, OBE, QX6392. (1st AIF: 9 Bn and BM 6 Inf Bde.) Comd 24 Bde 1940-41, Rear Echelon AIF ME 1941, 25 Bde 1941, NSW L of C Area 1943-46. Regular soldier; of Brisbane; b. Charters Towers, Qld, 23 Apr 1890. Died 17 May 1950.

[7] Maj-Gen J. J. Murray, DSO, MC, NX365. (1st AIF: Maj 55 Bn.) Comd 20 Bde 1940-41; GOC 4 Div 1942-44. Company director; of Mosman, NSW; b. Sydney, 26 Apr 1892. Died 9 Sep 1951.

[8] Lt-Gen Sir Stanley Savige, KBE, CB, DSO, MC, ED, VX13. (1st AIF: 24 Bn 1914-17; Comd Urmia Force, Persia 1918.) Comd 17 Bde 1939-41; GOC 3 Div 1942-44, I Corps and NG Force 1944, II Corps 1944-45. Manufacturers' agent and company director; of Melbourne; b. Morwell, Vic, 26 June 1890. Died 15 May 1954.

The first Japanese blows at the Philippines had destroyed half the defending air forces and shown that the attackers were free not only to land there but to move southward with every chance of isolating the Philippines before American reinforcements could arrive. President Roosevelt and his military leaders, however, were agreed that they must accept the risks of trying to reinforce the islands while there was any chance of success and that the United States must not withdraw from the South-West Pacific. Logically then they decided to establish an advanced American military base in Australia and to keep open the Pacific line of communication. On 17th December General George C. Marshall (Chief of Staff of the United States Army) approved Brigadier-General Dwight D. Eisenhower's plans for the establishment of this base which was, first of all, to be an air base and commanded by a senior Air officer (Lieut-General George H. Brett). But, though the forces to be sent to Australia were to be part of the United States Army Forces in the Far East, with the prime task of supplying the Philippines, almost at once "it was evident that the establishment of this new command implied a more comprehensive strategy in the Southwest Pacific than the desperate effort to prolong the defense of the Philippines".[9]

On 22nd December 1941 four American ships (escorted by the American heavy cruiser, *Pensacola*) arrived at Brisbane. They carried some 4,500 men of field artillery units and the ground echelon of a heavy bomber group, munitions, motor vehicles, petrol and 60 aeroplanes; they had been on their way to the Philippines when the Japanese attacked and had then been re-routed from Fiji by way of Brisbane. They were being followed closely by four other ships carrying an additional 230 fighter aircraft. But by that time the isolation of the Philippines was nearly complete and, on 15th December, all that remained of the Philippines heavy bomber force—fourteen Flying Fortresses (B-17s)—were ordered south to the Netherlands Indies and Australia on the ground that there was insufficient fighter protection to enable them to operate from their own bases. It was then clear to President Roosevelt that the chance of reinforcing the Philippines had gone and he directed that the reinforcements then on their way should be used "in whatever manner might best serve the joint cause in the Far East".

By this time the projected Australian base had become a major American commitment. "The immediate goal was to establish nine combat groups in the Southwest Pacific—two heavy and two medium bombardment groups, one light bombardment group, and four pursuit groups. . . . This force represented the largest projected concentration of American air power outside the Western Hemisphere . . . and a very substantial part of the fifty-four groups that the Army expected to have by the end of the winter."[1]

On 23rd December the British Prime Minister, Mr Churchill, and President Roosevelt, with their Chiefs of Staff, began strategic and military

---
[9] M. Matloff and E. M. Snell, *Strategic Planning for Coalition Warfare 1941-42* (1953), p. 88, a volume in the official series *United States Army in World War II*.
[1] Matloff and Snell, p. 95.

discussions in Washington. By the end of the first week of these discussions the British staff began to share something of the American concern regarding the northern and eastern approaches to Australia and New Zealand. As a result agreement was reached regarding the diversion of shipping necessary to permit reinforcement of the South-West Pacific. The major shipments were to be to Australia and to New Caledonia, which the American planners regarded as a tempting objective for the Japanese, partly because of its strategic position on the Pacific supply line and partly because of its chrome and nickel deposits. There was, however, an increasingly obvious need for the establishment of other island garrisons throughout the Pacific. By the closing stages of the conferences some 36,000 air, anti-aircraft and engineer troops were listed for Australia, and about 16,000 infantry and service troops for New Caledonia. It was planned to get these on the water during January and February 1942 though the shipping position was such that it remained uncertain when the necessary equipment and supplies for them could be transported. No decision was taken, however, to send army ground forces to Australia.

Among the most important results of the December conferences was agreement between Britain and America regarding the machinery to be set up for the strategical command and control of their military resources. This machinery was to be based on the Combined Chiefs of Staff Committee composed of the American Joint Chiefs of Staff and four representatives of the British Chiefs of Staff. The first expression of this principle of unity of command was to be in ABDACOM (American, British, Dutch, Australian Command) under General Wavell.[2] The course of events in the ABDA Area was, however, short and unfortunate, and, as the situation in Malaya rapidly deteriorated, a revision of planning in relation to the disposition of ground forces became vital. On 13th February Wavell cautiously but plainly foreshadowed the loss of Sumatra and Java and opened the question of the diversion to Burma of either the 6th or 7th Australian Divisions (then bound for Java and Sumatra respectively) or both. Before this question was decided, however, and on the day after Wavell's warning, the American War Department abruptly decided to send ground combat forces and their ancillary services to Australia as well as air and anti-aircraft units. Almost at once movement orders were issued to the 41st Division and supporting troops. By 19th February shipping for the move was available.

This decision implied a new development in American strategy. When the question of the diversion of the Australian divisions to Burma was raised both Churchill and Roosevelt urged agreement upon the Australian Prime Minister, Mr Curtin. But Curtin, advised by his Chiefs of Staff, was resolute in his refusal. The wisdom of his decision was to be underlined by events which followed in Burma and by events later in the year in New Guinea. However, in his exchanges with Curtin, the President

---

[2] The Australian Government would have preferred an American commander. On 26th December, in a cable to President Roosevelt, Mr Curtin said: "Should the Government of the United States desire, we would gladly accept an American commander in the Pacific area."

defined his understanding that the maintenance of one Allied flank based on Australia and one on Burma, India and China must call for an Allied "fight to the limit" and he declared that "because of our geographical position we Americans can better handle the reinforcement of Australia and the right flank. I say this to you so that you may have every confidence that we are going to reinforce your position with all possible speed."[3]

Meanwhile, in the Philippines, General Douglas MacArthur, commander of the United States Army Forces in the Far East, had withdrawn his forces to the Bataan Peninsula by early January and the end of large-scale resistance was in sight. On 22nd February, with Singapore surrendered, ABDACOM disintegrating, and plans for the firm definition of the Pacific as an area of clear American responsibility within the Allied strategic pattern taking shape in his mind, Roosevelt ordered MacArthur to Australia with a view to having him accepted "as commander of the reconstituted ABDA Area".[4]

While these events were developing the Australian leaders had become increasingly dissatisfied with the lack of voice accorded them in the determination of strategic decisions which affected Australia vitally. They felt that there was reluctance, on the part of Great Britain particularly, to grant to Australia any real part in the direction of policy. When ABDACOM was created they were disturbed by the fact that they were not represented on the Combined Chiefs of Staff Committee from which Wavell would receive his orders and dissatisfied with the scanty Australian representation on ABDA Headquarters. On 5th February, only partly placated by a limited form of representation in the United Kingdom War Cabinet and only because of the urgency of the situation, the Australian War Cabinet approved proposals for the establishment of a Pacific War Council (on which Australia would be represented) in London and for direction of the Pacific war by the Combined Chiefs of Staff Committee in Washington—while still requesting the establishment in Washington of a Pacific War Council with a constitution and functions acceptable to Australia.

On 26th February the Australian and New Zealand Chiefs of Staff reviewed the situation in the Pacific. They declared that their countries were in danger of attack, emphasised the need to plan for an offensive with Australia and New Zealand as bases and recommended the establishment of an "Anzac Area" with an American as Supreme Commander (to replace one which had already been defined on 29th January as an area of joint naval operations under Vice-Admiral Herbert F. Leary, United States Navy, and to include not only most of the Western Pacific but also New Guinea, Ambon, Timor and the sea within about 500 miles of the Australian west coast). These proposals were cabled to the Dominions Office and to President Roosevelt on 1st March together with proposals for Australian and New Zealand representation on the Combined Chiefs of Staff Committee. A few days later the Australian Government decided that it would welcome the appointment as Supreme Commander of General Brett,

[3] Matloff and Snell, p. 131.
[4] Matloff and Snell, p. 165.

who had returned to command of the American forces in Australia after the dissolution of the ABDA Headquarters where he had been deputy to Wavell.

Concurrently Roosevelt and Churchill had been planning a world-wide division of strategic responsibility and, by 18th March, had reached general agreement on the establishment of three main areas: the Pacific area; the Middle and Far East area; the European and Atlantic area. The United States would be responsible for operations in the Pacific area through the United States Joint Chiefs of Staff who would consult with an advisory council representing Australia, New Zealand, the Netherlands Indies, China and possibly Canada. Supreme command in the area would be vested in an American.

In anticipation of this agreement the Joint Chiefs of Staff had been planning the subdivision of the Pacific area. On 8th March, after studying the Australian and New Zealand proposals, they accepted instead the view that the navy was primarily concerned with protecting the Pacific lines of communication and that New Zealand belonged within those lines; they regarded "the Australian continent and the direct enemy approaches there" as a separate strategic entity. They defined Australia and the areas to the north and north-east as far as and including the Philippines as the South-West Pacific Area (S.W.P.A.) which would be an army responsibility under General MacArthur as Supreme Commander, and designated most of the rest of the Pacific as the Pacific Ocean Area for which the navy would be responsible and in which Admiral Chester W. Nimitz would be Supreme Commander.

This was the stage of planning when, on 17th March, after a hazardous dash by torpedo boat and aircraft, General MacArthur arrived at Darwin, and, immediately, General Brett telephoned Mr Curtin and read him a letter which he had prepared in the following terms:

The President of the United States has directed that I present his compliments to you and inform you that General Douglas MacArthur, United States Army, has today arrived in Australia from the Philippine Islands. In accordance with his directions General MacArthur has now assumed command of all United States Army Forces here.

Should it be in accord with your wishes and those of the Australian people, the President suggests that it would be highly acceptable to him and pleasing to the American people for the Australian Government to nominate General MacArthur as the Supreme Commander of all Allied Forces in the South-West Pacific. Such nomination should be submitted simultaneously to London and Washington.

The President further has directed that I inform you that he is in general agreement with the proposals regarding organisation and command of the Australian Area, except as to some details concerning relationship to the Combined Chiefs of Staff and as to boundaries. These exceptions he wishes to assure you, however, will be adjusted with the interested Governments as quickly as possible.

The President regrets that he has been unable to inform you in advance of General MacArthur's pending arrival, but feels certain that you will appreciate that his safety during the voyage from the Philippine Islands required the highest order of secrecy.

On the same day the Prime Minister informed the War Cabinet which agreed that he should cable London and Washington:

General Douglas MacArthur having arrived in Australia, the Commonwealth Government desires to nominate him as Supreme Commander of the Allied Forces in this theatre. His heroic defence of the Philippine Islands has evoked the admiration of the world and has been an example of the stubborn resistance with which the advance of the enemy should be opposed. The Australian Government feels that his leadership of the Allied Forces in this theatre will be an inspiration to the Australian people and all the forces who will be privileged to serve under his command. If this nomination is approved might I be informed of the text and time of any announcement.

Next day—18th March—Mr Curtin announced the news to the Australian people, who greeted it with enthusiasm. They were soon to find that MacArthur's reputation lost nothing in the man. Alert and energetic, with an air of command, lean, his face combining the intellectual, the aesthetic and the martial, he was outstanding in appearance and personality. He was proud and, with skilful publicity measures, was soon to build himself into a symbol of offensive action and final victory.

He had been one of America's leading soldiers for many years. Son of General Arthur MacArthur he was born at a frontier post in 1880 and had shared the lives of soldiers as a boy before he entered West Point in 1899. He served in the Philippines and went to Japan as his father's aide when the old soldier was sent as an observer to the Russo-Japanese war in 1905. He was in France in 1918 as chief of staff of the 42nd (Rainbow) Division, became commander of the 84th Brigade in that division, and commander of the division itself from 1st November to the Armistice on 11th November 1918. After that war the highest offices in the United States Army came quickly to him. He became Superintendent of the Military Academy at West Point in 1919 and then served again in the Philippines for some five of the years 1922-30. In November 1930, he became Chief of Staff of the United States Army and remained in that post for five years (his original term having been extended). He was then appointed Military Adviser to the Philippine Commonwealth Government and later was made a field marshal in the Philippine Army. At the end of 1937 he was retired from the United States Army at his own request but remained with the Philippine Army to continue his ten-year plan for building military strength in the Philippines to a point where they could hope to defend themselves. In July 1941 he was recalled to service with the United States Army, with the rank of lieutenant-general, as commander of the United States Army Forces in the Far East.

But if MacArthur's record was, in many respects, brilliantly impressive, it was by no means uniformly so. As Chief of Staff he had initiated vigorous and practical reforms in army organisation; but these reforms were an insufficient basis for the demands of the multi-theatre conflict which developed in 1941. He laid the foundation for the development of an American armoured force; but he gave no evidence, for example, of possession of the vision of the British and German tank enthusiasts. He foresaw that "the airplane, the physical embodiment of the spirit of speed, has become an indispensable member of the military team"; but one of his reforms, the establishment of the General Headquarters Air

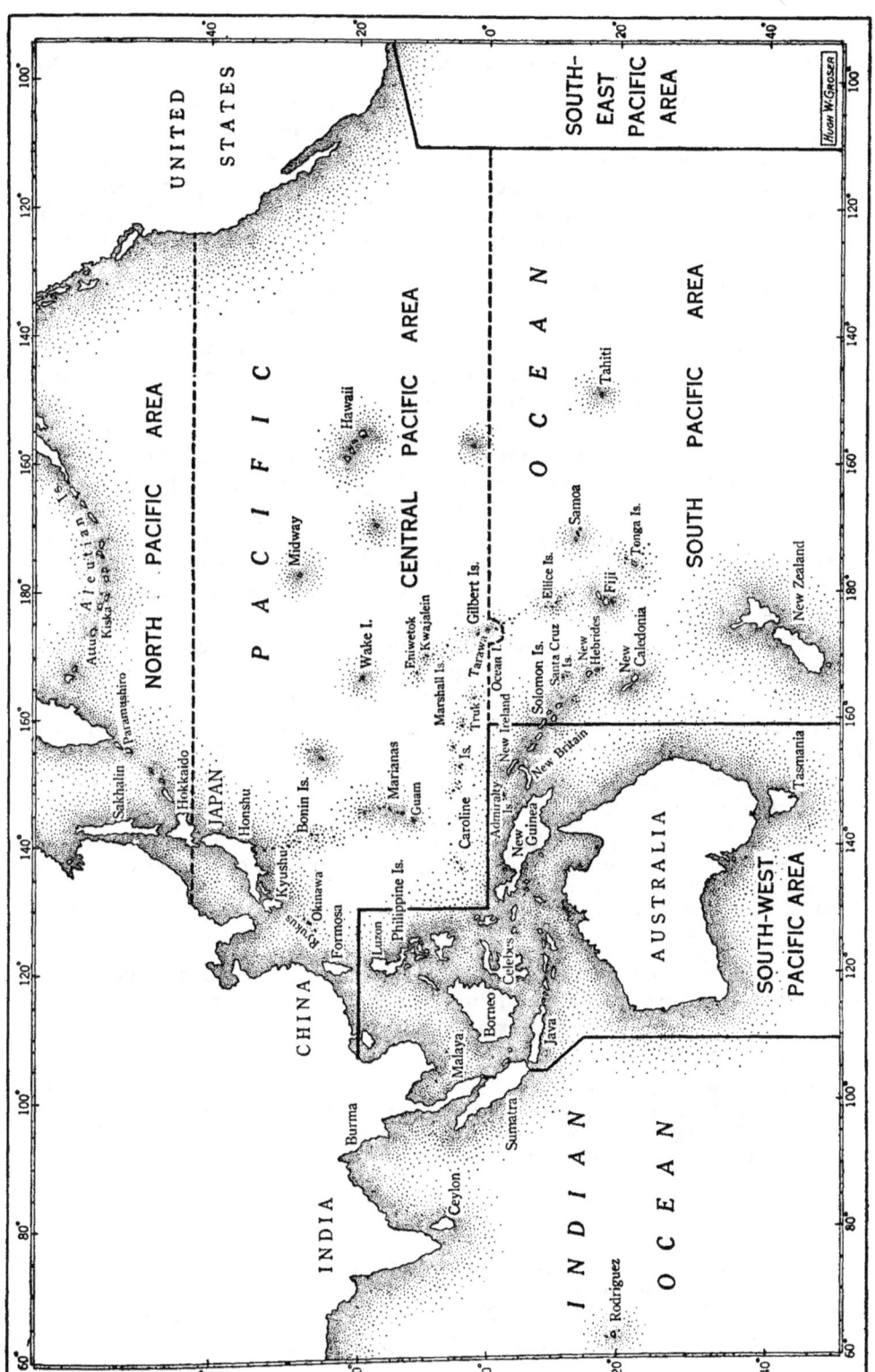

The Pacific Theatre

Force in 1934, proved inadequate for the needs of the new war—nor did he handle his air force effectively in the Philippines. He appreciated the fundamental importance of speed and mobility in war; but the Japanese caught him off balance in the Philippines with the speed of their own movement and destroyed a large part of his air forces on the ground. As the attack by the Japanese in December was being prepared he miscalculated their intentions and timing and was over-confident of his powers to check them in the Philippines where they quickly defeated him.

In his personality and actions there were contradictions. He stirred the profoundest admiration and loyalty in many; but provoked resentment, dislike and outright hostility in others. He had physical courage; but from the time the withdrawal to Bataan was completed (about 6th January) until he departed from Corregidor on 12th March he left that fortress only once to visit his hard-pressed troops in Bataan.[5] He was resolute; but when President Quezon of the Philippines shocked the American leaders in Washington by proposing that the Philippines be granted immediate and unconditional independence and forthwith be neutralised by agreement between the United States and Japan, MacArthur himself was prepared to consider Quezon's proposals. He was uncompromisingly loyal to many of his associates; but, in conversation with Brett after his arrival in Australia, he heaped abuse on his Philippine Air Force and its commander (whom Brett from long personal knowledge and a fighting association in Java considered a proved "energetic and capable officer" and whose own version of events was quite different from MacArthur's) and asserted that Admiral Thomas C. Hart (commanding the United States Asiatic Fleet) "had run out on him". A few days after his arrival in Australia he announced:

> My faith in our ultimate victory is invincible and I bring to you tonight the unbreakable spirit of the free man's military code in support of our just cause. . . . There can be no compromise. We shall win or we shall die, and to this end I pledge you the full resources of all the mighty power of my country and all the blood of my countrymen.

But there is evidence that, in those early days, he was not only dismayed but aghast at the situation in which he found himself. Brett, who knew him, served under him, and suffered much from his moods, wrote of him:

> a brilliant, temperamental egoist; a handsome man, who can be as charming as anyone who ever lived, or harshly indifferent to the needs and desires of those around. His religion is deeply a part of his nature. . . . Everything about Douglas MacArthur is on the grand scale; his virtues and triumphs and shortcomings.[6]

When MacArthur arrived in Australia he found an unbalanced assortment of less than 25,000 of all ranks and arms of the American forces;

---

[5] J. M. Wainwright, *General Wainwright's Story* (1946), p. 50.

[6] Brett, "The MacArthur I knew" (*True*, Oct 1947).
   It was unlikely from the outset that MacArthur's relations with Marshall would be entirely smooth. "At an early date MacArthur and George C. Marshall became identified with opposing groups within the Army. During and after World War I a rivalry, fed by a series of incidents and misunderstandings, developed between them. Eisenhower was an aide to MacArthur while

of the Australian forces, on whom he would have to depend chiefly for some time to come, many of the main "cutting edge"—the tried A.I.F.— were still overseas.

As a result of the revised planning which had followed the collapse of ABDACOM the 7th Australian Division had been diverted to Australia and would disembark at Adelaide between 10th and 28th March. Two brigades of the 6th Division had been diverted to Ceylon and only the headquarters and the 19th Brigade of that division were then on their way to Australia. The 9th Division was still in the Middle East—and was likely to remain there since the British leaders considered its retention of the highest importance, and, at Mr Churchill's suggestion, early in March the United States had offered to send a second division to Australia if the Australian Government would agree to leave the 9th Division temporarily where it was. The offer was accepted and on 28th March the 32nd Division, then preparing to move to northern Ireland, was ordered to prepare for movement to Australia.

Soon after MacArthur's arrival the Australian and New Zealand Governments were informed of the detailed proposals for the division of the world into three Allied strategic theatres and the proposals for the subdivision of the Pacific. They united in their protests, seeing themselves and their adjacent islands as one strategic whole. They were over-ruled on the grounds that the division was one of convenience only and did not mean that there would be any absence of joint planning and cooperation.

On 1st April the new Pacific War Council, which President Roosevelt had planned would act in a consultative and advisory capacity to the Chiefs of Staff, was constituted in Washington with Great Britain, Australia, New Zealand, Canada, China and the Netherlands represented. On 3rd April Dr Evatt (the Australian representative) cabled to Curtin the full text of the directives which had been framed for issue to General MacArthur and Admiral Nimitz and asked for formal approval to be given as soon as possible. These defined the Pacific Theatre and, within it, the South-West Pacific Area, the South-East Pacific Area and the Pacific Ocean Area, within the last-named defining also the North Pacific, Central Pacific and South Pacific Areas.

The instructions to General MacArthur were:
1. The South-West Pacific Area has been constituted as defined.
2. You are designated as Supreme Commander of the South-West Pacific Area, and of all Armed Forces which the Governments concerned have assigned or may assign to this Area.
3. As Supreme Commander you are not eligible to command directly any national force.

---

the latter was Chief of Staff from 1930 to 1935 and military adviser to the Philippine government thereafter. Eventually, however, Eisenhower, too, broke with MacArthur, returning to the United States in 1939. In due course, he came to the attention of Marshall, now himself Chief of Staff, and was rapidly advanced on the career which eventually led to his appointment as Supreme Commander of the European invasion. In this process Eisenhower became completely identified with the Marshall group. His rapid promotion and the priority given to the European theater over the Pacific necessarily drew the ire of the MacArthur supporters. The emergence of Eisenhower and MacArthur as the two popular military heroes of the war projected the essentially intramilitary feud upon the larger framework of national politics."—S. P. Huntington, *The Soldier and the State* (1957), pp. 368-9.

4. In consonance with the basic strategic policy of the Governments concerned, your operations will be designed to accomplish the following:
   (a) Hold the key military regions of Australia as bases for future offensive action against Japan, and strive to check Japanese aggression in the South-West Pacific Area.
   (b) Check the enemy advance across Australia and its essential lines of communication by the destruction of enemy combatant, troop and supply ships, aircraft, and bases in Eastern Malaysia and the New Guinea-Bismarck-Solomon Islands region.
   (c) Exert economic pressure on the enemy by destroying vessels transporting raw materials from recently conquered territories to Japan.
   (d) Maintain our position in the Philippine Islands.
   (e) Protect land, sea and air communications within the South-West Pacific Area and its close approaches.
   (f) Route shipping in the South-West Pacific Area.
   (g) Support operations of friendly forces in the Pacific Ocean Area and in the Indian Theatre.
   (h) Prepare to take the offensive.
5. You will not be responsible for the internal administration of the respective forces under your command, but you are authorised to direct and coordinate the creation and development of administrative facilities and the broad allocation of war materials.
6. You are authorised to control the issue of all communiqués concerning the forces under your command.
7. When task forces of your command operate outside the South-West Pacific Area, coordinate with forces assigned to areas in which operations will be effected by Joint Chiefs of Staff, or Combined Chiefs of Staff, as appropriate.
8. Commanders of all armed forces within your area will be immediately informed by their respective Governments that, from a date to be notified, orders and instructions issued by you in conformity with this directive will be considered by such Commanders as emanating from their respective Governments.
9. Your staff will include officers assigned by the respective Governments concerned, based upon requests made directly to national Commanders of the various forces in your area.
10. The Governments concerned will exercise the direction of operations in the South-West Pacific Area as follows:—
    (a) The Combined Chiefs of Staff will exercise general jurisdiction over the grand strategic policy and over such related factors as are necessary for proper implementation, including the allocation of forces and war materials.
    (b) The Joint United States Chiefs of Staff will exercise jurisdiction over all matters pertaining to operational strategy. Chief of Staff of the whole Army will act as executive agency for Joint United States Chiefs of Staff. All instructions to you to be issued by or through him.

The most important parts of Admiral Nimitz's directive were:

In consonance with the basic strategic policy of the Governments concerned, your operations will be designed to accomplish the following:
(a) Hold the island positions between the United States and the South-West Pacific Area necessary for the security of the lines of communications between those regions; and for the supporting naval, air and amphibious operations against the Japanese forces.
(b) Support the operations of the forces in the S.W.P.A.
(c) Contain the Japanese forces within the Pacific Theatre.
(d) Support the defence of the Continent of North America.

(e) Protect the essential sea and air communications.
(f) Prepare for the execution of major amphibious offensives against positions held by Japan, the initial offensives to be launched from the South Pacific Area and South-West Pacific Area.

Mr Curtin, still not completely satisfied with the boundaries proposed, now, however, acquiesced in the proposals for subdivision, in view of the urgency of the situation. But he insisted that any power to move Australian troops out of Australian territory should be subject to prior consultation and agreement with the Australian Government and pointed out that, in this respect, the limitations imposed by existing Commonwealth defence legislation should be borne in mind constantly. He also demanded clarification of the powers of the Commonwealth concerning the direction of operations in the South-West Pacific Area, while making it clear that he disapproved of political intervention in purely operational matters; a demand which he considered was completely justified by the fact that Australia was not represented either on the committee which controlled strategical policy or the one which controlled operational strategy.

A partial solution, at least, to these problems was achieved by recognition of the right of appeal of a local commander to his own government, and through the definition of the following principles in a note to the President by the United States Chiefs of Staff:

Proposals of United States Chiefs of Staff (for operations in the South-West Pacific Area) made to the President as United States Commander-in-Chief, are subject to review by him from the standpoint of higher political considerations and to reference by him to the Pacific War Council in Washington when necessary. The interests of the Nations whose forces or land possessions may be involved in these military operations are further safeguarded by the power each Nation retains to refuse the use of its forces for any project which it considers inadvisable.

Such was the singleness of purpose, however, of both the Prime Minister and General MacArthur in pursuing their common aim of driving back the Japanese that the problems which had loomed large on paper rarely occurred in practice to disturb the close relationship which grew up between the two men. MacArthur never yielded in his attitude that the Pacific was the main war theatre and offered the best opportunities for opening a "second front" which would help the Russians. To this end, he reiterated, the first step was to make Australia secure; the second was to organise Australia as a base for a counter-stroke. And he asked Mr Curtin to secure from outside, particularly from the United States, the maximum assistance that was available. This the Prime Minister attempted —a task at which he never slackened.

In his preliminary comments on the text of MacArthur's directive Curtin had asked, on 7th April, for additional naval and air forces, particularly aircraft carriers. On 23rd April he was told that the total strength of the American forces, ground and air, allotted to the S.W.P.A. was 95,000 officers and men. After discussions with MacArthur he then cabled to Evatt that MacArthur was "bitterly disappointed", that the proposals regarding the air forces, together with the fact that there was no increase in the naval forces, produced a situation in which MacArthur could not carry out his directive and which "leaves Australia as a base for operations in such a weak state that any major attack will gravely threaten the security of the Commonwealth. Far from being able to take offensive action . . . the forces will not (repeat not) be sufficient to ensure an adequate defence of Australia as the main base."

At the same time Curtin was mindful of a promise which Churchill had made on 17th March: "the fact that an American Commander will be in charge of all the operations in the Pacific Area will not be regarded by His Majesty's Government as in any way absolving them from their determination and duty to stand to your aid to the best of their ability, and if you are actually invaded in force, which has by no means come to pass and may never come to pass, we shall do our utmost to divert the British troops and British ships rounding the Cape, or already in the Indian Ocean, to your succour, albeit at the expense of India and the Middle East." Curtin therefore requested assistance from Britain, by the diversion of two divisions whose movement East was projected for late April and early May, and by the allocation of an aircraft carrier "even of the smallest type". Churchill, however, refused, saying: "No signs have appeared of a heavy mass invasion of Australia", and "the danger to India has been increased by the events in Burma as well as by an inevitable delay, due to the needs in home waters, in building up the Eastern Fleet". As far as aid from Britain was concerned, then, Curtin was left with what gloomy comfort he could draw from a further promise made by Churchill on 30th March:

> During the latter part of April and the beginning of May, one of our armoured divisions will be rounding the Cape. If, by that time, Australia is being heavily invaded, I should certainly divert it to your aid. This would not apply in the case of localised attacks in the north or of mere raids elsewhere. But I wish to let you know that you could count on this help should invasion by, say, eight or ten Japanese divisions occur. This would also apply to other troops of which we have a continuous stream passing to the East. I am still by no means sure that the need will arise especially in view of the energetic measures you are taking and the United States help.

Meanwhile Australia's agreement to the detailed arrangements under which MacArthur would work had become effective from midnight on 18th April. MacArthur's growing ground forces in Australia then totalled some 38,000 Americans, 104,000 of the A.I.F., and 265,000 in the militia. Before his arrival integration of American and Australian forces had been achieved through a system of joint committees. He now established a General Headquarters in Melbourne and organised his forces into five subordinate commands: Allied Land Forces, which included all combat land forces in the area, under General Blamey; Allied Air Forces under Lieut-General Brett; Allied Naval Forces under Vice-Admiral Herbert F. Leary; United States Army Forces in Australia, responsible for the administration and supply, in general, of American ground and air forces, under Major-General Julian F. Barnes; United States Forces in the Philippines, a fast-wasting asset, under Lieut-General Jonathan M. Wainwright. All of these commanders, except Blamey, were Americans (and MacArthur had agreed to the appointment of an Australian to the combined ground command only at the insistence of the War Department in Washington).

By this time Blamey already had a radical reorganisation of the Australian Army under way. On 2nd February, then in Cairo, he had proposed to Curtin that he should move to the Far East as soon as the Middle East situation was sufficiently clear. On 18th February the War Cabinet had decided that Blamey should return to Australia, and Lieut-General L. J. Morshead should command the A.I.F. in the Middle East. With the air link to Australia then disrupted Blamey flew from Cairo to Capetown early in March and took ship to Australia on the 15th. On the voyage he heard the announcement of MacArthur's appointment and commented: "I think that's the best thing that could have happened for Australia." When he reached Fremantle on 23rd March he was handed a letter from Curtin telling him that the Government proposed to appoint him "Commander-in-Chief, Australian Military Forces".

The War Cabinet had made this decision on 11th March, appointing Lieut-General Lavarack of the I Corps to act until Blamey's arrival. On the 16th the Military Board recommended that the Australian Commander-in-Chief should become "Commander-in-Chief Allied Armies in the Australian Area" upon the appointment of a Supreme Commander in the Anzac Area; that, until the appointment of the Supreme Commander, the Board should cease to function but, on the appointment being made, should be reconstituted as the senior staff of the Commander-in-Chief. The Minister for the Army, Mr Forde, declined to submit these proposals to the War Cabinet until after Blamey's arrival. On 26th March the War Cabinet considered them and, on Blamey's advice, decided that the Military Board would cease to function and the heads of its Departments would become Principal Staff Officers under the Commander-in-Chief. On the same day Blamey assumed his appointment.[7]

On 9th April Blamey issued the orders which defined the main lines of his reorganisation. Army Headquarters were to become General Headquarters (Australia). (In late May they were redesignated Allied Land Forces Headquarters—L.H.Q.) The land forces in Australia were to be organised into a field army and lines of communications. A First Army (Lieut-General Lavarack) was to be created and located in Queensland and New South Wales, absorbing Northern and Eastern Commands. A Second Army (Lieut-General Mackay) was to be located in Victoria, South Australia and Tasmania, absorbing Southern Command. (Not long afterwards, however, the Second Army took over also most of the troops in New South Wales.) The field troops in Western Australia (Western Command) became the III Corps (Lieut-General Bennett). Headquarters and some of the units of the 6th Division which had arrived in or were

---

[7] Blamey did not then cease to be the nominal Deputy Commander-in-Chief, Middle East. Curious though it may seem the termination of this appointment was not notified until the *London Gazette* of 27th November 1942.

immediately returning to Australia (two brigades, as mentioned, having been ordered to remain in Ceylon) were to move to the Northern Territory where the 6th Division would absorb the 7th Military District. (Shortly afterwards this command became the Northern Territory Force.) The troops in Papua and New Guinea (8th Military District) were to become New Guinea Force (Major-General Morris[8]). Except in the Northern Territory and New Guinea the fixed coastal defences, anti-aircraft units and garrison battalions were to be under the lines of communications area commanders.

Command was to pass from the home forces commander to the two army commanders at 6 p.m. on 15th April; the headquarters of the various commands and military districts were to cease operating from the same time.

Within this organisation on 15th April there were ten Australian divisions—seven infantry, two motor (formerly cavalry), one armoured; the Northern Territory and New Guinea Forces, each with a numerical strength roughly equivalent to that of a division; and one incomplete American division—the 41st. (Most of the 32nd Division was scheduled to arrive by mid-May). Of these divisions, the First Army included the following: 1st (Major-General Clowes); 2nd (Major-General Lloyd[9]); 3rd (Major-General Savige); 5th (Major-General Milford[1])—newly formed in Queensland from the 7th, 11th and 29th Brigades; 7th (Major-General Allen); 10th (Major-General Murray)—newly formed from the Newcastle Covering Force; 1st Motor (Major-General Steele[2]). The First Army was organised into two corps: I Corps (Lieut-General Rowell); II Corps, under Lieut-General Northcott who, for the past seven months, had commanded the 1st Armoured Division. The Second Army comprised three formations; the 2nd Motor Division (Major-General Locke[3]); the 41st U.S. Division (Major-General Horace H. Fuller); the 12th Brigade Group. (The 32nd U.S. Division would go to the Second Army on arrival.) In Western Australia the III Corps included the 4th Division (Major-General Stevens[4]) and a number of unbrigaded units. As his reserve Blamey temporarily retained the 1st Armoured Division (Major-General Robertson) and the 19th Brigade. (The 19th Brigade, however,

---

[8] Maj-Gen B. M. Morris, CBE, DSO. (1st AIF: 55 Siege Bty; 5 Div Arty 1917-18.) Comdt Aust Overseas Base ME 1940; Aust. Mil Liaison Offr India 1940-41; Comdt 8 MD 1941-42; Comd NG Force 1942; Angau 1942-46. Regular soldier; of Upper Beaconsfield, Vic; b. East Melbourne, 19 Dec 1888.

[9] Maj-Gen H. W. Lloyd, CB, CMG, CVO, DSO, ED. (1st AIF: Comd 12 AFA Bde 1918.) GOC 2 Div 1940-43; 1 Div 1943-45; Admin Comd Second Army 1943-46. Of Darling Point, NSW; b. Melbourne, 24 Nov 1883.

[1] Maj-Gen E. J. Milford, CB, CBE, DSO, VX12014. (1st AIF: Maj 4 AFA Bde.) CRA 7 Div 1940; MGO AHQ 1941-42; GOC 5 Div 1942-44, 7 Div 1944-45. Regular soldier; of Melbourne; b. Warrnambool, Vic, 29 Oct 1894.

[2] Maj-Gen W. A. B. Steele, CBE, DX906. (1st AIF: 2 LH Regt; S-Capt 13 Bde.) Comd 1 Motor Div 1942, 3 Armd Div 1942-43; DQMG LHQ 1944-45. Regular soldier; b. Gympie, Qld, 4 Feb 1895.

[3] Maj-Gen W. J. M. Locke, MC, NX198. (1st AIF: 4 Inf Bde; BM 3 Inf Bde.) Comd 2 Armd Bde; GOC 2 Motor Div 1942-43; Chairman LHQ War Establishments Investigation Cttee 1943-44; Chairman permanent Post-War Planning Cttee (Army) 1944-46. Regular soldier; of St Kilda, Vic; b. St Kilda, 11 Aug 1894.

[4] Maj-Gen Sir Jack Stevens, KBE, CB, DSO, ED, VX17. (1st AIF: Spr 2 Div Sig Coy; Lt Aust Corps Sig Coy.) Comd 6 Div Sigs 1939-40; Comd 21 Bde 1940-42; GOC 4 Div 1942, NT Force & 12 Div 1942-43, 6 Div 1943-45. Public servant; of Melbourne; b. Daylesford, Vic, 7 Sep 1896.

soon went to the Northern Territory and, on 19th May, Blamey was to write to General Bennett that he proposed to add the armoured division and an infantry division to the latter's command, "keeping in mind the possibility of an eventual offensive to the north from the area of your command".)

The main troop movements resulting from these groupings involved the 7th and 4th Divisions. The former, disembarking at Adelaide, was to be concentrated in northern New South Wales by 27th April (and it moved to southern Queensland soon afterwards). On 1st April there were only two infantry brigades in Western Australia. To build up the strength there of the 4th Division, 6,000 men were to move from Victoria.

On 10th April, Blamey issued his first Operation Instruction as Commander-in-Chief to the commander of the First Army. He stated that the retention of the Newcastle-Melbourne area was vital but the probability of a major attack thereon was not then great because the enemy's main concentrations were in Burma and the Indies. The enemy's first effort southwards from the Mandates would probably be "an attempt to capture Moresby followed by a landing on the north-east coast with a view to progressive advance southwards covered by land-based aircraft". He added:

In view of the limitations of resources, it is not possible at present to hold the coastline from excluding Townsville to excluding Brisbane. As our resources increase it is intended to hold progressively northwards from Brisbane.

On 18th April, after Blamey's reorganisation of the army had become effective, MacArthur formally assumed command of Australian forces. Curtin had written to him on 17th April:

I refer to . . . your directive, regarding the assignment of Forces to your Command and notification to local commanders as to the date of commencement of the Supreme Command.

2. In accordance with the terms of your directive, taken in conjunction with the official memorandum by the United States Chiefs of Staff, which forms part of your directive, I would inform you that the Commonwealth Government assigns to the South-West Pacific Area under your command all combat sections of the Australian Defence Forces. These Forces are as follows:

Navy—The Naval Forces at present operating under Admiral Leary.

Army—The 1st Army
The 2nd Army
the 3rd Corps
the 6 Division (Darwin)
the New Guinea Force

Air—All Service Squadrons but not including training units.

3. In accordance with Article 8 of your Directive the Commonwealth Government is notifying its Commanders of the Forces assigned to the South-West Pacific Area that, as from 12 midnight on Saturday 18th April 1942, all orders and instructions issued by you in conformity with your directive will be considered by such Commanders as emanating from the Commonwealth Government.

At this stage it was obvious that the changes brought about by MacArthur's appointment were more sweeping even than had first appeared. It was reasonable to expect that the Supreme Commander would work through a headquarters which, throughout its various layers, would represent in due proportion the Australian as well as the American forces under his command; the Australian far outnumbered the American and seemed likely to continue to do so for a long time. (That such integration was practicable was to be demonstrated later in the European theatres.) But no such development took place in Australia although the Australians were to be represented on MacArthur's headquarters by a rather shadowy liaison organisation and their own Army Headquarters, under General Blamey, was to remain intact, though as an entirely separate and virtually subordinate entity. The absence of a combined staff was the more remarkable because of the existence, from the beginning, of the following factors (other than those which related to mere numbers): General Blamey was far more experienced in actual war than any of the American commanders, including MacArthur. Blamey's experience in the 1914-18 War had been long and varied and he had emerged from that war with a glowing military reputation. His service between the wars was of a high order. His leadership of the Second A.I.F., and his discharge of responsibility as Deputy Commander-in-Chief in the Middle East, had brought him valuable experience and had shown that he, probably more than any other high-ranking officer in the Australian Army, could combine military skill and political shrewdness in the degree demanded in a Commander-in-Chief. Blamey's subordinate commanders in the Australian Army and his senior staff officers had had far wider experience of war than their American counterparts. Inevitably their service in the 1914-18 War had, as a rule, been far longer; and of the seventeen army, corps, divisional and force commanders, eleven were fresh from hard-fought Middle East campaigns, and one had fought the Japanese in Malaya. These, and the other Australian leaders, had evolved a staff organisation which functioned efficiently under the direction of highly-trained and experienced staff officers in key positions. The headquarters of the First Army, for example, was formed by enlarging that of the I Corps, an expert team which had controlled operations in two Middle East campaigns.

General Marshall had suggested to General MacArthur on 9th April that all the participating governments should be represented on his staff, and informed him that a number of the higher positions on the staff should go to Dutch and Australian officers and particularly to Australians.[5] On 19th April, the day after MacArthur assumed command, MacArthur announced the heads of the branches of his staff. All were Americans; eight had served with him in the Philippines.[6]

Marshall again pressed MacArthur to include Allied officers in his staff in senior appointments but MacArthur did not do so. On 15th June

---

[5] S. Milner, *Victory in Papua* (1957), a volume in the official series, *United States Army in World War II*, pp. 22-3.

[6] The senior staff officers were: Maj-Gen Richard K. Sutherland, Chief of Staff; Brig-Gen Richard J. Marshall, Deputy Chief of Staff; Col Charles P. Stivers, G-1 ((Personnel); Col Charles A. Willoughby, G-2 (Intelligence); Brig-Gen Stephen J. Chamberlin, G-3 (Operations); Col Lester J. Whitlock (Supply); Brig-Gen Spencer B. Akin, Signal Officer; Brig-Gen Hugh J. Casey, Engineer Officer; Brig-Gen William F. Marquat, Anti-aircraft Officer; Col Burdette M. Fitch, Adjutant-General; and Col LeGrande A. Diller, Public Relations Officer.

he informed Marshall that the Australians did not have enough staff officers to meet their own needs. "There is no prospect," he said, "of obtaining qualified senior staff officers from the Australians."[7]

There is no record of MacArthur having asked Blamey to provide senior staff officers; yet there were in the Australian Army many senior specialists in each branch of staff work who were at least the equals of the Americans in military education and had the advantage of experience in recent operations in Africa, Europe and Asia.

On 25th April MacArthur issued his first directive relating to a general plan. It proposed no alteration of Blamey's dispositions, and gave the Allied Land Forces the task of preventing "any landing on the north-east coast of Australia or on the south-western coast of New Guinea". So far, however, there was no proposal to send more infantry to New Guinea. On 28th April when Mr Curtin, at MacArthur's request, told Dr Evatt that additional forces were required for the South-West Pacific and that MacArthur was fearful that he would not be able to guarantee the security of his main base, he also said:

MacArthur considers as highly dangerous the many references which have been or are being made to offensive action against Japan from Australia as a base, if there is reluctance or inability to carry out these intentions which have been referred to in the many communications since the establishment of the ABDA Area.

MacArthur's ground forces in Australia could be grouped under three headings: A.I.F.; Australian militia; Americans. Of the A.I.F. the 6th Division (which would be concentrated again in Australia by August) and the 7th were highly-trained volunteers with recent and varied experience in battle—desert warfare in North Africa, mountain warfare in Greece and Syria, operations against German, French and Italian troops. Leaders had been tested and staffs were of the first order. There were then no formations facing the Japanese, except the 7th Armoured Brigade in Burma, which were the equal of these in training and experience. The 1st Armoured Division (although deficient in armoured equipment[8]) was manned by volunteers who, up to that time, had been trained to match themselves against the German panzer divisions.

At this time and later it was customary for some Australian and American military and political leaders to refer to the militia in such terms as "home defence troops", "inefficient and undisciplined", "second-line", "only partially trained and equipped". But such terms are imprecise and relative, leave crucial questions unanswered, and invite closer examination. In December the state of training of the militia had varied widely, unit strengths were low and fluctuating. The militia, however, contained a solid core of outstanding officers and N.C.O's, the officers somewhat older than

---

[7] Milner, p. 23.
[8] In April 1942 there were in Australia 185 tanks: 89 M3 Light; 30 M3 Medium; 12 Matilda; 2 AC1 (the Australian tank); 52 two-man tanks (from Java). On order were 149 M3 Light, 100 M3 Medium, 240 Matilda, 114 AC1, which were expected to have all arrived by October 1942. By 22nd May the six armoured regiments of the 1st Armoured Division (5th, 6th, 7th, 8th, 9th, 10th) had between them 142 tanks of various types; the three regiments of the 6th Armoured Brigade (12th, 13th, and 14th) had no tanks. In the 3rd Army Tank Brigade the 2nd Battalion had 20 Matildas while the 1st and 3rd Battalions had no tanks.

those of the A.I.F. but including a higher proportion who had served in 1914-18. Among them were such men as Freeman,[9] Holland,[1] Langley[2] who, in their twenties, had commanded battalions or light horse regiments in the old A.I.F. H. W. Murray[3] was commanding a battalion in Queensland with another Victoria Cross winner, Major Towner,[4] as his second-in-command. Leaders of this type were not likely to leave training and spirit at "second-line" standard. Since January, as mentioned earlier, the divisional commanders had included a group fresh from North Africa, Greece and Syria—Robertson, Clowes, Savige and Murray. By April a large-scale injection of A.I.F. officers of all ranks into the militia formations was under way (in May, for example, six of the militia infantry brigades were led by former battalion commanders of the 6th and 7th Divisions). The militia formations by that time were fully embodied, fit, and engaging in fairly elaborate unit and brigade exercises.

The scale of equipment of militia units was improving rapidly during the early months of 1942 as the factories began to reach full production. At the end of February (that is, after the fall of Singapore and before General MacArthur's arrival in Australia) the numbers of certain basic weapons on hand in Australia and the monthly rate of their local production were:

	On Hand	Monthly Production
Rifles	294,000	8,000-12,000
Bren light machine-guns	1,590	300
Other light machine-guns	3,038	Nil
Anti-tank guns	493	80
3-inch mortars	854	240 (by April)
25-pounders	195	40-80
18-pounders and 4.5-inch howitzers	349	Nil
3.7-inch anti-aircraft guns	145	8
40-mm anti-aircraft guns	16	Nil

The supply of ammunition for most weapons was adequate: from 1,000 to 2,400 rounds a field gun, 80 per cent of total requirements of ball ammunition for small arms, only 179 rounds a gun for anti-tank guns but this was being produced at the rate of 7,500 rounds a week.[5] It will be recalled that these arms were then divided among the equivalent of ten divisions. Week by week the Chief of the General Staff presented to the War Cabinet a statement showing the deficiency in the supply of each standard weapon. At first glance these tables were alarming. They showed on 28th February a deficiency of 32,000 rifles, and a far higher figure if

---

[9] Brig N. M. Freeman, DSO, ED. (1st AIF: CO 31 Bn 1918.) Comd 4 and 6 Inf Training Bdes. Barrister and solicitor; of Geelong, Vic; b. Geelong, 21 Apr 1890.

[1] Brig A. C. S. Holland, CBE, VD, NX101314. (1st AIF: CO 54, 53, 55, 56 Bns.) Comd 9 Bde 1940-43. Company director; of Mosman, NSW; b. Sydney, 20 Sep 1889.

[2] Brig G. F. Langley, DSO, ED, VX133472. (1st AIF: CO 14 LH Regt 1918.) Comd 2 Bde 1942-44; Commissioner for Aust Red Cross UK and ME 1944-46. Schoolmaster; of Warrnambool, Vic; b. Melbourne, 1 May 1891.

[3] Lt-Col H. W. Murray, VC, CMG, DSO, DCM, QX48850. (1st AIF: 13 Bn; CO 4 MG in 1918.) CO 26 Bn; VDC 1942-44. Grazier; of Richmond, Qld; b. near Evandale, Tas, 1 Dec 1885.

[4] Maj E. T. Towner, VC, MC. (1st AIF: 2 Bn.) 26 Bn 1942-44. Grazier; of Longreach, Qld; b. Glencoe, Qld, 19 Apr 1890.

[5] The returning AIF formations were to bring home with them from 12,000 to 15,000 tons of ammunition.

"reserves" were taken into account, of some 250 heavy and 1,000 light anti-aircraft guns, of some 7,000 light machine-guns and so on. On the other hand the lists of basic weapons on hand and coming from the factories in substantial numbers showed that the Australian militia divisions were as well armed as the general run of Allied forces which had so far been in action and far better than some. Local production of the principal weapons had reached so high a rate as to ensure that within a few months there would be few serious deficiencies. Not all the 18-pounder field guns would be replaced with 25-pounders, not all the older machine-guns with Brens; there would not be in each section a sub-machine-gun (a weapon adopted in British armies only in 1940); there would be some shortages of technical gear, but, judged by the standards of even a year earlier, the Australian home forces would be fairly well armed and with a higher proportion of modern weapons than American divisions then held. The returning A.I.F. formations did not dip deeply into the local pool of weapons since they arrived fully armed.

What were the reasons why then and later the effectiveness of the militia, which formed the greater part of this army, was under-valued and leaders in a theatre that was somewhat over-insured in ground troops (not sea or air) persistently sought reinforcement? One factor seems to have been the traditional Australian prejudice against conscript forces and the traditional adoption, as the standard of military efficiency, of her own volunteer expeditionary forces or the British regular army. Any force of lower standard was rated as no more than second-class. Military reputation was a source of great national pride and there was fear that conscripted troops might lower that reputation. The American leaders, arriving in a remote British country of which they had hitherto known little or nothing and at a time when the Japanese had defeated them in the Philippines and were winning successes on every front, were more than ready to accept a low valuation of the Australian militia. Reinforcing these tendencies was the natural desire of General MacArthur and the Australian Ministers to persuade Washington to reinforce their armies. Their argument was strengthened if the Australian militia were written about in somewhat nebulously disparaging terms. But surely it would be surprising if, in the test that seemed to lie ahead, the militia divisions fell so far short as such labels suggested they would; if the force that had chiefly provided the leaders and doctrines of the A.I.F. had while so doing deprived itself of all vigour and skill; if the 265,000 in the militia proved of such different calibre to the 170,000 in the expeditionary force.[6] The actual performance in battle, however, of parts of each main contingent of General Blamey's army of May 1942—the three A.I.F. divisions, the eight divisions of the home forces and the two American divisions—will be described in the following chapters.

If the Australian militia really lacked effectiveness it was likely that the

---

[6] The strength of the AIF still in the Middle East on 2nd May 1942 was 35,622; in the United Kingdom 584; in Ceylon 12,417; at sea 5,156; in Australia 110,337. An additional 3,000 were distributed between New Caledonia, Port Moresby and Portuguese Timor.

third main component of MacArthur's ground forces—the Americans—would be at least equally lacking, for both the 32nd and 41st Divisions were formations of the National Guard (the American equivalent of the Australian militia) and many of the factors in the background of their development were similar to those in the background of the Australian Army.

The 1914-18 War had demonstrated to the United States that their military organisation badly needed overhaul and, after that war, they had set about the task. But other factors hindered this development: the traditional democratic distrust of military preparations; the ceaseless activity of "isolationists"; and lack of money. In 1935, however, War Department expenditure for national defence began a slow upward climb. But Hanson W. Baldwin[7] (an American observer) noted that "the growth of our military and naval forces in these years did not equal the rapid deterioration in the world situation. . . . The progress in quantity was not matched by the progress in quality." By August 1940 only eight infantry divisions, one cavalry division and the elements of a second, and one armoured division were on an active basis and these were all below strength. During June the authorised enlisted strength of the Regular Army had been expanded from 227,000 to 375,000. On 16th September the Selective Service Bill (conscripting citizens for a year's service) became law and, on the same day, National Guard units began to be inducted for active service with the result that, by November, 278,526 men had been enlisted in these units. When the critical international situation demanded the retention of these men and the *Selective Service Extension Act* was passed in late August 1941 "the Army of the United States consisted of a partially equipped force of 28 infantry divisions, a newly created armoured force of 4 divisions, 2 cavalry divisions, the harbour defences of the United States and an air force of 209 incomplete squadrons", representing a total strength of approximately 1,600,000 men. On 31st December, a little more than three weeks after the attack on Pearl Harbour, the entire strength of the United States Army was 1,657,157 men. By the end of April 1942 the total was about 2,500,000. In such a rapid mobilisation the necessary processes of training and equipment lagged.

The 32nd and 41st Divisions had been on full-time duty since October and September 1940, respectively. Under fully-trained officers and senior N.C.O's such a period of training should produce an expert force, but the United States lacked what other combatant Allied nations possessed—long experience in the previous war and the reserve of experienced officers and the store of practical knowledge of the realities of warfare which such experience produced. American participation in 1917 and 1918 had been brief, particularly for the National Guard divisions. To Australian eyes there was some lack of realism in the outlook of the newly-arrived formations, staff work seemed defective and training methods somewhat unpractical. The Australian soldier lived hard during training; in battle he was

---

[7] Hanson W. Baldwin, *Defence of the Western World* (1941).

in many respects no more uncomfortable than he had often been before. The American formations on the other hand tended, in Australian opinion, to clutter themselves up with inessential paraphernalia, and thus to increase the difference between camp life and battle conditions to such an extent that contact with the latter was bound to produce a rude shock, even to the most high-spirited. Their equipment was adequate—partly of last-war types and partly of later models. They were equipped with field artillery on a lighter scale than the Australian divisions—at this stage thirty-six 105-mm and twelve 155-mm howitzers against the seventy-two 25-pounders of a fully-equipped Australian division. The American divisional reconnaissance troop was a smaller unit than the Australian divisional cavalry regiment, and the American division lacked the pioneer and machine-gun battalion normally attached to an Australian division. The rearming of the American Army with new weapons was then far from complete. The historian of the 41st Division has recorded that in August 1941 the division was exercising with wooden machine-guns and trucks labelled tanks.[8]

The bulk of the 41st Division arrived in Australia on 6th April, the 32nd, plus the remainder of the 41st, on 14th May. After they had been training in Australia for some months Lieut-General Robert L. Eichelberger arrived in late August as the American Corps commander. He noted later:

> In Washington I had read General MacArthur's estimates of his two infantry divisions, and these reports and our own inspections had convinced my staff and me that the American troops were in no sense ready for jungle warfare. It was true that we were newcomers, but I had expected to learn lessons in jungle training in Australia. And it seemed to me that our troops in training were just being given more of the same thing they had had back home. . . . I told Generals MacArthur and Sutherland that I thought the 32nd Division was not sufficiently trained to meet Japanese veterans on equal terms. After an inspection . . . I gave the 32nd Division a "barely satisfactory" rating in combat efficiency. . . . I was to lead these troops later, and I recall one soldier who told me that in twenty months of service he had had only one night problem. He asked how he could be expected to be proficient in night patrolling against the Japanese under those conditions.[9]

Eichelberger reached the conclusion that many of the Australian commanders whom he met

> though they were usually too polite to say so, considered the Americans to be—at best—inexperienced theorists.[1]

Whatever the defects or virtues of the various components of MacArthur's army it was nevertheless a formidable force. The events which had been developing in the islands north-east of Australia and along the north-western approaches while this army was being organised indicated that it would soon be put to the test.

---

[8] William F. McCartney, *The Jungleers* (1948), p. 11.

[9] Robert L. Eichelberger, *Our Jungle Road to Tokyo* (1950), pp. 11-12.

[1] Eichelberger, p. 7.

CHAPTER 2

THE ISLAND BARRIER

FOR many years Australians, uneasily peering northward, had comforted themselves with the contemplation of the great arc of islands which stretches from the Pacific by way of the island mass of New Guinea and beneath the centrepiece of the Philippines, through the East Indian archipelago to the Indian Ocean. These islands, particularly in the northeast, seemed a barrier to invasion. But few Australians had much knowledge of them, and the military leaders mostly shared the general ignorance. After the fall of Java in March 1942, the only places where fighting was taking place along this island barrier were Timor, where an Australian Independent Company was at large, and the Philippines.

When General MacArthur left for Australia on 12th March there was confusion in the Philippines over the command arrangements. He did not tell the War Department in Washington that he had divided the forces in the Philippines into four commands, which he planned to control from Australia, and of which Major-General Wainwright was to command only one—the troops on Bataan and small pockets holding out in the mountains of Luzon. Both President Roosevelt and General Marshall assumed that Wainwright had been left in overall command. He was accordingly promoted lieut-general and moved to Corregidor on the 21st. On the same day MacArthur informed Marshall of his own arrangements. Marshall considered them unsatisfactory and told the President so. Roosevelt thereupon made it clear to MacArthur that Wainwright would remain in full command.

Major-General Edward P. King took over Luzon Force from Wainwright. The total strength was then 79,500 of whom 12,500 were Americans. On 3rd April General Homma's *XIV Army* fell upon them with reinforced strength. The defence crumbled, and on the 9th King surrendered his force. On the same day Wainwright wrote to MacArthur that he considered "physical exhaustion and sickness due to a long period of insufficient food is the real cause of this terrible disaster". Some years later he wrote:

> I had my orders from MacArthur not to surrender on Bataan, and therefore I could not authorise King to do it [but he] was on the ground and confronted by a situation in which he had either to surrender or have his people killed piecemeal. This would most certainly have happened to him within two or three days.[1]

Up to this time the island fortress of Corregidor, where Wainwright had his headquarters, had been under heavy but intermittent aerial and artillery bombardment. The aerial bombardment had begun on 29th December but waned after 6th January, when Homma was left with only a small air force which he could spare for use against the island only in sporadic

---
[1] L. Morton, *The Fall of the Philippines* (1953), p. 456, a volume in the official series *United States Army in World War II*.

New Guinea

small attacks; the artillery bombardment began on 6th February from guns sited on the southern shore of Manila Bay. On 15th March it entered a new phase with thickened fire aimed at the four fortified islands in the bay, particularly the two southernmost ones. The shelling decreased once more as the Japanese prepared their final concentrations against

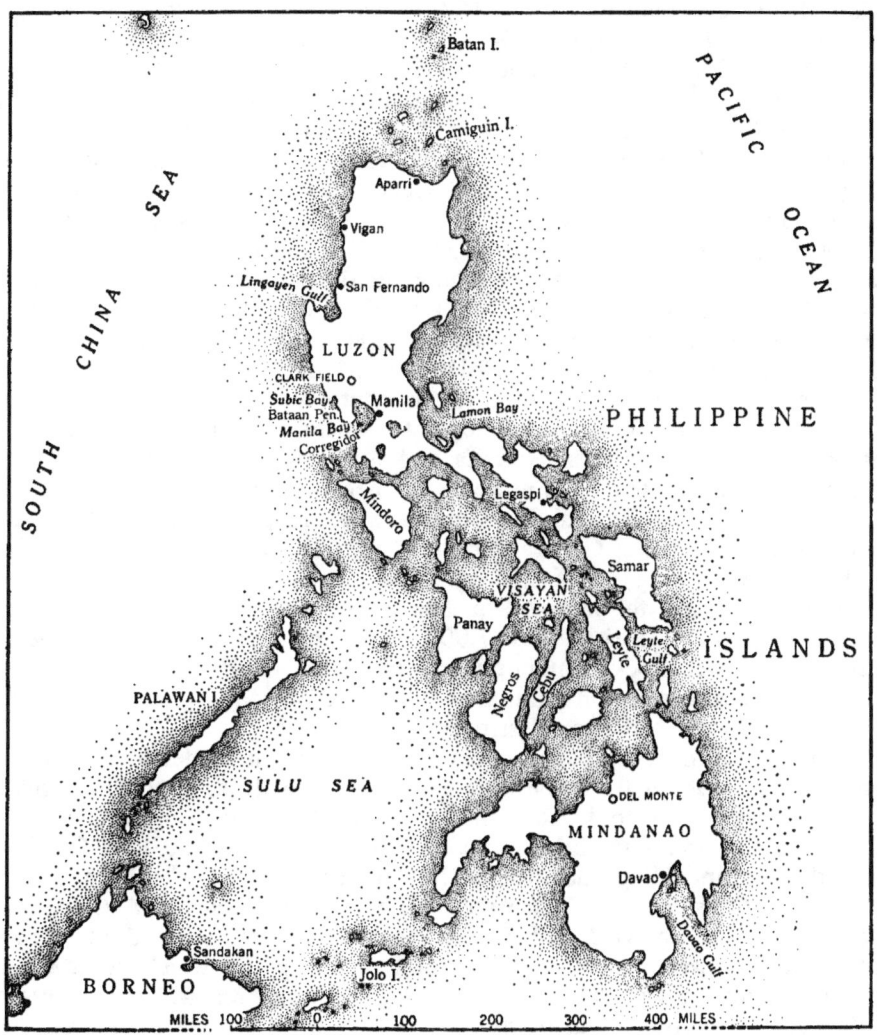

Bataan, there was a period of intensified air attack when air reinforcements reached Homma, then, with the beginning of April, there came a temporary respite for the island garrisons as the Japanese moved into Bataan. From the 9th onwards, however, Homma was free to throw all his weight against the islands, with guns sited on both sides of the bay.

The shelling never really stopped. With over one hundred pieces ranging in size from 75-mm guns to the giant 240-mm howitzers, the Japanese were able to fire almost steadily. They destroyed gun emplacements, shelters, beach defenses, buildings—almost everything on the surface—at a rate that made repair or replacement impossible.[2]

At the beginning of May the Japanese guns and aircraft let loose their final fury. On the 4th some 16,000 shells fell on Corregidor from Bataan. The defenders (11,000-12,000 effectives after the Bataan surrender) had suffered 600 casualties since 9th April, and were shocked and weak; most of their coastal guns were destroyed. But on 5th May they sustained "the most terrific pounding" they had yet received. "There was a steady roar from Bataan and a mightier volume on Corregidor." That night Japanese troops landed on Corregidor. Though they fell into confusion during their approach and were met with stout resistance at some points, Wainwright decided on the morning of the 6th that further resistance would result in a wholesale slaughter of his men, particularly 1,000 who were lying wounded and helpless. He sent a message to President Roosevelt that he was going to meet the Japanese commander to arrange for the surrender of the fortified islands in Manila Bay.

This proposal left the position in the south unresolved. There, beyond small landings and the establishment of a fairly static garrison at Davao, in Mindanao, in December, Homma had not been able to make any move. On the morning of the 10th, however, he began a series of landings with a force under Major-General Kiyotake Kawaguchi playing a leading part. By 9th May Brigadier-General Bradford G. Chynoweth's forces on Cebu (about 6,500 strong) were scattered and Chynoweth himself was in the mountains hoping to organise further resistance from there; on Panay Colonel Albert F. Christie with 7,000 men had fallen back in an orderly fashion into well-stocked mountain retreats from which he was preparing to wage guerilla war; on Mindanao the bulk of Major-General William F. Sharp's forces had been destroyed.

Wainwright made desperate efforts to avoid the surrender of the troops in the south. About the same time as he first broadcast a surrender offer from Corregidor he told Sharp that he was releasing to the latter's command all the forces in the Philippines except those on the four fortified islands in Manila Bay and ordered him to report at once to MacArthur. Almost at the same time Sharp received a message from MacArthur himself (sent in the knowledge of the Corregidor surrender but without knowledge of Wainwright's action in relation to Sharp) in which MacArthur assumed command of the Visayan-Mindanao Force. But when, in the late afternoon of the 6th, Wainwright was taken to meet Homma, the Japanese refused to treat with him except as the overall commander in the Philippines and sent him back to Corregidor to think the matter over. Late that night Wainwright told the local Japanese commander that he would surrender all the forces in the Philippines within four days. This decision inevitably led to great confusion in the south. Sharp, bewildered as to

---

[2] Morton, p. 538.

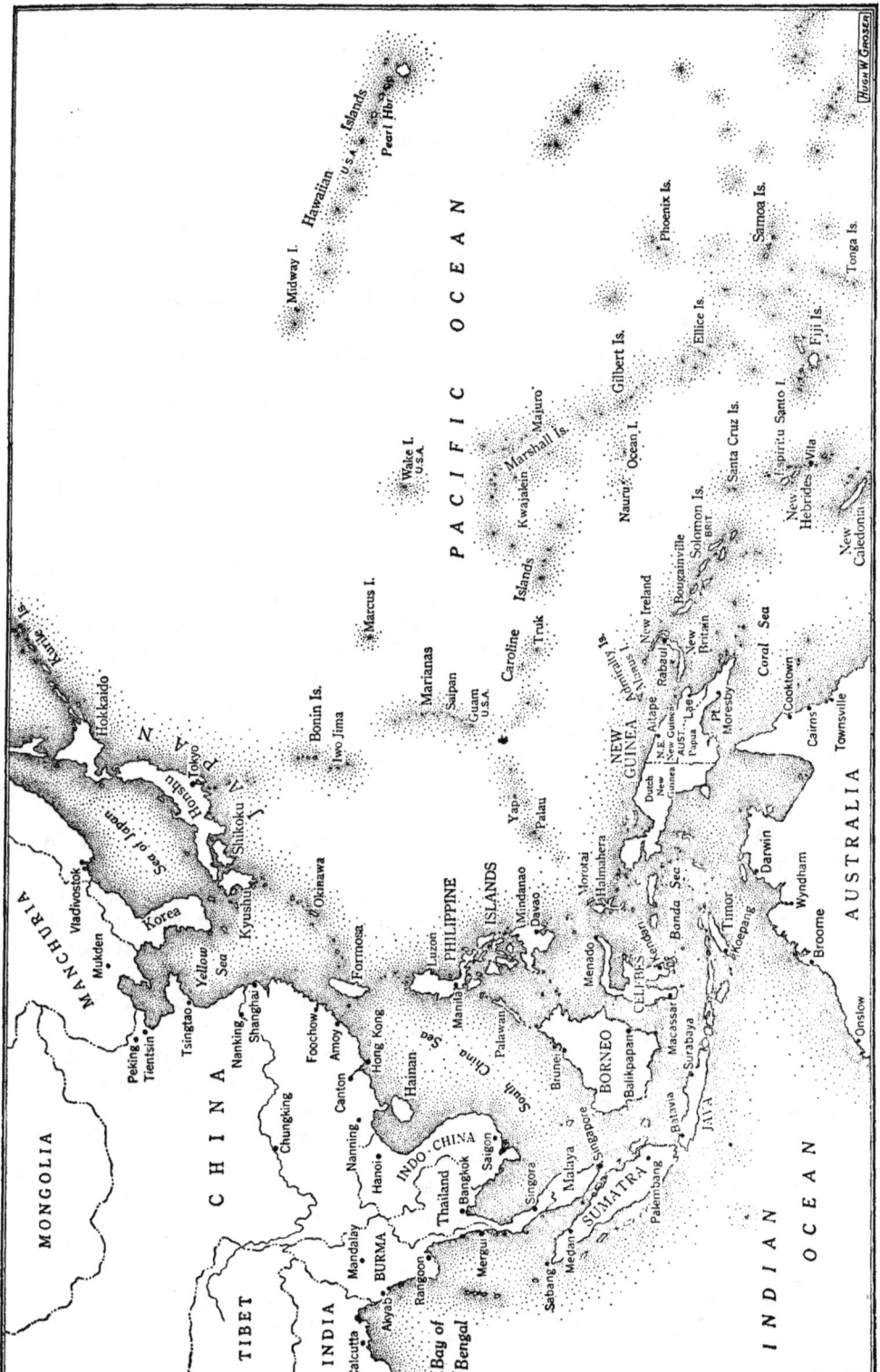

The Eastern Theatre

where his duty lay, finally made his own difficult decision and directed his subordinates to capitulate. Chynoweth was reluctant to do so and Christie, who was in a particularly strong position, bluntly questioned Sharp's authority to issue a surrender order and asserted that he did not see

"even one small reason" why he should surrender his force, because "some other unit has gone to hell or some Corregidor shell-shocked terms" had been made.³

In the final event, however, the general surrender became effective, though the wide dispersal of all the defending forces throughout the islands delayed the process.

Although the reduction of the Philippines and the defeat of the American-Filipino army of 140,000 men, took far longer than the Japanese had planned, they did not allow the delay to hold up unduly their plans for a southward advance. Their main movement had swept round the archipelago and, by the time Wainwright surrendered, they were firmly established in New Guinea and at other points in the South-West Pacific adjacent to Australia.

Australia's main interest in the Pacific war was to be directed towards Papua and New Guinea in which, apart from their strategic importance, she had a direct interest through her responsibility for their government, but there were other Pacific islands to which she also had a responsibility, or which were of such significance in her planning that she was forced to interest herself in them.

Of these New Caledonia had seemed in 1941 and early 1942 to be one of the most important. The 2/3rd Australian Independent Company (21 officers and 312 men), which had been sent there in December, was powerfully reinforced on 12th March with the arrival of the major part of an American task force, commanded by Major-General Alexander M. Patch, consisting of two infantry regiments, a regiment of artillery, a battalion of light tanks, an anti-aircraft regiment, a battalion of coast artillery and a squadron of fighter aircraft. (Later, when the South-West Pacific Area was defined, New Caledonia was not included in it and the responsibility for its defence shifted entirely to America and New Zealand.)

Still farther out in the Pacific, about 2,200 miles north-east of Sydney and some 200 miles apart, lay Ocean Island and Nauru, both rich in phosphate deposits. Late in February Australian field artillery detachments which had been stationed there in 1941 were withdrawn in the Free French destroyer *Le Triomphant,* which made a quick dash first to Nauru and then to Ocean Island, took off those who were to leave and trans-shipped them to the Phosphate Commission ship *Trienza* which was standing by in the New Hebrides. The *Trienza* then cleared for Brisbane.

Small parties of Europeans remained on both islands—six on Ocean Island, seven on Nauru. The Administrator of Nauru, Colonel Chalmers,⁴

---

³ Morton, p. 579.
⁴ Lt-Col F. R. Chalmers, CMG, DSO. (South African War: Tpr 1st Tasmanian Contingent, Lt 4th Contingent.) (1st AIF: CO 27 Bn 1917-18.) Administrator of Nauru 1938-43. Of St. Helens, Tas; b. Hobart, 4 Jan 1881. Executed by Japanese 26 Mar 1943.

did not leave. He had served in the South African War, and in the 1914-18 War with the 27th Battalion which he commanded from October 1917 onwards. In a letter which he sent out by *Le Triomphant* to his Minister he wrote: "We will do our best here whatever may happen." Although his whole Administration staff volunteered to remain he kept with him only Dr B. H. Quin (Medical Officer), W. Shugg (Medical Assistant) and two volunteers from the Phosphate Commissioners' staff—F. F. Harmer and W. H. Doyle. Fathers Kayser and Clivaz, missionaries, also remained.[5]

South and south-west of Nauru and Ocean Island are the New Hebrides (under joint British and French control) and the Solomon Islands (a British Protectorate) where detachments of the 1st Independent Company had been stationed during 1941 to protect aerodromes and seaplane-alighting bases and to man observation posts; a secondary task was to train local inhabitants including natives to undertake these duties. In January 1942 the line manned by these detachments and the rest of the Independent Company ran in a north-westerly direction from Vila (New Hebrides), through Tulagi and Buka (Solomons), Namatanai and Kavieng (New Ireland) to Manus Island in the Admiralty Group. Thus, with the garrison at Rabaul, the 1st Independent Company constituted the Australian "advanced observation line".

After the war with Japan had begun the men of this company found themselves working closely with the well-planned naval coastwatching network in the islands—an organisation whose task in time of war was to report to the Navy Office instantly any unusual or suspicious happenings, such as sightings of strange ships or aircraft, floating mines, and other matters of defence interest. Among the coastwatchers were included District Officers, Patrol Officers, other officials, and planters, of the Territories of Papua and New Guinea and the British Solomon Islands.

Throughout these areas the occupation of Rabaul on 23rd January was the pivot on which the whole Japanese movement swung. The invaders had made air reconnaissance of the islands of practically the whole Territory of New Guinea—and much of the protectorate—beforehand. On the 21st they bombed Kavieng in New Ireland, Lorengau in the Admiralties, and Madang, Lae, Salamaua and Bulolo on the New Guinea mainland. On the same day that they landed at Rabaul they occupied Kavieng, and their aircraft raided the Trobriand Islands, off the south-eastern tip of the New Guinea mainland. On 3rd February they first raided Port Moresby from the air.

Bougainville Island in the northern Solomons, New Ireland, New Britain, the Admiralty Islands, and the eastern half of the mainland of New Guinea, with their many hundreds of adjacent small islands, were Australian territory. The south-eastern part of the New Guinea mainland and the

---

[5] The Japanese occupied Nauru and Ocean Island on 26th August 1942. They brutally ill-treated the native populations and massacred some. On Ocean they murdered the six Europeans. Of the Nauru party they murdered Chalmers, Quin, Shugg, Harmer and Doyle in March 1943. Kayser and Clivaz were taken to Truk with some of the natives. Kayser died of his privations; Clivaz survived.

smaller islands off its coast formed the Territory of Papua. In 1884 Great Britain proclaimed a Protectorate over this area, and it became Australian territory in 1906. In the first weeks of the 1914-18 War an Australian military force had taken from the Germans the northern part of the eastern half of the New Guinea mainland, New Britain and the arc of islands running from the Admiralties to Bougainville. At the Peace Conference Mr Hughes had demanded possession of these island "ramparts" for Australia to keep them from "the hands of an actual or potential enemy". Australia was given a Mandate over them in 1920, and in 1921 a civil administration was established.

Papua included some 91,000 square miles of country, the Mandated Territory 93,000, lying completely within the tropics with the characteristic high tropical rainfall and hot-moist climate, though conditions in the high valleys and plateaus of the hinterland may be cool and bracing and the highest mountain areas are bitterly cold. The mainland is dominated by towering and broken mountains, the lower and middle slopes of which are covered densely with rain forests, the higher blanketed with moss. The backbone of the mountain system is the great central spine which runs in a general east-west direction and rises to 15,400 feet. A few of the islands are atolls but most are of the "high" type and share the mainland features—mountains, dense vegetation and rushing river systems.

In 1939 the European population of these Territories, living almost entirely on the coastal fringes, was about 1,500 in Papua and 4,500 in the Mandated Territory, their respective centres being Port Moresby and Rabaul. The native population was probably in the vicinity of 1,800,000 —mostly primitive tribesmen, separated by a multiplicity of languages, cultures and social organisations; inter-tribal fighting was the rule among them and ceased only as European influence spread.

When the war came the local administrations in the two Territories, though separate, were similar in form. There were nine magisterial divisions in Papua, each under a Resident Magistrate with a small staff of Assistant Resident Magistrates and Patrol Officers to assist him. In the Mandated Territory there were seven Districts each under a District Officer assisted by Assistant District Officers and Patrol Officers. Although the local officials exercised both administrative and judicial powers over all individuals and activities within their districts, their most important and extensive duties related to natives and the development of areas of European control. Each Territory maintained a native police force officered by Europeans.

Thus far the comparatively short period of Australian administration in both Papua and New Guinea, the tremendous physical difficulties of the country, and the comparative slenderness of the Australian resources had combined to prevent the whole area from being brought under effective control. By 1939, for example, less than half the Mandated Territory was officially classified as "under control", about 18,000 square miles were considered to be "under influence" in greater or less degree, and some 5,500 of the remaining 36,000 square miles were classed as having been "penetrated by patrols". But exploration and the spread of influence was being persistently carried out by hardy officers who had built up a fine record of peaceful penetration:

> The patrols showed great restraint—the orders were rigid—in the face of frequent native hostility. Not a few officers and police were killed in open fights and ambush. Drawing-room pioneers understress the natural savagery of the New Guinea scene. The relatively peaceful spread of white influences over both areas was a remarkable achievement.[6]

Economic development was substantially limited to copra and rubber production in Papua, copra production in New Guinea and mining in both Territories—with the greatest mining development on the goldfields of the Bulolo Valley in New Guinea. There were more than 500 coconut plantations in New Guinea which produced 76,000 tons of copra for export in the peak year 1936-37. That year Papua exported 13,600 tons. In its best years the Papuan rubber industry could produce about one-eighth of Australia's requirements; in 1940-41 exports were 1,273 tons. Gold production in the two Territories between 1926 and 1941 was valued at about £22,580,000. Of this £19,000,000 was won in the Mandated Territory, most of it from the Bulolo Valley fields, which were almost completely dependent for service and maintenance upon aircraft, the use of which had been developed to a degree probably unparalleled in comparable circumstances elsewhere in the world.

For unskilled labour, economic enterprises of all kinds relied almost completely upon the natives. Although there was a small body of casual labour working under verbal agreements most natives worked as indentured labourers under voluntary contracts of service (usually for three-year periods in New Guinea; 18 months to 2 years in Papua) which defined the conditions of their work and depended upon penal sanctions for their enforcement. In 1940 there were about 50,000 indentured labourers at work in both Territories—under a system, incidentally, which, it was becoming increasingly clear, would have to be superseded by a free labour system, despite the fact that

> the protective legislation was of good model and by far the most important and well-policed body of civil law in the territories. Working under indenture was agreeable to the natives and had become of some positive social and economic importance to them. An increasing volume of labour offered itself without direct compulsion.[7]

There was little real general Australian interest in Papua and New Guinea before the war; little general appreciation of the fact that Australia was the major colonial power of the South-West Pacific; and virtually no military knowledge of the region and no appreciation of the tactical and logistical problems it would pose in war.

As far back as 18th March 1941, the War Cabinet had approved that women and children not engaged in any essential work in New Guinea and other Territories should be encouraged to leave unobtrusively for

---
[6] W. E. H. Stanner, *The South Seas in Transition* (1953), p. 23.
[7] Stanner, p. 46.

Australia. In November it was decided that further encouragement should be given to these people to leave, with a strong warning that it might not be possible to make any special arrangements in the event of war. On 11th December, the War Cabinet endorsed a decision of three days before that there should not yet be any compulsory evacuation of women and children from Papua and New Guinea. Next day they reversed this decision, and by 29th December about 600 women and children had left the islands and it was considered that the evacuation had been substantially completed. None the less a number of women (other than missionaries and nurses to whom the orders did not apply) still remained. As for the civil male population, a proportion was, for some time after the occupation of Rabaul, to constitute something in the nature of a leaderless and difficult legion although many civilians, both from inside and outside the Administration, were to render heroic service and those who were fit and eligible were gradually called up, or voluntarily enlisted, in various branches of the three Services.

On 8th December 1941 Brigadier Morris who commanded the 8th Military District (i.e. all troops in Papua and New Guinea) had been authorised to call up for full-time duty the New Guinea Volunteer Rifles (N.G.V.R.), a force manned by some of the local European inhabitants of the Mandated Territory. On 25th January, two days after the fall of Rabaul, the War Cabinet decided that all able-bodied white male British subjects between the ages of 18 and 45 should be called up immediately for service. But by this time civil control throughout the Mandated Territory had been disrupted and the Administrator, Sir Walter McNicoll, was on his way to Australia.

By this time also a difficult situation was developing in Port Moresby between the Administrator of Papua (Mr Leonard Murray[8]) and the army commander. Murray had been in the Papuan Administration for more than 30 years and was a nephew of the distinguished former Lieutenant-Governor of Papua, Sir Hubert Murray, who had built most carefully between 1908 and 1940 the form and tradition of the Papuan Service which his successor was now understandably reluctant to see submerged beneath the weight of a military administration. Morris was a regular soldier who had been in the Middle East in charge of the Australian Overseas Base before his appointment in May 1941 to command the 8th Military District. A gunner by training he was an unassuming and courteous man with a strong sense of duty and much sound common sense. He recognised bluntly the military necessities of the circumstances which had now developed.

The situation which arose between Morris and Murray was best exemplified by the difficulties which manifested themselves late in January over the calling up for military service of the local white residents. When, on 27th January, Morris issued the call-up notices to men in the 18 to 45

---

[8] Hon H. L. Murray, CBE. Private and Official Secretary to the Lt-Gov of Papua 1916-40; Administrator of Papua 1940-42; attached Allied Geographical Section GHQ SWPA 1942-45. B. Sydney, 13 Dec 1886.

years age group his action inevitably caused the closing of the commercial houses and, just as inevitably, signified the actual if not the legal end of the civil administration and the substitution of the military commander as the supreme authority in Papua. The difficulties of divided control became accentuated and the processes of civil administration rapidly became more and more confused, particularly after Japanese air raids on Port Moresby on 3rd and 5th February which caused panic among the natives. After the second attack the civil administration was unable to maintain order in the town. On the 6th the Administrator was told that the War Cabinet had approved the temporary cessation of civil government in Papua. This decision was gazetted in Canberra on the 12th. The Administrator published a *Gazette Extraordinary* on the 14th stating that civil government had ceased at noon that day; he left for Australia on the 15th and, that day, Morris issued an order by which he assumed all government power.

Many of the functions of civil administration had to be maintained and it was necessary particularly to preserve, as far as possible, control of native labour. The authority of both the Government and the private employers had already broken down, or was fast doing so, in many areas, so that conditions of anarchy quickly developed among the natives of those areas. It was also most desirable that the Territories' production of copra and rubber should continue to the greatest possible extent. Early in March Morris posted most of the officers of both civil administrations, and many other men experienced in the Territories, to two new units—the Papuan Administrative Unit and the New Guinea Administrative Unit. Lieutenant Elliott-Smith[9]—formerly Assistant Resident Magistrate at Samarai who had been called to Port Moresby late in January to work on Morris' staff as a link between the military and civil authorities—organised the Papuan, and Captain Townsend,[1] formerly a senior District Officer in the New Guinea Administration, the New Guinea Administrative Unit. The two units were merged on 21st March and became the Australian New Guinea Administrative Unit—Angau—to function as a military administrative unit for both Territories. At that time Angau was divided into a headquarters and two branches: District Services—to police the Territories and maintain law and order, regard the welfare of the native people, and to provide and control native labour; Production Services—to provide the food required by the natives, transport for the men of the District Services and those working the plantations, and technical direction for production.

The other forces which Morris commanded consisted in the main of the 30th Brigade Group. In February 1941 the Australian Chiefs of Staff had directed attention to the possibilities of a Japanese advance by way of New Guinea. Out of that had come a decision to send the 49th (Queens-

---

[9] Lt-Col S. Elliott-Smith, PX134; Angau; CO 1 Papuan Inf Bn 1944-46. Resident magistrate; of Samarai, Papua; b. Ulverstone, Tas, 10 Aug 1900.

[1] Lt-Col G. W. L. Townsend, OBE, VX117176. (1st AIF: Lt 3 Army Bde AFA.) Angau and FELO. District officer; b. Sandgate, Qld, 5 Apr 1896.

land) Battalion to Port Moresby, where one of its companies had been since July. This battalion had been formed as a result of the division of the 9th/49th Battalion into its two original components; each battalion then completed its establishment with volunteers for islands' service. But the 49th contained a great many very young soldiers and, until well into 1942, was considered to be neither well-trained nor well-disciplined. At the time of the main party's arrival in March 1941, the Port Moresby defence plans centred on the Paga Coastal Defence Battery of two 6-inch guns. The defence of these guns was the basic task of the 1,200 men of the garrison. After the warning on 8th December by the Australian Chiefs of Staff that the Japanese would soon attempt to occupy Rabaul and Port Moresby, General Sturdee's assessment that the minimum strength required at each of these two places was one brigade group, and a decision that Port Moresby (and Darwin) must be considered second only to the vital Australian east coast areas, efforts were made to reinforce these outposts. The 39th and 53rd Battalions, and other units of the 30th Brigade, arrived at Port Moresby on 3rd January. But these reinforcements were also very raw and very young. (One calculation later placed their average age, excluding officers, at about 18½.[2])

The 39th Battalion was a Victorian unit which had been formed in September 1941 from elements of the 2nd Cavalry and the 3rd and 4th (Infantry) Divisions; some units had sent good men to the new battalion, but others had taken the opportunity to "unload" unwanted officers and men. The commander, Lieut-Colonel Conran,[3] who had served in the 1914-18 War, had tried to ensure that each of his companies would be commanded by an old soldier who would also have another veteran as his second-in-command. He had been vigorous in training. In November a spontaneous and widespread move by men in the battalion to enlist in the A.I.F. had been frustrated because recruits for that force were not then being accepted.

The 53rd Battalion, however, had had rather a different history. Up to November 1941 it had been part of the composite 55th/53rd (New South Wales) Battalion, but was then given separate identity, "specially enlisted for tropical service", and marked for movement to Darwin. In developing its separate form, however, it was made up from detachments from many units in New South Wales and (as often happened in such cases) was given many unwanted men from those units. At the time of its formation most of the men had had three months' militia training though about 200 of them had been called up as late as 1st October. As its embarkation date approached towards the end of December many of its members were illegally absent, bitter because they had been given no Christmas leave, so that, just before it sailed, its ranks were hastily filled with an assortment of rather astonished and unwilling individuals gathered from widely varied sources. Consequently it was a badly trained, ill-

---

[2] Report of Barry Commission on Cessation of Papuan Civil Administration in 1942.
[3] Col H. M. Conran, ED, V50227. (1st AIF: Lt 23 Bn.) CO 39 Bn 1941 to May 1942; OC of Troop trains 1943-45. Horticulturalist; of Red Cliffs, Vic; b. S.S. *Gallia*, Irish Sea, 9 Jul 1889.

disciplined and generally resentful collection of men who landed at Port Moresby on 3rd January as the 53rd Battalion.

These three inexperienced and ill-equipped battalions—39th, 49th and 53rd—had the 13th Field Regiment and the 23rd Heavy Anti-Aircraft Battery to support them. (The original establishment of the anti-aircraft battery was increased by the diversion to Port Moresby of additional anti-aircraft guns which had been destined for Rabaul so that, by March, it was organised on the basis of a fixed station of four 3.7-inch guns at Tuaguba Hill and three mobile 3-inch gun stations whose positions were changed frequently.)

Morris also had two units of local origin which spread wide as a reconnaissance screen. The first was the Papuan Infantry Battalion (P.I.B.), consisting of Papuan natives, led by Australian officers and a number of Australian N.C.O's. The nucleus of this battalion had been formed as one company in June 1940, through the efforts of Major Logan,[4] a Papuan police officer, who became its first commanding officer. Soon after Japan came into the war Logan was succeeded by Major Watson,[5] a bluff outspoken man, quick in thought and speech, who had been with the P.I.B. since its formation. He had served as a young artillery officer in the old A.I.F. and had won a reputation for great personal courage. He was one of the old hands in New Guinea, had "made his pile" in the gold rush days and was disappointed that only a few of his junior leaders were New Guinea identities. Most of them had been brought in from various units serving in the Moresby area—notably from the 49th Battalion—as the second and third companies were formed during 1941. Since the value of this unit was seen to lie chiefly in its knowledge of local conditions, and its main role would be scouting and reconnaissance in which the bushcraft of the natives could be used to the fullest extent, the disadvantages of having officers and N.C.O's who were not experienced in the country were obvious. Morris, however, soon had the Papuans operating in the role for which they had been enlisted and, by February, Lieutenant Jesser[6] and his platoon were patrolling the Papuan north coast from Buna to the Waria River, while other platoons were screening lines of possible approach closer to Port Moresby.

The second local unit was the New Guinea Volunteer Rifles. So scrupulous had the Australian Government been in observing its undertakings to the League of Nations that, until the beginning of war in 1939, it had refrained from making any defence preparations whatever in the Mandated Territory. Shortly before that, however, returned soldiers took a vigorous lead in demanding that at least some effort should be made to arm and train those residents who wished to be better prepared to defend themselves and their homes. Colonel J. Walstab, the Chief of Police, was

---

[4] Maj L. Logan, P3. (1st AIF: Lt 1st Div Train.) CO 1 PIB 1940-42. Government official; of Port Moresby, Papua; b. Maidstone, Kent, England, 7 Feb 1892.

[5] Maj W. T. Watson, DSO, MC, DCM, NX144850. (1st AIF: AN&MEF; Lt 6 Bty 2 AFA Bde.) CO 1 PIB 1942-44. Gold miner; of Columbiano, Ohio, USA; b. Nelson, NZ, 10 Nov 1887.

[6] Maj H. J. Jesser, MC, QX53205; 1 PIB. Railway employee; of Brisbane; b. Rockhampton, Qld, 11 Apr 1917.

one of the leaders of this movement and, largely because of his efforts, it was finally decided to form a militia-type battalion in New Guinea.

Army Headquarters issued the necessary authority on 4th September 1939 for the raising of what was to become known as the N.G.V.R. But the members were to be volunteers, who would be unpaid until they were mobilised, and warlike stores would not be issued to them direct as to an army unit but through the Administration police force. Nor was their strength to be more than about half the normal strength of a battalion although the original limit of 20 officers and 400 other ranks was raised to 23 and 482 by June 1940. These numbers were to provide for a headquarters, headquarters wing, machine-gun section and one rifle company (less two platoons) at Rabaul; a rifle and a machine-gun company at Wau; one rifle company each at Salamaua and Lae; machine-gun sections at Kokopo (near Rabaul), Kavieng and Madang.

The early days of the battalion were marked by vigour and enthusiasm with the old soldiers taking a leading part. Two regular instructors were sent from Australia and travelled from centre to centre introducing modern training methods. By mid-1941, however, the battalion had lost much of its zest. Many of the youngest and most ardent members had gone away to the war. Particularly on the goldfields, those who remained were finding the difficulties of getting from their scattered and often remote homes to the training centres increasingly irksome, and were disappointed at the seeming scarcity of stores and ammunition for training.

In September, Captain Edwards,[7] who had been one of the most enthusiastic of the mainland volunteers since the creation of the battalion, was promoted to command the unit and set up his headquarters at Bulolo. He was already on full-time duty and so could concentrate on his unusual task which required him to be adjutant as well as commander. To help him Warrant-Officer Umphelby,[8] one of the regular instructors, was promoted lieutenant and made quartermaster. Several of the men (notably Sergeant Emery[9] and Rifleman Vernon[1]) were available full time. By December Edwards' mainland strength was 170 to 180. Although immediately after Japan entered the war Morris was authorised to place the battalion on full-time duty only a comparatively small group was then called up and it was not until 21st January that the battalion was actually mobilised.

At the beginning of January the air force based on Port Moresby had only two squadrons of flying-boats, with a protective reconnaissance role. At the end of the month there were only 6 Hudsons, 4 Wirraways and 2 Catalinas there and General Wavell would not, either then or in mid-February, consent to divert American Kittyhawk fighters (P-40s) then

---

[7] Col W. M. Edwards, CMG, MBE, NGX455. (1st AIF: 13 Bn; Capt British Army.) CO NGVR 1941-44; Comd Pacific Islands Regt 1944-45. Labour superintendent; of Lae, TNG; b. Enmore, NSW, 27 Feb 1896.
[8] Maj D. H. Umphelby, VX114300. NGVR and various Base Sub-Area appts. Regular soldier; of Toorak, Vic; b. Toorak, Vic, 10 Oct 1905.
[9] Lt R. E. Emery, MM, NG2001. NGVR and Angau. Planter; of Madang, TNG, and Campbelltown, SA; b. Kapunda, SA, 19 Nov 1908.
[1] Rfn R. E. Vernon, NG2003; NGVR. Prospector; of Black Cat Creek, TNG; and Brisbane; b. Brisbane, 20 Nov 1909. Killed in action 19 Jul 1942.

available in Australia and destined for ABDA Command. At this same time the naval organisation in Papua-New Guinea consisted of shore installations only. In the wider naval plan it seemed unlikely that a sufficiently powerful naval force could be concentrated off the east coast of Australia to prevent a Japanese move against Port Moresby.

Fortunately for the Australians there came a pause in events between late January and early March while the Japanese organised their next major moves forward. In New Guinea the obvious immediate objectives were the four most important European centres along the mainland coast —Wewak, Madang, Lae and Salamaua. In all of these the bombing of the three last-named on 21st January set off a series of extraordinary events.

Wewak was the administrative centre of the Sepik District (the largest of the New Guinea Administration districts) which stretched from the Dutch border eastward along more than one-third of the Mandated Territory coastline and south as far as the Papuan border. It took its name from the Sepik River which flowed through its centre from Dutch New Guinea to the sea between Madang and Wewak. Between the coast and the river the country was made forbidding by the rugged Bewani and Torricelli Mountains. South of the river lay the almost unknown heart of New Guinea, shut in by the Central and Muller Ranges running from east to west, heaving their broken heights to 13,000 feet and more, enclosing the Papua-New Guinea border between them. But it was the river itself which gave the district its distinctive character. In its course of some 700 miles it spread into seemingly limitless swamps, flowed deeply through a main channel a quarter of a mile or more wide in places, and bore with it masses of debris and floating islands of tangled grass and scrub. Crocodiles infested it, and hordes of mosquitoes bred there. The sago-eating people who lived along the river were of smouldering temperament and oppressed with witchcraft and superstitious fears. Traditionally they were head-hunters. In the big houses which were the ceremonial centres of each village, they hung by the hair long rows of heads, each head dried and smoked and with the features modelled in painted clay.

District Officer Jones[2] was in charge of the Sepik District. He had been an original Anzac at 19 years of age, and had gone to New Guinea soon after his return from the 1914-18 War. He was a big man with a ruddy complexion and an unhurried manner. At the beginning of January he had worked out an escape route for the people of his district to follow if they were cut off by sea and air: by way of the Sepik, the Karawari (a tributary of the Sepik), overland to the Strickland River and on to Daru on the south coast of Papua. In determining this route he heeded the advice of J. H. Thurston, who had been one of the pioneers of the Morobe goldfields and later pioneered the fields near Wewak, and Assistant District Officer Taylor,[3] who had already, on a great patrol, covered much of the country through which the proposed route passed.

[2] Lt-Col J. H. Jones, PX128. (1st AIF: Sgt 2 Fd Amb.) Angau. District officer; of Sepik River District; b. Liverpool, Eng, 7 May 1895.
[3] Maj J. L. Taylor, PX68; Angau. Assistant District Officer; b. Sydney, 25 Jan 1904.

After the news of the bombings of 21st January most of the 30 or 40 private European people in the district gathered in the camps which Jones was preparing and stocking on the Karawari and there awaited further instructions about evacuation. By mid-February, however, they were restless and began to leave the Karawari for Angoram, the Administration post on the Sepik, about 60 miles from the river mouth. Most believed the overland trip which Jones had planned for them to be impossible. About this time some hopes developed that it might be possible for them to be flown out to safety, but these were disappointed. On the 19th Jones ordered Rifleman Macgregor[4] (of the N.G.V.R. Madang detachment), a pre-war Sepik recruiter and trader who had been using his two schooners on the river on evacuation tasks, to take the Administration launch *Thetis* and four schooners out to Madang. This Macgregor did, accompanied by four other Australians (to supplement the boats' non-Australian crews). They reached Madang safely and, under orders from Sergeant Russell[5] who was in charge of the N.G.V.R. there, worked bravely from that point, either crossing to New Britain to assist survivors from Rabaul or building up stores along the route to the Ramu and assisting parties into that area. Jones meanwhile had sent word to Angoram that he proposed remaining at Wewak with some of his staff and that the rest of the Administration staff would remain on duty in the district.

At this time the behaviour of the Assistant District Officer at Angoram began to disturb Jones and, on 10th March, he told Taylor to take over. The Angoram officer's mind had, however, become unhinged. He refused to leave his station, and armed and entrenched about 40 of his native police; on the 20th he fought a pitched battle for more than two hours with Taylor and the party with him, shot Taylor and drove him and the rest of the Europeans away from the station.

Next day Jones arrived on the river. He then planned to attack the station with the help of seven other Europeans and seven natives. On the 23rd they closed in on the station. But the Assistant District Officer there had shot himself dead and his police had fled. Jones then left Assistant District Officer Bates[6] in charge at Angoram and departed for Wewak on the 24th.

Scarcely had Jones gone than Bates had word that some of the rebel police had killed Patrol Officer R. Strudwick on his way down from the Karawari to Angoram. Later rebel police also killed three European miners, two Chinese and many natives, ravaged a wide area, fomented local uprisings at some points and caused serious disorders among the natives generally before they themselves were finally killed or apprehended.

Meanwhile practically all the other European residents of the district,

---

[4] WO R. Macgregor, NG2168. (1st AIF: Pte 36 and 34 Bns.) NGVR and Angau. Recruiter and trader; of Madang, TNG; b. Parish of Cumberland, NSW, 13 Jan 1893.

[5] Lt G. Russell, NGX425. NGVR; Angau. Business manager; of Madang, TNG; b. Darlington, Eng, 6 Jun 1904.

[6] Maj C. D. Bates, MC, PX129; Angau. Assistant District Officer; of Rabaul, TNG; b. Uitenhage, South Africa, 4 Aug 1907. Died 1 Jan 1954.

except the Administration staff, had set out finally to get clear of the approaching Japanese. On his arrival on the river Jones had sent about 12 of them off in the schooner *Nereus* with instructions to land at Bogadjim and make their way overland to safety from that point. After the fight at Angoram Thurston took a party as far as they could travel by water up the May River to start overland thence for Daru through the mysterious breadth of New Guinea. At the end of April, 8 Europeans and 82 natives, they struck into the mountains on foot.[7]

Jones and his men then busied themselves with the long task of bringing the renegade police to book and restoring order among the natives who had become disaffected—and with the general task of maintaining their administration.[8]

Meanwhile, in the adjoining Madang District, the civil administration was interrupted by the bombing of Madang on 21st January. Most of the civil population of the town then gathered at a pre-arranged assembly point about two miles to the south. Next day they set out on foot along an evacuation route which had been planned previously. Within a fortnight most of them arrived at Kainantu (in the Central Highlands due south of Madang). There they remained, comfortably situated, until the fit men of military age among them were ordered to report for military service and the others went on to Mount Hagen to be flown out to Australia.

When Madang was thus evacuated Sergeant Russell assumed control of the town, but he and his few men were in a most difficult situation after the civil authority over the natives disappeared and when several more bombing raids during the ensuing weeks intensified the confusion. When District Officer Penglase[9] arrived to take charge of the district on 24th May he noted:

> Natives [had] found themselves in circumstances to which they were not accustomed. Overnight, the Government, with its benevolent policy in which they had the greatest confidence and respect, no longer functioned. Roads, gardens and villages were neglected, and some natives, hitherto residing in villages near Madang, evacuated and moved to safer locations in the bush. Vast numbers were passing through the district from Morobe and other places of employment, whilst others were travel-

---

[7] Thurston and his whole party arrived safely at Daru on 21st September.

[8] On 19th May Jones heard that the Japanese had occupied Hollandia, the capital of Dutch New Guinea. He decided to visit the area and discover the exact position for himself. On 25th May, with three NGVR men (Sergeant Russell and Riflemen J. West and A. W. Esson) who had come from Madang, and ten native police, he left Wewak in a small motor vessel. From Wutong (on the border) he sent scouts towards Hollandia. On their return these reported that the Japanese had been at Hollandia but had gone again. Jones and his party then sailed into Hollandia Harbour on the afternoon of the 28th. They set up a flagpole on the jetty and ceremonially hoisted the Australian Blue Ensign. "The local populace appeared to be impressed with this ceremony," Jones wrote later. "Our reception could not be termed cordial, in fact their general demeanour appeared sullen, but this may be a wrong impression as it is possible that our appearance was such a surprise that they were, shall we say, flabbergasted and were in doubt as to what was going to happen." The Australians then began a tour of inspection of the town while "a large crowd of Asiatics followed in our wake". A Javanese medical officer told them that the Japanese had come there on the 6th in an aircraft carrier and two destroyers and landed several officers and about 200 marines. The Japanese raided the Government stores, killed all the livestock they could find, "drank the town dry" and then went away taking with them the Dutch Controleur, his wife and child and a Dutch priest, and saying that they would be back in three weeks. The Australians hauled down their flag at 6 p.m. with the same formality with which they had raised it and sailed at 7 p.m. They narrowly escaped capture by a Japanese destroyer on their way back to Wewak.

[9] Maj N. Penglase, NGX301; Angau. District officer; of Wau, TNG; b. Echuca, Vic, 23 Jan 1902.

ling to the Markham, Finschhafen and Waria, spreading the most impossible rumours. Japanese bombs had struck fear into their very hearts and they were bewildered and apprehensive about the future. In addition the town had been looted, plantations were deserted and practically every unprotected home had been ransacked. In this connection it can be said that the natives were not only responsible. The District Office had been demolished, all records destroyed and the safe blown open and robbed of its entire contents of value. Missionaries, however, had remained at their respective stations and were exercising their influence in an endeavour to maintain control of the natives, and members of the New Guinea Volunteer Rifles also did good work in this respect. . . . The only [Administration] officers remaining in the District on the 24th May were Lieutenant J. R. Black[10] at Bogia, who had not received any instructions and decided to remain at his post, and Lieutenant R. H. Boyan who was actively engaged assisting in the evacuation of troops from New Britain.

During this January-May period events in Lae and Salamaua moved more swiftly than elsewhere in the Mandated Territory. The Japanese needed Lae to build into a forward air base and they needed Salamaua to make Lae secure. The two towns were the air and sea points of entry into the forbidding country of the great goldfields area of New Guinea.

The inland town of Wau was the centre of that area. Primitive tracks converged on it from the mouth of the Lakekamu River on the southern coast of Papua and from Salamaua and Lae on the north-east coast. But the country through which these tracks passed was an upheaved mass of twisted mountains, rising and sprawling seven and eight thousand feet above the level of the sea, the peaks cloud-covered, mists swirling away from the slopes and summits as the sun rose. Lonely winds blew among the trees which spread like a tumultuous ocean of green as far as the eye could reach. There was the noise of many waters falling or hurrying through deep ravines. The mountains were the homes of wild tribes.

On the southern coast the Lakekamu River mouth was 150 miles north-west of Port Moresby, 12 to 15 days' journey by land, up to 24 hours' by small lugger or schooner. Bulldog was 50 miles up river, slightly east of north from the mouth. Then over broken ridges and mountain crests and slopes, a difficult way wound generally still northward to Kudjeru, 35 miles as the crow flies, but up to a week of exhausting climbing and walking.[1] From Kudjeru to Wau by way of Kaisenik was two days' fairly comfortable walking. This was the only feasible overland route from Port Moresby to Wau. But the general area through which it passed from Bulldog to Kudjeru was the sinister "Baum country", scarcely known,

---

[10] Lt-Col J. R. Black, PX130. Angau and BBCAU. Assistant District Officer; of Bogia, TNG, and Mount Compass, SA; b. Adelaide, 12 May 1908.

[1] The mountains in New Guinea were so rough and the tracks so primitive that the only practicable way generally of indicating distance was through "walking time". This would, of course, vary greatly according to the capacity and condition of the walker and the load he carried. In pre-war New Guinea, however, it was rare for a European to carry anything except perhaps a stick and a firearm when he travelled in the bush. Where walking times are referred to throughout this narrative, therefore, they are (unless it is otherwise stated) intended to indicate the times which would be taken by an unburdened European, used to walking in the mountains and travelling at what would be regarded by pre-war residents as an average rate. Heavily burdened soldiers, not used to the New Guinea mountains, might normally take about three times as long to cover the same distances. When moving tactically through areas where enemies were present, or sick or exhausted by operations, bad food or lack of food they would probably take much longer again.

and what knowledge there was of it had been gained from events which marked well its own savage nature and that of the people who lived there.

Hellmuth Baum was a German who refused to surrender when the Australians first seized New Guinea. He disappeared into the mountains where he wandered barefoot for years among the natives, learned their ways and languages and prospected for gold. He reported himself when the war ended and then continued his wanderings and prospecting. He was a gentle and just man. In 1931 Kukukuku natives, welcome in his camp at the headwaters of the Indiwi River (a tributary of the Lakekamu), treacherously killed him. One struck him a terrible blow on the head with a stone club. They cut off his head with one of his own axes and then disembowelled him and sang over the remains. Quite methodically they began clubbing his carriers to death. They killed seven of these but a number escaped. When the District Officer (Eric Feldt—who later directed the coastwatchers after the Japanese invasion began) received this news, he took a patrol towards the scene of the murders but the country largely defeated him. Penglase, then an Assistant District Officer, led a series of remarkable patrols into the area during the year October 1931-October 1932 to try to arrest the murderers and find practicable routes through the baffling country. His patrols were attacked by the natives and suffered hardships among the rugged and inhospitable mountains but, as a result of these trips, Kudjeru was established as a "jumping-off" point from the Wau side and the line of a primitive route between Kudjeru and Bulldog was established.

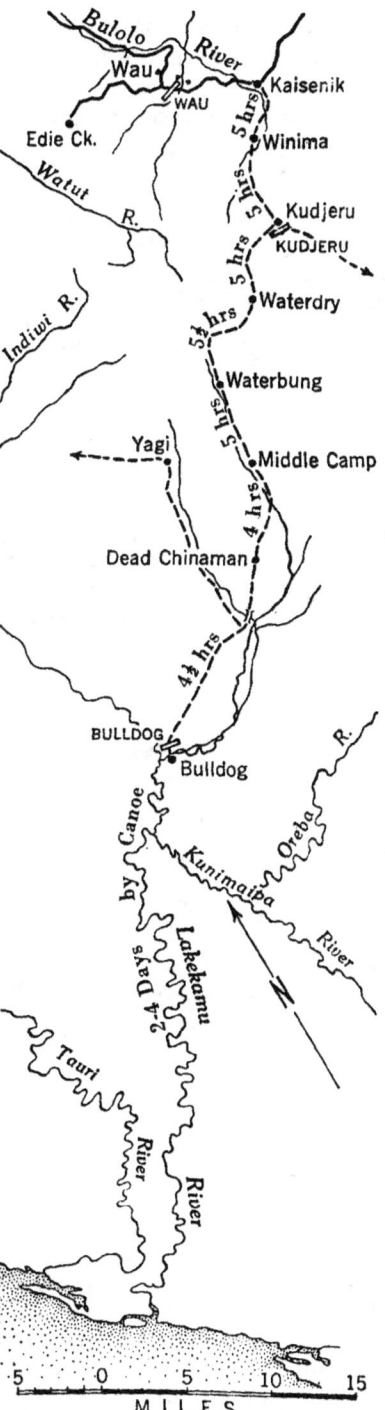

To the north-east of Wau was the Buisaval Track, which followed the surveyed route of a proposed road from Wau to Salamaua. First it led south-east along the Bulolo River to Kaisenik then swung north-east to Ballam's, climbing a steady grade which passed over dry and sun-drenched

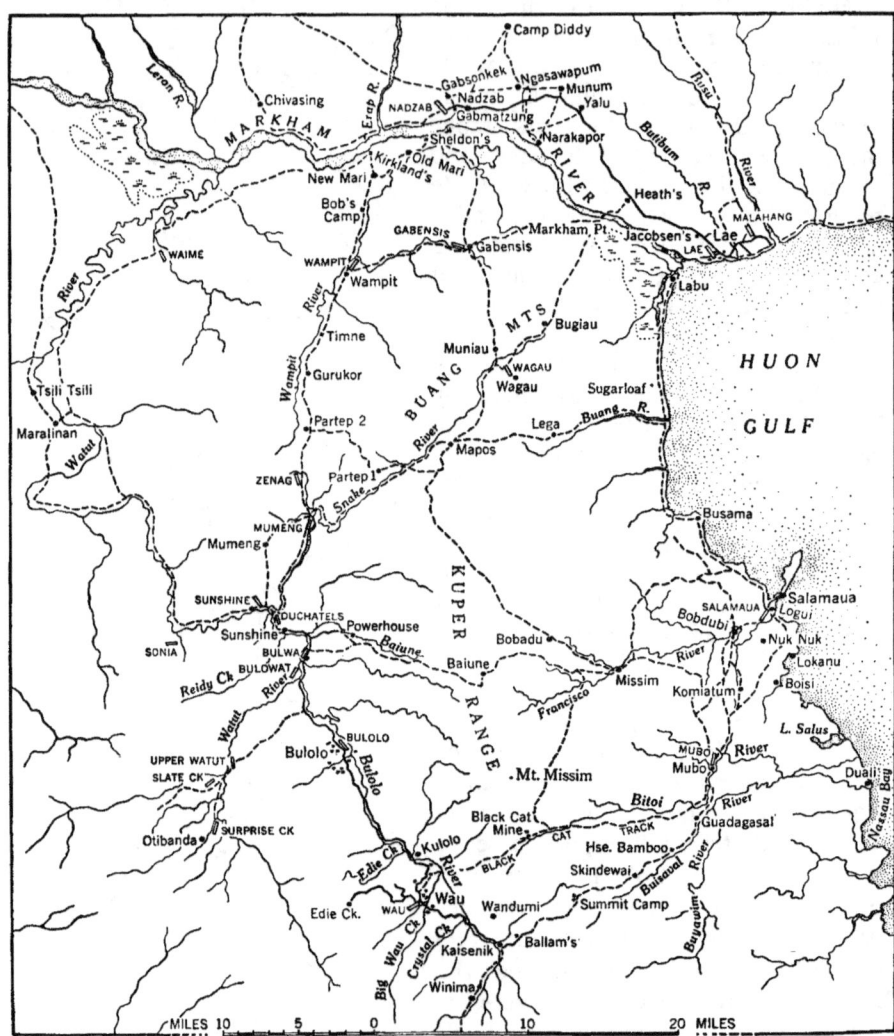

Wau-Salamaua-Lae area

kunai ridges. It was three to four hours' walk from Wau to Ballam's. From Ballam's to the summit of the main range lying between the Bulolo Valley and the coast it was about three hours' comfortable climbing, for the first hour over more dry kunai ridges but then through cool, damp mountain bush. From the summit the track dropped for three hours in a steady downhill grade to the north-east, through bush and over many sparkling streams to Skindewai. Thence it continued for three to four hours to House Bamboo, over rougher ways and precipitous mountain sides, falling down to the deep valley of the Buisaval River which the track paralleled. Then it climbed sharply to the Guadagasal Saddle, precipitously below which on the east, down the tangled and rushing mountain, the Buisaval raged into its junction with the Buyawim River and, equally close in the plunging depths on the other side, the Bitoi River swept into the so-called Mubo Gorge (a valley of narrow river flats between steep mountains). From the Guadagasal Saddle the track leaped down into the Mubo Gorge, and within 40 minutes, crossed the Bitoi by a swaying kunda[2] bridge and junctioned with the track which ran from Wau to Mubo by way of the Black Cat Creek and the Bitoi River. The village of Mubo was less than half an hour's walking along the bed of the Bitoi. From Mubo the track turned due north out of the depths of the Bitoi River system, over three to four hours of exhausting climbing, before it broke forth into the harsh kunai country, into sight of the sea far below, and into the village of Komiatum. There was then nearly two hours' travel down and across hot and thirsty ridges before the track ran into the steaming, green, flat country at Nuk Nuk, and so quickly down the last reaches of the Francisco River, across it into the village of Logui and on to the narrow isthmus on which Salamaua lay.

The Black Cat Track left the Bulolo River just north of Wau, climbed to the head of the Black Cat Creek, then followed the Bitoi River to junction with the Buisaval Track near Mubo. It had been the original route from the coast into the goldfields of the Bulolo Valley but, by the time the war came, was rarely used. A little farther down again along the Bulolo was the beginning of another track, but this was even more undeveloped and more rarely used than the Black Cat Track. It struck north from Wau to the village of Missim then turned east to follow the Francisco River to its mouth less than two miles from Salamaua.

From Wau a motor road ran north-west down the valley of the Bulolo River, after about twelve miles passing through the Bulolo Gold Dredging Company's township of Bulolo, running on to Bulwa and thence to Sunshine. From that area two main tracks branched. The one turned north-east over scorched and broken kunai ridges, becoming alternative tracks which followed either the valley of the Snake River or the high ground east of it and converged at Mapos. The Snake Valley provided easier going, the alternative route a good path but arduous travelling over timbered ranges, down and up steep gorges. From Mapos the track provided hard climbing over the Buang Mountains, then fell steeply to Lega and down the valley of the Buang River to the river's mouth. Generally these tracks would mean five or six days' strenuous walking from Wau. They had been favoured routes into the goldfields when gold first boomed at Edie Creek and along the Bulolo.

The second track led to Lae over some 80 miles. After crossing the

---

[2] A type of very strong vine, very common in the mountains of New Guinea. It is the rattan of commerce.

Snake it climbed steeply over grass ranges to Zenag, then dropped down the divide between the watersheds of the Snake and Wampit Rivers. It followed the course of the Wampit to its junction with the Markham, but threw off a branch at Wampit which struck east to the Markham through Gabensis. Down the broad Markham Valley from Nadzab a road some 26 miles long ran to Lae, through sun-drenched kunai grass and stony river flats.

On 21st January, just about noon, Patrol Officer Pursehouse[3] reported from Finschhafen that some 60 Japanese aircraft were headed towards Lae and Salamaua. These divided and simultaneously struck hard at the two little towns, and at Bulolo, where five fighters, flying just above the ground up the valley, destroyed three Junkers, but, turning east again before they reached Wau, missed five aircraft on the field there.

The people at Lae got Pursehouse's warning and took cover, but the attackers left destruction and confusion behind them. As they flew away two Australian Wirraways from Rabaul dropped down out of the clouds where they had remained concealed and landed on the airfield among the wreckage of seven civil aircraft which had been on the ground when the Japanese arrived. Half an hour after the raiders went, Major Jenyns,[4] second-in-command of the N.G.V.R. who had arrived just before the raid, went to see the Administrator, Sir Walter McNicoll, who, with a small group of senior officials, had been working from Lae for some time in anticipation of the final transfer of the capital from Rabaul. The Administrator was sick and weak from a difficult and protracted illness. He agreed with Jenyns that a state of emergency existed and told him to "take over" with his soldiers. Most of the civilians then moved out of the Markham Valley.

At Salamaua (where Pursehouse's report had not been received) the raiders took the town completely by surprise. They destroyed one R.A.A.F. and 10 or 12 civil aircraft on the ground. Despite the intensity and efficiency of the attack, however, there was only one Australian casualty. Kevin Parer (member of a well-known goldfields family and brother of Ray Parer who had been one of the England-Australia air pioneers) was in his loaded aeroplane, its engine running ready for take-off to Wau, when the Japanese struck. He was shot dead. Another pilot had just landed and, all unsuspecting, was taxiing to the hangar. Suddenly bullets were ripping through his plane and it was on fire. He dropped out of it and rolled into the kunai grass. After the raid all business in the town stopped and most of the European population (of whom there were probably 70 to 80 left at this time) "adjourned to the pub" to discuss the situation.[5]

---
[3] Capt L. Pursehouse, PX178. Naval Intelligence (Coastwatchers); Angau; "M" Special Unit 1943-44. Patrol officer; of Finschhafen, TNG and Goulburn, NSW; b. Goulburn, 4 Nov 1912. Killed in action 17 Jan 1944.
[4] Maj E. W. Jenyns, NGX350. (1st AIF: Lt 26 Bn.) NGVR and Angau. Gold miner and planter; of Lae, TNG; b. Beaudesert, Qld, 7 Sep 1893.
[5] Account by Rfn H. W. T. Forrester.

Penglase, District Officer in charge of the Morobe District, whose headquarters were at Salamaua, had with him at this time R. Melrose, the Director of District Services and Native Affairs in the Administration. The Salamaua people heard nothing from Wau and Bulolo and feared that those centres had suffered heavily. They saw black smoke rise and hang over Lae but could not get in touch with the people there. They expected further attacks and, on the night of the 22nd, the civil population withdrew to a camp previously prepared in the bush outside the town. On the 23rd Melrose picked up enough news on a small wireless set to know that the Japanese were then at Rabaul.

There was general agreement that a Japanese landing at Salamaua was imminent and that all civilians should leave as soon as possible. But Penglase and Melrose were in a difficult position. Assuming, as they did, that all air traffic out of Wau had been immobilised, they decided that there were only two ways of escape: on foot, south to Port Moresby—and Penglase, one of the very few men who had experienced the rigours of that terrible country south of the Bulolo, felt that the old and the sick among them would never survive the journey; or by sea, down the coast, in the only two small craft and canoes available—a risky prospect in view of the known presence of large numbers of Japanese aircraft and the probable presence of hostile surface craft. Finally, however, they decided that Melrose, who was himself suffering from heart trouble, would take out by sea those who were obviously unfit for the overland trip (and the one woman among them, Sister Stock from the Salamaua hospital, who had been most steadfast) while Penglase led the rest towards the Lakekamu. The two parties set out on 24th January.

After their departure the only Europeans left in the town were six air force men, who were manning a signals station, and five or six of the N.G.V.R. with Sergeant Phillips[6] directing them. Among the N.G.V.R. was Rifleman Forrester,[7] who, with two or three others, had been on full-time duty in Salamaua since about mid-December preparing barbed wire and machine-gun posts.

In the days immediately after 21st January Phillips and his men were kept busy refuelling R.A.A.F. aircraft of which about four or six called most days. This was hard work as they had to do it from drums and natives were not always available to help them. The raid had frightened the natives, Administration control had disappeared, prisoners had been released from the gaol and some of them had secured arms, disorder was rife. Some little time after the civilians left, one of the R.A.A.F. pilots reported Japanese shipping which might have been moving towards Lae and Salamaua. When the N.G.V.R. relayed this to Port Moresby they were told to destroy all they could of Salamaua but not to leave until they were sure that occupation was imminent. That evening they threw petrol over the main offices, the stores and the hotel and burnt them.

[6] Capt R. H. D. Phillips, NG2296. NGVR and Angau. Cashier; of Kila, TNG; b. Sydney, 12 Sep 1904.
[7] Rfn H. W. T. Forrester, MM, NG2053. (1914-18: 3rd Canadian Div Sig Coy.) NGVR and Angau. Gold miner; of Salamaua, TNG; b. London, 9 Aug 1891.

Meanwhile, a scratch N.G.V.R. platoon under Lieutenant Owers,[8] a surveyor with New Guinea Goldfields, had set out from Wau soon after the raid by way of Mubo, not knowing whether the Japanese had landed at Salamaua. As these men plodded towards the top of the range they passed groups of dispirited civilians making a slow way inland through the mountains and bleak bush which were foreign to most of them. With these were some N.G.V.R. men who, confused as to where command lay in the suddenly changed circumstances, had joined the civilian exodus. Corporal McAdam,[9] a large, quiet forester with a battered nose who considered a man a weakling who could not do twenty miles a day in the mountains for days on end, pushed ahead of the rest of the platoon. From Salamaua he sent word of the situation back to Owers and some days later the platoon arived at the isthmus to find the small group there in difficulties among disorderly natives.

Behind Owers' platoon Umphelby set out over the Buisaval Track about mid-February with the rest of his company (which included a medium machine-gun platoon). Before leaving Wau they requisitioned anything they thought might be useful to them. In appearance they were a motley group, wearing a medley of their own clothing and army uniforms, their equipment mostly of the 1914-18 War leather type, emu feathers in their hats. They had no steel helmets, no entrenching tools, and, except for a few made at the Bulolo workshops, no identity discs. All carried packs and haversacks, their packs weighing between 40 and 50 pounds. None of them had ever carried such loads before in their walking through New Guinea; in pre-war days, it had not been considered possible (or seemly) for a white man to carry even the smallest load in the mountains. Even in war many of them considered that they could not operate without their "boys" and so, when they reported in for service, brought their "labour lines" with them. Umphelby's company formed a "pool" of such natives and thus 70 "boys" or more moved with them in a long line. The company was typical of the N.G.V.R. They had knowledge of the problems of New Guinea, the terrain and of natives. Like the Boers in South Africa nearly half a century before, they had come together from their isolated homes to fight, but each yielded only as much of his own individuality as he thought fit. There were many of enthusiasm and great courage among them, but they had had little training which would fit them to operate as a coherent unit; their average age was about 35; their supply services were sketchy, and to provide food was always a problem.

Umphelby made Mubo his headquarters. He mounted two Vickers guns on a ridge commanding the entrance to the valley from Salamaua. In the days which followed he kept one platoon at Salamaua, changing it from time to time, disposed the rest for the protection of his base, and kept them at hard training and reconnaissance patrolling. One task of the Salamaua platoon was to watch for the approach of the Japanese. They

---

[8] Capt N. Owers, NGX369. NGVR; Survey Corps; IORE NG Force, I Corps, II Corps. Licensed surveyor; of Wau, TNG; b. Inverell, NSW, 12 Apr 1907.

[9] Maj J. B. McAdam, MM, NGX431. NGVR; Angau; CRE NG Forests 1944-45. Forestry officer; of Wau, TNG; b. Lancs, England, 6 Feb 1910.

manned Lookout No. 1, a camouflaged platform in a lofty tree on Scout Ridge (as it later came to be known), just south of the mouth of the Francisco River; this had been established immediately after the raid. Other tasks were to collect information and gather stores from the abandoned town—sugar, rice, tobacco and tinned goods—to send back to Komiatum and Mubo where supply dumps were being established.

At the beginning of March there came to the platoon at Salamaua a grim little band led by Captain A. G. Cameron. They were thirteen survivors from the 2/22nd Battalion which had been at Rabaul. Their leader was a ruthless and able soldier who, as a fugitive after the fall of Rabaul, had been in touch with General Morris' headquarters at Port Moresby, giving news of the disaster and of the movements of his fellow fugitives. Morris had ordered him to come out of New Britain if he felt sure that he could not engage in guerilla activities there, and Cameron had done so in a 21-foot boat with a two-stroke engine, bringing twelve men with him.

Meanwhile Edwards had increased his small local detachment at Lae to a company with Captain Lyon,[1] who had recently returned from a school in Australia, in command. Lyon spread three platoons from Lae to Wampit building up stores dumps. On 7th March five aircraft raided Lae, which had been laid waste and was almost empty. Lyon then got word that a big convoy was headed in his direction. He himself stayed in the town with four men to await events while the rest of his men, making for Nadzab, prepared to destroy the one remaining petrol dump—at Jacobsen's Plantation, about two miles from Lae in the Markham Valley, where 15 cars also awaited destruction. At 4.45 a.m. on the 8th Lyon was awakened to hear the noise of Japanese coming ashore. He had a lorry waiting. He and his men, accompanied by three natives, then turned their backs on the lost town, and went up the main road towards Nadzab.

That morning the Japanese landed also at Salamaua, where the bulk of the N.G.V.R. platoon fell back across the Francisco River leaving behind a few men, with whom were Cameron and several 2/22nd Battalion survivors, to demolish the aerodrome and fire the petrol dump. As Cameron and his runner, Lance-Corporal Brannelly,[2] were falling back, Brannelly shot an enemy soldier at point-blank range—probably the only Japanese casualty from land action in the landings either at Lae or Salamaua. After the rear party had crossed the bridge over the Francisco, and when the Japanese appeared on its approaches from the Salamaua side, the N.G.V.R. men destroyed it. Most of them then took the track back to Mubo.

From late January to early March Wau had become an evacuation centre. After the January bombings most of the European and Asian civil population of the goldfields gathered there feeling that they had only a limited time to get out of the threatened area. They were joined by the

---
[1] Maj H. M. Lyon, NX151701. NGVR; Angau; 1 NGIB. Store manager; of Lae, TNG; b. Glasgow, Scotland, 14 Aug 1907.
[2] L-Sgt T. A. V. Brannelly, VX12987; 2/22 Bn. Labourer; of Clifton Hill, Vic; b. Bacchus Marsh, Vic, 21 Dec 1918.

civilians from Lae who came in on foot under the leadership of E. Taylor[3] (Assistant Director of District Services and Native Affairs in the Administration) and the overland party from Salamaua whom Penglase had diverted to Wau when he discovered, after pressing ahead of the rest, that that town was still intact. On his way out by air the Administrator had appointed the senior Assistant District Officer there (McMullen[4]) Deputy Administrator, and Assistant District Officer Niall[5] was helping McMullen. They managed to get some of the displaced people out to Port Moresby by air with hardy pilots flying aircraft which, in some cases, they would not normally have been permitted to take into the air. Soon, however, it was evident that no more unescorted air traffic could be allowed in and out of New Guinea; the R.A.A.F., hard pressed, could not supply fighters to assist and the air line closed.

After the arrival of the Lae party Taylor took charge of an improvised refugee camp which was set up at Edie Creek. He was a man highly respected and of great experience in New Guinea. As the senior Administration official on the spot he felt a deep responsibility for the people in his care and was determined to prevent them falling into the hands of the Japanese. And most of these people themselves were restless and were ready to face the hardships of travelling over unknown or little known country rather than accept capture. The advice of Penglase and three local surveyors (Ecclestone,[6] Fox[7] and G. E. Ballam) was therefore sought. They decided that Fox and Ballam should head a party to blaze the track to Bulldog and locate and build camps between Wau and Bulldog each capable of housing 40 people; that, three days in their rear, parties of carriers, each under an Administration official, should begin leaving Wau daily to build up food stocks at each camp. In the meantime the authorities at Port Moresby had been asked to arrange to provide food at, and sea transport from, the mouth of the Lakekamu for 250 people from 25th February. Fox and Ballam led their party out on 9th February. There were three other Europeans, 70 native carriers and five native policemen. They carried out their task but the plan to maintain supplies along the route was not realised and the parties of evacuees leaving Wau subsequently carried their rations with them and supplemented them from a dump which had been built up at Kudjeru. Penglase and Ecclestone led one of these parties to Bulldog and then returned to Wau. Taylor took approximately 60 European and Chinese men out from Edie Creek on 7th March. In this fashion all the refugees reached Port Moresby safely.

March, however, brought other troubles to the goldfields. On the morning of the 1st, nine bombers struck at the centres there, and, heavily, at

---

[3] Lt-Col E. Taylor, MBE, NX163949; Angau. Assistant Director of District Services and Native Affairs; of Lae, TNG; b. Mt Morgan, Qld, 25 Sep 1889.

[4] Col K. C. McMullen, NGX371. Angau; Directorate of Research LHQ; BBCAU. Assistant District Officer; of Wau, TNG; b. Sydney, 17 Nov 1904.

[5] Maj H. L. R. Niall, CBE, NGX373; Angau. Assistant District Officer; of Wau, TNG; b. Coolah, NSW, 14 Oct 1904.

[6] Capt J. W. Ecclestone, NG3501. Angau; RAE (Forestry) 1944-45. Surveyor; of Lae, TNG; b. Carlsruhe, Vic, 15 Apr 1898.

[7] Maj C. W. G. Fox, P454. Angau; RAE (Forestry) 1944-45. Surveyor; mining warden and forestry inspector; of Wau, TNG; b. Albury, NSW, 8 Dec 1901.

Wau. When, a week later, news of the landings at Lae and Salamaua reached Major Edwards at N.G.V.R. Headquarters, he moved from the Bulolo to the Watut and reported to Port Moresby that he was preparing to destroy all the important installations from Wau to Baiune (the great Bulolo Gold Dredging "power house" area on the Baiune River). Because of his lack of suitable portable radio equipment the move cost him communication with both his forward positions and Morris' headquarters and he remained out of touch until the 16th. The drone of many aircraft passing above him but hidden by rain and low clouds suggested the possibility of parachute attacks, of which very lively apprehensions were common throughout the whole valley at this time. On the morning of the 9th he gave orders for demolitions to begin. The two main power stations at Bulolo and Baiune and the main bridges at Wau and Bulolo were then put out of action. (Bombs had previously set off demolition charges which had been placed ready in the main Bulolo workshops.) Vehicles throughout the valley which might be useful to the invaders were immobilised.

During the next week Edwards had no news until the 16th. On that day a runner came to him with news from the coast (which he believed) that the invaders were preparing to move out from Lae up the Markham and that a platoon which had previously been sent from Lae to the mouth of the Buang River to cover that line of advance had been surprised by Japanese raiders. Thereupon he ordered his forward men to fall back. When, however, he realised that he had made a mistake he sent Umphelby and his company back to Mubo, established N.G.V.R. Headquarters firmly at Reidy Creek (four miles from Bulwa) with Jenyns in charge, and himself took command at the Lae end where his main centre was set up at Camp Diddy.

But the Japanese, it seemed, were in no hurry to push inland. Their first definite move in that direction came from Salamaua on 18th March, ten days after the landings. That day about 60 Japanese led by 4 natives, marched to Komiatum, destroyed the N.G.V.R. stores dump there, and returned to Salamaua. On the Lae side the invaders kept to the township area for several weeks, getting the aerodrome into order and establishing base workshops and dumps.

The Japanese pause gave the New Guinea men time to meet new problems. Their supply systems which depended on long carrier lines began to work better, communications, medical and other services were put on a sounder basis, a school of instruction was established at Wau, scouting parties began to slip up to and through the fringes of the Japanese positions, and vitally important observation posts, some of which had been prepared and were operating before the invasions, were manned.

In the Salamaua area Lookout No. 1 which had been abandoned after the Japanese arrival was reoccupied in April by the men of one of the newly-formed N.G.V.R. scout sections, under McAdam, now a sergeant.

When the first confusion which followed the arrival of the Japanese was dying down Edwards had told McAdam that information of what the invaders were doing at Salamaua was vital. McAdam said he would get it if he were allowed to pick his own men. He chose Jim Cavanaugh,[8] a forester like himself but younger in the service, fair haired and blue eyed; Geoff Archer,[9] a welder with the Bulolo Gold Dredging Company and a wanderer by instinct; Bert Jentzsch,[1] older than the others, a mine manager; Gordon Kinsey,[2] Bob Day,[3] and Jim Currie.[4] These were all men who loved the bush and had an instinctive understanding of its ways.

McAdam began his move forward on 30th March. He made very quick time to Mubo and went on to get the latest information from Pilot Officer Leigh Vial,[5] a promising young Assistant District Officer who had escaped from New Britain after the occupation of Rabaul, became one of the coastwatchers, and was installed by Umphelby's men in a lofty lookout about eight miles in a beeline south-west of Salamaua. (For some six months his quiet voice was to be heard regularly at Port Moresby reporting full details of Japanese aircraft landing at, taking off from and passing over Salamaua.) Leaving Vial, McAdam then began to edge his lookouts and his base camps closer and closer to the Japanese until within a short time his men were on

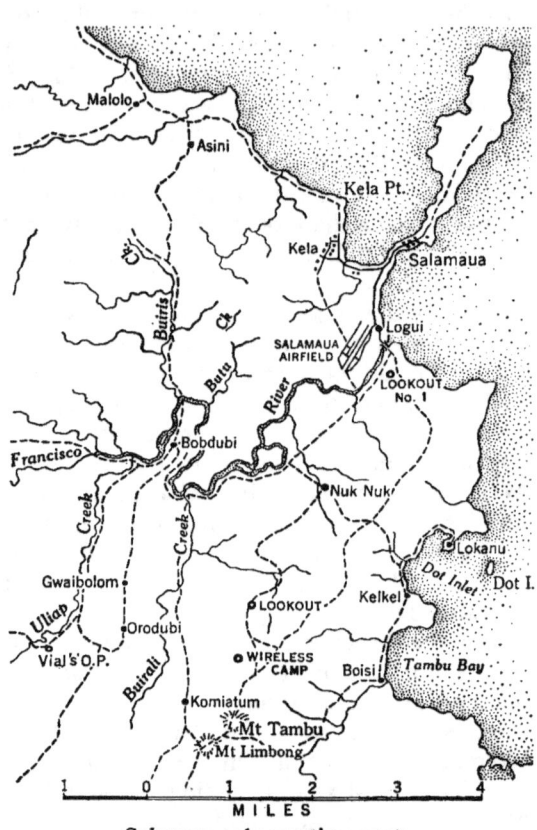

Salamaua observation posts

the watch from the original Lookout No. 1 just below the mouth of the Francisco. Although scarcely a movement in Salamaua escaped them, for

[8] Lt J. Cavanaugh, NGX276. NGVR and RAE (Forestry). Forester; of Wau, TNG, and Lismore, NSW; b. Murwillumbah, NSW, 3 Jun 1914.
[9] Capt G. R. Archer, MC, NGX257. NGVR; "Z" and "M" Special Units. Gold miner; of Hampton, Vic; b. Murrumbeena, Vic, 7 Dec 1913.
[1] Cpl A. E. Jentzsch, NG2235. NGVR; Amenities Service. Mine manager; of Wau, TNG; b. Wycheproof, Vic, 24 Apr 1893.
[2] Lt J. G. Kinsey, NGX362. NGVR and Angau; 1 NG Inf Bn. Building contractor; of South Johnstone, via Innisfail, Qld; b. Geelong, Vic, 10 Feb 1912.
[3] Lt P. R. H. Day, NGX453. NGVR and Allied Geographical Section. Gold miner; of Bulolo, TNG; b. Fremantle, WA, 28 Feb 1904.
[4] WO2 J. W. Currie, NG2183. NGVR and Angau. Gold miner; of Wau, TNG; b. Barwon Downs, Vic, 6 Nov 1901.
[5] F-Lt L. G. Vial. RAAF (Coastwatchers) and FELO. Assistant District Officer; of Rabaul; b. Camberwell, Vic, 28 Feb 1909. Killed in action 30 Apr 1943.

some time they were hard put to make the best use of the information they gained because their communications system was primitive. In their early days their nearest wireless was at Mubo. Ingeniously and, having no maps, through the exercise of magnificent bush sense, notably on Cavanaugh's part, they linked their various lookouts and camps with a telephone network contrived mostly with salvaged wire taken from abandoned camps, and burnt transformers from Wau, and sent their reports back to Mubo by runner. (Later the wireless was brought from Mubo to Wireless Camp—just forward of Komiatum—and information from the observation posts was telephoned to Wireless Camp and radioed back to Port Moresby in a few minutes.)

They were continuously watching, scouting tirelessly into the very fringes of the garrison area itself. They survived by adapting themselves completely to their new circumstances, with cool courage, intelligence, physical hardihood and superb bushcraft. McAdam said later:

We only used our own tracks and we took pains never to mark the main tracks so that, whenever we saw them, they were a book telling us what the Japs had been doing. . . . Our tracks were so lightly marked that it took a good bushman to find them. We left no marks in that forward country. We walked carefully on roots, stones. We had the heels taken off our boots. Where necessary we walked our natives behind us to put their tracks over ours. . . . We went there with three automatic revolvers only one of which we could rely on. We couldn't carry our rifles because they caught in the bush so, in forward scouting in pairs, we took a pistol each, the good one and one uncertain one. Our sole defence was our speed. We could see a Jap before he could see us and if we had 10 yards' start we could get away. What I wanted was a Tommy-gun so that our forward scouts could put the Japs flat and so get a 10 yards' start on them. All the four months I was there we were unable to get a Tommy-gun. There were about six in N.G.V.R. but we didn't have one.

The Japanese, however, knew they were there and after scouts (mainly Currie and Archer) had operated from the old Lookout No. 1 for about a month a Japanese patrol came searching for them. The searchers actually passed beneath the telephone line but did not see it. They condemned the local natives for assisting the Australians. Mainly to avoid further trouble for the natives McAdam withdrew his men from the old No. 1 soon afterwards.

At Lae less spectacular but more important work of a similar kind was going on—more important because Lae was the main Japanese base on the Huon Gulf and from it the main Japanese air strength operated. Before the Japanese occupation Sergeant Mitchell,[6] an amateur wireless operator, had been installed on Sugarloaf, a conical hill overlooking the Huon Gulf, 9 miles south of Lae. On his set, which had been built up from civilian sources, he was in touch with both Wau and Port Moresby. He wirelessed to Port Moresby a full description of the landings on the 8th March. About noon that day, however, he saw a Japanese gunboat patrolling below him and, suspecting that it was using direction-finding apparatus to pinpoint his position, then closed his station.

---

[6] WO2 D. McR. Mitchell, NG2129; NGVR. Mine manager; of Bankstown, NSW; b. Parramatta, NSW, 24 Apr 1911.

After 8th March when Captain Lyon was established at Kirkland's, on the south bank of the Markham, he sent a party to find a suitable site for an observation post on Markham Point, a high bluff on the opposite side of the Markham from Lae and about 8 miles from the town. It offered excellent observation of Lae and of the whole Huon Gulf area, marred only by the fog and cloud which closed Lae for days at a time.

Other watching posts were established along the Markham which, although of briefer life, provided more excitement for the men manning them.

Early in April the N.G.V.R. built and manned a post just north-east of Heath's Plantation which was about seven miles from Lae on the road to Nadzab. About the middle of the month they ventured as far as Jacobsen's Plantation. Thence, from a near-by post, they could watch Japanese moving along the road and keep the aerodrome under observation. But as there was no signalling equipment at the observation post, and it took about nine hours for a runner to reach Camp Diddy by a back route through Yalu, the observations from Jacobsen's lost much of their value.

Individuals of the N.G.V.R., however, were thrusting even farther forward than this. Phillips (who had come across from Salamaua) and Corporal Clark, one of five New Guinea Volunteers of that name, actually entered Lae itself. While Phillips lay on a terrace on the western side of the strip, counted more than thirty aircraft arriving and watched where they were hidden, Clark circled the airfield and examined ammunition dumps. As proof of what he had done he brought back tags from some of the bombs which he had found. Acting on the reports of these two, Allied airmen were later able to destroy a number of the aircraft and several of the dumps.

While the men of the N.G.V.R. were thus settling to their lonely work General Morris, back in Port Moresby, could, at that time, do little to help them. Not only was he worried about the security of the Bulolo Valley and the threat of a Japanese approach to Moresby by the Bulldog Track but he was finding the maintenance of the N.G.V.R. most difficult. As soon as its existence was established he began to use the Bulldog Track for this purpose but his best efforts could keep only a trickle of supplies moving over it. Engineering improvements necessary to the track represented a Herculean task which he had not the men to attempt.

To increase the security of this troublesome but vital route, to form a base at Kudjeru for patrols and air observation, and to provide a link with the N.G.V.R., he decided to send forward a group of reinforcements who had been bound for the 1st Independent Company and who now could not join their parent unit. Even before he had left Australia Lieutenant Howard,[7] in charge of these men, had been instructed

You will . . . take immediate steps to organise the reinforcements as one independent platoon of three sections with a view to its employment in 8 MD on tasks for

---

[7] Capt N. R. Howard, NGX174. 1st and 2/4 Indep Coys; 2/1 Cdo Sqn. Gold miner; of Wau, TNG; b. Brisbane, 20 Mar 1910.

which the special training given to Independent Companies makes it particularly suitable.

He was ready, therefore, when Morris gave him his orders and the first of his men left by sea for the Lakekamu on 29th March.

By the time Howard himself arrived on the Markham about 25th April to get first-hand experience of what was happening, the Japanese were beginning to react in protest against the presence of the Australians both at Salamaua and at Lae.

From Salamaua a fighting patrol, about 65 strong, which had crossed from Lae on 23rd April accompanied by two Europeans dressed in white, set out along the track to Komiatum. One European seemed to be acting as a guide. But from their observation posts some of Umphelby's men had seen them coming and three of them lay waiting in ambush at Komiatum. They reported later that they killed five of the Japanese and wounded others before they themselves, unharmed, left Komiatum. As on the occasion of the previous visit the strangers did not linger unduly and soon returned to Salamaua.

From the Markham the N.G.V.R. men reported on 24th April that a Japanese outpost had been established at Heath's Plantation and, a little later, that a small gun had been sited there facing north-west along the road.

While this interesting situation had been building up in the Lae-Salamaua-Bulolo area during the period January to April, the Japanese had been on the move elsewhere throughout the Mandate and along the island arc from Vila to the Admiralties.

The New Hebrides positions remained comparatively unmolested but at Tulagi Captain Goode[8] of the 1st Independent Company who had moved forward from Vila, was watching the rapid approach of the Japanese. Goode stood by while the Resident Commissioner of the Solomons Protectorate evacuated the north-west of his islands, retaining only a small staff in the south-east, and turned his civil administration into a military administration as the British Solomon Islands Protectorate Force. The A.I.F. and R.A.A.F. detachments—some 50 all told—remained on Tanambogo Island in Tulagi Harbour. Soon after the fall of Rabaul the Japanese began desultorily to bomb Tulagi. The bombing grew more purposeful towards the end of April when, on the 25th, eight bombers carried out a determined raid.

On Bougainville and Buka coastwatchers and soldiers had been having a rather more difficult time. When Rabaul was occupied it seemed that invasion of Bougainville was imminent. Kieta, the administrative centre of the District, was at once abandoned but Lieutenant Mackie,[9] who commanded the section of the Independent Company at Buka Passage, did not allow that to move him to hasty action. He was working closely

---

[8] Maj A. L. Goode, SX3711. 1st and 2/4 Indep Coys; "M" Special Unit; OC 2/10 Cdo Sqn. Agent; of Port Pirie, SA; b. Port Pirie, 17 Sep 1915.
[9] Maj J. H. Mackie, VX39164. 1st Indep Coy; "M" Special Unit. Electrician; of Kyabram, Vic; b. Kyabram, 1 Feb 1919.

with Assistant District Officer Read[1] and the two were preparing to continue to operate on Bougainville after the arrival of the Japanese. Mackie moved to Bougainville and, on 24th January, a small rearguard and demolition party which he had left on the airfields at Buka engaged strafing Japanese aircraft (one of which they claimed to have shot down into the sea) and blew up the fuel supplies and bombs before they too left for the larger island.

The position at this time was an extremely complicated one for the young A.I.F. officer and for Read, who was still a civilian. The abandonment of Kieta had meant a serious breakdown in the civil administration and this had been followed by disorder among the natives and confusion among the civil European population, a number of whom, including some women, still remained on the island. Out of this Mackie, Read and Paul Mason[2] of Inus Plantation, a capable amateur wireless operator and engineer, who, as a civilian had been part of the coastwatching organisation since 1939, emerged as three determined figures who were to keep resistance alive on the island and maintain Bougainville as an invaluable reporting centre. They now set up coastwatching posts, each with a teleradio, at Buin, Kieta, Numa Numa, Aravia, and near Kessa on the north coast of Buka. On the 8th March six Japanese cruisers and two destroyers anchored in Carola Haven near Kessa. Shore parties drove out the four soldiers manning the watching post near by and killed Percy Good, an Australian planter, who had been acting as one of the coastwatchers. After a short stay the ships left. On the 30th March more Japanese came, occupied Buka Passage and sent parties ranging over the north coast of Bougainville. Mackie himself, visiting his watching post which had been re-established near Carola Haven, was cut off by this occupation. Read sent him warning in a message bravely carried by a native policeman. Mackie's position was now extremely perilous. He reported the arrival of more Japanese warships in Carola Haven, however, before he led his men in darkness aided by the Reverend Usaia Sotutu, a Fijian missionary, from one small island to another until finally they reached Bougainville again.

The Japanese were now on the move all round that island. They had occupied Faisi in the Shortland Islands on the same day as they had settled at Buka Passage. About the same time they raided Kieta, drove out the few soldiers who were still there, and caused Mason, watching from a near-by lookout in the hills, to move farther south to a supply dump which he had established. He was joined later by the four hungry and tattered soldiers from the post at Buin for, about a week after their occupation of Faisi, the Japanese had moved against the Australians at Buin and destroyed their camp and equipment and the Administration buildings there. Soon afterwards Mason, with two soldiers who had been detached to him by Mackie, set up another post in the vicinity of Buin.

By May Mason was settled near Buin, Mackie had his main camp at

---

[1] Maj W. J. Read, DSC, VX95356. Lt-Cdr RANVR; Angau 1944-46. Assistant District Officer; of Buka Passage, Bougainville; b. Hobart, 18 Sep 1905.
[2] Lt P. E. Mason, DSC; RANVR. Plantation manager; of Bougainville.

Aravia, and Read was established overlooking Buka Passage. Japanese parties were searching the island more and more thoroughly and the Australians had placed their lives completely in the keeping of the natives who surrounded them, and they were living out lonely days of constant watchfulness; to the Allied forces as a whole they were merely voices speaking of the Japanese movements from the centre of Japanese-occupied territory.

On 8th April attacking forces arrived at Lorengau on Manus Island in a troop-carrying ship and a destroyer. Tupling,[3] the coastwatcher in the Ninigo Group to the west, had warned Lieutenant Palmer[4] of the Independent Company, and Assistant District Officer Vertigan,[5] of the coming of the ships. Palmer and Vertigan had planned against such an eventuality, and, before they withdrew to the south coast, the commandos destroyed everything that might be of use to the Japanese and left booby-traps at the landing places. Off the south coast a schooner was ready and Palmer and his men, with Vertigan and the rest of the civilians, set sail for the mainland. They made their landfall at Bogadjim just south of Madang, then pushed inland through the mountains and bush to Bena Bena. Aircraft later picked them up and flew them to Port Moresby. Palmer and Vertigan had planned well and had been capable and unhurried in the execution of their plans.

By the end of April, having thus gathered into their net all the strategic points on the approaches through the Mandated islands, the Japanese seemed to be in a strong position to attack Port Moresby itself, possibly as a preliminary to attacks against the Australian east coast. In that town the early February air raids had been followed by widespread disorder and looting and Morris found it difficult to prevent his unseasoned soldiers from taking a leading part. He had insufficient provost troops and, of those he had, some were themselves unreliable.[6] Two more raids followed before the month was out during the second of which (on 28th February) possibly 124 bombs were dropped in the vicinity of the Seven Mile airfield, and the air force hangar on the shores of the harbour, and two R.A.A.F. Catalinas were sunk and one damaged. The anti-aircraft gunners, however, got their first kill during this raid when they shot down a Japanese fighter, the pilot of which was taken prisoner by the 39th Battalion.

These gunners were keen and efficient though many were mere boys who had already sweated out many weeks of waiting and discomfort and suspense. A picture of their battery in action in a later raid has been given by two of them:

---

[3] Petty Officer W. L. Tupling; RANVR (Coastwatcher). Plantation manager. Missing presumed dead 20 Mar 1943.

[4] Maj A. S. Palmer, MC, SX6543. 1 Indep Coy; LO NG Force 1942-43; 2/5, 2/6 Cdo Sqns; Directorate of Public Relations. Journalist; of Broken Hill, NSW; b. Adelaide, 9 Dec 1911.

[5] Maj D. H. Vertigan, MBE, VX112276; Angau. Assistant District Officer; of Manus Is; b. Forth, Tas, 27 Aug 1906.

[6] Although Morris was vehemently criticised for the disorders General Blamey was to judge later: "General Morris set about his impossible task with courage and determination. The responsibility lies less with the commander on the spot than with those responsible for providing him with inadequate and incompetent forces."

The terrific crash, crash of the guns shattered the quietness of the morning as sweating gunners, stripped to the waist, hurled shells at the invader. One of the shots which pitted the sky all around him apparently took effect as the plane dropped sharply to 11,000 feet causing the station to "Cease loading" as he turned homeward. The plane, a Mitsubishi-96, was destined never to reach home, however, as once again he met a terrific fire which this time effectively sealed his fate, one shell scoring a direct hit on the cabin. Men cheered wildly as the plane roared into its last dive towards the mountains.

It was of the men of this battery that a war correspondent later wrote:

Some of the youngest of them were inclined to be "windy" in the early days when they were almost the only anti-aircraft gunners on New Guinea and the Japanese planes came often and flew low. They will tell you now how one of the regular sergeants, who has been the backbone of this battery from the beginning, used to cuff the youngsters on the ears when some of them showed signs of taking shelter until they were more afraid of him than of the Japanese. After the first three or four raids, however, all of them were hardened soldiers, down to the 16-year-old boys who had falsified their ages to get into this militia battery and suddenly found themselves right in the firing line. . . . This is not an A.I.F. but a "chocko" battery although I know of only one A.I.F. "ack ack" battery that has fired so many rounds or scored so many hits, or been in action so long, and that is one that served at Tobruk during the siege.[7]

At the end of February the Australian defence leaders saw Port Moresby as a strong position on the flank of the Japanese movements from either the Mandate or the Netherlands Indies, and also as a threat to the Japanese base at Rabaul. Its security lay initially with the navy and the air force. In the air, they said, they would require for the effective defence of Moresby two fighter-interceptor squadrons, one long-range fighter squadron, one dive-bomber squadron, two general-reconnaissance flying-boat squadrons and one general-reconnaissance torpedo-bomber squadron; and an increase in airfields would be needed. With regard to the army they thought that:

Given reasonable naval and air protection which would make the approach and landing of a combined expedition a very dangerous operation, we consider that the land forces at Moresby are an adequate garrison for the defence of this important base. The present situation is that while we possess suitable naval forces, their operations are restricted by a lack of suitable bases, and available air forces are much below the required strength. We must consider therefore:

(a) Whether, if available, an increased army garrison would make for greater security.
(b) Whether Moresby is to be regarded as indefensible and the present garrison withdrawn.

Reinforcement is at present out of the question since we have inadequate forces for the defence of the east coast, and this is the only area from which reinforcements can be drawn. In any event, unless we have adequate naval and air support, the enemy could always produce an attacking force superior to the garrison and covered by powerful air forces.

In our view withdrawal is equally out of the question. Quite apart from the potential effect on public morale of withdrawal before attack, we must hold on to this important base as long as possible, and exact a heavy toll from the enemy if he should attack it. The garrison is well provisioned and we see no reason to assume that we cannot continue to maintain it.

---

[7] *The Sydney Morning Herald*, 8 Aug 1942.

(Australian War Memorial)

Darwin, 19th February 1942. Bombs fall on the Post Office during the first Japanese air attack on the Australian mainland.

(Cdr J. C. B. McManus, R.A.N.)

The Darwin jetty during the raid. The Australian ships *Barossa* and *Neptuna* are alongside.

(Australian War Memorial)

Major-General B. M. Morris, G.O.C. New Guinea Force, and some of his staff, at Port Moresby, July 1942. *Left to right*: Lieut-Colonel E. T. Brennan, A.D.M.S.; Lieut-Colonel D. D. Pitt, G.S.O. 1; Lieutenant A. B. Luetchford, A.D.C. to General Morris; Lieut-Colonel E. B. Serisier, A.A. & Q.M.G.; and General Morris.

(Australian War Memorial)

Port Moresby, 1942.

(Australian War Memorial)
Japanese bombs burst along the Port Moresby waterfront.

(Australian War Memorial)
The anti-aircraft defences of Port Moresby were strengthened from April onwards by the arrival of A.I.F. batteries, newly-returned from the Middle East. An anti-aircraft position at Port Moresby, July 1942.

(*Australian War Memorial*)

Salamaua, viewed from an observation point above Nuk Nuk. The airstrip is the cleared area in the centre of the picture, with the mouth of the Francisco River to the right. Salamaua itself was situated on the flat isthmus linking the promontory and the mainland.

(*Australian War Memorial*)

Kudjeru (looking north), where a section of the 1st Independent Company was established in April 1942 to guard against possible Japanese movement south of Wau along the Bulldog Track.

Though there was, therefore, no increase in Morris' field force during March, and though that month brought seventeen more heavy air raids on Port Moresby, there were improvements in the Allied naval and air position. The American Navy was recovering from the blow which had been dealt it at Pearl Harbour. At the end of January Vice-Admiral William F. Halsey had ventured with some success against the Marshall Islands (in the Japanese Mandate itself) and the Gilberts which lie southeast of the Marshalls. Vice-Admiral Wilson Brown was then detailed to try an air and surface attack on Rabaul which was rapidly becoming the main Japanese base in the South-West Pacific. Discovery by Japanese airmen of the aircraft carrier *Lexington,* round which the task force was mustered, caused the project to be abandoned. Later in February Halsey sailed against Wake Island and, at the beginning of March, aircraft from his carrier *Enterprise* bombed Marcus Island. Two days after the Japanese landings at Lae and Salamaua Brown sent aircraft from the carriers *Lexington* and *Yorktown* against the Japanese concentrations there. They sank a number of Japanese ships and did not lose heavily themselves.

Air strength at Port Moresby was increasing. On 21st March the first fighters of No. 75 Squadron R.A.A.F. arrived. They swept low over the trees without warning and the infantry machine-gunners, who had come to accept the fact that all the fighters they saw were hostile, fired at them and damaged three. It was an eventful day. Little more than two hours later an unsuspecting Japanese reconnaissance plane fell to the eager airmen's guns. The soldiers' spirits rose high.

With aircraft now actually arriving, work on the airfields went ahead with increased vigour. By the middle of April General Morris was able to report that airfields had been built or were nearing completion at the Seven Mile, Kila, Bomana, Rorona and Laloki. By May American engineers had begun to help with these undertakings. A company of the 43rd Engineer Regiment and two negro units—the 96th Engineer Battalion less two companies and a section of the 576th Engineer Company—were sent to Port Moresby.

The anti-aircraft defences were also strengthened. On 11th April, less than four weeks after its disembarkation at Port Adelaide from the Middle East, the 2/3rd Light Anti-Aircraft Battery (Major Kelso[8]) began to arrive. On 23rd April it was in action against Japanese aircraft for the first time. In May the American 101st Coast Artillery Battalion, armed with .5-inch anti-aircraft machine-guns, reached Moresby.

By that time also a small but positive offensive movement by Australian land forces was being prepared. General Blamey had decided that Lae and Salamaua might be the scene of a profitable minor and local offensive. So, on 17th April, the 2/5th Independent Company (Major Kneen[9]) arrived at Port Moresby with the warning that they might expect instructions from Morris to cooperate with the N.G.V.R.

---
[8] Lt-Col P. W. A. Kelso, NX391. 2/1 Lt AA Regt; CO 109 Lt AA Regt 1942-43, 54 Composite AA Regt 1943-45. Commercial traveller; of Mosman, NSW; b. Harrow, England, 29 Jul 1908.
[9] Maj T. P. Kneen, NX65838; OC 2/5 Indep Coy. Officer of Colonial Administration Service; of Guadalcanal, Solomon Is; b. Douglas, Isle of Man, 18 Jun 1914. Killed in action 1 Jul 1942.

It was now clear, however, that the major crisis could not be long delayed. On 26th April Morris was warned that Japanese operations, intended to be decisive, were pending along the north-east axis.

At this time, also, there was an uneasy position along the north-west axis where Darwin had been under air attack since 19th February. Immediately after 8th December 1941, emphasis had been directed towards the north-west approaches to Australia by the vigour of the Japanese attack on Singapore and by the way the invaders crashed through the ABDA Area. On the Australian mainland Darwin rapidly became the key-point on these approaches.

It was the remote northern gateway to Australia, built on the shores of a busy harbour sheltered to the north by Melville and Bathurst Islands, and 2,000 miles or more by air from most of the State capitals. Immediately to the east and west of the town, in the 1,000 miles of coastline which lay between the Queensland and Western Australian borders, beaches alternated with mangrove swamps and, when the level of the sea dropped many feet at low tide, mud flats lay bare. To the south lay first the bush-covered and pleasant country of north Australia, watered by swamps and billabongs and rivers—notably the Roper and the Daly— flowing east and west. Then the tropical north merged into central Australia which was arid and thinly settled. Most of the country was given over to cattle runs some of which were up to 3,000,000 acres in extent.

There was a road travelling the 1,000 miles from Darwin south to Alice Springs, but when the rains came much of it became impassable. There was a railway running south from Darwin for about 300 miles to Birdum (its capacity then not more than 80 tons a day) and then a gap of about 600 miles to Alice Springs whence another line linked "the Centre" with Adelaide.

In the dry season the weather in the Darwin area was calm and shining. During "the Wet", from October to March, the whole of north Australia was drenched by daily rains and steamed with an enervating heat. Vehicles could move only short distances off the main roads. Either the thick dust which accumulated during the dry months turned to impassable bogs or the deceptively hard-looking, gravelly surface of the roads and tracks broke through beneath a slight pressure to a grey morass beneath.

On 11th December 1941 the Chiefs of Staff had underlined their uneasiness about Darwin. Next day the War Cabinet decided that, in general, women and children should be forced to leave the area (although this decision was not then fully acted upon). At the end of December the 27th and 43rd Battalions joined the 23rd Brigade to replace the 2/21st and 2/40th which, as mentioned earlier, had gone to Ambon and Timor. The 19th Light Horse Machine Gun Regiment (dismounted) followed in January to replace the 2/4th Machine Gun Battalion which went to Malaya.[1] Early in the New Year the 147th and 148th U.S. Field Artillery

---
[1] The only front-line AIF units which then remained in the area were the 2/4th Pioneer Battalion and the 2/14th Field Artillery Regiment. The latter unit, resentful of being left in Australia, severed its colour patches down the centre and declared that it would wear them that way until re-united with the 8th Division.

Regiments (from the *Pensacola* convoy) arrived, although a battalion of the 148th went on to the Indies soon and was lost there. During February the 2/4th Independent Company prepared to move from Victoria to Katherine; the 808th U.S. Engineer Battalion arrived at Batchelor and brought the total of American forces in the Darwin area to 2,601; the 7th and 8th Battalions reached Darwin and the field force was then constituted as two brigades—the 23rd and 3rd.

On 17th February when Mr Curtin asked Mr Churchill for the diversion of the returning A.I.F. to Australia, he said that Darwin was the first place which should be reinforced; on the 18th, when the Chief of the Air Staff told the War Cabinet that the first six squadrons of American fighters to be assembled in Australia were to go to ABDA Command, the War Cabinet decided to ask General Wavell that some at least of these machines be retained in Australia for the defence of Darwin, as well as for the defence of the east coast areas and Port Moresby. The events of 19th February were to give a sharp point to their request.

At the end of January Wavell had asked for more troops for Koepang, Dutch Timor. This was at first refused on the grounds (*inter alia*) that Darwin itself still needed reinforcing and the forces required to protect Australia's other vital areas had already been reduced to a minimum. On 15th February, however, the 2/4th Pioneer Battalion, the II/148th U.S. Field Artillery Battalion and a troop of Australian anti-tank guns set out for Koepang in five transports, escorted by the American cruiser *Houston*, the American destroyer *Peary*, and the Australian sloops *Swan* and *Warrego*. No air cover for the convoy was available. Approaching Timor the ships were attacked by 35 bombers and 9 flying-boats. The warships fought back vigorously. An Australian army officer said later of the *Houston*:

> She spun on her heel, every gun was blazing. She kept the Japs right up in the sky and they could not get down to bomb us.

The convoy, however, on Wavell's orders, turned back to Darwin where it arrived on the 18th.

At 9.35 on the morning of the 19th the Catholic Mission on Bathurst Island radioed that a large number of aircraft had just passed overhead travelling south at a great height. The mission wireless was then jammed. Within two minutes of its receipt the warning was passed to the R.A.A.F. Operations Centre, but the air force did not at once accept that these aircraft were hostile; they could be ten American Kittyhawks under Major Floyd J. Pell which had landed at Darwin unexpectedly on the 15th, had set out for Timor that morning, and were returning because of bad weather; or an American group retreating from the Indies—sometimes American ships and aircraft arrived without warning.

None of the Australians could know at that time that the aircraft were from a fleet of four carriers (supported by battleships, cruisers and destroyers) which Vice-Admiral Kondo had led in a night approach through the Banda Sea. At daylight on the 19th probably 54 bombers and 27 fighters were launched by this fleet against Darwin. In the Kendari area to the north-west the *First Air Attack Force* prepared to send off 54 medium bombers.

Meanwhile Pell's ten machines were back over Darwin about the same time as the warning from Bathurst Island arrived. Pell dropped down to the airfield with four others to refuel and left the remaining five Kittyhawks aloft as air cover. As these were climbing to 15,000 feet nine Japanese fighters, which had been detached from the main flight in the vicinity of Bathurst Island to close the target directly, drove at them. Lieutenant R. G. Oestreicher (the most experienced of the five American pilots) shouted "Zeros! Zeros!" into his radio and, with his companions, dived away, dropping his bellytank as he did so. The others were shot down but Oestreicher got into cloud cover, from which he later shot down two bombers, and brought his bullet-marked machine home.

Still no warning was sounded at Darwin. Finally the alarm went at 9.58 a.m. just when the army's heavy anti-aircraft guns (sixteen of 3.7-inch and two of 3-inch) opened up as the main attacking force finished its sweep from the south-east down the sun at 14,000 feet and reached the bomb-release point. Columns of water leaped from the harbour as the bombs hit. The anti-aircraft fire was uncertain at first and then settled among some of the formations. Fighters, dive bombers and high-level bombers attacked the airfield, the harbour and the town.

From the airfield Pell and his four pilots raced to get the only available fighters into the air. One pilot was killed on the ground. Pell himself parachuted from 80 feet and was killed. The other three machines were picked off as they rose (but the pilots survived parachute or crash landings). Dive bombers and fighters then attacked the airfield systematically. Some of the strafing planes were so low as they raced up and down the airstrip that the faces of the pilots could be clearly seen from the ground. Soon many of the buildings were shattered or in flames. Machine-gunners and riflemen fired into the attackers from the ground.

There was great destruction in the harbour. One bomb hit the jetty near the shore end, shattered an entire span, hurled a locomotive into the sea, killed a number of wharf labourers and left some marooned on the jetty's seaward end. Many ships were soon hotly beset. Anti-aircraft fire from ships mingled with the army fire. Oil took fire on the water. At 10.15 the Chief Officer of the hospital ship *Manunda*

looked round and saw what had happened. . . . The wharf was burning near its inner end; *Barossa* and *Neptuna* at the wharf both appeared to have been hit and *Neptuna* appeared to be on fire. *Zealandia*, about 500 yards away, was on fire. *British Motorist* was sinking by the head. *Meigs* was on fire and sinking aft. *Mauna Loa* was down by the stern with her back broken. *Tulagi* was nowhere to be seen. *Portmar* was in trouble. . . . On the naval side a Catalina flying-boat was ablaze, an American destroyer [actually the tender *Preston*], ablaze aft, went dashing across our bows, missing us by inches and steering with her engines. Another American destroyer [*Peary*] was on our port side, a solid mass of flames with burning oil around her and what was left of the crew jumping into the burning oil.

Army machine-gunners from Stokes Hill (the site of the oil storage tanks near the jetty) fired steadily. They engaged one bomber which dived straight at the tanks. The pilot missed his aim and inflicted only minor damage—on two tanks.

Damage to the town itself was caused mostly by fifteen large bombs. The hospital was hit and the Administration offices, police barracks and post office were shattered—the lastnamed by a direct hit which disrupted all telephone communications and killed the postmaster, his family, and the girls at the switches.

The raiders broke away at about 10.30 a.m. and the "all clear" was sounded at 10.40 a.m. But just before midday the 54 bombers from the Ambon bases arrived, pattern-bombed the airfield and set a seal to the destruction the carrier aircraft had caused.

The raiders sank eight ships in the harbour and destroyed two near Bathurst Island (the *Florence D* and *Don Isidro* which were setting out to try to run the blockade into the Philippines); three ships were driven ashore but later salvaged; ten other ships were damaged. Twenty-four American and R.A.A.F. aircraft were destroyed and two were damaged. Probably about 250 people were killed and some 320 others received hospital treatment for wounds. The attackers were definitely known to have lost five aircraft and five "probables" were claimed by the defenders.

After the raids confusion developed among the townspeople and some sections of the R.A.A.F. By the middle of the afternoon of the 19th many of the civilians were seeking to leave the town by any available means and a long string of vehicles was already moving southwards down the main road to Adelaide River. Later some looting both by servicemen and civilians began and it continued sporadically for some time afterwards. Soon after the raids those women—except hospital nurses—who still remained in the area were sent to the south, but able-bodied male civilians of suitable age were drafted into the army. Indeed the disorders were not finally eliminated until Major Simpson[2] was brought to Darwin in April. He reorganised the provosts and did outstanding work in restoring order and discipline.

When Mr Justice Lowe completed the investigation which, soon after the raids, the Government appointed him to make into the circumstances at Darwin on the 19th February, he reported of the army:

> The evidence before me was all to the effect that the anti-aircraft batteries operated efficiently and that the personnel of the A.M.F. performed very creditably in their baptism of fire. . . . The only part of the Military Forces required for action in the raid itself were anti-aircraft equipment and personnel; as I have already indicated . . . the conduct of the personnel is to be highly commended.

The 19th February 1942 will be remembered as the first time in the history of Australia that the blows of war actually fell on Australian soil. But, at the time, the historic importance of the occasion was of less moment than the interpretation of the intention behind these blows. It later became clear that the Japanese object in bombing Darwin was to take advantage of the opportunity target offered by the shipping in the harbour and to

---

[2] Lt-Col C. L. Simpson, VX66. 2/8 Bn; DAPM NT Force; APM Qld L of C Area. Police constable; of Box Hill, Vic; b. Leeds, England, 21 Apr 1909.

neutralise a base which might prove troublesome to them in their attacks on Timor and Java. But it was understandable that there should have been many who saw the raids as the beginning of a "softening up" process preliminary to Japanese landings, particularly as they were followed within two days by the invasion of Timor. Such swiftness would not have been out of keeping with the Japanese methods. The invaders had not waited for the fall of the Philippines before they pushed on to occupy Rabaul nor for the fall of Singapore before they struck into Burma. Then again some noted that the raiders had seemed to spare certain important installations, such as the oil tanks, and inferred that they wanted them for their own future use.

Before the end of the month National Security Regulations were invoked to vest the administration of the Northern Territory north of Birdum in the military commander (in the same terms as those by which General Morris in Port Moresby had been given similar authority). On the 9th March after noting Lowe's interim report the War Cabinet decided that the whole area north of Alice Springs should be placed under complete military control. On the 24th the appointment was approved of Major-General Herring,[3] who had returned from the Middle East as commander of the 6th Division only a few days earlier, to command the forces in the Darwin area in place of Major-General D. V. J. Blake.

The air raids had highlighted Darwin's supply problem. Supply by sea by orthodox means was now hazardous and regular supply by air was not yet practicable, while the problems of overland supply were legion. But the army was forced to try to exploit both the overland and sea routes. Immediately after the first raids an additional 385 lorries and 40 trailers were hastily made available in an attempt to increase the road-carrying capacity to 250 tons a day. Previously the daily capacity of the road link had been 150 tons which provided only for the daily consumption by the force of rations, petrol, aviation spirit and road material. On 19th March a sum of £1,481,080 was allotted to increase the capacity of the Central and North Australian railways. To augment the road and rail overland routes, a service which it was hoped would consist ultimately of nine small vessels, each of a carrying capacity of 400-500 tons, on 9th March began to shuttle cargo from Cairns to Darwin.

At the same time steps were taken to build up actual strength in the Darwin area still further. Lowe had been rather diffidently critical of the density of the anti-aircraft guns at Darwin. The army, however, had believed that the eighteen guns in operation there at the time of the raids were the most which it could make available in the light of other commitments. But as March advanced plans were pushed ahead for a stronger concentration of anti-aircraft artillery, both American and Australian, including batteries of the 2/1st Anti-Aircraft Regiment (Lieut-Colonel Gib-

---

[3] Lt-Gen Hon Sir Edmund Herring, KCMG, KBE, DSO, MC, ED, VX15. (1914-18: RFA in France and Macedonia.) CRA 6 Div 1939-41; GOC 6 Div 1941-42, NT Force 1942, II Corps 1942, I Corps and NG Force 1942-43, I Corps 1943-44. Chief Justice of Victoria since 1944, Lt-Gov since 1945. Of Melbourne; b. Maryborough, Vic, 2 Sep 1892.

son[4]) back from the Middle East, and the American 102nd Coast Artillery Battalion armed with heavy machine-guns. Soon after Gibson's arrival in the Territory as regimental commander, he was also appointed Anti-Aircraft Defence Commander, Northern Territory Force, and the regimental headquarters carried out this function until August 1943, when it left the Territory.[5] By the 19th, too, an American Kittyhawk fighter squadron was on its way to Darwin and two more such squadrons were scheduled to move there. By 28th March the total strength of the forces in the area was: Australian Navy 1,002; Australian Army 14,082; R.A.A.F. 857; United States forces 3,200; and it was planned to increase the Australian Army figures by 10,000 and those of the United States Forces by 3,000.

This was the day on which General Herring virtually took over the Darwin command. Such was considered to be the urgency of the situation that Herring and some of his staff officers had left Adelaide for Darwin by air on the 27th March, little more than a week after they arrived back from the Middle East.[6]

Herring's strength at this time did not lie in the extent of his military experience, which in higher command had been limited. He had distinguished himself during long service in the British Army in the 1914-18 War, first as a trooper and then as an artillery officer. He had commanded the 6th Divisional Artillery in North Africa and Greece but his command of the 6th Division itself had dated only from the beginning of its period as part of the garrison of Syria. His strength was to be found in the depth of character of this small and quiet man, in his ideals of service which enabled him to give all about him something of his own quality.

And all the strength of his purpose was required in his new command. It had been clear for some time before that all was not well with the army in the 7th Military District. It was true that those sections from whom action was demanded in the 19th February raids had acquitted themselves well. It was equally true that in some other units there was high-spirited resolve, allied with efficiency in training, which augured well for their conduct in action. But well before 19th February, indeed during 1941, some troops in the Darwin area had become restless and discontented—a result of the general effects of tropical service; of a feeling among some officers and men that Darwin was being used as an Australian military Siberia; of a policy of placing two different classes of soldiers—A.I.F. and militia—side by side for a common task, in trying and monotonous circumstances, under different conditions of service, and of retaining in what they regarded as a backwater soldiers who had enlisted for service overseas; and of certain deficiencies in leadership. In addition it was likely that the raids of 19th February and their attendant circumstances

---

[4] Lt-Col A. R. M. Gibson, ED, NX381. CO 2/1 Hvy AA Regt 1940-41, 2/1 Lt AA Regt 1941-43; Comd AA Defences NT Force 1942-43; Comd Brisbane AA Gp 1943-44, Fremantle AA Gp 1944-45. Solicitor; of Gordon, NSW; b. Lindfield, NSW, 25 Feb 1903.

[5] During this period the 2/1st Lt AA Regt was responsible for the anti-aircraft defences of all Northern Territory areas, and particularly airfields, outside the area of the Darwin Fortress. Within the fortress area the anti-aircraft defences, including the defence of the RAAF aerodrome, were under the command from August 1942 of Major (later Lt-Col) R. M. Ford.

[6] These were: Colonel R. B. Sutherland, Colonel R. Bierwirth, Major A. E. Bamford, Major A. W. Sheppard, Captain D. McCarthy.

had disturbed the minds of some of the men. So Herring found to some extent a dejected force.

The troops were deployed on the coast in the immediate vicinity of Darwin itself which, with its fixed defences of ten guns, was constituted a "fortress area". These deployment positions were tactically unsound and offered a chance of successful action only in the unlikely event of the enemy landing in the particular areas.

Herring found also a disturbing supply position. The lines of communication were functioning only with difficulty, adequate daily maintenance of the force over a period was not assured, and reserves of all kinds were below the margin required for the present strength and the reinforcements which had been promised. Because of this he was forced to have the movement to Darwin of the veteran 19th Brigade deferred at this critical time.

The new commander was given very wide powers, even wider than those implied in the fact that the area north of Alice Springs had been placed under complete military control. On the grounds that Darwin was the most vulnerable area on the Australian mainland, that its retention was of great importance for future offensive operations and that its loss would give the enemy control of the whole north area of Australia, he was instructed to prevent its seizure and occupation. To this end he was ordered:

> You will command all Australian Military Forces in the Northern Territory and such U.S. land forces as are assigned to your command. You will coordinate the defence plans of all three Services at all times. When a land attack on the Northern Territory has started, or in your judgment is clearly imminent, you will assume absolute control over Naval, Military and Air Forces.

His first step was to revise the tactical plans on the premise that he could not deny to the enemy the whole of the coastline within striking distance east and west of Darwin and that, therefore, he must deploy his field force in the locality from which he could move most readily and effectively toward any area where the enemy might land, and to the assistance of Darwin Fortress itself to which a separate force was necessarily allotted. Thus he disposed the 3rd and 23rd Brigades along the main road, south of Darwin and planned similarly to site the 19th Brigade on its arrival.

Then began a period of intense testing, training, indoctrination and reconnaissance, of rapid construction, and of detailed organisation in an endeavour to provide for the maintenance of the force. A number of officers were replaced by young veterans from the Middle East. Lieut-Colonel Dougherty,[7] young, cool, practical, who had shown his worth in North Africa, Greece and Crete, was brought from the 2/4th Battalion to command the 23rd Brigade; King,[8] quick-witted and ruthless, an experienced professional soldier, was given the 3rd Brigade; Major McCarty,[9]

---

[7] Maj-Gen I. N. Dougherty, CBE, DSO, ED, NX148. CO 2/4 Bn 1940-42; Comd 23 Bde 1942, 21 Bde 1942-45. Schoolteacher; of Armidale, NSW; b. Leadville, NSW, 6 Apr 1907.
[8] Maj-Gen R. King, CBE, DSO, VX20315. CO 2/5 Bn 1941-42; Comd 16 Bde 1943-45. Regular soldier; of Newcastle, NSW; b. Newcastle, 27 Aug 1897.
[9] Lt-Col J. McCarty, MC, NX61. 2/4 Bn; CO 2/4 Pnr Bn 1942-45. Salesman; of Kensington, NSW; b. Tamworth, NSW, 31 May 1910.

of the 2/4th Infantry Battalion took over the 2/4th Pioneer Battalion; other A.I.F. officers were promoted to command the 7th, 8th and 19th Battalions. Although the wholesale replacement of officers represented by such appointments as these (which by no means exhausted the process) was ruthless, and certainly unduly harsh in some cases, the effect was electric, particularly as it was accompanied by corresponding staff changes. The 6th Divisional staff replaced the old "7 M.D." Headquarters almost completely and was rapidly augmented by more officers from the returning A.I.F.

The new commanders drove the units relentlessly, concentrating first on physical hardening, on revised minor tactics to meet a form of warfare not hitherto foreseen, and on the consolidation of their elementary training as a basis for later intensive exercises in swift movement, and deployment as battalions, brigades, and finally as a force. Lines of possible Japanese approach were explored and mapped and, in the light of this constantly increasing topographical knowledge, and as training became effective and as airfields developed south of Darwin, the general strategical plans for the area were revised. These tended to shift the centre of gravity of the force farther south and the units were ultimately sited to meet what was considered to be the most likely invading action—coordinated drives, or separate thrusts, from the Bynoe Bay and the Anson Bay-Daly River areas.

Meanwhile a watch was developing over the empty spaces of the hinterland and the extended coastline. Efforts had previously been made to coordinate the pedal wireless sets of north Australia into a reporting network; Squadron Leader Thomson[1] in his ketch *Aroetta* had, for some months, been operating among the natives of the Gulf country. The 2/4th Independent Company, based on Katherine, was to keep in touch with Thomson and fulfil a guerilla-reconnaissance role in the triangle Birdum-Groote Island-Anson Bay. To augment these plans the North Australia Observer Unit was formed under Major Stanner,[2] like Thomson an anthropologist.

The construction and maintenance program was speeded up. The arterial roads from the south and from Mount Isa were improved and tactical laterals developed; engineers worked on aerodrome construction both by day and, in the light of blazing flares, by night; air services were augmented; the small ships began to creep in with supplies and relieve the strain on the overland route.

The background to all this was one of constant watchfulness and almost hourly expectancy of sighting an invasion fleet. Air raids became common and, though they caused few casualties, and, in general, only minor material damage, provided the undertones of real war. As each developed it did so with the promise that it might be the beginning of the pre-

---

[1] W Cdr D. F. Thomson, OBE, 250194; RAAF. Anthropologist; of Melbourne; b. Melbourne, 26 Jun 1901.

[2] Lt-Col W. E. H. Stanner, VX89030. OC North Australia Observer Unit 1942-43; Assistant Director Research (Territories Admin) LHQ 1943-44; Civil Affairs Offr, Aust Army Staff UK 1944-45. Anthropologist; of Sydney; b. Sydney, 24 Nov 1905.

invasion "softening-up". But the Japanese air efforts were curiously spasmodic.

Soon after midday on 31st March seven heavy bombers, escorted by 12 to 15 fighters, attacked the R.A.A.F. aerodrome. At 10.30 p.m. the first night raid began. On 2nd April the town was further damaged by raiders and 60,000 gallons of aviation spirit were lost from a badly-holed storage tank. Seven bombers, escorted by fighters, were over again on the 4th; six of the bombers and two fighters were shot down, one bomber and two fighters were probably destroyed, for the loss of two American Kittyhawks and one pilot. After this flare-up came a lull, with only Japanese reconnaissance aircraft flying over, until the afternoon of 25th April when twenty-four heavy bombers with a fighter escort attacked the R.A.A.F. installations. Eight bombers and three fighters were destroyed and a number of others were badly damaged. On the 27th seventeen or eighteen bombers, with eighteen escorting fighters, appeared; three bombers and four fighters were shot down for the loss of four Kittyhawks. After this another period of quiet followed for some weeks.

By the beginning of May, the effort that had been put forth was beginning to show results. Operationally there was an increasingly efficient force, more alert, more confident and far readier to meet invasion. It had been learned with amazement that the Australian commando forces on Timor were fighting on; they were now being directed and assisted from Darwin.[3] The veterans of the 19th Brigade and 2/6th Cavalry were preparing to move north to give a sharper edge to the field force. Engineer and ordnance units were also moving north. Supplies were beginning to flow in through a maintenance system which was working at a pitch of efficiency not considered possible previously.

Emptier and more vulnerable, however, than the Northern Territory was the adjacent country in the north of Western Australia. Dangerously open also were the more southern areas of Western Australia where Fremantle formed the Australian terminal of the Indian Ocean sea routes, the main sea lines of communication with the Middle East and Great Britain, and where American submarines were already based.

In January 1942, the Minister for the Army had announced that henceforth there would be two commanders of the Home Forces. Lieut-General Mackay would remain responsible for eastern and southern Australia, but Major-General Plant (who had just been appointed to Western Command) would be responsible for the remote force in Western Australia.

The Japanese soon showed that there might be cause for concern about the north-west. On the morning of 3rd March numerous small craft were lying at anchor in the harbour at Broome and fourteen flying-boats were moored there. Most of these aircraft had just arrived from the Indies carrying refugees who were still aboard them. There was no defence when Japanese aircraft arrived and proceeded systematically to attack the flying-

---

[3] See Appendix 2 for an account of the operations in Timor subsequent to March 1942.

boats and the land planes which were on the near-by aerodrome. All the flying-boats were destroyed and six large aircraft ashore (including two Flying Fortresses and two Liberators). Women and children were among those cast into the water dead or wounded, or uninjured but struggling to keep afloat. Captain Brain[4] of Qantas Empire Airways, who was responsible for saving several lives, estimated that 35 to 40 people were killed and probably as many again wounded.

Wyndham was also attacked that day but there was little to be damaged there except the town itself. Broome was raided again on the 20th and Derby was raided on the same day. On the 23rd Wyndham was raided for the second time.

The Chiefs of Staff then decided that Broome was important only as an R.A.A.F. refuelling station and that Wyndham could not be linked effectively into any defence plans; that they would, therefore, concentrate their forces at Darwin and make it the centre for both the north and north-west of Australia. Broome and Wyndham were then left undefended except for about 80 and 30 members of the V.D.C. at each place, an overlap of the Northern Territory coastwatching services to Wyndham, and small detachments of engineers who were stationed at each place to carry out demolitions in the event of invasion. Australia would have to accept enemy occupation of the north-west if the Japanese decided on it.

However, despite the threat to the north of Australia that seemed to be developing at this time, the most vigorous Japanese activity in the sector north-west of Australia was being manifest in Burma.

The rapid march of events there posed a threat to India and Ceylon, exposed British weaknesses and led to the retention in Ceylon of part of the returning A.I.F. Hitherto there had been only two brigades of an Indian division and one brigade of local troops, with detachments of supporting arms, in Ceylon. One brigade group of the 70th Division, the only British division in India, was marked as reinforcement for the garrison but, even after its arrival, the weakness of Ceylon's defences would remain a matter of concern. There was no other source of rapid reinforcement except the returning A.I.F. At length it was decided that the garrison would be reinforced with the 16th and 17th Brigade Groups of the 6th Division which were still at Suez.[5] Orders at once went out for this to be done, and Brigadier Boase,[6] then commanding the 16th Brigade, was promoted to the rank of major-general to take command of the A.I.F. in Ceylon, and Lieut-Colonel Lloyd[7] of the 2/28th Battalion, was promoted to command the 16th Brigade.

---

[4] W Cdr L. J. Brain, AFC; RAAF. Airlines pilot and Operations Manager with Qantas 1924-46; General Manager TAA 1946-55; Managing Director de Havilland Aircraft Pty Ltd since 1955. Of Sydney; b. Forbes, NSW, 27 Feb 1903.

[5] The discussions leading up to this decision are described in the previous volume of this series.

[6] Lt-Gen A. J. Boase, CBE, NX366. (1st AIF: Maj 9 Bn.) AA&QMG 7 Div; Brig i/c Admin Base & L of C Units ME 1940-41; Comd 16 Bde 1941-42 and GOC AIF Ceylon 1942; MGGS First Army 1942-43; GOC 11 Div 1943-45, Western Command 1945. Regular soldier; of Brisbane and Sydney; b. Gympie, Qld, 19 Feb 1894.

[7] Brig J. E. Lloyd, CBE, DSO, MC, ED; WX3346. (1st AIF: Lt 23 and 24 Bns. Indian Army 1918-22.) CO 2/28 Bn 1940-42; Comd 16 Bde 1942-43, 2 Aust PW Reception Gp 1945. Secretary; of Perth; b. Melbourne, 13 Apr 1894.

When Boase arrived on 18th March he found that few preparations had been made for the reception of his force, that there was a serious shortage of stores and equipment of all kinds and a lack of balance in the allotment of units to the garrison, and that defence plans were only just beginning to develop. On 21st March the *Otranto,* carrying most of the

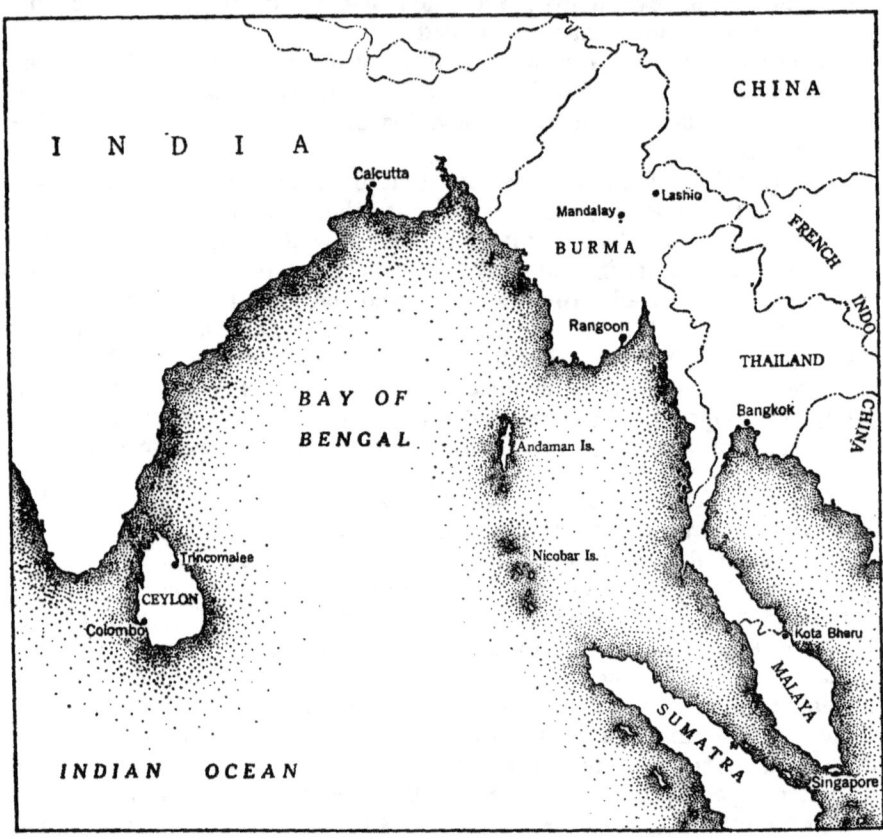

17th Brigade Group, berthed at Colombo and the *Orontes* and *Westmoreland* arrived soon afterwards with the balance of the force. The Australians then found that they were responsible for the defence of the south-west corner of Ceylon which, until the south-west monsoon broke, was considered to be the sector in which the Japanese would be most likely to land.

It seemed that reinforcements for Ceylon had arrived only just in time when a strong Japanese naval force appeared in Indian waters, and Colombo and Trincomalee were heavily attacked by carrier-borne aircraft on 5th and 9th April respectively. Though little damage was done on land the defenders lost heavily in the air and at sea. Standing on to the north-west after raiding Colombo, the Japanese force sank the cruisers *Cornwall* and *Dorsetshire*. On 9th April, the aircraft carrier *Hermes* and the Australian destroyer *Vampire* were also sunk by dive bombers.

Though the Japanese sustained heavy aircraft losses that was not sufficient compensation to the British for their own losses. If the raiders had renewed their attacks these would have been difficult to meet. The position was gloomy as the Japanese were moving purposefully elsewhere in Indian waters. There was nothing much to hinder them since they had destroyed or driven out the combined ABDA fleet by the beginning of March, and the Commander-in-Chief of the British Eastern Fleet, as he told Wavell, could do nothing to prevent the invasion of southern India or Ceylon. Nor could he send naval forces into the Bay of Bengal to protect shipping or the east coast of India. So the Japanese ranged unchecked through the Bay of Bengal where, during this same period, with light naval forces and aircraft, they sank just on 100,000 tons of merchant shipping and caused panic on the east coast of India. "This was India's most dangerous hour," Wavell said later. "Our Eastern Fleet was powerless to protect Ceylon or eastern India; our air strength was negligible and it was becoming increasingly obvious that our small and tired force in Burma was unlikely to be able to hold the enemy."

By this time it was clear to the Australians that, if land fighting were going to take place in Ceylon, it would be a type different from that to which they were accustomed. The south-west area of the island was almost entirely covered with coconut, rubber and tea plantations and areas of thick bush. Generally the only open parts of the country were given over to rice-fields. The interior roads were not suitable for heavy military traffic. So the veteran campaigners began to discard those of the lessons of the Middle East which obviously would not apply in the Far East and to search for and apply the lessons of Malaya. Much of their time was taken up with engineering tasks—strengthening bridges, widening roads, and developing tracks—but from the beginning they were training in the new methods. They built up a supply of bicycles to enable them to move rapidly and silently on tracks where motor transport could not travel, modified the design of their Bren gun carriers to protect the crews from explosives which could be thrown into the vehicles from the thick scrub, and improvised weapons for bush warfare. They concentrated on moving through thickly-wooded country, physical hardening and developing the ability to live for long periods on simple and limited rations. The 17th Brigade established a "Jungle Warfare School" (along lines which were to become well defined in similar schools in Australia as the war with Japan developed) and the whole trend of training reflected a ready adaptability.

Thus the beginning of May found the Japanese vigorously on the move through the whole area north of Australia. At Corregidor the end was coming for Wainwright and his men; in Burma the British-Indian force was being pushed back to India. In the islands closer to Australia some sort of climax was obviously approaching; in the Solomons the Japanese air attacks on Tulagi were intensifying; behind Lae and Salamaua the men of the N.G.V.R. were hanging grimly to the edges of the Japanese occupation; at Port Moresby General Morris had been warned that a "decisive" moment was at hand. On the mainland itself General Herring was still racing time at Darwin; north-west Australia was open for a series of progressive Japanese steps towards Fremantle. In the east the First Army had been told by the Australian leaders that probable moves by the Japanese would be the capture of Port Moresby followed by a progressive advance south under cover of land-based aircraft; that the whole coastline from Brisbane to Townsville could not then be held; that the First Army's tasks were to defend Thursday Island with the existing garrison, to defend Townsville with a garrison which would be built up to one division at an early date, to defend the Brisbane area.

In the Solomon Islands the Japanese attacks on Tulagi mounted vehemently until 2nd May when eight heavy raids took place between 6 a.m. and 5 p.m. That day coastwatchers reported the approach of Japanese ships, whereupon Captain Goode and the soldiers and airmen with him coolly carried out their demolition program and the glow of their fires rose high that night. Then they put off in their small boat for Vila in the New Hebrides. They could scarcely have timed their escape more finely, for the Japanese began the occupation of Tulagi next day.

By this time reports gathered by Australian and American Intelligence made a definite pattern. Japanese naval forces were on the move southward, Japanese aircraft concentrated in New Britain were ready to support this movement.

Warned well in advance Rear-Admiral F. J. Fletcher of the United States Navy, who had been cruising in these seas, on 1st May brought his force to a rendezvous south of the Solomons with Rear-Admiral A. W. Fitch, fresh from re-fitting at Pearl Harbour. Fletcher had with him the aircraft carrier *Yorktown,* the heavy cruisers *Astoria, Chester,* and *Portland,* six destroyers and the tanker *Neosho.* Fitch brought to the rendezvous the carrier *Lexington,* the heavy cruisers *Minneapolis* and *New Orleans,* and five destroyers. Fletcher took command of the combined force and Fitch's ships began to re-fuel at sea from an oiler, guarded by the heavy cruiser *Chicago* and the destroyer *Perkins.*

On the 2nd Admiral Fletcher received reports that the Japanese were preparing to move on Port Moresby. He himself at once set a course for the north-west, leaving Fitch to move to a meeting on the 4th with the Australian heavy and light cruisers *Australia* and *Hobart* (Rear-Admiral J. G. Crace).

Fletcher had news on the evening of the 3rd that the Japanese were landing at Tulagi. After a high-speed run he launched his attacking planes from the *Yorktown* early in three separate attacks on the Japanese in Tulagi Harbour. The target was disappointingly meagre but the Americans smashed a destroyer and a cargo ship, five seaplanes and a number of small craft, and damaged other ships. One American pilot was lost.

By the 5th Fletcher had rendezvoused again with Fitch. Soon he knew definitely that a strong Japanese force of troop-carrying ships was moving down from Rabaul to Port Moresby under naval cover which included the aircraft carrier *Shoho*. It seemed likely that the force would make for Port Moresby by way of the Jomard Passage in the Louisiade Archipelago. A separate striking force, built round the carriers *Shokaku* and *Zuikaku*, was moving into the Coral Sea round San Cristobal in the southern Solomons.

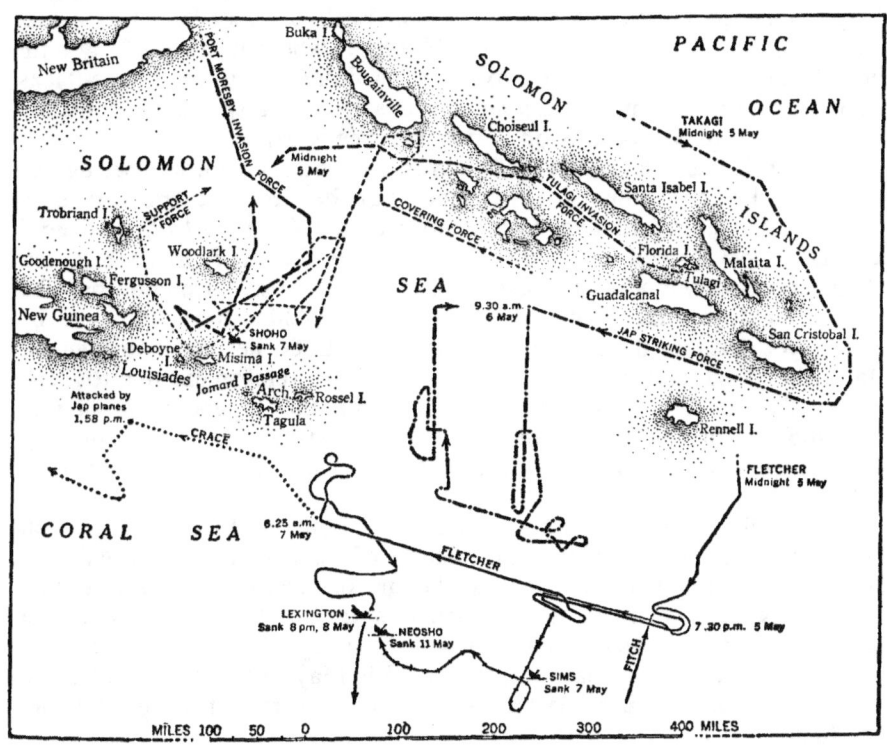

Coral Sea Battle, 5th-8th May

On the morning of the 7th May each force knew where the other was. At 9 a.m., the transports were ordered to turn back and, for the time being, the threat to Moresby ceased. The *Shoho* was picked up by scouting aircraft near Misima. Aircraft from the *Lexington* and the *Yorktown* sank it. About the same time Japanese aircraft from the *Shokaku* and *Zuikaku* attacked and sank the *Neosho,* mistaking it for an aircraft carrier. It was a costly mistake for them.

Next morning the main action was joined off the Louisiades. Japanese aircraft from Rabaul flew down to take part in it. From their bases in the Cairns-Townsville-Cloncurry area Australian and American pilots hurried to join the battle. The opposing aircraft carriers manoeuvred strenuously to avoid the attacks levelled at them as they sent their own aircraft into the air. Not a single shot was exchanged by opposing surface craft. It was a fitting culmination to the first months of this new war of which sea-air movement had been the dominant feature.

But, from the Allied point of view, the destructive results of the aircraft attacks on the Japanese ships were disappointing. Other than the *Shoho* no Japanese ships were sunk although a number, including the other two carriers, were damaged. The Americans lost the *Lexington,* the destroyer *Sims* and the *Neosho,* and the *Yorktown* was badly damaged. Despite this the Japanese turned and went back the way they had come, postponing their attempt to take Port Moresby, where from 6th May until the 9th the garrison had been anxiously awaiting heavy bombing attacks followed by the landing of Japanese troops from transports and possibly the descent of paratroops, as on Timor ten weeks earlier.

Whether it was the sighting of Admiral Crace's squadron barring the way of the Japanese convoy or the sighting of the aircraft carriers, or both that caused Admiral Inouye, Commander of the *Fourth Fleet,* in overall command from Rabaul, to order the convoy to turn away remains in doubt. There can be no doubt, however, that it was most fortunate that the efficient American naval Intelligence enabled the Allied naval forces to be on the spot and that the convoy was turned back. So hesitant had General MacArthur and General Blamey been to send reinforcements to New Guinea that on 10th May, the day on which the Japanese planned to land round Port Moresby, the defending garrison was not materially stronger than the one which General Sturdee had established there early in January.

The Coral Sea battle caused keen anxiety both in Washington and in Australia. At a meeting of the Joint Chiefs of Staff on 11th May Admiral Ernest J. King pointed out that until the end of June there would be only two serviceable American aircraft carriers in the Pacific, whereas the Japanese had from seven to ten, and radio intercepts indicated that a large naval force was due to leave Japan on 20th May and could be at some point on the line joining Alaska, Hawaii and Australia between 1st and 5th June.

In Australia on 12th May MacArthur sent Curtin a gloomy appreciation in the course of which he said that he believed the enemy could strike "a new blow of the most dangerous potentialities against the S.W.P.A. or against India", and that a Japanese offensive against the S.W.P.A. should precede a movement against India. He urged haste in developing the Australian "defensive bastion". "We have . . . in this theatre at the present time all the elements that have produced disaster in the Western Pacific since the beginning of the war." He informed Curtin that he had cabled to General Marshall a request for two aircraft carriers, a corps of three divisions, and a first-line strength of 1,000 aircraft.

However, not only did the Battle of the Coral Sea stave off attack on Port Moresby (and air attacks on the Australian north-east coast, for both the *Shokaku* and *Zuikaku* had been detailed to press on to Townsville and destroy there the assemblage of Allied shipping and aircraft), but it helped to dislocate a wider and more ambitious plan.

The rapidity of the advance southward of the Japanese up to the end of January made it necessary for them quickly to establish a firm perimeter in the New Guinea-Solomons area. They needed this to enable them to consolidate their gains and to build up their strength to seize key-points farther south and sever the Pacific lines of communication. Airfields were the vital links. Port Moresby, Salamaua, Lae and Tulagi were therefore obvious points at which to aim.

The invasion of Lae and Salamaua had been carried out by a combined navy-army group totalling about 3,000 men. These gathered in Rabaul, left there with a strong naval escort and, as they approached their destination on 7th March, divided into two groups. A strong battalion group of Major-General Tomitaro Horii's *South Seas Force* landed at Salamaua. Naval troops occupied Lae. As soon as it was clear that the land defence of the two points was secure Horii's men withdrew from Salamaua leaving about 1,500 naval troops in the whole Lae-Salamaua area to build up and defend the Lae air base which was their chief concern.

The Japanese Imperial General Headquarters discussed operations against Australia on 15th March. The army staff were opposed to an invasion of Australia which they said would require ten divisions or more. Both army and navy confirmed a plan formulated in February to take Port Moresby, and isolate Australia by occupying Fiji, Samoa and New Caledonia. The convoy turned back in the Coral Sea carried a force including the *114th Regiment* and the *3rd Kure Naval Landing Force*. The seizure of Port Moresby was to be followed by that of Midway Island in order to force a decisive engagement with the American fleet. The Japanese would also invade the western Aleutians to secure their defences in the north. Despite the setback in the Coral Sea General Hyakutake, commanding the *XVII Japanese Army,* was ordered from Tokyo on 18th May to press on towards New Caledonia, Fiji and Samoa, and to resume the advance on Port Moresby in July. The successful execution of these plans, the Japanese hoped, would prevent the concentration in Australia and New Zealand of forces sufficiently strong to wage an offensive war. From New Guinea, New Caledonia, Fiji and Samoa sustained neutralising attacks would be levelled at key-points of Australia and New Zealand. Sheltered within the outer rim of the defences thus established the development of the Greater East Asia Co-Prosperity Sphere was to proceed.

CHAPTER 3

KANGA FORCE

IN the weeks following his arrival in Australia General MacArthur found himself hedged about by those same circumstances which had prevented the Australian military leaders from planning to offer strong opposition to the Japanese in the islands to the north. General Blamey's reorganised army was only beginning to take shape; American ground troops were only just arriving and the stage of training they had reached did not yet fit them for active operations; the Allied air forces in Australia were still inadequate and sufficient airfields were not available for them to operate far afield; the British Far Eastern Fleet could not hope even to prevent Japanese naval domination of the Bay of Bengal still less to play an effective part elsewhere; and the American Navy was still on the defensive in the Pacific, probing tentatively against the Japanese in a series of hit-and-run raids, and able to guarantee no measure of security for Allied forces which might be sent outside the main base, or even for Australia itself. In very similar circumstances MacArthur had already fought and lost a major campaign in the Philippines. During his first months as commander of the South-West Pacific Area he was in no position to try to force an issue with the Japanese. Even in mid-May, when examining the possibility of an approach towards Japan through New Guinea and New Britain to the Philippines, MacArthur's Chief of Staff, Major-General Sutherland, wrote:

... the Japanese have, at present, sea and air superiority in the projected theatre of operations; and the Allied Forces, in the South-West Pacific Area, will require local sea and air superiority, either for participation in the general offensive, or for any preliminary offensive undertaken when opportunity offers. Sea control would rest primarily on air superiority.

Until June, at least, MacArthur lacked the forces needed for large-scale operations outside Australia, but, while he was waiting for his air and naval strength to be reinforced, there was one minor way in which the Australians could worry the Japanese on land in the islands—by guerilla action.

In the Australian Army at this time there were Independent Companies which had been specially formed for such operations; some of these have already been mentioned. Their immediate origin was to be found in ideas which developed in England in the early and difficult months of the war, although the basic idea on which they were founded went back as far as the history of war itself, and had found modern expression in the Peninsular War, after the main Spanish armies had been driven from the field; in the tactics of the Boers who, their formed strength broken, had tied up 250,000 British troops for two years by the skilful use of small bands of well armed and highly skilled bushmen whom they called "commandos"; in Palestine during 1936-37. When the German armies extended themselves along the coast of Western Europe some British leaders became interested in plans whereby British commandos might strike them small but stinging blows, and they set about the formation of small units of bold men in whom would be "a dash of the Elizabethan pirate, the Chicago gangster and the Frontier tribesman, allied to a professional efficiency and standard of discipline of the best regular soldier".[1] Thus, by early 1940, the British Army had formed (from Territorial battalions) ten such companies to supplement the Royal Marines in landing operations. By June of that year five were fighting in Norway and, on the 24th of that month, men of No. 11 Commando carried out the first raid across the Channel. Other such raids (by Special Service Troops as the British came to call them) followed, and then Independent Companies began to operate in the Middle East.

Late in 1940, a British officer (Lieut-Colonel J. C. Mawhood), with a small specialist staff, arrived in Australia to initiate training designed to produce a high standard of efficiency in irregular warfare. The original Australian intention was to form four Independent Companies in which each soldier should be a selected volunteer from the A.I.F. aged between 20 and 35, and of the highest medical classification and physical efficiency.

The organisation of a training school (No. 7 Infantry Training Centre) began in February 1941. It was sited on Wilson's Promontory, Victoria, in an isolated area of high, rugged and heavily timbered mountains, precipitous valleys, swiftly running streams, and swamps. Its winter climate was harsh (and prolonged periods of wet weather were later to impede training and affect the health of the trainees). By October the 1st, 2nd and 3rd Independent Companies had been formed and trained, each commanded by a major and consisting of 17 officers and 256 other ranks, divided into company headquarters, engineer, signals and medical section, and three platoons each of three sections. The nucleus of the 4th Company was then at the centre when it was decided to discontinue training because specific tasks for additional companies could not be envisaged. In December, however, after the outbreak of war with Japan, the school was reopened as the Guerilla Warfare School, the training of the 4th Company was completed, and the 5th, 6th, 7th and 8th Companies were rapidly formed.

From the beginning the army was not single-minded in its attitude towards Independent Companies. There was a feeling among some officers that well-trained infantry could do all that was expected of the commandos, and that the formation of these special units represented a drain on infantry strength that was out of proportion to the results likely to be achieved. The supporters of the commando idea replied that the new companies would relieve the infantry of the task of providing detachments for special tasks.

While the war with Japan was looming, and in its early months, the Independent Companies were scattered round the fringes of the Australian area with the intention that they should remain behind after any Japanese occupation and harry the invaders. Thus, as mentioned earlier, the 1st

---

[1] D. W. Clarke, *Seven Assignments* (1948), p. 219.

Independent Company was spread from the New Hebrides to the Admiralties, the 2nd went to Timor, the 3rd to New Caledonia, and the 4th to the Northern Territory.[2]

In April, when the New Guinea Volunteer Rifles were observing the Japanese at Lae and Salamaua, General Blamey thought that there was an opportunity to use independent troops to develop a minor and local but profitable offensive. Thus Major Kneen's 2/5th Independent Company arrived at Port Moresby on 17th April on the way to cooperate with the N.G.V.R., to keep close to the Japanese in the Markham Valley, and to raid the Japanese installations there with the main purpose of hindering their air operations from the local aerodromes.

During 21st-24th April Generals Vasey and Brett were at Port Moresby. Among the decisions reached during their visit was one to form a guerilla group to be known as Kanga Force. This was to consist of a headquarters, to be raised from details in the Port Moresby area, the N.G.V.R., Lieutenant Howard's platoon which was now in the Wau area, the 2/5th Independent Company, and a mortar platoon which was to be raised from the 17th Anti-Tank Battery and other units in Port Moresby. Immediately Howard's platoon was to reconnoitre the Markham Valley with a view to later offensive action against Lae; the N.G.V.R. was to reconnoitre the Lae and Salamaua areas and carry out restricted offensive action there. Neither the commandos nor the N.G.V.R. were to take any action that would "prejudice the main role of Kanga Force, which will be the attack of Lae and of Salamaua, making the most use of the factor of surprise".

MacArthur wrote to Blamey on 1st May that he hoped an opportunity would soon occur to take "a limited offensive"; the chance might present itself to raid Lae and Salamaua, or even to retake them, by an overland advance from Port Moresby.

Blamey replied that he entirely agreed and that tentative plans for such an operation had been made during the visit of Generals Brett and Vasey to Port Moresby; aeroplanes would be needed to transport the new troops and then to maintain them; a raid on Lae could produce very good results, but he doubted whether the forces available would be able to retake and hold the town; the 2/5th Independent Company was being held at Port Moresby in view of the threat of a Japanese attack but, if that threat were removed, he would order the operation to be carried out if air transport could be arranged. MacArthur then asked Blamey to carry out his plan as soon as the position justified it and said he was asking Brett to provide aircraft for the operation and maintenance of the force.

While this exchange had been taking place there had been little movement round Salamaua since the Japanese raid on Komiatum in late April. There had been brushes along the Markham, however. On 1st May near Ngasawapum (about four miles east of Nadzab) an enemy patrol surprised three Australians who were driving along the road in the ration truck. Suddenly, some distance ahead, a native sprang on to the road waving his

---

[2] These Independent Companies will henceforward be referred to as the 2/2nd, 2/3rd, 2/5th, 2/6th Independent Companies, etc., as they later became known.

lap lap—a recognised danger signal. Between him and the truck, Japanese were waiting in ambush. The Australians escaped into the kunai and their enemies started towards Nadzab in the truck. Farther along the road Sergeant Mayne[3] of Howard's platoon was on his way to join his officer at Diddy, with a signaller, McBarron,[4] and two riflemen. The Japanese in the truck overtook them and made Mayne and McBarron prisoners though the two others escaped.

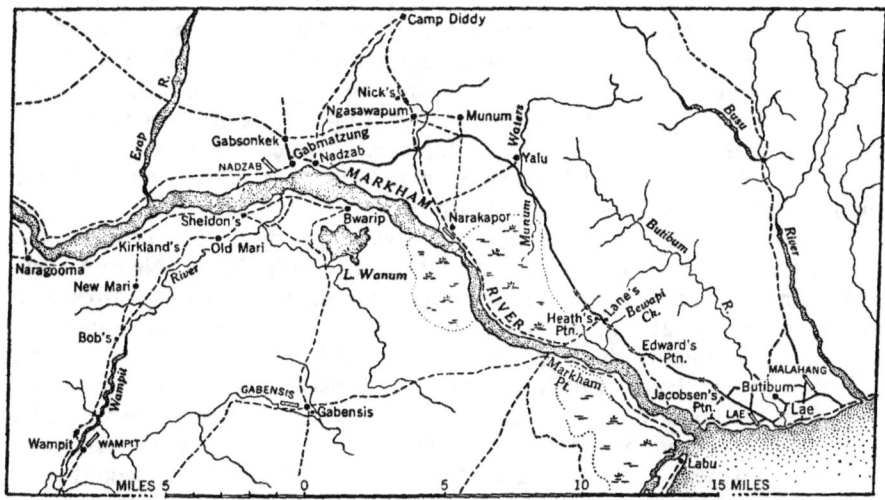

Two days later a Japanese patrol about 15 strong surprised Howard and other men camped in the timber behind Jacobsen's Plantation. The Japanese began to fire wildly before they got close enough for accurate shooting. Thus the Australians escaped, though they lost most of their clothing and all of their equipment and Jacobsen's was closed as a forward post.

Following this raid an aeroplane strafed the mission at Gabmatzung, near Nadzab, on 6th May and, on the same day, that aircraft or another flew low for half an hour over Camp Diddy apparently examining this area where Major Edwards had all his wireless equipment, most of his stores and 16 sick men. Edwards therefore withdrew most of his men across the river but soon afterwards Captain Lyon began to operate regularly once more from Diddy as an advanced base and Ngasawapum and Munum as forward posts, with telephones connecting the three.

On 21st May Lieutenant Noblett,[5] with a detachment which included Lance-Corporal Anderson[6] and Rifleman Emery,[7] reoccupied the post near

---
[3] Sgt R. C. Mayne, VX64256; 1 Indep Coy. Draughtsman; of Edwardstown, SA; b. St Peters, SA, 24 Feb 1920. Missing presumed dead 1 Jun 1942.
[4] Sig Artificer L. J. McBarron, QX64904; Fortress Sigs 8 MD. Clerk; of Cairns, Qld; b. Herberton, Qld, 24 Feb 1921. Missing presumed dead 1 Jun 1942.
[5] Capt K. E. Noblett, NGX268. NGVR; OC 43 and 23 Sqns Air Liaison Sec 1943-45. Clerk; of Bulolo, TNG; b. Adelaide, 3 Aug 1908.
[6] L-Cpl F. T. Anderson, NGX460; NGVR. Electrician; of Bulolo, TNG; b. Rockhampton, Qld, 24 Aug 1911. Missing presumed dead 1 Jun 1942.
[7] Rfn J. R. Emery, NGX284; NGVR. Commercial artist and plantation manager; of Campbelltown, SA; b. Henley Beach, SA, 10 Oct 1916.

Heath's and made a camp in the creek-bed about ten minutes' walk away. At dawn the next morning Emery guided Anderson towards the post, and left him within a few yards of it. Scarcely had he turned when he heard a shot. He waited. There were no more shots but he heard Japanese talking. He hurried back to warn Noblett and the rest and found that they also had heard the shot. They hid themselves in thick bush along the track and waited. Sergeant R. Emery shot the first Japanese to appear and the other attackers began to fire wildly—even the field gun at the plantation joined in with a few rounds—and most of the Australians began to make their separate ways out of the area as the firing died down. Noblett, however, waited in the bush for about seven hours and a half, watching the Japanese. When he saw one alone he shot him. While he was cutting off the dead man's badges four other Japanese arrived. "I was very lucky to get out of it," reported Noblett, who thought that natives had told the Japanese of the presence of the Australians.

It was now clear that some natives were giving information to the invaders. The N.G.V.R., however, continued to use Diddy, Ngasawapum and Munum. They watched the road, made regular visits to Heath's area and sent occasional patrols as far as Lae itself. At Narakapor, south of Ngasawapum and off the main road, on the 27th May, two of them met a native named Balus who had given the Australians much help in the past. He told them that the Japanese had told the Butibum natives, who were friendly to the invaders, that reinforcements would shortly arrive and that the Japanese, led by natives from Butibum and Yalu, would then move up the Markham Valley and into the Bulolo Valley. (Butibum was close to Lae on the north-western side.)

It must have been difficult for the natives to decide whom they should help. The Japanese were in a commanding position at Lae and Salamaua and the Australians were homeless in the bush—a compelling argument to simple minds. In addition the Japanese did not merely ask but demanded cooperation from the villages and the consequences of refusal were harsh, the burning, or air bombing and strafing of a reluctant village being routine procedures. (The villages of Munum, Guadagasal and Waipali were all burned by the Japanese at various times.) It was understandable that even many villages which had no love for the Japanese, no desire to aid them, and were loyal to their former masters, would greet the Australians with little enthusiasm when they came. But even so the attitude of the natives to the Australians was generally one of friendly helpfulness largely due, no doubt, to the fact that the men of the N.G.V.R. were skilled in handling them and many were well known to some of the villagers. Many natives indeed went beyond an attitude of sympathy and friendliness and passed on information at considerable risk to themselves, or patrolled deep into Japanese territory as guides or on other missions. Some, however, were prepared to aid the Japanese, whether from feelings of resentment dating from pre-war times, from hope of gain, or for personal reasons of various kinds it is hard to say.

The men of the N.G.V.R. had filled a large gap in the period up to late May. Under difficult conditions they had carried out a task of watching and keeping touch with the invaders, and of letting the bewildered natives within the Salamaua-Wau-Lae semicircle see that the Australians had not been driven completely from the area. They had done this within a spidery organisation and largely through their own ability to improvise; through knowledge, experience and common sense which had to serve instead of the benefits of training; through individual courage and patient watchfulness instead of as part of an integrated machine. Now they were to take their place in a more ambitious organisation, which brought some benefit to them and some disadvantages.

When the Battle of the Coral Sea was over Blamey and MacArthur agreed that the "limited offensive" they had planned could be got under way. On 12th May Major Fleay[8] was appointed to command Kanga Force and was ordered to concentrate his force in the Markham Valley "for operation in that area", his task, as more specifically defined earlier, "the attack of Lae and of Salamaua, making the most use of the factor of surprise".

Fleay, only 25 at this time, had been an original member of the 2/11th Battalion. His task now obviously called for coolness and mature judgment, experience in handling men so that the diverse elements under his command could be alternately driven, coaxed and inspired into overcoming the difficulties of the lonely and dangerous days which lay ahead of them and so that they could draw from their commander a strength which would make up for the lack of an orthodox military organisation behind them. But Fleay's own experience was limited and in particular he lacked knowledge of tropical conditions.

It was planned now to fly the reinforcements into the Wau area. Transport aircraft were very scarce, however, and, with Zeros operating from Lae, strong fighter escort for any troop movements by air was essential. Unfavourable weather also hindered the planes so that it was not until 23rd May that the movement of Kanga Force began. Then the headquarters, most of the Independent Company and the mortar detachment were flown to Wau. This was the first substantial movement of troops by air in New Guinea—a form of troop transport which was to become commonplace later.

By 31st May Fleay was able to report that his own headquarters and his mortar detachment were at Wau. Kneen's men were spread down the Bulolo Valley as far as Bulwa, Howard's headquarters were at Bulwa, with one of his sections at Kudjeru, one at Missim, and one preparing to take over from the N.G.V.R. at Mapos. The N.G.V.R. still had Captain Umphelby's company watching the Salamaua sector from Mubo, and Lyon's company covering the routes inland from the Markham with a rear headquarters at Bob's Camp, south of the junction of the Markham and Wampit Rivers, and a forward headquarters still at Camp Diddy.

Fleay then prepared to give the weary men of the New Guinea unit

---
[8] Lt-Col N. L. Fleay, DSO, WX361. 2/11 Bn; CO Kanga Force 1942-43, 2/7 Cav (Cdo) Regt 1944-45. Printer; of Maylands, WA; b. Wagin, WA, 2 Dec 1917.

some respite, and ordered one of Kneen's sections under Lieutenant Doberer[9] to move to Bob's on the 6th June to come under Lyon's command for forward reconnaissance, and a second section, under Lieutenant Wylie,[1] to move similarly on the 10th.

By now Fleay's instructions had been finally clarified. He defined his object as "to harass and destroy enemy personnel and equipment in the Markham District" (including Salamaua in that area). With this object in view he summed up the position as he saw it about 10th June.

He considered that there were 2,000 Japanese at Lae and 250 at Salamaua as against 700 men under his own command of whom only 450 were fit for operations: the threat of Japanese entry into the Bulolo Valley committed him to the protection of the numerous tracks which led there from the Salamaua and Lae areas and of the overland route from Wau to Papua by way of Bulldog; the threat of air invasion forced him to provide for the defence of the most likely landing points—Wau, Bulolo, Bulwa and Otibanda; to a considerable extent he was in the hands of the natives, firstly because he had to rely on them to maintain his supply line and secondly because the pro-Japanese activities of some of them gave him little chance of surprising his enemies at Lae or Salamaua with large forces. He concluded that the only course open to him was to maintain as large a force as possible for the defence of the Bulolo Valley and the overland route to Papua and to engage the Japanese by raids designed to inflict casualties, destroy equipment and hamper their use of Lae and Salamaua as air bases. He decided that these raids should be on Heath's Plantation (where the Japanese formed an obstacle to any large-scale movement against Lae); on the Lae area to destroy aircraft, dumps and installations and to test the defences with a view to operations on a larger scale in the future; on the Salamaua area to destroy the wireless station, aerodrome installations and dumps; that they should take place in the order indicated and should be prepared rapidly, as the need for action was urgent.

Accordingly he at once issued orders for the raid on Heath's and that preparations be made for the attack on Salamaua. As it transpired, however, the Salamaua raid was made first. It could be planned in great detail as a result of the work of Sergeant McAdam's scouts, by whom scarcely a movement in Salamaua went unnoticed. From one of their posts the bell sounding the air raid alarm on the isthmus could be clearly heard. They watched working parties, vehicle movements, officers and men entering and leaving buildings. They built up a complete picture of all strongpoints and weapon positions and knew the purposes for which the various buildings were being used. They reconnoitred all the tracks leading into the town.

In his initial orders for the attack on Salamaua Fleay named Umphelby as the commander and told him that, in addition to his own men, he would have two sections (each of one officer and 18 men armed with

---

[9] Lt F. W. Doberer, NX72209; 2/5 Indep Coy. Accounts clerk; of Artarmon, NSW; b. Grafton, NSW, 19 Apr 1911.
[1] Lt M. W. Wylie, WX11075; 2/5 Indep Coy. Clerk; of Cottesloe, WA; b. Claremont, WA, 17 Jan 1917.

rifles, 1 Bren gun and 3 sub-machine-guns), a mortar detachment and 3 engineers from Kneen's company. His objects were to destroy aerodrome installations, particularly the wireless station and dumps; to kill all Japanese who were met, and to capture equipment and documents so that identifications could be made.

Captain Winning[2] of Kneen's company led the commandos into Mubo on the 15th June. With him were Major Jenyns and three N.G.V.R. men under Sergeant Farr[3] to control the native carrier lines. Jenyns, Umphelby and Winning then went on to the forward observation areas where they learned that the estimated Japanese strength in Salamaua had risen to 300 men. At a conference of the officers and Sergeant McAdam on the night of the 17th it was decided that Mubo was too far back for a base camp and Winning and McAdam were to reconnoitre for a new advanced base.

On the 18th, therefore, these two and Rifleman Currie went out on a three-day reconnaissance. They chose a forward base about three miles in a direct line from Salamaua, crossed the Francisco River and selected as the assembly point for the raid the site of the old civilian evacuation camp at Butu, entered the aerodrome area and examined the Japanese dispositions and activity, and reconnoitred Kela village area as far as the Japanese wire.

Selected men from the N.G.V.R. and the commandos were given brief training together. From an aerial photograph of Salamaua a sand-table was built and on this model tactics were planned, the N.G.V.R. men supplying minute details of location and layout.

But some of the preparations were troubled ones. Supply, as always in this difficult country, was a particular problem. At Mubo there were no reserves to meet the sudden accretion of A.I.F. troops and the newcomers had to draw heavily on the small N.G.V.R. dumps. The move forward from Mubo had been timed for 23rd June but the late arrival of supplies meant that the force did not arrive at the forward camp until just before dark on the 25th. The carriers were behind them again and so it was not until the 27th that the Butu assembly area was reached. The time for the beginning of the raid was then fixed for 3.15 a.m. on 29th June.

For a short period there was difficulty also regarding the command. Although Umphelby had been nominated by Fleay in his written orders as commander, Winning said that he himself had been instructed to take command. Finally Fleay ruled in favour of Winning, a tough, active, sandy man, dynamic, unorthodox, shrewd; his self-confidence inspired confidence in others.

The raiders spent the afternoon of the 27th and the whole of the 28th in briefing and rehearsal, and in consolidating the work which had been done on the sand-table at Mubo. During this preparation they kept a close

---

[2] Maj N. I. Winning, MBE, NX65553. 2/5 Indep Coy; OC 2/8 Cdo Sqn. Planter; of Java, and Pymble, NSW; b. Oban, Scotland, 27 May 1906. Killed in Java 3 Dec 1950.
[3] WO2 H. J. W. Farr, NG2211. NGVR. Angau. Engineer; of Forest Lodge, NSW; b. Emu Plains, NSW, 8 May 1911.

watch from the observation posts on the Japanese who showed no signs of uneasiness or awareness.

The tactics of the raid were determined by the peculiar topography of the Salamaua area. There the main coastline ran roughly north-west. From it a narrow isthmus thrust out to the north-east, not more than a mile long, only a few feet above sea level, generally less than 300 yards wide and spreading into the solid mass of a heavily timbered hill at its northern end. On the southern side of the junction of the isthmus with the main coastline, and about a mile and a quarter below it, the Francisco River, flowing roughly north-east reached the sea. Less than half a mile from the river, on the Salamaua side, was the airfield. Almost due north of the aerodrome, across a swamp, was the village of Kela from which the coastline ran due north again for less than a mile and turned sharply west to form Kela Point. The whole Kela and Kela Point area was fairly thickly covered with houses—native, Chinese, European—stores and administrative buildings.

The aerodrome, Kela and Kela Point areas were all strongly held by the Japanese and McAdam's men had noted which houses had the most important occupants. The plan was to attack selected objectives roughly along the line from the aerodrome to Kela Point, with the mortar detachment in position to break up any attack which might develop from the isthmus and fan out towards the aerodrome on the south and the Kela area on the north.

The raiding troops were divided into seven parties. The first, under Lieutenant Kerr[4] (of the Independent Company) with Lieutenant Lane[5] of the N.G.V.R. and 17 men, including the guide, Kinsey, was the aerodrome party. Its task was to destroy three red-roofed houses—where the Japanese had their billets and aerodrome headquarters east of the hangar—and kill the occupants. The second party, under Sergeant O'Neill[6] with McAdam as guide, was to blow up the two steel wireless masts and wireless equipment on the southern fringe of the built-on Kela area, and the bridge just to the north-east by which the coastal road crossed a tidal stream feeding into the swamp. This party was also to hold the road against reinforcements from the isthmus. O'Neill and McAdam had five other men with them, two of them engineers. The third party, four men under Lieutenant Leitch[7] and guided by Cavanaugh, had the medical assistant's former house, just west of the wireless masts, as its objective. A little north of this house was one which had formerly belonged to the "policemaster", near it a white-roofed house where a sentry was known to be stationed. Winning and Umphelby, with Cavanaugh guiding them also and accompanied by five other soldiers, were to move against these

---

[4] Capt J. S. Kerr, VX36699. 2/5 Indep Coy; Directorate of Armament LHQ 1943-45. Timekeeper; of South Yarra, Vic; b. Clifton Hill, Vic, 8 Feb 1906.

[5] Lt A. W. Lane, DCM, NG2091. (1st AIF: WO1 1st Div Train.) NGVR and Angau. Gold mining manager; of Wau, TNG; b. Newtown, NSW, 19 Dec 1890.

[6] Lt W. O'Neill, DCM, WX13036. 2/5 Indep Coy; 2/12 Cdo Sqn. Shop assistant; of Claremont, WA; b. Southern Cross, WA, 21 Dec 1916.

[7] Lt J. C. Leitch, NX76247; 2/5 Indep Coy. Wool clerk; of Neutral Bay, NSW; b. Brisbane, 27 Feb 1921. Killed in action 11 Jan 1943.

buildings. A fifth party, its total strength ten, guided by Currie, was to be led by Corporal Hunter[8] against opposition in the Morobe bakery area which was among bush between Kela and Kela Point. Lieutenant O'Loghlen[9] of the N.G.V.R., with Archer as guide and six other men under his command, was to destroy houses and Japanese in the Kela Point area. The seventh party was under Lieutenant D r y s d a l e,[1] guided by Private Suter[2] (the only guide not from the N.G.V.R.) who had Gomari, Cavanaugh's personal boy, to assist him. This was the mortar party and consisted of its leader and ten men (not including Gomari).

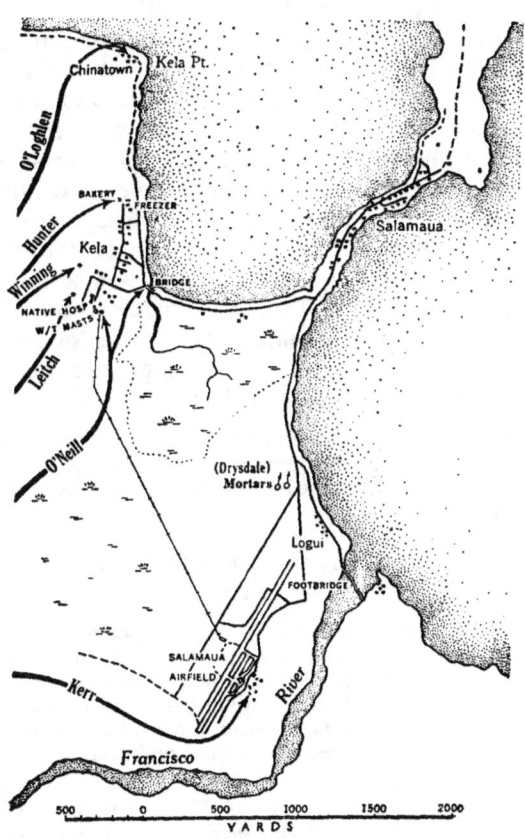

The raid on Salamaua.

Originally it had been hoped that the raiders might be able to clean up the outer areas quickly and then advance along the isthmus. But that required effective air support beforehand to neutralise the isthmus defences, and two night raids before the 28th had not been well executed and a daylight raid requested for the 28th did not take place.

At 2 p.m. on the 28th the various parties began to move out from Butu for their starting areas. Drysdale's men moved first and settled at Logui village on the Salamaua side of the Francisco River. The other parties followed at times arranged in accordance with the distances they had to travel. Each rifleman carried at least 60 rounds, each Tommy gunner 150 rounds. Every man carried as well a pistol and two hand grenades. For each house to be demolished one sticky grenade, reinforced with two one

---

[8] L-Sgt W. M. T. Hunter, WX13683. 2/5 Indep Coy; Adv LHQ. Mill hand; of Fremantle, WA; b. London, 23 Feb 1918.
[9] Capt C. M. O'Loghlen, NGX303. NGVR and Angau. Solicitor; of Wau, TNG, and North Balwyn, Vic; b. Melbourne, 6 Apr 1916.
[1] Lt W. Drysdale, VX39455; 2/5 Indep Coy. Student; of Sandringham, Vic; b. Edinburgh, Scotland, 1 Jan 1921. Killed in action 1 Oct 1942.
[2] Pte D. H. Suter, VX71823; 2/5 Indep Coy. Gold miner; of Springvale, Vic; b. Sandringham, Vic, 14 Aug 1912.

pound slabs of T.N.T. wrapped in a hessian bag, was carried. Bundles of two to four flares with instantaneous fuses were taken for setting fire to other houses and prepared charges were carried by the sappers for destroying the bridge and wireless masts.

The early part of the night was driven through with heavy rain, but this cleared and left Salamaua bathed in bright moonlight.

Before nightfall Kerr's party was looking over the aerodrome from a position 500 yards from the south-west corner of the strip. Most of them slept while Kinsey reconnoitred an approach in the darkness. He could hear a Japanese sentry singing quietly to himself. At 1.40 a.m. the main body began to move forward. Kinsey took them through bush, pit pit[3] and bamboo on the eastern side of the strip until they were roughly opposite their objectives. There was a little delay in finding the track through the last 200 yards of thick scrub and they were barely in position when the sound of sudden fire and a louder explosion from the direction of Kela village shattered the night. Japanese poured out of the houses towards shelters and trenches.

> The enemy must have had a defence plan at the drome which made our job harder than that of the other groups (Kerr said later). They must have had alert sentries, because they ran—or tried to run—to their defensive positions as soon as the firing opened up at Kela.

The Australians shot most of them down, then charged to their demolition tasks. Kinsey described what they did.

> We used one sticky bomb and two pounds of T.N.T. on each building. We raced up the steps, dropped bombs into the centre of the house, and retreated, covered by rifle and Tommy-gun fire and grenades. Some houses had three or four Japs, some more. The house I went to—some of the Japs had got out into dugouts—I got at least five Japs. After the explosions there was much wild shooting from the Japs. . . . We fired into bushes and houses.

Kerr put a Bren gun team on the edge of the strip, near the hangars, to cover the rear of the houses and sweep the area. Several Japanese fired at intervals from an air raid shelter and occasional bursts of fire came from the corners of damaged buildings. Towards dawn Japanese reinforcements began to arrive. The Australians dropped back to the hangars and tried to fire the charges but they would not ignite. As daylight was breaking Kerr led most of his men back into the bush. They waited for some hours while Kinsey searched for four missing soldiers but finally they left without them and arrived back at Butu about 5 p.m.

When the firing from Kela started O'Neill's demolition party was about 80 yards from the bridge. They raced along the road, fired a Tommy-gun burst into a sentry post, threw a grenade into an air raid shelter where they thought Japanese were hiding, then the engineers went to work with their charges while the rest of the group covered them. The charges were almost set when mortar bombs began to fall, first round Kela Point, then near the bakery and then on the bridge itself and the near-by road junc-

---

[3] A species of tall grass not unlike sugar cane.

tion. One bomb, exploded squarely on the bridge, set off the charges. The bridge was blown to bits. Machine-guns, firing a large proportion of tracer, began to range on the road junction and one of the engineers was wounded. A large gun, or mortar, began to drop missiles on the hills behind Kela. By this time Winning's group had joined O'Neill. They had found the houses which had been their objectives empty so had ranged through the village killing any Japanese they saw. A man came running along the road and was brought down. He was a Japanese airman and they took documents from him.

The firing and the explosion which had startled the other parties into action a minute or two before the time actually fixed had come from Leitch's and Hunter's parties. Hunter's raiders had run into an alert sentry near the bakery which sheltered the men they had been detailed to kill. They had to shoot him with a sub-machine-gun and thus the alarm had been given. Other Japanese leapt from their sleep. The Australians killed them but Currie was wounded. Hard after Hunter's first burst of fire Leitch's men had thrown a "reinforced" sticky grenade into the medical assistant's house. Bewildered survivors rushed out. But sub-machine-gunners were waiting at two diagonally opposite corners of the house. One gunner said he shot six of these Japanese, the other said he shot one. Leitch's men thought that, all told, they killed twenty of the enemy in and around that house, including three officers.

Meanwhile O'Loghlen's party was busy at Kela Point. Its initial approach had been hampered by the presence of native dogs. Archer had then crept through the shallow water of the ocean's edge, under cover of a three-foot sea wall, along the whole line of houses. He could hear the voices of the Japanese inside or alongside the houses which were thought to be occupied. O'Loghlen decided to attack from the seaward side. Scarcely did he have his men in position, only five yards from where two Japanese sentries were sitting, when the firing at Kela village began. His men, Archer said later, hurled their bombs into the two houses which they thought contained Japanese and destroyed them. They thought also that they damaged three other houses with flare bombs but in five or six others the flares failed to ignite. The raiders were satisfied that they killed fifteen Japanese and they captured a sub-machine-gun and three rifles. As they began to withdraw they came under machine-gun and mortar fire and had one man wounded.

From Logui Drysdale heard the first shots and had his mortar in action within fifteen seconds. After four ranging shots every bomb fell on the isthmus. All told Drysdale's men fired 36 bombs. One of them fell directly on the most important target, a strongpost at the neck of the isthmus, soon after the garrison there had opened fire. Fifteen men were thought to have been in this post. When two red Very lights were fired as a distress signal by some of Kerr's opponents on the aerodrome about 4 a.m. Drysdale thought that Winning had fired them since this had been agreed upon as the withdrawal signal. He therefore ceased fire and prepared to get his men out. But a Japanese mortar was dropping its bombs at the Francisco

River mouth where they were to cross; the tide was high and the crossing deep and dangerous. The Australians therefore hid their mortar to give them a better chance to get clear. Finally they crossed safely.

By 11 a.m. all the raiders were back at Butu except Kerr's party. The Japanese were still shelling, mortaring and machine-gunning Kela village and the point. Aircraft strafed the bush and bombed what the pilots thought might be the withdrawal tracks. About midday Winning began to lead his men back to the forward base camp, passing through a defensive post of N.G.V.R. men under Lieutenant Hitchcock[4] waiting for the Japanese to follow up. But pursuit did not come. By the following day when all of Kerr's men, including those four who had been missing at the time of his withdrawal from the aerodrome, had reported back it was seen that the raiders had suffered only three casualties—the men who had been wounded. None of the wounds were serious.

In reporting the results of the raid Winning estimated that a minimum of 100 Japanese had been killed, 25 by Kerr's men, 7 by his own and O'Neill's, at least 20 by Leitch's men, at least 20 by Hunter's, 15 by O'Loghlen and his party, possibly 13 by Drysdale's mortar. He claimed six houses certainly destroyed, three trucks, one bridge and a bicycle. He said: "I and my fellow officers consider this estimate to be very conservative." One of the few particulars in which the raid was not successful was that the charges laid at the wireless masts did not explode.

Up to the time of the Salamaua raid practically no Japanese equipment or documents had been taken by the Australian Army. Winning sent back a sub-machine-gun, a rifle and bayonet, ammunition, shell fragments, a waterproof cape, an airman's helmet, goggles and gloves. Documents taken included a number of marked maps and sketch maps, a diary, copies of orders and other material which produced valuable information. Badges collected by the raiders assisted materially in building up an Order of Battle.

The raid made the Japanese at Salamaua very nervous. During the 29th they shelled the vicinity of Kela and Kela Point. Aircraft flew low over the mountain trails. Some days later, fighting patrols up to 90 strong scoured the foothills. The Butu camp was found and some stores were destroyed. An estimated 200 reinforcements were seen to come from Lae between 29th June and 8th July. Watchers thought that others might have come unseen by night. Kela village was converted into a strongly-held perimeter position.

On the same day as he had ordered Umphelby to prepare for the attack on Salamaua Fleay had told Kneen to prepare to attack Heath's with a raiding party formed from Doberer's and Wylie's sections, a mortar detachment, and Lyon's N.G.V.R. company. He was to destroy the Japanese soldiers and equipment at the plantation, capture documents and equipment.

---

[4] Capt E. P. Hitchcock, MC, DCM, NG2076. (1st AIF: 2 Fd Amb; Lt 6 Bn.) NGVR and 1 Papuan Inf Bn. Gold miner; of Wau, TNG; b. Omeo, Vic, 10 May 1892.

By 15th June the commandos and the mortarmen were operating with Lyon's men from Diddy. They took over the standing patrol at Ngasawapum and patrolled down the Markham Road gathering information for the raid. One of their reports suggested that part of the Heath's area had been wired and that possibly there was a Japanese position at Lane's Plantation near Heath's. Kneen himself patrolled deeply to the Lae side of Heath's and Doberer was active in the same area. They decided that the high ground on that side offered the best jumping-off place for the raid.

It was about this time (mid-June) that Sergeant Emery and Rifleman Murcutt[5] attempted an exploit that was hazardous by any standards. They floated on a raft down the Markham from Nadzab intending to land in the darkness about three miles from Lae and work through to the aerodrome, but found it impossible to stop at their intended landing place. Faced with the prospect of being carried out to sea in full view of their enemies, they capsized the raft and made their way ashore, losing all their stores. They then made a long, dangerous trek back through an area thick with Japanese. Their trip was not entirely fruitless, however, for they noted eight new houses at Jacobsen's and later informed the air force of these as possible targets.

Kneen now planned to lead Lieutenants Doberer, Wylie, Phillips and 54 men along a track which followed closely the north bank of the Markham between the river and the road, assemble at Bewapi Creek about a mile south-east of Heath's, move up the creek and then along the road and attack Heath's from the Lae side. To cause confusion and hinder reinforcements coming from Lae he would blow up the bridge (30 to 40 feet long and supported by two heavy beams) by which the road crossed the creek. After the raid he would withdraw his force along the road past Munum Waters (some four miles north of Heath's) where Captain Shepherd[6] of his own company would cover him through. Air support was promised in the form of attacks on Lae between 6 and 9 on the morning after the raid to disorganise Japanese counter-measures.

About 2 p.m. on the 29th the raiders left Diddy for Narakapor where they spent the night. They were a formidable force; 21 of them carried Tommy-guns, 37 had rifles, most of them had revolvers as well, and each carried two grenades. They had no sticky grenades or T.N.T. but they carried explosive charges to destroy the bridge and the gun.

On the 30th they travelled the overgrown track along the Markham bank and finally broke through swamp and bush to reach about 4 p.m. the small cleared patch on Bewapi Creek which was their rendezvous. Over them as they walked a Zero had dived and twisted, giving them anxious moments, but apparently the pilot did not see them.

Kneen took with him his Intelligence sergeant, Booth,[7] and Privates

---

[5] WO2 W. M. Murcutt, NGX283. NGVR and Angau. Native labour overseer; of Lae, TNG, and Sydney; b. Brisbane, 2 Sep 1907. Killed in road accident 5 Dec 1946.

[6] Lt-Col A. E. T. Shepherd, NX72826. 2/5 Indep Coy; 1 Parachute Trg Centre. Lecturer in mathematics; of Duntroon, ACT; b. Sydney, 5 Sep 1910.

[7] Sgt R. D. Booth, NX48924; 2/5 Indep Coy. Solicitor; of Dubbo, NSW; b. Dubbo, 20 Feb 1911. Died 3 Sep 1943.

Murray-Smith[8] and Hamilton[9] who had volunteered for the task of destroying the bridge, and moved up the creek to the road. From there Booth went on alone while the others determined how the bridge should be blown. He crawled round the southern edge of Lane's clearing until he reached the boundary between Heath's and Lane's. Then he wriggled forward until he could see his objective clearly. He lay concealed behind a log. Two Japanese sentries came and sat on the log for a long time. Booth could not move an inch. Insects bit him and he burned and itched. He did not arrive back at the assembly point until 10.30 and the start-time, originally fixed for midnight, had to be put back in consequence.

It had been raining but the same moon as had lighted the way for the Salamaua raiders was flooding the valley when Kneen began to lead his men forward at 11.30. Sergeant Booth remained at the bridge as cover for the two dynamiters while the rest moved on to the line of kapok trees which paralleled the road on the left and formed Heath's front boundary. There they were to divide, Wylie's section—trailed by Kneen, and Phillips with the N.G.V.R. group—to follow the line of trees and, concealed in their shelter from the road, kill the sentries at the top of the drive and move down the drive to cover the front of the house from the northern and western sides. Kneen and Phillips were to slip into position on Wylie's left, help him cover from the north and themselves cover the eastern side. Doberer's section and the mortarmen (without their mortar) were to strike diagonally across the property from the beginning of the kapok trees directly towards the house, killing any sentries they might meet on the way. Wylie was to open the attack by throwing hand grenades under the house. Booth, Murray-Smith and Hamilton were to rush forward after destroying the bridge and blow up the gun.

All went well. Doberer's men were well on their way across the cleared area making for a few trees near the house. Then a dog began to bark from the drive. The men froze. The dog stopped barking. The men began to move and the dog began to bark. The dog woke the Japanese in the house and the raiders heard one shout as though to quieten it.

Meanwhile two men who had been detailed to kill the sentries near the entrance to the drive had found them in weapon-pits on the opposite side of the road. They stalked to within ten yards of them but could get no closer in the bright moonlight. They waited until they thought the main parties had had time to reach their positions, not knowing that Doberer's men had been held up by the dog. Then they shot the sentries down and threw a grenade into their pits for good measure. It was 2.20 a.m. on 1st July.

The drive parties were almost in position but Doberer's group was thrown off balance and moved back to the road. They joined Kneen in a

---

[8] Sgt S. Murray-Smith, VX69849. 2/5 Indep Coy; 1 Cipher Sec LHQ 1943-45. Student; of Mt Eliza, Vic; b. Toorak, Vic, 9 Sep 1922.

[9] Sgt R. N. Hamilton, VX69850. 2/5 Indep Coy; "Z" Special Unit. Student; of Toorak, Vic; b. Melbourne, 12 Jan 1923.

ditch on the Lae side of the drive. From this ditch fire was poured into the house and some of Wylie's men were throwing grenades in and around the building. The steady crackle of fire filled the night. During lulls the raiders could hear groans and bumping noises from inside the house. Japanese trying to get clear were picked off. Then 15 or 20 of them broke out and made for the bush. They were allowed to go because, in a steadily settling mist, it was thought that they were some of Doberer's men trying to improve their position. Through the rattle of the small-arms fire came a deeper explosion as the shattered bridge settled into the creek bed.

The Japanese gun opened fire. The first three or four shots passed over the raiders' heads and fell in the vicinity of the Bewapi Creek bridge, but the next shot appeared to strike Kneen full in the chest and he fell dead. No provision had been made for the leader's death and some confusion followed before Wylie took over. It was reported that a Japanese machine-gun was firing from the opposite side of the road and there seemed to be other indications that Japanese were at large in the area. The attackers withdrew after action had been joined for 15 to 20 minutes though little fire had come from the house itself. Orders for a special party to silence the gun were cancelled. There was no pursuit as the Australians fell back helping two of their men who had been wounded but leaving Kneen's body behind.

Next morning bad weather hampered the attempts to strike Lae from the air and confuse Japanese retaliatory action against the raiders. Marauders (B-25s) attacked the town between 5.25 and 5.40 a.m. Of six Mitchells (B-26s) sent from Port Moresby three failed to find the target but three dropped bombs between 5.40 and 6.10 a.m. Despite these attacks Japanese fighters were busy strafing the road as soon as daylight came but they did no damage to the returning Australians. On the 2nd they made direct attacks on the Ngasawapum and Nadzab areas where some of the Australians were hiding but, in spite of some very narrow escapes, there were no casualties. There were further bombings again on the 3rd (at Gabmatzung and Gabsonkek) and strafing aircraft swept the roads.

The raid was not the success which had been hoped for. Heath's still remained an obstacle to any large-scale movement against Lae although the house itself had suffered virtual destruction. The threatening gun remained in position. None the less an unexpected blow in the guerilla tradition had been struck at the invaders. Fleay reported that the spirit of the men was excellent, that they had answered every call and had stood up extremely well under fire. He reported also "42 enemy killed, many others wounded" (but although an intense fire was poured into Heath's for some twenty minutes and the occupants must have suffered heavily, there could have been no certain basis for this claim).

In anticipation of retaliatory action the Australians closed Camp Diddy and began to operate from a forward base south of the Markham—at Sheldon's Camp, opposite Nadzab. The expected immediate movement by Japanese ground forces did not take place along the Markham, however, but the invaders were active on the Salamaua side as July came.

By the 16th Kanga Force estimated that the Salamaua garrison had been increased to 400 or 500. Patrols continued to scour the foothills looking for the guerillas and it became too dangerous for the Australians to retain the most forward observation posts. The old secret N.G.V.R. tracks were secret no longer and it was difficult for the scouts to move at all. The Japanese air forces were now sweeping wide and it seemed that a direct threat to the Bulolo Valley was growing. Komiatum and Mubo were bombed and strafed a few hours after the Salamaua raid. Nine bombers hit Wau on 2nd July. Next day the town was again bombed and strafed and five bombers also attacked Bulolo scoring a direct hit on one of the dumps, where two soldiers were killed and stores were destroyed. This loss, combined with large-scale desertions by carriers who melted away to the hills in face of the raids, seriously affected supply, and, among other things, caused the relief of the N.G.V.R. men still in the forward Markham area to be delayed.

On the 5th July Fleay ordered that the actions of Kanga Force be restricted to extensive patrolling and observation, except when Japanese patrols were met, presumably because his troops were tired and sick (particularly the men of the N.G.V.R.) and because of the shortage of supplies in forward areas. But now his men did not have to patrol to find action for it was coming to them.

On the 21st July McAdam's men reported that a force about 100 strong was crossing the Francisco at the bridge near the airstrip. They were lightly equipped and were moving fast, guided by four or five natives —Tapi, a former police sergeant, Malo of Wanimo, Tuai of the Sepik, and Abalu of Busama. Above these men three seaplanes were making a close reconnaissance of the trail towards Komiatum. By 4.55 the leading troops were entering the Mubo strip clearing, having covered the distance from Salamaua in nine hours—fast going.

There were 64 Australians at Mubo, about half of them commandos and half N.G.V.R. The rest were on patrol or were maintaining the Mount Limbong lookout. The 64 waited for the Japanese on the high ground overlooking Mubo village and the airstrip. When the Japanese entered "the gorge" they did so without any attempt at deployment and made a good target. The Australians engaged them with machine-guns from the heights and struck many of them down. The Japanese fire was erratic and caused no casualties among the defenders. By last light the invaders had had enough and fell back the way they had come, carrying their dead and wounded with them.

A captured document gave the original strength of the patrol as 136 and reports of the return of the Japanese to Salamaua indicated that they then numbered only 90. Malo and Tuai, who had been captured, said that the raiders had been recent arrivals at Salamaua and were naval troops. Both natives told of the presence of a European in Salamaua who had been working with the Japanese since before the Australian raid. Lieutenant Murphy[1] of Angau, a former patrol officer, was convinced that he knew the man.

> He is particularly well acquainted with all the country between the coast and the Bulolo Valley and knows the Waria backwards. He is familiar with many out-of-the-way bits of the country and tracks, and is well known to the natives in the villages.

The attack on Mubo was apparently synchronised with a movement against the Australians along the Markham for the Japanese pushed out from Heath's also on the 21st July. This sally followed a clash on the 19th.

The Moresby headquarters had asked Kanga Force for a prisoner. Two patrols crossed the Markham from Sheldon's on this errand. One, consisting of Sergeant Chaffey,[2] Privates Gregson[3] and Pullar,[4] and Rifleman Vernon, went past Heath's along the river track then cut back on to the road to set an ambush between Lae and Heath's, planning to cut off a supply truck and capture the driver. Chaffey had a Tommy-gun, the others had revolvers and grenades. About 2 p.m. a lorry came slowly up the road but bogged just short of the ambush position. Chaffey opened fire on two guards standing on the back of the truck. He killed one but the other dropped on the tray and opened fire with a machine-gun which he had set up there. Vernon came from behind a stump, dropped on one knee to steady his revolver, and received a burst of machine-gun fire in the chest. Chaffey fired the rest of his ammunition and thought he got two out of three men sitting in the front seat—but the revolvers of the others were of not much use against the machine-gun. Gregson went to help Vernon who said that he was done for and told the others to get out. He was bleeding badly and seemed to Gregson to have not much longer to live. As the other three dropped back into the bush they heard a single revolver shot and then a burst of fire. It sounded like Vernon having one last shot at the Japanese before he died. He had been one of the outstanding N.G.V.R. men on the Markham side.

Two days later came the Japanese thrust up the valley. The Australians had been keeping a standing patrol at a camp called Nick's, close to and slightly west of Ngasawapum. Shortly before 21st July Lieutenant Noblett had established a new camp about 1,000 yards south of Ngasawapum and just off the Markham Road. Usually 16 to 20 men at a time worked from there patrolling the tracks to Narakapor, Munum and the Yalu area. On the 21st a relief was being carried out and there were two patrols at the new camp with weapons only for one as it was the custom of the relieving patrol to take over the weapons of their predecessors. About 1.30 p.m. two shots were heard from the direction of the Markham Road

---

[1] Capt J. J. Murphy, NGX310. Angau and "M" Special Unit. Patrol officer; of Otibanda, Papua, and Brisbane; b. Gympie, Qld, 12 Mar 1914.
[2] Capt W. A. Chaffey, NX78912. 2/5 Indep Coy; "Z" Special Unit. MLA (NSW) since 1940. Farmer and grazier; of Tamworth, NSW; b. Tamworth, 18 Feb 1915.
[3] L-Cpl J. K. Gregson, VX70223; 2/5 Indep Coy. Station overseer; of Hay, NSW, and Kew, Vic; b. Kew, 15 Apr 1917.
[4] Pte W. J. Pullar, QX27036. 2/5 Indep Coy; 2/5 Cdo Sqn. Prospector; of Townsville, Qld; b. Invercargill, NZ, 7 Aug 1908.

and parties went out to investigate. Corporal Jones[5] took two men down a "short cut" but ran into a Japanese party led by a native. Both groups opened fire and the native was one of the first casualties. Outnumbered, Jones' men made their individual ways back to Nadzab, but he himself was cut off and forced to hide in the thick growth.

Fire was opened on the camp from several different directions. It was obvious that the Japanese were there in force and the Australians fell back in small groups to Nadzab and Sheldon's, leaving most of their gear behind them. Jones was the last man back. He said that he had counted two parties, one of 81 and the other of 53, both led by natives. It was thought that the Japanese had suffered 6 casualties and two of their native guides had been wounded.

Private Underwood[6] was wounded and missing. Warrant-Officer Whittaker,[7] formerly an Administration Medical Assistant, who was running a small hospital at Bob's, heard this. As far as anyone knew the Japanese were still at Nick's. Whittaker said later:

> I went back and got Bill Underwood out after he was wounded. I had to go six hours to get him. I set out at 1730 and got to Ngasawapum hours later, went into the bush in the area where he was shot, went into the camp, called quietly, and he answered. I bound him up. I walked him back to Nadzab to where a canoe was waiting, got him to Sheldon's and on to Bob's Camp at 0730.

Natives said afterwards that the Japanese burned Munum village on their way up the valley to punish the inhabitants for "going bush" when they arrived; that before the raid four Ngasawapum and three Gabsonkek boys had been closely questioned by the Japanese so that the latter must have known a good deal about the activities of the Australians before they started out. It was also said that four natives captured at the camp during the raid were flogged and threatened and then allowed to go.

From this time forward the fortunes of Kanga Force suffered a marked decline. This was due to a number of causes—the effects of sickness and strain among the troops, vigorous Japanese efforts to rid themselves of their turbulent neighbours and their constant threat of advance over any of seven or eight routes, lack of reinforcements, a threatening new crisis with regard to supply. The last three at least were conditioned to a large extent by Japanese action elsewhere for, on 21st July (the same day as the raids on Mubo and Nick's had taken place) invading forces landed on the north coast of Papua and began to push vigorously over the Owen Stanley Range, constituting a threat which bore daily more heavily on the maintenance plans for Kanga Force—plans which even under the most favourable conditions had never produced a smooth flow of supplies to the guerillas.

The supply line through Bulldog had failed to come up to expectations.

---

[5] Sgt L. G. Jones, NX43289. 2/5 Indep Coy; "M" Special Unit. Clerk; of Manly, NSW; b. Strathfield, NSW, 23 Jul 1922.

[6] L-Cpl D. W. Underwood, WX18564. 2/5 Indep Coy; 2/5 Cdo Sqn. Labourer; of Gooseberry Hill, WA; b. Leicester, England, 31 Jan 1920.

[7] Capt G. K. Whittaker, MBE, NGX280. NGVR and Angau. Optometrist and planter; of Lae, TNG; b. Chillagoe, Qld, 16 Jan 1904.

By improving the track, building bridges and rest camps, and reorganising the carrier lines, it had been hoped to make the track carry 6,000 pounds daily, but it never provided anything like that figure. Aircraft could have been used either to supplement deliveries over this track or replace them almost completely, but General Morris did not have aircraft. As late as early August he had none stationed permanently at Port Moresby and, in his efforts to get some, did not hesitate to say that, through their lack, his forward troops were "liable to starvation". Nor, when they did begin to be available, did Kanga Force figure largely as a commitment for their services as, by that time, a far more urgent need had developed in Papua.

So the outbreak of serious fighting elsewhere increased Kanga Force's difficulties. Even after the raid on Salamaua Winning's men had to rely to a large extent on Umphelby's rapidly diminishing reserves as Winning said that he had then, at one time, only 11 tins of soup and 7 pounds of rice to feed 72 men, with no tea or sugar. On 10th July he and Umphelby went to Wau to stress the difficulties of their food situation, largely responsible, he claimed, for the fact that only 23 of his 49 men then at Mubo had been reported fit for duty on the 5th. Considerable improvement in the circumstances of his own group followed this visit but elsewhere in the forward areas bad conditions had prevailed and the men, besides becoming rapidly weak and unfit, found their tempers fraying and their spirits drooping.

An example was a message sent back to Howard by one of his officers, Lieutenant Littlejohn,[8] who was watching the Mapos Track. It was dated 16th June and was written in pencil on a piece of paper six inches by four.

> To us the tobacco position is still most unsatisfactory. You tell us 82 tins have been sent and more were sent to make up a three weeks' supply. Then you say our issue is 70 tins. Also that 14 tins went forward with Private Pearce.[9] Pearce denies this. I am not interested in how much we should have but where is it? To whom was the mythical 82 tins of tobacco given? Where is the 70 tins (2 weeks' supply)? Who gave Pearce the tobacco to bring out here? The fact remains that we have no tobacco (not even stock tobacco), have received none and want some badly. If 82 plus 14 tins have gone astray it is time somebody found out where it has gone to.

This question of supply pivoted on the evergreen problem of securing and keeping native carriers—one which had been aggravated by the early July air raids and which, particularly in the forward areas, became more acute as July advanced. Japanese intimidation tactics and the difficulty of getting native rations forward to feed carriers had a cumulative effect. Patrols had to be restricted, reliefs and other troop movements could not take place.

On the 27th July Captain Lang,[1] who had succeeded Kneen and was

---

[8] Capt R. A. Littlejohn, NX77259. 1st Indep Coy; 2/3 Cdo Sqn. Grazier; of Crowther, NSW; b. Sydney, 13 Sep 1915.
[9] L-Cpl A. W. Pearce, QX15827. 2/5 Indep Coy; Angau. Truck driver; of Cairns, Qld; b. Ayr, Qld, 20 May 1921.
[1] Maj P. S. Lang, VX39041. 2/5 Indep Coy, 2/7 Cav (Cdo) Regt and various base and area commands. Research officer and lecturer; of Lismore, Vic; b. Melbourne, 22 Jul 1912.

in charge of the Markham area, reported that 40 boys had deserted from Bob's the previous night and that lack of carriers was holding up his patrols. On the 28th he reported the desertion of 40 more carriers—from Partep 2 (on the Wampit River Track forward of Zenag)—and said that the Japanese had threatened to bomb Old Mari village (south of the Markham between Bob's and Sheldon's) if Australian patrols crossed the river. In consequence the local natives were reluctant to supply labour and he had to rely entirely on overworked mules to supply outposts at Sheldon's and Kirklands.

The position is therefore very serious (he wrote). Any Jap bombing or strafing along our L of C will disrupt our supply line for some time. This may even occur as a result of threats and rumours, and we have no permanent line of labour. We cannot use force since we have none. . . . We can do nothing to protect these natives who help or have helped us in the past largely on promises.

We now cannot obtain labour on the north side of the Markham and we are now seeing a rapid, inevitable and progressive diminution this side. The Jap technique with natives has never been bad and is improving. Moreover they are not even trying yet, since no bombs have fallen this side.

Partly as a result of all these problems of supply, partly through the general strain of warfare in the country where Kanga Force was operating, weakness and sickness rapidly thinned the ranks of the guerillas. Naturally the men of the N.G.V.R. were suffering most. McAdam's scouts, most active and successful of all groups under Fleay, had worked themselves to a standstill and had to be relieved. A 2/5th Independent Company party took their places, led by Sergeant O'Neill who had developed into an outstanding scout in the N.G.V.R. tradition. By 7th August Fleay told General Morris that all troops forward of Bulolo and Wau were A.I.F. (although this was not entirely correct as some individuals, like Rifleman Pauley[2] at Mubo and Sergeant Emery at Sheldon's, remained to act as scouts, observers and contact men with the natives, and the N.G.V.R. was to be represented in some form in the area until the guerilla period finally ended). But even the relatively fresh A.I.F. men were suffering badly. By early August Fleay had found it necessary to relieve Howard's detachment at Mapos as there were not sufficient fit men left there to send out a patrol. On 31st August headquarters at Moresby were told that the total effective strength of the 2/5th Company had been reduced to 182 although the company had come into the area 303 strong.

This dreary situation had been partly relieved by some attempts to make life easier for the force during July and August. Accommodation at Mubo was improved by the erection of huts, a forward hospital unit was opened at Guadagasal on the 2nd August, an attempt was made to establish a canteen at Wau. But the history of that canteen probably provided the perfect example in miniature of the failure to keep Kanga Force supplied, for it was able to remain open for only a fortnight. At the end of that time all stock had been sold and the canteen closed.

---

[2] Lt A. E. Pauley, NGX361. NGVR and 1 NG Inf Bn. Gold miner; of Otago Central, NZ; b. St. Bathans, NZ, 19 Oct 1912.

Although the background picture was thus darkening there were men in the force who refused to be depressed. One of them was the energetic Winning who was not content to sit idle at Mubo. For some time reports had been coming of a Japanese gun sited at Busama and Winning determined to investigate them. On 19th August he took a patrol out from Mubo. He found that the natives at Busama were very pro-Japanese and had warned his enemies of his coming. He saw 60 Japanese disembarking from three barges soon after his arrival, but found no gun and no evidence of Japanese concentration. His observations at Busama convinced him that the village was the centre of a deception plan, "that the Jap during the day as a blind merely moved up and then moved back under cover of darkness". He had been uneasy before this about possible large-scale movements against Mubo where he had left 49 men under Captain Minchin,[3] and had sent a note to Minchin telling him not to move out with a patrol as he had proposed to do. Now he sent Minchin a second note stressing that the Japanese activity was "a blind" and followed it with a third, while, with his party, he struck out through the Buangs for Bulwa.

Meanwhile both Fleay, back at Wau, and Minchin, had been reacting to reports of Japanese movements which had reached them. Heeding, apparently, a report from Mubo about 27th August, Fleay informed Moresby that 200 Japanese had moved to Busama. By the 29th he was reporting that the numbers had grown to 300, that the Japanese were concentrating stores at Busama, and had obtained natives to guide them thence to the Bulolo Valley.

But even more disconcerting news was at hand. A 6,000-ton transport, with a destroyer for escort, was in the harbour at Salamaua on the 27th. Several hundred troops and stores, including motor vehicles, were unloaded on the night 28th-29th August. Next, Kanga Force informed Moresby that three sampans had been carrying an estimated 200 to 300 troops to Lokanu, a coastal village a few miles south of Salamaua.

Fleay decided that simultaneous attacks on Mubo from Lokanu, and on the Bulolo Valley from Busama, were likely. He asked for reinforcements, knowing that the 2/6th Independent Company had arrived at Port Moresby on the 7th August and had originally been intended to augment his force. But Lieut-General Rowell, who had taken over from Morris at Moresby about two weeks earlier, was watching an uneasy situation develop just south of Kokoda where a mixed force was fighting hard to stop the Japanese penetration which had developed from landings at Gona on the 21st July, and was apprehensive of the consequences of a Japanese assault on Milne Bay which had started on 26th August. Fleay was told, therefore, that he would have to do the best he could with what he had and that there was little prospect of the other company joining him.

At Mubo on the 29th Minchin received news that 130 Japanese had been seen entering the valley of the Francisco River. He then left Mubo with a patrol of 20 men meaning to intercept the Japanese near Bobdubi.

---

[3] Capt L. J. Minchin, NX12579. 2/5 Indep Coy; HQ 3 Div. Clerk; of Strathfield, NSW; b. Burwood, NSW, 19 May 1916.

On the way, however, he saw the Japanese approaching Komiatum by another track. Hastily he warned Wau by radio from the near-by observation post where Pilot Officer Vial had originally been established[4] and, assuming that he was cut off from Mubo, set out for the Bulolo Valley across the main range.[5]

By the morning of the 30th Fleay had made up his mind that Mubo was about to be attacked from three sides—from Komiatum frontally, from Lokanu on the right, and from Busama on the left. He reported later:

> We had only a small garrison at Mubo, and orders were issued to this party that if forced to withdraw they were to fall back on Kaisenik. No defensive position is possible between Mubo and Kaisenik owing to the nature of the country.

His feeling of insecurity was strengthened by uncertainty concerning the actual numbers advancing on Mubo; he estimated that there were about 1,000 Japanese in that vicinity. Whatever the number was it was obviously too many for Lieutenant Hicks,[6] who had been left at Mubo with 29 men. By 2 p.m. Hicks had reported that his enemies were closing in on him. Now Fleay made up his mind.

> It appeared obvious that the Japanese would continue their advance to the Bulolo Valley (he wrote subsequently). If so the enemy could reach the Kaisenik area by the night of the 31st August, thereby cutting off our planned move to the defensive position near Winima [two hours' walk south of Kaisenik].
>
> It now became apparent that the movement of troops and stores to the Kaisenik area would have to proceed with all speed. It was decided to carry out demolitions under cover of darkness and as twelve hours was required for the completion of demolitions, orders were given to commence at nightfall 30th August 1942.

At 3 p.m. on the 30th Fleay issued instructions for the "scorching" of the Bulolo Valley and withdrawal to Winima and Kudjeru. His plan was to form a line in the Kaisenik-Winima area and carry out his secondary role—to hold the Bulldog Track. Troops from along the Bulolo Valley were ordered to report at once to No. 6 Camp near Wau. There rations for the march were handed out, arms and ammunition were distributed for carrying.

As darkness fell the camp buildings and any others still standing in Wau township were set alight. Equipment, stores, ammunition that could not be carried, blazed in great fires. At Bulolo, Bulwa and Sunshine, the demolition parties worked steadily with petrol and dynamite. The night resounded with explosions and demolition charges were blown on the Wau and other aerodromes, roads were cratered and bridges shattered.

---

[4] Then known as Moy's Post, after Lt F. H. Moy of Angau, who had been manning the post since Vial's departure earlier in August.

[5] After climbing to 10,000 feet and suffering great privations Minchin's patrol turned back and returned to the observation post. On 2nd September the post was abandoned. Moy assumed leadership of the party and, greatly helped by Rifleman Forrester who was with Minchin's party, and loyal natives, led them to Boisi village, on the coast about eight miles south of Salamaua. They were then in country and among natives known to Moy. Travelling by canoe at night and lying hidden in daylight they made a leisurely journey to Morobe. Thence they journeyed inland, and on 5th October reached Garaina where they found an aircraft establishing a supply dump and whence they were flown to Moresby, having been wandering at times in very bad country for five weeks.

[6] Lt D. S. Hicks, NX53090; 2/5 Indep Coy. Barrister-at-law; of King's Cross, NSW; b. Sydney, 1 Aug 1911.

By midnight the main body of troops was clear of the smoke and glowing embers that marked Wau. Trucks could be used to Crystal Creek, three to four miles south-east of Wau. After that the job was a marching and carrier-line one. Confusion manifested itself for a time, with a growing and untidy accumulation at Crystal Creek, equipment abandoned along the track, carriers deserting.

Not all of Fleay's men, however, took the track through Kaisenik during the main movement. Lieutenant Hicks did not report at Blake's Camp (one hour and a half south of Winima) until 2nd September. He had sent a runner before him to say that the Japanese, 900 strong, had entered Mubo from three sides at 2.30 p.m. on 31st August. He had withdrawn before the Japanese, his men carrying what weapons they could and hiding the rest. His force was intact and had inflicted some casualties on the Japanese. They had not suffered casualties themselves. On their way down they passed a patrol of 20 under Lieutenant Wylie who, Fleay said later, had been sent to reinforce the garrison. But Wylie and his men went on alone to keep contact with the invaders. On the night of the 5th-6th September one of their small patrols got close enough to Mubo to observe the Japanese dispositions and two nights later another patrol found the enemy in considerable strength on Garrison Hill, just west of the village. The Japanese were at Mubo to stay.

Farther down the Bulolo Valley Winning and his patrol from Busama arrived at Bulwa on the 3rd and found the area burnt and their friends gone. They came up the valley some days in the wake of the main body.

But the men whose position gave real cause for anxiety were those elements of Lang's company which were still operating in the Markham area. Earlier they had been concerned about the spread of Japanese influence south of the river. Their own patrolling during August, however, had suggested that this concern might have been over-emphasised and by the end of the month a patrol which had been across the river was of the opinion that the time was favourable once more for an attempt by some of the former Administration officers to re-establish contact with the natives there and for the establishment of a permanent patrol east of the river. The withdrawal of the main body from the Bulolo Valley, however, gave them rather more urgent matters to attend to since their supply line was broken and it seemed likely that the line of their withdrawal was also to be severed.

Thus, with the end of August, came to an end the first phase of the irregular operations in the Salamaua-Lae-Wau area. The Japanese were poised at Mubo within easy striking distance of Wau and the Bulolo Valley but had not yet thrust up the Markham in any force; the Australians had abandoned the Bulolo Valley and the town of Wau, left them smoking behind them, and were hastily preparing to fight at the head of the Bulldog Track.

CHAPTER 4

THE JAPANESE ADVANCE TO KOKODA

KOKODA lay in the green Yodda Valley, 1,200 feet above sea level, on the northern foothills of the massive Owen Stanley Range. It contained a Papuan Administration post, a rubber plantation, and the only aerodrome in Papua between Port Moresby and the northern coast. A primitive foot track crossed the mountains from Port Moresby and then ran east-north-east from Kokoda to the Buna-Sanananda-Gona area by the sea. Much of the Port Moresby-Kokoda sector was merely a native pad. Few passed over it—only the barefoot natives, or occasionally a missionary, a patrolling officer of the Administration, or some other wandering European. Aeroplanes served the Yodda Valley. The infrequent travellers whose business took them to the north-east coast generally went by sea, or flew to Kokoda and walked down.

A road climbed 25 miles or so from Port Moresby up to the Sogeri plateau and across it to Ilolo on the edge of the plateau facing into the main ranges. These rose turbulently to the clouds. Forests covered them densely with seas of green. Winds moaned through them. Rains poured down upon them from clouds which swirled round the peaks and through the valleys. Torrents raged through their giant rifts and foamed among grey stones. Among the mountains native tribes made their homes.

From Ilolo the track fell easily through the bush for three or four miles. Then it plunged down mountainsides through dense forests where afternoon rains drummed into the green canopy above it. There was a sound of water rushing far below. There was a twilight gloom among the trees and in the depths. There was a brawling stream and a bridge of moss-grown logs and stones. After that the track climbed a short distance up a steep slope to the village of Uberi round which mists swirled in the mornings and evenings. From Uberi to Ioribaiwa it was a hard day's walk. The track toiled up a long mountainside. It was smooth and treacherous, hemmed in by dark trees, beaten upon by rain. It seemed to pause on the crest before it leaped down the other side of the mountain by dim ways to pass over Imita Ridge, and so into the bed of a rushing stream along which it splashed for about three miles. It climbed out of the stream on to a spur of sunlit kunai grass and upwards to the crest of the 4,000-foot Ioribaiwa Ridge. From Ioribaiwa to Nauro was a shorter day but still hard going. The track went down and up again until it overlooked Ioribaiwa from the Nauro side. From that point on to Nauro there were some hours of slippery walking generally downwards but with stretches of hard climbing over ridges and spurs. Nauro lay in a pleasant valley on the edge of the Brown River. Menari was some hours farther on. The track to it first passed along the river valley through bush which dripped with rain and over carpets of dead leaves which were soundless underfoot. From the valley it strained up and over a towering mountain and fell swiftly down on to the flat ground where Menari lay. Leaving Menari it began the long, upward climb towards the crest of the main Owen Stanley Range by way of precipitous slopes and broken ridges. Often torrents of rain beat a dull tattoo against the broad leaves which roofed much of it. Near Efogi it broke out into the open country of a large river valley in which the village was sited. On the opposite side of the valley Kagi seemed almost to hang from the open mountainside, clearly seen through the thin mountain air but still a weary climb distant. Above it rose the main crest line of the range. The track passed over it at about 6,500 feet through a wide gap on either side of which, as far as the eye could reach, the broken skyline rose some thousands of feet higher into the clouds or lost itself in swirling mist. Here the moss forests—soft and silent underfoot—began. Streamers of moss hung from the trees.

After crossing the crest of the range above Kagi the track dropped easily enough through the bush and over the moss for an hour or two. But then its downward trend grew quickly steeper and steeper. The ground fell away precipitously on either side, dense bush pressed in, the track seemed almost to plunge headlong so that a walker slid and fell and clutched at hanging branches for support. In the silence of the bush and the moss there first welled and then rushed the roar of a torrent far below. High on moss-covered logs the track edged across a number of feeder streams, and then, suddenly, broke out on to the brink of rushing, twisting water thick with white and yellow spume, boiling in whirlpools round grey stones as big as small houses and disfigured with moss and pallid fungus.

This was Eora Creek. It rose high on the northern slopes of the mountains east of Kagi. Its course determined the way of the track from the top of the range down to Kokoda. Where the two met was the beginning of a gigantic V-shaped rift through which the waters raged down to the Yodda Valley, tearing deeper and deeper into the bases of the mountains as they did so until the sides of the V rose in places a full 4,000 feet on either side of the torrent, so steeply that in places they had to be climbed almost hand over hand.

The way ahead which the track now followed did not lead upwards, however, but, clinging like a narrow shelf to the left hand side of the V, followed the torrent along until, after about another hour's walk it dropped again to the very edge of the water and crossed it. (This point was to become well known during the fighting in the mountains as Templeton's Crossing.) A small cluster of huts which formed the village of Eora Creek lay about three hours' walk farther on. The track to the village climbed high along the right bank until the roar of the torrent could be heard no more. Then a ridge thrust down to the creek like a sharp tongue and the track followed its narrow crest from which both sides fell away like a precipice. As the track descended there came from the right the distant whisper of a tributary torrent unseen in the mountain depths below, rushing to join Eora Creek whose muted roar was being borne up from the left. Suddenly the track went over the point of the spur, plunging and slipping down an almost sheer slope which ended in a flat platform (the site of the few huts of Eora Creek village) overhanging the creek below which filled the air with sound. Below raged a whirlpool formed by the junction of the two creeks, a turbulence spanned only by slippery logs. The track crossed these and continued on for about two more hours of walking to Alola, climbing the left hand side of the V. High along a narrow pinch which clung about 2,000 feet above the creek bed it made its way to the village of Isurava. From Isurava it ran steadily downhill for about two hours with sharp rises over spurs which it crossed at right angles and quick, slippery descents down the other sides of them. It still hung to the side of the valley, was broken by juts of pointed rock, tangled with masses of roots which wove through it, splashed through little streams and passed by waterfalls. So it came to the village of Deniki, whence the Yodda Valley came into sight below, stretched out like a garden, the Kokoda airstrip plainly to be seen, the Kokoda plateau thrust like a tongue from the frowning mountain spurs. Into this green valley the track quickly descended, crossed it in about three hours of walking, leaving the bleakness of the mountains behind and running into steamy warmth, and came to Kokoda itself.

When the Japanese first landed in Papua there was much talk of "the Kokoda Pass". But there was no pass—merely a lowering of the mountain silhouette where the valley of Eora Creek cut down into the Yodda Valley south of Kokoda.

From Kokoda the track slipped easily down towards the sea for three full days of hot marching. First it passed over undulations fringed by rough foothills and covered with thick bush. It forded many streams, passed through the villages of Oivi and Gorari, went on down to the Kumusi River which, deep and wide and swift, flowed northward and then turned sharply east to reach the sea between Gona and Cape Ward Hunt.

This was the country of the fierce Orokaivas, unsmiling men with spare, hard, black bodies and smouldering eyes. They were still greatly feared by all their neighbours although it was many years since Europeans first came and forced peace upon them. They suffered at the hands of the Yodda Valley gold-seekers at the end of the nineteenth century and the severity of the magistrate Monckton at the beginning of the new century, and it was said that they had not forgiven either occasion. Their kinsmen, the coastal Orokaivas farther on, were of the same type.

The track crossed the Kumusi by a bridge suspended from steel cables. The place of crossing came thus to be known as Wairopi (the "pidgin" rendering of "wire rope"). A little farther on, in the vicinity of Awala, began a network of tracks which passed over tropical lowlands through or past Sangara Mission and Popondetta into spreading swamps and thus reached the coast on which were the two little settlements of Buna and Gona—the former the administrative headquarters of the district, the latter a long-established Church of England mission.

Up to July 1942 Australian military interest in this lonely coast and the even lonelier track which linked it with Port Moresby was of slow growth.

On 2nd February Major-General Rowell, then Deputy Chief of the General Staff, had signalled Major-General Morris:

> Japanese in all operations have shown inclination to land some distance from ultimate objective rather than make a direct assault. This probably because of need to gain air bases as well as desire to catch defence facing wrong way. You will probably have already considered possibility of landing New Guinea mainland and advance across mountains but think it advisable to warn you of this enemy course.

Morris, with a difficult administrative situation on his hands, only meagre and ill-trained forces at his disposal and more likely military possibilities pressing him, that month sent a platoon (Lieutenant Jesser) of the Papuan Infantry Battalion to patrol the coast from Buna to the Waria River, the mouth of which was about half-way between Buna and Salamaua, and watch for signs of a Japanese approach.

On 10th March a Japanese float-plane swept over Buna about 11 a.m., bombed and machine-gunned two small mission vessels there, then settled on the water. However, it was promptly engaged with rifle fire by Lieutenant Champion,[1] the former Assistant Resident Magistrate, and the small group with him, who were staffing the Administration and wireless station on the shore, and it quickly took the air again.

At the end of March the Combined Operations Intelligence Centre, in an assessment of the likelihood of Japanese moves to occupy the Wau-Bulolo area after the seizure of Lae and Salamaua, had suggested the possibility of a landing at Buna with a view to an overland advance on Port Moresby. But little serious consideration seems to have been given to this suggestion.

The Japanese expedition against Port Moresby, turned back by the Allied naval forces in the Coral Sea, had underlined the need to reinforce the troops and air squadrons in New Guinea. On 14th May MacArthur wrote to Blamey that he had decided to establish airfields on the south-east coast of Papua for use against Lae, Salamaua and Rabaul, that there appeared to be suitable sites between Abau and Samarai, and he wished to know whether Blamey had troops to protect these bases. (The 14th was the day on which the ships containing the 32nd American Division and the remainder of the 41st arrived in Melbourne.) Blamey had already ordered the 14th Brigade to Port Moresby and it embarked at Townsville on the 15th. He replied, on the 16th, that he could provide the troops, and MacArthur, on the 20th, authorised the construction of an airstrip in the Abau-Mullins Harbour area. At the same time he ordered that the air force bring its squadrons at Moresby up to full strength and that American anti-aircraft troops be sent from Brisbane to the forward airfields at Townsville, Horn Island, Mareeba, Cooktown and Coen.

The 14th Brigade, with only about five months of continuous training behind it (although most of the individual men had had more than that), was thus the first substantial infantry reinforcement to reach Moresby since

---

[1] Capt F. A. Champion, P375; Angau. Assistant Resident Magistrate; of Buna, Papua, and Kalinga, Qld; b. Port Moresby, 27 Apr 1905.

General Sturdee had sent two battalions there, making a total of three, on 3rd January, four months before the Coral Sea battle.² When the inexperienced 14th Brigade was sent forward there were, in eastern Australia, three brigades of hardened veterans—the 18th, 21st and 25th—but unwisely none of those was chosen.

On 24th May Morris was instructed to provide a garrison for the new airstrip but was told that if the enemy launched a major attack it was to withdraw after having destroyed all weapons and supplies. A reconnaissance of the proposed area, however, had led to the conclusion that it was unsuitable; Morris, on the advice of Elliott-Smith, then of the Papuan Infantry Battalion, emphasised that there were better sites at Milne Bay and on 12th June G.H.Q. authorised the construction of an airfield there.

MacArthur could now proceed with greater confidence because of a great defeat that the Japanese Navy had suffered in another hemisphere.

After their occupation of Tulagi on 3rd May the Japanese quickly spread to the neighbouring island of Guadalcanal and began the construction of an airfield there. On 5th May the Japanese High Command had ordered Admiral Yamamoto, Commander-in-Chief of the Japanese Combined Fleet, to take Midway and the Aleutians. On 18th May, as mentioned

---

² On 18th March 1943 the newspaper correspondents at MacArthur's headquarters were told that: "when General MacArthur first came to Australia, the defence plan for the safety of this continent involved North Australia being taken by the enemy. This was based on the conception of the 'Brisbane Line' of defence. It had been drawn up on the fundamental that the littoral of islands to the north of Australia would be taken by the enemy, and that Northern Queensland and Darwin area would be overrun by the Japanese. It was the intention of Australia to defend along a line somewhere near the Tropic of Capricorn, which would be known as the Brisbane Line. At that time the role of Port Moresby was to 'hold the enemy to enable mainland defences to be brought into action'. It was General MacArthur who abandoned the 'Brisbane Line' concept and decided that the battle for Australia should be fought in New Guinea."

On 1st November 1943 Curtin wrote a letter to MacArthur in the course of which he referred to the effects of the return of the A.I.F. and the arrival of the United States Forces in Australia and said: "The additional forces enabled a transformation to be made in your strategy from a defensive one on the mainland, to a defence of the mainland from the line of the Owen Stanley Range."

MacArthur, in his reply, wrote that: "The statement that the additional forces enabled a transformation to be made in *my* strategy from a defensive one on the mainland to a defence of the mainland from the line of the Owen Stanley Range is incorrect. It was never my intention to defend Australia on the mainland of Australia. That was the plan when I arrived, but to which I never subscribed and which I immediately changed to a plan to defend Australia in New Guinea."

Thereupon, on 16th November, Curtin wrote to Blamey asking him what were the plans of the Australian General Staff early in 1941. What changes were made and on whose authority, and what instructions were issued by General MacArthur after his arrival and the date of same. Blamey described how Moresby had been reinforced soon after the Japanese declaration of war, and plans made to reinforce Darwin, Western Australia and Townsville; quoted MacArthur's "first directive relating to a general plan" (issued on 25th April) which prescribed the "entirely defensive role" for Allied Land Forces of preventing "any landing on the north-east coast of Australia or on the south-western coast of New Guinea and made no alteration in the existing dispositions of the forces". The 14th Brigade was moved to New Guinea in May under orders issued by Allied Land Forces.

If MacArthur had a radical change of policy in mind immediately after his arrival Curtin and Blamey were not made aware of it, and the steps taken to reinforce Port Moresby were singularly cautious. On 3rd January when Sturdee sent two battalions to Port Moresby he had few units which had had more than a few weeks' continuous training. By 15th May when, after the Coral Sea battle, Blamey sent an additional brigade to Port Moresby, a battle-tried Australian corps including one division, part of another, and corps troops and two American divisions were in Australia, the training and equipment of the ten infantry and motor divisions of the home army and of the 1st Armoured Division had greatly improved, and air reinforcements had been received. Relatively the two battalions which General Sturdee sent to Port Moresby in January were a greater proportion of his strength than the three battalions—militia, not A.I.F. —were of MacArthur's and Blamey's, yet the need throughout March, April and May was far more urgent.

The maintenance of G.H.Q. at Melbourne until 20th July 1942 seems hardly consistent with MacArthur's statement of November 1943. Melbourne is 2,000 miles from Port Moresby; it was as though a headquarters in London was conducting a battle in Egypt.

Statements similar to those made in the G.H.Q. press statement of 18th March 1943 and MacArthur's letter in November 1943 have appeared in a number of books and it is for that reason that this question is discussed here in some detail.

earlier, it issued orders for attacks on New Caledonia, Fiji, Samoa and Port Moresby to cut communications between America and Australia.

Early in June, eluding an American naval force which had been sent into those cold seas to intercept them, the Japanese landed at Kiska and Attu in the west of the Aleutians. At the same time they made their advance against Midway.

Although, after the encounter, they had lost touch with the heavy Japanese forces which they had met in the Coral Sea, the American naval staffs had correctly deduced from their Intelligence that the next major Japanese move would be against Midway, and the Aleutians. They therefore quickly concentrated near Midway a fleet consisting of 3 carriers (the *Enterprise, Hornet* and *Yorktown*—the last-named having been hastily patched up), 7 heavy cruisers, 1 light cruiser, 14 destroyers and 25 submarines. Marine Corps and army aircraft were based on the island itself.

On the morning of 3rd June Japanese forces, on an easterly course, were sighted several hundred miles south-west of Midway. Army aircraft engaged them. Next morning Japanese aircraft raided the island and the Americans located the centre of the concentration of their enemies. The Japanese were out in strength with a striking force of 4 carriers, 2 battleships, 2 cruisers and 12 destroyers. A support force and an occupation force followed, the former containing 2 battleships, 1 heavy cruiser, 4 cruisers and 10 destroyers, the latter consisting of transport and cargo vessels escorted by 3 heavy cruisers and 12 destroyers. The Americans attacked with both land-based and carrier-borne aircraft during the 4th and the following two days in an engagement which was primarily an air-sea one (though not entirely so as in the Coral Sea).

When the smoke of the battle cleared it was obvious that the Japanese had suffered very heavily. They lost their four carriers, one cruiser and one destroyer, while a number of the other ships were damaged. They lost probably about 250 aircraft; the Americans lost 150 aircraft and the aircraft carrier *Yorktown.*

This decisive battle redressed the balance of naval power in the Pacific which had been so dangerously shaken for the Americans at Pearl Harbour; it marked the point at which the Allies might begin to turn from defensive to offensive planning. Despite this, it did not yet mean that the Allies had command of the Pacific seas nor alter the fact that there were dangerous groupings of Japanese forces available for operations particularly in the South-West Pacific.

These had already begun to concentrate.[3] Lieutenant-General Harukichi Hyakutake's *XVII Army* was the instrument being prepared. Its main force was then being drawn from the *5th, 18th* and *56th Divisions*, which

---

[3] These plans apparently never contemplated invasion of Australia and New Zealand. Later, when asked if the Japanese had ever planned such invasion, General Tojo replied: "We never had enough troops to do so. We had already far outstretched our lines of communication. We did not have the armed strength or the supply facilities to mount such a terrific extension of our already over-strained and too thinly spread forces. We expected to occupy all New Guinea, to maintain Rabaul as a holding base, and to raid northern Australia by air. But actual physical invasion—no, at no time."

were concentrated mainly at Davao after the end of the fighting in the Philippines; but Hyakutake was gathering elements also from Java, and Major-General Tomitaro Horii's *South Seas Force,* built strongly round the *144th Regiment,* was still at Rabaul after its successful assault there in January and the capture of Salamaua by one of its battalion groups. Formidable naval support for Hyakutake was planned to come from Vice-Admiral Kondo's *Second Fleet* (13 heavy cruisers, 2 light cruisers, 24 destroyers), Vice-Admiral Nagumo's *First Air Fleet* (7 carriers, 11 destroyers) and Vice-Admiral Mikawa's fleet which included the four battleships *Hiyei, Kirishima, Kongo* and *Haruna.*

A few days after the Midway battle indications of a renewed thrust by the enemy in the South-West Pacific were accumulating. On 9th June MacArthur wrote Blamey that there was increasing evidence of Japanese interest in developing a route from Buna through Kokoda to Port Moresby and that minor forces might try to use this route either to attack Port Moresby or to supply forces advancing by sea through the Louisiades.[4] He asked what Morris was doing to protect the Kokoda area.

On 6th June Morris had given the Papuan Infantry Battalion (30 officers and 280 men) the task of reconnoitring the Awala-Tufi-Ioma area. On 20th June General Blamey ordered him to take steps to prepare to oppose the enemy on possible lines of advance from the north coast and to secure the Kokoda area. Thereupon on 24th June Morris ordered that the 39th Battalion (less one company), the P.I.B., and appropriate supply and medical detachments should constitute Maroubra Force, with the task of delaying any advance from Awala to Kokoda, preventing any Japanese movement in the direction of Port Moresby through the gap in the Owen Stanleys near Kokoda, and meeting any airborne landings which might threaten at Kokoda or elsewhere along the route. One company of the 39th Battalion was to leave Ilolo on 26th June.

Many changes had taken place in the 39th Battalion during its five months in Papua. Some of the men had had experience of action against raiding Japanese aircraft. At the airfield at the Seven Mile, one of the principal targets of the raiders, they had claimed at least one Zero as a "certain kill" and others as "probables". Reinforcements which arrived in March were all A.I.F. enlistments (and were resentful at having to serve with a militia unit). Brigadier Porter,[5] who had taken over the 30th Brigade on 17th April, had driven the battalion hard in common with the other units of the brigade. Porter was active, keen and receptive of new ideas. He had been an original officer of the 2/5th Battalion and later commanded the 2/31st in the Syrian campaign. While he was critical of his brigade in some respects he considered that they had been shabbily treated in many ways and worked hard to overcome disadvantages which they suffered. By

---

[4] This plan resembled so closely one which the Japanese definitely formulated a few weeks later that it seems probable that the Intelligence was based on intercepted Japanese wireless messages.

[5] Maj-Gen S. H. W. C. Porter, CBE, DSO, ED, VX133. 2/5 Bn; CO 2/6 Bn 1941, 2/31 Bn 1941-42; Comd 30 Bde 1942-43, 24 Bde 1943-45. Chief Commissioner of Police, Victoria, 1954- . Bank official; of Wangaratta, Vic; b. Tintaldra, Vic, 23 Feb 1905.

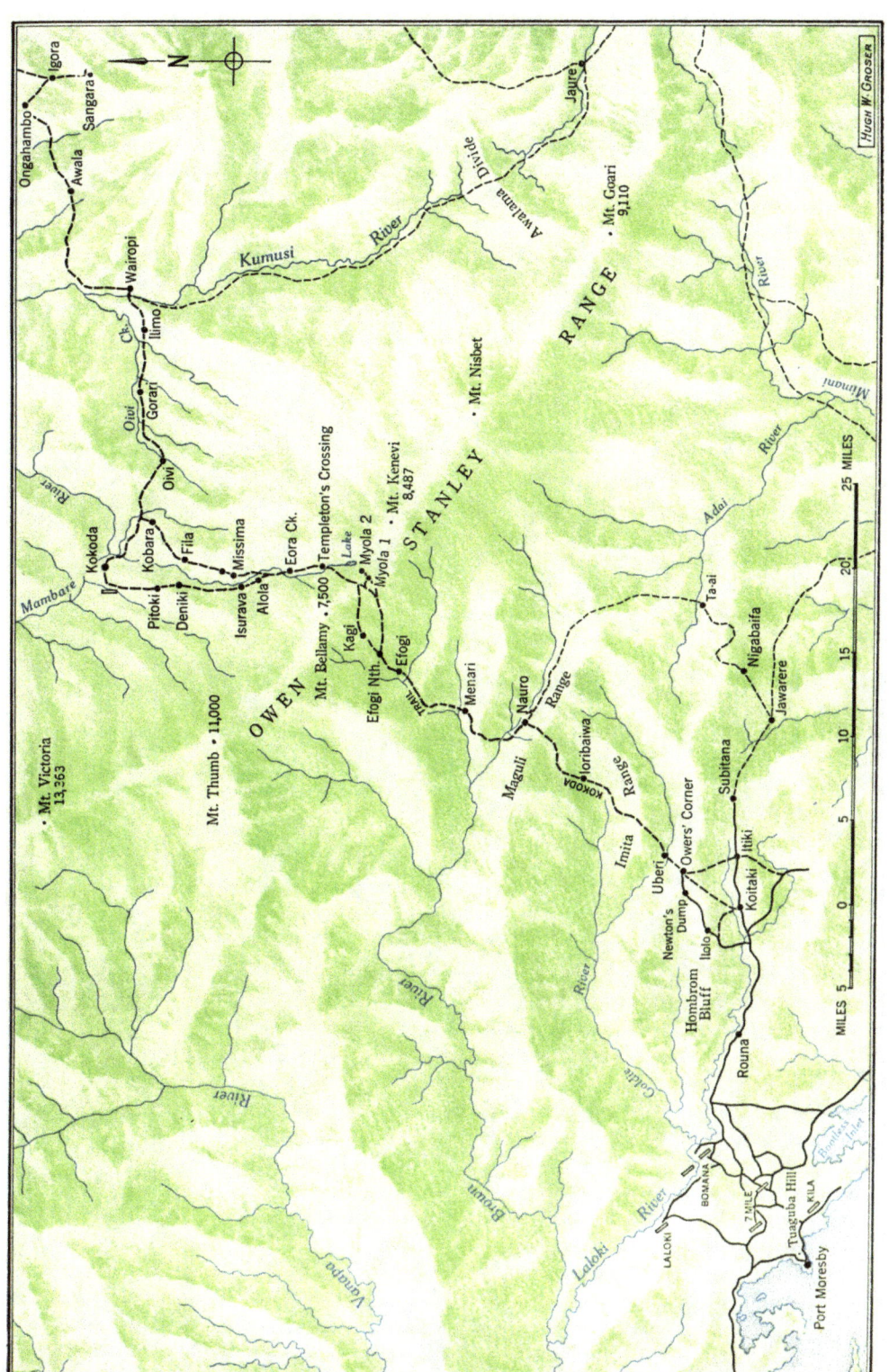

The Kokoda Track

the beginning of July he had sent back to Australia about 20 officers from his brigade and had managed to get forward approximately 30 A.I.F. officers, and A.I.F. men who were commissioned in his units. The 39th Battalion received a strong leavening of these and a survivor of the 2/22nd Battalion, Lieut-Colonel W. T. Owen, took over command. After the reshuffle the only 1914-18 War veteran remaining in commissioned rank was Captain Templeton,[6] who retained "B" Company. Templeton was reputed to have served in submarines in the earlier war and had fought in Spain during the Civil War. When the new war came he was rejected as medically unfit for the A.I.F. because he had "flat feet" and consequently he burned to show his fitness at almost any cost. Among his troops he was known affectionately as "Uncle Sam".

With this battalion preparing to cross the range Morris was faced with new problems. He still had the defence of the Port Moresby area to worry him and had been understandably loath to throw off detachments which would weaken his main force.[7] But the problem which was now to loom larger than any others was that of supply. Because of that problem, if for no other reasons, Morris considered the Kokoda Track impassable for any large-scale military movements; and that in such country the force with the longer supply line would be at a very great disadvantage.

Therefore (he had said) even if the Japanese do make this very difficult and impracticable move, let us meet them on ground of our own choosing and as close as possible to our own base. Let us merely help their own supply problem to strangle them while reducing our supply difficulties to a minimum.

Now, however, he was in a position where, if his men met the enemy, the very advantage he sought would not only be denied them but, initially at least, would rest with their opponents. The Australians would be separated from their base by roadless mountains which were impassable to wheeled vehicles. They had no transport aircraft based at Port Moresby. For their main supply line they would have to depend upon native carriers.

Porterage by natives was the traditional method of transporting supplies and equipment in New Guinea from the time when Europeans first began thrusting inland from the coasts. Although the use of natives for carrying was almost always arranged on a casual and day-to-day basis, the general recruitment of native labour and the conditions under which such labour might be employed were rigidly prescribed in both Papua and the Mandated Territory. Regulations limited the number of natives who might be recruited from any area at any time, provided for employment, in most cases, in accordance with contracts which obliged employers to return indentured labourers to their villages at the end of a limited term of service and imposed detailed conditions of service which employers must observe.[8]

---

[6] Capt S. V. Templeton, V50190; 39 Bn. Manager; of East Brighton, Vic; b. Belfast, N. Ireland, 21 Jan 1901. Killed in action 26 Jul 1942. (Templeton was probably older than here stated.)

[7] At the end of June the total strength in the whole of New Guinea was: A.I.F. 1,098; militia 12,273; American 2,208. The Americans were mainly "service", and not "combat" troops. A heavy proportion of the Australians were in lines of communication, maintenance, fixed defence and anti-aircraft units.

[8] These conditions covered rates of cash payment (a minimum of 10/- per month in Papua, 5/- in the Mandated Territory), scales of issue of food, clothing and other necessities, and standards of accommodation.

Penal sanctions (gaol sentences or fines) could be imposed to force the natives to fulfil the terms of their contracts. At the beginning of 1942 there were about 10,000 indentured labourers in Papua and 35,000 in the Mandated Territory.

On 15th June the hand of military authority fell heavily on the native labour force of the two Territories. Morris invoked the National Security (Emergency Control) Regulations to terminate all existing contracts of service in Papua and New Guinea and provide for the conscription of whatever native labour might be required by the Services. He ordered that "the Senior Military Officer or any District Officer" might employ any native upon such work and subject to such conditions not inconsistent with the order as he might think fit; that all natives so employed should enter into a contract of employment for a period not exceeding three years; that no labourer duly engaged for or in any such employment should:

1. Neglect to enter into a contract of employment;
2. After he has entered into such contract—
    (a) desert from such employment;
    (b) absent himself without leave;
    (c) refuse or neglect to perform any work which it is his duty to perform;
    (d) perform any work in a careless or negligent manner.

Rates of pay were set at not less than 8/- and not more than 15/- a month for "skilled labour"; not less than 8/- and not more than 10/- a month for "heavy labour"; from 5/- to 10/- a month in certain other circumstances. Food and certain personal necessities were to be provided.

On 3rd July Lieutenant Kienzle[9] arrived at Ilolo with orders to take charge of all Angau personnel and native labour working on the construction of a road from Ilolo to Kokoda. The work was to be completed by the end of August. But Kienzle was not optimistic enough to hope that he might achieve this. In civil life he was a rubber planter in the Yodda Valley and he was one of the few men in Papua with an intimate knowledge of the country between Ilolo and Kokoda.

At Ilolo he found pack animals at work and about 600 native labourers. The native labourers (wrote Kienzle afterwards) were:

> very sullen and unhappy. Conditions in the labour camp were bad and many cases of illness were noted. Desertions were frequently being reported. The medical side was in the capable hands of Captain Vernon,[1] AAMC. I commenced reorganising and allotting labour to various jobs. One of the first tasks was to erect quickly sufficient clean, dry buildings to house the labour adequately. Plenty of native material close at hand enabled this to be done rapidly. The consideration shown and an address to the natives had the effect of bringing about a better understanding and appreciation of the task ahead.[2]

The pack animals were horses and mules of the 1st Independent Light Horse Troop (1 officer and 20 men). This troop had been working round

---

[9] Capt H. T. Kienzle, MBE, PX177; Angau. Miner and planter; of Yodda Valley, Papua; b. Levuka, Ovalau, Fiji Is, 15 May 1905.
[1] Capt G. H. Vernon, MC, P390. (1st AIF: RMO 11th LH.) Medical practitioner and planter; of Daru, Papua; b. Hastings, England, 16 Dec 1882. Died 16 May 1946.
[2] Report by Lt H. T. Kienzle in Angau War Diary, Sept 1942.

Port Moresby on track reconnaissance and the location of crashed aircraft and began to pack between the jeep-head and Uberi on 26th June. When they moved up to the beginning of the Kokoda Track they sent six men to trap wild horses in the Bootless Inlet area and break them in. Until the arrival of these horses, however, the main body impressed horses, mules and pack saddlery from the plantations on the Sogeri plateau. They soon found that mules were the best pack animals for their purposes, with the small brumbies from Bootless the next best. The bigger feet of the plantation horses were ill-suited for the narrow mountain tracks. The men found also that the narrowness of these tracks made control of the animals difficult and so they taught them to follow one another in single file, one man riding at the head of the column and one at the rear. As standard practice, loads were made up to 160 pounds for each animal, and to save weight, supplies were packed in bags—an expedient which also facilitated the transfer to native carriers at the end of the packing stage.

At Ilolo Kienzle also found Templeton's company of the 39th Battalion waiting for someone to guide them across the mountains. At once he began to organise carriers and stages for their march. On 7th July he sent Sergeant-Major Maga, of the Royal Papuan Constabulary, to Ioribaiwa with 130 carriers to erect a staging camp there. On the 8th he led Templeton's men out from Uberi, with 120 natives carrying rations and the soldiers' packs. At Ioribaiwa they found that Maga had done his work well and had grass shelters ready for the carriers and tents for the troops. They went on to Nauro the next day, with 226 carriers. On the 10th, while the soldiers rested at Nauro, Kienzle sent forward one of his own men, a native policeman and 131 carriers to Efogi carrying rice and Australian food. On the 12th he led his charges into Kagi and found Lieutenant Brewer,[3] the Assistant District Officer at Kokoda, and 186 carriers, waiting there. Thereupon he sent his own carriers back along the way they had come with orders to start building up supplies at the various depots of which the foundations had already been established along the track. (He had formed the opinion that it was best to have the carriers based on definite points with the task of carrying only over the next two stages.) By the 15th the troops had reached Kokoda. Thence Kienzle, after gathering supplies of food for the carriers, mainly sweet potatoes and bananas from his own plantation at Yodda, and handing over to Templeton his own personal stores which were still there, started back again towards Port Moresby. As he went he noted:

> The establishment of small food dumps for a small body of troops was now under way as far as Kagi. This ration supply was being maintained by carriers over some of the roughest country in the world. But with the limited number of carriers available maintenance of supplies was going to be impossible along this route without the aid of droppings by plane. A carrier carrying only foodstuffs consumes his load in 13 days and if he carries food supplies for a soldier it means 6½ days' supply for both soldier and carrier. This does not allow for the porterage of arms, ammunition, equipment, medical stores, ordnance, mail and dozens of

---

[3] Capt F. P. Brewer, PX76; Angau. Patrol officer; of Port Moresby; b. Sydney, 15 Dec 1907. Killed in aircraft accident 20 Oct 1944.

other items needed to wage war, on the backs of men. The track to Kokoda takes 8 days so the maintenance of supplies is a physical impossibility without large-scale cooperation of plane droppings.[4]

By the time these comparatively modest plans for defence against any landings which might take place on the north coast had thus developed, events elsewhere, and planning on the highest Allied levels, had resulted in far wider plans being formulated in relation to that area.

For the Allies the victory at Midway had shed a ray of light upon an otherwise sombre scene. June was elsewhere a month of great anxiety. The Allied forces had been driven out of Burma and there were fears that China might lose heart. In North Africa Tobruk had been surrendered on 21st June and the Eighth British Army had fallen back to El Alamein. Malta was facing starvation. In Russia the defending army had been pushed back across the Don and now faced the German summer offensive. In June, losses of British, Allied and neutral shipping reached a higher total than in any previous month.

One outcome of the reverses in the Middle East was that the prospect of obtaining the return of the 9th Division to Australia became remote. Late in June it was hurried from Syria to reinforce the Eighth Army, and by 7th July was in action. Moreover in June the 16th and 17th Brigades were still in Ceylon, so that of eleven brigades that Australia had sent overseas only four had returned. When, on 2nd March, Mr Curtin had offered to allow the 16th and 17th Brigades to be added to the garrison of Ceylon, it was on the understanding that they would soon be relieved by part of the 70th British Division, due in a few weeks. Mr Churchill, however, intended to hold them in Ceylon for a longer period; on 4th March he had written to the Chiefs of Staff in London that the brigades

> ought to stay seven or eight weeks, and shipping should be handled so as to make this convenient and almost inevitable. Wavell will then be free to bring the remaining two brigades of the 70th Division into India and use them on the Burma front. . . .[5]

The brigades had been in Ceylon almost five weeks when, on 28th April, Mr Curtin, on General MacArthur's advice, asked Mr Churchill to divert to Australia a British infantry division rounding the Cape late in April and early in May, and an armoured division that was to round the Cape a month later. These, he proposed, should remain in Australia only until the return of the 9th Division and the 16th and 17th Brigades. Churchill replied that this would involve "the maximum expenditure and dislocation of shipping and escorts". He hoped to relieve the brigades in Ceylon with two British brigades about the end of May. At the end of June, however, the 16th and 17th Brigades were still in Ceylon. On the 30th of that month the Australian Government, having agreed not to continue seeking the return of the 9th Division for the present, again asked for the return of the 16th and 17th Brigades. At length, having been in

---

[4] Report by Lt Kienzle.
[5] W. S. Churchill, *The Second World War*, Vol IV (1951), p. 154.

Ceylon not "seven or eight weeks" but sixteen, the brigades sailed from Colombo on 13th July. They disembarked at Melbourne between 4th and 8th August.

In the Central Pacific the success at Midway was followed by the reinforcement of the garrison of the Hawaiian Islands. By early October there were four divisions there—a relatively heavy insurance when it is recalled that there were only four American divisions west of Hawaii.

In the South-West Pacific Midway was followed by an ambitious proposal by General MacArthur. On 8th June he suggested to General Marshall that he should attack in the New Britain-New Ireland area preparatory to an assault on Rabaul. To achieve this he asked for an amphibious division and a naval force including two carriers. With it he would recapture the area "forcing the enemy back 700 miles to his base at Truk".[6] On the 12th Marshall presented a plan to Admiral King. It required a marine division to make the amphibious assault and three army divisions from Australia—presumably the 32nd and 41st American and 7th Australian—to follow up; and three carriers and their escort. To succeed, Marshall emphasised, the operation must be mounted early in July. In retrospect, these plans reveal an inadequate appreciation by the Staffs concerned of the complexity of amphibious operations on the scale proposed, the unreadiness of the American Army divisions, and the naval implications. The Navy Staffs objected on the grounds that they would have to expose their carriers to attack by land-based aircraft in a narrow sea where they would have no protection from their own land-based aircraft, and that MacArthur would be in command.

Finally King informed Marshall of his own plan for a drive north-west from the New Hebrides by forces under naval command. MacArthur protested at the prospect of "the role of Army being subsidiary and consisting largely of placing its forces at the disposal and under the command of Navy or Marine officers".[7] The outcome was a directive by the Joint Chiefs of Staff, issued on 2nd July, their first governing the strategy of the war in the Pacific:

> The objective of this directive is the seizure and occupation of the New Britain-New Ireland-New Guinea area, in order to deny those regions to Japan. Task I is the conquest and garrisoning of the Santa Cruz Islands, Tulagi and adjacent positions; Task II involves taking and retaining the remainder of the Solomons, Lae and Salamaua, and the north-eastern coast of New Guinea; and Task III is the seizure and occupation of Rabaul and adjacent positions in New Ireland-New Guinea area. . . . Forces to be committed are ground, air and naval strength of SWPA, at least two aircraft carriers with accompanying cruisers and destroyers, the SOPAC [South Pacific] Amphibious Force with the necessary transport divisions, Marine air squadrons and land based air in SOPAC, and Army occupational forces in SOPAC for garrisoning Tulagi and adjacent island positions plus troops from Australia to garrison other zones. Command for Task I will be a CTF [Commander Task Force] designated by the C-in-C PAC [Commander-in-Chief Pacific] assumed to be Admiral Ghormley who is expected to arrive in Melbourne for conferences.

---

[6] Matloff and Snell, *Strategic Planning for Coalition Warfare*, p. 259.
[7] Matloff and Snell, p. 262.

C-in-C SWPA is to provide for interdiction of enemy air and naval activities westward of the operating area. Tasks II and III will be under the direction of C-in-C SWPA.

Both Ghormley and MacArthur protested that the date (early August) projected for the embarkation upon Task I, did not allow them sufficient time for preparations. On 8th July they sent a joint dispatch to Admiral King (the American naval Commander-in-Chief) and General Marshall.

> The opinion of the two commanders, independently arrived at, is that initiation of this operation, without assurance of air coverage during each phase, would be attended with the greatest risk (demonstrated by Japanese reverses in the Coral Sea and at Midway). The operation, once initiated, should be pushed to final conclusion, because partial attack leaving Rabaul still with the enemy, who has the ability to mass a heavy land supported concentration from Truk, might mean the destruction of our attacking elements. It is our considered opinion that the recently developed enemy positions, shortage of airfields and planes and lack of shipping make the successful accomplishment of the operation very doubtful.

The Chiefs of Staff replied, however, that not only did the threatened complete occupation of the Solomon Islands group offer a continual threat to the mainland of Australia and to the 8,000-mile-long sea route to the United States, but also, through the building of air bases on Guadalcanal, to the proposed establishment of American bases at Santa Cruz and Espiritu Santo. They appreciated the disadvantages of undertaking Task I before adequate forces and equipment were available for continuing with Tasks II and III, but it was imperative to stop the enemy's southward advance.

Ghormley was thus committed to a task he mistrusted and MacArthur's own forebodings were soon to be realised.

In July MacArthur had begun moving forces nearer to the threatened areas. Early in the month he ordered the 41st American Division northward from Melbourne to Rockhampton and the 32nd from Adelaide to Brisbane. They were to form a corps, the command of which was given to Major-General Robert C. Richardson, but Richardson objected to serving under Australian command and was replaced by Major-General Robert L. Eichelberger of I Corps.[8] On 20th July MacArthur moved his own headquarters from Melbourne, 2,000 miles from Port Moresby, to Brisbane, 1,300 miles from it.

On the 15th July he had issued an outline plan for the development of an Allied base in the Buna area, as one of his first steps in preparing to carry out the directive of the Joint Chiefs of Staff. Australian infantry and American engineers were to move overland from Port Moresby "to seize an area suitable for the operations of all types of aircraft and secure a disembarkation point pending the arrival of sea parties". A force of approximately 3,200 was to be established at Buna early in August. The

---

[8] Milner, *Victory in Papua*, p. 50. Eichelberger, Harding of the 32nd Div and Fuller of the 41st had been classmates at West Point. All were born in 1886, and thus were older than every Australian commander except Blamey, Lavarack and Mackay.

rapid development of airfields for use by both fighter and bomber aircraft was to follow.

The development of this base would complement preparations which were already advanced for the construction of airfields at Milne Bay—part of the third step of a plan which MacArthur was to describe to the American Chiefs of Staff on 2nd August:

> My plan of operations to prevent further encroachment in New Guinea has been and still is affected by transportation problems and lack of assurance of naval assistance to protect supply routes; before augmenting defences in New Guinea it was necessary to build a/ds [aerodromes] progressively northward along the north-east coast of Australia, since the then existing development at Moresby was too meagre and vulnerable to permit keeping AF [Air Force] units therein; first step was to develop the Townsville-Cloncurry area; engineers and protective garrisons and finally AF units were moved into that area and Moresby used as an advanced stopping off a/d; the second step was then instituted by strengthening Port Moresby garrison to two Australian infantry brigades and miscellaneous units, moving in engineers and AA units to build and protect a/ds and dispersal facilities, developing fields further northward along the Australian mainland through York Peninsula and movement forward thereto of protection garrisons and air elements; this step was largely completed early in June although some of the movement of engineers into undeveloped areas of the York Peninsula and the construction of airfields was incomplete, but rapidly progressing; the first two steps were primarily defensive, the succeeding steps were to prepare for offensive executions; lack of amphibious equipment limited offensive steps to infiltrations; the third step was to build airfields at Merauke, 150 miles NW of Torres Strait, to provide a protective flank element to the N of that strait; to secure the crest of the Owen Stanley Range from Wau southward to Kokoda; to provide an airfield at Milne Bay to secure the southern end of the Owen Stanley Range bastion.

On 25th June a small force from Port Moresby had disembarked at Milne Bay to protect the new airfield site, and on the 29th a company of American engineers had landed. These troops consisted principally of two companies and one machine-gun platoon of the 55th Battalion, the 9th Light Anti-Aircraft Battery (less one troop) with eight Bofors guns, one platoon of the 101st United States Coast Artillery Battalion (A.A.) with eight .5-inch anti-aircraft guns, No. 4 Station of the 23rd Heavy Anti-Aircraft Battery with two 3.7-inch guns, and one company of the 46th United States Engineer Battalion. Their task was to construct and defend at Gili Gili an airstrip from which heavy bombers could operate and, the day after they landed, they were told that the work must be completed at the earliest possible moment, the target date being set at the 20th July. They had not been long at work, however, before it was decided to build up a much stronger garrison. So, on 11th July, Brigadier John Field[9] arrived at Milne Bay with advanced elements of his 7th Brigade Group. He was to command "Milne Force" which, in addition to the troops already in the area, would consist mainly of the 9th, 25th and 61st Battalions of his own brigade, Australian artillery and engineers (4th Battery of the 101st Anti-Tank Regiment, 6th Heavy Anti-Aircraft Battery, 9th Light Anti-Aircraft Bat-

---

[9] Brig J. Field, CBE, DSO, ED, TX2002. CO 2/12 Bn 1939-42; Comd 7 Bde 1942-45 (Admin Comd 3 Div Mar-Jul 1944). Mechanical engineer and university lecturer; of Hobart; b. Castlemaine, Vic, 10 Apr 1899.

tery, 24th Field Company), and an additional American anti-aircraft battery and "Service" units. As soon as the airfield was ready one Australian fighter squadron would be sent to Milne Bay. Field was to operate directly under Blamey's headquarters: he would not be subject to control by New Guinea Force, and was to exercise "operational control" over all land, sea and air forces in his area.

His task was defined in the following terms:

(a) To prepare and defend an aerodrome at the upper end of Milne Bay for the operation of all types of aircraft.
(b) To preserve the integrity of south-east New Guinea by
   (i) Preventing hostile penetration in the area.
   (ii) Denying, by air attack, Japanese use of the sea and land areas comprising the D'Entrecasteaux, Trobriand and Louisiade Islands Groups.
(c) To maintain active air reconnaissance of the above areas in conjunction with the Allied Air Forces.[1]

The maintenance of Milne Force would be an American responsibility.

Despite great natural difficulties significant advances were being made at Milne Bay as July went on. If the proposed Buna base could be pushed ahead rapidly the Allies would soon be set fair to fend off any Japanese attempts to land in Papua. But their enemies forestalled them.

About 2.40 p.m. on 21st July a float-plane machine-gunned the station at Buna. Perhaps two hours and a half later a Japanese convoy, reported at the time to consist of 1 cruiser, 2 destroyers and 2 transports, appeared off the coast near Gona. It was part of a concentration of shipping which Allied airmen had detected gathering at and moving south from Rabaul during the preceding days. About 5.30 p.m. the Japanese warships fired a few salvos into the foreshores east of Gona. The convoy was attacked first by one Flying Fortress without result and then by five Mitchell bombers which claimed to have scored a direct hit on one of the transports. Air attacks continued as landings began on the beaches east of Gona. Darkness then shut off the ships from further attack and the whole scene from further observation. At 6 next morning a cruiser and two destroyers shelled Buna, and the landings near Gona, which had apparently been going on through the night, were seen to be continuing at 6.30. The defending aircraft reported a direct hit on the transport which was thought to have been hit the previous day, and the sinking of a landing barge. Meanwhile more warships and transports had been sighted off the Buna-Gona coast.

As a result of the landings Morris was instructed on the 22nd to concentrate one battalion at Kokoda immediately, to prevent any Japanese penetration south-west of that point and patrol towards Buna and Ioma. He was also told that arrangements were being made to fly across the mountains 100,000 pounds of supplies and ammunition but that it was unlikely that any troops could be similarly transported. On the same day he ordered Lieut-Colonel Owen of the 39th Battalion to leave for Kokoda

---

[1] LHQ Operation Instruction No. 27 of 18 July 1942.

on the 23rd and take command of Maroubra Force. If Owen failed to block a Japanese advance to Kokoda he was to retire to previously prepared positions in the vicinity and prevent any further penetration towards Port Moresby. At the same time (so deep rooted was the belief in the effectiveness of the mountains as a barrier against invasion) he was told that an attempt to move overland against Port Moresby was not likely and that the Japanese intentions were primarily to establish an advanced air base in the Buna-Gona area.

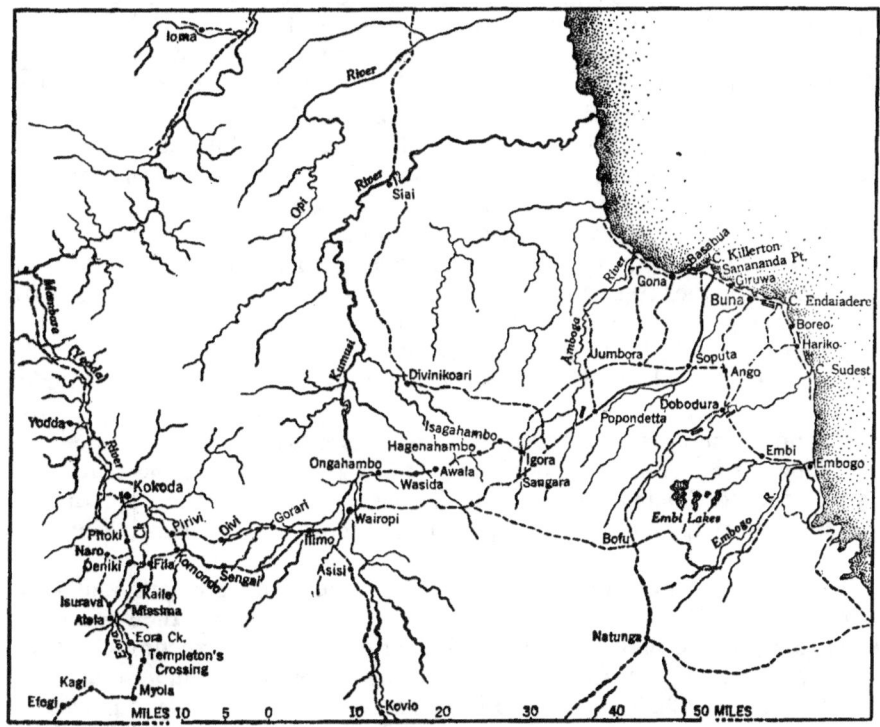

Kokoda-Buna area

In the vicinity of Buna and Gona themselves there was inevitable confusion after the attacks. At Buna, Lieutenant Champion, and Lieutenant Wort[2] of the Papuan Infantry Battalion with some of his men, watched the approach of the attackers. They left Buna for Awala about 6 p.m. At Gona the Reverend James Benson of the Anglican Mission there and two mission sisters waited until the landings were actually beginning before they also took the track towards Kokoda with a few possessions hastily thrown together.

Meanwhile Major Watson of the Papuan Battalion was uncertain what was happening. On the day the landings began 105 of his natives, under

---

[2] Lt W. F. Wort, QX42199. 1 Papuan Inf Bn; Angau. Farmer; of Wynnum, Qld; b. Caboolture, Qld, 20 Jun 1919.

three Australian officers and three Australian N.C.O's, were spread from Ioma to the Waria; Lieutenant Smith[3] and Sergeant Hewitt[4] with 30 natives were in the vicinity of Ambasi, near the mouth of the Opi River, Wort's detachment was in the Buna area; the remainder of Watson's force was round Kokoda-Awala. He himself, with Captain Jesser, was moving down from Kokoda to Awala. Late that afternoon and early next morning he had reports from Captain Grahamslaw,[5] the senior Angau officer in the area, of Japanese action off Buna but the reports were necessarily vague and Grahamslaw himself had gone forward towards Buna before Watson arrived at Awala early in the morning of the 22nd.

Grahamslaw took with him Lieutenant McKenna,[6] Warrant-Officer Yeoman[7] and 9 police. At Isagahambo Warrant-Officer Bitmead,[8] assisted by Warrant-Officer Barnes,[9] was running a hospital with 300 native patients in it. Grahamslaw told Bitmead to pack his drugs and fall back to Awala. Bitmead, however, said that he would send Barnes back while he himself remained to do what he could for his patients until the last moment. He said that he had a guard posted about a mile down the road and would thus have sufficient warning of the approach of the Japanese. Grahamslaw and his party then pushed on towards the coast but were surprised by the advancing Japanese soon after midday.

About 9.30 a.m. Watson had received news from Wort at Awala, and then thrust forward patrols, the strongest consisting of 35 natives under Jesser. These left Awala at 11.15 a.m. on the 22nd and, early in the afternoon, came up with Bitmead who told them that he had natives scouting along the Sangara-Buna track and felling trees to block the road. The patrol reached Sangara but later withdrew again before the approach of the Japanese who had, unknown to Jesser, engaged Grahamslaw earlier in the day.

That night Lieutenant Chalk[1] took four men into Sangara and confirmed that the Japanese had camped there. Jesser's party then withdrew to Hagenahambo, tearing up small log bridges and obstructing the road as they went, for the Japanese were using bicycles. About 4 p.m. next day (the 23rd) Chalk was in position approximately 1,000 yards east of Awala when the Japanese appeared moving behind a screen of natives. Chalk's men engaged them; the Japanese, armed with mortars, machine-

---

[3] Lt A. A. Smith, Q30; 1 Papuan Inf Bn. Truck driver; of Balmoral, Qld; b. Brisbane, 23 Dec 1920. Executed by Japanese 28 Aug 1942.

[4] Sgt L. R. Hewitt, V47951; 1 Papuan Inf Bn. Painter; of Ascot Vale, Vic; b. Ascot Vale, 21 Mar 1921. Killed in action 20 Sep 1942.

[5] Lt-Col T. Grahamslaw, OBE, PX123; Angau (Regional Comd HQ Southern Region 1944-45). Civil servant; of Port Moresby; b. Townsville, Qld, 3 Mar 1901.

[6] Capt J. B. McKenna, PX168; Angau. Assistant Resident Magistrate; of Port Moresby; b. Albury, NSW, 26 Apr 1912.

[7] Lt S. H. Yeoman, PX137; Angau. Accountant; of Salamaua, TNG; b. Bega, NSW, 14 Jan 1904.

[8] WO2 H. F. Bitmead, P448; Angau. Medical assistant; of Isagahambo, Papua; b. Wallaroo, SA, 18 Oct 1910.

[9] WO2 D. S. Barnes, SX31210; Angau. Pharmaceutical chemist; of Kensington Park, SA; b. Bute, SA, 28 Feb 1922.

[1] Capt J. A. Chalk, QX42213. 1 Papuan Inf Bn; 57/60 Bn. Warehouse assistant and relieving commercial traveller; of Eagle Junction, Qld; b. Brisbane, 27 Jul 1916.

guns and a field piece accepted action immediately it was offered. Chalk withdrew and most of his native soldiers melted away into the bush.

Just at this time the first of the 39th Battalion men (Lieutenant Seekamp's[2] platoon) were arriving as a result of quick movement by Captain Templeton. On the 21st Templeton had been in the Buna area where he had gone on a reconnaissance and to ensure that the unloading of stores which had come round by sea had been completed. He had hurried back towards Awala where he had arrived next day. He had ordered Seekamp's platoon forward to Awala. He then had his second platoon between Awala and Kokoda and his third at Kokoda for the defence of the airfield there. He himself returned towards Kokoda to meet Owen.

Watson now ordered Seekamp to hold at Awala for thirty minutes while the remnants of the Papuan Battalion established themselves at Ongahambo, two or three miles back along the track. Some confusion followed, however, and Seekamp withdrew to Wairopi. Watson then destroyed his stores and the buildings at Ongahambo and fell back to Wairopi himself. By this time his force was woefully reduced and consisted of a few European officers and N.C.O's and a mere handful of natives, the rest of the Papuans having "gone bush".

By the early morning of the 24th Seekamp's men and Watson's small group were on the western side of the Kumusi and had destroyed the bridge behind them. At 9 a.m. they received a message from Templeton:

Reported on radio broadcast that 1,500-2,000 Japs landed at Gona Mission Station. I think that this is near to correct and in view of the numbers I recommend that your action be contact and rearguard only—no do-or-die stunts. Close back on Kokoda.

At 10.30 Captain Stevenson,[3] Templeton's second-in-command, arrived at Wairopi. He said that Lieutenant Mortimore's[4] platoon was waiting near Gorari. He ordered Seekamp to prepare to fight a rearguard action as he withdrew along the track and to leave a lookout on the west side of the Kumusi. About midday Jesser, tireless and intrepid, who had been scouting round the Japanese advance, swam the river and reported that the Japanese had spent the night at Awala and had made no forward move from there by 7 a.m. He reported also that he had been in touch with the mission people from Sangara, who like those from Gona, were refugees in the bush. But the Japanese were not far behind him and by 2.30 appeared on the east bank of the river. Fire was exchanged and then once more the Australians fell back and took up a position in rear of Mortimore's men near Gorari. There Owen and Templeton found them about 2 a.m. on the 25th.

---

[2] Lt A. H. Seekamp, WX1192. 39 Bn; 2/6 Bn 1943-45. Labourer; of Berri, SA; b. Berri, 20 Feb 1916.
[3] Capt C. M. Stevenson, VX14385. 2/14, 39 and 2/2 Bns. Clerk; of Armadale, Vic; b. Alexandra, Vic, 13 Jan 1918.
[4] Lt H. E. Mortimore, VX16042. 2/14 and 39 Bns. Bread carter; of Red Cliffs, Vic; b. Warburton, Vic, 10 May 1914.

Owen decided to make a stand 800 yards east of Gorari and dispersed his Australians beside the track with some of the Papuans in the thick bush on their flanks. He himself returned then to Kokoda to meet reinforcements who were expected by air and so was not present when the Japanese walked out of the silence of the bush track into the ambush which had been laid. The Australians claimed that they shot down fifteen of their enemies before they themselves withdrew to Gorari. But the invaders were swift and determined in pursuit, and by 4.45 p.m. they were again engaging the Australians. They forced them back to Oivi—two hours' march east of Kokoda. The Australians were very tired then and six of their men were missing.

Owen, disturbed about the state of his men and by the fact that there were no other forces between Kokoda and his "C" Company (Captain Dean[5]), which had left Ilolo on the 23rd and was moving up the track, asked that two fresh companies of his battalion be flown in. General Morris, however, had only two aircraft serviceable, out of four which arrived at Port Moresby on the 25th and 26th, and the best he could do was to get two aircraft in to Kokoda on the 26th, each carrying fifteen men of Lieutenant McClean's[6] platoon.

McClean, eager for action, hurried forward to Oivi with those of his men who arrived in the first lift. He was with Templeton's two platoons and the Papuans when the Japanese attacked at 3 p.m. The attackers were halted at first by the fire of the forward section, then outflanked it and forced it back to the main positions on the plateau on which Oivi stood. The defenders then went into a tight perimeter defence of diameter about 50 yards. The two opposing groups maintained a desultory fire during the afternoon, the Japanese sometimes pressing to within a few yards of the perimeter before they were killed. About 5 o'clock Templeton went to examine the rear defences and to warn the second half of McClean's platoon, under Corporal Morrison,[7] whom he thought to be about to arrive. There was a burst of fire from the gloomy forest. Templeton did not return.[8]

As dusk was falling the Japanese finally encircled the tired men on the plateau and moved in for the kill. Watson, commanding both Papuans and Australians, estimated that the enemy was strongest in his rear and that the attackers were bringing fire to bear from about twenty light machineguns. Their shooting, he marked, was high and wild—fortunately, because he felt his force to be greatly outnumbered, although their machine-gun fire continued to hold the attackers outside the perimeter. McClean and Corporal Pike[9] temporarily lessened the pressure on the rear positions

---

[5] Capt A. C. Dean, SX2643. 2/27 and 39 Bns. Regular soldier; of Adelaide; b. Parkside, SA, 26 Jun 1915. Killed in action 8 Aug 1942.
[6] Maj D. I. H. McClean, MC, VX100098. 39 Bn and 1 Para Bn. Furrier; of Melbourne; b. Oakleigh, Vic, 9 Jul 1915.
[7] Sgt E. J. Morrison, MM, VX117697; 39 Bn. Farmer; of Foster, Vic; b. Chiltern, Vic, 5 Mar 1919.
[8] There is evidence to suggest (but not prove) that Templeton was wounded and then was given first aid and later killed by the local Orakaivas.
[9] Cpl T. H. Pike, VX132479. 39 Bn; NG Force Special Wireless Coy. Storeman; of Brighton, Vic; b. Caulfield, Vic, 21 Jun 1921. Died 12 Dec 1945.

about 8 p.m. when they crawled to the perimeter edge and engaged their enemies with hand grenades. The groans and cries of pain from the victims of this sally were plainly heard within the defences, and were of different tone to the coaxing "Come forward, Corporal White!" and "Taubada me want 'im you!" and similar invitations with which the Japanese were trying to trick the Australians out of cover.

But the militiamen were approaching a state of exhaustion. Stevenson showed Watson some of his men falling asleep over their weapons even as their enemies pressed them closely. At 10.15, therefore, guided by Lance-Corporal Sanopa (a Papuan policeman), Watson led the whole group out to the south where the fewest Japanese were thought to be. He intended to circle back across the Kokoda path and re-engage at daylight. But there was no track. It was very dark and heavy rain was falling. The men struggled towards Deniki (as easier to reach than Kokoda). They stumbled into creeks, slipped on the steep hillsides. The bush tore at them. When daylight came they were still only two miles from Oivi.

Meanwhile there had been uncertainty at Kokoda where Owen was waiting with Lieutenant Garland's[1] platoon and, among others, Brewer, who had two signallers operating his wireless set in the bush outside the settlement and had been building a supply dump at Deniki. Owen had no news of the fighting at Oivi until some of Morrison's men reported about 2 a.m. on the 27th that Oivi had been surrounded and cut off from their approach. Later he decided that, failing more news from Oivi by 11 a.m., he would then leave for Deniki. At dawn he ordered most of his little force to withdraw. He and the few who remained then stacked into the houses as much as they could of the material they could not carry away, and at 11 a.m. set out for Deniki leaving the houses burning. To their surprise they found, when they reached Deniki, that Watson and Stevenson and most of their men had arrived there an hour or two before. Early next morning a small group of McClean's men, who had become separated from the main force, reported in with the news that they had slept at Kokoda the previous night and that there had been no appearance of the Japanese before they left. Owen then realised that he had erred. He had told Port Moresby that he had left Kokoda and was thus cut off from supplies and reinforcements which could have been landed there (and which, in fact, were ready at Port Moresby to be sent in to him). He at once hastened to retrieve the situation. Leaving McClean and two of his sections at Deniki he hurried back to Kokoda with the balance of the 39th men and the P.I.B. (the latter now including about 20 Papuans). All told the force numbered some 80 men.

With them went Captain Vernon, who had served as a medical officer with the 11th Light Horse in the first war. He had become an identity in Papua where he had been making a living for some years, partly as a medical officer, partly as a planter. He was deaf. Early in July he had been sent to Ilolo to act as a medical officer to the carriers there. Soon

---

[1] Lt A. G. Garland, VX114258; 39 Bn. Commercial traveller; of Parkdale, Vic; b. Richmond, Vic, 25 Feb 1920.

afterwards his duties were extended to cover all the carriers along the track to Kokoda. He left Ilolo on 20th July on his first forward tour of inspection and arrived at Deniki just in time to accompany Owen on his return to Kokoda. Owen was particularly pleased to see him as there was no other doctor available at the time. Warrant-Officer Wilkinson,[2] assisted by Warrant-Officer Barnes since Bitmead had sent the latter back from Isagahambo, had been doing the medical work for the forward troops up to that time. He was an "old hand" in New Guinea where he had been mining and "knocking round" from 1930 to 1940. He had served with the A.I.F. in the Middle East and was now a member of Angau.

By about 11.30 a.m. on the 28th Owen was disposing his force round the administrative area on the extreme tip of the tongue-shaped Kokoda plateau which poked northward from the main range. The administrative area was about 200 yards from east to west at its widest and not much more from north to south. The eastern, northern and western sides of the plateau fell away sharply for about 70 feet to the floor of the valley of the Mambare River which flowed roughly east and west in front of the settlement. At the southern end of the administrative area a rubber plantation began and stretched over level ground back towards the mountains and Deniki. The track from Oivi ran in from the east to the tip of the plateau. As he faced down this track, along which he felt attack would come, Owen posted Garland's platoon on his right flank with most of the Papuans on their left. Seekamp's platoon was round the tip of the plateau with Morrison's section on their left. Behind Morrison the regimental aid post was set up at the northern end of the rubber. Mortimore's men dug in among the trees and astride the track to Deniki.

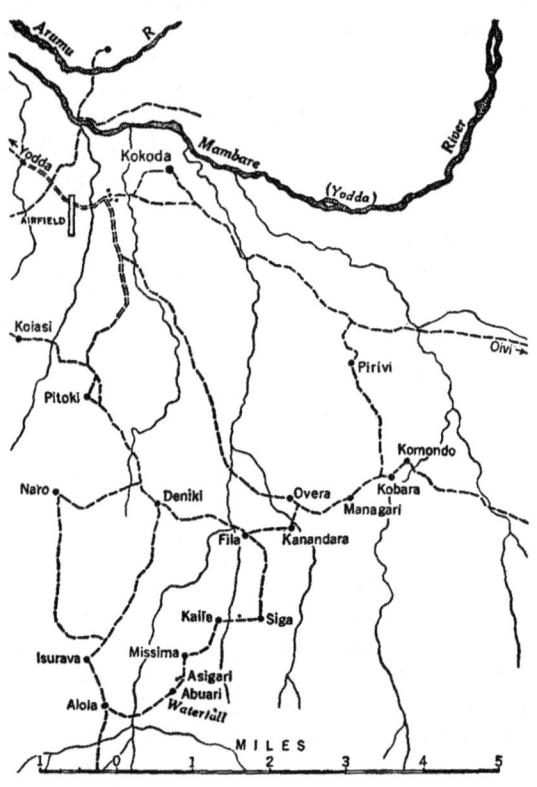

About midday two aircraft circled the field. Owen's men hastened to try to remove the obstructions which they had placed there but finally, on

---

[2] WO2 J. D. Wilkinson, PX11. I Corps Tps Supply Column; Angau. Shift-boss and miner; of Misima, Papua; b. Stawell, Vic, 3 Nov 1907.

instructions from Port Moresby, where naturally General Morris was ill-informed about the position at Kokoda, the aircraft did not land the reinforcements they were bringing and made back the way they had come.

During the rest of the day disquieting signs of Japanese movement were seen but there was no attack. Darkness came. About 2 o'clock in the morning of the 29th the Japanese began to lay down machine-gun and mortar fire. Half an hour later, through the moonlight, they launched an emphatic attack up the steep slope at the northern end of the area where Seekamp was waiting. The attack pressed in. It was close fighting with the Australians beating the attackers back with grenades. Owen was in the most forward position at the most threatened point in Seekamp's sector, on the very lip of the plateau. He was throwing grenades when a bullet struck him above the right eye. Watson sent for Vernon, deaf and unconcerned, who was asleep at the R.A.P. which had now been moved forward of Morrison's section. The two carried Owen back to the medical post.

Watson now took command of the force which, as the night wore on and the Japanese pressure continued, was becoming separated and confused. He ordered Morrison's section forward to Seekamp's assistance but soon defenders and attackers were so intermingled that it was difficult to tell friend from foe in the misty moonlight. About 3.30 Brewer and Stevenson moved out from what had been the Assistant Resident Magistrate's house—about 40 yards below the centre of the mêlée—towards a group of men over whose heads Stevenson threw a grenade as he called upon them to assist in repelling what seemed to be a new facet of the attack. Then a cross-fire from both defending flanks swept the group while, from their right, someone began to throw bombs at the two officers. The men Stevenson had called to were Japanese.

Soon it was clear that the attackers were through the northern positions and both flanks. The Australians were falling back, leaving Owen unconscious and with only a few minutes to live. Watson, Stevenson, Brewer and Morrison were among the last to withdraw. Just behind them were a Bren gunner named "Snowy" Parr[3] and his mate, reluctantly giving ground. A group of 20 or 30 of their enemies appeared in the cleared area close to Parr. He blasted them deliberately at close range. Brewer said later "I saw Japs dropping". Parr thought he got about 15 of them. "You couldn't miss," he said. Vernon was smoking behind a tree at the edge of the plantation. They left Kokoda and about them was

the thick white mist dimming the moonlight; the mysterious veiling of trees, houses and men, the drip of moisture from the foliage, and at the last, the almost complete silence, as if the rubber groves of Kokoda were sleeping as usual in the depths of the night, and men had not brought disturbance.[4]

The men were jaded and very dispirited when they arrived back at Deniki. Their actual casualties at Kokoda had not been heavy (about 2 killed, 7 or 8 wounded) but some men had been cut off in the fighting

---
[3] Pte W. Parr, VX60779. 39 Bn; 2/15 Fd Coy. Textile worker; of Wonthaggi, Vic; b. Kaitangata, NZ, 8 Apr 1922.
[4] Report by Captain Vernon, in Angau war diary.

and were missing and a few had fled. Most of the Australians were very young (the average age of one of Templeton's sections, for example, was only 18) and the closed green world into which they had been suddenly cast was strange to them. They felt very isolated. Their enemies were the best soldiers in the world at that time in jungle warfare.

The week after their return to Deniki, however, brought both respite and assistance to the forward Australians. By midday on the 30th Dean and his company had arrived with supplies and ammunition. On 1st August Captain Symington,[5] thickset and volubly confident, who had fought with the 2/16th Battalion in Syria, arrived with his "A" Company and took over as second-in-command to Watson. Two other companies and other details were moving up the track. Major Cameron, who had been appointed brigade major of the 30th Brigade after his return to Port Moresby from Salamaua, was now hurrying to the front to take temporary command of Maroubra Force.

Better organisation was now developing along the lines of communication. After Kienzle had arrived at Uberi from his trip across the mountains with Templeton he had started more carrier trains forward to Nauro, with four days' supplies for 120 men, and to Efogi with similar quantities. On 24th July he sent Dean's company off with 135 natives carrying packs and supplies of various kinds and 22 carrying rice. He then went quickly back to Port Moresby and there stressed to Morris the need for more carriers, for the development of a supply-dropping program with aircraft possibly using Efogi and Kagi initially as dropping areas, and for a telephone line across the mountains. Next day he set off again from Ilolo with Symington's company, Warrant-Officer Lord[6] and 500 carriers. Three days later the first air drops began; rice was dropped at both Efogi and Kagi. But when Kienzle arrived at Isurava on the 31st he had word from Watson that the latter's need for both food and ammunition was urgent as the supplies at Kokoda had been lost and no reserves were held. Kienzle then decided that the only solution was to find a dropping ground reasonably close to the front.

He remembered that on flights from Kokoda to Port Moresby before the war he had noticed a clear area on the very crest of the range which looked as though it might be the bed of a dry lake or lakes. On 1st August, therefore, accompanied by four natives, he set out from Isurava to look for this. About the point where the track topped the range he struck eastwards cutting through a tangle of dense bush and vines, and moss. Early on 3rd August he emerged from the bush on to the edge of the smaller of the two old lake beds which lay close to one another but separated by a mountain spur. It was set like a saucer in the high mountain tops, was well over a mile long and up to half a mile wide. The ground was flat and treeless and covered with rippling fields of kunai grass. A sparkling stream (part of the headwaters of Eora Creek) cut across its centre.

---

[5] Maj N. M. Symington, MC, WX2719. 2/16, 39 Bns; LO 6 Div. Clerk; of West Perth, WA; b. Mosman, NSW, 17 Oct 1917.

[6] WO2 F. A. Lord, P1354; Angau. Plantation assistant; of Pilliga, NSW; b. Sydney, 27 Nov 1910.

(Australian War Memorial)

Members of the New Guinea Volunteer Rifles display a Japanese flag captured at Mubo on 21st July 1942. The group includes some of the outstanding N.G.V.R. scouts. *Back row from left*: G. R. Archer; J. Cavanaugh; L. E. Ashton: H. M. Shutt; J. G. Kinsey; F. L. Leather; J. B. McAdam; S. F. Burns; I. H. Patterson; J. C. Shay. *Front*: J. A. Birrell; R. Napier; C. L. Cavalieri (behind Napier's left shoulder); H. L. Harris (lying); A. McA. Graham; R. W. Doyle; H. J. W. Farr; W. Allen; G. R. Rayner (seated); A. R. Sheath.

(Australian War Memorial)

Lieut-Colonel O. A. Kessels, C.O. 49th Battalion; Brigadier S. H. W. C. Porter, commanding 30th Brigade; Lieut-Colonel N. L. Fleay, O.C. Kanga Force; Lieut-Colonel W. T. Owen, C.O. 39th Battalion; and Major J. A. E. Findlay, Owen's second-in-command. Port Moresby, July 1942.

Gona Mission, 31st July 1942, ten days

(Allied Air Forces S.W.P.A.)

after the Japanese landings in that area.

(Australian War Memorial)
Native stretcher bearers negotiate the swift waters and rocky bottom of a creek in the Owen Stanleys.

(Australian War Memorial)
A wounded infantryman receives a light from a Salvation Army officer at a staging post in the Owen Stanleys. A stick such as that carried by the wounded soldier on the left was an essential part of equipment in the mountain ranges.

Bright sunshine was dissipating the last of the morning mists. Quail started up from the coarse grass and the harsh cry of wild duck broke the silence. But Kienzle did not linger. The place had no name (it was forbidden ground to most of the natives who lived in those areas) so he called it Myola.[7] He sent word to Sergeant Jarrett[8] at Efogi to come forward and establish a large camp at Myola as quickly as possible; then he blazed a new trail back to Eora Creek on the 4th and the point where it met the old track on the banks of the creek he called Templeton's Crossing. By that time the laying of telephone lines across the mountains to Deniki was just being completed; next day, Kienzle told the supply officer at Ilolo of his discovery and of the acute supply position and asked for air dropping to begin at Myola. That day an experimental drop was made.

At this time, however, no effective air dropping technique had been developed. At the beginning of the Kokoda fighting, when the Australians still held the Kokoda airfield, lacking transport aircraft they used fighters to drop supplies. The belly tanks of these were slit along the bottom, filled with stores and then cast loose over the strip. But this was an expedient which could not be widely used. Practically the only guidance up to this time was to be gained from pre-war New Guinea days when supplies had sometimes been dropped to isolated individuals or parties. Following the practices then developed stores were dropped enclosed in two, or more, sacks, the outer sack being considerably larger than the inner. While the inner one would usually burst on impact with the ground the outer one would sometimes hold and prevent the contents from scattering. But not much accuracy could be achieved and, unless the area over which the stores were cast was clear and level, much of the cargo was lost, since many of the bundles could not be found in the thick bush or retrieved from rugged slopes; even in those bundles which were picked up most of the contents might be damaged beyond use; and the types of materials which could be supplied were severely limited.

Nevertheless Myola was quickly to develop as a main base in the mountains. Despite this, however, there was still a long carry of two or three days forward to the front. Over that stage everything—ammunition, rations, medical supplies, blankets—had to be transported by natives. To Kienzle, therefore, fell the task of establishing staging points and dumps at Templeton's Crossing, Eora Creek, Alola and Isurava. At each of these places Angau men were in charge of carriers and, for some time, of stores also.

At the same time as these supply arrangements were developing the medical position also improved. On 30th July Captain Shera[9] arrived at Deniki as medical officer to the 39th Battalion. Next day, therefore, Vernon started back along the track. At Isurava on 1st August, however, Captain McLaren[1] of the 14th Field Ambulance on his way forward asked Vernon

---

[7] The name of the wife of his friend and commanding officer, Elliott Smith. Myola is an Australian aboriginal word meaning "dawn of day".
[8] WO2 H. E. Jarrett, PX184; Angau. Engineer; of Ramsey, Vic; b. Kyneton, Vic, 26 Sep 1911.
[9] Capt J. A. McK. Shera, MBE, QX54836. RMO 39 Bn and 2/3 Pnr Bn. Medical practitioner; of Brisbane; b. Rockhampton, Qld, 9 Aug 1913.
[1] Capt W. W. McLaren, NX126922. 14 Fd Amb and Angau. Medical practitioner; of Chatswood, NSW; b. Cowra, NSW, 24 May 1914.

to look after the wounded at Eora Creek until other assistance arrived. This Vernon did until Captain Wallman[2] marched in on the 6th "with ten orderlies and a good supply of comforts". Although the day was far spent Wallman himself insisted on pushing on to Isurava but he left his team at Eora Creek and thus freed Vernon for his proper duties.

There was plenty of work for him to do among the carriers. On his forward journey he had found a small hospital full of sick carriers at Ioribaiwa with an ominous threat of dysentery to come; at Nauro the Angau representative was spending most of his time doctoring the carriers and local natives; at Efogi the carriers, though well cared for by Jarrett, were showing very positive signs of hard work and exposure; they were feeling the cold acutely and lacked even one blanket a man. At the beginning of his return journey Vernon noted:

> The condition of our carriers at Eora Creek caused me more concern than that of the wounded. . . . Overwork, overloading (principally by soldiers who dumped their packs and even rifles on top of the carriers' own burdens), exposure, cold and underfeeding were the common lot. Every evening scores of carriers came in, slung their loads down and lay exhausted on the ground; the immediate prospect before them was grim, a meal that consisted only of rice and none too much of that, and a night of shivering discomfort for most as there were only enough blankets to issue one to every two men.

At Kagi he met Warrant-Officer Rae[3] of Angau

> who was one of the best fellows on the line. . . . He and I had a long talk over the troubles of the carriers and the upshot was that I sent a message to Angau to say that less than half had blankets and none a liberal enough diet. We added that a day of rest once a week was becoming a necessity and that overwork and exposure was playing havoc with the [native] force. Indeed at this period I thought that our [native] force was rapidly deteriorating; later on I considered it almost at breaking point.[4]

Meanwhile, at Deniki the spirits of the Australians were rising once more. They were rested; their isolation was lessened by the completion of the telephone line on 4th August. Cameron arrived to take command of them the same day and they felt his vigour. They were reinforced. When Captain Bidstrup,[5] with the remainder of his "D" Company, arrived at Deniki on the afternoon of the 6th, all companies of the 39th Battalion were represented in the Deniki-Isurava area and the total strength was 31 officers and 433 men; there were also 5 Australian officers, 3 Australian N.C.O's and about 35 natives of the Papuan Infantry Battalion; there was a small group of Angau leaders with 14 native police. Cameron's plans for an attack on Kokoda—where it was thought there were 300-500 Japanese—were then well advanced.

The 7th August was the day of final preparation. One of Symington's

---

[2] Capt D. R. Wallman, S30945. (1st AIF: Pte AAMC 1915; Capt AAMC 1918.) 14 Fd Amb. Medical practitioner; of Adelaide; b. 4 Mar 1896.

[3] Capt J. I. Rae, PX149; Angau. Field assistant; of Gulargambone, NSW; b. Dubbo, NSW, 27 Mar 1914.

[4] Report by Captain Vernon.

[5] Capt M. L. Bidstrup, MC, SX4500; 39 Bn. Chemical works manager; of Wallaroo, SA; b. Adelaide, 6 Oct 1911.

patrols reported that they had killed eight and wounded four of an opposing patrol for the loss of one man wounded. Cameron sent Brewer and Captain Sorenson,[6] with Sanopa and another policeman and two local natives, to reconnoitre a track along which he hoped to send Symington's company into the assault. Sanopa, keen of sight and hearing, moved warily in front of the patrol all the way, a rifle swinging loosely in one hand, the other hand holding a grenade. The patrol reached the edge of the rubber just south of the station and saw no Japanese on the plateau.

In the early morning of the 8th three companies moved out for the attack. Bidstrup left at 6.30 for the vicinity of Pirivi where he was to hold any Japanese movement from Oivi against the right flank of the attack. With his company went Warrant-Officer Wilkinson, Sergeant Evensen[7] and 16 Papuans. Half an hour later Symington moved out, Brewer with him and Sanopa heading the forward platoon. Symington's men were to drive into Kokoda by way of the track which Brewer and Sorenson had explored the previous day and which ran between the track to Oivi on the right and the main track from Deniki on the left. They constituted the central pivot of the assault. At 8 o'clock Dean's company, with the task of attacking along the main Deniki-Kokoda track as the left flank company, started for their forming-up area. They took with them four Australians and 17 Papuans of the P.I.B.

On the right Bidstrup's company met opposition near Pirivi and lost 2 men killed and 2 wounded (including Lieutenant Crawford,[8] the platoon commander). Sergeant Marsh[9] took over this platoon and Bidstrup sent Crawford back to Deniki for treatment with an escort of two men. (Later Crawford told the men to leave him and return to the company; he was not seen again.) This fighting delayed Bidstrup's ambush which was planned to be in position by 11 a.m. at the junction of the track the Australians had followed from Deniki and the Oivi-Kokoda track. None the less Bidstrup had his ambush in position by the time a strong Japanese party from Oivi, warned by escapers from the clash at Pirivi, came questing carefully up the track. McClean's platoon, in the right-flank positions on the southern side of the track, poured telling fire into them and shot many Japanese before they could get to cover. Australians and Japanese then engaged one another in the thick bush. But Marsh's platoon, just getting into position 100 yards or so to the left, had been set upon by a party of Japanese coming down from the Kokoda side. Almost at once they lost 2 men killed and 2 wounded and, as some of the Japanese from the Oivi side joined in the fight, were very hard pressed. They were forced into a tight perimeter defence and could get no word to Bidstrup, who had been trying, just as anxiously, to get in touch with them. He sent two

---

[6] Capt H. N. Sorenson, VX117106; 39 Bn. Truck driver; of Oakleigh, Vic; b. Maryborough, Vic, 2 Sep 1917.

[7] Capt M. G. Evensen, NGX189. 1 Papuan Inf Bn; 39 Bn; OC 28 Sqn Air Liaison Section. Plantation manager; of Rabaul, TNG; b. Geraldton, WA, 15 Aug 1905. Killed in action 25 Oct 1944.

[8] Lt H. W. Crawford, SX1034. 2/10 and 39 Bns. Waterside worker; of Port Adelaide, SA; b. Adelaide, 4 Jun 1908. Missing presumed dead 8 Aug 1942.

[9] S-Sgt H. W. Marsh, VX103134; 39 Bn. Grocer; of Traralgon, Vic; b. Traralgon, 10 Feb 1919.

runners out but neither was seen again. At 4.30 p.m., therefore, with darkness approaching and knowing that Marsh had been ordered to make his own way back to Deniki if cut off, he withdrew his main force, harassed by energetic attacks from the front and flanks as he did so. He had heard no firing from Kokoda so, feeling that the attack had not gone according to plan, made for the village of Komondo where he bivouacked for the night. He knew that he had lost 11 men killed, wounded or missing, but did not know what losses Marsh had suffered.

While Bidstrup's company was thus engaged Symington, on the central axis, was having an easier time. At noon he and his men had moved north from the rubber plantation, their advance preceded by bombing and strafing by 16 Airacobras (P-39s). They found only four or five Japanese in Kokoda and these fled. They ranged through the settlement area and to the northern end of the airfield and then, having taken a small quantity of Japanese equipment, dug in for the night.

Moving down the main track Dean's men quickly ran into trouble. First they clashed sharply with a Japanese patrol and then came against well-sited machine-gun positions commanding a creek crossing in a steep gully. Though they fought hard, and Cameron strengthened them with some Headquarters Company men, they could make little progress. Sergeant Pulfer[1] was killed trying to bring in a wounded man. Cameron himself went forward to study the position and discuss it with Dean. Dean then moved across the creek and was shot. Shera hurried forward to help him but Dean was dead before he arrived. The company then attacked so vigorously that they drove the Japanese out of their most forward positions and killed a number of them. As they pressed on, however, they came hard against other positions. The day wore on and Cameron realised that his men could not advance and he broke off the attack. As the troops fell back they picked up their wounded. (Chaplain Earl,[2] who had moved out with the company at the beginning of the day, had been caring for eleven of these in a little clearing among what had been the foremost Japanese positions; he gave them cigarettes taken from the pockets of dead Japanese.) But the Japanese followed the withdrawal and began firing on the front of the Deniki positions at about 5.50 p.m. Their fire continued intermittently until about 9 p.m.

During the night of the 8th-9th August, therefore, the position was that Bidstrup's company (less Marsh's platoon) was bivouacked at Komondo on their way back to Deniki; Marsh's platoon, unknown to Bidstrup, was in a tight perimeter defence just south of the Oivi-Kokoda track (and they lost another man during the night when Private Joe Dwyer[3] slipped quietly away to try to find water for the wounded and was never seen

---

[1] Sgt C. Pulfer, V37803; 39 Bn. Machine operator; of Footscray, Vic; b. Richmond, 1 Aug 1915. Killed in action 8 Aug 1942.
[2] Rev Fr N. J. Earl, MBE, PX195. Padre 39 Bn and 109 CCS. Catholic priest; of Kensington, NSW; b. Sydney, 2 Mar 1911.
[3] Pte J. D. Dwyer, VX103108; 39 Bn. Farmer; of East Bairnsdale, Vic; b. East Bairnsdale, 21 Apr 1910. Missing presumed dead 8 Aug 1942.

again); Symington was passing an undisturbed night at Kokoda; "C" Company, now commanded by Captain Jacob,[4] was standing-to at Deniki.

On the 9th the Japanese began to attack Deniki again about 7.45 a.m. and continued their attacks sporadically until the early afternoon. During these attacks Jesser shot a native whom he saw guiding a Japanese party into the battalion position but, in doing so, was wounded himself. About 1.30 Bidstrup and his main body began to arrive. Bidstrup still had had no word of Marsh's platoon. (Marsh and his men arrived next day, the two wounded men carried by the others. They had slipped out of their perimeter position near Pirivi in the dull dawn of the 9th, concealed in the half-light and thick bush.) The attacks on Deniki waned as the afternoon advanced and night settled quietly over the Deniki area.

Little of this quiet was shared by Symington's men, who were being gradually beleaguered at Kokoda. News of them had been brought to Deniki on the morning of the 9th by the indefatigable Sanopa who, with another policeman, had then brought out some captured maps, probably the first taken in this campaign, and a request for aircraft to drop food and ammunition as each man was carrying only two days' dry rations, about 100 rounds, and two grenades. The two policemen had then returned to Kokoda.

By that time events were moving fast there. The morning of the 9th had found Symington's men dug in in the old Australian positions. In the rubber at the south-east end of the administrative area Lieutenant Neal[5] had his platoon. About 11.30 a.m. he detected Japanese, smeared with mud and hard to see among the trees, creeping stealthily forward to his position.

He was reinforced with another section and drove his enemies to the ground with fire. Intermittent weapon engagements took place during the afternoon. Towards evening the attackers gathered a force which Symington estimated to be about 200 strong and struck violently at Neal's position. The Australians flayed them with fire. In the early evening quiet figures crept towards the defence and there was close fighting with grenades and bayonets. Going up to Neal's position later in the night Sorenson found two of the men lying in a forward position with their throats cut. It was hard to see the enemy in the darkness and the rain. Firing continued, and in the early morning of the 10th, another attack was beaten off.

Commenced a night attack at 10.20 (a Japanese officer wrote in his diary). Advanced stealthily on hands and knees and gradually moved in closer to the enemy. Suddenly encountered enemy guards in the shadow of the large rubber trees. Corporal Hamada killed one of them with the bayonet and engaged the others but the enemy's fire forced us to withdraw. The platoon was scattered and it was impossible to repeat our charge. . . . The night attack ended in failure. No. 1 Platoon also carried out an attack about 0300 but it was unsuccessful. Every day I am losing my men. I could not repress tears of bitterness. Rested waiting for tomorrow, and struggled against cold and hunger.

---

[4] Capt K. R. Jacob, SX1157. 2/10 and 39 Bns. Clerk; of Unley Park, SA; b. Kadina, SA, 1 May 1920. Killed in action 30 Aug 1942.
[5] Lt F. R. Neal, VX117104; 39 Bn. Storekeeper; of Caulfield, Vic; b. Leongatha, Vic, 26 Apr 1920.

Again, before midday on the 10th, Japanese attackers were harshly handled by the defence, but the Australians' food and ammunition were now running low. Wounded were lying at the medical centre where Corporal Smith,[6] the company clerk, was caring for them, cooking what food he could lay hands on (including Japanese rice), and doing his best to keep up the strength and spirits of his companions with "something hot". But the most he could gather was all too little. Symington decided that if no supplies and ammunition had been dropped by 7 o'clock he would retire along the Yodda Track where the Japanese seemed to be fewest. He and his men had done well. The Japanese had not gained an inch.

About 5.30 a loud chanting welled out from the Japanese positions. As it died down a Japanese called out in English "You don't fancy that, do you?" The Australians informed him that they had "Never heard worse". Then the Japanese launched the most vehement of their attacks. One of them noted: "The enemy violently resisted with rifle fire and grenades." Mortars, smoke, heavy and light machine-guns, rifles and grenades confused the scene and, about 7 p.m., according to his plan, Symington began to move his company down the western side of the area. But there had been some confusion in notifying the plans for withdrawal and Neal and his platoon were still fighting hard. Staff-Sergeant Cowey,[7] the company quartermaster-sergeant, who had served on Gallipoli, volunteered to remain with two sub-machine-gunners to help them to get clear. But when Neal's men tried to disengage soon afterwards they were so pressed that the Japanese were moving close after them as they fought back towards the western edge of the plateau. Most of them, however, finally got clear.

Meanwhile the main body of the company, about 46 strong, had slipped into the bush at the edge of the aerodrome. They slept there and climbed the foothills on the 11th, and camped about 4.30 p.m. in a garden. From the garden they heard shots below them and, about a quarter of an hour later, Cowey and four or five men appeared. Cowey said they had run into a Japanese outpost containing three men. They had killed the three men. From the garden Symington's men could then see enemy soldiers in a small village about 800 feet below, but the Australians were too tired to be unduly disturbed. As the evening fell they lit a fire and the smoke was lost in the swirling mist; they cooked bananas and pumpkins and sugar cane in a stew and then slept.

While these men were struggling towards their garden, patrols from their battalion had been trying to get through to Kokoda where the company was thought still to be invested. On 10th August the Deniki force had had a quiet day but Cameron had worried about Symington's company, from whom he had had no news since that which Sanopa had brought, and had asked Moresby to fly a mission to locate the men. Nothing had been learned from that search, however. On the 11th, therefore, Cameron

---

[6] Sgt A. T. Smith, VX128770; 39 Bn. Clerk; of Kilsyth, Vic; b. Kew, Vic, 22 Jul 1921.
[7] S-Sgt J. P. Cowey, MC, V5493. (1st AIF: Lt 46 Bn.) 39 Bn. Orchardist; of The Patch, Vic; b. Brunswick, Vic, 23 Feb 1890.

sent out his patrols but still had learned nothing. Weather had prevented air drops on these two days and it was known that the Kokoda garrison must be in sore straits. On the 12th, however, drops did take place, but then, of course, the effort was wasted. Late that day a native from a village about three hours' walk from Deniki delivered a note to Cameron from Symington. The company had been befriended by the natives and was moving back. Symington thought that there were from 1,000 to 2,000 Japanese in the Yodda Valley. His company was in need of rest. Cameron sent Wilkinson out with a party of Papuan soldiers. Night was coming as Wilkinson's men left and rain was falling. In the darkness and the rain they passed through Japanese positions. It was so dark the patrol had difficulty in keeping together. Wilkinson said "you had to hold on to the native in front". He reached Symington at midnight and told him of the Japanese dispositions as he knew them, and that it looked as though an attack on Deniki was imminent. Next day (the 13th) he led the company to the track between Deniki and Isurava, from which point they went back to Isurava to rest. Neal had rejoined the main body on the previous day and Symington's losses were now known to total 10 killed and 11 wounded.

On that day the lull which had prevailed at Deniki broke, as all signs on the previous day had pointed to it doing. In the morning of the 12th Sergeant Irvine[8] of the Papuan Battalion, with Wilkinson, two 39th Battalion men, and two Papuan soldiers, had patrolled forward towards Kokoda—it had been a busy day for Wilkinson. Irvine reported that his patrol killed six Japanese. (Wilkinson said later that Irvine had shot them all himself with a sub-machine-gun.) Other reports indicated increasing Japanese activity and during the afternoon troops were seen marching out from Kokoda towards Deniki. Cameron ordered Captain Merritt's[9] "E" Company forward from Isurava, where they had been for about a week, and sent the remnants of "B" Company to replace them at Isurava. He reported to Port Moresby that he was expecting attack and that 1,000 to 2,000 Japanese were massing in the valley below him. At 5.30 on the morning of the 13th the attacks began.

Bidstrup's company was in the right forward position, Jacob in the centre front with "C" Company, and Merritt on the left. The main force of the attack fell on Merritt with lighter attacks on Jacob. Merritt lost nine of his men in the first hour and said later of the Japanese: "They came up the hill, four or five abreast, in shorts and helmets. Lieutenant Simonson's[1] platoon beat them back with grenades and Tommy-guns." During a lull at midday, Simonson heard mess tins rattling; he crept forward, saw Japanese sitting about eating, and knocked out two machine-guns and a number of men with grenades. All day the attackers probed

---

[8] Lt D. L. Irvine, NX130656. 53 Bn; 1 Papuan Inf Bn; 49 Bn. Truck chaser; of Warrawong, NSW; b. Jamberoo, NSW, 29 Oct 1916.
[9] Maj W. G. T. Merritt, VX60848. 39 Bn; 7 MG Bn; LO 3 Div 1944-45. Assurance agent; of Dandenong, Vic; b. Colac, Vic, 8 Dec 1911.
[1] Capt D. J. Simonson, MC, VX117109. 39 and 25 Bns. Clerk; of Malvern, Vic; b. Melbourne, 21 May 1920.

and drove at the front. Night followed behind drifting rain and mist, wet and swirling darkness which was broken by bursts of fire until about 1 a.m.

The fighting began again in the dim dawn of the 14th, concentrating still on Merritt. The Japanese got behind him and he withdrew one of his platoons. His men were now holding an area of about 250 by 60 yards on a feature. Simonson was then forced back. The company was reduced from 78 to 65 men but were still resisting stoutly when the Japanese pressure eased and the attacking fire died away. With the lull, however, Cameron decided to withdraw and, in the confusion of the urgent and unexpected move, the men left most of their equipment, and some of their own numbers, including men of Lieutenants Dalby's[2] and Pentland's[3] platoons, were also left. When the main body dug in at Isurava they used bayonets, steel helmets and bully-beef tins as tools. They formed a perimeter there with Jacob's company on the right front, Merritt's on the left front, "B" Company supported by Bidstrup's 17 Platoon on the left flank, Symington on the right flank. Bidstrup himself, with the main part of his company, was in ambush between Isurava and Deniki where an enemy patrol of ten men, carrying two light machine-guns, approached him on the morning of the 15th. He reported later that Corporal Boland[4] killed the two men carrying the machine-guns and fire from the rest of the patrol killed six others before the ambush was moved back some thirty minutes' walk along the track.

However, though these men of the 39th Battalion were thus hard pressed at the end of a most difficult three weeks, there were other Australians, forward of them and isolated in the coastal country which the Japanese had overrun, who had been or still were in even more difficult circumstances.

When Captain Grahamslaw's party was surprised by the Japanese on 22nd July they scattered in the bush. Grahamslaw found himself quite alone. He watched the invaders go past for some hours as he lay hidden beside the track. He was in great danger and then, and some little time afterwards, had narrow escapes. Later he linked again with Lieutenant McKenna. Unable to reach Kokoda by the direct route the two then set out to skirt round the south-eastern slopes of the Owen Stanleys to Abau and return thence to Kokoda by way of Port Moresby. About the 28th a native overtook them with a note from Bitmead who, despite his precautions, had been taken by the Japanese. They had tortured him, more than once, by leading him out before a firing squad and then, just as he was braced to receive the shock, marching him back again to the hut which was his prison. But he had escaped and, with two American airmen

---

[2] Capt H. Dalby, MC, SX4130. 2/27, 39 and 2/14 Bns. Bank officer; of Campbelltown, SA; b. Corryton, Magill, SA, 28 Mar 1914.

[3] Capt W. C. Pentland, VX117100. 39 Bn, 2/1 Gd Regt. Salesman and buyer; of Hawthorn, Vic; b. Melbourne, 5 Dec 1914.

[4] Cpl J. W. Boland, V65593; 39 Bn. Furniture assembler; of South Melbourne, Vic; b. Moonee Ponds, Vic, 23 Jan 1919.

who had survived when their bomber was shot down by a Japanese fighter, was following Grahamslaw and McKenna. One of the airmen was badly wounded so Grahamslaw pushed on over the mountains alone to send medical assistance back, leaving McKenna to wait for Bitmead and the Americans. Grahamslaw reached a mission station near Abau about 4th August, after suffering considerable hardship, and then sent back help for the others.

The people from the Sangara and Gona Missions were less fortunate. From Sangara the plantation manager, two Anglican priests, two mission sisters, a lay mission worker, a half-caste plantation assistant with his son (aged 6) and a young half-caste woman, moved into the bush out of the way of the advancing Japanese. But natives later seized them, subjected them to great indignity and then handed them over to the Japanese who beheaded them all on the beach at Buna on 13th or 14th August.[5]

Fleeing from Gona Father Benson, Miss Mavis Parkinson and Miss May Hayman were forced off the track by a Japanese patrol which passed them early in the night of 21st July. They wandered in the bush for the next two days and nights. They were then guided by friendly natives to Siai on the Kumusi River where they rested comfortably. On 10th August they joined a party of 5 Australian soldiers and 5 American airmen lower down the Kumusi. Lieutenant Smith of the Papuan Battalion was the leader. He and his sergeant, and three spotters who had been manning a wireless reporting station at Ambasi, had retreated inland when about 100 Japanese landed at Ambasi at the end of July. One of the Americans had a bad leg wound and one had both hands badly burned. Smith had decided to lead the party south-east across the line of the Japanese movement inland and then swing south across the lower parts of the Owen Stanleys to Rigo which was within easy walking distance of Port Moresby.

Two days later they were ready to set out. Benson said later: "The boys asked for a service and a blessing; so I said the short office of the Itinerarium."[6] Then they started. Benson wore a pair of Smith's shoes with the toes cut out. Miss Parkinson wore thin shoes quite unsuited for walking. Miss Hayman was almost barefoot. The wounded American "hopped along bravely with the help of his crutch".[7] After some days of painful travel they reached the vicinity of Dobodura, where natives betrayed them and Japanese attacked them. Four of the Australian soldiers were killed. Benson found himself alone in the bush and, after much suffering, fell later into the hands of the Japanese who treated him reasonably well. The two girls were first captured by natives and then handed over to some Japanese who murdered them. Smith, searching for them, was also taken by natives. He too was killed. The five Americans together tried to continue their journey. Natives speared and clubbed them to death.

---

[5] Those executed included: Lt L. Austen; Rev Henry Holland; Rev Vivian F. B. Redlich; Miss Margery Brenchley; Miss Lilla F. Lashmar; Anthony Gors and his young son; and Louis Artango.
[6] James Benson, *Prisoner's Base and Home Again* (1957), p. 35.
[7] Benson, p. 35.

As the vigour of the Japanese thrust into the mountains became apparent perturbation grew at Port Moresby and in Australia itself. Morris' requests for transport aircraft to be based at Port Moresby had become more vehement. On 3rd August he signalled to Army Headquarters:

> Supply situation Maroubra and Kanga most serious. Must repeat must have transport planes with parachutes stationed here immediately. Failing this operations will be jeopardised and forward troops liable to starvation.

On the 5th the only two aircraft available for supply work returned to Australia but Allied Air Force Headquarters stated that one was due to be stationed permanently at Moresby. Morris signalled tersely:

> Transport planes previously made available all returned to mainland. . . . Kanga and Maroubra personnel cannot be fully maintained by native carriers and latter will desert in large numbers if tracks subjected to air attack. Weather conditions over mountains usually difficult and planes have to stand by for long periods awaiting breaks. Procedure for obtaining transport planes outlined is too slow and has already cost us Kokoda. Consider two machines permanently based here is minimum requirement.

By that time, however, plans were developing in Australia for the deployment in Papua of additional forces (and this deployment would pose vastly greater problems of supply than any the Allied leaders had yet considered). On 11th August Lieut-General Rowell, who had been commanding I Corps since April, arrived at Port Moresby and formally took over command in New Guinea from Morris on the 12th. At the same time the 7th Division was hastily preparing to move from Queensland to New Guinea.[8]

The Japanese advance into the Owen Stanleys had caused concern at Washington, and on 31st July Admiral King had asked General Marshall to ascertain MacArthur's plans to check it. On 2nd August, in the course of a message to Marshall (part of which is quoted earlier), MacArthur explained that his plan to prevent further encroachment in New Guinea had been greatly hampered by "a critical shortage of transportation, especially sea transport, and by dearth of naval convoy ships to protect his supply routes". He said that, before the defences of New Guinea could be improved, it had been necessary first to complete a series of airfields in the Townsville-Cloncurry area and develop Port Moresby as an advanced air base; as a second step the garrison of Moresby had been increased to two brigades and engineer and anti-aircraft units sent forward. Finally airfields were built at Milne Bay and Merauke and troops ordered forward "to secure the crest of the range at Wau and Kokoda". The 7th Division would begin moving to New Guinea in a few days.[9]

In retrospect, however, all this seems an inadequate explanation why infantry reinforcements were not sent to New Guinea sooner or why, when

---

[8] Between July and September General Blamey had instituted a reorganisation of the Australian Army and had made some new appointments. He had proposed and the Government had adopted a plan whereby to save manpower he abolished one infantry division—the 10th. He also converted the two motor divisions into armoured divisions. He appointed General Sturdee as Head of the Australian Military Mission in Washington and made General Northcott Chief of the General Staff. General Herring succeeded Northcott in command of II Corps and General Stevens took command of Northern Territory Force.

[9] Milner, pp. 72-3.

they were sent, the inexperienced and poorly-trained 14th Brigade was chosen and not a brigade or brigades of the 7th Division, now, at last, on its way to the front.

That there was, at G.H.Q., inadequate knowledge of conditions in New Guinea was demonstrated on 13th August when General Sutherland, on the advice of Major-General Hugh J. Casey, the Chief Engineer at G.H.Q., wrote to General Rowell proposing that "reconnaissance be made of critical areas on the trail through the Owen Stanley Range for the selection of points where the pass may be readily blocked by demolition, and that the necessary charges be emplaced in the most forward areas and assembled for ready installation in the rear areas". In the course of a tart reply, Rowell wrote:

> The amount of explosive which could be carried by native porters for the five days' trip at present needed to reach the top of the Owen Stanley Range would hardly increase the present difficulties of the track. Some parts of the track have to be negotiated on hands and knees, and the use of some tons of explosives would not increase these difficulties.
>
> It is respectfully suggested that such explosives as can be got forward would be better employed in facilitating our advance than for preparing to deny the enemy!

On the same day as Rowell assumed command Brigadier Porter was ordered to move across the mountains and take command of Maroubra Force to which a second of his battalions (the 53rd) had by then been allotted. The first company of that battalion had already left Ilolo on the 11th, another was starting out from Ilolo on the 12th and the whole of the unit was expected to be concentrated in the forward area by the 20th. At the same time ambitious supply plans were being made. They were designed to stage 40,000 pounds forward daily from Uberi by means of native carriers and to build up large stocks of ammunition along the route. Kienzle was to control all native carriers forward of Kagi.

Before events had reached this stage, however, Lieut-Colonel Honner[1] had been flown from Western Australia to command the 39th Battalion. In civil life he was a lawyer and had formerly been a schoolmaster. He was one of the original captains of the 2/11th Battalion. He was quiet and unassuming in appearance and manner, but, in the Libyan desert, Greece and Crete, had emerged as an outstanding company commander of the most calm and intrepid personal courage. He arrived at Isurava on 16th August and took over from Cameron at once. "B" Company of the 53rd Battalion marched into Alola on the same day and "C" Company was only one day's march behind them. Honner, knowing that Porter was on his way, decided to keep the 53rd intact for him to employ as he would and to use the 39th Battalion to keep in touch with the Japanese. He therefore left the 53rd Battalion companies at Alola with the Papuans to patrol the tracks running east and west of the main northward Kokoda Track and converging on Alola from Kaile and Missima on the right and from Naro on the left. Later he wrote:

---

[1] Lt-Col R. Honner, DSO, MC, WX15. 2/11 Bn; CO 39 Bn 1942-43, 2/14 Bn 1943. Lawyer; of Nedlands, WA; b. Fremantle, WA, 17 Aug 1904.

Isurava provided as good a delaying position as could be found on the main track. To the front and to the rear, tributary creeks flowed eastwards, down into the Eora Valley, providing narrow obstacles with some view over them. They were bordered by a belt of thick scrub, but between them were cleared spaces either side of the track. In a flat clearing on the right was Isurava village, commanding a track dropping steeply down to Asigari in the Eora Valley. Above the more extensive rolling clearing of long grass on the left was timber thickening into almost impenetrable jungle beyond. Forward of the front creek, and to the left of the northward track to Deniki, was an overgrown garden through which a path from the main track ran westwards towards the Naro Ridge. If the enemy wanted to advance along the main track they would have to dislodge us. If they should try to outflank us they would face a stiff uphill climb from the Eora Valley on our right or a tedious struggle through the dense jungle round our left. And if they should choose the easy way in from the flanks . . . they would walk into our waiting fire.

Physically the pathetically young warriors of the 39th were in poor shape. Worn out by strenuous fighting and exhausting movement, and weakened by lack of food and sleep and shelter, many of them had literally come to a standstill. Practically every day torrential rains fell all through the afternoon and night, cascading into their cheerless weapon-pits and soaking the clothes they wore—the only ones they had. In these they shivered through the long chill vigil of the lonely nights when they were required to stand awake and alert but still and silent. Only the morning brought a gleam of comfort—a turn at sleeping and forgetting, a chance, perhaps, to lie and dry in the warmth of the glowing day. But little light filtered through the leaf-marked murk where Merritt's men guarded the front creek cliff, pale ghosts crouching in the damp-dripping half-dark, hidden from the healing of the searching sun.

Wounded spirits rather than wan bodies lay in need of healing where the downhearted remnant of "B" Company held the high ground on the left. Weary from the longest fighting, it had lost its first two commanders and, through the defection of those unhappy "deserters" now back in its ranks, its good name. Cameron recommended that it should be disbanded and its men allotted to other companies because, in his view, its morale was so low that it was finished as a fighting force. It stood where the main attack could be expected to fall. . . . Should I leave the key to our stronghold in such frail hands? I felt that to replace these unfortunates with another company could be the final lethal act of contempt, destroying where I should be building. I appointed Lieutenant French[2] to command and made it clear to him and his men that they now had the most dangerous sector to hold—the post of honour. When the testing hour did come "B" Company bore the heaviest burden and held on doggedly to erase for ever that early slur.

Already there was a burgeoning confidence born of the first scattered battles which had exploded the myths of Japanese super-soldiers currently used as bogies to frighten young Australians. And the men of the 39th saw themselves for the first time as parts of a united battalion ready to do battle on an organised plan, as schemes for mutual support and local counter-attack were evolved and practised. They were cheered, also, by the return of comrades given up as lost; Dalby had come in from Deniki before my arrival, Pentland soon after it, five more struggled in on the 17th and another six on the 19th. Finally there was a promise of relief on the 21st. All the news seemed good news, and courage feeds on hope.

But soon there was disquieting news too—of heavy enemy reinforcement ahead of us, of grave supply difficulties behind us. I knew that relief could not come for many days and I was determined never to ask for it. I was equally determined that there should be no more precipitate retreats—that we should "stand and fight"— orders I had heard myself at more than one pass in Greece, including famed Thermopylae.[3]

---

[2] Maj B. J. French, VX117110. 39 and 2/6 Bns. Grazier; of Derrinallum, Vic; b. Warragul, Vic, 17 Apr 1918.

[3] R. Honner, "The 39th at Isurava" in *Stand-To*, July-August 1956.

When Porter arrived at Isurava on the 19th he found the 39th Battalion thus awaiting the main Japanese onslaught. But only minor skirmishes disturbed the peace of the next few days. One of these centred on the forward patrol position on the main track where Honner had replaced Bidstrup's men with one of Jacob's platoons (then siting Bidstrup's company between Symington's and French's).

The standing patrol lost one man killed and one wounded but slew at least two of their enemies whose corpses lay in view along the track. Chaplain Earl went to the forward patrol position, a spade over his shoulder. He then found that an Australian was dead in a listening post well forward of the main patrol positions. But the brave priest went alone through no-man's land where he knew there were many Japanese, dug a grave and reverently buried the dead soldier. Soon after his return the Japanese reopened fire and appeared again within 100 yards of the patrol.

Except for such occasions Porter's command of Maroubra Force was uneventful. He handed over to Brigadier Potts[4] of the 21st Brigade on 23rd August. By that time the Australians had learned a good deal of the Japanese tactics and no longer deluded themselves that this was a mere foray into the mountains to cover a base at Buna. The Japanese were moving on Port Moresby as purposefully as soldier ants moved through the South American forests—and with similar tactics.

They were brave and strong of purpose. They were trained and experienced in this type of warfare. They were hard and enduring, lived on simple foods and were not tied by their own supply lines. When they met opposition they felt for the flanks and then spread to move round and envelop it before they tried to move over it. In attacking prepared positions they came back again and again to the same point—although they might switch temporarily—trying to create a weakness through which they could break. They followed any withdrawal so closely that their opponents found it difficult to make a clean break and to regain the initiative in patrolling. They used the high ground off the tracks to great advantage. They used camouflage well. Their weapons and equipment were light, their communications good. They adapted local devices and conditions to their own use.

They were acting in accordance with well-prepared plans. Although the Allies at this time did not know the details of these they were becoming aware of the general shape of them.

The defeat at Midway Island had caused the Japanese to abandon their wide plans to occupy New Caledonia, Samoa and Fiji. They did not, however, abandon their plans to take Port Moresby. On 14th June General Hyakutake, commander of the *XVII Army,* whose headquarters were then at Davao, had been ordered to prepare an overland attack on Port Moresby. He was not to launch this, however, until he was satisfied that the track from the Buna-Gona coast via Kokoda (of the existence of which the Japanese had been well aware for some time) was passable for a

---
[4] Brig A. W. Potts, DSO, MC, WX1574. (1st AIF: Capt 16 Bn.) CO 2/16 Bn 1941-42; Comd 21 Bde 1942, 23 Bde 1942-45. Farmer; of Kojonup, WA; b. Peel, Isle of Man, 16 Sep 1896.

sufficient force. If the attack were finally judged feasible it was to be carried out by Major-General Horii's *South Seas Force*. When his preparations for this new venture were well advanced, however, Horii learned that the deployment of his men was to be part of a larger movement than he had expected. On 18th July Hyakutake issued orders for the employment against New Guinea of almost the whole force available to him. Colonel Kiyomi Yazawa's *41st Infantry Regiment Group* (*Yazawa Force*), veterans of Malaya and the Philippines, would come down from the Philippines to support Horii's advance over the Papuan mountains. Major-General Kiyotake Kawaguchi's *124th Infantry Regiment Group* (*Kawaguchi Force*), which had served in Borneo and the Philippines, would come down from Palau and cooperate with the navy in an attack on Milne Bay. Since long before the war the impression had been formed in Australia that the Japanese had been assiduously collecting Intelligence about Australia and the islands to the north-east. According, however, to General Yoshiwara, chief of staff to General Adachi of the *XVIII Army* from 1942 to 1945, major operations in New Guinea had not been contemplated and little was known of that "dark, uncivilised place".[5]

The task of making the initial examination of the Kokoda Track was allotted to Colonel Yosuke Yokoyama who arrived at Rabaul about 14th July with the *15th Independent Engineer Regiment*. His report was to reach Horii early in August and on that report would depend whether or not the main movement was put in train. Yokoyama was ordered to land near Basabua (about a mile and a half east of Gona), advance rapidly to the "mountain pass south of Kokoda" and examine the track leading to Port Moresby. He was to prepare the coastal section of the track for motor traffic and make the mountain sections passable for pack horses at least. Even if he found it was not practicable to advance beyond Kokoda he was to hold the area between the coast and the ranges.

On 19th July Yokoyama left Rabaul in command of a force which included not only a large part of his own regiment but the *I Battalion* (Lieutenant-Colonel Tsukamoto) of Horii's *144th Regiment*, detachments of the *55th Mountain Artillery* and *47th Field Anti-Aircraft Artillery*, a company of the *5th Sasebo Naval Landing Force* to a total of some 2,000 men. With him also he had 100 Formosans of the *15th Naval Pioneer Unit*, about 1,200 Rabaul natives who had been conscripted as carriers and labourers, and 52 horses. Once he got most of his force ashore Yokoyama lost no time in pressing inland. Tsukamoto led the advance with his *I/144th Battalion*, his orders to "push on night and day to the line of the mountain range", and he it was who drove the Australians back to Kokoda and occupied that area on the morning of 29th July. His men then began ranging wide on reconnaissance while the forward Japanese strength built up to about 1,500. By the morning of 8th August Tsukamoto had about three companies in front of the main Australian positions and they were

---

[5] Yoshiwara, *Southern Cross, an account of the Eastern New Guinea Campaign*. This and later quotations are from a translation made for the Australian Official War History Branch by Miss Doris Heath.

the men who killed Captain Dean and drove his company back to Deniki. They had moved out from Kokoda only that morning and so left it vacant for Captain Symington's entry. Symington's occupation of the place forced one reinforced company hurriedly to return to a hard fight.

During this period there had also been much Japanese activity on the coast. Soon after Hyakutake arrived at Rabaul from the Philippines on 24th July he found that Yokoyama was sending most hopeful reports to Horii. On the strength of these Tokyo ordered Hyakutake on the 28th to put the main plan into effect. Hyakutake then at once completed his planning with Vice-Admiral Tsukahara and Vice-Admiral Mikawa, commanders respectively of the *XI Air Fleet* and the *Eighth Fleet*. These final plans closely followed the pattern which had already been developed. The *Yazawa Force* would join Horii and the combined forces would cross the mountains to Port Moresby. The *Eighth Fleet* and the *Kawaguchi Force* would take Milne Bay and then coordinate a landing at Port Moresby with Horii's debouchment down from the mountains. The naval troops at Lae and Salamaua would sally against the local defenders in a diversionary role as the main movement overland and against Milne Bay got under way. As a first step in the major part of these proposed operations Mikawa's men would land in the Buna area, build airfields there and lay the foundations for the development of a main base. Hard after this would come Horii's main landings.

Meanwhile attempts to land additional equipment and supplies for Yokoyama and the balance of his reconnaissance force had been proceeding. In spite of the Allied air watch one transport (loaded mainly with supplies) got in on 25th July. But two other transports, running in on the 29th, were less fortunate. One, carrying some 263 men (the balance of the *15th Independent Engineers*), was sunk though most of the troops managed to get ashore in motor boats. The other was forced by the attacking aircraft to sheer off back to Rabaul still carrying its cargo of vehicles and supplies. On 31st July another convoy was forced back to Rabaul before it reached Gona. On 13th and 14th August, however, Mikawa's construction men got through. Bad weather and Japanese fighters held the Allied airmen off so successfully that some 3,000 Japanese, Koreans and Formosans of the *14th* and *15th Naval Construction Units,* together with their equipment and supplies, got ashore without any loss of shipping.

After these landings Horii got the main body of his *South Seas Force* away from Rabaul on 17th August. He then had with him his own headquarters, the remaining two battalions of the *144th Regiment* with their gun, signals and ammunition detachments, the balance of the *55th Mountain Artillery* and *47th Field Anti-Aircraft Artillery,* a company of the *55th Cavalry* with an anti-tank role, lesser ancillary detachments, more of the *5th Sasebo,* 700 Rabaul natives and 170 horses. Hard behind these came the bulk of the *Yazawa Force.* On 21st August two battalions of the *41st Regiment* landed at Buna with strong supporting arms (including a regimental gun unit, a mountain battery, a quick-firing gun detachment), about 100 of the *5th Sasebo,* 175 Rabaul boys, and 230 horses.

Horii was thus at the head of a formidable and confident force. About 13,500 troops had been landed in Papua of whom some 10,000 formed a well-balanced fighting group. The rear echelon of the *South Seas Force* and one of Yazawa's battalions was still to come. Only the mountains and a thin Australian force were between the invaders and Port Moresby. But a new set of circumstances had already begun to affect the Japanese planning. American marines had landed in the Solomons on 7th August and were diverting some of the Japanese attention from New Guinea.

(Australian War Memorial)
Members of "D" Company, 39th Battalion, on their way back to the base area.

(Australian War Memorial)
A parade of the 39th Battalion at Menari, where they were addressed by their commanding officer, Lieut-Colonel R. Honner, on 6th September.

(Australian War Memorial)

Major-General C. A. Clowes, commanding Milne Force.

(Australian War Memorial)

Lieut-General S. F. Rowell, G.O.C. I Australian Corps.

(Australian War Memorial)

Milne Bay.

CHAPTER 5

MILNE BAY

THESE American landings in the Solomons which, for the Australians, most immediately were to affect the course of events at Milne Bay, had been prepared hastily.

In June Major-General Alexander A. Vandergrift had arrived at Wellington, New Zealand, to prepare his 1st Marine Division for action about the beginning of 1943. The United States Marine Corps had been founded in the 18th century on the model of the British marines. The possession of its own troops enabled the navy to conduct operations ashore without calling upon the army, and the marines were proud of their record of service in every corner of the American empire. They were volunteers and credited themselves with a greater degree of dash and enterprise than the army. In December 1941, there were seven infantry regiments in the corps which, like the navy as a whole, was in process of large expansion. Three of these regiments were included in the 1st Division, three in the 2nd, and the seventh regiment was in the Philippines.

As a result of the rapid expansion of the corps a large proportion of the 1st Division consisted of young soldiers. On 8th December 1941, the division numbered only about 7,000 officers and men—little more than a third of its full strength. In common with the corps as a whole it had to fill its ranks with recruits and at the same time provide cadres for new formations. Consequently experienced soldiers were thinly spread through the regiments. Until 1941 no formation as large as a division had existed in the Marine Corps and thus officers had had little opportunity to gain experience in higher command and staff work.

The corps was intended primarily for amphibious operations—to win beach-heads under the guns of the navy and hold them until the arrival of the army. However, before the war broke out, the Americans had done little to develop landing craft. In 1940 the corps had no ramp boats; at an exercise in August 1941, five such boats and 16 tank lighters had been available. In that month the first tracked landing vehicles came from the factories and 200 were then on order for the Marine Corps. Fortunately for the Allies the British had been more active in producing landing craft. They had developed some efficient boats before the outbreak of the war with Germany and, in 1940 and 1941, had tested their L.S.I. (Landing Ships Infantry) and several other types of craft in Norway, Greece, Crete, Syria and elsewhere. American manufacturers were building to British designs when Japan attacked and production increased rapidly in the first half of 1942.[1]

Late in June Admiral Ghormley, aware of the planning that the Joint Chiefs of Staff were then completing, told Vandergrift that it was proposed to attack the Japanese in the Tulagi-Guadalcanal region. The attacking

---
[1] See L. E. H. Maund, *Assault from the Sea* (1949).

force would consist of the 1st Marine Division (less one of its "combat teams"—the equivalent of a British brigade group—which then was, and would remain, in Samoa), a combat team of the 2nd Marine Division (then at San Diego), the 1st Marine Raider Battalion (then in New Caledonia) and the 3rd Marine Defence Battalion (then at Pearl Harbour).

If Vandergrift were taken aback by these instructions he could have been forgiven. He had not yet seen his division assembled. The three combat teams were half trained, incompletely equipped and only one had then

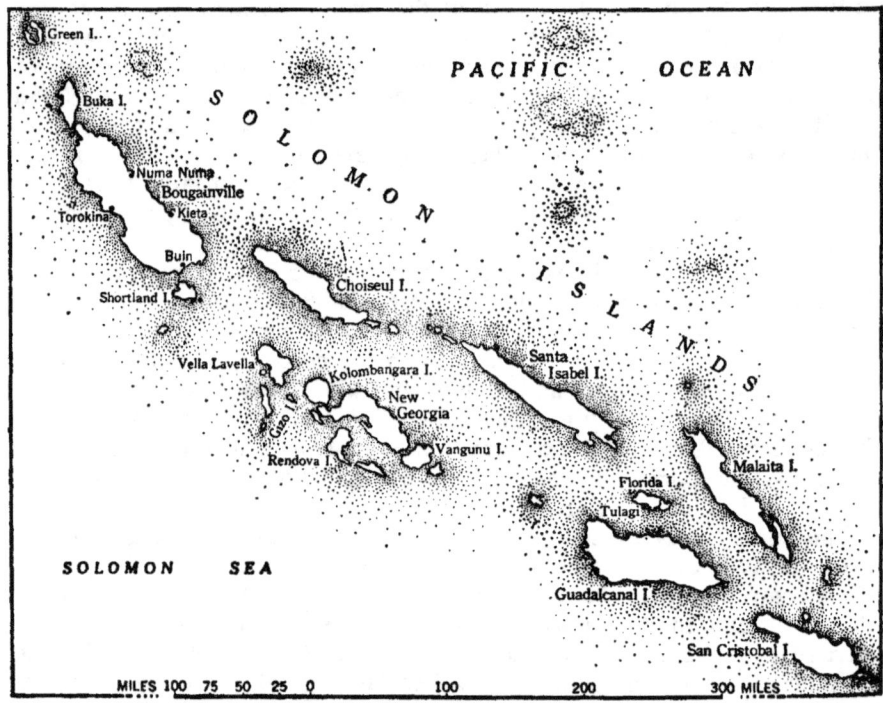

arrived in New Zealand. In addition Vandergrift had very little information about the area he was to attack. His documentary references were scanty both in numbers and detail. His Intelligence officers began to search for New Zealand residents who had formerly lived in the Solomons. His chief Intelligence officer flew to Australia on 1st July to get information from General MacArthur's headquarters and to interview in Sydney and Melbourne people who had knowledge of the Solomon Islands. Eight of these were subsequently attached to the marines as guides and advisers. From the information of the enemy strengths given them by MacArthur's headquarters, and from their own sources, the marines decided on 20th July that there were 8,400 Japanese on Guadalcanal and Tulagi (as against Ghormley's estimate of 3,100).

On 28th July Vandergrift's men from New Zealand arrived in Fiji, D-day having been put back from 1st to 7th August. There they met the remainder of the force and rehearsed the landings. There also the leaders of the various main components of the force met as a group for the first time: Vice-Admiral Fletcher, in command of the entire expedition; Rear-Admiral Richmond K. Turner, commander of the Amphibious Force; Rear-Admiral Crutchley[2] of the Australian Squadron, who was second-in-command to Turner and would command the screening naval force which would include three Australian cruisers; Vandergrift, who was to

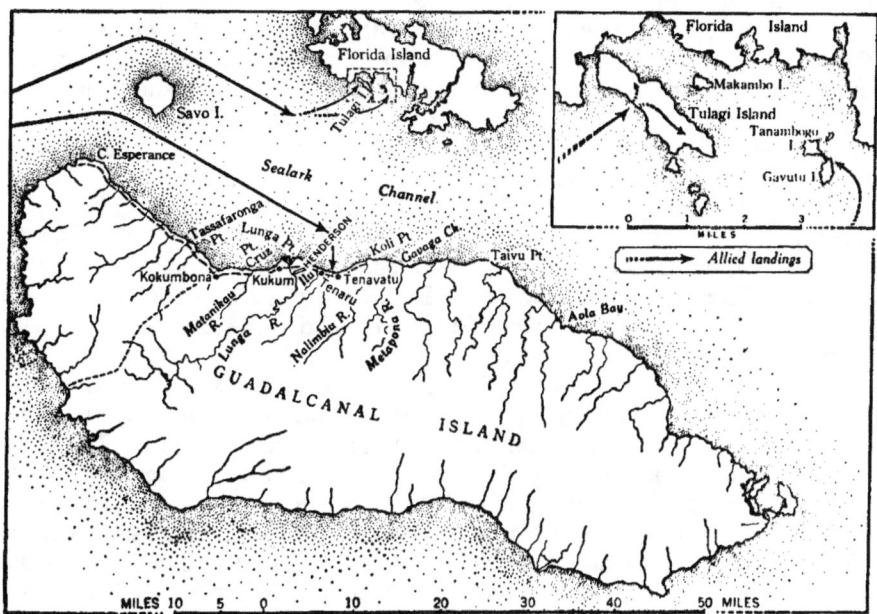

command ashore. At this stage it became clear that there was a basic misunderstanding between Vandergrift and the naval commanders. Vandergrift had based his plans upon the assumption that the Allies would firmly control the sea and air routes to the Solomons. He found that this was far from being so. The admirals were well aware that they were open to heavy Japanese air and sea attacks and had planned to get most of their ships well clear of the Solomons as soon as possible after the landings were made.

After preliminary bombardments, landings took place on the morning of 7th August on Guadalcanal, Tulagi and Gavutu. The two last-named huddled close to the south coast of Florida, an island about 20 miles north of Guadalcanal. Tulagi was an island ridge running east and west, two miles long, half a mile wide. Tulagi Harbour was the stretch of water between Tulagi itself and Florida. In the harbour and near its eastern

[2] Admiral Sir Victor Crutchley, VC, KCB, DSC; RN. Comd HMS *Warspite* 1937-39. Australian Squadron 1942-44; Flag Officer Gibraltar and Mediterranean Approaches 1945. B. 2 Nov 1893.

entrance were the smaller islands of Gavutu and Tanambogo, connected by a causeway.

Guided by Sub-Lieutenants Horton[3] and Josselyn[4] of the Australian Navy (formerly officers of the protectorate administration) the boats carrying the first of Lieut-Colonel Merritt A. Edson's 1st Marine Raider Battalion grounded at exactly 8 a.m. on Tulagi Island. The rest of the battalion quickly followed and after them came the II/5th Battalion. The attackers pushed straight across the island before turning south-east along the northern shore. But they met determined opposition and were still fighting at nightfall.

The Japanese were even more intransigent on Gavutu where the 1st Parachute Battalion had gone ashore from small boats about noon, and lost quite heavily during the actual landings, caught in a punishing fire from the shore. After they landed fire from near-by Tanambogo harried them despite naval gunfire and bombing attacks directed at it. Attacking reinforcements landed on the 8th but still the fighting was hard.

Finally, however, by nightfall of the 8th, the harbour islands and Tulagi itself were in the marines' hands. Tulagi cost 36 marines killed and 54 wounded; about 200 Japanese were killed there, 3 surrendered, about 40 swam to Florida. On Gavutu and Tanambogo the Americans lost 108 killed or missing, and 140 wounded, and killed some 500 Japanese (the whole garrison).

Meanwhile, on Guadalcanal itself, the Americans had landed on the north coast to the east of Lunga Point and pushed cautiously westward on the first day. Japanese bombers appeared soon after noon. They paid only perfunctory attention to the troops ashore, however, and went looking for the carriers, but did not find them. More aircraft came later in the afternoon and hit the destroyer *Mugford*. By that time confusion was setting in at the beach-head where so much material had already been landed that it could neither be handled nor added to. The marines bivouacked for the night having suffered no casualties.

When the advance continued on the 8th one or two prisoners were taken. From them it became clear that the Americans had over-estimated the numbers of the defenders. It seemed that the Japanese force did not exceed 700 fighting men and these had fled westward when the first bombardment began. The advance became more rapid after that and the marines cleared quickly some isolated resistance which developed. During the afternoon they occupied the airfield.

The unloading, however, was not proceeding smoothly although General Vandergrift had opened a second beach-head farther west. Material was coming ashore much faster than it could be handled. The position in the air, too, was giving cause for concern. The American carrier-borne aircraft found themselves at a disadvantage against the highly manoeuvrable

---

[3] Lt D. C. Horton, DSC. BSIP Def Force 1939-42; RANVR 1943-46. District Officer; of British Solomon Islands; b. Calcutta, India, 2 Mar 1915.
[4] Lt H. E. Josselyn, DSC. BSIP Def Force; RANVR; RNVR. District Officer; of British Solomon Islands; b. Newark, Notts, England, 24 May 1913.

Zeros, although the Australian coastwatchers throughout the Solomons were greatly assisting the Americans by warning them of the approach of Japanese aircraft.

From Paul Mason on Bougainville had come warning of the first raid on the 7th about two hours and a quarter before it developed over the invasion fleet:

> . . . time for ships to disperse in readiness, for carrier-borne aircraft to be refuelled and reammunitioned and to take off and be at high altitude in waiting for the bombers, for guns to be manned; all without haste and without undue interruption to the task of unloading the supplies; in fact, sufficient warning to defeat the attack. On board H.M.A.S. *Canberra,* for instance, the bos'n's mate piped over the loud-speakers: "The ship will be attacked at noon by twenty-four torpedo-bombers. Hands will pipe to dinner at eleven o'clock."[5]

At 8.40 a.m. on the 8th, W. J. Read watched 45 bombers pass over his position on the same island and straightway went on the air, his call sign compounded from the initials of his daughter Judy. "From JER. Forty-five dive bombers going south-east." By the time these arrived over Guadalcanal all the ships were under way and manoeuvring at top speed. The raiders suffered heavily. So too, however, did the Americans. A blazing bomber dived on to the deck of the transport *George F. Elliott* and set it on fire. Almost at the same time the destroyer *Jarvis* was hit by a torpedo and, a little later, went down with all hands.

Fletcher had been operating his carriers south-west of Guadalcanal in support of the landings. He had, however, lost 21 of his 99 carrier-borne planes; fuel was running low; he was worried by the number of Japanese aircraft operating in the area. On the 8th, just as night was coming, he asked Ghormley for permission to withdraw his carriers. Ghormley agreed. When he was told of this Turner called Vandergrift and Crutchley aboard his flagship. He told them that the proposed withdrawal of the carriers would leave his ships without effective air protection and that he had decided, therefore, to withdraw his fleet at dawn next morning. He was uneasy about a report that Japanese surface forces had been sighted approaching his area.

Vandergrift was seriously disturbed. He had 7,500 men ashore at or near Tulagi, 11,000 on Guadalcanal. He could not withdraw even if he wanted to. Not all his material had been unloaded. He would soon be short of all essentials including food and ammunition. He would be alone on a hostile shore whose surrounding waters would be under virtual command of his enemies. Counter-invasion seemed a certainty.

But, bad as the situation was, that same night was to see it worsen drastically. Just as the conference on board Turner's flagship broke up the first sounds of the Battle of Savo Island came rolling over the rain-drenched waters from the north-west. There Crutchley's screening force was patrolling between Florida and Guadalcanal where Savo Island lay midway between the western extremities of the two. The screening ships were surprised by a Japanese naval force and thrown into confusion. As

---
[5] E. Feldt, *The Coast Watchers* (1946), p. 115.

a result the American cruisers *Quincy, Vincennes, Astoria,* and the Australian cruiser *Canberra* were sunk, the heavy cruiser *Chicago* and the destroyers *Ralph Talbot* and *Patterson* were damaged. The Japanese lost no ships and indeed, as was subsequently learned, suffered hits by only two shells which struck their flagship *Chokai*. But, fearing attack in the morning by American aircraft which they knew to be in the area, and the *Chokai's* charts having been destroyed by the two shells which struck her, they did not proceed to engage the transports.

Glumly Vandergrift now went into a defensive position. He had only five battalions of infantry on Guadalcanal and, until he could provide air cover for the move, would not transfer his forces from the Tulagi area to the larger island. He organised his defences to extend from the Ilu River, east of Lunga Point, to the village of Kukum just west of the point. They circled the vital airstrip which the Americans named Henderson Field and which they hurried to complete so that they could base aircraft on the island. Vandergrift was afraid that the Japanese would concentrate on his beach-head and destroy his stores, piled in confusion, before he could get them inside the perimeter.

About a week after the landings on Guadalcanal the District Officer, Martin Clemens, reported in through the American lines. During the Japanese occupation he had remained on the island in accordance with the decision of the Resident Commissioner (W. S. Marchant[6]) to maintain his administration despite the presence of the invaders. From his position on the north coast, east of Lunga, Clemens had watched the initial American landings and hurried to contact the newcomers. He had with him a detachment of the Solomon Islands Defence Force—nearly 60 native volunteers—who had watched and patrolled extensively during the occupation and whom Clemens now placed at Vandergrift's disposal.

On the 19th a company of marines patrolling eastward engaged a Japanese patrol. From examination of the Japanese dead it was clear that they were newcomers to the island, well fed and well found. Vandergrift decided that they were the spearhead of the counter-attacking force which he had been expecting. As he prepared on the 20th, however, to meet the shock he was cheered by the arrival at Henderson Field of Marine aircraft—No. 223 Squadron (Wildcat fighters) and No. 232 Squadron (Douglas dive bombers)—which had been catapulted in from an escort carrier. That night much enemy activity was reported from the perimeter at the Ilu. At 3.10 a.m. on the 21st Japanese attacked across the sand-bar at the river's mouth. By the time night came, however, the attacking force had been almost completely destroyed. Nearly 800 had been killed and 15 taken prisoner for the loss of 35 marines killed and 75 wounded.

It was learned later that the American landings in the Solomons caused a revision of the Japanese planning for the proposed attack on Port Moresby. Lieut-General Hyakutake was then ordered to make the recovery of Guadalcanal the mission of his *XVII Army*. Hyakutake's formations

---

[6] Lt-Col W. S. Marchant, CMG, OBE. Resident Commissioner British Solomon Islands Protectorate 1939-43. Chief Native Commissioner Kenya Colony 1943-47. B. 10 Dec 1894. Died 1 Feb 1953.

were still widely scattered, however. One of the most immediately accessible was a balanced group about 2,000 strong built round the *II Battalion of the 28th Regiment* and commanded by Colonel Kiyono Ichiki. The Japanese had planned that this *Ichiki Force* would land at Midway but, after the defeat there, Ichiki had taken his men back to Guam and they were at sea bound for Japan when they were recalled for an attack on the American positions at Guadalcanal. Ichiki himself and his first echelon, about 1,000 strong, landed at Taivu Point (east of Lunga) about 18th August at approximately the same time as some 500 men of the *5th Yokosuka Naval Landing Force* landed at Kokumbona (west of Lunga). The rest of the *Ichiki Force* were following in slower transports. Hyakutake, however, under the misapprehension that the American forces on Guadalcanal were comparatively small and were disintegrating in the face of adverse conditions, believed that Ichiki and his first echelon alone might be able to take the airfield. Ichiki agreed. So he attacked across the mouth of the Ilu River on 21st August. When he realised that the day was lost and his force destroyed he burnt his colours and killed himself on the battlefield.

In anticipation of further Japanese efforts to recapture Guadalcanal American carrier groups including the *Wasp, Saratoga* and *Enterprise* were concentrated in the waters south-east of the Solomons in the days following Ichiki's abortive attack. Admiral Fletcher was in command. Hearing that all the Japanese carriers were north of Truk he sent the *Wasp* and some other ships south to refuel. But on the morning of 23rd August a searching American aircraft located a Japanese transport group moving south. The combined *Saratoga* and *Enterprise* groups moved to meet them. The following afternoon they located a strong Japanese fleet built round the carriers *Ryujo, Shokaku* and *Zuikaku*. In the engagement which followed —the Battle of the Eastern Solomons—the Japanese lost the *Ryujo* in addition to some smaller ships and many aircraft. They then turned back. Further, on the 25th, marine flyers from Henderson Field, found a transport group, escorted by a cruiser and four destroyers, approaching along the strait between Florida and Santa Isabel Island to the north-west of it. They damaged this group and turned it back also while Flying Fortresses, coming up later, sank a destroyer which was standing by a transport going down from the marine attack. (The destroyer's captain was greatly disgusted. When he was picked up later from a raft he said, "I suppose even a B-17 has to hit something sometime, but why did it have to be me?")

The *Enterprise,* however, was seriously damaged and the Americans were worried about their ability to provide air cover for Vandergrift's forces.

Soon it became apparent that the Japanese were adopting new tactics to get attacking forces to Guadalcanal; they were moving troops in barges under the lee of the islands, travelling by night and hiding by day. Vandergrift knew that forces were building up against him in this fashion and was worried. Japanese ships were running along his shores in the night and bombarding him from the sea.

Among the Americans themselves malaria was becoming a cause for concern and fatigue was noticeable. A thin trickle of supply ships was getting in (seven during the first month of the marines' occupation) and food and ammunition supplies were adequate. Other items of equipment remained short, however, as few of the ships could remain until they were fully unloaded. Most serious of all was the growing shortage of aircraft. Although the marine aviators were claiming five Japanese aircraft for every one they lost themselves the Japanese seemed able to replace their losses. By 11th September Vandergrift's air strength was almost exhausted.

Early on the night of the 12th a Japanese bombardment from the sea began. Almost at the same time a Japanese attack flung forward on the southern perimeter on what was to become known as Bloody Ridge. There was hard fighting but the Americans were still holding with the morning. The following night furious attacks opened again. The Americans were hard pressed but finally broke the attacks. When Japanese ships arrived offshore about 11 p.m. they shelled the defenders from the sea but, by that time, the impetus of the Japanese land attack had been lost. A fresh attack went in on the eastern side of the perimeter later in the night but that too was broken by marine artillery fire. There were other attacks, in the early morning and during the daylight hours of the 14th, but it was clear that the new Japanese bid to recapture Guadalcanal had failed.

At sea, however, the position for the Americans was not so satisfactory. On 31st August the carrier *Saratoga* had been damaged by a torpedo leaving only the two carriers *Wasp* and *Hornet* to cover the transport of reinforcements to Guadalcanal. On the afternoon of 15th September, as these moved into the waters south of Guadalcanal, a Japanese submarine pack met them. The battleship *North Carolina* was torpedoed and had to steam out of the area for repairs. The destroyer *O'Brien* was also hit and sank later. Three torpedoes hit the *Wasp* and, burning, she sank. The way was open, therefore, for further Japanese attacks which were sure to come.

Hyakutake had still not mounted against the Americans the strongest attack of which he was capable. The original Japanese plans for the attack on Port Moresby had envisaged the use of Major-General Kawaguchi's *124th Infantry Regiment* group in a seaborne attack on Milne Bay in coordination with the overland advance by way of Kokoda. After *Ichiki Force* was destroyed on Guadalcanal, however, Kawaguchi was ordered to move against the Americans. *Kawaguchi Force* would then consist of the *124th Infantry Regiment* group, the *II/4th Battalion* and the second Ichiki echelon. Kawaguchi's main group was moving down to Guadalcanal with the *First Fleet* when it was turned back as a result of the Battle of the Eastern Solomons. The Ichiki group, moving separately, was checked by the marine flyers on 25th August. The whole *Kawaguchi Force* then reorganised in the Shortland Islands and moved down to Guadalcanal, principally in barges. The main body landed to the east of the American positions but one battalion group of the *124th Regiment* under Colonel Oka landed at the mouth of the Matanikau River west of the American positions.

The operations on the night of 12th September were not part of the main attack but were simply preparations for it. By nightfall on the 13th Kawaguchi was satisfied that he was in position for the attack which would retake the island. He probably used three battalions in the main attacks from the south on Bloody Ridge and one against the Ilu River defence from the east. It is likely that Oka was to attack the Americans' western defences simultaneously with the main attacks. He did not, however, move until the afternoon of the 14th—and then with little determination and as little success.

Kawaguchi lost heavily in his attacks. About 600 of his men were killed on Bloody Ridge itself (where the marines lost 31 killed, 103 wounded, and 9 missing). Later the Japanese themselves reported that they lost 633 men killed and 505 wounded. After their repulse they retreated in disorder. Of the main attacking force some went eastward but the larger number cut a difficult track round to Kokumbona.

The use of *Kawaguchi Force* against the Americans on Guadalcanal, and its defeat there, did not, however, mean that the Japanese had abandoned their plans to attack Milne Bay. When they diverted *Kawaguchi Force* to Guadalcanal they gave another force the task of capturing Milne Bay where the Australians and Americans had been hard at work since the arrival of Brigadier Field and his 7th Brigade in July and early August.

Milne Bay was shaped like a semi-ellipse. From China Strait on the east the sea flowed—through an entrance approximately seven miles wide —westward for some twenty miles. Gili Gili was near the head of the bay. Heavily wooded mountains pressed in from three sides, leaving only a narrow coastal strip, soggy with sago and mangrove swamps; bush-covered except where a few coconut plantations stood in orderly rows. On the north shore the mountains came down almost to the sea leaving only a ledge which was rarely more than a mile wide and in places narrowed to a few hundred yards. Along the coast, never more than a hundred yards from the sea, a 12-foot track, crossing many streams, ran for nine or ten miles from Ahioma, through K.B. Mission to Rabi, whence it rounded the north-west corner of the bay and travelled to Gili Gili. In the vicinity of Gili Gili, and at the head of the bay, the coastal plain was at its broadest but even there densely bush-covered spurs ran down from the main 5,000 feet summits only a few miles away. On the southern shore the mountains rose steeply and again there was a narrow strip of flat land edging the sea, with mangrove swamps and native coconut plantations, and traversed by a track which ran west then north to Gili Gili. Almost the entire coastline offered suitable landing places, though the mangroves of the low-lying south-west corner of the bay would make landing operations more difficult than elsewhere. The place was notorious for torrential rains during the months just beginning and was a malarial pest-hole.

It must have seemed to Field on his arrival at Milne Bay that the possibility of a battle might be the least of his worries for he faced a big engineering and construction project under the most unfavourable condi-

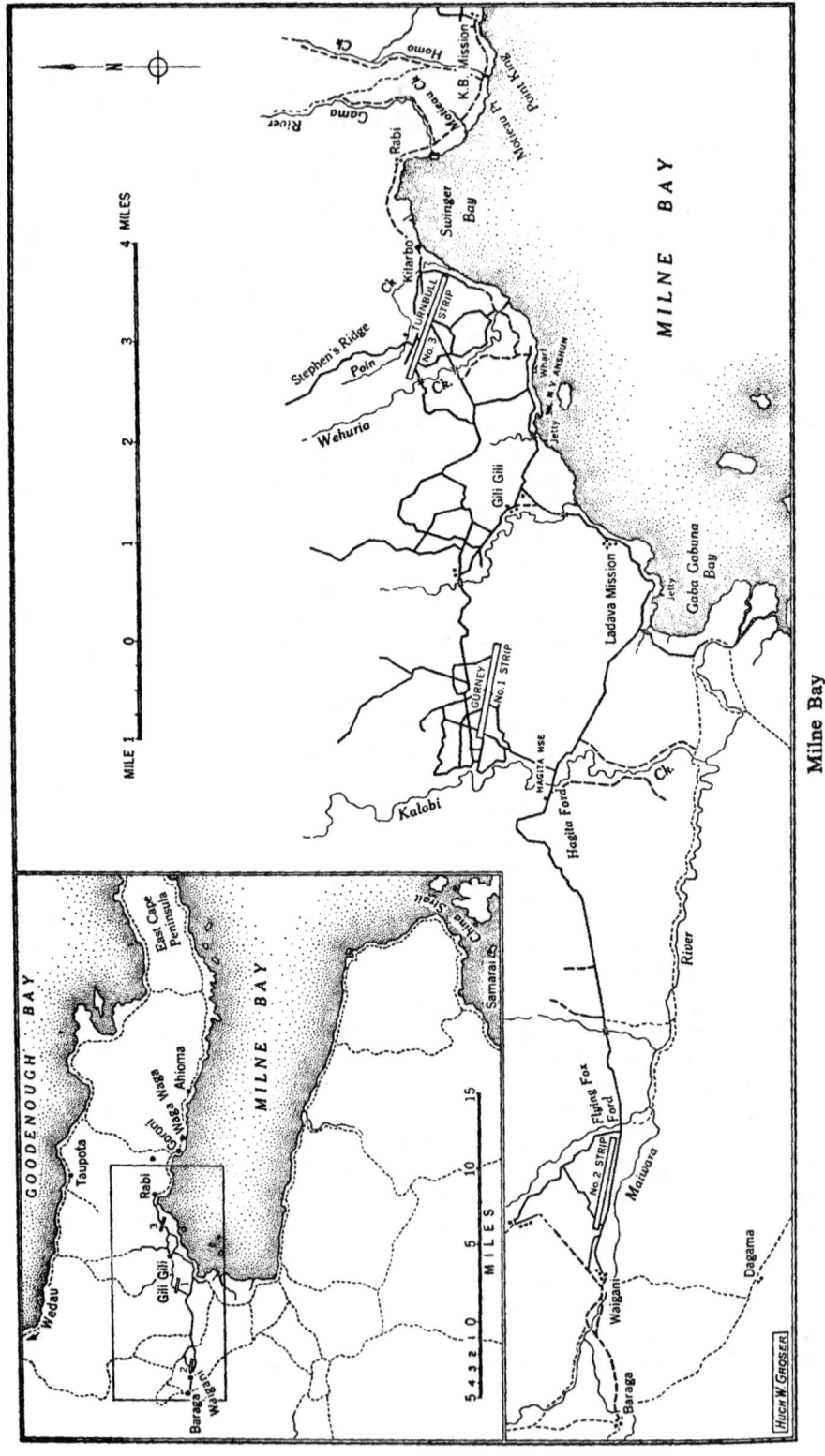

Milne Bay

tions. He was, however, well chosen for the task ahead of him. He was a steadfast and able soldier, by nature courteous, kind and unassuming. He had had over 16 years' commissioned service in the militia when he was given command of the 2/12th Battalion on its formation in 1939. He had led his battalion with quiet capability through the desert fighting in Africa and had left it for command of the 7th Brigade only a few weeks before his arrival in Papua. In civil life he was a mechanical engineer and university lecturer in Tasmania.

He found work on the airfield well advanced, with the first strip almost at the stage when the laying of steel mats could begin. But within a few days of his arrival on 11th July he was told to reconnoitre a site for a second strip. The actual construction of these fields, however, primarily the responsibility of the American engineer company, seemed to be the easiest of Field's engineering tasks. The road system in the area totalled only about twenty miles of formed surface, only about ten feet wide. Without any heavy equipment he had to set his men to the building of new roads, and the construction of passing places and loops on existing roads. He found that the bridges, of which there were about seventeen in the main area, were all of light timber and would have to be strengthened or replaced to meet the needs of military traffic, and that the selection of a site at Waigani for the new airfield—No. 2 Strip—involved the building of at least two new 60-foot bridges in addition to other preparatory work. Further a large wharf construction program was an immediate necessity since no wharfs for deep-sea vessels existed. A coral shelf made it possible to bring ships of 4,000 to 5,000 tons to within 40 feet of the shore from which point they were unloaded on to pontoons. As these pontoons did not enable vehicles to be filled directly from the ships the work of unloading was slow and required many men. There were also the accommodation needs of the garrison itself.

As Field's only engineers were the Americans and the 24th Field Company, his battalions, as they arrived, had to become builders and engineers, and labourers, working side by side with such natives as were available. With the patience and ready adaptability which marked the Australian infantrymen, they set to work; and, at the same time, they prepared to fight, patrolling far afield to familiarise themselves with the surrounding country, digging and wiring, siting their weapons, fitting in what training they could (though needing much, they had very little time to spare for it). In those tasks they needed all their ingenuity for there were no maps. They mapped their own areas as they settled in them, named tracks and features as they explored them, and numbered the roads for ease of reference.

These men were part of an army which had yet to learn to adapt itself to tropical island conditions. They wore shorts and the sleeves of their shirts were rolled to the elbows and thus they were vulnerable to the attacks of malarial mosquitoes. Most of them landed without mosquito nets, which generally had been stowed in inaccessible places on the ships. The mosquito repellent cream which was issued to them was commonly considered to be ineffective. For some reason they were ordered not to begin taking quinine until they had been in the area for seven days. Thus they soon began to find that malaria might be their greatest enemy. In order to carry out the allotted tasks some hundreds of native workers had to be brought into the area and these inevitably constituted a reservoir of malarial infection. Torrential rains threatened to turn the area into seas of water and mud.

Field believed that his men would do well in action but reported that, if he were to face invasion, he would like the support of some A.I.F. troops. The only officer in the brigade who had seen active service in the present war was Field himself. Only four officers had served in the 1914-18 War.

Signs of Japanese interest in Milne Bay manifested themselves rapidly as the 7th Brigade settled to work. On the very day that Field landed a hostile aircraft had reconnoitred the area. The landings at Gona and Buna on 21st and 22nd July increased the Australians' expectancy. On the 24th Lieutenant A. T. Timperly, the Angau officer in charge of the Trobriand Islands, told Field that between the 13th and 22nd hostile aircraft had carried out wide searches over his group and the D'Entrecasteaux Islands, examining areas for up to an hour at a time from low altitudes and probably photographing them. On 4th August Milne Bay had its first air raid. Four Zeros then swept along the strip strafing the aircraft of Nos. 75 and 76 Squadrons, R.A.A.F., which had arrived eleven days before, the original allotment of one squadron having been increased to two. A number of "alerts" followed on succeeding days culminating in a second actual raid on 11th August when six Zeros were engaged first by the anti-aircraft defences and then by Squadron Leaders Jackson[7] and Turnbull[8] with their R.A.A.F. fighters.

Field drove his men hard. By the end of July, following instructions, he had planned a site for a third airstrip and, when the II Battalion (less one company) of the 43rd United States Engineer Regiment arrived with modern equipment on 7th August, he put one of the companies to work at once on this No. 3 Strip which would run north-west from the water's edge between Gili Gili and Kilarbo. He had studied the situation outside his immediate boundaries and asked leave to place detachments on airfield sites at Goodenough Island and Wanigela. As a precaution he had stocks of fuel laid down at both places for use by aeroplanes making emergency landings there. He sent a platoon of the 61st Battalion to Taupota to cover the overland approaches to Milne Bay. A little later, still uneasy about those approaches, he sent one company and a machine-gun platoon of the 25th Battalion to Wedau. Closer in, he had "D" Company, of the 61st Battalion at Ahioma and Captain Bicks'[9] "B" Company of the same battalion at K.B. Mission.

---

[7] W Cdr L. D. Jackson, DFC. 23 and 75 Sqns (Comd 75 Sqn 1942-43); Wing Leader 78 Wing 1943-44. Garage proprietor; b. Brisbane, 24 Feb 1917.
[8] Sqn Ldr P. St G. B. Turnbull, DFC. 3 and 75 Sqns; Comd 76 Sqn 1942. Electrician; of Glen Innes, NSW; b. Armidale, NSW, 9 Feb 1917. Killed in action 27 Aug 1942.
[9] Maj C. H. Bicks, DSO, Q27624. 61 Bn; HQ SHAEF NW Europe 1945. Meat inspector; of Brisbane; b. Kneller Hall, Twickenham, Middlesex, England, 10 Oct 1902.

Field's task was complicated by the nature of the orders he had been given by G.H.Q. As mentioned earlier these provided that in exercising his authority he was not to "disturb execution of general plan local commands naval, air and U.S.A.F.I.A. forces except when attack imminent". In effect this gave American troops and some others an excuse for not contributing to the general defence or the protection of their own localities. When the first air raids occurred some of these troops had not even dug slit trenches.

Milne Force grew rapidly. On 8th August it numbered 265 officers and 5,947 men of all arms and services when Field heard that it was to be increased still further. On the 12th Brigadier Wootten[1] and advanced parties of the veteran 18th Brigade arrived and units of the brigade group followed, including the 9th Battery of the 2/5th Field Regiment, but it was 21st August before the whole brigade had arrived.

Wootten was a heavily-built man who had served as a regular officer with the first A.I.F. and in 1923 left the Army for the Law. He had sailed with the 6th Division in 1940 in command of the 2/2nd Battalion. Subsequently he took command of the 18th Brigade and led it in the Middle East desert fighting. He had a reputation as an able and resolute leader, for an energy which belied his bulk, and for a quick and discerning eye.

On the same day as Wootten arrived control of Milne Force passed to New Guinea Force as part of the reorganisation which had brought General Rowell to New Guinea to take over from General Morris and which envisaged the employment in New Guinea of the whole of the 7th Division. As part of this reorganisation Major-General Clowes was to command the augmented Milne Force. On the 13th he arrived at Milne Bay with some of his chief staff officers, after a hazardous flight with an inexperienced American pilot who got lost in rain and clouds and finally landed with his petrol almost exhausted. But most of his staff was still to come and it was not until the 22nd that he was able formally to assume command of ground forces which, by the 28th, numbered 8,824 (Australian Army 7,459; United States Army 1,365); the infantry, however, numbered only about 4,500.

Clowes was a regular officer, learned, cautious and taciturn. He had served through the 1914-18 War as an artillery officer and on the staff and had commanded at Darwin for three years between the wars. In 1940 he had been chosen as Corps artillery commander, and in 1941 led the Anzac Corps artillery in the campaign in Greece. His task was, in conjunction with the Allied air forces, to deny to the enemy the area occupied by Milne Force and vital outlying sea and island areas and to protect and assist the Allied air forces operating from Milne Bay. The staff which he assembled was headed by an able citizen soldier, Colonel Chilton,[2] who had led the 2/2nd Battalion in Africa and Greece. The

---

[1] Maj-Gen Sir George Wootten, KBE, CB, DSO, NX7. (1st AIF: 1 Bn and BM 11 and 9 Inf Bdes.) CO 2/2 Bn 1939-40; Comd 18 Bde 1941-43; GOC 9 Div 1943-45. Solicitor; of West Wyalong and Mosman, NSW; b. Marrickville, NSW, 1 May 1893.

[2] Brig F. O. Chilton, DSO, OBE, NX231. CO 2/2 Bn 1940-41; GSO1 NG Force 1942; Comd 18 Bde 1943-45. Solicitor; of Warrawee, NSW, and Sydney; b. Sydney, 23 Jul 1905.

more junior staff officers, however, were largely untried, most having been previously on the staff of the 1st Division which Clowes had been commanding in the Sydney area.

After a reconnaissance of the area Clowes began to readjust the dispositions of his force and, by the 25th, the 7th Brigade was responsible substantially for the eastern sector, with Lieut-Colonel Meldrum's[3] 61st Battalion in position round No. 3 Strip, Lieut-Colonel Miles'[4] 25th Battalion about three miles west of that area with one troop of the 2/5th Field Regiment near by, and the 9th Battalion (Lieut-Colonel Morgan[5]) some two miles to the south, on the western shores of Milne Bay. The 2/10th Battalion (Lieut-Colonel Dobbs[6]) was inserted into the Gili Gili area between the 61st and 25th. To the west, on the road to Waigani, was the remainder of the 18th Brigade, with the 2/9th Battalion round Hagita House and the 2/12th near Waigani itself, and Milne Force Headquarters

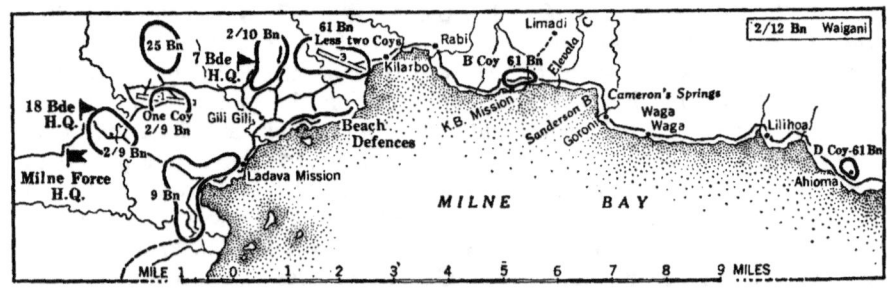

Dispositions, 6 p.m. 25th August.

on the Waigani Road between the two. A beach defence area stretched round the coast for about a mile on both sides of the Gili Gili wharf with medium machine-guns from the 7th Brigade, Bofors, and one troop of 25-pounders sited there, and American maintenance units allotted beach-defence roles.

In thus deploying his force Clowes considered that a landing was possible either on the north or the south of the Gili Gili plantation area or actually in the centre of it where the wharf was located; that possible lines of approach were from either the north-west or the south-west; that the north shore offered the most feasible line of approach. He provided that the inexperienced 7th Brigade should hold in the Gili Gili area from static positions, covering the approaches to it and also covering the beach, with its 25th Battalion in reserve. The 18th Brigade was to be used in a counter-attack role or such other mobile role as developments might

---

[3] Lt-Col A. Meldrum, DSO, QX55238. (1st AIF: Lt 2 LH Regt.) CO 61 Bn 1941-43; Comd Moresby Port Sub-area 1943-44, Murchison PW Gp 1945. Conveyancer-at-Law and Valuer; of Balmoral, Brisbane, Qld; b. Law Junction, Lanarkshire, Scotland, 23 Aug 1892.

[4] Lt-Col E. S. Miles, DSO, QX36371. (1st AIF: Lt 49 Bn.) CO 25 Bn, 15 Garrison Bn. Accountant; of Toowoomba, Qld; b. Laidley, Qld, 22 Jul 1896.

[5] Lt-Col H. D. Morgan, QX36567; CO 9 Bn 1942. Regular soldier; of Maryborough, Qld; b. Woonona, NSW, 11 Oct 1898.

[6] Lt-Col J. G. Dobbs, SX2929. (1st AIF: Pte 25 MG Coy.) 2/27 Bn; CO 2/10 Bn. Accountant; of Mitcham, SA; b. Prospect, SA, 28 Oct 1899.

require, with the 2/10th Battalion sited to cover the left flank of the 61st Battalion and to move quickly as required if anything should go wrong at the tactically important No. 3 Strip; the other battalions were tactically disposed to cover what appeared to be important localities. No. 3 Strip had so far only been cleared of jungle and was not yet in use.

On the afternoon of 24th August a coastwatcher at Porlock Harbour, just west of Collingwood Bay, reported seven barges moving east. A later report stated that they had put in at Fona. Clowes asked Nos. 75 and 76 Squadrons to deal with these, but an air raid that afternoon engaged all their attention. Next morning the coastwatcher at Cape Varieta on Goodenough Island told of seven barges landing troops on the south-west coast of the island. Bad weather prevented the air force from attacking the troops as they landed but later attacks by the fighters destroyed the barges drawn up on the beach.

Meanwhile, on the 25th, more reports of Japanese shipping movements came in. At 10.10 a.m. Clowes was told that aircraft had sighted a Japanese force of 3 cruisers, 2 transports of about 8,000 tons each, 2 tankers or vessels resembling tankers, each of about 6,000 tons, and 2 minesweepers. Soon it was clear that this force was headed for Milne Bay. Clowes, deciding that invasion was imminent, assumed active command of all Allied land and air forces in the Milne Bay area, in accordance with his directive. He also placed all unbrigaded units, including American and R.A.A.F. ground troops, under command of the brigadier in whose area they were situated and placed one of the 2/10th companies under Field.

At this time Field was worried about the company at Ahioma which Clowes had previously ordered him to bring back but for whose return boats had not been available until that day. Major Wiles,[7] Meldrum's second-in-command, left for Ahioma with two luggers, *Elevala* and *Bronzewing,* to assist this company; only three boats with engines were available in the area, and they were small and their engines unreliable. At 1.15 a.m. on the 26th the crew of the R.A.A.F. tender which Clowes had sent to patrol the bay and give early warning of the entrance of any hostile ships, reported that, at 11.40 p.m., they had sighted four ships in the bay about eleven miles east of Gili Gili wharf. Less than an hour later heavy and continuous gunfire was heard from the sea.

For Clowes the night was thus clouded with uncertainty: he had no naval forces, coastal guns or searchlights with which to dispute the entrance of Japanese ships; they could roam his waters and effect landings where they wished, and darkness curtained them from Allied air attack. Soon, however, some definite news began to come through from the 61st Battalion. Captain Bicks' company was reported to be engaging Japanese at K.B. Mission.

From the mission, by the night of the 25th, Bicks had sent forward to Cameron's Springs, about a mile and a half along the track, a standing

---

[7] Lt-Col H. J. Wiles, DSO, QX54945. (1st AIF: Lt 41 Bn.) 61 Bn (CO 1943-44). Salesman; of Brisbane; b. Bedford, England, 15 Nov 1894.

patrol of 14 men under Lieutenant Robinson[8] and another patrol up the dry bed of the near-by Homo Creek; a third party of eleven men was absent on a long patrol. About midnight Bicks heard a burst of firing from the direction of Ahioma. He was anxious about the Ahioma company to whom he had sent a runner earlier but of whom he had had no recent word. About 1 a.m. four Japanese reached Robinson's position moving from the direction of Ahioma. Uncertain in the rain and darkness, Robinson's foremost sentry, Private Whitton,[9] challenged the newcomers. They shot him. In turn the Australians shot the four Japanese. When, however, some twenty minutes later a column of about 100 men appeared out of the darkness, Robinson was still uncertain at first whether they were the men from the missing company or invaders. He called to them. Excitedly talking they gathered round the body of one of their scouts. The Australians began shooting into the centre of the group. The Japanese returned the fire and some spread into the water on the Australian right flank and, neck deep, began to work round the defended position. Robinson then ordered his little band to fall back about 200 yards. As they did so one group of three men disappeared; they were not heard of again. A second group, under Lance-Sergeant Ridley,[1] also disappeared.

When Robinson made a fresh stand in his new position, a Japanese tank advanced down the road firing into the bush on both sides and then fell back to make room for advancing infantry. So the grim game went on until about dawn when Robinson and his men were back in the main company area. But the tank commander overreached himself. As he tried to negotiate a log bridge across a creek he stood up in his turret. Robinson shot him from 150 yards. The tank seemed to fall into the creek and ceased to trouble the Australians for the rest of the day.

As the morning advanced Bicks' men settled into a defensive position along the line of a creek a few hundred yards east of K.B. Mission, skirmishing forward and killing a number of their enemies. It then seemed that the Japanese had withdrawn temporarily. Bicks sent a reconnaissance patrol forward but its leader was killed and the patrol brought back little information. By this time Bicks thought that his men had inflicted about 40 casualties. Soon another patrol made contact some hundreds of yards east of the Australian positions.

About midday Wiles and two men walked into Bicks' area from the north. Wiles had sent off part of "D" Company from Ahioma the previous night in *Bronzewing* and *Elevala* and with one other section and some sick men had followed in a small boat; the rest of the company were on foot. The *Bronzewing* had run into the Japanese landing parties, had been engaged with heavy fire and forced ashore. Wiles, who heard the firing, was doubtful if many of the men in it had survived as they seemed to

---

[8] Lt H. D. Robinson, QX19919; 61 Bn. Saw sharpener; of Imbil, Qld; b. Southport, Qld, 12 Mar 1911. Killed in action 1 Feb 1945.

[9] Pte W. C. Whitton, QX36055; 61 Bn. Clerk; of Yeerongpilly, Qld; b. Brisbane, 7 Oct 1916. Killed in action 26 Aug 1942.

[1] WO2 D. R. Ridley, QX49636; 61 Bn. Builder's labourer; of South Brisbane; b. Huonville, Tas, 29 Jan 1913.

have beached about the point where the Japanese had landed and where, he estimated, their craft had already made two or three trips. The *Elevala* managed to evade the Japanese, landed its complement and was then abandoned. Wiles, having beached his boat, sent the balance of his party into the hills and, with two men, detoured to rejoin the battalion. Later, however, two more men, clad only in shorts and with bare and bleeding feet, passed through Bicks' headquarters and told him that they had been on the *Bronzewing* and had seen many of their comrades drowned or killed. Bicks had first thought that he was fighting 100 to 150 men. After talking with Wiles he increased that estimate to about 1,000.

Meanwhile, back in the main area, some of the uncertainty had cleared with the passing of the darkness. From their positions on the western shore the 9th Battalion reported that the Japanese ships were leaving the bay at dawn and being assailed from the air as they did so. The Australian Kittyhawk fighters were also attacking the landing points, destroying empty barges as they rested on the beach, setting fire to dumps of petrol and stores, and blazing at the area of the landings and along the track to the forward Australian positions. They kept at this throughout the day.

While the air force was thus harassing the invaders the ground forces were moving to help Bicks' men. It was impossible to move anti-tank guns forward through the mud of the tracks but stocks of anti-tank mines and sticky grenades were hastened to the 24th Field Company, the grenades for distribution by the engineers to the forward troops. Field had moved the 25th Battalion to help the 61st as soon as the direction of the Japanese movement was clear and Captain Steel[2] of that battalion took out two of his platoons to reinforce Bicks, followed by Captains Gowland[3] and Campbell[4] with the two remaining rifle companies of the 61st Battalion. Lieutenant Klingner,[5] with Meldrum's mortars, was also hurrying forward.

Bicks was now anxious to disorganise the Japanese, if possible, destroy the tank which had worried him the night before and secure a better defensive position farther east. Field arranged artillery and air support for him and, at 4.45 p.m., with the Kittyhawks blasting the track ahead, Bicks pushed forward with his own men and Steel's platoons. The attack drove the Japanese out of screening positions about 600 yards east of the mission. It then advanced a further 200 yards through thick secondary growth and very hard going before coming under heavy fire from other Japanese strongly sited along the line of a creek with their right flank resting on a swamp and their left on the sea.

Bicks' men were now very tired, and the Japanese positions were strong. Night was coming on. The Japanese had tanks and the Australians had no anti-tank guns or even anti-tank rifles. Bicks decided to withdraw to Motieau, west of K.B. Mission, where he had asked Campbell to estab-

---
[2] Capt P. J. Steel, QX35560; 25 Bn. Grazier; of New Farm, Qld; b. Blackheath, NSW, 24 Jan 1907.
[3] Capt R. E. Gowland, QX48865; 61 Bn. Salesman; of Brisbane; b. Brisbane, 25 Mar 1922.
[4] Capt K. C. Campbell, QX36033; 61 Bn. Manager; of St Lucia, Qld; b. Brisbane, 20 Oct 1912.
[5] Lt L. M. Klingner, QX36036; 61 Bn. Accountant; of East Brisbane; b. Norman Park, Qld, 7 Oct 1914. Killed in action 27 Aug 1942.

lish a defensive position and where he hoped to be able to form a firm base. The thick country hampering them, Bicks with some of his own men and Steel's two platoons fell back first, leaving Robinson to fight a rearguard action. The Japanese followed closely and Robinson's men said that they killed about a dozen who came carelessly along the track. When the rearguard itself came in Bicks passed them through Gowland's, Campbell's and Steel's positions and then faced them back along the track. Some confusion followed as a result of which Steel led his platoons out and left the three 61st companies settled on the west bank of Motieau Creek. Bicks now commanded the whole advanced force. He knew that the creek was not a tank obstacle but felt that it would slow down the movements of armoured vehicles. He commanded a good field of fire across the low, open plantation country leading up to the mission. The sea was on his right, his left flank was guarded by swamp.

As the last light was slipping away Bicks and Robinson took two of their men and moved quietly forward a few hundred yards to their old headquarters with the intention of salvaging the company records and a vehicle which they had left there. They killed two enemy soldiers who were poking about the old camp. They secured the records but the vehicle was bogged and they could not move it. As they were departing a Japanese patrol loomed up from the seaward side of the track, led by a tall soldier who seemed to be over six feet. Robinson, brave and alert and a fine marksman, shot this man and the little Australian group returned to Motieau, under fire.

As darkness settled Bicks had his men fed and tried to rest them in positions taken up in depth along the track. Early in the evening, however, shell fire from hostile ships in the bay began to fall round the area, but it was not accurate and caused no casualties. Then, about 10 o'clock, the Japanese launched an attack in dim moonlight. There was confused fighting. The bullets made a curious "plopping" noise as they passed through the palm leaves and undergrowth. Grenades often rattled through the stiff fronds before they exploded. Gowland's company, which had moved forward earlier across the creek to meet the Japanese, began to give ground. Lieutenant King[6] of Campbell's company took his platoon forward in support. Behind him Lieutenant Tomlinson,[7] already wounded, dashed forward with another platoon until stopped by the mission fence. King and Tomlinson took up positions on either side of the track and there were joined by Gowland with some of his men. Events were quickening now. The Australians could see the Japanese round the mission, Klingner's mortar bombs falling (fired from Motieau) and 25-pounder shells from near Gili Gili ranging around them. King was shot through the jugular as he sighted from behind a palm and, bleeding badly, refused a stretcher saying that there were others more in need than he. A com-

---

[6] Lt E. W. King, Q27752; 61 Bn. Sheet metal worker; of Alderley, Qld; b. Enoggera, Qld, 9 Feb 1919. Died of wounds 27 Aug 1942.
[7] Lt C. B. Tomlinson, QX51718; 61 Bn. Clerk; of Windsor, Qld; b. Brisbane, 8 Sep 1921.

panion ran beside him holding a pad to his neck to stop the bleeding, but he died later.

The fight went on. One of Tomlinson's Brens heated badly. Quickly a soldier urinated on the hot barrel to cool it. Suddenly, from just right of his position, Tomlinson saw a sheet of blinding fire: a Japanese flamethrower was in action. He waited for the next spread of flame. When it came he deluged with grenades the area from which it originated. The flame-thrower went out of action. But the forward positions were becoming untenable. The men fell back to the main positions on the western side of the creek assisting their wounded as they went.

Quiet followed, broken at intervals by sporadic attacks until about 4 a.m. on the 27th. By that time the Japanese were moving vigorously round the Australian positions, trying to work through the sea (up to their necks) on the one side and wading through the morass on the other. As they moved some of them called loudly in English to the Australians to withdraw. About 50 men from the three companies were genuinely deceived by these orders and began to move back to Gili Gili by way of the beach. By 4.30 Bicks' strength was so depleted, his men—many of whom had had no sleep for 48 hours—so worn, and his anticipation of dawn tank attacks which he could not hope to hold seemingly so well founded, that he held a conference of officers and decided to withdraw to the Gama River, a mile farther west. There he hoped to hold the tanks behind that more effective obstacle.

A covering patrol, moving forward, reported that the Japanese had apparently fallen back beyond K.B. The Australians gathered a quantity of Japanese equipment and weapons, including automatic weapons and a flame-thrower, and then withdrew. Passing through Motieau they found the body of Lieutenant Klingner. He had been shot dead earlier in the night as he fought his mortars. They settled on the banks of the Gama. As Bicks inspected his positions there he discovered a number of men suffering so acutely from wounds, malaria, exhaustion and bad feet that he had to send them back.[8]

In the morning the Australians patrolled up the Gama River and as far forward as the mission without meeting the enemy. There was considerable air activity above them after a raid by eight bombers and twelve fighters on No. 1 Strip. About 10.30 a patrol from Dobbs' 2/10th Battalion reached them. The sergeant in charge said that his battalion was moving forward. Then the company commander from Ahioma appeared from the hills with some 40 men. These were the part of the company which had not embarked at Ahioma in the *Bronzewing* and *Elevala*. The officer said that he had seen about 5,000 Japanese taking part in the original landings in the vicinity of Lilihoa. He had avoided any contact by travelling through the rough country to the north of the track.

At 1 o'clock Meldrum telephoned Bicks that the 2/10th would soon reach him. About an hour later the A.I.F. veterans began to arrive and

---

[8] Feet remained a major problem in the whole force. There was no chance of getting them dry. The Japanese also suffered badly.

passed through on their way to K.B. Mission. Dobbs apparently accepted the information brought by the men from Ahioma and passed the news on to his officers that the Japanese numbered about 5,000.

At 6 p.m. Bicks was ordered to bring his men out to the rest area near Gili Gili. Gowland and Campbell left first and then Bicks' company followed about 9 o'clock numbering then only 2 officers (Bicks and Robinson) and 32 men. They sank over their knees in the mud of the track in places, each man holding the equipment of the man in front to save himself from being lost in the darkness.

By nightfall on the 27th the 61st Battalion had lost 3 officers and 12 men known to have been killed, 2 officers and 14 men known to have been wounded (not including any casualties in the Ahioma company). The 25th Battalion had lost 3 killed and 2 wounded. An uncertain number of men from the 61st was missing. (Among these, however, Lance-Sergeant Ridley and the three men who had been cut off with him when the Japanese surrounded them during Robinson's initial encounter were no longer listed, for they had reported in that morning. Ridley told how they had pretended to be dead; that, lying on the track, they had actually been handled by the curious Japanese and he himself had been pricked with a bayonet. When the Japanese left them they escaped through the foothills.)

During the two nights and days when the Australians on the north shore had been having their baptism of fire General Clowes had been haunted by uncertainty regarding his enemies' intentions. On the 26th the approach of an additional convoy was reported by the air force. The convoy was said to consist of six ships, at least three of them warships. On both nights Japanese ships had come into the bay in the darkness, moving to plans at which the Australians could only guess, and fading away before the dawn. Gunfire had come from the dark waters, the sound of barges, and the busy noise of launches plying between ships and shore. What did all this movement mean? Were fresh forces being landed? And, if so, where? Were the Japanese embarking the forces which had already been landed on the north shore to land them again closer in? The rain shrouded the scene, drumming through the trees and over the grey sea, turning the roads into morasses. The tropical mists added their gloom to the scene so that the whole encounter seemed unreal and unpredictable.

This atmosphere of uncertainty was deepened for the Australian commander because he had no maps. He and his staff were using a rough sketch which had been produced in one of the 7th Brigade battalions by compass and pacing and had been dye-lined at Milne Force headquarters. Consequently they were not able accurately to assess information as it came back or plan operations in any more than a very general sense.

The problem which Clowes faced was how far and where to commit his main force. His vital area was Gili Gili which contained all his supplies and installations including the wharf and the airstrip. He had so far successfully blocked the approach from the north shore of the bay. He had, however, to consider the possibility of further landings—south of Gili Gili along the thinly defended beaches of the plantation front or even overland from the north-west or south-west. At all costs, he thought, he must maintain a large reserve until the Japanese showed their hands clearly. Finally, however, he decided to commit another battalion and had placed Dobbs under Field's command at 2.30 on the morning of the 27th. Major Miethke's[9] "B" Company, already under 7th Brigade, had taken up a defensive position at No. 3 Strip on the previous day and, early on the 27th, had pushed out to Kilarbo, some little distance along the road to Rabi.

At a conference with Field on the morning of the 27th Dobbs decided to move with his battalion equipped lightly "as a large-scale fighting patrol" to Rabi, thence north-east for some miles by way of a back track and finally strike down to K.B. He borrowed additional sub-machine-guns, stripped Captain Brocksopp's[1] "C" Company (whom he intended to use in the van) of all their Brens, reduced the complement of Brens in Captains Matheson's[2] and Sanderson's[3] companies to one a platoon but left Miethke's company with their full complement; despite the knowledge that the Japanese had at least one tank he discarded all his anti-tank rifles, thinking, probably, that 20 sticky grenades which he had issued would be an effective substitute. He set out with his battalion streamlined to an approximate strength of 500.

When he accepted the reports that possibly 5,000 Japanese had landed, he revised his planning and moved directly along the coastal track towards K.B. Mission. Bicks says that he warned Dobbs that he thought it would be unwise for him to site his battalion at K.B. as the country there was not suitable for defence and could be seen from the sea, and that the Japanese had tanks which they could use in that area. But the 2/10th settled into a loose perimeter defence at the mission just as night was falling.

The men were tired and hungry. Since the first reports of the approach of Japanese ships had been received many of them had made a number of moves as they adjusted their positions, they had had little sleep for two nights, their meals had been unsatisfying and irregular, rain for seven days previously had filled the track deep with mud which pulled hard at their feet. Now they had no tools with which to dig in and they settled in groups of three to await the coming of their enemies.

Brocksopp's company was in the right sector, Lieutenant Brown's[4] platoon holding on the right, flanked by the sea, and the two other platoons,

---

[9] Maj G. R. Miethke, MC, SX1461; 2/10 Bn. Civil servant; of Alberton, SA; b. Woodville, SA, 27 Jun 1916.
[1] Maj J. E. Brocksopp, SX1430; 2/10 Bn. Solicitor; of Adelaide; b. London, 4 Jul 1913.
[2] Maj H. R. Matheson, SX1441; 2/10 Bn. Telephone mechanic; of Port Pirie, SA; b. Two Wells, SA, 15 Apr 1912.
[3] Capt R. W. Sanderson, ED, SX1469; 2/10 Bn. Life assurance inspector; of Glenelg, SA; b. Glenelg, 12 Jun 1912.
[4] Maj M. J. Brown, MC, SX1017; 2/10 Bn. Draughtsman; of Adelaide; b. Adelaide, 2 Jun 1919.

under Lieutenants Mackie[5] and Lethbridge,[6] with Brocksopp's headquarters, actually inside the perimeter as battalion reserve. Miethke's company formed the left forward positions of the perimeter. Matheson's and Sanderson's companies (each less a platoon patrol watching flanking tracks) occupied the two rear positions.

At 7.45 the noise of an engine was heard, and a tank approached through the darkness and the rain, its lights shining brightly. "Put out that —— light!" yelled an Australian, who has never since been allowed to forget it.

At 1950 hours (wrote the historian of the 2/10th Battalion) the silence was again broken, this time by a high-pitched voice chanting in Japanese from the depths of the jungle. The one voice (and a beautiful voice it was) would recite for about one minute, after which the chant would be taken up by a number of other voices, rather nearer to where the 2/10th lay quietly waiting. Upon the second group completing their recitation, a third group, obviously comprising some hundreds of the enemy, and closer again, would sing in sonorous unison. This procedure was repeated three times. Whether it was some form of religious rite, or merely a boasting recital calculated to inspire courage in the chanters and despair in the hearts of the listeners is not known, nor did the battalion ever again hear this type of musical performance.[7]

At 8 p.m. the fight began. The tank engaged Miethke's company and about twenty minutes later was joined by a second tank. Meanwhile Japanese infantry were pressing. The strain fell heavily both on Miethke's and Brocksopp's men. The tanks cruised among them, flooding each other with their lights and thus each guarding the other against close attack. Tracer and fireflies streaked the darkness and a hut in Miethke's arc was set alight. The exchange of fire was intense, shells from the 25-pounders back near Gili Gili screamed over, and the din of battle grew steadily. The tanks moved backwards and forwards through the Australians until about midnight though they never troubled the two rearward companies. They were impervious to small arms fire, tried to run down individuals, paved the way so that their infantry came right among the defenders. In Miethke's company Lieutenant Scott[8] attacked one with a sticky grenade which failed to explode. (Mould had grown inside these grenades.) In Brocksopp's positions Mackie and Sergeant Spencer,[9] a soldier of unwearied courage, made similar attacks but the grenades would not stick. Spencer, however, then hurled hand grenades into the following infantry.

It was fortunate that the Japanese were firing high and inaccurately or few could have survived in the Australian positions. Since the Brens seemed to draw fire Miethke had them passed from one position to another, never leaving them in one place for more than a few minutes at a

---

[5] Capt C. H. Mackie, SX1198; 2/10 Bn. Nurseryman; of Kensington Park, SA; b. Scotland, 11 Feb 1911. Killed in action 29 Dec 1942.

[6] Lt S. D. Lethbridge, SX11766; 2/10 Bn. Railway porter; of Kapunda, SA; b. Port Pirie, SA, 13 Dec 1912.

[7] E. F. Allchin, *Purple and Blue* (1958), p. 252.

[8] Lt A. R. Scott, VX6330; 2/10 Bn. Regular soldier; of Frankston, Vic; b. Gibraltar, 22 Oct 1914. Killed in action 27 Aug 1942.

[9] Sgt G. G. Spencer, DCM, SX1193; 2/10 Bn. Labourer; of Maggea, SA; b. Hamley Bridge, SA, 8 Nov 1909.

time. Private Abraham,[1] manning one, had his leg riddled with bullets. Private Kotz,[2] in charge of a second, was indefatigable in engaging the attackers from one position after another, and, at one stage charged headlong at a Japanese position fifteen yards ahead and wiped it out with grenades.

Brocksopp's men were equally determined. At one stage Private McLennan[3] of Brown's platoon leapt from his firing position and bayoneted between five and eight Japanese. In the same platoon Corporal Schloithe[4] found his section illuminated by a blazing hut as they fought. He led his men into the sea, away from the light, and they fought on grimly from there.

But the battle was going against the defenders. As midnight approached Miethke had beaten off four separate frontal attacks launched by chanting Japanese. Strong attacking groups were fighting the Australians from many points inside their own defences, however, and the numbers of these groups were constantly increasing. The Australian casualties were mounting, among the killed being Lieutenants Baird[5] and Gilhooley,[6] the artillery observation officers (and with their deaths the rearward communications were lost). In Brocksopp's right front positions Brown had been wounded and evacuated, a sergeant who then took over had been killed, the men were being forced into a desperate position; on the left Mackie was fighting hard with his platoon. He prepared to counter-attack with Lethbridge's platoon. But confusion was setting in. There seemed to be no contact with Miethke and little with the rest of the battalion. Brocksopp ("the coolest man you ever saw", one of the other officers said; "you'd have thought he was at a garden party") began to feel that there was no position left for a counter-attack to restore. Dobbs told him to withdraw to the line of scrub 300 yards in rear. This he attempted but began to lose touch with many of his men. He returned to his former positions with a patrol, but was recalled by an order from the colonel for a complete withdrawal into the bush. Then he found that he had lost touch with the rest of the battalion. The adjutant, Captain Schmedje,[7] who had joined him a short while before and had been trying to find the other companies and the colonel, said to him "You're on your own! What are you going to do?" They gathered 51 of the company together, cut through the scrub and emerged again on the road a few hundred yards east of the Gama River.

---

[1] Pte A. J. Abraham, DCM, SX10515; 2/10 Bn. Canister maker and farm labourer; of Semaphore, SA; b. Broken Hill, NSW, 26 Feb 1918.

[2] Pte J. A. Kotz, MM, SX9891; 2/10 Bn. Labourer; of Adelaide, SA; b. Saddleworth, SA, 25 Jul 1914.

[3] Pte W. McLennan, SX11741; 2/10 Bn. Labourer; of Broken Hill, NSW; b. Peterborough, SA, 5 Jan 1912.

[4] Cpl C. E. Schloithe, SX5895; 2/10 Bn. Labourer; of Renmark, SA; b. Loxton, SA, 8 Oct 1918. Died of wounds 1 Jan 1943.

[5] Lt A. C. Baird, NX56438; 2/5 Fd Regt. Insurance clerk and accountant; of Beecroft, NSW; b. Dubbo, NSW, 20 Apr 1916. Killed in action 27 Aug 1942.

[6] Lt G. J. E. Gilhooley, NX56439; 2/5 Fd Regt. Clerk; of Burwood, NSW; b. Hunter's Hill, NSW, 11 May 1916. Killed in action 27 Aug 1942.

[7] Lt-Col T. J. Schmedje, MC, SX649. 2/10 Bn; BM 15 and 16 Bdes. Regular soldier; of Melbourne; b. Echuca, Vic, 25 Mar 1915.

While they were doing this Miethke, in the darkness and rain, was undergoing a similar experience. He had not had the order to retire. His company was breaking up. His second-in-command was dead. He had only about five rounds a man of ammunition left. He mustered about thirty men and, stopping to fire from successive positions, made his way back to Homo Creek and thence moved through the bush to the Gama where he expected to find the rest of the battalion holding.

Ahead of Miethke Brocksopp had linked at the river with Matheson. At K.B. Matheson had been able only to lie listening to the sounds of battle. He saw many of the rest of the battalion go back, waited until it seemed that they were all clear, then moved back himself to Homo Creek. There, trying to do what he could in the confusion, he, with a small composite group, became separated from the rest of the unit. Then he moved back and at length joined Brocksopp, Schmedje and the others with them. Among these was Corporal O'Brien[8] of his own company who had secured an anti-tank rifle and four boxes of sticky grenades which had hastily been sent forward by a launch service, as the road was impassable past Rabi. Lieutenant Teesdale-Smith,[9] the Intelligence officer, who had been trying to arrange the reception of the launches, said that two militia platoons were coming forward to help.

Brocksopp and Matheson organised a position on the west bank of the Gama River. Scarcely had they done so when the Japanese came surging down the track, about 2 a.m., led by a tank on which a number of infantrymen were riding. The Australians engaged them, O'Brien coolly getting off three shots with his anti-tank rifle before he was wounded by a grenade burst. It was difficult to see what was happening in the darkness. The tank was raking the bush with fire, and mortar bombs—or grenades fired from a discharger—were falling among the defenders. Then the Japanese seemed to be well across the river, both on the road and on the flanks. Brocksopp, still thinking that they represented a force of 5,000, decided that the rest of the battalion had probably reorganised for the defence of No. 3 Strip and told his men to go back. He himself and Schmedje stayed near the river hoping to collect any stragglers from their battalion who might be in the vicinity. They watched what seemed to be a continuous stream of the invaders pouring along the track towards the airfield. They thought that, in ten minutes, a whole battalion passed. A little later they started westward, picked up some of Brocksopp's company, and linked up with Miethke and his company and other components of their battalion. The whole party detoured through the difficult country where the mountains pressed down. They were very cold and wet, worn with lack of sleep, and hungry, with only one small tin of dehydrated emergency ration between every two or three men. They supplemented these with the inside of palm trees and, on their last day out, some taro

---

[8] WO2 J. F. P. O'Brien, DCM, SX1603; 2/10 Bn. Slaughterman; of Minnipa, SA; b. Adelaide, 20 Nov 1912.

[9] Lt-Col P. S. Teesdale-Smith, SX622. 2/10 Bn; Staff and Int appointments 1943-45. Combustion engineer; of South Plympton, SA; b. Port Lincoln, SA, 3 Feb 1914.

and sweet potato which native women cooked for them. They reached the main areas again on the 30th.

While they were carrying out this difficult movement the other components of their battalion had made their way back to the Force area. Matheson had gone back by way of the beach. Colonel Dobbs, with most of the unit, had moved north along Homo Creek and had waited there for daylight to come, subsequently skirting the track and later re-forming in the Force area those of his men he could muster.

During his efforts to assess the situation in the early morning of the 28th he had sent back a patrol under Lieutenant Wilson[1] to the K.B. area. This patrol found Private Abraham who had been so badly wounded fighting with Miethke's company. His platoon, withdrawing, had not been able to find him as he lay unconscious. Five times during the fighting in the night a tank had charged him trying to run him under. Unable to use his legs he had evaded it by rolling aside. When the patrol found him he was holding off four Japanese who were engaging him from the cover of a hut. They had originally been ten. He had killed six. Wilson's men killed the other four. Then it took them three days to get him back to Gili Gili. During that whole time, Wilson said, he remained cheerful.

But, despite such deeds as this, the 2/10th Battalion, a proud and experienced battalion of volunteers, had been thrust back in their first fight with the Japanese—and by forces which, as it was learnt later, were not overwhelmingly superior but which were made of brave and determined men whose plan of attack, centring on the use of their two tanks, worked well. In this fighting the 2/10th lost 43 killed and 26 wounded. About 23 of Miethke's company were among the killed and approximately 20 of his men were wounded.

Colonel Miles' 25th Battalion were left facing the Japanese after the 2/10th had been pushed back. The previous day Miles had taken over the defence of No. 3 Strip and arrangements had been made to send the 61st Battalion back to the Gili Gili area to rest there in reserve. Miles then had two companies thrust forward of the strip—Captain Ryan's[2] company at Rabi and beyond, Captain Steel's company round Kilarbo. A minefield had been laid in the vicinity of Kilarbo and one, farther back, covering the strip itself. As the night of the 27th and the early morning of the 28th advanced Ryan had a platoon towards the Gama River, a platoon at Rabi with his own headquarters, and Lieutenant Schlyder's[3] platoon along the track in the rear, between Rabi and Diura Creek which crossed the road about half-way between Rabi and Kilarbo. Captain Steel had Sergeant Ludlow's[4] platoon backing Schlyder behind Diura Creek, a platoon in the area of Kilarbo village itself, covering the road and the

---
[1] Lt K. R. E. Wilson, SX1597; 2/10 Bn. Farmer; b. Rajrot, India, 3 Aug 1912. Died of wounds 27 Dec 1942.
[2] Capt B. T. Ryan, Q21621; 25 Bn. Bank officer; of Stanthorpe, Qld; b. Christchurch, NZ, 31 Oct 1906.
[3] Lt E. L. Schlyder, QX34428; 25 Bn. Commercial artist; of Warwick, Qld; b. Wollongong, NSW, 8 Jan 1917. Died of wounds accidentally received 30 Mar 1944.
[4] Lt J. J. Ludlow, MM, Q22716. 25 and 22 Bns. Orchardist; of Glen Niven, Qld; b. Stanthorpe, Qld, 29 Oct 1915.

minefield, with his own headquarters and two sections of the anti-aircraft platoon under Sergeant Parkinson[5] also there, and Sergeant Steele[6] was back towards the strip, adjacent to Poin Creek. The move of the 61st back into reserve was proceeding (but slowly) until only small elements, including battalion headquarters and a detachment of five Vickers guns, were left on the strip. On the airfield itself considerable fire-power was concentrated with Americans integrated with other defenders at the seaward end.

When the men of the 2/10th began to come back the Japanese were hard behind them. Some passed through Ryan's forward platoon and then, before the attack of two Japanese tanks, that platoon fell back to Rabi. There the tanks and accompanying infantry threatened Ryan again so that, after a brief encounter and because he was being assailed from the rear, he moved his main force north-west into the hills.

Meanwhile, Brigadier Field had sent forward to Kilarbo an anti-tank gun from the 101st Regiment to cover the minefield and was trying to get a vehicle laden with sticky bombs, Molotov cocktails, and extra ammunition along the road to Rabi; but the road was a morass and rain poured down. The truck bogged hopelessly between Kilarbo and Rabi. Its crew disabled it and made it into a road-block.

After Ryan had been forced into the hills Schlyder tried to make a stand round this road-block. But as the Japanese worked round him he fell back to Kilarbo and joined Steel's company. The pursuers followed quickly and confused fighting set in. Ludlow's men, who had been detailed to cover the gun, were forced away from it. The Japanese took it, but not before Acreman,[7] the lieutenant in charge, had rendered it useless. The fighting was close before Steel's company fell back, so close that Sergeant Parkinson was mortally bayoneted while manning a machine-gun.

Now Sergeant Steele took a hand. Earlier he had cut a field of fire from the road to the coast and had prepared also to fire down a clearing intended for use as an aeroplane bay. He held his ground with about sixteen men. Ludlow, with some of his platoon, joined him and a few other men were gathered. Farther back, as the order for artillery fire was about to be given, there came the sound of fighting from about 400 yards forward. The artillery held their fire. Steele and Ludlow were holding firm, cutting down the attackers as they pushed into the cleared areas. They held from about 5 a.m. until nearly 8. Steele thought that his men killed 40 or 50 Japanese. While Steele and Ludlow thus took toll of their enemies other men from their company were falling back across the strip to the beach, some of them covered by the steady Bren gun fire of Lance-Corporals Jorgensen[8] and Wise[9] and Private Davis.[1]

---

[5] Sgt J. H. Parkinson, Q22366; 25 Bn. Shop assistant; of Toowoomba, Qld; b. Oakey, Qld, 1 Oct 1916. Died of wounds 16 Sep 1942.
[6] Lt S. D. Steele, MM, Q22003; 25 Bn. Labourer; of Stanthorpe, Qld; b. Sydney, 15 May 1918.
[7] Maj K. A. Acreman, MC, QX48827. 101 A-Tk Regt; GHQ SWPA 1944-45. Clerk; of Stafford, Qld; b. Brisbane, 12 Sep 1920.
[8] Sgt E. N. Jorgensen, MM, QX57206; 25 Bn. Fibrous plasterer; of Toowoomba, Qld; b. Toowoomba, 29 Oct 1920.
[9] WO2 L. G. Wise, QX62382; 25 Bn. Station hand; of Liston, via Stanthorpe, Qld; b. Stanthorpe, 22 May 1918.
[1] Sgt R. J. Davis, QX31222. 25, 2/6 Bns. Stove repairer; of East Brisbane; b. Brisbane, 9 Sep 1919.

A quiet day followed as the Japanese maintained the tactics which they had not so far varied at Milne Bay. They rested by day and fought by night.

By nightfall on the 28th General Clowes' dispositions had been somewhat changed. In the early morning, as the situation had grown tenser, Field had started to bring forward the 61st Battalion again—a slow process because transport was short, rain was still falling heavily, and the roads were bogs. By late afternoon, however, the movement was complete and the battalion was covering the north-western end of No. 3 Strip. At its south-east end the 25th Battalion had been re-settled between the sea on the right, the strip itself on the north and Wehuria Creek to the south of it. Across the creek a composite company was in position, formed from elements of the 25th, Australian maintenance units, and some Americans. Thus depth was given to the defence of No. 3 Strip. The

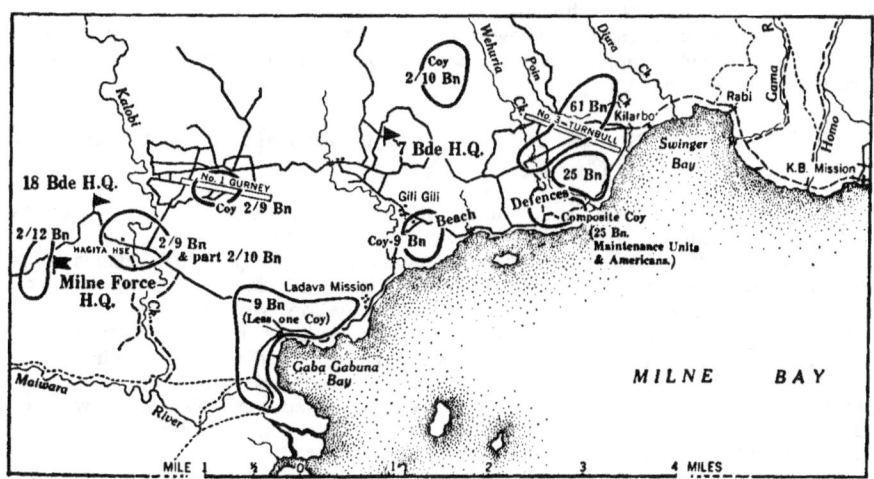

Dispositions, 6 p.m. 28th August

2/10th Battalion—except for a force of about company strength which had been formed the previous night under Matheson and now was disposed for the defence of 7th Brigade Headquarters, to the right of the 61st—was re-forming in the 18th Brigade area. The 2/9th Battalion positions were substantially unchanged but the 2/12th had been moved in from Waigani to an area immediately west of Milne Force Headquarters to be ready to initiate an advance along the north shore by the 18th Brigade. The 9th Battalion remained in its original area except for one company which was covering the Gili Gili wharf area.

By this time Clowes and, above him, Rowell, who, in the short time he had been in New Guinea had not been able to visit Milne Bay, knew that the higher headquarters were feeling considerable concern about the course of events. On the 26th, the first day of the fighting, Blamey had urged on Rowell the need for offensive action on Clowes' part. Rowell's reply, not sent for some days, had shown a sympathetic appreciation of Clowes' difficulties.

> Feel sure that complete freedom sea movement enjoyed by enemy compelled Clowes retain considerable portion forces in hand to meet landing south coast of bay. State of few tracks available such that movement forces from one flank is difficult and considerable degree dispersion inevitable.

On the 28th MacArthur expressed to Blamey his dissatisfaction with the scanty nature of the information coming out of Milne Bay and with the progress being made there. General Sutherland, his Chief of Staff, wrote curtly:

> The Commander-in-Chief requests that you instruct Major-General Clowes at once to clear the north shore of Milne Bay without delay and that you direct him to submit a report to reach General Headquarters by 0800K/29 [8 a.m. 29th] of the action taken together with his estimate of the enemy's strength in the area. Please further request General Clowes' opinion as to the possibility that a second movement of enemy shipping into Milne Bay was for the purpose of withdrawing forces previously landed.

On the same day the Deputy Chief of the General Staff, General Vasey, who was at G.H.Q., wrote Rowell a personal letter.

> The lack of information from you on the operations at Milne Bay has created a very difficult situation here. GHQ get through air sources various scraps of information. The source of these is usually not given, and they generally indicate a lack of activity on the part of our troops in the area. Our view is that these are not worth anything, but in default of authentic information from you we are not in a position to combat GHQ, whose outlook is based on these sundry reports.
>
> Only two minutes ago I have been phoned by Sutherland asking me what reports I had, and what offensive action had been taken by Cyril [Clowes]. I was compelled to answer that I was unaware. Sutherland stated that MacArthur was very concerned about the apparent lack of activity on Cyril's part. I replied that it was not necessarily lack of activity, but lack of information. . . .
>
> You possibly do not realise that for GHQ this is their first battle, and they are, therefore, like many others, nervous and dwelling on the receipt of frequent messages. . . .
>
> MacArthur is determined to fight in New Guinea and on the evening of the 26th August we had a conference to formulate a plan for sending 25 Bde to Milne Bay. Now a definite direction for that has been received, and the bde gp. in accordance with the attached Staff Table is now under orders to embark.
>
> By the tone of this morning's conversation with Sutherland, I feel that a wrong impression of our troops had already been created in the minds of the great, and it is important for the future that that impression be corrected at the earliest possible moment.

Immediately after writing this letter, on the same day, Vasey scribbled an even more personal note to Rowell, in his own hand. He referred to his previous letter, written in General Blamey's absence.

> I have sent him [Blamey] a copy of my letter to you as I feel a matter of major policy with GHQ will come out of it. It boils down to the question of who is commanding the army—MacArthur or T.A.B. [Blamey] and it seems the sooner that is settled the better.

My view is that the decision to send 25 Bde to Milne Bay is either precipitate or too late. Precipitate because no one knows it is necessary and we have continually said Cyril and his army will soon clear up what is there. Too late because if we are to lose the place it will be gone before the bde can get there. Anyway if as soon as the Jap attacks and does what we expected of him the plan is to be changed, it's obviously a bum plan. At the conference I insisted on

(a) adequate naval escort
(b) land only at Milne Bay or Moresby. A suggestion was made it might be put somewhere on the South Coast. "We want to fight the Japs" is the only known expression at GHQ.

I am now awaiting the result of Cyril's activities yesterday. I'm dying to go to these b——s and say "I told you so—we've killed the b——y lot." . . . One of MacArthur's troubles is that all his navy has gone to the Solomons and he wants information on which to base a request, or demand, on Washington to get it back.

MacArthur's staff lacked experience in war, especially at the tactical level; they almost completely lacked knowledge of the terrain over which the fighting was taking place, and could therefore make no proper appreciation of the conditions at Milne Bay; it was not the Australian practice to send long "ball for ball" descriptions of battle to higher commands, especially when those higher commands could do nothing to influence the battle, while the Americans seemed to expect such reports, and, especially, detailed accounts of enemy casualties. Added to all of this was the fact that it was extremely difficult for Clowes to get a complete picture of what was happening; the Australians could not see anything of their enemies; they did not know what the Japanese ships were doing each night when they entered the bay; they lacked maps, had difficulty in maintaining signals communications and, because of lack of experience in the headquarters of his battalions, Field was poorly informed of what was happening on his front. It seems also that unauthorised messages were sent out from air force sources and, at the best, these were ill-informed, and often based on nothing more than rumour. Nevertheless Milne Force *did* send out the usual situation reports.

With this situation developing far to the rear, Clowes was still handicapped by uncertainty regarding the Japanese intentions. Half of his force had already been committed to action and, if other landings were to be made elsewhere, he would need the remainder of his troops to deal with them. However, in view of the quietness of the day on the 28th, he planned to move Field's brigade again to K.B. at dawn on the 29th. But indications of further attack on No. 3 Strip on the night 28th-29th stayed his hand. No attack came. The 29th was a day of sporadic action and alarms and patrol activity highlighted by the discovery of two Japanese tanks, bogged and abandoned on the track west of the Gama River. At 4.33 p.m. aircraft reported a cruiser and nine destroyers headed for Milne Bay. The commander, new apprehensions of landings on the southern or western shores springing to life, cancelled instructions he had given to Brigadier Wootten to attack along the north shore as far as K.B. with a view to later mopping up the whole of the East Cape Peninsula. Shelling came again from the bay just before and after midnight though it was comparatively light and caused no casualties.

The 30th was a day of new patrolling. The most extensive task was undertaken by the indefatigable Bicks and his equally indefatigable henchman, Robinson. These two, with four others, including that same Lance-Sergeant Ridley who had previously shammed death in the midst of the Japanese, set out about 9.30 a.m. Captain Campbell with some of his men was to follow.

Dead men lay on and beside the track, and scattered Japanese equipment. Bicks passed the bogged tanks. He said later:

> With Robinson and 2 OR's I went on, finding a Jap hospital at Gama River. Here I saw evidence that they'd killed their wounded. Several men, neatly laid in a row and naked with bandaged legs and in one case a head wound, had bullet wounds in the vicinity of the heart. We pushed on across the Gama River to Motieau Point without seeing any live enemy. Here we saw the first dead native who'd obviously been taken prisoner by the Japs as his hands were tied behind his back with sig wire. Shot and bayoneted! We were at K.B. about midday and gained first-hand information of Thursday night's fight there when the 2/10th were overrun. Many of our dead and enemy dead! We found the bodies of two FOO's [Forward Observation Officers] of the 2/5th Field Regiment. Also found several of *my* battalion men (who were in shorts) their features no longer recognisable. They may have been from "D" or "B" Company. Their hands were tied behind their backs, arms had been broken by gunshot wounds and they'd been bayoneted. Pushing on . . . we approached 11 Platoon's old bivouac position. Here we encountered three enemy moving towards a hut there. Robinson and I killed two at 40 yards but the third got away.

That day General MacArthur was seeing the Milne Bay picture in rather a different light, anxiety still gripping him. He signalled Washington:

> . . . this is first test of Australian troops under my command; the Australians claim the Commander is excellent and rate half his troops as good; the other half from the 7th Australian Division they rate excellent; the strength of Japanese forces that have landed not known, but am convinced it is very much less than that of Australian combat troops at Milne Bay; with good troops under first class leadership would view the situation confidently, unless enemy reinforcements are landed, but as I have previously reported am not yet convinced of the efficiency of the Australian units and do not attempt to forecast results.

And, again on the same day, another commander was seeing through different eyes again. Rowell wrote to Vasey:

> It is perilously easy to criticise a commander for his actions at a distance of 250 miles. To my regret I have not been to Milne Bay. . . . And so I've no first-hand knowledge of conditions. . . . But it must be emphasised that movement is difficult and ability to concentrate equally so. In addition our inability to sink ships and lack of naval cover, must have made Clowes anxious about the possibility of future landings. So there it is. His first attack with 61 Bn was stopped, and when he relieved 61 by 2/10, the latter got cut up before it could go in. However, I ordered Cyril, late on 28 Aug to put everything in, but I sincerely doubt whether in the conditions, anything but a small force can be deployed. It is true, of course, that if he pulls everything eastwards, he may be able to get some momentum.
>
> I'm sorry that GHQ take a poor view of Australians. In some cases that is all too true, but I wish Chamberlain [Chamberlin—MacArthur's senior Operations officer] & Co. could visit the jungle to see what conditions are, instead of sitting back and criticising. It is obvious also, that the Japs are the very highest class of troops, as the 2/10 were well above the ordinary.

Bicks' patrol penetration as far as K.B. did not mean, however, that the Japanese had been cleared from the area. About 3 a.m. on the 31st the dark morning silence was broken by the sound of a heavy "clang". Startled the Australians fired flares and attacking forces were revealed grouped round the eastern side of No. 3 Strip—the seaward end. Defensive artillery fire crashed among them, and mortar fire controlled by Lieutenant Acreman from a forward post. Stupidly the Japanese bunched themselves in groups, which offered tempting targets to the defenders firing across the open areas of the field and, apparently to encourage themselves, shouted loudly. Three times they formed up and attacked and three times fell before the hail of fire which caught them. They re-formed once more in the shelter of Poin Creek from which they made their way towards Stephen's House—some 200 yards north of the strip and near its northwestern end—and tried their now rather feeble strength against Meldrum's waiting 61st Battalion. But Meldrum had foreseen such a move and had had some of his men placed along the high ground known as Stephen's Ridge which commanded any flank approaches to the north-west end of the strip. As the Japanese advanced they came mainly against Robinson's platoon and withered. In the lull which preceded the dawn three bugle calls rang loud and clear from the darkness of the Japanese positions. It seemed as though the invaders were being plucked back by the shrill notes.

The comparative silence which came with the new day was broken by the sound of occasional sniping and, at first, the groans and cries of the Japanese wounded lying round the strip. But, about 8 o'clock, the sound of what seemed to be revolver shots broke above the other sounds. The voices of men in pain were not heard after that. The Australians considered that the Japanese had shot many of their own wounded.

During the fighting in the darkness Lieut-Colonel Arnold's[2] 2/12th Battalion had been struggling forward to the strip, up to their knees in mud along the roads, the first of Wootten's brigade to move in accordance with Clowes' orders to him to attack along the north shore—initially as far as K.B. Mission. Arnold's leading company, under Captain Swan,[3] passed through the forward positions at 9.9 a.m. on the 31st closely followed by the battalion's battle headquarters, Lieutenant Steddy's[4] recently formed "Commando Platoon"[5] and the other companies. They met resistance immediately they crossed the strip. Swan was wounded and Captain Ivey[6] took over his company. He pushed on while Arnold's headquarters, Steddy, and the other leading elements destroyed the opposition which came from snipers in the trees, and desperate Japanese soldiers who lay

---

[2] Lt-Col A. S. W. Arnold, OBE, ED, SX1468. 2/10 Bn; CO 2/12 Bn 1942-43. Public servant; of Kensington Gardens, SA; b. Tumby Bay, SA, 18 Apr 1906.
[3] Maj R. G. Swan, TX2017; 2/12 Bn. Farmer; of Richmond, Tas; b. Hobart, 1 May 1910.
[4] Lt E. M. C. Steddy, QX6234; 2/12 Bn. Grazier; of Ascot, Qld; b. Townsville, Qld, 17 Sep 1914. Killed in action 1 Jan 1943.
[5] Each of the 18th Brigade battalions formed a commando platoon at Milne Bay from within the battalion. Each such platoon had the normal strength in men and arms. Members were selected for their willingness to take risks, among other qualifications. This arrangement was designed to enable the commander to provide for the protection of his headquarters and to keep a force available for special missions which might otherwise disorganise a company.
[6] Capt C. H. V. Ivey, DSO, TX2018; 2/12 Bn. Orchardist; of Cygnet, Tas; b. Cygnet, 22 Oct 1913.

motionless among their own dead and when the advance had passed over them rose to fire into the Australians from the rear. As Arnold's men went ahead they saw that the Japanese were remaining close to the road, rarely spreading more than about 80 yards from it. Ambush parties in groups of 3 to about 14 were found in small lanes cut into the bush at right angles from the road. Soon it was clear that the secret of the advance lay in beating the Japanese "to the draw"; that no recumbent form could be accepted as that of a dead man. So Arnold's men developed an extraordinary quickness in their reactions and were merciless in ensuring that everybody really *was* dead.

Progress was necessarily slow and it was not until the early afternoon that the leading elements reached the Gama River. By 4 p.m. Arnold had reported that he himself was at the Gama and he estimated that his men had killed 70 Japanese. His own casualties were light and had been reported some forty minutes earlier as one officer killed and Swan and 9 men wounded.

By 5 p.m. Arnold had established his headquarters at K.B. which Ivey and his men had stormed at the point of the bayonet, killing or wounding, they reported, some 60 of their enemies. Captain Suthers'[7] company, which had been following them, dug in with Arnold and Ivey. Later Suthers described his progression from the Gama forward, over ground which had already been traversed by the others.

On the way up I met an "I" Section man who said the track to K.B. was clear. As he said this our leading platoon did over an L.M.G. and five men! They spotted them first. A man saw an apparently dead Jap move and shot him. Others came to life and they shot them and found an L.M.G. mounted. They were lying on their faces and backs as though dead. There were 12 to 20 really dead Japs lying about.... At Point King [less than half a mile west of K.B.] we saw the first Japanese brutalities—found a native boy mutilated. They tied him with sig wire and put a bayonet up his anus and burnt half his head off with a flame-thrower. Nearby a native woman was pegged by the hands and legs with sig wire and they cut her left breast off. The boy had been dead about six hours and the woman the same. I saw two . . . A.M.F. men, one bayoneted with his hands tied with sig wire. The other was tied to a tree with his hands bound in front and he had bayonet thrusts in his arms and a bayonet sticking in his stomach.

But while Suthers was settling to a relatively undisturbed night with Ivey's company and the colonel, others of the battalion, back on the Gama River, were having a more strenuous time. There Captains Kirk[8] and Gategood,[9] with their companies and a detachment of Headquarters Company under Captain Boucher,[1] had been strengthened by the arrival in their area of two companies of the 9th Battalion. The first of these, under Captain Hyde,[2] had been told to cover the road in the vicinity of

---

[7] Capt A. G. Suthers, QX6040; 2/12 Bn. Engineering clerk; of Dover Heights, NSW; b. Gympie, Qld, 25 Mar 1918.
[8] Capt C. S. Kirk, MC, QX3817; 2/12 Bn. Bank clerk; of Toowoomba, Qld; b. Goondiwindi, Qld, 10 Jul 1915. Killed in action 1 Jan 1943.
[9] Maj K. A. J. Gategood, QX6026. 2/12 Bn; Chief Instructor HQ Jungle Warfare Trg Centre 1945. Salesman; of New Farm, Qld; b. Newtown, NSW, 13 Nov 1905.
[1] Maj M. C. W. Boucher, TX2014. 2/12 Bn; Staff and Base Area appts. 1943-45. Production manager; of Hobart; b. Hobart, 27 Feb 1910.
[2] Maj G. R. Hyde, QX40828; 9 Bn. Business manager; of Lutwyche, Qld; b. Kensington, Vic, 6 May 1905.

(Australian War Memorial)
Japanese light tanks bogged and abandoned at Milne Bay, September 1942.

(Australian War Memorial)
M.v. *Anshun*, lying on her side at Gili Gili, where she was shelled and sunk by Japanese naval gun-fire while unloading on the night of 6th September. The *Anshun* was later salvaged.

(Australian War Memorial)
In accordance with Allied plans to develop Australia as the major Pacific base, American forces began to arrive in increasing numbers. Newly-arrived American troops during kit inspection.

(Australian War Memorial)
In addition to the militia and the returning A.I.F. divisions, the Australian Army possessed its own highly-trained 1st Armoured Division, A.I.F. General Grant (medium) tanks, armed with 75-mm and 37-mm guns and machine-guns, at rest during training manoeuvres in **Australia.**

Rabi and to block off the tracks coming in from the north. The second, Captain Williams'[3] company, had a similar task along the road between Rabi and K.B.

Night was coming. About 300 Japanese suddenly debouched from one of the densely wooded valleys on to the main track and flung themselves against the 9th companies, which Hyde had just joined. A savage mêlée lasted for about two hours. Then the Japanese retired having lost some 90 men, the Australians claimed. The remnants of the band moved east where Williams' men mauled them later in the night.

Dispositions, 6 p.m. 31st August

Next day Wootten asked Clowes if Field could take over responsibility for the area up to the Gama. Clowes agreed. So a company from each of the 25th and 61st Battalions relieved Arnold's companies on the river and these then moved forward to K.B. and established themselves as part of the perimeter defences.

During 1st September the Australians patrolled forward up to a mile east of the mission. They were assisted by the willing fighter pilots whose zeal so outran their knowledge of the ground positions that Arnold's diarist wryly recorded: "Planes strafed enemy positions and also own troops." With the night small Japanese parties caused unrest around the perimeter and killed and wounded a number of the defenders.

One of the company commanders told later of a mine-laying patrol he sent out from K.B. The night pressed blackly.

Sergeant Jim Hosier[4] was there and someone ran a hand over his face. Jim cursed him and a *Jap* jabbered. . . . We lost three men and found them dead next day. It was so dark men walked holding on to the next man's scabbard. They walked

---

[3] Capt E. A. Williams, Q16720. (1st AIF: Lt 41 Bn.) 9 Bn. Telephone mechanic; of Clayfield, Qld; b. Birmingham, England, 21 Feb 1896.

[4] Sgt J. O. Hosier, QX20636; 2/12 Bn. Tram conductor; of New Farm, Qld; b. Richmond, Qld, 19 Mar 1914. Killed in action 9 Jan 1943.

right through "D" Company and a platoon of "A" Company before they knew where they were. The sergeant, Hosier, heard a man speak quietly, recognised the voice and then knew where he was.

With the 2/12th thus established at K.B. on the 1st September Clowes arranged that Wootten should land there the 2/9th Battalion (Lieut-Colonel Cummings[5]). But he received a signal from MacArthur at 9 p.m. (one of a number of "flap" messages which hindered him in the execution of his plans) to "Expect attack Jap ground forces on Milne aerodromes from west and north-west supported by destroyer fire from bay. Take immediate stations." As a result of this misinformation all units were ordered to "stand-to" throughout the night and Clowes told Wootten that he could not count on the 2/9th being available for operations on the north shore next day.

On the 2nd the 2/12th pressed forward with Kirk, Gategood, Boucher and their men while Steddy's "commandos" worried the Japanese, drove them from some smaller positions and killed nine of them. When night fell Kirk and Gategood were settled on the fourth ford east of the mission and the rest of the battalion was at K.B. There they had been joined during the afternoon by Colonel Cummings and his first two companies as, after the previous quiet night at Gili Gili, Clowes had told Wootten to send the 2/9th forward across the bay in the two small boats then available.

On the morning of the 3rd Kirk and Steddy went ahead along the shore until they came against Japanese defences about 800 yards ahead of the fourth ford and centred round another little stream just west of Elevala Creek. Their men killed about 20 of their opponents, as nearly as they could estimate, but suffered rather severely themselves. Two companies of the 2/9th then arrived—Captain Marshall's[6] as advance-guard, and Captain Anderson's.[7] Marshall found that the Japanese positions covered the track from the coast to about 150 yards north in close bush, a machine-gun and a 20-mm field piece commanding the main approach. The position seemed to be a delaying one, strong in fire-power. He sent Lieutenant Fogg's[8] platoon to attack on the right of the road and Lieutenant Heron's[9] on the left. The attack went in with about 60 men at 10 a.m. and, within three minutes, 34 of those had been shot down, the stream, two feet deep, slowing them up as they entered the final 30 yards of their charge. Fogg was struck in the head and was at first left for dead in the creek. But his batman, Private Reid,[1] dragged him from the water and dressed his wound though his own right arm was shattered by a bullet as he did so. Heron,

---

[5] Col C. J. Cummings, DSO, OBE, ED, QX6011. 2/12, 2/33 Bns; CO 2/9 Bn 1941-44, 1 Beach Gp 1944-45. Accountant; of Cairns, Qld; b. Atherton, Qld, 25 May 1908.

[6] Maj A. Marshall, MC, QX4398. 2/9 Bn and HQ 18 Bde. Jackeroo; of Stanthorpe, Qld; b. Melbourne, 18 Sep 1919.

[7] Maj A. J. Anderson, MC, QX6003. 2/9 Bn; Staff appts. LHQ 1944-45. Schoolmaster; of East Brisbane; b. Clifton, Qld, 28 Feb 1912.

[8] Lt C. H. Fogg, QX21387; 2/9 Bn. Bank clerk; of Clayfield, Qld; b. Rockhampton, Qld, 29 May 1916.

[9] Lt R. A. Heron, QX157; 2/9 Bn. Salesman; of Brisbane; b. Bowen, Qld, 16 Sep 1914. Killed in action 18 Dec 1942.

[1] Pte C. W. Reid, QX23808; 2/9 Bn. Labourer; of Rockhampton, Qld; b. Rockhampton, 12 Aug 1917.

leading his platoon, was wounded, as were his sergeant and a number of men. Corporal Gordon[2] took over the platoon and, with his own section, fought a grim battle with the Japanese on the eastern side of the creek, he himself, with his sub-machine-gun, killing about six including one soldier with whom he duelled at about five yards' range, each of them behind a tree.

Notable among the many brave men in that company were the giant Lance-Corporal John Ball[3] and Lance-Corporal Allen.[4] Ball's body was found later 25 yards across the stream, right among the Japanese machine-gun positions—so far across, indeed, that he had outstripped all others and none had seen him die. There was no mark on him and it was thought that he had thrown an anti-tank bomb and that the blast had killed him. Allen lay dead almost at the muzzles of the guns.

At this stage Captain Hooper[5] came forward with the third company of the 2/9th. He led his men up the steep slope to Marshall's left then came down in the rear of the Japanese positions. His men killed one of their enemies. The others had gone. Hooper's and Anderson's men then pushed on about half a mile to Sanderson Bay where they went into peri-meter defence for the night. Behind them the rest of the battalion formed another perimeter.

So the night came. It brought Japanese ships into Milne Bay again. Shells fell on the north shore area but caused no casualties.

On the 4th Colonel Cummings of the 2/9th planned that Hooper should move astride the road to a point where the coastal strip widened and then swing out to the left flank to search the bush and give flank protection to Major Peek's[6] company. Peek was to advance astride the track. Little over an hour after he had set out, however, Hooper came up against Japanese positions at Goroni. He swung wide to the flank but then with-drew, having lost contact with Lieutenant Scott[7] and his platoon. Cummings then ordered him to move north for some 600 yards, with his two remaining platoons, then east for a similar distance, and fall upon the Japanese right rear, expecting this attack to take place between 11 and 11.30. But at 12.30, having heard nothing of Hooper, he called Anderson forward and planned to attack with Peek's company and Anderson's. Scott meanwhile had appeared out of the rough country to the north of the track and was to strengthen the attack.

Shortly before the assault was due to go in Hooper arrived back and reported that he had penetrated between one and two miles to the Japanese

---

[2] Sgt J. Gordon, QX1236; 2/9 Bn. Grazier; of Glenmorgan, Qld; b. Talbot, Vic, 7 Dec 1907. Killed in action 18 Dec 1942.

[3] L-Cpl J. J. Ball, QX284; 2/9 Bn. Labourer; of Maroochydore, Qld; b. Biggenden, Qld, 16 Sep 1919. Killed in action 3 Sep 1942.

[4] L-Cpl B. E. Allen, QX16772; 2/9 Bn. Labourer; of Dubbo, NSW; b. Dubbo, 25 Mar 1908. Killed in action 3 Sep 1942.

[5] Capt R. C. Hooper, QX6082. 2/9 Bn; Staff and Base Sub-Area appts 1943-45. Bank officer; of Windsor, Qld; b. Richmond, Qld, 18 Jul 1903. Died 30 Mar 1957.

[6] Maj E. J. F. Peek, QX6036. 2/9 Bn and trg appts. Printer; of Mackay, Qld; b. Townsville, Qld, 5 Jul 1906.

[7] Capt D. C. J. Scott, QX1188; 2/9 Bn. Grazier; of "Ballancar", Inglewood, Qld; b. Painswick, Gloucestershire, England, 7 Aug 1912.

rear, had found supply dumps, had been fired on and had withdrawn. Cummings decided to press home the attack with the other two companies and, from Scott's platoon position, preliminary artillery and mortar fire was brought down. At 3.15 p.m. the attack drove forward, Peek astride the road and Anderson to cross the river which fronted the Japanese positions in an attempt to take the Japanese positions from their right rear. Peek made some progress but Anderson fared badly. His men crossed the river, through five feet of water about 20 yards wide. They turned to go downstream through coarse kunai grass and scrub, which rose above their heads. As they moved on they encountered Japanese sentries. Lieutenant Paterson[8] shot two of these men and the Australians advanced against the main positions, but were beaten back. With Anderson wounded, Paterson, assisted by Warrant-Officer Boulton,[9] took over the company and left Sergeant De Vantier[1] to lead his platoon. They reorganised 100 to 200 yards back, on the edge of the kunai and scrub which they had left to make the attack over comparatively open ground. They attacked again, and again they were beaten back. But, as the Japanese came out of their positions to harry them, the Queenslanders moved forward to meet them and a heavy fire developed from both sides.

The advance of the section of which Corporal French[2] was in command was held up by fire from three enemy machine-gun posts, whereupon Corporal French, ordering his section to take cover, advanced and silenced one of the posts with grenades. Armed with a Thompson sub-machine-gun he then attacked the third post firing from the hip as he went forward. He was seen to be badly hit by fire from this post, but he continued to advance. The enemy gun was heard to cease fire and the section then pushed on. It was found that all members of the three enemy gun crews had been killed and that Corporal French had died in front of the third gun pit. By his cool courage and disregard of his own personal safety this non-commissioned officer saved members of his section from heavy casualties and was responsible for the successful conclusion of the attack.[3]

On this day, also, the Australians had the final news of another loss which saddened them. A patrol from the 2/12th Battalion, led by Lance-Corporal Allan,[4] found Squadron Leader Turnbull's[5] body among the crashed remains of a Kittyhawk in the bush near K.B. Mission. The soldiers much admired and appreciated the work of the two R.A.A.F. squadrons and, for them, the gallant Turnbull had epitomised the courage and skill of all the airmen.

On the 5th patrols of the 2/9th Battalion were early astir. One, led by Scott, found Paterson who had been lying wounded in the bush all night.

[8] Capt J. Paterson, MC, QX1254; 2/9 Bn. Dentist; of Dalby, Qld; b. Brisbane, 11 Sep 1909.
[9] WO2 W. S. Boulton, QX4436; 2/9 Bn. Master drover; of Toowong, Qld; b. Toowoomba, Qld, 13 Mar 1896.
[1] Lt R. De Vantier, MM, QX415; 2/9 Bn. Schoolteacher; of Gympie, Qld; b. Esk, Qld, 14 Dec 1918. Killed in action 18 Dec 1942.
[2] Cpl J. A. French, VC, QX1071; 2/9 Bn. Hairdresser; of Crow's Nest, Qld; b. Crow's Nest, 15 Jul 1914. Killed in action 4 Sep 1942.
[3] From the citation in the recommendation that French be awarded the Victoria Cross.
[4] L-Cpl R. B. Allan, QX8242; 2/12 Bn. Farm labourer; of Finch Hatton, Qld; b. Homebush, Qld, 8 Mar 1919.
[5] After Turnbull's death on 27th August Squadron Leader K. W. Truscott took command of No. 76 Squadron.

One reported having reached Waga Waga without incident. At 9.15 Lieut-Colonel Cummings began to advance once more with his main force. After Arnold's men had taken over their position Hooper's company, with Captain Barnes[6] now in command, went forward astride the road with Peek on their left, while Marshall occupied Waga Waga. At 11.20 Barnes' men clashed with Japanese in positions near a creek crossing about half a mile beyond Waga Waga.

Lieutenant McDonald[7] led his platoon forward across the creek. When he was about 80 yards beyond the stream he found himself in the centre of Japanese positions and under attack from about 80 of his enemies. For about five minutes the two opposing groups beat at each other with heavy fire. On McDonald's left Sergeant Roberts'[8] platoon, and on his right Lieutenant Scott's, were also fighting. The Australians were losing men fast and were ordered back about 400 yards. McDonald had lost 4 men killed and 15 wounded and had only eleven men left in his platoon. In Scott's platoon seven men had been wounded including himself.

Cummings now brought Marshall's company forward again and planned that Marshall and Barnes would attack later in the day with Peek moving round the flank to come against the Japanese right rear. R.A.A.F. fighters made strafing and bombing runs until about 2.30 after which the artillery and mortars began to plaster the track. At 3.10 the attack went in. But the opposition had melted away.

Although, as a quiet night now settled over the forward Australian positions, there was every reason to believe that the Japanese strength on the north shore had been completely broken, General Clowes' worries were not over. At 9 p.m. he received a signal from Blamey which told of expectations that the Japanese would land more troops in Milne Bay that night and that more Japanese reinforcements would arrive on the 12th. Little more than an hour later he was told that the remnants of the Japanese forces would be withdrawn in the darkness and that he could expect a fresh landing by two hostile battalions on the 10th. As the night went on Japanese ships came again to Milne Bay and the busy sound of boats hurrying between ships and shore was heard by the forward troops.

On the 6th the 2/9th fought isolated skirmishes. They were now in the middle of what was obviously the Japanese main base area, from Goroni to Lilihoa. Dumps and base installations and all the scattered paraphernalia of a broken force marked the area. Patrols went as far as Ahioma without hindrance.

Dramatic action came again with the night—but from the sea. The motor vessel, *Anshun*,[9] was unloading at Gili Gili. The hospital ship, *Manunda*, lay in the bay, its white and green hull illuminated with lights.

---

[6] Lt-Col E. Barnes, QX3615. 2/9, 8 Bns; CO 19 Bn 1945. Clerk; of Cairns, Qld; b. Ingham, Qld, 31 May 1914.

[7] Capt D. J. McDonald, QX2571; 2/9 Bn. Accountant; of Rockhampton, Qld; b. Wagga Wagga, NSW, 22 May 1907.

[8] Capt D. J. Roberts, QX4799; 2/9 Bn. Grazier; of Toowoomba, Qld; b. St. George, Qld, 12 Oct 1911.

[9] This ship, with urgently needed ammunition and stores, had been standing by at Port Moresby for some days awaiting an opportunity to come into the bay.

About 10 o'clock Japanese ships once more sailed up the bay. They flooded the *Anshun* with light and, as shells struck her, she heeled and sank at the wharf.[1] The *Manunda* was likewise lit up, but the hospital ship was not fired at. A searchlight played over the forward Australian positions and shells fell at many points round the foreshores. Again, just after midnight, the *Manunda* was bathed in the searchlights and once more the shore positions were shelled. Some of the soldiers were hit, Arnold's battalion, which lost 2 men killed and 12 wounded, suffering most.

Next day (the 7th), spurred by the warnings he had received regarding the Japanese intentions, Clowes began to concentrate the 18th Brigade once more in the Gili Gili area, having instructed Arnold and Cummings to destroy all Japanese material which they could not quickly salvage. With the night Japanese naval forces were again in the bay. There was shelling for about fifteen minutes, near midnight, mostly of the Gili Gili wharf and No. 1 Strip areas, and the Australians suffered some casualties. Again the searchlights played on *Manunda* but no harm was offered her.

The 2/9th completed their movement by sea on the 8th and, late that day, the last of the main elements of the 2/12th, who had been left to complete the demolition of the Japanese stores and equipment, marched in from K.B. in the darkness.

For the moment, at least, organised fighting was finished. Only isolated killings marked the succeeding days as Japanese survivors were hunted down, or headed off as, desperate and starving, they tried to make their way generally north-west towards Buna. But even this "mopping up" was dangerous work.

On the 7th, from K.B., where he had been left while the rest of his battalion moved in the wake of the 2/9th, Suthers took most of his company to Limadi, a village in the rough mountain country a few miles north-east of K.B. where he had been told some 250 Japanese were in hiding. He found a small but determined party there with two machine-guns in position. His men killed about 5 Japanese and some escaped. Lieutenant Brown[2] was killed at the head of his platoon. That day Corporal Condon,[3] forward with Ivey's company, was attacked by two Japanese armed with rifles while he himself had only a machete as he went about his work. He was said to have killed both of them with this primitive weapon.

In the 2/9th Corporal MacCarthy[4] and three of his friends caused a minor alarm when they poked forward looking for souvenirs just before the battalion returned to Gili Gili. No one else knew that they had gone. Suddenly the quiet was broken by sounds of fighting so that other men,

---

[1] HMAS *Arunta*, which was escorting the *Anshun*, in accordance with orders went outside the bay during the night. She returned next morning to find only the upper works of her charge above water.

[2] Lt K. R. Brown, TX185; 2/12 Bn. Insurance clerk; of Launceston, Tas; b. Scottsdale, Tas, 13 Sep 1915. Killed in action 7 Sep 1942.

[3] Sgt J. Condon, QX3596; 2/12 Bn. Labourer; of Rockhampton, Qld; b. Charters Towers, Qld, 26 Nov 1910.

[4] WO2 T. E. MacCarthy, QX2653; 2/9 Bn. Bridge carpenter; of Mackay, Qld; b. Childers, Qld, 21 Jun 1907.

swimming or working, leaped to their arms thinking a new attack had begun. But MacCarthy's party had merely "flushed" five Japanese whom they killed.

By the time they were concentrated again at Gili Gili Wootten's two battalions had suffered some 200 casualties. Of these the 2/9th had lost approximately 30 killed and between 80 and 90 wounded; the 2/12th had had 35 killed and 44 wounded.

Clowes then busied himself with preparations for the new attacks he had been told to expect, but which never materialised. Thus far the defence of Milne Bay had cost the Australians 373 battle casualties. Of these 24 were officers; 12 officers and 149 men were either killed or missing. Of the Americans one soldier of the 43rd Engineers was killed and two were wounded in the ground actions; several more were killed or wounded in air raids.

Of the Japanese casualties Clowes reported: "It is conservatively and reliably estimated . . . that enemy killed amount to at least 700. A large proportion of this total was actually buried by our troops; others had been buried by the Japanese. This number does not include any of the enemy who may have been lost with the merchant ship *Nankai Maru*, sunk in the bay by our aircraft. One P.O.W. stated that 300 men had been lost with the ship. It is not possible to estimate the number of enemy wounded."

The Japanese landed a total of 1,900 to 2,000 troops, thinking that 20 or 30 aircraft were based at Milne Bay and that the ground forces numbered two or three companies deployed for the defence of the airfield. They had planned to use both soldiers and marines in the attack. After the Kawaguchi units were diverted to Guadalcanal they intended to use troops of the *4th Infantry Regiment (Aoba Force)* against Milne Bay. But they could not get *Aoba Force* down from the Philippines in time and so determined to rely on naval forces only. When Milne Bay had been occupied they proposed to capture Port Moresby "with one blow", in a combined land, sea and air attack in full strength.

Their convoy left Rabaul on 24th August and, on the morning of the 26th, landed Commander Hayashi's *5th Kure Naval Landing Force,* about 600 strong, *10th Naval Labour Corps* numbering some 360, and possibly about 200 of Commander Tsukioka's *5th Sasebo Naval Landing Force.*

Although initially the landings were unopposed the Japanese plans miscarried from the very beginning. The balance of the *5th Sasebo* approximately 350 strong who had embarked at Buna, were to disembark at Taupota and cooperate with the main landings by moving across the mountains to Milne Bay, but became marooned at Goodenough Island through the destruction of their barges by Allied air attacks on 25th August. Then the main invasion forces landed at the wrong place. They had intended to land closer to the airfield and, indeed, could have done so with very little opposition. The well-directed R.A.A.F. attacks on the 26th caused disorder and casualties amongst them. Their own lack of air support hindered them. They knew little or nothing of the country over which they had to advance, sharing with the Australians the disadvantages of having no satisfactory maps. Nor did the natives cooperate with them. The relentless rains hampered their movements and weakened many of their men. The increasing resistance they met as they pushed on towards the partly-prepared No. 3 Strip, culminating in their disastrous attacks on the strip itself—in which they lost heavily—wore them down. Reinforcements were not available in sufficient numbers to enable them to maintain the impetus of their attack or to restore the position in any measure once it began to slip from their grasp.

Probably on the night 29th-30th August the whole of Commander Yano's *3rd Kure Naval Landing Force* and about a third of the *5th Yokosuka* were landed but they were too late to affect the issue. Apart from the landing of these companies, which together would have totalled about 770, it seems that the main task of the Japanese ships that arrived at night was to take off wounded. The last such evacuation took place on the night of the 6th and the morning of the 7th September when the cruiser *Tenryu* and two corvettes were in Milne Bay and lifted some 600 wounded and unwounded survivors.

We now know that Commander Hayashi and most of his staff were killed, as well as most of his *5th Kure* which headed the original landing; that most of the *5th Yokosuka* were killed; that Yano was wounded and taken off by sea and that probably his company of the *3rd Kure* suffered rather less than the other units. We know also that few of the remnants of the invasion force succeeded in making their way overland to rejoin their comrades at Buna. In a final summing up it seems safe to conclude that the Japanese sustained probably four times the casualties of the Australians.

Afterwards, consideration of the relative strengths involved in this engagement led to criticism of Clowes' handling of the operations—particularly by General MacArthur and, to a lesser extent, by General Blamey. After his peremptory instructions to Blamey on the 28th August, and the doubts he expressed in his message to Washington on the 30th, MacArthur, in a personal appeal to General Marshall for more naval forces to enable him to redress a general situation which he considered was going badly for his forces, made the following ungenerous comment:

> The enemy's defeat at Milne Bay must not be accepted as a measure of relative fighting capacity of the troops involved. The decisive factor was the complete surprise obtained over him by our preliminary concentration of superior forces.

Later, in considering General Clowes' report in October, he criticised both the report and Clowes' conduct of the operations.

Blamey wrote guardedly to Rowell on the 1st September:

> It, of course, is extremely hard to get the picture of the whole of the happenings, but it appeared to us here as though, by not acting with great speed, Clowes is liable to have missed the opportunity of dealing completely with the enemy and thus laying himself open to destruction if, after securing a footing, the enemy were able to reinforce their first landing party very strongly.
>
> I think it was this that give rise to some anxiety on the part of Headquarters, South-West Pacific. However, Clowes is to be heartily congratulated on the success of his first action command.

Rowell replied:

> You will probably have seen my letter to Vasey on the matter of Clowes' handling of the show, and after visiting Milne Bay myself, I'm sure that he was right. Inability to move except at a crawl, together with the constant threat of further landings, made it difficult for him to go fast or far.

Appraisal now of all the circumstances involved seems fully to justify Rowell's summing up. Clowes did what he was sent to Milne Bay to do. He completely defeated the Japanese invasion at comparatively light cost to his own forces. In deciding how best to do that he had to make a choice: on the one hand to attempt a spectacular stroke which might smash the initial landings quickly but elsewhere would leave him open to attack which he had every reason to expect as a result of Japanese control of the sea; on the other hand, to tread warily, as he did, waiting until the general position cleared before he delivered his main stroke. Had the torrential rains not clogged all roads and tracks, he could have struck a series of swift, clean blows with his main force, trusting to his mobility to enable him to switch to meet any attack which might develop from another quarter.

There was one factor, however, in the defeat of the Japanese which Clowes controlled only incidentally—the work of Nos. 75 and 76 Squadrons R.A.A.F. He wrote himself:

> I wish here to place on record my appreciation of the magnificent efforts on the part of our R.A.A.F. comrades. The success of the operations was in a great measure due to their untiring and courageous work which has earned the admiration of all who have been associated with them here.

Writing of the operations to General Blamey Rowell said:

> I . . . think that the action of 75 and 76 Squadrons R.A.A.F. on the first day was probably the decisive factor.

And it is now quite clear that the sinking of Japanese barges by the airmen on the morning of 26th August was of great importance; it deprived the Japanese of the means of turning the sea flank of the defenders by moving troops along the coast in the darkness, and prevented these barges being used to ferry men and equipment ashore on later visits by invading naval forces.

The Milne Bay operations were important in their results. Strategically they confined the main Japanese operations in Papua to the Buna-Kokoda area and spelt failure for the Japanese plans to capture Port Moresby. This first land victory over the Japanese since December 1941 had a tonic effect not only for the Australians, but farther afield.[5] Australians had been able to take the measure of the invaders and found them far less formidable in many respects than they had been led to believe, though they recognised that they were brave and determined fighters. Accurate appraisal of Japanese weaknesses and strengths emerged; much was learnt about their equipment.

Of particular interest was the fact that militiamen had taken the first shocks on an uncertain occasion and had shown that they could fight well. Many of them were resourceful and determined soldiers although, as units, they probably lacked that experience and *élan* which enabled the 2/9th and 2/12th Battalions quickly to sum up the strengths and weaknesses of

---

[5] "We were helped, too, by a very cheering piece of news that now reached us, and of which, as a morale raiser, I made great use. In August and September 1942, Australian troops had, at Milne Bay in New Guinea, inflicted on the Japanese their first undoubted defeat on land. If the Australians, in conditions very like ours, had done it, so could we. Some of us may forget that of all the Allies it was Australian soldiers who first broke the spell of the invincibility of the Japanese Army; those of us who were in Burma have cause to remember."—Field Marshal Sir William Slim, *Defeat into Victory* (1956), pp. 187-8. Slim was then commanding the XV Indian Corps in Arakan.

the invaders, adapt themselves to counter the one and exploit the other, and to drive home a series of attacks.

However, although September thus saw the Japanese attacks thrown back both at Milne Bay and on Guadalcanal it was by no means certain that the Allies could continue to hold either place, and, at the same time, the Japanese thrust across the Papuan mountains was developing successfully for the invaders. From the beginning of the Guadalcanal fighting MacArthur had been left with virtually no naval strength at all. After the Japanese landed at Milne Bay he had to weigh the necessity for reinforcements against the risk of sending them under the protection of a single destroyer, *the only sizeable surface craft then available in the South-West Pacific Area.* On 6th September he radioed General Marshall personally.

> Due to lack of maritime resources, I am unable to increase ground forces in New Guinea as I cannot maintain them . . . it is imperative that shipping and naval forces for escort duty be increased to ensure communication between the Australian mainland and the south coast of New Guinea. With these additional naval facilities I can despatch large ground reinforcements to New Guinea with the object of counter-infiltration towards the north, and at the same time make creeping advances along the north coast with small vessels and marine amphibious forces. Such action will secure a situation which otherwise is doubtful. If New Guinea goes the results will be disastrous.

But MacArthur had little chance of getting the naval forces he sought while the struggle for the Solomons continued. And in any event Admiral King was unwilling to entrust his precious aircraft carriers to the command of MacArthur or any other army officer who might commit them to unjustifiable risks. This was a main reason why the first offensive had been undertaken under Admiral Ghormley in the Solomons and not under General MacArthur in New Guinea.[6] However MacArthur's efforts to get additional forces of all kinds were continual. In these efforts he had the unfailing support of Mr Curtin who was disturbed at what seemed to be the lack of appreciation on the part of Britain and America of the importance of the South-West Pacific. This lack seemed to him to stem from the policy "Beat Hitler first". On 28th May Dr Evatt had cabled to Curtin the text of an agreement between Great Britain and America expressing this policy and then wrote:

> The existence of this written agreement came as a great surprise to myself and, I have no doubt, to you. We were not consulted about the matter.

He quoted a document relating to the grand strategy which had been agreed upon, which set out the reasons why the British and American leaders considered that full-scale invasion of Australia was unlikely. He doubted the cogency of some of the arguments used and concluded that the document revealed the background against which MacArthur's directive was drafted; the strategy it defined was primarily defensive in character; the offensive was to take place in the future. He said that General Marshall

---

[6] For a well-documented discussion of this problem see J. A. Isely and P. A. Crowl, *The U.S. Marines and Amphibious War* (1951), pp. 87-8.

was the main protagonist of the grand strategy which had been defined; that Admiral King was sceptical of it and resolved to concentrate on the Pacific war against Japan.

Evatt also repeated hearty assurances by Mr Churchill of British support to Australia if that should become necessary. Apparently as evidence of his good faith, Churchill had arranged to ship to Australia in June three squadrons of Spitfires and fully maintain them. By the end of June, however, in view of the deterioration of the British position in the Middle East, he had decided to postpone fulfilment of that offer. Curtin demurred without avail. On 27th August he asked Churchill what his plans were for the concentration of a naval force in the Pacific so that the Allies might bring to bear at a vital point forces superior to those of their enemies, stating that it would be evident from the Coral Sea, Midway and Solomon Islands naval engagements that operations in the Pacific were leading to a naval clash which might well decide the course of the conflict in the Pacific. Churchill replied that a Japanese incursion into the Indian Ocean was still possible; that the British had had to move a division and one armoured brigade from India to the Persia-Iraq command; the flow of shore-based aircraft into the Indian Ocean had been affected by the position in the Middle East; the British plans for reinforcement of the Eastern Fleet had had to be postponed because of Malta's needs and because of operations which were contemplated for the near future. He concluded that the time was not opportune for the transfer of British naval forces from the Indian Ocean to the Pacific.

Before he received this reply Curtin was informed by MacArthur that 30 fighter planes, all bombers which were then en route to the S.W.P.A., and the ground forces intended for the S.W.P.A. during the next two months had all been diverted elsewhere. MacArthur had protested to the Joint Chiefs of Staff and he asked Curtin to make representations himself to President Roosevelt. This the Australian Prime Minister, a harassed suppliant, did, pointing out that 607,000 of 1,529,000 Australian men between the ages of 18 and 45 had been enlisted in the fighting forces, and saying:

> In the absence of knowledge of what is contemplated in the SWPA in the general scheme of global strategy, we feel apprehensive regarding the capacity of the Forces assigned to the SWPA to ensure the security of Australia as a base. . . .
> We have two of your splendid American Army Divisions in Australia. . . . The total number of United States Army and Air Corps troops is 98,000. We are deeply grateful for their presence but on the general question of the strength necessary for the SWPA, I would respectfully point out, Mr President, that Australia's capacity to help herself has been limited by that fact that 48,000 men are still serving overseas [Middle East] and our casualties in dead, missing and prisoners of war total 37,000 or an aggregate of 85,000.

The President's reply, however, was no more encouraging than Mr Churchill's had been.

> I have given very careful consideration to the situation in the SWPA as presented in your two messages . . . and fully appreciate the anxiety which you must naturally feel with regard to the security of Australia.
> It would appear from your messages that Mr Churchill has already communicated

to you the decisions of the Combined Chiefs of Staff in regard to the immediate employment of the British Eastern Fleet. This employment precludes reinforcement by British forces of the United States Pacific Fleet at the present time. Since it is clear that the United States Pacific Fleet is unable to provide a superior naval force solely concerned with the defence of Australia and New Zealand, the Combined Chiefs of Staff have carefully considered the necessity for and possibility of increasing the ground and air forces required for the territorial defence of Australia. . . .

After considering all the factors involved, I agree with the conclusions of the Combined Chiefs of Staff that your present armed forces, assuming that they are fully equipped and effectively trained, are sufficient to defeat the present Japanese force in New Guinea and to provide for the security of Australia against an invasion on the scale that the Japanese are capable of launching at this time or in the immediate future.

The present operations in the Solomons area are designed to strengthen our position in lines of communication leading to Australia and therefore, if successful, should contribute to its security. Projected reinforcements for these operations will further strengthen the Allied position in the SWP and will create favourable conditions for more extensive operations against the enemy as appropriate means become available.

Present commitments of shipping are such that it is not possible to move additional troops to Australia now or in the immediate future. Every effort is being made to ensure uninterrupted flow of supplies, equipment and forces committed to your area. . . . I am confident that you will appreciate fully the necessity of rigidly pursuing our overall strategy that envisages the early and decisive defeat of Germany in order that we can quickly undertake an "all-out" effort in the Pacific.

The logic of the general stand taken by Churchill and Roosevelt—particularly in the light of later events—is difficult to assail. More open to criticism, however, is the summary manner in which they relegated Australia to a position of ignorance and voicelessness in relation to their planning. Not only was Australia an active and effective belligerent in her own right but, in particular, she was a loyal and spontaneous supporter of Great Britain—and deserving, therefore, at Mr Churchill's hands at least, of more considerate treatment. A fuller confidence would have allayed in some measure the alarm of one devoted Allied leader and secured an easier unfolding of Allied strategy.

It would no doubt have comforted the leaders in the South-West Pacific to know that, as a result partly of the opposition of the United States Navy to the decision to concentrate against Hitler first and partly of the need to oppose the renewed Japanese thrusts, far more American troops were overseas in the Pacific than in the Atlantic zones at this time. By the end of September five American divisions were in the South and South-West Pacific areas and four more in Hawaii. Only four were overseas in the Atlantic—two in Northern Ireland, one in England and one in Iceland. By early December of 57 United States Army Air Force groups deployed outside the American continents 23 were in the Pacific areas or the China-India theatre, and in addition nearly all the American naval air arm overseas was concentrated in the Pacific.

However, by September 1942, there was still cause for unease on the north-east approaches to Australia. What of developments in the north-west where the Japanese had reached Timor in February and where, in April, India had been facing her most dangerous hour?

In Timor Japanese activity did not seem to presage movement towards Australia. There were no unduly large concentrations of forces there, although this in itself was not necessarily significant since an invasion force would probably assemble farther north in the Indies. The Australians of Sparrow Force, who had dramatically broken their silence in April, were active in harassing their enemies and were a fruitful source of information. Nevertheless the proximity of Japanese forces facing Darwin from Timor constituted an uneasy situation for Australia and, at the least, the Japanese occupation of the island facilitated air attacks on northern Australia.

By mid-September, however, a virtual stalemate still existed on the immediate north-west approaches. But these approaches were only the southern extremity of a line which extended north-west through the Indies, Malaya and Burma to the north-eastern borders of India—a line which, after the Burma Army had completed its withdrawal across the Indian frontier into Assam by the 20th May, was held by the Japanese throughout its entire length. And developments elsewhere along that line, particularly in Burma where events so closely affected India, were of great importance to Australia.

By June there was some improvement in the situation in Burma and India which had looked so grave a short time before. The Japanese had shown no signs of mounting a seaborne attack against India and monsoon weather made it improbable that they would attempt this for some months, if at all. The capture of Madagascar, though it had delayed reinforcements for India, had removed a potential menace to her lines of communication with Great Britain.

As the year went on, however, the Congress-inspired disturbances of August tied up a great deal of the army strength in India on internal security duties. Another major cause for concern was the deterioration of the Allied position in the Middle East. An offer of assistance there by General Wavell was accepted. An even greater threat to India than that of a German advance through Egypt, however, was the German advance to the Caucasus which menaced Persia and Iraq. In September the 5th Indian Division and the 7th Armoured Brigade left India for Iraq.

Nevertheless Wavell was not without hope of being able to launch an offensive into Burma. As a preliminary he had determined in June to reoccupy Fort Hertz in the extreme north of Burma. Because of the lack of roads this had to be an airborne operation. A small parachute detachment was dropped by air to prepare the landing ground and the occupation took place in September. The latter part of 1942 saw Wavell in a far more favourable position than could have been hoped for in the earlier part of the year with Japan temporarily extended to the limit of her reach.

In the face of extraordinary difficulties, effective steps had begun on 8th April to substitute an air route over the Himalayas for the Burma Road. This "air lift" operated in reverse in a most interesting fashion. The Japanese advance into Burma had cut off part of the Chinese forces which had been fighting there. These were then concentrated in India for re-equipping and training by the United States. As this project got under way additional equipment for the Chinese Army accumulated. It was found impracticable to transport this to China. It was decided, therefore, to move the Chinese troops to the equipment rather than follow the more usual procedure of moving the equipment to the troops. This "reverse" procedure was so successfully carried out that, as 1942 advanced, General Joseph W. Stilwell, the American Chief of Staff to Generalissimo Chiang Kai-shek, had built a Chinese corps of approximately 30,000 men round the original nucleus in India.

In general, then, by September of 1942, it was clear that the Japanese inability or reluctance to attempt to reach beyond the north-western borders of Burma, and the growing Allied strength in that area, meant that the decisive battles during the next few months would probably be fought in the South and South-West Pacific. There the Japanese were still on the move, and there a grim struggle of attrition at sea had already developed which was to determine the shape of the future. It was not merely a question of which side would lose the most ships and aircraft. The vital question was going to be which side could build replacements more quickly. At the time, however, most Australians knew little of the true significance of this struggle. The Japanese advance over the mountains of Papua held their attention.

CHAPTER 6

WITHDRAWAL TO IORIBAIWA

WHILE the militiamen of Maroubra Force, fighting hard, were being pushed back along the Kokoda Track towards the crest of the mountain range as the difficult days of August advanced, A.I.F. veterans from the Middle East were hurrying to their assistance. Since early in May the 7th Division had been concentrated in south Queensland. There, their commander, Major-General Allen, had had them at work preparing to meet possible invasion and training in what were conceived (largely from the lessons of Malaya) to be the elements of the new kind of warfare in which they expected later to engage. Allen had been driving them hard in rough tropical country near Brisbane. He was an able soldier with wide infantry experience in two wars: Gallipoli and France in the first; North Africa, Greece and Syria in the second. In 1939 and 1940 he had raised and trained the 16th Brigade; when it was put into the field in the Middle East in 1940 it was the best trained of the 6th Division's formations. Allen was animated at all times by a burning loyalty to his officers and men.

Except among the key men there was no knowledge that the 7th Division was setting out for New Guinea when, on 3rd August, the units of the 18th and 21st Brigades were given embarkation orders. They were told—and accepted—that they were going farther north by sea as part of their training. But they moved with remarkable efficiency for, after a difficult journey by road, the first flights of both brigades had streamlined themselves into ships which were waiting at Brisbane and were at sea by the early afternoon of the 6th. Later the convoy split and while the ships carrying the 2/10th Battalion of the 18th Brigade sheered off to Milne Bay those bearing the 2/14th and 2/16th Battalions of the 21st Brigade continued northwards to Port Moresby.

Brigadier Potts and his brigade major, Challen,[1] who arrived at Port Moresby by air on 8th August, had only four clear days in which to prepare for the arrival of their 21st Brigade. And they needed every moment since apparently New Guinea Force had received little warning of the brigade's coming and had made few preparations to receive it. Potts, who had been warned what his role was to be, had his brigade staged into the Itiki area when the battalions began to arrive on the 13th. There he was within easy distance of the end of the motor road, just past Ilolo, and the beginning of the mountain track which led onward and upward to Kokoda.

On the 15th his instructions were confirmed and amplified. He was told that an estimated 1,500 Japanese had so far opposed the Australian forces in the Owen Stanleys and that some 3,000 reinforcements had been landed at Gona on the 13th, although what proportion of fighting troops

---
[1] Lt-Col H. B. Challen, MBE, VX138. 2/8 Bn; CO 2/14 Bn 1942-43; GSO1 (Liaison) I and II Corps, NGF during 1943-45. Manufacturer's agent; of Melbourne; b. Daylesford, Vic, 26 Nov 1906.

was in that total was not known; that the Japanese obviously intended either to advance on Port Moresby or hold the Kokoda Pass to prevent an Allied advance on Buna and Gona; that the 39th Battalion and the Papuans had withdrawn to Isurava, and that the 53rd Battalion was then moving up the track and was due to be concentrated in the Isurava area by the 20th. He was ordered: "21st Brigade will recapture Kokoda with a view to facilitating further operations against Buna and Gona." On his arrival in the forward area he was to assume command of Maroubra Force.

By this time (15th August) the brigade was assembled at Itiki, the 2/27th Battalion having arrived on the 14th. It was only as they settled in their camp area that the men began to form some idea of what lay ahead. Their camp was an open area of ground in which they could sort themselves out, and ahead of them the mountains rose. They heard something about the fighting; the reflective purposefulness of men going into battle settled over them. They discussed and experimented with the arrangements and composition of the loads which they must carry and from this evolved a standard pack. All they could learn of the country and conditions before them came from disconnected scraps of information, from the study of a single air photograph which had been made available to the brigade, from a track graph which they later proved inaccurate, and from Major Elliott-Smith who had just come back down the track.

On the 16th Lieut-Colonel Key[2]—quietly confident, an original officer of the 2/8th Battalion who had served in Libya, Greece and Crete and had taken command of the 2/14th just as the battalion was preparing to leave the Middle East—got his men moving from Itiki, the first of the 21st Brigade to start across the Kokoda Track. They numbered 24 officers and 517 men, their carrier platoon and most of the mortar platoon having been left behind with the normal "Left out of Battle" component of the battalion and certain other elements which could not be used in the mountains. (Some of these, with portions of similar groups left by the other battalions of the brigade, were formed later into the 21st Brigade Composite Company.) They left the motor transport just past Ilolo and set out for Uberi. Many of them were carrying loads of up to 70 pounds. This was the easiest part of the track, but the mud dragged at them and their heavy burdens pressed them down so that soon they could feel their knees shaking. The late afternoon, however, found them at Uberi and in high spirits.

The next day tried them sorely, as they began to climb the "golden stairs" which had been cut into the long mountainside leading upwards from Uberi. The track rose 1,200 feet in the first three miles, dropped then some 1,600 feet, rose about 2,000 feet in the last four miles. Of this stretch the 2/14th's historian later wrote:

> The golden stairs consisted of steps varying from ten to eighteen inches in height. The front edge of the step was a small log held by stakes. Behind the log was a puddle of mud and water. Some of the stakes had worked loose, leaving the logs

---

[2] Lt-Col A. S. Key, VX148. 2/8 Bn and CO 2/14 Bn 1942. Assistant sales manager; of Armadale, Vic; b. Hawthorn, Vic, 1 Jul 1906. Presumed died in 1943 while prisoner of war.

Near Owers' Corner the road ended and the track across the Owen Stanleys zigzagged in its sharp descent to Uberi.
(*Australian War Memorial*)

Native carriers on the Kokoda Track with a two-man load weighing about 70 lbs.
(*Australian War Memorial*)

Kokoda village and

(Allied Air Forces S.W.P.A.)

airfield, 14th July 1942.

(*Australian War Memorial*)

A 25-pounder of the 14th Field Regiment. The gun was eventually hauled into position for firing on the Japanese at Ioribaiwa. September 1942.

(*Australian War Memorial*)

Native carrier line at Eora Creek village. The four natives on the right carrying rifles are members of the Royal Papuan Constabulary.

slightly tilted. Anyone who stood on one of these skidded and fell with a whack in the mud, probably banging his head against a tree or being hit on the head with his own rifle. Those who had no sticks soon acquired them, not only to prevent falls, but to allow the arms to help the legs, especially with the higher steps. After the first half dozen steps, it became a matter of sheer determination forcing the body to achieve the impossible. It was probably the weight more than the climb, though the climb would have been enough to tire even a lightly loaded man. The rear companies, where the going is always hardest, took twelve hours to complete the nine miles.[3]

Another officer[4] of the battalion said:

Gradually men dropped out utterly exhausted—just couldn't go on. You'd come to a group of men and say 'Come on! We must go on.' But it was physically impossible to move. Many were lying down and had been sick. . . . Many made several trips up the last slope helping others. We began to see some of the tremendous efforts the troops were going to make to help the lesser ones in. Found many of the battalion [at Ioribaiwa] lying exhausted, some ate, others lay and were sick, others just lay. Some tried to eat and couldn't.

Early next morning the battalion was on the move again, less only one man (an appendicitis case).

Ahead lay the Maguli Range, a climb of two thousand two hundred feet, of which the track report said, "Impossible for white men carrying loads; natives may carry up to fifteen pounds." Loads were hoisted on and the thin line of slowly moving khaki started up the range.

By five o'clock in the afternoon the last man had reached Nauro. Some considered that the eighteen hundred foot drop into Nauro was as bad as the climb. Under the heavy loads the jolting caused by steps often more than a foot in height made shin muscles red hot, while knees threatened to give way, and stomachs were churned up.[5]

At the end of the sixth of such days (from Efogi following the new track which Kienzle had opened) the 2/14th settled at Myola where, two days later, Lieut-Colonel Caro's[6] 2/16th Battalion joined them.

Brigadier Potts was sharing equally with his men the toil of the journey. There was great strength in his thick-set frame, despite his 46 years, an even greater strength of spirit behind the round, cheerful English face, the blue eyes which smiled from beneath grey hair cut *en brosse*. He had served through Gallipoli and on to the end of the Great War, settled on a Western Australian farm between the wars, joined the 2/16th Battalion as a company commander on its formation, distinguished himself in Syria, and been promoted to command the 21st Brigade early in April.

With characteristic energy, Potts had overtaken the 2/14th Battalion at Menari by the evening of the 19th although he had not left Ilolo until the 17th. By that time he was beginning to feel uneasy about supply. He had been told that 1,000 rations would be available at the end of each daily stage—Uberi, Ioribaiwa, Nauro, Menari, Efogi—and 40,000 at

---
[3] W. B. Russell, *The Second Fourteenth Battalion* (1948), pp. 124-5.
[4] Capt P. E. Rhoden.
[5] Russell, pp. 125-6.
[6] Lt-Col A. E. Caro, WX3373; 2/16 Bn (CO 1942). Accountant; of Nedlands, WA; b. Maylands, WA, 29 Jun 1905.

Myola and forward. As he went on he found that not only was this not so but—and the bitterness of his words was foreign to his character:

> At the stations at the end of the daily stages arrangements for our reception varied considerably but never at any time were they even satisfactory. The staffs of these stations had in most cases not been notified of our impending arrival and, where they had been, displayed little interest and gave the minimum of help. This was particularly so at Myola where the cooperation of the staff was so important. Prompt action was taken to remove the existing staffs and replace them with efficient personnel. A particularly bright exception to the above criticism was the experience at Menari where everything possible was done to assist the troops, despite the lack of warning.[7]

Potts found also that, although the cold was severe, only 80 blankets were available at Efogi and forward although he had been assured that adequate supplies of these had been laid down. Pushing on to Myola on the 21st his worst fears were confirmed when he found a completely inadequate reserve of rations and ammunition there and that nothing had been dropped since 16th August although the weather had been good. He determined to hold his brigade at and in rear of Myola until the supply situation had cleared.

Meanwhile headquarters of the 7th Division had been established at Port Moresby on the 18th and Potts informed them of his supply difficulties. Then he himself, with his brigade reconnaissance party, went on by way of Kienzle's track past Templeton's Crossing and found Brigadier Porter and Maroubra Force Headquarters at Alola. He took over command of Maroubra Force on the 23rd. At once he sent Major Cameron back to divisional headquarters to stress his supply needs. On the same day he ordered the 2/16th Battalion forward to Myola, so as to have his two battalions as far forward as possible.

Meanwhile the A.A.S.C. and ordnance officers at Myola had been feverishly checking their stocks, having, they asserted, not been told that the 21st Brigade was arriving in the area. Major Fargher,[8] the New Guinea Force representative, arrived at Myola on the 23rd, took charge, and told headquarters that only four days' rations were held there. Potts confirmed this and added that only two days' reserves were held forward of Myola. He then had a supply plan drawn up on the basis that he required seven days' reserve rations for 2,000 troops and 80 natives at Alola and one day's reserve at Eora Creek and Templeton's Crossing for the same number of troops and for 250 and 270 natives respectively. His staff told him that it would take seven days to build up such reserves and that 800 more native carriers would be needed forward of Myola.

Thus was brought to a head at a most critical time the greatest single problem of the campaign in the Owen Stanleys—supply.

It will be recalled how, up to that time, Lieutenant Kienzle and Major Elliott-Smith had been working hard and effectively to build up and operate

---

[7] 21st Brigade, Report on Operations—Owen Stanley Range.
[8] Col D. B. Fargher, OBE, NX400. (1st AIF: Pte 39 Bn.) DAQMG I Corps 1942; AQMG II Corps 1943-44, First Army 1944-45. Insurance inspector; of Goulburn, NSW; b. Melbourne, 5 Jan 1899.

native carrier lines across the mountains. Although Kienzle's discovery of Myola had given rise to high hopes that aircraft might be used to carry the main burden of supply, Potts had now revealed that the performance had fallen far short of hopes. Nevertheless it was clear to the men on the spot that only aircraft could save the situation for the carriers clearly could not carry the load required.

General Rowell soon afterwards told General Blamey that, at 29th August, the daily maintenance requirement of Maroubra Force was 15,000 pounds (and that of Kanga Force 5,000 pounds). To meet the Maroubra Force requirements, with native carriers on the basis of a six- to eight-day carry of a maximum of 40 pounds a native, would necessitate the use of at least 3,000 carriers, without allowing for the porterage of their own rations, wastage among them and other possibilities. Unless this number could be greatly increased the forward force could not be strengthened nor could even the smallest reserve of supplies be built up. But Rowell wanted to build up 20 days' reserves and that would require the transport of 200,000 pounds more of rations and ammunition. Such a carry, spread over 20 days, would demand the use of at least an additional 2,000 natives and still would not allow for any increase in the strength of the force. Clearly the entire Australian operations in the Owen Stanleys would bog down completely unless effective alternative or supplementary means of supply could be found.

Maintenance by air had already been limited by the lack of landing grounds and dropping areas, by the problem of developing efficient dropping methods, and even more by the shortage of aircraft. General Morris had struggled with these problems. On 16th August Rowell had emphasised to Blamey how lack of air transports was a limiting factor. Blamey wrote at once to General MacArthur and General Sutherland. On the 23rd, before Blamey had received a reply, Rowell pressed him again, saying that, since 17th August, only one plane had been available, and that one for the two preceding days only. On the 24th MacArthur told Blamey that he had arranged to place at Port Moresby six Douglas Dauntless dive-bombers (A-24s), one Flying Fortress and two transports. He wrote:

> With these planes it is estimated that a minimum of 20,000 pounds of supplies per day can be delivered to Kagi and Wau. There are available in Australia only thirty transport planes at the present time. Of these an average of not more than 50 per cent are available at any one time. Air supply must necessarily be considered an emergency rather than a normal means of supply. Consequently every effort should be made by the GOC, NGF, to develop other means of supply.

The figure of 20,000 pounds used by MacArthur was that which Rowell had recorded as his daily maintenance requirement for both Maroubra and Kanga Forces. Even with the additional aircraft operating, therefore, he would still require the services of some thousands of carriers if his force were to be increased in the Owen Stanleys or his reserves built up there. However, stores could not be delivered by air beyond Myola because there was no place at which they could be landed or even dropped at that time. Even, therefore, if sufficient aircraft could be provided to fulfil all the supply commitments as far as Myola a long line of carriers would have to continue to operate forward of it. Again a serious complicating factor was that, even under the best conditions, air supply in New Guinea was chancy and unreliable. Rowell signalled Blamey on the 30th:

> Weather and flying conditions into Myola which impose severe strain on pilots prevent more than total number of daily trips (by any one aircraft) of two to Kanga or three to Myola. Difficult to operate at will to either place owing to details loading aircraft and need to arrange fighter cover. . . . Position can deteriorate very quickly if aircraft damaged or bad weather prevents operating for period of few days as has happened recently.

Such, in outline, was the background of the problem which Potts exposed on his way to assume his new command. His revelations caused consternation both at the 7th Division, where General Allen, newly arrived, had been assured by New Guinea Force that supplies had been arranged, and at Force Headquarters, where Rowell himself had been mistakenly secure in his estimate, based partly on information which had been given him on his assumption of command, that by 16th August 25 days' supplies for 2,000 men, together with adequate small arms ammunition, were available at Myola. Rowell's own investigations then confirmed what Potts said. He could explain the lack of air droppings between the 16th and 22nd August because an air raid on the 17th had destroyed or severely damaged the five available transport aircraft. (At the time the hiatus had not appeared to be unduly serious in view of what had been thought to be the satisfactory supply position at Myola.) He could not, however, explain the failure to build up reserves before the 16th and could only report finally:

> The closest inquiry disclosed that the rations . . . had, in fact, been dispatched from Moresby and it can only be assumed that, from causes unknown, they were dropped elsewhere than at Myola and were not recovered.

It is likely, however, that the rations were never dropped at all and the explanation lay in faulty work by an inexperienced staff. New Guinea Force should never have remained in ignorance of the true position for a day. As it was, the real state of affairs had remained unknown for a week and had then been revealed only through an agency outside the Force organisation itself. Potts was observing basic principles in testing his supply system before he committed his forces. He should not have been given orders which, through no fault of his own, he could not fulfil. His initial orders had been for offensive action. Now, on the 24th, Rowell ordered Allen to withdraw the 39th Battalion as soon as possible so as to relieve the supply situation, and to undertake no forward offensive movement until 30 days' reserves had been built up for him at Myola. Rowell added that only 300 of the 800 carriers asked for by Potts could be spared from the Moresby-Myola Line of Communication until the Myola reserve was in sight and air deliveries were more reliable; that there could be no question of sending forward the third battalion of the 21st Brigade until the supply situation was sufficiently secure to enable offensive operations to be undertaken. Such security, his written instructions stressed, was "NOT in sight".

Thus maladministration of supply undermined Potts' position even before he met his enemies and had the effect of cabining and confining all his activities in the forward areas. Immediately, by causing his role to be changed from an offensive to a defensive one, it lost him the initiative; it reduced his force below the minimum he required and to a strength, he claimed, inferior to that of the Japanese opposing him; it delayed the arrival in the actual battle area of his tried 2/14th and 2/16th Battalions; it denied him the use of his 2/27th Battalion at a crucial time.

He now considered three plans: to leave the 53rd and 39th Battalions in position at Alola and Isurava respectively and the 2/14th and 2/16th in position covering Myola until supply was assured; to relieve the worn but courageous 39th Battalion with one of the 21st Brigade battalions, leave the fresh 53rd in position and hold the other A.I.F. battalion as a reserve; to leave both militia battalions in position and deploy the 2/14th and 2/16th on the high ground east and west of them. He rejected the first plan because it would mean exposing the exhausted and depleted 39th to a strong attack and the third because of insufficient supplies. He adopted the second—with the untried 53rd Battalion as one of its pivots.

It will be recalled that Lieut-Colonel Honner had found this battalion moving up the track as he himself went forward and had left them at Alola. Porter, in his turn, had also left them there. When Potts arrived at Alola their "B" Company was on the right of the track, "D" Company was on a ridge forward of Alola, "C" Company was responsible for the high ground on the left of Alola, "A" Company had the task of covering the track from Eora Creek in the rear. The battalion had been told to patrol to the right along the branch track which led from

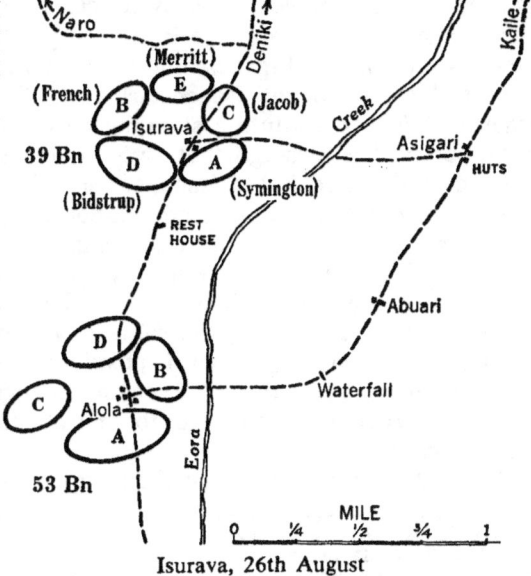

Isurava, 26th August

Alola through Abuari and Missima to Kaile; forward through the 39th Battalion's positions to Deniki; along the track to Naro on the left. By dusk of the 23rd they had had two minor contacts only—one on the track to Deniki and one near Kaile. The track leading to Kaile was particularly difficult. From Alola it plunged 1,000 feet or more down a bush-covered, rugged, 45-degree slope to the bed of Eora Creek. It crossed the torrent by way of a slippery log bridge. Its way up the opposite side of the great V of the Eora Creek was closed in by bush, was treacherous and so steep that in places a climber must use his hands. About 1,500 feet above the creek bed was the Abuari waterfall, where a mountain stream plunged over a rock face which rose almost sheer for about 100 feet; its spray veiled the hillside and the falling water made a great noise. The track passed just in front of the main fall and through the spray over a slippery ledge of rock. On the other side of the fall it edged round a wall of sheer rock which rose high above it. Soon afterwards it came to the little village of Abuari and went on through the bush and over the rough mountainside to Missima and thence to Kaile.

In accordance with the plan he had decided upon Potts proposed to leave the 53rd Battalion's role unchanged, to relieve the 39th with the 2/14th and hold the 2/16th in reserve.

On the morning of the 24th Lieutenant MacDonald[9] of the 53rd, with 20 of his men, moved forward through Honner's positions towards Deniki. He was engaged by a Japanese patrol one hour's walk along the track. He reported later that the Japanese let his men pass their most forward elements before they fired and killed his leading scout, Private MacGraw;[1] that Private Bostock,[2] the second scout, then took cover and killed four Japanese as they moved towards MacGraw's body while the rest of the patrol engaged other Japanese in dug in positions. MacDonald later withdrew his men as the Japanese moved around them.

Next day Lieutenant Isaachsen[3] and 20 men, with Captain Ahern[4] attached, left to constitute a standing patrol at Kaile. That night the battalion received a message that two Japanese platoons had attacked the patrol at Kaile, had killed Isaachsen and had wounded one man. Lieut-Colonel Ward,[5] the battalion commander, signalled orders that the party was to fall back on Missima and remain there as a standing patrol but the message did not get through as by this time the wireless set which had been established at Missima was off the air.

On the track to Deniki, the same day, Sergeant Meani[6] took 20 men out through Honner's forward positions. He found MacGraw's body propped against a tree in such a way as to suggest that he had been merely wounded. When his men tried to recover the body they were attacked and scattered.

By the 26th it was clear that the comparative quiet of the preceding few

---

[9] Capt N. A. W. MacDonald, NX119142; 53 and 55/53 Bns. Accountant; of Lithgow, NSW; b. Petersham, NSW, 11 Jul 1906.

[1] Pte D. J. MacGraw, N38257; 53 Bn. Labourer; of Concord, NSW; b. Auburn, NSW, 27 Sep 1918. Killed in action 24 Aug 1942.

[2] Pte H. C. Bostock, N23043. 53, 39 Bns. Banana worker; of Carool, NSW; b. Murwillumbah, NSW, 3 Aug 1915.

[3] Lt A. Isaachsen, SX2769. 2/10, 53 Bns. Bank clerk; of Hawthorn, SA; b. Minlaton, SA, 4 Feb 1918. Killed in action 25 Aug 1942.

[4] Maj F. J. Ahern, NX127372. 53, 36 Bns. Public servant; of Woollahra, NSW; b. Sydney, 10 Jun 1920.

[5] Lt-Col K. H. Ward, NX127633; CO 53 Bn. Clerk; of Old Guildford, NSW; b. Balmain, NSW, 5 May 1903. Killed in action 27 Aug 1942.

[6] Sgt F. W. Meani, N18111. 53, 39, 2/4 Bns. Clerk; of Botany, NSW; b. Botany, 8 Oct 1921.

days was breaking along the whole front. On the right MacDonald moved out along the Kaile Track with 20 men but returned in the evening and reported that the wireless set at Missima had been smashed and there was no trace of the men who had been manning it, that his patrol had killed three Japanese, and that Japanese had penetrated forward along the track toward Abuari. As darkness was falling Captain Cairns'[7] "B" Company were ordered forward to meet the enemy penetrations.

While the 53rd was thus occupied action was flaring on the 39th Battalion's front. There Lieutenant Simonson's platoon, constituting the forward patrol some 40 to 50 minutes out along the track to Deniki, was attacked during the morning. They were quickly reinforced by Lieutenant Sword's[8] platoon while Lieutenant Clarke,[9] the "next for duty" in the forward position, stood by. After a five-hour fight the attackers withdrew. Later in the afternoon Clarke, returning down the track from a reconnaissance to the forward patrol position, routed an enemy party at the Deniki-Naro track junction. Apparently he hunted down the remnants of the broken group with cold-blooded purpose for he later reported that he and one of his men had killed eight of them in a native garden as darkness was falling.

The remainder of the battalion was not unmolested during this period. Simultaneously with the opening of the attack on the forward patrol, a Japanese mountain gun bombarded the main positions and killed two of the defenders. It opened fire again as the afternoon waned. But by that time new hope had come to Honner's weary men for the first of the 2/14th battalion were arriving. About 5 p.m. Captain Dickenson[1] with his "C" Company relieved Captain Jacob in the right forward position at Isurava. At the same time Captain Nye[2] was leading the second company of the 2/14th into the Alola area where they bivouacked for the night.

That morning Potts had signalled Allen that the relief of the 39th Battalion by the 2/14th was to begin that day and

> Condition of 39th Battalion men weak due continuous work lack warm clothing blankets shelters curtailed rations and wet every night monotonous diet combined with comparative static role last fortnight.

Later in the day he signalled:

> 53rd Battalion training and discipline below standard required for action. Only use for holding objective aerodrome etc. For these reasons consider it imperative 2/27th move to Myola as my only fighting reserve.

At 6.15, with an intensified threat from the right and from the front, and with his own headquarters, at Alola, under shell fire, he repeated his

---
[7] Capt T. F. Cairns, NX140277. 53, 55/53 Bns. Clerk; of Queanbeyan, NSW; b. Newstead, Vic, 27 Oct 1900.
[8] Lt R. H. Sword, VX100093; 39 Bn. Traveller; of Box Hill, Vic; b. Blackburn, Vic, 20 Feb 1914. Killed in action 9 Dec 1942.
[9] Lt D. R. Clarke, VX16944. 2/14, 39 and 2/2 Bns. Clerk; of Wagoora, Qld; b. Lauriston, Vic, 16 Apr 1916.
[1] Capt H. E. Dickenson, VX14110; 2/14 Bn. Bank clerk; of Sale, Vic; b. Sale, 20 Feb 1913.
[2] Capt C. C. P. Nye, VX14096; 2/14 Bn. Railway employee; of Ormond, Vic; b. Port Melbourne, 1 Nov 1916. Killed in action 8 Sep 1942.

request for the 2/27th. In reply Allen, responsible for the defence of Port Moresby itself from seaborne and airborne attack, referred to the Japanese landings which had taken place early that morning at Milne Bay, under instructions from New Guinea Force stated that it was inadvisable to send the 2/27th yet, and suggested that the relief of the 39th and their return to Port Moresby be expedited.

As the morning of the 27th advanced Potts was growing anxious about the position in the 53rd Battalion sector. At 8 a.m. he ordered Colonel Ward to retake Missima and Ward told Captain King[3] to move his "D" Company through Cairns' position for that purpose. King did not start until nearly 10. By 2 p.m. he was moving round Cairns' right flank to attack high ground south-east of Abuari from which fire was reported to be holding up Cairns' advance. At 3.30 Ward reported to Potts that the two companies were moving on to Missima and, believing this to be correct, himself set out along the track with Lieutenant Logan.[4] But the two forward companies had failed in their tasks because (the battalion diarist records) of

(1) Nature of country (2) Heavy MMG fire by enemy which could not be located (3) Lack of offensive spirit and general physical condition of troops.

At 3.45 a runner reported to battalion headquarters that Ward and Logan had been ambushed and killed. Soon afterward Major Hawkins,[5] administering command of the battalion, told brigade headquarters that the Japanese had come round the waterfall near Abuari and were making for the creek crossing between Abuari and Alola and for Alola itself. He was ordered to hold Abuari, the waterfall area and the crossing, pending the arrival of the 2/16th Battalion which, by that time, was moving forward behind the 2/14th. As Hawkins moved another company forward to hold the creek crossing Captain Buckler's[6] "A" Company of the 2/14th took over their old positions.

While the right flank was thus threatened the forward and left flank positions were hard pressed. At first light the Japanese had reoccupied the area which had been cleared the previous evening by Clarke and had cut off the two forward platoons, now commanded by Sword. (Simonson had been wounded fighting off attacks during the night and had been sent back.) These platoons fought on. Honner, on Potts' instructions, then attempted to relieve a patrol from Jacob's company, under Lieutenant Pentland, which Potts had ordered the previous day to go out to guard the Isurava-Naro track and bar any enemy approach towards Alola. Lieutenant Davis'[7] platoon from Dickenson's company went, guided by

---

[3] Capt C. J. T. King, NX127375; 53 Bn. Valuer; of Arncliffe, NSW; b. Wagga Wagga, NSW, 3 Jan 1912.

[4] Lt R. L. Logan, NX127634; 53 Bn. Clerk; of Randwick, NSW; b. Glebe Point, NSW, 17 Sep 1918. Killed in action 27 Aug 1942.

[5] Maj C. J. T. Hawkins, NX127370. 53 Bn; 7 MG Bn. Public servant; of Wilberforce, NSW; b. Canterbury, England, 15 Jan 1908.

[6] Lt-Col S. H. Buckler, OBE, VX13637. 2/14 Bn; Staff appts LHQ. Regular soldier; of Coff's Harbour, NSW; b. Coff's Harbour, 12 Feb 1919.

[7] Lt A. J. Davis, VX52941; 2/14 Bn. Noxious weeds inspector; of Leongatha, Vic; b. Yarram, Vic, 7 Jan 1907. Died of wounds 28 Aug 1942.

Sergeant Buchecker,[8] the Intelligence sergeant of the 39th. Davis met heavy opposition. He himself was last seen, wounded, trying to make his way back alone, one of his men was killed, and Sergeant Buchecker was badly wounded. Chaplain Earl and Captain Shera moved out into the dangerous bushland and carried the wounded sergeant back. Captain Nye's company arrived later in the afternoon with orders to push out along the Alola-Naro track. (But Japanese and thick bush prevented their movement and when night came Honner used them to thicken his defences.)

Meanwhile, about 4 p.m., there was a crescendo of Japanese mortar and machine-gun fire, prelude to furious attacks of which the brunt fell on Honner's two left forward companies—Merritt's and French's.[9]

> Across the creek they [the Japanese] swept in a swift thrust that sliced through "E" Company's thin front line, cut off [Lieutenant] Dalby's left platoon and a section of the right platoon and, swarming behind them, forced them forward out of their posts. Through the widening breach poured another flood of the attackers to swirl round the remainder of the right platoon from the rear. They were met with Bren-gun and Tommy-gun, with bayonet and grenade; but still they came, to close with the buffet of fist and boot and rifle-butt, the steel of crashing helmets and of straining, strangling fingers. In this vicious fighting, man to man and hand to hand, Merritt's men were in imminent peril of annihilation. But two quick counter-attacks turned that furious tide. [Sergeant] Kerslake's[1] counter-penetration platoon drove out the enemy breaking through the gap and closed it against further inroads. [Sergeant] Murray's[2] mobile reserve raced up to recapture Dalby's position and was immediately successful. The intruders were hurled back towards the creek, but the relentless conflict in the shadows went on through the waning afternoon until . . . contact was re-established with Dalby's lost platoon which, encircled and outnumbered, had gallantly carried on the fight.[3]

French was now seriously threatened, his men reeling under a series of hammer blows. But they shot their attackers down until bodies cluttered the small open space in front of them. The first of Nye's platoons to return had been sent to strengthen Merritt's left and the second to Bidstrup's right (on the other side of French) so that the reinforced jaws of the companies on French's right and left could force out his assailants. The pressure was already easing when Nye's third platoon was placed under French's command and Captain Cameron's[4] "D" Company of the 2/14th arrived about dark further to strengthen Honner's hard-pressed defences and back up Merritt's tired men.

By nightfall on the 27th, on the right, Cairns and King of the 53rd were out of contact with their battalion and a third company was at the

---

[8] Sgt A. V. Buchecker, VX117676; 39 Bn. Storeman; of Irymple, Vic; b. Mildura, Vic, 22 Jan 1920.

[9] "I was shaving in a river behind the perimeter when the attack came in," said Merritt afterwards. "The CO, also washing there, grinned and said: 'Captain Merritt, will you go up to your company when you've finished your shave? The Japs have just broken through your perimeter.' Honner was the coolest man I've ever seen."

[1] Sgt K. R. Kerslake, VX105399; 39 Bn. Explosives worker; of Lilydale, Vic; b. Lilydale, 12 Feb 1920.

[2] Sgt W. Murray, VX117698. 39 Bn; 2/7 Fd Amb. Draper; of Ballarat, Vic; b. Ballarat, 22 Dec 1914.

[3] "The 39th at Isurava" (*Stand-To*, July-August 1956).

[4] Maj R. W. C. Cameron, VX14030. 2/14 Bn; Movt Control Staff 1944-45. Clerk; of Brisbane; b. Brisbane, 30 Nov 1911.

creek crossing. With Buckler's company of the 2/14th, the rest of the 53rd, except for about 70 men who had not reported in from patrol and some of whom were later found to have taken to the bush, was in position round Alola and patrolling to the left flank. The day had cost the 53rd five killed (including Ward and Logan) and two wounded. On the left Honner's battalion was still holding at Isurava with the three companies of the 2/14th. From the rear the 2/16th Battalion was moving forward with Lieutenant McGee's[5] "A" Company at Eora Creek and Captain Sublet's[6] "B" Company following closely.

On the 28th there was little action on the right flank although from Alola Japanese could be seen moving in the vicinity of Abuari. By 8 a.m. 67 men of Cairns' and King's companies had regained touch with the 53rd and were in position on the track to Abuari patrolling forward to the village. At 11.30 a.m. McGee arrived and at 2 p.m. was pushed across the creek towards Abuari while Buckler led his men forward to Isurava. By nightfall McGee's patrols had entered Abuari without opposition and Sublet was watching his rear.

Just before dark Captain Ahern reported in from Kaile with eighteen men. He stated that, after Isaachsen's death on the 25th, he had held Kaile until dark and had seen the Japanese carry away fourteen of their dead before he withdrew to an ambush position back along the track from which he ultimately made his way back through the 39th positions. His men were exhausted and hungry.

On the left, however, the 28th was not such a quiet day. It had been preceded by desultory bayonet fighting during a night of heavy rain. Japanese fire from dawn until about 8 a.m. prepared the way for a morning attack, probing and testing round the positions. First, two assaults were made on Dickenson's positions. His company thought that each was made by about 100 men. The attackers, soldiers of powerful physique, were supported by wild screeching as they advanced. Dickenson's men thought that they inflicted about 90 casualties. Cameron, Dickenson on his right and Nye on his left, also sustained attacks during the morning and made the Japanese suffer heavily. Savage and continuous thrusts were made at Nye's company, directed mainly at Lieutenant Moore's[7] platoon. Moore beat them back but was killed in doing so.

At the end of this busy morning Colonel Key arrived and took over command of the whole area from Honner (although the latter, knowing the weight of the Japanese thrust and reluctant to leave, convinced Potts that he and his men should remain with Key). As the afternoon advanced Key maintained Dickenson on the right of the track Isurava-Deniki, forward of Isurava, Cameron in the forward and central position, and Nye

---

[5] Capt G. M. McGee, WX3250; 2/16 Bn. Regular soldier; of Launceston, Tas; b. Lemana, via Deloraine, Tas, 20 Nov 1913. Died 7 Sep 1943.
[6] Lt-Col F. H. Sublet, DSO, MC, WX1598; 2/16 Bn (CO 1943-45). Public servant; of Victoria Park, WA; b. Meekatharra, WA, 13 May 1910.
[7] Lt G. G. Moore, VX37973; 2/14 Bn. Clerk; of South Melbourne; b. Newcastle-on-Tyne, England, 6 Jun 1917. Killed in action 28 Aug 1942.

covering the battalion's left flank. The 39th, now only about 250 strong, was disposed to cover Key's rear.

Dickenson and Nye sustained the main afternoon attacks until about 3.30. Then the Japanese rushed Cameron's positions and overran part of Lieutenant Pearce's[8] platoon. But Pearce's men fought back grimly until Lieutenant Hutchison's[9] platoon from Buckler's company in reserve to the east of the track, counter-attacked across their positions and swept away the remaining Japanese.

A clear night found Key's men in good heart, confident of their superiority and adeptly meeting Japanese attempts at infiltration. The battalion had lost one officer and 2 men killed during the day and 12 men wounded. But the Australians considered that they had inflicted far heavier casualties on their enemies.

Next day, the 29th, a difficult position developed on both the right and the left. On the right McGee was in contact by 9 a.m. in the vicinity of Abuari, trying to encircle a Japanese force which he estimated to be about 100 strong. The Japanese were stubborn. They seemed to have at least two heavy machine-guns well dug in and protected. Sublet moved to support McGee and took command of both companies. His men inflicted casualties but suffered themselves and could not advance. At 2.15 Sublet asked that a company of the 53rd go round the waterfall in an attempt to fall upon the Japanese rear. Captain King's was sent. Meanwhile McGee was heavily engaged but the fighting died down later in the afternoon and King

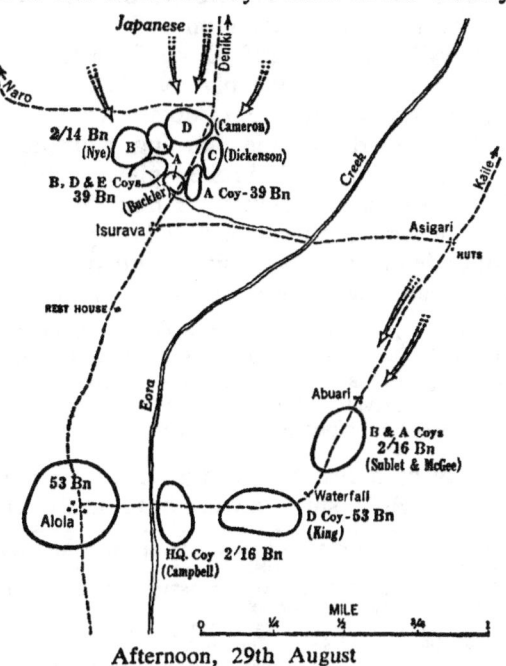

Afternoon, 29th August

reported that he would be in a position to attack at dawn next morning. The day ended in a stalemate with Sublet and McGee withdrawn into a perimeter, King moving on the right, Lieutenant Campbell[1] with Headquarters Company of the 2/16th holding at the creek crossing. During

---

[8] Lt G. E. Pearce, MC, VX52829; 2/14 Bn. Orchardist; of Shepparton, Vic; b. Peebles, Scotland, 17 Oct 1909. Died of wounds 6 Dec 1942.
[9] Capt I. McL. Hutchison, VX13966. 2/14 Bn, Mil Hist Section. Draftsman; of Toorak, Vic; b. Kew, Vic, 19 Dec 1917.
[1] Capt R. P. Campbell, WX2734; 2/16 Bn. Clerk; of Merredin, WA; b. Day Dawn, WA, 13 Dec 1913.

the day the 2/16th companies had lost 7 men killed and one officer and 22 men wounded (mostly from McGee's company) in exchange for an estimated 40 Japanese casualties.

Although the position on the brigade's right was therefore most uneasy none the less the Japanese stroke there seemed to be perhaps in the nature of a diversion to draw away attention from the main thrust on Key's front. There heavy attacks on all companies began early in the morning.

Dickenson, holding Key's right, early beat back a forceful sortie. But the Japanese there thrust again with even greater determination. Lieutenant Cox[2] of Buckler's company came forward with his platoon. He was killed and his platoon was mauled. Corporal Bear[3] took charge of his remaining men and was reported himself to have killed at least 15 Japanese with his Bren gun at point-blank range. But the Japanese still drove hard at Dickenson's company. Lieutenant Boddington[4] and 4 men were killed, many Australians were wounded, and the attackers smashed through the positions which Boddington and Lieutenant Clements[5] had held. Privates "Snowy" Neilson[6] and Bowen[7] of Clements' platoon coolly stood firm to give the rest of the platoon a chance to re-form. Sergeant Thompson[8] led forward a party from Captain Rhoden's[9] Headquarters Company which had arrived during the morning. Corporal Bear and Privates Avery[1] and Kingsbury[2] of Cox's broken platoon insisted on attaching themselves to Thompson and fought with him. Soon after midday the break-through was menacing the whole battalion position. Clements drove in a counter-attack leading a composite group of his own men, Thompson's men and what had been Cox's platoon. As the counter-attack moved Kingsbury

> Rushed forward firing the Bren gun from his hip through terrific machine-gun fire and succeeded in clearing a path through the enemy. Continuing to sweep enemy positions with his fire and inflicting an extremely high number of casualties on them, Private Kingsbury was then seen to fall to the ground shot dead by a bullet from a sniper hiding in the wood.[3]

Mainly as a result of Kingsbury's action the position was then restored.

Meanwhile, since dawn, Cameron's men, on Dickenson's left, had been

---

[2] Lt W. P. Cox, VX32903; 2/16 Bn. Trust officer; of Flemington, Vic; b. Unley, SA, 24 Dec 1913. Killed in action 29 Aug 1942.

[3] Lt L. A. Bear, DCM, MM, VX17821; 2/14 Bn. Die cast operator; of Moonee Ponds, Vic; b. Spotswood, Vic, 26 Nov 1921.

[4] Lt W. G. Boddington, VX39187; 2/14 Bn. Banker; of Auckland, NZ; b. Amberley, NZ, 22 Feb 1909. Killed in action 29 Aug 1942.

[5] Lt J. G. Clements, VX52850; 2/14 Bn. Clerk; of St Kilda, Vic; b. Melbourne, 13 May 1920. Killed in action 28 Nov 1942.

[6] Pte A. J. Neilson, MM, VX51865; 2/14 Bn. Farm labourer; of Albury, NSW; b. Wodonga, Vic, 5 Oct 1919. Died 18 Jan 1943.

[7] Pte L. J. Bowen, VX60124. 2/14 Bn; 2/6 Fd Coy. Timber cutter; of Red Cliffs, Vic; b. St Kilda, Vic, 19 Jun 1919.

[8] Maj R. V. Thompson, VX15269. 2/14, 2/15 Bns. Farmer and grazier; of Moorooduc, Vic; b. Frankston, Vic, 8 Dec 1917.

[9] Lt-Col P. E. Rhoden, OBE, VX14250; 2/14 Bn (CO 1943-45). Solicitor; of Essendon, Vic; b. Essendon, 23 Dec 1914.

[1] Lt A. R. Avery, MM, VX17772; 2/14 Bn. Nurseryman, of Prahran, Vic; b. Armadale, Vic, 7 Apr 1917.

[2] Pte B. S. Kingsbury, VC, VX19139; 2/14 Bn. Real estate sub-agent; of West Preston, Vic; b. Armadale, Vic, 8 Jan 1918. Killed in action 29 Aug 1942.

[3] From the citation notifying Kingsbury's posthumous award of the Victoria Cross.

fighting hard, assisted by one of Buckler's platoons. As the pressure increased Buckler himself hurried forward with another platoon. His men beat at the Japanese with grenades and then drove them back with bayonets.

Farther left Nye was sustaining a series of most determined assaults on his three platoons. Lieutenant Bisset,[4] in the most forward position where Moore had been killed the previous day, beat off attack after attack while Lieutenant Treacy,[5] who had taken over Moore's platoon and was on Bisset's right rear, most skilfully parried every thrust levelled at him.

The afternoon came. The Japanese continued to attack. Dickenson gave ground. Potts ordered "C" Company of the 53rd forward to strengthen Dickenson's stand. The platoons of the 39th Battalion under Sword and Pentland, which had just reported at Alola after having been cut off since the actions of the 27th, hurried back to form a reserve for Key although they were hungry and sick. ("When I saw those poor bastards, tottering on their bleeding, swollen feet, turn round and go straight back to Isurava, I knew they were good," said a member of the 2/16th Battalion afterwards.) Lieutenant Johnston[6] (without orders to do so) led forward a party of physically unfit volunteers from the same battalion and reported that he passed 53rd Battalion men on the way. He told Honner simply, "We heard the battalion was in trouble so we came back".

Elsewhere the defences were yielding. Cameron's company had been broken by heavy attacks which began about 3 p.m. There Private Wakefield,[7] almost single-handed, with his Bren gun disorganised several attacks and inspired all about him. But the Japanese came through and swung to the rear of Nye's position. Treacy's men swept down and drove them back. Bisset, with Lieutenant Thurgood[8] and some of the fragments of Cameron's company in touch on his right, was heavily assailed about 5. All told that day his men repulsed eleven separate attacks, each, they estimated, of a company strength. They calculated that they struck down at least 200 Japanese. But, in the latest attack, Bisset himself was hit by a burst of machine-gun fire. On his left rear Lieutenant Mason's[9] platoon was being beaten back. Mason's men had taken part in four counter-attacks during the afternoon, swaying and surging in bitter defence and counter-thrust. In that platoon acting-Corporal McCallum[1] had been the dominating figure. Now, with a Bren in one hand, a Tommy-gun in the other, he flailed his attackers from their very midst, covering the withdrawal of his

---

[4] Lt T. H. Bisset, VX14631; 2/14 Bn. Clerk and jackeroo; of Surrey Hills, Vic; b. Albert Park, Vic, 30 Jun 1910. Killed in action 29 Aug 1942.

[5] Capt M. A. Treacy, MC, VX15489; 2/14 Bn. Shop assistant; of Mildura, Vic; b. Nathalia, Vic, 24 Nov 1915. Killed in action 29 Nov 1942.

[6] Lt S. B. Johnston, WX4349. 2/16, 39 Bns. Farmer; of Dardanup, WA; b. Bunbury, WA, 23 Mar 1915. Died 18 Oct 1956.

[7] Cpl H. C. Wakefield, MM, VX30922; 2/14 Bn. Wool worker; of Sydney; b. Melbourne, 3 Dec 1916.

[8] Capt J. G. Thurgood, VX15868; 2/14 Bn. Salesman; of Glenbrook, Tenterfield, NSW; b. Ararat, Vic, 17 Sep 1914.

[9] Lt L. F. Mason, VX18727; 2/14 Bn. Clerk-draftsman; of Albert Park, Vic; b. Williamstown, Vic, 2 May 1919.

[1] Cpl C. R. McCallum, DCM, VX15241; 2/14 Bn. Farmer; of Tarra Valley, Sth Gippsland, Vic; b. Foster, Vic, 24 Jul 1907. Died of wounds 8 Sep 1942.

comrades, the Japanese literally reaching for him so that part of his equipment was wrenched off in their hands as he smashed them down. His friends said that he killed 40 Japanese and saved a third of the platoon before he himself came back.

Key was in a most serious position as night came. He had been forced to re-form his positions and his enemies were menacing him gravely from the high ground on his left. At 7.30 p.m. Potts who, in view of the desperate circumstances, had decided merely to hold on the right flank and commit all his reserves to help Key, told Key that he would counter-attack with two companies of Lieut-Colonel Caro's 2/16th Battalion at first light. But Key could not hold and at 8.45 p.m. asked permission to withdraw to Isurava Rest House ridge (a little less than half-way back to Alola). Honner was sent back to reconnoitre the position to which the withdrawal would take place. Captains Goldsmith[2] and Langridge[3] moved their 2/16th "C" and "D" Companies forward to cover Key's withdrawal, which was carried out during the night, the men bearing their wounded with them in conditions of the greatest difficulty. Among these was the dying Lieutenant Bisset, one of the best-loved officers of the battalion.

During the day Key had lost 2 officers and 10 men known to have been killed, 3 officers and 45 men wounded, while the numbers "missing" were high. Among the missing were Lieutenants Pearce and Gardner[4] with portion of Cameron's company. They and their men had last been heard of, isolated and fighting hard forward of the main company positions. Key claimed some 550 Japanese casualties for the day's fighting.

While events were pressing thus heavily on Brigadier Potts he had signalled Allen that he could not extricate the 39th from the forward area (without leaving the 2/14th dangerously alone) and that both Key and Honner reported the Japanese attacking in superior numbers. The previous day he had told Allen that the 53rd was badly disorganised and that he was convinced that they could not be relied on to fight, had repeated his request for the 2/27th and had said that he would return the 39th to Myola next day. Now he asked again for the 2/27th and for more carriers and air drops to ease his wretched maintenance position. Just before midnight on the 29th Allen replied that battalion headquarters and two companies of the 2/27th would go forward under Lieut-Colonel Cooper[5] next day and that he would let Potts have a decision regarding the remainder of the battalion when the operations at Milne Bay had crystallised. He was anxious about the number of carriers but said that he was arranging for an additional 500 to go forward and that considerable air drops had taken place during the day. He stressed the need to send the 39th back to Myola as soon as possible to ease the supply problem, told Potts that he was hoping to get the 53rd out at an early date and

---

[2] Capt D. K. Goldsmith, WX1586; 2/16 Bn. Bank clerk; of Northam, WA; b. Pingelly, WA, 13 May 1918.
[3] Capt B. D. N. Langridge, WX1599; 2/16 Bn. Bank clerk; of Inglewood, WA; b. North Perth, WA, 10 Feb 1919. Killed in action 8 Sep 1942.
[4] Lt V. G. Gardner, VX51106; 2/14 Bn. Grocer; of Mildura, Vic; b. Euston, NSW, 14 Feb 1920.
[5] Lt-Col G. D. T. Cooper, MBE, SX1435. 2/10 Bn; CO 2/27 Bn 1942-43; and training appts. Mechanical engineer; of Leabrook, SA; b. Adelaide, 2 Apr 1912.

that, meanwhile, Major Cameron had been promoted and was coming forward again to assume command of that ineffective unit.

With the withdrawal to the Rest House the first phase of the campaign of the 21st Brigade came to an end in temporary defeat. But lack of fighting quality on the part of the brigade was not one of the reasons. The delay which was forced on the newcomers at Myola through the supply situation was certainly one of the prime reasons since Potts, never able to develop a firm base, was forced to commit his brigade, company by company, as they arrived, in an effort to extricate the 53rd and 39th Battalions. Thus he was never able to regain the initiative lost before the arrival of his men. Another reason was weak patrolling particularly by the 53rd Battalion who, by half-hearted reconnaissance and fighting on both the right flank and to Naro Ridge on the left flank, allowed their enemies to secure the high ground on both flanks from which Potts, because of the commitments he was forced to make as his companies arrived, was never able to dislodge them. If another reliable battalion had been available to him he could probably have secured his main positions by using it to drive the Japanese from these commanding locations. Contributing minor factors were the disadvantage at which the Australian battalions were placed through lack of equipment of various kinds. They had no green uniforms and so were easy targets for enemies whom they could not see until they were almost face to face with them. They were forced to use bayonets, steel helmets and empty tins with which to try to dig positions which could give them little protection.

Well-trained, aggressive and hardy Japanese closely followed the withdrawal on the 30th. About 9.30 a.m., from the right, they opened fire on Alola with machine-guns sited in the vicinity of Abuari. There McGee was again held in a clearing above the village with Sublet's company, temporarily under Captain Wright,[6] trying to work round him. They waited for King's attack to develop but, at midday, that 53rd Battalion officer reported that he could make no progress in the rough country and had gone into a defensive position. Sublet, still feeling unsuccessfully for his opponents' flanks, had reported at 11.30 that the Japanese had infiltrated to the area between the waterfall and Alola. Now, when he heard that he could expect nothing from King, he and McGee attacked. They were not successful. They persisted, but lost men and made no progress. As men fell wounded Private Myhre,[7] in great personal danger, was assiduous in caring for them.

During this fighting Lieutenant Gerke's[8] platoon was ambushed as they moved into the attack through dense and confused country. A burst of machine-gun fire killed Corporal Clarke.[9] Private Maidment[1] coolly col-

---

[6] Maj G. W. Wright, WX3253; 2/16 Bn. Regular soldier; of Leederville, WA; b. Perth, WA, 29 Apr 1911.
[7] Pte J. F. Myhre, MM, WX14367; 2/16 Bn. Sailor; of Larvik, Norway; b. Larvik, 31 Aug 1919. (Myhre was discharged in 1943 for service with the Norwegian mercantile marine.)
[8] Maj J. Gerke, WX7309; 2/16 Bn. Fitter; of Cottesloe, WA; b. Claremont, WA, 7 Jun 1915.
[9] Cpl M. T. Clarke, WX5693; 2/16 Bn. Farmer; of Burekup, WA; b. Bunbury, WA, 17 Aug 1919. Killed in action 30 Aug 1942.
[1] Pte G. Maidment (correct name A. G. Thornton), DCM, WX4227; 2/16 Bn. Labourer; of East Ryde, NSW; b. Sydney, 29 Jun 1914. Died of wounds on or after 1 Sep 1942.

lected grenades from Clarke's pouches, and, disregarding heavy rifle and machine-gun fire, dashed up the slope towards the Japanese positions. He was badly wounded in the chest almost at once, but destroyed several posts and continued throwing grenades until none were left. The Japanese immediately began to press forward, but Maidment seized Clarke's sub-machine-gun and, standing in the centre of the track, engaged the Japanese and halted them. When Maidment had emptied his magazine Sergeant Morris[2] continued firing into the Japanese. The two saved many lives and were largely instrumental in extracting the platoon from a most difficult position, although it was now cut off from the rest of the company.

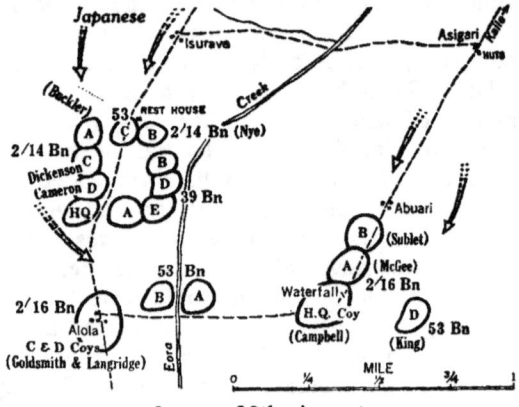

3 p.m. 30th August

Late in the afternoon the forces on the Abuari Track were ordered to withdraw to the main track where Goldsmith's company, less a platoon, and Langridge's were now in position round Alola. But Sublet and the others with him found the going hard. The cliffs and crags among which they had been fighting beetled behind them, dark, wet bush pressed about them, only a few logs spanned the creek as a bridge, the track to Alola was just a faint mark merged with the bush on the steep hillside. Those who crossed the bridge did so by crawling on their hands and knees. On the other side many lost the track and blundered in circles back to their starting-point. Some reached Alola; others began to fumble back up the line of the creek; a stretcher-bearer, Private Roy Turner,[3] carried a wounded man on his back. The orders to withdraw had not reached Captain Wright and some of his men, and Gerke and his platoon, were still out of contact.

There was an even more rapid deterioration on the left. Morning had found Key in perimeter defence at the Rest House. He had the 39th Battalion—numbering only 150 fighting men at midday after the most unfit had been started back to Myola—"C" Company of the 53rd, his own battalion, and one platoon from the 2/16th in the forward left flank position. He did not have enough men to cover the high ground on the left. Early in the afternoon the Japanese pressed down from that direction and forced the platoon of the 2/16th back into the perimeter. They were by-passing the most forward positions and driving at Key's rear where Cameron and Honner's men were holding. At 3 p.m. Potts ordered a

---

[2] WO1 G. E. Morris, MM, EM, WX4356; 2/16 Bn. Farmer; of Harvey, WA; b. Montgomeryshire, North Wales, 30 Apr 1911.

[3] Pte R. L. Turner, WX3682; 2/16 Bn. Miner; of Perth; b. South Fremantle, WA, 24 Nov 1911.

(Australian War Memorial)

The troops in the forward areas depended for supplies largely on air drops and the native carrier-line. General Blamey watches ammunition wrapped in blankets for dropping being loaded into an American transport plane.

(Australian War Memorial)

A Douglas transport plane drops supplies near Nauro in the Owen Stanleys.

(Australian War Memorial)

Brigadier A. W. Potts (left), commander of the 21st Brigade; Corporal R. Simpson, Potts' driver; Captain J. K. Murdoch, staff captain 21st Brigade; Lieutenant A. L. Salom, liaison officer, 30th Brigade; and Captain C. L. Thompson, adjutant 2/14th Battalion.

(Australian War Memorial)

The Owen Stanleys, looking north from a high point near Nauro.

withdrawal to Eora Creek; Dickenson's company and Cameron's (the latter now consisting only of 2 officers and 32 men), with the 2/16th platoon, were to clear any Japanese there off the track to make this withdrawal possible. As they swept forward at 4.50 p.m. the Japanese flung themselves against Buckler and Nye, who were holding the rear, and against battalion headquarters. A mêlée ensued in the small area which Key had been holding. As Key with his headquarters was ready to move, fire swept across the track and forced him and his group down the side of the precipitous V of Eora Creek.

Two companies of the 2/16th commanded by Captains Goldsmith and Langridge covered the withdrawal of the main 2/14th Battalion force out of the Alola area. McGee and Sublet were still out along the Abuari Track. Key himself, Captain Hall[4] (adjutant), Lieutenant S. Y. Bisset[5] (Intelligence officer), Warrant-Officer Tipton[6] (regimental sergeant major), and men of battalion headquarters, did not pass through with the rest. Neither did a group of Nye's men under Lieutenant Treacy who had remained to attend and bring out the wounded, nor Captain Buckler and some of his company who also had remained to protect the casualties and fight any necessary rearguard action. It was almost an hour after Nye's departure that Buckler, now in charge of the whole party which consisted of himself, Lieutenants Treacy and Butler[7] and 41 men began to move back. But the Japanese had closed in on the track. Sergeant Gwillim[8] patrolled forward in the darkness to clear the way out. He was ambushed. Three of his men were killed, Gwillim himself, Corporal Metson[9] and Corporal Dick Smith[1] were wounded.[2]

This bitter 30th day of August cost the 2/14th dear. As it passed it was definitely known that 10 men had been killed and 18 wounded on the day; 172 were "missing" (including the commander, the adjutant, the Intelligence officer, the regimental sergeant major, Captain Buckler, Lieutenants Treacy, Butler, Pearce, Gardner, and Davis).

By the morning of the 31st August the remnants of the 2/14th were in position about a mile south of Alola, the brigade headquarters had been set up half-way between Alola and Eora Creek, the 53rd Battalion, sent out of battle, had been ordered to return to Myola, Goldsmith's and Langridge's companies and the headquarters of the 2/16th had passed through the forward positions and were astride the track near brigade.

---

[4] Capt T. Hall, VX52875; 2/14 Bn. Bank officer; of McKinnon, Vic; b. Colac, Vic, 9 Nov 1910. Missing presumed dead 2 Sep 1942.
[5] Capt S. Y. Bisset, MC, VX21199; 2/14 Bn. Clerk; of Surrey Hills, Vic; b. Balaclava, Vic, 27 Aug 1912.
[6] WO1 L. E. Tipton, VX14386; 2/14 Bn. Motor driver; of North Carlton, Vic; b. Carlton, 25 Jun 1911.
[7] Capt C. G. D. Butler, VX14598; 2/14 Bn. Quantity surveyor; of Melbourne; b. Melbourne, 10 May 1917.
[8] Maj J. E. Gwillim, VX22526. 2/14 Bn; Mil Hist Section. Bank clerk; of Caulfield, Vic; b. Melbourne, 7 Jan 1920.
[9] Cpl J. A. Metson, BEM, VX15796; 2/14 Bn. Salesman; of St Kilda, Vic; b. Richmond, Vic, 1 Aug 1918. Killed in action 4 Oct 1942.
[1] Sgt W. R. D. Smith, VX13452; 2/14 Bn. Farm hand; of Longford, Vic; b. Corringham, England, 6 Jul 1911.
[2] The story of the subsequent adventures of Buckler and his men is an heroic one. See Appendix 1 in this volume.

By 8.30 a.m. McGee's, Sublet's and Campbell's men who had been withdrawing along the creek bed to the east of the track were beginning to come in. By early afternoon the 2/14th were moving back again (through the 39th Battalion which was holding at Eora Creek) to positions just south of Eora Creek with Potts' headquarters near by. While they did this the 2/16th Battalion maintained their positions, with elements of the companies from the Abuari Track still coming in, but moved back about three-quarters of an hour's march at nightfall.

During this period the Japanese showed every evidence of preparing for a large-scale advance, working hard themselves and driving the natives to widen tracks and make them more passable, establishing camps within sight of the Australians. Potts asked for air attacks on these tempting targets but effective support of that kind was difficult in such country. He asked also for evacuation by air of the wounded, whose increasing numbers were becoming as much of an anxiety to him as his lack of adequate supplies. But this could not be arranged. He had, however, the support of a loyal and able medical team headed by Major Magarey.[3]

Magarey had landed at Port Moresby on 14th August with the 2/6th Field Ambulance, and four days later had set out for the front accompanied by Captain Oldham[4] and 31 men. On his way he established medical staging posts, each manned by two orderlies, at Uberi, Ioribaiwa, Nauro, Menari and Efogi, a holding post under Oldham at Myola, and then, accompanied by a medical N.C.O., went on towards Alola. At Templeton's Crossing Magarey ordered that the holding post be reduced to a staging post and 36 sick and lightly wounded men be sent back to Myola, where Oldham would hold such men likely to be fit to return to their units within a week or ten days, and arrange the evacuation of the remainder to Moresby.

By the time Magarey arrived at Alola late on the 24th an R.A.P. of the 39th Battalion under Captain Shera was established just forward of Isurava; Captain Hogan[5] of the 53rd had a post at Alola; an improvised advanced dressing station under Captain Wallman was operating at Isurava, while Captain McLaren was in charge of a miniature A.D.S. at Eora Creek and up till that time had been overseeing the convalescent camp at Templeton's Crossing. Most of the wounded appeared to Magarey to be capable of walking, but what stretcher cases there were had been carried by native bearers or natives of the P.I.B. to Isurava, where essential surgery was being performed by Wallman.

> In any case casualties appeared to be very light (noted Magarey) and few serious wounds had reached medical aid. No fractures had been met with. The general condition of wounds was good, probably owing to the extensive use of sulphanilamide, both locally and orally.

---

[3] Maj J. R. Magarey, SX3668. 2/6 Fd Amb; 2/4 AGH; 105 CCS. Medical practitioner; of Adelaide; b. Adelaide, 21 Feb 1914.

[4] Maj J. M. Oldham, NX34762. 2/6 Fd Amb; 102 AGH. Medical practitioner; of Sydney; b. Melbourne, 14 Oct 1912.

[5] Capt A. B. Hogan, NX140503; RMO 53 Bn. Medical practitioner; of Sydney; b. Mayfield, NSW, 5 Oct 1920.

The medical plan which Magarey then clarified after close consultation with Brigadier Potts had the unusual feature of depending on evacuation forward, based as it was on Potts' plan to retake Kokoda. If that hope was realised casualties could be flown out over the mountains. Hence casualties were held as far forward as possible to minimise the labours of regimental and native stretcher bearers.

On the 26th August, however, fire falling at Isurava Rest House forced Wallman to withdraw his patients and installations to Eora Creek, a long carry from the forward posts of some nine hours. Meanwhile the R.A.P. of the 2/14th Battalion under Captain Duffy[6] had been established at Isurava, and on the 27th that of the 2/16th Battalion under Captain Steward[7] was set up at Alola where Steward, in addition to receiving casualties from his battalion in the Abuari area, would assist Hogan in his dual role of staging through casualties to Eora Creek. Major Watson of the P.I.B. made available four teams of native stretcher bearers each under a European, and two of these were sent to Duffy at Isurava whither Captain Shera was now preparing to withdraw with the 39th Battalion, and two were based at Alola to help with casualties from Abuari.

With the intensification of the fighting on the 28th Duffy reported increasing numbers of casualties passing through his post but, as yet, no serious overstraining of the evacuation line. The carry from his post to Alola, however, was only some two to three hours while that from Alola to Eora Creek was about 6 hours. This position was aggravated by the fact that different supply lines were operating over the two stages with consequent greater difficulties in arranging for the return of the wounded from Alola. One result was that casualties began to bank up at Alola and the position was made more difficult as an inflow of wounded from the 2/16th Battalion began. This position was nevertheless not unduly serious as long as sufficient overhead cover for the patients was available. But next day (29th) searching machine-gun fire from across the valley swept over Hogan's and Steward's posts wounding 5 and killing one. The youthful Hogan, shot through both legs, was himself among the wounded. Later in the day Brigadier Potts told Magarey that the 2/14th had been outflanked and his own headquarters was under fire from the high ground north of Alola. He was moving his force back and this involved moving all wounded out of Alola. At the time there were 12 lying cases being held there. By using all the available carriers, some of the Papuans and some 39th Battalion men, the medical people got all these cases moving out of Alola, but the progress of the stricken men along the congested track was slow—particularly that of those being borne by Australians who found that they could neither carry with the same speed or the same ease as the sure-footed natives, became more exhausted and could not carry the wounded men in the same comfort. The stretcher cases therefore

---

[6] Maj D. G. Duffy, VX14867. RMO 2/14 Bn; 2/3 CCS, 102 AGH. Medical practitioner; of Melbourne; b. Mourilyan, Qld, 1 Jan 1915.
[7] Maj H. D. Steward, VX14709. 2/6 Fd Amb; RMO 2/16 Bn; 2/8, 2/11 AGHs. Medical practitioner; of Melbourne; b. Eaglehawk, Vic, 2 Jun 1912.

spent the night on the track to Eora Creek. On the morning of the 30th Captain Grahamslaw sent 140 natives forward from Eora Creek under Warrant-Officer Lord. But by the time Lord reached the stretchers (now increased in numbers by fresh 2/14th Battalion casualties) he found that he had only about 20 natives with him, sufficient in fact to carry only two stretcher cases. The indefatigable Lord, however, ranged wide in search of his carriers and finally got all the stretchers moving back once more.

It quickly became clear that the withdrawal would continue and that all stretcher cases would have to be carried to Myola. Because it seemed likely that aircraft could land there a request was sent to divisional headquarters to arrange air evacuation from that point. Magarey was working then on information from Potts that he would probably have up to four days to clear Eora Creek and planned to make the fullest possible use for medical evacuations of the native carriers bringing supplies forward—since no natives were available exclusively for medical work. The plan was operating on the same day and, by about 2 p.m., 10 stretcher cases were moving from Eora Creek to Templeton's Crossing, leaving about 25 still to be moved with two or three days still in hand. But about 4.30 p.m. on the 30th the medical officers were told that the 2/14th was even then falling back to a position behind Eora Creek and, by the next morning at the very latest, the 2/16th would be coming back through the 2/14th. As the Eora Creek village was in a very exposed position it was essential to get the wounded at least some of the way up the hill in their rear before dark. By this time more than 30 stretcher cases were at the medical post. By an extraordinary effort these were all moving along the track by nightfall—a few walking, each held up by two other soldiers walking beside him, some being carried by men of the P.I.B., some borne by natives who had been carrying supplies.

> While this was going on (wrote Magarey afterwards) Captain McLaren reported that there were 3 patients—two with abdominal wounds and one with a sucking chest wound—who were extremely unlikely to live. . . . Because of the extreme shortage of labour, Captain McLaren was instructed to give each of these patients morphia.... As Captain McLaren was leaving with the remainder of the personnel and equipment the advisability of a further dose was considered, but as all of them appeared moribund, and supplies of morphia were getting low, this was decided against. . . . As dusk approached the three patients . . . were again examined and it was considered probable that none would live for more than half an hour. As no more patients were likely to arrive in Eora Creek, it was decided to move up the hill to make sure that all patients had reached the staging post and were being adequately attended to. This was found not to be the case; several stretcher cases were found abandoned two or three hundred yards up the hill. An attempt was made to reach the staging post to get natives to return for these cases; but this was eventually abandoned owing to the inability to see or keep on the track in the dark. After some time a group of PIB with a European in charge was found with three stretcher cases somewhere above brigade headquarters. A torch was borrowed from Sigs and PIB sent down to bring up the abandoned stretchers, which they did. . . . [On 31st August] the three patients left for dead in Eora Creek were examined. Two were dead but the lower abdominal wound . . . asked whether he was to be left behind!! Arrangements were made with W.O. Lord to get him out, which was done. This man lived for several days but died before reaching the road-head.

As darkness approached on the 31st all the stretcher cases, except a few late arrivals, were on the way from Templeton's Crossing to Myola, a special relay of 300 native carriers having been sent down from Myola for them. Wallman and his team moved with them, the orderlies distributed on a basis of one to every two or three stretchers. McLaren and a few orderlies remained at Templeton's Crossing to handle any new arrivals there and a special band of natives was made available for evacuation from the most forward positions. These were in the charge of two competent warrant-officers, Preece[8] and Davies[9] of Angau who continued their work throughout the whole of the withdrawal. At 5.30 p.m. Magarey received a message from Colonel Norris,[1] the senior medical officer of 7th Division, that air evacuation from Myola was impossible. Magarey at once ordered Oldham to send out overland from Myola to Moresby as many as possible of the casualties he was holding. Next morning, when Potts told Magarey that he could not hold Myola and that Magarey would have to clear all his patients from Myola as quickly as possible, the latter arranged for Major Brummitt,[2] who had just come forward with a second detachment of the 2/6th Field Ambulance, to set up an Advanced Dressing Station at Efogi. He was merely to stage patients through to the main medical post at Menari which Wallman and McLaren were to run until Oldham, who was moving back with the patients, arrived there.

By the morning of 1st September Caro of the 2/16th had his men in a new position farther back toward Eora Creek with Goldsmith's company forward. Goldsmith was under increasing stress when the battalion began to withdraw again through Honner's front to the high ground above Eora Creek, and was subsequently cut off with 75 of his troops. Fire whipping the crossing killed Lieutenant Paterson[3] of Langridge's company and wounded several of his men after they had covered the passage for others of their battalion. By midday the main body of the battalion was overlooking the village, where Lieutenant Gerke and his platoon, who had been missing since 30th August, rejoined them; they reported that they had killed several Japanese on their way back and brought with them the 53rd Battalion signalmen who had been surprised at Missima on the 24th and had been wandering in wild country, bootless, without arms and very hungry.

During the day the Japanese toiled increasingly against the 2/16th who, on the high ridges, were cut off from the water below and suffered greatly from thirst. Most of the weight of the attacks was directed towards

---

[8] Lt R. Preece, MM, PX183; Angau. Plantation manager; of Rigo District, Papua; b. Ayr, Scotland, 8 Feb 1918.

[9] Capt J. B. Davies, PX213; Angau. Native labour superintendent; of Port Moresby and Hunters Hill, NSW; b. Stanmore, NSW, 24 Jun 1914.

[1] Maj-Gen Sir Frank Kingsley Norris, KBE, CB, DSO, ED, VX221. (1st AIF: 2 AGH; 1 LH Fd Amb.) CO 2/1 CCS; ADMS 7 Div 1940-43; DDMS II Corps 1943-44; DGMS AMF 1948-55. Medical practitioner; of Melbourne; b. Lilydale, Vic, 25 Jun 1893.

[2] Lt-Col D. W. Brummitt, SX1433. RMO 2/10 Bn; 2/6 Fd Amb; 2/1 AGH; CO 15 Fd Amb. Medical practitioner; of Dulwich, SA; b. Adelaide, 12 May 1913.

[3] Lt D. A. Paterson, WX11085; 2/16 Bn. Accountant; of South Perth, WA; b. Geraldton, WA, 18 Aug 1918. Killed in action 1 Sep 1942.

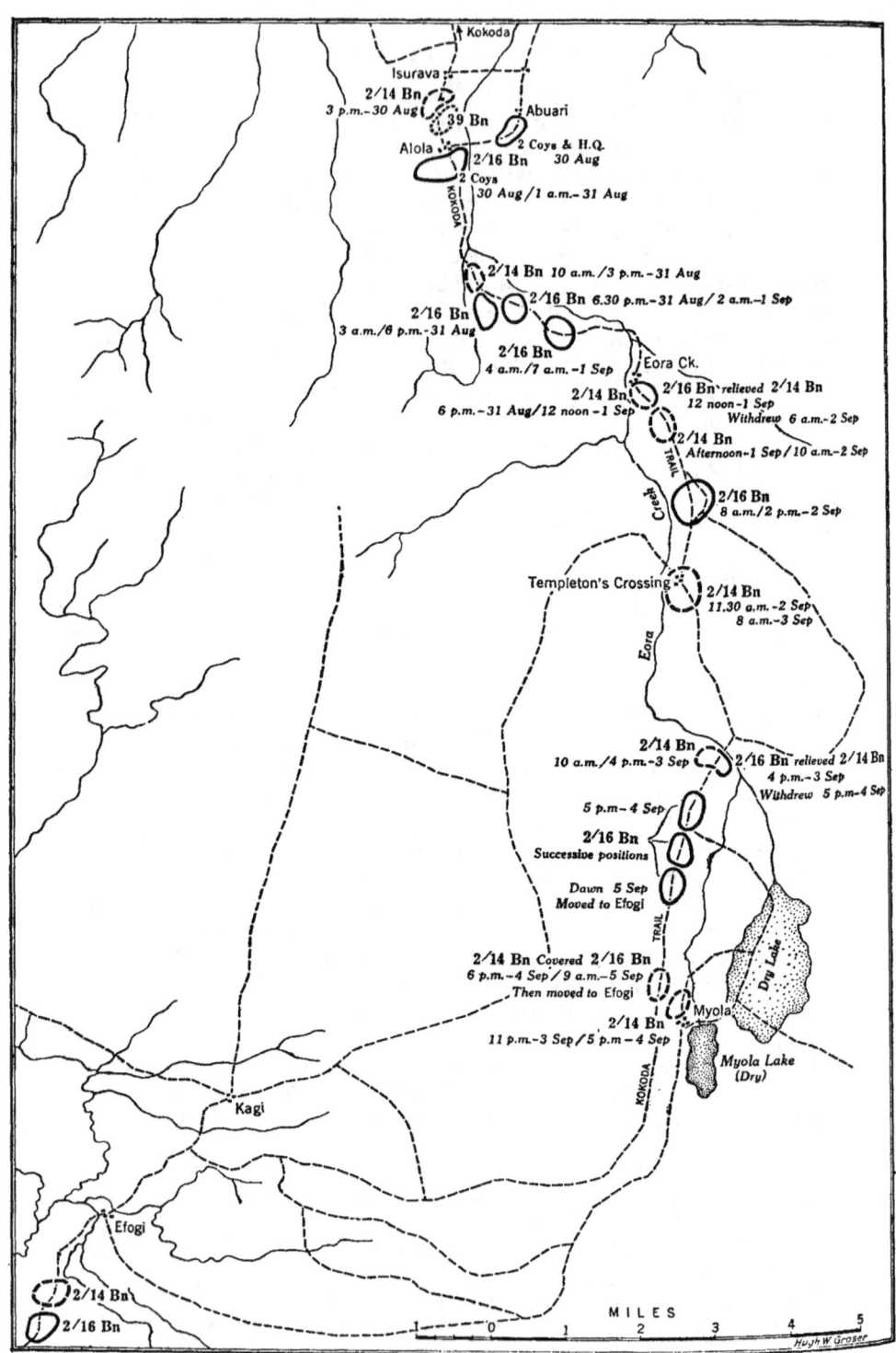

The withdrawal from Isurava, 30th August to 5th September

Langridge's company in the right forward positions. The Japanese stormed at them again and again until midnight. There Sergeant Duncan[4] and his platoon bore much of the brunt and Warrant-Officer Haddy[5] proved himself a cool leader. The 2/16th held, as ordered, until 6 o'clock next morning.

For the other battalions the day was fairly quiet. The 2/14th (Captain Rhoden now acting as commander) had fallen back behind Caro's battalion and was half-way between Eora Creek and Templeton's Crossing. From that point Rhoden sent out Lieutenant McIlroy[6] and 20 men to watch the old track along the ridge west of Eora Creek to Kagi. They were to remain in position there for three days or until relieved, whichever was the sooner.[7] Honner had been ordered to Kagi to reconnoitre and cover the tracks leading through there and was moving his men rapidly in a forced march. The 53rd were making a dispirited way to Myola where, on arrival on the 2nd, they were to be relieved of all automatic weapons, rifles and equipment and whence, leaving one company for carrying and guard duties, they were to continue to Port Moresby.

At this stage Potts considered his position afresh. His brigade was pathetically depleted. They had had nearly a week of constant fighting and during that time most of them had been unable even to brew themselves a mug of tea and certainly had not had a hot meal. Now, shelterless, their feet pulpy and shrivelled from the constant wet, they were soaked by continuous rain. They were worn out by fighting in a country where movement alone for even unencumbered men was hardship. They were burdened by their own wounded; desertions by carriers aggravated that difficulty and the supply problem. Potts felt that he could not hold any position for long unless he was heavily reinforced and until the Japanese lines of communication and supply were so extended as seriously to embarrass them. He told Allen this and of his intention to withdraw to Templeton's Crossing. He felt that he must soon establish a firm base from which he could hold and considered that a position half-way between Myola and Efogi, with the Kagi track junction held, was the most suitable.

Accordingly, at dawn on the 2nd, the move to Templeton's Crossing began. By 8 a.m. the 2/16th was settling one hour's march north of Templeton's Crossing with the 2/14th forward of it. The 2/16th had been strengthened once more by the return of Goldsmith's men who had been cut off the previous day. Rhoden led the survivors of the 2/14th through the 2/16th about 10 a.m. without having been in contact. About 11 a.m. their pursuers were seen moving towards a standing patrol consisting of Corporal Willis[8] and six men who had been sent out by Sublet from the

---

[4] Lt W. J. Duncan, WX3280; 2/16 Bn. Warehouse assistant; of North Perth, WA; b. Perth, 4 Jul 1919.

[5] Lt A. C. Haddy, WX3636; 2/16 Bn. Maltster; of Perth, WA; b. Laverton, WA, 16 Jun 1912. Killed in action 7 Dec 1942.

[6] Lt R. M. McIlroy, VX39721; 2/14 Bn. Clerk; of Newtown, Geelong, Vic; b. Bendigo, Vic, 4 Jul 1911.

[7] It was not until 6th October, that McIlroy again linked up with the main Australian forces. See Appendix 1.

[8] Cpl J. H. A. Willis, WX3571. 2/16 Bn; Torres Strait Pioneer Coy 1943-44. Truck driver; of North Perth, WA; b. Waroona, WA, 22 Sep 1910.

left forward positions where he was holding. Willis reported back that his patrol had shot ten of the Japanese. Soon Sublet announced that his main positions were in contact and that the Japanese were moving round his left flank. Caro decided that they were coming in behind him and prepared to move out by leaving the track and following the ridges to the east. This he achieved as the day was dying although disaster nearly overtook him at the last moment. Evidently the Japanese saw the Australians moving. Quickly they plunged forward. Their officers stood with drawn swords directing and encouraging their men who screeched as they attacked. The Australians yelled insults and stood their ground. Sergeant Duncan and his platoon, assisted by Sergeant Morris who rushed his men down the track to join in, stopped the rushes as they came. The Australians lost 2 men killed and one wounded at this awkward time but thought that they saw some 30 Japanese fall.

The 2/16th struggled over the rough country as Rhoden waited between Templeton's Crossing and Myola. They were nearly exhausted. Hunger worried them. They had to tear their way through thick bush. They drank the water which oozed from the moss-covered trees. About 4 p.m. on the 3rd they emerged into the 2/14th area whereupon that battalion fell back on their way to Myola. With them went Lieutenant Bisset, Warrant-Officer Tipton and 11 men, all of whom arrived in the wake of the 2/16th after having been missing since the 30th August when they were swept off the track with Colonel Key. Of the other members of Key's[9] party they brought little news because they said it had split into small groups soon after its initial misfortune.

Rhoden's men rested at Myola on the morning of the 4th September while he himself reconnoitred the area. They had a hot meal. They washed and were given clean clothes to replace the stinking garments which had remained unchanged on most of them since they had first set out over the mountains. They exposed their puffed and leprous-looking feet to the sun. From some the socks had to be cut away. Corporal Clark,[1] the unit chiropodist, pared off rotten tissue. But their break was short lived. Word came that the 2/16th was heavily committed and Rhoden moved to cover Caro's attempts to extricate his unit.

The 2/16th had been engaged again almost before the 2/14th had left the area on the previous day—the 3rd. A wet and only mildly disturbed night followed. About 2 p.m. on the 4th Lieutenant Hicks[2] who had been patrolling to the west reported that Japanese were rounding the left flank. Soon afterwards McGee's company, in the forward position, was fighting hard. Sublet, in the absence of Caro and his second-in-command,

---

[9] Colonel Key was the third battalion commander lost in these operations within a matter of weeks. An interesting pointer to the different nature of the fighting in New Guinea is provided by the fact that up to this time only one Australian battalion commander had been killed in the Middle East in the five campaigns that had been fought there by the A.I.F. or in the sixth that was proceeding.

[1] Cpl G. K. Clark, VX15860; 2/14 Bn. Window dresser; of Hampton, Vic; b. Moonee Ponds, Vic, 18 Apr 1915. Killed in action 2 Jul 1945.

[2] Lt G. T. Hicks, WX7841; 2/16 Bn. Tailor and mercer; of Angaston, SA; b. Collie, WA, 15 Jan 1916. Died of wounds 5 Dec 1942.

Major Hearman,³ who were back at Myola on reconnaissance, decided to withdraw to better positions. He seemed to be beset by about 300 determined men. As he withdrew, his two rear companies (Goldsmith's and Langridge's) were ambushed, but McGee, who had been waiting, helped them through. Their pursuers lunged again when the Australians had scarcely reached their new positions. Darkness broke the contact and Hearman, who had now returned, led the men towards Myola. They slipped and fell in the night. They struggled to get their wounded back. Each man held the clothing or the bayonet of the man in front so that he would not lose his way, but finally they had to stop and wait for the daylight to come. At first light on the 5th they went on to Myola where the 2/14th covered them. There they were refreshed as the other battalion had been, and ate their fill of the stores which were being destroyed and which littered the area as the work of demolition went on. Then, crawling, sliding and edging their difficult way through the rain, they took the road to Efogi where they began to arrive in the early afternoon of the 5th September. The 2/14th followed and the two battalions, too worn to travel farther, bivouacked with protective patrols out.

The abandonment of Myola must have sickened Potts. More than any other man he knew its importance. On the 2nd he had reported to Allen that his men were in good heart and he considered ("conservatively", he said) that they had inflicted over 700 casualties. He stated that all stores at Templeton's Crossing had either been removed or destroyed and that he had made provision for the removal to Efogi of the supplies at Myola. In reply he was told that the 21st Brigade Composite Company were available as reinforcements whenever he required them, the importance of holding Myola was urged on him, and his attention was directed to the desirability of assuming the offensive. It was ironic that that note should have been struck at a time when his force was exhausted and at a fraction of its original strength while, with his brigade fresh and intact, he had been ordered *from* the offensive at the beginning of his operations. At Myola he had hoped to retrieve the situation with the first two companies of the 2/27th Battalion, which had arrived at Kagi on the 4th. The weight of the latest assaults on the 2/16th, however, and the lack of promise which the Myola area offered for defence, complicated by the fact that the old track from Kagi offered the Japanese the opportunity to reach Efogi without going near Myola at all, forced him to abandon the plan. He was a gallant and ambitious soldier and, in leaving Myola, he was not only relinquishing his main supply point but was also disregarding the latest expressed wishes of his commander; and at a time when the supplies which had meant so much to him originally were now coming from the air with some regularity and a real beginning had been made with air support attacks which could have done much to help the ground forces resume the offensive for which they had been longing—if that resumption had been possible.

---

³ Maj J. M. Hearman, WX1593. 2/16 Bn; Comd 1 Rft Trg Bn (JW) 1944-45. Farmer; of Donnybrook, WA; b. London, 10 Nov 1910.

His only consolation was his confidence that, from the time his brigade had begun operations, they had inflicted perhaps 1,000 casualties on their enemies.

While the 2/14th and 2/16th Battalions were withdrawing from Myola on the 5th they made contact with the most advanced forces of the 2/27th Battalion which Colonel Cooper had been moving into position. Cooper himself, with Captain Sims'[4] "A" Company and Captain Lee's[5] "B" Company, had arrived at Kagi on the 4th and found Honner there with his battalion, then numbering 185. From that point, on orders from Potts, Cooper moved back to high ground just south of Efogi, linked there with the balance of his unit and had his whole battalion (approximately 28 officers and 560 other ranks strong) in position on Mission Ridge by 2 p.m. on the 5th. He then took over the automatic weapons and other equipment of the 39th Battalion and Honner moved his men off for Port Moresby.

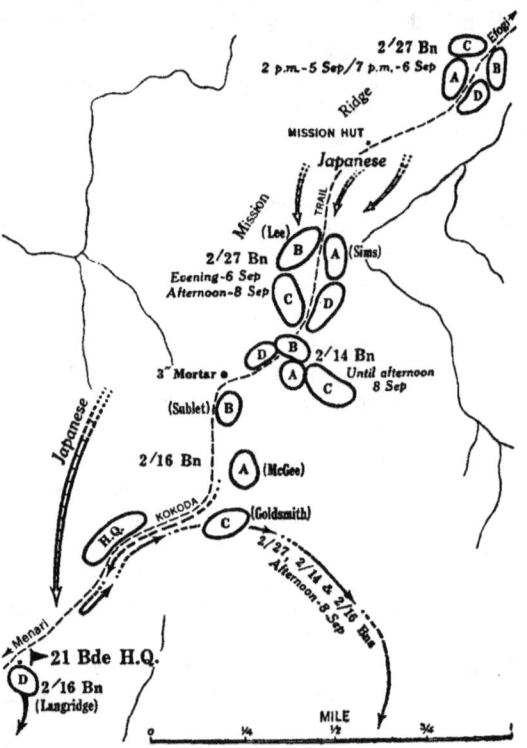

On the morning of the 6th Caro and Rhoden led their weary men through the fresh battalion and occupied a position in rear, Rhoden forward of Caro. (Here Rhoden was rejoined by Lieutenants Pearce and Gardner — the latter wounded — and some of their men. They had been missing since the fighting at Isurava on 29th August. Pearce reported that they had beaten off a number of attacks, had killed Japanese in doing so, and that he had sent Sergeant Irwin[6] ahead with the main party while he had fought a rearguard action himself to enable the others to get clear; but there was no word of Irwin.)

At 7 a.m. on the 6th Cooper sent Lieutenant Bell[7] with a patrol to the junction of the Kagi-Myola tracks. He was to replace a patrol from

---

[4] Lt-Col C. A. W. Sims, MC, SX9455; 2/27 Bn. Electrical fitter; of Wallaroo, SA; b. Sydney, 12 Jul 1916.

[5] Lt-Col A. J. Lee, MC, SX2917, 2/27 Bn; 2/16 Bn 1943-44; CO 2/9 Bn 1944-45. Company director; of Glenelg, SA; b. Adelaide, 30 Jul 1912.

[6] Sgt W. H. Irwin, VX17786; 2/14 Bn. Labourer; of Seddon, Vic; b. Carlton, Vic, 5 Mar 1913.

[7] Lt F. D. Bell, VX41615; 2/27 Bn. Grazier; of Denman, NSW; b. Baerami, NSW, 16 Dec 1914.

part of the 53rd Battalion which had been left in the area originally for supply duties. Through an error the 53rd patrol was pulled out before Bell arrived. Bell's patrol was ambushed, Bell was wounded, and, when he arrived back at the battalion about 3.30, he reported that one of his men had certainly been killed, one other was believed to have been killed, 3 others had been wounded and 8 were missing. He said that he had counted seven Japanese platoons moving down the Myola-Efogi track. Soon afterwards Cooper, on Potts' orders, drew his men back a little to a position with less exposed flanks.

The column which Bell had seen moved on to occupy Efogi and from 9 p.m. on the 6th to 5 a.m. on the 7th a procession of lights moving down the track from Myola and Kagi indicated that a stream of Japanese was flowing to a concentration in front of the Australians. Early in the morning of the 7th eight Marauder aircraft strafed and bombed the Japanese positions. But the Japanese probed and felt for the Australians as the morning went on, and subjected them to fire from what Potts' men thought to be a long-range mortar or a field piece. The Australians patrolled but with largely negative results until a party of the 2/27th under Sergeant Johns[8] reported at 5 p.m. that they had killed 6 Japanese and captured a light machine-gun and grenade discharger, without loss. The long-range fire opened again about 5.30 and killed 2 men and wounded 5.

The expected Japanese attacks came in the dead hours before dawn on the 8th and continued with the morning. The main strength was estimated to be five companies (in addition to an unknown patrol strength). Captain Sims' company beat the attackers back with rifle fire and grenades but the Japanese drove in again and again. Each time fire tore the attacks apart. But the assaulting troops were very determined. Six of Sims' Brens were knocked out. The company had gone into action with 1,200 grenades and with each man carrying 100 rounds of ammunition. The men used this entire supply, the whole battalion reserve, and much of the reserve companies' stocks. Finally the attackers withdrew.

While they had been charging the front with such determination the Japanese had been following their usual practice of working round the flanks. Soon after dawn they were assailing brigade headquarters and Langridge's company of the 2/16th which was guarding the brigade's rear and the supply dumps there. The brigade headquarters people and Langridge found themselves heavily engaged, the conflict developing almost into hand-to-hand fighting. Before his wireless failed soon after 10 a.m. Potts gave Caro instructions that he was to take command of the brigade if the headquarters were wiped out, and withdraw the force to Menari. Meanwhile he was to attack back along the track towards Potts' headquarters (some 700 yards in his rear) assisted, if necessary, by the 2/14th whose flanks Cooper was instructed to cover.

Caro himself, however, was deeply involved. He had been under heavy

---

[8] Lt R. D. Johns, MM, SX3078; 2/27 Bn. Bank clerk; of St Peters, SA; b. Glenelg, SA, 8 Oct 1920.

attack from the rear since 6.30 and his own headquarters had been in great danger. He had tried to relieve Potts by pushing Sergeant Morris and a platoon down the track but Morris had been squeezed out. With the position getting more serious every moment, the 2/14th was ordered to withdraw to the 2/16th area with a view to a combined sally down the track, and the 2/27th also closed back. By 2 p.m. Rhoden had made the necessary adjustments with Cooper and was back in Caro's area. It was now planned that three companies would attack back towards brigade headquarters—Nye's company from the 2/14th, Sublet's and Goldsmith's from the 2/16th. At 2.45 the attack went in with Nye on the right of the track, Sublet on the track itself with McGee moving behind him, and Goldsmith to the left of the track. On the right Nye struck the heaviest opposition, his enemies dug in in front of him and reinforcing strengths attacking from his flanks. Warrant-Officer Noble[9] with 8 men, some of them wounded, finally stormed through to the brigade area. Behind him, however, the gallant and lively Nye lay dead with 16 of his men, among them the heroic Corporal McCallum. At the end of the two hours' fighting Sergeant Matthews[1] and the few survivors of the main part of the company, out of ammunition, retired. Eight of the few of the company who remained were wounded (and one of these died next day).

On the track itself Sublet's company was suffering similarly to Nye's and found that it could not progress against an enemy strongly entrenched and waiting. On the left two platoons drove through to Potts' headquarters. When he informed Caro of this (the wireless was working intermittently) Caro replied: "Enemy being heavily reinforced. Can you assist battalions to get forward?" Potts replied that it was imperative for Caro to get through and that he would try to assist from his end. Captain Langridge then thrust back towards Caro's battalion with Lieutenants Grayden[2] and Lambert[3] and their platoons (Grayden's men had fought their way in in the previous attack). The Japanese, however, killed Langridge and Lambert, struck down a number of their men and held the rest under intense fire. Not only, therefore, was Potts still separated from his main force but he and the few men with him were in acute danger. At this critical time Major Challen, who had been at Menari on reconnaissance, arrived back with 30 men from the Composite Company whom he had found at Menari moving forward. With him also was Captain Lyon[4] from divisional headquarters. As darkness was falling Potts was able to disengage and move back to Menari, having been told by men of the attacking force who had got through from Caro of the battalions' plans

---

[9] WO2 W. A. Noble, VX14780; 2/14 Bn. Traveller; of Brighton, SA; b. Hindmarsh, SA, 31 Mar 1917. Killed in action 11 Sep 1942.

[1] Sgt J. M. Matthews, VX15185; 2/14 Bn. Slipper maker; of Fitzroy, Vic; b. Carlton, Vic, 22 Dec 1918. Missing presumed dead 9 Sep 1942.

[2] Capt W. L. Grayden, WX8868; 2/16 Bn. MLA WA 1947-49; MHR 1949-54. Mechanical engineer and journalist; of South Perth, WA; b. Bickley, WA, 5 Aug 1920.

[3] Lt H. Lambert, WX11368; 2/16 Bn. Farmer; of Burracoppin, WA; b. Perth, WA, 16 Feb 1913. Killed in action 9 Sep 1942.

[4] Maj G. E. Lyon, VX43185. 2/14 Bn; BM 21 Bde 1942-43, 25 Bde 1943-45. Accountant; of Brighton, Vic; b. Caulfield, Vic, 19 Oct 1914.

to make for that point by a circuitous route if the main attacks failed, as they had done.

Meanwhile Caro, Cooper and Rhoden had been planning how best to extricate their men. Finally they decided that they would try to move out by way of a narrow track, steep and closed in with dense bush, through the rough country to the east and swing back on to the main track at Menari, in the order 2/16th, 2/14th and 2/27th. Although still under fire Caro moved his men between 4 p.m. and 5 p.m. in accordance with this plan and successfully broke contact. Progress was painfully slow in that terrible country. The men cut and slashed at the scrub. Their hearts seemed to be bursting as they struggled to help their wounded, hoisting, lowering, pulling and pushing the clumsy stretchers on which the worst cases had to be carried.

Behind the 2/16th followed the 2/14th with the 2/27th holding the Japanese to give the other battalions a chance to get clear. Captain Lee's company of the 2/27th fended off attacks as the rest of the unit moved. About 5.30 he thrust the Japanese into temporary confusion with a short, sharp counter-attack, and before they recovered led his company in the wake of their fellows.

Potts was waiting anxiously at Menari on the morning of the 9th with no further word from his battalions. By 11.30 a.m., however, the 2/14th and 2/16th were arriving, already under fire from Japanese mortars and machine-guns and a quick-firing field piece. While Captain Russell[5] and a small group of men who had come up with the Composite Company held north of Menari, and McGee's company held at Menari itself, Caro settled his men in position south of the village and Rhoden moved through to Nauro over a track knee-deep in mud. (Rhoden was less Lieutenants McGavin,[6] Clements and Greenwood[7] and their men who, with parties from the other two battalions, had been left behind to carry the wounded while the main bodies pushed on to beat the Japanese to Menari.) Potts still had no word of Cooper so, reluctantly, having sent a small Angau party out to try to contact the missing battalion, he left Menari at 2.30 p.m. since the Japanese commanded it from the high track to Efogi. A little later in the day when Russell, in accordance with his instructions, began to to move back in short bounds, he was ambushed and forced off the track losing 2 men killed by a vicious cross-fire which swept their path.

On the morning of the 10th the advancing Japanese brushed against the forward position of Caro's battalion which then broke contact cleanly and began to go back once more. By early afternoon they were in position with the 2/14th, which Challen was now commanding, on the Maguli Range between Nauro and Ioribaiwa. There the two battalions, their

---

[5] Maj W. B. Russell, VX14035; 2/14 Bn. School teacher; of Highett, Vic; b. Creswick, Vic, 3 Mar 1911.
[6] Capt A. S. D. J. McGavin, VX14106; 2/14 Bn. Student; of Black Rock, Vic; b. Calcutta, India, 25 Jul 1920. Killed in action 28 Nov 1942.
[7] Capt J. R. Greenwood, VX38847; 2/14 Bn. British regular soldier; b. Sunderland, England, 25 Apr 1917.

combined strength now only 307 all ranks, were formed into one composite unit with Caro in command and Challen as second-in-command.

That day, Brigadier Porter took over command of the force from Brigadier Potts, who returned to Port Moresby to report. Porter's orders were to take control of all troops from Uberi forward, to hold the Japanese, to stabilise the position and to gain what ground he could. In addition to the 21st Brigade he was to command also, as the most important additions to his force, the 3rd Battalion (less one company), the 2/1st Pioneer Battalion (less one company), and patrols of the 2/6th Independent Company which were to work from Ioribaiwa. He had been told that the 25th Brigade would soon arrive to spearhead the operations which were designed to stabilise the position in the Owen Stanleys.

Porter decided to withdraw his force to the main Ioribaiwa feature. In the light of the experiences of the 8th and 9th he was not confident of clearing the Japanese from the track if they got behind the 2/14th and 2/16th Battalions and, besides, he was more impressed by the tactical advantages of the Ioribaiwa area than those of Nauro Ridge.

Early on the 11th the Japanese were attacking elements of the 2/14th as the 2/16th began to move back through the 3rd Battalion. These 2/14th men held temporarily the attack which fell upon them from three sides but in doing so Warrant-Officer Noble and several men were killed and a number were wounded. Sergeant Sargent,[8] a brave and resourceful young leader, was cut off caring for a wounded man and with him two other men.

The Japanese followed up and fell into an ambush which the 2/16th had left and lost possibly ten of their number. This checked them and, by the afternoon, the Composite Battalion was in position on the ridge half an hour north of Ioribaiwa, sited along the track in great depth, McGee's company forward. On the right and on the track in rear the 3rd Battalion was located, and patrols of the 2/6th Independent Company were working to the left.

McGee had placed an ambush party forward of his area where a creek crossed the track. Later in the afternoon this party, under Corporal Moloney,[9] watched with interest while thirty to forty Japanese moved down the creek bed and began to rummage among the shelters which the Australians had left standing. While the Japanese were fighting over tins which they found, twenty to thirty of them, Moloney claimed, fell before the fire which the Australians then poured into them.

On the 12th the Composite Battalion's positions were reorganised, the 3rd Battalion's positions were adjusted, and orders were issued that Ioribaiwa was to be held until relief came. The Japanese were losing some of their aggressiveness, no doubt feeling the strain of the long-drawn-out fighting and handicapped by the extension of their own supply lines just as the Australians had been in the earlier days of the campaign. They

---

[8] Lt A. L. Sargent, VX15290. 2/14 Bn; "Z" Special Unit 1943-45. Transport driver; of Wangaratta, Vic; b. Wangaratta, 3 Nov 1918. Executed by Japanese 7 Jul 1945.

[9] Lt B. W. Moloney, MM, WX4210; 2/16 Bn. Miner; of Kalgoorlie, WA; b. Bullfinch, WA, 23 Sep 1915. Killed in action 20 May 1945.

engaged the Australians with fire late on the 12th but a quiet night followed as tired troops on each side took stock of the position. On the 13th Japanese mortar fire, and shelling from what was thought to be a mountain gun, killed and wounded some Australians. The Japanese probed the area. Some of them blundered into booby traps which Sublet's company, now forward, had set. Lieutenant Watts[1] reported that his patrol which had gone forward to the river crossing had shot down five or seven of their enemies.

Night came with no further action. With the 14th the 2/31st and 2/33rd Battalions deployed, the one moving forward along the track, the other (which had arrived in rear of the 21st Brigade the previous day) moving on the Australians' right flank.

The arrival of these battalions of the 25th Brigade was one of the results of the concern which was being felt on the highest military plane about the results of the operations in the Owen Stanleys. That concern was sober and controlled on Rowell's part. (He said later—and Allen was of like mind—"At no time did I consider that the capture of Moresby by the enemy from the north was possible.") Rowell's and Allen's concern was based on a true appreciation of the difficulties which Potts' men were facing but MacArthur's concern was founded on lack of knowledge of the conditions of the campaign, and of the quality of the Australian troops who were involved. At this time MacArthur was very worried about the whole of the Pacific situation. On 30th August he had radioed the Joint Chiefs of Staff:

> Unless the strategic situation is constantly reviewed in the light of current enemy potentialities in the Pacific and unless moves are made to meet the changing conditions, a disastrous outcome is bound to result shortly; it is no longer a question here of preparing a projected offensive; without additional naval forces, either British or American, and unless steps are taken to match the heavy air and ground forces the enemy is assembling, I predict the development shortly of a situation similar to those that have successfully overwhelmed our forces in the Pacific since the beginning of the war.

With the issue of Milne Bay only then being decided and the operations in the Owen Stanleys assuming the nature of Allied reverses, MacArthur and his own headquarters were very fidgety. In a personal letter to Rowell on 1st September, General Vasey wrote: "GHQ is like a b——y barometer in a cyclone—up and down every two minutes. . . . They're like the militia—they need to be blooded."

On the 6th September MacArthur (completely disregarding the facts) told General Marshall in America: "The Australians have proven themselves unable to match the enemy in jungle fighting. Aggressive leadership is lacking." Next day he conveyed similar sentiments to Vasey with a request that Vasey inform Rowell of the necessity to "energize combat action". This Vasey did and, writing to Rowell personally, he referred also to a complaint by Rowell that the news being given out regarding the fighting in New Guinea did not satisfactorily represent the

---

[1] Capt R. D. Watts, WX9138; 2/16 Bn. Farmer; of York, WA; b. Perth, WA, 28 Sep 1916.

position. He said that this was due to two reasons: firstly the time-lag between the actual events and the issue of communiqués (which MacArthur wrote himself), secondly "General MacArthur's own personal outlook and actions". Of the latter he wrote:

> My information . . . comes from Howard[2] our Press Relations L.O. [Liaison Officer] at GHQ. He says that MacArthur will not admit that any serious operations are going on in New Guinea and, as you probably know, all press articles must bear out the tone of the official communiqué. . . . The reasons for this attitude of MacArthur I do not know—nor does Howard.

Against this rather uncertain background Rowell was trying to solve two different aspects of the one problem. He felt that he could not rely on the militia forces which formed the bulk of the strength available to him both for the defence of Port Moresby and for operations in the mountains; he was trying to get additional A.I.F. forces allotted to him. Of his militia the 14th Brigade had not yet been committed. On the 29th August, after he had been told that the 25th Brigade was going to Milne Bay, he had signalled Blamey:

> Allen has now had good chance to see 14 Infantry Brigade and is by no means impressed with their efficiency and general standard of training. This is no reflection on their courage but units contain a large number of young men not yet properly developed or trained. His view with which I concur is that 25 Infantry Brigade is required here if this place is to be regarded as reasonably secure from major seaborne attack. . . . Your decision will naturally depend on the outcome of the operations now in progress at Milne Bay. But bearing in mind the difficulties of quick reinforcement I submit that it is advisable to spare no sacrifice to collect ships to bring these seasoned troops in now.

The decision stood, however, to send the 25th Brigade to Milne Bay. Rowell again emphasised his need for this A.I.F. formation saying: "After the experience of the 53rd Battalion I can have NO repeat NO confidence that any A.M.F. unit will stand." Finally his representations, the pressure of circumstances, and the passing of the crisis at Milne Bay, bore fruit, and he was told on 3rd September that the destination of the 25th Brigade had been changed to Port Moresby. Shipping to transport them represented a serious problem, however. Rowell urged that their arrival be hastened, saying of Potts, on the 8th: "Emphasise that during past week he has been heavily outnumbered and has suffered considerable casualties including half 2/14th Battalion."

By this time Blamey had become alarmed and had told Rowell that both the 16th and 17th Brigades, which had just arrived from Ceylon, were available if he required them.[3] Rowell replied that he would like the 16th Brigade sent forward, but then found himself fighting to retain both the 14th and 30th Brigades since it was then proposed that the 16th Brigade should relieve one of them and should not be additional to his existing force.

---

[2] Lt-Col F. J. Howard, VX12841. Hist Records Offr, HQ AIF ME 1940-41; LO Press Relations GHQ SWPA 1942-43; ADPR NG Force 1943-44. Author and journalist; of South Yarra, Vic; b. London 17 Oct 1904. Author of *No Music for Generals* (1952), and other novels.

[3] The 17th Brigade arrived Melbourne on 3rd August, the 16th on 8th August.

A further proposal which was to be the forerunner of important events emerged at this time. Major-General Sutherland, MacArthur's Chief of Staff, had visited New Guinea early in September and, as a result, it was decided that American fighting troops should be sent into Rowell's area. These were to consist initially of one regiment, and MacArthur directed that they be used to find a new track across Papua over which they could pass and strike the Japanese in the rear.

While these high-level discussions were going on Rowell had to face problems arising on the spot. He had to check the Japanese advance but he felt that his main danger might come through the infiltration of Japanese parties which would work down into the Moresby area via the Brown, Goldie and Laloki Rivers—a threat which he thought would become very lively when his opponents reached Ioribaiwa since they would then have a feasible route down the Goldie River.

Inserted between Rowell and Potts was Allen's headquarters. Allen himself had been in a most invidious position. He had been able to do little to influence actual operations in the mountains, and Rowell's headquarters had been responsible for supply—the factor on which the operations so largely depended. Conscious of the responsibility he had been given for the defence of Port Moresby itself from seaward attack he had had an exasperatingly impotent time, with the Japanese on the move round the south-eastern extremity of the island at Milne Bay and advancing so aggressively overland. What he could do to assist Potts he had done loyally and energetically. Now Rowell freed him from the responsibility for the defence of Port Moresby so that he could give his undivided attention to the forward operations.

So, as September advanced, a rearranged stage was being set. The 3rd Battalion of the 14th Brigade had been ordered forward on the 5th under Lieutenant-Colonel Paul,[4] a devoted and admired leader but not young enough to climb the mountains. After a few days, Cameron, twenty years younger than Paul, took command of the 3rd after his brief period with the 53rd. At the same time the 2/1st Pioneer Battalion which had arrived in Port Moresby on the 6th was sent to Ioribaiwa. The 2/6th Independent Company was based on Laloki with orders to patrol deep up the Goldie River to Ioribaiwa and as far as Karema on the Brown River. A special force under Colonel Honner, about 500 strong, was formed of a company from each of the 36th, 49th and 55th Battalions, and elements of the 2/6th Independent Company, to advance by way of the Goldie River to cut the Japanese line between Nauro and Menari. An increase in his air strength and the lengthening lines of Japanese communication enabled Rowell to begin a series of effective air strikes against his adversaries from about 6th September onwards. By the 14th the 25th Brigade was concentrated in the Ioribaiwa-Uberi area, and that day Porter handed over command of operations in the forward areas to Brigadier Eather.[5]

---

[4] Lt-Col A. T. Paul, MC, DCM, NX129432. (1st AIF: 6 Bde AFA.) CO 3 Bn 1938-42; Comd Aust Sigs Second Army 1943-44. Public servant; of Canberra; b. Melbourne, 4 Nov 1889.
[5] Maj-Gen K. W. Eather, CB, CBE, DSO, ED, NX3. CO 2/1 Bn 1939-41; Comd 25 Bde 1941-45; GOC 11 Div 1945-46. Dental mechanic; of Bankstown, NSW; b. Sydney, 6 Jun 1901.

At that time the Japanese were still in sufficient numerical strength to constitute a force to be gravely reckoned with. The main body of Major-General Horii's *South Seas Force,* which had landed near Buna on 19th August was built round the two fresh battalions of the *144th Regiment*—Major Horiye's *II Battalion* and Lieut-Colonel Kuwada's *III Battalion.* Horiye and Kuwada at once hurried forward to the front where they joined Lieut-Colonel Tsukamoto's *I Battalion* on the 24th. The Japanese plan then was that Tsukamoto and Kuwada, strengthened with engineers, dismounted cavalry and mountain gunners, would attack along the axis represented by the Deniki-Isurava track and spur, Kuwada leading his battalion in an outflanking movement along the high ground west of Isurava, while Horiye's battalion circled by way of the east side of Eora Creek along the Missima-Abuari track. Thus the attack began to develop on the 26th, Tsukamoto and Kuwada trying themselves first against the tired and depleted 39th Battalion and Horiye developing his threat to the ill-prepared 53rd Battalion on the Australian right flank. The fighting did not reach its peak, however, until after the arrival in the forward area of two battalions of *Yazawa Force*—Lieut-Colonel Koiwai's *II/41st* and Major Kobayashi's *III/41st.* These had landed at Buna on 21st August and pushed straight inland, Horii himself going with them to direct the battle from the front. At once upon their arrival he had Koiwai's battalion committed and held Kobayashi's battalion in reserve.

Horii thus had five battalions, strongly reinforced with engineers, artillery and service troops of various kinds. They had not yet run into the supply difficulties which were vexing their opponents, they had only a comparatively short and easy journey behind them, they held the initiative. Against these Potts was matching the worn-out militiamen of the 39th Battalion, whom he was trying to extricate even as the battle was developing, companies of the 2/14th and 2/16th Battalions as they arrived in sub-unit groups after a hard struggle across the mountains, and the 53rd Battalion on whom he already knew he could not depend. His A.I.F. battalions had an average strength of about 550 before they set out and were without artillery support.

Scarcely had Horii got the Australians off balance at Isurava and started them moving back along the track looking for a point on which they could firmly base themselves and launch forward into a counter-move, than the Japanese strength was further increased. On the night 2nd-3rd September a convoy made an unhindered landfall at Basabua and disembarked at least 1,000 fresh troops, mainly Colonel Yazawa's *I Battalion.* Major Miyamoto at once took this battalion forward to join the rest of the regiment. Horii was thus able then to use the equivalent of two brigade groups (up to strength in infantry, well balanced with engineers and service troops, and supported by two mountain guns). As he thrust forward he used these two groups alternately, Colonel Kusunose commanding one, Yazawa commanding the other. Battle casualties and sickness cut down his strength daily but, as late as 12th September, it probably numbered about 5,000 fighting men.

CHAPTER 7

IORIBAIWA: AND A COMMAND CRISIS

THE 25th Brigade had done well to begin its deployment for action on 13th-14th September. It had not arrived at Port Moresby until the 9th, after eight days at sea. Next day, before dawn, the first company—one from Lieut-Colonel Buttrose's[1] 2/33rd Battalion—was moving up the track. It was followed on the 11th by the rest of the battalion and Lieut-Colonel Dunbar[2] with his 2/31st Battalion. On the 12th Lieut-Colonel Withy's[3] 2/25th moved in the wake of the other two battalions. The whole brigade wore the new "jungle green" uniforms, the first Australian formation to be so equipped.

On his way to Ioribaiwa Brigadier Eather of the incoming brigade passed Brigadier Potts coming down, Potts having handed over to Brigadier Porter. Impatient for action, however, he did not stay to hear Potts' story. He was an energetic leader, 41 years of age at this time, who had commanded militia battalions before the war, and had sailed with the 6th Division in command of the 2/1st Battalion. He had been marked early by General Allen, then commanding the 16th Brigade, as his most promising battalion commander and, after watching Eather's showing in Libya, General Mackay had supported Allen's judgment.

Eather was ordered to halt the enemy advance towards Port Moresby by offensive action as far forward as possible; to regain control of the route to Kokoda, through the Isurava-Deniki area, with a view to the recapture of Kokoda. He was warned that the Nauro, Menari and Efogi air-dropping areas were *absolutely vital* to him in order to maintain his supply and to permit of further advance beyond them. He was told that the 21st Brigade had been instructed to hold a defensive position north of Ioribaiwa and that Lieut-Colonel Honner, with Honner Force, would move from Laloki on or about the 12th, under command of New Guinea Force, in an effort to cut the Japanese lines of communication.

Eather himself reached Uberi on the 11th. He then telephoned Porter who had just moved his force back to Ioribaiwa. After discussion with Porter he decided to send the 2/33rd Battalion round the right flank of the 21st Brigade (where Lieut-Colonel Cameron was holding with part of his 3rd Battalion), to send the 2/25th Battalion forward along the main track from Porter's rear and so through Ioribaiwa to Nauro, and the 2/31st round Porter's left flank to swing in on Nauro from that direction.

When Buttrose bivouacked on the night of the 13th-14th, some 500 yards in rear of Porter, the 2/33rd Battalion suffered the 25th Brigade's

---
[1] Brig A. W. Buttrose, DSO, ED, SX1434. 2/33 Bn (CO 1942-43); CO 2/5 Bn 1944-45. Wool expert; of Woodville, SA; b. Glenelg, SA, 18 Nov 1912.
[2] Lt-Col C. C. Dunbar, ED, QX6332. 2/25 Bn; CO 2/31 Bn 1942, 16 Motor Regt 1942-43. Insurance representative; of Warwick, Qld; b. Rockhampton, Qld, 15 Jun 1902.
[3] Lt-Col C. B. Withy, DSO, MC, QX6291. (1st AIF: Capt 1 Bn.) Company manager; of Ascot, Qld; b. St Leonards, NSW, 30 Jan 1893.

first New Guinea casualty: a two-man Japanese patrol threw grenades into their lines in the darkness and killed an officer.[4] Next morning the battalion left the track and began the flanking movement towards Nauro. By early afternoon they had reached Captain Boag's[5] position (the right flank company of the 3rd Battalion), on a ridge above Ponoon. They went into defence on the forward slope below Boag without having contacted the Japanese.

That day the composite 2/14th-2/16th held astride the main track, losing several men killed and wounded by Japanese gunfire. Night found them still there with the 2/25th in rear and Japanese creeping about their foremost localities.

On the left, however, more positive action boiled up during the day. The 2/31st swung off the track in the morning, through the 2/16th and on to a side track which ran north-west from Ioribaiwa along a ridge. The top of the ridge had an average width of only some twenty yards, narrowing into five-yard bottlenecks in some places, so that only a cramped field of advance was open. With his leading company under fire there Dunbar essayed a flanking movement with two other companies but the steep sides of the ridge, and nests of well-placed snipers, curtailed this movement. Heavy rain set in, shot through with sporadic fire. In the late afternoon Dunbar recalled his companies to the crest of the ridge. The Japanese followed them in with a strong thrust which raked the ridge with fire, but the men settled in a tight perimeter for the night.

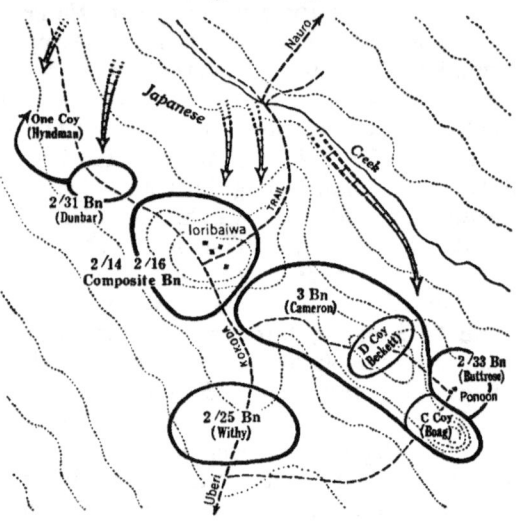

Noon, 15th September

On the 15th at 2 p.m. a hostile patrol was wedging itself between the left flank of the 2/33rd and Boag's company of the 3rd Battalion. Eather, then, having shifted one of Cameron's companies (Captain Beckett's[6]) to strengthen his centre, ordered Withy of the 2/25th to attack towards the high ground on the right with two companies while Buttrose of the 2/33rd drove to the left with one company, the whole effort being designed to pinch off the intruding force. But the ruggedness of the country defeated Buttrose's movement while Withy's companies, in hostile contact from

---

[4] Lt G. M. Barclay, a platoon commander in "B" Company.

[5] Capt T. C. Boag, NX128779. 3 and 2/5 Bns. Public servant; of Canberra, ACT; b. Harden, NSW, 9 Jul 1914.

[6] Capt J. S. Beckett, NX128775; 3 Bn and AEME. Motor car salesman; of Queanbeyan, NSW; b. Candelo, NSW, 28 Dec 1907.

3.30, could not dislodge their enemies from the high ground and were losing men. At 5.30 Buttrose sent Captain Clowes'[7] company against the Japanese positions but it could make little headway, lost one officer and two men killed and had five men wounded, and finally withdrew. Soon afterwards the intruders surprised one of Beckett's platoons and forced it back. The end of the day, therefore, found Eather's right flank penetrated.

Meanwhile the centre was under pressure from Japanese who had crept closely upon the 2/16th and dug in during the night. The most advanced elements gave a little ground early in the day. Then the tired remnants of the 21st Brigade were swept by destructive machine-gun, mortar and mountain gun fire which killed 7 and wounded 19 of the 2/14th, and killed 4 and wounded 10 of the 2/16th. Late in the day Private ("Pappy") Ransom[8] of the 2/14th reported in and stated that he and Private (Bill) Edwards[9] had been left behind earlier; that Edwards had been killed and that he himself had watched the Japanese setting up weapon positions within 50 yards of his concealment. He had sniped four of them before leaving his position in the late afternoon. Acting on Ransom's information Lieutenant Jefferson[1] of the 2/25th then took a patrol out into the night and attacked the weapon posts with grenades and sub-machine-guns. He lost none of his own men but considered that he inflicted fifteen casualties on the Japanese.

While all this was happening Dunbar, on the left, was finding the going difficult. With first light he had patrols out. But intermittent mortar and machine-gun fire troubled him. This, with a skilful enemy who avoided the open and sniped from the cover of trees and bushes, together with the rugged nature of the country, slowed movement. A Japanese sortie in the late forenoon cost him some casualties. Lack of water was becoming serious. Despite their determination, active patrolling, and the effectiveness of their mortar fire the position of the Australians when night fell was uneasy.

That night Eather told General Allen by telephone:

> I think his [the enemy's] action today is the culmination and putting into effect of a plan based on information he has collected about Porter during the last two days. I consider I have just arrived in time. I think it is going to take me all my time to stabilise the position for the present. Porter agrees.

He also said that he had sent out 180 carriers with stretcher cases and had none left for forward support. He wanted a minimum of 200 sent forward at once and said that air supply was not feasible in his present position.

With the morning of the 16th the attackers strained harder at the Australian positions. Buttrose thrust through Boag's positions with Captain

---

[7] Capt T. M. Clowes, QX6232; 2/33 Bn. Regular soldier; of Warwick, Qld; b. Warwick, 4 Sep 1918. Killed in action 22 Nov 1942.
[8] Pte L. F. Ransom, VX23199; 2/14 Bn. Labourer; of Regent, Vic; b. Clifton Hill, Vic, 4 Dec 1904. Died 16 Mar 1957.
[9] Pte L. Edwards, VX15508; 2/14 Bn. Labourer; of Red Cliffs, Vic; b. Mildura, Vic, 1 May 1921. Killed in action 15 Sep 1942.
[1] Capt K. M. Jefferson, QX17291; 2/25 Bn. Bank clerk; of Hawthorne, Qld; b. Crow's Nest, Qld, 24 May 1918.

Archer's[2] "B" Company, and gave Clowes the task of ambushing the Japanese if they withdrew. Archer had some local success but lost two men wounded. At the same time Withy's two companies, temporarily under Buttrose's command, continued their pressure from the right; but the position was not noticeably eased.

In the centre the composite battalion, still holding forward, came under heavy fire at 8.30 a.m., and a determined attack half an hour later forced the defenders back some distance. These men were now very battle-worn, after continued bitter, defensive fighting for over three weeks under the most appalling conditions of hardship. The 2/14th Battalion diarist recorded:

> The strain was beginning to tell on all members of the unit, and some of the lads in forward positions who had stood up to it well and had done a wonderful job right through, began to crack up. Enemy mortar, MG and field piece continued to do deadly work on our forward positions all morning and our casualties mounted.

A day or two before one of the officers had noted in his diary:

> This evening in the twilight I buried two Headquarters Company chaps. A very sad business as they had been terribly knocked. A shell had caught them in their slit trench. One of the chaps lending a hand fainted for a moment or two at the graveside. No one said a word—we just helped him to his feet. I noticed tears in the eyes of quite a few of the troops.[3]

On the left the progress of the 2/31st Battalion was still slow in the face of determined opposition. The leading company, Captain Hyndman's,[4] which had sustained much of the pressure since the battalion had begun its move, beat off a small but spirited Japanese attack soon after 8 a.m., causing fourteen Japanese casualties, it claimed, for the loss of two men wounded.

Even the usually imperturbable Eather was taken aback by the situation which was erupting so quickly round him. At 8.15 a.m. on the 16th he signalled to Allen:

> Enemy feeling whole front and flanks. Do not consider can hold him here. Request permission to withdraw to Imita Ridge if necessary. Porter concurs.

In a telephone conversation with Allen, which followed at 9.30 a.m., he said that he had no indication of the enemy strength but it was greater than he had anticipated; nor could he give any accurate indications either of his own or the Japanese casualties. He said that the Japanese were moving round his flanks and he did not think that he could hold them at Ioribaiwa but would do so if possible. He asked Allen whether he felt that if he could not hold at Ioribaiwa he might withdraw to Imita Ridge? Allen replied that he must keep on the offensive and must hold the enemy as long as possible. He impressed on Eather the importance of retaining Ioribaiwa but left to him the final decision whether he should withdraw or not.

---

[2] Maj T. E. Archer, VX12008; 2/33 Bn. Wool classer; of Brighton, Vic; b. Melbourne, 15 Apr 1916.
[3] Quoted in Russell, *The Second Fourteenth Battalion*, p. 170.
[4] Maj C. W. Hyndman, QX6153; 2/31 Bn. Regular soldier; of Ivanhoe, Vic; b. Melbourne, 6 Aug 1913.

Eather then decided to move back, reasoning that if he continued to hold the Ioribaiwa position he would soon have committed all his force to defensive tasks and would have lost any freedom of movement to adopt the offensive; that, as he was obliged to cover Port Moresby, he must keep his force intact; that his supply position was precarious, dependent upon native carriers who would be dispersed by any threat to his lines of communication; that a withdrawal to the line of Imita Ridge would give him time to establish patrols well forward with a view to advancing again as soon as he had established a firm base.

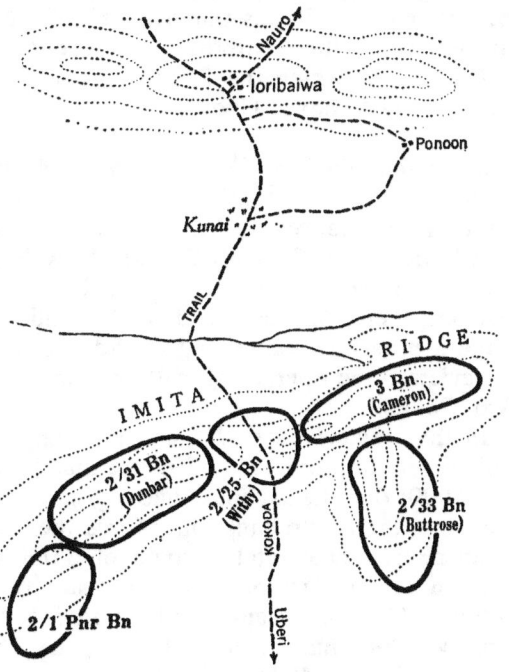

Dispositions, 20th September

With Buttrose still holding on the right Withy began to relieve the composite battalion in the forward positions about 11 a.m. and the small group of men who represented the 2/14th and 2/16th Battalions moved back. The 2/25th then remained firm while the other two battalions struck inwards on to the track in their rear. The 2/31st then dropped back. At 4.30 p.m. the last of the 2/25th left Ioribaiwa Ridge and passed through the 2/33rd which was thus left on the track as rearguard. As night came Captain Miller's[5] company of the 2/33rd formed a rearguard while the rest of the brigade struggled wearily over a slippery track through a night that was made more dark by heavy rain.

Late in the afternoon Allen told Eather that he must fight out the battle on the Imita Ridge. General Rowell, in turn, underlined those instructions in a message to Allen which read:

> Confirm your orders to Eather. Stress the fact that however many troops the enemy has they must all have walked from Buna. We are now so far back that any further withdrawal is out of question and Eather must fight it out at all costs. I am playing for time until 16 Inf Bde arrives.

Next morning Miller's men were still waiting in carefully-arranged ambush. They held their fire when the Japanese first appeared then poured volleys into an advancing group. As the platoons afterwards "leapfrogged"

---

[5] Capt L. Miller, TX2007. 2/33, 12/50 Bns. Librarian; of Launceston, Tas; b. Launceston, Tas, 2 Aug 1918.

back the pursuing Japanese were fairly caught by mortar fire. When the Australians finally broke contact they estimated that they had shot down fifty Japanese without loss to themselves.

By 11 a.m. on the 17th the main deployment on Imita Ridge had been completed. The 3rd Battalion was on the right of the track, the 2/25th in the centre, the 2/31st on the left. The 2/1st Pioneers were on the left rear and it was planned that the 2/33rd would fill the right rear position when their withdrawal was complete. The composite battalion, 272 strong of which the 2/14th provided only 10 officers and 77 men, was moving to cover Uberi.

Meanwhile the War Cabinet and the Advisory War Council had become anxious about the situation in New Guinea and, on 9th September, the Minister for the Army, Mr Forde, had asked General Blamey to go to Port Moresby, confer with General Rowell and report to the War Council. Blamey arrived at Port Moresby on the 12th, had discussions with the commanders there, and returned to Australia on the 14th. On the 16th he made a broadcast expressing confidence in the outcome and on the 17th he reviewed the operations in Papua and New Guinea before the Advisory War Council.

In that review he said that the strength of the Allied forces in New Guinea was approximately 30,000, that of their opponents estimated at up to 10,000; that the Japanese had a greater number of troops in the forward area than the Australians, their force there considered to be two regiments of an approximate total strength of 6,000; that this Japanese preponderance in forward strength was a result of Allied supply difficulties. He outlined his reinforcement plans saying that, in addition to the 25th Brigade which had recently arrived, the 16th Brigade was on the water, one squadron of light tanks was soon to be sent to Port Moresby with another squadron scheduled to follow; three field regiments, a mountain battery and one horse pack-transport unit were also being sent. In addition "a regiment of U.S. troops (approximately 3,500) was being sent to Port Moresby in accordance with the desire of the Commander-in-Chief S.W.P.A. that American troops should obtain experience in operations and in the development of supply arrangements in this area". He concluded by saying "Lieut-General Rowell, Major-General Allen and the troops are confident that the Japanese will not be able to take Port Moresby from the land", and that he shared their confidence.

It must have been a shock to Mr Curtin, therefore, when on the evening of the same day General MacArthur spoke with him by secraphone from Brisbane and told him that he was worried by the situation in New Guinea. MacArthur said that he considered that the real reason for the unsatisfactory position there was the lack of efficiency of the Australian troops; that he was convinced that the Australians were in superior numbers to the Japanese in the Owen Stanleys, but despite that, were, as at the beginning of the campaign, still withdrawing; that the Japanese, for their part, must be having similar difficulties to the Australians but they were *not* withdrawing. MacArthur felt that, if the Japanese penetration continued, the Allies in New Guinea would be forced into such a defensive concentration as would duplicate the conditions of Malaya. The invaders, he said, had not pushed across the mountains with a serious force and the fact that a small force could press such a situation on the defenders was causing him serious unease.

The American was at pains to point out that his view of the matter was not the view of the Australian military leaders. They were confident of their ability to meet the situation. But so far was he from sharing that confidence that he proposed to send American troops to the area by air or sea in order to do everything possible to stem the attack. Within a week he expected to have 40,000 men in New Guinea and, if they fought, they should have no trouble in meeting the situation. If they would not fight, he said, 100,000 there would be no good. He had been told that he could expect very substantial air reinforcements in the future but the commitments of the British and American fleets had left him without adequate naval support. He was affected by the American position in the Solomons which he thought was not favourable. On the whole, he considered, his problem was reduced to one of fending off the Japanese for some months, and the fight to this end must be made in New Guinea.

MacArthur's most immediate point was that General Blamey should go at once to New Guinea, personally take command there and "energize the situation". Not only did he consider this a military necessity but, for Blamey, he thought it was a personal necessity since, if the situation became really serious, it would be difficult for the Australian leader to meet his responsibility to the Australian public. MacArthur said he would speak to Blamey in these terms, although he had no authority actually to direct him. He asked if the Prime Minister would follow by speaking to the Australian general himself.

Mr Curtin said that he would tell General Blamey that he considered he should go to New Guinea and take command there. This he did by secraphone that day. Blamey agreed.[6]

The Australian commander was thus faced with a situation in which, pressed as he was both by the Commander-in-Chief of the South-West Pacific Area and the Prime Minister, no compromise was possible. He was solely responsible for the military leadership and organisation of all the Australian forces in the South-West Pacific, the bulk of which were *not* in New Guinea and were not yet fully efficient; and for all military aspects of the defence of the great land mass of Australia. It was a tribute to his self-control and sagacity that he had thus far refrained

---

[6] A passage in *MacArthur: 1941-1951*, published in 1956, by Maj-Gen Charles A. Willoughby, who was MacArthur's senior Intelligence Officer, and John Chamberlain, suggests that MacArthur himself moved to Port Moresby at this time or earlier. In p. 83 they write: "There remained the overland threat to Moresby: Intelligence reports soon made it plain to MacArthur that the Japanese planned to cross the 14,000-foot Owen Stanleys along the Kokoda Trail. Thus 'the Papuan peninsula would be stitched into the Japanese pattern of quick conquest'. MacArthur determined to prevent this at all costs. He moved into Port Moresby personally, along with his staff, to join a handful of Australians and local Europeans who had come to New Guinea to prospect for gold and who remained to fight."
In fact MacArthur moved to Moresby with an advanced echelon of GHQ on 6 Nov 1942.

from intervening personally in the control of forward operations; and to his ability to delegate responsibility and refrain from interference. As a soldier it would no doubt have been a relief to him to transfer temporarily to a field command.

In his address to the Advisory War Council there had been no hint of lack of confidence in his subordinate generals, no suggestion that he wished to take the conduct of operations out of their hands. Nor did Blamey hasten to comply with the Prime Minister's instruction. It was not until 20th September that he informed Rowell of it and not until the 23rd that he arrived in Port Moresby. In his letter to Rowell on the 20th he was frank in his criticism of the "politicians", and at the same time showed that he was aware of the practical and personal difficulties of the somewhat amateurish arrangement that had been forced upon him.

The powers that be (he wrote) have determined that I shall myself go to New Guinea for a while and operate from there. I do not, however, propose to transfer many of Adv HQ Staff and will arrive by aeroplane Wednesday evening, I hope with Hopkins.[7] At present I propose to bring with me only my PA, Major Carlyon,[8] two extra cipher officers and Lieut Lawson.[9] I hope you will be able to house us in your camp and messes.

I hope you will not be upset at this decision, and will not think that it implies any lack of confidence in yourself. I think it arises out of the fact that we have very inexperienced politicians who are inclined to panic on every possible occasion, and I think the relationship between us personally is such that we can make the arrangement work without any difficulty.

When, however, the Commander-in-Chief arrived at Port Moresby at 5 p.m. on 23rd September Rowell met him, quickly made it clear that he did not welcome him, and it soon became painfully evident that "the arrangement" would not work as Blamey had hoped. Rowell recorded later:

On 21 Sep 42 I received a semi-official letter from the C-in-C advising that he was proceeding to MORESBY on 23 Sep 42 to operate from there.

I met the C-in-C at the aerodrome at 1700 hrs on 23 Sep 42. During the evening of that day, and once on each of the two days following, we had a full and frank discussion of the position of the G.O.C. NEW GUINEA Force in view of the C-in-C's arrival. At times the discussion was acrimonious as I then believed, and still do believe, that the C-in-C's confidence in me, expressed in broadcast of 16 Sep 42, no longer existed.

The main theme of these discussions, apart from the question of loss of confidence, was an endeavour to find a working arrangement suited to the circumstances. The fact that General Blamey had no staff with him made it inevitable that my own staff would, sooner or later, be called on to serve two masters and that I would gradually become a figure-head.

The C-in-C suggested that I should become a deputy to him but I demurred at this as it would have merely made me a staff officer with all vestige of command authority removed.

---

[7] Maj-Gen R. N. L. Hopkins, CBE, NX392. (1st AIF: Lt 6 LH Regt 1918.) CO 7 Cav Regt 1940; GSO1 1 Armd Div 1941-42; DMO LHQ 1942; BGS HQ NG Force 1942-43; LO between LHQ and 7 Amphibious Force US Navy 1943-44. Regular soldier; b. Stawell, Vic, 24 May 1897.
[8] Lt-Col N. D. Carlyon, OBE, VX11996. ADC to GOC I Corps 1940-42; PA to C-in-C AMF 1942-44; Mil Asst to C-in-C 1944-45. Managing director; of Melbourne; b. Ballarat, Vic, 4 Sep 1903.
[9] Maj R. A. Lawson, MBE, VX398. Staff of Gen Blamey 1939-43; Mil Sec Branch AHQ 1944-45. Clerk; of Sandringham, Vic; b. Melbourne, 22 Feb 1913.

I submitted a proposal, which was not acceptable to the C-in-C, that the size of the force either in NEW GUINEA or under orders to move warranted the establishment of an Army Headquarters under which myself and my staff would have been responsible for the defence of MORESBY and for operations in the OWEN STANLEY Range. The superior Headquarters would then have had general responsibility for the whole area, as well as the detailed control of MILNE BAY and Commando units at WAU.

Later (1st October) Blamey wrote to Curtin:

I would like to say that the personal animus displayed towards me was most unexpected. . . .

In regard to his [Rowell's] . . . claim that I had failed to safeguard his interests in accepting the direction of yourself and the C-in-C, S.W.P.A., I informed him perfectly frankly of the exact incidence of events which led me to come to New Guinea, and there appears to be no ground for any resentment or objections on his part. It seemed to me when I received your directions and those of the C-in-C, S.W.P.A., that it behoved me to carry out those instructions, and there can be no doubt that when the consequent instructions were given to General Rowell, it was his duty also to carry them out without question, cheerfully and cooperatively. I endeavoured to induce him to see this point of view, but his resentment was too deep.

I informed him that I did not propose to make any alteration in the method of command, and I would do nothing that would derogate from his authority. He asserted his intention of refusing to accept the situation and remain in New Guinea. I pointed out that such an attitude would be unacceptable to any Government and that it would certainly mean his retirement from the Forces. . . . This was the substance of my interview with him on the day of my arrival on the 23rd September.

A very strained situation continued between the two men on 24th September. On the evening of that day Blamey asked Major-General Burston[1] (the head of the army's medical services, and an old friend of Rowell's) to speak to Rowell and try to make him see the situation as Blamey saw it. This, however, apparently did nothing to ease the tension. On the 25th Blamey went to Milne Bay and, apparently, without reference to Rowell, gave orders to Major-General Clowes for the dispatch of a force to Wanigela:

On the second day after my arrival I visited Milne Bay accompanied by Brigadier-General Walker, US Forces, temporarily commanding the air forces in New Guinea. From our discussions there it appeared that we might develop close cooperation between the air and land forces and overcome the difficulties of movement to some extent by the transport of land forces and supplies by air. This necessitated the finding of landing grounds. An examination of the landing ground at Wanigela Mission, approximately 100 miles north-east of Milne Bay, made it appear possible that the first step might be made in this way, and it was ultimately decided to fly the 2/10th Battalion, A.I.F., to Wanigela from Milne Bay.[2]

Next day Rowell addressed this minute to Blamey:

1. By the terms of para 3 of LHQ Operation Instruction No. 30 dated 9 Aug 42,

---

[1] Maj-Gen S. R. Burston, CB, CBE, DSO, VD, VX2. (1st AIF: 7 Fd Amb; SMO AGB Depot 1917-18.) DDMS I Corps 1940; DMS AIF in ME 1940-42; DGMS LHQ 1942-45, AMF 1945-47. Physician; of Adelaide; b. Melbourne, 21 Mar 1888.

[2] Commander Allied Land Forces, Report on New Guinea operations—23rd September 42-23rd January 43.

GOC 1 Aust Corps, which appointment I was holding at the time, was designated Commander "New Guinea Force".

2. Para 4 of the same instruction authorised me to exercise operational control over all military forces constituting New Guinea Force at that time and such other troops as may have been subsequently assigned thereto.

3. Your arrival at Moresby to operate as Commander-in-Chief from here will inevitably vary my authority and it is submitted that the position needs to be defined so that all concerned will know what variation is contemplated. This applies particularly to Allied formation commanders now exercising command under my orders as well as the joint service aspect of Navy, Army and Air cooperation. In this connection I instance your verbal orders to Commander Milne Force at Milne Bay on 25 Sep 42 regarding the despatch of a detachment to Wanigela.

4. The question of the exercise of powers of the Authorised Person under National Security (Emergency Control) Regulations will also need to be determined. By the terms of para 18 of LHQ Operation Instruction No. 30, the powers of the Authorised Person are vested in me. The wording of the regulation is as follows:

'The Senior Officer of the Military Forces for the time being present and having the operational command of the Military Forces serving in that part.'

It would now appear that this authority should pass to you and that fresh delegations be made to replace those already issued to me.

Blamey did not reply directly but, later in the day, issued the following directive to Rowell:

I have been directed by the Prime Minister and the Commander-in-Chief, South-West Pacific Area, to take control of the forces in the New Guinea area.

For the present it does not appear necessary or desirable to set up an additional headquarters staff. Therefore I propose to exercise command through yourself and the present staff.

I will be glad if you will direct that arrangements are made to furnish me promptly with all tactical and other information and alterations in the functions, allocations, dispositions and location of troops.

I will be glad if you will ensure that all messages and information for Headquarters Allied Land Forces or Headquarters Australian Military Forces are submitted to me, including Situation Reports, before dispatch.

In the event of my absence from Headquarters, where it is apparent that such absence would cause undue delay in furnishing such information, you will forward it direct, at the same time taking such action as is necessary to ensure that I am kept fully informed.

The above applies also to matters of Administration of any importance. . . .

Rowell then set the necessary processes in train to these ends. On the 27th he and Blamey discussed and decided upon certain arrangements which they would follow. It seemed that a *modus vivendi* had been arrived at, but later that day Blamey decided that New Guinea Force was not making adequate efforts to provide him promptly with information, though he did not tell Rowell this. At 9 a.m. on 28th September, he told Rowell that he had decided to relieve him of his command and that he had telegraphed an "adverse report" on him to both the Prime Minister and General MacArthur. He did in fact send two reports to both that day in the second of which he asked that Lieut-General Herring be sent to Port Moresby as Rowell's successor. In justification of his decision he referred in a letter to Curtin[3] to what he called Rowell's "non-cooperative attitude" and said:

With reference to the statement in my message that I was not satisfied that necessary energy, foresight and drive had been shown, the following items are cited—
(i) The capacity to drive the Japanese from New Guinea depends on our capacity to place sufficient forces in suitable tactical positions to do so.
The present line of advance via Kokoda is so difficult that it will be months before a force of 2,000 men could be supplied by this route. There is no hope of achieving victory along this route alone.
I had urged on my previous visit, a fortnight earlier, that the route north from Abau should be examined energetically. No action was taken by General Rowell to do so. It was left to GHQ SWPA to direct their Chief Engineer, General Casey, to make such an investigation.
I took immediate action to energize this effort.
(ii) A second instance is the lack of effort to take advantage of our success at Milne Bay.
Details of an operation about to take place for this are contained in another communication.
General Rowell's attitude to this operation was expressed in his own words in the presence of myself and another officer—'If we take it on it will only lead to the Japs sending more in.' He said, however, he was prepared to direct General Clowes to carry out the operation.
It was clearly a case that demanded vigorous action by the Commander of the Force. I took such action and went to Milne Bay with the American Air Force Commander, and, in consultation with General Clowes, outline of the operation was decided.
General Rowell, however, held that I had taken the command out of his hands.

Blamey's letter continued:

On the other side, I would like to say that the effort that has been put into this locality has produced most striking results and that General Rowell has cooperated in the development of this area with the Air Force splendidly.
Apart from his insubordinate attitude, my principal criticism is a lack of appreciation of the need for seeking out energetically the possibilities of developing aggressive action. This, I think, is due mainly to limited experience of command.

Rowell had left New Guinea before this letter was written and he was given no opportunity of replying to the charges it contained. It is most difficult now to determine how well-founded they might have been. Despite Blamey's assertion that it would "be months before a force of 2,000 men could be supplied by this [the Kokoda] route", nevertheless the 16th and 25th Brigades (numbering substantially more than 2,000) were fighting and being maintained along this route during October-November. As for "the route north from Abau"—an attempted advance by Americans over this route later was only partially successful and had no practical result. Furthermore, Rowell was later to deny that Blamey had directed him to examine this route, writing:

When Blamey made his first trip, MacNider [commanding the first troops of the 126th U.S. Regiment to arrive in Port Moresby] was already in Moresby. I had talked with MacNider and expressed my views as to sideshows. I said that, as he was acting on G.H.Q. orders, I couldn't veto his proposals, but I made it clear

---
[3] Dated 1st October 1942.

that there would be no diversion of facilities from the main task. I discussed this with Blamey when he came in and he was in complete agreement.

In respect of the Wanigela move Rowell was later to write:

In my period of command the role of Milne Force was never changed. This Wanigela concept was all of a pattern with the American idea of outflanking the mountains. . . . Blamey certainly did raise it with me and I probably answered as I did. The test of the Wanigela move is an assessment of what it actually achieved in the overall plan.

In reporting the situation to the Advisory War Council on 1st October Mr Curtin said

He did not believe . . . that Lieut-General Rowell had been transferred because of any lack of confidence by General Blamey in General Rowell's decisions on operational matters.

In a later report to the Council on 15th October

the Prime Minister referred to his interview with Lieut-General Rowell on 3rd October, and said that he had formed the impression that the difficulties had arisen out of a clash of personalities and temperaments.

This episode, set in motion by MacArthur's ill-advised proposal and ill-informed criticisms of 17th September, was an unhappy one for the army in general, for the Australian Commander-in-Chief, and for General Rowell. The Commander-in-Chief had fostered Rowell's great promise and now, a strong man, found a seriously estranged subordinate unexpectedly and starkly opposing him at a critical time. Rowell, high-principled and proud, having allowed personal feelings temporarily to cloud his judgment, was called upon to hand over his command just as his cool and patient planning seemed about to bear fruit. Had Blamey been patient a little longer, had Rowell been less open and direct, the moment would have passed.[4]

General Rowell left New Guinea on the 28th. On the same day General Blamey issued an Order of the Day stating that he had assumed command of the forces in New Guinea on the 24th. What was the general position in New Guinea when General Blamey thus assumed command in his own person?

After issuing instructions on 9th September which had freed the 7th Division to concentrate on operations north of Port Moresby, General Rowell had, on the 14th, precisely defined the forward area for which the division was responsible. This was the region of the Kokoda Track north and north-east of the Laloki River which ran roughly parallel with the coast and some ten miles north of it, east of an imaginary line through Hombrom Bluff which lay about half-way between Port Moresby and Owers' Corner. The main units allotted to the division were those of the 21st and 25th Brigades, the 3rd and 55th Battalions, 2/1st Pioneers, 2/6th

---
[4] A detailed account of the sequels to this episode appears in J. Hetherington, *Blamey* (1954), pp. 166-70.

Field Company, 2/14th Army Field Company, and 2/4th and 2/6th Field Ambulances.

On the same day the 30th Brigade had been ordered to stop any penetration which might develop by land into the Port Moresby base area through the country from Hombrom Bluff west to the Brown River, which flowed roughly south from the mountains to join the Laloki some nine miles north-north-west of Port Moresby. Within that area the Goldie River ran south-west to the Laloki from the vicinity of the Kokoda Track. Additionally the brigade had been given a defence role against landings in the Port Moresby area. To carry out all these tasks it had the 39th, 49th and 53rd Battalions (with the 53rd, however, allotted the work of unloading ships), Honner Force, and the 2/6th Independent Company less detachments.

The rest of the field force had been organised into three groups: the 14th Brigade in a coast-defence role at Port Moresby, with only the 36th Battalion under command at the time; an artillery group—including the 13th and 14th Field Regiments—given defensive tasks against attack from both the land and the sea; the New Guinea Force Composite Carrier Group, made up of the bulk of the carrier and mortar platoons of the 21st and 25th Brigades, as a reserve designed to act as a mobile striking force.

A minor aspect of the planning on the formation level during this mid-September period, was that which involved the operation of two separate small forces wide on the east and west of the Kokoda Track. On the east General Allen had established a detachment of company strength made up from the rear details of the 21st Brigade and commanded by Major Robinson[6] of the 2/16th Battalion, with orders to prevent any Japanese advance south from Nauro by native tracks which led through many miles of broken country to Jawarere. This constituted Jawforce. On the west was Honner Force. It constituted an interesting experiment, and represented recognition of the fact that, in the form of warfare which had developed in the mountains, an enemy could and should be struck along his vital supply and communication lines. Unfortunately plans to maintain Honner by means of horse transport and air drops could not be realised for lack of enough horses and lack of suitable dropping grounds. Honner was told, therefore, that he was not to go beyond the limits of the rations which he carried and, about the 17th, he was approaching that limit without having encountered Japanese.

This same period saw the first arrival of American infantry in New Guinea in accordance with General MacArthur's directions that, initially, one regiment should be used to find an alternative track across Papua by which they could strike the Japanese on the Kokoda Track in the rear. The plan was, in fact, an extension of that which Rowell had attempted to put into operation with Honner Force.

On 12th September a small advanced party, under Brigadier-General Hanford MacNider, arrived in Port Moresby to make preliminary arrange-

---

[6] Maj A. Robinson, DSO, WX1589; 2/16 Bn. Hotel keeper; of Geraldton, WA; b. Prescot, Lancs, England, 13 Apr 1906.

ments for the American operations. After consulting with Rowell, MacNider decided on the route which the Americans would follow. They would go by way of Rigo, a coastal village 40 or 50 miles south-east of Port Moresby, up the valley of the Kemp Welsh River which flowed almost due south from the mountains, thence to Dorobisolo on the southern slopes of the main Owen Stanley Range. They would strike then north-east across the range itself to Jaure on the headwaters of the Kumusi River. From Jaure they would probably follow the line of the Kumusi, flowing north-west, to Wairopi on the Buna side of Kokoda. Over this proposed route a small reconnaissance patrol started on the 17th, guided by Lieutenant Sydney Smith[7] of Angau.

The previous day an advanced detachment of the 126th Infantry Regiment, from the 32nd U.S. Division, had arrived at Moresby. It consisted of one company of the II Battalion and a company of the 114th Engineers. By the 25th this detachment had built a motor road to Rigo and had begun the establishment of a base. The main body of the 126th arrived at Moresby on the 28th.

But these were not the only American infantry being sent to New Guinea at this time although the original plans for the drive to the Kokoda Track from the south-east had envisaged the use of only one regiment. On the 18th September two companies of the 128th Regiment arrived at Moresby by air and the rest of the regiment followed in the next few days. The decision to send in this formation and its accelerated movement once that decision had been made, were obviously the results of the unease which MacArthur had expressed to Curtin on the 17th.

On the 20th September Rowell had assessed the position, as he saw it, in a letter to headquarters in Australia.

> 1. The main reasons for the success of the Japanese in forcing the Owen Stanley Range and advancing on Moresby are as follows:—
> (a) Superior enemy strength at the decisive time and place.
> (b) More simple administrative needs of the Japanese soldier and his better clothing and equipment particularly in respect of camouflage.
> (c) Lack of reinforcing troops to restore a situation where the enemy was gaining superiority e.g. at Isurava and Efogi.
> (d) Higher standard of training of enemy in jungle warfare. Our men have been bewildered and are still dominated by their environment.
>
> 2. A stage has now been reached where there is every prospect, owing to the enemy administrative difficulties and to the very considerable reinforcements arriving for us here, that any further deep penetration, other than by small patrols, can be stopped. The problem now to be solved is what is to be the future role of New Guinea Force in the Moresby area.
>
> 3. The primary task, as I see it, is the retention of Moresby as an Air Operational Base. This now demands adequate protection against seaborne attack as well as defence against further enemy inroads, either by the direct route into Moresby or by side-tracks and trails such as those down the Goldie and Brown Rivers.
>
> 4. Until recently, the only form of defence considered here was that against seaborne attack, but the needs of the situation to the north have forced me to draw away more and more troops until today there is only one battalion [53rd] of

---

[7] Capt S. S. Smith, NX151299; Angau. Civil servant; of Port Moresby; b. Cooktown, Qld, 7 Mar 1916.

(*Australian War Memorial*)

The so-called "Golden Stairs", rising towards Imita Ridge, each step battened at its edge by a rough log, sometimes broken and therefore treacherous, and cradling mud and water from the afternoon rains.

(*Australian War Memorial*)
Brigadier K. W. Eather (left), commander of the 25th Brigade, and Major-General A. S. Allen, G.O.C. 7th Division. September 1942.

(*Australian War Memorial*)
The 2/33rd Battalion crossing the log bridge over the Brown River on the way from Nauro to Menari. October 1942.

indifferent fighting quality available for direct defence, and that is employed entirely on unloading ships. There are, in addition, certain beach defence guns and MMGs in more or less permanent locations. This stage of affairs should not be permitted to persist and I consider that a garrison of not less than one division with a complement of tanks should be located here for this role alone.

5. The defence of Moresby from the north can be best achieved by operations which will force the enemy further and further back. The projected move of 126 US Infantry Regt may conceivably help to achieve this, but it will take some little time to stage and its effect will not be felt immediately. It may, of course, merely have the effect of forcing the enemy to reinforce the Buna area to meet the threat, a move for which he presumably has adequate troops at Rabaul. It is not proposed to allow 126 US Regt to commence its move from Moresby until the local situation is stabilised. Present plans are based on its moving via Rigo, but I consider that base should be moved to Abau, subject to satisfactory results of recoe [reconnaissance] by the Engineer in Chief at GHQ.

6. Operations astride the Myola-Kokoda track will be costly, both in combat troops and administrative effort. I consider the best results are likely to be obtained by applying steady pressure on the main track as far to the north as possible, and relying on exploitation by side-tracks to cut into the enemy L of C and so force him to withdraw. Possibilities in this regard are, up the Goldie River into Ioribaiwa, and from Itiki through Jawarere to Nauro.

7. The limiting factor in these proposals is always administrative. Lack of pack transport and continual decrease in availability of native porters will restrict the size of flanking forces which can be employed. Improvement of tracks and arrival of pack transport companies will, however, increase the probable scope of such moves.

8. Defensive requirements to the north, together with provision of adequate troops for offensive operations, will call for a division. This does not need to be organised on standard lines—in fact, such an organisation is wasteful here. For example artillery is not necessary, but infantry units should have a very much larger number of personnel in rifle companies.

9. In this regard there are two important factors to be stressed:
 (a) Wastage of manpower in jungle and mountain warfare.
 (b) Training in this type of warfare.
 (a) MANPOWER
  The wastage of personnel from battle casualties and physical exhaustion is extremely high. This demands greater infantry W/Es [War Establishments] as well as reserves of fresh units to replace those temporarily depleted in numbers or otherwise battle weary.
 (b) TRAINING
  Training as known in Queensland bears no relation to jungle conditions. The Port Moresby area itself is just as bad a training ground. It is essential that troops get into actual jungle and learn to master its difficulties of tactics, movement and control.

10. These two factors, taken together, postulate the need for a second division of the special type that can be always available for active operations, and the other for re-fitting and training. There would accordingly always be the equivalent of a division available here, specially organised and trained for operations outside the Moresby area, if and when the occasion arises.

11. The question of personnel replacement requires urgent attention. All except one of the AIF Bdes, are now in, or en route to New Guinea, and they all need reinforcements to a greater or lesser degree. If personnel are not available these formations will merely waste away, and there are not unlimited troops (US) to take their place.

Rowell's statement in the fourth paragraph of that letter—"the needs of the situation to the north have forced me to draw away more and more troops until today there is only one battalion of indifferent fighting quality available for direct defence [against sea-borne attack]"—was well illustrated by the command groupings which existed on 23rd September (the day of General Blamey's arrival). By that time Rowell had in operation a two-divisional organisation, following the opening in Port Moresby on the 19th of the headquarters of the 6th Division, under General Vasey.[8] The 6th Division itself had never existed as such since its departure from the Middle East, because of the retention of two of its brigades in Ceylon and the posting of the third brigade to the Northern Territory. Now, although its headquarters had been re-established, its 16th Brigade had disembarked at Port Moresby only on the 21st, the 17th was bound for Milne Bay, and the 19th was still in the Darwin area.

Within the 7th Division were the 25th Brigade Group (including, in addition to its normal battalions, the 3rd and 2/1st Pioneer), the 14th Brigade (36th, 39th and 55th Battalions), and the 16th and 21st Brigades. The role of the 25th Brigade was unchanged, the 14th Brigade had the task of keeping secure the lines of communication between Ilolo and Uberi, the 16th Brigade was to cover the approaches to Port Moresby through the Eilogo-Hombrom Bluff area, and the 21st Brigade was scheduled for relief.

The 6th Division for the moment comprised the 30th Brigade (49th and 53rd Battalions and Honner Force), the 2/6th Independent Company less detachments, the 128th American Infantry Regiment, the New Guinea Force Carrier Group, the 13th Field Regiment, 2/6th Field Regiment and one battery of the 14th and some anti-tank artillery. On their relief the 21st Brigade and the 39th Battalion were to come under command, as also on arrival were the 7th Divisional Cavalry and 2/1st and 2/5th Field Regiments which were moving to Port Moresby. General Vasey had been ordered to stop penetration into the Port Moresby base area through the country west of Hombrom Bluff, to patrol offensively to the Japanese west flank and to defend Port Moresby against seaborne attack.

But all this organisation and preparation was secondary in importance to the operations at the front. When it had been determined on the 17th that Blamey would go to New Guinea Eather had been seeking a firm base at Imita Ridge. There his men, lacking shovels, dug in with bayonets and steel helmets, screened by the offensive patrolling which he had put into operation. The patrols were about 50 strong, all ranks. They carried five days' rations, a Bren gun and at least seven sub-machine-guns, and were ordered to harass their enemies, particularly along the lines of communication. As they began to operate Eather was getting the breathing space he needed for the Japanese had not followed his withdrawal. Nor had his losses been heavy: 8 had been killed, 84 wounded in exchange, he estimated, for some 200 Japanese killed.

One of the first of the strong patrols to go out on the 18th was led

---

[8] The post of Deputy Chief of the General Staff, hitherto held by Vasey, was filled by Major-General F. H. Berryman, who, since April, had been Major-General, General Staff of the First Army.

by Captain Dodd[9] of the 2/25th Battalion. Between Imita Ridge and Ioribaiwa Dodd located a Japanese post in the course of preparation. Before dawn on the 19th he rushed this with grenades, sub-machine-guns and bayonets. On the morning of the 19th he continued skirmishing and then, still forward, rested in ambush waiting for night to come again. Apart from this small action the day was uneventful except that the 2/33rd Battalion entered the main positions. Eather's force was then concentrated and firm, its main strength (excluding the headquarters of the 21st Brigade and the composite 2/14th-2/16th Battalion which, by this time, were back at Uberi) numbering 132 officers and 2,492 men made up as follows:

HQ 25th Brigade	8 and 70
2/25th Battalion	27 and 520
2/31st Battalion	26 and 502
2/33rd Battalion	28 and 490
2/1st Pioneer Battalion	20 and 540
3rd Battalion	22 and 347
2/6 Independent Company Patrol	1 and 23

The 20th passed quietly. Dodd reported from his forward position that, with the dawn, he had discovered a slight Japanese recession but much activity in the vicinity of the track. He waited until the day was late but the Japanese showed no signs of advancing. He then started back while a similar patrol from the 3rd Battalion under Captain Atkinson[10] and Lieutenant Dullard[1] moved forward. Other patrols had little to report. Farther back Porter was ordered to return his headquarters to the base area on the 21st while the 2/14th and 2/16th Battalions resumed their separate identities at Uberi and readjusted their positions.

The next three days were marked by Japanese passivity under bombardment from guns of the 14th Field Regiment, sited at Owers' Corner, in the face of questing Australian patrols, and on the 22nd, by a cautious movement forward along the track by the 2/25th Battalion. Withy met no opposition although, ahead of him and west of Ioribaiwa, Atkinson's patrol lost Dullard and three men killed.

By the evening of the 23rd, therefore—the day of General Blamey's arrival—Eather had already begun to edge forward again against a supine enemy whose numbers west of Ioribaiwa his patrols had estimated at about 600.

On the 24th General Allen conferred with Eather at Imita Ridge. Withy's forward platoons, under Lieutenants Steel[2] and Walker,[3] engaged

---

[9] Lt-Col R. W. P. Dodd, MC, QX6337; 2/25 Bn. Theatre manager; of Toowoomba, Qld; b. Kerang, Vic, 17 Mar 1913.

[10] Capt W. J. S. Atkinson, MC, NX12877. 3 and 2/4 Bns. Clerk; of Canberra, ACT; b. Skipton, Vic, 7 Dec 1910.

[1] Lt E. A. Dullard, NX76318; 3 Bn. Public servant; of Canberra, ACT; b. Melbourne, 30 Dec 1916. Killed in action 24 Sep 1942.

[2] Lt H. W. Steel, QX5502; 2/25 Bn. Stock and station agent; of Stanthorpe, Qld; b. Sydney, 10 Jan 1913.

[3] Capt B. G. C. Walker, QX7214; 2/25 Bn. Clerk; of Clayfield, Qld; b. Brisbane, 7 Sep 1918.

entrenched Japanese and then Captain O'Bryen's[4] "B" Company took over. O'Bryen pushed hard on the 25th, gained a little ground and captured some equipment and Withy began recasting his position to assist O'Bryen and maintain the pressure. Eather planned now to hold with Withy in the centre and move Buttrose's and Dunbar's battalions round the right and left flanks respectively. He began this manoeuvre on the 26th with Withy still in contact. By nightfall on the 27th, with the Japanese positions under artillery bombardment, Buttrose and Dunbar were closing in on Ioribaiwa from the flanks while Withy's men, who had pressed slowly forward, had penetrated barriers and defence works which blocked the track and were in fleeting touch. Eather proposed to launch his men at the Ioribaiwa positions next day.

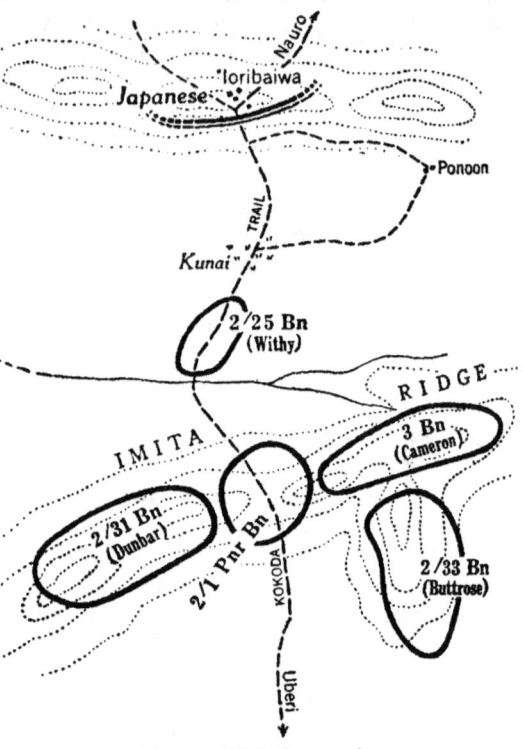

Noon, 23rd September

On the 28th the attack went forward as planned but there was no opposition. The Japanese had abandoned their positions and much equipment. By the end of the day the three battalions were in occupation of the Ioribaiwa area. There the 3rd Battalion joined them on the 29th. By that time offensive patrols were already pushing forward towards Nauro where one of them, under Captain Andrew[5] of the 2/25th, arrived on the 30th to find that it too had been abandoned.

It seemed now that all the factors which had operated so adversely against the Australians at the beginning of the mountains campaign were now operating, even more effectively, against their enemies. But none of those who had fought the Japanese doubted that much desperate fighting still lay ahead even though the immediate overland threat to Port Moresby seemed to have been removed. During the process of removing that threat, however, a rather bitter judgment had been brought to bear on some of the leaders and men of the Australian Army. How far did a clearer perspective now enable those judgments to be sustained?

[4] Maj T. J. C. O'Bryen, QX6305; 2/25 Bn. Branch manager; of Emerald, Qld; b. Townsville, Qld, 27 Jun 1906.

[5] Maj C. S. Andrew, QX6336; 2/25 Bn. Assistant agriculturist; of Crow's Nest, Qld; b. Crow's Nest, 23 Mar 1920.

To Mr Curtin on the 17th September General MacArthur had said the Australian commanders had the utmost confidence in their ability to deal with the situation but that he did not share that confidence. The stage which had been reached by the end of September, however, vindicated the Australians. But there were many who accepted General Blamey's presence in New Guinea from the 23rd onwards as the obvious reason for this improvement. Clearly this could not have been the reason. Eather's withdrawal to Imita Ridge had been the immediate cause for the Commander-in-Chief's presence in New Guinea. But, before he arrived, Eather was already on the move forward once more. There was no new circumstance associated with Blamey's arrival which affected the events of the next few days in the slightest. Those stemmed from three main sets of conditions: the exhaustion of Japanese men and means as a result of the Australian resistance, particularly by Potts' brigade, and as a result of the difficulties of the Kokoda Track; the presence and skill of Eather and his men at a critical time; General Rowell's planning.

Potts was transferred to another command. But Eather's first tactical move after he had been committed was to continue the process of withdrawal which had been forced on Potts—and he had then a completely fresh brigade, at the beginning only of the notorious Kokoda Track and therefore not drained of strength by a long and rigorous approach to battle, while, in addition, he had the remnants of the 21st Brigade, the 3rd Battalion, the 2/1st Pioneers. He had been able to accept battle as a formation. Potts, on the other hand, had had only four battalions initially, one of which (the 53rd) was soon sent out of battle. His men had walked over the mountains to be committed company by company on arrival. He had met the Japanese in the full impetus of their advance when they were fresh, vigorous and well found, and when there was no strength to fight forward from behind him. Although Eather had to rely on pack transport and native carriers, his supply line was a short one. Potts was at the uncertain end of a long and most uncertain line, bogged in the soft sands of other peoples' logistical errors. Eather withdrew in order to establish a firm base and sent forth strong, offensive patrols. But the Japanese gave him the pause he needed to achieve this. Potts withdrew, again and again, with a similar purpose, but his pursuers kept at him and denied him the opportunity he needed so desperately. The climactic affair at Efogi might have happened earlier had his men not fought vigorously and manoeuvred swiftly.

From these, and additional analogies, it is difficult to escape the conclusion that Eather, or any other leader in Potts' circumstances, would have had to follow precisely the line of action which the latter had followed. It was unfortunate for Potts, therefore, that Blamey thought it desirable to transfer him to Darwin (a comparative backwater) soon after the 21st Brigade was relieved. Rowell and Allen had not wished him to go. Blamey and Herring, who did not at that time understand so well the circumstances in which Potts had found himself and the way he had acquitted himself, genuinely misjudged him.

What of the judgments which had weighed the men and professed to find them wanting? Stronger than his statement to Mr Curtin regarding "lack of efficiency" were General MacArthur's reports to the military leaders in America. His lack of confidence was certainly justified in the case of one militia battalion, but the connected story of the others testified that his strictures were quite unwarranted. In the beginning the lack of confidence undoubtedly arose from lack of knowledge of the nature of the country and of the problems of a form of warfare with which he was not familiar. Perhaps, too, he did not understand the Australians' day-to-day account of operations. At the beginning of September, and referring particularly to reports of the Milne Bay operations, General Vasey had written to General Rowell:

. . . I am more convinced than ever that our reports need to be written in Americanese. They [the Americans] don't understand our restrained English.

The remark points to the whole field of difficulties implicit in the integration of the forces of two or more nations. Further, MacArthur was struggling for additional forces of all kinds to enable him to begin his offensive. By depreciating the quality of the forces he already had, he could underline his needs. But, however critical their American leader might be of them, the men of the 21st Brigade felt that they had justified themselves.

Both the 2/14th and 2/16th Battalions had started over the trail in the second half of August approximately 550 strong. On 19th September they numbered only 101 and 143 respectively. Since that date they had not suffered casualties, and small bands and individuals had rejoined them. But they were pathetically reduced both numerically and physically when, on relief by the 36th Battalion, they left Uberi on the 26th. They still had their "left out of battle" personnel as a nucleus on which to rebuild, and many men would return from hospital, but, for some time to come, they could not be considered a fighting force. Nor could the third battalion of the brigade, the 2/27th, whose story had been a separate one after they had been cut off at Efogi.

Between the time of the arrival of the 25th Brigade and the relief of the 2/14th and 2/16th Battalions, individuals or small parties had reported in to the Australian positions with news of the main body of the 2/27th Battalion which had been missing since the night of 8th September.

When they broke off the track between Menari and Efogi in the wake of the other two battalions Colonel Cooper's men found, like the others, that the going was very difficult. In addition their wounded slowed them down—some walking, twelve being carried on stretchers by soldiers themselves since the native bearers had deserted during the fighting. A black night, overcast and drizzling with rain, added to their difficulties so Cooper decided to bivouac until dawn.

On the morning of the 9th he sent ahead those of the 2/14th and 2/16th Battalions who had stayed with him, and the fittest of the walking wounded, proceeding more slowly with the rest of his battalion. The men were breaking their way through the bush, pulling themselves painfully up the steep slopes by means of trailing vines and trees, crawling on their hands and knees, dragging the clumsy stretchers with them. In the early afternoon Captain Smith,[6] the staff captain from brigade, met them with seventy native bearers and that eased the situation although the soldiers themselves still had to carry five of the stretchers.

Shortly before that Captain Sims with his company and Lieutenant Sandison[7] with two platoons of another company had been ordered to push ahead more swiftly to Menari, reconnoitre the situation there and assist, if necessary, to hold that position open until the rest of the battalion arrived.

Sims found Japanese in possession at Menari. The nature of his approach was such that he considered that to attack would mean committing his men two at a time over open ground. By this time he had lost all contact with the rest of the battalion so decided to withdraw under cover of darkness south-east along a creek bed below the Japanese positions to a point at which he calculated Cooper would strike the creek. But he could not regain touch with his unit. Next day, after spending much time cutting a track through lawyer vine, bamboo and secondary growth of all kinds, his men found themselves overlooking Nauro just as evening was falling. A patrol sent forward reported the Japanese in possession. Sims felt that attack was out of the question. His men had had little food since the 6th. It was now the 10th. Their ammunition was low. He conferred with his officers and they decided that they would have a better chance of survival if split into platoon groups. They therefore broke up and set out once more.

Sims' own story indicates what was, in greater or less degree, the experience of all the groups during the days which followed:

We had our first meal when we shot a pig in a village on the 14th September.... Most of the troops had dysentery and were very weak and emaciated. We'd go from daybreak till sunset. We burnt the pig meat on our bayonets. We were going to put a piece in our haversacks for the next day but, as we were going, two other groups came in and we gave it to them. They ate everything to the brains, eyes, intestines and broke the bones for marrow. On the 14th a chap shot a cockatoo and every bit was eaten including the bones. In the late afternoon we went up a steep spur and bivouacked opposite a waterfall where we had a shower. I had pneumonia and tropical ulcers. By the time I got back I had dengue too. Every man in the company lost 2½ to 3 stone.... We met patrols from the 2/14th and 2/16th cut off at Templeton's Crossing and Myola—six or seven in each. It was the survival of the fittest. We'd separate and go on. Whoever could go on without calling a halt would get ahead.

It was not until the 17th that this group arrived back in the brigade area. Other groups continued to arrive during the next two weeks.

While these men were thus beset by a harsh country Cooper, with his

---

[6] Maj P. S. Smith, MBE, WX3396. Staff Capt 21 Bde 1941-42; DAQMG 7 Div 1942-44; DAQMG (Maint) Adv LHQ 1944-45. Manager; of Peppermint Grove, WA; b. Melbourne, 12 Nov 1912.
[7] Capt C. H. Sandison, SX2893; 2/27 Bn. Sales superintendent; of Glenelg, SA; b. Adelaide, 1 Sep 1914.

main battalion group, was faring no better. He had waited for a reconnaissance report from Sims but, having had no word by 5 p.m. on the 9th and having seen the Japanese at Menari, he set out to skirt the village leaving a platoon to direct Sims and Sandison on their return.

When there was no news on the 10th his men continued on their painful way. As with Sims' company food was scarce since the most any one man had had when the battalion left the track on the 8th was a tin of bully beef and an emergency ration. On the 13th, however, they ate yams which they collected from a native garden, rested and checked their arms, ammunition and numbers. At that stage there were 18 officers and 293 men, including 12 stretcher cases and three men from the 2/16th.

They paused next morning to bury one of the wounded who had died in the night. The country tested them sorely again that day. At five o'clock they halted on high ground overlooking Nauro and cooked their yams as the daylight was fading. They made for Nauro next morning but, finding it occupied by their enemies, struck back into the bush once more.

On the 16th they reached a grassy plateau about three miles south-east of Nauro. They had left the stretchers east of Nauro in the care of Captain Gill[8] and a strong party. That night they found more yams, and taro, in a deserted hut and ate them. When Cooper sent

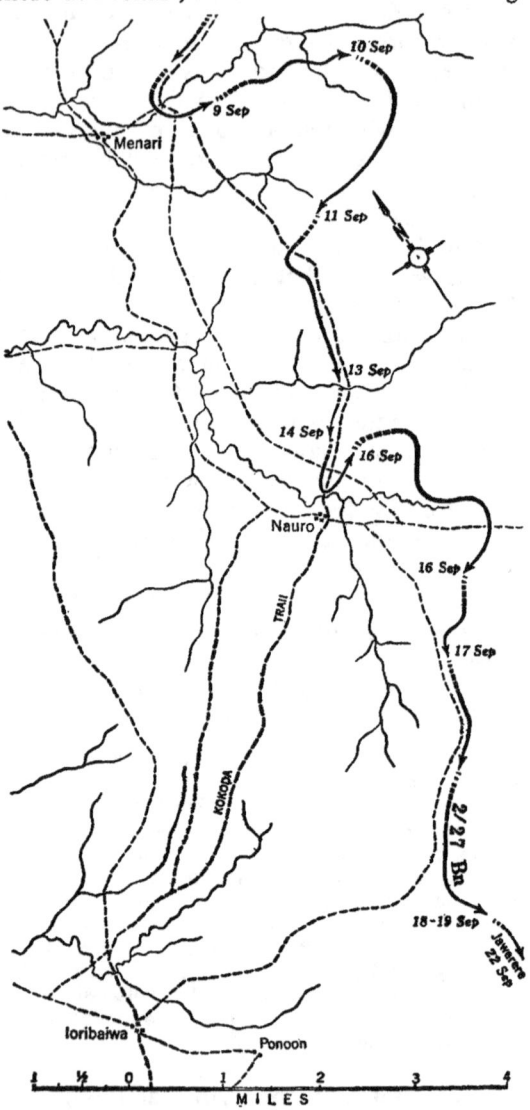

Route of 2/27th Battalion's withdrawal

---

[8] Capt T. F. Gill, SX4550. 2/27 Bn; Air Liaison Group. Chartered accountant; of Largs Bay, SA; b. Largs Bay, 18 Aug 1914. Missing believed killed 9 Sep 1943.

Corporal Penney[9] and Private Ramsey[1] to the stretcher parties next morning to tell them that yams and taro were being sent to them, the two men ran into a Japanese patrol. Ramsey was killed.

That morning, the 17th, Cooper sent six men on ahead to make all haste to get a message through to Port Moresby concerning his whereabouts. The following afternoon this party met the Intelligence officer of the 2/16th Battalion and, through him, the message was received at divisional headquarters soon afterwards; but the rest of the battalion, struggling along behind the messengers, was still finding the journey arduous, suffering from the cold and wet and lack of food. It was not until midday that they reached Jawarere where Major Robinson, commander of Jawforce, gave them food and made them as comfortable as he could. On the 22nd they were on the last stage of their journey and when they struck the road were met by trucks which moved them quickly to a convalescent camp on the outskirts of Port Moresby.

For the stretcher parties, however, the ordeal was not yet over. On the 18th Colonel Cooper had sent a message to Captain Gill that he was to move the stretchers to a near-by garden and then leave them there to be picked up later. Gill then provided what food he could for the sick and wounded, settled them in a cultivated area several miles east of Nauro, and on the morning of the 19th left them in the care of Corporal Burns[2] and Private Zanker[3] who had volunteered to stay.

By that time Burns and Zanker had seven stretcher cases and nine walking sick and wounded to care for, their sole supplies being ten shell dressings, a bottle of morphia and a syringe—and a garden of yams. They made crude shelters but, despite them, sweltered in the heat and were soaked by the afternoon rains. Aircraft flying above their positions raised their hopes but they could not attract their attention. There was firing near by. Burns wrote later:

> Monday [21st September] arrived after a terrifically cold night. The boys were very restless all night especially Corporal Williams[4] and I sat with him for the best part. The heat and flies were so bad that they almost drove us to the first stages of insanity. The heat was terrific and the flies—I think we had all that were in New Guinea. The lads all received a wash and shave this morning, my shaving gear, facewasher and toothbrush serving everyone. Corporal Williams and Private Burke[5] felt the going very hard from this stage on. We had to be with them day and night. . . . Wednesday 23rd was one of our hardest days. The sun was fiercer than ever and it took a lot out of the lads. Corporal Williams spent a terrible night and when Zanker and I had washed the lads we decided to put him on a new stretcher and put the first fresh dressings on his wounds. It was a terrific job but

---

[9] Sgt E. M. Penney, SX3572; 2/27 Bn. Labourer; of McLaren Flat, SA; b. McLaren Flat, 1 Jul 1918.
[1] Pte C. R. Ramsey, SX13905; 2/27 Bn. Farmer; of Cowell, SA; b. Cowell, 16 Sep 1918. Killed in action 17 Sep 1942.
[2] Sgt J. H. Burns, MM, SX4556; 2/27 Bn. Baker; of Waikerie, SA; b. Renmark, SA, 14 Oct 1919.
[3] Pte A. F. Zanker, SX4984; 2/27 Bn. Labourer; of Wild Horse Plains, SA; b. Two Wells, SA, 26 Jan 1915.
[4] Cpl L. T. Williams, SX3723; 2/27 Bn. Clerk; of Linden Park, SA; b. Norwood, SA, 3 Jan 1901. Died of wounds 24 Sep 1942.
[5] Pte J. T. Burke, WX3156; 2/16 Bn. Farmer; of Hyden, WA; b. Adelaide, 22 Jul 1917. Died of wounds 27-28 Sep 1942.

we succeeded in the end. Both Zanker and I had a couple of blackouts during it. We had now used two of our last three dressings. . . . The lads had run out of smokes too and I collected a few likely looking leaves but I'm afraid they weren't quite the right type. Diarrhoea broke out during the day and we were lifting the poor lads for the next twenty-four hours without respite. After spending most of the night on the go Friday dawns with a blazing hot sun and millions of flies. Again I spent the night with Corporal Williams and at 0800 hours he had a drink and at 0810 hours we found him dead. We immediately dug a grave approx three feet deep by means of a tin hat and a machete. It was a hard hour's work. At 0930 we buried him with just a little prayer. . . . The 25th arrived. . . . Private Burke of the 2/16th Bn had taken a definite step towards the end at this stage and he lapsed into semi-consciousness. He was in a bad way. There was nothing we could do for him except a dose of morphia to put him out of agony every now and then.

On the 27th Burns sent off the strongest of the walking cases with a native who had promised to guide them to Itiki. There were five of them. Later in the day the men who had remained became alarmed to see Allied planes strafing the track only 200 yards from them. Heavy rains soaked them. Many of the wounds were fly-blown. At midnight Private Burke died and Burns and Zanker sadly buried him beside Corporal Williams. All were feeling the strain badly now:

We read the New Testament as much as possible and had general discussions on different subjects to try and keep their minds occupied. . . . The 30th September finds the boys' morale and spirits very low. We shave and sponge the lads again but the smell was getting too strong to stay beside them too long. If only we could have had some dressings for them! . . . Heavy rains in the afternoon almost flooded us out. Private Martlew[6] took a turn for the worse and we had to watch him very closely. The flies were worrying Corporal Roy McGregor[7] very much and we spent the hours of daylight taking it in turns to keep them away from him. The yam stock was beginning to run low so we were praying for help more than ever.

On 2nd October one of the four separate patrols which had been looking for them found them. There was a medical officer with the patrol, Captain Wilkinson[8] of the 2/4th Field Ambulance, and Warrant-Officer Preece of Angau was there with a carrier party. But much hard travelling still lay before them. They did not reach hospital in the Port Moresby area until the evening of the 7th. Later Burns wrote:

No tribute can be paid which is too high for those native bearers, for without them it would have been impossible to have reached safety in time to save the lives of two of our men. And to their master WOII Ron Preece of NGF—his name will be a byword to the boys of the stretchers for a long time.

In the whole operation the 2/27th Battalion lost 39 men killed and 2 missing, believed killed; 3 officers and 43 men were wounded. These figures were naturally lighter than those of the other two 21st Brigade battalions which were in action much longer than the 2/27th. The 2/14th suffered a total of 244 battle casualties—6 officers and 75 men killed

---

[6] Pte R. G. Martlew, SX9413. 2/27 Bn; 2/1 Composite AA Regt. Tractor driver; of Bordertown, SA; b. Bordertown, 19 Mar 1921.
[7] Cpl R. G. McGregor, SX4941; 2/27 Bn. Cellar hand; of Berri, SA; b. Waikerie, SA, 4 Feb 1919.
[8] Maj R. S. Wilkinson, SX3630. RMO 2/4 Fd Regt; 2/4, 2/7 Fd Ambs. Medical practitioner; of Rose Park, SA; b. Mt Barker, SA, 23 Jan 1911.

or died of wounds, 2 officers and 29 men missing, 6 officers and 126 men wounded. In addition four men died from sickness and other causes. The 2/16th battle casualties were 4 officers and 65 men killed or died of wounds, and 4 officers and 90 men wounded. The proportion of "sick" to battle casualties was estimated at 2 to 1.

The men of the 21st Brigade had set an example of gallantry and endurance that the incoming brigades might well follow.

CHAPTER 8

TO TEMPLETON'S CROSSING

AT the beginning of October the Australians were pushing once more across the Kokoda Track after the advance of the 25th Brigade from Imita Ridge to Ioribaiwa. As they pressed on into the mountains intense fighting continued on and round Guadalcanal, 770 miles to the east. It was clear that the Japanese had decided to finish the Guadalcanal campaign before reinforcing New Guinea substantially; equally clear that Japanese capture of the smaller island would be followed by swift concentration against the larger one, although it was not then known that the Japanese had actually planned to take Port Moresby by the end of November.

Despite the worrying naval situation created by the torpedoing of the battleship *North Carolina* and the destruction of the aircraft carrier *Wasp* on 15th September, the Americans had succeeded in running in to Guadalcanal a large convoy which landed useful reinforcements (notably the 7th Marine Regiment) and much needed material of all kinds on the 18th. They were still not strong enough, they considered, to attempt to drive their enemies off the island and remained on the defensive round the vital Henderson Field.

This primitive strip

lacked adequate dispersal facilities, revetments, fuel storage tanks and machine shops. All aircraft had to be loaded with bombs by hand, and refuelled from gasoline drums by hand pumps.[1]

None the less, Brigadier-General Roy S. Geiger, commanding the 1st Marine Aircraft Wing, was maintaining an average of about fifty operational aircraft at the field by the beginning of October. Japanese ships hesitated to come within their radius by day. Japanese destroyers took to running down the coast by night and landing troops under the lee of the island in small groups to make their way overland to join the force concentrated against the American defences.

These defences took the form of a 22,000-yard perimeter which enclosed Henderson Field by running south along the Ilu River on the right, then turned west through roughly-wooded ravines and ridges south of the airfield, crossed the Lunga River at right angles, and touched the coast between Kukum and the mouth of the Matanikau River.

After a sharp repulse to probing American forces round the mouth of the Matanikau late in September General Vandergrift began to fear that that area, outside his perimeter, might become an "Achilles heel". He therefore thrust sharply into it early in October but news of impending major Japanese operations caused him to withdraw his main attacking

---

[1] J. Miller, "Crisis on Guadalcanal", *Military Affairs*, Vol XI, No. 4, p. 195. (Miller is author of *Guadalcanal: The First Offensive* (1949), a volume in the official series *United States Army in World War II*.)

force (which had lost 65 killed and 125 wounded) on the 9th. His men counted 253 Japanese dead but learned later that they had inflicted heavier casualties than those.

Now the navy, on which the stranded marines depended completely, again entered the Guadalcanal scene.

It is necessary to remember that as of October 10, 1942, there seemed a very good chance that we would lose [the war]. Coral Sea and Midway, yes; our naval air fought those and it covered itself with glory. The submarines were doing well. But the rest of the Navy, in fact the Navy as a whole, had not looked good. *Oklahoma* and *Arizona* had left the fleet forever at Pearl Harbour; *Lexington*, *Yorktown* and now *Wasp* were gone, *Saratoga* and *North Carolina* were in for repairs. In the Java Sea we had lost a heavy cruiser and a whole division of destroyers; at Savo three cruisers more, and our destroyer loss now stood at fifteen ships. What had the Japs paid for this? The carriers of Midway, another one at Coral Sea, two cruisers downed by submarines and a few destroyers—not a Jap ship was sunk by the surface Navy. They were ahead.[2]

The navy determined to attempt to stop the nightly naval bombardments which were trying the Americans in the Henderson Field area and to give some pause to the flow of reinforcements. For this purpose, and to protect the left flank of a convoy carrying the 164th Regiment—an army formation—into Guadalcanal, Rear-Admiral Norman Scott, with 4 cruisers and 5 destroyers, put out from Espiritu Santo in the New Hebrides. Scouting aircraft reported to him on 11th October that they had discovered a Japanese naval force moving south to Guadalcanal. Sailing to intercept, Scott was off Cape Esperance, the northernmost tip of Guadalcanal, just before midnight—in the waters of the disastrous Savo Island Battle of the night 8th-9th August. Pips, representing Japanese ships, leaped on to the American radar screens. Scott's ships gained a seven-minute advantage as they opened fire over the dark waters. On the islands the marines, remembering the previous battle, listened apprehensively as the noise of gunfire rolled across the sea. But this time the ships which burned high into the night were Japanese. Of the heavy cruisers *Furutaka* was sunk and *Aoba* badly damaged. (In *Aoba* the Japanese force commander, Admiral Goto was mortally wounded.) The destroyers *Natsugumo* and *Fubuki* went down. Scott lost only the destroyer *Duncan* and had two cruisers and one destroyer damaged. Next morning Dauntless dive bombers plummeted down on the big destroyer *Murakumo* as she struggled to help the badly mauled *Aoba* and sank her.

But, in tune with the see-saw nature of the war's fortunes at Guadalcanal, the high American excitement which followed this battle was quickly sobered. While the 164th Regiment was landing at noon on 13th October Japanese airmen rained bombs on Henderson Field from a height of 30,000 feet. Surprised, the American fighters could not reach interception level. More bombers struck again at 1.30 while the defending fighters were being refuelled and further serious damage resulted. But worse came with the night. A naval force, including two battleships, stood offshore and pounded

---

[2] Fletcher Pratt, *The Marines War* (1948), pp. 78-80.

the American positions. The attackers reported that explosions were seen everywhere and the entire airfield was a sea of flame.

Forty-one Americans were killed, over half the 90 aircraft operating from Henderson Field were destroyed or damaged and the field itself was smashed into temporarily unusable rubble. After the warships had gone Japanese 15-cm howitzers ("Pistol Pete" to the Americans) which, despite the naval and air opposition, had been landed west of the Matanikau, continued to register on the airstrip.

Still staggering from this onslaught the defenders had news on the 14th that seven 9,000 to 10,000-ton transports, escorted by warships, were bound for Guadalcanal. Fortunately they had by this time laid down a smaller strip, which, though rough and grassy and unmatted, was to serve them well while the main field was out of action. From this the surviving planes took off to meet the new threat. By the night of the 14th they had sunk one transport and the darkness was shot through with flames from another as it burned on the surface of the sea. But dawn of the 15th showed the remaining transports and their escorts unloading off Tassafaronga Point, some ten miles west of Lunga Point. General Geiger then had twenty-seven planes operational but scarcely enough fuel to get them into the air. His men scoured the surrounding bush for small supplies which might have been overlooked, and drained the wrecks of aircraft which lay about. Their search yielded about 400 drums which represented approximately two days' supply. By 11 a.m. they had sunk another transport and set two more afire. The rest of the ships then put out to sea once more but, it was clear, not before they had landed much material and many additional men.

The first of the land actions which all these preparations had presaged opened on 20th October. The Japanese then struck vigorously at the Matanikau positions on the 21st and 23rd but were repulsed for the loss of 25 marines killed and 14 wounded. Early on the 25th they attacked again—but on the south of the perimeter this time. There the I/7th Marines were holding a long front thinly, but though a few of their positions were overrun in the first wild minutes they broke the initial attacks. Reinforced with infantry the marines held against a series of new attacks until dawn.

The 25th was a day of heavy air raids and bombardment of the American positions by "Pistol Pete". Rains had turned the airstrips into bogs and Geiger's men were earthbound during the first part of the day. Japanese warships ranged up and down the shore. As the day went on, however, the sun dried up the worst of the mud and the defending planes could take the air. By last light they claimed to have shot down twenty-two of their attackers. Then the Japanese land forces struck again, but, broken, the attackers withdrew again at dawn.

The failure of these attacks marked the end of the ground phase of the Japanese October offensive, for the attackers withdrew east and west soon afterwards. They had suffered heavily. Vandergrift's headquarters estimated that some 2,200 had been killed although other estimates placed the Japanese casualties as high as 3,568 in two regiments alone.

Over 1,500 stinking Japanese corpses lay in front of the 1st Battalion, 7th Marines, and the 3rd Battalion, 164th Infantry. The latter regiment reported that it had completed the nauseous task of burying 975 enemy bodies in front of K and L Companies. . . . American losses had been light by comparison. The 164th Infantry lost 26 men killed and 52 wounded throughout October.[3]

But before the Americans had time to savour this victory—before, indeed, it was assured—events at sea seemed once more to swing the balance. While the Japanese land forces were still attacking, news came that their navy was out in force, manoeuvring off the Santa Cruz Islands. The ships (as was subsequently learned) numbered 4 aircraft carriers, 4 battleships, 8 cruisers, 1 light cruiser, 28 destroyers, 4 oilers and 3 cargo ships. At Pearl Harbour Admiral Nimitz had received Intelligence of their approach and had sent Rear-Admiral Thomas C. Kinkaid racing to the Santa Cruz waters. When Kinkaid finally stood out to meet the Japanese he was commanding two carrier groups. In one force he had the carrier *Enterprise,* the new battleship *South Dakota,* one heavy cruiser, one light anti-aircraft cruiser, and eight destroyers; in another, round *Hornet,* two heavy cruisers, two light anti-aircraft cruisers, and six destroyers. Kinkaid's strength was therefore considerably inferior.

On the morning of 26th October his searching aircraft located the main enemy forces but not before the Americans had themselves been picked up by the Japanese scouts. In the Battle of Santa Cruz which followed Kinkaid lost *Hornet* and the destroyer *Porter,* and *Enterprise, South Dakota,* the light cruiser *San Juan* and the destroyer *Smith* were damaged. He lost also 74 aircraft. On the other hand no Japanese ships were sunk although several (including two carriers) were damaged and more aircraft than the Americans had lost were probably destroyed. Although the Japanese fleet then returned to Truk that was because of the failure of the operations on land.

General Hyakutake's plans for the use of his *XVII Army* had continued to be based on an underestimate of the American strength on Guadalcanal which, after the arrival of the 164th Infantry, numbered more than 23,000. His basic concept was that Major-General Kawaguchi's forces still remaining on Guadalcanal would secure the area of the Matanikau mouth and enable the establishment of artillery positions from which Henderson Field could be bombarded. Additionally he played with the idea of an amphibious assault. His men would "capture the enemy positions, especially the airfield and artillery positions, at one blow". After the reduction of the American positions the Japanese would seize other islands in the southern Solomons, intensify their attacks on New Guinea and take Port Moresby by the end of November.

---

[3] Miller, "Crisis on Guadalcanal", in *Military Affairs,* Vol XI, No. 4, p. 211.

Hyakutake's main strength for the Guadalcanal operations would be drawn from the *2nd* and *38th Divisions*. The *2nd Division* contained the *4th, 16th* and *29th Regiments*; the *38th* contained the *228th, 229th* and *230th*.

By mid-October most of the *2nd Division* and two battalions of the *38th Division* were on Guadalcanal in addition to the veterans of the *Ichiki* and *Kawaguchi Forces*. The total Japanese strength there then numbered some 25,000 men including field, anti-aircraft and mountain artillery, a company of tanks, and ancillary units.

The Japanese Navy was cooperating with the army to the fullest extent. The force which Admiral Scott had mauled off Cape Esperance on the night of 11th-12th October had been running down to neutralise Henderson Field to provide greater safety for the landing of more troops and supplies. But meanwhile the greatest naval force the Japanese had assembled since Midway was gathering at Truk and Rabaul.

On land Hyakutake's plans were nourished by the belief that American spirit and strength were waning. He told Lieut-General Masao Maruyama, commander of the *2nd Division,* to attack the American positions from the south with his main force on a date tentatively fixed as 18th October. While Maruyama pushed inland from Kokumbona (west of the Matanikau) to his start-line Major-General Tadashi Sumiyoshi, the *XVII Army's* artillery commander, would operate in the Matanikau area a force consisting of the *4th Infantry* and two battalions of the *124th*, tanks and field and mountain artillery. And at that time plans were still extant for a landing through the American seaward defences by the *228th Infantry.*

General Kawaguchi would command Maruyama's right wing consisting of one battalion of the *124th Infantry,* two battalions of the *230th Infantry,* mortars, guns and ancillary detachments. Major-General Yumio Nasu would command the left wing made up of the *29th Infantry* with support in mortars, guns and the like similar to that allotted to Kawaguchi and the *16th Infantry* in reserve. Kawaguchi and Nasu would attack northward simultaneously from east of the Lunga to capture the airfield and annihilate the Americans.

The Japanese, however, made a whole series of costly errors in executing these plans: their attacks were not coordinated; when Sumiyoshi attacked in the Matanikau corner, Maruyama, preparing for the main attack in the south, was still struggling into position over a difficult track which exhausted his men and denuded him of all his heavy support weapons; when Maruyama himself attacked, Kawaguchi's battalions on the right wing lost direction in darkness and rain and crossed behind the *29th Regiment* which formed the left wing. Several of the senior Japanese commanders were killed. But perhaps the greatest Japanese mistake was their underestimate of the strength of the forces opposed to them. Certainly they outgunned the Americans from their positions west of the Matanikau and had the almost unhindered nightly assistance of naval units; the majority of their men were fresh while Vandergrift's forces (with the possible exception of the new arrivals) were weakened by malaria, dysentery, malnutrition and arduous service. But the Americans were waiting in positions they had been preparing for more than two months; they had local air superiority which hindered Japanese preparations and limited the amount of material they could land; they had had time to prepare elaborate artillery support programs covering the lines of approach to their positions; roughly equal in numbers to the attackers they would normally be able to smother any break-through which shattered their perimeter at any point.

The failure of the ground operations cut the substance from beneath all the Japanese naval planning. The large force to which Admiral Kinkaid had given battle off the Santa Cruz Islands had been waiting to exploit and consolidate General Hyakutake's success ashore. But Hyakutake's delay in getting into position for the final assaults had so worried the naval commanders that they had sent an anxious message on the 24th or 25th saying that the fleet would be forced to retire for lack of fuel if the attack were not carried out immediately. When the assault was broken the navy had no alternative but to cancel their own plans.

It was in the light of the situation which developed in Guadalcanal during this difficult month of October that General MacArthur and General Blamey had to plan their operations in New Guinea. Even if the Guadalcanal forces continued to hold they had to be prepared for a Japanese change of plan which would aim merely to contain the Americans in the south while changing the emphasis to the New Guinea axis. Much more likely, however, was an American collapse in the Solomons.

On 16th October General Marshall radioed MacArthur:

Have examined charts of Japanese naval surface concentrations in Bougainville ports and to the south, especially the Shortland Islands—Faisi area, totalling 5 or 6 BBs [Battleships], 3 carriers, many cruisers and DDs [destroyers]; another Carrier Task Force operating south and southeast of Guadalcanal not located; we have only 1 carrier at present in SOPAC; Japanese outranged our artillery on Guadalcanal, keeping airfield under constant bombardment from land, with occasional bombardment from ships; their naval superiority is preventing reinforcement and re-supply, especially gasoline; situation most critical. . . .

In his reply on the 17th General MacArthur reviewed the operations in his own area and concluded:

It is now necessary to prepare for possible disaster in the Solomons; if we are defeated in the Solomons as we must be unless the Navy accepts successfully the challenge of the enemy surface fleet, the entire SWPA will be in the gravest danger. . . .

President Roosevelt himself was even more outspoken. The Pacific War Council, in a record of its meeting on the 21st October, noted:

The President said that in the Solomons it was no use saying we were not in a hole. There had been excellent cooperation from the services in Australia, and the New Guinea area under the Australian command had become more and more tied in with the other command. Actually cooperation between MacArthur and Ghormley was not very good. The attack in August had been brilliantly carried out but, looked at now, it seemed questionable whether it was not too far from a supply base to be permanently tenable. Further, only one air field had been occupied, and perhaps an attempt should have been made to secure another on the north side of New Guinea. The United States had a large number of troops in Guadalcanal, but the Japanese had launched a major operation with far greater forces than we could put there or maintain.

Even at the beginning of October MacArthur knew that every day saved in New Guinea was important. On the 1st he defined his plans:

... Our Forcès in the Southwest Pacific Area [will] attack with the immediate objective of driving the Japanese to the northward of the Kumusi River line.

The New Guinea Force will:

1. Advance along the axes Nauro-Kokoda-Wairopi and Rigo-Dorobisolo-Jaure-Wairopi and/or Abau-Namudi-Jaure-Wairopi with the objective of securing the line of the Kumusi River from Awalama Divide to the crossing of the Kokoda-Buna Trail, both inclusive.

2. Occupy and hold Goodenough Island and the north coast of Southeastern New Guinea south of Cape Nelson in such force as to deny these areas to the Japanese forces.

3. Upon securing these objectives, all land forces will prepare for further advance to secure the area Buna-Gona upon further orders of this Headquarters.[4]

On 5th October Blamey wrote to MacArthur throwing a hard light on the pivotal problems of the New Guinea operations:

The object of the New Guinea Force is to drive the enemy out of Southeastern New Guinea and Papua. The capacity of the force to do this is limited mainly by two considerations—

(a) communications to permit the movement of the necessary troops

(b) supply.

Preparation of adequate communications is a matter involving the making of roads under the most difficult conditions of terrain and requires time. Supply is dependent—

(i) on the development of communications

(ii) on the amount of sea supply which can be made available

(iii) on the amount of air supply which can be made available.

For the moment air supply is paramount.

The first line commitments are—

(a) *Wanigela*—one infantry battalion (720 troops);

(b) *Kokoda front*—one infantry brigade (front line), total 4,600 troops;[5] one infantry brigade in reserve; 2,000 native carriers.

(c) *Kanga force*—650 troops; 1,300 native carriers.

(d) To this should be added the troops of the 32nd US Div advancing along the Rigo-Abau route. It is proposed to press the advance with a force of approximately 1,000 troops and 600 native carriers.

Every effort will be made by these means to press the advance on BUNA on all three fronts.

The total number therefore to be supplied by air are—

(i) troops—approximately 7,000

(ii) native carriers—3,900.

---

[4] GHQ Operation Instruction No. 19 of 1 Oct.

[5] This figure appears to be incorrect. It is considerably in excess of the 25th Brigade Group's strength.

Difficulties of supply and communication may make it impossible to coordinate the advance in the three directions. The order of priority will therefore be—
(a) Advance Kokoda Route—7th Australian Division.
(b) Hatforce 24 [the Wanigela force principally 2/10th Battalion].
(c) 32 United States Division.

The effort which can be made by Hatforce will of course be small and the difficulties of terrain which face the 32nd United States Division are very considerable.

The calculated weight required to be dropped by air is at the rate of 10-lbs per man per day. As a result of experience this includes 30 per cent estimated losses and a proportion for carriers and includes necessary general supply and ammunition. When landing can be substituted for dropping, the calculated weight is 6.6 lbs per man per day. The calculations of the United States and Australian forces approximate very closely.

In addition to this daily requirement, it is essential that reserve supplies be gradually accumulated. First to a total of 21 days and later to 30 days. It must be foreseen that there will be frequent days, particularly during the wet weather, when air supply will not be possible at all. This may extend to a considerable period.

Details of requirements in air transport are summarised below. These details were determined at a conference attended by—
CG Adv Ech 5 AF [Commanding General Advance Echelon 5th Air Force] (Brig-General Walker).
CG 32nd US Div (Major-General Harding).
GOC NGF (Lieut-General Herring).
Brig-General MacNider.

General Walker authorised me to say he concurs in these conclusions.

Effect of Roads. The speed with which roads can be pushed forward to take jeeps or 1½-ton four-wheel drive trucks is a material factor in reducing requirements for air supply. For example, the completion of the road OWERS' CREEK-NAURO, by-passing UBERI and the IMITA Ridge, will reduce requirements for 7th Australian Division by nearly half, i.e., to a daily total of approximately 25,000 lbs.[6]

32nd US Division is commencing reconnaissance to extend roads towards their objective.

Effect of landing instead of dropping. If aircraft can land instead of dropping supplies, a saving in weight to be transported by air of about 30 per cent is to be anticipated.

The ability to land at KOKODA a/d will reduce 7th Australian Division requirements by 16,000 pounds to a total of 32,000 lbs daily (not including reserves).

Supply by sea. Every effort is being made to establish a small craft supply route from MILNE BAY to WANIGELA. The success of this will reduce air transport requirements by 5,000 lbs daily (not including reserves) but it may be some time before it is effective, and it may always be precarious.

Employment of carriers. Native carriers are required to lift supplies forward between air dropping grounds and forward troops. The number of carriers required is based on lifting supplies for two daily stages. The number of carriers available are only sufficient for this purpose, and the heavy wastage rates, together with the increasing difficulty of collection and distribution, makes it virtually impossible to maintain sufficient carriers in the field to carry from road or pack-head and so reduce air transport requirements. Certain stores, including fuse caps and other

---

[6] Late in August Lieutenant Owers, with a small survey party, was looking for an alternative route forward of Ilolo by which the troops on the Kokoda Track might more easily be supplied. With Owers working ahead of them the 2/14th Field Company and other engineer units then became responsible for the construction of a jeep track from Ilolo to Nauro. The point where this proposed road left the mule track to Uberi they named Owers' Corner. The ruggedness of the country, however, made their task one of surpassing difficulty. Subsequently they had to abandon it in the face of the Japanese advance. Although they resumed work again as soon as possible (on 28th September, with the help of the 2/1st Pioneer Battalion) it soon became clear that, having regard to the time factor as well as the difficulties, the project should be abandoned. This was done early in October.

explosives, wireless spares and medical equipment cannot be dropped. These of course are carried throughout from road or pack-head to forward troops. As an example of the impossibility of materially affecting air transport requirements, it is calculated that the maintenance of troops between UBERI and KOKODA without any supply by air, would require 10,000 carriers.

Summary of Air Transport requirements in New Guinea area

	Total maximum daily weight in lbs (not including reserve)	Minimum daily weight in lbs (not including reserve)	Remarks
Wanigela	5,000	Nil	5,000 lbs including additional weight for AA ammunition. Nil after establishment supply by sea.
32nd United States Div.	10,000	5,000	5,000 lbs up to LARUNI; 10,000 lbs on arrival JAURE.
7th Australian Division	48,000	32,000	Reduction on employment of KOKODA drome for landing aircraft.
Kanga Force	5,000	4,300	Minimum estimated for present force with aircraft landing at Wau. Maximum including 7th Independent Company.
Total	68,000	41,300	
Daily average increase to build up reserves	34,000	20,600	
Grand total average daily air transport requirements	102,000	61,900	Reserves on basis 21-30 days.

To give effect to General MacArthur's intentions General Blamey planned to maintain General Rowell's intention that the Australian 25th and 16th Brigades would continue the advance across the Kokoda Track with the successive objects of capturing Kokoda and the aerodrome there to facilitate reinforcement and supply; of securing the line of the Kumusi River; and of closing on Buna. At the same time one battalion of the 126th United States Infantry Regiment would strike up from the southeast, by way of Jaure, either to Wairopi or Buna (in accordance with the developing situation) and another force would move on a third axis Wanigela-Pongani (on the coast between Wanigela and Buna)-Buna. The main force on the third axis would be a battalion of the 128th Infantry which, having been flown to Wanigela, would press on along the coast to Pongani to join there with two battalions of the 126th Regiment which would be flown direct to Pongani or its immediate vicinity. The three forces would converge on the Japanese positions in the Buna-Gona area.

At the beginning of October action in accordance with these intentions was, naturally, most advanced along the first axis—the Kokoda Track. Patrols had already found Nauro unoccupied and had gone on toward

Menari. The 3rd Battalion led the advance of the main body on the 1st. Behind it the 2/25th moved out from Ioribaiwa on the 2nd with Major Marson[7] in command. The other two battalions were to follow on succeeding days.

The 3rd Battalion found evidence of hasty Japanese withdrawal: bodies and equipment lay along the track. By the early afternoon of the 2nd the leading company was at Menari and was continuing to Efogi without opposition. Colonel Cameron reported that the area between Ioribaiwa and Nauro seemed to have been occupied by some 2,000 men; that his troops had buried twelve Japanese on whom there were no signs of wounds; that there was evidence that the invaders had been reduced to eating wood, grass, roots and fruits which were known to be inedible, and that dysentery was rife among them. He found the bodies of two Australians, one bound to a tree, one decapitated.

The 3rd Battalion, except for Captain Boag's company which went ahead towards Efogi, spent the 3rd and 4th clearing dropping grounds at Nauro. Marson passed through to bivouac half-way between Nauro and Menari. On the afternoon of the 4th Boag reached Efogi and reported it clear. He said that carriers who had been working for the Japanese told him that their most recent masters had fallen back to Kokoda. Cameron's main body reached Menari on the 5th and, by the end of the next day, Marson was pressing on towards Efogi. Both battalions had patrols working well ahead and on the flanks. On the 5th Marson had sent out Lieutenant Barnett[8] and Lieutenant Cox[9] with 53 men, carrying five days' rations, to try to reach Myola, contact the Japanese if possible and determine their strength. Cameron's patrols were working round towards the Myola-Templeton's Crossing area through Kagi on the left.

The men of the 2/33rd Battalion, moving behind Marson and Cameron, were clearing distressing evidence of the fighting which had taken place between Menari and Efogi nearly a month before. On the 7th they buried there the bodies of some 55 Australians as well as many Japanese dead; next day they buried 20 more.

On the 8th it seemed that the Australians had overtaken the Japanese rearguard. Both Barnett, and a patrol from the 3rd Battalion under Sergeant Tongs[1] which had moved via Kagi, encountered Japanese between Myola and Templeton's Crossing. Barnett was not successful in dislodging what he estimated to be a Japanese platoon holding astride the track. Wounded himself and having lost two other men wounded and one killed, he fell back on Myola. Tongs, with only a section on a purely reconnaissance mission, likewise fell back.

By this time Eather had the main strength of all four of his battalions disposed along the track between Menari and Efogi. Menari was in use

---

[7] Col R. H. Marson, DSO, ED, QX6378; CO 2/25 Bn 1942-45. Dairy farmer; of Toogoolawah, Qld; b. Wiltshire, England, 21 Jun 1904.
[8] Maj A. Barnett, MC, QX4914; 2/25 Bn. Clerk; of Lismore, NSW; b. Taree, NSW, 18 Mar 1919.
[9] Capt D. L. Cox, QX7326; 2/25 Bn. Clerk; of Chelmer, Qld; b. Brisbane, 9 Dec 1913.
[1] Capt B. G. D. Tongs, MM, NX126952. 3 and 2/3 Bns. Carpenter; of Queanbeyan, NSW; b. Narrandera, NSW, 27 Jun 1920.

as a dropping ground and one of Cameron's companies had already prepared an area at Efogi for the same purpose. Eather ordered the remainder of the 3rd Battalion to join this company at Efogi North on the 9th; Lieut-Colonel Buttrose would lead his 2/33rd Battalion through Efogi that day to cover the main track from Myola; on the morning of the 10th the 2/25th would swing left to Kagi to cover the approaches through that area and the 2/31st would come forward to Efogi North.

Eather's battalions seemed to move slowly after this contact. By nightfall of the 10th Lieutenant Cox (who had taken over Barnett's patrol) was still not making progress against the Japanese rearguard. The 3rd Battalion was in a defensive position at Myola; the 2/33rd was in the same area; the 2/25th was bivouacked at the Kagi-Myola turnoff; the 2/31st, in rear, had arrived at Efogi.

The slowness of the 25th Brigade was due mainly to two factors. Firstly, Eather was trying to nurse his men against the heavy demands the nature of the country itself was making on them; secondly he was greatly worried about supply.

Shortage of carriers remained one of the biggest problems. The effects of this were not so grave while the 25th Brigade was operating in the Imita Ridge-Ioribaiwa area, despite the fact that no air dropping grounds were available and not merely because the supply line was so much shorter, because the Pack Transport unit was at work forward from the jeephead to Imita Ridge. When, at the end of August, reserve supplies along the track fell very low, special efforts were made to increase the carrying capacity of the troop. It was then reorganised as a section of a Pack Transport company, and did excellent work until the end of the packing period despite difficulties of track maintenance, shortages of men, exhaustion of animals, epidemics of strangles and infectious nasal catarrh among horses imported from Australia, and shortage and disrepair of pack saddlery (which, until 60 new saddles arrived from Australia about mid-September, consisted mostly of plantation equipment held together only with great difficulty as the work went on[2]).

When Eather's advance began he tried to build up dumps as he went forward but only 900 natives were available forward of Uberi from the beginning of October and sickness and desertions decreased this number daily. The supply of carriers was running out, although the men of Angau were doing all they could to maintain it, casting away the pre-war principles which restricted the numbers of natives who could be recruited for work from particular areas, and building up a vast problem of native administration for the future. The maximum recruitment figure permissible in pre-war days from some of the areas from which recruits might most conveniently be fed on to the Kokoda Track was 8,830. By 9th October Angau was already maintaining 9,270 from the same districts and had to undertake to provide 4,000 more. The drastic recruiting policy bore

---

[2] By the end of October the unit had packed payloads of 1,418,310 pounds forward of jeep-head, working from mid-October 43 mules and 135 horses with 1 officer and 110 men. In November the packing period came to an end.

heavily not only on the conscript carriers themselves but on their family, village and tribal groups. Food production fell away and the many tasks which were normally the lot of the able-bodied men remained undone.

In the early stages of the 25th Brigade's advance carriers were usually allotted on the basis of 90 to brigade headquarters and 40 to each battalion, with a large pool which worked under divisional arrangements. One Angau representative moved with brigade headquarters and one with each battalion, to control and work the carriers. In the units the natives carried the heavy weapons and their ammunition, reserve ammunition, medical gear, and signals equipment; they assisted to supply the battalions from the forward supply dump, which was usually about half a day's march to the rear.

After a battalion was committed to action the strain on the carriers increased. Each stretcher case required 8 natives to move him back to the nearest advanced dressing station. This probably represented half a day's work. While the natives were carrying wounded they could not, of course, carry supplies. Action also interfered with their work in other ways. Carriers could not then be sent right forward to battalions, and this obliged the units to draw supplies themselves from dumps established in their rear. During the nightly halts the carriers had to be camped as much as 2 or 3 hours' walk to the rear where they were not open to Japanese attack, where their noise could not be heard nor their fires seen by the Japanese.

The soldiers themselves were generally more burdened than the carriers. In the 25th Brigade each man carried up to five days' rations (2 days' hard and 3 emergency), half a blanket, a groundsheet, soap, toothbrush, half a towel, half a dixie, a water-bottle, his weapon and ammunition. One shaving kit was usually carried by each three men. Within each battalion weapons and ammunition were usually carried as follows: each rifleman carried his own rifle and 100-150 rounds of ammunition; one 3-inch mortar with 15 bombs was carried by natives when these were available, at other times by the mortar crew assisted by other Headquarters Company men and sometimes by men of the rifle companies; one Vickers machine-gun, with 2 or 3 belts of ammunition, was carried similarly to the mortar; one Bren gun a section was carried in turns by each member of the section with 10 magazines a gun distributed among the members of the section; 2 sub-machine-guns a section were carried by the gunners with 5 magazines and 150 loose rounds a gun; one 2-inch mortar to each platoon was carried by the mortar members with 12 rounds a mortar distributed throughout the platoon; 2 grenades were carried by each man. Each battalion carried with it also 5 carrier loads of medical gear; cooking gear; 2 picks and 2 axes; 1 machete and 1 spade a section; and signals equipment consisting basically of six telephones and six 108-wireless sets.

The demands thus made on soldiers and carriers alike, and the slow toilsome nature of maintenance by purely human means, would have crippled the Australians had they not been able to look for supply from the air as they advanced deeper into the mountains.

Very early in the Papuan operations it became clear that supply by air demanded an integration of effort by three main groups—the forward ground forces; the base supply organisation; the aircrews. To the first of these fell the tasks of selecting the dropping areas and (where necessary) clearing them, devising and utilising appropriate signals to guide the aircraft, gathering the stores which were dropped and distributing them as required.

In the base supply organisation appropriate forms and recognised procedures were developed rapidly. The use of air transport demanded administrative organisation to handle the assembly of bulk stores in depots, transport to airfields, loading of planes, staffing of supply dumps, calling forward of stores and personnel at correct times together with the checking and clerical work necessary to such projects. No precedent was available on which to base a system or organisation but, as the campaign developed, so did a satisfactory system evolve, mainly through trial and error. This necessitated the cooperation and combined working mainly of the Staff Duties section of the General Staff, the Quartermaster-General's Branch, Supply and Transport, Ordnance, Engineer Stores, Medical and Salvage Services, and the Transport Group of the Advance Echelon of the Fifth Air Force.

The combined method of working which developed depended initially upon the receipt at the base each day of an urgently signalled statement of holdings, of demands in order of priority for the next day, from the forward formations. Staff Duties then decided the priorities, balancing the daily demands of the forward formations with all other relevant factors. "Q" Branch calculated on that basis the number of plane-loads involved. If the total number of aircraft could not be made available by Fifth Air Force, appropriate adjustments were made by Staff Duties to their priorities. "Q" Branch then prepared plane-loading tables and an outline plan for air supply for the following day. Various supply agencies (Army Service Corps, Ordnance, Medical Stores and Engineer Stores depots) were then ordered to have the necessary stores ready for dispatch at an airfield rendezvous by a certain time. At the loading points personnel of special detachments loaded and checked the stores on to the aircraft, posted a guard in each and prepared the necessary manifests. As each aircraft took off its departure was notified to Headquarters New Guinea Force over a direct line from the airfield.

Theoretically, the time program involved in this procedure allowed for the receipt of demands from the forward formations in the afternoon of each day, the completion of the Staff Duties calculations by the late afternoon, the completion of the initial "Q" estimates and lodgment of demands for aircraft by the early evening, and the preparation of the loading tables and outline plans for flying by the late evening. More often than not, however, the staff work involved went on at a frenzied pace almost to the moment of the departure of the aircraft in the early mornings and, as the campaign mounted towards its successive climaxes, the demands made on the staffs involved (particularly the Staff Duties and "Q" personnel) were so intense that many of the officers were worn out by the strain of the responsibility and long hours of work.

In these early days the difficulties which were continually manifested seemed limitless. Troubles associated with the nature of the transport medium itself were constant: there were always too few transport aircraft and the numbers available not only varied from day to day but could vary from hour to hour; the numbers available were in turn conditioned by the availability of fighter escorts, by the weather, and by enemy air activity. Communications channels from forward areas were limited and always overloaded so that there were serious delays in the exchange of vital supply information between the New Guinea Force Headquarters and the forward headquarters. Rapid changes in the operational situation constantly necessitated last-minute changes in the involved supply arrangements and plans. The percentages of recoveries from air droppings were low, varying from a maximum of about 80 per cent to a minimum of 10 per cent. About 20 per cent of the tins burst when tinned meat was dropped in cornsacks. Biscuits packed in blankets, shattered on impact. Every round of small arms ammunition dropped had to be laboriously tested when recovered to ensure that it would not jam in the breech of a weapon during action; premature explosions by dropped mortar bombs caused such frequent casualties that, for a time, the dropping of these bombs was discontinued.

Important factors in the preparation of supplies for air dropping were the availability of packing materials, simplicity of packing procedure, protection of supplies and the effect of the weight of packing on the effective payload of transports. Blankets were sent forward as wrappings on some commodities. Copra sacks were sometimes used for packing until regular supplies of corn sacks arrived from Australia. The type of packing materials governed the procedure of packing, which in turn dictated the labour requirements. Because of shortage of labour the packing procedure had to be as simple as possible. Cumbersome and heavy wrappings did not necessarily prevent damage from the first impact with the ground. The principal value of wrapping was as binding for the contents. Effective binding reduced the subsequent damage from bouncing and simplified recovery.

In the final analysis, however, the success of the air-dropping programs depended upon the skill and courage of the aircrews who carried out this monotonous and dangerous work. Their first task was to locate the actual dropping area. In the early stages pilots made many mistakes because they could not recognise ground features from the sparsely detailed maps which were all that were available. Such mistakes were later lessened, however, through the use of Angau guides who had worked in the areas involved and through the development of very simple methods of ground to air communication; e.g. burnt patches on the ground or the use of logs in the formation of leading or dropping marks. In similar fashion the actual technique of dropping developed through trial and error. In this connection the most important factors were the nature and condition of the dropping ground, the speed and height from which packages were dropped, the accuracy of dropping and the packing and wrapping of items. The most effective height for air dropping from Douglas transports was found to be between 300 and 400 feet. Dropping from lower levels at high speed resulted in excessive smashing of packages and heavy losses through the scattering of stores over wide areas.

Ideally, it was learned, cargo should be stacked in the open doorways of Douglas aircraft from which the entire door-pieces had been removed, with the heavier and more bulky items placed at the bottom of the stack. As the aircraft made successive runs over the dropping areas, at the most effective heights, "pusherouters" (who had safety belts fastening them to the interior of the aircraft) thrust the stack outwards with their feet on the flashing of a signal from the pilot.

On 2nd October Eather had told General Allen that a program of air droppings must be quickly instituted. This had begun on the 4th with drops at Nauro but the percentage of supplies lost was high. By the end of the 5th Eather's instructions to retake Kokoda had been modified by reference to maintenance as a limiting factor. He was told to concentrate on covering Kagi and Myola; that his brigade would be relieved by Brigadier Lloyd's 16th Brigade as soon as possible after he was in position beyond those areas. Lloyd himself arrived forward on the 5th to discuss plans with him.

On the 7th Allen signalled Lieut-General Herring (who had arrived at Port Moresby on the 1st in succession to General Rowell):

> Implementation of air-dropping programme causing gravest concern. Under present system it would appear that air force cannot supply planes necessary to assure dropping of 50,000 pounds daily weather permitting. (2) 50,000 pounds daily covers maintenance only and does not repeat not provide for building up a reserve. It does however allow for 30 per cent wastage due to destruction by dropping. Actual daily requirements for delivery to units etc for maintenance is 35,000 pounds. (3) Understood it is intention to build up 21 days' reserve supplies ammunition etc forward under existing system. This is quite impossible as supplies etc dropped during first two days of programme less than 50% of requirements for daily maintenance only. (4) Unless supply etc dropping of 50,000 pounds daily plus additional to build up reserve is assured complete revision of plans will have to be made and large proportion of troops withdrawn to Imita Ridge position. Any attempt then to hold a determined enemy advance Kagi-Templeton's Crossing-Myola area and to occupy Kokoda will be jeopardised beyond all reason.

The next few days saw an accelerated program of air supply and, on the 11th, Eather ordered Buttrose of the 2/33rd to seize Templeton's Crossing. Buttrose sent Lieutenant Innes[3] forward with a platoon to relieve Cox but Innes reported the Japanese positions too strong for him to handle. Captain Copp[4] then moved forward with the rest of the company. On the same day, guided by Sergeant Tongs to the point of Tongs' previous

---

[3] Capt W. T. D. Innes, ED, NX12360; 2/33 Bn. Pharmacist; of Narromine, NSW; b. Paddington, NSW, 19 Jan 1906.

[4] Maj W. D. Copp, MC, VX11589; 2/33 Bn. Regular soldier; of Rutherglen, Vic; b. Corowa, NSW, 24 Nov 1918. (Served also as H. D. Cullen.)

contact, Lieutenant Heron,[5] with a platoon of the 3rd Battalion, was repulsed by the Japanese south of Templeton's Crossing, losing two men killed.

At this moment there came to General Allen at his Command Group headquarters at Menari a sharp reminder that General Blamey was growing restless:

> Your order definitely to push on with sufficient force and capture Kokoda. You have been furnished with supplies as you requested and ample appears to be available. In view lack of serious opposition your advance appears much too slow. You will press enemy with vigour. If you are feeling strain personally relief will be arranged. Please be frank about this. Dropping arranged only at Myola 12 rptd 12 Oct. As soon as you can assure more advanced location will arrange to drop there.

Next day Allen replied:

> My outline plan . . . is designed to capture Kokoda as soon as possible. Apparently it has been misunderstood. Nothing is being left undone in order to carry out your wishes and my brigade commanders have already been instructed accordingly. The most serious opposition to rapid advance is terrain. The second is maintenance of supplies through lack of native carriers. Reserve supplies have not repeat not been adequate up to 11 Oct. Until information of recoveries today am unable to say whether they are yet adequate. Rate of advance does not entirely depend on air droppings. Equal in importance is our ability to carry forward and maintain our advanced troops. Notwithstanding that men carry with them up to five days' rations maintenance forward of dropping place is still necessary. This country is much tougher than any previous theatre and cannot be appreciated until seen. From all reports the worst is north of Myola. The vigour with which we press the enemy is dependent on the physical endurance of the men and the availability of supplies. Our men have pressed so far with vigour consistent with keeping them fit to fight. With regard to my personal physical fitness I am not repeat not feeling the strain. I never felt fitter nor able to think straighter. I however feel somewhat disappointed on behalf of all ranks that you are dissatisfied with the very fine effort they have made.

While this exchange was taking place Allen told Eather to aim to keep in touch with the enemy by patrols; to consolidate in the area Eora Creek–Myola–Kagi with one battalion disposed at Eora Creek, two at Templeton's Crossing and one at Kagi; to secure Alola as quickly as possible for use as a dropping ground. The 16th Brigade was to defend Myola, to prepare there a landing ground for light aircraft, and to be ready to move through the 25th Brigade to take Kokoda.

On the 12th the 2/33rd and 2/25th Battalions were converging on Templeton's Crossing, the one along the main track, the other along the track which ran forward from Kagi. In rear Dunbar was moving his 2/31st towards Kagi and Cameron was holding the 3rd Battalion at Myola.

Soon after midday Buttrose arrived at the point where the Japanese had been holding across the track between Myola and Templeton's Crossing. There the track passed along the crest of a narrow ridge, densely covered with thick bush of which bamboo was the main constituent. This

---

[5] Capt H. A. Heron, NX141441. 3 and 2/3 Bns; HQ 6 Div 1944-45. Railways employee; b. Wagga Wagga, NSW, 22 Jan 1918.

dense growth was almost impenetrable except by means of a few narrow pads which the Japanese had well covered. The defenders held tenaciously from one-man pits which were effectively camouflaged with branches, leaves and grass. Only a well-placed grenade could be relied on to silence the occupants of these pits and, since each pit was only about 2 feet 3 inches across, a direct hit by a grenade was difficult to make. The Japanese moved their automatic weapons frequently from one position to another and the Australians found the origins of hostile fire hard to pin-point.

Buttrose found that Copp had driven his enemies back about 300 yards for the loss of three men wounded. Two of his platoons were then holding across the track while Lieutenant Innes was trying to move through the dense bush and rugged country on the left flank. Soon Innes returned, one of his men dead, and said that he had come against about 20 Japanese digging in some 300 yards in rear of their forward positions. Buttrose was planning now that Captain Archer should move frontally with his company against the defenders while Copp held where he was and Captain Clowes' company broke a way round the left flank to take the obstructing positions in the rear. But, by nightfall, little progress had been made against the stout defences, which were so sited on the narrow ridge as to force any attack to be a laborious up-hill climb. Archer's assaults had failed to move the defenders and darkness found him still facing them with Copp to his rear. There was no message from Clowes although Archer reported that his men had heard firing from the Japanese rear. Four men had been killed and nine wounded in addition to the earlier casualties. Meanwhile the 2/25th had bivouacked between Kagi and Templeton's Crossing.

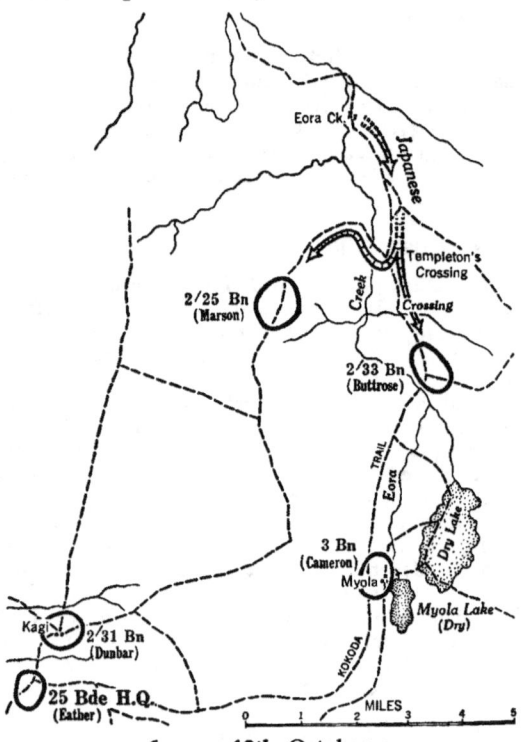

6 p.m., 12th October

On the morning of the 13th Archer began once more to probe. Still there was no word from Clowes. Late in the morning Lieutenant Power[6] took a platoon along a track on the southern side of the Japanese and

---

[6] Capt K. Power, MC, VX12699; 2/33 Bn. Regular soldier; of Hawthorn, Vic; b. Casino, NSW, 31 Jul 1911.

surprised them. His men captured a heavy machine-gun and estimated that they shot 30 Japanese for the loss of 1 man killed and 4 wounded. But again Archer was held. Early in the afternoon Clowes reported back with the news that he had met opposition the previous day. He had attacked at dawn of the 13th along the ridge which was lightly but effectively held for about a mile from Templeton's Crossing. Night brought cold rain driving across the gloomy mountain sides and dripping from the bush. Buttrose had lost another man killed, one officer and 11 men wounded and one man missing; but he was determined to clear the ridge next day. He would use Copp's men to attack along the track while Power attempted to repeat his brilliant little performance of that day.

While the 2/33rd was thus trying to claw the Japanese out of their holes the 2/25th had met opposition. Thrusting forward from Kagi towards Templeton's Crossing their forward scouts were fired on. Captain O'Bryen's company and Captain Butler's[7] then pressed up to find that sharpshooters, accurately sniping, screened holding positions and that steep ridges hindered their attempts to outflank. Butler's men forced some of the holding strength off high ground on the left of the track but did not win much ground.

A grim aside that day focused attention on the savagery of the Owen Stanley fighting and the desperate plight of the retreating Japanese. A section leader[8] of the 2/25th, on patrol, found a parcel of meat which inspired in him distasteful suspicions. He brought it back to be examined by Captain Donnan,[9] the battalion's medical officer. Donnan reported:

> I have examined two portions of flesh recovered by one of our patrols. One was the muscle tissue of a large animal, the other similar muscle tissue with a large piece of skin and underlying tissues attached. I consider the last as human.

Two days later Lieutenant Crombie[1] signed the following statement:

> I was the officer in charge of the burial party of two 3 Battalion militia personnel killed on 11 Oct 42 and, on examination of the bodies, found that one of them had both arms cut off at the shoulders and the arms missing and a large piece cut out of one thigh as well as one of the calves of one of the legs slashed by a knife. The other body also had a large piece cut out of one of the thighs. These mutilations were obviously made by a sharp knife, and were not caused by bullets or bayonets. The men's deaths were caused in one case by a burst of MG fire in the chest and the other in the head.

Buttrose, despite his determination, had not been faring well on the 14th. Profiting by their lesson of the previous day the Japanese anticipated Power's move and blocked him. Before midday Copp was back in Archer's holding position reporting that two of his platoons on the right of the

---

[7] Maj W. G. Butler, MC, QX6349. 2/25 Bn; HQ 7 Div; BM 7 Bde 1945. Grazier; of Longreach, Qld; b. Southport, Qld, 3 Oct 1912.
[8] Cpl F. T. Cook.
[9] Capt M. G. F. Donnan, QX19164. RMO 2/25 Bn; 112 AGH, 113, 110 Mil Hosps. Medical practitioner; of Brisbane; b. Mackay, Qld, 23 Aug 1915.
[1] Capt W. M. Crombie, QX6414; 2/25 Bn. Station overseer; of Longreach, Qld; b. Brisbane, 12 Mar 1914.

track had been strongly counter-attacked while Lieutenant Warne's[2] platoon on the left had been held early and, trying to edge forward, Warne himself had been killed. The climax to Buttrose's troubles came when heavy rain prevented the air strafing attacks which had been planned. He had lost 4 more men killed and 19 wounded and his strength was steadily draining. But new hope arrived with the 3rd Battalion; it would attack from the left flank next morning.

It seemed that the 2/25th Battalion was settling to a similar experience to the 2/33rd's. It was sparring for an opening in the wild bush and, although Captain O'Grady[3] with his fresh company took over from Butler, no progress was made.

The 15th, however, opened more brightly. On the main track the 3rd Battalion swung round the left of the 2/33rd as planned, but only the hot ashes of recent fires remained in the Japanese positions. Captain Beckett then hurried on towards Templeton's Crossing with instructions to swing back from there on to the Kagi Track and fall on the rear of Marson's enemies.

The afternoon saw the 2/33rd Battalion ploughing and slipping a burdened way through mud towards Templeton's Crossing, with the 3rd Battalion men sliding behind them. They brushed with an enemy ambush party then bivouacked at the first crossing of Eora Creek where the track was sunk deep in the stream's gloomy rift. They lay among the strewn bodies of the 21st Brigade's dead in the cold, wet night.

Forward from Kagi, Marson was heartened by the news that Buttrose's way was now clear. Eather ordered him to push on. But, almost immediately he attempted to do so, with O'Bryen's company leading, O'Bryen was checked. Butler drove on through O'Bryen's holding position with mortar support. (Of the twenty-seven mortar rounds which were fired, however, eight failed to explode, additional proof to that which had been furnished earlier within the brigade by the killing of mortarmen through premature bursts that many bombs dropped from the air became defective.) Butler's way was then barred by barricades of timber and wire. He fell back having lost men for no gain.

Bombs from friendly aircraft were falling ahead of them when the 2/33rd prepared to press on to Templeton's Crossing on the 16th. Soon after midday Clowes, who had led his company forward earlier, reported that he was half-way between the previous night's bivouac area and Templeton's Crossing, and hard on the heels of the enemy, the ashes of whose fires seemed to have lost only about one hour's warmth. Buttrose then led the rest of his men on. He was with Clowes again at Templeton's Crossing before the middle of the afternoon and found that that vigorous officer had been pushing a small delaying party of Japanese before him from ridge to ridge. Soon after 4 p.m. Marson's leading elements affected

---

[2] Lt H. A. Warne, NX59611; 2/33 Bn. Agriculturist; of Richmond, NSW; b. Tweed Heads, NSW, 3 Dec 1916. Killed in action 14 Oct 1942.

[3] Maj O. J. O'Grady, QX6334. 2/25 Bn; Army Labour Service 1944-45. Accountant; of Brisbane; b. Warwick, Qld, 24 Oct 1910.

the convergence on Templeton's Crossing which had been aimed at earlier. On moving into attack in the morning Marson had found—as Cameron had done on the main track on the previous day—that the opposition had melted away.

In conference, Buttrose, Marson and Cameron now decided that Cameron would take his battalion forward some hundreds of yards from Templeton's Crossing and cover the track, Buttrose would place his battalion to the right and Marson would cover the left flank. Thus Cameron sent Captain Beckett's company forward as a leading patrol. By 5.30, however, Beckett was closely held and was digging in before Japanese waiting about 500 yards farther on. Cameron then moved the rest of his men to Beckett's rear. While this was happening the 2/25th had come under mortar fire and Marson himself and two of his men were wounded.

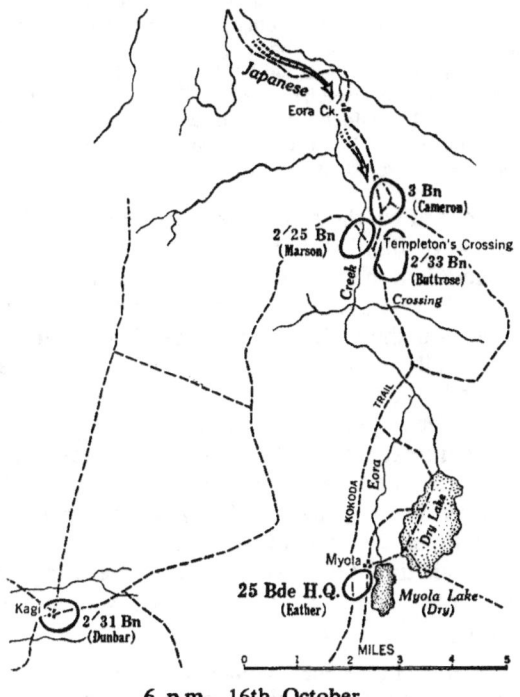

6 p.m., 16th October

The 3rd Battalion had an uneasy night. Then, on the morning of the 17th, Captain Atkinson's company struggled over ridges and broken hillsides through hampering bush growth to attack round Beckett's right flank. When his men were almost in position soon after 1 p.m.

> They had first to dispose of a machine-gun and Tongs did it. He crawled up a fire lane, under fire, and tossed a grenade which lobbed right in the pit. The two Japs in the pit were blown clean out and sprawled one on each other—dead. That started the ball rolling. The men got excited and began yelling and whooping.[4]

So they burst their way into a strongly defended position, capturing arms, equipment and documents, and consolidated on Beckett's right. Atkinson told later of two soldiers who went about their radically different tasks with courage and coolness. One of his platoon commanders, Lieutenant Richardson,[5] was shot through the chest and lay huddled behind a tree breathing through the hole the bullet had made:

---

[4] Interview with Captain Atkinson in 1943.
[5] Lt C. H. Richardson, NX141420; 3 Bn. Public servant; of Canberra; b. Sydney, 7 Aug 1920.

When Richardson was shot, Downes,[6] a country lad, always with his pipe in his mouth, tried to spot the sniper. I went down to bandage Richardson. The sniper had a go at me. The bullet went between my pack and my back and hit my dixie. Downes saw the muzzle blast, moved out into the open to see better, and shot him. Then he calmly went back behind a tree, took his pipe from his mouth, turned round to the boys and said "Well, I got the bastard!"

We had one stretcher bearer, Dwight,[7] and he used to go out whenever anyone was hit and would go where others wouldn't go. He got one man out of a forward pit, going under fire for some yards, lifting him, putting him on his back, and then running 150 yards under fire.

Soon after they had pressed home their successful attack Atkinson's men were fighting hard against counter-attacks. By 6 p.m. Atkinson and Beckett had had 7 men killed and 11 wounded. By that time the other two rifle companies, under Captain Boag, were in position for the night farther on the right of the track. They had made a wide encircling movement, fell on a surprised enemy late in the afternoon, and killed, they claimed, thirty.

For the other two battalions the day was fairly uneventful under spasmodic mortar fire. Brigadier Eather established his headquarters within Buttrose's perimeter. From the 2/25th Marson was sent out with his wounds leaving Major Millroy[8] commanding a battalion with a total strength of 25 officers and 401 men.

By this time General Allen was operating from an advanced headquarters at Myola. There, on the 17th, he was stung by a message from General Blamey:

> General MacArthur considers quote extremely light casualties indicate no serious effort yet made to displace enemy unquote. You will attack enemy with energy and all possible speed at each point of resistance. Essential that Kokoda airfield be taken at earliest. Apparent enemy gaining time by delaying you with inferior strength.

Allen replied at once:

> 25 Bde has been attacking all day and enemy is now counter-attacking. Will advise when situation clarifies. Serious efforts have been made to dispose of enemy and energetic steps have been taken at each point of resistance. This action will continue. Battle casualties since contact with enemy are killed Offrs 5 ORs 45 wounded Offrs 10 ORs 123 but I respectfully submit that the success of this campaign cannot be judged by casualties alone. Lloyd's 16th Brigade starts move forward 18 Oct to continue pressure. Until dropping ground further north is established possibly Alola there is no alternative once Lloyd's brigade is forward but to base Eather on Myola and Efogi North. In short with the carriers available I can only maintain three battalions forward in contact with enemy. Respectfully suggest you defer judgment until you receive Minogue's[9] report or until a more senior staff

---

[6] Pte D. D. Downes, NX19501. 3 and 22 Bns. Grazier; of Blanket Flat, NSW; b. Blanket Flat, 17 Feb 1910.

[7] Pte G. E. Dwight, NX78237; 3 Bn. Fruit grower; of Maleny, Qld, and Lindfield, NSW; b. Randwick, NSW, 30 Mar 1914. Killed in action 29 Nov 1942.

[8] Maj A. J. Millroy, QX6418. 2/25 Bn; Trg appointments 1943-44. Company director; of Rockhampton, Qld; b. Rockhampton, 8 Jul 1904.

[9] Lt-Col J. P. Minogue, VX108096. GSO2 (Liaison) HQ I Corps 1942; GSO1 Staff Duties NG Force 1942-43, LHQ 1943-44; GSO1 Aust Mil Mission, Washington, 1945. Barrister-at-Law; of Melbourne; b. Seymour, Vic, 15 Sep 1909.

(Australian War Memorial)

Survivors of the 2/27th Battalion at Itiki. This group had been out of touch in the Owen Stanleys for thirteen days.

(Australian War Memorial)

The march of the 16th Brigade through Sydney on 5th September was a tumultuous affair of cheers and drifting paper. Eight days later the brigade sailed for New Guinea.

(Australian War Memorial)

On 2nd October the 16th Brigade began to move forward from Owers' Corner towards Templeton's Crossing. A halt on the track between Nauro and Menari.

(Australian War Memorial)

Members of the 16th Brigade reaching the crest of a ridge on the way forward to Templeton's Crossing.

officer can come forward and discuss situation with me.[1] The severity of the conditions under which the troops are operating is emphasised by the fact that the net wastage by sickness alone in 25 Bde is Offrs 24 ORs 706 and 16 Bde Offrs 1 ORs 38.

On the same day Allen had ordered the 16th Brigade to relieve the 25th. Lieut-Colonel Edgar's[2] 2/2nd Battalion was to relieve the 2/33rd, which was to return to Myola and take over there from the 2/1st (Lieut-Colonel Cullen[3]) which would then move forward. The balance of the relief was to be arranged mutually between the two brigades.

But the events of the 18th rather forced a modification of that planning. On the 3rd Battalion front Boag's two companies lost direction in a further movement and emerged into Atkinson's area. An active enemy kept Cameron on the alert throughout the day consistently testing and probing at his front and harassing him with effective sniping. Boag was to form a firm base on the battalion's right flank for an attack by two companies of the 2/25th Battalion under Captain Blundell[4] but some lack of coordination manifested itself and the attack did not take place. Blundell had two men killed during his manoeuvrings.

During the day the 2/2nd began to relieve the 2/33rd. Eather became uneasy, however, seeing the Japanese pressure on the 3rd Battalion as a prelude to an attack on the right flank. As night came therefore he decided that the relief of the 2/33rd would not continue as arranged, and Edgar was warned by Lloyd to be ready to move at first light on the 19th to high ground to the right of and slightly forward of the 2/33rd. It was arranged that the 2/33rd would remain in position until the afternoon of that day by which time the 2/1st, of which an advanced party had already arrived, would be forward to take over from him.

On the 19th the position threatened to become acute. In the vicinity of Atkinson's right flank positions Boag lost 2 men killed and 5 wounded in hard skirmishing. Cameron hoped to gain some relief by attacking with elements of Captain Jeffrey's[5] company from Atkinson's general area. Although, however, Jeffrey's men thought they had silenced some machine-guns and put about fifteen of their well-concealed enemies out of action, 4 of them were killed and 6 were wounded and they achieved no finality.

Lieut-Colonel Edgar, at this stage, was manoeuvring on to the right flank of the 2/33rd Battalion with the dual purpose of extending Buttrose's

---

[1] Lieut-Colonel Minogue, liaison officer from New Guinea Force Headquarters, was then moving up the track to visit Allen's headquarters. He arrived there on the 20th. Allen said later: "General Blamey had two courses open to him on receipt of my signal—(a) To have confidence in my judgment which, in view of my past experience, I claim he was justified in having. (b) Come forward himself or send General Herring or a senior staff officer forward to discuss the situation with me and appreciate the position on the spot personally.
"It was not necessary to urge me or the troops under my command to capture Kokoda. We were more anxious to get there than he was. It was a considerable hardship living and fighting in that country. Had I pressed the troops harder than I was doing at this stage the operation could have resulted in failure to reach the objective and an unnecessary loss of life. I knew the capabilities of my brigade and battalion commanders and had confidence in them. Therefore I did not repeat this message to them."

[2] Brig C. R. V. Edgar, CBE, DSO, ED, NX140. CO 2/2 Bn; Comd 4 Inf Bde 1943-45. Bank officer; of Manly, NSW; b. Wedderburn, Vic, 9 Jul 1901.

[3] Lt-Col P. A. Cullen, DSO, ED, NX163. 2/2 Bn; CO 2/1 Bn 1942-45. Accountant; of Woollahra, NSW; b. Newcastle, NSW, 13 Feb 1909.

[4] Capt P. L. Blundell, QX6368; 2/25 Bn. Grazier; of Stanthorpe, Qld; b. Brisbane, 13 Feb 1909.

[5] Maj J. S. Jeffrey, NX128780. 3 Bn; HQ 16 Bde. Bank officer; of Merewether, NSW; b. Nyngan, NSW, 18 Jun 1910.

right and pushing forward strong patrols to give some protection to the strained right of the 3rd Battalion which was still resisting counter-attacks. It was obvious that it would be difficult for Cameron's men to hand over and extricate themselves. Lloyd planned with Eather to relieve them with the 2/1st Battalion while the 2/2nd Battalion attacked. By nightfall Cullen had arrived in the 2/33rd Battalion area in preparation for the execution of this plan. The 25th Brigade diarist recorded:

2/25, 2/33 and 3 Bn personnel now quite exhausted and relief almost imperative.

At 7 a.m. on the 20th Brigadier Lloyd became responsible for operations in the forward areas. That day, while the 2/2nd launched fierce attacks which were designed to clear the position, the 2/1st took over from the 3rd, but it was not until almost nightfall that the 2/1st was in a position finally to accept responsibility for the area. Even then rest for Cameron's tired men who had fought so well did not follow immediately as they remained in reserve behind the 2/1st ready to play a further part if the still confused situation made that necessary. The 2/33rd and 2/25th were more fortunate, although the 2/25th lost a number of men wounded during the day from enemy mortar fire. By 5 p.m. Lieut-Colonel Stevenson's[6] 2/3rd Battalion had relieved both these units. The 2/33rd moved back at once to an A.A.S.C. dump area near the first crossing of Eora Creek; the 2/25th was ordered to follow them next morning.

Plans for the employment of individual battalions fluctuated somewhat in the next few days. Eather's brigade remained in position in the area just to Lloyd's rear. The 3rd Battalion was held forward on attachment to the 16th Brigade, waiting to protect Alola after it had been captured and prepare dropping grounds there; the 2/25th remained at the A.A.S.C. dump; the 2/33rd was hard at work on supply duties in the Myola area; the 2/31st was held forward of Kagi on the junction of the Alola and Templeton's Crossing tracks, ready to move forward at short notice. All four battalions were seriously depleted in number, the strengths of the three 25th Brigade battalions on the 23rd October being:

	Officers	Other Ranks
2/25th	22	394
2/31st	20	451
2/33rd	20	366

On the 20th October (on relief by the 16th Brigade) the total casualties in the 25th Brigade were listed as:

	Officers	Other Ranks
Killed	5	63
Wounded	11	124
Sick	28	743

The care of these sick and wounded men was a heavy task.

In preparation for the advance of the 25th Brigade the jeep-head near Uberi had been developed as the basic divisional medical post. Lieut-

---

[6] Maj-Gen J. R. Stevenson, CBE, DSO, ED, NX49. CO 2/3 Bn 1941-43; Comd 11 Bde 1943-45 and Merauke Force 1943-44. Parliamentary officer; of Lakemba, NSW; b. Bondi, NSW, 7 Oct 1908.

Colonel Chenhall[7] used the headquarters group of his 2/6th Field Ambulance to set up a main dressing station there with one surgeon—Captain Leslie[8] from the 2/9th General Hospital—attached, and accommodation for 200 light casualties. The remainder of the 2/6th were allotted to forward posts to serve the advance as far as Nauro. From that point on to Myola, it was planned, Lieut-Colonel Hobson[9] and his 2/4th Field Ambulance, who had arrived from their training areas in Queensland on 17th September, would take over the forward duties. As a preliminary they became responsible for staging duties at Ilolo until relieved by a detachment of the 14th Field Ambulance. Major Vickery,[1] one of the 2/4th officers, relieved Major Humphery[2] (who had taken over from Major Magarey earlier) on 25th September as senior medical officer to the forward troops.

As planned, Hobson took over from Chenhall when the advance reached Nauro. By that time, however, since there had been no battle casualties and there were then comparatively few sick or injured men on the track, the extensive arrangements which Chenhall had made at Uberi were seen to be unnecessary. Chenhall then prepared to move his field ambulance forward to assist Hobson's.

When the 25th Brigade and the retreating Japanese had clashed vigorously south of Templeton's Crossing, wounded men poured into Hobson's main dressing station now established at Myola. It was still hoped that many sick and wounded men could be flown out from that area where engineers had been hard at work improving the strip at Myola No. 2. The airmen were reluctant to use the strip, however, their leaders claiming that the hazards were too great. The landing ground was rather short in comparison with those used for the larger type of transport and, facing the take-off end and not far from it, was a hillside which forced a quick climb and sharp banking. In the mountains swirling thrusts of air up and down were common and an aircraft, caught by one of these at a critical moment, had little chance of avoiding a crash. So the available hospital accommodation at Myola was severely taxed as casualties mounted and Leslie, who had come forward, and the other medical officers were committed to extensive major surgery for which they had insufficient facilities.

While events along the Kokoda Track had thus progressed to a stage which looked like being climactic in the Templeton's Crossing-Eora Creek area, considerable movement had been taking place along the two other axes which General Blamey had defined as lines of advance on Buna from the south-east and south-west.

---

[7] Lt-Col F. N. Chenhall, NX452. 2/4 Fd Amb; CO 2/6 Fd Amb 1942-43, 114 Con Depot 1943. Surgeon; of Sydney; b. Corowa, NSW, 30 Dec 1902.

[8] Maj D. R. Leslie, VX39117; 2/9 AGH. Medical practitioner; of Melbourne; b. Hitchin, England, 23 Feb 1914.

[9] Col A. F. Hobson, OBE, NX454. 2/4 Fd Amb (CO 1942-44); ADMS 7 Div 1944-45. Medical practitioner; of Rose Bay, NSW; b. Strathfield, NSW, 5 Sep 1907.

[1] Maj I. F. Vickery, NX473; 2/4 Fd Amb. Medical practitioner; of Cronulla, NSW; b. Bellevue Hill, NSW, 29 Jul 1914. Killed in action 27 Nov 1942.

[2] Lt-Col R. J. Humphery, NX446. RMO 2/33 Bn 1941; CO 2/6 Fd Amb 1943-45. Medical practitioner; of Fairfield, NSW; b. Lismore, NSW, 30 Jun 1912. Accidentally killed 2 Jul 1945.

During his period of command General Rowell had written to General Blamey's headquarters on 20th September:

> The question of any move along the north coast towards Buna is directly associated with the provision of landing craft and continuous fighter cover during movement.

Blamey's visit to Milne Bay on the 24th September had, however, resulted in an attempt to overcome such difficulties by flying troops to Wanigela (and later he planned a more extensive project than the one he had originally considered). On 5th October 61 plane-loads of men and material were flown to Wanigela and a force (Hatforce) which consisted mainly of 2/10th Battalion and a battery of American .5-inch anti-aircraft guns was established there. This was doubly interesting—as a forward step and as the first large-scale operational move of ground troops by air in the Pacific war.

To link the operations of the 126th and 128th United States Regiments with this venture, and to provide for the American overland advance which had been planned, the task of the 32nd U.S. Division was formally defined by New Guinea Force on the 8th October:

> The role of 32 Div is to attack the enemy at Buna from the east and south-east.

The division was immediately to reconnoitre and develop the routes leading to Jaure from Rigo and Abau, connecting laterals between the main routes from each of the two latter points, an overland route from Abau leading to Wanigela by way of the Musa River. It was to establish a system of supply by means of small watercraft through Abau. It was to locate and maintain at Jaure a force not exceeding two battalions (since maintenance difficulties precluded the establishment there of greater strength). The definition of its action beyond Jaure was left until later. It was to leave one regiment at Port Moresby—to fill an emergency role there—which would be available later for the execution of the main divisional plan.

These instructions were altered somewhat and added to within a week. Brigadier-General MacNider was appointed to command the Wanigela force. He was ordered to consolidate Wanigela as a sea and air base for supplies, to exploit forward to Buna by sea and land, to institute and develop small craft supply routes from Wanigela to Pongani.

On 14th October the air move from Port Moresby to Wanigela of Colonel Alexander J. MacNab's 128th Regiment and the 2/6th Australian Independent Company (less patrol detachments operating in the vicinity of the Kokoda Track) began. Within two days the movement of most of the American regiment, and the Independent Company, had been completed. A troop of the 2/5th Field Regiment with four 25-pounders, a light anti-aircraft detachment of 6 Bofors and an American platoon with three .5-inch anti-aircraft machine-guns were warned for movement by sea to Wanigela as soon as transport became available.

Upon arrival at Wanigela Major Harcourt,[3] who commanded the Independent Company, lost no time in pushing his men off on the overland route to Pongani. Harcourt was an intrepid officer whose forty-seven years seemingly had done nothing to lessen his zest for living, his energy, or his physical endurance.

Scarcely had Harcourt with his men crossed the Musa River than that stream flooded widely. The trails foundered in the several miles of water which spread near its mouth. MacNab's battalions were cut off from the overland route. They began then to ferry to Pongani in 20-ton supply luggers of which the first two had arrived at Wanigela about the middle of the month. The leading luggers, however, which arrived off Pongani on the morning of the 18th, were bombed there by American aircraft which mistook them for Japanese and some casualties resulted. Despite this the ferry movement continued during ensuing days.

Meanwhile the difficult movement of the 126th Regiment over the third axis which led through the wild mountains of the centre of Papua had begun. An advanced detachment of the II Battalion had followed the reconnaissance party over the Jaure Track early in the month. About a week behind them went the rest of the battalion which was arriving at Jaure by the 22nd. They were accompanied by 200 native carriers in charge of Sergeant Smith[4] of Angau, who also acted as a guide. These Americans had no contact with any Japanese and found no indication that they were exploring that flank. The difficulties of the Jaure Track were such, however, that no move was made to send any additional units of the 126th behind the II Battalion.

Thus, as the end of October approached, the Australians and Americans were definitely, if still slowly, converging on the Buna-Gona area along three lines of advance. Whether they would achieve their purpose of driving the Japanese out of Papua before the Japanese strength then levelled at Guadalcanal could be diverted against them was another matter.

---

[3] Maj H. G. Harcourt, DSO, OBE, MC, TX2156. (1914-18: Maj Royal Dublin Fusiliers; MG Corps.) OC 2/6 Indep Coy; 2/7 Cav (Cdo) Regt. Civil servant; of Hobart; b. Westcliffe, England, 13 Feb 1895.

[4] Capt R. A. Smith, P394; Angau. Trader; of Wainapune, Papua; b. Tamworth, NSW, 21 Jul 1905.
  Smith wrote afterwards: "The natives in my team across the ranges deserve the credit for the arrival of the U.S. troops we convoyed. . . . There is a point which should not be forgotten regarding these boys. . . . They felt instinctively that the U.S. soldier did not possess the hardihood of the Aussie and so knew that with them they did not have the protection their fellow carriers with the C.M.F. enjoyed. This being so made their effort in crossing the range and their front-line work at Buna all the more meritorious."

CHAPTER 9

EORA CREEK

WHEN he set out on 3rd October to take over from Brigadier Eather, Brigadier Lloyd was eager for action, his men no less so. Their desire to measure themselves against the Japanese had been sharpened by the importance of the occasion. They passed General MacArthur near Owers' Corner on their way forward. He said then: "Lloyd, by some act of God, your brigade has been chosen for this job. The eyes of the western world are upon you. I have every confidence in you and your men. Good luck and don't stop." MacArthur was making his first visit to New Guinea. He arrived on 2nd October, spent about an hour at Owers' Corner on the 3rd, and thus was able to see from a distance the country in which the troops were operating, and departed on the 4th.

Lloyd was a genial leader with something of the manner of an English regular officer. He was well into his forty-ninth year at this time; the New Guinea mountains might prove too much for him physically. He took care to know personally as many of his officers and men as he could and let them see that he was interested in them and thought they were grand people. They returned his respect and liking. He was a veteran of the 1914-18 War, during which he had proved himself an able and high-spirited young officer, and he had rounded off his service with a term in the Indian Army. In 1940 he took the 2/28th Battalion away, led it during the siege of Tobruk and later succeeded to command of the 16th Brigade. As recently as the second week of August he and his brigade had arrived from Ceylon, so that they had had little time to savour their return home before they were committed once more to an overseas venture. The British Prime Minister and General Wavell had been unwilling to release them and the 17th Brigade from the garrison of Ceylon. The fact, however, that these troops were urgently needed at home was demonstrated when only 36 days elapsed between the disembarkation of the 16th Brigade at Melbourne and its re-embarkation for New Guinea. The men were not unready for jungle warfare, having trained for it strenuously in Ceylon.

The 16th Brigade had been tried in the desert and Greece, and, in part, in Crete and Syria. General Allen, who now commanded the 7th Division of which it had just become a part, had been its original commander and expected much of it. Eather, whose brigade it now relieved, had been one of its original battalion commanders and was watching it with critical anticipation.

The brigade had arrived in New Guinea on 21st September. On 3rd October the 2/3rd Battalion (30 officers and 587 men) began to move forward from Owers' Corner. Next day the 2/2nd Battalion followed with 26 officers and 528 men. Two days later 27 officers and 581 other ranks of the 2/1st took the track. In addition to his arms and ammunition, each officer and man carried three days' emergency and three days' hard rations, with the inevitable "unconsumed portion of the day's ration". His haversack contained his toilet gear, a change of clothing, sweater and dixie. Half a blanket rolled in his groundsheet and strapped on to the back of his belt, a gas cape (as protection from the weather) and a steel helmet completed his outfit. With each company went the normal complement of light machine-guns and sub-machine-guns, rifles and bayonets, a liberal supply of grenades, ammunition and machetes. For each battalion one 3-inch mortar with twenty-four bombs and one Vickers machine-gun with 3,000 rounds was carried.

Quickly the men settled to conditions along the track. On the 6th, when a prisoner was handed over to them at Menari by the 25th Brigade, they saw their first Japanese and found him "an unprepossessing specimen". With the eager boyishness which remained with so many Australian soldiers in spite of their grimness in action, they took a dump of discarded felt hats which had been torn almost in halves when they were dropped at Menari and sewed them into raffish shapes to wear in styles varying from light-hearted Alpine to rakish Mexican "Viva Villa". They reacted sombrely to the atmosphere of the Efogi battle-ground where the 21st Brigade had fought so desperately.

> Along the route (wrote the diarist of the 16th Brigade) were skeletons, picked clean by ants and other insects, and in the dark recesses of the forest came to our nostrils the stench of the dead, hastily buried, or perhaps not buried at all.

At Myola, where they guarded the dropping areas and gathered the stores, they began to appreciate fully the supply difficulties they would face and the problems their wounded would represent to them.

By the 19th their last illusions about the difficulties which faced them vanished as they tried to relieve the 25th Brigade forward of Templeton's Crossing in the midst of an engagement. In the afternoon of that day, among other patrols, one led by Lieutenant Ryan[1] went out from the 2/2nd Battalion to the ridge east of Templeton's Crossing. He came against a strong position, his patrol was badly mauled, and he himself, shot in the stomach, was barely able to drag himself into the nearest Australian positions.

By the early evening Eather and Lloyd had planned that, next day, the 20th, Lieut-Colonel Edgar would send his 2/2nd Battalion from the Australian right flank against the Japanese who were savagely thrusting at the 3rd, Eather's most forward battalion, while Lieut-Colonel Cullen would try to relieve the 3rd with his 2/1st Battalion and Lieut-Colonel Stevenson's 2/3rd Battalion would take over from both the 2/25th and 2/33rd.

It will be recalled that the track from Templeton's Crossing followed the right-hand side of the great Eora Creek ravine, over about two hours and a half of difficult going for an unburdened man, before it reached Eora Creek village; that first it rose high up the mountainside through

---

[1] Lt W. P. Ryan, NX8752; 2/2 Bn. Shop assistant; of Armidale, NSW; b. Armidale, 15 Sep 1921.

the dripping bush until even the roar of the torrent below could be heard no more. Nothing could then be seen from the track except the rain forests pressing in. It was broken by upward-rearing ridges which cut across it at right angles as it made its way over the torn side of the mountain and before it fell steeply down again to the water. Japanese were now bitterly blocking this track immediately beyond Templeton's Crossing.

When Edgar (a composed and experienced soldier) was ordered to push the Japanese from these positions he planned to do it with four companies. Two would swing wide to the right of the 3rd Battalion, move northward along the heights of the main ridge which paralleled the track, and then turn left to drive down parallel spurs at right angles to the track in front of the 3rd Battalion's positions. The other two companies would thrust forward at the closer reaches of the track, also from right of the 3rd Battalion, to sustain that flank and to support the rear of the foremost attackers.

On the morning of the 20th a cold gloom hung over the mountains. Water was dripping from the sodden trees and falling soundlessly on a sodden carpet of mould. Captains Ferguson[2] and Baylis,[3] whose companies were to do the wide outflanking movement, were on the move from 8 a.m., Ferguson leading. The 3rd provided guides to pilot them clear of its right. Ferguson moved then on a bearing of 70 degrees, his men behind him in single file as they made their difficult way up the slope through the cold, wet bush. The dank odour of tropical decay hung heavy in the air. High up the slope they swung left and moved painfully towards their assembly area. By 11 a.m. Ferguson was in position on the most forward spur, Baylis ready on the parallel spur on his left as they faced west towards the Japanese positions. On the hour the two companies went into the attack, moving deliberately down the slope over broken ground and through thick bush.

In Ferguson's company Lieutenants Hall[4] and Blain[5] had their platoons forward, Hall on the right. Ferguson, with a runner and an Intelligence man, was advancing between the two. Sergeant Barnes'[6] platoon was in reserve, on loan from Headquarters Company to replace Ryan's platoon which had been cut about the previous day.

In Baylis' company Lieutenants Tanner[7] and Wickham[8] were on the right and left of the advance respectively, Lieutenant Goodman's[9] platoon

---

[2] Lt-Col I. B. Ferguson, DSO, MC, NX2654. 2/2 Bn; GSO2 1 Combined Ops 1944-45. CO 3 Bn RAR, Korea, 1950-51. Journalist; of Potts Point, NSW; b. Wellington, NZ, 13 Apr 1917.
[3] Maj C. F. W. Baylis, MC, NX1800. 2/2 Bn; 1 Reception Gp 1944-45. Bank clerk; of Uralla, NSW; b. Killara, NSW, 6 Jul 1913.
[4] Lt W. D. Hall, NX57864; 2/2 Bn. Clerk; of Manly, NSW; b. Footscray, Vic, 27 May 1917. Killed in action 20 Oct 1942.
[5] Lt R. N. Blain, NX1951; 2/2 Bn. Grocer; of Glen Innes, NSW; b. Emmaville, NSW, 13 Nov 1917. Killed in action 20 Oct 1942.
[6] Sgt M. R. Barnes, NX13475; 2/2 Bn. Station hand; of Moree, NSW; b. Huntly, NZ, 1 Jan 1917.
[7] Lt R. R. Tanner, NX1746; 2/2 Bn. Butcher; of Wallabadah, NSW; b. Wallabadah, 13 Nov 1917. Killed in action 20 Oct 1942.
[8] Lt H. G. Wickham, NX59872; 2/2 Bn. Clerk; of East Hills and Picton districts, NSW; b. East Hills, 15 Oct 1920.
[9] Lt P. Goodman, NX28904; 2/2 Bn. Articled clerk; of Chatswood, NSW; b. Richmond, NSW, 5 May 1920.

in reserve. The platoons were moving still in single file, scouts well ahead, ready to fan out into open formation on contact.

The Australians went forward with slow care in the eerie mountain silence. A twig cracking sounded loud and sharp. About 200 yards down the most forward slope Hall and Blain came against the Japanese outpost positions, and then noises of battle rolled out, and the advance passed on. A further 100 yards and the attackers were against the first of the main enemy positions—about fifteen pits round perhaps four light machine-gun posts and spreading over both company features. These pits were well concealed and almost the first intimation Ferguson had of their presence was a devastating fire which swept through his little force. Among others Hall fell dead but his men encircled the position and gradually rooted the defenders out of their holes. Again the slow advance went forward, this time to come up against a line of main Japanese positions. When the defenders were forced out of these Ferguson had come to the end of his spur. He swung left then across to Baylis' feature where he brought his depleted force in behind the other company as support. By that time the other forward platoon commander, Blain, was dead, with a number of his men, and Barnes, leader of the third platoon, was wounded.

Baylis' men had been engaged simultaneously with Ferguson's. First they came against a forward Japanese platoon but, covering behind trees, supported by light machine-gun fire and grenading, they drove ahead at a cost of only two men. After they had fought forward for about another 100 yards heavy machine-gun fire swept them. Tanner fell there, with several of his men. Quickly Baylis ordered Goodman to leapfrog through the leaderless platoon which would then become the reserve. As Goodman's first section moved down it was pinned by machine-gun fire. The other two sections swung out of the fixed lines. Corporal Roberts[1] closed his section on to a machine-gun post and bombed it into silence. The Australians kept pressing against the remaining strength of this position, able to see little in the thick bush but firing at the bases of trees and other likely targets. Finally the surviving Japanese broke and fled from these second strongpoints leaving equipment and rifles behind them. But after the attackers had followed on for about another 150 yards heavy fire smashed into them again and held them close to the earth. At Baylis' request Colonel Edgar then turned the mortars on to the Japanese but with little apparent effect. Later Baylis asked the colonel if he could arrange for an attack from the other side by a company of the 2/1st Battalion so that, between them, the two companies could squeeze the defenders out. When Edgar told him, however, to press on alone Baylis sent his second-in-command, Captain Blamey,[2] round the left flank with the remnants of Tanner's platoon while the other two platoons harassed the

---

[1] Cpl G. K. Roberts, NX4360; 2/2 Bn. Labourer; of Tucabia, NSW; b. South Grafton, NSW, 23 Jun 1916.

[2] Capt J. M. Blamey, NX34853; 2/2 Bn. Solicitor; of Manly, NSW; b. Dulwich Hill, NSW, 17 Jan 1914. Died of wounds 26 Nov 1942.

Japanese with fire. In the face of this threat their enemies withdrew as darkness lowered. Baylis thought his men had killed at least 12 of them in the day but he had lost 5 men killed and 10 wounded.

The two companies then dug in together for the night in box formation. In describing the scene later, two officers wrote:

> As we dug a two company perimeter for the night a desolate scene was presented: our own and enemy dead lying in grotesque positions, bullet-scarred trees with the peeled bark showing ghostlike, our own lads digging silently. And with the coming of darkness came the rain, persistent and cold, and in this atmosphere we settled in our weapon pits for the night. At night we could hear the Jap chattering and moving about.[3]

While Baylis and Ferguson had been thus engaged Captains Fairbrother[4] and Swinton[5] had been moving the other rifle companies into action. Fairbrother issued his final orders in the dim mountain dawn and then, at 8.30, with guides from the 3rd Battalion, led out through that battalion's right, north along the main ridge, to turn against the Japanese positions which lay astride the track and between the 3rd Battalion and Baylis' and Ferguson's objectives. Approximately where he would hit the main track a small pad crossed it at right angles.

At 10.18 a.m. the forward scouts of Lieutenant Smith's[6] platoon, which was leading, came under fire. Smith's men pushed on until machine-gun fire whipped them to the ground. Although unable to locate his enemies or decide their strength Fairbrother then sent Lieutenant Hodge's[7] platoon wide to the right and, after that, on to the track in the rear of Smith's assailants. There Hodge held although he was flailed from farther ahead.

Meanwhile Swinton had been moving on the flanks and rear of Fairbrother's advance. Learning of Hodge's difficulties he sent Sergeant Lacey's[8] platoon round the right flank to try to help him. But Lacey had gone only about 300 yards when his men began to fall to a heavy fire. Swinton then ordered Lieutenant Coyle's[9] platoon to circle round Smith's left and fall upon the holding forces from that direction. This Coyle did with some success and without loss. Meanwhile Swinton had sent Lieutenant Irvin's[1] platoon to help Lacey, but Irvin's men, in their turn, found themselves beaten at by fire.

Night was coming now and, as the two companies farther forward had done, Fairbrother and Swinton dug into a perimeter defence for the

---

[3] "The Kokoda Trail" by Capts H. G. McCammon and C. H. Hodge in *Nulli Secundus Log*, a journal of the 2/2nd Battalion.
[4] Maj D. N. Fairbrother, MC, NX1274; 2/2 Bn. Fitter's assistant; of Hamilton, NSW; b. Adelaide, 25 Dec 1910.
[5] Capt C. N. Swinton, NX1837. 2/2 Bn; F-Lt RAAF 1945. Bank officer; of Uralla, NSW; b. Casino, NSW, 24 Aug 1918.
[6] Capt H. C. Smith, NX1408. 2/2 Bn; 1 Reception Group 1944-45. Farm employee; of Denman, NSW; b. Gloucester, England, 24 Jan 1908.
[7] Capt C. H. Hodge, MBE, NX60545; 2/2 Bn. Bank officer; of Murwillumbah, NSW; b. Mullumbimby, NSW, 3 Jun 1912.
[8] Lt A. R. Lacey, MM, NX2389; 2/2 Bn. Clerk; of Ballina, NSW; b. Sydney, 1 Jan 1912.
[9] Capt G. Coyle, NX1250; 2/2 Bn. Shop assistant; of Newcastle, NSW; b. Toowoomba, Qld, 3 Oct 1922.
[1] Lt O. B. Irvin, NX70737; 2/2 Bn. Clerk; of Bondi, NSW; b. Bombala, NSW, 13 May 1919.

night. Fairbrother had lost 6 men killed and 10 wounded, Swinton 4 killed and 4 wounded.

While the 2/2nd Battalion had thus been leading the 16th Brigade's initial attack the 2/1st had been "doubling up" in the 3rd Battalion area, its orders being to continue the advance when the 2/2nd had cleared the track. The companies were all in position before 10.30 a.m. on the 20th, trying to support the 2/2nd's attacks with mortar and light machine-gun fire. But this task proved most difficult as, though the foremost Japanese were less than 100 yards in front, they were not visible, nor could the fall of fire be observed. When the attacking forces were held in the afternoon it was decided that Captain Catterns'[2] company of the 2/1st should attack from the right of the main Australian positions early on the 21st and move forward down the main track.

Now, also, Lloyd's third battalion was entering the scene. As Edgar and Cullen were manoeuvring in the face of the Japanese Lieut-Colonel Stevenson was bringing his 2/3rd forward from Myola. By 3.30 p.m. it had arrived at Templeton's Crossing and relieved the 2/25th and 2/33rd.

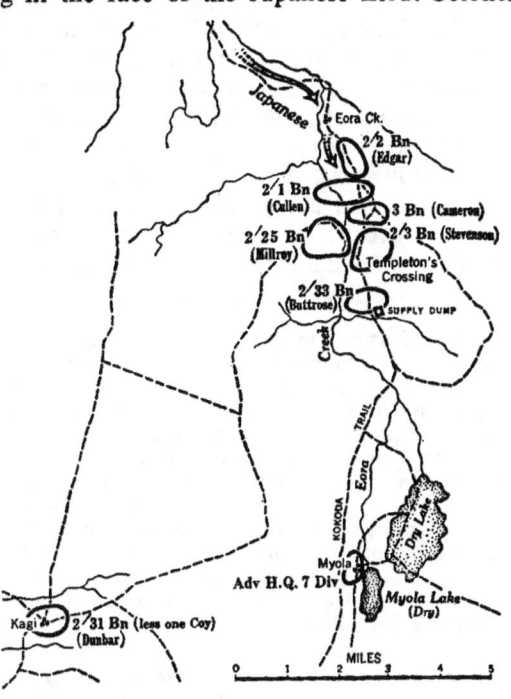

6 p.m., 20th October

When the night came, on 20th October, therefore, Lloyd's brigade was concentrated at Templeton's Crossing and in close contact with the Japanese. Backing it closely was the 3rd Battalion (which was remaining in the area on attachment to protect Alola after its capture and prepare the dropping grounds there) and a platoon from the 2/33rd Battalion was in position to strengthen the right flank.

On the morning of the 21st the Australians were early astir. Catterns moved his company round the right flank through Ferguson's and Baylis' positions. Soon after 10 a.m. the three companies were advancing down the slopes towards the track. But the Japanese had gone. The Australians estimated that they had been holding there with at least a battalion, and Baylis himself thought that the positions his men had actually cleared the

---

[2] Maj B. W. T. Catterns, MC, NX342; 2/1 Bn. Newspaper reporter; of Sydney; b. Balmain, NSW, 11 Aug 1917.

previous day were of company strength. Abandoned equipment and papers lay about. After they had combed the area across the track and down to the creek the two companies of the 2/2nd rejoined their battalion higher up the slope while Catterns' men pushed on along the track.

Meanwhile the other companies had been having a similar experience. Fairbrother's early morning patrols found the track clear immediately in front of them. There the Japanese had been fighting from what appeared to have been a platoon position in which 14 dead men now lay among scattered rifles and equipment. At 9.30 Captain Brown[3] of the 2/3rd led his company into Fairbrother's position and then moved eastward towards the crest of the ridge along the small cross-track. He was to clear positions the Japanese had been holding on the higher ground. But those positions too had been abandoned.

With the afternoon a new brigade movement was under way. Brown's company was moving along a narrow, slippery track high up the slope to the right of, and parallel with, the main track, in places deep in morasses of foul smelling mud, hemmed in by tall trees and dripping bush. Major Hutchison[4] joined him there with another company of the 2/3rd and took command of both. By that time one of Brown's patrols had already brushed with a Japanese light machine-gun post on a minor footway leading back towards the main axis and killed one of its crew. The two companies continued a laborious advance until about 5 p.m. when a sudden fire swept over the leading platoon. It killed Private Fernance[5] (the first man of the battalion to die in action in this campaign) and wounded two other soldiers. Of that incident Lieutenant MacDougal[6] later said:

> On the afternoon of the first day out from Templeton's Crossing, as the leading company was moving along the track with the two forward scouts out in front, there was a sudden burst of fire and the scouts and one man farther back were hit. The company stopped on the track and in the bush on either side while the commanders of the two leading platoons went forward cautiously. Suddenly they were shot at by unseen Japanese evidently dug in at the foot of trees; but, though the shots came from a range of only ten yards—they stepped it out next day—neither of them was hit. As they lay low in the bush they could hear the butt swivel of the Japanese sniper's rifle clicking as he moved. They went back, under cover. The company camped that night about sixty yards from the Japanese post, spread out across the track ready for attack from any direction. After dark, one of the platoon commanders went out and brought in one of the scouts who had been wounded by the sniper's first shots.[7]

MacDougal went on then to speak of the intrepid men who became forward scouts. These led the advance in this bush fighting where there was room along the tracks for men to move only in single file. Normally

---

[3] Capt C. K. Brown, NX4867; 2/3 Bn. Solicitor, of Wollongong, NSW; b. Los Angeles, California, USA, 7 Nov 1909.

[4] Lt-Col I. Hutchison, DSO, OBE, MC, ED, NX100. 2/3 Bn (CO 1943-45); CO 1 Bn RAR Korea, 1952-53. Shipping clerk; of Mosman, NSW; b. Sydney, 2 Aug 1913.

[5] Pte D. J. Fernance, NX39546; 2/3 Bn. Labourer; of Grafton, NSW; b. South Grafton, 14 May 1916. Killed in action 21 Oct 1942.

[6] Lt B. H. MacDougal, DCM, NX572; 2/3 Bn. Salesman; of Mosman, NSW; b. Mosman, 11 Apr 1915.

[7] Interview in *The Sydney Morning Herald*, 30 Jan 1943.

they did not expect to see the Japanese who were lying in wait until the ambushers fired. And to that sudden fire the scouts were almost certain to fall, to lie dead on the track, or wounded at the mercy of their enemies, while the rest of the company or platoon, who had been filing behind, fanned out through the thick bush to try to outflank the obstruction. MacDougal said:

> On the march during the next weeks each leading company had to send scouts out ahead on the track. It was almost a certainty that once, or perhaps more often, a day the forward scouts on the track, or scouts exploring the Japanese positions across the track, would be killed or wounded by unseen snipers, who would wait until they were twenty yards away or less before firing. Yet there was never any difficulty in finding men for the job. Before the leading platoon moved off in the morning or after a spell, the commander might say: 'We'll need two forward scouts.' Three or four men would begin to collect their gear and come forward. These three or four would arrange among themselves who would go out in front. One would say to another 'You did it yesterday', and there would be some quiet discussion until, in a few seconds without any more orders or suggestions from the platoon commander or sergeant, two scouts would be selected and ready.

During that same afternoon of the 21st the 2/1st and 2/2nd Battalions had been moving along the main track in that order, with Catterns' the vanguard company for the brigade, Captain Sanderson's[8] company following closely and the commanding officer, Cullen, himself moving in rear of Sanderson. At about 2 p.m. the forward scouts came against a Japanese position on a ridge up which the track climbed. Catterns' men thrust against it but lost 2 killed and 4 wounded. He was trying to outflank round his enemies' left. But the bush was thick, the upward slope steep and broken. It was 7 p.m. before he was in position to attack. In the fading light the Australians therefore bivouacked. They would attack at first light on the 22nd.

So night came again. The fight for Templeton's Crossing had ended but it was clear that the fight for the main Eora Creek crossing was only beginning. At that crossing place the country offered what were possibly the most favourable conditions for defence along the whole length of the track between Port Moresby and Kokoda. There, it will be remembered, the main stream, after flowing down an ever-deepening valley from near Templeton's Crossing, had gouged a deeply sunken and gloomy gorge and was joined by a tributary which flowed in from the south-east. The swirling waters of the two had churned what was almost a great pit around the point of junction. Massive boulders lay in the bed of the stream and the waters rushed round them foaming. Just above the junction a bridge crossed the tributary and just below it a second bridge crossed the main flow. As the track, after rising and falling over humps and razor-back spurs, approached the first crossing, it passed over a bare ridge and through a few miserable native huts—the village of Eora Creek—plunged precipitously down the forward slopes, crossed the first bridge, then followed the echoing floor of the gorge briefly before it twisted west to

---

[8] Capt A. G. Sanderson, NX7567; 2/1 Bn. Accountant; of Croydon, NSW; b. Claremont, WA, 7 Mar 1908. Killed in action 23 Oct 1942.

cross the second bridge. It scrambled north again, crossing a slight widening of the creek valley through broken ways, and, a little farther on, thrust up the scarred side of a mountain so steep that the crags seemed to overhang it. To the right of the track as it crossed the creek forbidding cliffs rose. To the left of the track and creek junction broken country

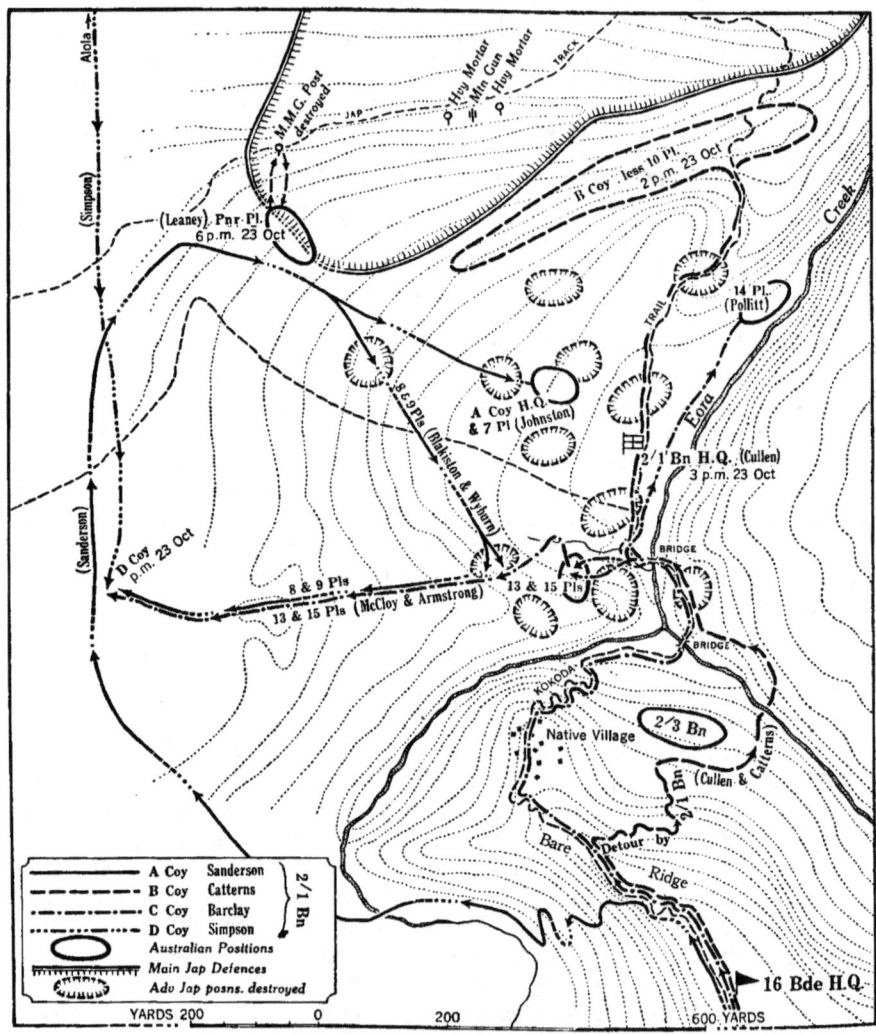

Eora Creek, 22nd-23rd October

reared high, tumbled and scrub covered, to sweep upwards in an arc of turbulent hills and crevasses into a thrusting feature north-west of that point and across the track farther on.

In the early morning of the 22nd both Hutchison and Catterns found that the Japanese had gone. They pushed forward, Hutchison still on the auxiliary track higher up the valley side and followed along that track by the 2/2nd Battalion, Catterns and the rest of the 2/1st on the main track, with the balance of the 2/3rd close behind. About 10.30 a.m. Brown's company, still leading Hutchison's detachment, swung on to the main track in front of the 2/1st and entered Eora Creek village. Then mortar and machine-gun fire raked them. Brown and some of his men were hit. They lay in the open for most of the day until, towards dusk, one or two began to struggle back up the slope and Sergeant Carson,[9] using his pioneer platoon as stretcher-bearers, made courageous efforts to bring some in, losing one of his bearers killed and one wounded in the process.

When Cullen arrived at the ridge overlooking the village about an hour after Brown was shot, he sent Captain Sanderson and his company across to the left bank of the creek with instructions to work up the ridge above the Japanese on the left and attack from that position.

By early afternoon most of the brigade was blocked on and behind the bare ridge which overlooked the village. Although they did not know it at first they could be seen there by the Japanese who began to shell, mortar and machine-gun them heavily. Lieut-Colonel Stevenson was struck in the ear and his medical officer, Captain Goldman,[1] was badly hit.

Goldman was working at the time with Captain Connell,[2] medical officer of the 2/1st Battalion, when the regimental aid post they were jointly manning came under heavy fire. Three of their men were killed and Lance-Sergeant Doran[3] was painfully wounded in the foot. Doran assisted Connell to carry on, however, and it was not until all the other casualties in the post had been treated that he reported that he himself needed attention.

As the daylight was beginning to fade Brigadier Lloyd studied the situation. It was becoming clear now that the Japanese were strongly entrenched at Eora Creek. On the right of the Australian positions the 2/3rd Battalion was deployed. All the men Cullen of the 2/1st could muster there were disposed about the track itself but he had less than half of his battalion with him; on orders from the brigadier, Captain Simpson's[4] company had swung off the track earlier to try to reach Alola by by-passing Eora Creek and most of Headquarters Company had followed in error and were not to rejoin the battalion until next day; Captain Sanderson's company were still out in the wild country to the left and nothing had been heard of them; one of Captain Catterns' platoons was

---

[9] Sgt A. L. Carson, DCM, MM, NX5027; 2/3 Bn. (1st AIF: Cpl 2 Bn.) Rigger; of Rozelle, NSW; b. Balmain, NSW, 2 May 1893. (Served in 1st AIF as Carlson.)
[1] Capt M. Goldman, WX11063. RMO 2/3 Bn, 111, 115 AGHs. Medical practitioner; of Double Bay, NSW; b. Cobargo, NSW, 16 Sep 1913.
[2] Maj J. F. Connell, MC, VX13901. RMO 2/1 Bn; 2/11 AGH; 2/8 Fd Amb. Medical practitioner; of Melbourne; b. Lockhart, NSW, 25 May 1913.
[3] L-Sgt J. Doran, MM, NX9045; 2/1 Bn. Labourer; of Neutral Bay, NSW; b. Bathurst, NSW, 6 Oct 1913.
[4] Capt A. M. Simpson, NX3863; 2/1 Bn. Journalist; of Sydney; b. Glasgow, Scotland, 1 Mar 1910. Killed in action 20 Nov 1942.

away on a special patrol. The 2/2nd Battalion was in reserve a little farther back along the track in the vicinity of brigade headquarters.

Lloyd decided that, although the Japanese had commanding positions covering them, he would have to attack across the bridges. There were only two other crossing places he could use, one to the right of the first bridge, the other well to the left where Sanderson had already crossed. Even if he did use the ford on the right his attacking forces would have to face the bottleneck of the second bridge; if he used the left-hand ford he felt that he might only be sending men in Sanderson's footsteps to no additional purpose. He therefore ordered Stevenson's battalion to secure the bridges themselves by 6 o'clock next morning so that Cullen could cross them and be free to concentrate on attacking the defences on the far side. If Stevenson could not force the bridgehead Cullen would still attack.

Neither of the battalion commanders liked the plan very much. Both were experienced infantry officers: Stevenson, 34 years old, a confident leader and smooth tactician; Cullen, four months younger than Stevenson, stocky, quick-witted, logical and aggressive. But it was difficult to frame an alternative, particularly as Lloyd was well aware of the need for haste.

This need was resulting in a pressure that was becoming increasingly irksome to Allen. On 21st October General Blamey had signalled bleakly:

> During last five days you have made practically no advance against a weaker enemy. Bulk of your forces have been defensively located in rear although enemy has shown no capacity to advance. Your attacks for most part appear to have been conducted by single battalion or even companies on narrow front. Enemy lack of enterprise makes clear he has not repeat not sufficient strength to attack in force. You should consider acting with greater boldness and employ wide encircling movement to destroy enemy in view of fact that complete infantry brigade in reserve is available to act against hostile counter-offensive.
>
> You must realise time is now of great importance. 128 US already has elements at Pongani. Capture Kokoda aerodrome and onward move to cooperate with 128 before Buna is vital portion of plan.

On the same day an even more galling signal arrived:

> The following message has been received from General MacArthur. Quote. Operations reports show that progress on the trail is NOT repeat NOT satisfactory. The tactical handling of our troops in my opinion is faulty. With forces superior to the enemy we are bringing to bear in actual combat only a small fraction of available strength enabling the enemy at the point of actual combat to oppose us with apparently comparable forces. Every extra day of delay complicates the problem and will probably result ultimately in greater casualties than a decisive stroke made in full force. Our supply situation and the condition of the troops certainly compares favourably with those of the enemy and weather conditions are neutral. It is essential to the entire New Guinea operation that the Kokoda airfield be secured promptly. Unquote.

Next day Allen replied:

> I was singularly hurt to receive General MacArthur's signal of 21st Oct since I feel that the difficulties of operations in this country are still not fully realised. This country does not lend itself to quick or wide encircling movements. In addition owing to shortage of carriers I have been confined to one line of advance. As is

already known to Commander New Guinea Force my available carriers forward of Myola are far below requirements. There is one line of advance which I would certainly have used had I the necessary carriers and that was the Alola-Seregina-Kagi. However, under the circumstances it was quite out of the question. I have complete confidence in my brigade commanders and troops and feel that they could not have done better. It was never my wish to site a brigade defensively in rear but the supply situation owing carrier shortage has enforced it. I fully appreciate the major plan and therefore that time is most essential. All my force are doing their level best to push on. I am confident that with the capture of the high ground at Eora Creek our entry into Kokoda and beyond will not long be delayed provided Alola is utilised as a dropping place. It is pointed out however that the track between Alola and Myola is the roughest and most precipitous throughout the complete route.

As cold and biting as this background which was developing on the highest military plane was the continuous rain which swept through the darkness above Eora Creek until 2.30 a.m. on the morning of the 23rd. Then a pale moon rose. Stevenson had sent Captain Gall,[6] now commanding Brown's company, to secure the bridgehead earlier in the night and Cullen took Captain Cox,[7] his adjutant, and cautiously reconnoitred over the first bridge. They drew no fire. Cullen, quick to see the advantage of the situation, decided to try to pass his attacking company, Captain Barclay's,[8] over the bridges in the moonlight so that they would be in position to assault the main Japanese defences across the creek in the period immediately before and after the dawn. He hoped that the attack would coincide with one by Captain Sanderson from the left since Sanderson's company had apparently not had time to get into position for an assault on the previous day. But he could not be sure that this would happen as his wireless sets were not working and he had no telephone cable. Thus Sanderson was completely out of touch as also was Simpson, struggling towards Alola.

On their reconnaissance Cullen and Cox had seen nothing of Gall's company and had to accept the fact that the bridgehead had not been secured. It transpired later that Gall had tried an outflanking approach from the left with two platoons, in preference to a direct approach over the bridges, and had sent his third platoon to try a crossing on the right of the bridges. But the Japanese had been too alert for him so that he had been forced to swing wider across the creek up to the high ridges on the extreme left. Of the right flank platoon one section had succeeded in crossing and, under intense fire, was left clinging precariously below the Japanese positions to the right of the second bridge. Private Richardson[9] of this section volunteered to carry back to Stevenson news of what had happened but was shot down before he had moved five yards towards the bridge.

---

[6] Capt J. M. Gall, MC, NX12174; 2/3 Bn. Station overseer; of Moree, NSW; b. Inverell, NSW, 16 Mar 1915.
[7] Brig G. S. Cox, DSO, MC, ED, NX8576. 2/1, 2/7 Bns; CO 2/4 Bn 1945. MLA (NSW) 1957- . Estate agent; of Sydney; b. Sydney, 4 Dec 1914.
[8] Capt P. Barclay, NX4142; 2/1 Bn. Station manager; of Chatswood, NSW; b. Wellington, NZ, 29 Apr 1914. Killed in action 23 Oct 1942.
[9] Pte F. L. Richardson, NX5054; 2/3 Bn. Railway shunter; of Glen Innes, NSW; b. Gunnedah, NSW, 4 Apr 1913. Killed in action 22 Oct 1942.

With Gall's company thus scattered Cullen pushed ahead his preparations for Barclay's attack. While Cox remained forward at the first bridge learning more of the land the Intelligence officer was marking the track down to the first bridge with pieces of paper struck through with upright sticks. Only through some such expedient could Barclay's men, heavily laden with weapons and ammunition, hope to make a reasonably silent way in the night down a narrow, steep and zigzag track which was alternately a clinging morass on the more level stretches and a treacherous slippery-dip on the slopes.

At 4 a.m. Barclay started downwards towards the creek. Apparently not expecting such an audacious manoeuvre the Japanese had relaxed their vigilance for Cox was able to guide the company across the first bridge safely. But only half were over the second bridge when the defenders woke to their presence. Now, however, the moon was down and it was dark. Sergeant Armstrong,[1] commander of the third platoon, waited until the two leading platoons were clear of the bridge on the other side and then hurried his men safely across through the bullets which were cracking down from the heights. Barclay was fortunate to lose only two men wounded from his whole company in the crossing. But he was not so fortunate on the other side where numerous paths the Japanese had made in moving about the area confused his men. He had planned to move with the track as his axis, one platoon holding to it, the other two platoons to the right and left respectively. But the leading platoon, Lieutenant McCloy's,[2] swung too far to the left and Barclay followed with part of his company headquarters. Lieutenant Pollitt's[3] platoon, trying to keep to the right of the track, drifted too far in that direction in the darkness, and Sergeant Armstrong, in the rear, made the same mistake as McCloy and yawed too widely to the left.

On the right Pollitt's men broke through a forward Japanese position and killed a number of the defenders. They continued then along the bank of the creek until the breaking dawn showed them moving into a dead-end defile. On their right the water foamed. On their left almost sheer rocks rose. They could do no more than cling to the positions they had won. This they did with the Japanese raining fire down on them and steadily wearing down their strength. And the fact that any continued to survive at all was probably due in large measure to the bravery of Lance-Corporal Hunt[4] who climbed the slope and stalked several Japanese like a solitary hunter after deer and killed two of them.

Meanwhile McCloy on the left had similarly smashed through Japanese opposition in his initial movement, forcing his way some distance westward up a spur which ran to the creek junction from that direction. But

---

[1] Lt R. J. H. Armstrong, NX5429; 2/1 Bn. Shop assistant; of Croydon, NSW; b. Grenfell, NSW, 26 Oct 1915.
[2] Capt J. B. McCloy, MC, NX2642; 2/1 Bn. Clerk; of Edgecliff, NSW; b. Sydney, 29 Feb 1916.
[3] Capt D. W. Pollitt, NX57454; 2/1 Bn. Bank officer; of Mosman, NSW; b. Dubbo, NSW, 28 Nov 1916.
[4] L-Cpl J. L. Hunt, NX10751; 2/1 Bn. Labourer; of Bathurst, NSW; b. Bathurst, 3 Oct 1912. Killed in action 23 Oct 1942.

Barclay was killed there and, when dawn showed Armstrong's platoon also on the lower slopes of the spur, McCloy assumed command of both platoons and prepared to attack northwards maintaining the direction which the track followed.

The ground was fairly open to the north, however, for some little distance—the floor of a basin which was enclosed on the east by the waters of the creek and, down the creek a little, by the craggy heights below which Pollitt's men were fighting for their lives; shut in on the north by a spur which swept southwards to back the cliffs which held Pollitt; pressed on the west by the semi-circular sweep of the rough ground rising upward from the spur McCloy was holding in the area of the creek and the track, and linking the two spurs. It was as though a space somewhat less densely bush-covered than most of the valley, on the western bank of the creek, a few hundred yards long by two to three hundred wide, were enclosed by a horseshoe of high ground both ends of which rested on the northward running creek. Pollitt was under the northern tip of the horseshoe, McCloy was preparing to take the shortest route across the open end of the horseshoe from the southern tip. But the Japanese had positions sited on the floor of the basin, running up to the high ground on the west, and, beyond those, their main line on the heights which hemmed the basin on the north. McCloy found that he could not cross.

Then the morning air carried down from the north-west the sounds of heavy firing. McCloy knew that Captain Sanderson's men, whose attack had been delayed from the previous night, were trying to fight their way through to the crossing. But the high ground and thick bush of the horseshoe's curve cut the newcomers off from sight and McCloy's two platoons could do nothing to help. Soon, however, they saw two other platoons moving down the ridge towards them and Lieutenants Blakiston[5] and Wyburn[6] with their men joined them. There was no sign though of Sanderson and the rest. This, as it was learnt a little later, was their story.

After Sanderson had crossed the creek on the 22nd he had led his men very wide to the left of the main crossing to come in behind the Japanese positions sited for its protection. But rough country hampered the Australians, they had difficulty in negotiating a waterfall and matted vines and bush dragged at them. So it was that they were not in position to attack until the early morning of the 23rd. By that time they were north-west of the crossing, on the right of the main Japanese positions which, from the high ground, faced southward across the basin towards the two bridges; and they were on the far side of the horseshoe from McCloy and his platoons. With the dawn they were moving down the heights towards the basin, a descent so steep that they had almost to swing down from tree to tree. Blakiston and Wyburn were on the right of the descent,

---

[5] Capt C. S. Blakiston, NX45564; 2/1 Bn. Insurance inspector; of Newcastle, NSW; b. Geelong, Vic, 25 Jun 1912.
[6] Lt R. J. Wyburn, NX40754; 2/1 Bn. Bank clerk; of Quirindi, NSW; b. Quirindi, 14 Dec 1917.

with Lieutenant Johnston's[7] platoon, with whom Sanderson himself was moving, on the left. The rough country separated Blakiston's and Wyburn's men from the rest and they drifted farther and farther to the right until they finished on the spur where McCloy was waiting. Sanderson and Johnston, meanwhile, had fought through opposition to reach the basin across which the forward Japanese positions were strung out towards the creek on the east. They engaged these but the Japanese held them off. As the fight went on more Japanese crept round the high ground above and behind the Australians until they were in such a commanding position that they could begin methodically to wipe them out with machine-gun fire. Sanderson, Johnston, and nine of their men were killed before the others of the platoon, most of whom were wounded, broke off the encounter and managed to make their way back into the rough country of the ridges. When Sanderson's body was found later it was lying ringed by over 300 spent shells from the German Mauser which he had brought back with him from the Middle East.

While his two attacking companies had been thus beset Cullen had been trying to reach them with the two platoons which Captain Catterns had available. The Japanese commanded the track to the bridges, however, in the daylight and so whipped it with fire that Catterns could not use it. He swung wide to the right and it was not until about 11.20 a.m. that he had crossed the creek into the area between the two bridges, laying wire as he went. He then managed to cross the second bridge and, just beyond it, found a dead man, a wounded man and two men unhurt of the 2/3rd Battalion section which Captain Gall had had to leave there the previous night. As Catterns pushed on then into the basin, from the floor of which the Japanese, cut about by Sanderson, McCloy and the rest, had now withdrawn, Lieutenant Pollitt joined him with the survivors of his platoon who had been caught by daylight in the defile on the right of the track. Pollitt himself had been hit badly and his men carried their other wounded with them.

About 12.45 p.m. word came back to Catterns from his forward platoon, Lieutenant Body's[8]: "The leading scout's been bowled." Body pressed doggedly on where the track rose steeply to cross the main ridge but soon had lost eight or nine men wounded. Catterns tried to outflank but could not do so. He could go no farther in the face of light and medium machine-guns, a mountain gun and mortars, firing from heights behind the northern side of the horseshoe. He spread his men across the track and well to the left of it where they began to dig in immediately below the defences.

Cullen then asked Lloyd for help. He said that a strong attack must be made on the Japanese right flank positions if his enemies were to be moved. Pending the arrival of this aid, he sent Lieutenant Leaney,[9] who

---
[7] Lt K. Johnston, NX7579; 2/1 Bn. Warehouse assistant; of Concord, NSW; b. Carlton, NSW, 29 Sep 1915. Killed in action 23 Oct 1942.
[8] Lt E. M. Body, NX3459. 2/1 Fd Regt, 2/1 Bn. Grazier; of Trangie, NSW; b. Sydney, 15 Sep 1915.
[9] Lt G. L. Leaney, MC, NX34302; 2/1 Bn. Farmer; of Nowra, NSW; b. Milton, NSW, 4 Dec 1918. Killed in action 20 Nov 1942.

joined him about 4 p.m. with the pioneer platoon, round Catterns' left to attack the Japanese right. Leaney's men did this although they numbered only eighteen. As Corporal Stewart's[1] section drove forward a medium machine-gun blocked them. One man fell dead, another wounded, to its fire. Stewart hurled a grenade into the position and plunged forward after the burst, pouring sub-machine-gun fire into the defenders, his men following him. He himself was wounded, but the section wiped out the gun crew, put the gun out of action, and held the ground for ten minutes afterwards in the teeth of a furious fire which killed another of them and wounded yet another, leaving only two men unharmed in the little band. They withdrew then, the wounded Stewart helping another wounded man as he went. Before Leaney finally quitted the scene with those who were left of his men, he himself returned alone into the position the Japanese now held again to bring out another wounded man.

By this time it was almost dark. It had taken Leaney a long time in the rough country to mount and deliver his attack. This determined the Australians to delay until next day a further attack they were planning with Captain Lysaght's[2] company of the 2/3rd Battalion which had arrived about 5.15 p.m.

While the 2/1st had been fighting hard during this busy 23rd October, the 2/3rd, waiting to move in their rear, had been having a comparatively uneventful but anxious day. Stevenson was out of touch with two of his companies until the early afternoon; one which he had sent wide on the right of his positions, and Captain Gall's. By nightfall, however, the right-flank company was on its way in without having come against any Japanese and it was known that Gall had linked with the remnants of Sanderson's and Barclay's companies. Meanwhile Lysaght had moved off at 4 p.m. to assist Lieut-Colonel Cullen under whose command he was temporarily placed.

The night of the 23rd-24th, therefore, saw something like stalemate threatening. Edgar was still holding his 2/2nd Battalion behind the high ground above Eora Creek village, waiting to advance when opportunity offered. He had lost men during the day from mortar fire. Stevenson, except for Lysaght's company and Gall's, was still holding forward to the right of Edgar and, like Edgar, had been enduring Japanese fire while he waited. Across the creek, and on the northern slopes of the basin, the 2/1st were in difficulties, tattered, and holding a position from which it seemed unlikely they could move forward and which was itself almost untenable. Their most forward troops, under Catterns, were almost under the very noses of the Japanese, not more than 30 yards from them and holed in like animals on a precipitous slope. From Barclay's and Sanderson's companies alone they had lost 3 officers and 17 men killed, and one officer and 25 men wounded. Even though they were strengthened during the night by the arrival of most of the balance of Headquarters

---

[1] Cpl J. A. Stewart, NX47465; 2/1 Bn. Farmer; of Nimbin, NSW; b. Nimbin, 17 Jun 1919.
[2] Maj N. H. L. Lysaght, NX101. 2/3 Bn; training and Staff appts. Assistant manager; of Wollongong, NSW; b. London, 5 Nov 1911.

Company (except for the mortars and medium machine-guns which remained on the ridge above the village to give fire support from that area), and had Captain Lysaght's company under command, they were still weak for any purposes and particularly weak for the circumstances in which they found themselves.

The night brought no rest. It was broken by intermittent firing and grenade bursts and covered desperate efforts to get rations and ammunition forward. The bulk of this work fell on those men of Headquarters Company who had been left back beyond the creek. All through the night these toiled forward and back again over a track that was narrow, slippery and steep, and swept by Japanese fire; on the return journeys they carried out the wounded.

That General Allen was hoping for a quicker result than now seemed likely was shown by the orders he had issued that day. He ordered Brigadier Eather to send the 2/31st Battalion on the way to Templeton's Crossing with instructions to move on to Eora Creek on the 24th and come under Lloyd's command. The 2/25th and 2/33rd were to be ready to go forward again next day. Allen's intention was to use both his brigades for the capture of Kokoda. When the 16th Brigade had cleared Eora Creek it would move forward on the right of that stream with the 25th Brigade moving on the left. The task of the 16th would be to secure and operate a supply dropping ground at Alola, to seize the commanding features at Oivi and then, after mopping up between that area and Kokoda, junction with the 25th Brigade. It would push on then to establish bridgeheads over the Kumusi River at Wairopi and Asisi. The 25th Brigade would capture and hold Kokoda, prepare the airfield and protect and administer the supply dropping area.

But the morning of the 24th brought no renewed hope of a speedy execution of Allen's plans. It confirmed Cullen's belief that his own men would be doing well if they merely maintained their positions. Some were being hit by the intermittent Japanese mortar fire which was coming from about 150 feet above their positions and 300 yards distant. The Japanese had only to drop their fire among the treetops below, which they knew sheltered the Australians. The bombs usually exploded in the foliage and then scattered like shrapnel. Although a large percentage were duds, the sound of a bomb plopping among the high branches and slithering through the leaves towards the slit trenches was a sickening one to the men crouched below.

Lieutenant Frew[3] provided an example of the difficulty of coming to grips with the enemy in that country. He sallied out with a patrol at dawn. As he climbed a ridge a rifleman was firing at him from above. So steep was the ridge that the first bullet, after just missing Frew's head, went through his foot. The second hit him in the other foot. Frew then shot his adversary.

Colonel Cullen decided that only an attack by at least two companies

---

[3] Capt J. McI. Frew, NX11545. 2/1 Bn; S-Capt SEAC 1945. Advertising; of Petersham, NSW; b. Balmain, NSW, 1 Aug 1916.

round the left flank offered any chance of success. He reported so to Brigadier Lloyd. About 10 a.m. he received word from Lloyd that Lysaght's and another company of the 2/3rd would be sent on this mission. Later in the morning Stevenson passed through Cullen's rear area with his own headquarters and Captain Fulton's[4] company and then, with Lysaght leading, moved round to the left to try to secure the high ground there. He was not long in provoking opposition and by 2.30 p.m. machine-gun and rifle fire was hampering his men. Lysaght's men pushed on, however, cleared the immediate vicinity, and captured two light machine-guns in doing so. About the same time Fulton's men brushed off a patrol and killed three of its members. Then Gall, who had linked his company again with the battalion, was pushed widest to the left. But the whole of the new movement having necessarily been slow and uneasy night came again without a decision.

For the men of the 2/1st Battalion the 25th was another day of holding on. It started badly. Back on the ridge above the village the medium machine-gun platoon had dug in their Vickers gun in the cold, wet darkness of the previous night with the intention of harassing the Japanese from that area. With the dawn, however, a Japanese field gun opened from the heights opposite and scored a direct hit on the Vickers, blowing the gun out of its pit and causing casualties among the crew—an additional lesson to the Australians of the completeness of the Japanese observation of even their rearward positions. Later in the morning two friendly aircraft tried to strafe the Japanese positions but their fire fell too far back to affect the immediate issue.

From their forward positions Catterns' men were sniping and grenading to the full extent of their limited supplies of ammunition. On the battalion's left Leaney was active. With his few men he drove at a forward Japanese post, killed three of the defenders and wounded others, and consolidated again in advance of his original positions.

During the afternoon a party which had been searching for a mortar observation post to the east of the creek located a suitable site. Line was laid and other preparations made to bring the mortar into action from the village ridge next day. Meanwhile, however, Japanese mortar fire continued to fall on the Australians in both the forward and rearward positions.

In the 2/3rd's area skirmishes and fire from both sides marked the day as the main body edged farther to the left and felt round the Japanese right flank, continuing the grim game which Gall's men had begun there after they had been forced wide on that side on the morning of the 23rd. A member of that company said later:

> The Japanese had the good sense to establish this forest fort on the only water to be found on the ridge. Consequently, for the four [sic] days before support arrived, the men of the company had to catch rain water in their gas capes and drink water from the roots of the "water tree". Their only food was dehydrated emergency ration, eaten dry and cold. Every time patrols from the company located one of the outlying Japanese machine-gun posts, scouts were killed or wounded.

---

[4] Capt I. C. Fulton, NX82; 2/3 Bn. Mechanical engineer; of Port Kembla, NSW; b. Sydney, 20 Feb 1912.

Then the post would be outflanked and overrun with Brens, Tommy-guns, and grenades, but each night the attacking parties had to withdraw to defensive positions, and, in the darkness, the Japanese would re-establish the posts or put out others. The Japanese snipers were alert and were good shots. When an Australian patrol had been pinned down by fire, it would not be long before a man would fidget, thrusting a hand or arm or leg out of the cover, and would be hit, perhaps from twenty-five yards.

The 2/3rd lost 4 men killed and 12 wounded on the 25th.

The next morning was marked for Cullen by a similar misfortune to that which had marked the 25th. Early in the day the mortar went into action. Though, as was subsequently discovered, the rounds fell with effect in the main enemy positions, the success was costly, for a Japanese mortar or gun replied almost at once and scored a direct hit on its target. Sergeant Madigan[5] then carried his wounded officer to the medical aid post under heavy fire, quickly secured another weapon, gathered replacements for others of the crew who had been badly hit, and continued the fight.

On this same morning of the 26th the two worn-out companies which Barclay and Sanderson had commanded in the original attack on the 23rd were once more with the battalion, and with them Captain Simpson's company which had set out for Alola on the 22nd. Simpson said that he had reached a position just above Alola and, with grenades and sub-machine-guns, had surprised Japanese there in a bivouac area. Although he had lost two men in the fighting which followed he knew that his company had killed at least six Japanese out of a larger number of casualties. A counter-attack from the flank and shortage of rations had forced his withdrawal. Cullen now sent him round to the extreme left of the positions beyond Leaney's pioneers (near whom Sergeant Miller[6] with a 2-inch mortar carried on a most effective little private war with the Japanese during the afternoon). With Simpson, went the company that had been Captain Barclay's, now commanded by Lieutenant Prior[7] and later in the day taken over by Captain Burrell.[8]

By that time, in his efforts to advance, Stevenson had moved the 2/3rd farther to the left and out of contact with the 2/1st. He was still struggling to round the flank and break into the main Japanese positions. But an attack by Lysaght thrust directly into medium machine-gun fire and could achieve no effect. Gall and Fulton swung round Lysaght later in the afternoon but made no marked gain. Sergeant Copeman[9] thrust into the Japanese positions with a patrol and cut a gap in their telephone line. Then, irritated by the Australian efforts, the defenders counter-attacked

---

[5] Sgt E. S. Madigan, NX1315. 2/2, 2/1 Bns. Clerk; of Newcastle, NSW; b. Newcastle, 2 Jul 1917.

[6] WO1 S. G. Miller, DCM, NX9615; 2/1 Bn. Grocer; of Darlinghurst, NSW; b. Stanley, Tas, 22 Jan 1906.

[7] Capt C. J. Prior, NX34872; 2/1 Bn. Bank officer; of Mosman, NSW; b. Eastwood, NSW, 12 Jun 1919.

[8] Lt-Col J. C. Burrell, NX2629; 2/1 Bn. Storeman-packer; of Strathfield, NSW; b. West Maitland, NSW, 3 Oct 1918.

[9] Maj J. Copeman, MC, MM, NX4545; 2/3 Bn. Dairy farmer; of Picton NSW; b. Ballina, NSW, 8 Dec 1919.

against Lysaght and Gall at last light. Although the attack achieved some little local success against one of Lysaght's platoons it lost its momentum and a quiet night began in the 2/3rd's area.

But, although the forward commanders might consider that their efforts to resolve their difficulties had been intense, neither General MacArthur in Australia, nor General Blamey in Port Moresby, shared their views. That day Blamey had signalled Allen referring to their previous interchange of messages:

> Your 01169 of 22 Oct does NOT confute any part of General MacArthur's criticism in his message sent to you on 21st. Since then progress has been negligible against an enemy much fewer in number. Although delay has continued over several days attacks continue to [be made] with small forces. Your difficulties are very great but enemy has similar. In view of your superior strength energy and force on the part of all commanders should overcome the enemy speedily. In spite of your superior strength enemy appears able to delay advance at will. Essential that forward commanders should control situation and NOT allow situation control them. Delay in seizing Kokoda may cost us unique opportunity of driving enemy out of New Guinea.

General Allen replied:

> One. Every effort is being made to overcome opposition as quickly as possible. Present delay has [caused] and is causing me considerable concern in view of its probable effect upon your general plan. Jap however is most tenacious and fighting extremely well. His positions are excellent well dug in and difficult to detect. I feel it will be necessary to dig him out of present positions since his actions to date indicate that a threat to his rear will not necessarily force him to retire. I have already arranged for 2/31 Bn to assist 16 Bde 27 Oct but it must be realised it would take 36 hours to get into position. Owing to precipitous slopes movement in this particular area is extremely difficult and a mile may take up to a day to traverse. I had hoped that 16 Bde would have been able to clear enemy position today. Two. As I feel that a wrong impression may have been created by our sitreps I must stress that throughout the advance a brigade has always been employed against the enemy but up to the present this has been the maximum owing supply situation. Three. Jap tactical position at present is extremely strong and together with the terrain is the most formidable up to date. No accurate estimate can be given of Jap strength except that commander 2/3 Bn reports that at least one battalion opposes him alone. Four. You may rest assured that I and my brigade commanders are doing everything possible to speed the advance.

Even had he known of this exchange Lieut-Colonel Cullen's mounting impatience with the delay could scarcely have been intensified. On the 27th he decided to move his own headquarters into the left flank area where Leaney, Burrell and Simpson were, with the intention of organising really heavy pressure there. But scarcely had his headquarters reached their new site than word came from Catterns that the Japanese had withdrawn on his front. Having ordered Burrell and Simpson to push hard on the left Cullen then quickly returned to the vicinity of the track intending to follow Catterns' advance. But it soon became clear that his opponents had merely pulled back some 500 yards to make their positions even more compact. Catterns was again held, and although Burrell and Simpson beat at the Japanese right flank, so that they killed and wounded numbers of the defenders, they made no substantial advance and lost men.

Thus the situation was growing hourly more wearisome. When a company from the 2/2nd took over their duties the details whom Cullen had left on the eastern bank of the creek came into the 2/1st area on the 27th, so that, for the first time at Eora Creek, almost the whole battalion was then concentrated. This was the first time, too, since the fighting on the 23rd that Captain Sanderson's old company was able to take the field again as a formed sub-unit. Now Lieutenant Wiseman[1] was in command.

As night came again Colonel Cullen knew that a kind of torpor was clogging the minds and bodies of his men. The will to fight and win, the intangible "morale" was still high, but worn bodies could no longer raise speed in execution of the plans which came only painfully and slowly to tired minds. Catterns' men, still in the most advanced positions, for they could not be relieved, were suffering most as they clung like leeches to the rough slope. They were always wet from the cold, driving rain and, added to the shortness of their rations, was the virtual impossibility of cooking food for themselves or making even a drink of hot tea. They were only 40 yards from their enemies and, if they ventured to light fires, the smoke drifted above the trees and became target indicators for the Japanese mortarmen. By day they could not move out of the two-man pits in which they crouched, and only at night could they go about their essential tasks of getting up food and ammunition; and darkness merely minimised and did not do away with the risks of movement in their bullet-swept areas. Their numbers were being reduced by the constant fire which swept their positions and the bursting of the grenades which their enemies rolled down on them from the heights. None the less they clung to their positions and resolutely beat back the frequent patrols which the Japanese sent to harass them.

Also, for the 2/1st, misfortunes were added to the normal hazards of battle. In the early hours of the 26th, when rain had lashed down in sheets and turned the already turbulent waters of the creek into a raging torrent, the bridge had carried away. But its broken timbers caught against some rocks a little farther downstream so that determined men could cross by bracing themselves against the wreckage. All supplies then had to come forward, all the dead weight of the helpless wounded then had to be carried back, through the bitterly cold mountain waters foaming down the cold and windswept darkness and whipped by plunging fire. Here it was that a brave priest, Chaplain Cunningham,[2] who joined the 2/1st only on the 27th, distinguished himself, helping to bear the wounded through the dangerous waters, comforting the dying and burying the dead regardless of creed.

While a sub-section of the 2/6th Field Company, helped by infantrymen, was still trying to repair the damage to the bridge, in the dusk of the

---

[1] Lt H. C. Wiseman, NX12458; 2/1 Bn. Pharmacist; of Wollongong, NSW; b. Cooma, NSW, 9 Oct 1911. Killed in action 20 Nov 1942.
[2] Rev C. W. J. Cunningham, MBE, WX17091. Padre to 2/1, 2/16 Bns; Senior Chaplain 7 Div 1944-45. Catholic priest; of Bunbury, WA; b. Smith's Mill, WA, 23 Oct 1904.

27th, another misfortune came. From its positions behind the village ridge the 3-inch mortar went into action. It quickly got thirteen rounds away but the fourteenth, the second of a supply that had been dropped from the air, exploded in the barrel and killed three of the crew.

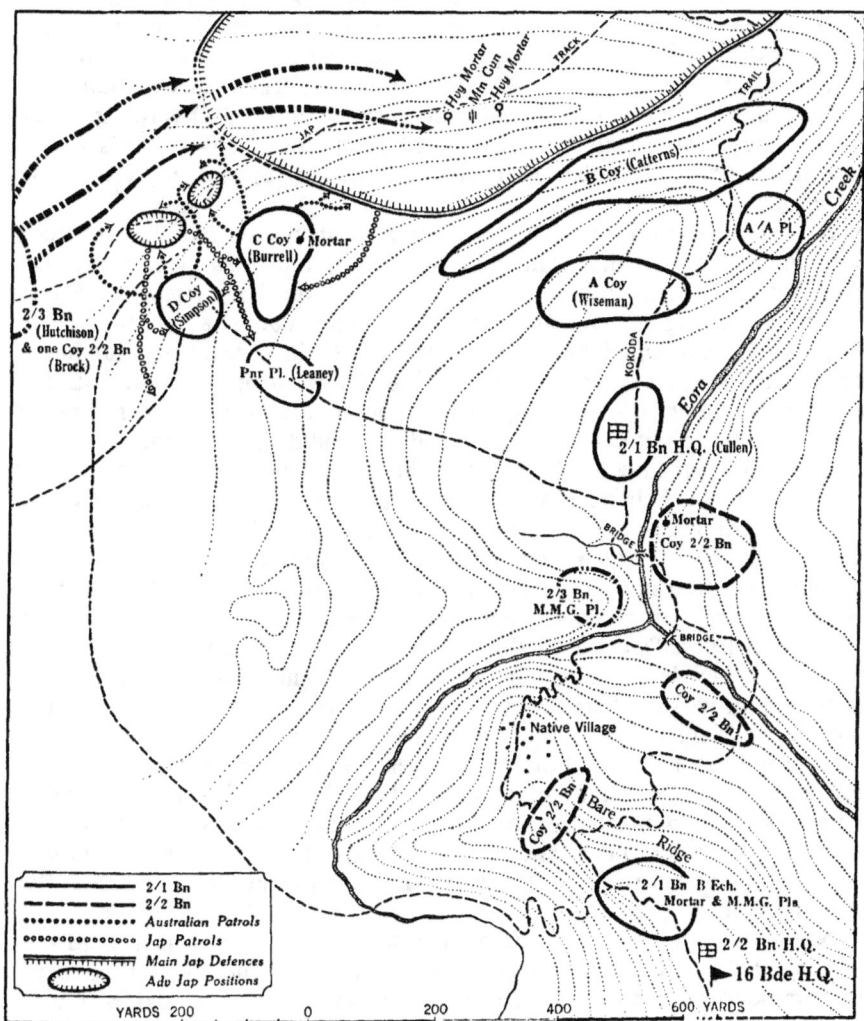

Eora Creek, 27th-28th October

Meanwhile the 2/3rd Battalion, still working round the high ground on the extreme left, were also chafing against the stubborn circumstances that were holding them. Early in the morning of the 27th Colonel Stevenson, suffering pain from his wounded ear, handed over his command to Major Hutchison. The latter, a short, thick-set young man who had been with the battalion from its inception, whose deliberate manner suggested the possession of a brain which, having decided upon a plan of action, would follow it through to the bitter end with bulldog fixity of purpose, decided then that he would resolve the situation. He determined that his men should comb the spur, methodically rooting out and killing any who barred the way into the main Japanese positions from the right of those positions. With Captain Brock's[3] company of the 2/2nd under his command, in addition to his own battalion, he formed three columns and ordered them to move forward at a distance of about 300 yards from each other. They would halt after they had gone about 1,000 yards and get in touch with one another so as to maintain an unbroken front in their advance.

At 8.50 a.m. on the 27th the movement began. At 11.30 Brock's column, moving on the right, met the enemy and lost men in the sharp give and take which followed. Then a patrol from Lieutenant McGuinn's[4] company, moving as the central column, clashed against a determined party and lost 1 man killed and 4 wounded. McGuinn, realising that he was up against a stronger position than he had at first appreciated, asked for assistance. Hutchison told Captain Fulton to attack in cooperation with McGuinn; but night came before the attack could go forward.

From first light on the 28th action began to boil along the whole Australian front. In their positions spreading from the track leftwards Catterns' dazed and hungry men could do no more than cling where they were. Grenades, bowled down from above, accounted for five more of them during the afternoon. Farther to the left Japanese were thrusting into Burrell's area with patrols which cut the company's telephone wires and stimulated Burrell's men to sharp reaction which flung the invaders out again. Farther left again Simpson's pressure had forced the Japanese back but provoked them to counter-attack which, although it cost them men, cost Simpson casualties also. As opposing patrols moved in and around both Burrell's and Simpson's areas, and in the open space between the two, a grim game of blind man's buff developed. The searchers on either side could normally not see more than some 10 yards ahead of them in the thick bush and neither of the two Australian companies concerned was sure of the other's position. So a sort of murderous confusion set in.

Meanwhile the 2/3rd made deliberate preparations, which were completed by the middle of the afternoon. Captain Fulton had been placed in command of a combined force consisting of his own and McGuinn's companies. At 5 p.m., after a barrage of rifle grenades, McGuinn struck downhill from the left and Fulton's own company, soon afterwards, struck from the right so that the Japanese right-flank positions were caught between the two. Despite a hail of defending fire from strong positions the Australians' ferocity increased.

---

[3] Capt B. Brock, NX239; 2/2nd Bn. Schoolteacher; of Woonona, NSW; b. Darwin, 31 Mar 1907.
[4] Lt-Col L. McGuinn, MC, NX5413; 2/3 Bn. Articled law clerk; of Dubbo, NSW; b. Dubbo, 1 Apr 1911.

We sailed into them firing from the hip (said Lieutenant MacDougal afterwards). . . . The forward scouts were knocked out, but the men went on steadily, advancing from tree to tree until we were right through their outlying posts and into the central position. Suddenly the Japanese began to run out. They dropped their weapons and stumbled through the thick bush down the slope, squealing like frightened animals. In a minute or two the survivors had disappeared into the bush. We buried well over 50 Japs next morning, though our own casualties were fairly light and there must have been other Japanese dead in the bush that we didn't find. Some of the dead Japanese were wearing Australian wrist watches. Before this Eora Creek fight the men had been saying that the Japanese wouldn't run. Eora Creek proved that he would.

During the action Corporal Pett,[5] "five feet of dynamite",[6] as a diarist described him, distinguished himself by knocking out four machine-gun posts single-handed.

Hutchison's men had leisure then to examine the positions which had held them up for so long. These were based on a sort of central keep about 300 yards across. Radiating from this central position in four or five directions were outlying machine-gun posts. Although the Japanese shrewdness in locating themselves on the only water to be found on the ridge had increased considerably the physical discomfort of the Australians during the preceding days, it had not represented all profit for the defence. For the first time in their struggle against the 16th Brigade the Japanese had not occupied the highest ground in the area and this had finally allowed Hutchison to get above them, an important factor in his final success. Obviously they had been in this position for a considerable time and, in a storehouse which it contained, the Australians found equipment of all kinds including machine-guns, mortars, a wireless set and informative papers. A physical check on the morning after the battle revealed 69 dead bodies and there were certainly others which remained unfound and unaccounted. The day cost the 2/3rd Battalion 11 men killed and 31 wounded.

The turning of the Japanese right flank by the 2/3rd Battalion meant the end of the Japanese resistance at Eora Creek. On the morning of the 29th patrols of the 2/1st Battalion found the defences down and they walked unopposed into the positions before which they had spent themselves so bitterly for almost a week. The battalion then took up the pursuit along the track with the 2/3rd moving on their left and the 2/2nd in rear. There would be no more fighting for either the 16th or 25th Brigades during the last three days of October, but that which they had already done was only a prelude to days of blood and battles which lay ahead.

The Japanese, although beaten in the mountains, were making for their base on the north coast and they could be expected to fight stubbornly there. By the time General Horii reached Ioribaiwa he was at the end of his resources and his thin supply line across the range could no

---

[5] Cpl L. G. Pett, MM, NX5337; 2/3 Bn. Carter; of Auburn, NSW; b. Condobolin, NSW, 27 Jan 1914. Died of wounds 6 Nov 1942.
[6] Capt T. B. Silk, "Kokoda Diary", in *Chocolate & Green*, Jul 1945.

longer support him, partly because the mountains were too rugged, partly because of the attacks by American and Australian aircraft, which did their most effective work at the Wairopi crossing where they destroyed the bridge as fast as the Japanese rebuilt it. At Ioribaiwa the Japanese commander received the last of a series of changing orders each of which had pared down his objective. When he developed his main attack before Isurava on 26th August he was told to press on to Port Moresby. Difficulties at Guadalcanal and disaster at Milne Bay, however, caused Imperial General Headquarters, at the end of August, to order General Hyakutake to instruct Horii to assume defensive positions as soon as he had crossed the main Owen Stanley Range and, in accordance with these orders, Horii selected Ioribaiwa as the area in which to stand. While he was approaching this point, however, the *Kawaguchi Force* was virtually destroyed on Guadalcanal. The Japanese High Command then felt that it should concentrate all its energies in the Pacific on retaking Guadalcanal particularly as the extent of the reverse at Milne Bay was then clear. In New Guinea, therefore, Horii's men were to fall back to the more easily defended Buna-Gona beach-head area. After the Guadalcanal situation was retrieved the main Japanese effort would be directed against New Guinea and, in concert with a fresh move to seize Milne Bay and another coastwise approach to Port Moresby, Horii would once more cross the mountains.

To implement this plan Horii allotted the rearguard role to Colonel Kusunose's *144th Regiment,* which prepared to hold at Ioribaiwa with two battalions and some supporting troops while the rest of the force fell back. The main body of the *41st Regiment* (less elements which were given a role along the track) were to fall right back to the coast to make firm there the positions to which the rest of the beaten troops could retire. In accordance with this plan Colonel Yazawa moved swiftly and was already back at Giruwa when the Australians struck their main blow at Ioribaiwa on 28th September. By that time also (for what reasons it is not certain but probably because the heart had gone out of them) the units of the *144th Regiment* had left their rearguard positions at Ioribaiwa and were intent on keeping as far ahead of the advancing Australians as possible.

Of the retreat across the Owen Stanleys a Japanese war correspondent (Seizo Okada) has written:[7]

> In one of the small thatched huts which we had hastily built on the mountain side [at Ioribaiwa], Sato and I had just finished our usual scanty evening meal of sweet potatoes, when we scented some important change in the situation. We hurried out to see Major-General Horii in his tent that stood on a little uncovered elevation. On a thin straw mat in the tent the elderly commander was sitting solemnly upright on his heels, his face emaciated, his grey hair reflecting the dim light of a candle that stood on the inner lid of a ration can. Lieut-Colonel Tanaka, his staff officer, sat face to face with him also on a mat. Two lonely shadows were cast on the dirty wet canvas. . . . The staff officer was silent, watching the burning wick of the candle as though to avoid the commander's eyes, when a rustling sound was heard in the thicket outside and the signal squad commander came in with

---

[7] Seizo Okada (special correspondent in New Guinea, 1942-43, for *Asahi Shimbun*): "Lost Troops."

another wireless message. It was an order from the Area Army Commander at Rabaul instructing the Horii detachment to withdraw completely from the Owen Stanleys and concentrate on the coast at Buna. This message was immediately followed by a similar order that came directly from the Imperial Headquarters in Tokyo. It was now beyond doubt that the order had been authorised by the Emperor himself. His Majesty's order had to be obeyed. It is true there was a strong body of opinion among the hot-blooded battalion commanders advocating a desperate single-handed thrust into Port Moresby. But Staff-Officer Tanaka remained cool, and reasoned with them saying that it was a suicidal action even if everything went well except the supply of food, which was in a hopeless condition.

The night was far advanced. It had begun to drizzle, softly. The headquarters was in confusion sending out messages to the front positions instructing them to make preparations for immediate withdrawal. . . . The order to retreat had crushed the spirit of the troops which had been kept up through sheer pride. For a time the soldiers remained stupefied among the rocks on the mountain side. Then they began to move, and once in retreat they fled for dear life. None of them had ever thought that a Japanese soldier would turn his back on the enemy. But they were actually beating a retreat! There was no denying that. As soon as they realized the truth, they were seized with an instinctive desire to live. Neither history nor education had any meaning to them now. Discipline was completely forgotten. Each tried for his life to flee faster than his comrades.

Our movement was evidently reported by a scouting plane. On the morning of the fourth day, after the front-line units had begun to move back, the Australians took up the pursuit. Our party, and small independent units, went down without bothering about anything; but the headquarters unit was constantly delayed by the sick and wounded whom they had to pick up on the way. At each key-point there was a platoon of the Yokoyama Engineer Unit, who waited for the last of our men to pass and blew up the cliffs or cut off the log-bridges to delay the Australians in pursuit. But the pursuit grew hotter every day, until the enemy were close upon our heels. At the same time, attacks from the air by American planes became more vigorous. . . . The roar of propellors that seemed to burst our eardrums and pierce our intestines, the ratatat of the machine-guns, the sound of cannon fire that streamed forth from tails of B-17s—these were nightmares threatening us in our miserable retreat. Moreover, the soldiers were short of food necessary to keep themselves from starvation. On our way forward we had gathered a pretty good crop of taroes, but now we could find none at all. Even the fields more than ten kilometres away from the track had been dug up all over almost inch by inch. From time to time we came upon large fields extending over the side of a mountain, but we could not find a single piece of potato in them. As for papayas, the stems themselves had been rooted out and bitten to the pith. Here and there along the path were seen soldiers lying motionless, unable to walk any longer in the excess of hunger and weariness.

One day, towards evening, we came to the ravine where the fierce fighting had taken place. It was in the remotest heart of great masses of mountains about midway across the Owen Stanley Range, and was deeper and larger than any other ravine we had passed. The dark path through the enormous cypresses . . . seemed to lead down to a bottomless pit. A rumbling sound like drumbeats came, it seemed, from somewhere deep underground. We rounded a rock, and saw a furious white serpent of water falling from a height of about a hundred feet and making roaring noises among the cavernous rocks below. The humidity here was very high, mosses hanging in bunches on the trunks of trees. We stepped across the edge of the seething basin, and followed the path leading further down through thick growths of bamboo-grass that glistened like wet green paint. The branches overhead were so closely interwoven that not a ray of sunshine came through. There was neither day nor night in that ravine; it was always pale twilight, and everything looked as wet as though it were deep under water. And in that eternal twilight lay numberless bodies of men scattered here and there. . . .

At Mount Isurava which stood at the northern end of the path across the Owen Stanley Range the narrow path was congested with stretchers carrying the wounded soldiers back to the field hospital on the coast. There were so many of them that they had been delayed here since the wholesale retreat began. Some of them were makeshift stretchers, each made of two wooden poles with a blanket or tent-cloth tied to them with vines and carried by four men. They made slow and laborious progress, constantly held up by steep slopes. The soldiers on them, some lying on their backs, emitted groans of pain at every bump. In some cases, the blood from the wounds was dropping through the canvas or blanket on to the ground. Some looked all but dead, unable even to give out a groan.

Nevertheless, whatever despondency may have been in the hearts of the retreating Japanese, their rearguards fought vigorously at Templeton's Crossing and Eora Creek once they had decided to make a stand. At Eora Creek the third battalion of their regiment joined them. Thus Kusunose mustered there a regiment, which had been much reduced by heavy casualties and sickness and weakened by the mountains and hunger, in strong and carefully selected defensive positions, and measured them against a fresh Australian brigade which had been weakened by the mountains but not yet reduced to any extent by battle.

By the time the Eora Creek fighting came to an end the 16th Brigade had lost between 250 and 300 officers and men killed and wounded.[8] For slightly more than every two wounded one was killed. This unusually high proportion of killed to wounded was the measure of the closeness of the fighting.

These casualties can be interpreted properly only in relation to the type of fighting which produced them. It was fighting in the now familiar pattern of bush warfare in tumbled mountains—by individuals pitted against one another, by small groups meeting and killing in sudden encounters among the silently dripping leaves and tangled quiet of the high rain forests; but with the first loud sounds of a new note being struck as Australians came against Japanese in ideal defensive positions which the latter manned strongly as a result of long preparation, and from which they fought most tenaciously. How effectively had Lloyd's men met the comparatively new challenge of ideally sited mountain defence? Certainly with courage and energy, as witness their frontal attack over the bridges which their enemies were sited to command. But it seems possible now that, in that manoeuvre, there was more courage and energy than skill;

---

[8] It is not possible now to determine the precise casualties suffered. The 16th Brigade War Diary for 28th October states that the total casualties to 1630 hours 28 October were:

	Killed	Wounded
Bde Hq	1 (attached)	2
2/1 Bn	33 (including 3 offrs)	62
2/2 Bn	28 (including 3 offrs)	49
2/3 Bn	10	41
	72	154

Figures from the War Diaries of the 2/1st and 2/2nd Battalions, and the accounts there of the various actions, are as follows:
  2/1st Battalion—Eora Creek: 3 officers and 41 men killed, 3 men missing, 5 officers and 83 men wounded. Total battle casualties for October 47 killed, 92 wounded, 3 missing.
  2/2nd Battalion—battle casualties for October: 3 officers and 31 men killed, 2 officers and 51 men wounded.
  In a post-war examination of casualty returns, Central Army Records Office, Melbourne, estimated that 99 were killed in action or died of wounds and 192 wounded in action in the three battalions during the period 19th to 29th October.

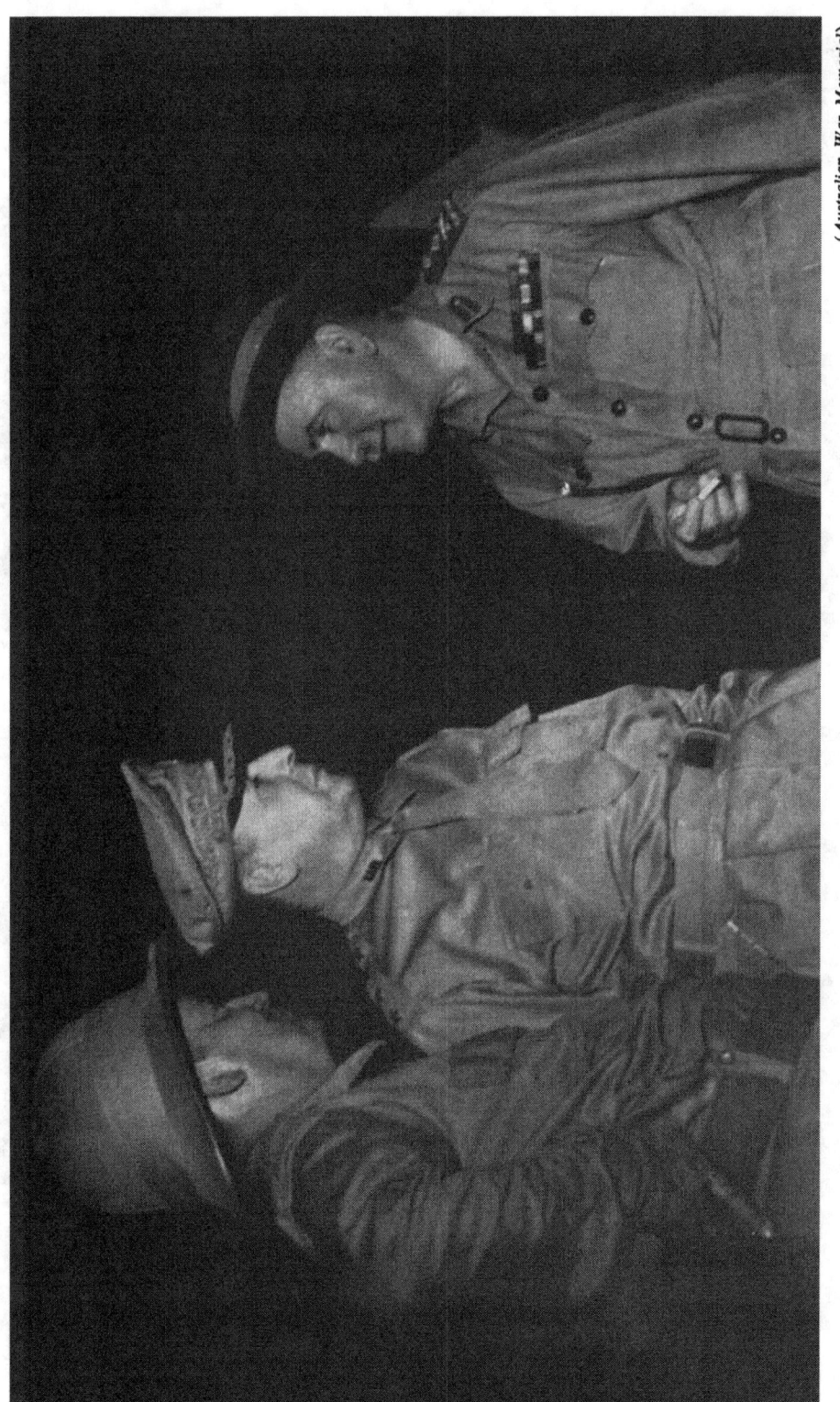

(Australian War Memorial)

The Minister for the Army, Mr F. M. Forde, General Douglas MacArthur, and General Sir Thomas Blamey. General MacArthur was paying his first visit to New Guinea. Port Moresby, 2nd October 1942.

(*Australian War Memorial*)

The ceremony of hoisting the flag, performed by Major-General G. A. Vasey, G.O.C. 7th Division, after the recapture of Kokoda on 2nd November 1942.

(*Australian War Memorial*)

The 2/10th Battalion was flown into Wanigela from Milne Bay on 5th and 6th October, followed by the 2/6th Independent Company and the 128th U.S. Regiment from Port Moresby in mid-October. This group at Wanigela includes (front row from left) Lieutenant P. C. Bennett, 2/6th Independent Company; Major H. G. Harcourt, O.C. 2/6th; Brig-General J. Hanford MacNider (seated on box); Major Chester M. Beaver of the 32nd U.S. Division's staff (kneeling); and, back row, standing, fourth from left, Lieut-Colonel J. G. Dobbs, C.O. 2/10th Battalion; Major J. H. Trevivian, 2/10th Battalion; Lieutenant F. W. G. Andersen, Angau; and Captain T. J. Schmedje, 2/10th Battalion.

that Stevenson's and Cullen's initial doubts about that plan were well founded. The positions had finally been turned from the Japanese right flank. Had one battalion, at least, followed in Captain Sanderson's path and felt out the Japanese carefully there for a day or two before attacking, it seems likely that the engagement at Eora Creek would have been less drawn out and less costly.

And then again, if Colonel Cullen had persisted with his plan on the 27th of driving against the Japanese from his own left-flank positions with all the strength that he could muster there, it is possible that immediate success would have followed. He found later that the point at which he planned to throw his men was merely a strong link between the main positions and the Japanese right flank positions which Hutchison's men overran the following evening. It was the Japanese recession which caused him to change his plans.

For the gallant and capable General Allen himself Eora Creek meant the end of his service in the mountains. This message from General Blamey reached him on the 27th:

> Consider that you have had sufficiently prolonged tour of duty in forward area. General Vasey will arrive Myola by air morning 28 October. On arrival you will hand over command to him and return to Port Moresby for tour of duty in this area. Will arrange air transport from Myola forenoon 29 October if this convenient to you.

Allen replied:

> It is regretted that it has been found necessary to relieve me at this juncture especially since the situation is improving daily and I feel that the worst is now behind us. I must add that I feel as fit as I did when I left the Base Area and I would have preferred to have remained here until my troops had also been relieved.[9]

But General Vasey arrived at Myola on the 28th and, on the 29th, Allen left for Port Moresby. Later, in Australia, he had the opportunity of speaking to General MacArthur to explain the conditions and he told MacArthur how much his signals had distressed him. In real or assumed surprise MacArthur said: "But I've nothing but praise for you and your men. I was only urging you on." Allen answered drily: "Well, that's not the way to urge Australians." He was cheered, however, by MacArthur's intimation that he had important work yet for him to do.

It was natural that Allen should feel aggrieved. He was a devoted soldier of wide experience in two wars who had demonstrated his ability in field command in every rank from that of platoon to divisional commander. He felt that neither MacArthur, nor Blamey, nor Herring could really

---

[9] In October 1944, Blamey wrote to the Minister for the Army to recommend that Allen should receive the knighthood of the Order of the British Empire. At that time Allen's command—Northern Territory Force—was being reduced to a brigadier's command and Allen had offered to relinquish his command and enter on a period of 12 months' leave without pay. Blamey cited Allen's distinguished service as a brigade commander in North Africa and Greece, and divisional commander in Syria and New Guinea where his division "stemmed the Japanese attack at Ioribaiwa Ridge and later moved to the attack" and where Allen "remained in command up to the time when the Japanese were driven over the top of the Owen Stanley Range". Blamey reminded the Minister that in the earlier war Australian major-generals who commanded divisions for periods not exceeding six months were knighted; Allen had commanded divisions for three years including two arduous campaigns.

appreciate the conditions under which he had been fighting as none had set foot on the Kokoda Track itself beyond the end of the motor road near Owers' Corner. Perhaps the disadvantages of that could have been overcome in some measure through the use of competent and experienced liaison officers—and indeed General Allen was too experienced a modern soldier not to realise that a theatre commander must rely largely on that and similar means to develop a picture denied generally to his own eyes by the demands of the desk from which necessarily he must discharge most of his responsibilities. But he noted that, up to 22nd October when Lieut-Colonel Minogue arrived at his advanced headquarters at Myola on a liaison mission, no senior staff officer from the headquarters of any one of his three superiors had visited his forward area to examine conditions at first-hand.

In explaining why his advance might have been termed "slow" he caused to be set down explanations of what he called the chief "retarding factors", under the following headings: Terrain; Transport of Supplies; Strength of Units; Condition of Troops; Evacuation of Wounded.

In relation to the terrain he pointed out that the primitive native tracks usually followed the tops of ridges, often knife-edged morasses in the constant rain, falling away into deep and gloomily wooded and tangled valleys. Such tracks offered ideal defensive positions which could be outflanked only by time-consuming and back-breaking climbs, often along paths which had to be hacked by the attackers through the tangled forest valleys and up thick and frowning mountain sides.

But even more serious were the always recurring supply problems which the nature of this country imposed. Allen estimated that, to supplement and complement the air dropping program, he required 3,000 native carriers to enable him to advance from Myola to Kokoda. Late in October only 1,250 were forward of Myola with none on the lines of communication in rear. He claimed that this shortage precluded his use of the second line of advance which he considered (Kagi-Seregina-Alola) and had forced him to hold one brigade in the Myola area while supplies were being built up forward. Beyond Myola he hoped to establish his first supply dropping area at Alola. With that in use he considered it would be possible to maintain two brigades forward, even though the use of dropping areas still left many supply problems unsolved as the percentage of recovery was sometimes as low as 40 per cent (with the total destruction of certain essential commodities), collection was a slow process and, on occasions, he asserted, his requisitions were not being fulfilled at all:

Instances have occurred where supplies requested to be dropped have not been forthcoming although the advance depended upon such droppings.[1]

Battalion and brigade records illuminate the dark picture of supply difficulties which Allen drew. They are full of references to hunger and to shortages of all kinds. Most explicit are the 2/1st Battalion's references culminating in the quartermaster's list of daily rations for the

---
[1] War diary, 7th Division.

period 23rd October-1st November, inclusive. It shows deficiencies against the battalion entitlement of 10 per cent in meat, 43 per cent in biscuits, 35 per cent in milk (tinned and powdered), 75 per cent in cheese, 40 per cent in sugar, 80 per cent in tea, 45 per cent in rice and 55 per cent in dried fruit.

To these circumstances were added the difficulties which Allen listed under the headings "Strength of Units" and "Condition of Troops". They arose from the reduction in the strength of the fighting infantry battalions for tropical bush warfare and from the heavy physical toll exacted from the troops by the nature of the country. The battalions of the 21st, 25th and 16th Brigades had averaged only some 580 all ranks when they started for the forward areas. Not only, Allen wrote, did the smallness of these numbers reduce his all-important "points of origin of fire" (as distinct from "fire power") but, in view of the lack of reinforcements, it caused him to be cautious of incurring unnecessary casualties lest his strengths should become so reduced that he would be unable to carry on the fight at all. And burdens of up to 60 pounds and more on the backs of his men, daily rains, cold, the fatigue of constant climbing and manoeuvring in the mountains, monotonous and insufficient food, drained the strength of his reduced battalions.

Finally, the prospect which faced wounded men was grim. The 2/4th and 2/6th Field Ambulances had staging posts at intervals along the track as links in an evacuation line which stretched back to the rearward areas. But these posts could do no more than hold a wounded man in only slightly less discomfort than he had endured on the actual battle front, or send him, a little less exhausted and ill, staggering and falling towards the next rearward post. Until the fighting passed Myola the worst cases had been carried back along the track by native bearers. After Myola, however, with the intensification of supply difficulties, the eight carriers which a stretcher case required, could not be spared to go farther back than that area.

From about 24th October Lieut-Colonel Chenhall had 5 officers and 68 men of his 2/6th Field Ambulance operating at the main dressing station at Myola No. 2. Soon afterwards Lieut-Colonel Hobson transferred his casualties (and the surgeon, Captain Leslie) from Myola 1 to Chenhall's M.D.S., and moved his 2/4th Field Ambulance to support the advance of the 7th Division. By midday on 1st November Chenhall had 438 cases in his care—212 battle casualties and 226 sick. He was becoming bitterly critical of the medical administration at the base and, a little later, sent urgent and strongly worded signals voicing his criticisms. He asserted that medical supplies were not only very short but bore little or no relation to the indents which he submitted; that, though air evacuation might not be possible, no proper alternative had been prepared for dealing with casualties; that no basic staff planning properly underlay the general medical situation.

Consideration of these particulars, and of the circumstances which prevailed from mid-August—when Brigadier Potts first led his 21st Brigade over the Kokoda Track—to the 29th October, when Vasey relieved Allen, makes it easy to understand Allen's disappointment when the task of driving onwards from Eora Creek was taken from him and fell to the vigorous, talented and picturesque Vasey.

Throughout it was at Brisbane and Canberra that there was lack of confidence, not at the front. As an outcome of the Government's anxiety, for example, the Minister for Air, Mr A. S. Drakeford, and the Minister for the Army, Mr Forde, had flown to Port Moresby on 1st October. Forde, who was accompanied by the Secretary of the Department of the Army, Mr F. R. Sinclair, spent 2nd October at Milne Bay. On the 3rd he was taken by jeep to the ridge overlooking Uberi, and spent about an hour there; on the 4th he flew back to Brisbane. One result of this visit was a 31-page report in which there was much emphasis on alleged wastefulness—Sinclair was a former Army Department accountant. Blamey, in November, wrote a commentary on the report's "numerous errors" and "theories contrary to the principles of war" and asked that his remarks should be shown to all members of the War Cabinet and Advisory War Council.

In October, Blamey was thinking ahead towards an offensive. On the 18th he wrote to MacArthur that plans must be developed to attack Lae and Salamaua. It might be possible to land troops from the air at Nadzab, in the wide Markham Valley, and advance thence on Lae. He proposed to use Australian troops for such an operation while he used Americans for an overland advance from Wanigela. MacArthur replied on the 20th that the enemy commanded the sea and could bring overwhelming force to bear on the north coast of New Guinea. Great caution was needed. The garrison at Milne Bay (where Blamey proposed to leave only one brigade) should not be reduced below two brigades.

CHAPTER 10

OIVI-GORARI

THERE was little that General Vasey could add immediately to General Allen's planning. Allen's efforts threw open the mountain paths for the new commander to follow to Kokoda almost at the moment he took over—just as General Rowell had started the Australians on the road back from Imita Ridge in September although to some it appeared that General Blamey had initiated the advance.

After Major Hutchison's 2/3rd Battalion had rolled up the Japanese positions at Eora Creek from the right flank late on 28th October, Lieut-Colonel Cullen led the pursuit on the 29th with his tired 2/1st Battalion, which was followed by Lieut-Colonel Edgar's 2/2nd Battalion.

On the same day General Vasey assumed formal command of the division as from 8 a.m. and General Allen left Myola for Port Moresby. Allen's latest orders for the capture of Kokoda could be sharpened a little now. Lloyd was told that his brigade would be retained complete as far as possible for the capture of Oivi and the establishment of a bridgehead on the Kumusi beyond. After he had secured Alola the 2/31st Battalion would revert to Brigadier Eather's command and the 25th Brigade would proceed intact against Kokoda. The 3rd Battalion would move forward to protect Alola and operate the dropping ground there.

By the early afternoon of the 30th, after deploying at the sight of distant enemy figures, the 2/1st had entered Alola without opposition and its leading men were thrusting towards Isurava. The forward company of the 2/2nd then took the right-hand fork of the track from Alola and went plunging down the mountain side to secure the bridge across Eora Creek (that same bridge across which Captain Sublet's men of the 2/16th Battalion had groped their way in the dark and difficult night of 30th August when the 21st Brigade was being beaten back). It will be remembered that this was the track which then led steeply up the eastern side of the ravine and passed beneath the Abuari waterfall, thence went by way of Missima, Kaile, Siga, Fila and Pirivi to join between Oivi on the east and Kokoda on the west the main track which led eastwards from Kokoda to the coast. Night found the 2/1st Battalion at Isurava Rest House patrolling forward to Isurava itself, with the main force of the 2/2nd camped in the Alola area (it was "insanitary and plagued by rats" they said), and the 2/3rd Battalion near by; the 2/31st was in rear.

Farther west of the creek the other two battalions of the 25th Brigade were making a difficult way. On the 29th the 2/25th was cutting a track over mountains so steep and thickly covered that, at one stage, the men made only some 600 yards in over two hours. They bivouacked that night among the dripping moss, on the cold wet crests of mountains which they estimated (having only sketchy maps) reached about 10,000 feet above sea level. Behind them the 2/33rd had reached Templeton's Crossing and been told to follow a hunting track wide on the west side of Eora Creek in order to close on the Japanese in the vicinity of Alola. Late on the 30th Lieut-Colonel Marson of the 2/25th received orders to try for Alola by the shortest and quickest route in view of the Japanese withdrawal from Eora Creek. Buttrose of the 2/33rd was then still searching the mountains for the track by which he aimed to strike eastwards.

From 7 a.m. on the 31st supplies were being dropped at Alola. But the small dropping area was on a ridge so that the percentage of recovery was low and many hungry men were disappointed. A little later the full-scale movement of the 16th Brigade along the right fork of the track got under way with the 2/2nd leading and 2/3rd following. And in their wake the 2/1st Battalion took the track to Missima after the 2/31st relieved them in the Isurava area in the early afternoon.

On the Alola-Isurava track the 2/31st was still forward when night came. Behind them the 3rd Battalion had all its companies at the Alola dropping ground. Near by General Vasey established his advanced headquarters in the last light.

The 2/25th and 2/33rd Battalions were still struggling in from the left. Weakness and weariness were bearing hard on them, the constant wet, cold and lack of hot and energy-producing foods, diarrhoea and scrub typhus, exacting a heavy toll so that the 2/25th diarist recorded:

> Many men in such condition that it was pitiable to see them struggle on—will power in many cases fighting against bodily exhaustion. . . . Frequently a day's hard march found the unit bivouacked for the night no further than one mile from the previous bivouac area.

Despite this slowness on the left, however, General Vasey did not wish to lose his impetus on the right-hand track. On 1st November he told Brigadier Lloyd to push on regardless of the situation in the Deniki area and this the 16th Brigade men did with light hearts:

> It was a happy sort of day (wrote the diarist of the 16th Brigade). The troops—or the majority of them—had a hot meal the night before—and hot meals had been rarities in the ranges. The track was drier and fairly easy and the country was becoming more and more pleasant—opening out into garden patches. The valley was widening, the pouring, dripping, misty ranges were being left behind. Everyone seemed to feel it; even the native carriers returning along the track had stuck gay yellow flowers in their hair, adding an air almost of festivity to the march.
>
> We had very little to eat, but we had some tobacco and the sun on our backs and so were happy. . . . It was fortunate that, with rations in the state they were, we were now entering into an area where there were plenty of vegetables in the native gardens. Marrow, yams and taro made a welcome change in the diet, as well as providing bulk to depleted supplies and giving us our first fresh vegetables for ages.

That night the 2/2nd camped near Missima village—"a pretty spot, full of flowers, a few huts, and we had our first view of Kokoda from there", they recorded. The 2/3rd passed through and its companies bivouacked along the track from Kaile to Fila.

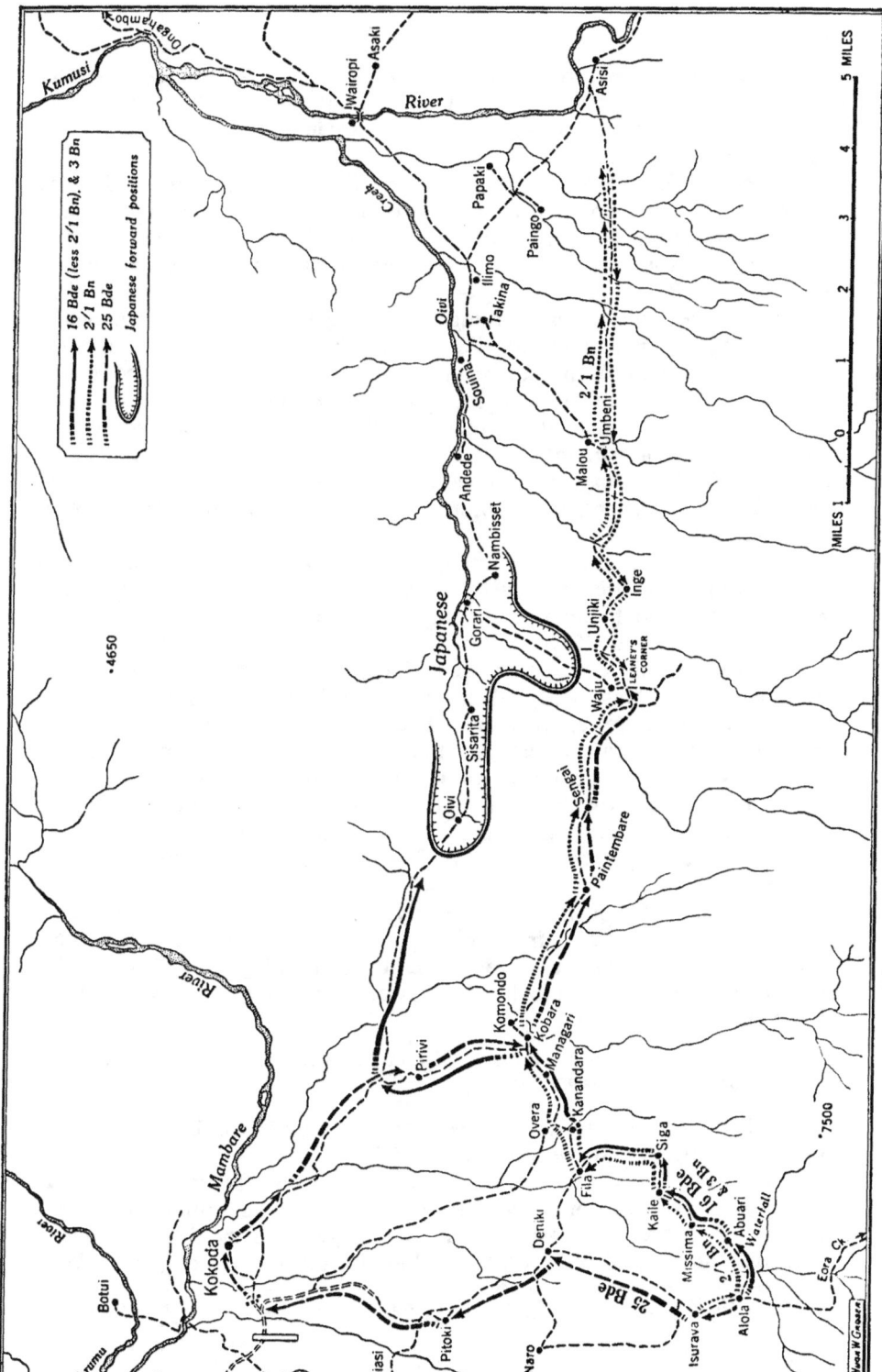

The approach to Oivi-Gorari, 31st October to 8th November

To the west the 25th Brigade was closing in. The 2/31st was still forward along the track, the other two battalions completing the circle of their wanderings with the 2/25th between Alola and Deniki and the 2/33rd at Alola.

On the eastern track, on the 2nd, the 2/3rd went forward to Kobara where the men began to prepare a dropping ground in an open kunai patch. One patrol quested as far as Pirivi—the area in which the 39th Battalion had fought to delay the Japanese approach on Kokoda on that 8th August, less than three months before. The whole brigade then camped in the Kobara region hungrily waiting for the food which would be dropped to them next day. Had it not been for the fruit and roots they had gathered from native gardens they would have fared badly. They made their evening meal from yams, paw paw, sweet potatoes, taro root and cucumber, all slightly green. But the going had been easier during the day—the track falling from Siga into the valley and, after passing through Fila, becoming well defined and level—so that, although the men were tired and hungry, they were not as distressed as they had been in the mountains.

There was good news from the western track. In the morning patrols of the 2/31st had been early astir. One, under Lieutenant Black,[1] entered Kokoda itself and found that the Japanese had been gone two days. By 11.30 a.m. the main 2/31st Battalion group was moving forward and had Kokoda firmly covered by the middle of the afternoon. By 4 p.m. Brigadier Eather was there with his advanced headquarters and the other two battalions were approaching. Preliminary engineer reconnaissance suggested that aircraft would be able to land after two days' work on the strip and dropping could go on from dawn of the 3rd.

So, quietly, the Australians re-entered Kokoda. Apart from its airfield its significance lay only in its name which would identify in history the evil track which passed across the Papuan mountains from the sea to the sea.

Vasey's new orders followed quickly. Lloyd was to prepare to move onwards to Wairopi and, from midday on the 4th, would be responsible for the whole area east of a north-south line running through Oivi. Nor did Vasey intend that the brigadier would lose sight of the need for haste. He signalled:

> I wish to see you moving towards Oivi in full strength at earliest. I feel your HQ and 2/1 Bn too far back.

That this urgency was not exaggerated was confirmed by air sightings of two destroyers and two transports off Buna.

On the 3rd Lloyd almost paid dearly for obeying the general too literally. Dropping began at Kobara early in the morning (although the percentage of recovery was disappointingly meagre) and the 2/2nd Battalion carrying three days' bully beef and biscuits moved out at 1 p.m. With

---

[1] Capt A. N. Black, QX19150. 2/31 Bn; NG Force, I Corps 1943-45. Schoolteacher; of Rockhampton, Qld; b. Rockhampton, 30 Mar 1912.

his leading company along the main track to Oivi—about 1,000 yards from the junction of that and the track from Pirivi—Edgar temporarily halted, awaiting additional supplies of telephone cable. Doubtless with Vasey's message well to the surface of his mind, Lloyd himself, as he talked, his arm lightly resting on the shoulders of Coloney Spry[2] (Vasey's senior General Staff Officer), moved beyond the forward scouts with a small party. The sudden rattle of machine-guns and the sharper notes of rifle fire broke about them. Spurred by quick concern Edgar had Captains Fairbrother and Ferguson whip a platoon from each of their companies wide to the right and left respectively and the small Japanese rearguard which had caused the trouble was driven in. By that time darkness was not far off and the battalion went into a defensive position astride the track with Fairbrother's patrols working forward on the right, Ferguson's on the left. Of the latter Staff-Sergeant Blackwell's[3] came against firm positions and lost two men wounded but brought back valuable information which enabled Edgar to make his plans for the next day. It seemed clear now that Oivi would be defended.

Back in Kokoda, meanwhile, the 25th Brigade was at work. Air droppings began about 8 a.m. but supplies rained down on the strip itself so that the task of repair and renovation was interrupted. The 2/6th Field Company, however, quickly got the task in hand again. The last elements of the brigade came in during the day and, just after midday, General Vasey, with ceremony, hoisted the Australian flag outside Eather's headquarters.

On the morning of the 4th the men of the 2/2nd moved forward warily to the point where Blackwell had been held the previous evening. But the Japanese were gone. Fairbrother led the new advance and, within less than a mile, his men began blasting Japanese before them. After another half mile, however, about 1.30 p.m., heavy and light machine-gun fire and the shells from a mountain gun were beating around them. Lieutenant Burke's[4] platoon could not advance. Fairbrother then, with an additional platoon under his command, moved the rest of his company by the flanks to take the Japanese positions in rear. By 5 p.m. his men had succeeded in cutting the track. But the Japanese had gone again and marks in the mud showed that they were dragging a mountain gun with them.

By this time the 2/3rd Battalion was in support and the 2/1st, with fresh supplies which had been dropped in the morning, were embarked on a new venture. This had been suggested by the run of the tracks for, from the vicinity of the dropping ground, a trail was found bearing almost directly east, below and roughly parallel with the main Oivi Track for some distance. Due south of Gorari it sent a lateral north to junction

---

[2] Brig C. C. F. Spry, DSO, VX7. I Corps; GSO1 7 Div 1942-43; DDSD LHQ 1943-45. Director-General Security Service 1950- . Regular soldier; of Brisbane; b. Yeronga, Qld, 26 Jun 1910.
[3] S-Sgt A. R. Blackwell, NX1864; 2/2 Bn. Wool classer; of Manilla, NSW; b. Manilla, 13 Sep 1915. Killed in action 5 Nov 1942.
[4] Lt J. K. Burke, NX717. 2/2 Bn; "Z" Special Unit. Agent; of Newcastle, NSW; b. Newcastle, 26 Jun 1906.

with the main track at that village. A little farther on it cast northwards two additional laterals which converged on the Ilimo area two to three miles along the principal route from Gorari.

In the late afternoon Cullen led his men eastward along this lower path. But wrong tracks confused them and, after about two hours' travelling, they found themselves back within a few hundred yards of their starting-point. They camped for the night. The 3rd Battalion, now under Lloyd's command, had relieved them at the dropping ground and had been told that, after that day, there would be no further droppings there and all units would be supplied from Kokoda.

In that area supplies had begun to build up. The first Douglas transport had landed about 9.45 a.m. and several other aircraft followed during the day with rations, clothing and medical supplies. Chocolate was issued to troops hungry for sweets and the men tasted bread for the first time in many days. From midday onwards the 2/4th Field Ambulance had a Main Dressing Station in operation, and thus, for the first time in the Kokoda campaign, the men could hope for reasonably comfortable conditions if they became casualties. So slender were the resources of the field ambulance at that time, however, that its performance fell short of expectations. As battle casualties and sick built up at the M.D.S. tented accommodation fell behind requirements, and for a time an area existed where sick men arriving at Kokoda built their own shelters and lay in cheerless circumstances on the ground. Nevertheless, for the first time, it was possible to fly the sick and wounded to hospital at Port Moresby, and with the consequent reduction in the number of patients at the M.D.S. conditions rapidly improved.

This, however, was little help to Lieut-Colonel Chenhall and his 2/6th Field Ambulance detachment at Myola. There, it will be recalled, Chenhall had had 438 sick and wounded men on his hands on 1st November, and was becoming critical of the general medical planning behind him. At the end of October a Stinson, the first of a number of small planes to land there, put down at Myola on a strip which the 2/6th Field Company had prepared. During early November several landings were made. On the morning of the 3rd the fourth patient was flown out and several cases were taken out on succeeding days. On the 7th Lieutenant Ronald E. Notestine, an American transport pilot, flew in and greatly impressed the Australians.

In all, however, only about 40 casualties were flown out of the mountains. Chenhall became increasingly outspoken. Colonel Kingsley Norris (the 7th Division's chief medical officer) wrote later:

> Two bombers, one loaded with stores . . . actually landed on the strip and after off-loading had taken off with no difficulty—the pilot remarking (among other things) "This is a grand little strip". In spite of every effort by Div and N.G.F., air evacuation was neglected. Why this was never adequately undertaken—why after three years of war no adequate ambulance planes were available—why certain casualties had to remain in a forward medical post for eleven weeks after being wounded—these and many other questions remain unanswered.

Brigadier Johnston[5] (Deputy Director of Medical Services at New Guinea Force Headquarters) has, however, left a rather different picture:

Unfortunately, when the possibilities of evacuating patients by plane were considered, all [the] practical difficulties were not at first realised and the belief became certain that planes would be able to accomplish the task satisfactorily. Such belief was confirmed by the action of two pilots in landing and taking off without mishap. But senior Air Force officers, including the Commander of the United States Air Force in New Guinea, refused to allow the attempt to be made with the planes then in use in that area. Despite the plight of those isolated in the midst of the Owen Stanley Range and the frequent appeals of many who, perhaps swayed by humanitarian feelings, were convinced that such attempt would be successful, the refusal was persisted in, unless suitable types of planes could be brought up. Of these about 5 were ultimately made available as a result of intensive search throughout Australia and surrounding areas. It is significant and confirmatory of the judgment of those responsible Air Force officers that two of these planes—a single-engined Stinson and tri-motor Ford—crashed while landing at Myola. Incidentally each of the other 3 planes (two single-engine Stinsons and one DH-50) crashed within a short time of arrival in N.G. from the mainland. However, before crashing at Myola, the Ford had evacuated 8 and the Stinson some 30 odd patients. Ultimately it became obvious that air evacuation had become out of the question. As the weeks went on certain of the remaining patients recovered sufficiently to be able to walk out.

For those still bedridden, native porters were finally obtained in sufficient numbers to act as stretcher bearers and after being shut up at Myola for some two and a half months, the last patients, together with the remainder of the unit, arrived back in the Port Moresby area, after their long trek, a day or two before Xmas.

There was nothing, however, that could be done about this situation from Kokoda, and the 25th Brigade did not expect, or desire, to remain on protective duties round the rapidly growing centre. Thus, without surprise, Eather received orders to get his battalions ready to move (on the morning of the 7th) to relieve the 16th Brigade.

That formation found itself heavily committed on the 5th. Edgar resumed the advance at 7.30 a.m., ready to test an extension of normal battle procedure. On meeting opposition his leading company would pin the front and begin a local encirclement. Automatically the second company would carry out a deeper encircling attack in an attempt to cut the track in the Japanese rear. (Although such a drill had become standard on the platoon level the colonel had never yet committed a second company in this fashion.)

So it was that, when Captain Ferguson's company, leading the advance, was engaged from the high ground fronting Oivi on either side of the track, before it had gone three-quarters of a mile, it deployed at once and Captain Brock's company manoeuvred deep on the right. But Ferguson's vanguard platoon was held on the track under destructive fire. Staff-Sergeant Blackwell's platoon, moving through bush on the right, found the way barred by lines of fire before they had covered more than 50 yards and Blackwell himself was killed. Lieutenant Moore,[6] Ferguson's

---

[5] Brig W. W. S. Johnston, CBE, DSO, MC, ED. (1st AIF: RMO 12 Bn.) CO 2/2 AGH 1939-41; DDMS I Corps 1941-42, II Corps 1942-43. Medical practitioner; of Melbourne; b. South Yarra, Vic, 21 Dec 1887.

[6] Capt R. McC. Moore, NX1916; 2/2 Bn. Grazier; of Boggabri, NSW; b. Sydney, 14 Apr 1907.

second-in-command, attacked round the left flank with the third platoon but could make little headway.

It looked now as though the Australians were coming against the main Oivi defences. Oivi itself still lay approximately a mile ahead—a few native huts set in a patch of young rubber—but the high ground which the Japanese were now holding controlled the approaches. This rose on either side of the eastward running track with a number of spurs thrusting westward as though to meet the advancing Australians—thickly-wooded approaches to the crests of the features. And soon the attackers were to learn that the Japanese had them well held, criss-crossing them with the fixed lines of light and heavy machine-guns. Snipers screened the defences, and mortars and one or two mountain guns supported them.

As the morning wore on Edgar, supporting Ferguson closely with Fairbrother's company, had reports from Moore of considerable strength on his flanks. He therefore sent Captain Gall's and Captain Walker's[7] companies of the 2/3rd Battalion, which had come forward under his command about 10.30 a.m., round to the left to assist Moore, relieve some of the pressure on Ferguson's company generally, and seize the high ground on that flank. A little later, having had no word from Brock who was relying on runners for communication, he pushed Captain Blamey's company of his own battalion up one of the spurs which the Japanese were holding on the right. Blamey moved strongly and gained some ground but then had to dig his men in to enable them to survive in the storm which was beating about them. Soon afterwards Brock returned to the track and reported that he had not been able to penetrate the Japanese positions which seemed to be in considerable width. Edgar therefore sent him to Blamey's right to lengthen the front at a dangerously open point and work the high ground there. Although the other companies tried to help him move forward by attempting to create a diversion with vigorous fire the Japanese effectively retaliated with heavy machine-guns and mortars. He was making slow headway against determined opposition when Edgar ordered him later to link with Blamey and hold.

As Edgar's difficulties were thus closing him in Hutchison was moving the rest of the 2/3rd forward in short stages. Late in the afternoon Edgar had him send his two remaining rifle companies (Lysaght's and Fulton's) round Brock's right in an effort to encircle the Japanese positions on the track in rear. But both were slowed by heavy machine-gun and mortar fire to which they began to lose heavily.

As night came both battalions dug in, the forward elements not more than 50 yards from their opponents. The 3rd Battalion had moved forward from Kobara and were in perimeter defence on the track in rear with one company farther in advance to protect Lloyd's headquarters and give depth to the 2/2nd and 2/3rd. So darkness settled on tired troops who had been able to achieve no decision.

There was little sleep for them during the night, however, and then,

---

[7] Maj E. S. Walker, NX261. 2/3 Bn; GSO2 Staff Duties and Trg, Aust Army Staff UK 1944-45. Bank officer; of Turramurra, NSW; b. Chatswood, NSW, 9 Oct 1917.

on the right of the track, a dawn patrol from Lysaght's company lost seven men within a short distance. A supporting patrol from Fulton's company was little more successful. Fulton then began to work round the flanks and he and Lysaght attacked at 2 p.m. In the fierce fighting which followed Lysaght's men were pinned to the ground although Fulton's drove hard and actually captured the highest feature on the crest of the ridge and a heavy machine-gun located there. But a destructive fire swept them off the ridge before they could consolidate. It looked as though the greatly weakened company might not be able to sustain the counterattack so Hutchison met the threat with Lieutenant Hoddinott's[8] anti-aircraft platoon which fought bravely and was largely responsible for holding the position. It seemed then that the Japanese were going to attack strongly between Edgar's companies and Lysaght. Captain Atkinson and Captain Jeffrey from the 3rd Battalion were therefore sent forward with their companies to Hutchison's command. They found Hutchison's men holding thinly and formed a perimeter with them. Scarcely were they in position, however, when the Japanese struck against the combined group with loud cries sounding through the last of the day. The Australians drove them back but, as darkness came, they knew that, though they had gained some ground, their general position was not greatly improved.

Considerable movement but less ferocity had marked the day for the companies on the left of the track. There Walker kept his company in holding contact while Gall tried to work the flank. But though Gall could hear the Japanese chattering and chopping as they built up their defences he could not locate their extreme right. He was told then to link with Walker and secure the Australian left.

At the end of the day Lloyd knew that he had lost at least 13 killed and 34 wounded from his two A.I.F. battalions while one man of the 3rd had been killed and two had been wounded.

After a quiet night the fighting on the 7th intensified the stalemate which was fast developing before Oivi. On the right of the track the Australians flung forward again at the high ground. Soon after 9 a.m. Lysaght's men went in with Jeffrey's of the 3rd supporting them, a crossfire from Fulton and Atkinson on the right, and Edgar's men on the left, beating their front. But four of Lysaght's remaining men were killed, one of his officers and eight men wounded, for no gain.

With ammunition coming forward from Kokoda now the Australians could try the effect of their mortars on the Japanese. They brought them into action but it was difficult to gauge results—except that every burst provoked the defenders to vigorous retaliation. Attackers and defenders lay dug in among the thick bush and flailed each other with fire.

This was a situation, however, which the resourceful Vasey had no intention of accepting, and already he had under way a movement to resolve it by means other than ram-like thrusts at the prepared Japanese positions. That movement had begun when Cullen led his 2/1st Battalion on 4th

---

[8] Capt F. J. Hoddinott, MC, DCM, NX4784; 2/3 Bn. Station overseer; of Glen Innes, NSW; b. Tambo, Qld, 31 May 1914.

November along the lower track which paralleled the main track for some distance before swinging north to junction with it near Ilimo. On the 5th progress had been easy at first. The men were on the move from 7.30 a.m. through villages and native gardens. In one of the villages, Sengai, they found the bodies of five Australians who had apparently been killed weeks before as they lay wounded on stretchers.[9] Pushing on in the afternoon they came upon signs of a recent Japanese reconnaissance patrol—footprints, cigarette packages, a small fire left burning—in whose steps they were apparently following as it returned to its base. About 5 p.m. they arrived at a track junction with a lateral turning north— the track to Gorari. Cullen had Lieutenant Leaney—now commanding "A" Company—send one of his platoons as a patrol along this track, in the obvious wake of the Japanese reconnaissance party. The platoon surprised three enemy soldiers sheltering in an old hut. The Japanese fled after a hot little encounter, two of them badly wounded, and leaving their weapons and equipment. The 2/1st Battalion bivouacked for the night.

They were on the move again early on the 6th, leaving Leaney with his company at the track junction (to be known to them now as Leaney's Corner) to secure their flank and rear and to establish a small supply base. Cullen told Leaney not to involve himself too deeply with any Japanese he might encounter. The main battalion objective was Ilimo and Cullen did not want to dissipate his strength with side issues. But the battalion made slow progress, crossing many streams and moving behind patrols which scoured the native gardens alongside their path. About 12.30 they came to a larger rushing stream through which they dragged themselves by means of a stout creeper which they flung across. While they were doing this their pioneers rapidly built a bridge as an important link in their supply line. On the other side of the creek a track ran northwards to Ilimo. But the Australians did not know this and were misled by confusing information given them in good faith by friendly natives. As a result they continued eastwards until the knowledge that they were obviously in error, rapidly failing supplies, and almost complete lack of communication with the main force (having no telephone cable they were relying entirely on a 208-wireless set which they had not been able to net in with the brigade set), caused them to retrace their steps towards Leaney's Corner on the 7th. While the main body camped just east of that junction at nightfall of that day Cullen himself, with Captain Cox, went on to meet Leaney. From him he learned of Brigadier Lloyd's difficulties in front of Oivi. He then made plans to attack northwards along the track to Gorari on the 8th. However, while the attack was being prepared that morning, he heard that the 25th Brigade was within an hour of his positions and hurried to meet Brigadier Eather.

With a firm base building at Kokoda after its reoccupation, the constant bully beef was being supplemented by varied and more attractive foods

---

[9] These were probably the bodies of five of the party Captain Buckler had left at Sengai on 21st September. See p. 211 and Appendix 1.

which the big transport aircraft were rapidly flying in: dried potatoes, meat and vegetable ration, baked beans, tinned fruit, sausages, tinned vegetables, jam, butter and sugar. But when the men began to eat even the small issues which were made to them the stomachs of most of them rebelled so that they lay retching and heaving.

With the Kokoda base secure behind him General Vasey was prepared to take risks which he could not otherwise have contemplated. In the early morning of the 6th Lloyd had summed up for him the situation as he saw it: he considered that the Japanese positions at Oivi extended over a three-mile front between the two main features, and might well be in considerable depth as the 2/1st Battalion had made contact near Gorari; that there were at least two Japanese battalions holding him up and possibly three; the 2/2nd and 2/3rd Battalions were wholly committed and half of the 3rd Battalion was ready for committal; the only reserves between Oivi and Kokoda were approximately 300 of the 3rd Battalion. All this Vasey considered and then, about 6 p.m., said that he was willing at that stage "to risk having no backstop on this front". The 16th Brigade was to maintain continuous pressure at Oivi and to consolidate on the Oivi position when the situation clarified; the 25th Brigade would achieve a position astride the Kokoda-Buna track in the vicinity of Ilimo, secure the area between Ilimo and Oivi, and establish the Kumusi bridgehead. To do this Brigadier Eather would try to take the Japanese in rear by moving down the lower track which the 2/1st had already opened up. On contact with the 2/1st Eather would assume command of that battalion.

Eather then ordered the 2/31st Battalion under Lieut-Colonel Miller[1]—until just previously second-in-command of the 2/1st and held in great respect and affection by those rugged men—to seize Gorari on 8th November. At the same time he told Buttrose of the 2/33rd and Marson of the 2/25th to move from the rear against the main Oivi positions. He planned also to have Cullen gain Ilimo with his 2/1st, prepare a supply dropping ground there, and patrol vigorously eastwards to Wairopi and west to Gorari.

In accordance with these plans the 25th Brigade moved swiftly from Kokoda by way of Kobara on the 7th, laying line as they went. The speed of the movement strained the men who were weakened by diarrhoea, the sickness which the new foods had brought upon them, and the unaccustomed heat of the lower country. But they camped for the night within perimeters not far west of Leaney's Corner.

On the morning of the 8th, on the way to Leaney's Corner, Miller of the 2/31st met and discussed the situation with Cullen, who was told by Eather soon afterwards to rest his men while the newcomers attacked up the track to Gorari. Miller then passed through Leaney's men who were in light contact some distance up the lateral, after which he sent

---

[1] Lt-Col J. Miller, NX124. 2/1 Bn; CO 2/31 Bn. Hospital attendant; of Gladesville, NSW; b. Glebe, NSW, 17 Apr 1904. Died 14 Dec 1942.

Captain A. L. Hurrell's[2] company on a wide right-flanking movement and by 11.50 a.m. his machine-guns and mortars were engaging the defenders. Forty minutes later Captain Beazley's[3] company began a fighting advance just to the right of the lateral. They were soon committed against positions on that axis. Then Captain Thorn[4] led his company round Beazley's right flank in the face of comparatively light opposition. Meanwhile A. L. Hurrell, in the wider right-flank movement, was faced by Japanese on a front of about 300 yards and, in the now familiar pattern, was groping for the elusive flanks and losing men quite rapidly as he did so. On the left edge of all this flurry Captain Upcher's[5] company of the 2/31st was maintaining the main axis along the track.

In the middle of the afternoon the 2/25th made contact with the 2/31st and then detoured to the right with the intention of swinging back on to the track between Gorari and the opponents of the 2/31st. By nightfall the 2/25th had begun to achieve this intention. On the 9th the 2/33rd would follow the same general detour, but moving a little wider, to cut the main Oivi-Ilimo track near Gorari.

With the coming of night the vigorous new stroke by the 25th Brigade was well under way, giving full promise of developing into a classical "pincers" movement. But it would be at a cost, for the 2/31st, even in that scattered fighting had already lost 28 men, including 7 killed.

At the opening of this new phase no appreciable change had taken place in front of Oivi. From the time they had begun the crossing of the mountains (up to but excluding 8th November) the 16th Brigade had lost 6 officers killed and 11 wounded, 101 other ranks killed, 1 missing and 267 wounded, a total of 386 battle casualties. In addition they had lost a very much higher percentage from sickness. So, weak in numbers and even weaker in physical strength, they could not force a final issue against the very determined defence.

Soon after dawn on the 8th the 2/2nd had their mortars at work and the forward men reported that "the enemy were heard squealing when the bombs burst". But the Japanese replied with heavy concentrations of mortar and mountain-gun fire. Not only did the 2/2nd have to endure that but, to their disgust, could not reply vigorously in kind after their early morning shoot. Vasey's headquarters told them that the mortar ammunition landed at Kokoda had been less than hoped for and they should conserve their stocks as much as possible. Their later shoots, therefore, had to resolve themselves into twenty-five rounds of harassing fire about 4.30 p.m.

At 8 a.m. Lloyd told his forward commanders that air support was coming up and two hours later low-flying fighters strafed the Oivi-Gorari

---

[2] Capt A. L. Hurrell, MC, NGX18. 2/31 Bn and Angau. Cadet patrol officer; of Salamaua, TNG; b. Wingham, NSW, 20 Nov 1916.

[3] Capt E. T. Beazley, VX6564; 2/31 Bn. Insurance agent; of Albury, NSW; b. Albury, 3 Jul 1912. Killed in action 22 Nov 1942.

[4] Capt C. R. H. Thorn, QX1210. 2/12, 2/31 Bns. Insurance agent; of Brisbane; b. Brisbane, 2 May 1913. Killed in action 19 Nov 1942.

[5] Capt R. R. Upcher, TX10. 2/1 A-Tk Regt, 2/31 Bn. Orchardist; of Dover, Tas; b. Dover, 7 Jun 1907.

(*Australian War Memorial*)
The Kokoda-Wairopi track, near Oivi.

(*Australian War Memorial*)
Wounded Australians from the Oivi-Gorari battle at the M.D.S. Kokoda, November 1942.

The destruction of the Wairopi bridge, 21st October 1942.

(*Allied Air Forces S.W.P.A.*)

(Australian War Memorial)
Lieut-General Robert L. Eichelberger, Commanding General I U.S. Corps.

(Australian War Memorial)
Brigadier J. E. Lloyd, commander of the 16th Brigade.

(Australian War Memorial)
Crossing the Kumusi River at Wairopi on a makeshift bridge constructed by Australian engineers. November 1942.

(Australian War Memorial)
Allied aircraft bomb Japanese positions in bush near Gona.

(Australian War Memorial)
An R.A.A.F. Wirraway comes in at tree-top level to machine-gun
Japanese positions at Gona.

track and dropped eighty 20-pound bombs in an attempt to soften the very tough defence. The effect was heartening to the Australians even though some of them were wryly non-committal in their recording of the occasion:

> One morning we got U.S. air support. We had been supported by them once before at Eora Creek, but they had frightened us more than they had the Japanese. Now we were to have help again. They bombed the feature with reasonable accuracy, and strafed Oivi village behind. The Japs, however, were so well dug in that we doubted whether the air support would be effective. But, in any case, the Yanks didn't hit *us* on this occasion.[6]

For the rest, the day was comparatively uneventful—one of test and counter-test. In these wary exchanges the Australians were sometimes caught by bold sharpshooters who had crept almost into their positions in the darkness. When morning broke these marksmen began to pick off some of the attackers from short range, and continued to harass them during the day. Mostly through them the 3rd Battalion lost 7 men killed and 5 wounded during the day.

And then it was night again, with torrential rain drumming through the darkness. When the 9th came, from the lower track the 25th Brigade was maintaining its impetus, enveloping the Japanese more firmly. The signal for more general pressure came when A. L. Hurrell's company of the 2/31st, after a sharp give and take, reported Japanese withdrawing north-east along the track. With low-flying aircraft gunning and bombing, the 2/31st edged ahead, Captain Upcher's men clearing out a small village which lay in their path. But by noon the advance was halted, with three companies astride the track in the order Captain A. L. Hurrell's, Captain Thorn's and Captain Beazley's from right to left, with Captain Upcher's company and Major Thorne's[7] Headquarters Company in reserve. Fronting them lay a dangerously cleared field of fire athwart the track, laced in depth with vine fences covered by fire. So the weary process of digging and feeling began again and by the end of the day the 2/31st had lost 9 more men killed and 9 more wounded.

But the 2/31st were an effective block against which, from the positions they had achieved in rear, the 2/25th could force the Japanese. And the 2/25th had begun to apply heavy pressure to that end about 9.30 a.m. when Captains O'Grady, Butler and Crombie swept their companies forward in a converging movement. Though they gained ground the defence not only held from well dug-in and barricaded positions behind cleared fields of fire and enfilading machine-guns, but twice during the day erupted into vigorous counter-attack. In the last light the 2/25th drove again, this time with all four companies. But the sullen defence again refused ground. The day cost Marson's battalion 37 casualties—4 officers and 10 men killed, 2 and 21 wounded—the most costly single day the 2/25th had so far fought.

---

[6] Capt H. G. McCammon and Capt C. H. Hodge, "The Kokoda Trail", in *Nulli Secundus Log*, p. 91.
[7] Maj E. Thorne, QX6058; 2/31 Bn. Regular soldier; of Kelvin Grove, Qld; b. Peckham, London, 2 Jul 1902. Killed in action 11 Nov 1942.

The day was not resting alone on the efforts of the 2/25th and 2/31st Battalion, however. The 2/33rd and the 2/1st were on the move once more. Colonel Buttrose moved the 2/33rd out of their bivouac area at 7 a.m. Soon he was in touch with the 2/31st and then ordered his men to move round that battalion and the 2/25th farther north, to cut the track to Gorari. They were astride the track north of the 2/25th by 10.20 a.m. Soon afterwards they were moving north towards Gorari itself. Captain Clowes' company, leading, brushed a small patrol out of their way but then struck dug-in positions which appeared to be protecting a dump or headquarters area of some kind. They believed the area might contain the junction of the Gorari lateral and the main Kokoda-Oivi-Gorari-Ilimo track, but a stubborn defence halted them there. Captain Clowes then led his company in a right-flank movement and fell upon what he considered to be a Japanese company in the outskirts of Gorari village. But not only were the invaders brave and determined

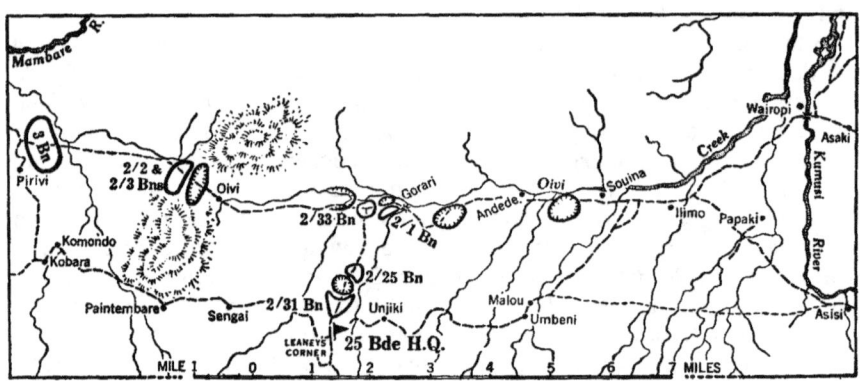

Oivi-Gorari, nightfall, 9th November

in defence, they struck back in turn at Clowes and drove his men to the protection of a near-by ridge. This was an ephemeral success, however, as Clowes then swept them out of his way and took the village so that Buttrose was able to form a perimeter in the village area for the night. While he was doing so the sound of fighting was coming down the evening air from farther east along the main track towards Ilimo where the 2/1st was committed.

Cullen had led that battalion in the wake of the 2/33rd, with orders to by-pass it to the east and gain the main track. About 5 p.m. the 2/1st swung east through the bush. Soon, however, a stream which they could not cross turned them north, as the sounds of the 2/33rd's engagement were reaching them. About 5.45 p.m., over the line his men were laying as they went, Cullen had news from Buttrose that the defenders of Gorari were moving eastward along the track (i.e. towards the 2/1st) as they gave to the 2/33rd assaults. He continued his northward movement, Lieutenant Leaney's company leading through the bush. About 6.30

Leaney's men met opposition which, however, they swiftly broke. And then the battalion debouched on to the main Gorari-Ilimo track, on their right a stout bridge spanning swift water, and across the bridge Japanese holding against Leaney's efforts to force a crossing and harassing him severely with sniper and mortar fire.

The 2/1st then dug in in the Japanese position which they had overrun. Among its defences were several huts which had been part of a headquarters and medical area of some kind. There were bags of rice and wheat, little barrels of plums pickled in brine, and medical stores which included quinine, morphia, bandages and crystals of mercurochrome—all very helpful to the Australians.

The night of the 9th, therefore, found a curious but swiftly developing situation on Eather's front. Three Australian battalions were spaced at intervals along the northward running Gorari lateral which linked the lower and upper tracks. The 2/31st was at the lower end (in the southernmost positions) hard against a solid Japanese pocket. Beyond that the 2/25th was astride the track trying to break into the pocket from the north and force the defenders against the waiting guns of the 2/31st. Beyond them again was the 2/33rd, holding Gorari at the northern end of the lateral against waxing pressure from Oivi towards which the 2/2nd and 2/3rd Battalions were still pressing. East of the 2/33rd the 2/1st was in a position to stave off any attack from the east across the bridge but was itself temporarily barred from crossing the bridge in continuance of the eastward movement towards Ilimo.

It was clear now that the next day or two must bring forth a slugging match. Desperate Japanese would try to fight out of the trap which had almost closed on them; the Australians were gathering themselves for the kill. The problem was whether the 2/33rd could hold against the tide that was setting in from the Oivi end as the Japanese learned that their main defence line there was sandwiched between Australians in front and Australians behind.

This tide promised to run strongly on the 10th. Early morning patrols of the 2/33rd estimated that at least two enemy companies were located only 400 yards to the west. Then Japanese attempts at infiltration were beaten back, although they cost Captain Brinkley,[8] the "B" Company commander, his life. In the early afternoon a determined threat seemed to be developing from the north-west supported by gunfire from close range and heavy small arms fire. A force of unknown strength tried to push in on the 2/33rd but the men were able to hold. They received no rations that day and were forced to fall back on their emergency rations.

From their more easterly positions the 2/1st undoubtedly diverted some of the pressure from the 2/33rd. Early in the morning Cullen sent Captain Simpson's company westward towards a higher feature which he imagined the Japanese to be holding against any eastward movement

---

[8] Capt P. L. Brinkley, WX462; 2/33 Bn. Public accountant; of Mosman Park, WA; b. Folkestone, Kent, England, 7 Apr 1916. Killed in action 10 Nov 1942.

by the 2/33rd. But Simpson's company, some fifty strong, met trouble and quickly lost sixteen of their number so that they withdrew to form the north-west corner of Cullen's perimeter. In their fighting Simpson's second-in-command, Lieutenant Wiseman, showed himself to be an outstanding leader, quite careless of his own life on at least two separate occasions as he tried to rescue some of his wounded men. And in this same engagement Private Ward,[9] company clerk and runner, fearlessly exposed himself to heavy fire in his efforts to assist the wounded and, stubbornly committed to his duty as he saw it, crossed and re-crossed the lines of fire of Japanese guns.

Lieutenant Powell,[1] commanding "B" Company, Captain Catterns being ill, was ordered to anticipate Japanese counter-attack from the west. As he waited, Leaney's company was settling to a day of vicious give and take of fire with Japanese engaging them hotly from scattered rocks in the vicinity of the track across the creek. Lieutenant Blakiston's platoon, right at the bridge, was the centre of this and the company lost three men killed as they exposed themselves to return the Japanese fire. Farther

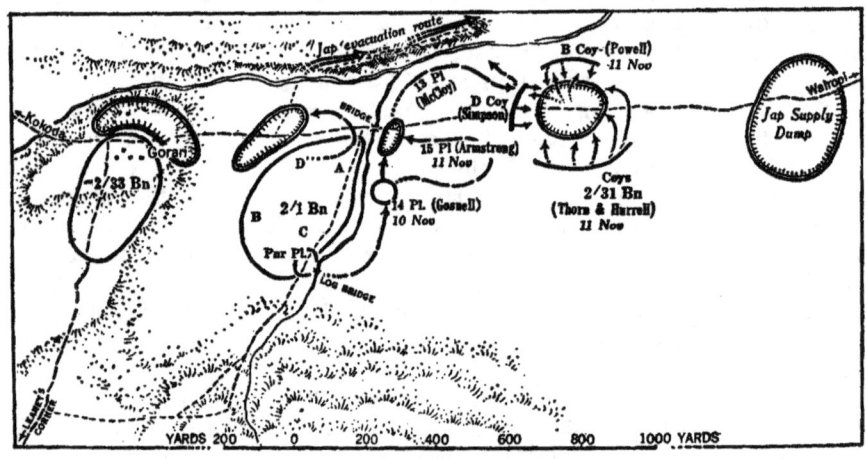

Gorari, 10th-11th November

south, from the southernmost corner of the perimeter, Captain Burrell's company were trying to cross the creek with the help of the pioneers. There Lieutenant Gosnell's[2] platoon, one by one, slowly levered themselves across three thin logs which had been placed across the creek at its narrowest point. Then they moved north along the creek, about the middle of the afternoon, killing three Japanese as they went, while the rest of the company continued the slow crossing in preparation for an attack on the 11th.

---

[9] L-Cpl C. W. Ward, MM, NX72951; 2/1 Bn. University student; of Broome, WA; b. Perth, WA, 4 Jan 1921.
[1] Lt R. E. Powell, NX11081; 2/1 Bn. Jackeroo; of Mosman, NSW; b. Perth, WA, 13 Jul 1913.
[2] Capt I. Gosnell, NX7627; 2/1 Bn. Commercial traveller; of Maroubra, NSW; b. Sydney, 2 Apr 1913.

On the 10th there was movement also below the 2/33rd and 2/1st as the 2/31st, pressing up the lateral from the south, and the 2/25th, bearing down the lateral from the north to crush the Japanese against the 2/31st, sparred for openings and felt round the Japanese positions to link with one another. During the morning, Crombie's company of the 2/25th thrust into the Japanese positions on the west of the track but were then held by Japanese fire sweeping open ground over which they had to advance. Then Lieutenant Mackay,[3] from Upcher's company of the 2/31st, linked with Crombie's company of the 2/25th and Upcher and Crombie planned a coordinated attack. But just as this attack was to start in the late afternoon the Japanese themselves struck and a wild mêlée began in the scrub off the track. Both Australian companies, however, broke through the outer crust of the Japanese defences, gouging at the Japanese pockets which barred their way. The end of the day found them digging in among the enemy positions.

Eather claimed 150 Japanese for the day's killing but the cost was beginning to worry him. From 8th November to 6 p.m. on the 10th, the 2/25th Battalion had lost 1 officer and 15 men killed, 1 and 30 wounded; the 2/31st had lost 1 officer and 16 men killed (with 4 others probably killed and 1 missing) and 44 men wounded; the 2/33rd had lost 5 men killed with 5 officers and 22 men wounded; the 2/1st had lost 6 men killed and 21 wounded.

The morning of 11th November saw early indications that the Japanese were struggling in frenzy to escape the trap which had closed round them. On the Gorari lateral a number of Japanese soldiers tried wildly to break through the Australian ring but were killed in their despairing attempts to do so. Then, at 6.30 a.m., Miller and Marson moved again in a coordinated plan to crush their enemies by moving simultaneously from the south and north respectively along the lateral. They had planned with care to avoid inflicting casualties on one another, telling their men to use their automatic weapons only in depressions and to go in with the bayonet and grenades, and fire single shots instead of bursts.[4]

The forest spaces became grim killing grounds in that early morning. As the 2/31st forced their way into the clearing which fronted them Captain Upcher's company on the left drove their broken enemies against Captain A. L. Hurrell's company on the right and the other two companies were thrusting up from the rear. Soon the 2/31st had counted 89 of their enemies dead in the little clearing alone and were in possession of a complete mountain gun, two medium machine-guns, many rifles and documents and much ammunition. This success cost them only 3 killed and 8 wounded. At the same time the 2/25th were crashing down the track from the north, leaving 54 Japanese dead in their path for

---

[3] Lt R. Mackay, NX31176; 2/31 Bn. Commercial traveller; of Campsie, NSW; b. Ashfield, NSW, 18 Feb 1915. Killed in action 11 Nov 1942.

[4] The Australian casualties through sickness and battle were now appreciable. Captain A. L. Hurrell of the 2/31st wrote later: "I remember Lt-Col Miller being annoyed when Lieutenant Mackay pointed that, with the much-depleted sections armed with a Bren and two Tommy-guns, there were barely enough bayonets to open our bully beef.'

the loss of 4 killed and 10 wounded. Mortars, machine-guns and much food and ammunition fell into their hands. Their trap thus sprung, the two battalions turned for the main track where the 2/33rd was having a comparatively quiet time but the 2/1st was busily engaged.

The 2/1st had spent a night of almost continuous fighting as Japanese attempted to break into their area with heavy fire, grenades and, on one occasion, bayonets. With the dawn Cullen was waiting for Burrell to complete his drive northwards along the far bank of the river and allow the rest of the battalion to cross. Lieutenant Armstrong, newly promoted, spear-headed Burrell's attack at 11.15 a.m. and finally cleared the defenders from their rocky positions which had commanded the bridge, killing nineteen stubborn soldiers on the objective itself. Burrell then sent patrols quickly eastwards on the north and south of the track—the one a platoon under Lieutenant McCloy, the other consisting of three of the battalion's commandos under Lieutenant Nathan.[5] Within less than 300 yards Nathan had lost his two men. He then returned to Burrell with his report.

McCloy also met effective opposition. With great courage he led his platoon against a position which later was found to have contained some 300 Japanese. Corporal Shearwin's[6] section pierced the opposing positions and were not driven to ground until they had killed eight Japanese who stood in their path. Shearwin, wounded himself, did not withdraw until greatly superior numbers were closing on him and three of his men had been killed and the remaining two wounded. He himself covered the movement of his little group back to the platoon.

At the same time Corporal Stoddart's[7] section was having a similar experience farther to the left. Stoddart struck boldly for the Japanese right flank and fell upon it with such force that his few men killed eighteen Japanese and seized their objective. Counter-attack in overwhelming strength later forced the section to withdraw, Stoddart, wounded in three places, shepherding out his men of whom only one remained unhurt.

By early afternoon Cullen was pushing his companies across the bridge as rapidly as possible. Powell was sent north from the track in an encircling movement, Captain Simpson led his men along the axis of the track itself. By mid-afternoon Powell had his men flung wide without being able to locate the Japanese eastern flanks as he tried to move in from the north, while Simpson was hard against the defenders on the track. Meanwhile the 2/31st Battalion had arrived in the area and Miller and Cullen planned a joint attack for 5.30 p.m. Miller would send two companies against the defended positions from the south; Cullen would have Powell and Simpson push in from the north and north-west.

And so it happened initially. But the Japanese, though surrounded, defended themselves savagely and aggressively. At one stage, against the

---

[5] Lt G. MacF. Nathan, NX50580; 2/1 Bn. Of independent means; of Burradoo, NSW; b. Sydney, 26 Nov 1917.

[6] Sgt H. J. Shearwin, MM, NX42526; 2/1 Bn. Truck driver; of Mascot, NSW; b. North Sydney, 10 Oct 1916.

[7] Sgt R. R. Stoddart, DCM, NX68711; 2/1 Bn. Grocer; of Mudgee, NSW; b. Mudgee, NSW, 7 Sep 1918.

full impetus of the Australian attack, they plunged westward along the track in a counter-attack against the junction of Powell's and Simpson's companies. The Australians stood closely against this recoil and an encounter between Corporal St George-Ryder[8] of Powell's company and a Japanese might have been almost typical. St George-Ryder emptied his sub-machine-gun from behind a tree into the counter-attackers, killing three of them. As he was changing his magazine he was furiously assailed by a Japanese with a sword who struck off his steel helmet and cut him badly about the head. The two closed. The corporal kneed his adversary and was twisting him down with his hands when a second Australian killed the swordsman.

As the impetus of the Australian attack was thus momentarily held, Major Robson,[9] second-in-command to Colonel Miller who had gone forward and been forced to ground by automatic fire and grenades, sent Captain A. L. Hurrell's company to assist Cullen's two hard-pressed companies, and sent Captain Thorn's company round the right flank. Except for small gaps through which a few fleeing Japanese filtered, the defenders were thus surrounded and the area they had been holding became another killing ground.

As darkness came the firing finally ceased. The Australian casualties in the encounter were comparatively light—the 2/31st, for example, lost approximately 7 killed and 7 wounded, but many dead and wounded Japanese lay on the track and in the bush. Within the perimeter they occupied Miller's men counted 74 dead and Cullen reported that his companies had killed more than 40 merely in repelling the counter-attack.

By this time it was clear that the Japanese Oivi-Gorari defences had been completely shattered. While the 25th Brigade had thus been engaged on the 11th the 16th Brigade had been able to move forward. The early morning patrols of the 2/2nd and 2/3rd Battalions found the Japanese positions on the Oivi features deserted and the battalions, with the 2/2nd leading, resumed their advance along the track. They found that very strong positions had been fronting them with well camouflaged weapon-pits, roofed with heavy logs and earth, in numbers which indicated that a large force had been opposed to them. Vines linking trees, and shielded candles every few yards along the main track, told a tale of stealthy night retreat. It was clear that the attacks which had made the night of the 10th-11th so restless for the 2/1st Battalion must have come from the main Oivi forces as they fell back.

Now the Australians began to reorganise preparatory to taking up the pursuit to the coast. On the afternoon of the 11th General Vasey had ordered Brigadier Lloyd to hold his brigade in the Oivi area for as long as possible to rest and refit. He wanted the 25th to prepare to advance eastward from the Kumusi River (which still lay ahead) on the 14th and Lloyd to follow on the 15th. From the Kumusi onward the brigades would

---

[8] Lt H. W. St George-Ryder, NX72954. 2/1, 2/32, 55/53 Bns. Clerk; of Suva, Fiji; b. Young, NSW, 1 Nov 1921. Died of wounds accidentally received 27 Jan 1945.
[9] Lt-Col E. M. Robson, DSO, NX349; 2/31 Bn (CO 1943-45). MLA (NSW) 1936-57. Solicitor; of Rose Bay, NSW; b. Ashfield, NSW, 7 Mar 1906.

advance to the coast by separate tracks. Although they were tired they felt that they had done well and were approaching the end of a long and difficult trail. Brigadier Eather expressed this in a message to his units:

I wish to congratulate all troops under my command on their splendid efforts during the last few days. To command such a body of troops is an honour and a privilege. Will commanders please convey this message to all ranks. Such fighting ability as that displayed in the recent action will surely enable us to complete the task allotted.

While the greater part of the two brigades rested and reorganised the 2/25th Battalion pressed on along the track on the morning of the 12th, through the 2/31st which followed later in the forenoon. As the 2/25th broke out of the bush on the banks of the creek immediately before Ilimo, however, they were met by sniping fire from across the bridge. Holding with some elements on the west side of the water, and with the 2/31st backing these elements on the approaches to the bridge, Marson tried a right flanking movement by having two companies ford the creek above the bridge. These two companies cut the track but darkness shut them off from their enemies, whom, once again, they had at an obvious disadvantage. The manoeuvre cost them 2 men killed and 4 wounded.

Dawn on the 13th showed that the Japanese had slipped out of their positions in the darkness and, on this new day, the 2/31st Battalion headed the Australian pursuit through the littered evidence of hasty retreat. With them went Major Tompson[1] leading a small engineer reconnaissance party composed of details from his 2/14th Army Field Company, the 2/5th Field Company, and the 25th Field Park Company. In the early afternoon they reached the site of the well-known wire bridge which had spanned the Kumusi until fire from Allied aircraft had razed it and which (from the pidgin) had given the name Wairopi to the spot. Like bird dogs the 2/31st men quested up and down stream but met no Japanese, although signs of desperate haste to cross the river by small rafts, abandoned as soon as the pursuers appeared, were numerous. Some 200 native carriers who had been pressed into the invaders' service welcomed the newcomers and told them that many of their quarry had crossed the river in two boats the previous night, struggling with the burden of their wounded and dumping rifles, ammunition and stores into the river as they fled.

Many of these were drowned, among them General Horii himself. After the encounter at Eora Creek he had readjusted his force, and brought Colonel Yazawa back from the coast and established him in strong, well-prepared positions on the high ground at Oivi with an infantry strength of about one strong composite battalion strongly supported by engineers and artillery. Later, to guard against an Australian breakthrough on Yazawa's left, he settled Colonel Tsukamoto at Gorari with strong elements of the *144th Regiment* (which Tsukamoto was temporarily commanding since Colonel Kusunose had become ill) and some support-

---

[1] Lt-Col R. A. J. Tompson, OBE, ED, NX70412. OC 2/16, 2/14 Fd Coys; CRE 7 Div 1942-44. Civil engineer; of Longueville, NSW; b. Ashfield, NSW, 30 Aug 1905.

ing troops. At Oivi-Gorari the 16th and 25th Brigades, however, destroyed probably about 600 Japanese on the spot and threw the survivors back along the main track to the coast or into the rugged country which flanked the left bank of the swift Kumusi. Most of Yazawa's surviving troops took the latter way out, Horii with them, their hope being to raft down the river to the sea. The turbulent waters, however, proved too much for many of them, and others were shot from the banks by P.I.B. patrols who were watching near the mouth of the river. Possibly several hundred, however, finally gathered with Yazawa himself at the river's mouth.

In the pursuit the 2/25th Battalion were hard behind the 2/31st. Colonel Marson had cast off a strong patrol early in the morning of 13th November to investigate native reports that a band of Japanese containing many wounded and numbering 150 to 200 had been seen making a difficult way to the north the previous night, obviously with the intention of trying to cross the Kumusi farther down. He had been ordered to reconnoitre and prepare a dropping ground in the vicinity of Wairopi and, in the middle of the afternoon, reported a suitable kunai patch some 200 yards west of the bridge itself. By that time, however, some supplies had already been dropped there, evidence of the fact that New Guinea Force Headquarters had profited by the experience of the campaign and were not only following the advancing infantry closely with supplies from the air but actually anticipating their demands.

Soon after 3 p.m. the 2/33rd Battalion had also reached the Kumusi and at once set about trying to secure the bridgehead. Before them now an 8 mile an hour current flowed in a river which was about 12 feet deep and 300 feet wide, set between banks perhaps 30 feet high. Only empty pylons rose where the wire bridge had stood and other bridges which had spanned the swift water had also been destroyed. Major Tompson had been examining the bridging problem which was obviously going to be most difficult. Late in the afternoon he was joined by Lieut-Colonel McDonald,[2] the division's Chief Engineer, and Major Buddle[3] with an advanced party of his 2/5th Field Company. But, although Buttrose got some strong swimmers from his battalion across the river, no means of making a battalion crossing were found and the battalion was forced to dig in on the near bank for the night. The next day, however, aeroplanes brought steel-wire rope and tools (in response to urgent requests which McDonald had made in advance after studying air photographs and maps which enabled him to forecast the difficulties of bridging the river); but the planes did not bring the empty drums which the engineers had particularly requested, as the pilots considered them dangerous to drop through their slip-streams. Buttrose's swimmers then got a steel cable across the water, and the engineers, who had discovered and repaired (with bullybeef boxes) a wrecked Japanese folding boat, attached the boat to this

---

[2] Brig W. D. McDonald, CBE, NX424. 2/6 Fd Coy; OC 2/5 Fd Coy, 2/25 Fd Pk Coy, 2/8 Fd Coy; CRE 6 Div 1942, 7 Div 1942-43; Comd HQ RAETC 1944-45; CE HQ II Corps 1945. Civil engineer; of Canberra; b. Penguin, Tas, 23 Sep 1901.
[3] Lt-Col B. H. Buddle, MBE, NX12340. OC 2/5 Fd Coy; Chief Instructor RAETC 1944; A/CRE 6 Div 1945. Civil engineer; of Sydney; b. Sydney, 22 Mar 1914.

with a block and tackle, and began to ferry the men of the 2/33rd across. By this means, approximately one company, crossing about eight at a time, reached the far bank and thus, although weakly, established the bridgehead—without enemy opposition. The boat then swamped, however, washed away, and was damaged beyond repair. But by that time both the 2/5th and 2/6th Field Companies had been hard at work developing other means of crossing. They had two flying-foxes ready for use by the early afternoon, and a small suspension footbridge ready by nightfall. Although darkness and heavy rain then put a temporary end to the infantry's attempts to cross, by that time the two flying-foxes had enabled Buttrose's main force to make the passage.

Thus the 14th saw the 25th Brigade substantially immobilised on the west bank of the river with the 16th Brigade resting and refitting behind them. Brigadier Eather's numbers were strengthened that day by the addition of the previously independent detachment known as Chaforce, formed from the fittest members of the 21st Brigade early in October under command of Lieut-Colonel Challen. Challen had Major Sublet of the 2/16th Battalion as his second-in-command and his force consisted of a company from each of the 21st Brigade battalions (each company a little over 100 all ranks strong), engineer, signals and medical detachments.

Chaforce had left for Uberi on 11th October so that most of the men in it had only a scant two weeks' rest after the early, difficult Owen Stanleys fighting. They had been ordered to harass the Japanese along their lines of communication between Buna and Kokoda but these instructions had been subsequently so modified that their main function had become a varied maintenance task in rear of the 16th and 25th Brigades. This had irked them, burning as they were to avenge the defeat they had suffered at the Japanese hands, and it is difficult to determine just why their role had been so emasculated. The original concept was bold and soldierly, and contemplation of such little epics as those of which Captain Treacy's was one of the best examples, suggests that its success could have been outstanding. Indeed, conditions of warfare in the mountains where the invaders' line was stretched most tenuously and precariously through wild and tumbled country were very suitable in places for the commando role for which Independent Companies had originally been formed and trained.[4] Presumably, rightly or wrongly, the Australian Command had felt that it could not spare an Independent Company for use in the Owen Stanleys at this time and thus Chaforce had been improvised as one. Any chance, however, of testing its value in that role disappeared on 14th November. By that time Challen had returned to his battalion—the 2/14th —leaving Sublet in command and the latter now became a liaison officer on General Vasey's headquarters. The three companies were allotted to

---

[4] For example, while the fighting at Eora Creek was in progress, a three-man patrol of the 2/6 Indep Coy led by Lt F. J. Winkle, based on Kambisi, about 80 miles west of Buna and with a forward base at Yodda, on the night 24th-25th October, entered Kokoda, observed Japanese seated round a camp-fire and a complete absence of guards or sentries. They withdrew, and next morning crossed the apparently unused airfield, and moved in the direction of the Owen Stanleys until they reached a point where intermittent small arms and mortar fire could be heard close by. They were fired on, reached the conclusion that they were moving among the front-line of Japanese, and on the night 25th-26th October withdrew to Yodda.

battalions, Captain Cameron's to the 2/31st, Lieutenant Haddy's to the 2/33rd, and Captain A. J. Lee's to the 2/25th.

The 2/31st and 2/25th, although temporarily checked in their main movement, were not idle on the 14th—nor had they completely lost touch with the broken Japanese elements—for the patrol which had left the 2/25th the previous day to pursue the party reported moving north returned to tell how they had been prevented from closing on this remnant, some 200 strong, by a determined and well-armed rearguard; Miller then sent three of his companies to take up the hunt while the 2/33rd and the engineers were continuing their attempts on the passage of the Kumusi.

On the 15th the crossing of the Kumusi continued—but slowly, although the engineers were at work by that time on a second bridge which they slung from the end of a partly destroyed Japanese trestle bridge. As the day wore on the 25th Brigade was still crossing. The flying-foxes could get only about 80 men across in each hour and not more than 150 could pass over the footbridge in the same time. But, in the afternoon, the 16th Brigade finally began the crossing in high spirits:

> The scene at the river bank was reminiscent of an old English fair or Irish market day (wrote its diarist). Battalions of heavily laden troops in their mud-stained jungle green shirts and slacks, carrier lines with the natives gaily caparisoned in bright coloured lap laps, bedecked with flowers and sprigs of shrubs stuck jauntily in leather bracelets, all mingled as they waited their turn to cross. The means used for crossing were both hazardous and adventurous but were attempted in something of a carnival spirit. On the one hand an extremely flimsy wire suspension bridge that gave all users a bath at its sagging middle and on the other a high strung flying-fox that, whilst efficient, occasionally stopped with the occupant swinging helplessly above the stream.

By the end of the 15th, although all of the first brigade was over the river, of the 16th only the headquarters and the 2/2nd had reached the far bank. It was not until late on the morning of 16th November that the rest completed the passage. Then the 3rd Battalion, which had taken over from the 2/31st pursuit of the Japanese remnants, abandoned its fruitless chase and followed on the 17th.

And so, nearly four months after it had begun with the Japanese landings at Gona on 21st July, the Battle of the Kokoda Track ended in the complete defeat of the invaders—as the other prong of the drive on Port Moresby had been broken at Milne Bay. But the Japanese stroke had been bold in concept and brave and vigorous in execution. It had narrowly failed not (as some military critics have claimed) because it was *bound* to fail, but for the sum of the following reasons: that the Japanese bungled badly their attempt to secure their southern flank by establishing themselves at Milne Bay; that the mountains drained their men and means as the wash of a rockbound coast drains the strength of a strong swimmer reaching in vain for the solid platform just beyond him; that the fighting on and around Guadalcanal denied them the support which had been planned for them and which would probably have enabled them to maintain—and perhaps to increase—the original impetus of their advance; that their opponents were among the most adaptable soldiers in the world who, having been seasoned already in war, could first match and then outmatch them in the special kind of warfare which the bush demanded.

From the beginning of the mountain campaign until its end the Japanese committed there at least 6,000 fighting men. Against them, though never more than one brigade at a time until the final clash at Oivi-Gorari, the Australians committed three experienced A.I.F. brigades. The 2/1st Pioneer Battalion was an additional A.I.F. infantry component but was virtually not committed to the actual fighting. Of the non-A.I.F. units the specially raised Papuan Infantry Battalion had performed with limited usefulness in a limited role in the early days of the invasion and three militia battalions had taken part in the campaign—the 39th, the 53rd and the 3rd.

The Australian soldiers killed and wounded in New Guinea (exclusive of Milne Bay and Goodenough Island) in the period from 22nd July to 16th November numbered about 103 officers and 1,577 men, of whom 39 officers and 586 men were killed. With the exception of very small casualties sustained in bombing raids at Port Moresby, by Kanga Force, and on isolated occasions, these figures represent the Australian losses during the Battle of the Kokoda Track.[5] In dissecting them further the interesting fact emerges that the three A.I.F. battalions of the 21st Brigade (of which the 2/27th was actually only committed for a few days) lost 26 officers and 470 men killed and wounded during the early days of the campaign—heavier losses than those of either of the two brigades which continued the fight.[6] With the 39th and 53rd Battalion figures added the cost of the first weeks became 40 officers and 617 men.

[5] The infantry losses during the period were:

	Killed in Action or Died of Wounds		Wounded in Action		Total Battle Casualties	
	Officers	Other Ranks	Officers	Other Ranks	Officers	Other Ranks
16th Brigade						
2/1st Bn	2	60	8	114	10	174
2/2nd Bn	2	42	2	91	4	133
2/3rd Bn	0	39	5	106	5	145
	4	141	15	311	19	452
21st Brigade						
2/14th Bn	8	111	6	131	14	242
2/16th Bn	4	67	4	75	8	142
2/27th Bn	1	42	3	44	4	86
	13	220	13	250	26	470
25th Brigade						
2/25th Bn	1	46	12	116	13	162
2/31st Bn	4	46	7	83	11	129
2/33rd Bn	3	26	4	75	7	101
	8	118	23	274	31	392
Militia						
3rd Bn	1	35	2	33	3	68
39th Bn	5	49	3	68	8	117
53rd Bn	3	10	3	20	6	30
	9	94	8	121	17	215

[6] On 9th November General Blamey addressed a parade of the 21st Brigade at the Koitaki cricket ground. During the course of his speech, he said that the Jap was like a gorilla; he would get into a hole and he would not surrender; while in his hole and protected by it he would kill; to be dealt with he had to be got out of his holes and put on the run. Blamey added that it was like shooting rabbits: while the rabbits were in their burrows they could not be shot; they had to be got on the run and then the man with the gun could get them.

"It never entered my head as I stood there on parade that the general had any idea he was being offensive, or that he intended to be so," wrote Brigadier Dougherty (then a newcomer to the brigade) afterwards. "But the brigade gave to what he said the interpretation that 'they ran like rabbits'. This interpretation of what he said spread throughout New Guinea and indeed

No accurate record exists of the casualties due to sickness during this period but between two and three men were hospitalised through sickness for every battle casualty. Perhaps the best picture of the sort of losses sustained in the campaign is given by study of the strength figures of a typical battalion—the 2/1st. It took the track on 6th October 608 all ranks strong. When it crossed the Kumusi on 16th November it numbered 355 all ranks. During that period it had received no reinforcements, many hospital cases had left and rejoined it again, individuals or small groups which had been detached for various reasons on 6th October had caught up with it again.

The major lessons of this battle were plain to General MacArthur and the Australian commanders, whose forces fought the ground battle as an exclusively Australian one, and were not to link with any American ground troops until after the crossing of the Kumusi on 16th November. First it was clear that bush warfare in difficult mountains demanded physical endurance and courage of the highest order, and an individual adaptability, skill and speed in offensive and defensive reaction, both to the enemy and the country, of a very special kind; and that, even among soldiers who developed these qualities to a high degree, the drain on mental and physical strength, and on numbers, was enormous. Second, the problem of supply had assumed a completely new guise. As petrol is to an internal combustion engine so is supply to any army in the field. But here the difficulties it could impose had to be realised afresh; and with that knowledge came a new emphasis on air power, for only through the air could supply be maintained and victory on the ground achieved.

---

back home, and resulted in bitter feelings. Following his address to the whole brigade [General Blamey] addressed the officers separately. He was direct with them and said that a few officers in the brigade had failed. This caused bitterness. But after both addresses Blamey told me that he thought highly of the brigade, and repeated to me what he had told the whole brigade—that I, as their new brigade commander, would be very proud of them."

". . . When the brigade was reorganising at Ravenshoe [in 1943] General Blamey's P.A. one day asked me if the general could speak to my officers. He had been genuinely upset at having hurt my brigade when he addressed them at Koitaki, as he had not intended to do so. When speaking to the officers on this occasion he referred to the Koitaki incident. He said he had then said certain things to the officers, and he meant all that he had said. He endeavoured to explain the meaning of what he had said then, and to put his remarks into their correct perspective. His comments on this occasion, frank and sincere, were well received."

CHAPTER 11

THE BUILD-UP BEFORE BUNA

AT the end of October General MacArthur's immediate plans were by no means precisely defined. He had attained his objects in preparation for offensive action in the South-West Pacific: his forces controlled the crest of the Owen Stanley Range from Wau to Milne Bay and had crept round the north coast of New Guinea to Cape Nelson; they had the islands surrounding Milne Bay under surveillance; their base installations at Port Moresby, Milne Bay and (in Australia) in the Cape York Peninsula, were essentially complete; air power was concentrating in New Guinea and northern Australia. But the general situation beyond those limits was such as to give the Allied commander cause for wary consideration.

The seas to the north of Australia, and the Pacific Ocean adjacent to the northern Solomons, the Gilberts, Marshalls, Carolines, Marianas and Philippines, were under undisputed Japanese control. The main Japanese fleet was concentrated in the Truk-Rabaul-Jaluit triangle. Large Japanese forces, mobile, well-equipped and experienced, were within striking distance of MacArthur's area. An intense offensive against the Americans on Guadalcanal was under way. The American fleet in the southern Solomons was weaker than the neighbouring Japanese fleet and needed the protection of land-based aircraft. It was unable—or unwilling—to assist in any action in the South-West Pacific at that time, and the naval forces available to the commander of that area were vastly inferior to those of his opponents in ships of all classes. The demands of Europe were not likely to permit replacement of heavy losses in MacArthur's personnel or equipment and would impose a long delay on any program for remedying existing deficiencies.

On the other hand the Japanese air forces which had been concentrated in great strength in the Rabaul-Kavieng-Buin area had suffered such heavy reverses that the Allies had aerial superiority over New Guinea and, usually, over the southern Solomons. They were able to deliver punishing attrition attacks to shipping and land objectives in the northern Solomons, New Britain and New Ireland. The Americans felt that they were superior to their opponents in both training and equipment; the Australian Air Force, while experienced and well-trained, did not have enough first-class aircraft. None the less Guadalcanal was demonstrating that air power alone could not prevent invasion by sea even though the Americans there, with a higher proportion than MacArthur of land-based dive bombers, were better fitted to deal with such manoeuvres than MacArthur was with his larger proportion of high-level bombers.

Generally the defenders of the South-West Pacific were not in a position to engage their enemies in a battle of attrition. It was clear that the invaders still had such impetus that they could strike heavy blows at Guadalcanal, or along the north coast of New Guinea or against Milne

Bay; or combine two of these courses; or combine a most exacting defence at either Guadalcanal or on the north coast of New Guinea with an attack, that would be most difficult to sustain, on the remaining area or at Milne Bay.

Having considered these circumstances General MacArthur decided on the 3rd November that he would immediately drive through the plan already under way in New Guinea—a three-column advance against Buna —provided that New Guinea Force could so order its supply program as to place ten days' supplies behind each column. The attacks would coalesce about 15th November (certainly not earlier than the 10th) but the actual date would depend upon developments. He reserved his decision whether he would attempt to consolidate and hold at Buna after its reduction.

This would depend to a large extent upon events at Guadalcanal. There it was still anybody's fight. Despite the failure of their October offensive, it was clear that the Japanese were still capable of carrying the American defences by storm; the naval battle of Santa Cruz had not strengthened the American position at sea; on 26th October only 29 American aircraft were operational at Henderson Field.

> Thus far in the campaign, Allied air and naval forces had fought valiantly, but had not yet achieved the result which is a requisite to a successful landing on a hostile island—the destruction or effective interdiction of the enemy's sea and air potential to prevent him from reinforcing his troops on the island, and to prevent him from cutting the attacker's line of communication.[1]

When, on 18th October, Admiral Ghormley had been replaced by the picturesque and forceful Admiral Halsey, the first decision Halsey had to make was whether or not Guadalcanal should be abandoned. General Vandergrift said that he could hold the island if he were given stronger support. This decided Halsey, who promised Vandergrift what he asked. One of his first actions was to send Admiral Kinkaid to fight the Santa Cruz battle.

Meanwhile the Joint Chiefs of Staff were preparing stronger air forces for the South Pacific and President Roosevelt himself had intervened. On 24th October he wrote to the Joint Chiefs that he wanted every possible weapon sent to Guadalcanal and North Africa even at the expense of reducing strengths elsewhere. Admiral King assured him that strong naval forces would meet his request. (These included twelve submarines from General MacArthur's area.) For the Army General Marshall replied that Guadalcanal was vital.

> The ground forces in the South Pacific were sufficient for security against the Japanese, he felt, and he pointed out that the effectiveness of ground troops depended upon the ability to transport them to and maintain them in the combat areas. Total Army air strength in the South Pacific then consisted of 46 heavy bombers, 27 medium bombers, and 133 fighters; 23 heavy bombers were being flown and 53 fighters shipped from Hawaii to meet the emergency. MacArthur had been directed to furnish bomber reinforcements and P-38 replacement parts to the South Pacific. General Marshall had taken the only additional measures

---

[1] J. Miller, *Guadalcanal: The First Offensive*, p. 169.

which, besides the possible diversion of the 25th Division from MacArthur's area to the South Pacific, were possible—the temporary diversion of three heavy bombardment squadrons from Australia to New Caledonia, and the release of P-40's and P-39's from Hawaii and Christmas Island.[2]

Halsey, therefore, was strongly backed as he pushed his plans ahead. Late in October he diverted the I Battalion, 147th Infantry, from another operation of dubious value to cover, with the 2nd (Marine) Raider Battalion and lesser elements, the construction of an air strip at Aola Bay, about 33 miles east-south-east of Lunga Point. (These made an unopposed landing there on 4th November, but the project was subsequently abandoned because of the unsuitability of the terrain.) In Vandergrift's original area two ships were to land more stores, ammunition and two batteries of 155-mm guns on 2nd November. These guns were heavier than any the garrison had yet possessed and would, for the first time, make effective counter-battery fire possible. On 3rd November the 8th Marines of the 2nd Marine Division were to land. More reinforcements would land about a week later—principally the 182nd Regimental Combat Team (less the III Battalion) from General Patch's Americal Division at Noumea, to which the 164th Infantry, already on Guadalcanal, also belonged.

These plans were still being executed when General Vandergrift thrust once again across the Matanikau River somewhat as the marines had done early in October. At daybreak on 1st November the first phase of a lavish support program opened: artillery, mortars, aircraft and naval guns combined to beat down opposition in front of the advancing marines. When light came the attack had made about 1,000 yards.

On the 2nd the advance continued and three marine battalions trapped the defending Japanese at Point Cruz. There was bloody work with the bayonet there before the surviving Japanese were driven into the sea, leaving behind some 350 dead, twelve 37-mm guns, one field piece and thirty-four machine-guns. Next day Colonel John M. Arthur pressed still farther ahead with two battalions of his own 2nd Marines and the I Battalion of the 164th Infantry. By the afternoon he was about 2,000 yards west of Point Cruz though still more than two miles short of Kokumbona. There Vandergrift halted him. East of the Lunga a new Japanese venture seemed to be burgeoning at Koli Point.

The Americans had correctly forecast this new move and the II Battalion of the 7th Marines, hastily moving eastwards, had established themselves east of Koli Point and just across the mouth of the Metapona River, by nightfall of the 2nd. They knew that some Japanese survivors of the previously unsuccessful attempts on the Lunga perimeter were already near by. In the rain and early darkness of that night a Japanese cruiser, a transport and three destroyers loomed offshore about a mile farther east and landed men and supplies. Next morning the II/7th Marines found themselves hard pressed by a westward thrust from that

[2] Miller, pp. 172-3.
In August and October the 40th US Division was sent to Hawaii and the 43rd to New Zealand. There were then ten US divisions overseas in the Pacific areas: in Hawaii the 24th, 25th, 27th and 40th; in the South Pacific Area the 1st Marine, Americal, 37th and 43rd; in the South-West Pacific Area, the 32nd and 41st.

position, fell back some distance, and crossed the Nalimbiu River to hold from its western bank. Meanwhile, American and naval units had been turned loose on this new threat; the I Battalion of the 7th Marines was hastily embarking on a small craft to the aid of the other battalion; the 164th Infantry (less a battalion) was preparing to set off overland from the Ilu River to contain the Japanese left south of Koli Point.

By 4th November Brigadier-General William H. Rupertus, who had been allotted immediate responsibility for the new sortie, had reached Koli Point with the water-borne reinforcements; the 164th and a company of the 8th Marines were moving eastwards; the 2nd Raider Battalion, just arrived at Aola Bay, was ordered to push westward towards Koli Point. The Americans thus, taking no chances, were in a most favourable tactical position, with a force strong enough to deal with a really serious threat.

Night of 7th November saw them defensively located about one mile west of the mouth of the Metapona. On the 8th the two Marine battalions and the II Battalion of the 164th located and almost encircled the main Japanese positions on the east bank of Gavaga Creek which paralleled the Metapona just to the east. General Vandergrift then withdrew part of the force, in order to press home new attacks he had planned against Kokumbona on the other side of the Lunga. As these left on the 9th, the remaining Americans closed their trap more firmly until they held a curved line from the beach on the east bank to the beach on the west bank of the sickle-shaped bend at the mouth of Gavaga Creek, with only one gap—at the southern extremity—where two companies of the 164th had failed to link. Through this gap many of the Japanese apparently escaped while others had withdrawn inland earlier. After another three days, however, the Americans had cleared the remaining pocket. They then reported that they had killed 450 for the loss of some 40 of their own men killed and 120 wounded.

Before this climax had been reached at Koli Point General Vandergrift had once more resumed his drive west of the Matanikau. On 10th November Colonel Arthur led out a strong force from Point Cruz (to which he had drawn back from the most westerly limit of his previous advance). By midday on the 11th they were just past the line of the penetration of 4th November. Vandergrift then had word that large, fresh invading forces were on their way by sea against him. He would need his whole force concentrated in the Lunga area. He therefore once more ordered Arthur to disengage. This the latter did so swiftly that his whole force was back across the Matanikau on the 12th. The Americans then destroyed their bridges and packed their ground forces tight within their main perimeter while they awaited the results of the efforts of their navy and air to keep the new invasion from the island.

By this time they had a fairly complete picture of the assemblage of ships in the harbours Truk, Rabaul, Buin—an unfailing barometer of Japanese intention. Scouting aircraft had reported a great many transports and cargo ships and, in addition, 2 aircraft carriers, 4 battleships, 5 heavy cruisers and 30 destroyers. In contrast Admiral Halsey's main force consisted of

24 submarines (which had destroyed a number of ships along the Japanese sea lanes to Guadalcanal), one aircraft carrier, 2 battleships, 4 heavy and one light cruisers, 3 light anti-aircraft cruisers, 22 destroyers and 7 transports and cargo ships. These were in two task forces, one under Admiral Turner responsible for the defence of Guadalcanal and the transport of troops and supplies to the island, and a carrier force at Noumea under Admiral Kinkaid (to support Turner as necessary) consisting of the carrier *Enterprise*, 2 battleships, one heavy and one anti-aircraft light cruiser and 8 destroyers.

Turner divided his force again into three groups. One, a transport group under his own direct command, moving out of Noumea to Guadalcanal with reinforcements and supplies, was to be covered by a second, under Rear-Admiral Daniel J. Callaghan, operating from Espiritu Santo. The third, under Rear-Admiral Norman Scott, like Callaghan's operating from Espiritu Santo, was to bring fresh troops and supplies from that island to Guadalcanal.

On 8th November Turner's four transports, escorted by two of Callaghan's cruisers and three of his destroyers, stood out from Noumea and rendezvoused with the rest of Callaghan's warships off San Cristobal on the 11th. Meanwhile, closely guarding three transports, Scott had arrived off Guadalcanal early that morning. Japanese bombers made the day an uncomfortable one for him and, with the coming of night, he withdrew from the immediate vicinity of Guadalcanal. Later he linked with Callaghan and Turner. Dawn of the 12th found all the transports busily unloading at Lunga Point with the warships standing offshore. Turner, expecting the arrival of a fresh Japanese fleet, was anxious to get the seven transports emptied and away again as soon as possible. But unloading was interrupted about the middle of the afternoon when some 25 torpedo bombers swept at the ships. Callaghan's flagship—the cruiser *San Francisco*—and the destroyer *Buchanan* were hit but none of the transports were damaged. Most of the attackers were shot down and unloading went on in the later afternoon.

The morning had brought news of the approach of a Japanese naval force which Turner assessed as 2 battleships, 2 to 4 heavy cruisers and 10 to 12 destroyers. These were obviously intent on the destruction of ships, or the bombardment of the airfield, or both. Turner, naturally anxious not to be caught by these purposeful craft, cut short his unloading at the end of the day (although it was still unfinished) and sent his soft-skinned vessels out of the danger area under a close escort. But, though the ships might elude the hunters, the shore defences could not. Callaghan therefore turned to protect the island, taking Scott with the latter's flagship *Atlanta* and two of his destroyers under his command. His whole force then consisted of 2 heavy and 3 light cruisers and 8 destroyers.

Headed towards Savo, Callaghan located the Japanese ships at 1.24 a.m. between Savo and Cape Esperance, but his radar was not strong enough definitely to find the position either of his own scattered forces or those of his enemies. The battle quickly became a mêlée, a naval free for all, with friend often not knowing foe across the dark waters. Both Callaghan and Scott were killed. But though the Americans were harshly handled the Japanese gave up their attempt to break through and withdrew. The new day, however, exposed crippled and rescue ships of both sides on the glittering sea between Savo and Guadalcanal. These still struck dying blows at one another. Among them was a stricken Japanese battleship. American airmen kept at her during the day and, when night came, her crew scuttled her. But not only the Americans had a sting left for, about 11 a.m., limping away from the battle scene where she had been almost sundered by a torpedo, the cruiser *Juneau* was torpedoed again—by a lurking submarine—and sank at the base of a great pillar of smoke with all but ten of her crew.

Twelve of the thirteen American ships which had been engaged were sunk or damaged. The cruisers *Atlanta* and *Juneau* had gone and four destroyers with them. The heavy cruisers *San Francisco* and *Portland*, with three destroyers, were seriously damaged. With the two remaining ships they made for Espiritu Santo after the battle. The Japanese lost the battleship *Hiyei* and two destroyers and had four destroyers damaged. But though numerically they fared the better, and lost far fewer men than the Americans, they failed in their object. This (it was learnt later) was to put Henderson Field completely out of action to give a run, clear of air interference, for an invasion fleet which was behind them.

To deliver this first blow Admiral Kondo, in command of the naval side of the new invasion, had sent Vice-Admiral Hiroaki Abe out from Truk on the 9th with the battleships *Hiyei* and *Kirishima* screened by light forces. Abe subsequently rendezvoused with more destroyers which put out from the Shortlands on the 11th. His group then consisted of the two battleships, the light cruiser *Nagara* and 14 destroyers, and this was the force which Callaghan met. (After the battle Admiral Abe was removed from his command, sent to a shore posting, and retired at an early age after a short "face-saving" period ashore.)

Before Callaghan and Abe clashed, Admiral Kinkaid, who had been racing time at Noumea where his carrier *Enterprise* was being repaired after the Santa Cruz battle, was boiling towards Guadalcanal although repair gangs were still hard at work on the ship. On the morning of the 13th, still between 300 and 400 miles from Guadalcanal, he flew off some aircraft to base them temporarily on Henderson Field since his carrier was still not able to operate with complete efficiency. The first target these sighted was the crippled *Hiyei* and they joyfully bore down on her. Meanwhile Admiral Halsey had ordered Kinkaid to cover, by remaining well to the south of Guadalcanal, the withdrawal of ships damaged the previous night. Later he told Kinkaid to have his heavy-gun vessels ready for a quick dash to Guadalcanal on orders from him—so Rear-Admiral Willis A. Lee waited at the alert with two battleships, *Washington* and *South Dakota*, and four destroyers. When, however, Halsey, having learned that a new bombardment force was on its way to pound Henderson Field on the night 13th-14th, sent orders for Lee to close on it, Kinkaid's group was still too far away to permit of this being done. Although Lee raced off he knew he could not reach Guadalcanal before about 8 a.m. next day.

Vice-Admiral Mikawa profited (although unknowingly) by this error. He had put out from the Shortlands about 6.30 a.m. with 4 heavy cruisers (*Chokai, Kinugasa, Suzuya* and *Maya*), 2 light cruisers (*Isuzu* and *Tenryu*) and 6 destroyers, as Kondo had planned to follow up Abe's initial attack on Henderson Field with lighter blows from Mikawa the following night. He saw no reason to change his orders to Mikawa simply because Abe had failed, and so, with Callaghan and Scott dead and their force broken, with Kinkaid and Lee far to the south, and with night keeping the airmen earthbound, there was little to hinder Mikawa when he arrived off Savo soon after midnight on the 13th. Peeling a patrol group off to westward under his own command he sent Rear-Admiral Shoji Nishimura to drench Henderson Field with high explosive. This the latter did, for thirty-seven minutes, with only two motor torpedo boats to worry him.

> Back in Washington it was still the morning of Friday the Thirteenth. Everyone hoped that Callaghan's sacrifice had stopped the enemy; it was a shock to hear that heavy surface forces had broken through and were shelling Henderson Field. And when, a few hours later, word came that Japanese transports were heading down the Slot unopposed by surface forces, even President Roosevelt began to think that Guadalcanal might have to be evacuated. "The tension that I felt at that time," recalled Secretary Forrestal, "was matched only by the tension that pervaded Washington the night before the landing in Normandy."[3]

Early on the 14th aircraft reported more fighting ships and some transports headed for Guadalcanal, and Mikawa's retiring Support Group some 140 miles north-west. Other aircraft then attacked Mikawa. They left *Kinugasa* burning and *Isuzu* smoking heavily. Shortly before 10 o'clock aircraft launched from *Enterprise* pressed the attacks home and saw *Kinugasa* sink. Before Mikawa got clear, he also suffered damage to *Chokai*, *Maya*, and a destroyer.

Unwittingly Mikawa had served as a decoy to draw attention from Rear-Admiral Raizo Tanaka's Reinforcement Group—11 merchantmen escorted by 11 destroyers. Tanaka, obedient to Kondo's orders for the third phase of his plan, was bringing these down to Guadalcanal laden with reinforcements. He had led them out from the Shortlands on the 12th. Sensibly he had sheltered on the 13th—in preparation for a dash on the 14th to enable him to discharge his troops under cover of darkness that night. But the gods were against him. Henderson Field, despite all Kondo's planning, was still very much alive; Kinkaid's carrier-borne aircraft fanned in high and fast from the south, and heavy aircraft from Espiritu Santo joined in. By the end of the day seven of the eleven transports had been sunk.

But still bigger events were pending. It will be recalled that Admiral Lee had left Kinkaid's main force early in the night of the 13th in a northward

---

[3] S. E. Morison, *The Struggle for Guadalcanal* (1950), p. 263, a volume in the series *History of United States Naval Operations in World War II*.

dash—though he was too far south to permit him to arrive off Guadalcanal in the darkness which had sheltered Mikawa's attack on the island. To avoid detection he had stood about 100 miles off shore during daylight on the 14th. He had listened with interest to the news of the fight with Mikawa and Tanaka but what really touched him closely was a report, about 4 p.m., that a large battle force was southbound from an area about 150 miles north of Guadalcanal.

Lee had very little detailed information of the composition of this force when he manoeuvred to intercept it. He was to learn later that it was Admiral Kondo's main force—the battleship *Kirishima,* 2 heavy cruisers (*Atago* and *Takao*), 2 light cruisers (*Nagara* and *Sendai*), and 11 destroyers. Prowling through the darkness round Savo, Lee made his first radar contact with these at 11 p.m. Seventeen minutes later he fired his opening rounds. Five minutes later the main battle was joined. But Kondo, cunningly deployed, soon had the Americans confused as to the relative positions of their own and the ships they were fighting. At 11.35 p.m. the opening phase of the battle ended with four American destroyers out of action without having launched a single torpedo, the battleship *South Dakota* blind through failure of power supply, the second battleship in confusion as it manoeuvred to avoid burning destroyers and found its radar echoes bouncing back off Savo. Only one Japanese ship—a destroyer —had been hit.

Soon afterwards Lee ordered his destroyers out of the engagement. Seven minutes later *South Dakota* was the centre of a concentrated torpedo attack. And then shells began crashing into her. But quickly *Washington* took up her cause. She engaged *Kirishima* as her primary target, and within seven minutes *Kirishima* was aflame and her steering gear was shot away. But *South Dakota,* badly battered, was also out of the fight. The outcome was still uncertain as the main battle flickered out. It was twenty-five minutes after midnight when Kondo ordered all ships not actively engaged to withdraw, eight minutes later when Lee, having observed the beginning of this retirement, ordered the withdrawal of his own forces.

In the small hours the Japanese, with vivid recollections of the ordeal the wounded *Hiyei* had suffered, scuttled their battleship *Kirishima* and the destroyer *Ayanami.* Three of Lee's destroyers went down, the fourth limped painfully to safety, the big *South Dakota* had been heavily hit 42 times, had lost 91 men killed or wounded.

Admiral Tanaka was still struggling on with his 11 destroyers sticking close to his four remaining merchantmen. When daylight came on the morning of the 15th it showed three of these four vulnerable ships unloading at Tassafaronga Point to the west of Kokumbona, with the fourth moving slowly offshore. The marines' artillery, the destroyer *Meade* from Tulagi, and swarming aircraft, destroyed all four while hundreds of sailors, shipwrecked in the battle of the previous night watched from the wreckages and rafts to which they clung. Then the aircraft began systematically to fire the beach stores until the shore seemed almost one long blaze.

This destruction marked the final failure of the Japanese attempts in November to put the issue at Guadalcanal beyond doubt. The whole failure cost the invaders two battleships, one heavy cruiser, three destroyers and 11 merchantmen sunk, and two heavy cruisers, one light cruiser and six destroyers damaged. Against that loss stood the sinking of ten American ships (one light cruiser, two light anti-aircraft cruisers, seven destroyers) and the damaging of one battleship, two heavy cruisers and four destroyers.

The Japanese plan for these two November weeks became known later. It will be recalled that, after the failure of the Ichiki and Kawaguchi formations, General Hyakutake had landed by mid-October the *2nd Division* and two battalions of the *38th Division*; that, in the ill-fated October ventures, General Maruyama had attacked the Lunga defences from the south in association with attacks from the Matanikau.

Subsequent to his failure Hyakutake decided to bring in more of his *XVII Army*; to convoy the balance (the major part) of the *38th Division* down from Rabaul in a single group of transports—although certain elements of the *228th Infantry* were trickled in to the beaches west of Kokumbona between 28th October and 8th November. His original plan envisaged a major landing at Koli Point and an attack from the Matanikau area. To prepare a clear run for the invaders the navy would bombard Henderson Field as a preliminary to the arrival of the convoy.

Subsidiary to the main plan was the minor operation to land supplies with a few additional troops at Koli Point to assist the survivors of the right wing of the Maruyama assault who had made their way to that point after the October disaster and were to build an airfield on the flat plain south of Koli Point. This landing took place as planned on the night of 2nd-3rd November, but was brought to nothing by the prompt American move westward to meet it under General Rupertus. Hyakutake thereupon abandoned his airfield-construction plans and ordered his men to circle back to Kokumbona by the inland route. Further disaster then attended them, however, for the larger part of the Koli Point force, having escaped the American trap there, were dogged in their retreat by the Raiders who had come in from the east. The Raiders hung like leeches from their flanks and claimed to have killed 400 for the loss of only 17 of their own men before they reported in to the Lunga on 4th December.

Admiral Kondo had planned the two successive blows at Henderson Field which Abe and Mikawa had attempted—the former without success, the latter with some immediate success for which, however, he paid dearly next day. The two later phases of Kondo's plan were the running in of some 10,000 *XVII Army* men (with all their heavy equipment) under Admiral Tanaka's protection, and his own main assault on the island. But Tanaka's merchantmen were destroyed; probably not more than about 2,000 men got ashore and only a small part of the equipment and stores survived the sinkings and the subsequent air attacks. Tanaka's decision to continue after the loss of his first seven ships on the 14th was a most courageous one. He could have turned back to his base and landed no reinforcements at all. But knowingly he traded his remaining ships for the chance of getting sufficient fresh troops ashore to give Hyakutake a chance of ousting the Americans. Kondo's own last effort, of course, was brought to nothing by Admiral Lee, and the last of Tanaka's ships were consigned to destruction.

With the naval-air battle of these November days the Guadalcanal campaign mounted its climax, for the success or failure of the fighting ashore at this critical time was almost entirely dependent upon it. The frustration of the Japanese attempts at sea meant that they must now mount another major naval effort before they could hope for the reconquest of the island. Whether they could do that, or whether they would be prepared to accept the risks of attempting it, was still to be seen. And since the hinge on which victory was swinging in the southern Solomons was a naval one, it is fitting that the summing up of this phase should be done by the American naval historian:

> Both fleets retired from the field of battle; both countries claimed a tremendous victory. In view of what each was trying to do, and in the light of future events, who really won?
> Both objectives were similar: to reinforce one's own garrison on Guadalcanal but deny it to the enemy by air and sea. With that yardstick the conclusion is unmistakable: Turner got every one of his troops and almost all his materiel ashore, while Tanaka the Tenacious managed to land only about 2,000 shaken survivors, 260 cases of ammunition and 1,500 bags of rice. The Americans dominated the air from start to finish and kept possession of Henderson Field. On the surface, Callaghan chased one force out of Ironbottom Sound, losing his life and several ships in the process, and Lee disposed of Kondo's second attempt to follow the Mahan doctrine. Air losses were far greater on the Japanese side. Of combat ships the United States Navy sustained the greater loss, but the elimination of two battleships and 11 transports from the Japanese Fleet was far more serious. The enemy could accept a heavy loss of troops because he had plenty of replacements, but he could not replace battleships or transports, and he depended on air and surface fleets to stop any American offensive against Greater East Asia. . . . In torpedo tactics and night action, this series of engagements showed that tactically the Japanese were still a couple of semesters ahead of the United States Navy, but their class standing took a decided drop in the subject of war-plan execution. Why was Admiral Mikawa permitted to abandon the area and the transports on the morning of the 14th? Without his muscle-men, the big-bellied transports waddled into a veritable slaughter-house. Again, with Henderson Field still a going concern and an American carrier snorting back and forth southward of Guadalcanal, why did carriers *Hiyo* and *Junyo* hang far back to the north-westward, instead of steaming down to square an unfavourable balance of air power? Lastly, why were the transports not recalled to Shortland to reorganise (as at Wake in December 1941) when it became apparent that the operation was not proceeding according to book? . . . a captured Japanese document admitted: "It must be said that the success or failure in recapturing Guadalcanal Island, and the vital naval battle related to it, is the fork in the road which leads to victory for them or for us."[4]

The same mid-November days which were thus proving critical ones in the Solomons saw a new phase opening in New Guinea. There, it will be remembered, in addition to the Australian forces pushing down to the Buna-Gona coast over the Kokoda Track, two columns (mainly American)

---

[4] Morison, *The Struggle for Guadalcanal*, pp. 285-7.

were approaching Buna from the south-east and the south, according to a plan which had developed chiefly from the Australian occupation of Wanigela in early October when the 2/10th Battalion was flown there from Milne Bay.

As a preliminary to this advance a small seaborne expedition was mounted against the Japanese survivors of the Milne Bay invasion force who had been marooned on Goodenough Island late in August. This, in its turn, however, had been preceded by a smaller expedition of a similar kind to Normanby Island.

There, survivors from a Japanese destroyer, which had been sunk by aircraft on 11th September, had been reported. While their presence did not constitute any military problem, Captain Timperly of Angau

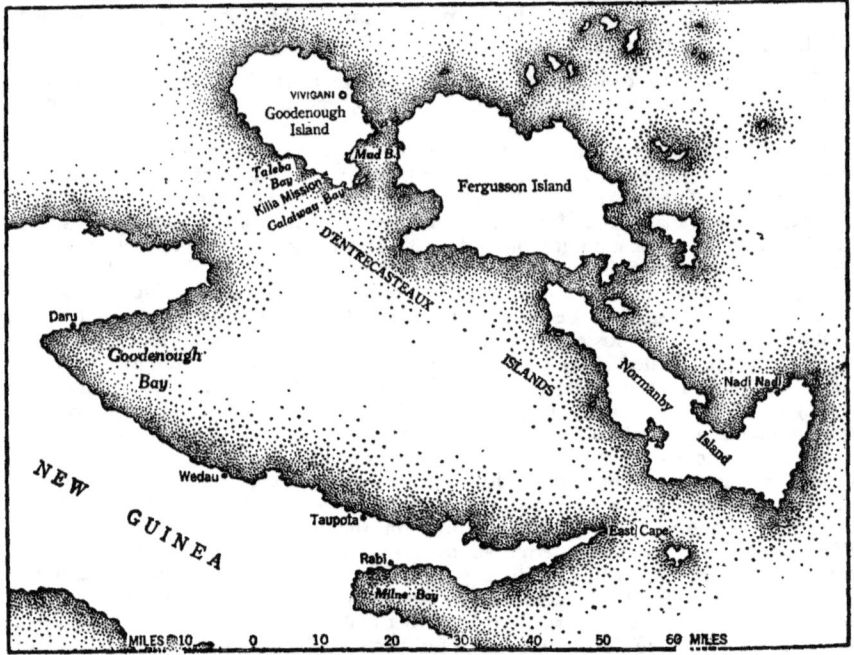

believed that their continued undisputed existence on the island was lessening Australian prestige among the natives and rendering administration difficult.

On 21st September, in H.M.A.S. *Stuart*, Captain J. E. Brocksopp of the 2/10th Battalion moved with his company, and certain attachments, against this shipwrecked group. He landed at Nadi Nadi at dawn next day. But the country was rough and tangled and Brocksopp was not able to bring the fugitives to battle. The natives were cooperative, and through them Brocksopp was able to take eight prisoners, all except one of whom were wounded. He found much evidence of Japanese occupation and the natives told him of parties living and moving in the area, the largest probably being about fifty to sixty strong. Two Japanese warships patrolled the coasts and turned searchlights on the shore that night but took no other action. Brocksopp embarked his party again on the *Stuart,* without incident, on the afternoon of the 23rd. He was convinced that the only way successfully to carry out such operations would be by using small craft in a series of little "aquatic hooks".

On 19th October Lieut-Colonel Arnold was told to take his 2/12th Battalion and certain attached troops to Goodenough Island; to destroy there approximately 300 Japanese marines whom native reports indicated were concentrated in the Galaiwau Bay-Kilia Mission area in the extreme south-eastern section of the island; to reconnoitre the approaches to the island and suitable sites for airfields and to re-establish coastwatching and air warning stations in the area.

Arnold planned to land his main battalion group (less one company group under Major Gategood) at Mud Bay, on the east coast. He would move slightly south of west to Kilia Mission, some four hours' march he was told, across the mountains which ran down the centre of the isthmus which formed the southern extremity of the island. Gategood and his men were to land at Taleba Bay, on the west coast of the isthmus immediately opposite Mud Bay and six miles distant as the crow flies. When the main thrust pushed the Japanese from Kilia they would tend to move north-west round the coast and come against the waiting Gategood some four miles only from the mission. Thus he would destroy them. After close scrutiny from the air of the area of their proposed operations by himself and his company commanders, Arnold embarked his main force in H.M.A.S. *Arunta* and Gategood's men in H.M.A.S. *Stuart.*

The landing at Mud Bay began soon after dark on 22nd October. Silence was to be one of its features as the soldiers trans-shipped to small vessels and went ashore through a beach-head made by Headquarters Company. But the rattle of racing chains as the destroyer cast her anchor echoed round the island, two landing craft collided with a crash in the darkness, and at least one other ran on a mud bank so that weapons and equipment clattered as soldiers fell heavily in the boat itself or into the water. There was some confusion on the beach as the companies sorted themselves out. Altogether the landing, planned as a standard amphibious operation on a small scale, did not go smoothly.

With his own headquarters and a lightly-equipped force of three companies Arnold pushed inland towards Kilia Mission at 11 p.m., guided by native policemen. But the Angau men who had described the approach had not taken into account their own practised ease in moving unburdened through the mountains when they had described the march as a four-hour one, a description which might have been applicable to their own movement on a fine day. The soldiers found the going most difficult. It was raining heavily.

This, in conjunction with the steep, slippery track, made the ascent of the intervening hills very difficult (said Arnold later). It was quite a common practice for men to slip back fifteen yards, to laboriously climb again, only to slide back once more. The men were soaked through and through by rain and perspiration. It was not till 0300 hrs 23rd October that the summit of the range was reached. Thereafterwards the descent became more hazardous than the climb.

Meanwhile Gategood's party, a little over 100 strong, had landed at Taleba Bay in the darkness of the early morning of the 23rd.

Arnold had timed his attack on Kilia for 6 a.m. but the slow and difficult going threw his plans out. It was not until 8.30 that his tired leading troops, Captain Ivey's company, met Japanese about half a mile north of the mission. The Australians found that their way lay through a narrow pass opening on to a stream which flowed at right angles to their line of advance. Beyond the stream a high feature, heavily wooded, rose steeply. Fire from positions which they could not locate, and grenades rolled down upon them, prevented Arnold's men from crossing the water. They were wearied by their march. Arnold decided that they should rest before attacking strongly on the 24th.

During this arduous day, try as he might, Arnold could not reach Gategood by wireless although, in the distance, he could hear firing at intervals. Actually, Gategood had struck determined opposition soon after his landing.

At first light he had moved inland along a native track. At 5.45 a.m. he encountered the Japanese, lightly at first but the resistance quickly grew. His men pushed on through waist-high grass, firing from standing positions as they advanced. They cleared the initial opposition and repulsed a sharp counter-attack about 9, but had difficulty in locating their opponents among the bush and were losing men. Company headquarters came under fire from what seemed to be a heavy mortar.

After the first encounter Gategood had tried unsuccessfully to get into wireless touch with Arnold. In the absence of news of any kind he began to fear that the drive from the other side of the isthmus had been delayed. His own position was worsening, with six of his men killed, and eleven wounded. At 10.45, worried by lack of news of the rest of the battalion, he began to withdraw towards the beach. But the cutter, approaching the shore to pick up the wounded, came under heavy fire and his difficulties were thus increased. Still lacking news of the main operations as the day went on, he feared they had miscarried so, moving to a more sheltered position, he embarked his company and set out for Mud Bay. He reported there next morning, the 24th.

By that time Arnold was just mounting his second attack. It met with no more success than that of the previous day. The Australians were unable to locate the Japanese positions. Arnold said "It was this inability to discover the firers that took the sting out of the attack". Captain Suthers, leading one of the attacking companies, gave an example of this difficulty:

> The country was so close that I got eight feet off a Japanese machine-gun and did not see it. I signalled to a signaller to put the phone on the wire. The moment I pressed the key he [the enemy] fired all he had, hit three of my men. The burnt cordite from the gun was hitting us in the face it was so close.

On the 25th Arnold had prepared an air support program and had two mortars forward. The aircraft did not arrive, however. Nevertheless, when he pushed forward he found that the Japanese had made off. His men moved down to the mission and the beach through an elaborately prepared (but unmanned) defence area. Later he returned part of his force to Mud Bay by sea and part returned over the mountains. The battalion then settled to work to build an airstrip in the Vivigani area, about halfway up the east coast.

In the entire operations the 2/12th lost 13 men killed and one officer and 18 men wounded. They took one prisoner and estimated that they killed 39 Japanese. What had become of the balance of the force they could still only guess.

It was learned later that approximately 350 Japanese of the *5th Sasebo Naval Landing Force* had originally been stranded on the island. At first they had been left without rations. They were supplied later, however, by submarines, which also took off about 60 sick and wounded. The Japanese had, in fact, been aware of the Australian landings from the time they began. In the fighting which followed they lost some 20 men killed and 15 wounded. All of the survivors were taken in two barges to Fergusson Island soon after they broke off the engagement. A cruiser picked them up there and took them to Rabaul.

After the Goodenough Island episode, only one battalion of the 18th Brigade was left at Milne Bay; and, after the development of the advanced base at Wanigela, the rest of the brigade had been ready to fly to Wanigela or elsewhere at short notice. This did not mean, however, that the Allied commanders were content progressively to weaken the Milne Bay base or did not fear further attacks there. Indeed, they were well aware of the necessity to secure the area against further Japanese attacks and to build it strongly as their own right-flank bastion. Other seasoned troops were, therefore, brought in to strengthen it. By the middle of October an advanced party of the 17th Brigade, newly returned from Ceylon, arrived at Gili Gili and the battalions followed closely.

The base at Milne Bay, the freedom of the flanking D'Entrecasteaux Islands from Japanese ground forces and airfields, and the development of their own forward airfield at Wanigela, meant that the Americans and the Australians could confidently plan supply by sea as their basic supply line for their coastwise movement. Responsibility for the development of the sea line (and supply generally) fell, early in October, to a Combined Operational Services Command (C.O.S.C.).

The maintenance of fighting forces in New Guinea (as elsewhere overseas) demanded the development of a base port with its many associated installations and facilities: docks; roads for the distribution of supplies to depots; buildings to protect stores against the weather, for camps and for hospitals; water-supply systems. Initially Milne Bay lacked all of these facilities; Port Moresby itself was only slightly less deficient. Administrative installations at these places had to be developed concurrently with offensive operations against the Japanese. The problem of supplying and servicing the Australian Army alone was difficult enough. In addition the United States Army and the Allied Air Forces had to be supplied and serviced, each with an administrative organisation and system differing from that of the Australian Army and from that of each other.

To meet the difficult administrative situation, and having conferred closely with General Blamey, on 5th October General MacArthur ordered the immediate establishment at Port Moresby of C.O.S.C.—to operate under the control of the Commander, New Guinea Force; to include all Australian Lines of Communications units and the United States Service of Supply; to be

> charged with the coordination of all construction and sanitation, except that incident to combat operations; and all Line of Communications activities including those listed below:
>
> a. Docking, unloading, and loading of all ships.
> b. Receipt, storage, and distribution of supplies and materials.
> c. Receipt, staging, and dispatch of personnel.
> d. Transportation in Line of Communications areas, or incident to Line of Communications or supply activities.
> e. The operation of repair shops, depots, and major utilities.
> f. Hospitalisation and evacuation.
> g. Such other activities as may be designated by the Commander "New Guinea Force".[5]

On 8th October Brigadier-General Dwight F. Johns, of the United States Army, assumed command of C.O.S.C. with Brigadier Secombe,[6] an Australian, as his deputy. The organisation the two were to build up was a radical departure from that which the Australian Army considered normal administrative procedure, but it was adequately to meet the novel demands of a campaign in a country lacking roads and railways, in which all transport had fundamentally to be by sea or air, and in which often the administrative or base areas coincided with the operational areas. Of the C.O.S.C. operations and organisation Johns was to report later:

> From its outset the Combined Operational Service Command was visualised and has been considered largely as a coordinating agency between the American and Australian Forces operating in the New Guinea theatre of operations. . . . It was organised on the bases of parallelism, representatives of the Australian and American Services handling the details of the various activities with respect of their particular Services, operating in close cooperation with each other and closely coordinating activities at all times. Following this general principle, for instance, practically all supervisory functions and command activities with respect to Australian units has been exercised by Brigadier Secombe and with respect to American units, by the undersigned. Detailed discussion on all problems arising and the agreement between Brigadier Secombe and myself as to the appropriate solution and action has, at all times, been arrived at as a basis for action and directives. In a similar way coordination between the American and Australian representatives on the Combined Operational Service Command staff having to do with supply, transportation, hospitalisation and evacuation, and construction has been attained. . . .

---

[5] New Guinea Force Report—COSC. G460.11.
[6] Lt-Gen V. C. Secombe, CB, CBE, VX12701. (1st AIF: Lt 15 Fd Coy.) CRE 7 Div 1940-41; AA&QMG 7 Div 1941; DDST I Corps and HQ AIF ME 1941-42; DA&QMG I Corps and NG Force 1943; DAQMG Adv LHQ 1944-45. Regular soldier; of Canberra; b. Glen Wills, Vic, 9 Jan 1897.

Perhaps the major feature with respect to transportation involved the provision of additional dockage and unloading facilities at Port Moresby and the coordination of unloading activities in order to increase the capacity of this port. This construction and coordination in activities resulted in the increase of the cargo handling record of the port from something under 2,000 tons daily to an average over a considerable period of time of approximately 6,000 tons daily with a peak day of just over 8,500 tons.

Other elements of the transportation responsibility of Combined Operational Service Command involved the coordinated utilisation of ocean shipping consisting of both large ships operated under the Army Transport Service of USASOS, and under Movement Control of the Australian Army, as well as small ships, trawlers, tug and harbour boats, operated under U.S. Advanced Base, the Australian Army Water Transport Group, and Angau. The action of C.O.S.C. with respect to large ships was concerned with coordination of shipping operations between New Guinea and the mainland of Australia, and of the employment on missions in this theatre of certain of these ships.[7]

Against the administrative background thus developing, the 126th U.S. Regiment, it will be recalled, had been given the task of crossing from the south coast of Papua overland by way of Jaure, but the difficulties of the track and the development of the airfield at Wanigela had combined to produce a change of plan. Only one battalion crossed the Jaure Track. The rest of the regiment was to be flown to the north coast to begin a landward advance on Buna from the south. Meanwhile, the 128th Regiment had been flown to Wanigela.

Both regiments belonged to Major-General Edwin F. Harding's 32nd Division, a National Guard (or, in Australian terms, a militia) formation from Michigan and Wisconsin, which had been on full-time duty for two years. Harding had landed his division in Adelaide in May 1942 and it had moved to Brisbane by August as the Allied emphasis began to shift northward. He said later:

From February when I took over, until November when we went into battle, we were always getting ready to move, on the move or getting settled after a move.

This, apparently, was considered the prime reason why an effective standard of training had not been reached by the time Lieut-General Eichelberger arrived in Australia to command the American Corps late in August.[8]

Not only was the 32nd Division's training deficient but, after their arrival in New Guinea, the men quickly found that some of their weapons, and much of their clothing and equipment, were unsatisfactory and that they had to modify many details of their organisation. The proportion of sub-machine-guns was increased; two platoons of each of the heavy weapons companies were issued with light machine-guns, the third with either two 81-mm or four 60-mm mortars; each Cannon Company had four 81-mm mortars. The divisional artillery was perforce left behind;

---
[7] New Guinea Force Report, COSC, G460.11.
[8] The AIF landed on Gallipoli in 1915 approximately 8 months after its formation in Australia; the 6th Division took part in the advance into Libya at the end of 1940, approximately 15 months after its formation in Australia; the 20th Australian Brigade repulsed General Rommel's first attacks on Tobruk in April 1941, approximately 9 months after its formation. During these months the battalions of the 20th Brigade either singly or as a formation served at Ingleburn, NSW; Bathurst, NSW; Brisbane, and Darwin, and in Palestine, Egypt and Libya.

the divisional engineers were too few in numbers for their many tasks and took only hand tools with them into the bush.

The Americans also underestimated the toll that the country would exact from them and the numbers and spirit of the Japanese they would meet. On 14th October General Harding had written to General Sutherland:

> My idea is that we should push towards Buna with all speed, while the Japs are heavily occupied with the Guadalcanal business. Also, we have complete supremacy in the air here, and the air people could do a lot to help in the taking of Buna, even should it be fairly strongly defended, which I doubt. I think it quite possible that we might find it easy pickings, with only a shell of sacrifice troops left to defend it and Kokoda. This may be a bum guess, but even if it proves to be incorrect I don't think it would be too much trouble to take Buna with the forces we can put against it.

He followed this on the 31st with:

> All information we have to date indicates that the Japanese forces in the Buna-Popondetta-Gona triangle are relatively light. Unless he gets reinforcements, I believe we will be fighting him on at least a three to one basis. Imbued as I am with considerable confidence in the fighting qualities of the American soldier, I am not at all pessimistic about the outcome of the scrap. . . . The health of the troops has been remarkably good. The sick rate is very low. If our luck holds in this respect, we should go into the operation with our effective strength reduced very little by sickness—less than four per cent, I would say.

His men shared their general's feelings for, when General MacArthur's order of 3rd November stipulated that ten days' supplies be built up in rear of each column before any further forward movement took place, an American observer noted:

> . . . Opinions were freely expressed by officers of all ranks . . . that the only reason for the order was a political one. GHQ was afraid to turn the Americans loose and let them capture Buna because it would be a blow to the prestige of the Australians who had fought the long hard battle all through the Owen Stanley Mountains, and who therefore should be the ones to capture Buna. The belief was prevalent that the Japanese had no intention of holding Buna; that he had no troops there; that he was delaying the Australians with a small force so as to evacuate as many as possible; that he no longer wanted the airfield there . . . that no Zeros had been seen in that area for a month; and that the Air Corps had prevented any reinforcements from coming in . . . and could prevent any future landing.[9]

By this time the triple overland-air-sea movement of the 126th and 128th Regiments had taken definite shape. After the 128th had been flown in to Wanigela in mid-October, had been prevented by floods from following the 2/6th Independent Company northward across country, and had had two boat-loads of their men attacked in error by an American aircraft as they were moving by sea to Pongani, they had finally slowly completed their seaward movement and were concentrated in the area from Oro Bay northwards to Cape Sudest by mid-November.

Meanwhile ill-fortune and some confusion had also attended the concentration of the 126th Regimental Combat Team. By the time the II Battalion had gathered at Jaure the Australian successes along the main

---

[9] Quoted in Milner, *Victory in Papua*, p. 138.

overland track suggested that a move by this battalion directly against Buna might profitably coincide with the Australian advance through Wairopi. The Americans therefore cast off a detachment under Captain Medendorp which left Jaure on 27th October, crossed the divide, and followed the Kumusi River down to Kovio to determine the Japanese dispositions and secure the battalion's advance against attack from the Wairopi flank. Although one of Medendorp's patrols had a brush with Japanese at Asisi, some 5 miles south of Wairopi, on 10th November, the latter showed no intention of moving up the trail through that area. Thus

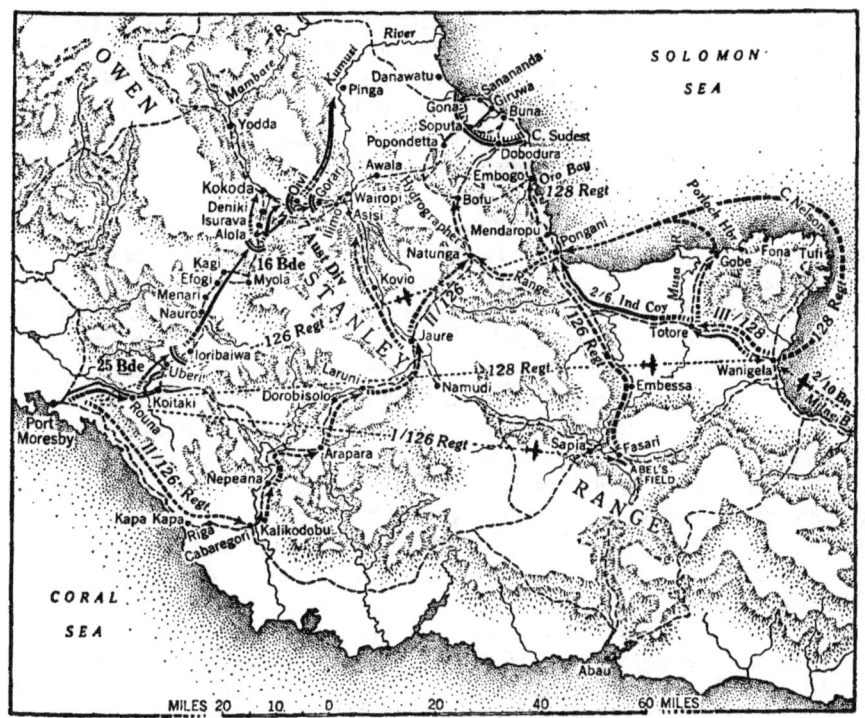

Allied advance across Owen Stanley Range towards Buna,
26th September-15th November

the battalion was able to travel eastward without incident, and on 14th November began to arrive at Natunga, about three days' westward march from Pongani and on the rugged slopes of the Hydrographer's Range.

Shortly before, however, Colonel Lawrence A. Quinn, commander of the 126th, surveying the difficult air dropping operations at Natunga and Bofu, had been killed when his supply plane, its tail fouled by a parachute, crashed in the mountains. Further setbacks followed within a few days. When the rest of the regiment was being flown across the mountains one transport crashed in the wild interior with the loss of all but six of the men it carried. (These six walked back to Abau and arrived there about a month later.) To complicate matters further some confusion developed as to whether the air movement should terminate at Pongani, where a landing strip had been completed early in November, or at Abel's Field in the mountainous country in the vicinity of Sapia, which, it was hoped, could be reached in four days by troops marching down from Abel's Field. As a result Colonel Edmund J. Carrier, the battalion commander, and most of I Battalion, were landed at Abel's Field, but regimental headquarters and III Battalion were put down at Pongani.

By mid-November detailed orders had gone out for a coordinated American-Australian advance on Buna. On the 14th General Herring told General Vasey that the Americans were spread along the line Oro Bay-Bofu. Between Bofu and Popondetta the Girua River flowed roughly north-east to the sea in the Buna-Sanananda area. Generally this river was to form the boundary between the American and the Australian forces. Buna was defined as the American objective, Sanananda and Gona as the Australian. The Americans were ordered to secure a crossing over the Girua near Soputa as soon as possible.

They planned to move northwards in two main columns—the 128th Regiment following the coastal track from the Embogo area to Cape Endaiadere, the 126th an inland axis to Soputa. The confusion whether the air move of the 126th should terminate at Abel's Field or Pongani twisted the plans for the inland move, however. On the 15th, with the general northward move timed to begin next day, Colonel Carrier's group were just marching into Pongani from Abel's Field, the II Battalion was at Bofu, and regimental headquarters and the III Battalion were at Natunga after a forced march from Pongani. It was decided then to ferry the I Battalion to Embogo and have them march thence west-north-west to Dobodura, where they would rejoin the regiment.

So the forward move began on the 16th; but further troubles came quickly. Ahead of the advanced base which had been established at Porlock Harbour the American supply line was an attenuated one composed of seven luggers, and a captured Japanese barge from Milne Bay. Late on the afternoon of the 16th, this barge, laden with two 25-pounders of Captain Mueller's[1] troop of the 2/5th Field Regiment (the troop had come round from Milne Bay to support the Americans), their crews and ammunition, left Oro Bay for Hariko, just north of Cape Sudest, in company with three of the luggers which carried rations, ammunition and men, each towing a boat or a pontoon. General Harding himself was on board one of the luggers, going forward to the front from the command post he had recently established at Mendaropu (just south of Oro Bay). As the little convoy rounded Cape Sudest fourteen Japanese Zero fighters came with the dusk. Soon all three luggers were blazing fiercely. Then the Australians on the barge watched their turn come.

> Three times a Zero made its swooping dives. Tracer bullets, leaving searing ribbons of flame in their paths, ripped into the hull of the barge and into the crouching bodies tightly packed aboard it. There was little that could be done

---
[1] Capt C. A. Mueller, NX12369; 2/5 Fd Regt. Accountant; of Sydney; b. Sydney, 10 Jan 1916.

in defence other than to keep cool and get behind anything offering a scrap of protection. These things the men did. A single light machine-gun had been set up on the stern. As the bright coloured rain of death poured down in graceful curves, Gnr A. G. King[2] stood to face the Zero. He fought the plane defiantly with this pitifully inadequate weapon. . . . Soon the barge was ablaze. Clouds of dense black smoke billowed upwards. Beneath this canopy the vessel was sinking fast.[3]

Five of the Australians were killed, sixteen wounded. In all, from the four craft, 24 men were lost, many more wounded. The survivors, including the general, swam ashore. Next morning more strafing Zeros put two more luggers out of action.

These misfortunes, besides resulting immediately in the loss of all the stores, including the two precious artillery pieces, completely disrupted the Americans' supply plans. Until they could establish an airfield at Dobodura, where one had been planned, they would be almost completely dependent upon supplies dropped from the air. General Harding, therefore, at once ordered General MacNider temporarily to halt the advance of the 128th Regiment until one of the remaining luggers could reach him; and set off on a 30-mile march with full packs the men who were still to be ferried forward from Pongani: Colonel Carrier's detachment of the I/126th Battalion, a company of the 128th Regiment, an engineer company, and the Australian 2/6th Independent Company.

Despite these checks, however, the combined Australian-American assault on the Japanese defences along the Buna-Gona coast was under way. About the same time as the Americans jumped off on their northward movement on the 16th the Australian veterans of the Kokoda Track crossed the Kumusi River to complete, they hoped, the last phase of their long fight. The 25th Brigade was advancing on Gona, the 16th Brigade on Sanananda. These advances, and the American advance on Buna, were to develop into three virtually separate fronts.

---

[2] Gnr A. G. King, MM, NX6271. 2/1 Fd Hyg Sec; 2/5 Fd Regt. Cost clerk; of Burwood, NSW; b. North Strathfield, NSW, 28 Oct 1918.
[3] J. W. O'Brien, *Guns and Gunners* (1950), p. 171.

CHAPTER 12

THE AMERICANS AT BUNA

UP to the time when they began their approach march on Buna on 16th November the Americans could have had little idea of the nightmare nature of the country into which they were moving. Their area, lying between the coast on the right and the Girua River on the left, formed a rough isosceles triangle, its apex among the several mouths of the Girua. Buna village lay near the beach about a mile south of that apex; "Buna Mission",[1] also at the beach, was a mile east of the village; and Cape Endaiadere was some three miles farther east.

Buna could be approached from the south-east along the very edge of the sea by way of a narrow strip of sandy soil passing through Duropa Plantation, across the bases of Cape Endaiadere, Strip Point and Giropa Point; or by a rough roadway, farther inland, which led in from almost due south through Dobodura and Simemi. Beyond Simemi this roadway narrowly separated two air strips, each running roughly east and west— New Strip on the right, Old Strip on the left. Between these the roadway crossed Simemi Creek by a stout bridge, then ran parallel to the creek north-west to Buna. Swamp and kunai stretched between these two lines of approach. West again, swamps, sluggishly heaving with the tides and foetid with rotten growth and sago palms, reached towards the Girua River line.

Using these two avenues in the coastal sector on the right of the 32nd Division's advance, Colonel J. Tracy Hale's 128th Regiment had already made flickering contact with the advanced Japanese elements by nightfall of the 16th. Along the coastline, the I Battalion, under Lieut-Colonel Robert C. McCoy, were reported to have found enemy outposts about 400 yards north of Hariko and to have gone into defensive positions. Lieut-Colonel Kelsie E. Miller's III Battalion, which had gone westward from Embogo to Dobodura to approach Buna from the south, claimed to have killed three and wounded one of five Japanese whom they met at Dobodura on the afternoon of the 16th. They then continued on towards Simemi. Behind them was Lieut-Colonel Herbert A. Smith's II Battalion, in reserve. It arrived at Dobodura with a company of engineers and at once all set to work clearing a landing strip.

On the 17th the I Battalion edged slightly forward along the shore and the III Battalion on the left entered Simemi. General Harding then prepared to attack simultaneously along the water's edge and the Simemi Track early on the 19th, with support from two Australian howitzers, his only available artillery. These were from the 1st Australian Mountain Battery, commanded by Major O'Hare,[2] a dashing young regular officer

---

[1] The so-called mission was in fact the Government Station; the mission station was at Gona.
[2] Lt-Col M. P. O'Hare, OBE, NX395. 2/1 Medium (2/13 Fd) Regt; OC 1 Mtn Bty. Regular soldier; of Cunderdin, WA; b. Nathalia, Vic, 26 Jul 1917.

who had seen service in the Middle East. The battery was armed with 3.7-inch howitzers, very accurate and fast weapons capable of getting off 12 rounds per gun per minute without undue strain on the crews. Their shells were most effective and they were very suitable for the type of country in which they were now deployed. The guns were worn, however, their connections so loose that closing a breech might throw a gun off line by as much as a degree. In temperate climates they could have been moved successfully by the pack horses of which the battery had about 150 at that time, but O'Hare had found that these animals became exhausted after packing the guns over about fifteen minutes of level going in the moist heat of New Guinea. Nor could native bearers solve the problem for about 90 were needed to carry one gun without ammunition. The guns' wheels, made of wood for lightness, bogged easily in mud or sand.

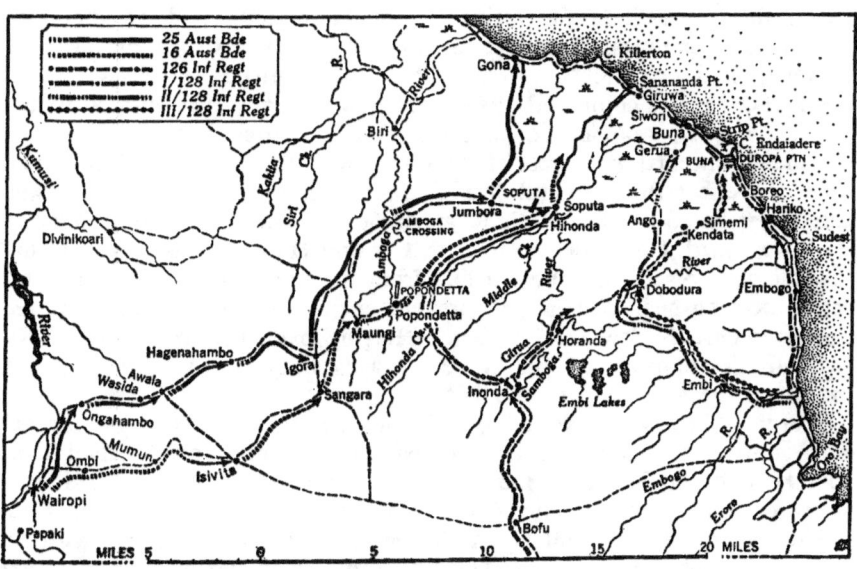

Routes of Allied advance towards Buna-Gona area from mid-November

In early November one section of these howitzers had been allotted to the 32nd Division, one to the 7th. The one for the Australians was flown in to Kokoda. O'Hare himself landed with the other at Pongani airfield on the 12th, and ferried it thence on a Japanese barge to a position about 1,000 yards north of Cape Sudest, where he brought it into action on the 16th. But he had fired only one round when American orders stopped him lest he draw counter-battery fire. Next day he mounted his guns some 600 yards north of Hariko, a position which he was to maintain for some time.

Meanwhile there had been some uncertainty on the inland route. There Colonel Tomlinson's 126th Regiment (less that part of I Battalion which was with Lieut-Colonel Carrier) had been pushing on from the Natunga-Bofu area to reach Dobodura by way of Inonda and Horanda and cover thence the left of the advance on Buna by following an alternative route west of Simemi through Ango and the village of Gerua. But, although an Australian wireless detachment had been attached to General Harding for the express purpose of keeping him informed of the progress of the Australians west of the Girua River, he could not establish radio contact with General Vasey during these early days of his advance, and thus was almost as ignorant of the whereabouts of his allies as of those of his enemies. Early on the 18th, therefore, he changed his plans slightly, telling Tomlinson, then at Inonda, to travel by way of Popondetta and Soputa and so forestall the possibility of the American left flank being peeled back by a thrust from the rear. Tomlinson then sent a strong detachment across the Girua River on the morning of the 19th. This found the Australian 16th Brigade past Popondetta and on their way to Soputa. Tomlinson then reverted to his original instructions. Scarcely, however, had he reached Horanda than he received news that he had been placed under command of General Vasey who wanted him at Soputa.

This was an outcome of a New Guinea Force decision to attack Japanese concentrations west of the Girua with the maximum force available. To effect this General Vasey was given the alternative of taking direct command of the 126th Regiment or shifting the American boundary westward. He chose the former. General Harding was then told that his role was to seize and hold a line from the Girua to the coast (including a crossing near Soputa), to prevent enemy penetration into his area, and to secure bridgeheads. General Herring overruled his protests. Reluctantly Tomlinson led his force towards Soputa where it began to arrive on the afternoon of the 20th.

Harding, however, still felt greatly put out by the alienation of such a large part of his force. In anticipation of Tomlinson's arrival there to take over he had sent the bulk of his reserve battalion (II/128th) forward from Dobodura to Ango, leaving one company to assist the engineers (more of whom had followed the original group in) with the construction of the strip. The II/128th Battalion would now have to take over entirely the left flank role which the 126th had been forced to relinquish, thus leaving, Harding considered, no reserve other than Colonel Carrier's small group which was following I Battalion along the seashore. And what disquieted him the more was news he had received from New Guinea Force that a battalion of Japanese reinforcements was thought to have been landed at Buna on the night 17th-18th and more were expected the following night.

This by-play had not prevented him, however, from going ahead with an attack which he had planned for the 19th, by the I/128th Battalion along the seashore and the III/128th Battalion along the track from Simemi. Rain poured down as the I Battalion sloshed forward along the track from Boreo towards Cape Endaiadere. On the fringes of Duropa Plantation, about a mile below the cape, they ran into machine-gun and rifle fire which, inexperienced as they were, threw them into confusion. The bush and long grass which closed off their view, together with clever Japanese tactics of concealment and swift changes to alternative positions which gave the Americans the impression of being literally surrounded by blazing weapons, bewildered them.

Out of rations, and with the greater part of its ammunition used up, the 1st Battalion ended the day a badly shaken outfit. The troops had entered the battle joking and laughing, and sure of an easy victory. Now they were dazed and taken aback by the mauling they had received at the hands of the Japanese.[3]

Even more abrupt was the III Battalion's baptism of fire. As they squelched forward from Simemi the trail became a narrow strip of corduroy against which the enveloping swamps oozed. As it approached the air strips this corduroy entered completely-cleared kunai grass country, little higher than the main swamp level. On the right New Strip was bathed in a blazing sun; the bridge between the strips lay ahead with Old Strip beyond it to the left, and, on the immediate left, a scarecrow growth marked the line of Simemi Creek with grey arms of dead wood. As they entered this inhospitable place such intense Japanese fire swept the Americans that, in Colonel Miller's own words, they were "stopped cold".

The next day saw a very slight improvement on Colonel McCoy's front. With assistance from the two mountain guns and several strikes by bombers, the men managed to edge ahead a further hundred yards before they were halted once more—an advance for which Lieutenant John W. Crow, who was killed, and one of his platoon commanders, Staff-Sergeant Paul Sherney, were chiefly responsible. But even this small gain was greater than anything Colonel Miller was able to achieve. Swamp and fire held his I Battalion men precisely where they had been beaten into immobility among the kunai approaches to the bridge the day before.

By this time, back on the highest military levels, General MacArthur, temporarily established at Port Moresby, was restlessly demanding a successful conclusion to the operations which had now developed not only before Buna but on the whole wide circle Buna-Sanananda-Gona, with the Australian 16th and 25th Brigades, respectively, bitterly committed at the two latter places. He told General Blamey that his land forces must attack the Buna-Gona area on the 21st November; that "all columns will be driven through to objectives regardless of losses". This was passed on to General Harding with information that heavy air support would be laid on for him at 8 a.m. He was to go forward immediately the air program concluded. If weather prevented the aircraft from assisting him his attack would go in just the same—about 8.10 a.m.

During the afternoon of the 20th Colonel Carrier's detachment and Major Harcourt's Independent Company, both of which groups, it will

---

[3] S. Milner, *Victory in Papua*, p. 175. This volume in the official series *United States Army in World War II* has been relied upon for the main thread of the following narrative, although much has been woven round that thread from Australian sources.

be remembered, had marched forward from Pongani, came up with General MacNider's headquarters near the edge of the water.

At this time Harcourt had 9 other officers and about 109 men with him. They had found conditions very trying since crossing the Musa in the middle of October, partly because of the difficult going and partly, Harcourt said, because the III/128th made no provision for supplying them after the Americans abandoned their own plans for an overland movement forward of the Musa River. Shortages continued to vex and weaken them and, during their stay at Pongani, a particularly virulent form of fever attacked many and left them weak. Then again although they did no fighting until they joined the Americans below Cape Endaiadere, they patrolled widely and arduously.

By the time Harcourt reported to Colonel McCoy at 7 a.m. on 21st November he had been told that that commander was holding a line from a point on the coast only some 600 yards south of Cape Endaiadere south-west to the eastern end of New Strip—a position which meant that his right was considerably above the line of the strip. Harcourt's own reconnaissance suggested that this was an error; that the American right was not nearly so advanced and probably little if at all above a line drawn due east from the strip. The reports of two patrols which he at once sent out tended to confirm this. However, the plan now explained to him was that, with McCoy on the extreme right and Carrier on McCoy's left, the Americans would advance on Cape Endaiadere on a 300-yard front. Harcourt would provide left flank protection, and oust the Japanese from their positions at the eastern end of New Strip, Colonel Miller would set his III Battalion once more at the bridge and, on the far left, Colonel Smith, with his II/128th, would push on from Ango, along the eastern bank of the river, over the four miles to Gerua and thence to Buna.

But confusion followed. Bombing aircraft assaulted the defences as planned at 8 a.m. Neither McCoy nor Miller had, however, received warning that this would be done. Neither did they receive their final orders for the attack until 8.50 a.m. and 8.40 a.m. respectively. And Miller's position was not improved when some of the bombs landed among his men killing four and wounding two. Then, as though to even matters along the front, after Harding had planned another air attack for 12.45 which did not develop, and another later which his men were to follow in, the bombers came again at 3.57, failed to disconcert the Japanese seriously, and dropped some bombs among McCoy's leading elements, killing 6 and wounding 12. Some of the remainder were so perturbed by this that they left their start-line and had to be coaxed by their officers to return.

Finally, however, the attack did go in but was shot ragged by the cool defence. The I Battalion scarcely improved its position. Harcourt's Australians, with Captain Belmer[4] in charge of the actual attack group, 50 to 60 strong, moved towards the strip, clearing several machine-gun

---

[4] Capt R. S. Belmer, NX76358; 2/6 Indep Coy. Regular soldier; of Sydney; b. Wellington, NZ, 15 Nov 1915. Killed in action 2 Dec 1942.

posts on their way and shooting snipers from trees. Among them, Private Martin[5] fought on after he had been shot in the arm, and shot again, in the leg, and shot a third time, in the stomach, only then leaving the fight on direct orders. But, having lost 2 officers and 3 men to the enemy fire, they halted within 58 yards of the strip, partly because of the opposition, partly because they were left up in the air by the American failure to get forward at all to the immediate right of them. On the Simemi Track Miller's III/128th Battalion was swept back from the bridge and, after 42 had been killed or wounded, sought shelter in bush below the western end of New Strip.

While this was happening Colonel Smith's II/128th Battalion, far to the left, had been advancing from Ango. Just after reaching Gerua village the main track forked, the right branch leading to the Buna Government Station, the left to Buna village. For a distance of 200 to 300 yards along the length of each from the point where they diverged, the two branches parted so gradually as to form an acute angle of only 20 to 30 degrees before they suddenly flung wide. The narrow space thus enclosed was to become known as the Triangle; the "Coconut Grove" lay just beyond, on the left-hand track.

As Smith approached the Triangle his leading company narrowly escaped an ambush. At once he attempted to outflank, facing the defences with one company on the track, holding a second in reserve, and sending one to either flank. But his flanking companies plunged deep into swamps in comparison with which the Japanese seemed almost a lesser evil. And so night overtook them.

When Harding received this news he knew that Smith could not hope to complete his mission with only one battalion. He therefore asked General Herring to return to him a battalion of the 126th. Herring left the decision to Vasey, who agreed that Colonel Tomlinson (by that time at Soputa with the 16th Brigade) should send his II Battalion off on the 22nd to join Colonel Smith.

At the same time Harding had been readjusting his coastal and centre positions. It seemed obvious to him that if Miller clung to his positions on the approach to the two strips, he would achieve no more in the future than he had been able to manage up to that time—almost nothing. He therefore told him to leave one company on the ground and bring the rest of his battalion round to the seashore to join McCoy and the others there. This Miller did on the 22nd, leaving Lieutenant Carl K. Fryday's company behind. By nightfall he had closed up on McCoy's rear. There were then only two main lines of attack in the American sector—along the shore and along the track to the Triangle.

Not only, however, did Harding readjust his forces at this time—he superimposed a rather curious readjustment in command on his already curious control system. He advanced Colonel MacNab, executive officer of the 128th Regiment, to operational command of the coastal drive over

---

[5] Pte S. A. Martin, SX17642; 2/6 Indep Coy. Stockman; of Victoria River Downs, NT; b. Darwin, 2 Jul 1922.

the head of MacNab's own commander, Colonel Hale. General MacNider, who had been the original commander of the mixed Australian-American force which had begun to build up at Wanigela on 14th October, remained as commander of Warren Force—the name which the Americans moving against Buna had apparently adopted some weeks before. Harding had thus inserted two other commanders between himself and his regimental commanders—in actual fact, since Tomlinson was not then under his command, between himself and Hale. That Hale felt the position was to be revealed by him much later in answer to a question put to him.

. . . while I commanded the 128th Infantry from 6 February 1942, until 3 December 1942, I was commander in name only from about mid-October until 23 November 1942.[6]

On the latter date MacNider, inspecting the forward lines, was wounded and Hale succeeded him, although MacNab remained in command of the actual operations.

By this time the Americans' situation had brightened from one aspect at least: they were more certain of getting supplies for, on the 21st, the Dobodura strip had been completed to a length of 1,000 yards and a width of 110 feet—a notable achievement on the part of the engineers in so few days. But other problems were now looming large for the 32nd Division. They needed to adjust their own approach to the task before them; and they needed further support, of greater weight than infantry alone could bring to bear. It was true that considerable air support had already been provided. But the nature of the close country which shut off the recognition signals made from the ground, the inexperience of the soldiers combined with the lack of practice and skill of some of the pilots in close-support operations, and the skilful construction of the defences which made them invisible from the air and almost impervious to bombing (except to a direct hit), rendered air attack largely ineffective. Aggravating that was the shortage of artillery. Although the two howitzers from the Australian mountain battery were in position above Hariko, no field guns were firing until the 22nd when Captain Mueller of the 2/5th Field Regiment brought into action the two 25-pounders which remained to his troop after the sinking of the barge on the 16th.

After that misadventure most of the surviving gunners had walked back along the coast to Oro Bay and then, with Mueller, retraced their steps to join the battery commander, Major Hall.[7] The latter, with the second troop of his battery, had left Milne Bay ten days after Mueller, his men and fifty sheep on the deck of one of the little ships which had been pressed into service, an ungainly barge towed behind them. At Wanigela, Hall rafted his guns and stores ashore on the 14th. Two days later he left them there in a beach and strip defence role under Captain

---

[6] In a paper, "Answers to questions by Historical Section GHQ as to certain phases of Papuan Campaign as applied to 128th Infantry".
[7] Brig W. H. Hall, DSO, ED, VX14684. 2/4 and 2/5 Fd Regts; Dir of Arty Eqpt LHQ 1945. Accountant; of Essendon, Vic; b. Aldershot, England, 5 Jan 1906.

Nix[8] while he himself went ahead to learn more of the American plans. At Hariko Mueller joined him, having left Lieutenant Marr[9] and a few helpers at Oro Bay to get his two remaining guns forward. Marr managed to do this by dismantling the guns and ferrying the pieces in a long-boat out to the lugger *Kelton* where, by delicate judgment, the heavy parts were hauled aboard on inadequate cargo gear. Scarcely had Marr achieved this when word was received from the Americans that no landing could be made through the surf at Hariko. He chose to ignore this warning and hurried his departure before it could be forbidden. Then, through pitch darkness and broken sea, in the long-boat and canvas assault boats, he and his men landed their guns on the night 21st-22nd. On the 22nd these, concealed beneath thick tropical growth, were in action just above Hariko.[1]

By that time more guns were on their way to the front. In Port Moresby Lieut-Colonel O'Connell's[2] 2/1st Field Regiment, veterans of the African desert and Greece, had been alerted. The 2nd Battery was standing by for final orders to move to Buna by sea, the 1st waited in hopeful expectancy, and the 51st was preparing to begin a flight to the coast on the 23rd. One troop of the 51st, constituting Blackforce under Major Hanson,[3] was to land at Popondetta and join General Vasey; the second troop, constituting Bullforce under Captain Manning,[4] was to land at Dobodura and join General Harding.

But more guns were not the final answer. Although the Australian commanders had generally shared the Americans' expectations that resistance in the Buna area would be light, some provision had been made earlier for support by tanks. It was now clear that these would be not only the ideal but perhaps the only answer to the solidly prepared and tenaciously held Japanese bunker defences. On 13th November General Clowes had been ordered to send from Milne Bay to Pongani or Oro Bay (as General Harding might desire) one troop of General Stuart tanks from a squadron of the 2/6th Armoured Regiment then arriving there. But lack of shipping defeated this plan for, when the first tank was loaded on the only available craft which might have been suitable (a captured Japanese landing barge), both barge and tank sank. Although they were subsequently salvaged it was clear that there was no immediate hope of moving the tanks. Instead, as a temporary measure, Clowes was told on the 21st to send a platoon of Bren carriers.

MacNab, therefore, lacked armoured support and had nothing like adequate artillery. Nevertheless he ordered the coastal drive to begin afresh

---

[8] Maj L. F. Nix, NX12377. 2/5 Fd Regt; 1 Aust Naval Bombardment Gp 1944-45. Solicitor; of Bondi, NSW; b. Brisbane, 8 Feb 1914.
[9] Capt W. R. Marr, NX17761; 2/5 Fd Regt. Reporter; of Dubbo, NSW; b. Homebush, NSW, 21 Dec 1919.
[1] The transport of their guns round this coast, and the landing of them, by the men of the 2/5th Field Regiment, ranks as a most notable achievement.
[2] Brig K. E. O'Connell, CBE, ED, NX104. CO 2/1 Fd Regt 1942-45; CRA 3 Div 1945. Loss assessor; of Ashfield, NSW; b. West Wallsend, NSW, 17 Sep 1908.
[3] Brig A. G. Hanson, DSO, ED, NX144. 2/1 Fd Regt (CO 1945). Clerk; of Killara, NSW; b. Hunters Hill, NSW, 13 Jul 1911.
[4] Capt H. A. Manning, NX149. 2/1 Fd Regt; 1 Aust Naval Bombardment Gp. Grazier; of Mendooran, NSW; b. Sydney, 14 Nov 1913.

on the 23rd. This McCoy and Carrier attempted by infiltration beneath the cover of artillery fire augmented by concentrated fire from heavy mortars which MacNab had had grouped as a battery. Lack of observation militated against both the artillery and mortars, however, and most of the artillery hits achieved were rendered comparatively ineffective by the fact that the instantaneous fuses with which the shells were armed caused them to explode on impact. Delayed fuses, to postpone the explosion until the projectile had buried itself deep in the target, would have been much more effective but none were available at the time. It was partly in consequence of this that McCoy and Carrier made very limited progress. "Line moved forward about 100 yards on coastal flank and centre but little on western or left flank."[5] This comparative failure inevitably reacted on the Independent Company, although it had been aggressively ranging round the eastern end of the strip, and, to its left, Fryday could not get forward although he remained firm on the approaches to the bridge.

Quiet then settled over the seashore for the next two days—except where Captain Belmer was still trying to track down Japanese posts at the eastern end of New Strip. Harcourt had planned a local attack there for the 24th but the Japanese posts were in even greater strength than the Australian reconnaissance had shown and Belmer lost six men for no gain.

On the Ango Track, however, these two days were more eventful. Major Herbert M. Smith, with his II/126th, had joined Colonel Smith's II/128th in front of the Triangle on the morning of the 23rd. The two battalions, widely separated by swamps from the main group, then assumed the name Urbana Force (the rest of the attackers retaining the name Warren Force which had previously been applied to all of them) with Colonel Smith commanding. But by that time the colonel was in difficulties. His own two flanking companies were still wide in the swamps with Company "G", on the right flank, in particular straits. After their initial plunge into the morass on the afternoon of the 21st, night caught them still floundering. They plunged deeper in the darkness, then halted about 10 p.m. with the more fortunate perched like birds in stunted trees, black slush beneath them. Most, however, just waited numbly for the new day to come, with the mud and water up to or above their waists. They pushed farther into the swamps on the 22nd and, about the middle of the afternoon, came to a stretch of kunai which rose slightly above the marsh level. It seemed that only about 200 more yards of swamp then separated them from the eastern arm of the Triangle. They were in a jumping-off position for attack if only they could be supplied. Colonel Smith, however, despaired of this. He planned to withdraw them and attack round the left where Company "F", although practically swamp-bound, had yet found the going slightly easier along Entrance Creek. He signalled Harding to this effect and that the line of supply was "neck-deep in mud and water". Harding, however, received the message as "knee-deep" and curtly replied that Smith was not to withdraw under any circumstances but to attack. He then overruled the latter's protests that he had in-

---

[5] War diary, 2/6 Independent Company.

sufficient knowledge of the terrain and virtually none of his enemies' dispositions, and his plea for an extra day or two to remedy both lacks. Aircraft would strike at the Triangle at 8 a.m. on the 24th, Harding said, and Urbana Force would follow the bombs in. Smith then took hasty counsel with his more junior namesake. The two decided to attack simultaneously from the right, with Company "G" of the 128th (already in position there) reinforced with Company "E" of the 128th; frontally with Company "F" of the 126th; from the left with Company "E" of the 126th which would relieve Company "F" of the 128th along Entrance Creek.

While the two American commanders were finalising their plans, last-minute arrangements for some artillery support were made. Early on the morning of the 23rd the Bullforce guns and gunners had begun arriving at Dobodura. Captain Manning, not being able to report direct to General Harding at Embogo, reported to Colonel Smith instead. But, in Manning's own words: "As he refused to adopt us had to wait to contact General [Albert W.] Waldron [the American artillery commander] by wireless." Waldron told him to support the attack of the two Smiths, and Manning then had two guns ready for action by nightfall.[6]

At 8 a.m. on the 24th attacking aircraft swept over the Urbana positions but they consisted merely of twelve fighters which not only missed their target area but were not followed by bombers. Smith held his hand and asked for a second attempt. It was arranged that this would be made again by twelve fighters as no bombers were available, but only four fighters kept the appointment. These left the Japanese untouched but strafed Smith's own headquarters. Apparently this persuaded the colonel to press on without waiting for further assistance from the air. So his men finally crossed their start-lines at about 2.30 p.m. supported, within a few minutes, by Manning's guns.

On the right Company "G" moved off as planned with Company "E" in a supporting position in the kunai. But the former ran into opposition about 200 yards from their start-line and were held on the slopes of a second strip of kunai. Soon the Japanese seemed to be concentrating a good deal of fire on Company "E". Although that company (and the heavy weapons platoon of Company "G" which had remained with them) lost only one man killed and five wounded, they became perturbed. Their own weapons seemed to be failing them through the effects of mud and water. Thereupon they fell back into the swamp and later, leaving some of their weapons behind them, stumbled to the rear. Not such disorder but an equal lack of success marked the frontal attack. Company "F" of the 126th, strengthened by Company "H" of the 128th, found barbed wire defences barring their way along the track. These, covered by heavy fire, effectively halted them both. On the left Company "E" of the 126th circled

---

[6] The transport of the Bullforce and Blackforce guns was the first move by air of 25-pounders in this theatre, and was a remarkable achievement in itself. Unlike the mountain guns the 25-pounders were not made to be transported in pieces. They had to be detached from their carriages and the pieces were then not only heavy but clumsy. It was then most difficult to load them into aircraft and the danger of them going through the floor was very great.

for some distance on Entrance Creek as a diameter swinging for the bridge on the track to Buna village. But accurate and heavy fire forbade their close approach to this. They dug holes and lay in them with swamp water seeping over them.

Mortified by this whole failure, and the nature of it, General Harding was not disposed to listen to Colonel Smith's explanations. Particularly was he incensed at the failure on the right wing. Smith had told him that he had ordered these companies to remain on the edge of the swamp until morning—and then Harding learned that they had straggled back to the rear. Smith said they were hungry and exhausted and incapable of further effort for the moment; that he was still of the opinion that no attack round the right could succeed. For those reasons he did not order the men back to their posts. He wanted to concentrate on the left and confine his activity on the right to patrols, and his patrol results during the next two days (25th and 26th) added weight to his arguments. Harding admitted it. On the 26th he told Smith to concentrate on the possibilities opened by the movements of the left flank company; to try to by-pass the Triangle completely and outflank the defences by getting his men on to a grassy strip which bestrode the left fork of the track—that which ran to Buna village.

On the afternoon of the 27th, however, Colonel John W. Mott, Harding's Chief of Staff, took over Urbana Force and Colonel Smith reverted to command of his own battalion. Mott at once relieved the commanders of the two companies which had failed on the right (although the Company "E" commander was reinstated soon afterwards) and ordered the companies to return at once to the positions they had abandoned and salvage their jettisoned weapons. By sundown all of them had been recovered except one of Company "E's" mortars. Mott at once sent that company back a second time and, when they returned again, they carried the missing piece with them. Meanwhile he had reached the same conclusion as Smith and Harding had done, substantially confirmed the former's plan for an outflanking move round the left, and proceeded to embellish it—particularly with certain ideas that Major Smith had developed. In reply to Harding's expressed desire for a night attack on the 28th, however, he asked for a little more time. Harding thereupon ordered him to attack the following night.

While Urbana Force had thus failed, and been gathering itself for an attempt to redeem that failure, the attack which Colonels Hale and MacNab had worked out in detail after Warren Force's lack of success on the 23rd, had taken place as planned on the 26th. By that day Colonel Miller's III/128th had relieved Colonel McCoy's I/128th in the most advanced positions along the water's edge. Forward of Miller, at 7.30 a.m., the Allied fighters opened what was to be the largest air attack yet undertaken on the coast. Bombers followed them in at 8 a.m., and the attacks continued until 9 a.m., fifty aircraft in all participating. Then the guns took over: O'Hare's howitzers concentrated on Cape Endaiadere; Manning's Bullforce, with four 25-pounders now in action round Ango, and Mueller's two 25-pounders from Hariko, brought their fire down along the western edge of New Strip and on the bridge between the strips. Twelve 81-mm mortars and four heavy machine-guns thickened the artillery fire.

At 9.30 a.m. Miller's battalion went in on the right to drive directly northward along the track to Cape Endaiadere. But the Japanese rose practically unscathed from their bunkers and strongpoints and stopped the Americans almost dead on the track and in the swamps which bordered it. Strafing aircraft which rushed down from Lae then completed Miller's discomfiture.

On his left Colonel Carrier's I/126th elements, aiming north-west for Strip Point, confounded the confusion. Carrier unknowingly went east instead of north-west. By 4 p.m. (still thinking he was headed aright) he had reported that there was little opposition ahead of him and he was nearing the sea. Harding, who had been forward with Miller and was now back at Embogo, not knowing of Carrier's error, and fearing that the latter was so far forward as to be in serious danger of being cut off, instructed him to come back until he formed an extension of Miller's left flank. Carrier thereupon emerged from a swamp which had stretched from his original right to Miller's left and which had been the scene of his day's hopeful but wasted manoeuvring.

This failure left the Australian Independent Company right out on a limb as they tried to seal Carrier's left flank. New Strip, which their patrols, skimming the southern edge, could not cross because of the commanding Japanese fire, was above them, swamp water was all about them, and either rain or blazing sun was beating on them. Left of them again Fryday's company, still in their position on the approaches to the bridge, had failed to secure the western end of the strip.

During the next few days Warren Force made no progress. General Harding then ordered another attack for the 29th but deferred it soon afterwards until the early morning of the 30th. Since Colonel Mott was preparing his Urbana Force attack for the night 29th-30th the effect would be an almost simultaneous attack on both flanks.

This was to be supported by more closely integrated artillery fire than any previously attempted, directed by General Waldron. The guns were still all Australian—Hall's two 25-pounders forward of Hariko, O'Hare's two howitzers in the same general area and Manning's four guns near Ango. One 105-mm howitzer of Battery "A", 129th U.S. Field Artillery Battalion was landed at Dobodura on the 29th but was not ready to support the attack on the 30th. The gunners were gradually lessening the problems which beset them in the flat coastal country. Manning reported that at first he had no accurate maps at all of his area but was able to construct a fairly satisfactory one from air photographs. His chief difficulty was observation. "No command at all, practically impenetrable jungle with open strips and all perfectly flat." He was at first forced to rely on information from the infantry and reports of sound bearings from listening observation posts. By the 29th or 30th he had been able to arrange only one observed shoot. Skilful calculations, however, enabled him to fire with sufficient accuracy to guarantee his shells falling within 200 yards of a given target. But even if that estimate were correct, it was not sufficiently accurate to give well-trained infantry the close artillery support they would look for; such men would advance as near as 30 yards to the fall of the shot.

A new artillery aid, however, was now beginning to lessen the disadvantages of lack of observation from the ground. On the 24th New Guinea Force had been able to arrange for No. 4 Army Cooperation Squadron R.A.A.F. "equipped with slow, almost weaponless Wirraways and manned by skilful pilots and observers",[7] to be made available for air spotting. On the 28th one of these aircraft was allotted to the 32nd Division, and one to the 7th Australian Division, to work with the artillery for two hours during the morning. Thereafter they were to play an increasing part in the coastal battle, at first landing at Dobodura for briefing before every mission, and later remaining at Dobodura and Popondetta for several days at a time subject to the demands of the artillery. Though the threat of Japanese fighters restricted their use to some extent they were handled so boldly that the soldiers soon became used to seeing them circling slowly, seeming almost to hover, over the Japanese lines and passing detailed directions to the guns.

They spotted shell bursts, lured enemy AA into disclosing their positions, reported Japs trying to escape; they were forced down and occasionally crashed in flames; and one daring Wirraway actually shot down a Zero. Their work according to the official artillery report, was 'superb'.[8]

During the later stages of the coastal battle, as these and other expedients increased the effectiveness of artillery fire and more guns arrived in the forward areas, the supply of ammunition became a great problem. At this stage, however, the problem was not so acute: shells were brought by air to Dobodura and then taken out along the track on four jeeps for Manning's guns at Ango; they were taken by sea to the guns on the shore. For the latter Hall's dump was well to the rear of his gun positions to which the shells then had to be manhandled.

At night, ammunition was loaded into canvas assault-boats which were then pushed and pulled along the surf. While so engaged, the men watched anxiously for aerial flares from Cape Endaiadere, for they would then be clearly visible to the enemy, who were strongly entrenched in that area. To pull an assault-boat along, one man had to walk in the water, chest-deep most of the way, well outside the line of breakers. There was about two miles to travel, and after a few hundred yards even the strongest was exhausted. Sometimes the boats would be swamped, and then it was a case of diving for the boxes which, when full of water, became harder than ever to handle. Once the ammunition was ashore, it would be carried to the guns through the dark jungle. The usual routine was for each man to hold the belt of the man ahead, the leader trying to follow the telephone line. If he lost the wire, the file would soon be off the track. Everyone would then crawl on

---

[7] *Army Air Forces Historical Studies No. 17*: "Air action in the Papuan Campaign 21 July 1942 to 23 January 1943."

[8] *Army Air Forces Historical Studies No. 17*.

hands and knees until the line was found again. Although this trip through the jungle was only about a mile, it took up to two and a half hours in the dark.[9]

Although, despite the difficulties still surrounding its use, General Harding could now hope for an increase in the effectiveness of his artillery, he was painfully aware that his men needed the kind of support which only tanks could provide, if they were to prevail against the solidly-entrenched Japanese. He had renewed his pleas for some of the tanks at Milne Bay. But still the lack of sea craft capable of carrying them prevented their dispatch. General Clowes (following his orders) had, however, been swift to get Bren carriers on the water (though he well knew that they could not be considered or used as substitutes for tanks). The first of these, with their crews, arrived at Porlock on the 27th. Harding was then told that at least four would reach him within the next two days and, in consequence, hoped to be able to use these new weapons on the 30th. But once again the lack of shipping nullified his hopes. Nor initially did he have the air support which he had confidently expected, for the approach to Buna of a Japanese convoy kept all available aircraft busy at a critical time.

Also, in the words of the American historian of this campaign:

> The men on both the Urbana and Warren fronts were tired and listless. They had not been sufficiently hardened for jungle operations and, with few exceptions, had not been fresh when they reached the combat zone. Thrown into battle in an exhausted state, most of them had had no chance to rest since. . . . The troops were half-starved. Most of them had been living on short rations for weeks and their food intake since the fighting began had averaged about a third of a C ration per day—just enough to sustain life. They were shaggy and bearded and their clothes were ragged. Their feet were swollen and in bad shape. Their shoes, which had shrunk in the wet, often had to be cut away so that the troops could even get their feet into them. . . . Morale was low. Instead of being met, as they had been led to expect, by a few hundred sick and starving Japanese, they found themselves facing apparently large numbers of fresh, well-fed, well-armed troops in seemingly impregnable positions, against whom in almost two weeks of fighting they had failed to score even one noteworthy success.[1]

At 6.15 a.m. on the 30th artillery and mortars opened a fifteen-minutes program in front of Warren Force. At 6.30 the attackers crossed their start-lines, McCoy's I/128th leading straight up the track. But within a hundred yards the vanguard company faced a big log barrier, which seemed to spout fire, thickened by a raking fire from the flanks. The artillery could not remove the barrier, nor could specially aimed concentrations from mortars and a 37-mm gun. The attack could not get round, over or through the main defence line of which this barricade was one of the pivots.

At the same time, on the left, with the Australian Independent Company on his own left, Carrier had been trying to lever an opening into the eastern end of New Strip. But well-directed fire swept his right company to ground near the north-east corner of the airfield. His left company got no farther than half-way along the field's southern edge before they

---
[9] O'Brien, *Guns and Gunners*, pp. 180-1
[1] Milner, pp. 196-7.

too took to the ground to survive the storm sweeping across and along the open spaces which had obviously been ranged as killing grounds. The Australians, handicapped by the American failure, gained no ground

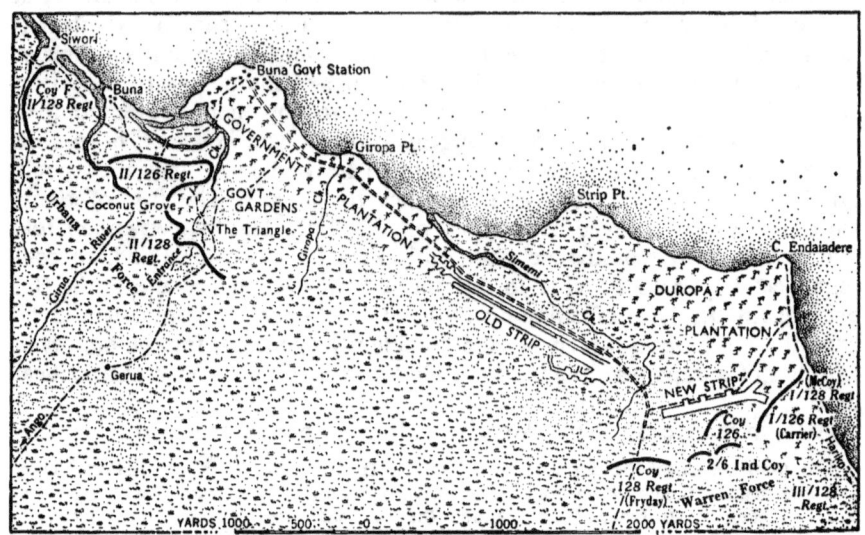

Evening, 30th November

though their patrols on the right located Japanese machine-gun positions to the north of the strip's east end and linked with Fryday below the bridge. They reported of the Japanese defences that:

> All emplacements appeared to be made of coconut logs laid lengthwise with others placed on bearers forming the roof. The whole was then camouflaged according to the country in which they were situated. In the case of those to the west of the strip kunai grass was festooned all over them with small bundles standing upright in front, while at the eastern end . . . [they] were covered with coconut leaves, bits of scrub and heaps of fallen coconuts or husks. In most cases the loopholes were hidden to view by the screen of bush or camouflage, although vision from inside out was still possible, and in nearly every case the pillbox or emplacement was not discovered until you were right on to it. The openings were difficult to see from the front and only in two cases—those near the bridge—were they located, nor could the width or size of the loopholes be ascertained.[2]

While Warren Force had thus stunned itself once more against the defences which stretched along New Strip and through the southern fringes of Duropa Plantation to the water's edge, Urbana Force had been similarly embroiled around the Triangle beyond the swamps which spread west of the strips. There, Colonel Mott had undertaken a most difficult task even before he joined battle: an approach march by ill-trained and apprehensive troops through darkness and swamps. It was true that the distance was short from the two grassy spaces which he had selected as his forming-up

---

[2] War diary, 2/6 Independent Company.

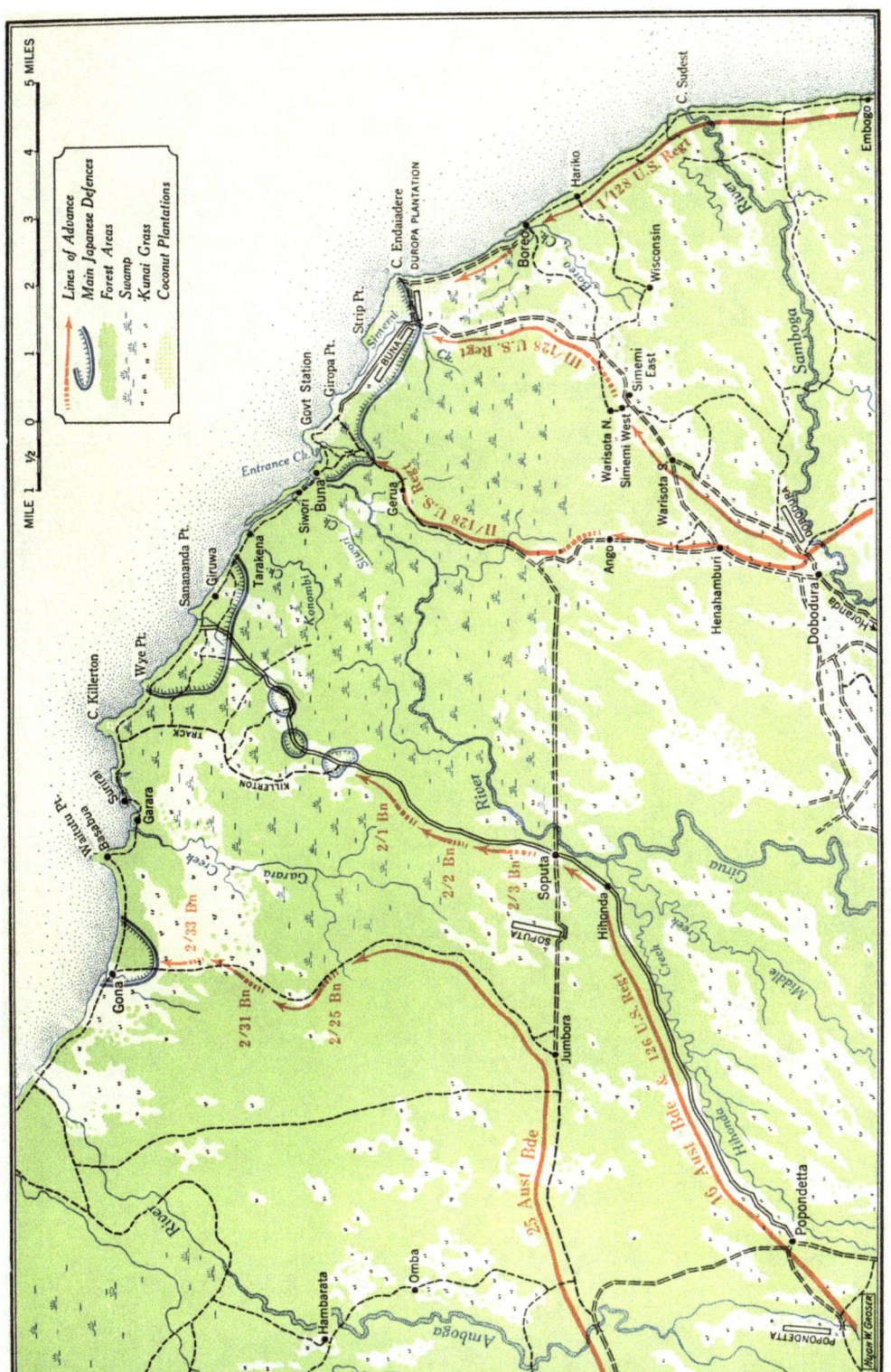

Allied advance on Buna, Sanananda and Gona, 16th-21st November

areas to the larger grassed area which lay astride the track to Buna village above the Triangle and which was his immediate objective. But a short distance under such circumstances can prove too much for even the best laid plans, and the Urbana plans, though bold, were far too intricate and ambitious—especially for their raw subjects. So it was that Mott's timetable was disrupted when his initial moves were scarce begun. He had planned to advance on to his objective as soon after midnight as possible and hard behind a small barrage from Manning's 25-pounders and his own mortars, both of which were ranged on the objective. But it was 4 a.m. before his men crossed their start-line.

Colonel Smith pitted his Company "G" against the apex of the Triangle and was to contain any Japanese sortie which might be made down the track. Companies "E" and "F" of the 126th pushed quickly through to the south-eastern edge of the objective, destroying a number of Japanese who tried to stop them, and carrying out their orders to secure first that part of it which was nearest the Coconut Grove and the Triangle. But Company "E" of the 128th, attacking forward then to clear the Coconut Grove, failed. Company "G" of the 126th likewise failed. They had jumped off on the left of the two leading companies with orders to wheel left again when they struck the track and take Buna village, but they became lost in the swamp. Mott quickly switched Company "E" of the 126th to this task (from consolidation on the original objective). These men hurried north-west along the track but burnt themselves out during the day, within 150 yards of the village, in two fruitless attacks. Wide to their left Company "F" of the 128th, after skirting the defences, flung as far as Siwori village and bestrode the track in the path of any attempt which might be made along it against their friends in the main area. Then, with the night, Mott lodged more firmly on and around the grassy area which had been his first target.

By this time General MacArthur was in the grip of great disquiet at Port Moresby. Nowhere round the new battlefront had his forces been able to achieve any decision. In the two weeks since they had started forward the 32nd Division had lost 492 men in battle—and had nothing to show for it.[3] The main Japanese line was still unbreached. At Sanananda and Gona the strength of the Australians was waning fast. In addition General Blamey had been outspoken to MacArthur in criticism of the American infantry. On 29th November MacArthur sent an urgent message to Lieut-General Eichelberger, the commander of I American Corps, to stand by at his headquarters at Rockhampton in Queensland. MacArthur's own aircraft followed hard on that message and landed Eichelberger in Port Moresby late on the afternoon of the 30th. Almost at once he and his Chief of Staff, Brigadier-General Clovis E. Byers, were summoned into the Commander-in-Chief's presence.

Byers and I were conducted to a sweeping veranda where General Sutherland sat at a desk, grave-faced (Eichelberger wrote later). He had just flown back over the Owen Stanley Mountains from Dobodura, and it was plain that his report on con-

[3] Milner, p. 195.

ditions at Buna was responsible for my abrupt summons. General MacArthur was striding up and down the long veranda. General Kenney, whose planes were to do so much to make the ultimate victory possible, was the only man who greeted me with a smile. There were no preliminaries.

"Bob," said General MacArthur in a grim voice, "I'm putting you in command at Buna. Relieve Harding. I am sending you in, Bob, and I want you to remove all officers who won't fight. Relieve regimental and battalion commanders; if necessary, put sergeants in charge of battalions and corporals in charge of companies—anyone who will fight. Time is of the essence; the Japs may land reinforcements any night."

General MacArthur strode down the breezy veranda again. He said he had reports that American soldiers were throwing away their weapons and running from the enemy. Then he stopped short and spoke with emphasis. He wanted no misunderstandings about my assignment.

"Bob," he said, "I want you to take Buna, or not come back alive." He paused a moment and then, without looking at Byers, pointed a finger. "And that goes for your chief of staff too. Do you understand?"

"Yes, sir," I said.

After breakfast [the following day] he put an arm around my shoulders and led me into his office. "If you capture Buna," the Allied commander said, "I'll give you a Distinguished Service Cross and recommend you for a high British decoration. Also," he continued, referring to the complete anonymity under which all American commanders in that theatre functioned, "I'll release your name for newspaper publication."[4]

Eichelberger arrived at the front on the 1st. There he was to be responsible directly to General Herring who had opened an advanced headquarters at Popondetta on the 28th. Herring had quickly found that he could get no accurate picture of what was happening on the American front. He therefore sent his senior liaison officer, Lieut-Colonel Robertson,[5] to visit Harding. Robertson flew to Dobodura and, at first, could see few signs of life as he looked about him after the aircraft which had brought him made a quick take-off. Then a wisp of smoke curling among the trees on the edge of the field attracted him. As he approached he could see a figure in American uniform bending over a fire and stirring a pot. Engaged upon this humble task he found a colonel, who told him that General Harding was just down the track and would be along soon. But he had a long wait before Harding appeared. Harding then could give him very few details of his infantry positions. He explained that he was quite out of touch with his forward troops. Nor could his signals officer give him much hope that early communication would be restored, saying that the signallers had found the going too hard to carry the divisional headquarters wireless set and had thrown it into the bush some miles back. Robertson, an officer of considerable experience, was astonished and dismayed and reported his impressions to Herring on the 30th. General Sutherland, who was with Herring at the time, listened gravely. Apparently Robertson's story capped his own impressions and possibly accounted in some measure for the report he made to MacArthur on his return—the

---

[4] Eichelberger, *Our Jungle Road to Tokyo*, pp. 20-2.
[5] Lt-Col W. T. Robertson, OBE, MC, VX213. 2/8 Bn 1939-41; GSO1 (Liaison) NG Force 1942-43; GSO1 (Ops) 7 Div 1943-44; GSO1 HQ Aust Army Staff UK 1945-46. Student; of Melbourne; b. South Yarra, Vic, 2 Feb 1917.

report which Eichelberger considered to be the reason for his almost immediate summons to MacArthur's presence after his arrival in Port Moresby and the haste with which he was then sent to the front.

On arrival Eichelberger found both Warren and Urbana Forces trying themselves once more against the defences. On the former's front, however, McCoy's men were soon hard held on the water's edge; while an attack by Carrier towards New Strip, coinciding with an attempt to push forward across the bridge by Lieutenant Fryday, was halted by a grass fire accidentally started in rear of it. The most that Carrier could then achieve was to have two of his companies circle the southern edge of the strip and join Fryday.

In the Urbana sector, after an uneventful but watchful night, Mott had got his men off the main track for a flanking attack on Buna village. Fire from Manning's guns and all the available mortars preceded the companies. But, just as the impetus was mounting, the leading company pulled back.

Whether it did so because there was a mix-up in signals or because the men were "jumpy" Colonel Mott was unable to ascertain.[6]

On the 2nd Eichelberger sent two trusted staff officers, Colonels Clarence A. Martin and Gordon B. Rogers, to observe Warren Force in action while he himself, with Generals Harding and Waldron, joined Colonel Mott.

The day was to see a shift of emphasis from the water's edge westward against New Strip. McCoy left only one company immediately below Cape Endaiadere—to feint along the track. The rest of his men would probe towards the eastern end of New Strip with one of Colonel Carrier's companies. At the same time the companies below the bridge would attack north and north-west. McCoy would command the east-west push, Carrier that from the south. Major Harcourt's Australians would link the two attacking groups although one of their patrols (under Lieutenant Blainey[7]) would operate on Carrier's extreme left, south-west of the bridge.

But, in the event, the attack seemed to jerk spasmodically into anticlimax: the supporting aircraft aimed their bombs and fire well but apparently did not signal the conclusion of their runs to the ground forces; in consequence the mortars and artillery did not open fire soon enough to maintain the shock of the bombardment unbroken; nor were the Japanese taken in by the feint along the track. Intense and skilful fire erased the Americans' intentions in their early stages. It stopped the Australians also, killing the constant Belmer, although, from the trees on the extreme left, Blainey's men got within 30 yards of the rear of some of the bridge defences—near enough to engage them with grenades.

A similar lack of success marked the Urbana Force attack that day although it was strengthened by additional mortars which Harding had rushed up, preceded by thick and well-aimed fire from these and the

---

[6] Milner, p. 206.
[7] Capt G. C. Blainey, NX76314. 2/6 Indep Coy; 2/6 Cdo Sqn. Assistant director and manager; of Bellevue Hill, NSW; b. Sydney, 12 Nov 1917.

original mortar battery and by "accurate, and, in general, beautifully executed" artillery fire from Ango. Of this day General Eichelberger wrote later:

> When I went to the front on 2 December I couldn't find a front. I had been told the day before that our men were within seventy-five yards of Buna village and attacking. I knew that four hundred artillery rounds had been laid into the troubled sector. When I came back that evening to my headquarters tent on a creek bank . . . I wrote to General Sutherland in Port Moresby.
> "The rear areas are strong and the front line is weak. Inspired leadership is lacking. In a circuit of Buna village I found men hungry and generally without cigarettes and vitamins. Yesterday afternoon the men immediately in contact with the Japanese had had no food since the day before. About four o'clock the rations arrived, two tins of C ration!"
> Here is what Colonel Rogers, then I Corps Intelligence officer, wrote me about his inspection trip [Rogers did not see the feint up the track nor the attempt on the bridges between the strips]:
> "The troops were deplorable. They wore long dirty beards. Their clothing was in rags. Their shoes were uncared for, or worn out. They were receiving far less than adequate rations and there was little discipline or military courtesy. . . . Troops were scattered along a trail toward the front line in small groups, engaged in eating, sleeping, during the time they were supposed to be in an attack. At the front there were portions of two companies, aggregating 150 men. Outside of the 150 men in the foxholes in the front lines, the remainder of the 2,000 men in the combat area could not have been even considered a reserve—since three or four hours would have been required to organise and move them on any tactical mission."
> . . . Our patrols were dazed by the hazards of swamp and jungle; they were unwilling to undertake the patrolling which alone could safeguard their own interests. . . . One result of . . . lack of communication and the density of the jungle was that companies and platoons were as scrambled as pied type on the floor of a printing office. . . . I stopped all fighting, and it took two days to effect the unscrambling of the units and an orderly chain of command.[8]

Eichelberger's comments on what he had seen led to an angry scene with Mott and later with Harding. He then relieved them both, giving the division to General Waldron and Urbana Force (after the lapse of another day) to Colonel John E. Grose. Colonel Martin replaced Colonel Hale in command of Warren Force. Both Grose and Martin were from Eichelberger's own staff, both had seen action in 1918. This was the new commander's first step in providing the leadership which he had decided was lacking. The task of straightening out the chaotic supply position he gave to Colonel George De Graaf, his own corps supply officer. Thus, with three of his own officers in the key positions under the already tried Waldron, he was now firmly in the saddle, and his was the responsibility for taking Buna.

In preparation for a major attack on the 5th Eichelberger gathered up the scattered bits and pieces of his command and formed them once more into homogeneous units. On the right of Warren Force, between the sea and the south-eastern end of New Strip, Colonel Martin placed McCoy's III/128th. Carrier's I/126th was re-formed south of the bridge between the strips. Miller's I/128th was in reserve behind McCoy. On the Urbana

---

[8] Eichelberger, pp. 24-7.

front Colonel Grose placed the II/128th on his right and the II/126th on his left, the two Smiths still commanding.

This 5th December attack would again follow the pattern which, up to the present, had been unsuccessfully laid down on the Buna front—a frontal assault with air and artillery support, mortars thickening the fire of the artillery. Lieut-Colonel O'Connell, of the 2/1st Field Regiment, who had flown from Port Moresby on the 3rd, was placed in charge of the guns. For the two near Hariko ammunition supply had recently been an acute problem which was relieved only just before the attack by the arrival of the little ships with 1,000 rounds and by the opening of a rough track from Hariko to Simemi. None the less delivery to the dump and gun positions was still slow and awkward. As the gunners manhandled the shells from the water's edge they stumbled over roots and collided with one another in the darkness. The track from Simemi provided only a trickle of ammunition. Over this track the gunners' only jeep, brakeless, running on kerosene, and missing with stuttering regularity, went bucketing to Dobodura to carry a mere forty rounds a trip.

One new feature, however, would mark the 5th December attack from those that had preceded it. Five Bren carriers had at last been got forward from Porlock Harbour. They were manned by men of the 17th Brigade who had reached Milne Bay during October. On 23rd November General Clowes had ordered Brigadier Moten[9] to man thirteen carriers supplied by the 18th Brigade. Each was then armed with two light machine-guns, each section with an anti-tank rifle in addition. Moten appointed Lieutenant Fergusson[1] to command this improvised platoon, mindful, no doubt, of the sound training that young officer had received in carriers as a trooper in his father's[2] 6th Divisional Cavalry Regiment, before being commissioned and posted to the 2/7th Battalion.

On 29th November Fergusson succeeded in landing five of his carriers at Oro Bay although the shipping and unloading difficulties, which had already delayed him seriously, forced him to return the other eight to Porlock from that point. He could then find no overland route by which to get farther forward. But while he himself was reporting to the front-line Americans, Lieutenant Walker,[3] his second-in-command, finally managed to get the carriers on to a barge which a small naval vessel then towed to Boreo. By the early hours of the 4th Walker had them ashore and in the afternoon they moved forward to an assembly area in preparation for the attack on the 5th. In that attack four would be manned by crews from the 2/7th Battalion, one by a 2/5th Battalion crew under Corporal Lucas.[4] One of the crews from the 2/7th was led by Sergeant "Jock"

---

[9] Brig M. J. Moten, CBE, DSO, ED, SX2889. CO 2/27 Bn 1940-41; Comd 17 Bde 1942-45. Bank officer; of Woodville, SA; b. Hawker, SA, 3 Jul 1899. Died 14 Sep 1953.

[1] Lt T. St D. F. Fergusson, VX6545. 6 Cav Regt; 2/7 Bn. Jackeroo and overseer; of Corowa, NSW, and Middle Brighton, Vic; b. Jerilderie, NSW, 30 Apr 1920. Killed in action 5 Dec 1942.

[2] Brig M. A. Fergusson, then commanding the 2nd Armoured Brigade.

[3] Lt I. W. Walker, VX4674; 2/7 Bn. Jackeroo and bookkeeper; of Sandringham, Vic; b. Essendon, Vic, 3 Sep 1919. Killed in action 5 Dec 1942.

[4] Sgt N. A. Lucas, VX3605. 2/5, 2/7 Bns. Cabinet worker; of South Perth, WA; b. Footscray, Vic, 3 Aug 1917.

Taylor,[5] who had shown himself in the African desert and Greece to be one of the outstanding fighting men of the A.I.F.

Although Fergusson's men eagerly faced the prospect of new action, private misgivings must have touched the hearts of any who had time to contemplate the nature of the country and the task which lay before them. The role for which carriers had originally been designed was reconnaissance and the rapid transport of troops and weapons across bullet-swept ground. What light armour they had was capable only of stopping small-arms fire—and even some of that was likely to penetrate at close range. Their sides were low and they were fitted with no overhead protection of any kind. A basic doctrine of infantry training had always been that carriers were not tanks and should not, indeed *could* not, be used as such. And yet this was the prospect, in the face of deeply-entrenched positions manned by soldiers of great endurance in defence, now ahead of Fergusson and his men—a prospect that could be justified only by a desperate need. That need was twofold: to adopt any expedient, however slender its chance of success, which might result in the prising of a hole through the Japanese casemates; to hearten the bewildered Americans whose first two weeks of warfare had been such a stunning shock to them.

From 8.20 a.m. to 8.35 on 5th December six twin-engined medium bombers gunned and bombed between Cape Endaiadere and Old Strip. Without waiting for the aircraft to finish, the artillery joined in at 8.30. At 8.42 Warren Force crossed their start-lines on the water's edge. There Fergusson and his carriers formed the spearhead of Miller's III/128th Battalion. On the left McCoy was trying to break through the eastern end of New Strip. From his positions south of the bridge Carrier was thrusting against the resolute defenders who had refused a passage there for so long. Between McCoy and Carrier, Lieutenant Fielding[6] was in charge of the most forward men of the Independent Company, whom Major Harcourt had instructed to provide contact patrols between the I/128th and I/126th and "to take any chance of inflicting casualties on enemy or opening avenues through which infantry advance could move".

American fire was whipping the tree tops for snipers when the carriers broke cover, each with a crew of four, their speed held down to two miles an hour, partly to allow the infantry to keep pace, partly because the ground was spongy under their tracks and littered with fallen logs over which creepers twined. Sergeant Taylor's and Corporal Lucas' vehicles were on the right, Fergusson's in the centre, Corporal Orpwood's[7] and Corporal Wilton's[8] on the left. A great volume of fire stormed about them

---

[5] WO2 D. R. Taylor, DCM, VX5449; 2/7 Bn. Labourer; of Melbourne; b. Aberdeen, Scotland, 14 Aug 1907.

[6] Capt G. A. Fielding, WX12059. 2/6 Indep Coy, 2/6 Cdo Sqn. Clerk; of Fremantle, WA; b. Fremantle, 6 Jun 1912.

[7] Cpl J. E. Orpwood, VX6912; 2/7 Bn. Factory employee; of Nagambie, Vic; b. Nagambie, 2 Dec 1918. Died of wounds 5 Dec 1942.

[8] Sgt C. H. Wilton, VX45098; 2/7 Bn. Grocer's assistant; of Orbost, Vic; b. Orbost, 22 Feb 1919.

as they moved into the cleared space over which they must advance. On the extreme right Lucas' carrier bellied on a log hidden in the long grass after it had travelled some 40 yards. The crew fought on from its shelter to give cover to Sergeant Taylor who was engaging a post about 50 yards to their left. Taylor had crossed about 75 yards of cleared space when a torrent of fire from a strong post just in front of him, heavily barricaded and camouflaged with palm fronds so that it was most difficult to locate, stopped him momentarily. He and his crew pounded it with grenades and flailed it with machine-gun fire. Then they circled to take it from the rear but not before a mortar bomb had exploded in the back of their vehicle, killing one of the crew. Just before they silenced this post a Japanese soldier attempted to grenade them. Taylor leaped from the carrier to meet him and killed him in the open. Swinging his vehicle to the right he then silenced a second post. As he was engaging a third post a burst shattered his left arm. With blood pouring from him he left the carrier to go to the assistance of Fergusson who was in difficulties farther to the left, while Private Locke's[9] fire covered him. Then as the carrier moved in to the post again, its damaged motor stopped. Desperately Private Cameron,[1] the driver, emptied his rifle into the Japanese until the rifle jammed and then struggled to right a stoppage in the Bren. As he was doing so he was hit in the head. Locke covered him out of the rear of the carrier and then, desperately wounded himself, fell among the torn scrub.

Meanwhile, in the third carrier, Fergusson had been heavily engaged by posts in front of him and sharpshooters commanding his open vehicle from the tree-tops. When his driver was hit he took over himself in the driving seat. He turned to look for the infantry who should have been supporting him and his carrier became jammed among fallen logs and trees. As he stood up to call to Taylor, near him on the right, a tree-top marksman shot him through the head. At once, from Taylor's carrier, Locke shot this sniper, but within seconds, Corporal Davies,[2] struggling to move Fergusson's body from the driving seat, was also shot dead. By this time, too, Corporal Orpwood in the fourth carrier had been wounded, mortally. After he had traversed about 100 yards on Fergusson's left a grenade burst over his vehicle's open top. Turning to crush the thrower, Orpwood became the target for a sharpshooter perched above him. He fell across the driver who temporarily lost control of his vehicle and then reversed into the cover provided by some bush and, under the protection of the forward infantry, removed his dying friend. Soon afterwards, however, his carrier stuck across a fallen log.

While he had been reversing he had passed Corporal Wilton's carrier, helpless astride a log which had lain across the path it was following to

---

[9] WO1 L. C. Locke, NX921; 2/7 Bn. Carpenter and joiner; of Grafton, NSW; b. Bellingen, NSW, 22 Jan 1917.
[1] Pte A. J. Cameron, VX57446; 2/7 Bn. Motor driver; of Beaumaris, Vic; b. North Carlton, Vic, 22 Oct 1910.
[2] Cpl F. G. Davies, VX2915; 2/7 Bn. Woodworker; of Richmond, Vic; b. Richmond, 3 May 1917. Killed in action 5 Dec 1942.

Orpwood's left rear. In a free-for-all with Japanese riflemen who engaged them from trees Wilton's two gunners were wounded. The crew then fought on for some time with the forward infantry. About midday Wilton sent the two wounded men back. A little later, however, on instructions from Lieutenant Walker who, hearing of the disaster, had hurried forward from the carriers' rear headquarters, Wilton attached himself and his remaining crewmen to the Americans with whom they remained until next evening. Walker, who, with a small party, searched for his dead and wounded and emptied the carriers of equipment which the crews had been unable to carry away (although each had taken with him all the weapons and ammunition he could bear) was mortally wounded during his brave search.

So, within half an hour, the five vehicles lay abandoned, proof of the dictum that carriers were not tanks. And, just in rear of them, Miller's leading company was shot to pieces from Duropa Plantation or from behind the log barricade. Miller's whole attack was halted before it was well begun; the blazing sun now sickened the discouraged survivors.

It was a similar story in McCoy's sector. There the men moved forward thirteen minutes after Miller's through coarse kunai grass and in heat which wilted them. As the long day waned they were still only on the fringes of the strip and any more positive achievements were quite beyond their reach. Farther left, and in the bridge area, however, Carrier's men had met with a little more success. The artillery, their own 37-mm gun, and the mortars, aided them in dislodging the defenders from about seven of the most forward positions, but when the Americans tried to close in on the bridge fierce fire swept them back. Night found them still some 200 yards south of the bridge.

Between McCoy and Carrier, commando patrols actually crossed the eastern end and centre of the strip, with most of the Japanese fire passing over their heads but, with no infantry up with them, they withdrew again later.

There was heartening news, however, from the Urbana front. Under the eyes of Generals Eichelberger and Waldron, Major Smith's II/126th Battalion moved against Buna village at 10.30 a.m. after nine Kittyhawks had attacked the Government Station to disorganise any move to send reinforcements from that area—the only area from which assistance to the defenders of Buna village could come—and the guns and mortars also bombarded the area. From almost due south of the village, the 126th companies tried to advance along three radial axes, Company "H" on the right, Companies "G" and "E" in the centre, with the Cannon Company of the II/128th on a fourth and most westerly radius.

Apparently the extreme right company's drive lost its force early. Next on the left two platoons of Company "G" went to ground under fire but the third platoon, Staff-Sergeant Herman J. F. Bottcher's, took quick advantage of an opening to overcome a number of enemy positions and halted only when they reached the sea at 1.30 p.m. There, with eighteen men and one machine-gun, Bottcher dug in on a narrow sand spit just east of the village and virtually commanding the line between the Government Station on the east and the village on the west. To the left again Company "E", largely as a result of the drive of two brave young leaders, Lieutenant Thomas E. Knode and 1st-Sergeant Paul R. Lutjens, both of whom were badly wounded, got within 50 yards of the village before they were stopped. On the extreme left, however, the Cannon Company of the 128th faltered below an open space in front of the village. Major Chester M. Beaver, a divisional staff officer, took command during the afternoon in an effort to get the company forward which, by that time, had been augmented by 2nd-Lieutenant Paul M. Schwartz's platoon of Major Smith's reserve company. Although Beaver and Schwartz then took a patrol to the very fringe of the village area the company itself did not move forward in their wake until darkness fell.

While this had been going on Colonel Smith had ranged along the western bank of Entrance Creek to such good effect that he could claim control of almost all its length on that side, except for the area of the Coconut Grove which was still strongly held. Smith's commanding position, Bottcher's break-through, and the close embrace of Major Smith's companies and the Cannon Company, meant that Buna village was fairly effectively cut off from landward help. It was clearly now only a matter of time before that stronghold fell.

None the less it seems that the success of this day on the Urbana front was much less than it should have been. Two factors had swung the delicate balance in the Americans' favour. First was Bottcher's brilliant and brave opportunism. Of him Eichelberger was to write:

On my recommendation the Allied commander commissioned Bottcher as a captain of infantry for bravery on the field of battle. He was one of the best Americans I have ever known. He had been born in Germany and still talked with a faint Germanic accent. A profound anti-Nazi, he came to [America] early in the 1930's, took out his first papers, spent a year at the University of California, and then went to Spain to fight against Franco. His combat experience was extremely useful in Buna, and his patriotism as a new American was vigorous and determined.[3]

Second was the heroism of certain individuals. These fell into two main groups: there were those who, like Bottcher, fought surpassingly well in their proper roles, and those senior and extra-regimental officers who assumed the mantles of junior and non-commissioned officers to lead the men forward.

I watched the advance from the forward regimental command post, which was about a hundred and twenty-five yards from Buna village (wrote Eichelberger). The troops moved forward a few yards, heard the typewriter clatter of Jap machine-guns, ducked down, and stayed down. My little group and I left the observation post and moved through one company that was bogged down.
I spoke to the troops as we walked along. "Lads, come along with us."
And they did. In the same fashion we were able to lead several units against the bunkers at Buna village.[4]

---
[3] Eichelberger, p. 32.
[4] Eichelberger, p. 28.

But the influence of such leaders as he could not restore to the men of Urbana Force the physical strength which the swamps and bush had drained out of them. Considering this Eichelberger laid down for the next few days a policy of "continued pressure and advance by infiltration" as a preliminary to the successive reduction of Buna village, the Coconut Grove and the Triangle. None the less Major Smith made careful preparations on the 6th for another attack on the village by his II/126th. And the day opened busily too for Sergeant Bottcher in his corner by the sea. He drove off a pre-dawn sally launched on him from the village and dealt similarly with one from the Government Station which followed. The next morning brought more determined attempts as the Japanese made another effort to pluck this thorn from their sides. But Bottcher's gun blew the station attack apart; then, as the village group closed in from the other side, Corporal Harold L. Mitchell, one of a small group of newcomers who had been sent to strengthen Bottcher's original garrison, overlooked them from a forward position. Single-handed he was suddenly among them with a bayonet, shouting aloud in fury to warn his fellows. Momentarily his assailants were disconcerted. That moment was all that Bottcher's skilful gun needed. But the Japanese came again later, in the gloom of the evening which the shimmer of the sea lightened so that the Americans saw that boats had put out from the Government Station to attack them from seawards. The American guns set the foremost craft afire and the attempt washed back with the tide.

Offensively, however, the day had not been so successful for the Americans. Colonel Tomlinson, with his 126th Regimental Headquarters, had just re-crossed the Girua to the American lines, since the temporary incorporation of those of his men who were with the Australians into the 16th Brigade had virtually deprived him of his proper command function. He had taken Urbana Force over from Colonel Grose on the morning of 7th December. He sent Major Smith and his battalion once more against the village in the afternoon. But the defenders beat them off for the loss of only a small forward trench on the south, wounding the intrepid Major Smith as he was encouraging his men. The dying hopes of the II/126th, now commanded by Captain William F. Boice, that they might yet take the village, flared again on the 8th but flickered out with the last weak trickles of fire from an ineffective flame-thrower which had been brought forward. Although the operator of this instrument got within 30 feet of the defences, when he stepped forward into the open, the fuel container on his back and the nozzle in his hand, his jet barely reached half the distance to his target. As he moved closer he and two of his covering party were shot down. His officer, going to his assistance, met a like fate.

The night brought the last Japanese attempt to break the American hold on the village. As the garrison sallied against the II/126th's left a small force from the Government Station fell on the American right but the effort failed.

By this time the II/126th was down to less than 300 men. But fresh troops were now available, for the 127th Infantry Regiment (the third regiment of the 32nd Division) which had arrived in Port Moresby on 26th November, was coming forward. Its leading battalion, the III/127th, landed at Dobodura on the 9th. Next day this battalion began the relief of the II/126th and had completed the take-over by the 11th.

During the six days since the attack of 5th December no gain had been made on the Warren Force front. There, acting on a suggestion made by General Herring on the 5th that he concentrate on pinching off individual posts, Eichelberger had declared against any more frontal assaults for the moment—reserving his main effort for the Urbana front. He ordered vigorous patrolling to pinpoint enemy posts and feel for weak spots. As these were located they would be deluged with artillery and mortar fire and so softened as to become a prey for the creeping infantry. But, in the event, though these tactics might have helped tire the defenders by keeping them on the *qui vive,* they did not advance the line very much, principally because the defensive positions remained substantially proof against shell fire. Only delayed-action fuses, still not available, were likely to be able to overcome this. Eichelberger, however, thought that he might get better results by moving some of his guns farther forward. He had hesitated to do this, fearing to lose any of the few he had by placing them within reach of stealthy attackers, but the arrival of two more guns of the 2/5th Field Regiment on the 8th gave him a little latitude.

These were two of those which Major Hall had left with Captain Nix at Wanigela in the middle of November. On the 27th Nix, eagerly accepting a rather vague order from somewhere farther forward, had loaded them on s.s. *Kuri Marau* and set out for Oro Bay. They arrived there in darkness at the beginning of a little odyssey which provided a good picture of the difficulties of coastwise supply at this time.

The skipper could get no response to his oft-repeated signals. Accompanied by Nix, he rowed ashore. After a search along the blacked-out beach, the pair stirred up the soundly sleeping members of an American defence post. They then located the much harassed Harbour Master, who, learning the nature of their cargo, cried "Hell, I want food, not guns and ammunition." . . . There was no way to get the guns ashore. The ship turned back, its cargo still aboard, to be clear of the danger area by dawn. On arrival at Porlock Harbour the *Kuri Marau* received orders to proceed immediately to Milne Bay. The guns had to come off. . . . The Harbour Master at Porlock was, like all of his kind on the New Guinea coast, very short on ships and very long on conflicting orders from above. Nix and company pestered him until he was glad to uphold their claim to a large, flat-topped barge, which they commandeered, so long as he got rid of them . . . when a ship could be got from somewhere to tow the barge.

Spirits were ebbing fast when the familiar *Kuri Marau* appeared on the scene again. At Milne Bay it was discovered that there had been a mistake; the vessel had been required at Porlock, of all places. Nix pressed his claims so vigorously that *Kuri Marau* soon started on its way to Hariko, the big, awkward barge blundering along in tow. . . . Just before dusk, three Jap planes came bombing and strafing. . . . The damage forced the ship to return to Porlock. Worse, it was ordered to Milne Bay again. The section seemed fated never to leave Porlock.

But new hope dawned the following day. Two small vessels were obtained to tow the barge in tandem. This time the journey was going to be done entirely in the dark. The barge arrived off Hariko on the night of 8 December without further mischance. . . . The waves were tossing the barge several feet up and down on the edge of the beach, and so landing the guns was a hazardous business.[5]

Major Hall now had four 25-pounders in action north of Hariko, and soon afterwards Major O'Hare, his strength recently increased by the arrival of an additional howitzer, moved to a new site on the Dobodura-Buna track, 2,000 yards south of the bridge between the strips.

General Eichelberger was now almost ready for what he hoped would be his final clearing attacks in the village area. The bewilderment, and reluctance of some of his troops was being replaced by a higher resolve and a feeling of greater confidence although, east of the Girua, 113 had been killed, 490 wounded, 64 were missing, 1,260 had been sent to hospital sick, leaving approximate effective strengths at 5 p.m. on 10th December of 55 officers and 1,062 men in Urbana Force, 114 and 1,955 in Warren Force; malaria, dysentery and scrub typhus were on the increase. The arrival of the 127th was heartening; more vigorous officers were re-infusing the men; under Colonel De Graaf's capable direction more food was being delivered and mail was beginning to come in; and word had gone round that Australian tanks and infantry would soon be joining them.

So it was with some feelings of exuberance that two companies of III/127th, which had been holding the village in a tight circle since they had taken over from II/126th, followed mortar bombs and shells into the Buna village at 7 a.m. on the 14th. But their birds had flown. After all the sound and fury, quiet lay over the shattered huts, the broken palms, the torn earth and fifty unburied dead. No one remained to dispute the American entry.

With the passing of the first blank feeling of anti-climax the attackers could turn to the real task: the subjugation of the Government Station area. But before that could be attempted again the Coconut Grove and the Triangle must be wiped out. Wise in his decision to exploit the physical uplift which followed on the capture of the village Eichelberger lost no time in turning to this.

Colonel Herbert A. Smith had earlier been warned for the task of clearing the Coconut Grove although his II/128th was scattered from the apex of the Triangle, along the west bank of Entrance Creek to Siwori. He had only some 84 of his 350 men available when General Byers, who had succeeded to the division when General Waldron was wounded on the 5th, told him to take the grove. But this small band plunged into the attack at 3 p.m. on the 16th. Fire swept them in their approach, wounding Byers among others, so that night found them still without the grove but lying closely round it. They hung on there through a night of drenching rain and went into the trees at 8.20 next morning with Smith himself at the head of one group, Sergeant Howard C. Purtyman at the head of another, Major Roy F. Zinser fearlessly at the head of another until he fell badly wounded. By noon the grove was in Smith's hands and with it quantities of rice, oatmeal, malt, barley, and some

---

[5] O'Brien, *Guns & Gunners*, pp. 174-6.

weapons and ammunition. The Americans buried 37 dead and others were uncounted.

Smith did not halt in the grove for, across Entrance Creek, the stubborn Triangle was still uncaptured. The skeleton of the bridge by which the village track had crossed the creek still held together and the attackers went with their own impetus across this and established themselves firmly on the eastern bank before they were checked. Smith then sent his men against the Triangle in a simultaneous movement from the bridgehead and from south of the apex of the Triangle where one of his companies had been lying for a long time to contain the defenders. But they provoked such a vicious recoil that it was clear that they could not hope for success with the strength available to them.

Now General Eichelberger, directly commanding since Byers had been taken to hospital, knew that the first phase of his Buna adventures had ended. Fresh forces were even then arriving in his area: Australian tanks and the experienced 18th Australian Brigade under Brigadier Wootten, who would initiate the second phase of the operations before Buna—with a comparatively detailed knowledge of the Japanese strengths and dispositions.

It was now known that, while the battle of the mountains was closing on the banks of the Kumusi River, not only had the remnants of the Japanese forces who had previously landed there been preparing to stand on the coast, but a Japanese reinforcement program was well under way. Two ships ran in at the beginning of November with fresh troops and supplies and another convoy landed a formidable group in the middle of the month consisting mainly of the *III Battalion, 229th Regiment,* and about 300 reinforcements for the *144th Regiment.* Major Hiaichi Kimmotsu was leading the *III/229th* which had won a reputation for hard fighting in China, Hong Kong and Java. With Kimmotsu came Colonel Hiroshi Yamamoto to take over the *144th Regiment.*

About this time, the Japanese were readjusting their command in the Pacific. The *Eighth Area Army* (Lieut-General Hitoshi Imamura) became responsible for operations in the Solomons and New Guinea on 16th November; Lieut-General Hyakutake, with his *XVII Army,* took over the Solomons battle; Lieut-General Hatazo Adachi arrived at Rabaul on 25th November and took over command of the *XVIII Army* and responsibility for the New Guinea theatre.

The Japanese on the Papuan coast were then organised into two main commands. East of the Girua River Captain Yoshitatsu Yasuda of the Japanese Navy, who had been responsible for the construction of the Buna airfield, was initially in command with about 500 marines (*5th Yokosuka* and *5th Sasebo*) and some of his construction troops in the Buna area itself—at the village, the Government Station and about the Triangle—and several hundred of the *15th Independent Engineers,* anti-aircraft gunners and army service troops of various kinds manning the defences from Cape Endaiadere to Giropa Point. Immediately after their arrival, however, on 17th November the *III/229th Battalion* joined him and Yamamoto took over command with Major Kimmotsu as his second-in-command. He left Yasuda in position with his marines and construction troops and added his newcomers to the Cape Endaiadere-Giropa Point sector. His force, all told, then numbered probably slightly more than 2,000. He was well served with artillery, mounting several 75-mm naval guns, some 37-mm pom poms, 5 heavy anti-aircraft guns and a few 13-mms. West of the Girua the Japanese were well entrenched in the Sanananda area and at Gona Mission where, at both places, the Australians, pressing on from the Kumusi, came hard against them while the Americans were bogging down in front of Buna.

CHAPTER 13

ON THE SANANANDA TRACK

A NETWORK of tracks covered the area between the Kumusi River and the coastline. From among them General Vasey selected two of the main threads, approximately parallel, as separate axes of advance for his two brigades. He told Brigadier Lloyd to make for the sea at Sanananda Point with his 16th Brigade, by way of Isivita, Sangara, Popondetta and Soputa; and Brigadier Eather to travel the left axis—to Gona, through Awala, Hagenahambo, past Igora Store, over the Amboga River at Amboga Crossing, and through Jumbora. The 25th Brigade crossed the river first and set out for Gona, but the 16th Brigade crossed hard behind them.

Lieut-Colonel Edgar's 2/2nd Battalion, spearheading Lloyd's advance, began to pass over the turbulent river just before midnight on 15th November, swinging high through the bush darkness on the two flying-foxes which the engineers had hastily erected, or gingerly picking a way across the single-log bridges above each of which a single wire provided a swaying means of balance. The whole battalion was across by 8 a.m. on the 16th. At 10.30 they moved forward for Popondetta from the point where the upper and lower tracks diverged beyond the bridge, with a section well forward and the companies following each other in single file. Brigadier Lloyd's headquarters marched behind them, followed by the 2/3rd and 2/1st Battalions in that order.

The day's slow march covered about six miles of foot track. The track crossed a number of small streams and deeper creeks, through which the men sometimes waded waist deep, and wound through forests which seemed to hold the heat and press down the humid air. The 2/2nd halted for the night at the little village of Mumun. The men of the three battalions were tired. A hungry, arduous, two-months-long mountain trail lay among the mists and cloud-tented crags behind them. Now they had had a night of hazardous river crossings and a day which had pressed down their sweating loads. Their food supply was uncertain as they had received no rations that day.

On the 17th, through seemingly virgin forests and secondary growth, the track undulated onwards in conditions similar to those of the previous day. Heavy afternoon rains made it a quagmire, turned the area into a vast steam bath, and so flooded the creeks as to change their crossing from an inconvenience into a positive hazard. These exacting coastal conditions told so heavily on the men in their weakened condition, which was aggravated by a shortage of food, for again no rations reached them in the day, that fifty-seven of the 2/2nd alone fell out gasping beside the track. Friendly natives helped where they could, handing fruit and sugar cane to the soldiers as they plodded through the villages and often assisting the weaker ones across the streams.

As the 2/2nd, still leading, bivouacked in a native village, with Sangara Mission still about an hour and a half ahead, torrents of rain swirled down during the hours of darkness.

That day General Herring had received some news from General Blamey of the climactic naval battle of Guadalcanal, which, spread over the period 12th-15th November, represented the peak of the naval war of attrition round the Solomons. Both Japanese and Americans sustained

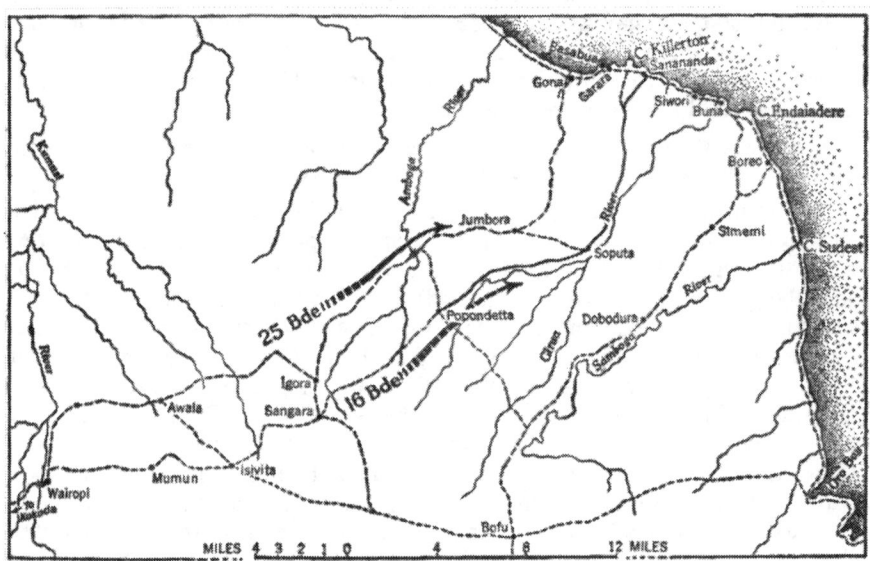

The Australian advance on Sanananda and Gona

heavy losses, but though the battle was later, in retrospect, seen to be decisive, its results were then still uncertain. Blamey wrote Herring that the Japanese were assembling air forces for attack; indications were that they were gathering troops and destroyers to land reinforcements at Buna. It was imperative that both the Australians and the 32nd American Division, then approaching Buna from the south, should push on with the greatest speed to seize the Buna sea-front and destroy the Japanese remaining in the coastal area.

Lloyd urged his brigade forward for Popondetta on the 18th. The rain had ceased. The streams had shrunk once more to fordable dimensions. Though the shortage of rations was becoming acute, promises of droppings at Popondetta heartened the men. Intelligence of fresh enemy landings seemed to have been borne out when news came during the day that about 1,000 additional Japanese were thought to have been landed in the Buna area the previous night and another 1,000 would probably land during the coming night.

Despite the need for haste, however, Edgar, canny from experience of this dangerous game of pursuing Japanese through the bush, did not relax his caution, and night was approaching as he reached Popondetta. Again heavy rain was falling as the 2/2nd tried to make camp, while the promise of food was beginning to dance like the Blue Bird before his men, as no supplies had been dropped at Popondetta but word came that some would be waiting at Soputa, a good seven miles ahead. With that news Lloyd had orders also to leave one battalion to guard the Soputa dropping ground while the other two pressed ahead to Sanananda to cut there the coastal track which led to Buna.

At this stage Edgar asked to be relieved of the lead in order to give his tired men some relief, and early on the 19th Major Hutchison led the 2/3rd through to form the new advance-guard. His role was unequivocal for, as one of his officers recorded later,

> Here it was that Brig Lloyd, standing like Napoleon, said, when asked the day's objective, 'The sea!' So the battalion started for the sea.[1]

The morning was not far advanced when the 2/3rd began to gather in Japanese stragglers. By 10.30 a.m. their first prisoner was being escorted back to brigade headquarters; soon another was being sent after him and the battalion diarist saw a third, "a naked, emaciated creature", squatting on the side of the road under guard. But these were mere flotsam and jetsam in an army's wake. It was midday before Captain Fulton's vanguard company caught their first sight of armed foes, who slipped swiftly out of sight. About the same time Fulton found four trucks abandoned on the road. Although the Japanese had tried to render these unserviceable some of the Australians had one in working order within an hour. Hutchison then halted his men for lunch. Soon after he resumed the advance he lost one man to sudden fire from the bush. Captain Walker swung his company to the right and Captain Gall broke bush round the left, in the quick attempt at envelopment which had now become classic in bush warfare. But the small rearguard evaporated and, more cautiously now, the Australians' advance was resumed at 2 p.m. Two hours later, however, Fulton's company, near Soputa, ran sharply against more defiant opposition. Once again Walker and Gall flung wide, but darkness caught their men still groping and, with practised speed, they dug in among the trees.

Early on the 20th, tentative Australian passes eliciting no response from what had been Japanese positions, the 2/3rd took up the pursuit once more and, after an uneventful half-hour, began breakfast. The smoke from their damp fires was rising when Lieut-Colonel Cullen, now ordered forward, led the 2/1st past them about 8.30 a.m., animated by fresh news that the 25th Brigade was only one mile south of Gona and that the Americans were approaching Buna. About a quarter of an hour later his leading men broke out of the narrow bush-enclosed track into a large, open kunai patch through which the track wandered northwards. Very soon afterwards volleys scattered them. Effective artillery fire quickly convinced Cullen that he was coming against strong positions and, when

---

[1] Capt T. B. Silk, "Kokoda Diary", in *Chocolate and Green*, July 1945, p. 44.

lack of telephone cable forced him to establish his headquarters on the track itself, in the timber just short of the kunai, shells slashed into his headquarters area, sending great divots of the damp earth flying.

Meanwhile, however, he himself had hurried forward to the leading company—Captain Burrell's. Quickly assessing the situation he told Burrell to try to maintain his thrust along the track; he would send Captain Catterns' company to test the Japanese left. But very soon afterwards, with his usual quick aggressiveness, he broadened his plan. He took Catterns away from his company, leaving Captain Prior to take charge of the right-flank quest, and placed Catterns in command of the two remaining rifle companies (Captain Simpson's and Lieutenant Leaney's), telling him to swing far to the left to clear the kunai patch completely and fully exploit the timber cover so that he could burst from the thick growth on to the rear of the Japanese positions and settle himself there astride the track. Success in such a move, he thought, would cause the defenders to fall back—as they usually did under such circumstances.

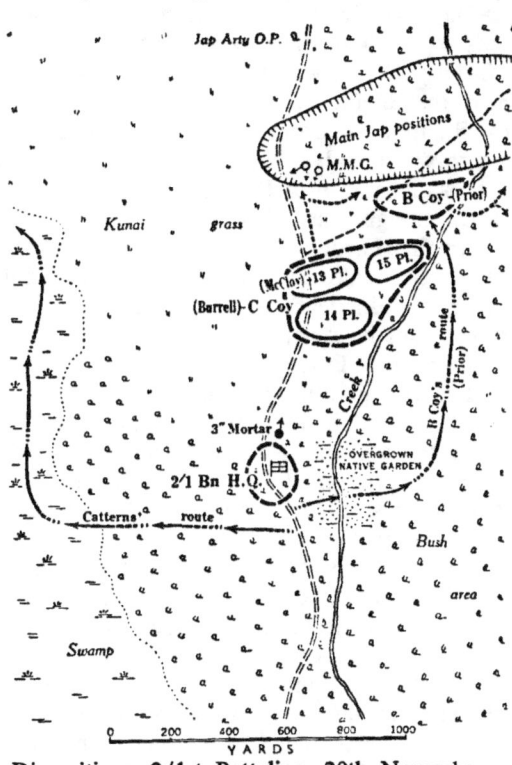

Dispositions, 2/1st Battalion, 20th November

As swift and determined in action as his commander, Catterns was on his way by 9.30 a.m. Whether or not he succeeded it was certain that this remarkable young leader, and his grim band of 90 men, would shock the Japanese.

With Catterns still deep in the undergrowth which framed the kunai, Burrell was gaining ground slowly along the track. Lieutenant McCloy's was his foremost platoon. Their skill and determination was hard for the Japanese to match. So careless was McCloy himself of what the enemy might do that, at one stage, observing from a distance of some 300 yards the movement of an enemy soldier who had escaped his forward scouts, and that this soldier was picking off his men, he stood among the plunging machine-gun and rifle fire to aim three carefully-considered shots. He killed with the third.

With three companies thus busying themselves Prior skirted Burrell's right, keeping to the thick bush, in execution of Cullen's earlier orders. His movement had been delayed and it was not until 11 a.m. that he was clear of Burrell's area and not until 12.30 that he came against the Japanese left flank. He proceeded then to smash through their outpost line but was finally held against their main positions, only some thirty yards separating attackers and attacked.

Close to Prior was the company quartermaster sergeant, Miller. When one of the riflemen was severely wounded and lying under heavy fire Miller brought him in. Later, a corporal, shot through the stomach, was lying in a forward and exposed position, beyond a bare area that was flailed by criss-crossing fire. It seemed impossible to help him while the daylight lasted, though the cries of the poor fellow's agony were demoralising even to that hardened company whom much fighting had taught to accept wounds or death as their lot. Not only did Miller go forward to what seemed certain death and give the wounded man morphia and dress his wounds, but he returned to cover, had a stretcher made and set off back again, with a brave stretcher bearer, Corporal Kemsley.[2] It took the two twenty minutes to crawl to the dying soldier, the stretcher dragging behind them. Then all three came back through the storm of fire. As though these deeds were not enough for him, Miller went out again in the late afternoon and brought back yet another wounded man. All the other soldiers felt the inspiration that flowed from him.

Soon after 2 p.m. Cullen told the brigadier that Prior and Burrell were in difficulties, that he considered the Japanese were employing two mountain guns, two medium machine-guns, one heavy and several light mortars, while he could not even guess at the number of light machine-guns. He began to worry about Catterns and asked Lloyd for more assistance. The latter said that he would send an American company (from Colonel Tomlinson's incomplete 126th Regimental Combat Team, the leading troops of which were then approaching Soputa) to help Catterns when it arrived. With this Cullen had temporarily to be content. He tried to strike a blow by bringing his 3-inch mortar into action about 2.15 p.m. Twenty-one accurate rounds silenced a medium machine-gun which had been firing from the edge of the kunai ahead, but a quick backlash whipped the Australians as twenty-nine artillery rounds fairly caught the headquarters group. (The victims were puzzled by the remarkable accuracy of this fire until they discovered later that it was directed from an observation post in a near-by tree.)

By this time the other two battalions of the brigade were backing Cullen closely. With alacrity Hutchison's men had doused their breakfast fires when the 2/1st had drawn such accurate shots so quickly after passing through them, and they were now dug in to give depth to the leading battalion. Farther back along the track the 2/2nd were relieved not long before 2 p.m. by the first Americans to arrive and the 2/2nd

---

[2] Cpl W. J. Kemsley, NX47317; 2/1 Bn. Labourer; of Macksville, NSW; b. Westmoors, Dorset, England, 27 Jul 1912.

then closed in on the 2/3rd's rear. Scarcely had they done so when Lloyd told Edgar to send two companies to help the 2/1st and these, commanded by Captains Bosgard[3] and Blamey, reported to Cullen at 4.30 p.m. Cullen sent them to his right to strengthen Prior's outflanking attempts there, but darkness forbade more than a mere link with Prior. As darkness approached echoes of heavy firing came from the closed northern reaches of the track. Then the listeners knew that their comrades, Catterns and his ninety, had closed in.

These had made a very wide detour to approach the main track at a point about two miles in rear of the Japanese front. Silently and in closed-up single file they forced their way through tangled undergrowth and swamp. The sound of Japanese guns and mortars warned them at first how wide of the open kunai to keep and then, as the day lengthened, guided them as they swung right towards the enemy positions. About 6 p.m. Corporal Albanese[4] and the leading section crossed a faint pad roughly parallel to the main pathway. The pad showed signs of recent use. Near by ran a small stream which was obviously being used as a watering place.

Stealthily Catterns and Albanese crept forward through the silent bush.

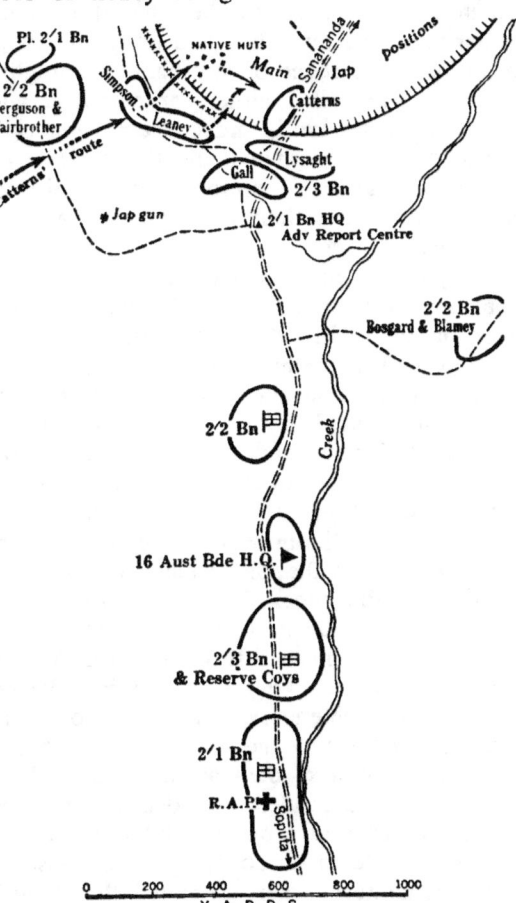

Forward positions, evening, 21st November

They stopped when they were overlooking a party of Japanese on their left. These were huddled over fires cooking their evening meal of rice. Some grass huts were near by and, through further trees, there was much movement on what was evidently the main track. From the right the

---

[3] Capt A. K. Bosgard, NX34874; 2/2 Bn. Bank clerk; of Mosman, NSW; b. Sydney, 8 Feb 1914. Killed in action 27 Nov 1942.

[4] WO2 R. H. Albanese, MM, NX68372; 2/1 Bn. Business manager; of Murwillumbah, NSW; b. Caboolture, Qld, 31 Dec 1919.

watchers could hear the gun which was causing the main Australian force so much trouble.

Catterns' group was a small one—ten officers and eighty men; it was too small to split, with one half going against the gun and the other on to the prime objective, the track. The Japanese were obviously occupying main positions and were therefore in strength. The Australians had no communication back to their battalion and so could not call for help either then or later. They had no means of getting the killed or wounded away from the scene of any fight that might develop. It was obviously a situation that called either for complete withdrawal or boldness of the most calculated kind, and concentration on one single purpose. Neither the leader nor his men could think easily in terms of withdrawal under any circumstances. Therefore they would attack. They would get the gun if they could, but their main object was to slash their way to the track and hold on there.

They were quiet, and still unseen by their foes, as they assembled, each company in extended order, five paces between each man. Leaney's men were on the right astride the little stream; Simpson's, on the left, used the foot pad as a start-line. At a sign from Catterns they began to move forward through the silent evening. Their slow advance through the darkening bush seemed implacable. They drew close to their unsuspecting enemies. Still they made no sound. Still their steps had a deliberate slowness, cat-like and intent. Scarcely 50 yards separated the two forces when suddenly the Japanese saw them.

So great was the impact on the Australians of the thunder of their own fire crashing into that silent place almost as one shattering report that, for a moment, the shock of it felled them to the ground. And then they were up again, hurling forward straight for the centre of a main defensive position. They smashed through apron fences of vines. They hurdled networks of trenches. They were fighting like wild cats in the very midst of the surprised defenders, some of whom, rallying, manned gun-pits and cut swathes through the attackers. But there was no stopping the assault and these Japanese died at their guns. Soon the huts were afire. They blazed high. Grenades exploded in the fires and scattered flames and sparks. Dead and wounded littered the area. Those of the defenders who were able to do so ran into the bush, some of them screaming.

Later, Catterns' men estimated that they killed at least eighty in that first assault. But they lost heavily themselves. Among their dead were five of the ten officers—Simpson and Leaney (the company commanders), Lieutenants Wiseman, Owen[5] and McClure[6]—all notable fighting men who had been foremost on almost every occasion of their battalion's long fight across the mountains. These, with the other dead and wounded, were gathered as the scattered attackers reassembled to the side of the

---

[5] Lt F. Owen, NX1249; 2/1 Bn. Panel beater and mechanic; of Croydon, NSW; b. Wallsend, NSW, 16 Dec 1918. Killed in action, 20 Nov 1942.

[6] Lt J. McClure, NX7639; 2/1 Bn. Salesman; of Vaucluse, NSW; b. Sydney, 16 May 1919. Killed in action, 20 Nov 1942.

main track where Lieutenant Murray,[7] who had taken Leaney's place, was already organising the defensive position. The wounded were laid round a big tree which had thick roots spreading out from it like little walls. Quickly the others began to dig in so that soon a sausage-shaped perimeter was developed with the remnants of what had been Simpson's company manning the northern end and Murray's men in the south.

As the night advanced they dug deeper. To the east they could hear more of their enemies in another main position. The noise of trucks slowly fading northwards told the story of the evacuation by the Japanese of their own casualties. And, during the night, the Australians increased these by another fifteen who were ill-advised enough to try to pass along the track in the dark.

With the dawn of the 21st the Japanese, now in possession of detailed knowledge of Catterns' positions, acted swiftly. They fell upon the Australians from three sides at once, having already harassed them throughout the night. The Australians, not only skilful and resolute in holding their fire until the most telling moment, but forced to do so because they had used up most of their ammunition in the previous evening's assault, broke the attacks.

Corporal Albanese, already marked for his contempt of danger in scouting ahead of the initial advance and a leading part he had played in the previous night's rout, was equally gallant in the defence. Corporal Ledden[8] was so aggressive in meeting the attackers that he was definitely known to have killed eight and was thought to have accounted for many more. Lance-Corporal Fletcher[9] was holding from a weapon-pit on the left flank. As the attackers pressed forward in the shadowy dawn he waited until they were a mere 10 to 15 yards away. Then he leaped from his pit to meet them, hurled a grenade, and as they fell or reeled from that explosion tore them with sub-machine-gun fire. During the next two hours the whole of his section was either killed or wounded. He was wounded himself. Wounded again he then lay in the open for half an hour, swept by fire, but still shouting encouragement to his fellows near by and urging them to positive and aggressive defence.

The Japanese, smarting under the blows already dealt them, and determined to clear this pocket from their midst, kept attacking throughout the day. They were like Red Indians circling a covered waggon.

In the crude daylight the Australian wounded, stacked round the big tree which had seemed to offer reasonable shelter the night before, were no longer protected from the encircling attacks. Many were wounded again from the fire which thudded intermittently round them as they lay. Some were killed.

---

[7] Lt A. D. B. Murray, MC, NX12590; 2/1 Bn. Bank officer; of Wentworthville, NSW; b. Walcha, NSW, 25 Oct 1906.
[8] Sgt J. P. Ledden, MM, NX11538. 2/3, 2/1 Bns; 33 Docks Operating Coy. Wharf labourer; of Paddington, NSW; b. Sydney, 11 Apr 1911.
[9] L-Cpl J. S. Fletcher, NX40507; 2/1 Bn. Labourer; of North Bingara, NSW; b. Bingara, 6 Jul 1908.

With the others round the tree was Private Soltan,[1] his leg badly broken by a gunshot wound the night before. When, however, during the darkness, a threat effervesced from the right flank, he dragged his roughly bandaged but unsplinted leg some 15 yards in that direction to lend his feeble strength to the defence. Throughout the entire day which followed he lay exposed, passing messages, hurrying ammunition along, reporting assaulting movements, urging his friends to greater efforts, and this though he was twice more wounded—in the other leg and in the body.

As this brave soldier endured the day on the one side of the defences, another, equally brave, was becoming a pivot on the opposite side. He was Private Varnum,[2] who by 10 a.m. was the only unwounded man along 30 yards of perimeter. A Japanese medium machine-gun was sited only 15 yards from him. It kept exploding almost in his face. He was later wounded, but he kept his Bren in action through all the hours of bitter daylight.

Catterns' men were not forgotten by the others farther back, however, as this desperate day progressed. Although he did not then know it, he had already done what he had set out to do, for the main Japanese force, outmanoeuvred and outfought, had fallen back during the night. The 2/1st followed behind them until 8.30 a.m., and was then ordered to halt to allow the 2/2nd and 2/3rd Battalions to pass through in that order.

Colonel Edgar sent Captain Bosgard groping to the right with two companies while Captain Fairbrother duplicated this movement on the left. Captain Gall's company of the 2/3rd came forward along the track in an attempt to push along that narrow cleared space to reach Catterns. Soon, however, the Australians found that the Japanese had resolved to give no more ground.

On the right Bosgard led his own and Captain Blamey's companies wide. Their way took them through some 3,000 yards of bush and swamp, although they were only about 400 yards from the main track. Though the Japanese fought them vigorously they pushed into a large supply dump area which contained about two tons of "good clean rice". After that, however, they were held. Then they dug their most advanced weapon-pits (only 30 to 50 yards from their enemies') in the comparatively open spaces of a derelict banana plantation on the forward side of a small stream.

On the left Fairbrother had been having a similar experience though his detour was rather more shallow. Of the events there Sergeant Caling[3] later wrote:

> We moved by dead reckoning through jungle, swamps and a belt of shoulder-high kunai grass to the forming-up place for the attack. The start time was 3 o'clock on a hot, muggy afternoon—November 21st, 1942. We advanced on compass bearing, but after about 100 yards we ran into a swamp, and were soon wading through

---

[1] Pte E. Soltan, MM, NX68683; 2/1 Bn. Labourer; of Botany, NSW; b. Botany, 21 Apr 1914.
[2] Pte A. J. Varnum, MM, NX45263; 2/1 Bn. Unemployed labourer; of Singleton, NSW; b. Singleton, 4 Mar 1917.
[3] WO2 G. J. Caling, NX1803; 2/2 Bn. Linesman; of Armidale, NSW; b. Sydney, 4 Apr 1917.

mud and slush up to our waists. Luckily, the Jap didn't get on to us while we were in there!

We eventually got through the swamp and hit low jungle again—and after about 100 yards of it we struck the Japs.

He was well prepared for us, being well dug in with fire lanes cut for his machine-guns. My platoon ran into a couple of these guns and we had to go to ground until the platoon commander decided to leave one section there to engage him, while he took the other two around on his flank. But he ran into further trouble; we suffered five casualties which we could ill afford . . . at this stage, as our platoon was only 18 strong. We then had word from company headquarters to withdraw about 40 yards and take our place in a two-company perimeter. It was at this stage that Pte Tom Harvey[4] showed outstanding courage and carried three wounded men out from right under the Japs' noses. . . .

We withdrew about 20 yards in the jungle and formed our perimeter. Then our mail came up while the wounded were evacuated back to the regimental aid post. I was particularly lucky with the mail as I received a parcel that contained 12 ounces of tobacco, together with papers and matches. At that time this was better than first prize in the lottery, as we had been weeks without a smoke.

The rain came with darkness and we spent a miserable night. 100 per cent security—that is, all hands awake and alert—was maintained all night.[5]

Meanwhile Edgar's men had made fleeting contact with Catterns' beleaguered companies, and Gall later renewed this contact as he pressed along the main axis. Though the whole area of the roadway was under Japanese fire a signals wire was run through from the main Australian positions, a telephone, ammunition and a small quantity of biscuits sent up. Soon the Japanese cut this wire, however, and so the main Australian force could not get sufficient information to form a true picture of Catterns' difficulties. But a message did get through to him to expect relief from 7.30 p.m. onwards.

When night came again (21st-22nd November) rain came with it, beating out of a sky which was split by lightning and shaken with thunder claps. By this time Captain Lysaght's company of the 2/3rd had moved forward to relieve Catterns and, in preparation for this, had joined Gall and Cullen's advanced headquarters which had been established in Gall's area. Soon after dark Catterns himself came out to meet Cullen. They discussed the situation and decided that the relieving company should not move into the area Catterns was vacating but settle just in rear of it. (As it transpired this was, perhaps, an unfortunate decision as the holding of Catterns' salient might have made subsequent operations easier. At the time, however, it seemed wise.)

In the early darkness Catterns' walking wounded began to come through. Lieutenant McCloy gathered all the men he could muster. They manned twelve stretchers. He led them forward into the position which had been so hard held. Three of them were lost as they moved through the bullet-swept night gently collecting the scattered wounded.

When the final cost of Catterns' little epic was tallied up it was found that, out of a total of 91 all ranks, five officers and 26 men had been

---

[4] Flying Officer T. C. Harvey, MM, NX1243. 2/2 Bn; RAAF 1943-45. Clerk; of Georgetown, NSW; b. Dudley, NSW, 19 Mar 1920.

[5] "The Sanananda Track", in *Nulli Secundus Log*, p. 94.

killed, 2 and 34 wounded, leaving only 24 unscathed. But the sortie had not only forced the defenders out of the positions where they had held the 2/1st initially on the 20th but also out of another completely prepared defensive position farther north (but still south of the termination of Catterns' dagger-like thrust). Indirectly, also, it resulted in the capture of the field piece which had so worried the Australians. Next day this was found buried where the Japanese had been forced to leave it when they withdrew, and there was ammunition buried near by. The Australians later used the weapon effectively themselves.

The position now, in the darkness of 21st-22nd November, was that Bosgard and Blamey of the 2/2nd were immobilised well to the right of the track. Their own right flank was completely in the air. On their left were some hundreds of yards of empty bush between them and Gall and Lysaght of the 2/3rd who were astride the main axis. Another gap, some hundreds of yards wide, intervened between the two latter and Fairbrother of the 2/2nd, who was out to the left with his own and Captain Ferguson's companies. The rest of the 2/3rd were crowding up behind the main positions to give depth. The remnants of the 2/1st were now in rear, their total strength reduced to 17 officers and 202 men.

During the day General Vasey had moved his headquarters from Popondetta to Soputa and had instructed Colonel Tomlinson to send a group of American officers forward to the 16th Brigade to get the picture from those hard-fighting men.

This 21st November was the day which MacArthur had set down for a forward movement on the whole front Buna-Sanananda-Gona; on which "all columns" were to be "driven through to the objectives regardless of losses". The Americans at Buna had not been able to comply with the orders. At Sanananda, for the moment, the Australians could do no more. Since starting across the mountains the 16th Brigade had lost almost one-third of their strength in battle alone—25 officers and 536 men (11 and 160 killed). Their losses had reduced their initial strength of 99 officers and 1,770 men to 67 and 974, and these were ill and worn and hungry.

It was now to be seen whether the fresh Americans of the 126th Regiment could change the course of events on the Sanananda front. Colonel Tomlinson set up his command post at Brigadier Lloyd's advanced headquarters. The plan was that the 16th Brigade would attempt no further move forward until the 126th Regiment had secured the Soputa-Sanananda-Cape Killerton track junction which lay ahead. And the Australians were content to sit back for a while and watch the Americans. There was a very real interest in their observation and a certain sardonic but concealed amusement. The Americans had told some of them that they "could go home now" as they (the Americans) "were here to clean things up".

Certainly Colonel Tomlinson's one thought was "to attack". He explained to Lloyd's liaison officer, Captain Williams,[6] that he proposed "a

---

[6] Maj D. E. Williams, NX4618; 2/3 Bn. Schoolteacher; of Canberra; b. Bargoed, Wales, 5 Feb 1918.

double enveloping movement" which would "squeeze the Japs right out". But he had little concept of the difficulties that would face his men in a flanking move through the swamp and bush. Nor did he realise (as the Australians did from bitter experience) how stubbornly the Japanese could refuse to be "squeezed".

Immediately before he actually entered the Sanananda fighting Tomlinson's II Battalion had been taken from him. In response to General Harding's request General Herring sent this battalion back across the Girua to strengthen the main American effort. They left Soputa on the 22nd. At 9.30 a.m. on the same day the III Battalion, Major Bond commanding, came up into the 16th Brigade area, detouring right and left to close on the Soputa-Sanananda-Killerton track junction by way of flanking tracks. Major Richard D. Boerem, with Companies "C" and "D" (less one platoon) of the I Battalion, pressed along the track itself to a point just beyond Lysaght's, the forward Australian company. From that time onwards for the rest of the day the position of the American companies became generally obscure. Captain Bevin D. Lee, with Company "L", had swung right. But his position was never as uncertain as that of the two companies on the left—Captain John D. Shirley's Company "I" and Lieutenant Wilbur C. Lytle's Company "K". Shirley swung wider than Lytle but, after the two left the main axis, nothing more was heard of them for the rest of the day by their worried colonel, or the watching Australians.

Tomlinson had planned his attack for the 23rd. But, as the day wore on, the positions of his companies were still unknown to him. On the right Lee was reported to be moving forward but enemy fire and sharp thrusts apparently disorganised him to some extent. He finally took up a position that was virtually an extension of the Australian right-flank positions where Bosgard and Blamey had their men dug in—and with whom one of his platoons had already joined after the company had been temporarily scattered.

The Australians themselves were not quite sure what was brewing. Bosgard had reported to Edgar that there seemed to be a stronger force opposite him than there had been the previous day, and that the volume of fire sweeping his positions seemed to have increased. He thought his opponents might have been reinforced the previous night. A vigorous assault on his positions (in which he himself was wounded in the face) lent colour to this theory, although the attackers were well held. Further than that, he was becoming uneasy about the volume of water gathering in his pits. He feared for the health of his men. But it was some consolation that the Japanese opposing him were on even lower ground. To the left there was greater uncertainty. Captain Fairbrother was acutely aware of extensive Japanese activity on his own left. But Edgar could do nothing to assist him, so Fairbrother's men patrolled or lay in their water-filled holes and shot at any Japanese who appeared.

And farther left again, apparently, the Americans under Lytle and Shirley, were groping into the thick and swampy bushland. During the morning Tomlinson had some news that these were approximately 1,000 yards north of the 16th Brigade and still moving northwards. The Australians doubted this. Later Tomlinson agreed that they should attempt to "fix" his companies with prismatic compasses bearing on signal lights fired by Lytle and Shirley into the air. They did this. Then it was revealed that the Americans had circled round in the swamp and bush and arrived back at a point less than 400 yards from 16th Brigade headquarters.[7]

Although they had planned an attacking movement on to the track for 3 p.m. this day they then had to abandon the project in favour of a continuation of their enveloping movement.

The entry into action of the Americans was not the only new development in the Sanananda area. The "Blackforce" detachment of the 2/1st Field Regiment (Major Hanson commanding) began to land at Popondetta on the 23rd, where the 2/6th Field Company had arrived on the 19th and, on a site selected by Lieut-Colonel McDonald, had at once set to work building an airstrip. At first they had no mechanical equipment to help them and

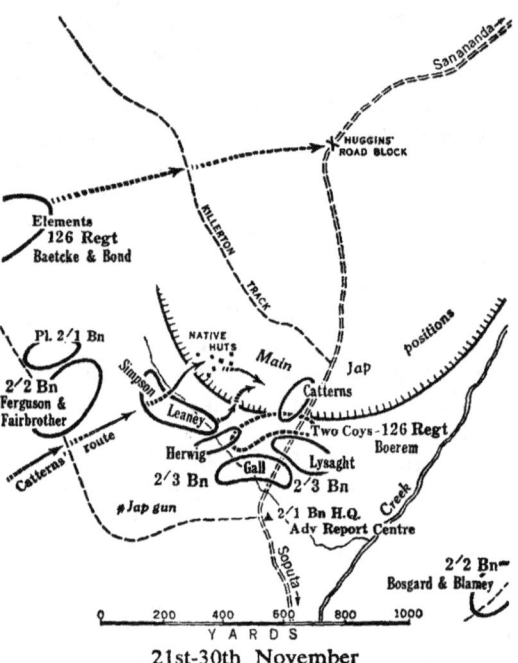

21st-30th November

faced the task of making a strip at least 1,400 yards in length on ground which was completely covered by kunai grass about 6 feet high. Colonel Canet[8] (Vasey's very able chief supply officer) loyally supported them by making available all the native carriers he could muster and, directed by the engineers, these worked so vigorously that in one day they cut a 1,600-yard swathe through the kunai. On the 21st the first Douglas transport touched down on the new strip, which made it possible to bring the field guns so quickly into action. So Hanson with Captain Wade,[9] Lieutenant Finlay[10] and 23 men, 2 guns, 2 jeeps, 200 rounds of ammunition and stores, landed in six transports about 9

---

[7] Interview, Maj D. E. Williams.
[8] Maj-Gen L. G. Canet, CBE, VX13430. HQ 7 Div (AA&QMG 1942-43); Col "Q" HQ NG Force 1943-44; D of Organisation "A" Bch LHQ 1945. Regular soldier; b. Shepparton, Vic, 1 Dec 1910.
[9] Capt E. R. Wade, NX831; 2/1 Fd Regt. Estate agent; of Hamilton, NSW; b. Lithgow, NSW, 4 May 1915.
[10] Maj W. M. Finlay, NX8708; 2/1 Fd Regt. Regular soldier; of Balgowlah, NSW; b. Edinburgh, Scotland, 30 Jul 1909.

a.m. on the 23rd. (Within a short time a complete troop was assembled and thus the artillerymen had four guns with them.) Immediately on landing Hanson assembled his guns and hurried them over the ten miles of track to the Soputa area. By 5 p.m. he had fired his registration shots and his men were eagerly accepting action. The infantrymen were pleased to see them. They had had no artillery support since the beginning of their journey across the mountains. They listened approvingly to the sharp "crack" of the 25-pounders and told one another that it was "like old times".

The 24th began auspiciously for the Americans and Australians. Allied aircraft assailed the Japanese coastal positions from Buna on the right through Sanananda to Gona on the left. The 16th Brigade diarist recorded that "the ground actually shook at times with the bomb blasts". His satisfaction was apparently a little tempered, however, when he had to record that "in one particular instance one stick of bombs actually fell behind our forward companies". But the error was quickly rectified, and the next run brought bombs crashing accurately down on their proper targets. Later Hanson's men harassed the Japanese with their artillery fire.

Still the infantry had to slog it out on the ground. On the right there was little change. Blamey took over the Australian command there from Bosgard. Captain Lee with his Americans accepted the sharp give and take of the skirmishing round the dump area. On the left Fairbrother's and Ferguson's men squirmed unhappily in their water-filled holes. A platoon from the 2/1st joined them in their misery. The Americans Lytle and Shirley were still struggling through the scrub and swamp somewhere near by. Later in the afternoon these two reported that they were in contact with one another. Plans were accordingly laid for them to attack the known enemy positions in their vicinity on the 25th. But late in the day probing enemy pushed them back into the swamp in some disorder.

Apart from this a separate new movement was now under way. The previous night a composite company from the 2/3rd Battalion had been formed under Captain Walker. Their orders were to break bush round the left flank until they cut the track which branched left to Cape Killerton. They would then swing right again to cut the main track about one mile north of its junction with the Killerton Track, which junction was the present American objective. From that position they would be able to lend strength to a hoped-for thrust by the 21st Brigade from the Gona side and to back up the American efforts. The patrol was to stay out for six or seven days if necessary. And with these instructions Walker set out at 9.45 a.m., Lieutenants Boyer[1] and Sayers[2] and ninety-one men constituting his party. They carried four days' hard and three days' emergency rations.

---

[1] Maj K. M. Boyer, NX9299; 2/3 Bn. Accounts clerk; of Homebush, NSW; b. Drummoyne, NSW, 7 Oct 1918.
[2] Maj H. T. Sayers, MM, NX5605; 2/3 Bn. Gold dredging employee; of Wellington, NSW; b. Sydney, 15 Jan 1916.

There was no significant tactical change on the 25th. On the divisional level much planning was going into the construction of airstrips so that more men and more materials could be flown in more quickly. Popondetta was emerging as the key airfield. General Herring passed orders on to Vasey to concentrate his constructional effort there for the present. He was to extend the existing strip and build three additional strips as quickly as possible. To enable this to be done and because of the bogginess of the site work on a strip at Soputa was to be discontinued temporarily.

On the battalion level a severe loss marred the day on the right of the track. The heavy mortars of the 126th Regiment were concentrating on the central Japanese area. One bomb, erratic in flight, landed squarely on Captain Blamey's headquarters. That brave young leader was mortally wounded, one of his men was killed, and five were wounded, including the brigade major of the 16th Brigade, Dawson,[3] Captain Lee (the American company commander), and two other American officers.

On the left the only movement of note was the continuing effort of Lytle and Shirley, their companies now merged, to reach the track. Major Bond, chafing against the indecisive nature of this movement and urged by Colonel Tomlinson, personally took command there himself, determined to force an issue.

On the 26th the American attack which had been working up since the 22nd moved forward behind an intense mortar and artillery barrage. It began in the morning as a coordinated drive from the right, along the track, and from the left. On the right Company "L", now commanded by Major Bert Zeeff, gained some 350 yards but lost heavily in doing so, and by 3 p.m. it was halted, with a heavy machine-gun firing into its left. On the track itself heavy machine-gun fire held Boerem as he tried with scant success to root out the defenders there. Behind him shells were chopping into the American rear echelon. Left of the track Bond's men still struggled with the bush and with vigorous feelers from the Japanese right.

For the Australians the day was marked by a loss similar to but even more extensive than that of the previous day. An American mortar bomb fell on a platoon in the forward central position. It killed five men and wounded eight; only two in the platoon were left unhurt.

At 5.30 p.m. Brigadier Lloyd had news from the special patrol of the 2/3rd which had set out round the left on the 24th. Lieutenant Boyer, who had carried on when Captain Walker was forced to return with a sprained ankle, sent word that he had reached the Killerton Track at 11.30 that day, but swamps blocked his eastward move. By this time, however, Lloyd had sent another patrol (from the 2/1st Battalion) into the same general area searching for additional information. General Vasey was chafing at the delay and was anxious to know whether he could get a really large body of troops round the left to cut the Sanananda Track in the vicinity of Cape Killerton.

---

[3] Lt-Col L. E. Dawson, DSO, ED, NX12330. 2/13 Bn; BM 16 Bde; GSO1 (Staff Duties) LHQ 1944-45. Buyer; of Chatswood, NSW; b. Killara, NSW, 4 Aug 1909.

Now illness was beginning to make even more alarming inroads than formerly among the Australians. Malaria was widespread and daily becoming more so. Scrub typhus, a killer, was almost common. Brigadier Lloyd determined that his "absolute maximum for any move forward but not for any sustained action that may be asked of them" was 79 officers and 942 men, including 4 officers and 91 men in "B" Echelon and 10 and 100 temporarily retained in the regimental aid post for the treatment of sickness.

The forward medical arrangements at this time were still in the hands of Lieut-Colonel Hobson and his 2/4th Field Ambulance. Until the crossing of the Kumusi River casualties were sent back to Kokoda where the 14th Field Ambulance took over the Main Dressing Station as the advance continued, whence the more seriously wounded and sick were flown to Port Moresby, and where the lighter cases were held for treatment and subsequent return direct to their units. Hobson's men established staging posts at intervals along the two routes of advance forward from the Kumusi (to Soputa and to Gona) and, on 21st November, formed a Main Dressing Station at Soputa to serve both the 16th and 25th Brigades. Within four days they were then holding at the M.D.S. and in their various staging posts 638 wounded and sick. They themselves were hard pressed for men and it was only by the exercise of much administrative ingenuity and by continued effort that they were able to meet their commitments. Their position improved greatly, however, after the beginning of air evacuation from Popondetta about the 23rd. Jeeps were landed for them, a captured sedan was converted into a motor ambulance and, for the first time in the Papuan campaign, motor vehicles were used for medical work forward of the road-head near Uberi. But the Japanese struck them a heavy blow on 27th November. After a low reconnaissance three days earlier of the areas near Soputa where the M.D.S. and the American Clearing Hospital were sited, 13 Zeros bombed and strafed each medical centre. At the M.D.S., sited in a clearing by the roadside and practically void of cover, 22 Australians were killed; about 50 were wounded including patients, members of the field ambulance, visitors to the hospital, and natives. Among the killed were two well-loved Australian medical officers, Majors Vickery and McDonald,[4] both of whom had done outstanding work during the campaign across the mountains. At the Clearing Hospital six Americans were killed.

A large part of the 27th was taken up with attempts to sort out confusion as to the exact positions of the American companies. The Americans themselves reported that Zeeff, on the right, having advanced some 350 yards, was in rear of the Japanese. Of Boerem's two companies in the vicinity of the track itself one was reported to be 100 yards forward of Captain Lysaght of the 2/3rd Battalion, and the other 200 yards to Lysaght's left front. But the Australians held rather different opinions.

---

[4] Maj H. F. G. McDonald, VX14704. 2/5, 2/4 Fd Ambs. Medical practitioner; of Canterbury, Vic; b. Queenscliff, Vic, 15 Mar 1912. Killed in action 27 Nov 1942.

Captain Herwig,[5] who had come forward with an additional company of the 2/3rd to strengthen the left front near Lysaght, suggested that Americans who had been digging in beyond him the night before had pulled out during the darkness without warning him. When this disturbing report was made to Colonel Tomlinson he at once sent staff officers scouring the bush to locate his companies. But some confusion must have continued for Herwig reported at 9 p.m. that the Americans had not advanced as they claimed and were to his rear.

Shortly before this, action had flared up once more on the right. There was fierce Japanese mortar and small-arms fire in the early darkness. Hanson's field guns added deeper notes to the uproar as they brought supporting fire down in front of the Allied infantry. The main volume of the Japanese attack fell on Zeeff's men but it also viciously flicked the Australian right and, in doing so, killed Captain Bosgard, who had taken over again on Blamey's death, as he lent his brave and experienced presence to his forward platoons. Thus, within three days, both of the Australian commanders in that area had been killed—a bitter loss which their battalion could ill afford.

At this time the movement over the range of General Herring's advanced headquarters was proceeding and it opened at Popondetta at 8 p.m. on the 28th.

On the actual front the infantry were still shaking themselves out and the commanders maturing their plans. The only sharp clash took place on the right where Americans of the III/126th Battalion ambushed and routed an enemy patrol killing, they thought, about eight. That morning Lieutenant Boyer brought in his special patrol from the Killerton Track. He confirmed the reports he had sent in previously. He said that he had paddled through swamps for two days before he cut the Killerton Track on the 26th. The spreading marsh prevented him from cutting across to the Sanananda Track. He had followed the Killerton Track southwards. Near the area where the Americans under Lytle and Shirley had clashed with the Japanese on the 24th four of his men fell to sudden fire from an enemy whom the Americans had apparently made watchful in that locality. The Australians carried the wounded back into the swamp. Just after midday on the 27th they struck the track the American wide left-flanking movement had followed and it led them back.

Boyer's discouraging news was confirmed by reports from the 2/1st Battalion patrol which Vasey had had sent into the same area on the 26th. Swamps and vine thickets had so hampered that patrol that it was now on its way back. Clearly no large body of troops could work round the left as General Vasey had hoped—certainly no farther to the left than the track which the Americans were using.

That night an extreme quiet settled on the Sanananda front. It was as though the opposing sides were brooding in the darkness. A red flare climbed high into the darkness from the coast's edge, hung and then

---

[5] Capt L. C. Herwig. NX4224. 2/3 Bn, HQ 11 Bde. Factory manager; of Arncliffe, NSW; b. Essex, England, 2 Dec 1900.

fell reluctantly. The rattle of spasmodic machine-gun fire welled distantly through the shades from the Buna front.

With the 29th another indecisive day passed. Then came the 30th, scheduled as the day for the culmination of the American efforts. This time the men of the 126th Regiment were to make their principal effort on the left of the track, with a coordinated attempt to move forward along the track itself, and a move in unison by Zeeff's Company "L" on the right.

The early morning was broken by small-arms fire from both sides, Australian artillery fire, and shots from a Japanese mountain gun. At 8.30 a.m. the Australian 25-pounders began their task of softening the Japanese defences. A Japanese gun opened in reply and small-arms fire began to whip more stingingly through the bush. Australian and American mortars added to the din. A few minutes after 9 the American attack began. For some little time the fire sounded intense to the Australians. Then it died to spasmodic bursts. It seemed as though the bush had swallowed the attack. But, as the 16th Brigade diarist recorded,

in this particular type of fighting the temporary [loss of] contact with companies was no new experience and news of the success or otherwise of our friends was eagerly awaited.

As the day waned, however, the anxious Australians knew that, on the right, there had been some edging forward but no marked progress; on the track itself Boerem's companies were stopped almost dead where they stood; but on the left there was more to record.

The previous day Major George Bond's men had been feeling the Japanese right flank about 1,000 yards west of the track. They were joined there then by the anti-tank and cannon companies under Captain Alfred Medendorp (who had come down from Wairopi) and by Major Bernd G. Baetcke, who was sent forward by Colonel Tomlinson to take over command and push through to the track next day. He began this movement, directly east, at 9.10 on the 30th with Major Bond in command of the main attacking force—Companies "I" and "K". Captain Shirley led the advance with Captain Roger Keast's anti-tank company assisting him. The second rifle company covered the movement, drawing heavy Japanese fire as they did so. The Cannon Company was in reserve.

The Japanese right flank gave to the initial assault. About that time Bond was severely wounded but the deliberate movement towards the track went on. A number of minor skirmishes followed. About 5 p.m. the leading scouts reported a Japanese bivouac area ahead of them and astride the track. Shirley led his company into a bayonet attack. Captain Keast was supporting him closely. Lieutenant Daniels,[6] a forward observation officer for the Australian artillery, thrust to the front. The attackers drove in strongly. After they had bayoneted a number of Japanese Shirley's men set up a perimeter defence astride the track. But the defenders took a toll. Daniels was among the killed.

---

[6] Lt A. N. T. Daniels, NX3380; 2/1 Fd Regt. Labourer; of Lidcombe, NSW; b. Lidcombe, 30 Jun 1919. Killed in action, 1 Dec 1942.

Thus, after more than a week of indecisive skirmishing through the bush, the position which was to become well known as "Huggins' Road-Block" was established on the Sanananda Track, just south of the Cape Killerton track junction. It was driven into a weakness between two main positions —the one immediately fronting the main Allied forces trying to push northward along the track, the other lying north again of the area in which Shirley established his perimeter.

The establishment of this road-block serves as a measure of the Americans' ability at this time. It had taken them nine days to achieve it. Their task was closely comparable with that which Captain Catterns had carried out in one day with roughly one-third the American strength, with no support, with very worn men and with the infliction of much greater casualties on the Japanese. And the Americans were fresh troops against whom the resistance on the track itself was only a fraction as strong as that which Catterns had met. But the latter's men had learned swiftness in action. They were the hardy and cunning survivors of many difficult days in North Africa, Greece, and the Owen Stanleys. They had confidence in one another. They were determined. Their leaders were tried men who held their appointments because they had been proved many times. They had learned to match the Japanese in the latter's chosen form of warfare. The bush was becoming their familiar habitat. By comparison the Americans seemed soft. They had had no opportunity to grow battle-wise in action. Some of their leaders were as bewildered as the men. Though many of the Americans were individually brave, as units they had neither the determination nor the skill to drive through difficulties to their objective. They, men of a nation which had grown great through self-reliance, had apparently to try to learn how to recapture this quality, which their machines (temporarily no use to them) had taken from them.

So December came with the stalemate on the Sanananda front barely eased—despite the arrival of the Americans. The main Allied positions resembled a horseshoe with the ends pointing northwards. On the right extremity Zeeff's company was still located, with the wasting remnants of the two 2/2nd Battalion companies to the left rear and closer to the track, on which Boerem's Americans were being closely backed by shadow companies of the 2/3rd Battalion (totalling 12 officers and 288 men). On the left extension of the horseshoe the two 2/2nd Battalion companies, also wasting fast, were still holding to their water-filled holes. To their left front was a platoon of the 2/1st Battalion. Slightly north of a line which might have been drawn from one extremity of the horseshoe to the other the road-block had been established. Major Baetcke, with Company "K" and the Cannon Company, was still in the bush 1,400 yards to the west of the road-block. And on the track which bisected the horseshoe's arc, enclosed but not sealed by these Allied positions, were the most southerly of the Japanese positions.

The first few days of December saw the road-block party holding fast against continuing Japanese attacks. It was in a precarious position. The garrison, consisting of Company "I" and the anti-tank company, with a light machine-gun section from Company "M" and a signals detachment, in all now numbering roughly 250, was in a relatively open space among bush and swamp, approximately oval shaped, some 250 by 150 yards in extent. Tall trees and thick bush surrounded it. Within this cover attacks could be mounted in safe concealment. From it they could erupt with stunning force. There was no supply line except that which could be driven by force and guile through Japanese-held territory. In some respects it was Catterns' story over again, with the defenders raked by fire and circling attacks exploding continuously in upon them, except that Catterns' ordeal had ended after one night and one day while that of the Americans was to drag out during a weary succession of days and nights.

Originally Baetcke had planned to settle his whole force in the road-block area, but Boerem's failure to progress along the track on the 30th had, in Baetcke's opinion, rendered this plan too risky. He therefore prepared to remain where he was (with Company "K" and the Cannon Company) as a base from which communications and supply to the almost beleaguered group might be maintained. On 1st December Captain Meredith M. Huggins in charge of a ration party reached him and Baetcke sent him on to the road-block next day. Scarcely had Huggins arrived there with his supplies, however, than Shirley was killed. Huggins at once took command.

Colonel Tomlinson hoped to be able to close the gap between his main force and the wedge formed by Huggins' force. But, for the present, his plan came to nothing. Major Zeeff, who was ordered forward on the right of the track, made ground by hard fighting but lost so many men that he was finally checked. Tomlinson then ordered him back. Simultaneously Boerem had been trying to make ground along the track, but again his men were stopped almost where they stood.

In this situation there was obviously little need for Tomlinson himself and his headquarters in front of Sanananda. General Herring therefore agreed that he might rejoin the main 32nd Divisional group. This he did on the 4th with most of his headquarters, leaving Baetcke in charge of the Americans on the Sanananda Track and under Brigadier Lloyd's command.

That day General Vasey came down to Lloyd's headquarters to discuss a further American attack planned for the 5th, and with him Lieut-General Eichelberger, who had then just taken command of the Americans before Buna; General Herring; and Brigadier-General Willoughby, chief of General MacArthur's Intelligence staff. It was decided that Boerem would lead frontally once more in an effort to clear the main axis and the country to the right. At the same time Baetcke would attempt to push through the Japanese right-flank positions to the track and then swing north to join Huggins. Captain Burrell of the 2/1st Battalion and Lieutenant MacDougal of the 2/3rd would accompany the Americans in the dual capacity of advisers and liaison officers. All the mortar and artillery fire which could be brought to bear would be laid down to cover the assault. The Americans would carry three days' hard and two days' emergency rations to be supplied by Lloyd. Their own supply arrangements were not considered suitable for the sort of operations which it was hoped would develop.

At 7.15 a.m. on the 5th the guns opened, and American and Australian mortars joined in. Soon afterwards the American movement began. The first report from them did not come until 9.40 a.m. A message then reached Lloyd from Boerem that the frontal attack had gone to ground along the rear line of the artillery concentration. Boerem said that he was trying to reorganise for a second attempt at his objective.

At 11.30 he expressed the opinion that

> his troops were somewhat disorganised. They had evidently become scattered in the thick undergrowth and it was taking some time to get them reorganised. They had passed through only one vacated enemy position, a LMG pit with timber overhead cover, but were now held up by a gun approximately 50 yards to his front whilst there was one LMG slightly further back and one on his right flank.[7]

Meanwhile Baetcke, having reached the limit of his northward movement through the bush parallel with the track, had swung eastward towards the track on a bearing of 110 degrees. But, for all practical purposes blind in the heavy kunai which closed round his men, after struggling on for about 200 yards on this bearing he was beaten by a destructive fire.

So once again the attack faded out. Two men were killed, 63 were wounded and 25 were missing at the end of the day. A bare 100 yards was gained near and to the right of the track by Boerem's men and the Japanese had fended off Baetcke's smaller band without undue disturbance to themselves.

The plight of Huggins and his men was therefore still as desperate as before. The Japanese were giving them no rest. On the same day as the main attack failed Huggins himself was badly wounded and a supply train, some 60 strong, was blocked by a determined Japanese ambush only 300 yards from the little garrison.

By this time the concern of the American high command about the apparent lack of decisiveness on the part of the American troops engaged was manifest. General Willoughby went forward during this day's attack to watch his countrymen in action. On his return he closely interrogated Lieutenant MacDougal who was not only an experienced and dashing officer, but an unusually outspoken one. MacDougal was very blunt regarding what he considered the Americans' lack of fighting qualities. Willoughby not only did not resent but appeared to appreciate the Australian's frankness.

Now, however, the struggle along the Sanananda Track was entering a third phase. First the tired 16th Brigade had used up its last dregs of strength against the stubborn Japanese. Next the fresh and confident Americans had drained both their freshness and their confidence. The Australians of the 30th Brigade, most of them still unblooded, would now

---

[7] War diary, 16th Brigade.

open the third round. Lieut-Colonel Kessels[8] had his 49th Battalion at Soputa by nightfall on the 4th, 24 officers and 481 men strong. The 55th/53rd Battalion landed at Dobodura and Popondetta next day, and by the morning of the 6th had completed their movement to Soputa. (The third battalion of the brigade—the 39th—had gone to Gona.)

The 49th and 55th/53rd Battalions were approaching their first action as units. The 49th, of course, was the original battalion of the Port Moresby garrison so that the period of its service in New Guinea went back to before the outbreak of the war with Japan. Despite this it had never yet been committed. It had been moved about in the changing plans for the defence of the Port Moresby area. This had involved it in monotonous months of labouring at the digging and building of defences of all kinds. Interspersed with this had been a total of some months of labouring on the wharfs and at varied maintenance tasks. Perforce training had been sporadic and incomplete. Only air raids, the promise of action as the Japanese threat had welled close through the mountain mists, and uneventful patrols had highlighted the long period. The temper of the men was uncertain, partly because of their history, partly because they had divided minds about the nature of the service that might fall to their lot. Their approach to the problem of enlistment in the A.I.F. well illustrated this.

On 28th August 12 officers and 138 men comprised the actual A.I.F. strength of the battalion. Twenty-five officers and 185 men had volunteered to transfer from the militia to the A.I.F. but the transfers had not yet been gazetted. The militiamen had received with resentment a notification, subsequently cancelled, that on enlistment in the A.I.F. the letter "M" would be inserted in their army numbers to mark them out from original members of the volunteer force. This alone held many back from offering for unrestricted service. By 9th September enlistment figures had not altered so that of a total battalion strength of 37 and 818, only 40 per cent were then serving members of the A.I.F. or volunteers for that force. (The officer response was 100 per cent.) By 28th October the percentage had increased only to 53 per cent.

The battalion commander, Lieut-Colonel Kessels, had had long militia training. He had been commissioned since 1922. Most of his commissioned service had been with the same battalion. A stiffening of experienced A.I.F. officers had come to him about the middle of the year and soon afterwards.[9]

Even more curiously composed and shaped was the 55th/53rd Battalion. This had been formed on 26th October by the amalgamation of the 55th and 53rd Battalions. The 55th had arrived at Port Moresby with

---

[8] Col O. A. Kessels, DSO, ED, QX36757; CO 49 Bn 1942-43. Railway control clerk; of Nundah, Qld; b. Sherwood, Qld, 4 May 1903.

[9] Among these were: from the 2/9th Battalion, Major E. W. Fleming (who became the battalion second-in-command), Capt W. H. Noyes ("D" Company commander), Captain R. W. Forster ("C" Company commander), Lieutenants W. K. Gillespie and I. W. Hill; from the 2/12th Battalion, Capt S. E. A. Pixley and Lieutenant S. W. Fernan; from the 2/25th Battalion, Captain J. W. Thorn ("B" Company commander) and Captain H. F. Shaw (Adjutant); from the 2/33rd, Captain J. K. Bryce ("A" Company commander), who had come by way of the 53rd Battalion with which he had served in the mountains.

the 14th Brigade at the end of May, had not been committed before and had suffered the boredom and frustration of Moresby garrison life. The second component of this composite unit had been the ill-starred 53rd Battalion which Brigadier Potts had sent out of action at the most critical stage of the mountain fighting. It had then done labouring work for a while before it went out of existence as a separate battalion—at which time it numbered 29 officers and 581 men. Some of these went to the new unit; others were allotted to other infantry units from their own States; others again, on the score of age or for similar reasons, went to service units then in New Guinea. Ninety-eight picked men had previously gone to the 39th Battalion.

Lieut-Colonel Lovell[1] led the composite 55th/53rd to the forward areas. Thirty years old, he had been a militia officer since 1935. An original officer of the 2/1st Battalion, he had been commanding the 55th for only a few weeks before the formation of the composite battalion. None of his company commanders had served overseas. Indeed, the 55th/53rd, as it approached its first action, lacked cohesion and training as a unit.

With this battalion and the 49th General Vasey proposed to relieve the worn 16th Brigade on 6th December. On 30th November the brigade had numbered only 67 officers and 795 men. Since crossing the Kumusi it had lost 13 officers and 143 men in action and the numbers of sick actually evacuated from the units totalled 18 and 344, although

it became a tradition that a man would not go back until his temperature rose to 103 degrees (wrote a member of the 2/2nd Battalion later). Even when a man was evacuated it involved an all day march back to the Popondetta airstrip.

Another recorded that

all had illnesses of one kind or another, mostly malaria; the physical hardships of the campaign, and the prolonged lack of sufficient food, had told on everyone. It was physical effort enough to walk around in safety at Battalion HQ; it required incomparable morale to stick day after day in the rifle company positions.[2]

An officer of the 2/3rd Battalion wrote:

One man arrived at the RAP looking very sick. The M.O., 'Aspro Joe' Joseph,[3] said 'How do you feel?' 'Not as hot as I was last night, Doc.' The M.O. then took his temperature. It was 106.2. This man had walked for 1½ hours to reach the RAP.[4]

Captain Dunlop[5] has left a general picture of some of the less spectacular sides of the 2/2nd Battalion's day-to-day routine, listing these among his chief impressions:

The weather, which alternated between hot sun and heavy rain. Both phases were uncomfortable everywhere; they were hell for the forward troops, who spent the three weeks either burning in hot sun (with no daytime shelter in forward pits) or in feet of water.

---

[1] Lt-Col D. J. H. Lovell, NX53. 16 Bde; 2/1 Bn; CO 55/53 Bn. Bank officer; of Haberfield and Bellevue Hill, NSW; b. Stanmore, NSW, 17 Dec 1911.
[2] Maj J. W. Dunlop, "The Sanananda Track" in *Nulli Secundus Log*, pp. 95-6.
[3] Capt L. H. Joseph, NX77338. 2/6 Fd Amb; RMO 2/3 Bn 1942; I and II Corps HQ 1943-45. Medical student; of Sydney; b. Sydney, 22 Feb 1919.
[4] Capt T. B. Silk, "Kokoda Diary" in *Chocolate and Green*, July 1945, p. 45.
[5] Maj J. W. Dunlop, NX3206. 2/2 Bn; GSO2 (Staff Duties) LHQ 1945. Paper merchant; of Sydney; b. Sydney, 20 May 1910.

The maintenance difficulties. Ammunition had constantly to be carried out, and a reserve built up with companies; hot food had to be cooked well in rear and got out to companies; the normal rations had to be distributed; stretcher parties were constantly needed—not only for wounded, but for the many men who refused to come in until too weak to walk. . . .

The team spirit of the whole Brigade at that time must be mentioned. Not only did HQ Company and Battalion HQ do more than ever before to help rifle companies, but carrying parties were provided by Brigade HQ, 2/1st and 2/3rd Battalions regularly and without question, and more than willingly.

That the Q arrangements mentioned briefly above worked as smoothly as they did was due to the efforts of Capt McPherson[6] and Lieut Richards,[7] both too ill to walk, with one stationed at one end of the supply line and one the other; Sgt Asher,[8] who established a kitchen in rear, and others such as Sgts McDonald,[9] Hain[1] and Cpl Brewer[2] who organised the supply and issue generally and handled the native carrier line. The last stage of the food's journey to forward companies was, of course, in the hands of the Companies' Q's, and S-Sgt Bright[3] (in bare feet because his feet were too sore to wear boots) and Sgt O'Donnell[4] in particular, were untiring.

No man will ever forget the fifty-bed hospital—there is no other way of describing it—run by the RAP just in rear of Battalion HQ, which looked after not only our own sick and wounded, but literally hundreds of US and other Australian troops who used it because of its position and because of its first-class organisation under Captain McGuinness[5] and Sgt Nicholas.[6]

Then there was the Salvation Army Coffee Stall run by Mr J. McCabe[7] a mile or so in rear; a fitting finish to the outstanding work that this Salvation Army officer did throughout the campaign.[8]

It was clear that this spent formation, willing though it still was, could do no more to affect the course of events along the Sanananda Track. Between 3rd October and 6th December (when its relief by the 30th Brigade began) it lost about 29 officers and 576 men in action.[9] Fifty-six

---

[6] Maj W. J. McPherson. MBE, NX12472. 2/2 Bn; BM 4 Bde 1944-45. Telegraphist; of Canberra, ACT; b. Maclean, NSW, 29 Nov 1912.

[7] Capt S. R. Richards, NX7159; 2/2 Bn. Farm hand; of East Maitland, NSW; b. Hurstville, NSW, 23 Jul 1917.

[8] WO2 M. H. Asher, NX8753; 2/2 Bn. Cook; of Narellan, NSW; b. Melbourne, 11 Nov 1905.

[9] Sgt F. M. McDonald, NX2335; 2/2 Bn. Labourer; of South Grafton, NSW; b. Wellington, NSW, 25 Aug 1905.

[1] WO2 A. D. Hain, NX7145; 2/2 Bn. Produce merchant; of East Maitland, NSW; b. West Maitland, 26 Jul 1910.

[2] Cpl C. B. Brewer, NX1452. 2/2 Bn; 2/7 Armd Regt. Labourer; of Nana Glen, NSW; b. Grafton, NSW, 14 May 1919.

[3] S-Sgt W. R. Bright, NX9642; 2/2 Bn. Gardener; of Turramurra, NSW; b. Hornsby, NSW, 18 Dec 1918.

[4] S-Sgt L. O'Donnell, NX1295; 2/2 Bn. Clerk; of Greta, NSW; b. Redhead, NSW, 3 Jul 1912.

[5] Maj A. E. McGuinness, MC, NX77381. Brit Army 1940-41; RMO 2/2 Bn; 2/9 AGH. Medical practitioner; of Penshurst, NSW; b. Arncliffe, NSW, 21 Feb 1911.

[6] Sgt T. Nicholas, NX9469; 2/2 Bn. Labourer; of Guilford, NSW; b. Parkes, NSW, 15 Oct 1905.

[7] J. F. McCabe. Attached 16 Corps 1941-43, II Corps 1944-45, BCOF 1951-53. Deputy Salvation Army Commissioner; of Bundaberg, Qld; b. Adelaide, 18 Jun 1914.

[8] "The Sanananda Track" in *Nulli Secundus Log*, pp. 96-7.

[9] The casualties suffered by 16 Bde units during the period 3 Oct-6 Dec 42 were:

	Bde HQ		2/1 Bn		2/2 Bn		2/3 Bn		Total	
	Offrs	ORs	Offrs	ORs	Offrs	ORs	Offrs	ORs	Offrs	ORs
Killed in action	—	3	6	69	4	48	—	35	10	155
Missing believed killed	—	—	—	—	—	1	—	1	—	2
Died of wounds	—	—	2	11	1	4	—	20	3	35
Drowned in action	—	—	—	1	—	—	—	—	—	1
Missing	—	—	—	2	—	—	—	—	—	2
Wounded in action	3	5	8	164	3	111	2	101	16	381
Accidentally killed	—	—	—	—	—	—	—	1	—	1
Accidentally wounded	—	—	—	—	—	—	—	3	—	3
Evacuated sick	3	46	15	282	18	290	20	304	56	922

officers and 922 men had been evacuated through sickness. The total of these figures represented approximately 85 per cent of the strength with which it had set out on the campaign.

By the evening of the 6th the 55th/53rd had relieved the 2/3rd Battalion except for a small party of thirty-three under Major Hutchison. The 2/1st Battalion was, however, still in a protective position round the guns and most of the 2/2nd still remained forward. These, together with the Americans in the area, Brigadier Porter was empowered to take under his command. It was envisaged that both of these groups would remain generally static while the two fresh militia battalions attacked on the 7th and, with this end in view, Porter placed the militiamen forward along the track. He planned to clear the Japanese from the area south of the roadblock with the 49th Battalion on the right of the track, the 55th/53rd on the left. In the absence of a third fresh battalion he would send only one battalion at a time into the actual assault while the other attempted to divert Japanese attention.

A night of drenching rain was followed on the 7th by morning sunshine which lighted the swamps and wet bush. After standing-to in the uncertain dawn the 49th Battalion pulled back along the track to allow the guns and mortars to register. There they waited to go in behind the barrage. Each man was carrying five days' rations (two days' hard, three days' emergency), two grenades and 100 rounds of ammunition, and a groundsheet. About two men in each section carried Owen guns; it was the first time the battalion had used them.

When the registration shoots were finished Colonel Kessels moved his men back to their previous positions. For a few minutes they waited while the barrage fell ahead of them. Through it the morning sun shone, and back through the exploding curtain Japanese fire whipped into the waiting men and struck a number of them down even before they began to move. At 9.45 a.m., as they went forward through the bush, Captain Forster's[1] company led on the right with Captain Bryce's[2] abreast on the left. Captain Noyes'[3] company followed behind Forster's and Captain Thorn's[4] behind Bryce's. All were quickly swallowed up in the bush.

Soon they began to lose very heavily. Forster's men pressed on for some hundreds of yards and overran a number of Japanese positions. Forster himself was wounded but Lieutenant A. R. Tolmer[5] (who had himself been slightly wounded the previous afternoon) carried on. He got one platoon some 700 or 800 yards forward until they linked with Lieutenant Moore's men of the 2/2nd, who had been forming the right forward extremity of the Allied horseshoe.

---

[1] Capt R. W. Forster, MC, QX1253. 2/9, 49 Bns. Share farmer; of Warwick, Qld; b. Clifton, Qld, 7 Nov 1914.

[2] Capt J. K. Bryce, VX12718. 2/33, 53 and 49 Bns. Commerce student; of Frankston, Vic; b. Alphington, Vic, 14 Feb 1920.

[3] Capt W. H. Noyes, MBE, MC, QX254. 2/9, 49 and 2/11 Bns; 19 Bde 1943-45. Car salesman; of Sydney; b. West Drayton, Middlesex, England, 2 Dec 1908.

[4] Capt J. W. Thorn, QX1397. 2/25, 49 Bns. Station manager; of Goondiwindi, Qld; b. Toowoomba, Qld, 23 Nov 1905. Killed in action 7 Dec 1942.

[5] Tolmer had served with the 2/22nd Battalion in New Britain, earlier in the year.

On the left Bryce's company were being badly torn by fire from Japanese positions sited on the left of the track; Bryce himself was wounded. Lieutenant Unsworth,[6] his second-in-command, took over, although wounded himself, and carried on until he was killed. Lieutenant Hughes[7] was killed at the head of his platoon. The company seemed to lose direction slightly and veered too far to the right in the shrouding bush until finally all their impetus was gone.

Between these leading companies and the second wave Colonel Kessels was moving. With him he had some of the pioneers and anti-aircraft platoon under Lieutenant Wylie.[8] He was the controlling link. But the most vital part of his system had failed. He had virtually only physical communication with his companies. It was originally intended that these should each have a 108-wireless set. When, however, five minutes before the start of the attack the sets had not arrived, the company commanders were told to take telephones and cable instead, but finally, though they had the instruments, at least three of the companies had to go forward without line. This lack of communications, the thick bush and the confusion of battle, made it almost impossible to synchronise the movement of companies as had been planned. As a result the gap between Forster and Bryce in front, and Noyes and Thorn in the rear, inevitably widened from the planned 200 yards. When Noyes and Thorn finally pushed ahead they were some 500 yards in rear of the forward companies and the Japanese had time to recover in some measure from the first onslaught before meeting the second.

On the right, part of Noyes' company tangled early with Thorn's men on their left. Both groups there were held and badly cut about. The rest of Noyes' company staggered ahead with a great volume of fire pouring into them from their left, although, strangely, few of them saw any Japanese. By the time they had covered about 800 yards only about 35 out of the original 98 in the company were still with the commander. All of the platoon commanders were down. But Noyes stayed in this new position for five hours until, having decided that the day was lost, he brought his men back.

In the vicinity of the track Thorn's men had at first pushed strongly ahead. Then fire slashed murderously through them from Japanese positions which had lain motionless beneath the first wave, and, in enfilade, from the left of the track where other positions commanded the left flank of the attack. Thorn himself was killed together with two of his lieutenants, Forster[9] and Morrison,[1] and many of his men.

And so the attack of these brave companies crumbled. But since the

---

[6] Lt G. G. Unsworth, QX14961; 49 Bn. Labourer; of Nambour, Qld; b. Wynnum, Qld, 26 Jul 1917. Killed in action 7 Dec 1942.

[7] Lt F. W. Hughes, VX2011; 49 Bn. Labourer; of Belmont, Vic; b. Maryborough, Vic, 30 Jul 1918. Killed in action 7 Dec 1942.

[8] Lt D. R. Wylie, NX54362. 2/33, 49 Bns. Auditor; of Sydney; b. Auckland, NZ, 15 Mar 1919.

[9] Lt C. E. D. Forster, QX36775; 49 Bn. Shop assistant; of Southport, Qld; b. Manilla, NSW, 24 Mar 1911. Killed in action 7 Dec 1942.

[1] Lt L. A. Morrison, QX36772; 49 Bn. Clerk; of Ascot, Qld; b. Brisbane, 13 Jul 1917. Killed in action 7 Dec 1942.

second phase of his plan was not necessarily dependent on either the success or failure of the first, and as indeed it might well redeem the position, Porter went ahead with his plans for an attack by the 55th/53rd Battalion.

While most of the remaining men of the 49th were still carrying on a scattered and flickering fight, about 2 p.m. Porter ordered Kessels to return. Kessels was then preparing to dig in his own headquarters group, some 40 strong, about 600 yards forward of his start-line, and still trying to establish firm contact with his companies. His own group had suffered with the rest. Lieutenant Wylie was among the casualties; he had been hit in the head and was missing. (Some ten days later he was to report back after wandering half-unconscious behind the Japanese all that time with Lance-Corporal Butler[2] helping him.) Kessels arrived back while Lovell was still finalising his plans for his own attack. It was agreed that the 49th companies would remain as they were while the 55th/53rd took a hand.

Lovell had already committed Captain Gilleland's[3] company well to the left of the track in a diversionary attack, synchronised with the 49th Battalion attack. It had gained approximately 80 yards. Now he ordered Captain Reid's[4] and Major Spring's[5] companies forward. He gave them their orders orally. He knew little of the Japanese dispositions and so these orders were simple: "55/53 Bn will attack enemy positions astride the road." He suspected that three machine-gun posts were sited near a "big white tree" which lay ahead of him and just to the right of the track. He could be quite certain that there were other posts to the rear of the tree. He told Reid, therefore, to go forward on a bearing of 20 degrees, clean out the positions to the right of and behind the "big white tree" and then exploit along the track. Spring was to follow the same bearing until he reached the track, cross, and range through the Japanese positions on the left of that vital cleared strip.

At 3.15 p.m. the two companies moved ahead through hampering undergrowth. Soon they were in the thick of fire from cleverly concealed positions. The heavy growth and their own inexperience caused them to bunch in little groups which made them good targets. Sharpshooters picked them off. Spring's men became confused and yawed to the right, where a number of them came up with what remained of Captain Thorn's company of the 49th. As a result only one section instead of the whole company crossed the track, and these few were held on the other side. This failure apparently laid Reid's men bare to fire which held them in scorching enfilade and struck many of them down, including Reid himself. Reid

---

[2] L-Cpl N. Butler, MM, V230062; 49 Bn. Station hand; of Balranald, NSW; b. Balranald, 24 Oct 1920.

[3] Capt J. R. Gilleland, NX143791; 55/53 Bn. Schoolteacher; of Hurstville, NSW; b. North Sydney, 25 Nov 1913. Died 5 Feb 1943.

[4] Maj W. C. Reid, NX127374. 53, 55/53 Bns. Shop assistant; of Macksville, NSW; b. Newcastle, NSW, 7 Jan 1908.

[5] Maj G. F. Spring, NX127369. 53, 55/53 Bns; Legal Corps. Solicitor; of Mudgee, NSW; b. Mudgee, 15 May 1905.

then sent his second-in-command (Lieutenant Dellaca[6]) back to Lovell with this news. To relieve the situation Lovell then ordered Gilleland to send his men diagonally across the road towards the white tree, from the position they had previously acquired well to the left of the track and in which Lieutenant Haan and some fifty Americans had relieved them about 4.15 p.m.

With night coming on the men of the 55th/53rd began to consolidate their slight advance approximately 100 yards in front of their morning positions. On this line the colonel regrouped the three companies, placing Gilleland in command of them. Their attack, like that of the 49th, had failed, and the cost was heavy. At the end of the day 8 officers and 122 men were listed as killed, wounded or missing, and, significantly in view of later developments within this battalion, the losses included 28 N.C.O's.

Now that it was clear that the day was quite lost, all the Australians could do was try to resolve the confusion as best they might. What was left of Kessels' companies came slowly back in bewilderment. None could say then just what their losses were but obviously only a threadbare unit was left. Those who could be reassembled were organised defensively into one company to the right of the big white tree under Captain Noyes. Early next morning Noyes was able to report that he was firming there with a total strength of 118—11 from Forster's company, 9 from Bryce's (the two companies which had led the assault), 60 from his own company, 38 from Thorn's. About 40 men were still out with Tolmer. Since the companies had each begun with 90 to 100 men it seemed that the casualties might total 250. (Much later a final tally set the figure at 14 officers and 215 men—between 55 and 60 per cent of the actual attacking force and nearly 48 per cent of the battalion.)

By that time Lovell had brought up his fourth rifle company, fresh and still whole, and had it astride the track on Noyes' left. Extending farther to the left was Haan's small group of Americans. Lovell had withdrawn Reid's and Spring's survivors well to the rear and had Gilleland protecting his own headquarters. As for the rest of the troops still in the area: wide to either flank the attenuated 2/2nd Battalion still formed the horns of the Allied crescent; ahead, through the country yet held by the Japanese, the road-block continued to endure; west of the road-block the two American companies still lay over the flanking track in the bush as a base from which to supply the road-block; the balance of the Americans were well behind the forward positions on the main track.

So the third round along the Sanananda Track opened much as the first two had done. The 16th Brigade operations had virtually ended in stalemate; the Americans had failed to resolve that; and now the militiamen had intensified it. Even for experienced battalions the heavy blows which the 49th and 55th/53rd had sustained would have been almost stunning. Their final effect on the previously untried newcomers

---

[6] Lt N. C. Dellaca, NX127387. 53, 55/53 Bns. Buyer; of Speer's Point, NSW; b. Helensburgh, NSW, 25 Aug 1905.

had yet to be revealed. Thus far what these had attempted, and the manner of it, was greatly to the men's credit.

The immediate effect, however, of the repulse of the latest Australian attacks, was to usher in a period of comparative pause and further preparation which was to last for about twelve days. Generals Herring and Vasey agreed that, apart from offensive patrolling, no further big-scale attacks should be undertaken for the time being.

Accordingly the 30th Brigade settled to a policy of patrolling and edging forward where possible. Of this period Brigadier Porter wrote later:

> Since our first assault, we have used a 'stalk and consolidate' type of tactics, combined with fire concentrations on enemy positions, as discovered. We have patrolled deeply and over wide areas. Several raids have had the effect of killing some enemy, but his well constructed MG positions defy our fire power and present a barrier of fire through which our troops must pass. We have attempted to seize these in failing light, but they are too numerous to deal with by other than an attack in great strength. One of these attempts silenced one MG but others supported from flank positions. On the latter occasion own troops avoided fixed lines by crawling back to cover in the bad light.

In these conditions a method used in the trench warfare of 1914-18 and earlier was introduced when the Australians tried sapping forward to known Japanese positions, though without any marked success. Also they tried the expedient of bringing forward a six-pounder gun (from the 2/1st Anti-Tank Regiment). They thought that perhaps it would damage the low, heavily-roofed and well-concealed strongpoints in a way which neither mortars, nor 25-pounders, nor aerial bombs, had done.

There was, however, no disguising the fact that temporarily the Allies were fairly held along the Sanananda Track. Brigadier Porter defined his intention as:

> To position minimum troops on present front for purposes of security and holding frontally. To maintain maximum troops in hand for mobile offence and for conservation of health and energy.

This he declared as being "based on a continuation of 'stalk and consolidate' plus holding present front with strong posts mutually supporting". Such orders from the dashing Porter were as expressive of baffled impotence as barley water is of the weakness of a sick man. And this temporary sense of bafflement could be detected from the highest to lowest levels in both Australians and Americans.

On the highest levels, it is true, some minor evidence of an aggressive policy could be assembled. The air forces could be turned loose with a certain vigour on the defenders; but the physical effects of these assaults on the stout front-line posts were small; nor could the pilots determine the general areas for attack with any certainty; on the 9th, for example, an ambitious program had to be called off after the first bombs had almost demolished the Salvation Army coffee stall nearly a mile behind the most forward Australian track positions. Again, the amalgamation of Numbers 1 and 2 landing strips at Popondetta on the 13th to create "Popondetta Main", providing four landing surfaces, seemed encouraging; but this was important only in relation to what could be achieved by the fighting troops actually in contact. Again, General Herring's rapidly maturing plans to fly over from Port Moresby the 2/7th Australian Cavalry Regiment and the 36th Battalion suggested the possibility of a decisive inflow of fresh troops; but, in bringing these units across, Herring was "scraping the bottom of the barrel" for the garrison commitments at Port Moresby and Milne Bay, and the front-line commitments at Buna, Sanananda and Gona, had almost exhausted his supply of infantry.

In the fighting units many of the troops were literally staggering from weakness as they tried to carry on the fight. Others, though not so weak physically, were beginning to show worrying signs of unwillingness to go forward.

The men of the 16th Brigade (now down to a fighting strength of 50 officers and 488 men) fell completely into the first group. On the 9th the 2/3rd Battalion, totalling a mere 130 all ranks, were ordered forward once again to relieve the 2/2nd, although their medical officer emphasised to Vasey that they were quite unfit for that service. The 2/2nd, still in the positions on either side of the track where they had been first stopped, were in even worse plight, the whole battalion being little more than 100 strong. The men themselves were so weak that, as they came slowly back on the 10th, they could not carry their automatic weapons. Lieut-Colonel Stevenson, who had returned to the 2/3rd Battalion a little time before, replaced them with two scratch companies formed from the survivors of his rifle companies. Major Hutchison took the right of the track with some 46 all ranks, Captain Herwig the left with about 59 all ranks.

Into the second group fell mainly an unduly large number of the 55th/53rd Battalion. In an attempted two-platoon attack in the early morning of the 13th the men were generally irresolute. The battalion diarist noted that their officers

had great difficulty in moving troops forward whilst dense undergrowth made maintenance of control and direction difficult. Troops were prone to go to ground and thus prevented themselves from being extricated by fire and movement.

Later in the day the platoon which had led on that occasion was sent again to attack a troublesome strongpoint. Within half an hour they had withdrawn. The attack had to be called off though the platoon had not sustained any casualties.

Nor did it seem that, as a group, the Americans outside the road-block were noticeably more resolute. Within the blockade the wretchedness of the men was increasing daily. On the 6th and 7th attempts to break through to them with supplies had failed. Early on the 8th, however, Lieutenant Peter L. Dal Ponte fought his way in. He remained in command then and sent the wounded Huggins back with the returning supply party that night. The latter reported from hospital that the Japanese had made frequent attacks on the garrison from different angles: that they were well clothed and in good physical condition; some of them got close enough to slit trenches during attacks to be grasped by the ankles and pulled in, and two Japanese officers had been killed in that fashion. He said that supplies were low and fever was raging; 225 men were left in the garrison of whom perhaps 125 were in fighting condition. When a second party got through to the road-block on the 10th Dal Ponte sent back word of increasing discomfort, although the Japanese determination seemed to have waned as no attacks had taken place in the preceding two or three days. After that no supplies reached Dal Ponte until the 14th. By that time he was almost out of ammunition.

How far this situation could have been relieved by more determined efforts on the part of the Americans outside the beleaguered area is a matter for conjecture. On the 12th Colonel Pollard,[7] who had taken over from Colonel Spry as General Vasey's chief staff officer after Spry had been wounded on 27th November, accompanied a supply party towards Dal Ponte's position. He reported subsequently that the party came under fire from light and heavy machine-guns and rifles about twenty minutes' march from their objective; that it then returned without delivering its supplies; that it made "no real attempt to force passage or overcome Jap opposition". Representations to this effect were made to Major Boerem who, since Baetcke had been sent back to hospital with fever on the 7th, was now commanding all Americans in the area.

On the same day Vasey seriously examined the entire question of holding the road-block.

> Question now arises regarding usefulness of road-block owing to the fact that American troops in occupation consider they no longer have necessary numerical strength to carry out offensive patrolling and for some days have been completely inactive. Whilst this continues main object of the post will be to deny its occupation to the enemy and obviate necessity of having to overcome further opposition in this area in subsequent operations. In addition, evacuation of the position would undoubtedly be retrograde step and would be a morale raiser for the Japs. The American forces in the positions on the western side have now been in occupation for some weeks and their physical condition is suffering as a result of fever and the fact that the whole force needs to be relieved in order that necessary reorganisation may be carried out. Whilst relief is highly desirable it is by no means a matter of necessity. Owing to the complete inactivity of these troops the occupation of these positions astride the L of C serves no useful purpose and could be dispensed with unless troops activated.[8]

Perhaps the implications concerning the two western companies were too harsh for the same pen continued:

> Positions on the western side of Soputa-Sanananda track occupied by American troops are all under water, the whole area now being a swamp due to heavy rains. Troops are unable to lie down on ground anywhere in position. Practically whole track used as L of C to road-block is through knee-deep marshes. With the coming of the wet season maintenance of any force operating to west of Soputa-Sanananda track would at best be most difficult and in all probability impossible.

None the less, whatever the reasons, Brigadier Porter did not find it

---

[7] Lt-Gen R. G. Pollard, CBE, DSO, NX70398. BM 25 Bde 1940-41; GSO2 7 Div (A/CO 2/31 Bn Jul 1941); GSO1 6 Div, and 7 Div 1942-43; DDMO LHQ 1945. Regular soldier; b. Bathurst, NSW, 20 Jan 1903.
[8] War diary, 7th Division.

easy to fit the Americans into his planning at this stage. In assessing the whole situation on 25th December he wrote:

> Huggins' Force is still in posn astride the road, isolated and severely dissipated. This force has accounted for numerous enemy *who attacked* it; but it is incapable of acting offensively. The whole of the remainder of US tps have been engaged in carrying rations to it—either as carriers, escort of picquets on the route in. At other times they merely occupy our rear perimeter. Any effort to induce them to occupy a forward position or take the offensive raises objections on the part of their commander.

Not only were these men tired and discouraged. Their numbers were sinking rapidly. On 10th December their entire "effective" strength west of the Girua was 635. They had lost 50 killed, 198 wounded, 80 missing and 249 had been evacuated sick. However grisly the comparison it is worthy of note that the losses in battle by the Americans in nineteen days were less than similar losses by the two Australian militia battalions in one day—on the 7th. And the total strength of these two battalions was little more than two-thirds that of the Americans.

It was clear that the Allied position along the Sanananda Track was one of wary discouragement when the 2/7th Australian Cavalry and more miiltiamen prepared to enter the scene about the middle of December.

The Australian leaders now well knew that there they were facing the main Japanese strength on the Papuan coast. In actual fact the Japanese probably were deploying about 5,500 men, including hospital patients, in front of Sanananda at the beginning of the coastal fighting. After the death of General Horii, command west of the Girua River had fallen to Colonel Yokoyama. On his right, at Gona, he sited an improvised force. On the Sanananda Track he gave the most forward positions, about the Sanananda-Killerton track junction, to Colonel Tsukamoto who mustered there about 1,700 men: the remaining strength of his own *I/144th Battalion*; a detachment of the *III/41st Battalion*; some of the *15th Independent Engineers*; about 700 Formosan naval labourers. Behind Tsukamoto, where Huggins' road-block was later established, were a company of *III/41st Battalion*, a battery of mountain gunners and some anti-aircraft gunners, and the main body of the *15th Independent Engineers*, about 300 strong. At Sanananda itself Yokoyama set up his headquarters, with him the balance of the *41st Regiment*, his cavalry troops, a mountain battery and some naval construction troops.

Strenuous efforts were made by the Japanese to reinforce these troops during late November and early December. On 22nd November the *21st Independent Mixed Brigade* (Major-General Tsuyuo Yamagata), its nucleus being the *170th Infantry Regiment*, arrived at Rabaul from Indo-China. Some 800 men of this force, mainly of the *I/170th Battalion*, set out from Rabaul in four destroyers on the night 28th-29th November. They lacked air cover, however, and, rounding the western tip of New Britain into Vitiaz Strait, fell a prey to Allied aircraft who drove them back to Rabaul. There Yamagata himself arrived in time to join his own second echelon, of which the *III/170th Battalion* was the main unit. They struck southwards through St George's Channel, covered by aircraft which managed to drive off several Allied air attempts to destroy the convoy, and reached Basabua early in the morning of 2nd December. Before they could unload, however, they were once more under heavy air attack and were forced northward in the darkness. At the Kumusi River mouth the ships began to unload but the aircraft kept at them. About 300 soldiers were lost in the landing but the remaining 500, with considerable supplies of ammunition and equipment, finally linked with those survivors of the Oivi-Gorari fighting who, having escaped down the river after their defeat and having been organised at the river's mouth by Colonel Yazawa, still remained there. Yazawa himself, with the greater part of his tattered force, had been picked up in barges which Yokoyama had sent along for them. Yokoyama realised that, ill, exhausted and with comparatively few weapons and no supplies, they were in no condition to fight their way down the coast to him at Sanananda. Although Allied aircraft inflicted some losses on this movement Yazawa himself got through to Sanananda with probably 400 to 500 men, and added these to the Sanananda forces. Soon a third attempt was made to land the *170th Regiment* on the Buna-Gona coast. The *I Battalion*, which had been driven back on its first attempt, set out once more from Rabaul on 9th December with the small balance of the *III Battalion* and some ancillary troops. Next day, however, Allied aircraft attacked with great determination, set fire to three of six destroyers making up the convoy, and shot down a number of the escorting fighters. The ships turned back again for Rabaul. On the 12th, however, the battalion started out once more, Major-General Kensaku Oda accompanying them to take over as Horii's successor. This time they made for the mouth of the Mambare River, 30 to 50 miles north of Sanananda, where, apparently, it had been decided to open a new beach-head: one to which ships could come without being forced into the narrow waters lower down the coast where an offshore reef almost paralleled the beach. There a well-concealed base could be established and small craft could ply with supplies and reinforcements to the main battle-front; and there sick and wounded could be staged. Bad weather covering them Oda and the *I/170th* reached the Mambare mouth without loss and there, with everything in readiness for a quick landing, rapidly unloaded in the darkness of the morning of the 14th. By the time the Allied aircraft located them after daybreak, all of the 800 men were ashore with most of their gear and most of the numerous small watercraft they had brought with them. The destroyers got clean away. Though the attacking aircraft managed to sink a few of the small craft and some of the supplies which, still wrapped in waterproof coverings and lashed to buoys so that they would wash in with the waves and the tides, were still floating about off shore, the Japanese losses were small.

So mid-December found the main Japanese force, now totalling about 6,000 men, including sick and wounded, remaining firm along the Sanananda Track. Although General Blamey was sending fresh units to that sector, he had decided to strike his next main blow at the Japanese before Buna to resolve that flank before attempting again to reduce the Sanananda positions. At the same time, however, a compact Japanese force was building up on the Australian extreme left flank, though events at Gona had markedly affected the way in which this force could be used.

CHAPTER 14

GONA

AFTER they crossed the Kumusi River on 15th November the 25th Brigade pushed on for Gona. About 40 miles of tropical lowland lay before them—a track alternately slopping through rank and steaming vegetation and winding through flats of coarse kunai grass on which the heat danced in visible waves.

At first Lieut-Colonel Buttrose led the way with his 2/33rd Battalion; Lieut-Colonel Marson's 2/25th was hard behind him. They saw signs along the track of hasty Japanese retreat and of developmental work and installations which the invaders had abandoned—permanent huts, large stables, dumps of rice and barley, formed roads, drains and cuttings. But soon they were too occupied with their own troubles to pay more than passing attention to these. The steaming heat, mud, fever and sore feet were quickly finding out the weaker ones.

By the mid-afternoon of 18th November the 2/33rd was at Jumbora where they stopped to prepare a dropping ground in open kunai country. Captain Clowes, with sixty men, pushed on, to occupy Gona if the Japanese had gone, or alternatively to report their strength. Lieut-Colonel Miller was preparing to pick up rations from Buttrose and pass the 2/31st Battalion through to take the lead. Brigadier Eather's headquarters was back at Amboga Crossing where the 2/25th Battalion had been held.

When Miller overtook him next morning Japanese riflemen were disputing Clowes' advance through a large kunai patch just south of Gona. Miller pushed Captain Thorn's company through but Thorn was barely clear of Clowes' positions when he ran into a regular fusillade. Miller then sent his other companies through or fanned them out on either side of the track. By late afternoon, however, all were held in a semi-circle before Gona: Captain Cameron's 2/14th Battalion Chaforce company on the right of the track on the outskirts of the village; Captain Beazley's company astride the track backed up by Captain Upcher's; Captain L. T. Hurrell's[1] company on the left, with Captain A. L. Hurrell's company to the left again, stopped on the edge of warding cleared areas; Thorn's company in reserve in the rear. A tenacious defence commanded the kunai clearings in front of and flanking the mission and took toll of the attackers as they emerged from the scrub and swamps of the main approaches, after tree snipers had already harassed them.

Eather told Miller:

> If you think you can clean up enemy use 2/33 Bn patrol also. Adv HQ 25 Bde and 25 Bn four miles in rear of you, and will move up in morning, situation permitting. No ammunition available until dropping commences which should be tomorrow.

---

[1] Capt L. T. Hurrell, NGX22; 2/31 Bn. Assistant agriculturalist; of Keravat, New Britain, and Cobargo, NSW; b. Comboyne, NSW, 22 Dec 1914. Killed in action 4 Dec 1942.

(Australian War Memorial)

An aid post erected by natives on the track to Gona. The smoke in the background is from camp fires.

(Australian War Memorial)

Corporal F. R. Smith and Private W. A. Musgrove, members of a company of the 2/33rd Battalion which had just withdrawn 100 yards from the front-line after two days and nights within grenade distance of the Japanese. The Australians are sheltering in five-foot kunai grass close to the fringe of bush surrounding Gona.

The remains of Buna Government Station, a desolate area blackened stumps of government buildings, after it was finally

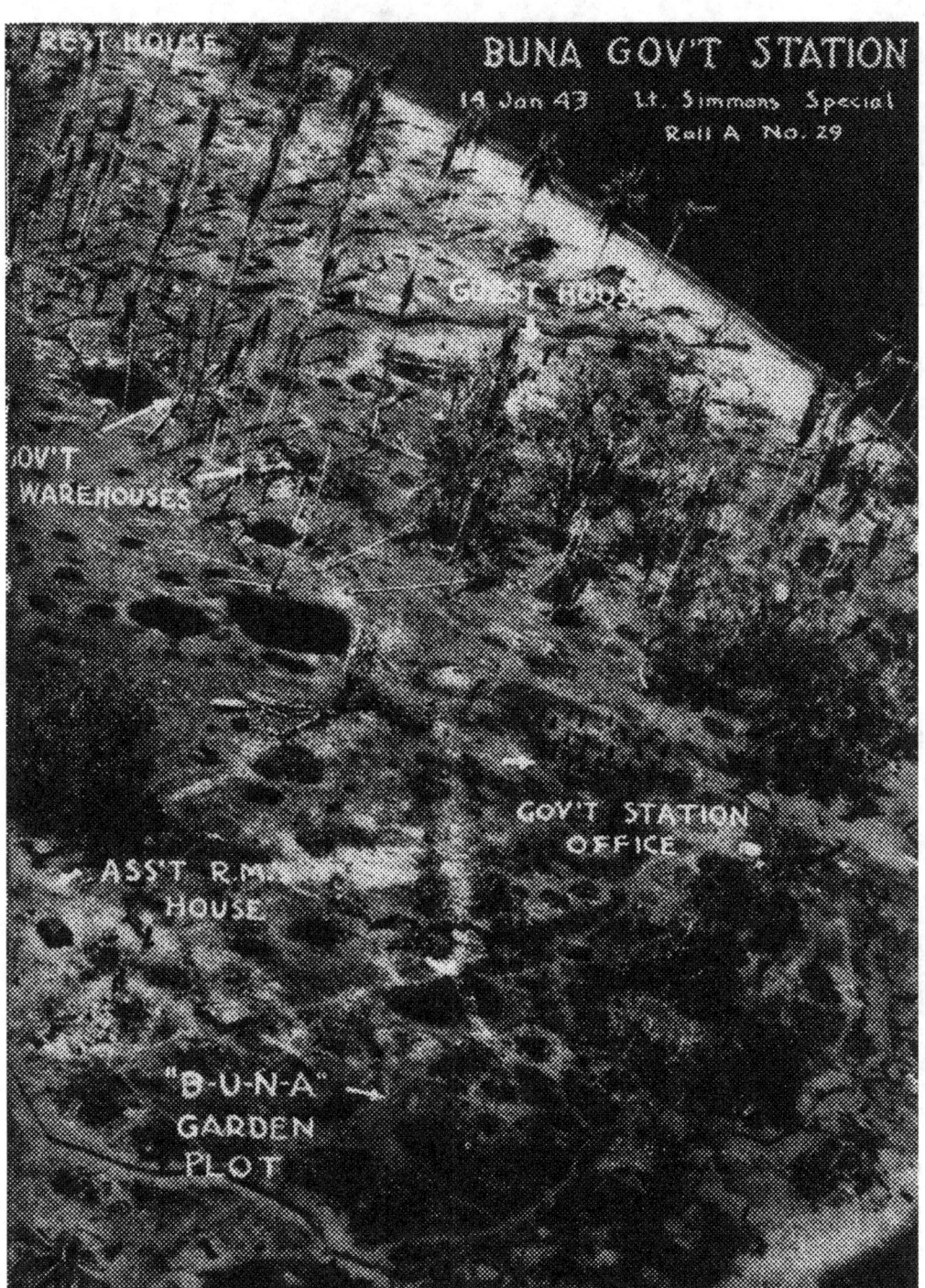

of bomb craters, twisted coconut trees, and the burnt and overrun by the 128th U.S. Regiment on 2nd January 1943.

(*Allied Air Forces S.W.P.A.*)

(Australian War Memorial)
The wounds of an Australian infantryman, hit by mortar burst in the head, thigh and arm, are dressed in the shelter of tall kunai grass at Gona.

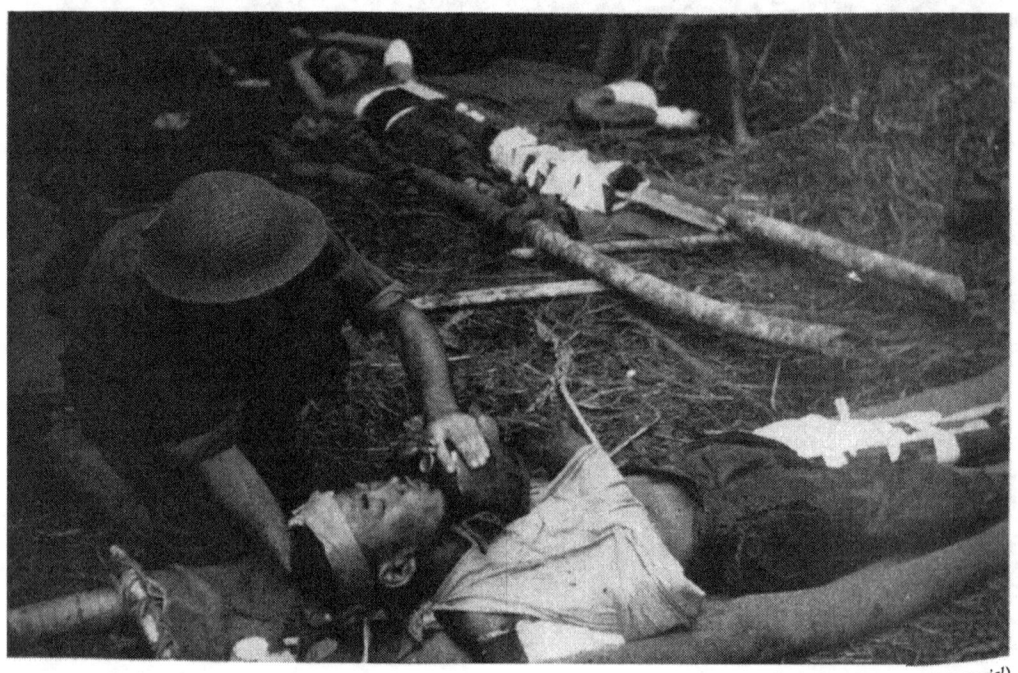

(Australian War Memorial)
Japanese, wounded in the final Australian assault on Gona, lie on rough bush stretchers, awaiting evacuation. An Australian raises a wounded prisoner's head to drink.

But as the night advanced Miller's position became too difficult. Both food and ammunition were low. Thorn was dead, Cameron and Lieutenant Pearce from the Chaforce company had been wounded, L. T. Hurrell and Upcher were down with raging fever. Miller had thus lost four of his company commanders, thirty-two of his men had been either killed or wounded, and the rest of the battalion was already wasting fast with malaria. Just before midnight Eather ordered him to break contact and fall back behind the 2/25th. This he did in the darkness through a protective position established by Clowes, with fortunate early morning rain pattering heavily on leaves and helping to cover the sounds of his men's movements. Although towards dawn the Japanese must have become aware of the move, because they then beat the bush with heavy fire, by 8 a.m. the bulk of the 2/31st was back behind the 2/25th. Their enemies had not followed them although Miller reported that, when he left, they were wakeful and active behind their own lines from which had come the sounds of busy trucks, a motor-boat plying to the shore, and men at work handling stores.

That all of their adversaries were not cooped up in front of them, however, was demonstrated to the Australians on this same day when the regimental aid post of the 2/31st reported that of two men who had fallen behind a sick party, one had been found strangled off the track near Awala, his rifle, ammunition and rations gone, and the other was missing. There were very dangerous stragglers in the bush and it behoved any man to walk warily along the silent tracks.

On the 20th Eather waited for supplies. There had been no planes over Jumbora. All of his units were down to their last emergency rations. On the 21st, however, supply aircraft came, dropping food, ammunition, quinine and tobacco. Eather then announced that the whole brigade would go forward on the 22nd except one company of the 2/33rd which was to guard the dropping ground. He proposed to attack Gona Mission with the 2/31st and 2/33rd Battalions, holding the 2/25th in reserve approximately two miles south of the village.

On the 21st Buttrose moved his 2/33rd Battalion to within two miles of Gona and sent patrols to approach from both the east and the west. Soon after 4 p.m. one patrol sighted Japanese as it was about to move off the track a mile ahead of the battalion. At 9.35 p.m. the other reported that it had reached the beach east of Gona with only minor contact.

At 6.30 a.m. on the 22nd Clowes started his company off along the track with the rest of the 2/33rd following half an hour behind him. Soon he was fighting about 1,000 yards south of Gona. Captain Power pressed his company forward in support. Clowes was losing men steadily, however, and about 10.50 a.m., this capable and devoted young regular who had taken a leading part in the fighting from the time his brigade first entered action in New Guinea in early September, was himself killed.

Soon Eather had the 2/31st working round the right of the 2/33rd to come against Gona from the east. (He was planning also to complete the movement by sending the 2/25th Battalion against Gona from the west. From that direction Lieutenant Haddy's 2/16th Battalion Chaforce company, under command of the 2/31st, was already firing into the defences, having crossed the creek which ran into the sea just west of Gona Mission and became known to the Australians as Gona Creek.) Lieutenant Hayes[2] (Thorn's successor) was leading the 2/31st Battalion's approach through the timber. Behind him Lieutenant Phelps[3] followed with Headquarters Company, and behind Phelps went Captain Beazley's company. As they approached the beach the timber country yielded to

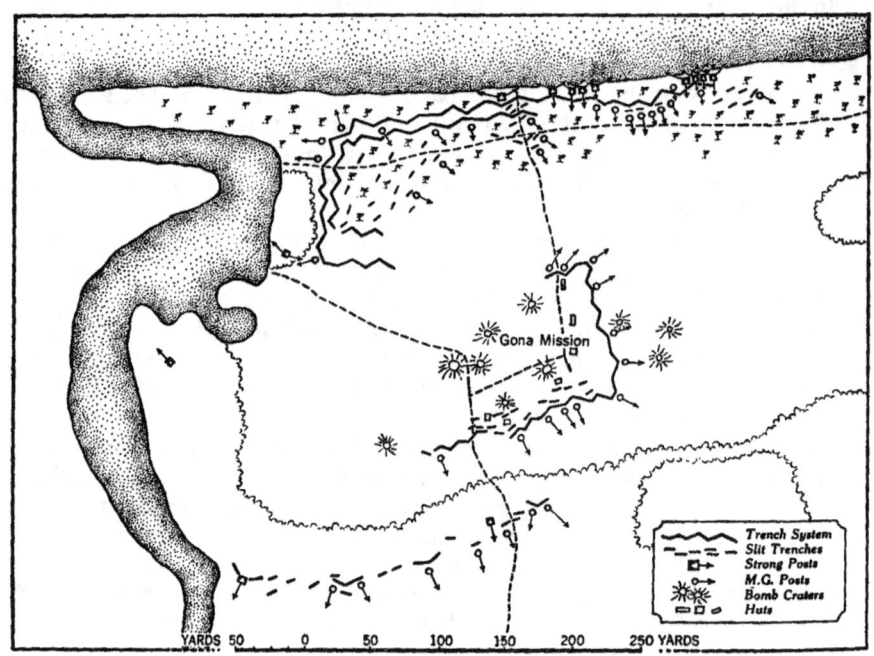

The Japanese defences at Gona

swamp and their detour led them through a kunai patch with the beach on their right and the swamp on their left. By 6 p.m. the whole battalion was in position on the edge of the kunai with Japanese defences fronting them about 300 yards ahead. With one company to guard their left flank as it rested on the swamp, and another to maintain their rear against any threat from the direction of Buna, Beazley, Hayes and Phelps prepared to attack in unison with the 2/14th Battalion's Chaforce company now led by Captain Thurgood. As Hayes' and Phelps' men broke cover for the assault they had to move half right to make room for Beazley's

---

[2] Maj H. F. Hayes, NX8077; 2/31 Bn. Regular soldier; of Bondi, NSW; b. Tyagarah, NSW, 2 Feb 1910.
[3] Lt R. S. Phelps, NX6845; 2/31 Bn. Carpenter; of Hurstville, NSW; b. Exeter, Devonshire, England, 29 Jun 1909. Killed in action 22 Nov 1942.

and Thurgood's as the frontage was too narrow to allow all to form up initially in the kunai patch.

Of the attack which followed the 2/31st diarist wrote later:

At zero the men rose and were immediately met by a most intense fire from the front and right flank. They cheered and yelled as they advanced and returned a heavy barrage of automatic fire. They reached the Jap pits but were not strong enough to continue as they were then enfiladed from both sides. Lieutenant Phelps was killed, Captain Beazley missing believed killed and Lieutenant Hayes wounded. The attack died down but the enemy continued a most intense rate of fire.

This unsuccessful action cost the 2/31st 65 casualties.[4] The remainder desperately formed a thin perimeter, backed by the swamp, waiting for the counter-attack which did not come, and desperately tried to gather in their dead and wounded under a heavy fire. Company stretcher bearers and aid posts attended the injured and Colonel Marson rushed forward parties to help them back through the swamp and bush. By midnight Miller felt once more that he could hold against any Japanese sallies that might still come, and Eather sent him word that the 2/25th would be forward to help him at first light.

Eather decided that his opponents, in greater strength than he had at first thought, were holding an area some 300 yards square against the sea on the north and Gona Creek on the west. From the creek's western bank Haddy's men were still watching and worrying the defenders. Buttrose's main force was still pressing close from the south. Eather therefore planned a new attack from the east with the 2/25th, and Marson led them to Miller's northern positions. At 4.30 a.m. on the 23rd he sent them westward along the shore with Miller's fire helping them. But, though they gained a little ground, generally they fared no better than the other battalion had done. They lost 2 officers and 62 men[5] and had to withdraw after dark to hold against the expected enemy counter-moves.

By this time it was clear that the smouldering defence was rapidly burning the Australians out. All three battalions had been badly mauled. From 19th November to 9 a.m. on the 23rd the thin 25th Brigade had lost 17 officers and 187 men in battle[6] and many others from malaria—and from sickness induced by the intense heat which shimmered around and above them as they lay in the open kunai. So Brigadier Eather had to plan afresh.

As darkness fell on the 23rd, and before the moon rose, he began to withdraw the 2/31st Battalion; without further loss, Miller brought his men back from within forty yards of the Japanese to the rear of the 2/33rd on the main track. Shortly before this Lieut-Colonel Cameron had led his 3rd Battalion into the area and, although their numbers were now only approximately 180, Eather proposed to use them to give a fresh twist to his tactics—to move them across Gona Creek and try the defences from the west. As an additional new factor he determined

---

[4] Killed 2 and 12; missing believed killed 1 and 7; wounded 1 and 42.
[5] Killed 12; wounded 2 and 50.
[6] Killed 7 and 53; missing 3; wounded 10 and 131.

fully to exploit the possibilities of the available air support. His request that the most intense air efforts which could be mustered should be levelled at the Gona area between 8 a.m. and 2 p.m. on the 24th was granted and he was told to withdraw his troops to a safe distance to allow the air attackers full play.

In reviewing the position in conference with his battalion commanders on the morning of the 24th Eather found that his weakened 2/25th, 2/31st and 2/33rd Battalions numbered only 15 officers and 277 men, 6 and 181, 14 and 243, respectively,[7] and thus were not strong enough to clear Gona of the Japanese who were well sited and well dug in. He gave orders for vigorous harassing patrols and a program of mortar and Vickers gun shoots and then awaited the results of the air bombardments. These began early in the morning. First, aircraft strafed the defenders and attacked with light bombs until about 11.30 a.m. Then the heavy bombers got to work between 1 p.m. and 2 p.m. with sorties so well directed that comparatively few bombs fell outside the target areas. These left the Japanese with little stomach for ground fighting during the day and gained a substantial rest for the tired Australians.

Late on the 25th Eather tried his new stroke (slightly modified) with the fresh 3rd Battalion. At 4 p.m. they attacked Gona from the south-west supported by machine-gun and mortar fire from the 2/25th and 2/33rd and by artillery fire from the four 25-pounders of the 2/1st Field Regiment sited forward of Soputa. Although they succeeded in penetrating the defences to a depth of some 50 yards at one point, strong positions, well dug and roofed, defied them; at 5.40 p.m. they withdrew, their casualties having been comparatively light.

It was now quite clear that Eather could hope for nothing more than merely to be able to contain his adversaries. And it looked for a short time as though these had no intention of sitting passive in besieged positions. As the evening of the 26th was lengthening, after a quiet day in the forward Australian positions astride the main track south of Gona, the men of the 2/33rd were vigorously assailed with the bayonet by a strong fighting patrol which advanced under cover of heavy machine-gun and mortar fire. Recoiling from an uncompromising reception the Japanese tried to make their way round the 2/33rd's right flank but were blocked by the 2/25th. As night settled Buttrose and Marson had their men cutting coordinated lines of fire in preparation for further attacks, and from the sea there came the sound of Japanese barges approaching the beach for purposes which the Australians could only guess.

Now, however, a new factor was entering the situation. On this same afternoon of the 26th Brigadier Dougherty had arrived at Brigadier Eather's headquarters. This quiet and experienced soldier, a simple and uncompromising sense of duty his greatest strength, had flown from Darwin to take over the 21st Brigade from Brigadier Potts when that brigade was reorganising at Port Moresby after its losses on the Kokoda Trail. His

---

[7] War diary, 25th Brigade.

arrival in the Gona area heralded that of his veterans who were anxious to avenge the reverses they had already suffered. At Soputa, the previous day, General Vasey had told him that he was considering two alternative roles for the 21st Brigade: to assist the 16th Brigade in its efforts to capture Sanananda by a wide movement to the sea between Sanananda and Gona, followed by an advance along the coast against the former; or to augment the 25th Brigade whom he described as "depleted and suffering from malaria and fatigue". As the 21st Brigade had yet to complete its forward move, Vasey continued, Dougherty should go to Gona and discuss the two alternatives with Eather. After that he would receive his orders.

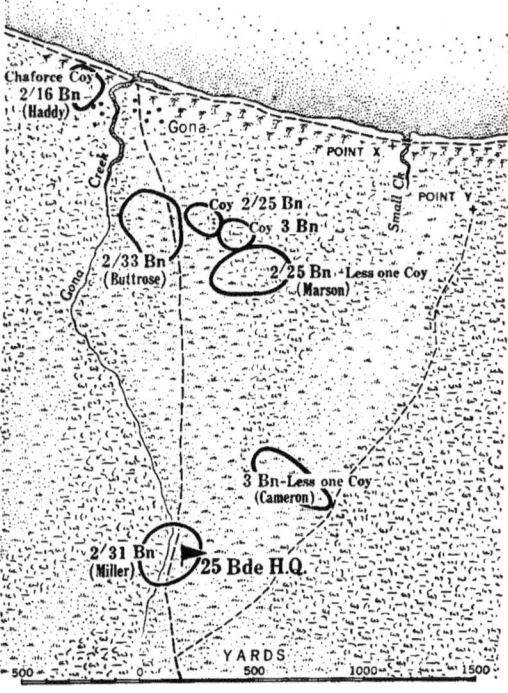

Dispositions 25th Brigade, 27th November

As he trudged from Soputa to Gona Dougherty pondered his problem. He had visited the 16th Brigade in front of Sanananda, knew that the Americans were struggling vainly to reach a decision at Buna, and had no illusions as to the condition in which he would find the 25th Brigade. Later he wrote of the ideas which came and went in his thoughtful mind:

> I set out for Gona, accompanied by Colonel Kingsley Norris (ADMS 7 Aust Div), my Brigade Major (Major Lyon) and two native carriers, walking from Soputa via Jumbora. The track at that stage had not been made jeepable. Coming back along the track through hot and steamy kunai patches, and along that very muddy stretch through jungle, were many sick and wounded men, aided only by means of the universal stick that was carried. The muddy stretch mentioned was about a mile and a half long, and the mud varied in depth from ankle to knee deep. After rain it became fluid and it was then easier to walk through than after a few days of dryness when it became like glue. In the jungle alongside this muddy stretch there were many paths which could be used as alternative routes, but they were perhaps equally tiring as the mud. They meant a longer journey— one's feet were continually slipping at all angles on greasy and twisted roots, and after a certain amount of use they became soft and gluey. . . .
>
> I had been giving consideration to the two probable roles which the General had indicated to me. I felt that concentration somewhere was necessary in order to eliminate some of the Japanese. At that stage our forces were split into three pieces

—Gona area, the Sanananda Road, and Buna. At no place did our strength appear to be sufficient to defeat the enemy. If 21 Aust Inf Bde was used to advance on Sanananda via the route suggested there was the possibility that it might meet opposition which it could not overcome—its strength was approximately a thousand only, not much greater than a full battalion. That would result in the allied force being split into four pieces instead of three. . . .

I felt that it would be much better to eliminate one lot of enemy opposition before proceeding further, and that the alternative task the General thought of giving us—the destruction of the enemy in the Gona Mission area, in cooperation with 25 Aust Inf Bde—was the desirable one.

I discussed the whole matter with Brigadier Eather. He agreed with my ideas as set out above. I became more convinced that those ideas were right when I saw how weary his brigade was.

During the afternoon of 26th November I rang General Vasey and told him of my views and those of Brigadier Eather. He agreed that the best course to take was the capturing of Gona Mission area before proceeding further, and I commenced consideration of plans for the attack.

The 29th was tentatively fixed as the date for the 21st Brigade assault on Gona. Dougherty wished to make it the 30th as the last of his battalions would not arrive until late on the 29th. Vasey agreed but then rang him early on the 28th with the news that General Herring, in view of certain information, insisted on the attack taking place as planned. Dougherty suspected that this information was that the Japanese were trying to land reinforcements.

From 9.30 a.m. to 10.11 a.m. on the 29th aircraft would concentrate upon a small rectangular space which surrounded Gona Mission. First twelve fighters would attack, each dropping a 300-lb bomb. Three Boston bombers would follow with parachute bombs and machine-gun fire. After that six Flying Fortresses would release eight 500-lb bombs and then three more Bostons would follow with bombs and machine-guns. Hard after these attacks the 2/14th Battalion would thrust along the coast from the east, the Blackforce guns, and the 25th Brigade from their positions astride the track south of Gona, supporting them with fire, with the 2/27th Battalion in brigade reserve pending the arrival of the 2/16th in the afternoon.

It was dramatically fitting that the 21st Brigade, rested in its major part and in some measure re-formed, should come to the assistance of the 25th Brigade when the latter formation was withering towards that ultimate exhaustion which it had barely staved off during the past weeks, for thus was the position at Ioribaiwa in early September reversed. And it was also dramatically fitting that the first of the 21st Brigade's battalions to move into this new action should be the 2/14th. This unit, it will be recalled, had opened the 21st Brigade operations in August when the Japanese were advancing from Kokoda, and had suffered more heavily than any other Australian unit in the entire mountain fighting. Now it was to open the brigade's operations in the new coastal fighting.

On 25th November Lieut-Colonel Challen, who had returned from Chaforce on the 2nd, had emplaned with the battalion at Port Moresby. (Ten days before it had moved to Ward's Field to take off but the move had been postponed at the last moment.) The battalion was not at full strength for 6 officers and 103 men were still detached to Chaforce. The total strength that Challen could muster at Port Moresby was about 19 officers and 450 men and of these some 350 all ranks were flown to the coast. The last of them reached Popondetta late on the 25th when the battalion was organised into three rifle companies, a Defence Platoon and Headquarters Company elements. Next day Challen led them on a tiring march to Soputa where they were told that they would move at 8 o'clock next morning to relieve the 25th Brigade. When they took the track early on the 27th they sank deep in mud which dragged heavily at their plodding feet until the last stages before they bivouacked, just before dark, between one and two miles south of Gona. In the late afternoon Japanese Zero fighters and dive-bombers stormed over them to strafe and bomb Jumbora and Soputa.

About midday on the 28th Challen told his company commanders that the battalion would leave the track just north of the 25th Brigade Headquarters and strike north-east through a long stretch of kunai running in that direction.[8] A few hundred yards south of the beach another spur of kunai, long, narrow and tapering, struck in like a spear from the east, its point almost resting on the original line of advance. This western extremity of the second kunai spur was "Point Y", the battalion's "lying up" position. Thence a patrol would push north-west to "Point X" at the mouth of the little stream which found the sea almost three-quarters of a mile east of Gona. (The Australians called this "Small Creek".) When the patrol reported "Point X" clear the battalion would assemble there to attack Gona from the east on the 29th, supported by the 2/27th Battalion.

In accordance with these plans the 2/14th halted in the shade of a belt of scrub about 3 p.m. and Lieutenant Dougherty[9] took his platoon forward to reconnoitre "Point X". A little later, when the rest of the battalion was waiting at "Point Y", news came from the 25th Brigade that "Point X" had been reported clear of the enemy.[1] Brigadier Dougherty thereupon ordered Challen not to await Lieutenant Dougherty's return. The 2/14th therefore moved on towards the beach through 300 yards of bush and then, in single file, through foul swamp, waist deep and fringed with prickly sago palms. Captain McGavin's company was advance-guard, Captain Butler's company, battalion headquarters, Lieutenant Rainey's[2] defence platoon and Captain Treacy's company following in that order.

Just before dark scattered shots and then heavy firing broke out from the head of the column. Confused reports began to come back to Challen

---

[8] Brigadier Dougherty had intended that the unit should move under cover of bush on the right-hand edge of the kunai and not through the kunai, where they could be seen. He did not discover Challen's mistake until it was too late to rectify it.

[9] Lt R. H. Dougherty, VX14647; 2/14 Bn. Iron moulder's apprentice; of Mordialloc, Vic; b. Richmond, Vic, 10 Aug 1919. Killed in action 11 Dec 1942.

[1] Brigadier Dougherty was to write later that the patrol to Point X was not in his plan; that the battalion should have moved towards that point with protective detachments out, instead of the patrol, and thus saved valuable time.

[2] Capt D. W. Rainey, VX14272; 2/14 Bn. Farmer; of Pyalong, Vic; b. Heathcote, Vic, 15 Oct 1920.

and he dispersed the rest of his battalion into the swamp slime. Captain Bisset, the adjutant, hurried ahead with Butler's rearmost platoon which had been called forward, and found that a difficult situation had developed in McGavin's company.

About 6.45 p.m. Lieutenant Evans,[3] with McGavin's leading platoon, had broken out on to the beach about 300 yards east of "Point X". Well-concealed Japanese briskly engaged them from underground, camouflaged, heavily-roofed strongpoints and, among others, killed McGavin himself. Evans took over and, while his own platoon continued to engage the defenders, he asked for Butler to make a flanking approach on his left, and told Lieutenant Clarke,[4] with the second platoon of his own company, to await Butler's attack before moving forward. About 7.20 p.m. he received news from Bisset that Challen had sent Butler to the right and Rainey was moving to the left. Later, through the night darkness hanging over the gloomy swamp, there burst the noise of Butler's attack. Clarke then tried to get forward but his platoon was cut about and he himself wounded. Butler's company was likewise held, Butler was badly wounded, Lieutenant Clements killed, Lieutenant McDonald[5] missing and almost certainly killed, and some sixteen others killed or wounded.

In the darkness which now hung like a thick curtain over scrub and swamp and sea it was impossible to locate the Japanese positions which had originally been picked up only sketchily in the last of the light. The confusion, arising largely from the fact that so many of the forward officers had been hit, was lessened by the rock-like Bisset. He with the wounded Clarke, who had taken over Butler's command, organised a holding line. Sergeant Coy[6] stood staunchly by until he fell unconscious from wounds. He had been with McGavin when that officer was killed, had shot the sniper responsible, had gone on to grenade two posts into silence, and had then dragged back two wounded comrades before rallying to Bisset. Working calmly among the scattered wounded Corporal Thomas[7] was killed and Private Brown[8] went on with the work of rescue with a wild storm of fire beating about him. As walking wounded or stretcher parties groped through the darkness Signalman Boys[9] met them and guided them to the telephone cable which they could follow through the bog, bush overhanging them and fire whipping in from the beach.

By 2 a.m. on the 29th the battalion had withdrawn to "Point Y" through an intermediate block which Captain Russell had established.

---

[3] Capt K. A. Evans, VX14028. 2/14 Bn; Staff appts LHQ. Articled law clerk; of Moonee Ponds, Vic; b. Melbourne, 12 Jan 1918.

[4] Capt E. R. Clarke, VX30930; 2/14 Bn. Salesman; of Bentleigh, Vic; b. St Kilda, Vic, 22 Aug 1913.

[5] Lt H. E. R. McDonald, VX24285; 2/14 Bn. Sales manager; of East Kew, Vic; b. Edenhope, Vic, 22 Jul 1914. Killed in action 28 Nov 1942.

[6] Sgt J. W. Coy, MM, VX17982; 2/14 Bn. Labourer; of Port Melbourne, Vic; b. South Melbourne, 26 Oct 1917.

[7] Cpl V. R. G. Thomas, VX15538; 2/14 Bn. Railways worker; of Reservoir, Vic; b. Chillingollah, Vic, 31 Jan 1912. Killed in action 28 Nov 1942.

[8] Pte J. A. Brown, VX22224; 2/14 Bn. Clerk; of Frankston, Vic; b. Ballarat, Vic, 3 Nov 1912.

[9] L-Sgt F. R. Boys, VX14698; 2/14 Bn. Storeman; of Golden Square, Vic; b. Bendigo, Vic, 4 Apr 1918.

Five officers and 27 men had been lost[1] for no gain and primarily through faulty patrol information that "Point X" was clear. Whether the 25th Brigade patrol, and one from the 2/14th itself which had broken out on the beach in the morning about half a mile east of "Point X", had missed picking up occupied positions in which Japanese were lying doggo by day, or whether the Japanese had been alarmed by the presence of the patrols and reacted by occupying the "Point X" area, is uncertain. The former was probably the case. (Lieutenant Dougherty might have supplied additional information but he and his men had swung much too far to the east and emerged towards Basabua where they surprised and killed approximately twenty Japanese. Runners with this news had missed the battalion and reached brigade headquarters about 7.15 p.m. but the patrol itself did not arrive back until the 30th.)

Brigadier Dougherty reacted to the misadventure by giving Challen new orders for the 29th: to swing east along the kunai spur from "Point Y" and then turn north for the beach, thence to follow it westward from his point of emergence ("Point Z") and pierce the Japanese left flank. Meanwhile the 2/27th Battalion would pass through Brigadier Eather's positions to debouch slightly to the west of "Point X" and take over the main attack on Gona.

This had been the second of the 21st Brigade units to move forward. Although most of the Owen Stanleys casualties who were to return to the battalion from hospital had done so by the 26th November, the unit was still nearly 300 under strength until 130 reinforcements from Australia joined it that day. About 6 officers and 105 men were still detached to Chaforce. Lieut-Colonel Cooper had begun to emplane on the 25th and on that and succeeding days 21 officers and 353 men had been flown into Popondetta. He left the usual nucleus of old hands behind at Port Moresby and, with them, the reinforcements. These latter were to receive more intensive training before going into action. When he moved his fighting strength from Soputa into brigade reserve at Gona on the 28th he was organised on the basis of a Headquarters, Headquarters Company (Captain Lee[2]) and three rifle companies (Captains Sims, Cuming[3] and Gill). Sims and Gill each had 4 other officers and 77 men with them, Cuming 3 other officers and 77 men.

Early on the morning of the 29th Cooper told his officers that Cuming would head the battalion move to the sea on the west side of Small Creek near "Point X". They would then move westwards on Gona in the wake of an air strike which was planned for 11 a.m. The artillery would fire concentrations on the Japanese positions just west of the creek until the infantry reached the beach and would then engage opportunity targets. Brigadier Dougherty had planned this merely as an insurance, feeling confident that the battalion would arrive at the beach unmolested.

---

[1] Killed 3 and 8; wounded 2 and 19.
[2] Capt J. D. Lee, SX2998; 2/27 Bn. Hotel manager; of Adelaide; b. Adelaide, 12 Jan 1911.
[3] Capt J. C. Cuming, SX2892; 2/27 Bn. Assistant works manager; of Leabrook, SA; b. Torrensville, SA, 22 Jul 1913. Killed in action 29 Nov 1942.

The move began at 10 a.m. But delay followed a guide's error which caused Major Hanson, the artillery observation officer, to miss his rendezvous with Colonel Cooper. Instead of pushing ahead in spite of this, Cooper delayed, looking for Hanson. Thus the original timings were thrown out and it was not until about midday that the battalion, having made the beach without opposition, swung west against the waiting Japanese who had had time to recover in large measure from the effects of the perfectly executed air strike which had taken place on schedule.

By 12.25 Sims' company, on the right among the coconut palms, and Cuming's, on the left in the kunai, had both been driven to ground by heavy fire and were losing men rapidly as they tried to edge forward. After a long three hours Cuming's company, some 75 yards in advance of Sims', drove north across the latter's front at a troublesome post near the water's edge. In a spirited dash his men burst out of the undergrowth straight into a withering fire which swept the open space over which they tried to advance. Cuming himself, seizing a Bren, plunged ahead of his company into the shadowed space of a Japanese post tunnelled under the spreading roots of a large tree. Firing and shouting, Captain Skipper,[4] his second-in-command, followed. (Later both their bodies were found at the foot of the tree ringed by enemy dead.) Though the company reached its objective it was cut about so badly that it had to withdraw to its original position in the secondary growth, temporarily officerless, as Lieutenants Caddy[5] and Bennie[6] had been wounded, Bennie mortally.

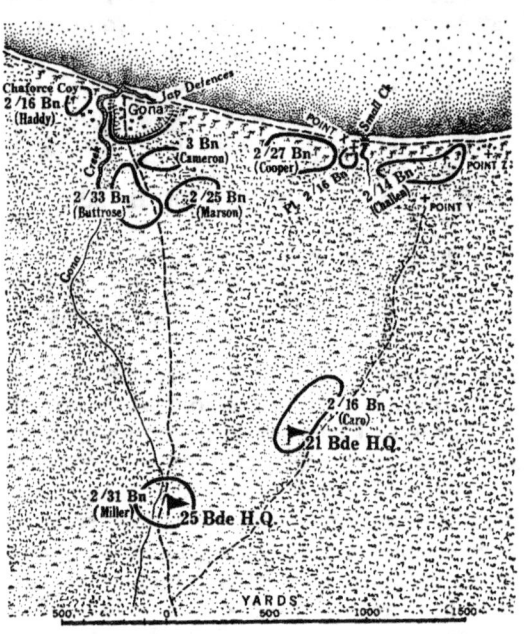

Dispositions, 6 p.m. 29th November

Cooper's men had done all they could for the day. In addition to the loss of Cuming and all his officers three of Sims' officers were casualties—

---

[4] Capt J. W. Skipper, SX2926; 2/27 Bn. Solicitor; of Walkerville, SA; b. Adelaide, 3 May 1914. Killed in action 29 Nov 1942.

[5] Lt. E. M. Caddy, SX9966; 2/27 Bn. Civil servant; of Adelaide; b. Norwood, SA, 24 Feb 1912.

[6] Lt J. S. Bennie, SX12507; 2/27 Bn. Civil servant; of Dunleath Gardens, SA; b. Mile End, SA, 9 Jul 1916. Died of wounds 30 Nov 1942.

Lieutenant Flight[7] killed, Lieutenants Johns and Sherwin[8] wounded. The killed and wounded (7 officers and 48 men) lay under Japanese observation and could be gathered in only under cover of night.[9] As this difficult task went on reconnaissance patrols went forward into the darkness.

But the 2/27th had not been the only battalion engaged that day. As the newcomers had pressed the main east-west attack along the shore, the 3rd and 2/33rd Battalions, from positions astride the track, had inched up from the south. On the right, for the loss of one officer and 11 men, the 3rd Battalion had finally dug in on the edge of the timber fronting the southern defences, after one platoon had broken into the village and been forced out again by heavy machine-gun fire. On the left the 2/33rd had been stopped by machine-guns and snipers. Both battalions had lost men from the effects of the heat on weakened bodies.

And to the east of all this flurry, the 2/14th had also been fighting. Colonel Challen had followed his new orders to attempt to clear the area east of Small Creek, in the rear of the 2/27th. At 9 a.m. on the 29th his battalion was on the move again, the courageous Evans once more leading the advance. They struck the beach about 11.30 without opposition. Evans then moved westward with a block established in his rear at "Point Z" to prevent any Japanese foray from the south or east. After advancing some 200 yards he came to a seemingly deserted village. He pushed cautiously onward through a tongue of scrub and then left the first of the houses behind him. Soon his men were vigorously engaged from well-concealed Japanese positions deeper in the village which extended about 400 yards along the seashore. Though Lieutenant Sargent hurried forward to direct mortar fire on to the opposition (almost on to himself, at extreme range), they could not make any substantial gains. Challen then ordered Captain Treacy's company to attack with mortar support through Evans' positions. Treacy showed the same grim courage that had carried him back across the mountains after he had been cut off at Alola at the end of August. His fine physique made him conspicuous as he coolly directed his attack to within thirty yards of the defending posts which were crossing each other's fronts with fire. Privates Valli[1] and Thompson[2] dashed into that fire, flailing the nearest strongpoints with Bren guns from only twenty yards' range. While the defenders cowered beneath this furious attack the company was able to continue the advance, but it was at the cost of the lives of these two brave soldiers for flanking fire finally caught them. About this time Treacy himself was killed.

In the thick of the fight Private Fyfe[3] was cursing the Japanese and

---

[7] Lt J. O. Flight, SX3217; 2/27 Bn. Civil servant; of Springbank, SA; b. Middle Brighton, Vic, 16 Jul 1918. Killed in action 29 Nov 1942.

[8] Lt A. B. Sherwin, SX2683; 2/27 Bn. Clerk; of Lower Mitcham, SA; b. Claremont, WA, 11 Jun 1916.

[9] Killed 4 and 11; wounded 3 and 37.

[1] Pte M. Valli, VX15286; 2/14 Bn. Labourer; of Wangaratta, Vic; b. Kilmore, Vic, 15 Aug 1918. Killed in action 29 Nov 1942.

[2] Pte G. F. Thompson, VX13877; 2/14 Bn. Tanner; of Alphington, Vic; b. Adelaide, 27 May 1919. Killed in action 29 Nov 1942.

[3] Pte A. F. Fyfe, VX59359; 2/14 Bn. Munitions worker; of Richmond, Vic; b. Richmond, 29 Oct 1920. Killed in action 29 Nov 1942.

yelling unprintable encouragement to his mates when a bullet struck him mortally. Lance-Corporal Weeks[4] tended him where he fell and then carried him carefully through heavy fire to a safer place. Lieutenant Young[5] went down wounded, and Rainey's platoon, skirting to the left, was forced to ground. Then Lieutenant Kolb,[6] with about sixteen men, moving further round the left, thrust in with the bayonet. But most of this determined little group were hit, Kolb fatally.

During this afternoon's fighting Lance-Corporal Davis[7] fell. Private Gaskell[8] rushed through sweeping bullets to help him, pausing in his dressing to fire again and again. Thus he kept the near-by snipers unsettled until he had bandaged Davis' wounds. After he had carried him to safety he similarly rescued two other wounded men before he received a death-wound himself.

About 4 p.m. Challen drew his men back a little. An hour later, behind a barrage of mortar bombs, he sent in a new attack under Sergeant Fitzpatrick[9] and Warrant-Officer Taafe.[1] Though it made some little progress it was then dourly held. After that the battalion withdrew to "Point Z" where they dug in for the night. Three officers and approximately thirty-five men had been lost in this second day's encounter.

Early in the night General Vasey approved Dougherty's plans for the 30th. The whole of the 21st Brigade was now in the area for during the day Lieut-Colonel Caro had led in his 2/16th Battalion, 22 officers and 251 men strong, formed into two rifle companies. Caro was given responsibility for the protection of brigade headquarters and also formed a patrol block between the 2/14th on the east and the 2/27th on the west, to stop any movement from the east towards the rear of the 2/27th. Now Dougherty allotted one company of the 2/16th to Cooper as from the early morning of the 30th to act as a reserve for a continuation of the 2/27th attack westward on that day.

Cooper then planned to fall upon the Japanese again at first light on the 30th. Captain Gill's fresh company would attack through the other two depleted companies which would then follow the new drive. So, at 6.15 a.m. on the 30th, Gill pushed ahead of the positions which Sims and Cuming had reached the previous day. But then heavy machine-gun and rifle fire began to mow his men down and the other two companies, moving to help him, were also checked, still 80 to 100 yards short of the

---

[4] Cpl S. Weeks, MM, VX13739; 2/14 Bn. Mill hand; of Bridgewater-on-Loddon, Vic; b. Bendigo, Vic, 19 Dec 1920.

[5] Capt N. H. Young, VX16157; 2/14 Bn. Agricultural student; of St Kilda, Vic; b. Elwood, Vic, 10 Dec 1918.

[6] Lt G. L. Kolb, VX44616; 2/14 Bn. Grocery manager; of Albury, NSW; b. Albury, 23 Aug 1917. Died of wounds 1 Dec 1942.

[7] L-Cpl V. C. Davis, VX60121; 2/14 Bn. Labourer; of Porepunkah, Vic; b. Bendigo, Vic, 28 Apr 1920. Died of wounds 29 Nov 1942.

[8] Pte W. H. Gaskell, MM, VX15293; 2/14 Bn. Labourer; of Mooroopna, Vic; b. Eaglehawk, Vic, 1 Jul 1918. Died of wounds 13 Dec 1942.

[9] Sgt C. H. Fitzpatrick, VX15291; 2/14 Bn. Farm labourer; of Byrneside, Vic, and Maryborough, Qld; b. Brisbane, 31 May 1918. Died 6 Dec 1958.

[1] Flying Officer E. J. M. Taafe, VX18815. 2/14 Bn; RAAF 1943-45. Of Seaforth, Vic; b. Ballarat, Vic, 7 Jul 1910.

Japanese. Captain O'Neill's[2] company of the 2/16th, moving up on the extreme left of the attack, suffered a like fate. The day then settled to an exchange of fire. Although Cooper planned a reorganised attack for the late afternoon he decided finally to hold it until next day. He had lost approximately a further 45, including three officers—Captain Best[3] (Sims' second-in-command) killed, Gill and one of his platoon commanders wounded. One officer and ten men of the 2/16th company had been hit.

Farther to the east the 2/14th were still embattled. The dark early hours of the 30th November had been disturbed when one of Challen's sentries, Corporal Shelden,[4] detected a patrol trying to slip past through the water on the seaward side. He killed five and wounded one of them. That ushered in a day of harassing patrols by the 2/14th (with a forward strength now of only 7 and 152) which culminated in a clearing attack westward along the shore by a platoon led by Corporal Truscott,[5] who had been prominent in the previous fighting both at Gona and in the mountains—a quiet, very religious man, held in great respect by his battalion. Skilfully and bravely Truscott moved his platoon in at 6 p.m. after Blackforce had given him five minutes of concentrated shell fire. He finally gouged the defenders out of their holes with 2-inch mortar and rifle grenade fire and his men shot them down as they fled along the beach or swam wildly out to sea. Captain Bisset, who had promoted this attack busily, then continued on across the creek at "Point X" and got in touch with the 2/16th and 2/27th Battalions.

The Australians now had a firm grip on a large section of the beach between Sanananda on the right (where the Japanese defences were still firm) and Gona on the left.

That evening Brigadier Dougherty agreed that the 2/27th should continue their westward assault next day. He told Caro of the 2/16th to transfer his second and only remaining rifle company (Major Robinson's) to Colonel Cooper's command by 5 a.m. on 1st December. Brigadier Eather agreed that the 3rd Battalion should move to protect the left flank of the 21st Brigade and Dougherty told Cooper to arrange for his companies, attacking westward along the shore, to link with that battalion, which would then move with them, extending their left flank. Cooper had already reported that he was in direct communication with Cameron.

At 5.45 a.m. on the 1st artillery and mortar fire began to crash down in the small area of the Japanese defences. At six, with bayonets fixed, the Australians entered the assault under the cover of mortar smoke. Cooper's three tattered companies were moving along the shore on the right of the attack, Captain O'Neill's 2/16th company formed the left flank with orders to link with the 3rd Battalion, Major Robinson's 2/16th

---

[2] Capt J. H. O'Neill, WX2731; 2/16 Bn. Bank clerk; of Subiaco, WA; b. Northam, WA, 30 May 1920. Died of wounds 5 Dec 1942.
[3] Capt E. W. Best. SX2933; 2/27 Bn. Civil servant; of St Peters, SA; b. Murwillumbah, NSW, 28 Sep 1917. Killed in action 1 Dec 1942.
[4] Lt E. T. Shelden, MM, VX16822. 2/14, 27 Bns, 1 NG Inf Bn. Farmer; of Little Hampton, Vic; b. Lyonville, Vic, 7 May 1916.
[5] Sgt J. H. Truscott, VX42435; 2/14 Bn. Farmer; of Welshpool, Vic; b. Foster, Vic, 26 Sep 1917. Killed in action 15 Dec 1942.

company was in reserve. But soon the attack seemed to be awry and there was confusion as to the cause. Along the beach the 2/27th men, after subduing the foremost position, were checked and withering, and for some time no one could say what was happening on the left. It transpired, however, that the 3rd Battalion had seen nothing of the left flank of the attack passing in front of them and had made no movement forward. But, soon after that, came the further news that O'Neill had indeed swept the 3rd Battalion front and, with part of Lieutenant Egerton-Warburton's[6] 2/27th company (previously Captain Gill's), was ravaging the central Japanese positions in the village of Gona itself. Lieutenant Mayberry's[7] platoon was the centre of O'Neill's attack and, by the time they reached the centre of the village, blasting the last of their way there with Brens and sub-machine-guns fired from the hip, had been reduced from eighteen to Mayberry himself and five men. These fought on from shell holes for some time although assailed from both north and south—the area Cameron's men were to have cleared—and, through some error of the gunners, under fire from the Australian artillery. Then as they tried to withdraw they clashed savagely with a party of Japanese moving back into positions after the bombardment, lost two more very brave men (Privates Sage[8] and Morey[9]), broke westward and crossed Gona Creek to join Lieutenant Haddy's Chaforce platoon on the far side.

Casualties were mounting fast. Most of the men who had entered the village were now either dead, wounded or missing (a few of the wounded and missing destined to get back when night came). O'Neill himself, badly hit, had been left lying on the eastern bank of the creek. Colonel Cooper was wounded and Major Hearman (second-in-command of the 2/16th) had taken over from him. About the middle of the morning more concentrated fighting boiled up when Major Robinson, with fifteen men from the reserve company, bravely assaulted a strong and troublesome post on the beach. They took the position, but a counter-attack forced them out soon afterwards. Wounded but resolute, Robinson was still fighting when he was again wounded.

For the Australians the rest of the day was one of sweat and hazard as they tried to clear their casualties from the battleground beneath a worrying fire from the main Japanese positions and unnerving shots from concealed snipers. With the night Corporal McMahon[1] and Private Yeing[2] of Haddy's platoon swam Gona Creek into Japanese territory and on a punt brought back the dying Captain O'Neill through the darkness

---

[6] Capt W. A. Egerton-Warburton, SX8029; 2/27 Bn. Shipping clerk; of Melbourne; b. Broken Hill, NSW, 4 Jan 1918.

[7] Lt L. P. Mayberry, MC, WX10392; 2/16 Bn. Regular soldier; of Perth, WA; b. Kalgoorlie, WA, 18 Mar 1912.

[8] Pte A. G. Sage, WX7689; 2/16 Bn. Farm hand; of Bilbarin, WA; b. Bristol, England, 3 Mar 1908. Killed in action 1 Dec 1942.

[9] Pte L. G. Morey, WX4202; 2/16 Bn. Truck driver; of Kalgoorlie, WA; b. Northam, WA, 17 Dec 1916. Killed in action 1 Dec 1942.

[1] WO2 W. T. McMahon, MM, WX4241; 2/16 Bn. Mining storeman; of Westonia, WA; b. Dwellingup, WA, 24 Sep 1915.

[2] Cpl E. Yeing, WX1879. 2/32, 2/16 Bns. Storeman; of Spearwood, WA; b. Palmyra, WA, 16 Apr 1919.

from the position in which he had been lying wounded all day. Through the same darkness came the wavering light of flares from far out to sea, and the distant echoes of heavy bombing, as aircraft attacked Japanese ships which had seemed to be moving in towards the shore but turned out to sea again under cover of smoke.

The day, which cost the 2/16th alone 3 officers and 56 men,[3] had once again hinged on a bitter mistake for the Australians—the failure of the 3rd Battalion to move forward and link with the westward attackers. This certainly demanded a nicety of timing and direction in manoeuvre very difficult to ensure in any attack, and certainly most difficult in the Gona country. The actual truth seems to have been, however, that the 3rd was not where Brigadier Eather had thought it to be, or indeed where Colonel Cameron thought it was, but farther south; that, instead of moving forward on its time schedule, it waited for the 21st Brigade's attack to become manifest, but inevitably saw nothing of it and was not waiting where O'Neill expected to make his junction. Here was a perfect example of the necessity for planning an attack in bush warfare even more carefully than elsewhere, mainly because of limited observation resulting in lack of information and faulty deduction. A major factor was also that the Gona maps were incomplete and inaccurate (despite the fact that air photographs could have been used to provide detailed information which was so urgently needed). But for this mistake the 1st December assault on Gona Mission might not have been another costly failure for the Australians.

Brigadier Dougherty was very worried. Early in the evening Vasey told him that too many casualties were being suffered at Gona; that he was considering leaving a force to contain the place while another force moved eastward in a flanking threat to Sanananda. The upshot was that Dougherty sent Challen along the coastal track to Sanananda next morning with instructions to maintain a firm base and confine his operations to fighting patrols. But scrub and mangrove swamp blocked Challen's main party beyond Basabua and he was forced to bivouac at Basabua on the night of the 2nd.

At Gona on the same day willing but tired men staged yet another attack as they tried to maintain pressure on their enemies. But its minor nature was indicative of the fact that they had temporarily exhausted their capacity for full-scale assaults. Lieutenant Hicks and twenty men of the 2/16th Battalion (a platoon of the 2/27th standing by to consolidate), supported by fire from the 3rd and 2/33rd Battalions, tried themselves against the most easterly of the Japanese positions which Major Robinson had tested the previous day. They came directly in from the east and pinched off the flanking defences but Hicks himself was mortally wounded and nine more men were shot.

By midday on the 2nd the troubled Vasey was conferring with three brigadiers at the 25th Brigade Headquarters below Gona: Dougherty,

---

[3] Killed 2 and 23; wounded 1 and 33.

Eather (whose men for the past few days had been able to do little more than merely hold their positions astride the track south of the village), and Porter (whose 30th Brigade was then entering the coastal scene). Vasey had planned to have Porter's brigade relieve Eather's but now he said that Eather must continue to contain the Gona garrison. The remnants of the 2/16th and 2/27th, forming a composite battalion under Lieut-Colonel Caro, would join the 25th Brigade. The first of Porter's battalions, the 39th, which was even then approaching Gona after flying in to Popondetta, would go to Dougherty's command and follow the 2/14th around the coast to Sanananda. This 39th was the proud militia battalion which had been the first Australian unit to be blooded in the Kokoda fighting. It was still led by the skilful and imperturbable Lieut-Colonel Honner. It was rested and reinforced; its reinforcements included about 100 of the 53rd Battalion who had joined it just before the amalgamation of the 53rd and 55th Battalions to form the 55th/53rd.

The new plan was operating on the 3rd. Wary fire from both besiegers and besieged marked the day in the main area. Eastwards Challen was finding no enemy to contend with but the country was unfriendly enough in itself. The coastal track shown on the map had faded into scrub and swamp and, as they milled about in this inhospitable region, the 2/14th held up Brigadier Dougherty's own group and portion of the 39th Battalion following behind them. Their difficulties were not lessened when one over-zealous R.A.A.F. airman swept low and strafed the whole force in error. It was clear that no line of approach could be established through this country, and Dougherty reported this to Vasey. Vasey then had no choice but to revise his orders. In the early evening he instructed Dougherty to resume command of his own three battalions and to include the 39th with them; to relieve Eather and the entire 25th Brigade (including the 3rd Battalion); and thus become responsible for the whole Gona area. The 49th Battalion, which had already begun to march in to Eather's command, was to return to Soputa and revert to command of the 30th Brigade which (less the 39th) would then resume action on the main track to Sanananda.

There was more than a hint of bewildered desperation in these rapidly changing plans. The opening notes of this last round, a mere fortnight before, had been confident ones for the Australians. Hot in pursuit the 25th Brigade had passed from elation to a sobered but confident assessment of the unexpected strength of the last-ditch opposition, to exhausted impotence, losing well over 200 officers and men in battle for little visible result just when it seemed that their long and bitter journey from the sea to the sea was at an end. Then the 21st Brigade, anxious to avenge the past, had seen their hopes fading when battle losses alone amounted to 340 out of almost an even 1,000 within five days of their entry into the new action. And still the end was not in sight.

Afterwards some veteran officers were critical of the Australian tactics in this tropical vignette of the trench warfare conditions of the earlier war. Major Sublet, a competent and experienced soldier, thought that one of the cardinal principles of war—concentration—had been lost sight of. He considered that, though the Japanese had been pounded from the air, with artillery and mortar fire, and flailed with small-arms fire, so that ultimately they scarce dared show themselves above ground, much of the advantage of this had been lost through the shifting emphasis of the Australian attacks. These had taken place on a number of different fronts and, in some cases, sufficiently limited objectives had not been defined. He wrote:

> In my opinion we would have gained more by pinching off one enemy strongpoint at a time by concentrating manpower with sufficient mortar fire, shell fire and small arms fire against each post in turn. The remainder of our forces could then have been disposed purely to arrest any attempt by the enemy to reinforce or to evacuate Gona.

On 4th December, however, Vasey's new plans came into operation. By 4.30 p.m. that day the 21st Brigade had completed the relief of the 25th Brigade.[4] Dougherty had his headquarters on the track about one mile south of Gona with Captain Thurgood's and Captain A. J. Lee's Chaforce companies there as protection. Honner had the companies of the 39th Battalion grouped round the track forward of brigade headquarters and below the Gona southern perimeter. On the seashore the 2/14th Battalion was in a defensive position in their old area just east of Small Creek. Linking with them on the west and reaching towards the eastern extremity of the Gona defences Colonel Caro had his composite battalion spread along the beach.

With the night came determined Australian patrol assaults on the most easterly of the Japanese positions. In this shadowy fighting a number of Japanese were killed and the Australians gained useful information.

Dougherty was content to spend the next day reshuffling his positions slightly as he brought the 2/14th in to change places with Thurgood and

---

[4] On relief by the 21st Brigade on 4th December, the 25th Brigade began to move off for Soputa preparatory to being flown out to Port Moresby. Its battalions had gone into action approximately 550 strong in early September and, on 19th September when they were consolidated at Imita Ridge, had averaged 27 officers and 504 men per battalion. On 2nd December, two days before they were relieved, the strengths of the battalions were:
  2/25th Battalion: 15 and 248
  2/31st Battalion: 9 and 197
  2/33rd Battalion: 8 and 170
In the next fortnight, while they waited to be flown out, sickness eroded their strengths still further so that, for example, 14 and 233 of the 2/25th finally returned to Port Moresby as a unit. (Among the casualties from that cause was the lion-hearted Lieut-Colonel Miller of the 2/31st who died from scrub typhus on the 14th.) The following figures, which may be taken as fairly typical, help to round off the picture.

The 2/25th, which was the strongest battalion when relieved, recorded these as its casualties (excluding non-fatal sickness cases) for the whole of the Owen Stanleys and Gona operations:—

	Offrs	ORs
Killed in action	4	40
Died of wounds	—	10
Missing	—	1
Died of illness	—	5
Accidentally killed	—	1
Wounded	13	115
Injured in action	—	1

The 2/33rd, the weakest battalion when relieved, recorded these casualties among its officers for the entire Owen Stanleys and Gona operations:—
  Killed in action   5
  Wounded in action 8
  Evacuated sick   13

On these figures, the 2/33rd suffered, from one cause or another, almost 100 per cent officer casualties.

Lee. Worrying news had come to him from General Herring that the Japanese would probably try to land reinforcements from destroyers at the mouth of the Kumusi River. He decided to send both the composite battalion and the 39th to attack again on the 6th, estimating that the total Japanese strength was now about 150. Silent patrols were to move forward

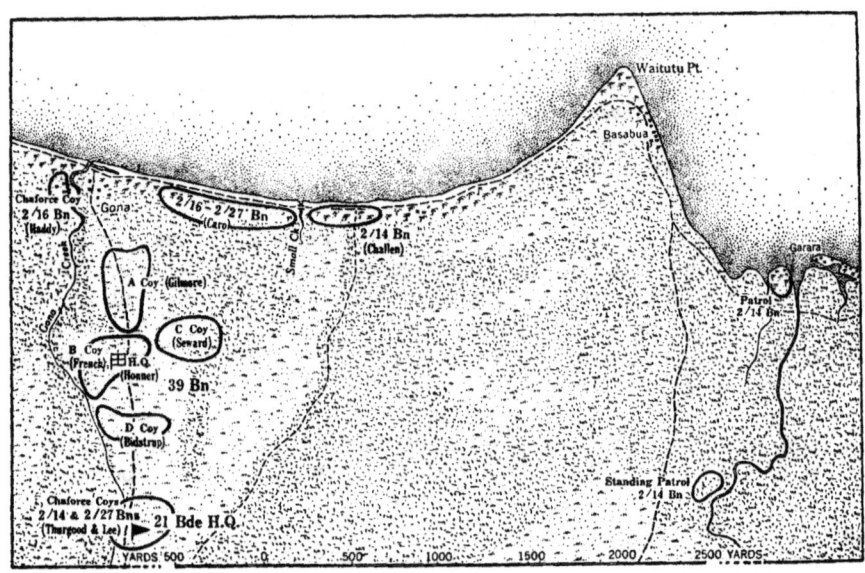

Dispositions, 6 p.m. 4th December

at 5.30 a.m.—Caro's against the most easterly Japanese strongpoint, Honner's against the south-west pivot and followed by the main weight of his attack on that axis to secure the fringe of timber, made up of trees four to five feet in diameter, with gnarled roots under and around which the Japanese were dug in. This ran in a line parallel to the beach.

But once again the Australian attack bogged down. Caro's men gained no real momentum along the beach although the leading platoon, Lieutenant White's,[5] reached within ten yards of their objective (the first post along the beach), where White was killed. In the 39th Battalion's sector Lieutenant Nelson[6] had led his platoon forward on the right of the track in the dark towards the centre of the Japanese southern defences. They were up to their shoulders in the water and slime of a sago swamp when heavy fire was encountered. Nelson was wounded and his men, unable to make the passage of the swamp, withdrew.

Meanwhile Colonel Honner's main movement, by Captain Bidstrup's company on the left of the road towards the timber line, was shot to

---

[5] Lt C. M. White, WX4832; 2/16 Bn. Bank clerk; of West Perth, WA; b. Perth, 3 Aug 1917. Killed in action 6 Dec 1942.

[6] Capt J. W. Nelson, NX135119. 39, 2/4 Bns. Regular soldier; of Rockdale, NSW; b. St Peters, NSW, 23 Oct 1915.

pieces. The smoke which had been laid to assist Bidstrup's men, and the half light of the fading night, shrouded their objectives—already well hidden, dug down almost to ground level and roofed—but they themselves loomed large through the murk to their waiting foes. Vicious crossfire from machine-guns struck them after they had gained only about 50 yards. Bidstrup would then have been quite out of touch with his left platoon had not Private Skilbeck[7] four times crossed open ground under intense fire to bring back reports to the company headquarters, each time helping wounded men on the way. Once he was asked to lead a reserve section forward and, while waiting for it, went back into Japanese fire to carry in another helpless and wounded man. Sergeant Morrison was another who refused to bend to the circumstances of that day. When his platoon commander was wounded he went forward through intense fire and, even above the din of the fighting, could be heard directing the platoon in its assault. He was wounded—first in the hand and then in the leg—but carried on, shouting orders as he lay on the ground. Fifty-eight of the company had been killed or wounded before the attackers withdrew to cover.

On the right of this main attack, however, some small and fleeting success had developed. The creek had protected Bidstrup's left. On his right flank Corporal Edgell's[8] section had been ordered to silence any posts in the area through which the attack would pass. Taking advantage of the noise and confusion of Bidstrup's attack he and his men rocketed to the objective through the gloom and a network of Japanese posts. Finding themselves alone there, however, this small group fought their way back again, Edgell himself (with a sub-machine-gun) and a Bren gunner beside him pouring such a storm of fire into a Japanese post that the two were credited with having killed 10 or 12 of the defenders before they went on their way leaving the final reduction of the post to Lieutenant Tuckey[9] and a patrol he had brought out with him.

By this time an uneasy situation had developed on the Australian extreme left—west of the main Japanese Gona Mission defences. It will be remembered that the 2/16th Battalion component of Chaforce had been established on the west bank of Gona Creek practically the whole time since 21st November, harassing the Japanese and watching the Australian left flank. Originally six officers and 103 men strong they had dwindled to a strength of 45 all ranks—in actual fact little stronger than a platoon—with Lieutenant Haddy commanding. Like the other Chaforce companies they had had virtually no rest since August when the 21st Brigade had first entered the battle in the mountains. The 45 who remained were gaunt and worn with strain and malaria. In an exposed and isolated flanking position at Gona they had been bombarded by Aus-

[7] Cpl A. J. Skilbeck, MM, VX149854. 39, 14/32 Bns. Hat maker; of Windsor, Vic; b. Footscray, Vic, 1 Apr 1921.
[8] Cpl R. G. Edgell, DCM, VX120253; 39 Bn. Hairdresser; of Moonee Ponds, Vic; b. Tungamah, Vic, 17 Sep 1912.
[9] Capt P. A. Tuckey, NGX391. NGVR; 39, 2/14 Bns; 1 NG Inf Bn. Winchman; of Springwood, NSW; b. Birmingham, England, 28 Feb 1909. Killed in action 11 Dec 1944.

tralian artillery and strafed by Allied aircraft several times, as they faced the Japanese. Always, his men recorded later, it was Haddy himself who met the varied occasions of their stress with quick presence of mind and unwearied courage, always first to test dangerous situations to protect his men. Several times the little band foiled Japanese attempts to land reinforcements in their vicinity. On such occasions (as in a normal harassing role) Haddy himself usually operated the 2-inch mortar with deadly effect, as implacable in defence as he was dashing in attack.

On the last day of November, with a Chaforce patrol, he relieved Lieutenant Greenwood of the 2/14th Battalion in a small village area, which became known to the Australians as "Haddy's village", between one and two miles west of his own Chaforce firm base and not far east of the Amboga River. In that position he beat off a Japanese attempt to seep eastwards towards the centre of operations. In doing so he lost two men killed but wounded a number of the attackers. From reports and observations he concluded that there were between 150 and 200 Japanese just west of the Amboga and native carriers who fell into Australian hands indicated that these were reinforcements for Gona who had been prevented from landing there by Allied air attacks. When, on 4th December, Captain L. T. Hurrell led a strong 2/31st Battalion reconnaissance patrol into this same area, Hurrell and three of his men were killed in a sharp brush with these dangerous elements. Soon, after certain other patrol manoeuvrings, Haddy returned to the village positions on the 5th with 20 volunteers. All were racked with fever and weak.

Just before a rain-driven midnight on the 6th the Japanese closed in. Feeling the aggressive strength opposed to him Haddy sent Private Bloomfield[1] back to his own main base for help. Bloomfield, weak with fever, staggered through the darkness with three wounded men, carrying one of them most of the way on his back. Finally he delivered his message to Sergeant Jones[2] who set out at once with the remainder of the Chaforce men, the whole band numbering fifteen. Soon Jones ran into four questing Japanese whom he shot but, before he was killed, the fourth bayoneted the sergeant. Corporal Murphy[3] then took over, encouraging his men and leading them so skilfully that they checked advancing Japanese until help came later on the 7th.

This was in the form of a 2/14th Battalion patrol, fifty strong, under Lieutenant Dougherty, whom Challen had sent on orders from Brigadier Dougherty after news of Haddy's plight had reached him. Dougherty found the Japanese in strength about half a mile east of Haddy's village. Always aggressive, he forced a violent clash in which he inflicted comparatively heavy casualties but in which a number of his own men were also lost. As the afternoon advanced he realised that he was being encircled

---

[1] Cpl C. A. Bloomfield, WX5668; 2/16 Bn. Shop assistant; of Albany, WA; b. Wokernup, WA, 8 Aug 1915.
[2] WO2 R. E. A. Jones, MM, WX4252; 2/16 Bn. Rockdrill miner; of Boulder, WA; b. Boulder, 11 May 1911.
[3] Sgt G. B. J. Murphy, MM, WX3006; 2/16 Bn. Clothing cutter; of Perth, WA; b. Boulder, WA, 18 Feb 1919.

by much stronger forces so reluctantly pulled back some 500 yards. The brigadier then ordered Colonel Challen to take the rest of his fighting strength (numbering some forty), link with Dougherty, and take charge of operations in that area. Challen achieved this in the early darkness and formed a perimeter for the night about one mile west of Gona Mission.

About 6.30 p.m. two of Haddy's men from the village reported at brigade headquarters and said that another six of their number were still in the scrub on their way in. (Sergeant Eric Williams,[4] leading these men, said the next day that he counted 400 to 500 Japanese moving east.) There was no sign of Haddy himself, however, and it later transpired that he had died as he had lived and fought.

Soon after he had sent Private Bloomfield for help he decided to try to extricate the rest of his men. They combined to write later:

> He ordered the withdrawal stating that he would stay to the last. It is mentioned by all his men that Haddy was always placing himself in such positions to enable his men to get out of tight corners irrespective of the risk attached. . . . From then until the 2/14th found the bodies of Lieutenant Haddy and Private Stephens[5] they were posted as missing. Stephens' body was in the hut underneath which Haddy had his HQ. At the time the Japs attacked he was on sentry duty and was hit with a grenade. Lieutenant Haddy's body was found under the hut and from the evidence around the hut it proved that Haddy had fought to the last, killing many Japs before they finally got him. . . . It was always Haddy who carried out tasks and volunteered for jobs which may have resulted in death for any of his men. On every patrol Haddy was in command of he insisted on being forward scout.[6]

Meanwhile, back in the main positions, after a night of determined harassing raids by Australian patrols, the 7th had been a comparatively quiet day. Brigadier Dougherty had arranged air attacks as a preliminary to another assault by the 39th. These proved disappointing, however, falling on the Australian rear areas and not near the Japanese. Honner (not prepared to send his men against an unshocked and alerted enemy) at once cancelled the ground program and Dougherty approved his action. That night General Vasey agreed with Dougherty's plans for the 8th, granted him 250 rounds for artillery support, and agreed to have surrender leaflets dropped on the Gona garrison next morning with the hope of white-anting their morale before an all-out assault by the brigade.

This was to be Dougherty's last throw. His fighting strength was down to 37 officers and 755 men (2/14th, 6 and 133; 2/16th, 5 and 99; 2/27th, 4 and 142; 39th, 22 and 381)—less than the full strength of one battalion.[7] Colonel Pollard, Vasey's chief staff officer, called on Dougherty on the morning of the 8th and told him that it might be necessary to withdraw the 39th Battalion and return it to 30th Brigade at Sanananda; that Vasey agreed with Dougherty's determination to liquidate Gona and, at the same time, investigate the Japanese force apparently based on the Amboga River, but that, if the impending attack were not

---

[4] Sgt E. F. E. Williams, WX4759; 2/16 Bn. Clerk; of Perth, WA; b. Northam, WA, 23 Jul 1918.
[5] Pte S. A. Stephens, WX13132; 2/16 Bn. Dairy farmer; of Cannington, WA; b. Spearwood, WA, 23 Jan 1910. Killed in action 7 Dec 1942.
[6] Appendix to 2/16th Battalion war diary, Dec 1942.
[7] War diary, 7th Division, Dec 1942.

successful, further attacks on Gona would be ruled out as being likely to be disproportionately costly; that Gona would then have to be merely contained while as large a force as possible moved to smash the Japanese concentration in the west.

Dougherty's plan now hinged on the 39th, his strongest battalion. After an artillery preparation it was to operate in three phases: to move north into the timber fringing the southern defences; to attack north-west into the village; to clear the timber belt on the east side of Gona Creek.

At 11.30 a.m. on 8th December Australian mortars and field guns began ranging. An hour later fifteen minutes of concentrated fire began, the gunners using delayed fuses so that the shells burst about two feet underground, actually boring into the dug-in positions with deadly effect. At 12.45 the 39th Battalion attacked, Captain Gilmore's[8] company on the right of the track, Captain Seward's[9] on the left. Anxious to come to grips Gilmore's men followed the barrage so closely that they were among the defenders before it had ended and while these were still reeling. On the company's right Lieutenant Kelly's[1] platoon lost men but smashed into the mission area itself. Undaunted by sweeping fire, Private Wilkinson[2] moved into the open, set up his Bren gun on a post about four feet high and, standing in full view of the Japanese, raked them with his fire. On the left of the company Lieutenant Dalby raced his men to the first post and was reported to have struck down the gunner manning a medium machine-gun and seven other defenders. Hard on his heels his men clawed out the remaining defenders of this big post, capturing a medium and three light machine-guns. Then Corporal Ellis[3] ranged hotly ahead and his fellows credited him with wiping out the next four posts single-handed.

On the left of the track Seward's company had been less fortunate. They were badly cut about by fire from the positions Captain Bidstrup's men had encountered on the 6th. Honner pulled out the survivors and left Lieutenant French's company to maintain the front there. Sound tactician that he was (and adhering to his own plan which he had made in expectation of success on the right) he then, as the afternoon advanced, sent Bidstrup's and Seward's men through the breach that Gilmore's men had made. They fought on through the afternoon and into the night until half the perimeter defences and the centre of the garrison area were in their hands.

Near the shore Major Sublet, who had taken over command of the composite battalion that morning, was not to be denied a share in this clash. He thrust his 2/27th component along the beach and Captain

---

[8] Maj J. C. S. Gilmore, QX3704. 2/12, 53, 39, 2/2 Bns. Farmer; of Cairns, Qld; b. Wolfram, Qld, 23 May 1913.
[9] Capt M. S. Seward, WX2902. 2/2 MG Bn, 2/16, 39, 2/11 Bns. Bank officer; of Perth, WA; b. Pingelly, WA, 2 Apr 1920.
[1] Capt H. H. Kelly, VX117105. 39, 2/2 Bns. Bank clerk; of Colac, Vic; b. Frankston, Vic, 24 Jul 1919.
[2] Cpl R. E. G. Wilkinson, MM, VX105413; 39 Bn. Labourer; of Fitzroy, Vic; b. Lucknow, Vic, 12 May 1910.
[3] Sgt S. J. Ellis, DCM, VX106080. 39, 2/8 Bns. Grocer's assistant; of Preston, Vic; b. Barongarook, Vic, 30 Mar 1911.

Atkinson[4] (with the company which Major Robinson had previously commanded) north-west from his command post. But they did not get far through the storm of machine-gun fire which beset them. Once again Lieutenant Mayberry shone out even in that brave company. With a scratch crew of six men he stormed headlong against a key position. Badly wounded in the head and right arm he still fought on and urged his men forward. His shattered right arm refusing its function, he dragged the pin out of a grenade and essayed a throw with his left hand. But the arm was too weak. He forced the pin back with his teeth and then lay for some hours in his exposed position before he was rescued. The other two platoon commanders also went down, Lieutenant Inkpen[5] mortally wounded.

As the day closed Thurgood and Lee of Chaforce covered the composite battalion from the east and Sublet set his men to digging in the small area they had gained.

The surviving Japanese were now pretty well enclosed in a much-diminished area. Between Sublet's positions on the right and Honner's on the left there lay a small corridor, possibly some 200 yards in width. Though this ground was swampy it was not sufficiently so to prevent the Japanese from traversing it at night. As darkness covered their desperate plight they tried repeatedly to make their way out through this corridor, or to break through the ring which Sublet and Honner had forged about them. At least 100 were killed in these attempts during the night, some by Honner's men, most by Sublet's, some mopped up by the Chaforce men to the east.

An atmosphere that was strangely macabre even for that ghastly place seemed to well out over the battlefield in the darkness that night, stemming from the despairing efforts of the Japanese to escape. A group, trying to steal along the seashore, was mown down by machine-gun fire from men of the 2/27th. Survivors, taking to the water and swimming for the open sea, illuminated themselves in ghostly light as the tropical, phosphorescent water boiled up around them and guided the merciless Australian fire. Into one of the 2/27th's company headquarters a Japanese officer burst with flailing sword and fell upon an Australian soldier there so that, to other Australians close by, there came the sudden sounds of two men fighting for their lives in the black night, of sword blows, shots, panting breaths and screams.

Early on the 9th, to clean out the remaining pockets of resistance, patrols from both the composite battalion and the 39th moved into the dreadful graveyard which Gona Mission had become for most of the 800-900 men of the improvised Japanese garrison who had been stationed there. In this work Lieutenant Sword, who had fought most bravely and tirelessly since the very beginning of the Japanese invasion, was killed.

---

[4] Maj W. M. Atkinson, MC, WX2846. 2/16 Bn; 1 Aust Para Bn. Businessman; of Merredin, WA; b. Cottesloe, WA, 1 Mar 1911.
[5] Lt. L. G. J. Inkpen, WX5678; 2/16 Bn. Clerk; of Bunbury, WA; b. Subiaco, WA, 13 Aug 1919. Killed in action 8 Dec 1942.

The grim search went on until the early afternoon when only isolated individuals, in some reckless last throw desperately starting up from the silence that was settling, remained of the Gona garrison.

> The afternoon was spent in burying, salvaging, and cleaning up the area (the 2/16th diarist wrote later). Gona village and beach were in a shambles with dead Japs and Australians everywhere. Apparently the enemy had made no attempt to bury the dead, some of whom had obviously been lying out for days. The stench was terrific. The Japs had put up a very stubborn resistance. They still had plenty of ammunition, medical stores and rice, although a large quantity of rice was green with mould. In one dugout rice had been stacked on enemy dead. More Japs had died lying on the rice and ammunition had been stacked on them again. 638 Japs were buried in the area.

Earlier in the day Honner had rung down the curtain over Gona Mission with a laconic message to Brigadier Dougherty: "Gona's gone!"

This was, however, in a sense an anti-climax as it meant only a very brief pause in the fighting in the Gona area. The 2/14th Battalion to the west across Gona Creek, had been having a lively time since it had settled into a perimeter about one mile west of the mission. Those three indefatigable young officers, Bisset, Dougherty and Evans, had harried the Japanese on the 8th and the equally indefatigable Truscott (now a sergeant) had led his men in the destruction of yet another post. The following day and night Challen's men had continued with a series of minor but aggressive passes against an enemy who was obviously in some strength.

It was clear to Brigadier Dougherty that his work was but half done until he had dissolved this very real threat, which the survivors from the mountains and some of the newly-arrived troops were posing. Late on the 9th, therefore, he ordered Honner to move the 39th westward. Honner then came into reserve for a night's rest preparatory to setting out on his new task on the 10th.

When Dougherty took stock of his strength on the morning of the 10th he found that his three original battalions had lost 34 officers and 375 men in battle and many through sickness. An additional 6 officers and 115 men had been lost in battle by the 39th.[6] These bitter losses represented more than 41 per cent of his strength and the engagement was still unfinished. They had been inflicted by an enemy who had seemed already beaten when the last round opened. The Australians had made several serious errors but had fought with dogged bravery, and undoubtedly the Japanese will to fight to the end was the major factor. For example, of the operations by the foremost clearing patrols on the last day at Gona Mission, the 2/16th Battalion diarist has recorded:

> Their task was to feel out enemy positions and if fired on go immediately to ground. The patrol following was to come forward and mop up post. At second Jap post along beach twelve Japs were encountered, at least nine of them were stretcher cases, but all opened fire on party with grenades and rifles. Party retaliated with grenades and killed seven Japs. A message was sent, brought patrol 2/27 Bn up and post was cleaned out.

---

[6] War diary, 21st Brigade, Dec 1942.

Quite obviously the Japanese were soldiers to whom, lacking a means of escape, only death could bring an acceptable relief.

Lieutenant Schwind[7] and Sergeant Iskov[8] of the 2/14th who, in the preceding days, had carried out a long and hazardous patrol in the area of the Amboga River, were guiding the 39th when that battalion moved westward on the 10th, parallel with the coast, and through scrub and swamp. The movement continued next day and, after he had crossed a creek which (it later transpired) flowed into the sea about two miles west of Gona Mission and one mile west of the 2/14th Battalion, Honner turned north towards the sea with Lieutenant French's company as advance-guard. In the early afternoon the leading scouts and Iskov killed a Japanese lieut-colonel and two other officers and documents were found on the bodies. Then the Australians, pressing forward into swamp, came hard against the southern defences of Japanese positions located in Haddy's village on the seashore. Corporal Edgell, the young but proved leader of the forward section, rushed the foremost post, into the muzzle of a machine-gun which wounded him badly in the right arm. Changing his own sub-machine-gun to his left hand he killed the three Japanese manning the gun and then, wounded as he was, assisted two other wounded men back. Lieutenant Plater,[9] a spirited young Duntrooner, maintained the impetus of the attack along the track, grenading and machine-gunning, and then personally striking down a number of Japanese officers and men in one foray after another as the day wore on. Just before nightfall one of his section commanders was wounded beside him and, as Plater dressed his wound, he himself was shot through the shoulder blade. But still he staggered at the head of the section to wipe out another obstructing post before he finally allowed himself to be carried from the field.

As Plater's platoon thus fought on, Lieutenants Mortimore and Gartner[1] had swung their platoons to the right and left respectively of the track. Gartner, already marked in the battalion as a skilful tree-sniper, fought hard for four hours until, through the scrub and swamp, he could see the village huts, tantalisingly close, on the seashore. By that time, however, his platoon had been reduced to approximately section strength. Sergeant Meani then led the ten remaining men to watch Mortimore's right flank while Gartner took over Plater's leaderless platoon.

Captain Seward tried to work his way wide round the left with his company (now only twenty-five strong), but a storm of fire stopped him. The whole battalion then dug in for the night. Rain came with the night, flooding tracks, weapon pits, latrines, so that the Australians were held in swamp and water before opposition sited on higher and drier ground. In the darkness and rain a determined attack overran Seward's forward

---

[7] Capt L. C. J. Schwind, VX15289; 2/14 Bn. Dry cleaner's assistant; of Wangaratta, Vic; b. Rutherglen, Vic, 15 Sep 1912.
[8] Lt R. F. Iskov, VX15237. 2/14, 2/23 Bns. Farm labourer; of Glenrowan, Vic; b. Glenrowan, 1 May 1920.
[9] Capt R. S. Plater, MC, NX148954. 53, 39 Bns. Regular soldier; of Edgecliff, NSW; b. Sydney, 5 Sep 1921.
[1] Maj P. E. Gartner, MC, ED, VX100096. 39, 2/2, 1 NG Inf Bns; Indian Army 1945-47. Student; of Canterbury, Vic; b. Surrey Hills, Vic, 5 Aug 1920.

platoon from which a handful of wounded survivors straggled in next morning.

During these days, from positions half-way between Gona Mission and Haddy's village, the 2/14th Battalion had been skirmishing along the coast. On the evening of the 11th Lieutenant Dougherty attempted an attack from the south on the Japanese holding in a cluster of huts just west of the 2/14th positions. But the enemy were not disposed to yield and killed the fearless young Dougherty as he came at them.

By the evening of the 12th Honner had lost 10 killed and 37 wounded in the new operations but had developed a clearer idea of what he was facing. Examination of the Japanese dead and their equipment suggested that his opponents were apparently portion of a freshly-landed force, well fed and well found, approximately equal in numbers, he thought, to his own. More precise information, hastily passed down from higher sources, then revealed that papers taken by Sergeant Iskov from the officers killed on the track on the 11th showed that possibly about 500 men of the *III Battalion* of the *170 Regiment,* had landed between the Kumusi and Amboga at the beginning of December from four destroyers which Allied aircraft had attacked on the night 1st-2nd December. Well-

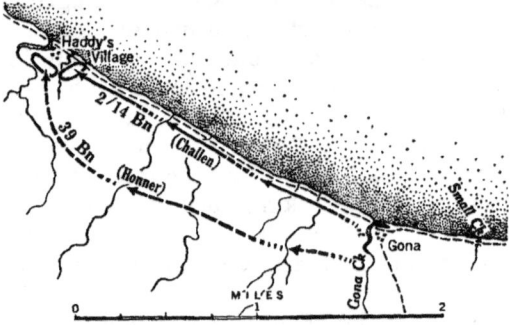

Nightfall, 15th December

founded estimates suggested that, allowing for casualties which had been inflicted in the fighting up to that time, the newcomers, together with survivors from the mountain fighting who had escaped down the Kumusi and congregated near its mouth, totalled some 600 in the Kumusi-Amboga area on 13th December.

For three days after the 12th Honner was striking for the sea west of Haddy's village to block off Japanese reinforcements from that direction. These were difficult days of small actions and skirmishes with the 39th edging slowly forward. By nightfall of the 15th, however, the battalion was not only pressing the defenders closely from the south but also closing in from the west where Captain Bidstrup's company, reinforced by the pioneer platoon, was then overlooking the beach.

During this period the 2/14th men had moved along the shore in the wake of an opposition which had melted grudgingly back into the main defensive area against which the 39th had been spending themselves. (The intrepid Sergeant Truscott was killed in this slow advance.) The Australian trap was slowly closing and, to ensure complete coordination, Dougherty then placed the skeleton 2/14th under Honner's command.

On the 16th the trap began to spring. On the main track from the south Lieutenant Gartner had given the Japanese no rest since he had taken over Plater's platoon five days before. He himself was never still. Among other responsibilities he made the 2-inch mortar his personal concern. Firing this from a shallow position he worried his antagonists constantly. As he worked this deadly little weapon he was the target for everything the Japanese could bring to bear on him until at last they got him about 9 a.m. on the 16th with a burst of machine-gun fire which drove through his hip. During the next six hours, with his platoon, he then fought forward about 40 yards crawling through thick bush. By 3 p.m. he could do no more and was carried from his post. Thirty-five Japanese bodies marked the little space over which his platoon had painfully edged.

On his right, Mortimore's men had similarly inched forward and, after dark, seized some huts in the south-east corner of the village. The same darkness brought a sally from the west by some thirty Japanese trying to reinforce the village. But they fell a prey to Bidstrup's waiting men.

The daylight hours had been ones of reconnaissance and scattered small clashes for the men of the 2/14th, sitting right on a little stream which marked the eastern edge of the village and waiting to link with the 39th advance. In the early night they then got Sergeant Shelden and Corporal Russell[2] across the stream with small parties, though the move cost Russell his life.

On the 17th the Australians drew their ring closer still. On the extreme left, near the water's edge, Lieutenant McClean's platoon of the 39th nipped off another post. Then two more sections of the 2/14th crossed the stream in a brisk little engagement in which Shelden personally knocked out two posts. That afternoon Captain Russell took command of the 2/14th from Challen who had returned with Dougherty to brigade headquarters. Shelden and Private Walters[3] did deadly work with rifle grenades, scoring a direct hit on a machine-gun group, destroying at a blow one heavy and two light machine-guns and some twenty-five Japanese.

In the dank darkness, about 2 a.m. on the 18th, Corporal Ellis of Captain Gilmore's company pressing from the south, wormed his way to within 10 yards of a medium machine-gun position and killed the crew with a shower of grenades. Thus he climaxed three days of lone-wolf activity in which he had searched for that post, crawling out into no-man's-land in the dark dawn and holing up through the day, showering with grenades what he judged to be the area of the post and sniping at any Japanese who appeared. He was credited with from twelve to twenty kills during those days. After his final exploit he returned to lead his section in the climactic assault.

Gilmore's and Seward's companies then inaugurated the last phase of this grim week's encounter. Soon after the 18th dawned they surged into the village, lashed by heavy fire, Lieutenant Dalby dashing ahead as he had done at Gona Mission and killing the gunner and six other defenders

---
[2] Cpl R. C. Russell, VX61384; 2/14 Bn. Tailor's cutter; of Hawthorn, Vic; b. South Melbourne, 17 Jun 1920. Killed in action 16 Dec 1942.
[3] Cpl L. A. Walters, VX15476; 2/14 Bn. Horticulturist; of Merbein, Vic; b. Lismore, Vic, 25 Nov 1920.

in a medium machine-gun position. The rest of the force then overran the defences.

They buried 170 Japanese at Haddy's village. Captured documents revealed that the wounded, and those known to have been killed in the early days of the engagement, outnumbered those finally buried by the Australians. The wounded had been evacuated across the sand bar at the mouth of the creek to the west, or taken off by barges at night.

Thus, for all practical purposes, there dissolved what could have been a major Japanese threat to the Australians, which had been presaged by the arrival at the Kumusi mouth of the *III/170th Infantry* on 2nd December. But the second failure of the *I/170th Battalion* to land (little more than a week later) had left Yamagata in a difficult position. He was not then strong enough to fight his way through the Australians who were just beginning to press him hard. He was under frequent air attack. He, therefore, cast aside all thoughts of doing more than maintaining his defence until more troops could reach him. These came soon afterwards. On the 14th the *I/170th*, it will be remembered, made a successful landfall at the mouth of the Mambare with about 800 men (with them Major-General Oda to take over as General Horii's successor).

Although the Japanese did not know it their new beach-head was under the eyes of watchers from the Papuan Infantry Battalion and some brave men of a new and special force.

In June 1942 an Allied organisation had been formed to coordinate espionage, sabotage, guerilla warfare and any other form of activity behind the enemy lines which might seem to offer success. This unit was the Allied Intelligence Bureau (A.I.B.) and came directly under Major-General Willoughby, General MacArthur's chief Intelligence Officer, with Colonel Roberts[4]—an Australian—as commander. The Coastwatchers in the South-West Pacific were incorporated into this force. So it was that, among other A.I.B. men, Lieutenant Noakes[5] and Sergeant Carlson,[6] his signaller, who had been sent to New Guinea to undertake sabotage tasks for which, in the event, opportunity was not offering, found themselves placed under Commander Feldt as Coastwatchers. Feldt left them at the mouth of the Mambare—and wrote later:

> The Mambare debouches into the sea between low, muddy banks along which nipa palms stand crowded knee-deep in the water. Behind the nipa palms, mangroves grow, their foliage a darker green dado above the nipa fronds. Here and there a creek mouth shows, the creek a tunnel in the mangroves with dark tree trunks for sides, supported on a maze of gnarled, twisted, obscene roots standing in the oozy mud. Branches and leaves are overhead, through which the sun never penetrates to the black water, the haunt of coldly evil crocodiles. Beyond the reach of high tide grow sago palms and jungle trees, with bushes and thorny vines filling the spaces between them. . . . Slim, boyish and enthusiastic, Noakes was the perfect terrier. Sneaking through the swamp, he arrived at the Jap encampment,

---

[4] Col C. G. Roberts, MC, V80016. (1914-18: Lt RE.) DDMI AHQ 1941-42; Controller Allied Intelligence Bureau 1942-44. Civil engineer; of Kew, Vic; b. Balmain, NSW, 31 Jan 1898.
[5] Lt L. C. Noakes, NGX253. NGVR; AIB ("Z" Special Unit 1942-43, "M" Special Unit 1944). Geologist; of Wau, TNG, and Pennant Hills, NSW; b. Epping, NSW, 9 May 1914.
[6] Sgt L. T. W. Carlson, NX143313. "Z" and "M" Special Units. Presser; of Paddington, NSW; b. Paddington, 3 Apr 1919. Killed in action 24 Oct 1943.

noted their tents and supply dumps and placed them in relation to a sand beach easily seen from the air. Back to camp through the jungle he made his way; then, with Carlson, he hastily coded a signal, which Carlson sent, giving the exact position of everything Japanese.[7]

Thus Noakes and Carlson brought Allied aircraft swarming about the ears of the Japanese, and continued to do so despite puzzled Japanese efforts at concealment. Partly as a result the Mambare beach-head fell far short of the Japanese expectations; although submarines from Rabaul ran there with supplies which were ferried down the coast on small craft, the volume was comparatively meagre.

Immediately, the Allied attacks delayed a projected movement south along the coast to assist Yamagata and limited its scope when it did come about. Although Oda finally managed to join Yamagata on the 18th it was with a portion only of the *I/170th Battalion* since his small craft had been too reduced in numbers to carry them all. By that time Yamagata was suffering severely from the pressure the 39th and 2/14th Battalions were bringing to bear on him and was also suffering heavy blows from the air. He therefore kept with him the men Oda had brought but Oda himself went down to Sanananda to take over from Colonel Yokoyama. He assumed the command there on 22nd December.

To face Yamagata the composite 2/16th-2/27th took over in the Haddy's village area on the 19th, at the end of a phase of operations which (west of Gona) had cost the Australians a further 129 casualties, of whom the 39th Battalion lost 2 officers and 105 men.[8]

These figures focus sharp attention on that battalion as they brought its total battle losses in the Gona area to 8 officers and 220 men for the sixteen-day period from the 3rd to the 18th. Their special significance lies in the fact that the 39th was a militia battalion. It is true that its commander, Honner, was not only a veteran A.I.F. officer but an outstanding leader, even in that tried force. Many of its other officers were also proved A.I.F. veterans. On the other hand, French's and Gartner's service had been entirely with militia battalions, as had Plater's (although he was a Duntroon graduate). And almost all of the men in the ranks were militiamen without previous experience of action before they arrived in New Guinea. A number of them steadfastly refused to join the A.I.F. under any circumstances, at least two of these being N.C.O's who were decorated for bravery and skill.

Although, therefore, undoubtedly much of the dash and devotion (perhaps the major part) of the men of this battalion could be attributed directly or indirectly to their A.I.F. leaders, just as obviously this could not have been the whole explanation. Perhaps the key lies finally in the fact that the 39th had already acquitted itself well in battle with the Japanese before its arrival at Gona. Had enough battle wisdom come from that experience to make the battalion the fighting force it proved itself to

---

[7] Feldt, *The Coastwatchers*, pp. 195-6.
[8] The casualties among the three groups were: 2/14th 1 officer and 2 men killed, 10 men wounded; 39th 31 men killed, 2 officers and 72 men wounded, 2 men missing; Chaforce 1 officer and 1 man killed, 7 men wounded.

be? Again a positive answer must surely be sharply qualified for the reinforcements who had built the battalion's shattered strength could, at the best, have been only vicariously battle-wise. Most significant, too, in this connection, is the fact that about 100 of those had come from the 53rd Battalion whose record had not been good. And high praise was given these men after Gona by the original members of the 39th! Surely the final element in the complex answer must be found in the pride with which the battalion remembered its earlier experiences and that it had been the first Australian unit to meet the invaders. From that recollection moral strength must have flooded in like a tide bearing with it a high purpose, a will to endure greatly, and a contagious inspiration for newcomers. So it was that this militia battalion became the pivot on which the capture of Gona finally swung, pressed to a successful conclusion a difficult and costly action after the fall of the main Gona bastion, and accepted losses which were remarkably heavy even for the type of warfare that developed in Papua.

Although (after a month of wearing operations, and at a heavy cost in casualties and the cost of the final exhaustion of the 21st and 25th Brigades) the Australians had destroyed the Japanese resistance in the Gona-Kumusi area before Christmas of 1942, they, and the Americans, were still at that time heavily committed both along the Sanananda Track and before Buna. In the latter area, however, the days before Christmas saw much stirring movement in which the fresh 18th Australian Brigade was the most vigorous element.

CHAPTER 15

THE AUSTRALIANS AT BUNA

ON 7th December General Blamey wrote from Port Moresby to the Chief of the General Staff, Lieut-General Northcott, in Australia: "We are now suffering the very common lot of armies who have advanced beyond the region of capacity for supply, and, as a result, are being held up by limited Japanese forces which are jammed in narrow areas on the north-eastern coast. Except at Sanananda, the Jap front is not more than half a mile from the coast anywhere, but he is covered in on his front by the filthiest country imaginable and by extraordinarily strong defences. . . . The bulk of our supply has to be taken in by aeroplane and landed on landing grounds that are not very good and sometimes are out of action on account of weather conditions. And while we have air superiority we are unable to utilise it to the full on the other side of the range, because as yet we cannot get strips strong enough to take fighter aircraft. The consequences are that as soon as our own protective umbrella returns, the news is flashed from Buna to Lae and the enemy comes out on strafing and bombing expeditions. We are unable to develop superior fire power because of the difficulty in getting guns across and maintaining the ammunition supply up to them."

Blamey then referred to instructions he had recently given for an examination of the Atherton Tablelands, in north Queensland, to determine their suitability for use as a large-scale training area. He said he had it in mind to send to Atherton soon the 16th, 21st and 25th Brigades, and possibly the 18th, so that these formations might rehabilitate themselves there; to bring over from Australia to Milne Bay a brigade of the 5th Division; to build up his coastal forces with a second brigade from the same militia division. But even as he pondered these plans he emphasised that they were "dependent upon circumstances". And indeed it was no later than the following day that he modified them.

Apparently he then recognised quite definitely that there was no promise of the Americans before Buna being able to force a successful issue, and so he determined to strengthen the attack there with Australians as soon as possible, thus realising a plan of which he had already given some notice.

Before arriving at this decision, however, he had considered the strength of the Australian Army generally, had forecast to the Prime Minister, in a letter on 4th December, the necessity for a further reduction of the Order of Battle by another division because of the lack of manpower and had asked for the return of the 9th Division from the Middle East. He wrote:

> I had hoped that our strategical plans would have been crowned with complete and rapid success in the tactical field. It was completely successful strategically in as much as we brought an American Division on to Buna and an Australian Division

on to Gona simultaneously. But in the tactical field after the magnificent advance through the most difficult area, the Owen Stanley Range, it is a very sorry story.

It has revealed the fact that the American troops cannot be classified as attack troops. They are definitely not equal to the Australian militia, and from the moment they met opposition sat down and have hardly gone forward a yard. The action, too, has revealed a very alarming state of weakness in their staff system and in their war psychology. General MacArthur has relieved the Divisional Commander and has called up General Eichelberger the Corps Commander, and sent him over to take charge. He informs me that he proposes to relieve both the regimental commanders, the equivalent of our brigade commanders, and five out of six of the battalion commanders; and this in the face of the enemy. I am afraid now that the bulk of the fighting will fall on our troops in spite of the greatly larger numbers of the 32nd U.S. Division.

The brigades that went over the mountain track are now so depleted that they are being withdrawn and I am utilizing the only remaining AIF brigade in Port Moresby and a brigade of Militia, that has been intensively trained here, and I think we will pull it off all right.

The Americans say that the other division which they left in Australia is a much better one than the one they have here, but since they chose this as number one, I believe their view to be merely wishful thinking. I feel quite sure in my own mind that the American forces, which have been expanded even more rapidly than our own were in the first years of the war, will not attain any high standard of training or war spirit for very many months to come.

This may appear to be a digression from the main subject, but it brings me to the point that in replacement of the 9th Australian Division we have been given two American Divisions, and as their fighting qualities are so low, I do not think they are a very considerable contribution to the defence of Australia. Of course, the American authorities will not admit this but will continue their attitude of wishful thinking. You will therefore see that if the 9th Australian Division is not returned for our future operations in this area we are going to be in a very bad way indeed. In fact I feel that our position will be definitely one involving considerable risk and danger.

The 6th and 7th Australian Divisions after the Buna operations are completed must have a prolonged rest out of action. They both have a very large number of reinforcements to absorb and a very large number of sick to return. This means that the defence of Papua will rest for a time mainly on Militia and American forces. My faith in the Militia is growing, but my faith in the Americans has sunk to zero. If the 9th Australian Division is not returned I fear very greatly that we will have to sit down for a very long time in this area in an endeavour to defend it, mainly by keeping the Jap flotillas away by air action.

At the time when the Australian Commander-in-Chief was writing in these terms, the position on the Papuan coast was that three of his veteran A.I.F. brigades and his two most seasoned militia battalions had capped their struggles in the mountains with bitter slugging matches against desperate Japanese who, their backs to the sea, were obviously preparing to fight to the last man. Also, along the Sanananda Track, a militia brigade was on the eve of a bloody entry into the coastal struggle and an A.I.F. cavalry regiment would soon be committed there. But, handily based at Milne Bay, the 17th and 18th Brigades of the A.I.F. and the 7th Brigade of militia were a pool from which rested and battle-tried units might be plucked for quick use against the stubborn enemy on the Buna-Gona coast. None the less, Blamey could not commit these formations lightly. He had a nice· balance to preserve between: the possible necessity for meeting fresh seaborne attacks against south-east New Guinea and the

(Australian War Memorial)
Major-General G. A. Vasey. G.O.C. 7th Division; Brigadier J. R. Broadbent, D.A. & Q.M.G. I Corps; Brigadier G. F. Wootten, commander of the 18th Brigade; and Lieut-General E. F. Herring, G.O.C. New Guinea Force, in Brigadier Wootten's tent at Sanananda.

(Australian War Memorial)
The advance of the 2/9th Battalion, supported by tanks of the 2/6th Armoured Regiment. to Cape Endaiadere, 18th December 1942.

(Australian War Memorial)

Giropa Point, 1st-2nd January. Australian Bren gunners fire on Japanese fleeing from a wrecked pill-box 100-150 yards ahead. The tank's identification sign and number have been deleted from the photograph by the wartime censor.

(Australian War Memorial)

Giropa Point. A close-up of the same tank (7 Troop, "B" Squadron, 2/6th Armoured Regiment) with a 2-inch mortar crew firing on the fleeing Japanese from the shelter of a torn coconut tree.

adjacent islands; a pressing need to resolve the coastal stalemate (but in face of the maintenance difficulties he had sketched for Northcott); a need for fresh and experienced troops to carry the fight deeper into Japanese-held territory after the Papuan phase was ended (for the preparation of whom he was planning to use the Atherton Tablelands). But events made the second of these needs so urgent that it demanded the quick use of experienced men.

On the 8th, therefore, Blamey sent a peremptory summons for Brigadier Wootten, commander of the 18th Brigade. At the time Wootten was visiting his 2/12th Battalion on Goodenough Island. As his 2/10th Battalion, the original nucleus of the force which had been flown in to Wanigela, was divided between that point and Porlock Harbour, Wootten had only the 2/9th Battalion immediately under his hand at Milne Bay.

Already this battalion had only narrowly escaped being committed at Buna in a hazardous venture. Blamey had planned to land them on the beach immediately east of Buna in coordination with an overland thrust by infantry and tanks from the south of Buna. But, to his intense chagrin, the navy had refused to make available the two destroyers and two corvettes which he needed, and he himself could muster only sufficient small boats to carry about 400 men. He was therefore forced to abandon his plan, after orders for the 2/9th Battalion had actually gone to Milne Bay and that unit had begun training for an opposed landing.

When Wootten arrived at Port Moresby on the 10th he was told by Blamey of the impasse at Buna, and that he was to take there the 2/9th Battalion and one battalion of the 7th Brigade, together with two troops of tanks from the 2/6th Armoured Regiment which had recently arrived in New Guinea. His task was to clear the Japanese from the area enclosed by Cape Endaiadere, New Strip, Old Strip, and Buna Government Station. Wootten, since he naturally preferred to work with his own men, requested that the 2/10th Battalion be substituted for the 7th Brigade battalion, which request Blamey readily granted, although it would involve a rapid move by the militia battalion to relieve the 2/10th. Wootten flew next day to Popondetta, where he discussed the position with General Herring, went on to Dobodura and met General Eichelberger, and spent the afternoon of this busy day in reconnoitring the situation in the New Strip area. On the 12th the framework into which the 18th Brigade would fit was hammered out in conference between Wootten, Herring, Eichelberger, Brigadier-General Byers, and Brigadier Hopkins (Herring's chief staff officer). It was decided that, after the arrival of his Australian troops, Wootten would take over the Warren Force sector including the Americans who were there. By this time a solid nucleus of his own staff had joined him, also Lieut-Colonel Hodgson[1] of the 2/6th Armoured Regiment and an engineer officer from the 2/4th Field Company; the 2/9th Battalion was boarding the corvettes *Colac, Broome* and *Ballarat* at Milne Bay; and

---

[1] Col C. R. Hodgson, DSO, NX70837. CO 2/6 Armd Regt 1941-42. Comd 2 Beach Gp 1944-45. Engineer; of Woollahra, NSW; b. Rotherham, England, 14 Dec 1903.

the first of Hodgson's tanks were already at Hariko. All of these preliminaries were swift, efficient and purposeful.

The corvettes, which, the preceding night when they were off Cape Sudest, had been so alarmed by a flare from an unidentified aircraft and a report of the approach of a Japanese naval force that their captains had thought it wise to return to Porlock Harbour, landed the infantry at Oro Bay on the night of the 14th-15th. These, in full battle order, followed the soft sea sand round the water's edge on the 15th, struggled chest deep across the Samboga River, and sweated through the muggy day to Hariko.

Ahead of them four tanks, from "C" Squadron of the armoured regiment, which Captain Whitehead[2] had brought round from Port Moresby in the *Karsik* a few days earlier, had already gone forward to a lying-up area in the rear of brigade headquarters. These, with four more, from Major Tye's[3] "B" Squadron which had gone direct from Australia to Milne Bay in early November, due to arrive from Milne Bay within the next day or two under Lieutenant McCrohon,[4] would constitute an improvised "X" Squadron under Whitehead's command.

The tanks were of the type known as American M3 Light or "General Stuart", each of 14 tons weight, 14 feet 7 inches long, 8 feet 8 inches high and 8 feet wide, propelled by a 250-horse power radial engine, capable of a maximum speed of about 40 miles an hour and armoured to an average thickness on the hull of 1 inch and 1.3/4 inches on the front of the turret. Each mounted co-axially in the turret a 37-mm quick-firing gun and one .30 Browning machine-gun, had a second Browning in front of the hull and carried a spare Browning inside. Each was fitted with a No. 19 wireless set under normal conditions providing internal communication from the tank commander to his four men, voice transmission up to about 10 miles, and communication with the standard infantry pack set (although in the tropical bush all wireless communication was, at the best, chancy and intermittent). The tanks' cross-country performance was good on suitable ground but could be limited severely by heavy timber, water, swampy or very rocky ground, and wide trenches. The crews would not normally use their vehicles at night (although they had powerful headlights). The smallest tactical unit was the troop consisting of three tanks, each with a crew of five. Within the troop, training stressed constant contact and mutual support.

The crews who manned these tanks were highly-trained men who had been carefully selected when the Australian armoured division had begun forming in 1941. The ambition of this division had always been to measure itself against the Germans in the Libyan desert. In August-October its training had been polished by three months of manoeuvres on the western plains of New South Wales, by far the largest and most elaborate military

---

[2] Capt N. G. Whitehead, MC, NX34954; 2/6 Armd Regt. Grazier; of Urana, NSW; b. East Melbourne, 15 Jul 1909.

[3] Maj K. F. Tye, NX71009; 2/6 Armd Regt. Meter inspector; of Concord, NSW; b. Croydon, NSW, 9 Sep 1906.

[4] Lt V. H. McCrohon, NX661. 6 Cav Regt, 2/6 Armd Regt. Engine driver; of Armidale, NSW; b. Hillgrove, NSW, 26 Oct 1916.

exercises carried out by Australian troops up to that time. And it was straight from that training that the 2/6th Armoured Regiment, a New South Wales unit claiming descent from the veteran 6th Light Horse, had gone to New Guinea, to a battlefield which, with its mud and reeking bush, was the complete antithesis of the setting for which they had trained. Though they did not know it then their detachment heralded the gradual break-up of their division for its units were destined to fight only piecemeal (and only in the Pacific), or never to fight at all, despite the fact that few critics would have quarrelled with this judgment of a newspaper correspondent after he had seen their manoeuvres end:

> It is very doubtful if [before going into action] there has ever been an Australian division fitter than this one, or prouder, or keener for action; or a division in which discipline has been crisper and the bearing of officers and men better.[5]

The four officers who, at Buna, were to take in the first troops of the armoured division to see action, were worthy representatives of the leaders of this formation. There was Hodgson, the 2/6th's commander, 39, formerly an English territorial officer, tall, spare, aloof, a cool and confident leader and hard taskmaster, greatly respected by his men; Whitehead, a massive fourteen and a half stone product of the land, broad shouldered and confident; Lieutenant Curtiss,[6] troop commander, just over 29, short and plump, determined not to fail those who looked to him; McCrohon, tall and straight, a veteran of the Western Desert where he had served in the 6th Divisional Cavalry.

The courage and ingenuity of such officers, and the men they led, were to be severely tried even before they entered action, merely in getting their clumsy 14-ton vehicles forward at all. It will be recalled that the mid-November attempt to do this had resulted in the only available craft sinking at its moorings at Milne Bay taking with it the first tank that was loaded. Though the availability of ships like the *Karsik* partly overcame this problem it did not solve it completely. Whitehead's and McCrohon's tanks (and those which followed later) were off-loaded at Oro Bay on to clumsy barges which they rode precariously, the water lapping a mere 2-inch freeboard. Motor launches then towed these through the reefs until they were off Hariko. There the launches, swinging as close inshore as possible, cast the barges off, of necessity leaving the tanks to get ashore as best they might. The crews then drove the tanks over the side with a lurch and a splash. Once ashore they followed the beach along to their assembly area with one set of tracks in the sea and the other just above the low water line so that the incoming tide would wash away the marks of their approach. "The transportation and landing of these tanks in and around Hariko, some few miles from the battlefield, was an amazing achievement in view of the equipment available to the men charged with the task," General Herring was to write later.

---

[5] *The Sydney Morning Herald*, 28 Oct 1942.
[6] Lt G. E. Curtiss, VX55589. 2/6 Armd Regt, 2 Beach Group. Clerk; of Elizabeth Bay, NSW; b. Strathfield, NSW, 20 Aug 1913.

By the 16th Brigadier Wootten's initial move was virtually complete. Of the Australians he then had immediately to hand the 2/9th Battalion, 26 officers and 638 men strong, including 127 reinforcements who had only just joined; the squadron of the 2/6th Armoured Regiment; five carriers of the 17th Brigade carrier group; detachments of the 2/4th Field Company and the 2/5th Field Ambulance. At Porlock some 34 officers and 648 men of the 2/10th Battalion were preparing to embark on the corvettes next day. The main artillery support would come from the Australian guns: the field gunners under Major Hall and Captain Manning, with Manning's four guns of the 2/1st Field Regiment still deployed off the track near Ango and Hall's four guns of the 2/5th still just forward of Hariko; the mountain gunners under Major O'Hare whose three 3.7's had been moved not long before by General Eichelberger to a position on the Dobodura-Buna track about 2,000 yards below the bridge which ran between the strips.

The Americans of Warren Force who would also come under Wootten's command included: the III/128th Infantry, now under Colonel MacNab, holding from the coast to the vicinity of the eastern end of New Strip; the I/128th Infantry extending westward thence below the southern edge of New Strip, with Major Gordon M. Clarkson, a dashing young regular, formerly of General Eichelberger's staff, commanding in place of Colonel McCoy; the incomplete I/126th Infantry still below the bridge which separated New and Old Strips but now led by Major Beaver, one of the divisional staff, who had proved himself a brave and resourceful leader when such were most needed. A little more American help would come to Wootten also from the one American artillery piece in the area: the 105-mm gun set up near O'Hare's three howitzers.

At 9 a.m. on the 17th Wootten, in accordance with General Eichelberger's direction, assumed command in the Warren Force sector, taking over from Colonel Martin who became in fact commander of Wootten's Americans. Wootten stated that his immediate intention was that the 18th Brigade Group should capture the area Cape Endaiadere-New Strip-Old Strip-Buna Government Station. But this obviously had to be carried out in phases. The first phase would be the capture of the whole area between the coast as far as the mouth of Simemi Creek on the right and, on the left, a line running from the east end of New Strip to the west end of Old Strip thence along Simemi Creek to its mouth. The 2/9th Battalion would be the striking force, supported by seven tanks, aircraft, artillery, and American mortars. One tank, the two battalions of the 128th Regiment, the 2/10th Battalion from the time of its arrival at Hariko, and the 17th Brigade carriers, would constitute the reserve.

In the last light of the 17th the seven tanks lumbered forward to their assembly area. In McCrohon's troop Corporal Evan Barnet,[7] a slight, dark, young man of 22, commanded one tank; Sergeant Jack Lattimore[8]—tall,

---
[7] Cpl E. H. MacD. Barnet, NX37404; 2/6 Armd Regt. Medical student; of Bellevue Hill, NSW; b. Warialda, NSW, 3 Jun 1920.
[8] Sgt J. Lattimore, NX42380; 2/6 Armd Regt. Process engraver; of Harris Park, NSW; b. Fairfield, NSW, 11 Jun 1919.

thin, highly-strung—commanded the third tank. In the other troop Curtiss had an unassuming but steady corporal named Cambridge[9] and a capable sergeant, John Church.[1] The seventh tank Whitehead proposed to take in himself.

Aircraft which, with the roar of their own engines, were to cover the noise of this moving armour, did not come over. In consequence the Australians feared that surprise might have been lost, but this was now a chance which had to be taken. Quietly, after the tanks, the men of the 2/9th Battalion made their way through the darkening bush by the sea to their own assembly area—a space near the water-line, less than half a mile below their start-line which had been marked with signal wire for 400 yards, bearing 240 degrees from a point on the water's edge which was east-south-east of the end of New Strip. A rusting carrier, relic of

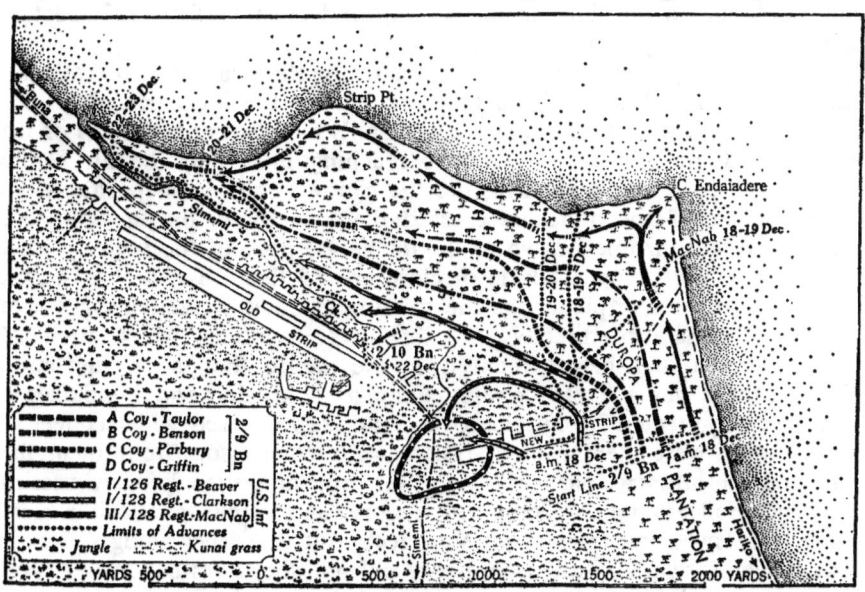

Advance of the 2/9th Battalion and supporting units,
18th to night 22nd-23rd December

Lieutenant Fergusson's ill-fated attack of 5th December, was a pointer to the course of this line, and a grim warning to the men of the 2/9th of what their own fates might be. Going into battle was for most of them not a new experience; they talked quietly in the night, and many were restless but did not care to show it, and each mentally prepared himself as he lay with his own thoughts through the long night.

They were early astir on the 18th, began to move to their forming-up place at 5.30 and, soon afterwards, MacNab drew his Americans back

---
[9] Sgt C. B. Cambridge, NX71581; 2/6 Armd Regt. Clerk; of Burwood, NSW; b. Bathurst, NSW, 27 Jun 1912.
[1] Sgt J. E. Church, NX19832; 2/6 Armd Regt. Stock agent; of Burren Junction, NSW; b. Wee Waa, NSW, 26 Mar 1916.

from the vicinity of the start-line to make way for them. Lieut-Colonel Cummings of the 2/9th was using three companies forward, aiming to capture first a strip of ground approximately 500 yards from the water's edge as far as Cape Endaiadere and continue thence over approximately the same width until he held the line of Simemi Creek: on the right Captain Griffin's[2] company, making for the cape itself on a 250-yard front, McCrohon's three tanks with them; in the centre Captain Taylor's,[3] extending the front for a further 250 yards—with Curtiss' armoured troop; turning about half left Captain Parbury,[4] with orders to establish his men firmly at a point some 200 yards roughly north of the eastern end of New Strip, where a grassy space ran up to the edge of the plantation, and protect the flank and rear of the main move against the most obvious possibility of Japanese reaction, at the same time determining the Japanese positions in the swamp and bush to the west. Captain Benson's[5] company was in reserve.

The weather prevented aircraft from assisting the attack but at 6.50 a.m. the guns opened, Manning's shells searching for the log barricade which had barred the Americans for so long, Hall's falling round the top of the eastern end of New Strip, O'Hare's reaching high into the air before they turned for their steep dive into the centre of the main positions.

Precisely at 7 the attackers crossed their start-line, the tanks spaced out in line and throttled down to the deliberate pace of the infantry who, for the most part, moved beside or close behind them. To the watchers it was an unforgettable picture as the three companies walked upright with seeming nonchalance directly at a line of strongpoints which stretched like an unseen bar before them from the sea to the end of the strip. Each of these was a small fortress, cunningly concealed and camouflaged; some were protected by interlaced coconut logs covered with six feet of earth, some were steel roofed, others were concreted. From them fire withered the infantry, particularly Parbury's unsupported leftward-veering men who fell among the long coarse grass as though an invisible giant hand were sweeping them from their feet. But the drive along the main axis carried forward with extraordinary phlegm, the tanks battering at post after post, the infantry closing in to hurl their grenades through the small openings, to kill the fanatic defenders to the last man with none asking quarter, to go on implacably from one post to the next, steadily beating the undergrowth as they went (they had learned the need for this at Milne Bay) to try to ensure that no living men remained in their path.

It was a spectacular and dramatic assault, and a brave one (General Eichelberger wrote later). From the New Strip to the sea was about half a mile. American troops wheeled to the west in support, and other Americans were assigned to mopping-up

---

[2] Capt R. R. Griffin, QX2786; 2/9 Bn. Clerk; of Clermont, Qld; b. Rockhampton, Qld, 4 Apr 1918. Killed in action 22 Dec 1942.

[3] Maj R. Taylor, MC, ED, QX1257. 2/9 Bn; OC 37 Sqn Air Liaison Sec 1945. Labourer; of Toowoomba, Qld; b. Seaham, England, 8 Jan 1914.

[4] Lt-Col C. B. Parbury, MBE, QX1148. 2/9 Bn; HQ 18 Bde. Grazier; of Tenterfield, NSW; b. Hobart, 22 Oct 1910.

[5] Capt A. M. Benson, QX6090; 2/9 Bn. Railways employee; of Tiaro, Qld; b. Gundiah, Qld, 3 Mar 1906. Drowned 25 Dec 1944, while on leave.

duties. But behind the tanks went the fresh and jaunty Aussie veterans, tall, mustached, erect, with their blazing Tommy-guns swinging before them. Concealed Japanese positions—which were even more formidable than our patrols had indicated —burst into flame. There was the greasy smell of tracer fire . . . and heavy machine-gun fire from barricades and entrenchments.

Steadily tanks and infantrymen advanced through the spare, high coconut trees, seemingly impervious to the heavy opposition.[6]

Swift-moving, even in this company, and with his way probably less densely disputed than that of the others farther inland, Lieutenant MacIntosh[7] was leading Griffin's right forward platoon along the edge of the coconuts and through the scrubby bush which fringed the sand sloping gently away to the water's edge. When he crossed his start-line he had Corporal Barnet drive his supporting tank directly for a strongly-logged post on his right which MacIntosh himself and Barnet had found by crawling forward from the American positions the previous night. There were two machine-guns there, five Japanese manning them. The tank blasted the post and MacIntosh's men closed in, grenading. Two of the defenders crawled out of the smoking wreckage into the two-foot-high grass which surrounded it. One wounded Lance-Corporal George Tyler[8] in the arm but the corporal then shot him dead at five yards' range. Just to the left Corporal Thomas'[9] section was hotly engaged from a post which MacIntosh had not seen the previous evening. Some of the defenders there were using a Bren gun and grenades which they had taken from Fergusson's carriers after they had been abandoned on the 5th. One of the grenades burst almost in Thomas' face as he dashed for the post, but, blood pouring from his face, he plunged on and killed two of the Japanese. A third fired at him with a Bren which stuck out between two of the logs walling the post. Seizing the gun by the muzzle Thomas wrestled for its possession and then dragged it through the opening and killed its previous user with it. Then he fought on (and for two more days, only leaving the field then on MacIntosh's orders). The platoon and the tank then beat down three more posts which disputed their way to the cape, and were first on the objective. By 8.10 a.m. they had turned westward along the sea line towards Strip Point.

Though MacIntosh's break-through had been swift, Griffin's other forward platoon, Lieutenant Sivyer's,[1] had been less fortunate. They were fighting their way through the long lines of coconuts and the kunai grass which grew between them. As they approached the cape, but still possibly 200 yards at least below it and the position MacIntosh had taken up, a concrete post stopped them with a well-aimed torrent of fire which took a heavy toll of them, although MacIntosh's men tried to help with machine-

---

[6] Eichelberger, *Our Jungle Road to Tokyo*, pp. 44-5.
[7] Capt W. F. MacIntosh, MC, MM, QX2163. 2/9 Bn; HQ 18 Bde. Clerk; of Townsville, Qld; b. Toowoomba, Qld, 22 Aug 1914.
[8] Sgt G. Tyler, QX5999; 2/9 Bn. Truck and tractor driver; of Killarney, Qld; b. Killarney, 22 Oct 1919.
[9] Sgt R. R. Thomas, DCM, QX11632; 2/9 Bn. Horse trainer, storeman and packer; of Townsville, Qld; b. Charters Towers, Qld, 22 Nov 1903.
[1] Lt T. R. Sivyer, QX15024; 2/9 Bn. Tin miner; of South Johnstone, Qld; b. Stannary Hills, Qld, 4 Apr 1917. Killed in action 18 Dec 1942.

gun fire from the seaward side. Sivyer himself was killed there, his sergeant, Prentice,[2] wounded. Griffin then sent Sergeant "Shorty" Walters[3] to take command. But Walters, crawling forward, was shot through the head, and the command fell finally to one of the corporals.[4]

Difficult though this day was, however, for these men of Griffin's, it was even more difficult for Taylor's company on their left. When Griffin first reached his objective about 8.10 Taylor's men had at least 200 more yards to cover before they lined up. But they had been so badly mauled that temporarily they could make no further progress. Griffin's left flank in consequence remained unsealed. Cummings therefore sited some machine-guns with the dual purpose of covering Griffin's weakness and thickening Taylor's toiling front.

Meanwhile, in his angled left-flank role, Captain Parbury was in even greater difficulties at the eastern end of New Strip. There his men had plunged into a regular hornet's nest. The company was being cut to pieces by both light and medium machine-gun fire from what seemed to be many immensely strong posts. Even before leaving the start-line they had begun to lose men and, as soon as they crossed the line, came under terrific small-arms fire. Without tanks, they had lost 46 out of 87 men in less than ten minutes in an advance of only about 100 yards. The commander of the right forward platoon, Lieutenant de Vantier, was killed with all his N.C.O's, except one who was wounded. (Among the killed was Sergeant J. Gordon who had been conspicuous in the fighting at Milne Bay.) Parbury then lost touch with this platoon and feared that it had been completely wiped out. He ordered his remaining men to ground so that some at least might survive and then the grass, two feet high, hid them. When he phoned the news to his commanding officer, Cummings suggested that he try infiltration tactics with one of his sections to see if it perhaps might be able to get through the barrier of Japanese posts which larger groups could not breach. Parbury thereupon sent Lance-Sergeant Morey,[5] from Warrant-Officer Jesse's[6] reserve platoon, on this mission. But Morey, one of the rapidly dwindling band of the battalion's "originals", was killed with all his men before they had gone 20 yards. The balance of the company, some 60 yards in front of the most forward Japanese positions and about 100 yards from the main bunker line, then lay waiting for tanks to come to their aid.

By that time, from his reserve position where he was ruthlessly destroying any Japanese remnants who had remained alive in Griffin's and Taylor's wakes and was trying to get at strongpoints which were biting at the edges of the forward companies, Benson had sent one of his platoons to thicken Parbury's small remaining numbers. Clarkson's

---
[2] Capt V. D. Prentice, MBE, MC, QX1476. 2/9 Bn; "Z" Special Unit. Farmer's assistant; of Southbrook, Qld; b. Southbrook, 24 Dec 1909.
[3] Sgt A. Walters, QX1221; 2/9 Bn. Labourer; of Berkshire Park, NSW; b. Wakefield, England, 19 Jul 1908. Killed in action 18 Dec 1942. (True name G. P. Armitage.)
[4] L-Cpl J. A. Rudd, QX1898. Of Mt Isa, Qld.
[5] L-Sgt G. W. Morey, QX2575; 2/9 Bn. Labourer; of Sydney; b. Murwillumbah, NSW, 21 Sep 1911. Killed in action 18 Dec 1942.
[6] Lt J. H. Jesse, DCM, QX3097; 2/9 Bn. Labourer; of Brisbane; b. Maryborough, Qld, 1 Jul 1917.

Americans were also trying to help in response to an appeal from Parbury to close in on his left flank. By crawling through the long grass they got some distance forward unscathed but then stopped some 30 to 40 yards in rear of the Australians whom they helped by passing wounded back.

To Parbury, thus held, the tanks seemed to be a long time coming. But they were having their own troubles. When they had crossed the start-line Captain Whitehead was in the centre of their formation and just behind the others, intending to keep himself free as far as possible to control his squadron and to give help himself quickly where it might most be needed. But almost at once he realised that he must leave his troop leaders and their individual tank commanders to decide for themselves how best they could help the infantry. So he became virtually a foot-loose fighting unit. And, from the beginning, his part was spectacular. Scarcely was he over the line before he spotted a marksman high in a tall palm ahead of him. He said to Trooper Gordon Bray,[7] his gunner, "Shoot him!" But Bray could not elevate his guns sufficiently. Whitehead then said "Shoot the tree down". So Bray aimed a solid 37-mm shot at the point where the thick butt narrowed to the tapering trunk. The first shot nicked the trunk, the second chopped it through like an axe. The sharpshooter tumbled headlong in a neck-breaking fall and Bray gave him a Browning burst for good measure as the tank passed on towards the main defences. Time ceased to have any meaning for the crew. It was probably a little more than an hour later, however, that Parbury's call for help first reached Whitehead. A soldier came knocking on his tank when he was somewhat to the north-east of the eastern end of the strip and he swung round and followed the man to the west until soon he found himself against three strongposts. He took on the most southerly of these first and silenced it with four or five shots. But, as the tank turned against the second, Bray's sights fogged over and, momentarily, a clutter of emptied shell cases blocked the swing of the gun. Whitehead himself was peering through the vision slit, his hands cushioning his forehead against the tank's wall, his face pressed to the slit, when a brave Japanese leapt on to the tank and thrust the muzzle of his rifle hard against the slit and fired. The bullet and splintered pieces of steel gouged through Whitehead's face and upraised arm from a range of only an inch or two. Blinded in one eye, dizzy and bleeding, he sat heavily on the floor of the tank, his good eye puzzled by flashing circles of light which went spinning crazily round his head. These (he was to learn later) were tracer bullets from a Japanese machine-gun which was set up a bare 10 feet away and firing directly into the vision slit. As his bewildered eye followed them round and round inside the tank his ear registered quick new hammering notes amid the already familiar clatter of bullets on the tank. Though he did not know it then these were from the spatter of fire which killed the soldier who had shot him. Two Australian infantrymen had been dogging the tank to pro-

---

[7] Tpr A. G. Bray, NX52708. 7 Cav Regt; 2/6 Armd Regt. Salesman; of Balgowlah, NSW; b. Waverley, NSW, 27 Sep 1919.

tect it. They saw Whitehead's assailant only after he leaped back from the attack, flinging his arms wide in a gesture of exultation. In that moment of triumph they killed him. A little later the tank turned to take the badly-wounded captain out. A Japanese was firing at it from behind a tree. Bray sent a 37-mm shot straight at the tree and had a fantastically-clear vision of a pair of boots at the foot of the palm and a piece of blood-stained rag fluttering foolishly—all that remained of what had been the man.

The bleeding Whitehead was scarcely clear of his tank before his colonel took his place. As he plunged into the fight, Hodgson, true to his own teaching, was looking out of the open turret of his tank to get a full view of what lay ahead. An inevitable fate overtook him when a machine-gun burst spattered his vehicle. He slumped back into the turret badly wounded. It was scarcely 10 o'clock and both the senior tank officers were out of action.

Meanwhile, from the right, Barnet had brought his tank into the vortex among the coconuts in the central positions, leaving his infantry on the objective. He saw Hodgson ride his tank in. He got a call from McCrohon, who had his hands full, to go to the assistance of Lattimore who was in trouble a little deeper in the coconuts. He heard Lattimore calling him on the radio. "Come on Splinter! Come on Splinter!" He saw Lattimore's tank bellied on a fallen coconut log. By this time, however, he was out of ammunition and wirelessed the stranded crew that he would be back. These, though their wireless could transmit, could not pick up his message and so were anxious and wondering as apparently he left them to their fate. But he filled up again quickly and was soon back. By that time the Japanese were lighting fires beneath the other tank in an attempt to roast the trapped crew who were squirting fire extinguishers through the apertures in a vain effort to scare their enemies off. To drive away the incendiaries Barnet then told his gunner, in whom he had great confidence, to aim as close as possible to Lattimore's tank. "Take the paint off," he said. Soon afterwards he left the vehicle the better to direct his successful efforts to "pluck the brands from the burning". (Later the tank itself was brought safely back.)

Though McCrohon's troop, thus in the thick of it, lost no tanks, Curtiss was not so fortunate. His own tank was the first casualty. About 8 or 8.30, fighting with Captain Taylor in the centre, Curtiss ran on to a stump, where he stuck. Like Lattimore's men he and crew narrowly escaped being cooked when their enemies lit a fire beneath them. But, under cover of shots from their infantry, they leaped unhurt through the hatch. By this time Sergeant Church was on the scene but all his determined efforts to move the stranded vehicle were in vain. It burnt out. A second tank (probably Corporal Cambridge's) was lost later in the day. McCrohon, by that time helping Taylor's company in the central sector, saw it hurry past him streaming smoke after a magnetic mine had exploded against it, its commander making for a position farther back where he and his men might hope to escape the bullets of their enemies as they fled the flames.

Out of the turmoil that all this represented Curtiss appeared to a thankful Parbury about 1 p.m., he himself having taken over Church's tank, and bringing two others with him. While the vehicles waited behind the infantry Parbury pointed out the opposing positions to the tank commanders. His plan was to have Warrant-Officer Jesse take his men forward in line with one section on either side of the two forward tanks and one moving between them. Jesse himself would move with the centre section to indicate the targets for the tanks by firing Very lights into them. From 30 yards forward and 70 yards to his right the eleven remaining men of de Vantier's platoon would give supporting fire for the new move. This Parbury had arranged with Private Logan,[8] a reinforcement who had joined the battalion only eight months before and now commanded what remained of the platoon. (Logan had reported back to him while Parbury was waiting for the tanks to come up.) The third platoon, Lieutenant Pinwill's,[9] would move behind Jesse's tank-infantry line. Bren gunners would spray snipers in the trees as the main movement went ahead. Even as Parbury was putting the finishing touches to this plan it might, however, have been brought to nothing by three Japanese who came sneaking forward through the long grass to set the right tank on fire with incendiary bombs. But Parbury's men riddled them before they could close.

About 2 p.m. the desperate move began. Jesse's Very lights streaked into the Japanese redoubts and tank shells seemed to follow the paths they made. Brens clattered. Every Australian weapon was running hot. Several posts blazed high as the dried coconut logs took fire. And then the Japanese cracked. Some of them leaped in panic out of their defences screaming in terror. Then the Australian foot soldiers were dragging out the core of the resistance, grenading right and left behind and beside the tanks. Within half an hour they had cleaned out eleven of the bunkers and, from the remaining five, the defenders soon ran away. It was over by 3 p.m. with the panting Australians facing west just above the eastern tip of the strip, Americans packing round on the right and left, between 80 and 90 of their enemies dead about them, and at least as many more interred in the broken casemates which the Americans, mopping up behind the Australians, blew down upon any of the unhappy survivors who remained within.

By the time Parbury's men had thus broken free of the defences on the left in which they had become entangled, Benson was swinging round his right, fighting to fill a westward facing line. Due north again of Benson, Taylor's men, lunging forward with some of the tanks in the late afternoon over the short but perilous yards they needed, at last succeeded in pivoting westward round the base of Cape Endaiadere, to bring themselves into line with Griffin and close the latter's left flank. Night found the Australians facing westward against the Japanese reserve line on a front which ran from the sea due south to the east end of New Strip.

---

[8] Lt L. G. Logan, MM, QX31184; 2/9 Bn. Station manager; of Cunnamulla, Qld; b. Brisbane, 12 Dec 1909.
[9] Lt F. S. Pinwill, QX3628; 2/9 Bn. Clerk; of Wolfram, Qld; b. Wolfram, 20 Aug 1917. Killed in action 20 Dec 1942.

Griffin was on the extreme right, his own right resting on the sea about 400 yards west of Cape Endaiadere, his front covering some 350 yards; Taylor held a 250-yard front on Griffin's left; Benson was on Taylor's left with an American platoon on his left; Parbury anchored the south, his left resting on the end of the pathway which ran north-east from the strip to the coast.

With dash and hardihood which boded well for the rest of Wootten's plans the 2/9th had thus completed their first task—for the loss possibly of 11 officers and 160 men,[1] more than one-third of their attacking strength. But resolute though they were, they owed much to the tanks. Two of these had been burnt out, and one needed repairs to the vision slit.

Probably the area of the day's operations was the most suitable for tanks in the whole Buna region. But even within that area the General Stuarts were like race-horses harnessed to heavy ploughs. Their speed had been designed as their protection and, since speed demands lightness, armour had been sacrificed to achieve it. In the plantation, however, among the high, coarse grass, through the swamp mud, over the bomb craters and shell holes in which viscous marsh liquid rose, they could merely grind in their lowest gear at the pace of a walking man, even if the necessity for cooperating with the foot soldiers had not demanded that they be kept down to this pace. They had not been designed as infantry tanks, and their crews had had no training for and experience of this role. Neither had the infantry been trained to work with tanks. So both had to improvise in the midst of fighting, even working out the details of their methods of communicating with one another as they went along. Although impromptu signals could be devised, the extent to which they could be used was small, for the tanks were almost blind in the Buna country, their vision, restricted at the best of times, being shut off by the tropical growth.

During the 19th the Australians finally cleaned up the area they had taken, adjusted their line, linked firmly with MacNab's right across the eastern end of the strip, and followed the abandonment by the defeated Japanese of the other posts in that area by occupying the whole region of the New Strip. By that time the 2/10th Battalion was sorting itself out at Hariko. Wootten decided then to send the tried 2/9th in again next day with Captain Matheson's company of the 2/10th to strengthen them. He told Cummings to complete the first phase of his previous orders, i.e. secure the whole of the area north of the strips and enclosed by the coast and Simemi Creek. Once again the guns and armour would support him. (Major Moss,[2] a dark, strongly-made man of more than average height whose thrusting approach to any problems which might beset him had earned him the nickname "Bull", was now in command of the tanks, having arrived that day from Port Moresby with Lieutenant Gunn[3] and

---
[1] War diary, 2/9th Battalion.
[2] Maj N. L. Moss, NX70817; 2/6 Armd Regt. Merchant; of Wahroonga, NSW; b. Wahroonga, 13 Sep 1909.
[3] Lt E. D. Gunn, NX32749; 2/6 Armd Regt. Insurance agent; of Orange, NSW; b. Broken Hill, NSW, 5 Aug 1912.

eleven men.) In addition to the guns and tanks whatever aircraft could be made available would help. The American ground forces would aid the new movement by sending MacNab's men forward to occupy the ground the Australians left when they went ahead and by pressing with Clarkson's from south of New Strip and Beaver's at the bridge area.

Three bombers dropped fifteen 500-pound bombs over Giropa Point at 6.30 a.m. on the 20th. Shells, mortar bombs and machine-gun fire then crashed and spun into the area over which the 2/9th had to advance before the infantrymen rose from their cover and walked steadily ahead at 7 a.m., with Lieutenants Gunn and McCrohon spacing four tanks among them. Griffin's company continued along the water's edge, Taylor's was still on Griffin's left, Benson's was to the left again and Parbury's survivors were in reserve with twelve men from the transport platoon added to make up some of their losses of the 18th. At Cape Endaiadere Cummings was holding Matheson's fresh company of the 2/10th pending the development of the battle pattern.

At first only sniper and harassing fire disputed the infantry's difficult passage through the tangled undergrowth among the coconuts. Then, almost three hours after they had begun beating their way forward from their start-line, they broke out from among the regularly-spaced palms into the stunted bush and kunai-covered marsh country almost due south of Strip Point which was most typical of the Buna region and which spread its inhospitable width as far as Simemi Creek beyond which ordered rows of plantation trees lifted again. There Parbury passed through Taylor's company (Taylor himself had just been wounded), which then fell back into reserve.

While Parbury and Benson now pushed across the 800 yards of the first of two clearly-marked patches of kunai, which proved to be rooted only in quaking ooze, and their men spread out across the base of Strip Point, Griffin, skirting the water's edge, rounded the point itself and reported it free of Japanese. Parbury's men then, with Benson's close behind, tramped through the swampy bushland which led on to the second kunai patch. But this treacherous country had proved too much for the tanks. Two of them were bogged so deep that they were held fast and only the beach now offered any chance of getting the tanks forward. So Parbury's company had no armour as they essayed the passage of the second kunai patch. Soon afterwards—it was now between 1 p.m. and 2 p.m.—these ill-fated men were once more in trouble. The right forward platoon was close against the seashore and Lieutenant Pinwill's platoon was on the left. Pinwill's platoon temporarily lost touch with the one on the right and, detached, plunged into the kunai where they came unexpectedly against a Japanese defence line which seemed to run north from the creek to the coast. Although Sergeant MacCarthy knocked out one post with a grenade Pinwill's advance was blown back by short-range machine-gun fire. He himself was killed with two of his men, four of the others (MacCarthy among them) were wounded and the remainder fell back upon the other forward platoon near the water. Private "Jock"

Milne[4] of the Intelligence Section, trying to reach the platoon from battalion headquarters, was cut down by a sniper. Crawling on, he then missed the platoon perimeter and found himself among Japanese who bayoneted him. Then it was, as the long day waned, that the dying Milne left messages which men of his battalion were later to find and preserve. They were written in a small notebook, crumpled and smudged with dirt, the letters formed so unevenly by the pencil in his dying hand as to make them appear like the painful script of a small child. On one page:—

Should I be dead when you find me search the surrounding bush carefully for wounded men. Jack Allen[5] is somewhere on my left.[6]

And on the opposite page:

Bombs are dropping all round me but somehow I feel quite happy about it.

Within about half an hour of Pinwill's trouble Cummings himself arrived, and, while he and Parbury were talking over the situation, Griffin's company, after following the coast-line round from Strip Point, joined them. Almost immediately the Japanese began to drop mortar bombs on them from 300 yards ahead. As the Australians were not dug in they were fairly caught and soon a number of them were hit, Parbury himself among them. The two companies then united under Griffin and covered Benson's men with Vickers and mortar fire while his men tried themselves against the new defence line. But they fared no better than the others. The Australians (having lost another 25 of their rapidly shrinking number) then formed a blunt arrowhead facing west and, from a point on the coast about half-way between Strip Point and the mouth of the creek, spanned the narrowing tongue of land marked out by the coast and the creek in their approach to one another. MacNab's Americans, who had been beating forward on the left of the Australians, then linked with Benson, and Australians and Americans thus faced the approaching night.

By this time it was clear that warding marshes and watchful Japanese were leagued to make a difficult business of any attempt to cross Simemi Creek. The most obvious crossing places were the mouth of the river, where the water was known to run shallow as it met the sea, and the point where the bridge spanned creek and fen between the strips. But the river's mouth had yet to be gained, and as for the bridge area, the continued lack of success there by the Americans since their very first approach a month before boded ill for any further attempts. Their latest disappointments were very fresh for only that morning an attempted crossing by one of Beaver's patrols had been blown apart when it was scarce begun; and an effort a little later by the 114th Engineer Battalion

---

[4] Pte W. F. Milne, QX2961; 2/9 Bn. Fruit farmer; of Aberdeen, Scotland, and Bowen, Qld; b. Longside, Aberdeenshire, Scotland, 21 Jan 1913. Killed in action 20 Dec 1942.
[5] Pte J. M. Allen, QX15349; 2/9 Bn. Watchmaker; of Tumoulin, Qld; b. Mareeba, Qld, 9 Sep 1918. Died of wounds 29 Dec 1942.
[6] The wounded Allen was later found on Milne's right.

to bridge the main gap in the decking under cover of smoke came to nothing. None the less Beaver was ordered to explore the creek line anew in the darkness of the coming night.

When the 21st came it was clear that the Americans had failed once more to find any solution to their problems. Brigadier Wootten then ordered the two battalions of the 128th and the main part of the 2/10th Battalion (which had concentrated round the eastern end of New Strip the previous afternoon) to search the creek for crossing places. The fresh Australians particularly set about this task with a will. They had old scores to settle with the Japanese, memories of their setback at Milne Bay to wipe out. So it was that neither the dirty, incredibly difficult, nor dangerous nature of the work deterred them, although they found it hard to locate the actual course of the creek itself in the spreading marshy bushlands, and many of the ways which their patrols followed led them through reeking mud and water up to their necks. In this wilderness the newcomers needed more than determination, however; they needed some lucky chance to aid them. Major Clarkson provided it. In reply to Lieut-Colonel Dobbs' anxious questioning he suggested that it might be possible to cross where the creek twisted itself into a U-bend a short distance north-east of the lower end of Old Strip. Dobbs at once detailed Captain Sanderson's company thoroughly to examine the area of the bend. But the first light of the 22nd found Sanderson tired and bewildered and no closer to getting across. With the light Dobbs came to him, avid for results. The unhappy captain said: "My platoons have patrolled all night, Sir, and found nothing." Dobbs replied very shortly "You know what to do when your platoon commanders can't manage a job!" and swung away. To Sanderson's deliberate brain this could mean only one thing. So he turned towards the marsh and creek and eased his thin length into the waste, now wading, now swimming, with two Brens covering him. At last he came out on drier, flat ground, which was covered by two-foot-high kunai. Rather doubtfully he concluded that he might be on the Old Strip and, a little later, reported as much. He had seen no Japanese save two fleeting figures which disappeared into the bush ahead of him. As quickly as possible he got one of his platoons across by the route he himself had followed. So Dobbs had his bridgehead by the late morning. Major Trevivian's[7] company then followed Sanderson's across and the two settled on the far bank for the night. In the dawn of the 23rd Captain Ifould's[8] company joined them.

Meanwhile the 2/9th, north-west of the other battalion, had been ordered to complete the capture of the tongue of land which was enclosed on the right by the coast and by the creek on the left. Cummings tried as far as possible to rest and reorganise on the 21st but the inevitable patrols had to be carried out and the last Japanese rooted out of the area which

---

[7] Maj J. H. Trevivian, SX1444; 2/10 Bn. Electrical engineer; of Adelaide; b. Broken Hill, NSW, 11 Jun 1913.
[8] Capt A. H. Ifould, SX4853; 2/10 Bn. Mining engineer; of Adelaide; b. North Adelaide, 17 Dec 1915. Killed in action 24 Dec 1942.

had already been taken. Warrant-Officer Donnelly[9] of Griffin's company, patrolling west along the creek, ran into almost point-blank fire from concealed positions. Donnelly himself, racing towards the origin of the fire, revolver in hand, was struck down by a bullet which penetrated his steel helmet. MacIntosh's platoon then tried to assist and found that the trouble emanated from a group of five Japanese who, with two machine-guns, were holed up under the spreading roots of a big tree. But so determined were these five, and so well planned their position, that immediately MacIntosh could do no more than cover Donnelly's platoon out and help the wounded back. Getting out one of the wounded, lying well forward and helpless, was a particularly ticklish task made possible only by the bravery of MacIntosh himself and Private Christensen,[1] and the extraordinary coolness of Corporal Thorne[2] who stood quite exposed to give them covering fire during their drawn-out task. This and other forays were a promise that there was still much fight left in the Japanese and the whole day, void though it was of any planned encounters, cost the 2/9th 4 killed and 6 wounded.

At 7.50 on the morning of the 22nd shells began to fall ahead of Cummings' battered battalion as they waited on a start-line running almost due south from the coast and nearly spanning the wedge of swamp and bush, which, little more than half a mile ahead, narrowed to a point at the creek mouth. Ten minutes after the barrage opened the companies crossed the line, Griffin's composite company on the right, "A" on the left (Lieutenant Thomas[3] now commanding) and Benson's in reserve slightly to the rear. Vickers machine-gun fire from their flanks whipped through the leaves of the trees and flailed through the long grass ahead of their wary and measured movement. They moved slowly, searching the long grass which closed them in and could hide any number of their cool enemies who would wait until the Australians were almost on top of them before they would disclose themselves. But at first only sporadic small-arms fire met the attackers until, shortly after 9, machine-gun fire caught Thomas' company in enfilade from the right. This checked the advance while the dangerous and cold-blooded business of winkling out the opposition got under way. But worse was to come for, barely half an hour later, shells from what was supposed to be a Japanese anti-aircraft gun turned to a ground defence role, began to fall with disconcerting effect in the vicinity of the Australian start-line. They caught the headquarters elements sited there and, within a very short time, 20 of these, mostly mortarmen and Vickers gunners, were struck down. Soon afterward the attacking companies solidified along a line that was still considerably less than halfway to their objective with MacNab's men, who had been moving up the line of the creek, closing on their left, and two tanks engaging the strong

---

[9] Capt V. J. Donnelly, QX3610. 2/9 Bn; HQ 18 Bde. Clerk; of Cairns, Qld; b. Cairns, 7 Apr 1918.
[1] Pte J. C. Christensen, SX4017; 2/9 Bn. Rigger; of Ottoway, SA; b. Adelaide, 23 Mar 1904.
[2] Sgt L. R. Thorne, MM, QX12767; 2/9 Bn. Salesman; of New Farm, Qld; b. Toowoomba, Qld, 21 Jan 1916.
[3] Lt V. F. Thomas, QX3050; 2/9 Bn. Salesman; of Gympie, Qld; b. Charleville, Qld, 23 Jan 1917.

(*Australian War Memorial*)

"Get down, you bloody fool. They've just got my cobber," the machine-gunner said to the photographer, George Silk, as he swung his Vickers viciously across the treetops to clear them of Japanese snipers. Silk, employed by the Australian Department of Information as an Official Photographer, took more than 20 of the photographs of the coastal battles used to illustrate this volume.

(*Australian War Memorial*)

Giropa Point. A dead Japanese lies in front of a smashed pill-box. The Australian on the right is Lieutenant D. S. Clarke of the 2/12th Battalion.

(Australian War Memorial)
An Australian uses a Bren gun to clear a coconut tree of a Japanese sniper.

(Australian War Memorial)
The sniper lies dead beside his smashed rifle and the tree-top.

posts on the right which were crossing the front with fire. By midday, however, the tanks had had to return to the refuelling point and the infantry, still behind the barrier thrown out by the searching machine-guns and with the grass ahead of them on fire, withdrew to the shelter of scrub. They were, therefore, little ahead in spite of a hard morning's work, and the well-placed Japanese shells had continued to fall in their rear areas. But by 1.30 the tanks were once more on the move and soon afterwards Griffin was reported to be progressing on the right. None the less

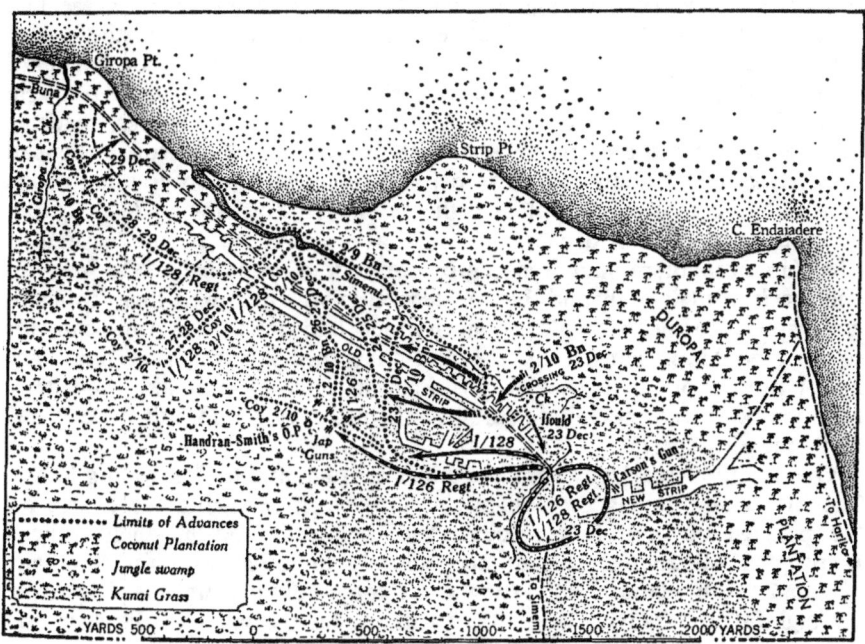

Advance of the 2/10th Battalion and supporting American units along Old Strip, 23rd-29th December

the new start was a difficult one for, less than half an hour after the resumption of advance was reported, both components of the composite company were denuded completely of their officers. MacIntosh was badly wounded by a shell burst, Griffin, a fine leader and athlete, hurrying to the spot, was killed, and his second-in-command, Captain Roberts,[4] had an eye blown out by a shell fragment. This left Sergeant McCready[5] in charge of Griffin's own remaining men and Warrant-Officer Jesse in command of the composite company. Later in the afternoon Major Parry-Okeden[6] (who took over when Cummings was wounded) gathered the

---

[4] Capt P. C. G. Roberts, QX1003. 2/9 Bn; HQ 18 Bde. Stock salesman; of Charleville, Qld; b. Goomburra, Qld, 25 Jul 1904.

[5] Capt S. P. McCready, QX10985; 2/9 Bn. Bank clerk; of Brisbane; b. Townsville, Qld, 20 Mar 1917.

[6] Lt-Col W. N. Parry-Okeden, DSO, QX6077. HQ 18 Bde; 2/9 Bn; CO 30 Bn 1943-45. Grazier; stock and station agent; of Chinchilla, Qld; b. Brisbane, 28 Sep 1910.

shreds of the three attacking companies into one and, with one tank remaining to assist him (the other was temporarily bogged), drove at the pill-boxes which were still holding out. So spirited was this move that, by 5 p.m., Parry-Okeden was able to report that the point area up to the mouth of the creek was in his hands although one strong position remained unsubdued on an island in the centre of the creek mouth. The 2/9th then settled to hold the ground they had won—at the end of a day which had cost them 8 officers and 50 men.

Thus six days of hard fighting had been needed to complete the first phase of Wootten's attack. The next step—the clearing of the bridge between the strips—was, however, unexpectedly easier. When the third of the 2/10th's companies, Ifould's, crossed the creek below the old strip in the dawn of the 23rd Dobbs swung it left towards the bridge, reaching for the Japanese there and to link with Beaver and Clarkson (who had themselves linked about two days before). The Australian crossing of the Simemi had completely nonplussed the defenders, however, and the 2/10th occupied the vital bridgehead by midday, with few, if any casualties. The Japanese there had apparently considered impassable the swamps and creek in their rear, and the consternation which caused them to abandon without further struggle the sites which had defied the Americans for so long could be gauged by the fact that this was the first time they had left any of their coastal positions in such a manner. And their abandonment was precipitate for, by staying, they could still have galled their enemies sorely.

Quickly the American engineers under a brave and tireless young leader, 2nd-Lieutenant James E. Doughtie, set to work repairing the bridge for the passage of both foot soldiers and armour. Wootten then ordered Beaver's 126th men across to keep closely in touch with the left flank of the 2/10th whom Dobbs now sent longitudinally up the Old Strip. By nightfall the 2/10th were 400 yards up on the right of the strip and 200 yards up the centre with Beaver on their left but angled back to the south-east, and Clarkson on Beaver's left barely across the bridge.

The night which followed was marked by an unusual alarm. About 10 p.m. two fast boats were reported off shore and soon it was clear that these were intent on mischief. Watchers from the Old Strip saw tracer reaching out from the shore and 37-mm's also took up the boat's challenge. Then flames leaped from the water at Hariko as one of the Allied supply craft took fire—the barge *Eva* laden with artillery, mortar and small-arms ammunition. Soon after 11 the marauders made off. But they were not long gone before suspicion began to grow in the minds of some of the leaders ashore. The attacking craft were very similar to American torpedo boats of which six had just been based at Milne Bay under American naval command, with their forward headquarters at Tufi. Their task was to prevent Japanese reinforcements landing in the area Buna-Mambare River and to assist in protecting Allied shipping. It was possible that these, new to the theatre, had mistaken their own forces for Japanese. And this indeed proved to be so. Writing back to Australia from Port Moresby on the 24th Major-General Berryman[7] referred to the difficulties of the campaign and recent attacks on small supply craft made in error by Australian Beaufighters. He continued:

> As if this is not enough, some motor torpedo boats attacked our small craft at Hariko last night and set one of them on fire which blew up. We strongly suspect that this was the first successful action of the PT boats which were operating, or supposed to be operating, in an adjacent area last night. However, keep this well under your hat and mention it to no one other than the CGS as it may not be true; even if it is we may never be able to prove it.

To this he added a little later "It is true and admitted".

Despite this irritating loss the fighting went on on the 24th as planned. Wootten had no intention of losing his advantage, and he told Dobbs to continue along the strip, with the assistance of one troop of tanks and with a fourth vehicle in reserve. These were the last serviceable tanks immediately to hand, the balance of the original eight; an additional eleven were only just leaving Milne Bay. Wootten was naturally wary of endangering the last of his armour, particularly as he knew that the Japanese had had in the area anti-aircraft guns capable of an anti-tank role. But these guns, in the face of air attack, had been silent for some days. Possibly they were out of ammunition; possibly the Australian gunners (who themselves inclined to this optimistic belief) had destroyed them; possibly their silence was merely the ruse of wily defenders. Whatever the brigadier's own misgivings regarding the third of these possibilities might have been, however, he did not communicate them to McCrohon who was to lead the tanks in. Both he and his Intelligence officer, in briefing McCrohon, told him that he could disregard any threat from these guns which were known to be sited on the left of the advance. Looking north-west along the strip, a rather indeterminate stretch of open ground covered with waving kunai and unevenly bush-fringed on either side, McCrohon asked to be allowed to take in all four tanks in his initial movement, saying that the front was too wide for only three. The brigadier was reluctant to concede this but finally McCrohon carried his point.[8]

At first, on the 24th, everything seemed to go smoothly. At 9.30 a.m., after a ten-minute barrage, the tanks went up the strip in line, 50 yards apart, with Church on the right, Lattimore on his left, Barnet on Lattimore's left and McCrohon himself on the extreme left of the line. The infantry were hard behind them with Trevivian's company on the right of the strip, Ifould's moving up the strip and to its left, Americans left of Ifould again, and Sanderson in reserve. A sniper was worrying Ifould's company, however. Right at the start the captain stood upright and engaged the marksman himself. But he lost the exchange, and his men, Lieutenant Brown leading them, left him dead as they crossed the line

---

[7] As mentioned earlier, Berryman had succeeded General Vasey as Deputy Chief of the General Staff. From 11th December he held also the appointment of MGGS HQ New Guinea Force.

[8] From interview with McCrohon, although the 18th Brigade account reads: "Alternatively it was realised that the enemy might be deliberately maintaining heavy and medium AA silence as a ruse. It was accordingly decided that until this position was clarified no greater tank force should be committed than the smallest tactical unit, i.e. one troop of three tanks while a fourth tank was held in immediate reserve." McCrohon's account has been preferred.

as part of a steady general advance which continued for half an hour with tanks and infantry combining to sweep the defenders from their path. Then the picture changed radically. McCrohon's tanks were concentrating on their front, searching for the pom-pom gun which was known to be sited off the end of the strip and which, they had been told, was the only gun they had to fear. They were still maintaining their original relative positions. Suddenly McCrohon saw a flash to his left front and then another; a hit followed, and the whole of the left side of the tank seemed to split. He told his wireless operator to warn the other tanks: "Get out! The ack-ack gun's operating." But the wireless was not working. The driver swung the tank round. McCrohon said "You're headed straight for a crater!" The driver replied "There's nothing you can do about it! I can't steer!" And then the tank fell into the crater. The Japanese gunner took Barnet's tank next. His shot crashed through the turret killing Corporal Jones[9] and mangling Barnet's arm. Then it was Lattimore's turn. The shot found the hull gunner's flap killing Trooper Forster,[1] mortally wounding Corporal Leggatt,[2] and blowing Lattimore's leg off. Lastly, in this quick and very ordered process of destruction, Church's tank was knocked out.

Now, denuded of their armour, the infantry were left bare to a destructive fire from the usual well-concealed and venomous strongpoints. Brown, in the centre of the Australian-American line, seemed to be in particular difficulties, faced by a redoubt about the centre of the strip, his men falling rapidly, uncertain as to the whereabouts of the Americans on his left whom he was asking to fire flares so that he might locate their flanks. It seemed too that the Americans had not been mopping up with thoroughness and the Australians were losing men to sweeping flanking fire from their rear and from trees. So the advance slackened after the loss of the tanks. In the early afternoon, however, Trevivian was able to advance a little more on the right until he approached the outskirts of the large coconut plantation which followed the coastline round from Buna Government Station and past Giropa Point, to end with its south-eastern tip lying against Simemi Creek on the one side and Old Strip on the other. There Trevivian was halted, and the rest of the day was given over to a policy of minor infiltration, and encirclement in the face of determined opposition, with the Australians having gained 500-700 yards for the day and lying in a backward-sweeping curve across the strip. To their left Beaver's Americans were watching the flank, farther forward than the two left Australian companies but not as far advanced as Trevivian. Backing Beaver's were Clarkson's men who had been combing the swamp on the extreme left during the morning but had bogged there and been pulled out to give Beaver depth.

---

[9] Cpl T. R. Jones, NX45073; 2/6 Armd Regt. Bank clerk; of Forbes, NSW; b. Dubbo, NSW, 28 Jan 1911. Killed in action 24 Dec 1942.

[1] Tpr F. F. Forster, NX96113; 2/6 Armd Regt. Salesman; of Manly, NSW; b. Holbrook, NSW, 19 Feb 1916. Killed in action 24 Dec 1942.

[2] Cpl R. G. E. Leggatt, NX48821; 2/6 Armd Regt. Clerk; of Coolabah, NSW; b. Nyngan, NSW, 10 Aug 1920. Died of wounds 25 Dec 1942.

Fighting patrols were out in the darkness but made no gains. Then, with the 25th, Dobbs made a new move. Wootten emphasised to him what he called "soft spot" tactics and directed his attention to the Japanese right, which, he thought, seemed most likely to yield to pressure. Dobbs then planned to use there Captain Matheson's company which had reverted to his command at first light, having previously been brought over from the 2/9th area to guard the bridge. He therefore sent them round the left of the Americans. But it was not until late in the day that Matheson found himself angled against strong Japanese positions which had stopped the Americans decisively earlier in the day. Beaver had come against these with a painful bump soon after 7 a.m. when he led off the new day's American movement. Colonel Martin's efforts to resolve the situation by a wide deployment of both Beaver's and Clarkson's men as the day went on achieved little more than to fold the Americans painfully against a number of harsh strongpoints. Nor had the Australians much more success to report. Trevivian had certainly gained a few yards but was hard held against one of the most outflung of the Japanese bunkers on the edge of the coconuts. Brown's remnants were behind him and Captain Sanderson had taken their place on the left of the strip and the right of the Americans where he, like Trevivian, had gained a few yards but had then been stopped.

Dobbs now proposed that his three companies on the strip should drive ahead on the 26th while Matheson's fresh men swept across from the left. The Americans would move forward on their flank against the positions which had been holding them up. But the day opened badly with a bootless foray at dawn by Lieutenant Rudall[3] from Matheson's company against one of the strongpoints which stood in the line of the company's advance. And when the main Australian movement began at 7 a.m., fifteen minutes after the first smoke shell had fallen, it made only local ground. On the extreme right Trevivian had some small success by driving into one of the dispersal bays near the end of the strip. To his left Sanderson's company seemed for a time to disappear into a welter of confused fighting as they tried to draw level and Dobbs temporarily lost touch with them. By mid-morning, however, they had burst through the positions which had been blocking them in the centre of the strip itself with Private Hughes,[4] an aborigine, outstanding even among his fiercely fighting comrades as he shot and grenaded the defenders out of their holes. But their left was still held by a machine-gun post integrated with the defences round the anti-aircraft gun which had destroyed McCrohon's troop and which was then giving Matheson pause about 100 yards to the south-west—the second of the two guns which had been a constant threat since the advance up the strip. The first, however, nearly 200 yards to the east of the second had just then ceased to be a problem as Beaver,

---

[3] Lt J. G. Rudall, SX10394; 2/10 Bn. Student; of Gawler, SA; b. Gawler, 20 Jun 1920. Killed in action 28 Dec 1942.

[4] Pte T. Hughes, MM, SX1570; 2/10 Bn. Labourer; of Stenhouse Bay, SA; b. Point Pearce, SA, 28 Apr 1919.

with one of Clarkson's companies helping him, had overrun it. It was silent as they closed in on it, its ammunition gone.

Towards noon Wootten grew impatient. He told Dobbs that it was absolutely necessary that Sanderson and Matheson should drive on with all their vigour in an attack which the battalion commander now proposed for them at 3 p.m.; that Sanderson should then take out the medium machine-gun position which was holding him up; that Matheson, who was not moving quickly enough, should clear the remaining anti-aircraft gun position which was now holding up both Australians and Americans.

Smoke covered the beginnings of this movement. On the right of the strip Trevivian inched a little farther ahead but Sanderson's attempted advance again lost its outlines in a savage flurry, with Lieutenant Gray[5] and his platoon pushing frontally into the muzzles of the weapons on the company's left front. Gray was wounded there with most of his men (only three of the platoon subsequently emerging unscathed). And still the defending post held out. At the same time Matheson was conducting a spirited encounter with the main gun position to the west. He had planned to smother the big gun with a sudden assault by two platoons under cover of 2-inch mortar smoke. But the thick smoke he had visualised became only wisps clinging about his men instead of hiding them, when Lieutenants Maclean[6] and McDougall[7] led them against the defenders. These, not to be stampeded, released a torrent of fire on the Australians, the core of it coming from a captured Lewis gun. Maclean and McDougall and a number of their men were hit when the issue was only just joined, though McDougall, who had previously been wounded on the 2/9th Battalion front and was concealing the fact, doggedly held to the last of his strength to remain with his platoon until they were dealing systematically with the enemy position. Some withdrew about 40 yards to engage the positions from the long grass while others, Sergeant Spencer directing them, stayed close about the posts. Something very like a particularly murderous brawl then developed. The Australians pounded grenades into the posts but several times Japanese hurled them back before they could explode within the defences. Wild-eyed but purposeful, one Japanese was firing blank rounds from the anti-aircraft gun as he tried to set fire to the grass and add flames to the confusion. Japanese riflemen kept popping stiffly up from the depths of the defences like marionettes and, as stiffly, sinking back into them again. The Australians called for petrol bombs but could get only one—which they splashed against the barriers. And then, almost suddenly, it was ended. The defenders were dead, with many dead and wounded Australians out of the 50 or 60 who had made the assault lying near them; Corporal Heron,[8] who had led his section bravely, was lifeless right upon the enemy post.

---

[5] Lt O. Gray, SX485; 2/10 Bn. Butcher; of Clare, SA; b. Dora Creek, NSW, 5 May 1914.

[6] Lt R. J. Maclean, NX113442; 2/10 Bn. Grocery carter; of Randwick, NSW; b. Waverley, NSW, 22 Aug 1918.

[7] Capt A. F. McDougall, MC, SX11003; 2/10 Bn. Cabinet maker; of Fullarton, SA; b. Adelaide, 28 Sep 1920.

[8] Cpl P. J. Heron, SX837; 2/10 Bn. Bank clerk; of Mt Gambier, SA; b. Shillong, Assam, India, 14 Jun 1918. Killed in action 26 Dec 1942.

Matheson then handed the gun in its concrete setting over to the Americans (much to Dobbs' subsequent annoyance) and ranged a further 300 yards north-west along the fringes of the strip before he settled for the night. To his right rear, however, the day was not yet spent; in the last of the light, the Japanese fell upon Trevivian's leading platoon on the right of the strip so savagely that the platoon had to give up the ground it had won and emerged with only four of its number left.

This painful progress up the Old Strip had not yet brought the attackers to the end of the runway proper, and it was clear that a considerable effort was still needed before their opponents could finally be dislodged. The 27th was therefore given over to consolidation and local sallies designed to trim the edges of the opposition and tidy the Allied lines. As a result of these Trevivian, now commanding his own few men, the men (about 20) which Brown still had left, and a group from Headquarters Company, swept away a Japanese position just off the end of the strip proper, to the right, and on the edge of the coconuts which still sheltered the hardest core of the Japanese resistance. By the early afternoon Sanderson, the positions which had taken so much of his blood and sweat the previous day having been abandoned during the night, had conformed to this adjustment and Americans were strengthening both his flanks. Wide to the left Matheson's men had also been astir, feeling their way along the edge of coconuts so far to the north-west that the strip now lay well behind them and they were more than 1,000 yards ahead of the main body. Matheson was not easy, however, about a southward-running track which he had picqueted the previous night and down which, he felt sure, there was a Japanese position. Though Americans had come up to seal it off he could not forget it.

As though to keep down any Allied hopes which might be rising during this fairly encouraging day, the Japanese struck in unexpected strength from the air. About noon some fifty of their aircraft stormed down upon the battle area. But the Allies, who could have been caught napping by this attack, escaped lightly, losing only eight men. Possibly the planes did more damage to their own forward troops than to their proper targets but, if so, they did not appreciably dampen the ardour of the dogged defenders, who fell upon the right flank Australians during the early part of the night in a vigorous local assault. The first warning Trevivian had of this was soon after 9 when a great commotion suddenly rolled up out of the darkness. Sergeant McAuliffe,[9] a calm leader who was now commanding Trevivian's left forward positions, telephoned him then to say that he thought the Japanese had overrun the right front. Trevivian at once hurried Lieutenant Brown and his men towards the threatened point. Brown found the right front staggering in some confusion, gathered them and drove the marauders off in a sharp clash. Although he was wounded himself (of all the officers and N.C.O's of what had been Ifould's company, only Sergeant Harrington[1] was now on his

---
[9] Sgt W. H. McAuliffe, MM, SX929; 2/10 Bn. Labourer; of Berri, SA; b. Adelaide, 16 Jul 1910.
[1] Sgt S. Harrington, SX196; 2/10 Bn. Mason's labourer; of Barmera, SA; b. Berri, SA, 15 Jun 1918.

feet) his crisp counter-blow took the Japanese before they had mounted machine-guns, otherwise the position could not have been restored that night.

The Australian and American efforts to adjust their own positions and finally squeeze their enemies off the Old Strip continued into the 28th. These now lacked any support from O'Hare's mountain guns which had been silent since the early morning of the 26th when they fired off the last of their ammunition. Their resulting ineffectiveness, however, was not as serious as it might have been earlier for more howitzers had recently arrived: four 4.5's of the 13th Field Regiment under Captain Stokes.[2] Two of these were flown to Dobodura on the 20th and moved up the track to a position about 500 yards south of O'Hare. The other two were taken round from Port Moresby by sea, landed at Hariko on the 23rd and thence were dragged inland to complete the troop. They were to prove most effective as a complement to the field guns.

One of the 25-pounders was now proving spectacularly successful in a boldly-experimental role. This was "Freddie One" of Major Hall's battery. It was hauled from the battery position near Hariko during the night 25th-26th December and sited forward of the bridge between the strips with (from the 27th) its observation post officer manning a look-out in a 70-foot high banyan tree some 1,300 yards ahead of the gun and in the bush off the southern side of the strip. Sergeant Carson[3] was in charge of the detachment manning this piece and from him it took the name by which it was to become famous at Buna—"Carson's Gun". From the very beginning of its operations when Hall himself "shot-in" Carson's gun its story was full of incident. The battery commander was ranging on a Japanese pill-box, using armour-piercing shot in preference to high explosive to lessen the danger to the Allied infantry spread close about his target area. His first shell disappeared through the 12-inch square embrasure of his target with the flash of its tracer flame bursting bright against the darkness of the aperture. (It was found later that this shot carried away the breech mechanism of a 75-mm gun which the strongpoint sheltered.) Soon afterwards the gun settled down to a two-day duel with a triple-barrelled 25-mm piece which, at first, gave back rather more than it took. But, on the 27th, after a ding-dong duel during which the war became a purely personal one for the opposing gunners and in which, Carson's men claimed, they eliminated three opposing crews, the 25-mm was completely silenced. This was merely a beginning, for Carson's men were to claim more sniping successes as the days went on. And they would dispute, with such stories as the following, any assertion that you could not "snipe" with a 25-pounder.

The deadly accuracy of the laying gave the O.P.O. the power of life and death over any individual Jap seen in the target area. Lieut . . . Handran-Smith,[4] the O.P.O.,

---

[2] Capt N. R. Stokes, SX24059; 13 Fd Regt. Clerk; of Unley, SA; b. Unley, 20 Jul 1918.

[3] Sgt R. G. Carson, NX18615; 2/5 Fd Regt. Wool expert; of Sydney; b. Pymble, NSW, 27 Apr 1902.

[4] Capt T. J. Handran-Smith, NX19286; 2/5 Fd Regt. Sales manager; of North Perth; b. Perth, 12 Jan 1907.

would sometimes nominate his targets. . . . When the Japs were withdrawing from the pill-boxes on the far side of the strip, Handran-Smith spied a Japanese giving orders to a couple of his men. The officer, or N.C.O., stopped momentarily in a short shallow trench. . . . This trench had been accurately registered, and many Japs had been killed in its locality by direct hits.

Said the O.P.O., "I nominate that bloke for the next round". Orders were quickly passed to the gun; all eyes were on the Jap. When the 25-pounder fired, the Jap appeared to sense that that round was meant for him. He jumped on to the parapet with the idea of making a dash. Foolish move! The onlookers assert that the shell hit him in the pit of the stomach. At all events he disappeared in instant disintegration.[5]

Such stories as these were borne out by the watching infantry: Major Trevivian said later that, when he and his men were fighting from the dispersal bays at the end of the strip, shells from the gun were clearing the tops of the bays by inches. "The draught wore a track across the top of the bays."

But far behind the vivid flash of Carson's gun the other gunners were going about their valuable but less spectacular work. Before almost every infantry and tank attack their shells streamed into the defences. And between these periods of high excitement they went on with their task of wearing down the Japanese will to fight on.

Each day brought heavy enemy fire. . . . Each night meant continuous harassing tasks against the enemy. Harassing fire exhausted the gunners; but it did much more to the enemy, and, happily, cheered the infantry immensely.

The gun detachments who produced this form of fire nightly almost came to believe that the only ones "harassed" by it were themselves. . . . From dusk to dawn the guns would fire irregular bursts at targets previously registered. Two or three men would work each weapon and the others of the detachment would lie close by, awaiting their turn. It is always a subject for amazement that a gunner can be sleeping soundly a few yards away from a 25-pounder in full blast, but yet be able to wake up immediately when an order is yelled to "Take post".

At Buna, a shift at the gun on harassing fire meant leaving a sodden "bed" on sodden ground to become even more sodden in the tropical nightly downpour. It would probably be a minute or so before the guns were about to fire on some timed program. Few men bothered about dressing for these series. The usual uniform was hat, boots, identity discs—and little else.

Numbers One quietly report their sub-sections ready to fire. The detachments stand still and tense. The command, "Fire" breaks the spell. Four rounds are on their way in a beautifully timed salvo. Before the smoke clears, the breeches have clicked shut and another round is in the bore; the layers are again peering through their sights. Again and again the same performance is repeated. There is a respite for perhaps an hour or less, and the gunners dash back to their crude shelters to snatch a little rest. This is harassing fire as the gunners know it; not just once in one night, but many times each night for many nights.[6]

Despite such willing support, however, the attackers were still finding the going along the Old Strip very hard on the 28th. Trevivian, with his 30 or 40 men, was still the right pivot among the coconuts off the upper end of the strip and the lower end of the dispersal bays. In their efforts to clear the defenders out of the bays his men and Sanderson's had drawn

---

[5] O'Brien, *Guns and Gunners*, pp. 189-190.
[6] O'Brien, *Guns and Gunners*, pp. 190-1.

somewhat apart and one of Clarkson's companies was filling the gap from the left of the strip to Sanderson's right. Sanderson was reaching to the north-west to a point about half-way up the line of the bays. Another gap then opened between his left and Matheson's right which was some hundreds of yards north-west again. As the morning advanced more Americans filled this gap and were told also to close Matheson's rear. Early in the morning, however, Dobbs complained to Wootten that the Americans were not keeping up with Matheson in his efforts to close more firmly on the Japanese and, about 8, Wootten told Martin that signs of resistance were being left behind by the Americans and that the employment of soft-spot tactics did not mean leaving centres of resistance of unknown strength behind. Out of this process of adjustment, however, the pattern that emerged on the morning of the 28th was that the Allied line stretched in an arc from Simemi Creek on the east for nearly a mile to a point less than half a mile due south of Giropa Point on the west.

The plan then was that Matheson's company on the western end of this arc would pivot north-east to the coast with Sanderson and the Americans conforming and supporting, and Trevivian forcing up from the other end of the arc. But though this purpose produced a day of bloody skirmishes and local forays, with numbers of Japanese appearing in American and Australian uniforms in attempts to mislead their opponents, there was little decision. As the Allies strained to tighten their grip their enemies strained to throw it off. Matheson had ventured far to the north-west, and actually crossed over Giropa Creek. Fire coming from the south began to fall near him there and he decided that he was in the path of the Urbana Force advance, an assumption which was soon confirmed by his meeting some Americans of that force whom he was able to inform that the way to the coast south of Buna on that axis was open. He was becoming dangerously detached from his own main force, however, and so returned across the creek. He was then ordered to get astride the track which ran north-west across his front to Giropa Point. Though he had strong misgiving about both the wisdom and necessity of this (since the cover of the grass and bush was to be preferred by both sides to the obvious temptation of the open pathway, movement off which, moreover, was not only concealed but almost as easy) he set Lieutenant Rudall's platoon the task. Rudall got across the track uneventfully—but then the Japanese closed on him. He lost men quickly; he himself was shot through the hip; to send the other two platoons to him would have been folly. So he had to bring his men out. Rudall himself, an heroic figure on this as on other occasions, then insisted on staying with Matheson until the last of his wounded was on the way to an American medical post in Clarkson's Company "C" locality. Only after that did he consent to set out for medical help himself.

The Japanese seemed now, however, to be thoroughly roused. Just before midnight they fell once more on Trevivian's long-suffering few men on the right. Trevivian, with one of Sanderson's platoons temporarily added to his group, beat them off. But roving bands of Japanese, the killer instinct strong within them and fanned to white heat by desperation, were intent on getting within the Allied defences under cover of darkness. One of these, possibly having stolen up the track which Matheson had seen running away to the south from near the end of the strip and had left to the Americans on the 27th, broke into the headquarters area of Clarkson's company (which was not far from the beginning of Matheson's track) and laid about them with such a will that dead and wounded Americans and Australians strewed their wake. Among these latter were Rudall and a number of his men, killed with other sick and wounded at the medical post.

With his opponents so savagely alive along the Old Strip Wootten sought Dobbs out on the morning of the 29th. He was "bouncing the ball" impatiently, critical of the efforts of Dobbs and his battalion. Dobbs was sick, worn with the strain, heart-broken over the loss of so many of his men, only his courage sustaining him. There was heat in some of their exchanges until Dobbs finally received Wootten's orders for the afternoon.

These centred on the use of additional armour—the balance of "B" Squadron which Major Tye had just brought round from Milne Bay. Tye himself, with four tanks, had preceded his main body. Having been warned by Wootten the previous night that his help would be needed he had these four tanks waiting near the bridge at 7.30 that morning. His other seven vehicles were with Captain May,[7] his second-in-command, in the New Strip area.

Wootten told Dobbs that, to help him in an attack that afternoon, he could have Tye's four leading tanks, and Lieutenant Emson's[8] company of the 2/9th who had been moved round to the bridge area a few days earlier to guard that vital link and act as brigade reserve. He was to drive north-east through the coconut grove to the coast between the mouth of Simemi Creek and Giropa Point. The left of the attack would be on the position then held by Matheson's company and the frontage sufficient to allow the attackers to settle so strongly on their objective as to be able to repel attack from either the south-east or the north-west. The guns would lay down shells along the beach running south-east from Giropa Point for ten minutes before the infantry went in and after that would concentrate on covering the left of the attack. Clarkson's Americans would maintain a rearwards guard as the attackers moved, facing west, south-west and south.

As Sanderson's company had moved across to Matheson's right in the early darkness of the morning Dobbs was using these two companies to give effect to Wootten's orders. To them he added one of Emson's platoons as a reserve to be used only as a last resort. That the attackers might need recourse to this, or some other, last resort Matheson for one had

---

[7] Capt R. E. G. May, NX70814; 2/6 Armd Regt. Industrial and designing gas engineer; of Bathurst, NSW; b. Singleton, NSW, 13 Nov 1915.
[8] Lt R. A. Emson, QX3550; 2/9 Bn. Insurance agent; of Sale, Vic; b. Maffra, Vic, 1 Oct 1905. Killed in action 29 Dec 1942.

little doubt. The unhappy memory of Rudall's experience over this same ground was still with him and, from the wide left flank positions to which he had ranged, he had actually looked so closely into the Japanese positions now fronting him that he had certain knowledge of their strength. But his orders were now clear and so, with 46 men, he waited in the early afternoon for the tanks to come up, and Sanderson, also with 46 men, waited on his right. They were ready at 2 p.m. in the stunted bush and long coarse grass, looking towards the coconuts over a belt of stumps some 40 yards wide—the butts of palms the Japanese had fallen to build their strongpoints. But no tanks came. Then the start-time was set for 4 p.m. That hour came but it also brought no tanks. It was difficult for the infantry to know what to do. Colonel Dobbs, inviting all the fire the Japanese could bring to bear on him, then set out to find the tanks. Soon afterwards one appeared in front of Matheson. But, even as his men rose to support it, it moved into the belt of stumps ahead of them and stuck fast on one of the butts. Once more indecision gripped the infantry and they sank again into their waiting positions. It was possibly about 5.30 that three more tanks appeared (whether directed by the brave colonel or whether because they had found their own way it is difficult now to determine) and went forward into the denuded area in front of and slightly to the left of Sanderson whose men rose and went with them. At the same time Matheson's forty-six started forward.

On the right the tanks soon came to a halt on the edge of the coconuts. Sanderson's men also found themselves stopped as they tried to cross the cleared area and came against positions of considerable strength sited not more than 15 feet in from the first line of standing palms. On the left, however, advancing against weaker opposition, Matheson's company kept on. Sergeant Mitchell,[9] who had taken over Maclean's platoon, then actually struck right through to the coast with Rudall's old platoon, Sergeant Fee[1] now commanding, covering his right rear and Sergeant Spencer's platoon (formerly McDougall's) similarly placed on his left. But just as it seemed possible that some good might come out of that day of errors—with Mitchell on his objective; with Fee backing him strongly; with Spencer's platoon warmly engaging a probable threat to Mitchell's left and Spencer himself, his tall, square figure planted firmly in the open, his square face unafraid, deluging converging Japanese with 2-inch mortar fire—the last error was played out. Confused tanks turned their guns on the foremost men. Matheson asserted that they gunned Mitchell's men off the objective and "practically wiped them out", striking down also some of Fee's platoon; that Private "Snowy" Evans[2] from the latter platoon raced across to one of the tanks and, springing on top of it with fire bursting all round him, hammered against the armour to attract the attention of the crew. But apparently they did not hear

---

[9] Sgt J. Mitchell, SX395; 2/10 Bn. Salesman; of Wayville, SA; b. Wellington, NZ, 21 Jul 1918. Killed in action 29 Dec 1942.
[1] Sgt R. C. Fee, SX190; 2/10 Bn. Labourer; of Semaphore, SA; b. Adelaide, 24 Jan 1913.
[2] Sgt A. A. Evans, DCM, SX10404; 2/10 Bn. Labourer; of Adelaide; b. Hilton, SA, 22 Oct 1920.

him and went on firing. In any case it was clear that the day was lost and, about 6.35, Matheson shot green Very lights (the agreed signal for withdrawal) into the darkening sky and brought what remained of his company back to their original positions, with only 3 men left of the 13 who had started off with Mitchell and about 22 all ranks left out of his original 46. His brave second-in-command, Captain Mackie, was among the killed, and Emson of the 2/9th, eager to be in the fight, though it was not properly his, had been shot dead.

Matheson then joined forces with Sanderson who was himself wounded (though still refusing to admit this fact) and who had lost a number of men. Then the full darkness came.

In it the last of the tanks were still collecting themselves, mortified officers and men aghast at their failure and anxiously seeking the causes. It was clear that their confusion went back to the very beginning of their movement when one or more of the first tanks to start out from the bridge area bogged almost immediately. Then worse followed so quickly that, as 4 o'clock approached, no one appeared able to say with certainty just what the detailed position was in respect of the eleven "B" Squadron tanks which then seemed to be churning round the whole area of both strips. Major Moss (from the tank replacement area near the bridge) reported the position at 3.45: that two tanks were at the rendezvous which had been fixed; two were still somewhere on the way up to that point; two were bogged on the lower end of Old Strip; two were in reserve at the bridge; three were still at New Strip. A later report from him, timed 6.25, did little more to sharpen the picture: that one tank was in action; two were out of ammunition; one was knocked out; one was unserviceable; one was on its way to the front; two were still bogged and two others were trying to help them out; one was still in the reserve area.

These messages are the early and late chapters respectively of an obscure story of which almost the only certain fact is that the infantry did not get the organised help they had been promised at the time it was due. Most probably this was due to the inexperience of the tank men and the failure of at least one individual; to faulty and insufficient reconnaissance so that tanks moving to the start-line missed their way and became lost and tanks which did enter action found themselves in strange ground. Probably also Tye, anxiously questing too far ahead, was not available where a more experienced commander might have anticipated difficulty and resolved confusion. But, whatever the difficulties, and disappointments, they arose from no lack of willingness or courage on the part of the majority. Conspicuous in trying to meet the need were the two lieutenants, McCrohon and Heap,[3] neither of whom were to have participated in the action. McCrohon, brave and experienced, saw the trouble begin and moving forward from the replacement area did what he could to reduce it. Heap, slim, deceptively mild in normal times, not

---

[3] Capt D. A. Heap, DX628. 2/6 Armd Regt; 2 Beach Group. Regular soldier; of Sydney; b. London, 16 Apr 1920.

yet tried in action, took over a returning tank late in the day and hurried it back into the fight. On the battleground, however, the tank which had first appeared before Matheson's company and was still fast on the stump, engaged all his attention. He did not succeed in salvaging the vehicle but finally got the crew out and left the field only when it was so dark that he had to walk ahead of his tank as he brought it back down the Old Strip. So he appeared finally to his anxious friend McCrohon who, back near the bridge, had seen all the other tanks in and feared that Heap had been lost.

The tanks, however, had no monopoly of mistakes that day. The attack was an error in itself. The waiting Japanese were too strong for two weak and tired groups, each much less than half a company in strength. And this was to be proved in very bloody fashion within a few days. But such a mistake could be explained by the necessity for finding out just how strong the opposition was. More difficult to explain is the decision to go ahead with the attack after the tanks first failed to appear, and night was fast approaching. An attack with such a background was foredoomed.

Through the darkness which settled over this unfortunate day, Japanese, still full of spirit, and true to what they had established as an almost nightly practice during the Old Strip fighting, sallied against the Australians' right flank. But Trevivian's men, adept now at meeting such dangers, shot high into the night 2-inch mortar flares which bathed the battlefield in a soft revealing glow. This flooded the startled raiders when they were only some 20 yards from the Australian positions. Four Vickers guns sited to the left of this front (near the Americans) to counter just such attempts then blew them into a twisting heap. The defenders pitched grenades into the mass of dead and dying men, while the aloof flares fell slowly towards the torn earth. When daylight came again Trevivian's men counted 42 dead in the grisly pile.

Nevertheless Dobbs' brave battalion was almost spent and it was well that new forces were arriving. Early in the morning of the 28th the 2/12th had left Goodenough Island and it arrived at Oro Bay that night. Colonel Arnold hurried ahead while the rest made their way up the coast to Duropa Plantation, the battalion's strength 33 officers and 582 men. Arnold, originally an officer of the 2/10th, was at Dobbs' headquarters well before lunch on the 30th, anxious to survey for himself the task he was about to undertake. By 8 p.m. he had issued orders to his battalion for their take-over next day of the area round the western end of the Old Strip where Sanderson's and Matheson's men were.

Wootten then told him to get ready to capture, on the first day of the New Year, that area of the coconut plantation which lay between the mouth of Simemi Creek on the right and Giropa Point on the left. He would maintain a frontage of 400 yards, taking off from the extreme west of the line the 2/10th and the Americans had established and striking north-east to the sea through the coconuts over a distance of some 600 yards. On his right the 2/10th and III/128th (Colonel MacNab had brought the latter round from the eastern bank of Simemi Creek on the

30th, changing places with the 126th elements) were to press into the coconuts in conformity with the main movement. After Arnold had consolidated along the coast he was to turn south-east along the plantation and thus exploit back towards the Old Strip. Fearful of confusion similar to that which had marked the 29th, Wootten issued particularly strict and detailed orders to Captain May to support the attack with six tanks. Three more tanks, Lieutenant Thomas who had taken over Emson's 2/9th company and been strengthened by the addition of another platoon (under Lieutenant Tippetts[4]), and a company made up of 4 officers and 74 men who had just arrived as reinforcements for the 2/10th, would constitute the brigade reserve. There would be full artillery support for the attack with Hall's troop firing on registered targets on the beach for ten minutes before the start time and Carson's gun engaging observed targets in the coconuts from first light until the attacking companies crossed their startline. Dobbs was to lay mortar smoke at Arnold's request and the 2/9th Battalion, from their positions on the eastern end of Simemi Creek, were to support the attack with fire along the beach east of Giropa Point.

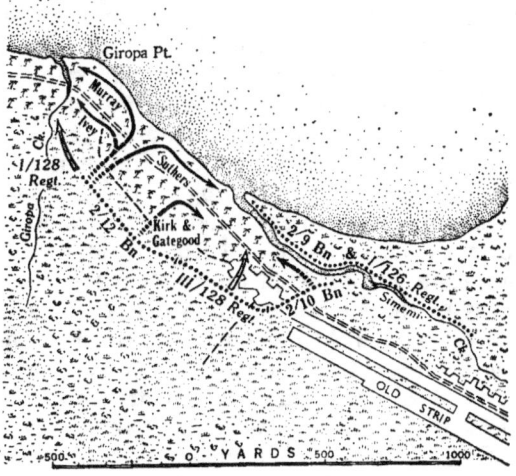

Giropa Point, 1st-2nd January

The two left companies of the 2/10th Battalion fell back as Arnold's men came forward on 31st December. Japanese marksmen picked off five of the fresh troops who exposed themselves as they moved into position and, intermittently, clusters of light mortar bombs fell among them. In his right forward position Arnold had Captain Kirk's company with Major Gategood's supporting them. On the left of the 400-yard line Captain Murray's[5] company was forward with Captain Ivey's supporting. (The task of the support companies was to kill small enemy parties who screened the strongpoints from pits and whom the tanks might leave behind.)

It was clear and fine with an oblique wind which had ruled out the use of smoke when Arnold sent these men into the attack at 8 a.m. on New Year's Day, one man in each of his sections carrying a prepared demolition charge made of two pounds of ammonal, a grenade and a piece

---

[4] Lt C. H. Tippetts, QX2692; 2/9 Bn. Truck driver; of Boronia, Vic; b. Hartshil, Warwickshire, England, 30 Jun 1911.
[5] Capt A. McL. Murray, TX334; 2/12 Bn. Farmer; of Kew, Vic; b. White Abbey, Co. Antrim, Ireland, 25 Apr 1907. Killed in action 1 Jan 1943.

of instantaneous fuse.[6] May, in a control tank with which the rest of his tanks were linked in a wireless net, was with him at the battalion headquarters. Arnold deployed six tanks in front of the infantry. Three others he kept under his own hand so that he might keep his forward strength constant as any vehicle came back for ammunition or fuel replenishment or was put out of action. The artillery, their fire quickened by that of mortars and twelve medium machine-guns, had prepared the way, the machine-gunners (applying the lessons of Milne Bay) firing remorselessly at the tops of the palms and beating out of them the snipers perched there.

The tanks crossed the open ground first. When they reached the standing palms the infantry then closed upon them fast, packing the rear and flanks of the armour which had orders to conform to the walking pace of the foot soldiers. May had his tanks moving with smoothly-controlled precision as they first took on the Japanese soldiers who, from pits, screened the strongposts, and then battered at the loopholes and doors before the attacking infantry rushed them with their ammonal charges. These, hurled into the breach made by the tanks, finished any post they struck. But the Japanese posts were thickly spread and well manned so that, on the right, Kirk and Gategood struck serious trouble quite early. Machine-gun fire slashed into their men and marksmen picked them off. By 9 a.m. the two companies were out of normal communication with the rest of the battalion and for a long time a killing fire frustrated all attempts to make this disadvantage good. Messages could only be passed to and from them by tanks. Arnold tried to aid them by sending a 3-inch mortar but again well-directed fire brought this attempt to nothing, striking down many of the men engaged. About 10.20 a.m., with Kirk killed, all of his officers wounded, and only a remnant of his company left; with Captain Curtis[7] the only unwounded officer in the other company and that company as a whole in only slightly better shape than Kirk's (Gategood himself having been badly hit making a valiant effort to gather together the remnants of both companies); with the wounded able to be got back only slowly and with the greatest difficulty; Arnold ordered Captain Suthers, with elements of Headquarters Company, to circle to the assistance of his right by following through initially in the wake of the two left-flank companies.

These two (probably breaking into the Japanese administrative area) had advanced quickly against fairly heavy but less intense resistance than Kirk and Gategood had met. Their success signal shot skyward from the beach at 8.51 a.m. Soon afterwards they turned north-west for Giropa Point itself with Murray's flanks closed by the sea on his right and Ivey on his left. Then ensued a struggle for the Giropa Point positions during which Murray and his second-in-command, Lieutenant Logan,[8] were both

---

[6] These were evolved from experiments conducted on the ground at Buna by Lt-Col A. F. A. Irwin, Chief Engineer of the 6th Australian Division.
[7] Capt O. A. Curtis, TX703; 2/12 Bn. Bank officer; of Hobart; b. Launceston, Tas, 13 Mar 1912.
[8] Lt T. T. Logan, QX1518; 2/12 Bn. Stockman; of Rockhampton, Qld; b. Ruiru, Kenya, 10 Feb 1913. Killed in action 1 Jan 1943.

killed and two of their two platoon commanders, Lieutenants Smith[9] and Clarke[1] were wounded—Clarke, none the less, taking over the company on Murray's death. In Ivey's company Lieutenant Elphinstone,[2] his second-in-command, and Lieutenant Silcock,[3] a platoon commander, were hit with a number of their men.

While this hot encounter was developing Suthers came through to the coast and then turned south-east to face towards the Simemi mouth, gather in what had been the two right-flank companies and clean up the area down to the creek, helped towards the end of the day by two platoons of the 2/9th under Lieutenants Tippetts and Thomas. There was brave and bloody work: against the strongposts which fringed the beachline, scrub and lawyer vine tangling them thickly round; among the coconuts falling away to the south-east; in the swamps which oozed into the creek. Where the tanks could work the infantry packed them closely, firing Very lights to guide the tank fire and then following that in with grenades and sweeping rushes. Where, in many places, the tanks could not work on the treacherous ground, the foot soldiers winkled out the posts alone. Lieutenant Bowerman[4] led the dismounted transport drivers of the 2/12th Battalion in a series of spirited assaults. By the end of the day the attackers had laid bare a network of posts over an area scored by radiating webs of crawl trenches. Some of the defensive positions they found to contain as few as 10 men, more seemed to average about 30, and in one about 70 men lay dead.

By nightfall the position had clarified both on the right and on the left. On the right only disconnected fragments of the defences held out. These were in a pocket contained by 100 to 200 yards of beach running north-west from the Simemi mouth, the line of the creek, Dobbs and MacNab crowding up from the south, and the line Suthers had established running southward to a point just above the end of the dispersal bays which opened off Old Strip. Farther up the coast the other two companies had made good the line of Giropa Creek except for one strongpost which was holding out at the very mouth. The darkness brought thunder and lightning and rain. Through it scattered Japanese groups and individuals tried to break their way out of the Simemi pocket. One such band came upon Captain Sampson's[5] medical post, laying about them wildly. But Sampson met them undismayed. The Australians, and MacNab's Americans whose only part in the day so far had been to follow on the rolling up of the defences, killed the fugitives in close, hard-fought clashes in the dark and dripping bush, and shot them down in the lightning flashes.

---

[9] Lt L. J. Smith, TX6014; 2/12 Bn. Accountant; of Hobart; b. Hobart, 26 May 1920.
[1] Capt D. S. Clarke, QX3502; 2/12 Bn. Insurance manager; of Cairns, Qld; b. Brisbane, 29 May 1915.
[2] Lt C. B. Elphinstone, TX2082; 2/12 Bn. Farmer; of Myalla, Tas; b. Penguin, Tas, 23 Aug 1907.
[3] Capt H. I. Silcock, NX12964. 2/12 Bn; Torres Strait Inf Bn 1943-45. Regular soldier; of Gymea Bay, NSW; b. Maclean, NSW, 8 Dec 1912.
[4] Lt W. P. Bowerman, MC, TX6013; 2/12 Bn. Clerk; of Hobart; b. Hobart, 6 Jul 1915.
[5] Maj V. E. Sampson, MC, VX39414. 2/6 Fd Amb; RMO 2/12 Bn, 1 Parachute Bn; 2/5 Fd Amb. Medical practitioner; of Corinth, Qld; b. Maleny, Qld, 19 Aug 1915.

The attackers were early at work again on the 2nd with two tanks each reporting to the Simemi and Giropa flanks and the 2/9th Battalion clearing the east bank of the Simemi. Most of the day was taken up in brief final encounters. In the late afternoon, after the tale was finally told along the Simemi, the 2/12th gathered at Giropa Point. There, although the last post had been reduced by 9.55 a.m., it had taken the Australians until the afternoon to hunt down the remnants of the defenders. Everywhere the Japanese fought virtually to the last man in the brave tradition they had observed at all points along this coast. On the 1st only 8 men allowed themselves to be taken prisoner and 6 of these were labourers. On the 2nd there was one prisoner.

Arnold himself had vivid personal experience of their fanaticism. He was with the foremost attackers in the last of the fighting along the Simemi. Two Japanese officers of its garrison emerged from the island post (which had been holding out against the 2/9th Battalion since 22nd December) set in one of the feeders to the creek mouth. With no stomach left for useless killing Arnold called to them to surrender, and called again. They gave no sign of understanding or even of hearing. One leisurely turned away. The other washed himself in the brackish water and drank some. Then, quite regardless of the silent watchers, he bowed very low three times into the sun. As he then stood erect and faced the Australians Arnold called "I'll give you until I count ten to surrender". With no word the other took a small Japanese flag and tied one end to his upraised sword and held the other end in his left hand so that it covered his breast. And so he faced his enemies still silent. Arnold counted deliberately. As he reached "Nine" the Japanese shouted in a loud, clear voice "Out!" Then the Australians riddled him. The other they found hanging by the neck, dead.

In this fighting the 2/12th Battalion lost 12 officers and 179 men (the larger part of them on ground across which less than half that number of the 2/10th had been started on the 29th). These casualties brought the total losses in the three 18th Brigade battalions to 55 officers and 808 men for the period 18th December to 2nd January inclusive—about 45 per cent of the numbers with which the units had first arrived on the Buna coast, although these numbers had been augmented during the sixteen days by the arrival of some reinforcements and the return of original members of the battalions.[6] It was a heavy cost by any standards, particularly so by those of bush warfare.

The Australians had, however, been fighting strong, well-entrenched and well-armed foes. It will be recalled that, after his arrival on 17th November with the *III Battalion* of the *229th Regiment*, Colonel Yamamoto had disposed in the whole Buna area probably a little over 2,500 men; that, of these, Captain Yasuda deployed about 500 marines and probably several hundred other men (mainly construction

---

[6] The battalion losses were:

	Killed		Died of Wounds		Wounded		Missing		Total	
	Offrs	ORs	Offrs	ORs	Offrs	ORs	Offrs	ORs	Offrs	ORs
2/9 Bn	8	70	1	16	14	233	—	32	23	351
2/10 Bn	7	91	1	11	12	170	—	6	20	278
2/12 Bn	5	49	—	8	7	121	—	1	12	179

troops) round the Buna Government Station-Triangle-Buna village area. Of the balance of the force Yamamoto sited more than 1,000 (including the fresh infantry) in Duropa Plantation, at Cape Endaiadere, and along the edge of New Strip, while, at the bridge between the strips and round the southern end of Old Strip, odds and ends of various army units were dug in with a strength of several hundred.

When, therefore, the 2/9th Battalion attacked on 18th December it is possible that they fronted up to twice their numbers, and the Japanese were in very strong and well prepared defensive positions. When Yamamoto was forced to yield to the pressure of their amazing feat of arms, he pulled his men back by degrees across the shallow mouth of the creek and across the bridge between the strips, having been holding firmly at the bridge for some time. He was then determined to prevent any crossing of the shallows at the creek mouth and commanded them from an island set there and from the western bank. Although it is not known how many men remained to him after he had made the crossing it seems likely that he still had a substantial part of his force intact. With these, he manned the defences which had been prepared on and about the Old Strip—a warren of trenches and bunkers, with several lines of bunkers across the strip, extending in one case to Simemi Creek on the right and in another to the swamp on the left; with bunkers in the dispersal bays above the strip, in the area below the strip, on the strip itself and in the coconut grove off its western end.

Integrated with these defences Yamamoto had machine-guns and mortars, at least two 75-mm mountain guns, two 37-mm guns, several 25-mm pom poms mounted dual and triple at the far end of the strip. About three-quarters of the way up the strip, and about 200 yards to the south, he had in position several 3-inch naval guns. To the north of the strip he had another 3-inch gun.

Despite the formidable nature of their defences, however, the Japanese forces east of Giropa Point were almost completely destroyed. Nine hundred were known to have been buried there and, as always, there were uncounted dead whose numbers could only be guessed at. With this destruction, though at a woeful cost in brave men's lives, the first period of the 18th Brigade's operations on the coast ended on 2nd January. Meanwhile the Americans of Urbana Force had been fighting to clear the area on the western side of Giropa Creek.

CHAPTER 16

BUNA GOVERNMENT STATION TAKEN

WHILE Brigadier Wootten's Australians, with American support from the I/128th Infantry, III/128th and the incomplete I/126th, had been fighting up the coast towards Buna from the south-east, the American infantry of Urbana Force were trying to break into the Buna area from the south.

Their failure to subdue the Triangle on 17th December had left them awkwardly placed. Their way led them north-east towards Buna Government Station, where the main Japanese resistance was still centred, but both flanks of that route were commanded by strong pockets. The Triangle was on the right; on the extreme left the Japanese held Musita Island, framed by the yawning mouth of Entrance Creek, and were facing the island in strength from the eastern side of the creek. Obviously one or both of these threats had to be dissolved if the American advance on the Government Station was to know any security, and the rear had to be blocked against any Japanese attempts at relief from the strongly-held positions towards Sanananda.

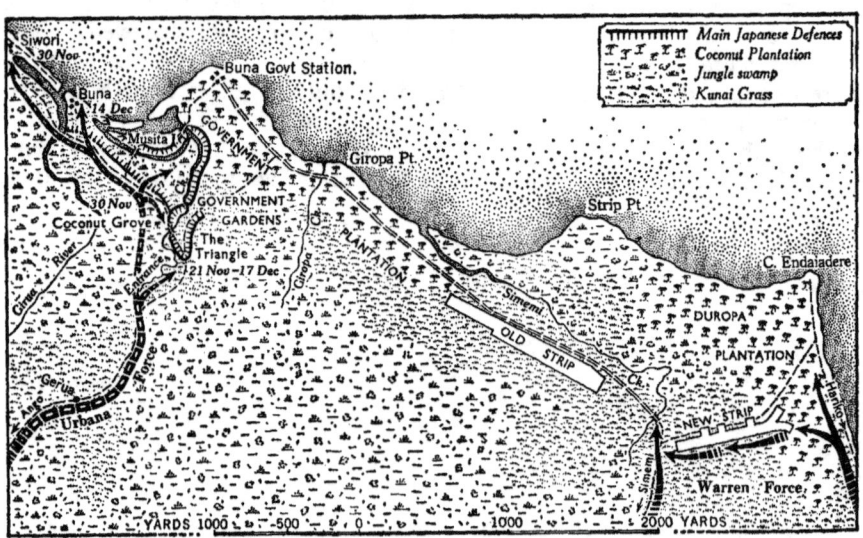

American operations before Buna to 17th December

To meet these circumstances, however, Colonel Tomlinson, the Urbana Force commander, would soon have fresh and comparatively well-found troops, for the movement of the incoming 127th was then well under way with the II/127th moving forward from Ango and the I/127th being flown across from Port Moresby. Tomlinson had the II/127th take over Smith's positions, after the failure to take the Triangle, sent the II/128th back along the track for a rest, and brought Captain Boice's II/126th back into the line, settling some of them into the Coconut Grove, clamping some about the Triangle and swinging two patrols from that battalion wide to his left rear, one under Lieutenant Schwartz to Tarakena and one under Lieutenant Alfred Kirchenbauer to Siwori village. He held as his reserve the first two companies of II/127th Battalion to reach the front.

As his first move in a new phase his plan now was to clear Musita Island on his left flank on the 18th. He proposed then to reduce the Triangle on the 19th thus giving his men a comfortable start through the Government Gardens to the coast south-east of the Government Station as an overture to an all-out attack on the station from that direction.

This plan went awry early, however. Unopposed, Captain Roy F. Wentland's company of III/127th had crossed the difficult stream by noon on the 18th. Still unopposed they then began moving towards the bridge which connected the northern tip of the island with the station shore. But soon they met Japanese who killed Wentland and four others, wounded six more and drove back the remainder to the mainland in some disorder.

Licking that wound, Tomlinson turned against the Triangle on the 19th. At 6.50 a.m. 9 Marauder aircraft bombed the Government Station and in less than an hour 13 Bostons followed. While the second wave of planes was pounding the station, two of Boice's companies (totalling 107) drove southward at the Triangle from the bridgehead leading down from the Coconut Grove. A heavy mortar barrage preceded them, and a third company (though mustering only 37) was stationed south of the road junction as a back-stop. But the day was a costly failure for the attackers and the end of it found forty of them killed or wounded for no gain, and the gallant Boice among the dead. Tomlinson, realising that he could expect no more from the 126th, pulled them back into reserve early next morning, except for the company at the tip of the Triangle. The 127th Infantry was to carry on.

Next day, shortly before 9 a.m., Captain James L. Alford's company of II/127th crossed the creek from the Coconut Grove under cover of mortar smoke and behind an elaborate artillery and mortar program. But then, unseasoned as they were, they fell into confusion and, by 11.30, all attacking movement had fizzled out. A very gallant attempt to retrieve the situation followed in the early afternoon when Lieutenant Paul Whittaker, 2nd-Lieutenant Donald W. Feury and Staff-Sergeant John F. Rehak, led a desperate attempt by a reinforced platoon to come to grips with the well-protected Japanese, but enfilade fire caught them, killing the three brave young leaders and four of their men and wounding twenty. So another unhappy day ended, at a total cost to Alford's company of 39 killed and wounded, and Tomlinson withdrew his men to the shelter of the Coconut Grove.

Thus, after three days fighting, no progress had been made towards clearing the way to the Government Station. The Japanese still held both the Triangle and Musita Island. Colonel Tomlinson, very tired and worn, asked to be relieved and General Eichelberger told Colonel Grose, commander of the 127th Infantry, to take Urbana Force over. This Grose did at 5 p.m. on the 20th, just in time to initiate a new phase, for Eichelberger was now planning to by-pass the Triangle, having already broached that idea to General Herring. Herring had agreed that, if the attack on the 20th failed, the Americans might feel for a way through the Government Gardens without first reducing the Triangle.

Eichelberger now decided that his best line of attack was through the north-west end of the Government Gardens—a line which would involve crossing Entrance Creek about midway between the Triangle and the island. The III/127th were to make the crossing—in canvas assault boats, each about 18 feet long and capable of carrying 10 men with their equipment. At 9.30 p.m. on the night of the 21st-22nd, therefore, the leading company put out into the dark stream in the wake of heavy mortar fire. By that time, however, their enemies were thoroughly alert and beat the black water with fire. The fire was so wild, however, that, by dawn of the 22nd, the company was firm on the opposite bank for the loss of only six men. In the early part of the day they covered the passage of a second company and by the early afternoon both companies were securely in position. They then selected a site for a bridge, about 200 yards upstream from their crossing place, and the engineers at once set to work there using the assault boats as pontoons. The bridge was finished on the 23rd and Eichelberger told Grose to send five companies forward from the bridgehead area on the 24th.

Meanwhile the island had not been forgotten. Strangely unmolested by the Japanese the engineers had been at work repairing a bridge which had previously linked the mainland with the western end of the southern side of the island. By the afternoon of the 22nd the work was done and a strong patrol from the III/127th Battalion crossed to the island without interference. Still unopposed, having traversed the island from west to east, it approached the second bridge, which linked the island with the Government Station area. Then it came under some fire and was strongly reinforced. Before midday on the 23rd, however, uneventfully enough, the Americans were in possession of the whole island and in a position to harass the Government Station with fire which included that from a 37-mm gun which they brought up. Eichelberger could now choose between trying to establish a bridgehead from the island or persisting with his plan to attack through the more southerly bridgehead which was already firm. Wisely, in view of the proximity of the main Government Station defences to the island, he continued with the latter course.

After a night of harassing and searching fire by both sides Grose sent the three rifle companies of the III/127th into the Government Gardens on the 24th with less than 1,000 yards to go to the sea along a line which ran a little north of east. But they were uneasily placed. Not more than 500 yards to their right the Triangle still smouldered corrosively against that flank. The ground ahead of them, though fairly flat, was covered with the tall, coarse kunai which rasped shoulder high in what had once been cultivated ground, and concealed bunkers and strongpoints. As this enclave of unfriendly grass, about 500 yards wide, approached the sea it came against the edge of the Government plantation which followed the water-line north-west to the point. The left of this "garden" sagged away into swamp which then, rather more than 100 yards northwards, yielded to the palm-covered higher and drier ground in which the Government Station itself was set.

Although only two companies, "I" on the right and "L" on the left, initiated this movement on a 450-yard front, behind a rolling barrage, almost at once Grose had to thicken the centre of the advance with a third company—"K". This, however, added little impetus to a movement that was grinding sluggishly in the lowest gear with the right flank barely clear of its start-line and under viciously effective fire from hidden positions. This fire so distorted Company "I's" strength and purpose, despite brave deeds by such individuals as Sergeant Elmer J. Burr, who threw himself on a Japanese grenade to smother its explosion with his own body, saving his company commander at the cost of his own life, that Grose pulled the company back at 9.50 a.m. and replaced it with Captain William H. Dames' company of the II/127th. Then, at first, it seemed that the vigorous Dames might regain the impetus which the right had lost. Inspired and led by Sergeant Francis J. Vondracek, who had been acting as a platoon commander in Company "I" and had remained in the line, the newcomers clawed out the most forward of the troublesome positions. Although they then went on to get astride the track which ran north-east through the gardens to the coast they were held there.

Disappointing though this day was on the right flank, and marked also by failure of the centre company to get ahead, the most bitter frustration was on the left. There Company "L" was strongly supported by the heavy weapons spread along the creek, mortars vigorously fought by Colonel M. C. McCreary and, after McCreary was wounded, by Colonel Horace A. Harding, Eichelberger's artillery commander, and by fire from the island and adjacent positions to the north. One of its platoons broke right through to the sea. Led by 2nd-Lieutenants Fred W. Matz and Charles A. Middendorf the platoon reached the edge of the plantation by 9.35 a.m. There two strongpoints halted them. Sergeant Kenneth E. Gruennert refused, however, to be stopped. Single-handed, he grenaded the defenders of the first post to death. Though wounded, he then pitted himself against the second, blasted his enemies out so that they could be shot down by the rest of the platoon, and then fell dead to a near-by rifleman. The rest of the platoon went ahead again behind his high example and by midday had reached the sea. There, however, the Japanese closed them in, and fire from the supporting gunners (who had no means of knowing that they were there since the platoon's communication had failed) fell among them. Middendorf was killed, Matz wounded. Finally Matz, with only eight men left, ordered most of the survivors out after an afternoon of bitter resistance and with darkness then about him. He and one of his men, too badly hit to march, remained behind and hid themselves among the Japanese positions.

Meanwhile, Grose, ill-informed about the left flank situation, did not follow up this success until it was too late. The waning day then found him with Company "K" (his original centre company which he had relieved with Company "I", from which Dames had taken over on the right) returning from a vain bid to assist Matz and Middendorf and the balance of his original left flank company, with Captain Byron B. Bradford's company of II/127th now on their right, hardly 100 yards from their morning's start-line.

Thus a well-planned, well-supported attack by adequate forces degenerated and was halted. General Eichelberger summed up:

> I was awakened on Christmas morning by heavy Japanese bombing from the air, and my Christmas dinner was a cup of soup given me by a thoughtful doctor at a trailside hospital. For the projected American advance had not proceeded as expected. Troops of Urbana Force bogged down in the kunai grass of Government Gardens and their commander lost contact with his forward units. . . . Next morning I wrote General MacArthur: "I think the low point of my life occurred yesterday."[1]

Distressed and off balance, Grose asked for a pause in which to reorganise on Christmas Day. Eichelberger told him to press on with the attack and gave him, in addition to the other two battalions of the 127th, elements of the I Battalion which were just arriving at the front—part of Captain Horace N. Harger's Company "A", and Company "C" under Captain James W. Workman. Grose then planned his initial movement round Dames on the right (trying to force a way along the track), "K" in the centre, Harger and Bradford on the left where the main emphasis would lie, Workman as reserve.

On this Christmas morning the Americans used heavy fire from the island and its vicinity to mask their intentions. Japanese attention was thus concentrated on the area which linked the island bridge with the Government Station. At 11.35 a.m. Harger and Bradford then began an unheralded advance through the gardens. At first Harger made slow progress but Bradford, on his left, struck vigorously through to the edge of the plantation to a point a mere 300 yards from the sea and only about 600 below the Government Station. There the Japanese, recovering from their disconcertment, encircled the company though Harger fought in to the little garrison during the late afternoon. But these two groups now formed but a precarious enclave. Not only were they some hundreds of yards in advance of any other companies but they were completely out of communication. So night found the Americans' left-flank thrust—their main one—hard against a foe who was now holding it as a man arrests the downward sweep of his attacker's arm and holds him then in a state of straining equipoise from which either might emerge the victor.

Meanwhile, on the right, Dames had made only slight gains after a hard day. In an effort to help him yet another attack had been made

---

[1] Eichelberger, *Jungle Road to Tokyo*, p. 47.

upon the Triangle—by Captain Workman, using one of his own platoons as the main component. But this, like those that had preceded it, was cast back, leaving Workman among the dead.

Grose was busy in the darkness reorganising his twisted line and marshalling assistance for Bradford and Harger. He ordered the main part of Company "C" to drive a corridor through from the left front to the beleaguered men. But this they failed to do on the 26th despite the strengthening of their front by the arrival of Company "B". Colonel J. Sladen Bradley, Chief of Staff of the division and acting as Grose's executive officer, and Major Edmund R. Schroeder, who had come forward the previous evening to take over the I/127th, then dashed through in the last of the light with the assistance of Lieutenant Robert P. McCampbell and one of the Company "C" platoons, briskly rebuffing sharp Japanese attempts to halt them. They found their comrades in a bad way.

> The condition of the companies on our arrival was deplorable (wrote McCampbell later). The dead had not been buried. Wounded, bunched together, had been given only a modicum of care, and the troops were demoralised. Major Schroeder did a wonderful job of reorganising the position and helping the wounded. The dead were covered with earth . . . the entire tactical position of the companies [was] reorganised and [they were] placed in a strong defensive position. . . .[2]

On the morning of the 27th Bradley returned to the main American positions leaving Schroeder in vigorous command of the forward positions. Captain Millard G. Gray, Eichelberger's aide-de-camp who had now taken over Company "C", spent the day drilling into the Japanese swamp positions on the American extreme left, while Lieutenant John B. Lewis, leading Company "B", skilfully took advantage of the Japanese absorption with Gray to edge closer and closer to Schroeder. By 5 p.m. he was through.

Apparently, however, this did not yet mean that the Americans were in any way firmly placed. Now the full story has been lost, but the impression is ineradicable: of a confusing array of infantry companies moiling in bewilderment amid the kunai grass; of unit and sub-unit commanders changing so rapidly that sometimes it is impossible now to determine who was locally in command at any given moment; of senior officers working as section, platoon and patrol commanders as the only means to drive their purpose through; of many very brave men fighting and dying to get results through their own individual courage which should have come through a cohesion of purpose and effort which was never present. An endless array of weary questions plods unanswered through the historian's mind. Consider only the sortie through the gardens and into the plantation of Bradford's and Harger's men (and the similar circumstances surrounding the earlier break-through on this same American left flank by Matz and Middendorf, and the still earlier one by Sergeant Bottcher near Buna village). Where was the crisp command which should have quickly exploited and reinforced these successes; the loyalty and cohesion and quick

---

[2] Milner, *Victory in Papua*, p. 300.

initiative which should have brought their fellows in the field hard in their wakes? If Bradley and Schroeder could get through what held back all the other companies in the small garden area? Why, having reached their summit with such fine touch, did Harger's and Bradford's men present such a sorry picture on the arrival of Schroeder and McCampbell? Why, with the position apparently so encouraging when night came on the 27th, did Eichelberger later write this?

> I was to explore the depths of depression . . . on the night of 27 December. . . . At two a.m. a conference took place in my tent. We heard the reports, and they were grave all right. Our troops, if the reports were to be credited, were suffering from battle shock and had become incapable of advance. A number of my senior officers were convinced the situation was desperate. I think I said, as I had said before, "Let us not take counsel of our fears". Nevertheless I was thoroughly alarmed.[3]

From all this, however, real achievement emerged on the 28th. That day Captain Dames, who had been slowly fighting forward up the track on the extreme right flank, and Gray, who had been whittling away at the left, closed in to the support of the beleaguered Schroeder. With the forward positions then strongly held the Americans were able to develop a corridor leading from their firm positions along the line of Entrance Creek to the plantation where Schroeder was now dominant. Before this reality the Japanese defenders of the Triangle unostentatiously drifted out of the positions they had defended so worthily for so long. The Americans, probing cautiously into the Triangle on the evening of the 28th, found a labyrinth of bunkers and strongpoints, littered with abandoned pieces of equipment and scattered ammunition, scored by shell bursts, with here and there fragments of human bodies.

Eichelberger, planning in anticipation of these heartening developments, had already decided to chop into the Government Station area from a new angle. To that end, early on the afternoon of the 28th, he had ordered Colonel Grose to get the III/127th Battalion marshalled on and in the vicinity of Musita Island. The plan was to force a crossing over the bridge which linked the northern tip of the island with the shore. To neutralise the fire of the strong Japanese positions which commanded the northern end of the bridge a fifteen-minute artillery and mortar barrage was arranged. Under cover of that barrage five assault boats would round the eastern side of the island, storm ashore at the northern end of the bridge and hold there while the main assault crossed the bridge itself, in the wake of a volunteer party whose task was to span with stout planks a 15-foot gap in the decking of the bridge.

But there was confusion in carrying out the plan. About 5.20 p.m. the protecting fire began to fall and the five boats put out into the stream, inadvertently leaving behind the officer-in-charge. Staff-Sergeant Milan J. Miljativich, to whom the command then fell, bravely tried to drive the venture home, but his boats were still in mid-stream when the barrage lifted and were caught there by the uncowed defence. Miljativich's was

---
[3] Eichelberger, pp. 47-8.

sunk under him and the other four washed back to the American shore. Meanwhile the bridge party, slow to assemble, had met with no more success. Six volunteers had succeeded in laying their planks in position and a few attackers crossed behind them. Then, however, the ricketty framework refused any longer to support the improvised decking and most of the few who had crossed were marooned among the enemy who killed or wounded all of them. (A patrol took off the surviving wounded the following night.)

The Americans spent the next day searching for a way out of their difficulties. That way opened on the night 29th-30th when a patrol, crossing the shallows from the narrow finger-like spit which projected eastward from Buna village to the Government Station shore, found no Japanese to greet them—the silence made tinglingly alive for the Americans by memories of the hot reception which had met an attempt to cross this way on the 24th. Thus the approach for which the attackers were searching was open and they planned now to use it to the full—by throwing a force through the shallows, simultaneously forcing the passage of the bridge and crowding up from the south where Major Schroeder was now in strength.

Schroeder by this time had gathered round him most of his own I/127th Battalion and some elements of the rest of the regiment just above the junction of the coastal and Gardens' tracks and, with Lewis' company, had closed the gap between the right flank and the sea. The right of that sector was therefore firm and the left echeloned back on to Entrance Creek. In the Gardens south of the track other parties were at work clearing out the remaining opposition isolated among the kunai and on the fringes of the Triangle.

This was then the plan: at dawn on the 31st Schroeder would intensify the pressure he was already exerting on the Government Station from the south-east; after an attack through the shallows on their left two companies of II/127th—Captain Dames', practised and assured after the determined part they had played in the Gardens' fighting, and Captain Edmund C. Bloch's—would cross the bridge from Musita Island and press towards the Government Station from the south; a third company of II/127th, under Lieutenant William W. Bragg, a young officer who had already shown his mettle, and Captain Jefferson R. Cronk's company of II/128th (the 128th and 126th men having been brought back from their rest area a day or two before) would ford the shallows. Bragg and Cronk were instructed to secure a firm enough footing on the hostile shore south-west of the Government Station to draw to themselves the main enemy attention and cover the right, thus enabling Dames and Bloch to establish the bridgehead and then try themselves against the south-west defences of the Government Station coincidentally with the forward thrust of the other two prongs of the attack.

This whole movement depended upon the left flank. There Bragg led his company, Cronk's following behind, into the ripples washing over the sandy bar, in the last of the darkness. Surprise was to be their most effective weapon. But this was thrown away by irresponsible firing as Bragg's company mounted the sandy spit, and suddenly a startled enemy seemed to have them bathed in light and blanketed in explosions. Bragg fell wounded.

Colonel Grose was waiting on the spit to hear news of the action from a man who was following the attackers with a telephone. The first information he received was that the lieutenant who had taken command when Bragg was wounded was running to the rear and others were doing the same.

I told the man (Colonel Grose said afterwards) to stop them and send them back. He replied that he couldn't because they were already past him. Then the man said, 'The whole company is following them'. So I placed myself on the trail over which I knew they would have to come, and, pistol in hand, I stopped the lieutenant and all those following him. I directed the lieutenant to return and he said he couldn't. I then asked him if he knew what that meant and he said he did. The first sergeant was wounded, and I therefore let him proceed to the dressing station. I designated a sergeant nearby to take the men back and he did so. I then sent the lieutenant to the rear in arrest and under guard.[4]

Fortunately the other company had been more resolute. By the time the sergeant got the wounded Bragg's men back to the scene of their panic, Cronk was fighting hard. He then took the whole group under his command and edged forward some little distance during the day. Nevertheless, the main object of the left-flank movement—to make possible the creation of the bridgehead—had not been achieved. And, from the south, Schroeder had little to report.

Despite this unhappy outcome it was clear that the Americans could not be kept out of the Government Station much longer. They had now only to keep pressing the beleaguered Japanese and the nut, tough though it was, must crack. Eichelberger, anxious to keep pace with the close of the Warren Force operations, ordered the full-scale clearing movement to begin on the first day of the New Year—to synchronise with the drive of the 2/12th Australian Battalion to clear the Simemi Creek-Giropa Point area. The Japanese, however, great defensive fighters as they had proved themselves at every point along the coast, still staved off the inevitable, grudgingly yielding only a little to the pressure from the south and holding Cronk fast on the spit. But with the evening there were unmistakeable signs that even their strong spirit was breaking: swimmers were seen striking out to sea from the Government Station area. And the morning of the 2nd saw the coastal waters from the Government Station to well past Buna village dotted with swimmers and desperate men clinging to anything that would float. Many sank, hit by fire from the shore. Enough remained within the Government Station defences, however, to make the 2nd a difficult day for the Americans. Captain Dames led the main movement off at 10.15 a.m., up the shoreline from the south-east and through the coconuts, with a second company—from the II/128th—hard behind. In the central sector Captain Gray's company reached the point, the

---
[4] Milner, *Victory in Papua*, p. 313.

men heaving themselves dripping out of swamps, where they had been working indefatigably for days, to clear the positions commanding the bridge and allow the long-sought passage from the island to open. From the spit Cronk was still straining inwards, but the advance was slow. It was not until 3.30 p.m. that Dames reached the tip of the bulge with which the coastline encircled the Government Station, to be joined there a few minutes later by Gray, whose task of clearing the approach over

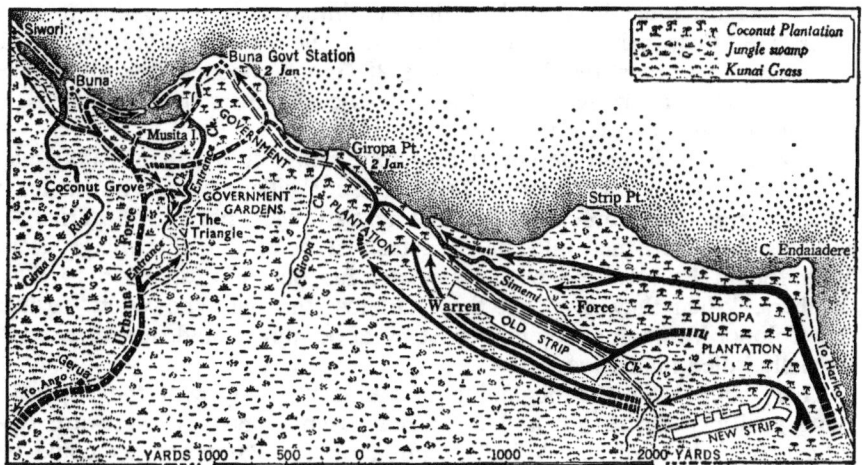

Lines of advance Warren and Urbana Forces, 18th December to 2nd January

the bridge was finished. By that time other companies, too, were packing round. Less than an hour later the passage over the bridge had been made good and by 4.30 p.m. the Government Station—an area of broken houses, splintered trees and blasted earth, strewn with the twisted shapes of the dead—was at last in American hands.

While the fierce, flickering encounters which always marked the mopping up of dogged Japanese went on around the Government Station, the Americans sent a second company south along the coast to assist Lieutenant Lewis who had been trying unsuccessfully for some time to break through to link with the advancing Australians. By the early evening this link had been forged and the Buna operations were virtually finished.

To the actual front-line had been drawn the whole of the 32nd American Division, except for the small parts of the 126th Regiment on the Sanananda Track, as well as Australian forces consisting of an infantry brigade, a commando company, two squadrons of armour, a separate Bren carrier component, artillery and engineers. Also the operation necessitated a wide and constant use of Allied air power and the build-up of an elaborate system of air-sea supply. It cost the Allies some 2,870 battle casualties, some 913 of them Australian. Of those casualties the three infantry battalions of the 18th Australian Brigade accepted 863—approaching a third of the American total for the employment of roughly one-third of the American strength for a third of the total time involved: a comparison which attests the vigour of this Australian brigade and the decisive nature of its entry into the struggle.

The Japanese are known to have lost a minimum of 1,390 men killed at Buna. These were counted dead: 900 east of Giropa Point, 490 west of that point including 190 buried at the Government Station itself. How many more, buried alive or dead in their strongpoints or uncounted for other reasons, must be added to that minimum it is impossible now to determine. Fifty prisoners were taken—on the Warren Force front 21 coolies and 1 soldier; by Urbana Force 28, mostly coolies, but with a few soldiers who were dragged naked and defenceless from the sea after they had swum hard for their freedom.

Captain Yasuda had deployed probably rather fewer than 1,000 men in the Buna Government Station-Triangle-Buna village area, with his main strength at the Government Station, his next strongest point at the Triangle, and less than 200 men allocated the task of defending the village itself. They fought bravely and exacted a cost far out of proportion to their numbers. When they saw that they had lost the fight, however, Yasuda and Colonel Yamamoto solemnly met by appointment and, together, ceremonially killed themselves.

Thus, soon after the beginning of January 1943, with the Japanese Buna positions destroyed, and the threat from Gona and westward dissolved, the whole of the Allied attention on the Papuan coast could be concentrated on Sanananda where a weary struggle was still going on.

CHAPTER 17

THE END OF THE ROAD

ABOUT mid-December when the 18th Australian Brigade was taking over from the Americans of Warren Force to sweep the coast as far as Giropa Point; when the Americans of Urbana Force were trying to clear the Triangle preparatory to closing in on the Buna Government Station; and when the Australian 21st Brigade and 39th Battalion, having just taken Gona, were cleaning up towards the mouth of the Amboga River, there began a new phase of the slow struggle among the swamps bordering the Sanananda Track in which first the 16th Australian Brigade, then the 126th American Infantry, and then the Australian 49th and 55/53rd Battalions had drained out their strength. Lieut-General Herring then possessed few infantry units which had not been committed at some stage of the New Guinea fighting. At Port Moresby there were the 2/1st Pioneers, the 36th Battalion and the 2/7th Cavalry Regiment (serving as infantry); at Milne Bay was the 17th Brigade. The pioneers had made a brief foray from Port Moresby along the Kokoda Track, but, for most of their time, had been labouring in the gravel quarry and on the roads at Port Moresby. General Blamey considered it necessary to hold the recently-arrived 17th Brigade at Milne Bay in case the Japanese attacked again. The 36th Battalion and the 2/7th Cavalry were the last Australian infantry to join the coastal forces.

The 36th, a militia unit from New South Wales, had arrived at Port Moresby late in May as part of the 14th Brigade. The 2/7th Cavalry was part of the 7th Division and had been formed in May 1940. Though the regiment had left Australia in that year, battle had so far eluded it. It trained in Palestine and Egypt, went to Cyprus in May 1941 to augment the slender garrison when that island was threatened with airborne invasion, and then rejoined its division in Syria. After their return to Australia with other units of the 6th and 7th Divisions early in 1942 the cavalrymen spent a period in south Queensland training in infantry tactics before they set out for New Guinea in September. Their work and training at Port Moresby continued into December and, when orders to move forward arrived, their spirits rose high. Some 350 of them were flown across the range.

On the 15th December, immediately before the concentration at Soputa of these two fresh units, Brigadier Porter considered the situation existing along the Sanananda Track. Excluding service troops, mortarmen and signallers, he had 22 officers and 505 men in the 49th and 55th/53rd Battalions; 9 officers and 110 men of the 2/3rd Battalion; 22 officers and 523 men of the 126th American Regiment. He noted, however, that the two last-named could be used only in a positional role, the 2/3rd because its men were sick and exhausted, the Americans "for various reasons" including sickness and fatigue. Of the strength opposed to this force he wrote:

> In actual numbers, it is difficult to estimate enemy strength but his state is such that he has undertaken locality defence with every available man and, as such, does not require personnel for the maintenance of a mobile force. All his strength appears to be devoted to occupying fixed positions, in which there are numerous alternative defences, for the purpose of staying indefinitely to impede our advance. His positions are in depth from our present position to a distance of 2,500 yards along the road—this information from our patrols—and probably all the distance to Sanananda. His strength in fighting personnel is probably 1,500 to 2,000 in the forward areas.
> . . . A policy of encirclement will enable us to capture and occupy localities further to the north and even on the road itself, at the expense of strength in hand and protection of our axis and vulnerable L of C installations. I am prepared to seize more ground, as such, but this will not reduce enemy localities other than by a slow policy of stalking and starving him. He must be attacked jointly and severally and this requires manpower. . . . Since our first assault; we have used a "stalk and consolidate" type of tactics, combined with fire concentrations on enemy positions, as discovered. We have patrolled deeply and over wide areas. Several raids have had the effect of killing some enemy but his well-constructed MG positions defy our fire power and present a barrier of fire through which our troops must pass. We have attempted to seize these in the failing light but they are too numerous to deal with by other than an attack in great strength.

Against this background Major-General Vasey planned an attack for the 19th December by the newly-arrived cavalry and the 30th Brigade, his orders, issued on the 17th, based on this summing-up of the Japanese situation.

> Our immediate enemy has been in position without reinforcement of personnel, material and supplies since 21-22 November. During the intervening period the enemy has been continually harassed by air, artillery or mortar bombardments and subject to infantry attacks and offensive patrols. From information obtained from prisoners of war and captured natives it would appear that he is now short of supplies.
> The enemy, therefore, should now be considerably weaker although his strength in automatic weapons has NOT been greatly reduced in the areas which he is still holding. However, in spite of great tenacity, past experience has shown he has a breaking point and it is felt that this is now close. Adverse local conditions and the ever present possibility of him receiving reinforcements makes it imperative that the complete and utter destruction of the enemy in the Sanananda area should be carried out at the earliest possible moment.

He said that the 2/7th Cavalry, skirting the most forward Japanese positions and starting from Huggins' road-block, were to push quickly along the track to Sanananda Point and seize the beach area there; while the 30th Brigade, moving initially in the cavalry's wake and destroying first the forces between themselves and the road-block, were to eliminate all the Japanese then remaining in the area from Giruwa to Garara.

In preparation for the 30th Brigade's part in this synchronised movement, Porter sent the 36th Battalion (Lieut-Colonel Isaachsen[1]) to take over on the 18th the positions astride the road which the other two militia battalions had been holding. Lieut-Colonel Kessels then swung the main

---
[1] Lt-Col O. C. Isaachsen, DSO, ED, SX2915. 2/27 Bn; CO 36 Bn 1942-45. Barrister and solicitor; of Malvern, SA; b. Mannum, SA, 5 Jun 1911.

(*Australian War Memorial*)

Strengthening a 25-pounder gun emplacement of the 2/5th Field Regiment at Buna. Known as "Carson's Gun" it was sited between the two strips and west of the bridge across Simemi Creek. *Left to right*: Gunner Mick Williams (on loan from the 2/1st Field Regiment); Gunners J. Webster, A. S. Meecham, Sergeant R. G. Carson, and WO2 J. Puxty (with binoculars) of the 2/5th.

(*Australian War Memorial*)

Major W. H. Hall, the commander of the 2/5th Field Regiment battery at Buna, observing from Captain T. J. Handran-Smith's O.P. in a 70-foot banyan tree sited about 1,300 yards forward of "Carson's Gun" and in the bush off the southern side of Old Strip

(*Australian War Memorial*)

Christmas Day at Buna 1942. A wounded soldier, Pte G. C. Whittington of the 2/10th Battalion, gropes his way to an aid station, guided by a Papuan boy. An emergency field dressing covers Whittington's wounds, from which he died later.

(*Australian War Memorial*)

Gona, during a lull in the fighting. A variety of mess equipment was used by the Australians. The Australian standing is holding the bottom portion of a Japanese mess kit; another is scooping water from the creek in a blackened tin probably used also as a billy-can; the soldier on the right is drinking from the corner of an Australian dixie.

part of his 49th Battalion away to the right and Lieut-Colonel Lovell took his 55th/53rd to the left. Porter's plans for the 19th were that Kessels should clear a way north-west to the road from the vicinity of the area which Major Hutchison was holding with a handful of weary men of the 2/3rd Battalion and establish himself at a point about 500 yards north of the Cape Killerton track junction; that the 55th/53rd should thrust almost due east from the position Captain Herwig was manning with the remainder of the 2/3rd to clear the major part of the road up to the Killerton Track; the 36th Battalion, in brigade reserve, was to be prepared to exploit the success of either of the other two battalions. Mortars and Major Hanson's four guns of the 2/1st Field Regiment would support the attack.

The guns opened at 7.22 a.m. on the 19th and the mortars joined in four minutes later. At 7.30 the two battalions began their closing movements towards the track. On the right Captain Noyes, commanding the 49th's attacking force which consisted of four groups each of approximately platoon strength, made good progress for slight loss by sweeping away two or three machine-gun positions which tried to bar them. Swift to reinforce this success Porter sent Major Douglas'[2] company of the 36th to the 49th Battalion's front. Before midday Douglas relieved Noyes of a troublesome position about 350 yards north-east of the track junction while Noyes' men went on through the bush. Late in the day Noyes found that he had skirted the defences which hugged the track and was able to contact Huggins'. After that he followed Porter's instructions and established a position in the bush a few hundred yards south-east of the road-block.

On the left of the brigade movement, however, the results of the attack by the 55th/53rd were disappointing. Captain Gilleland's company on the right flank of that battalion was in trouble early. They came against a strongly-held area from which two machine-guns and stubborn riflemen refused to be dislodged. Although they cleaned out one of the machine-gun positions the other defied them, and the end of the day found them still struggling with it. On their left Captain Coote,[3] his company heavily embroiled when it had gone little more than 100 yards, was mortally wounded, his second-in-command was shot near by, communication with the company was substantially lost, and, though Sergeant Poiner[4] stayed with his wounded commander and made brave efforts to maintain control, the company disintegrated into a number of small groups. The loss of two of the platoon commanders and a large proportion of brave N.C.O's increased the confusion. As the morning went on Lieut-Colonel Lovell sent in a third company with orders to go through close on Coote's right. They were slow. In the early afternoon Captain Henderson[5] came forward

---

[2] Maj C. D. Douglas, NX141454; 36 Bn. Clerk; of Darling Point, NSW; b. Sydney, 8 Nov 1915.
[3] Capt F. G. Coote, NX143794; 55/53 Bn. Engineer; of Lakemba, NSW; b. Leichhardt, NSW, 10 Oct 1916. Killed in action 19 Dec 1942.
[4] Lt H. J. Poiner, NX80471. 55/53, 2/4 Bns. Stock and station agent; of Ganmain, NSW; b. Junee, NSW, 29 Sep 1915.
[5] Capt H. K. Henderson, N23072. 53 and 55/53 Bns. Tailor; of Casino, NSW; b. Christchurch, NZ, 16 Jun 1905. Killed in action 19 Dec 1942.

to hurry them along. But some of the men were reluctant to advance and Porter wrote bitterly later:

> Captain Henderson lost his life as he bombed an enemy LMG post. The remainder of his party left him to the task without aiding him.

Finally it became clear that confusion was general and the attack was called off. The battalion assessed its losses at 6 officers and 69 men (including 18 N.C.O's) and had achieved little. Porter told Lovell to take over the positions Herwig's men of the 2/3rd had been wearily but doggedly manning, and one south of Herwig which Lieutenant S. W. Powers'[6] company had been manning as the left flank of the 36th. Powers thereupon went to the position occupied by the 49th, broke bush westward to the track on Douglas' right and began moving south to clear the roadway to the track junction and thence back to the main Australian positions. Night overtook him, however, when he was near the junction and he settled there.

While the small remainder of the 49th relieved the remnant of the 2/3rd, Powers and Douglas (under Kessels' orders) set about carrying on the fight on the 20th. Powers, however, had barely recommenced his southward movement soon after dawn when Japanese positions astride the track halted him. While he was held there Douglas' men thrust hard at the positions round which they themselves had been lying, but fared no better than Powers had done. Brigadier Porter, never dilatory, then instructed the Americans to take over from the rest of the 36th and ordered the 36th to attack next day the positions which had stopped Douglas (and of which, obviously, those which had held Powers formed a part). Isaachsen hurried to Kessels' headquarters in the late afternoon, planned his attack, took Powers' and Douglas' companies back into his own command, moved the former back to the vicinity of his own headquarters and made ready to receive the other two companies next morning. When these arrived about 9.40 a.m. on the 21st they were shown the ground, moved out to an assembly area north-west of the position Hutchison had been holding, and were ordered to fall upon the Japanese from the north. Captain Moyes[7] was to take the right, Captain A. M. Powers[8] the left; Lieutenant S. W. Powers' company was to be the reserve. Moyes and A. M. Powers then led off at 3 p.m. behind the artillery and mortar fire. Moyes got forward about 250 yards in the teeth of mounting fire but, for a time, no news came from A. M. Powers. The rattle of heavy machine-gun fire was heard from his flank, however, and soon Isaachsen learnt that one platoon had lost direction and become separated from the company, that the remainder were held under a most resistant fire, and that the company commander himself was missing and was probably dead. Soon the company withdrew; Moyes found it necessary to conform;

---

[6] Capt S. W. Powers, N91701; 36 Bn. Manager and secretary; of Chatswood, NSW; b. Fremantle, WA, 17 Aug 1904.
[7] Capt G. E. Moyes, NX141455; 36 Bn. Chemist; of Castle Hill, NSW; b. Sydney, 9 Feb 1920.
[8] Capt A. M. Powers, N91607; 36 Bn. Manager; of Bardwell Park, NSW; b. Fremantle, WA, 17 Aug 1904. Killed in action 21 Dec 1942. The Powers were twin brothers.

and night found the battalion dug in with little to show for the loss of 55 killed, wounded or missing.

By this time Brigadier Porter had become bitterly critical of both the 36th and 55th/53rd Battalions. He said that any success which was theirs was "due to a percentage of personnel who are brave in the extreme"; and "the result of unskilful aggression". He was caustic in referring to their deficiencies of training and spirit. Nevertheless, it is very doubtful if any Australian units could have suffered the same percentage of losses in their first action and done much better (and the final tally of casualties at Sanananda was to show that the militia losses were almost one-third of the total Australian-American casualties suffered there).

However, rightly or wrongly, Porter lacked confidence in two of his battalions. On 22nd December, the 49th was placed under Brigadier Dougherty (21st Brigade) who, with his brigade headquarters and the 39th Battalion, came over from the Gona area to take command at Huggins' and forward. The Americans, who made up the rest of Porter's force, were unlikely to gain ground, although, their force west of the road-block having been relieved by the 39th, they were concentrated once more. They were losing men in action daily trying to do what was expected of them, but were quite spent. Major Boerem was anxious to have them relieved and, on the 27th, he wrote:

> This unit arrived on 21st Nov with 56 officers and 1,268 enlisted men. The total strength to date is 20 officers and 460 enlisted men.

Porter could achieve little more than active patrolling during what remained of the year. To add to the Australians' worries, a very positive Japanese thrust at the four field guns developed. On the night 28th-29th, a raiding party fell upon the gun positions in determined style, exploded a charge in the barrel of one gun and destroyed it. Thenceforward the gunners could never feel safe.

This unsatisfactory state developed behind the 2/7th Cavalry Regiment after it had launched its own movement along the Sanananda Track.

On 16th December Lieut-Colonel Logan,[9] with Lieutenant Barlow's[1] troop of Major Strang's[2] "A" Squadron of the 2/7th Cavalry, set out along the pathway which came in from the west to cut the Killerton Track and then passed on to join the Sanananda Track at Huggins' road-block. This pathway had developed into the supply-line to the road-block and along it Logan now proposed to pass his regiment to avoid the Japanese positions still separating the 30th Brigade from Huggins'. The cavalry would launch their clearing attack towards Sanananda Point from the firm base which Huggins' represented. Logan returned late the same day leaving Barlow at the road-block to gather information. In the late afternoon of the 17th Strang, with his two other troops, moved along the supply trail

---

[9] Lt-Col E. P. Logan, NX12339; CO 2/7 Cav Regt. Company director; of Lindfield, NSW; b. Mosman, NSW, 26 Dec 1903. Died of wounds 19 Dec 1942.
[1] Lt E. D. Barlow, QX5580; 2/7 Cav Regt. Pastoralist; of Toowoomba, Qld; b. Toowoomba, 2 Aug 1913. Killed in action 19 Dec 1942.
[2] Maj M. R. Strang, NX12410; 2/7 Cav Regt. Secretary; of Haberfield, NSW; b. Glebe, NSW, 17 Sep 1909. Killed in action 19 Dec 1942.

to secure a dangerous kunai area in the vicinity of the Killerton Track, and thus enable the main body to carry out unmolested the approach march to the road-block on the 18th. In this, however, he was not successful although he claimed to have killed eight of a Japanese group who refused to be dislodged from a small flanking perimeter commanding the kunai clearing and who, in turn, killed two of his men before the main body of the Australians approached. None the less the latter went through the kunai without loss and the regiment was concentrated at the road-block when night fell, heartily welcomed by the Americans there. In the miasmic darkness Logan told his men that they would set out the next day at 6 a.m. to push along the track with all possible speed to Sananada Point; they could expect to be cut off from the main Australian force for some time; Strang's "A" Squadron would lead, with Logan's fighting headquarters, Captain James'[3] "B" Squadron, Captain Cobb's[4] "D" Squadron, Major Wilson[5] (Logan's second-in-command) with the rear headquarters, and "C" Squadron following—in that order.

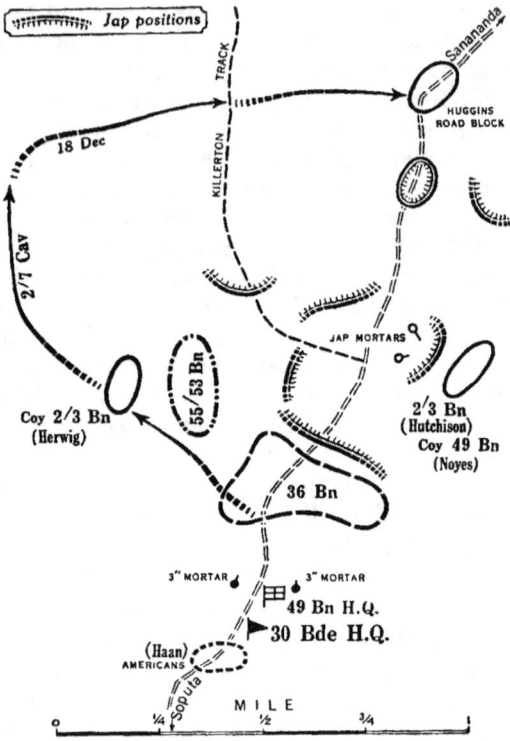

Dispositions prior to attacks of 19th December

It was still dark next morning when the guns from Soputa opened on the Japanese positions forward of Huggins' and Strang's men led off close behind the bursting shells. Dazed after the long night and the savage bombardment, the Japanese allowed the squadron to advance for about 450 yards without hindrance. Six of them then started up from the centre of a dump area and two were killed as they fled. Their blood hot, Strang's men followed with great dash—but ran headlong into the main Japanese positions which were now thoroughly alert. Strang himself was mortally

---

[3] Brig J. A. James, ED, NX12291. 2/7 Cav Regt; 2/31 Bn 1943-45. Sawmiller; of Mayfield, NSW; b. Stockton, NSW, 7 Mar 1919.
[4] Capt H. W. A. Cobb, QX6313; 2/7 Cav Regt. Bootmaker and saddler; of Caboolture, Qld; b. Kadanga, Qld, 2 Apr 1915. Killed in action 21 Dec 1942.
[5] Maj W. J. R. Wilson, QX6331; 2/7 Cav Regt. Grazier; of Lancefield, Vic; b. Melbourne, 2 Apr 1909.

wounded and all his troop leaders were killed, leaving Sergeant Oxlade[6] (bravely assisted by Trooper Hooke[7]) commanding the most advanced troop, in which four men were killed and the officer and six men wounded; the second troop suffered least (it lost its officer and one other man only); only three men were alive in the third troop. By about 9 a.m. squadron headquarters and the second troop were coming back to the dump area and re-forming there, but Oxlade's men and the three survivors of the other troop were still forward.

The whirlpool thus suddenly formed across the track washed back against Colonel Logan and Captain James' men (in Strang's immediate rear) and the rest of the regiment waiting to go forward from Huggins'. The forward Japanese, who had allowed "A" Squadron through, squeezed in on those who sought to follow. Logan ordered James to make a left flanking sweep with Captain Cobb, who was behind James, moving similarly to the right. The rearmost squadron was to follow Cobb. This whole deployment, however, was necessarily slow if only because, by this time, Logan could reach only Cobb by wireless and had to rely on runners to carry orders to the others.

When James led this outflanking attempt, he found the Japanese vigorously opposed to it. They forced his men back into the narrow confines of the roadway and there pressed them so closely that one Australian, Corporal Sanderson,[8] killed three of them in hand-to-hand fighting before he was killed himself. By the early afternoon it was clear to James that he would be doing well merely to maintain his position. He therefore gathered his men into a perimeter defence which the adjutant, Lieutenant Faulks,[9] had established on the site of Strang's first encounter after the loss of his colonel. Logan had been badly hit about 11 a.m. His leg was shattered; he attempted to crawl the 500 yards back to the road-block but died in the bush beside the track.

Night found about 100 men in James' perimeter some 400 yards forward of Huggins'. Most of James' squadron were there, with the remnants of Strang's, the fragmentary headquarters group and a few men from "C" Squadron who had outstripped the rest of their squadron in their efforts to get forward. The main group from "C" Squadron, having failed to make any appreciable progress, fell back on Huggins'. Ahead of them Cobb's squadron, frustrated in their efforts round the right, had twisted about the track in day-long efforts to advance, losing, among other brave men, Corporal Connell.[1] When Connell was shot down he called to his mates to keep clear of him, but they kept on in the hope

---

[6] Capt L. M. Oxlade, MM, QX5730. 2/7 Cav Regt; 2/9 Cdo Sqn. Clerk; of Chinchilla, Qld; b. Brisbane, 12 Jun 1918.

[7] Tpr P. W. Hooke, MM, QX6898. 2/7 Cav Regt; 2/4 Fd Regt. Farmer; of Gundiah, Qld; b. Rockhampton, Qld, 30 Jan 1916.

[8] Cpl O. K. Sanderson, QX10004; 2/7 Cav Regt. Labourer; of Tweed Heads, NSW; b. Parkes, NSW, 15 Sep 1914. Killed in action 19 Dec 1942.

[9] Capt L. G. Faulks, MBE, NX47806. 2/7 Cav Regt; HQ 29 Bde. Accountant; of Sydney; b. Sydney, 6 Sep 1917.

[1] Cpl E. D. Connell, QX5335; 2/7 Cav Regt. Engine driver, butter grader and cream tester; of Monto, Qld; b. Kingaroy, Qld, 7 Jun 1913. Killed in action 19 Dec 1942.

of reaching him. So he raised himself from the ground with one last effort to draw the fire which he knew was waiting for them, deliberately threw himself into it and fell dead. Later, approaching darkness finally forced most of the squadron back on Huggins' but Cobb himself, Captain Haydon[2] (his second-in-command) and the rest of the squadron headquarters, and Lieutenant Frank Baker's[3] troop were still somewhere out along the track—probably about 100 yards south of James'.

The main efforts of the cavalry on the 20th were directed towards assessing their position. By wireless James was able to direct artillery and mortar fire on the Japanese ahead of him and give an outline of his circumstances to Major Wilson who, from the rear headquarters still at Huggins', was temporarily commanding the regiment. About 11 a.m. James was in brief communication with Cobb who, with one of his troops, was still somewhere in the vicinity. Cobb asked for his other two troops to be sent forward from Huggins' to join him but Wilson replied that heavy machine-guns commanding the road ruled out any immediate hope of this. James then gave Cobb details of his location and Cobb replied that he would try to join the forward garrison, but no further word came from him. Later it was learnt that, in the darkness of the next dawn, he and his men had begun a wary movement towards James along a drain which bordered the road. The Japanese had this covered, however, shot four of the men, split the little group and pinned all motionless under a merciless sun for the rest of the day. When darkness came again Cobb got his wounded back along the drain. He himself remained alone at the most forward point and his companions never again saw him alive.[4] Command of the little group then fell to Captain Haydon.

Meanwhile James had been settling his men more firmly within their defence and laying out ground strips to guide the aircraft which he hoped might bring him ammunition, batteries for his wireless, and food (his men had only two days' rations with them). Wilson got orders through to him about 4 p.m. to try to send back a patrol to Huggins' with details needed to fill out the scanty picture which the wireless painted. When darkness came James therefore sent off Corporal Morton[5] and Troopers Chesworth[6] and Hancox[7] to swing wide on the western side of the track and then strike eastwards into the road-block. The three men, apprehensive in the midst of the Japanese positions, made slow progress through the dark bush and swamp. By 2 a.m., however, they calculated that they were

---

[2] Capt F. B. Haydon, NX12255. 2/7 Cav Regt; 2/25 Bn; OC 40 Sqn, Air Liaison Sec 1945. Jackeroo-grazier; of Blandford, NSW; b. Murrurundi, NSW, 26 Jun 1916.

[3] Lt F. A. Baker, NX13882; 2/7 Cav Regt. Head storeman; of Bexley, NSW; b. Kogarah, NSW, 2 Nov 1917.

[4] They heard firing and grenading from the point where he was last seen by Trooper E. R. Ebner (of Toowoomba, Qld), Cobb's orderly room clerk. Almost a month later his body was found, with a dead Japanese beside it and a haversack which contained maps and plans, buried beneath Cobb's head, evidently his dying action to prevent these falling into Japanese hands.

[5] Cpl H. A. Morton, MM, NX15895; 2/7 Cav Regt. Jackeroo; of Narrabri, NSW; b. Wahroonga, NSW, 16 Sep 1917. Killed in aircraft accident 2 May 1953.

[6] Tpr G. Chesworth, NX16267; 2/7 Cav Regt. Farm hand; of Williamtown, NSW; b. Williamtown, 15 Aug 1919. Killed in action 21 Dec 1942.

[7] Tpr F. C. G. Hancox, QX38208; 2/7 Cav Regt. Labourer; of Wooloowin, Qld; b. Proserpine, Qld, 3 Jan 1921. Killed in action 21 Dec 1942.

then close to Huggins'. They turned due east on the last short lap of their cat-like journey. But luck then failed them and they stumbled over unseen Japanese positions. A grenade exploded at their feet, its burst smothered by the thick mud. Throwing caution to the winds they plunged ahead behind their own fire. Answering fire met them. Chesworth and Hancox went down before it, but Morton, though hard hit, went leaping on like a stag through the enemy ring. Then, behind the burst of one of his own grenades, he was hit again. "Huggins, are you there? Ham Morton here!" he called despairingly. Friendly voices answered him, the fusillade stopped, and hands dragged him within the Huggins' defences; unknowingly, he had made his last attack on one of the outer American positions and it was American fire which had inflicted his second wound.

The news which Morton brought, and vigorous patrolling from both Huggins' and James' on the 21st and 22nd, added much to the Australians' knowledge of the Japanese dispositions. Nevertheless no junction was made between Huggins' and James', and Haydon's little group remained isolated among the Japanese. James, however, had his men hard at work preparing additional positions to be occupied when the rest of the regiment broke through to him and was most successful in directing artillery and mortar fire on the besieging positions.

At this stage General Vasey brought Brigadier Dougherty of the 21st Brigade across from Gona. In that area, it will be recalled, Dougherty had halted his main operations after the seizure of Haddy's village on the 19th and had settled down to aggressive patrolling to prevent any further Japanese attempts to move east once more from the mouth of the Kumusi.

On the 21st Vasey told Dougherty to leave Lieut-Colonel Challen in command in the Gona area (the troops there to be known as Goforce) and bring his own headquarters and the 39th Battalion across to the Sanananda Track. Dougherty took over Huggins' from the Americans next day, and also took into his command the 49th Battalion and the cavalry. The men of the 39th (temporarily commanded now by Major Anderson[8] while Lieut-Colonel Honner was ill with malaria) were weary and reduced in numbers and could not be expected to do more than garrison Huggins'; the 49th, reduced to a skeleton, were still in the bush a few hundred yards south-east of the road-block, astride the new supply line; the cavalry, although still fresh and eager, had not been much more than half the strength of a battalion when they first arrived, had taken a hard knock and had yet to be concentrated again. The role given to Dougherty was, therefore, a limited one: to maintain the two road-blocks, build up reserves of ammunition and rations, and patrol aggressively; he was not to attempt any large-scale operations.

After Dougherty's arrival Lieutenant Hordern[9] completed his preparations for a strong sortie to James' with "C" Squadron and the two troops

---
[8] Lt-Col A. J. Anderson, DSO, WX1590. 2/16, 39 Bns; CO 24 Bn 1944-45. Gold refiner; of Fimiston, WA; b. Boulder, WA, 19 Nov 1912.
[9] Maj S. Hordern, CMG, OBE, NX34918. 2/7 Cav Regt; 1 Armd Regt. Stock and share broker; of Bellevue Hill, NSW; b. Sydney, 16 May 1910.

which had become separated from Captain Cobb on the 19th. Early on the 23rd these set out to extend the line of approach laid down by the 49th Battalion by swinging wide to the right after they left Huggins' and later chopping westward across the track into James'. Their movement was slow, small patrols feeling ahead of them like questing antennae to find a way through the maze of Japanese defences. When he was about a third of the way out Hordern cast off a troop under Sergeant Davis[1] to form a small perimeter and act as a firm base for patrols to keep sweeping the line which was being opened. A little farther on he established a second such position under Sergeant Batchelor.[2] The main movement then continued, still through a network of abandoned Japanese positions, until finally, with Trooper Pearlman[3] (who had done outstanding scouting work during the whole of the day) probing ahead, Hordern crossed the road and entered James' perimeter — without having lost a man. He found the garrison in excellent heart although they were down to half a tin of emergency rations a day.

On the 24th Hordern returned to Huggins' and it was then decided that the balance of the regiment should move forward to James', leaving at Huggins' the mortar detachment and the medical post. This they did without incident that afternoon, although the passage of the new route was still a nerve-racking experience.

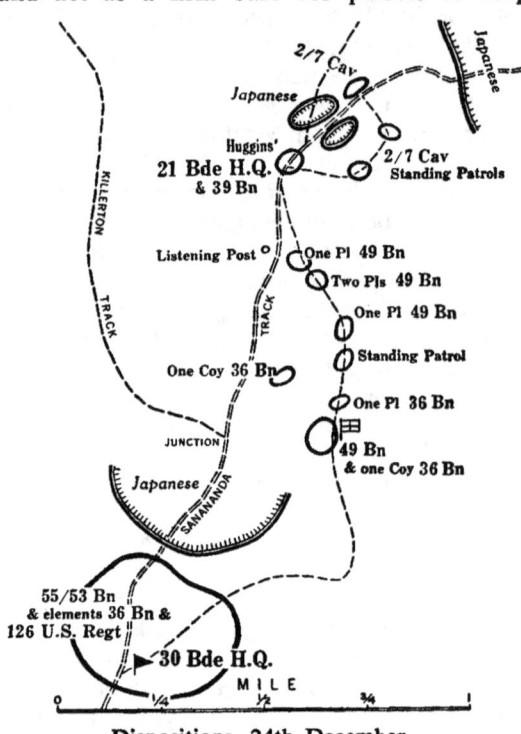

Dispositions, 24th December

It seemed an age before we passed Batchelor's perimeter (wrote Chaplain Hartley[4] afterwards). This little citadel of safety seemed very strange, perched on a small piece of higher ground in the midst of dense undergrowth. They reported all clear as we silently passed. The wink of an eye, the raising of a hand was greeting and

---

[1] Sgt E. J. Davis, NX37219. 2/7 Cav Regt; 2/13 AA Regt, 2/1 Med Regt. Commercial traveller; of Cremorne, NSW; b. Sydney, 12 Jul 1917.
[2] Lt O. H. Batchelor, NX52014. 2/7 Cav Regt; 2/8 Bn; Papuan Inf Bn. Bank officer; of Cronulla, NSW; b. Sydney, 30 Jul 1918.
[3] Tpr H. Pearlman, NX22740. 2/7 Cav Regt; 114 AGT Coy. Wool classer and farmer; of Boggabri, NSW; b. Boggabri, 18 Jan 1913.
[4] Rev F. J. Hartley, VX39632. Chaplain 2/7 Cav Regt, 116 AGH; Senior Chaplain (PD) HQ 7 Div 1943-44. Clergyman; of Ormond, Vic; b. Rutherglen, Vic, 11 Mar 1909. The quotation is from his book, *Sanananda Interlude* (1949), p. 31.

encouragement enough for these silent watchers. . . . As we neared James' the track wound in and out Japanese defences that had been abandoned after James' perimeter had been consolidated. This maze of bunkers and foxholes made us realise how impossible it would have been to supply our perimeter if Nippon had held on to these nests. The strength of these dug-in positions revealed how futile it would have been to try to drive out the enemy without long and sustained attacks. It made us aware too of how precarious was our life line. If the Japs decided to reoccupy their vacated holes the situation would become very critical indeed. The machine-gun nests came right to the road directly opposite the perimeter.

Although the cavalrymen were now concentrated once more, with 19 officers and 205 men at James', their position was most discouraging. After six days of hard fighting they had advanced only some 400 yards and lost 7 officers and 33 men killed with about as many more wounded. But, pending the development of a new battle pattern, they set about fixing themselves more firmly in their new position, actively reconnoitring, and harassing their enemies. Their first job on Christmas Day, however, was to get out the wounded. There were thirteen of these at James', eight of them lying cases for whom rough stretchers had to be made on the spot. Chaplain Hartley wrote later:

> We were astir early and cooked our breakfast. We got over the problem of smoke from our fires by using cordite from the captured enemy shells. . . . It was a slow, tedious and nerve-racking journey. The patients were heavy. Four men were required for each stretcher. These bearers had to carry their arms in their free hands. . . . There were times when, to our strained hearing, the noise along the track sounded like a herd of elephants crashing through the undergrowth. . . . Whenever there was a stop for rest, armed men would penetrate the jungle off the track and silently watch against a possible ambush. . . . As we came nearer to Huggins' it became easier going. . . . We now came into view of the Jap camp that had been shot up on 1st December [30th November]. . . . There were mangled and rotting corpses scattered everywhere. Blank-eyed skeletons stared with sightless eyes from beneath broken shelters. Bones of horses with their saddles and harness rotting round them shone white as the morning sun peering through the creepers caught them in her beams. We actually welcomed this gory sight. It was to us a sign post. It meant that Huggins' was but a hundred yards beyond.[5]

After this party had delivered their wounded at Huggins' they returned to the forward perimeter carrying with them Christmas cheer and mail. The small comforts (including sweets for men who were hungry for sugar) gave the soldiers new strength, and letters from home gave them new heart.

One small group, however, still had no share in even this simple Christmas. Haydon's few men had all this time remained precariously alive in the ditch beside the track forward of Huggins'. The captain, seeing no other way of getting his wounded out of the hornet's nest in which a number had already been killed, had set his men painfully to work, some days before, at digging a narrow crawl trench back to Huggins' under the noses of the enemy. With extraordinary patience the soldiers went on with this work, steadily growing weaker from lack of food and their exertions, but they finally got back to Huggins' on the evening of the 26th after almost eight days of danger and privation.

---

[5] Hartley, p. 35.

At first light on the 29th a sortie took place which was to lead to the only event of more than patrol significance between the time James' perimeter was established and the end of the year. Lieutenant Capp,[6] with a reinforced troop, sallied against a Japanese post sited in the deep bush east of the track, roughly midway between Huggins' and James', and offering a constant threat to the supply-line. Capp's men went in with great dash, cleared trip wires, and took the two outer lines of earthworks in the face of well-directed fire. Then, however, the Japanese opposed them so effectively that they had to withdraw—losing 5 killed and 4 wounded.[7]

When Capp reported that he thought he could have taken the position with more men, Lieut-Colonel C. J. A. Moses, a former officer of the 8th Division who had shared General Gordon Bennett's escape from Singapore earlier in the year, and had arrived on the 27th to take temporary command of the cavalry regiment, told Hordern to take his squadron against the post. Dougherty arranged artillery and mortar support and the start-time was set for 10 a.m. on the 30th. Although the shells fell as planned, the mortar fire was both late and inaccurate. After a revised mortar program Hordern took his men forward at 11. But, no novices at reading signs, the Japanese were ready. They shot 16 of the attackers, all three troop commanders among them, and Hordern knew it would be folly to press the attack further.

New plans were again being made to end the ghastly nightmare which the Sanananda affair had become. The primaeval swamps, the dank and silent bush, the heavy loss of life, the fixity of purpose of the Japanese for most of whom death could be the only ending, all combined to make this struggle so appalling that most of the hardened soldiers who were to emerge from it would remember it unwillingly and as their most exacting experience of the whole war.

After the 19th December had made it clear that the arrival of the two fresh units would still not enable the Australians to sweep a way clear to the sea, Herring visited Vasey on the 20th. The two generals agreed that further major offensive action on this front was not possible with the troops available. Herring said that he would try to bring tanks and fresh infantry into the fight, but that could not happen before the 29th at the earliest. How necessary these were was shown by the figures which Vasey's headquarters prepared three days later as an approximate summary of the strength on the 7th Division's front. They showed that the division had received from 25th November to 23rd December 4,273 troops

---

[6] Lt C. Capp, NX16269. 2/7 Cav Regt; 2/16 Bn. Station hand; of Quirindi, NSW; b. Leura, NSW, 5 Nov 1919.

[7] Among the killed were Tprs W. M. Gray (of Kurrajong, NSW) and T. B. Macadie (Cowra, NSW). After the attack penetrated the perimeter Gray went to help Tpr M. G. Coppock (Moree, NSW), who had been badly hit and had fallen helpless into a hole. As he tried to pull Coppock out Gray was then hard hit himself. Macadie hurried to help them both but was shot down in his turn. The rest of the troop managed to get Coppock clear but the other two died in the hole into which Coppock had first fallen. When, almost a month later, the chaplain buried them he inscribed a rough cross above their bodies "Two Australians who died to save a friend".

to replace 5,905 lost to its front from all causes. Thus Vasey's force was about 1,632 weaker than at the outset.

These figures were particularly disturbing against the background of the entire scene at that time on the Buna-Gona coast. On the right, before Buna itself, the 18th Brigade still had much fighting ahead of them and none could forecast exactly when the situation would be cleared; in the Urbana Force sector the Triangle was still to be reduced and the difficult way through the Government Gardens to the sea lay ahead; Vasey's figures, and the experiences of the 2/7th Cavalry and the 30th Brigade, told the story of Sanananda; on the left the little Goforce could no longer guarantee its ability to carry out even the limited tasks allotted to it. Vasey considered air action the only real protection for his left flank. No further Australian help could come from Port Moresby where no other infantry were left. Possibly the 17th Brigade might come round from Milne Bay but not only would such a move leave a vital point and its adjacent islands and coasts to the protection of one widely-flung brigade, but it would also leave Blamey entirely without means quickly to counter any fresh jab the enemy might make at New Guinea. Could Australia provide more infantry? Of the three A.I.F. infantry divisions the 9th was still in the Middle East; the 7th had been wholly committed in New Guinea and depleted by battle losses and sickness; of the 6th the 16th Brigade had been worn to a shadow in New Guinea, the 17th was at Milne Bay, and the 19th formed the core of the Northern Territory garrison. The militia infantry numbered 18 brigades at this time (two of them of only two battalions). Of these, three brigades had been committed in New Guinea, and three more were destined to arrive there early in 1943; five were in Western Australia, and two in the Northern Territory, forming part of the sparse garrisons of the broad and empty areas from which threats of Japanese landings had not yet lifted. Only five remained to meet military commitments which stretched from the islands north of Cape York (and included the protection of the vital air bases in that northern tip) to Tasmania in the south.

Since, therefore, General Vasey could not finish the fight at Sanananda with what he had, he was compelled to await the end of the Buna fighting so that he might get a transfusion of Australian and American strength from the coastal right flank, or to look for help from American infantry not yet thrown into New Guinea.

At the beginning of the year (as previously mentioned) when the Japanese menace first developed, the first American ground formation sent to Australia had been the 41st Division, and the 32nd Division had followed to compensate for the continued absence from Australia of the 9th Division. The 163rd Infantry—a Montana regiment—of the 41st was on its way to New Guinea in December.[8] The Americans rated the regiment

---

[8] The 1st Montana Volunteer Infantry had served under General Arthur MacArthur in the Philippines at the turn of the century. Subsequently it alternated between State and Federal forces, serving on the Mexican border and, during the 1914-18 War, as a training organisation in France. Its latest entry into Federal service was in September 1940, and it landed in Australia some 18 months later.

"well-trained, and the men, fresh, ably led [by Colonel Jens A. Doe, 'noted for his aggressiveness'] and in superb physical condition, were ready for combat".[9] Blamey was directed that the 163rd should go to the Buna front. He promptly told General MacArthur that it was a pity that he had interfered in a matter within Blamey's sphere; that he did not "for one moment question the right of the Commander-in-Chief to give such orders as he may think fit" but that he believed that nothing could be "more contrary to sound principles of command than that the Commander-in-Chief . . . should [personally] take over the direction of a portion of the battle". The 163rd went to the Sanananda front. Future developments before Sanananda thus depended on the entry into action of these fresh Americans and the successful clearing of the Buna sector. The one might be looked for by the end of the year; the other, it seemed likely, could not take place until early in the New Year and some little time would be required after that for necessary regrouping. Herring wrote an appreciation:

> Enemy is reduced in numbers, short of ammunition, food and supplies, whilst our Air Force and PT boats are preventing any large reinforcements or delivery of supplies. He is weak in artillery, has no tanks and has suffered a series of defeats. He has been attacked by our Air Force and artillery and has no adequate countermeasures. He has had over six weeks to develop his defences and along all good approaches we can expect timber pill-boxes in depth which can only be located by actual contact. He is a determined defensive fighter and fights to the death, taking a heavy toll of attacking troops. He has used guns and Molotov cocktails in the jungle effectively against our tanks. . . . We have practically unchallenged air superiority, whilst our PT boats are effectively protecting our convoys of small craft to Oro Bay and forward to Hariko. Owing to the jungle it is not possible to derive adequate direct and close air support.

A few days later General Berryman wrote down his thoughts—and concluded: "We have air superiority, and are superior in numbers, guns, mortars and tanks. The problem is to use them to the best effect in the jungle." He added that Giruwa-Sanananda appeared to be the main Japanese base—with a hospital at Cape Killerton. Against this main area were three major lines of approach: along the sea shore from Tarakena—but this was reputedly a swamp-bound line which, in places, allowed a passage only a few yards wide, with the sea washing one side and mangrove swamps, deep and stagnant, against the other; along the main road to Sanananda—but this was held in depth by obstinate, entrenched and concealed Japanese; along tracks branching westward from the main road towards the coast west of Sanananda—but these were unfamiliar and the country they traversed was known to be largely covered by rotting marshes.

Herring defined his plans on the 29th December. He wrote that it was his intention to resume intensive operations against the Sanananda-Cape Killerton positions as soon as Buna was reduced. Against Sanananda his fighting formations would be the 7th Division and "Buna Force". To the 7th Division he allotted the 14th, 18th and 30th Brigades and the 163rd Infantry. The three regiments of the 32nd Division would constitute Buna

---

[9] Milner, *Victory in Papua*, pp. 329-30.

Force. The task of the 7th Division would be to capture the Sanananda Point-Cape Killerton position and contain the Japanese in the Amboga River-Mambare River area. Buna Force was to defend the Cape Endaiadere-Buna area from seaborne attack and advance up the coast against the Sanananda defences by way of Tarakena. Additional guns were to be moved across to the Sanananda Track from the Buna area and eight more guns of the 2/1st Field Regiment were to come from Port Moresby by sea. Most of the tanks were to join the 7th Division as soon as the Buna operations ended.

On 4th January, having conferred with Generals Eichelberger, Vasey and Berryman, Herring issued his orders. These required Vasey to begin carrying out his role after two battalions of the 163rd had arrived, but obliged the 32nd Division to begin pressing against Tarakena at once with a view to pushing on along the Tarakena-Giruwa axis.

The Japanese, however, were themselves already forcing something of an issue in the Tarakena area. At dusk that day they rose from the swamps and fell upon the most advanced American positions, which Lieutenant Louis A. Chagnon commanded forward of Siwori, and which, only a few hours before, fresh arrivals had brought up to a strength of 73.

The Americans opened fire blindly and in thirty minutes had exhausted their supply of ammunition. They then withdrew in disorder.[1]

Chagnon's men, having taken to the sea, counted themselves fortunate that all but four were later able to reassemble at Siwori village.

By this time Eichelberger had made Colonel Grose responsible for the westward push, with the 127th Infantry as his main striking force. Grose at once sent Lieutenants McCampbell and James T. Coker with their companies to make good the Tarakena loss. These, after a difficult crossing, were on the west bank of Siwori Creek by 9 a.m. on the 5th and closed with the Japanese, McCampbell following the water-line, Coker wallowing bravely through the swamp on his left. Despite Japanese delaying tactics, they slowly advanced on that and the following days, Lieutenant Powell A. Fraser's company having come forward to help them on the 7th. By nightfall on the 8th, after difficult going (particularly along Coker's axis which still led through clogging swamp) and crisp encounters, the three companies had their enemies at bay at Tarakena. Two fresh companies then came through these tired but satisfied men, and reduced the village before the night was far advanced. Konombi Creek, a tidal stream some 40 feet wide, lay ahead and offered no ready means of crossing. On the 9th Japanese on the far bank successfully disputed the passage and, during the darkness which followed, the swift current frustrated new American attempts. Some brave volunteers then swam the creek in broad daylight and made fast a guy wire on which the two available boats could be warped across. Lieutenant Tally D. Fulmer then led his company over the water, the other company followed, and the bridgehead was

---
[1] Report of the Commanding General Buna Forces on the Buna Campaign, December 1, 1942-January 25, 1943 (General Eichelberger's official report).

firm by the end of the 10th. But this well-earned success turned a little sour when the 11th revealed what lay ahead—"a section where the mangrove swamp comes down to the sea. At high tide the ocean is right in the swamp. . . ."[2] Eichelberger thereupon decided to allow Grose to wait until the drive up the Sanananda Track drew aside the curtain which still concealed what Grose might expect farther on.

Meanwhile, within the framework which Herring had formed, Vasey had elaborated his plans. On 31st December these depended mainly on the arrival of the 163rd Infantry, but the 14th Brigade Headquarters was also arriving from Port Moresby. Lieut-Colonel Matthews,[3] then commanding the 9th Battalion at Milne Bay, was to become temporary commander of 14th Brigade with only the depleted 36th and 55th/53rd Battalions (which properly belonged there) constituting it, the former already reduced by battle and sickness to some 16 officers and 272 men. Vasey planned that, on the 2nd and 3rd January, the 163rd would relieve the headquarters of the 21st Brigade, the 2/7th Cavalry, 39th and 49th Battalions (in and around the road-blocks). The three last-named would then take over from the 36th and 55th/53rd by 3 p.m. on the 4th and make up the 30th Brigade to which the remnants of 126th Infantry were also allotted. After this relief by 6th January, Matthews would move his two thin battalions west of Gona to relieve what remained of the 21st Brigade. Thus, on the 27th December, after disembarking his I/163rd at Port Moresby, Lieut-Colonel Harold L. Lindstrom flew them across the range. By the time the planned regroupings and reliefs were complete the II/163rd (Major Walter R. Rankin)—whose movement over the mountains had been delayed by bad weather—had also arrived; and the 18th Brigade, their task before Buna completed, had crossed country to the vicinity of Soputa. The 18th Brigade numbers were being quickly made up from about 1,000 fresh troops who were being flown in, and though, after their Buna experiences, the "old hands" were under no illusions as to what lay ahead of them, their spirits were high. By the evening of the 7th three tanks, under Captain May and Lieutenant Heap, had arrived at a bivouac area about three miles south of Soputa (with a fourth soon to arrive from Popondetta). The rest of the tanks were weatherbound at Cape Endaiadere by incessant rains and were to move across to the Sanananda Track as soon as possible. The same rains prevented the artillery moves which had been planned but, mainly to lessen the problem of ammunition supply by getting the weapons as close to the sea as possible, the guns of the 2/5th Regiment and the 4.5's were concentrated near Giropa Point, and on the 7th, Major Vickery[4] landed at Oro Bay eight more guns of the 2/1st, which he later brought into action in the Strip Point-Giropa Point area.

---

[2] Milner, p. 338.
[3] Lt-Col G. R. Matthews, DSO, ED, SX1442. 2/10 Bn; CO 9 Bn 1942-45 (Admin Comd 14 Bde Jan-Feb 1942). Public servant; of Hazelwood Park, SA; b. Stepney, SA, 12 Oct 1910.
[4] Brig N. A. Vickery, MBE, MC, ED, NX130. 2/1 Fd Regt; 1 Naval Bombardment group. Clerk; of North Sydney; b. Lakemba, NSW, 28 Jul 1917.

Vasey now planned to have the two newly-arrived American battalions in the road-blocks and astride the Killerton Track (about three-quarters of a mile above its junction with the main track) by nightfall on the 9th, to cut off the most forward Japanese zone (south of Huggins' and north of the 30th Brigade) and harass the Japanese lines of communication. That done he proposed to destroy all the Japanese thus hemmed in. In order to achieve this the 18th Brigade was to take the 2/7th Cavalry under its command and relieve the rest of the 30th Brigade by the morning of the 10th. Vasey directed also that the remnants of the 126th were to be relieved; this was done by the afternoon of the 9th, battle casualties, sickness and the transfer of regimental headquarters to the Buna front having reduced their original 1,400 to a mere 165.

Before that date, however, eager to come to close grips with the Japanese, Colonel Doe asked to be allowed to try to overcome the main positions between the two road-blocks. Forward at James' he had one company plus a platoon; the rest of Lindstrom's battalion was at Huggins'. Now Doe proposed that the company from James' should fall from the north-east upon the Japanese left flank and a company from Huggins' should circle his own left flank and then launch themselves from the west against the Japanese on that side of the road. General Vasey, having dispatched Colonel Pollard to the road-block to ensure that this sally of Doe's would not commit Rankin's II/163rd Battalion, or prevent that battalion from carrying out their Killerton Track role on the 12th, assented to Doe's proposals. When, in the wake of Major Hanson's artillery fire about midday on the 8th, Lindstrom's men went into the attack, they had their first taste of the quality of their opponents, who not only refused to budge but flung back the attackers. A little sobered by this efficient hostility Doe then proceeded to follow the main plan. On the morning of the 9th he sent Rankin to strike across country towards the Killerton Track. Rankin was almost at the trail before he met opposition. Some fire from a near-by strongpoint troubled him, but not sufficiently seriously to retard him, and, as the day advanced, he sited his battalion across the track. Next day the regiment's third battalion marched into the battle area and Doe spread some of the men across the east flank supply-line to Huggins' and settled the rest in the road-block itself.

The practised Wootten, now busy taking over from the 30th Brigade, had set up his headquarters on the road about three-quarters of a mile below the Cape Killerton track junction. On his right Major Parry-Okeden settled the 2/9th Battalion in the area the 49th had been holding, lying in bush and swamp a quarter to half a mile about east and east-south-east of the junction and roughly parallel with the track. Lieut-Colonel Arnold linked the 2/12th's right with Parry-Okeden's left, extended to the track and deployed south-west along it. From Arnold's rearmost position the cavalry then closed the left flank with a series of positions running almost due north on the west of the road to just short of the Killerton Track, half to three-quarters of a mile above the junction. Lieut-Colonel

Geard,[5] who had taken over from Lieut-Colonel Dobbs when the latter went to hospital after Buna, had the 2/10th in reserve in the brigade headquarters area. Thus the Australians closely cupped the Japanese position astride the main road just south of the track junction, while to the north the Americans blocked both escape routes.

The forward battalions tested the defences on the 10th and 11th when patrols probed for information and the commanders tried to crowd some of their men even closer to the Japanese; but these reacted sharply and flicked the patrols back with minor but stinging losses (9 killed and 19 wounded). Wootten's immediate plan was to have the 2/9th and 2/12th clear the junction and the road to about a quarter of a mile beyond. Knowing his opponents, however, he entertained few hopes that he might achieve this with one blow and planned, therefore, for separate phases. The first, on the 12th, envisaged a closure towards the junction — a simultaneous attack by the two battalions on opposite sides of the Japanese defences with, on the right, the 2/9th thrusting southwest, and on the left the 2/12th closing on to the road from the east and driving along it at the same time. Three tanks were to

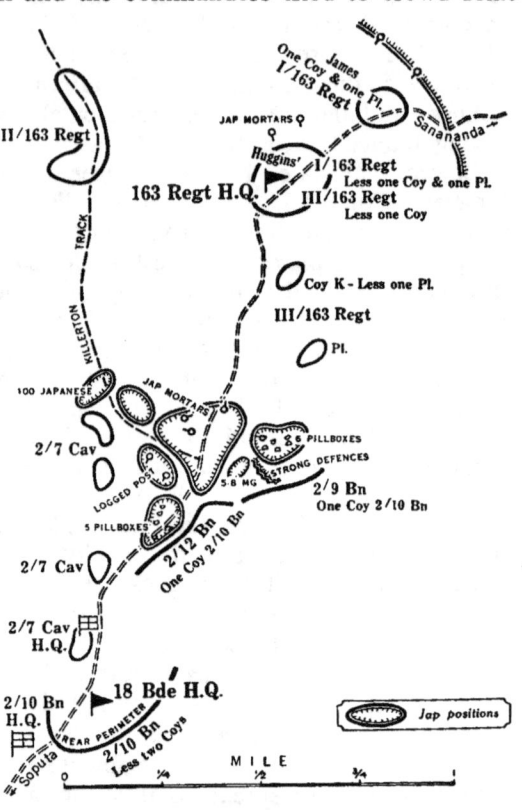

Dispositions, 8 a.m. 12th January

help the 2/12th, a company from the 2/10th would strengthen each of the attacking units, while the rest of the battalion, the cavalry, one tank and the mortars of the two battalions would be a reserve.

In the morning mist on the 12th, through the swampy bush, Parry-Okeden sent his two attacking companies of the 2/9th, Lieutenants Jackson's[6] and Lloyd's,[7] to circle his own right flank and get into position

---

[5] Lt-Col C. J. Geard, TX2013. 2/12 Bn; CO 2/10 Bn 1943-44. Farmer; of New Norfolk, Tas; b. New Norfolk, 8 Jun 1910.

[6] Lt G. K. Jackson, QX372; 2/9 Bn. Naturalist; of Brisbane; b. Sth Brisbane, 12 Jun 1914. Killed in action 12 Jan 1943.

[7] Lt P. A. Lloyd, NX103594; 2/9 Bn. Wool classer; of Darling Point, NSW; b. Richmond, Surrey, England, 23 Nov 1918. Killed in action 12 Jan 1943.

Australian infantrymen move forward through a group of Americans to take up the fight at Sanananda.

(*Australian War Memorial*)

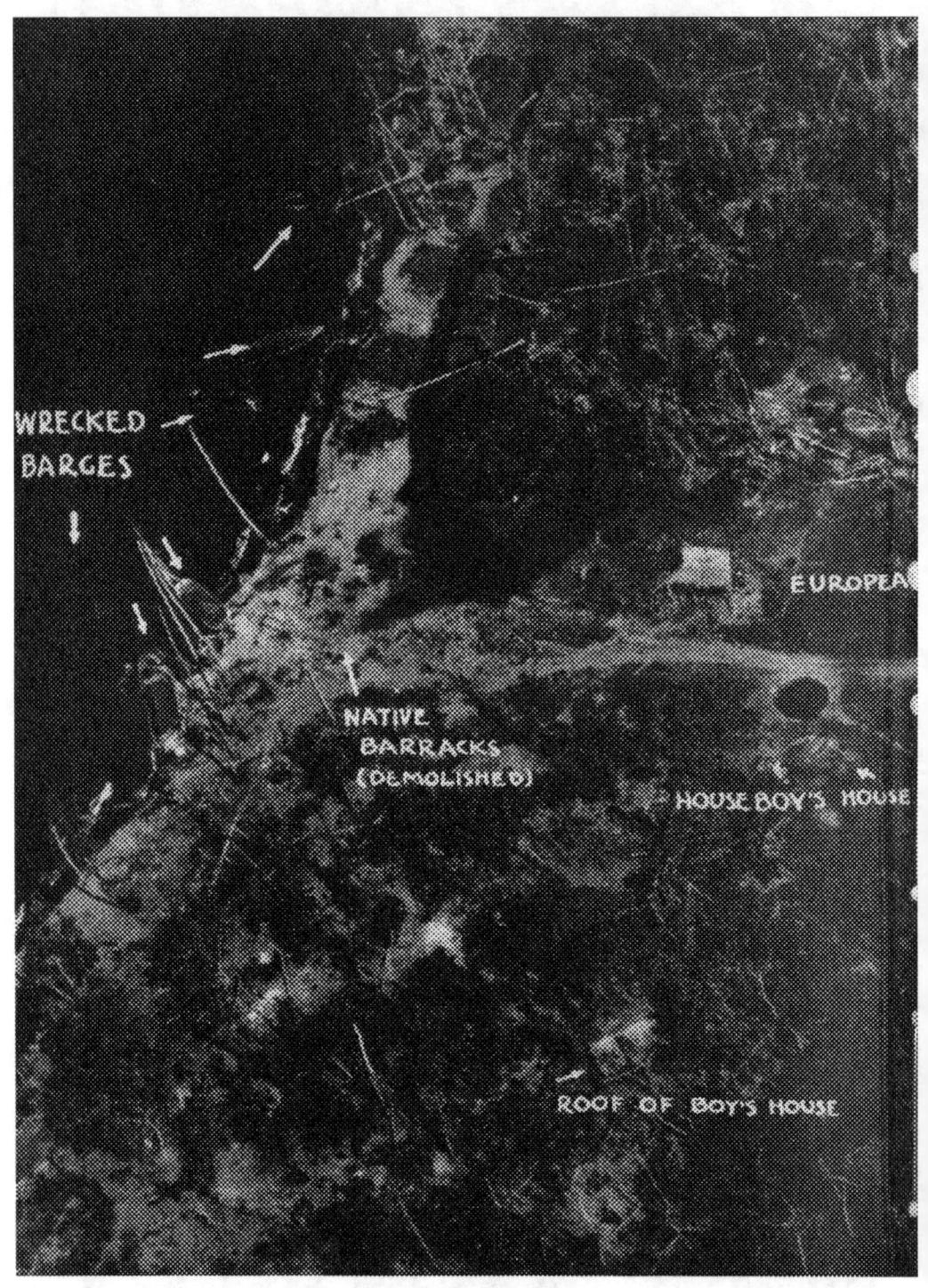

Sanananda. Its fall marked the end of the fighting in Papau
soldiers who survived

(Allied Air Forces S.W.P.A.)

and the end of an experience which none of the hardened
it will ever forget.

(*Australian War Memorial*)

An Australian section post on the Sanananda Track, less than 30 yards from Japanese positions.

(*Australian War Memorial*)

Water, mud and slush were inseparable companions of the Allied troops during the advance on Sanananda.

roughly north-east of the road junction. The other two companies remained generally east and south-east of the junction, their initial task being to support the attack with fire to the west, their later task to close the left flank and harass the Japanese ahead of them. At 8 a.m. Jackson crossed his line, precisely on time, and his men started killing the scattered outer defenders. On his left, however, Lloyd was delayed a little at first and then found his way very difficult in the face of a punishing fire. For a time Jackson held back his advance to allow the other company to keep pace but, despite that, was among the line of trees which constituted his objective by 9.30 a.m. Lloyd then succeeded in getting farther forward and linked with Jackson's left. The other two companies maintained the battalion front by pressing forward on Lloyd's left. The men dug in, having substantially achieved their object for the day (although the hard core of the defences was still solid on the track) for a loss of 6 officers, including Jackson and Lloyd who were both killed, and 27 men. They were still linked on the left with the 2/12th.

That battalion's day, however, had gone wrong from the beginning, when the tanks began to cross the start-line at one minute past eight. The tank crews had been told that there were no anti-tank guns to hinder them and that their task was to knock out the Japanese bunkers, but no one could tell them where those bunkers were. The road ahead was a narrow defile through the swamps, the ground flanking its raised surface so soft that no tank could travel on it, the track itself so narrow that there seemed to be no hope of any tank turning once it had crossed the line. Thus there seemed to be one way only for them—straight on—when Lieutenant Heap led his troop out in line ahead, with Corporal Boughton's[8] tank some 20 yards behind him, and Sergeant MacGregor's[9] following at the same interval. After he had gone about 60 yards Heap stopped, peering left towards a point where he had been told he might find a bunker, his tank's gun traversing slowly to the left. A shell struck the front of his tank, ricochetted on to the driver's flap—which it sprung wide—and stunned the driver, whose forehead was pressed against the wall just above the aperture. Heap then saw the gun flash (though he was never able to see the gun itself) from a concealed position about 40 yards to his right front and a second shell struck the track. A third hit followed, springing the hull gunner's flap and stunning the gunner. By this time Heap had swung his own gun round and was briskly engaging the enemy, though he still had only a general idea of where the other gun might be. A fourth shell then smashed through the vehicle and burst inside it. The only way Heap could now escape was to take the risk of getting off the track. He therefore wirelessed Boughton that he was doing this and plunged into the bush on his left. Boughton's tank then went ahead but, in its turn, was hammered badly by the enemy gun before it could get

---

[8] Cpl C. G. Boughton, NX38452; 2/6 Armd Regt. Labourer; of Pallamallawa, NSW; b. Moss Vale, NSW, 19 Feb 1914. Died of wounds 12 Jan 1943.
[9] Sgt K. A. MacGregor, NX56166; 2/6 Armd Regt. Barrister and solicitor; of Wollstonecraft, NSW; b. Newcastle, NSW, 5 Jun 1912. Killed in action 12 Jan 1943.

off a shot at its unseen enemy, and Boughton was mortally wounded. It now seemed that, blinded and partly crippled and caught within the narrow confines of the track, the tank was doomed. But the driver, Lance-Corporal Lynn,[1] was brave and cool. He peered through a gaping shell hole in the broken vehicle and performed the seemingly-impossible feat of turning about on the roadway, and the tank limped out of the fight. Undaunted, Sergeant MacGregor next closed in. He was not long engaged, however, before flame exploded round his vehicle, probably in part at least from a mine pushed beneath it on the end of a forked stick, and the tank itself was seen to be on fire. It was gutted and the crew perished, but precisely how each died is uncertain still for the fog of battle then closed them round and when the burnt-out tank was examined later no trace of their bodies was found.

These misfortunes stamped out the day's pattern for Arnold's infantry. His plan had been that Captain Trinick's[2] and Captain Curtis' companies should attack up the road with the tanks, with the other two companies moving forward in support from the right of the road. But Trinick himself (who had just "wangled" his way back to the battalion after he had been declared medically unfit for front-line service) was mortally wounded, and his company was unable to advance. On the left, Curtis, whose company's movement was to be the major one, made three desperate attempts to get ahead, but each time his men were driven back beyond the startline. The tangled branches of trees which had been torn and twisted by artillery fire proved one of their greatest obstacles; they were caught in these as though in masses of barbed wire. So the 2/12th had scarcely advanced at all by the end of the day, and had lost 4 officers and 95 men. They were so close to the Japanese that carrying parties had great difficulty in getting food to them. When hot food was brought forward much of it had to be thrown into the forward pits from a point near company headquarters.

The Australian commanders were bitterly disappointed at the apparent failure of this day. Vasey wearily took counsel with Wootten at 18th Brigade Headquarters in the evening. As a result he decided to seek the views of General Eichelberger to whom had passed the command of the force in the forward area.[3] Next day Eichelberger, Vasey, Berryman (who was acting as Eichelberger's chief of staff) and Pollard discussed the situation and sharp differences of opinion seem to have developed as various ways out of the impasse were examined. Vasey himself had decided that:

> As a result of the attack by 18 Aust Inf Bde on 12 Jan 43, it is now clear that the present position which has been held by the Jap since 20 Nov 42 consists of a series of perimeter localities in which there are numerous pill-boxes of the same type as those found in the Buna area. To attack these with infantry using their

---

[1] Cpl F. R. T. Lynn, MM, NX43691; 2/6 Armd Regt. Farmer and grazier; of Glen Innes, NSW; b. Glen Innes, 20 Jan 1910.
[2] Capt J. A. J. Trinick, VX9548; 2/12 Bn. Commercial artist; of Camberwell, Vic; b. Hawthorn, Vic, 15 Jan 1918. Died of wounds 26 Jan 1943.
[3] Herring had returned to Port Moresby that day; and on the 13th Blamey returned to Australia.

own weapons is repeating the costly mistakes of 1915-17 and, in view of the limited resources which can be, at present, put into the field in this area, such attacks seem unlikely to succeed.

The nature of the ground prevents the use of tanks except along the main Sanananda Track on which the enemy has already shown that he has A-Tk guns capable of knocking out the M3 light tank.

Owing to the denseness of the undergrowth in the area of ops, these pill-boxes are only discovered at very short ranges (in all cases under 100 yards) and it is therefore not possible to subject them to arty bombardment without withdrawing our own troops. Experience has shown that when our troops are withdrawn to permit of such bombardment, the Jap occupies the vacated territory so that the bombardment, apart from doing him little damage, only produces new positions out of which the Jap must be driven.

Vasey considered it best either to advance to Cape Killerton and thence eastwards along the coast by the Killerton Track, provided supplies could be landed by sea, or to land additional troops in some strength from the sea in the Killerton area, although he realised that he lacked the resources to carry out such a plan.

Berryman on the other hand was convinced that a close blockade of the Japanese positions south of the road-blocks was the most practicable solution. Eichelberger, though generally in agreement with this view, approached this proposal rather more cautiously, and Vasey and Pollard shied away from it. Nevertheless, preliminary orders to establish the blockade were issued and, next day, Berryman had prepared detailed orders (which, however, Eichelberger held over pending the receipt of detailed reconnaissance reports from Vasey's patrols on the 15th). On the 14th Vasey wrote unhappily to Herring:

> Doubtless you have heard of the lack of success of the attack of 18 Aust Inf Bde on 12 Jan and also of my interview with Eichelberger and Berryman yesterday.
> The position is that George's [Wootten's] attack drove in all the outposts in front of the enemy pill-boxes and has disclosed some of them to our sight. 30 Aust Inf Bde, unfortunately, was unable to do this. In view of this situation I feel that it is useless carrying out further attacks supported by tanks (for use of which the country is quite unsuitable, as evidenced by the very early loss of two out of the three employed) and in an area where the distance between our foremost troops and these pill-boxes varies from 20 to 80 yards. It was in view of this that I asked Eichelberger to come and see me yesterday. I attach some notes which I prepared for him. From these you will see that the present intention to encircle closely the Jap opposite 18 Aust Inf Bde is not one of the courses which I thought open to me. While I agree that this course may in time succeed in reducing those immediately in front of us, I feel that it is hardly within the spirit of my instructions which were and, as far as I know, still are to capture Sanananda beach area.

However, the situation was being resolved. A sick and bedraggled prisoner reported on the morning of the 14th that on the night of the 12th-13th (i.e. immediately after the Australian attack) the Japanese defenders of the position south of the road-blocks had been ordered to withdraw all their fit men leaving only the sick and wounded to hold the positions to the last. On the 13th, however, further orders followed: that the positions should be completely abandoned during darkness on the 13th-14th. This information was already being confirmed by the lack of opposition to Australian patrols; and Wootten's men were seeping so quickly into the area that, by nightfall of the 14th, the entire road junction area was in their hands. Vasey at once ordered Wootten to pursue his retreating enemies with speed; to push down the Killerton Track to the coast and seize the Cape Killerton area with a view to attacking Sanananda and the track from the west. Doe's Americans were to destroy the Japanese in their immediate vicinity and then advance directly along the Sanananda Track. Behind these main movements the cavalry were to clean up, and the 30th Brigade was to protect the Soputa-Jumbora dumps. The 14th Brigade was to continue to hold the left flank and cut off any Japanese moving westward.

The 14th Brigade men had had a strange week in the Gona area. They were deployed from Garara on the east of Gona to the mouth of the Amboga River, leaving the 21st Brigade free to move out on the 7th to Popondetta, from which point, and Dobodura, they emplaned for Port Moresby with only 217 left in the whole brigade. When the 36th Bat-

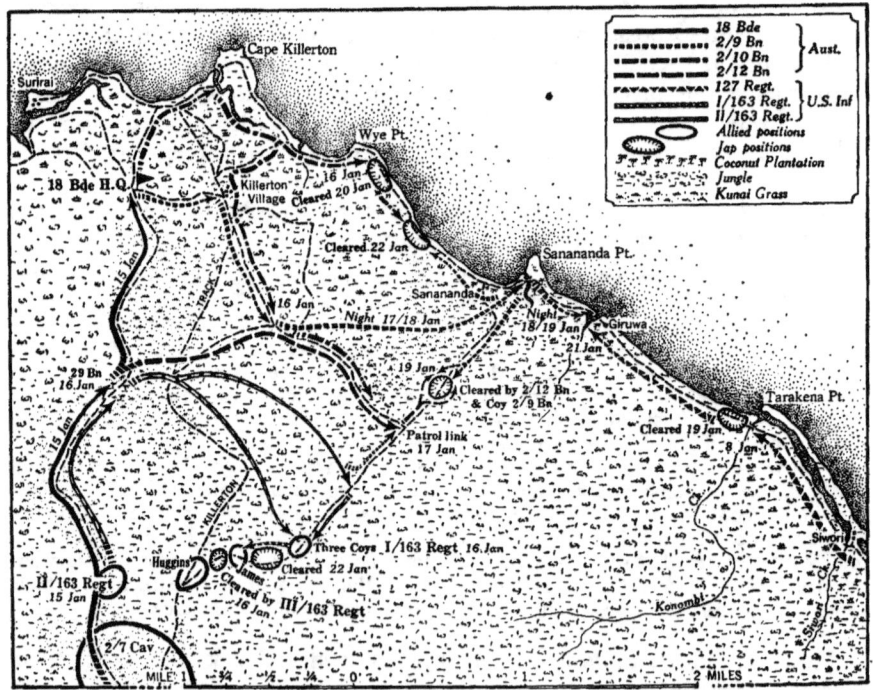

Final operations along Sanananda Track, 15th-22nd January

talion took over along the Amboga River they were told that the Japanese had an observation post across the river from Haddy's village and probably 300 men a little farther back on the western side of the Amboga; the Japanese were passive and made no attempt to fire on the Australians unless they tried to cross the river. A reconnaissance patrol of the 36th attempted this on the night of the 4th-5th January but found the Japanese wakeful and lost one man. A fighting patrol, rafting across the river next day, found the defenders still alert and lost several men killed and wounded. The 36th then settled down to harassing their enemies with fire and patrolling widely for flanking approaches. But though they crossed the river several times the spreading swamps blocked their closing movements. On the 12th, however, a determined patrol crossed at the river's mouth, met no opposition and pushed on some distance along the coast. Their way led them through defensive positions and freshly-abandoned camps, which they estimated had been occupied by at least a battalion, but they met no Japanese. Other patrols followed on the 13th and 14th, but all returned with reports that the Japanese were leaving the Kumusi regions also. Barges were taking them away, the natives said, aircraft were bombing them and P.T. boats were attacking them at night. It was clear that any threat on the left flank had dissolved. There was, therefore, no risk when Lieut-Colonel Isaachsen, in obedience to orders received on the morning of the 14th, pulled back the bulk of the battalion to defend the Gona-Jumbora track against Japanese fleeing from the main battle area. North of them the 55th/53rd, who had already collected more than fifty Rabaul natives who had abandoned the Japanese, were awaiting Japanese moving along the coast.

Swift in execution, Wootten began his approach on Cape Killerton at 7 a.m. on the 15th, the 2/10th Battalion forming his advance-guard. Until shortly before noon the 2/10th moved fast along the track until it petered out among bush and swamp. The companies wallowed separate ways in search of it and Killerton village, which was lost to them in the forbidding marshes and tangled scrub. Nightfall found them still below the coast, perched in trees like wet fowls, or lying in water.

> Next morning (as Major Trevivian recalled it) we pushed on through the bloody mangrove swamps. It was the hardest job I ever had in the army. Sometimes the water was over our heads, most times up to our arm-pits. Our rate of progress was about 100 yards an hour and we had to cut down pieces of mangrove to get the stores across. At that stage we were carrying ammunition, mortars and the heavy stuff—and I would like to record the sterling job that the mortar chaps did in that show. If there is one bunch of fellows I had respect for it was the mortars. Eventually we struck a track which ran along the beach and ultimately into Killerton village. We came on to that right by a Japanese position. The Japs were sunbaking at the time and it was a toss-up who got the biggest surprise. . . . In the meantime, while the battalion was pushing along the coast, Cook's[4] company was sent off to find Killerton village. Until we found it we couldn't accurately determine where we were. Nothing seemed to make sense as far as our maps and photographs were concerned. Eventually an aircraft was sent out to help but by that time we were on the objective and the thing was plain sailing.

The battalion (less Captain Cook's company) then combed the coastline across the cape, struck at one or two isolated enemy parties and camped for the night with their most advanced company, Captain Wilson's, at

---

[4] Lt-Col F. W. Cook, DSO, MC, SX1225; 2/10 Bn. Laboratory assistant; of Firle, SA; b. Southampton, England, 12 May 1918.

Wye Point (a little more than a third of the way from Cape Killerton to Sanananda Point) and Wilson's patrols flicking at Japanese outposts 200 to 300 yards farther along the coast. These were obviously guarding strong positions for, when Trevivian's company passed through Wilson's in the dawn of the 17th, they were sharply checked after 200 or 300 yards and drew back in the afternoon to allow the mortars to drop 45 rounds on the defences.

By this time the whole brigade was closing in on the main defence area. After Cook of the 2/10th had left his battalion on the morning of the 16th he led his company to a point almost two miles south-east of Killerton village from which he felt eastward for the Sanananda Track. By evening he was close to it. Wootten thereupon decided that the 2/12th should strike at the road along that line, and Arnold, with two companies, should thrust eastward from the Killerton Track through the last light and early darkness and come up with Cook about 8.30 p.m. and take him under command. Drenching rain fell during the night, with lightning hurtling through it, striking into the swamp water and shocking some of the men sharply. It so raised the level of the swamps that water lapped high about every movement of the Australians next morning. In the early light the rest of Arnold's battalion joined him, leaving at the coconut grove the 39th Battalion which had come forward as the pivot in the communications line. The quest for the track then got under way again in a neck-deep torrent. By 11.30 a.m., however, Captain Ivey's company were through this and astride the road, firing intermittently at Japanese who tried to pass them, and Cook's men were astride it a little farther to the south, shooting their way northwards to link with Ivey. During the remainder of the day most of the rest of the battalion reached the road and, when night came, they were holding about 300 yards of it.

Not only did nightfall of the 17th find the 2/12th (with Captain Cook's company) in position on the track above the Japanese who were still holding the Americans farther south, and the main body of the 2/10th pressing down the coastline from Wye Point to Sanananda Point, but it also found the 2/9th significantly poised. As with the 2/12th, Wootten used the 2/9th to penetrate through country which could reasonably be regarded by the Japanese as a sufficient obstacle in itself and which he could, therefore, expect to be less heavily defended than other lines of approach. Accordingly he sent Major Parry-Okeden south-east from brigade headquarters, just west of the village, on the 17th and then, from the area where Cook had bivouacked on the 16th, north-east towards Sanananda Point itself. With the darkness Parry-Okeden then settled his men defensively in a large kunai patch about three-quarters of a mile in a straight line south-west of Sanananda Point. Next morning, after a night in which some ten inches of rain poured down, his men ploughed through mud and water up to their waists, crushed two strongpoints, cleared Sanananda village and point, and established one company ("A") at the mouth of the river at Giruwa, for the loss of one killed and two wounded. They killed 21 of their enemies, made prisoner 22 Japanese and Koreans and 21 coolies (most of them forced labourers from Hong Kong). "C" Company then swung southward along the Sanananda Track to help the 2/12th, cleared out two separate foci of resistance, but were held by a third with night coming on.

Reaching towards these men along the track from the south Arnold had opened the day by starting Curtis' company of the 2/12th up the right of the track and Lieutenant Clarke, now commanding the company in place of Trinick, up the left. They advanced a cautious 200 to 300 yards without interference, but then Clarke's men came against such determined opposition that, although they tried themselves against it in three distinct movements during the day, it remained obdurately in their path. And, on the right, although at first an easier passage than the left had seemed to be offering, Arnold deployed his other three companies without success during a day which cost him thirty-four casualties.

When his patrols reported early on the 19th that all the Japanese positions fronting them were still manned in strength, Arnold planned to use Cook's company to try to break the deadlock on his left flank. Cook thereupon led his men forward at 8.50 a.m. and soon afterwards shot his success signal into the sky. Arnold himself wrote admiringly of this exploit:

> The successful attack by "A" Company 2/10th Battalion on left flank was one of the outstanding features of this phase of the campaign. The position held by the Japs was almost entirely surrounded by water more than shoulder deep, except for small tongue of dry land about 15 yards wide and which was covered by enemy LMG fire. Under cover of a mortar bombardment this company infiltrated by twos and threes along this tongue forming up within 25 yards of the enemy. On a given signal they pushed forward with the bayonet under their own hand grenade barrage. The enemy resistance collapsed and the company advanced 500 yards killing 150 Japs many of whom were hiding in huts and captured three large dumps of medical and other stores. As in many other cases enemy wounded engaged our troops and had to be shot. This may give rise in the future to Jap propaganda but they are doing it so consistently that our troops cannot take any chances.

After this skilful action Arnold pressed forward west of the road to make contact with "B" Company of the 2/9th, which had taken over the forward positions from "C" Company early that morning. On the east of the road, however, the Japanese still refused to give way despite thrusts from the north by the 2/9th men and from the south by Captain Harvie's[5] and Ivey's companies of the 2/12th.

These closing stages of the Sanananda struggle were made more horrible by the drenching rains and swollen swamps. Only the raised surface of the track rose above loathsome mud and water through which every movement had to be made. The struggle went on with movement on either side slowed as if by the leaden weights of a nightmare. With such movements did the men of the 2/12th and the 2/9th seek to link on the 20th. About the middle of the morning each of these groups drew back to allow the gunners to try to smash the defences. After that "C" Company of the 2/9th pushed once more through the slime from the north against the

---
[5] Capt T. G. A. Harvie, ED, QX6137; 2/12 Bn. Shop assistant; of Mackay, Qld; b. Mackay, 30 Jul 1910.

remaining track positions while Arnold sent in Harvie's and Ivey's companies from the south and, when they could make little headway, pushed Cook's company through them. But Cook likewise was checked and, although night found a ring closed round the Japanese defences by the linking of the two battalions on the east of the road, the last of the defenders still refused to die or yield. The toll they were exacting was mounting in a ghastly fashion, for the Australians along the track were losing some 50 or 60 men in killed and wounded each day, Cook's company alone having lost 51 in his attacks of the 19th and 20th. On the 21st, however, Arnold rang down the curtain over this scene of mud, filth and death. His patrols reported early that morning that there was little opposition to be met, and then an emaciated prisoner confessed that only sick and wounded remained within the defences. The Australians closed in and 100 Japanese fell before them, while swollen and discoloured corpses of a hundred previously killed bumped against them in the swamp water or protruded from the obscene mud. The sickened Arnold wrote:

> Since January 17 the battalion has been working in the worst possible country. Both flanks of the MT road are running rivers beyond which is nothing but jungle swamp. The road has been built up several feet with the surface of corduroy. In most places it becomes a causeway. As the result of our aircraft bombing large gaps occur through which the rivers run making all movement difficult particularly the supply of food and evacuation of wounded. The whole area, swamps and rivers included, are covered with enemy dead and the stench from which is overpowering. It is definitely the filthiest area I have ever set eyes upon. In a great many cases the Japanese bodies have been fly-blown and others reduced almost to skeletons.

The Australians had no wish to linger. In the early afternoon they went on up the road to the Sanananda-Giruwa coast where the 2/9th and 2/10th were still at work, while, from the east, the Americans were closing in.

A long pause had followed the crossing of Konombi Creek, before the Americans tried to resume their advance on the 16th under Colonel Howe. But the Japanese were still alert and stopped them with well-sited weapons which commanded the narrow approaches, and the whole surrounding country remained most inhospitable.

> This damn swamp up here (said Howe) consists of big mangrove trees, not small ones like they have in Australia, but great big ones. Their knees stick up in the air . . . as much as six or eight feet above the ground, and where a big tree grows it is right on top of a clay knoll. A man or possibly two men can . . . dig in a little bit, but in no place do they have an adequate dug-in-position. The rest of this area is swamp that stinks like hell. You step into it and go up to your knees. That's the whole damn area, except for the narrow strip on the beach. I waded over the whole thing myself to make sure I saw it all. . . . There is no place along that beach that would not be under water when the tide comes in.[6]

Eichelberger, considering these and other remarks of Howe's, told him that he might bring forward practically all of the 127th if he desired, and Howe set about pressing forward again on the 17th. But still he could measure his advance in yards only. Next day, however, resistance

---

[6] Quoted in Milner, *Victory in Papua*, pp. 353-4.

weakened, and, on the 19th, with the aid of a 37-mm gun, the Americans virtually broke what opposition remained. On the 20th they took several machine-guns and a number of emaciated and dysentery-racked prisoners, and the late afternoon found them approaching Giruwa while, beyond it, they could see Australians of the 2/9th Battalion who had been at the river's mouth since the 18th. Only sporadic shots met the Americans as they walked into Giruwa on the 21st. All about them in this part of the main Japanese base was death and desolation. In what had been the Japanese 67th Line of Communications Hospital

> the scene was a grisly one. Sick and wounded were scattered through the area, a large number of them in the last stages of starvation. There were many unburied dead, and . . . "several skeletons walking around". There was evidence too that some of the enemy had been practising cannibalism. Even in this extremity the Japanese fought back. Twenty were killed in the hospital area resisting capture; sixty-nine others, too helpless to resist, were taken prisoner.[7]

While the Americans had been approaching Giruwa, "A" Company of the 2/9th had been killing fugitives attempting to cross the river by night and had seen barges coming in the darkness and taking off detachments of the garrison. Two of Parry-Okeden's other companies (as has been seen) had been attacking alternately down the track while the fourth had been probing westward to help the 2/10th whose attempts to clear the coastline from Wye Point had been bitterly contested since the 17th.

On the two following days Trevivian, leading the forward company, found himself trying to edge ahead along a narrow strip of beach with the sea on one side and impenetrable swamp on the other. At high tide the strip might be twelve feet wide; at low tide it shrank to about two. The Australians found it impracticable to dig themselves in because seepage filled the holes almost as soon as they got beneath the surface of the sand. A man seeking cover would find himself with his head under water. The patrols were constantly at work trying to go round the right flank but the swamps defeated them. Typical was one fine attempt which progressed almost precisely 100 yards in four hours. The gunners did what they could but most of their shells fell into the sea or uncomfortably close to the Australian infantry. The only really effective help Trevivian could get was from the mortars. These were being fought with grim determination by Lieutenant Scott,[8] a recently-arrived reinforcement officer. His bombs, which had to be carried forward from the village, were rationed, but he and Trevivian developed a technique of movement which alone enabled the advance to continue. Scott would lay down his bombs, Trevivian's men would seize another few yards of ground in their wake and then lie pinned beneath the Japanese fire until more bombs were brought forward. Two days were thus consumed. On the 20th, however, behind an effective mortar and artillery barrage Trevivian's men gained about 500 yards, capturing several machine-guns, with their ammunition, and killing

---
[7] Milner, p. 363.
[8] Capt R. J. Scott, SX13538. RAAF 1939-41; 2/10 Bn. Assistant buyer; of Glenelg, SA; b. Sydney, 31 Aug 1915.

some 40 Japanese, though the Australian losses about equalled those of their enemies. Among the Japanese dead was the lieut-colonel who had been commanding a dual-purpose gun which had been the Australians' chief worry. Trevivian killed him as he stood dazed beneath a small Japanese flag which he had tacked to a mangrove, his sword at the ready. Although the Australians did not get the gun itself it worried them less after that. None the less they were well held again from 8 a.m. onwards. Then, as the morning advanced, they withdrew to allow Parry-Okeden's mortars to come into play from the other side of the sorely-beset Japanese pocket. These still did not break the Japanese will and, in trying to move forward, Trevivian's company were once more blocked although, tantalisingly, they could see men of the 2/9th less than 300 yards away. Geard then brought forward Captain Matheson's company and got them round his right flank to come under Parry-Okeden.

Brigadier Wootten now planned the destruction of the men he had at bay. He ordered Parry-Okeden to push his own men into the pocket from the south-east next day while Matheson's men converged from the north-west. A carefully planned artillery program was to precede the movement, which Wootten timed to begin at 9.30 a.m. on the 21st. These plans went awry, however, when the guns failed to find the target area, and it was not until the 22nd that the two battalions swept the last resistance away and reported at 1.15 p.m. that they had joined forces and organised resistance along the coast was ended.

During this week, it will be recalled, the Americans of the 163rd Regiment had been operating on the track in the rear of the 2/12th Battalion. On the 15th Colonel Doe had some of his men at work trying to clear out the main Japanese pocket beside the track between Huggins' and James'. But, despite the Americans' best efforts and the fact that they got right among the defences, these were still untaken when Vasey arrived at Huggins' about noon. He had been expecting Doe to thrust northward along the track but had waited in vain for news that this was happening —or indeed for any news at all of the American intentions. Now he came to find out for himself. He felt that Doe had been slow and urged more decisive action, saying that this would result in fewer casualties than a hesitant approach. He hoped that the northward advance would begin not later than 7.30 a.m. on the 16th. Doe thereupon proceeded to arrange his companies in the area of the road-blocks into battalion groups so that he had the I and III Battalions concentrated there. His II Battalion was still on the Killerton Track which it had followed in the wake of the Australians to the vicinity of the coconut plantation. His orders for the 16th envisaged a drive up the west of the road from James' by Lindstrom's battalion, a flanking thrust south-east to the Sanananda Track by Rankin from his positions near the Killerton Track, and reduction of the remaining Japanese positions between Huggins' and James' by his third battalion. He looked for artillery support from Manning and Hall, mortar support from fifteen 81-mm's which he had massed in Huggins', and assistance from two of the tanks which had arrived from Cape Endaiadere.

But these anticipations were not very soundly based because the first intimation that the staff of the 7th Division had of Doe's requirements was when they received a copy of his orders late on the 15th. Lieutenant McCrohon of the tanks was sent forward to the Americans late that day to reconnoitre the area of the attack at first light on the 16th. It was at once clear to him, however, that no tanks could move through the bogs and water along the line that Doe was to follow.

Thus without tanks, but after a night of harassing artillery fire on the Japanese positions north of James' and in the immediate wake of fifteen minutes of an intense artillery and mortar bombardment, Lindstrom sent three companies northward round the western edge of the Japanese positions. Although one was quickly forced to ground and was being torn by a vicious fire, the other two got clear of opposition, rounded the defences and established themselves on the road north of these. There the third company later joined them in a perimeter position. Meanwhile Rankin's battalion, breaking bush from the north-west, had cleared out a number of isolated parties and settled on the track—some north of Lindstrom's three companies, some south. And to the rear of both of these units the III Battalion completed the reduction of the pocket between Huggins' and James' from which most of the defenders had flown. This, and the completion of mopping up by the Australian cavalry, finally cleared the whole area south of James'. The entire day cost the 163rd 22 killed and 27 wounded which brought their casualties for the 16th and 17th to 29 killed and 37 wounded.

At 8.30 that night Vasey sent Colonel Pollard to Doe to tell him of the results of the day's movements by the 18th Brigade. That brigade was then closing on the track and the coast farther north, and Vasey was anxious to use the M.T. road to supply them, instead of the difficult and circuitous tracks to the west. He told Pollard, therefore, to urge Doe to get on with all speed. The Americans, however, did not gain any ground next day, though they lost only one killed and three wounded. This annoyed Wootten, and news during the afternoon that one of the patrols of the 163rd had come up with the 2/12th Battalion, by that time straddling the track north of the Japanese fronting Doe, provoked him to telephone divisional headquarters.

> He [Wootten] stated that he understood the role of this regiment was to protect his right flank and rear in his advance on Sanananda and not that his units were responsible for protecting them overnight while they bivouacked. He requested that action be taken immediately to see that the regiment carried out its role and relieved his troops for the task allotted them.

Next day Vasey discussed with Eichelberger what he considered to be a "lack of offensive spirit of 163rd", and the point beyond which he did not feel it his duty to push his authority over them. Then the two set out to see Doe. Eichelberger wrote later:

> We went up the Sanananda Trail. American soldiers were lying across the road and firing; there was also American and Japanese firing behind us. . . . Vasey and I . . . crawled down into a trench. This was Doe's command post. It had a roof

of sorts and revetments to protect it. I said, "Where are the Japs?" Doe answered, "Right over there. See that bunker?" I saw it and Vasey saw it, and it was only fifty yards away. Doe was in the front line and so were we. He gave us some hot tea and then went on with the attack. Vasey was satisfied with Doe's determination and so was I.[9]

However, although they lost thirty men, the American position was little improved by the end of the day, and it was not until midday on the 22nd, after savage fighting and for the loss of nearly 100 more men, that they eliminated the Japanese who remained so stubbornly between James' and the positions Rankin and Lindstrom had established on the 16th.

Though the 22nd thus saw the end of the Sanananda struggle, Japanese still remained in the area. Many had been taken off by barge during the preceding nights, some had swum or drifted round the Australian coastal forces, some hundreds broke westward through the bush and escaped through the net which the 14th Brigade had spread for them. Though the 14th Brigade had been very much on the alert since they had redisposed themselves on the 14th, sharp clashes with roving bands of Japanese in the Amboga River areas indicated that large numbers of fugitives were getting past them or round their seaward flank. On the 16th a 36th Battalion patrol, thrusting westward from the Amboga mouth, encountered some 250 of them in one group, well armed and ready to fight. They killed one of the Australians and wounded two, and ate the man they had killed. The 36th generally took a heavy toll during these last days of the coastal battle, and after the fighting round the track was over. As the month went on they became almost casual in their killing—as an entry on the 26th by Colonel Matthews in his diary indicates:

Conversation heard on telephone today. Capt Smith at Native Compound interrupted while speaking to Staff Capt by a voice speaking in a whisper:
"Is that you, sir?"
"Yes! What is it?"
"There are a lot of Japs here, sir."
"Where are you?"
"The post just up the road."
"How many Japs?"
"Just a minute. How many, Bill?"
(Mumble, mumble.)
"Eight, sir."
"How far away?"
"How far off, Bill?"
(Mumble, mumble.)
"About thirty yards away in the grass, sir."
"Well, what are you doing about it?"
"What are we doing about it, Bill?"
(Mumble, mumble.)
"Nothing, sir."
"Well go to town with them can't you?"
"He says to go to town, Bill."
(Mumble, mumble.)
Sudden fusillade of Tommy guns and grenades for about five minutes.
"We got 'em, sir! Six killed and two prisoners."

---

[9] Eichelberger, *Our Jungle Road to Tokyo*, pp. 60-1.

Although such killings might suggest that the Japanese fared badly in comparison with the Allied forces who defeated them along the Sanananda Track, this was far from being so. In that area alone the Australians and Americans lost in killed and wounded between 2,000 and 2,100 officers and men—with an additional 86 if the cost of the 127th Regiment's drive from Tarakena is added. Of these more than 1,400 were Australians (634 from three militia battalions—39th, 49th and 55th/53rd —and 426 from the three 18th Brigade battalions). Almost 600 Australians and some 274 Americans were killed or missing. On the other hand, probably 1,500-1,600 Japanese were killed along the track, though many of these were wounded who had been left to die or fight to the death. The Japanese took off by sea probably about 1,200 sick and wounded during the period 13th-20th January, and about 1,000 escaped overland to the west of Gona.

Their losses at Sanananda were therefore not as heavy as they might well have feared they would be. On Major-General Oda's arrival there on 22nd December he had found the situation discouraging. The Japanese were still inflexible in defence and the positions they had so cunningly sited were immensely strong. Their supplies, however, were down to a mere trickle. In the most forward positions Lieut-Colonel Tsukamoto was desperately short of food and ammunition. In the intermediate positions (two perimeters, one on either side of the road, between Huggins' and the newly-established James' road-block and, fronting James', a convex system of perimeters across the track) which Oda took over himself, the situation was little better. Each man was down to a handful of rice a day; all were eating roots, grass, and crawling things; some ate the dead.

Back at Rabaul, General Adachi was most anxious about the plight of his forces on the Papuan coast. In the teeth of the Allied air attacks there was little he could do to improve the supply situation. And a new factor had developed to hinder his coastwise movements since the torpedo boats from Tufi had begun ranging the offshore waters at night and disrupting not only the movements of his small craft but striking at his submarines, his main supply link. Uneasily mindful of the lack of success which had attended his earlier attempts to land reinforcements he was then apparently less inclined than ever to commit the balance of the *21st Independent Mixed Brigade* to the perilous voyage from Rabaul. On 26th December, however, he sent orders to Major-General Yamagata to move his forces from their positions west of Gona to the Sanananda area, with the rescue of the Buna garrison, now in their last straits, as Yamagata's first task. Yamagata at once undertook the move to Sanananda and, leaving a rearguard to occupy the Australian left flank, ferried 700-800 men successfully into the main beach-head within a week.

While this move was still in its early stages Colonel Yazawa had been ordered to cut his way down to Buna through the American left flank and withdraw the garrison to Giruwa. Yamagata's move, however, was slowed apparently through shortages of petrol for his small craft and

Yazawa, awaiting the arrival of these comparatively fresh troops to assemble his Buna relief force, was not able to get his thrust on the move before the evening of 2nd January. By that time the Buna garrison no longer existed as a force, however, and Yazawa's task became simply to succour as many of them as possible. To assist those who were skirting the American positions by sea he required the Tarakena spit as a landing place for them. For that main reason he struck hard at Lieutenant Chagnon on the 4th and drove him off the spit. Subsequently he was able to gather there almost 200 survivors of the Buna garrison.

As the Japanese position thus declined in Papua similar difficulties closed them round on Guadalcanal, where, since the American landings at the beginning of August, the fighting had so vitally affected events in New Guinea.

After the mid-November naval battles it soon became clear that, though hard fighting still lay ahead, the Americans were no longer in danger of being ousted, despite the fact that they still did not occupy a much larger area than that in which they had first established themselves after their initial landings. They had, however, been able to enlarge their Lunga perimeter slightly during November to include the Matanikau River and the area west to Point Cruz. The Japanese then began developing Mount Austen, its apex a 1,514 foot summit dominating the surrounding area, as their pivotal positions.

In the first half of December it was clear that fresh American troops would have to be brought in to replace those who had borne the brunt of the fighting and seen the longest service. Most urgently in need of relief was the 1st Marine Division, although their battle casualties had not been excessive. Of some 1,300 American dead from all causes between August and 12th December the Marine division had lost over 600, their total battle casualties numbering 1,472. But fatigue and illness were greater weakening factors than battle, with malaria as the arch-enemy.[1]

On 30th November the Joint Chiefs of Staff decided to send the 25th American Division to the South Pacific. (It had begun moving from Hawaii to Australia on the 25th.) Pending its arrival on Guadalcanal the rest of the Americal Division would be fed in from Noumea (the 164th and 182nd Regimental Combat Teams of that division having already arrived on Guadalcanal) and the 1st Marine Division would leave for Australia for rest and refit. The Marines began to leave Guadalcanal on 9th December and, the same day, Major-General Patch took over from Major-General Vandergrift tactical command of the troops on Guadalcanal. The Americal Division, however, numbered only some 13,000 men at 11th December and, after the departure of the 1st Marine Division got under way, the Americans became alarmed at their own

---

[1] The malaria rate rose from 14 cases per 1,000 in August to 1,664 per 1,000 in October, 1,781 in November, 972 in December and 1,169 in January 1943.—Miller, *Guadalcanal: The First Offensive*, p. 227.

apparent weakness. They, therefore, hurried the arrival of the 25th Division and the landing of these troops was substantially completed by the beginning of January. There were then three divisions on the island and XIV Corps was formed with Patch in command. It consisted of the Americal and 25th Divisions with the 2nd Marine Division and other Marine ground forces attached. By 7th January the American forces on Guadalcanal totalled 50,000.

During this same period there had been a marked increase in air strength. On 23rd November there were 84 American Army, Navy, Marine Corps and Royal New Zealand Air Force aircraft operating from Guadalcanal. By the end of the month there were 188 aircraft of all types. By December Henderson Field could be used as an all-weather strip. The construction or improvement of three other strips on Guadalcanal was well advanced.

As the American position on Guadalcanal thus improved the Japanese position worsened rapidly. The Japanese operations in the air, on the sea and on land, had cost them dear. Malnutrition and disease exacted an even greater cost. By December the Japanese strength on the island was not more than 25,000; in the face of American air and naval power almost no reinforcements could be got in; supplies were so scanty that many soldiers were literally starving; it was impossible for the Japanese to undertake any offensive operations. Nevertheless they continued to resist the American attacks with tenacity and skill from mid-December when Patch set out to pave the way for a corps' offensive in January by seizing Mount Austen. The end of December found the American attempts on the Mount Austen positions only partially advanced and the attacking 132nd Regiment mauled and dispirited. Though this regiment continued its attacks during the first days of January they could not oust the defenders from the most important of their Mount Austen positions. Nevertheless the Americans felt themselves to be in a position to begin on 10th January a major offensive designed to clear the Japanese finally from Guadalcanal. This offensive, however, developed against a dwindling enemy, for on 15th January orders from General Imamura reached General Hyakutake on Guadalcanal to withdraw his *XVII Army* from the island. Soon afterwards, therefore, Hyakutake began moving his troops westward towards Cape Esperance from the lines to which they had by that time been forced back westward of Point Cruz. Japanese destroyers ran down the Slot and began lifting the defeated troops on the night of 1st-2nd February. About 13,000 Japanese were then taken back to Buin and Rabaul.

On 9th February General Patch informed Admiral Halsey that the Japanese forces on Guadalcanal had been totally and completely defeated. In bringing this about the Americans had deployed about 60,000 men on Guadalcanal. Of these some 1,600 were killed by the Japanese and 4,245 were wounded. On the other side about 36,000 Japanese fought on Guadalcanal of whom probably about 14,800 were killed or missing, 9,000 died of disease, and about 1,000 were taken prisoner. More serious for the Japanese, however, were the heavy shipping losses which they suffered and the loss of probably more than 600 aircraft and their pilots.

As the inevitability of this defeat became apparent so also did the inevitability of defeat in Papua. When, therefore, the Japanese decided early in January to lift the survivors from Guadalcanal, they decided at the same time that the Papuan troops would make their way overland and by sea to Salamaua and Lae after fresh troops from Rabaul had reinforced the two latter points. When General Imamura told General Adachi of these plans the latter at once ordered the *102nd Regiment* of the *51st Division* to Lae. It ran the gauntlet of the Allied air forces and arrived safely on 7th January, although two of the four transports which five destroyers convoyed were sunk after their arrival at Lae and the Japanese air forces sustained heavy losses in trying to beat off the Allied attacks.

Adachi was not so prompt, however, in ordering the evacuation of the Papuan coastal positions though the failure of the Mambare beach-head had finally sealed their fate. By 12th January their last grain of rice was gone and they were literally starving; their medical supplies had long been exhausted and their sick and wounded were either dying fast or becoming living skeletons with swamp water awash about them as they lay; ammunition was low. On the same day Oda radioed Adachi.

Most of the men are stricken with dysentery. Those not . . . in bed with illness are without food and too weak for hand to hand fighting. . . . Starvation is taking many lives, and it is weakening our already extended lines. We are doomed. In several days we are bound to meet the same fate that overtook Basabua and Buna.

Next day Adachi told Yamagata that he could prepare to move his forces from Sanananda to the area of the Kumusi and Mambare mouths and travel thence, overland or by sea, to Salamaua and Lae; the movement of the sick and wounded by small water craft could begin at once; as many whole men as possible would also be taken out by launch but the rest would have to break overland to the west; this overland movement was not, however, to begin until the 25th. But Yamagata knew that he could not hold on to his positions until the 25th. On the 18th, therefore, he advanced the date for the clearance of the Sanananda positions to the 20th and prepared orders for his men to break westward, assemble on the coast some miles beyond Gona and be picked up there by launches. He himself got clear away on the night of the 19th-20th. The following night large sections of the force still remaining in the area began to break away in accordance with their orders, Oda and Yazawa with them. Both of these officers were killed, however, by the Australians who were watchful for the escape attempts.

In the opening stages of the Sanananda affair there were probably about 5,500 Japanese troops of all kinds in the area, perhaps some 1,800 of them hospital patients at that time. During the operations their strength was possibly increased by about 500 of the troops whom Yazawa had brought down the Kumusi, about 800 newcomers of the *170th Regiment* and possibly 200-300 escapers from the Buna area. It is likely, there-

(*Australian War Memorial*)
Wrecked Japanese barges, pieces of equipment and the bodies of the dead littered the beaches at Buna when the fighting ended.

(*Australian War Memorial*)
An Australian padre, Chaplain A. E. Begbie, erects a temporary wooden cross over an Australian grave at Gona.

(*Australian War Memorial*)
An aerial view of Wau airfield during the Japanese attack, January 1943.

(*Australian War Memorial*)
The 17th Brigade was flown in to defend Wau. These infantrymen are leaving a transport plane to go into action.

fore, that a maximum of 7,000 might have been through the area between mid-November and 22nd January, and this figure is certainly well above the maximum for any given time. Of these a minimum of 1,600 are known to have been buried by the Australians and Americans, some 1,200 sick and wounded were taken out by barge between 13th and 20th January, about 1,000 are known to have eluded the final sweep and got clear to the west of Gona whence many subsequently made their way to Salamaua and Lae. At least 3,200 therefore remain unaccounted for. Of these a considerable number must have been dead on sea and land and uncounted, while sick and wounded from among them must have been taken off between mid-November and 13th January —but many must also have escaped.

The Japanese at Sanananda performed a remarkable feat. Far in advance of their own main base, their line of supply never more than a thin and wavering one and for the last month almost non-existent, starving, sick, short of almost every physical and warlike need, the larger part of them exhausted from their struggles in the mountains, they held the Australians and Americans in almost baffled impotence for some time and inflicted on them well over 2,000 casualties in battle.

It is difficult to say exactly how many men the Japanese employed in the Kokoda and Buna-Gona coastal operations. It seems certain, however, that the figure was about 18,000. Of these more than 12,000 died. About 3,400 escaped on foot from the actual battle area and 2,000 were taken off by sea before the fighting began.[2] In addition about 1,900 men were landed at Milne Bay and some 300 were stranded on Goodenough Island. Between 600 and 700 of these were known to have been killed. The total Japanese force committed in the whole of Papua probably numbered, therefore, a little over 20,000 of whom about 13,000 remained dead on the battlefields and about 7,000 survived. The invaders inflicted total casualties on the Australians and Americans in Papua of 8,546 between 22nd July 1942 and 22nd January 1943.

The question arises as to the necessity for the Buna-Sanananda-Gona campaign—whether the Japanese garrison in that area could have been left to "wither on the vine" as some island garrisons were left later in the war.

Airfields on the Buna-Gona coast were vital for the development of Allied offensive operations farther to the north and were necessary for the effective defence of Port Moresby. The scowling Owen Stanleys not only prevented the Allied aircraft, for much of their time, from venturing out on attack or reconnaissance but shielded the approach of raiding Japanese from visual or even radar detection almost to the time of their arrival at their bomb-release line. Until radar and fighter aircraft could

[2] In *Southern Cross, an account of the Eastern New Guinea Campaign* (1955), published in Japanese only, General Yoshiwara, who was Adachi's chief of staff, gives the strength in the coastal area as 11,880 and the casualties there as "about 8,000". The figures in this paragraph are in general agreement with those in Yoshiwara's book and in *The Complete History of the Greater East Asia War* (1953), by Colonel T. Hattori of Imperial GHQ, Tokyo, a typescript translation of which is in the library of the Australian War Memorial.

be firmly based north of the mountains, Moresby could not be regarded as a satisfactory air base, and indeed it was not capable of housing more than a limited number of squadrons.

With the clearing of the Japanese from the north coast came the building of the great Dobodura air base. This followed the development first of Oro Bay into a forward Allied port. Over the road system springing from this port went the machinery and material for the construction of the airfields and then the ammunition and fuel for the aircraft themselves and the supplies for the men who kept them in the air. The later development of Buna as a port allowed the build-up of supplies for the operations which followed in the Huon Peninsula area. From the Dobodura fields flew out the aircraft (except for the heavy bombers which could operate from Moresby) which made those operations possible.

Did the ground fighting, however, need to continue to the knock-out stage to enable this development to take place? By mid-December General MacArthur might have asked himself seriously whether he had substantially gained his physical objectives. But clearly, it seems, there were then still so many Japanese spread strongly and widely from Cape Endaiadere north-westward that the security and most efficient use of the Allied airfields could not have been guaranteed and the ground fighting had to be continued to a further stage.

Not only, however, was this a necessity for security. It was also necessary for more intangible reasons. Primarily, perhaps, the Allies had not yet taken the true measure of the Japanese in their defence system on the coast and it was too soon for them to be able to justify a decision not to eradicate the Japanese completely. Before Buna it was perhaps also of importance that the Americans had been beaten—and they could not be allowed to remain beaten in this first action. Nor could MacArthur himself, with the knowledge that one more major defeat might spell the end of his military career, afford to allow any appearance of victory to remain with the Japanese. The employment of the 18th Brigade was necessary, and once this superb formation was committed the operations at Buna could not stop short of the capture of that area by the Australians and the Americans.

On the Sanananda Track the issue was not quite so clear cut. The ineffectiveness of the Americans, and doubts regarding the quality of the Australian militia, clouded the issue there. These circumstances, allied with the facts that information regarding the Japanese strength and potential was still not clear in mid-December, that there was still a less than complete appreciation that the Japanese were probably the world's most resolute soldiers in prepared defences, and that the fighting before Buna had to continue, made it reasonable that a fourth round should be initiated along the Sanananda Track (with the arrival of the 36th Battalion and 2/7th Cavalry).

The situation became markedly different, however, by 2nd January. By that time the airfields could definitely be secured and the threat to Papua was gone. The almost superhuman quality of the Japanese in defence was obvious. Looking back now it is clear that the Japanese at Sanananda *could* have been sealed off at that time and thus allowed to perish. This, it will be recalled, was the course which Major-General Berryman advocated. It was a course which might have been followed later in the war under similar circumstances—as an outcome of ways of thought which developed with increasing success and confidence. At the stage, however, which the Sanananda operations represented for the Allies —with the Japanese obviously almost at the end of their endurance; with a necessity for clearing the path as completely as possible in the initial stages of an offensive advance; with the desirability present of lifting the Allied morale as high as possible by finishing the operations in Papua decisively and completely—the decision to press the coastal fighting to the bitter end was probably inevitable.

CHAPTER 18

WAU

WHILE the campaign in the Owen Stanleys was waxing and waning during the period from July to November 1942; the threat to Milne Bay was mounting and being destroyed in August and September; the fighting in Papua was drawn to its dreary close among the swamps of the Buna-Gona coast during the last of 1942 and the first month of 1943; then, during all that time, the small band of guerillas which was Kanga Force was hanging close about the Japanese in the Wau-Salamaua-Lae area.

It has been told how the New Guinea Volunteer Rifles, after the Japanese landed at Salamaua and Lae in March 1942, established themselves in the bush about the Japanese positions and, in late May, were absorbed into Kanga Force after the arrival at Wau of Lieut-Colonel Fleay, the 2/5th Independent Company and the lesser elements of the force; how the first phase of the Kanga Force operations ended with the arrival of a strong Japanese group at Mubo on 31st August; and how, anticipating that these Japanese would continue from Mubo to Wau, the Kanga Force men laid waste the Bulolo Valley and moved their centre to Kudjeru at the beginning of the Bulldog Track.

After Lieutenant Wylie with a small band of commandos and New Guinea Riflemen passed the last of the Mubo garrison coming down the track on 1st September he advanced warily until his men had the Japanese at Mubo under close observation. Three uneventful weeks then passed and it became clear that it was not the immediate intention of the Japanese to press on to Wau. Thus Fleay had been precipitate in devastating the Bulolo Valley.

The considerations which led up to this decision were based initially on the judgment that the Japanese were concentrating strength at Busama. The situation was exacerbated by reports of landings of men, supplies and vehicles at Salamaua itself and of troop movements in the vicinity of Lokanu. After the event it became clear that these reports were exaggerated. Fleay's concern, however, was natural enough and was increased by advice from New Guinea Force that he could expect no early reinforcement. His crowning difficulty then was that both Captain Winning and Captain Minchin were absent from Mubo as the Japanese approached it and had left only about thirty men there astride what had become the line of the main Japanese approach. Fleay was conscious of the fact that he could impose only limited delay at Mubo. He estimated that Japanese, to a strength of about 1,000, could enter Mubo during the late daylight of the 30th or during the night 30th-31st and be at Kaisenik some 24 hours later. So his orders for the "scorching" of the valley went out—at 3 p.m. on the 30th. But the occupation of Mubo did not take place until about the same time next day. And as for the estimate that the Japanese could reach Kaisenik within 24 hours of taking Mubo—an assessment of a hard two-day march for burdened troops expecting ambush or attack would have been more realistic. We know now that Wau was not then the Japanese objective. Their move to Mubo was part of their plan to threaten the Australians in concert with the main landings on the Buna-Gona coast and to place at Mubo the most forward defences of their

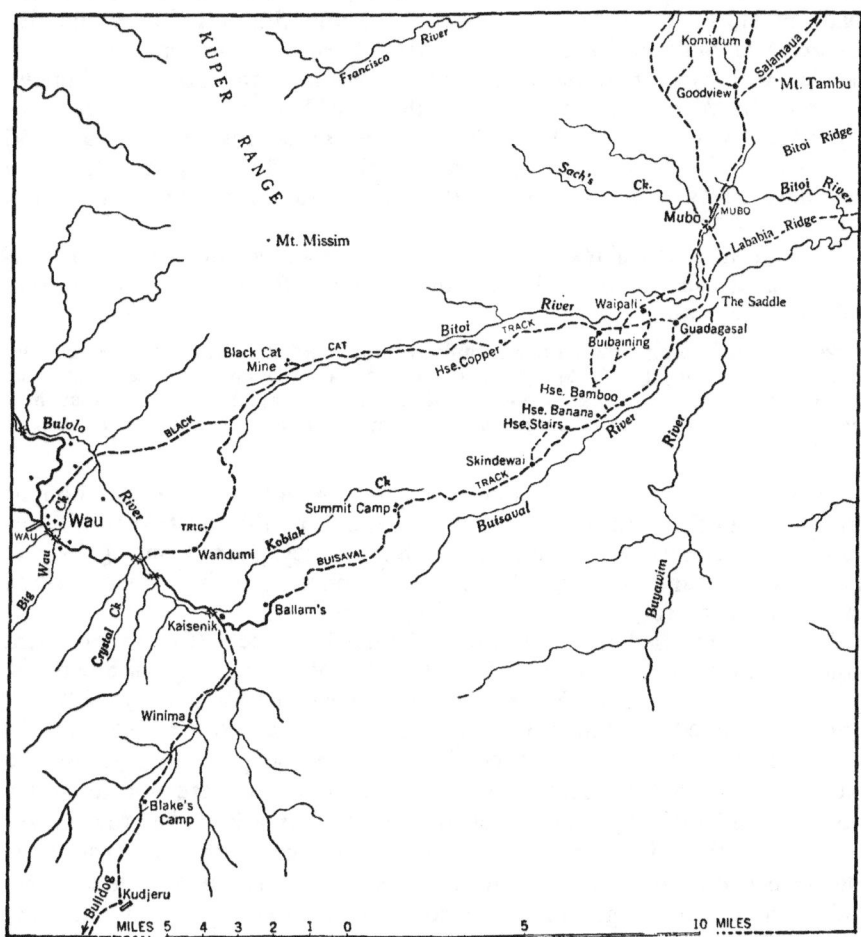

The Buisaval and Black Cat Tracks

Lae-Salamaua bases. But Fleay could not know this at the time and his decision, though premature in execution, was understandable. Had the Japanese advanced nothing could have excused an Australian failure to "scorch".

Initially, however, the consequences were not only the destruction of the facilities and installations in the Bulolo Valley but general confusion and uncertainty among the Australians. For some little time after his move began Fleay was out of touch with New Guinea Force, which was puzzled by his silence and by reports from aircraft crews (who had been sent to Wau with supplies) that the aerodrome there had been made unusable and the township gutted by fire. After contact was regained on 2nd September, however, order began to develop once more. The following day 140 Papuan carriers arrived at Kudjeru with food. Twelve planeloads of stores were dropped on the 4th and 5th. Gradually the disordered accumulation of stores at Crystal Creek was sorted out and the usable portions carried back to Blake's, Winima and Kudjeru. Supply-dropping at Wampit for the men at the Markham end of the area was organised. A special effort on the Bulldog Track resulted in about 50 boy-loads daily coming into Kudjeru that way by 15th September. About that date Fleay was able to report that the ration position was "most satisfactory".

Though the Australians were as unaggressive as the Japanese during this period Lieut-General Rowell was not impatient, for he reported to Australia on the 20th:

> Work is proceeding slowly on the Bulldog Track and it is now possible to move small sub-units through gradually. Supply can be assured either by sea and river, or by air droppings. Kanga Force is performing a valuable task in that it is engaging the attention of a considerable enemy force and is ensuring a flow of valuable information.

Two days later, however, it looked as though action might be looming once more in the Kanga Force area. On the 23rd the most forward Australians—at Guadagasal—were forced back. They pushed out again next day, however, and by nightfall were once more in their former position as a standing patrol; more uneventful days followed.

It will be recalled that a small detachment of the 2/5th Independent Company and a few individuals from the N.G.V.R. were still at Sheldon's, on the south bank of the Markham River, when the main body of Kanga Force evacuated the Bulolo Valley. In the quiet which followed the Mubo incident these men settled down to routine patrolling across the river and towards Lae. They found that the Japanese were not venturing much beyond their perimeter post at Heath's Plantation, that the natives were losing their fear of being caught fraternising with the Australians and were willing to talk to them and even to supply them with carriers. This encouraged the guerillas to send a small harassing patrol down the river as far as Heath's. On the night of 12th-13th September this patrol laid booby traps across a well-used track near Heath's. A Japanese party blundered into it early the next afternoon. The alarmed garrison then opened blindly with their field gun and beat the bush with rifle and machine-gun fire. The guerillas quietly withdrew unharmed. After that, however, there were few highlights for the Australians along the Markham. They kept touch with the natives (notably through the work of Sergeants Emery and Booth of the N.G.V.R. and 2/5th respectively) and kept track of the main Japanese movements. But these movements were neither bold nor extensive.

Back at Mubo the Australians decided to break the peace that seemed to have descended. In the early morning darkness of 1st October Captain Winning led a band nearly 60 strong against the main Japanese camp at Mubo. With him went Fleay "as a rifleman". Winning's intention was to approach the stronghold by way of an old overgrown trail but he could not find it in the darkness. The raiders therefore followed a track which led into Mubo from the south-west by way of high ground known as Mat Mat Hill. Lieutenant Drysdale, who was leading, was, however, wounded by a booby trap. The defenders were aroused. Another booby trap gave urgency to the initial alarm. Japanese poured out to meet the attack. Winning's men, heavily outnumbered, fell back carrying the dying Drysdale and two other wounded men. Sergeant O'Neill, already recognised as a skilful scout and daring leader, with two other soldiers covered part of the withdrawal by holding a track along which the Japanese threatened to outflank the retreating Australians. It was said later that 16 Japanese suddenly appeared in front of O'Neill; that he met them with such a volume of accurate sub-machine-gun fire that he killed all 16. But the main party was broken up during its withdrawal and small groups were rejoining the parent body for some days afterwards. (Fleay himself and a soldier formed one such group.) When reports from all of these were finally checked the Australians estimated that they had caused some 50 casualties among the Japanese.

Corporal Kinsey watched Winning's ill-fated attack from a perch in a high tree only some 700 yards from Mubo, where he and Rifleman Leather[2] had been manning a lookout for some time. Later, in the Japanese camp, they observed a slow-moving sequel to the attack.

> We watched a procession of 100 men (said Kinsey later) carrying a corpse from the headquarters building to the south-west corner of the 'drome where they prepared a log base and much firewood and had a burial service with men in three platoons in U shape round the spot. The body was put on the logs, a pile of wood put on it and the pile set fire to. Later we found that this body was the O.C. of the Mubo company.

Some days later, after the scattered raiders had been drawn together again, this remarkable scout and his friend Leather set out for Salamaua. Winning had asked them to try to get into one of the old observation posts. They carried 14 days' rations with them. Well before the main track reached Mubo they plunged into the mountain and bush forsaking *all* tracks. Up and down tangled mountains they went as they headed due north. They watched the Japanese from the old No. 2 Lookout, questioned the natives, satisfied themselves that there were not many more than about 1,000 Japanese in the vicinity of Salamaua, absorbed a most detailed picture (day-to-day movements by the garrison, numbers, shipping, gun

---
[2] Rfn F. L. Leather, NG2113; NGVR. Dredge oiler; of Bulolo, TNG; b. Mt Pirie, Qld, 30 Dec 1912.

sites) and left again after five days. Kinsey said later: "I didn't stay longer because I was coughing and was afraid this would give me away."

Meanwhile the long-awaited reinforcements had reached Kanga Force. On 4th October Major MacAdie[3] arrived at Port Moresby with some 290 all ranks in his 2/7th Independent Company. MacAdie was 23 years old at this time, only two years out of Duntroon and fresh from an instructor's post at the Guerilla Warfare School. He was well over 6 feet tall, thin and strangely hawk-like, with curiously flecked eyes set deep above a high-bridged nose. The company flew to Wau on the 8th and 9th and came under Fleay's command. At the same time New Guinea Force re-defined Fleay's instructions, ordering him to continue to harass the enemy in the Mubo-Salamaua-Lae area with the objects of reporting their activities and holding the aerodromes in the Bulolo Valley. Fleay accordingly spread the bulk of his two companies from Kudjeru through the Bulolo Valley and up the mountains towards Mubo with the Markham Valley detachment still operating from Sheldon's. MacAdie, believing that his unit was not properly efficient despite the fact that it was considered to have completed its training, drove his men hard. He flung them wide on patrols both as an operational and training necessity, developed intensive weapon training programs and stressed the need for sound training in basic infantry techniques. From the beginning he recognised the particular value of Intelligence in the type of operations for which Independent Companies were designed, increased the strength of his Intelligence Section from two (the authorised number) to six and modified the standard Intelligence training to lay less emphasis on orthodox map reading (finding the standard maps insufficient in number and inadequate in quality) and develop bushcraft. At the same time, after the devastation of the valley in late August, he found himself with a large reconstruction program on his hands. His energetic engineer officer, Lieutenant Sheridan,[4] worked his section hard. They rebuilt hangars and workshops, restored power and lighting to the Wau Valley after 14 days' hard work on the Mount Kaindi Power House, improved tracks and roads, in twelve days rebridged the Bulolo near Bulwa with a 146-foot-span suspension bridge which had a normal load capacity of 10 tons and a safe overload capacity of 15 tons, rebuilt the Kulolo suspension bridge across the Bulolo giving it a 90-foot span and a 5 tons' capacity, and carried out various other building tasks with thoroughness and speed.

With the emphasis on rebuilding and patrolling November and December passed quietly enough for the men of Kanga Force. Evidently neither Blamey nor Herring was pushing them into any very active offence, possibly having no desire to sting the Japanese into retaliation in New Guinea while the Papuan battle was still being so bitterly contested, and certainly wishing to avoid having to divert from the main front in any extraordinary

---
[3] Col T. F. B. MacAdie, DSO, VX85235. OC 2/7 Indep Coy 1942-44; CO Bena Force 1943-45, 3 NG Inf 1945. Regular soldier; of Melbourne; b. Williamstown, Vic, 22 Sep 1919.
[4] Lt D. M. Sheridan, NX66090; 2/7 Indep Coy. Steel rigger and machine miner; of North Bondi, NSW; b. Hamilton, Ontario, Canada, 3 Sep 1915.

effort aircraft and other sorely needed means of supply. Thus, on 12th November, Fleay was reminded that his main role was a watching one. He was to hold the Bulolo Valley airfields, and was told specifically that his men on the Markham should undertake only limited reconnaissance north of the river and should avoid detection by the Japanese. Although his supply to the Kudjeru-Wau area was assured (particularly as far as Wau was concerned, through the Wau airfield which had once more been opened) the men on the Markham were only precariously maintained. The picture which Captain Stout,[5] medical officer of the 2/5th, had painted on 11th October when he was in charge of the hospital at Bobs, remained fairly constant throughout the rest of their period there.

> The general health of the troops in this area is rapidly deteriorating due to an inadequate diet . . . not only inadequate but unbalanced, and the constant tinned meat is resulting in a high percentage of . . . gastritis and diarrhoea. They are developing a [distaste for] tinned foods generally, and many of them cannot stomach tinned meat and simply "go without". . . . Troops are becoming desperately short of shirts, shorts, etc. Clothes become saturated with sweat and dirt each day; an inability to change into clean, dry clothes is causing an epidemic of contagious skin troubles. In spite of the above inconveniences and discomforts morale is generally good.

In the Mubo region Winning had established his most forward point near the Saddle, just forward of Guadagasal, where the track dipped between two long spurs approaching it from either side and the area between the Buisaval River on the east and the Bitoi on the west was narrowest and fell precipitously away to the river on either side for 1,000 feet or more. He kept his patrols always busy among the hills and gorges between the Saddle and Mubo itself. They scoured the adjacent tracks, booby-trapped those most favoured by the invaders, and set up observation posts from which they overlooked the Japanese movements in the main Mubo camps. Mostly these posts were manned by N.G.V.R. men, true to the tradition they themselves had established: Archie Graham,[6] Albert Pauley, Bruce Fraser[7] and Geoff White[8] were there (with O'Neill of the Independent Company) overlooking Mubo for many weeks. The natives knew where they were but were loyal to them. The Japanese knew they were about. White cockatoos would fly round them sometimes when they moved. Then the tree-top watchers would see the Japanese pointing towards their positions. But the Japanese never found them. They slept soundly at nights. They cooked their food under cover of the night fogs, and kept water beside them in bamboos. They were calm, brave and always watchful.

At one time in early December it seemed to the Kanga Force men that they had so irritated the Japanese that the latter might be preparing to move forward from Mubo. But the portents faded and the Australians

---

[5] Capt E. W. Stout, NX77294. RMO 2/5 Indep Coy; No. 1 Orthopaedic Unit 1943-45. Medical practitioner; of Cooma, NSW; b. Whitehaven, NSW, 9 Apr 1911.
[6] WO2 A. McA. Graham, NG2022. NGVR; Angau. Miner; b. West Wyalong, NSW, 18 May 1898.
[7] Sgt B. Fraser, NGX419. NGVR; HQ 6 Div 1945. Alluvial miner; b. Brisbane, 19 Aug 1914.
[8] Lt G. J. White, NG2390. NGVR; Angau. Miner, assayer and planter; of Slate Creek, TNG; b. Hobart, 10 May 1914.

themselves then prepared to strike a hard blow in the most ambitious military operation planned for the Wau-Salamaua-Lae area up to that time. It would involve the use of more than 300 troops and about 400 native carriers. The supply, organisation and control of carriers would be arranged, as usual, by the Angau men in the area—Major Penglase, recently returned from Madang; Captain Niall, in charge at Wau; Warrant-Officers Watson,[9] and White,[1] with the forward troops. Penglase, knowing both the area and the natives extremely well, warned Fleay that there was no guarantee that the natives would remain fast under fire, but Fleay asserted, "They'll have to stay". Fleay's intention was to destroy as many Japanese as possible and, if the encounter developed favourably, to take and hold Mubo. MacAdie would command the attack, with Winning as his second-in-command, and they would muster all available troops of both Independent Companies. The plan provided for the seizure and maximum use of the boldest features surrounding the Mubo gorge. MacAdie himself, with 60 officers and men, was to seize Vickers Ridge which dominated the eastern side of the gorge, dropping 1,000 feet in half a mile and falling sharply then to the river bed over its next 500 feet. Captain Finch[2] with 40 all ranks was to take and hold the kunda bridge which crossed the Bitoi to link Vickers Ridge with Mubo. Captain Bowen[3] and Lieutenant Wylie, with some 80 all ranks from both companies, were to retain the Saddle as an extricating position. Winning's tasks centred on the high ground on the western side of the gorge. He himself was to take 100 of his own officers and men (with Warrant-Officer White of Angau and 162 carriers) to Mat Mat Hill which overlooked Mubo by 1,000 feet from the south-west. Lieutenants Ridley[4] and Leitch would lead another band of 2/5th men, 50 strong, northward from Mat Mat Hill to Observation Hill which thrust steeply down towards Mubo airstrip from the north. The actual attack was to begin at 9.30 a.m. on 11th January.

MacAdie brought his company forward from Wau (except for one platoon which was already at Skindewai) and linked with Winning's company on the 8th. Soon afterwards he and his men moved out towards their forming-up place high on the Buisaval Track above Vickers Ridge, which they reached on the evening of the 10th. Below them they watched the unsuspecting Japanese going about their normal duties and looked north-west across the basin to the crest of Mat Mat Hill. Winning's men were, however, having difficulty in reaching their positions there. Their leader had wanted more time than the two days allotted to him to get them into position but, the schedule remaining unaltered, had to drive

---

[9] Capt R. Watson, MBE, NX49798; Angau. Clerk; of North Bondi, NSW; b. Brighton-le-Sands, NSW, 18 Jun 1916.

[1] Lt S. W. White, NGX279. NGVR; Angau. Salesman; of Biggenden, Qld; b. Lismore, NSW, 11 Jan 1908.

[2] Capt N. D. Finch, NX5190. 2/4 Bn; 2/7 Indep Coy. Salesman; of Epping, NSW; b. Cootamundra, NSW, 10 Aug 1916.

[3] Capt G. T. Bowen, NX55542; 2/7 Indep Coy. Accountant; of Kogarah, NSW; b. Port Kembla, NSW, 18 Aug 1919. Killed in action 16 Jan 1943.

[4] Capt W. L. Ridley, NX57733; 2/5 Indep Coy. Farmer and grazier; of Forbes, NSW; b. West Wyalong, NSW, 20 Dec 1912.

his men into a searing march and climb of 10 hours and a half on each of those two days. Even so they could not keep to the start-time, which they were to signal themselves with a long burst from their one Vickers

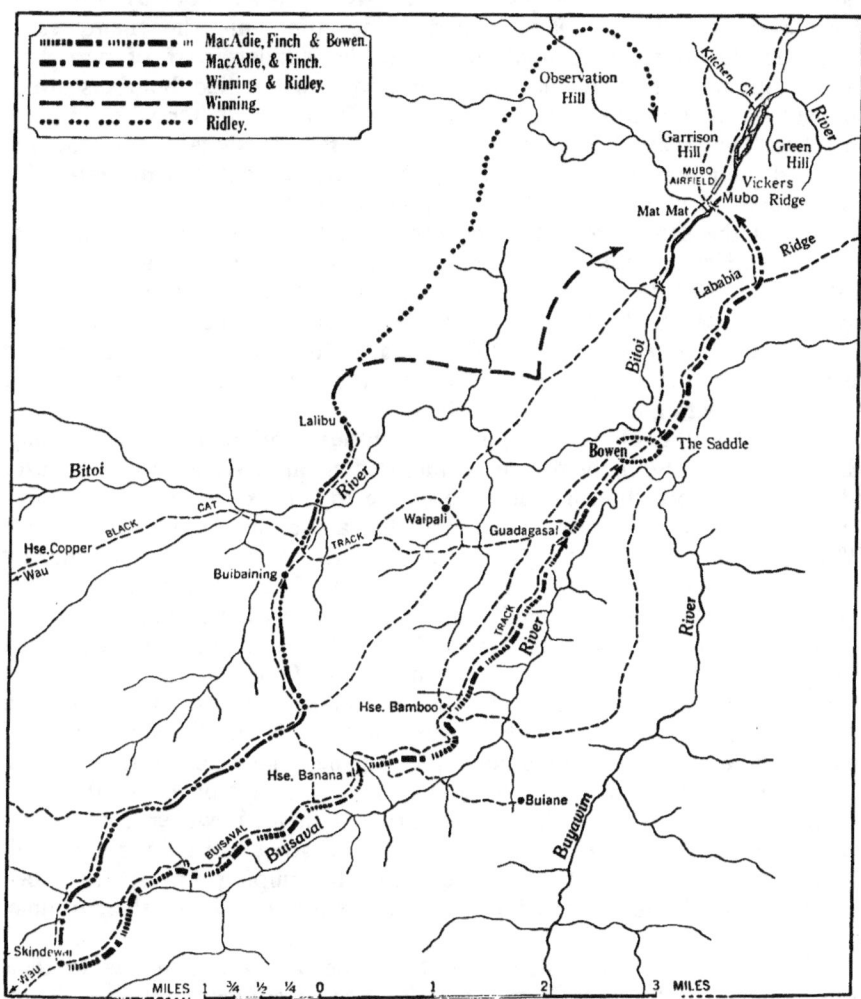

Routes of advance on Mubo, 11th January

gun. The morning of the 11th, after a night of drenching rain, brought swirling fog. This was fortunate for Winning as his weary men were still scrambling into their positions when the attack should have been opening, struggling to get their 3-inch mortar and Vickers gun into positions which were still unreconnoitred (the reconnaissance party having been held up by the flooded Bitoi) and which, when occupied at last, were found to be shut in by the bush.

Meanwhile MacAdie's men above Vickers Ridge had breakfasted on hot coffee and food which Watson and his natives had brought down from a supply point not far to the rear. After that they moved to their previously reconnoitred attack positions and were settled there by 8.30 a.m. They watched a long Japanese carrier line come into the enemy camp from the direction of Komiatum, heard the sudden roar of aeroplane motors among the misty mountains and saw two Allied bombers sweep suddenly over the Japanese. They saw the Japanese scatter wildly for slit trenches. They waited in vain for some time for the signal from Mat Mat Hill and their wireless failed to bring them into touch with the labouring parties there. But the long Vickers burst at last broke out—at 1.20 p.m. Almost at the same time plunging fire from MacAdie's men struck into the completely surprised Japanese on Garrison Hill below them. The Australians claimed 20 or 30 for their first bursts. They saw Winning's mortar bombs explode off the target and in their own area but, just at the right time, found wireless touch with him, and from their own grandstand seats, directed the mortar fire. Whenever the Japanese broke cover their machine-gunners got fairly among them.

But on the other side of the gorge difficulties continued to dog Winning. His own party found themselves committed to an advance down a razor edge seldom more than 8 feet wide at the top, rocky, overgrown, falling away so steeply at the sides that only the actual profile was negotiable. While Winning himself fought the mortar and Vickers gun, Lieutenant Kerr was looking after the actual movement, but the country defeated him. As the afternoon dragged on, the weariness of his men (they were weak from being too long on tinned food), the inimical terrain, and the well-placed Japanese kept his men out of the fight.

Meanwhile more success had attended Ridley's thrust at Observation Hill. After the general firing started he burst out of the thick growth near his objective and got right among the Japanese gun positions. His men killed the Japanese who tried to stop them and swept on down the slope towards Garrison Hill. Their advance brought them, however, into danger from MacAdie's fire and so they pulled back some distance up the hill. There they remained, effectively engaged by sniping fire which killed Leitch, until Winning, preparing to get his own party out of their trouble, recalled them.

When Winning and Ridley went MacAdie was uncertain as to their future plans. He decided, therefore, to hold his positions on Vickers Ridge and the Saddle (Finch having rejoined him during the afternoon as apparently no action was threatening in the kunda bridge area). His men lay quiet during the wet night and the next morning, until they saw their enemies going about their normal occasions in the obvious belief that the Australians had all gone. Then they opened sudden and effective fire. As the morning went on they shot at whatever targets were offering and, in their turn, were vigorously engaged by the Japanese. Night found them miserable beneath more rain, mortar bombs bursting among them. But they were plaguing the Japanese again in the early daylight hours of the

13th. About 11.30 a.m. they counted 126 fresh troops approaching Mubo from Komiatum. As these came straight on down the valley the Australian fire cut numbers of them down. MacAdie, however, was still uncertain whether the attack from Mat Mat Hill was to be renewed. The only instructions he had were to "withdraw to the Saddle if in danger". He therefore sent Finch back to the Saddle for more definite orders. By this time too he was worried particularly about his right flank which was most vulnerable, and during the afternoon he sent Captain Lowe[5] and Sergeant Jubb[6] to reconnoitre that area. Lowe returned about 5, shot through the back, with the news that a band of about 100 were outflanking the Australians round their right and others were closing in from lower down the slope. One of the latter had wounded Lowe and killed Jubb. MacAdie then gave Lowe's platoon to Lieutenant Lade[7] and sent them off to intercept the outflankers. Afterwards, with Lade covering them, the rest of the group began a steady movement uphill towards the Lababia Track. By that time it was dark. It was raining again. The uphill slope was steep and muddy as the hungry men dragged their gear up with them. On the track at the top they formed a defensive position and without food or definite orders waited for the next dawn. After it came they patrolled to find the Japanese and bring in the gear they had been unable to carry the previous night. Then Finch returned with orders to retire to the Saddle. They did this. The main body regrouped (Lade was still out) and nightfall found MacAdie busily organising the defences. He knew that there were strong forces out after him by this time and he waited for the counter-thrust which he felt sure would come.

It came late on the 16th and fell first on Captain Bowen's platoon in the most forward position along the main track. Bowen himself was killed and the attackers pressed so close in the early darkness to Lieutenant McKenzie's[8] section (who were credited with killing eighteen in their first burst) that in places only a few yards separated attackers and defenders. After the attack died down the Australians "stood to" in their positions throughout the night and were closely engaged again next morning by (they estimated) about 350. As the attack pressed more and more heavily (with McKenzie bearing the brunt) the Australians began to fall back in a well-controlled movement and nightfall found them comfortably settled at House Banana. There MacAdie found Major Jones,[9] commander of "B" Company of the 2/6th Battalion, who told him that his company was farther back along the trail and would reach Skindewai next day. They were the most forward troops of the 17th Brigade which had begun

---

[5] Capt H. Lowe, NX120832. 2/7 Indep Coy; 2/7 Cdo Sqn. Grazier; of Manildra, NSW; b. Penrith, NSW, 10 May 1910.

[6] Sgt L. C. Jubb, QX20457; 2/7 Indep Coy. Station hand; of Wilmot, Tas; b. Sheffield, Tas, 8 Jul 1921. Killed in action 13 Jan 1943.

[7] Lt N. A. Lade, TX5452. 2/7 Indep Coy; 2/7 Cdo Sqn. Farm labourer; of Sulphur Creek, Tas; b. Penguin, Tas, 26 Nov 1915.

[8] Maj N. B. McKenzie, MC, QX24484. 2/7 Indep Coy; 2/7 Cdo Sqn. Clerk; of Auchenflower, Qld; b. Brisbane, 7 Sep 1921.

[9] Lt-Col J. S. Jones, VX181. 2/6 Bn; CO 4 NG Inf Bn 1945. Textile manufacturer; of Ballarat, Vic; b. Ballarat, 7 Jul 1915.

flying into Wau three days before. The Kanga Force period of guerilla autonomy was ended.

How well had Fleay's commandos done their job during almost seven months of independent activity? They had one outstanding success to their credit—the Salamaua raid on 29th June. Apart from that they had done little to harass the Japanese at their Salamaua and Lae bases. By contrast with the Salamaua raid, the attacks on Heath's, the October attack on Mubo, and even the ambitious January attack on Mubo were not well carried out. The Kanga Force commander was young and inexperienced in command, and few senior officers from New Guinea Force had visited the area to help him. Nor did he have sufficient help on his own headquarters. There he had one officer only—and the supply problem alone was sufficient to tax a separate maintenance staff. The actual operation of supply from Port Moresby was frequently faulty, based as it was on over-much reliance on the Bulldog line without detailed knowledge of the capacity of that line. The result was often a hand-to-mouth existence for the troops who were sometimes more concerned to know where their next meal was coming from than with the discomfiture of their opponents.

The Kanga Force men, however, neglected in the matter of supplies and relief and reinforcements, had posed a constant threat to the Japanese at Lae and Salamaua without provoking these to large-scale retaliation which might well have meant an entry into the Bulolo Valley when the Allies were fully and desperately engaged elsewhere; and which could conceivably have meant a threat to Port Moresby from the north when the eastern flank was being cleared only with the greatest difficulty. Additionally they ensured a flow of valuable information during critical months. They did what they were sent to New Guinea to do.

The troops who were now arriving to augment Kanga Force were infantry veterans of the North African desert and Greece, some of whom had fought also in Crete, others also in Syria. They had arrived at Milne Bay in October. Despite the demand for experienced infantry during the Papuan coastal fighting General Blamey had held them there, partly because that base was still open to threat, partly because he foresaw the possibility of the thrust at Wau which was now developing, partly because he wanted to keep them intact for the retaking of Lae and Salamaua.

The Japanese underscored his prescience with their decision of 4th January to withdraw from Guadalcanal and Papua and build up their Lae-Salamaua garrisons. General Adachi was then quick to get reinforcements under way from Rabaul for Lae. But the Allies had been expecting some such move, warned by the shipping concentrations which had built up at Rabaul—91 vessels, including 21 warships, and some 300,000 tons of merchant shipping on 30th December. Their aircraft picked up the convoy of 10 destroyers and transports off Gasmata (on the south coast of New Britain) on 6th January and broke through the escorting fighter planes. However, despite their best efforts then and next day (which accounted for at least two of the ships and possibly about 50 aircraft for the loss of 10 Allied planes), the major part of the force landed at Lae on the 7th.

In a letter to Herring on the 8th Blamey referred to these fresh troops:

Whether the intention of this force is to push forward from the Lae and Salamaua area towards Wau remains to be seen. This event has always been present in my mind and I have kept the 17th Brigade A.I.F. intact either to meet this threat or as the spearhead of an advance in this area.

He then outlined his immediate plans for the disposition of his forces in New Guinea, stating that, after the Japanese Sanananda positions had been reduced, the 41st American Division would be sufficient for the defence of the Buna area. He would then withdraw from the Papuan front the 32nd American Division and all the Australian units there and bring two fresh Australian brigades from the mainland. One of the fresh Australian brigades (the 29th) would replace the 17th at Milne Bay.

Next day Blamey warned Brigadier Moten that he was to take over Kanga Force. Although Moten had been commanding the 17th Brigade now for a year he had not yet led a brigade in action. He had taken the 2/27th Battalion away in 1940, had proved himself an able commander in Syria. At this time he was 43 years old, big and well fleshed, with a florid face, a slow and lazy manner, not given to words. Moten flew to Wau on his initial reconnaissance on the 10th and returned to Port Moresby on the 14th to find his written instructions waiting for him. He was to take over all troops in the Wau area as from the 15th. The force there would continue to be known as Kanga Force. Its role would be to ensure the security of the Bulolo Valley as an advanced base with aerodrome facilities suitable for future operations which would "be facilitated if the enemy can be induced to believe that Salamaua is a future objective"; to collect and forward information regarding enemy strength, dispositions and movements; to facilitate the operations of coastwatching and air warning stations in the area.

Meanwhile the 17th Brigade had been moving from Milne Bay to Port Moresby. The 2/6th, the first battalion to move, completed its journey by the 13th and got its leading elements away to Wau next day. With them went their commander, Lieut-Colonel Wood,[1] and, although the move was hampered by unfavourable weather and an accident to one of the troop-carrying aircraft, nightfall found Wood settling a solid nucleus of his battalion at Wau and the 17th Brigade advanced headquarters functioning there. Next day ten more planes flew in with more of the 2/6th and Wood's major deployment was prepared. Major Jones was ordered to place his company in a defensive position on the track in the vicinity of Mubo and he set off at once with his reconnaissance party; Captain Dexter,[2] ordered to settle his company in a similar position on the Wau-Lae track near Timne, likewise got his reconnaissance quickly under way.

---

[1] Brig F. G. Wood, DSO, ED, VX166. 2/6 Bn (CO 1942-45); Comd 25 Bde 1945. Manager; of Oakleigh, Vic; b. St Kilda, Vic, 4 Mar 1906.

[2] Lt-Col W. R. Dexter, DSO, VX5172. 2/6 Bn; CO 61 Bn 1944-45. Stock auctioneer and agent; of Geelong, Vic; b. Melbourne, 5 Jan 1914.

The next week was marked mainly by the build-up at Wau of the 2/6th Battalion. Although, as the earlier fighting had so vividly demonstrated, air transport of men and supplies was the key to mobility and success in New Guinea, and although it was now making possible the rapid reinforcement of the Wau theatre, it was particularly susceptible to the vagaries of the weather. Civil flying in pre-war days had shown that the clouds hanging and twisting over the mountains which hemmed in the Bulolo Valley imposed particular hazards; indeed, sometimes made the passage of aircraft into the valley impossible for days at a time and could shut out the valley or roll back from openings into it at a few minutes' notice. This was now being demonstrated to the army (and was to be demonstrated even more vividly in the days to come). On 15th January six aircraft (carrying among others Moten and the main part of his headquarters) left Port Moresby for Wau with a fighter escort. All were forced back. The next day only small elements (Moten himself among them) were able to get through and four aircraft were forced back to Moresby. On the 18th ten transport aircraft with their fighter escort were over the town soon after 9 a.m. The third one to come in crashed on the outskirts of the airfield killing 8 of the passengers and crew. All told the planes brought in only 49 men and Moten complained that the emplaning arrangements were uneconomical and haphazard. But the 19th was a more fruitful day and 111 of the 2/6th were safely landed bringing the battalion's total strength at Wau to 28 officers and 535 men.

By that time the deployment of the battalion was wide and well advanced; Jones had linked with MacAdie and had his company at Skindewai; Captain Sherlock,[3] with his "A" Company, had also set out along the Buisaval Track—to base his company on Ballam's, patrol the Wandumi area and the eastern entrance to the Wau Valley; Dexter had moved to Timne; one platoon had been sent to the Black Cat Mine as a standing patrol on the old mining track which followed the Bitoi River west from Guadagasal through Waipali, north of Buibaining and past House Copper, then ran up the Black Cat Creek, by way of the Black Cat Mine, to the Black Cat Gap where the main mountain skyline dipped slightly and, from the Gap, fell south-west to Wau. So far, however, the Australians had observed no positive indication of the next Japanese move. Herring wrote to Blamey:

> We are sending Moten's second battalion forward to him as soon as air transport can carry it, but I feel that Jap action in the [Guadagasal] Gap area is defensive rather than offensive and there is no need to worry about Kanga at the moment. The raid on Mubo has undoubtedly disturbed him and I feel he fears that it may be a preliminary to an attack on Salamaua similar in strength to those which have defeated him at Buna and Sanananda.

But this complacency was soon to be shattered. On the 20th MacAdie sent Lieutenant Dunshea[4] with a patrol towards Buibaining to look for

---

[3] Capt W. H. Sherlock, VX3561; 2/6 Bn. Grazier; of Coleraine, Vic; b. Malvern, Vic, 20 May 1908. Killed in action 29 Jan 1943.

[4] Capt C. J. P. Dunshea, MC, QX16381. 2/7 Indep Coy; 2/8 Cdo Sqn. Motor transport driver; of Mitchell, Qld; b. Wellington, NSW, 24 Apr 1917.

any signs of Japanese movement in that direction. Next day Dunshea saw 50 Japanese moving past Buibaining along the Black Cat Track and watched another party bathing in the Bitoi River. MacAdie at once intensified his patrolling of this area (sending Lieutenant Lade out with 54 others) and subsequent observations not only confirmed those initially made but also established that larger parties were on the move along the track past Buibaining.

When (on the 22nd) Moten had the news of the first sightings he had a second platoon from the 2/6th warned for movement to the Black Cat Mine. But he cancelled this order next day and sent instead Captain Winning (who had recently returned to Wau leaving only some 55 of his company out with MacAdie) with about 30 of his men. Nevertheless the position was still by no means clear and the precise axis of the Japanese thrust at Wau (if one were coming) was still undefined. But each day's delay meant that the Australians would be in a stronger position: on the 23rd 31 air transports arrived at Wau bringing additional men of the 2/6th Battalion and more supplies; on the 24th 34 planes brought more stores again, the leading elements of the 2/5th Battalion (some 81 all ranks including the commander, Lieut-Colonel Starr[5]) and engineers of the 2/8th Field Company.

At this time Moten intended Starr to take over the defence of the Mubo-Wau area while the 2/6th Battalion moved down the valley for the defence of the Bulolo area. Accordingly Starr was early on the move on the 25th along the track to Mubo, approximately half of his party moving behind him and the other half remaining at Wau. But the weather disappointed him on the 26th, no aircraft were able to land and the main body of his battalion was earth-bound at Port Moresby.

By that time the pattern of the Japanese movements and intentions was becoming clearer. On the 24th Winning had indications that the Japanese were on the move in the vicinity of the Black Cat and, next day, reports from a patrol he had out along the track towards House Copper indicated more definitely what he had already begun to suspect—that the invaders were cutting their way along a long-disused track from House Copper south-west to Wandumi. This was roughly parallel with and between the Black Cat Track on the Japanese right as they advanced and the Buisaval Track on their left. It was soon to become known to the Australians as the "Jap Track". By the 26th Moten felt reasonably sure that this new track had developed as the main axis of the advance. With his main deployment hinged on the Buisaval Track on his right, and a small deployment on the Black Cat Track (which now seemed to offer the best chance of striking at the attackers) he reported that day to Headquarters New Guinea Force that any movement out of Wau would leave him with an insufficient reserve there. However, he decided to take the risk and use the 2/6th Battalion (less Jones', Sherlock's and Dexter's companies) in an aggressive movement through the Black Cat area on

---
[5] Lt-Col P. D. S. Starr, ED, VX46. 2/5 Bn (CO 1942-43); CO 58/59 Bn 1943. Bank clerk; of Williamstown, Vic; b. Townsville, Qld, 20 Mar 1910.

the assumption that his essential reserve would arrive at Wau by the 27th (Herring having promised that he would hasten the concentration of the 2/5th Battalion). This decision involved the temporary abandonment of his plans to move the 2/6th to Bulolo and the cancellation of orders which had already gone out to that effect. On the 26th, therefore, Wood, with two platoons already at the Black Cat, one having followed Winning there, regrouped his main local strength into two companies, one under Captain Gullett[6] and one under Captain Stewart,[7] and set out along the Black Cat Track next day with 110 native carriers—a steep, slippery climb of about 8 hours for the laden soldiers whose sojourn at Milne Bay had not left them in good condition for mountain work.

At that time Moten's intention was to destroy all the Japanese between the Black Cat and House Copper. To this end he planned that, having taken Winning's group into his command, Wood would attack from the Black Cat towards House Copper on the 28th. At the same time Jones, having moved "stealthily" the previous day to the track east of House Copper, would sally towards the Black Cat and fall upon the rear of the Japanese being assailed by Wood, his own rear protected by Lade and his patrol (who had now been in an ambush and watching position near Buibaining since the 22nd) and additional men brought forward by MacAdie blocking the Mubo-House Copper track near Waipali. Sherlock, having previously concentrated his company at Wandumi, would attack up the Jap Track towards House Copper. As a preliminary Winning and Sherlock would scout offensively on the 27th.

On the 27th the main body of the 2/5th Battalion was arriving at Wau. By noon 9 officers and 204 men had landed. Captain Bennett's[8] company set out at once to stage the night at Ballam's and move on to Skindewai on the 28th, on which day Major Rowan's[9] company would concentrate at Ballam's. Starr was to take command of all troops on the Buisaval Track from the beginning of the 28th.

Although it looked, therefore, as though the course of events was set fair for the Australians, the energy of the Japanese forestalled the planning. About 10 a.m. on the 27th Sergeant Wild[1] of Sherlock's company, patrolling the Jap Track between Wandumi and Wandumi Trig, clashed with Japanese whom he thought to be setting booby traps. On hearing the exchange of fire Sherlock moved calmly. He was older than the average company officer, a man with a strong sense of duty, a disciplinarian (but one who shared his tobacco with his men), a leader since his schooldays when he had stroked the Geelong Grammar School eight in three successive

---

[6] Maj H. B. S. Gullett, MC, VX3511; 2/6 Bn. MHR 1946-55. Journalist; of Melbourne; b. London, 16 Dec 1914.
[7] Lt-Col H. McB. Stewart, VX3837. 2/6 Bn (A/CO during 1945); CO 2 NG Inf Bn 1944-45. Estate agent; of South Yarra, Vic; b. Yass, NSW, 18 Jan 1908.
[8] Maj A. C. Bennett, VX7499; 2/5 Bn. Station overseer; of Hamilton, Vic; b. Orange, NSW, 12 Apr 1915.
[9] Maj A. T. Rowan, VX158. (1st AIF: Pte 8 Bn.) 2/5 Bn; CO 1 Recruit Trg Bn. Schoolteacher; of Burwood, Vic; b. Euroa, Vic, 1 Sep 1899.
[1] Sgt J. Wild, VX5096; 2/6 Bn. Coach builder; of East Geelong, Vic; b. Oldham, England, 9 Dec 1916. Died of wounds 20 Jun 1943.

years. Now he settled his company (and 2 officers and 20 men of the 2/5th Independent Company) in positions he had prepared on the kunai slopes forward of Wandumi village and waited for more news. Later he sent Lieutenant Kerr of the Independent Company to try to supplement Wild's report. When Kerr returned later in the afternoon he had little to add except that he had lost one of his men to a sniper. Sherlock then decided to make no further move until the following morning and camped in the village for the night, his men remaining quiet in the face of questing bursts fired blindly by the Japanese. At 4 a.m. on the 28th they were astir in preparation for their move towards House Copper. Ten minutes later, however, the Japanese attacked them and when Sherlock moved them back at 5 a.m. into positions on the track some 300 yards

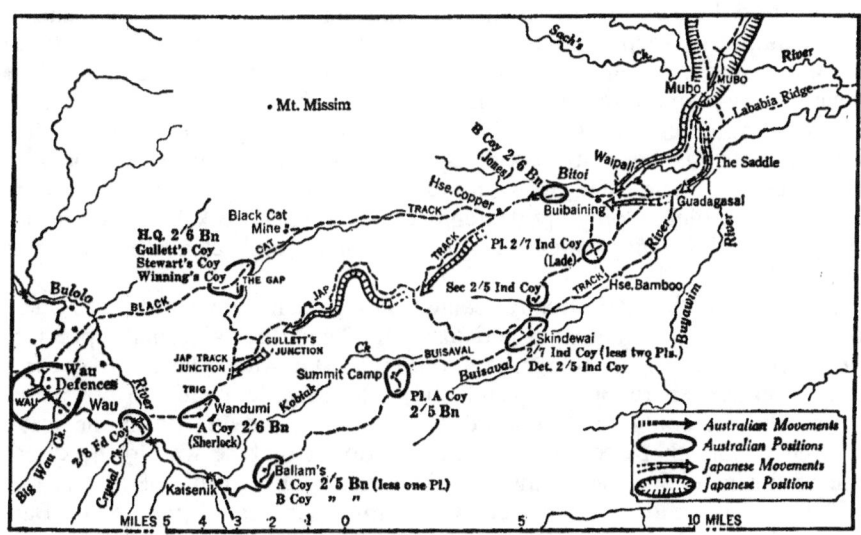

Dispositions, dawn, 28th January

south-west of the village they had lost one killed and 4 wounded. In the new positions Lieutenant St John's[2] 9 Platoon, which had already borne the brunt of the attack on the village, was on the right and on them fell the main force of the new attack. St John's men, however, inspired by their brave leader and Sergeant Gray[3] (the latter not only supporting his officer in all his efforts but fearlessly going out under heavy fire to bring Corporal Noble[4] in from a forward slope where he was lying wounded) resisted all the Japanese attempts to oust them during the morning. They still held their ground as the early afternoon wore on.

---

[2] Lt E. R. St John, MC, VX4456; 2/6 Bn. Salesman; of Elwood, Vic; b. East Malvern, Vic, 1 Jan 1909.
[3] Sgt J. G. Gray, MM, VX38792; 2/6 Bn. Stock and commission agent; of Holbrook, NSW; b. Kalgoorlie, WA, 2 Nov 1909.
[4] Cpl J. W. Noble, VX1154; 2/6 Bn. Grazier; of Geelong, Vic; b. Geelong, 31 May 1913.

Meanwhile, about 12.30 p.m., Lieutenant Cameron's[5] platoon of Bennett's company of the 2/5th Battalion had arrived after a quick movement early that morning down from Ballam's to Kaisenik and a gruelling forced march from Kaisenik over the scorched kunai ridges. After only a few minutes' rest Corporal Wilkinson's[6] section moved to support the right front, a second section went to the left front to stiffen there the Independent Company men, and a third section covered the left flank.

Until about 2.30 p.m. the Japanese repeatedly attacked the Australian positions frontally with mortar and machine-gun support. But, as fast as they formed up to charge, cool and well-directed Australian fire broke up the attacks. Then the Japanese changed their tactics. Crawling through the high kunai grass under cover of machine-gun fire they got well among St John's foremost positions. Sherlock himself, with the survivors from the infiltrated positions, his own headquarters, two or three commandos and Wilkinson's section, then drove with the bayonet in a demoralising counter-attack, overwhelmed the intruders and restored the positions (the tireless Gray—among others—being hit during this movement). At 6 p.m. the sweating defenders were still holding firm, though they had lost five more men in the later afternoon. By that time their mortar bombs were exhausted and their small-arms ammunition was failing (though engineers from a 2/8th Field Company detachment at Crystal Creek had been bringing ammunition and water forward to them, and carrying out their wounded).

Moten, however, had already reacted, though somewhat tardily, to Sherlock's reports. Apparently he had discounted Sherlock's earlier reports of the strength moving in along the Jap Track. But when the intrepid company commander reported by telephone to brigade headquarters about 3 p.m. that he could see "hundreds" of Japanese moving down the track in front of him there could be no further doubt that he was in the direct line of the main Japanese advance. Apparently as a result of that report "C" Company and Headquarters Company elements of the 2/5th Battalion who had landed at Wau only that morning were started out under Major Duffy[7] to reinforce the hard-pressed Wandumi force. They came up with Sherlock about evening. Sherlock and Duffy then decided that, since they could not hope to hold the hundreds of Japanese closing in upon them and, in any case, these would flow round any position the Australians took up between Wandumi and the river, they would draw their force back to the river. This movement was already under way when Major Muir,[8] Moten's brigade major, arrived. He informed Moten at once of the position and the latter ordered him to take command of the whole force. Muir then decided to hold on one of the lower features in rear

---

[5] Capt L. A. Cameron, MC, VX3347; 2/5 Bn. Clerk; of Warracknabeal, Vic; b. Warracknabeal, 17 Mar 1918.

[6] L-Sgt L. A. Wilkinson, MM, VX36351; 2/5 Bn. Labourer; of Deniliquin, NSW; b. Deniliquin, 28 Oct 1911.

[7] Maj J. W. Duffy, VX71; 2/5 Bn. Bank officer; of Balwyn, Vic; b. Dublin, 31 May 1905.

[8] Lt-Col R. A. C. Muir, QX6236. 7 Cav Regt; 25 Bde 1941; BM 17 Bde 1941-43, and staff appts. Chartered accountant; of Brisbane; b. Perth, WA, 20 Jun 1910.

of the former position. He reasoned that, although the nature of the country (of which sharp kunai-clad ridges falling down towards the river were the main feature) foredoomed either holding or attack forward towards Wandumi to ultimate failure since the Japanese were always commanding the higher ground, the force should try to hold the track until morning at least and give the 2/7th Battalion time to build up at Wau on the 29th. Sherlock and Duffy agreed. But the Japanese were all round them in the darkness and so they felt their way back to a conical-shaped hill below which, in their rear, the ground sloped down to the river. There, with bursts of fire from attackers already spread along the river in their rear breaking spasmodically over them, they waited for the new day. The last message Moten received from them was at 3 a.m. on the 29th. Muir signalled that there were 300-500 troops fronting them; large numbers were moving round their left flank; if Moten decided they should move to the Wau side of the Bulolo they would do so, but otherwise they would hold on. Moten replied that they were to withdraw but they never received the message.

This situation which developed at Wandumi on the 28th was the key not only to the ultimate outcome of the fight for Wau but to immediate events in the closely adjoining sectors—particularly the Black Cat one. At 6.45 a.m. Lieut-Colonel Wood was told by Moten of the Wandumi attack and ordered to send a party down. He instructed Winning to go. Winning set out from the Black Cat Mine at 8.15 a.m. with 4 other officers and 87 men to march to Wandumi by way of a track which struck south from the Gap. Wood estimated that the party should reach Wandumi by noon. But they found the going slow and, near the junction of the track from the Gap with the Jap Track, began to meet opposition. As they swung south-west towards Wandumi pressure on their rear so increased and hampered them that, by 5.15 p.m., they were but three-quarters of a mile below the track junction. By this time communications with Wood had failed. Winning reported later that it seemed to him that the sounds of fighting which had been coming from Wandumi had swung towards the Crystal Creek-Wau area; that he therefore left the track and turned in that direction. And so he arrived at Wau the following day. Meanwhile, spurred by a message in the later afternoon of the increasing seriousness of Sherlock's plight, Wood had tried (but failed) to get in touch with Winning by runner to hasten him to Sherlock's aid.

Soon after sending Winning off that morning Wood had sent Stewart out along the track to House Copper to link with Jones advancing from Buibaining. Stewart (his party totalling 5 officers and 99 men) left the mine at 8.45 a.m. and soon found that the well-defined native track from Wau which had held that far deteriorated rapidly. Carpeted with moss it plunged into tall timber which shut out the light and held the damp and made the difficult track drear and depressing. By 1 p.m. Stewart's three wireless sets had failed. About 4 p.m. heavy rain began to sheet his force and night found his men huddled under kunai shelters with nothing achieved. About noon on the 29th they reached the intersection of the

Black Cat Track and the Jap Track. They then scouted as far as House Copper without incident, lay in ambush for two hours, and then Stewart, having no news of Jones, decided to lead his company down the Jap Track to Wandumi. He saw no Japanese until about 6.30 p.m. when two passed through the bivouac and ambush position he had taken up for the night. He let them go hoping to trap a larger force—but none came. Next morning, in obedience to orders he had received by runner late the

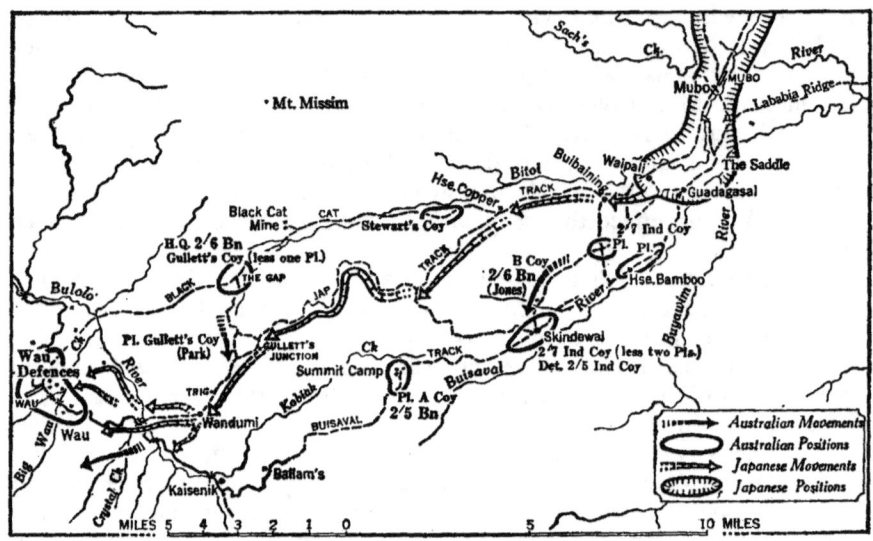

Dispositions, dawn, 30th January

previous evening, he began to retrace his steps up the track, arrived at the junction about 10.30, found that Jones was not there and moved on to House Copper. When there was still no indication of what had happened to Jones, and with his rations very low, he decided to return to the Black Cat area. He and his men, tired, many of them with bad feet and sore legs, arrived back late the following day.

While this was happening Jones was in trouble. He had brought his company to a position on the track about four hours and a half east of House Copper by the evening of the 27th. On the morning of the 28th he began his move onwards but quickly ran into stiff opposition. He lost a number of men, could not progress and, by midday on the 30th, was back at Skindewai, his men tired, footsore and hungry.

While the three groups under Jones, Stewart and Winning thus fruitlessly exhausted themselves (and one of Gullett's platoons—under Lieutenant Park[9]—which had been sent on the 29th to hold the Wandumi Trig had been forced out of touch and was not to be heard of again until they arrived at Wau a few days later); while Wood was standing fast

---

[9] Lt J. W. Park, VX51193; 2/6 Bn. Clerk; of Balwyn, Vic; b. Bendigo, Vic, 14 Feb 1910. Killed in action 9 Feb 1943.

at the Black Cat with the small numbers left to him; and while Sherlock's men were in straits at Wandumi; it was clear to Moten that Wau was in jeopardy. At 3.35 p.m. on the 28th he signalled Herring:

> Enemy attacking in force Wandumi about four hours from Wau. Our company isolated this area. Sending company from Wau to Wandumi to support. No reserve force left in Wau. You must expedite arrival of troops this area.

He was looking now not only for the arrival of the rest of the 2/5th Battalion but also for that of the 2/7th Battalion. But the weather was against him. The first flight of planes (4 of 30 which left Port Moresby that morning) had arrived at 9 a.m. with the additional 2/5th Battalion men, most of whom were rushed out to Wandumi during the afternoon. But these were all who did arrive that day as the weather closed in after their landing. Thus, although the balance of the 2/5th were ready to leave Port Moresby, the leading elements of the 2/7th Battalion had been standing by since the night of the 26th and the main unit group was not

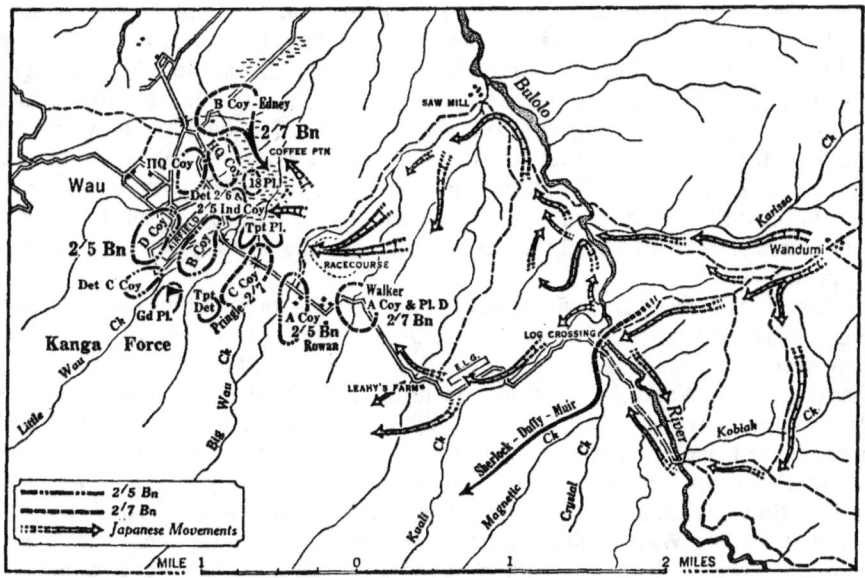

The Japanese attack on Wau, dawn, 30th January

only waiting at the Port Moresby strips from dawn of the 28th but actually got many men airborne at 8 only to see them flown back again, there was nothing anyone could do to get them to Wau. By the end of the day, therefore, Moten had only scratch groups on the ground at Wau itself and, although Sherlock was still fighting, it was clear not only that it was merely a matter of time for his force but that part of the Japanese drive had flowed round it, for a transport driver reported to Moten at 7 p.m. that he had seen a body of Japanese troops marching down the road to Wau at a point not more than two miles south-east of the aerodrome.

In a desperate effort to get some substance back into his actual Wau defences Moten ordered Starr to bring his two companies in from Ballam's. They left there in a forced march at 10 p.m., their vanguard arrived in the Crystal Creek area about 4.30 a.m. on the 29th, in the confused darkness actually passing almost unchallenged through the Japanese who were astride the road, and arrived to man the aerodrome defences at 7 a.m.

By that time Japanese small arms and mortar fire from the south-east was falling on the outer defences of the airfield and it continued intermittently until 8.15 a.m. But by 9.15 Australian reinforcements had begun to land, heralding a record arrival of 60 planes with 814 troops—the remainder of the 2/5th Battalion (making that unit's total strength 35 officers and 580 men) and Lieut-Colonel Guinn's[1] 2/7th Battalion.[2] Moten then disposed closely about the airfield the forces immediately available. As the situation clarified a little during the day he ordered Guinn to send Major Walker[3] with his company in a sortie out along the road towards Crystal Creek. Walker ("Luger Joe" to his men), a brave and resourceful young leader, came sharply against the Japanese in the vicinity of Leahy's Farm (south-east of the airfield), killed about 15 of them, he estimated, for the loss of four of his own men, and settled for the night facing the enemy, Rowan's company of the 2/5th to his immediate and right rear, Captain Pringle's[4] company of the 2/7th backing Rowan and holding the Big Wau Creek crossing. More of Guinn's battalion packed the eastern end of the airfield in the native hospital area with the balance of the battalion (Captain Edney's[5] company) holding the north-eastern approaches. Men of the 2/5th Battalion held the north-west and western approaches.

Except for sporadic rifle shooting and bursts of machine-gun fire the night was uneventful. In the dark hours before the dawn of the 30th, however, the Japanese made their bid for the airfield. At 4 a.m. they fell heavily upon Walker's positions fronting Leahy's Farm. Though part of the company was able to hold fast Walker himself and some of his men were forced back and to the right on to Rowan's position. In the darkness Walker's group were about to assail the 2/5th company with the bayonet before they realised that they were friends. Soon afterwards Pringle's company at the Big Wau crossing were fiercely set upon by Japanese advancing along the road. Those of Walker's company, however, who had remained in their original positions, were flailing at these Japanese from their rear, Rowan and the group with Walker himself assailed them from their left flank, and Pringle's men met them with calculated fire which took a heavy toll. Then, when the attackers tried to work round Pringle's left,

---

[1] Col H. G. Guinn, DSO, ED, VX33; 2/7 Bn (CO 1941-44). Commercial traveller; of East Malvern, Vic; b. Carrum, Vic, 21 Mar 1900.
[2] The battalion was less Lieutenant A. N. Rooke's platoon which had flown on the 23rd to Bena Bena, in the highlands between Lae and Madang, to protect the airfield there.
[3] Maj K. R. Walker, DSO, VX4740; 2/7 Bn. Motor car salesman; of Mildura, Vic; b. Essendon, Vic, 25 Aug 1917.
[4] Capt F. B. Pringle, VX14161; 2/7 Bn. Dairyman; of Windsor, Vic; b. Terang, Vic, 3 Sep 1914.
[5] Capt W. K. Edney, VX7224. 2/7 Bn; training appts 1943-45. Ticket writer; of Camberwell, Vic; b. Gardenvale, Vic, 11 Sep 1916.

fire from the band which Winning had led down from the Black Cat (in his fruitless attempt to help Sherlock at Wandumi) cut deeply into them. Meanwhile Edney set out to patrol the line of the Big Wau Creek preparatory to moving southward by way of the racecourse and joining Walker's left flank, but a brief movement brought him against hard fighting Japanese who stopped him among coffee trees. While he was thus held Walker had reorganised his company, and, only lightly opposed, was firm again in his original positions by 10 a.m.

As the morning advanced some of the fog of battle cleared and Moten planned to capitalise the advantage he now felt was his. His position was strengthened by new arrivals during the morning—most importantly a section (two guns) of the 2/1st Field Regiment. Captain Wise[6] landed his gunners at 9.15 a.m. with Japanese fire falling among the big aircraft as they rolled to a standstill. Some rifle shots fell among the gunners as they unloaded their stores and prepared to deploy. Wise was told at once that he was in support of the 2/7th Battalion's operations, was put in touch with Guinn, to whom Moten had given the striking role leaving Starr responsible for the actual aerodrome defences, and then went forward to Walker's positions to establish his observation post. Already the reconnaissance for the gun position was going ahead and the 25-pounders themselves were being assembled at the airfield. By 11.30 a.m. they had got their first round away.

At 2 p.m. Moten, at Guinn's headquarters, gave the battalion commander his orders for the advance. Guinn then allotted Pringle the key task of capturing the high ground on Walker's right, almost due west of Leahy's Farm, and commanding the proposed axis of advance. Immediately upon the completion of this task Walker was to push up the spur, strongly held and covered, which rose just ahead and to his right. The artillery and mortars would support him. Edney, relieved of his responsibility in the coffee plantation, was to hold the crossing of the Big Wau Creek in Pringle's place.

About 4.15 p.m. Pringle set his men to their task. Ahead of them the high feature rose, the slopes of black earth leading up it made treacherous by rain and commanded by a hot fire which struck into the attacking Australians as they worked their way up towards the bush-covered crest with the aid of vines and shrubs by which they swung and tufts of grass round which their seeking hands closed. At 4.50, the dash of Pringle's men had placed the objective within their grasp, but Walker, beginning his movement up the spur which fronted him, was being chopped at by a medium machine-gun above him and heavy fire from light machine-guns and tree-top riflemen. Just then 300-400 Japanese appeared along the road which led from Leahy's Farm. They seemed unaware of the presence of Walker's men until they were a mere 200 yards from them. The Australians then poured their fire into them and Wise brought his shells crashing fairly among them with such effect that there was suddenly a

---

[6] Maj R. J. Wise, NX142. 2/1, 14, 2/8 Fd Regts. Flour miller; of Narrandera, NSW, and Sydney; b. Mosman, NSW, 26 Feb 1916.

major burst at the farm as a shell set off a supply of explosives. The ground rocked, a great cloud of billowing smoke rose, and many Japanese were killed. Wise wrote later:

> ... approx 400 Japs advanced in "column of lumps" along the road right in front of me . . . and I had a field day with them.

A few minutes later Australian Beaufighters swept low with a whispering roar, gunning the confused Japanese into greater confusion. None the less those on the spur fronting Walker held their positions and stopped the Australians with sweeping machine-gun fire. Pringle's men, from their vantage points, were prevented by the thick scrub from bringing effective supporting fire to bear and so the night came with the intractable Japanese positions marked as artillery targets for the following day.

At Wau itself the 31st was a day of extensive patrolling and small clashes resulting in little change in the relative positions of the opposing forces. More fresh Australians flew in. Among them were Captain Hay[7]

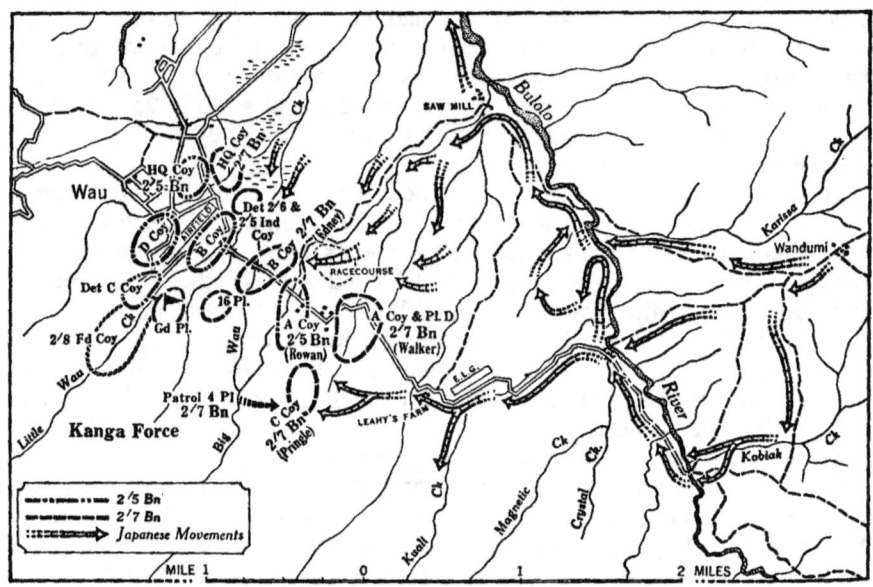

Dispositions Wau-Crystal Creek area, dawn, 31st January

returning to the 2/6th Battalion with 100 reinforcements for his unit and Major Warfe[8] (an original officer of the 2/6th Battalion) with his 2/3rd Independent Company. Warfe, a builder in civil life who had found soldiering much to his liking, was a hard, able and energetic officer who killed his King's enemies with a cold-blooded purpose and apparently no regrets. He had been commanding this company since September after

---

[7] Lt-Col D. O. Hay, DSO, MBE, VX9890; 2/6 Bn. Public servant; of Canberra; b. Corowa, NSW, 29 Nov 1916.

[8] Lt-Col G. R. Warfe, DSO, MC, VX186. 2/6 Bn; OC 2/3 Indep Coy; CO 58/59 Bn 1943-44, 2/24 Bn 1945. Joiner and shop-fitter; of Caulfield, Vic; b. Leongatha, Vic, 27 Jul 1912.

its return from garrison service in New Caledonia. There was news from New Guinea Force that two composite companies formed from 21st and 25th Brigade carrier platoon personnel, each 172 all ranks strong and consisting of 3 rifle platoons and 2 medium machine-gun platoons, would begin to arrive at Wau next day. They were to be used for the close defence of the aerodrome and Wau township and were not to be employed offensively outside that area.

Just after dark Muir, St John and 26 survivors of the Wandumi fighting arrived back in the Australian positions. Although their arrival had been preceded by that of other and smaller parties from Wandumi, Muir was able to give a fuller account of the events there than any received up to that time. He related how the Japanese made a very strong attack with up to 500 troops from the direction of the village on the early morning of the 29th and, at the same time, pushed hard from the direction of the river. It was clear to the Australians that they would not only be overwhelmed at any moment but could serve no further useful purpose by staying where they were. They therefore broke their way through the bush on the right flank (where there seemed to be the fewest enemy) and made for the Bulolo River just above its junction with Crystal Creek. There they found a single log bridge spanning the river and crossed it safely though they knew the Japanese had seen them. They decided then to try to circle the Japanese positions by following the creek's course up into the hills and so make their way back to Wau. But soon afterwards disaster overtook them. As they were crossing the creek the watching Japanese cut into them with machine-gun fire, killed the gallant Sherlock and wounded several others (including St John), cut Muir and his party off from Duffy and the rest, and thereafter harassed the fugitives with patrols and dogs. Then, hungry and harried, carrying their wounded with them, Muir and his men finally got back to Wau. Others of the Wandumi force returned much later, among them Duffy and a few of the 2/5th Battalion men who did not arrive until 4th February. It seemed that the 2/6th Battalion troops had sustained most of the casualties and a final tally placed their losses at one officer and 4 men killed, one and 14 wounded, 2 men missing.

So nightfall of the 31st found the garrison at Wau in strong positions and good heart with every hope that the crisis had passed. Out in the hills there was no development of great moment although movement was taking place there. The commandos and the 2/6th Battalion company along the Buisaval Track were watchful but not threatened. In the Black Cat area Stewart's patrol had just returned in a state bordering on exhaustion but others had struck out into the region of the Japanese advance. At 10.15 a.m. Captain Gullett, stocky, dynamic and brave, took 37 men out towards the junction of the track from the Gap with the Jap Track. They settled in ambush about half a mile on the Gap side of the junction but were too weak to attack the much stronger Japanese forces which were in the vicinity. Wood, who had received orders from Moten in the early afternoon to prepare the Gap positions as a base from which parties approximately 50 strong could harass the Japanese lines of communication, signalled that he would attack the junction forces when Winning and the company with him arrived back.

The comparative quiet for the 2/7th Battalion continued on 1st February after a fairly undisturbed night. During the day Pringle beat off a vacillating attack without loss; Walker's men edged up the remainder of the high ground immediately fronting them; Edney's company (now without their commander who had been missing since a patrol clash on the previous day and was soon to come in wounded) patrolling towards the Bulolo, found their movement checked in its early stages by a well dug-in position which they estimated to be manned by about 50 men; Warfe (having sustained his first losses in the darkness of the preceding night when two of his men were killed) set his whole company patrolling the area between the Bulolo River and Wau Creek. This they did without incident until, in the last of the daylight, they came against Japanese positions (some of which Edney's men had already tested) in a thick copse about half a mile north-north-east of the junction of the Big and Little Wau Creeks. They dropped mortar bombs into these and then returned to the Wau defences for the night where both supplies and strength had built up further during the day. Fifty-three transports landed a total payload of 26,612 pounds, including a company of the 7th Machine-Gun Battalion and 50 reinforcements for the 17th Brigade. That day the strength of Kanga Force totalled 201 officers and 2,965 men.

With the dawn of the 2nd the 2/7th patrols were on the move. On the right flank Pringle's patrol ran into sharp opposition and, when he sent another platoon to help, the fighting flared high with the Japanese, from well-dug and well-concealed positions, pouring a hot fire from machine-guns and grenades into the Australians. This lasted well into the day and cost Pringle one killed and 2 officers and 7 men wounded. When the fighting died down to a tense quiet only a few yards separated the opposing positions. During this period Pringle, having lost all his officers, owed much to the steadfast support of his Company Sergeant Major, Doran,[9] and to the tireless and cheerful bravery of Corporal "Stumpy" Carter[1] who formed his link with the foremost sections, wriggling beneath the fire which constantly swept over the ground which he crossed and re-crossed.

While this was going on Major Muir led over a flight of Boston bombers from Port Moresby to indicate to them the main Japanese positions in the Crystal Creek area. Clouds defeated him, however, and his bombers transferred their attention effectively to the Buisaval Track. There supply aircraft had preceded them, dropping rations to MacAdie and his men, a fairly successful venture which followed several failures of the days immediately preceding.

On this same day Warfe's commandos had been trying to clear the copse where the opposition had manifested itself the previous day. After

---
[9] WO2 R. N. Doran, VX8889; 2/7 Bn. Transport driver; of West Brunswick, Vic; b. Carlton, Vic, 17 Apr 1911. Killed in action 19 Aug 1943.
[1] Sgt S. R. Carter, VX15081; 2/7 Bn. Farm labourer; of Patchewollock, Vic; b. Ballarat, Vic, 9 Mar 1919.

an artillery bombardment Captain Russell[2] (with Captain Tancred[3] attached) led his platoon into the copse. When they came under telling medium and light machine-gun, rifle and mortar fire, Russell, taking Tancred, Lieutenant Lewin[4] and four sub-machine-gunners with him, went scouting ahead. They killed several Japanese who tried to bar them but, in pressing further ahead, Russell and one of the men were killed. Tancred then held with one section and ordered Lieutenant Cobb[5] and his men forward on the right flank. Cobb was struck down and, dying, ordered Corporal Brown[6] who was beside him "Carry on Corporal! Keep going forward." But Tancred judged the opposition too strong, waited for the coming darkness and then withdrew his men.

Before dawn on the 3rd Major Nelson[7] (who had taken over Edney's company after the latter was wounded on the 1st) led his men to their

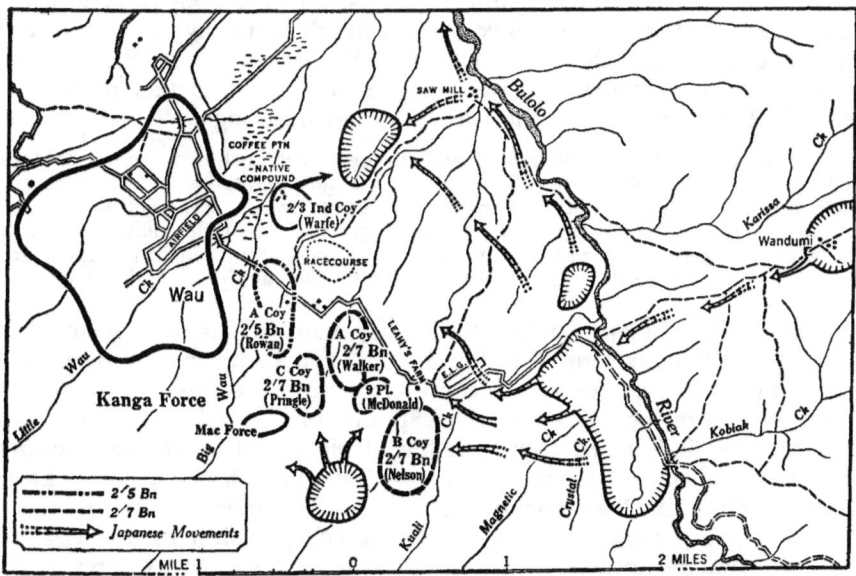

Dispositions Wau-Crystal Creek area, nightfall, 3rd February

forming-up position for an attack through Leahy's Farm to the high feature beyond, known as Bare Knoll. After an artillery and mortar barrage they began their advance at 8 a.m., Lieutenant McDonald[8] ("Meggsie"—much

---

[2] Capt D. McR. Russell, VX44768; 2/3 Indep Coy. Clerk; of South Yarra, Vic; b. Adelaide, 22 Jul 1919. Killed in action 2 Feb 1943.

[3] Lt-Col P. L. Tancred, NX117028. 2/3 Indep Coy; OC 2/3 Cdo Sqn. Regular soldier; of Queenscliffe, Vic; b. Toowoomba, Qld, 14 Mar 1919.

[4] Capt J. E. Lewin, NX76248. 2/3 Indep Coy; 2/3 Cdo Sqn. Paymaster; of Berala, NSW; b. Bexley, NSW, 15 Jun 1919.

[5] Lt F. P. Cobb, QX42392; 2/3 Indep Coy. Station hand; of Winton, Qld; b. Winton, 29 Oct 1921. Killed in action 2 Feb 1943.

[6] WO2 F. J. Brown, MM, QX16132. 2/3 Indep Coy; 2/3 Cdo Sqn. Freezer; of Townsville, Qld; b. Cairns, Qld, 6 Apr 1921.

[7] Maj St E. D. Nelson, VX237; 2/7 Bn. Law clerk; of Geelong, Vic; b. Caulfield, Vic, 18 Mar 1919.

[8] Lt A. J. McDonald, VX5554; 2/7 Bn. Butcher; of Box Hill, Vic; b. Fitzroy, Vic, 25 Sep 1919. Killed in action 3 Feb 1943.

loved for his bright and buoyant personality), with a platoon from Walker's company covering their right flank from a high feature (McDonald's Knoll) just south-west of Leahy's Farm. By 10 a.m., having taken the Japanese by surprise, they were digging in on Bare Knoll. For McDonald's men on their right the day was uneventful until the afternoon when three of their number, returning with water from the stream which ran below them, were surprised by a concealed Japanese party and two of them were shot down. McDonald brought one in but, returning for the other under heavy machine-gun fire, was himself killed. The remainder of his platoon hotly engaged the enemy pocket. Walker himself, coming to assist them, was wounded by one of the Australians' own booby traps but continued on to direct the action, and the encounter concluded with the death of 13 Japanese. But the day was marred for the Australians by their losses of McDonald's men, the two brave officers, and five men from Pringle's company who, patrolling to link with Walker's company, were wounded by the booby traps the latter had set. The casualties in that difficult country, however, threw into relief the bravery of the battalion stretcher bearers. Their work, wrote the battalion diarist, during

"C" Company's clash of yesterday and during today's action is typical of their conduct all through the action. They have won the admiration of all ranks and their N.C.O., Sergeant "Lofty" Vaughan,[9] is liked by all. His unchanging good nature can be expressed always in his cheery greeting of "Hello mate". Whatever the work—fatigue, ration party, or stretcher bearing—his magnificent strength and big heart are always ready to help and encourage his men and those in the companies.

Although the Japanese were still fighting hard in this main sector they were obviously weakening. But that they still retained plenty of vigour was being attested elsewhere—in the copse area, along the Buisaval Track and in the vicinity of the Black Cat. At 9.30 a.m. on the 3rd Warfe assembled to reduce the first-named. Behind falling shells he put Lieutenants Lewin's and Barnett's[1] and Corporal Brown's sections into the attack with Lieutenant Hortin's[2] medium machine-gun section in a defensive role. Barnett's men shot and grenaded their way into the copse against increasingly hot machine-gun fire until Barnett himself was wounded with several of his men, including Corporal Parker,[3] and two of his men were killed. The main body then withdrew about 100 yards and reorganised under Lieutenant Lamb.[4] But they left Parker lying before a stubborn machine-gun position. Sergeant Littler[5] then moved in alone to help him. He was bringing Parker out under heavy fire when he was hit himself. Despite that

---

[9] Sgt R. R. Vaughan, MM, NX30624; 2/7 Bn. Labourer; of Urunga, NSW; b. Urunga, 16 Aug 1912.

[1] Lt G. W. Barnett, NX26665. 2/3 Indep Coy; 2/3 Cdo Sqn. Wool sorter; of North Fitzroy, Vic; b. South Melbourne, 11 Oct 1915. Died after discharge.

[2] Maj S. E. B. Hortin, VX85203. 2/2 Indep Coy; Water Tpt 1944-45. 3 Bn RAR, Korea, 1950-53. Regular soldier; of Parkville, Vic; b. Mordialloc, Vic, 13 Jun 1918.

[3] Cpl R. P. Parker, WX12270; 2/3 Indep Coy. Sampler; of Northam, WA; b. Pingelly, WA, 22 May 1917. Died of wounds 6 Feb 1943.

[4] Lt J. D. Lamb, VX5116. 2/6 Bn; 2/3 Indep Coy; 2/3 Cdo Sqn. Jackeroo; of Geelong, Vic; b. Geelong, 15 Aug 1920.

[5] Sgt W. A. Littler, MM, NX57124. 2/1, 2/3 Indep Coys. Baker; of Marrickville, NSW; b. Marrickville, 8 Sep 1917.

he continued his efforts to help the other wounded man, and later both were rescued. Meanwhile Brown linked with Lamb's right under heavy fire. Warfe himself then examined the situation and later set Brown's men at the main Japanese positions with Lamb trying to cover them with fire. They broke through the first line of opposition but then they (and Lamb's section) were sheeted with fire which they estimated to be coming from two medium and seven light machine-guns, thickened by rifle fire and grenades. With darkness coming on and the Japanese pressing in Warfe withdrew his men to their defensive positions at the compound, having lost two killed and four wounded. Among the wounded was Lance-Corporal Las Gourgues,[6] already marked by his dashing bravery, who leaped into a Japanese weapon pit in the closing stages of the attack although he was badly wounded in the chest, seized the machine-gun which was there, turned it against its owners and, when told to withdraw, brought the machine-gun out with him and then collapsed.

Warfe was, however, in a strong position for a further attack. By this time he had detailed information of the Japanese dispositions in the copse. At 2.45 p.m. next day the 25-pounders, medium machine-guns and 3-inch mortars began to drench the copse with explosions and fire. At 3 o'clock Warfe's men moved into the attack in perfectly controlled formation. The main groups of the defenders withdrew before them—acting on the warning provided by the barrage—although those who remained shot down ten of Warfe's men before the commandos fired their success signal into the air at 4 o'clock to indicate that the copse had been cleared. Twenty-five Japanese were killed.

Out along the Buisaval Track during these days food threatened to become almost a greater problem to MacAdie than the Japanese. On the 30th he had decided to put all troops on a reduced ration scale with the prospect even then that his rations would be exhausted by 2nd February. He told his men at Ballam's to catch any mules they could and use them to bring food from Kudjeru. That same day 26 mules became available to carry stores to the Summit but even they could do little to ease the situation because of the difficult nature of the country and the wide deployment of the force which then had 25 all ranks at Ballam's, 202 at Skindewai, 42 between Skindewai and Guadagasal and 92 in the Buibaining and Waipali areas. Next day a test supply aircraft circled the Australians' positions but made no droppings. Meanwhile Lade, near Buibaining, was warned that the Japanese were believed to be withdrawing and to attack them when the opportunity offered. On the 1st MacAdie reinforced him with a section bringing his strength to 90 all ranks and 21 native carriers. That same day Lade reported that he had located several Japanese posts manned by an estimated 20 to 30 men. He would attack these on the 2nd. As he was preparing to get under way on that day, however, the Japanese moved in on one of his parties. Although the result was no more than a skirmish it determined MacAdie to reinforce Lade's positions with Jones'

---

[6] L-Cpl L. Las Gourgues, DCM, NX53016; 2/3 Indep Coy. Clerk; of Melbourne; b. London, 4 Jul 1901.

company. But soon he revised his plans on an estimation that there were at least 250 Japanese in the Buibaining area, that a direct attack on them would be too expensive, that his whole force was required to concentrate on the main task of holding the Skindewai-Mubo track, that he had insufficient carriers to supply a large force in the Buibaining-Waipali area, and that the evacuation of wounded from that region was impossible. On the 5th, therefore, he withdrew Lade and Jones to Skindewai and replaced them with 47 all ranks from "A" Platoon.

Round the Black Cat positions there had been more action. On the 1st Gullett reported that he had had a quiet night but that the Japanese were concentrated on a ridge south of the Jap Track Junction. On the morning of the 2nd his watchful men who were forward along the Jap Track ambushed and killed eight big, well-built Japanese. Meanwhile Winning (who had arrived back from Wau the previous afternoon) had moved with some 60 infantry and commandos to a position near the junction, his task being to hold it while Gullett; with 40 of his own men and Lieutenant Blezard[7] commanding a 2/5th Independent Company group and a few 2/6th Battalion men, deployed to take the Japanese from the north-east. As there were no suitable observation posts, the whole movement was preceded by blind and (as was later discovered) largely ineffective fire from two mortars. Winning had a brisk set-to near the junction and Gullett's group launched themselves upon the Japanese at about 3 p.m. Blezard and two men were killed, three others were wounded, but Winning's encounter and Gullett's attack between them probably accounted for 50-60 Japanese. Then, with night coming on, the Australians withdrew towards the Gap, leaving two ambush parties in positions beside the track, estimating that there were 200-300 Japanese between the Jap Track Junction and Wandumi.

On the 3rd, Wood had his men again early astir. His plan was that, after air attacks, the mortars would deluge the main Japanese positions and, after that again, two attacking groups would thrust in—one under Winning and one (Gullett's company) under Captain Laver.[8] Shortly after 8 o'clock Captain Hay (then adjutant) was out on the Jap Track putting strips in position as indicators to the aircraft and preparing Very signals. A little later a scouting Wirraway was over. It was back again at 1.20 p.m. circling, and the forward troops fired flares to indicate their positions. The soldiers knew that the pilot had seen their signals because they picked up his reports on one of their wireless sets. He was back again at 2.39, machine-gunning as he came and leading in Beaufighters which attacked the Japanese with cannon and machine-gun fire. Only two of the aircraft, however, appeared to be near the target. When the airmen ceased firing at 2.55 the mortars got into action and Laver and Winning edged closer to their objectives, ready to go in when the mortars stopped. Once again

---

[7] Lt J. W. W. Blezard, VX114273; 2/5 Indep Coy. Secretary; of Jerilderie, NSW; b. Moama, NSW, 23 Jul 1906. Killed in action 3 Feb 1943.
[8] Maj H. L. Laver, MC, VX3829. 2/6 Bn; 2/7 Bn 1944-45. Stock and station agent; of Caulfield, Vic; b. Caulfield, 4 Apr 1915.

(Australian War Memorial)

A section of the Wau-Bulldog road.

(Australian War Memorial)

Australian troops on the move forward from Wau.

(Australian War Memorial)

A line-up of native boys in Portuguese Timor, October-November 1942. They are being paid for building a hut for the Australians. The survival of the guerillas in Timor depended largely on the friendliness and cooperation of the native population.

(Australian War Memorial)

An Australian patrol in Portuguese Timor, October-November 1942. *Left to right*: Corporal J. H. Sargeant, 2/1st Fortress Sigs; Privates J. B. Williams, C. Chopping, W. A. Crossing and Sergeant A. E. Smith, 2/2nd Independent Company.

AERODROME SECURE

Winning was to hold the Jap Track Junction; Laver was to take the Japanese positions south of the junction and exploit forward to the Wandumi Trig. But Winning was set upon in the vicinity of the junction, though Laver got well south of it, some confusion developed and both groups broke off the track into the bush and subsequently made their way to Wau having lost 7 men killed, 2 wounded and 4 missing. (Wood was critical of the conduct of the 2/5th Independent Company troops on this occasion and, keeping only eight, sent the remainder to Wau to rest.)

The 4th was a comparatively quiet day in the Black Cat area. The gunners at Wau shelled the Japanese positions and, with the night, the mortars harassed the Japanese. On the 5th Wood signalled Moten that he had a new plan. He proposed to cut a new track east to the Jap Track above the junction, from a position a little more than half-way along the track from the Gap to the junction, and use this as an approach for his attackers. But, in the later afternoon, Moten told him to do no more than patrol and rest next day in preparation for an attack on the main enemy positions on the 7th in the wake of artillery and air assaults. In readiness for this Wood reorganised his force into three companies (Laver having returned on the afternoon of the 5th) each of an approximate strength of 40 with Stewart, Gullett and Laver commanding. The proposed new track was cut and became known as Gullett's Track. Its junction with the Jap Track was called Gullett's Junction.

Before these latest developments out at the Black Cat it was quite clear that the critical period at Wau itself had passed. Late on the 3rd Moten signalled Lieut-General Sir Iven Mackay (who had temporarily relieved Herring in command of New Guinea Force at 9 a.m. on 30th January) that he considered the Wau aerodrome to be now secure. He said that, when the companies formed from the 21st and 25th Brigade carrier platoons arrived, he would be able to release for offensive operations the 2/5th Battalion, the machine-gun company and that part of the 2/7th Battalion he had not yet committed. The carrier companies landed on the 4th and he was thus free to reorganise his attack on the Japanese remaining in the valley. That day all three forward companies of the 2/7th Battalion were engaged in minor affrays, Nelson's men burnt the buildings at Leahy's Farm to remove cover which the Japanese might use, but the only major change in the dispositions was the relief of Pringle's tired men by "D" Company Headquarters (Captain Smith[9]) and Lieutenant Thomas'[1] platoon. The carrier companies took over the aerodrome defence role completely from the 2/5th Battalion and Starr was preparing to set Bennett's and Captain MacFarlane's[2] companies moving up the west bank of the Bulolo River.

A quiet night followed. The 5th was another day of small patrol clashes for the 2/7th Battalion marred, however, by the loss of two brave men

---
[9] Capt A. Smith, VX3927; 2/7 Bn. Clerk; of Kew, Vic; b. Toowoomba, Qld, 17 Apr 1914.
[1] Lt P. C. Thomas, VX3852. 2/6, 2/7 Bns. Warehouseman; of Malvern, Vic; b. Prahran, Vic, 30 May 1912.
[2] Maj R. H. MacFarlane, VX5338; 2/5 Bn. Bank officer; of Deniliquin, NSW; b. Thursday Is, 28 May 1917.

from Thomas' platoon. Sergeant Ciddor[3] took a patrol westward to try to get in touch with Lieutenant McIntosh[4] who, with an improvised group of Headquarters Company men (Mac Force), for some days had been occupying and patrolling from a position far out on the Australian right flank. When Ciddor met a small enemy party he himself killed two of them but was in turn mortally wounded. Corporal Robinson,[5] trying to cover his withdrawal, was shot down in his turn. Later, in the early darkness, the Japanese launched a small but vigorous foray on McDonald's Knoll. They tangled with the Australian booby traps, however, and these and a willing fire threw them into confusion and killed a number of them.

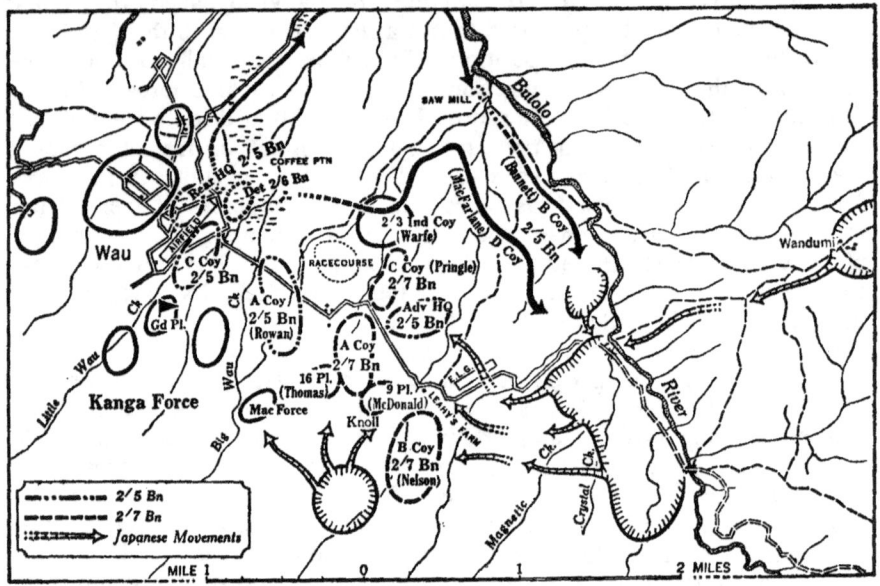

Dispositions Wau-Crystal Creek area, dawn, 6th February

The 6th was marked for the Australians by painful losses. With the new day a youthful N.C.O., Sergeant Birrell,[6] took a patrol forward of McDonald's Knoll to the ground over which the Japanese had sallied the previous night. He found Japanese dead there, litter and signs that wounded had been dragged away. He also found Japanese there who were still full of fight. His patrol killed four of them but he himself was mortally hit and one of his men was wounded. Farther out to the right there were also other Japanese whose spirit was still high. Early in the morning the Intelligence officer had gone out to McIntosh's positions with detailed

---

[3] Lt M. M. Ciddor, VX15617; 2/7 Bn. Storeman; of St Kilda, Vic; b. Manchester, England, 14 Apr 1919. Died of wounds 6 Feb 1943. His commission later came through dated 4 Feb 1943.

[4] Lt D. B. McIntosh, VX23387. 2/8 Fd Coy; 2/7 Bn. Warehouse manager; of Glen Iris, Vic; b. Nhill, Vic, 12 May 1908. Killed in action 6 Feb 1943.

[5] Cpl B. C. Robinson, VX33802; 2/7 Bn. Farmer; of Goroke, Vic; b. Goroke, 22 Nov 1916.

[6] Sgt D. Birrell, VX20085; 2/7 Bn. Farm hand; of Tumbarumba, NSW; b. Wagga Wagga, NSW, 3 Oct 1923. Died of wounds 15 Feb 1943. Birrell had become an infantry sergeant in 1941 at the age of 18.

instructions for a patrol McIntosh was to carry out behind the Japanese front. After the patrol had left the Mac Force base an air raid began. Then, as though at a signal, a strong band of Japanese rose from the thick country, moved in on the base, and laid out an air strip. Sergeant Lang[7] shot two of the men who were busy with the strip and that precipitated "an encounter of ferocity not yet equalled in the fighting" as the Australians fell upon the intruders with such determination that they took from them a medium and two light machine-guns. But even in that grimly fighting group Sergeants Lang and Hall[8] and McIntosh himself were outstanding. At the conclusion of the action, however, the brave young officer lay dead with three of his men, and six others were wounded.

The air raid which formed part of the background for this savage and isolated fight was spectacular. About 10.30 a.m. nine Japanese bombers escorted by about 20 fighters appeared over Wau. Four Douglas transports were unloading on the field, five others were making their approach and the Allied fighter umbrella was up. Bombs began to fall and a furious dog-fight ensued. A Wirraway was destroyed on the ground and one stick of bombs fell fairly along the strip. Although they did comparatively little material damage they caused a number of casualties of whom three were killed in the Air Cooperation Signals hut which received a direct hit. But the score was more than evened in the air where the fight waxed furious over the township itself and then swung off down the Bulolo Valley and out over the mountains. In their final tally the Allied airmen estimated that, for the loss of the Wirraway and one Douglas missing, 3 bombers and 15 fighters were shot down. Of these the 156th Light Anti-Aircraft Battery, two troops of which had arrived at Wau on 1st February, was officially credited with 2 Zeros and one bomber. Out along the Black Cat Track the 2/6th Battalion had a grandstand view of the fight as they perched above the valley. They saw 3 Japanese fighters and 2 bombers shot down during the dog-fight, watched 2 other aircraft crash into the surrounding hills as they limped for home.

The Australians greatly needed the air superiority which this fight demonstrated. On the actual day of the raid Major-General Berryman told Brig-General Ennis C. Whitehead, commanding the advanced echelon of the Fifth Air Force, that the force at Wau required 23 planes every day or 70 every three days for ordinary daily maintenance and to build up reserves. Whitehead agreed to work on this basis and (two days later), being informed that it seemed likely that the Japanese might attack into the Bulolo Valley from the north, he promised to reconnoitre these approaches and harry any attack from the air. In general, indeed, his support for the Australian operations was so unstinted that Mackay wrote to Blamey on the 4th:

I have found Brigadier-General Whitehead of the U.S.A. Air Force extremely cooperative. In fact there is no question of asking for help—he takes the initiative.

---

[7] Sgt H. Lang, VX5801; 2/7 Bn. Farmer; of Beaconsfield Upper, Vic; b. Beaconsfield Upper, 6 May 1916.
[8] Sgt F. J. Hall, MM, VX5823; 2/7 Bn. Labourer; of Notting Hill, Vic; b. Notting Hill, 2 Jul 1917.

After 6th February the 2/7th Battalion entered a period of isolated patrol contacts with Japanese who were withdrawing completely from that front and the further fighting round Wau fell to the lot of the 2/5th Battalion and the 2/3rd Independent Company.

The 2/5th had moved out on the 5th with orders to clear the area south of the Wau creeks and west of the Bulolo River. They met no opposition that day and their leading companies (Captain Bennett's and Captain MacFarlane's) bivouacked that night on the west bank of the river northeast of Leahy's Farm. They did not get much further on the morning of the 6th before they came hard against entrenched Japanese. On the right of their advance Lieutenant Toland's[9] platoon was heading Bennett's movement astride the road to Crystal Creek. Suddenly machine-gun fire from both sides of the road cut down three of Toland's men. Bennett, recognising that strong Japanese positions sited in depth along the road and in the dense bush on either side of it would exact a heavy toll of any frontal attack, discussed the position with Colonel Starr who then brought Major Rowan's company forward to hold the road and sent Bennett's company wide through the bush to circle the Japanese positions and come in upon them from the south by way of a dominating ridge. Nightfall then found Bennett's men about 1,000 yards south of Crystal Creek at the end of an afternoon during which their only contact had been with a Japanese patrol of whom they killed one man. Rowan, however, had lost men during his forward movement and MacFarlane's company (on the left of the road) had run into well camouflaged defences and hot fire to which ten of them fell.

The morning of the 7th found the Australians pressing hard against the Japanese, however. On the right flank the 21-year-old Lieutenant Reeve[1] and his platoon headed the movement of Bennett's company. They burst into a Japanese position on the eastern edge of the high ridge which overlooked Crystal Creek. The startled Japanese had time for only a few scattered shots before Reeve and his men were among them, killing many. The surviving Japanese fled in disorder leaving Reeve's men in possession of a medium machine-gun, much ammunition and many papers. The Australian platoon then moved westward for about 200 yards, clearing more Japanese posts as they went. Toland's platoon then came forward to exploit the ridge westwards during the afternoon and they and Reeve's platoon grimly set about destroying Japanese positions as the afternoon wore on. When they were held later by fierce fire Bennett brought his third platoon forward in an effort to clear the entire ridge before night fell. The Japanese refused to be silenced, however, and darkness came with the Australians in a company perimeter for the night and the last of the Japanese positions on the ridge still holding out.

Equally hard fighting but no such obvious success marked the day for MacFarlane's company on the left. Though they pressed hard against the

---
[9] Lt D. J. Toland, VX8969; 2/5 Bn. Woollen spinner; of Paddington, NSW; b. Stockton, NSW, 4 Dec 1917.

[1] Capt E. R. Reeve, MC, VX1017. 2/5 Bn; 2 NG Inf Bn. Carpenter; of Kew, Vic; b. Birregurra, Vic, 5 May 1921.

Japanese they could make no significant advance. MacFarlane himself, among others, was wounded during the afternoon and the command then fell to Captain Scott.[2]

It was little wonder that the Australians were finding the going difficult; it was now becoming apparent that they had come against the Japanese headquarters area and the defences surrounding the junction of the Wau road and the track to Wandumi; the enemy numbers were swelling even as the Australian movement was under way. During the day the 2/7th Battalion reported about 150 Japanese moving east across their positions and these must have joined the defences that night.

Early on the 8th artillery and mortar fire hammered into the Japanese positions. On the right Bennett had given Lieutenant Cameron's platoon of the 2/5th the task of clearing the western end of the ridge. Cameron's men circled widely through thick and clinging bush and over rough country to come at the main Japanese positions from below the western edge of the ridge about 11 a.m. Then Cameron himself led the attack in, with his own sub-machine-gun fire and fire from a Bren gunner close beside him cutting down about a dozen Japanese before the rest of the platoon came up with him. Completely nonplussed at being attacked from the steep and densely covered hillside the defenders broke and fled. Some of them rallied, however, and drove back with a short counter-attack which felled several of the Australians before it was repulsed. By midday Bennett's company was in possession of the whole of the high ridge overlooking Crystal Creek. During the afternoon, from Bennett's headquarters, the forward observation officer was able to harass with artillery fire Japanese retreating up the track towards Wandumi. At the same time Reeve and his men, with the Japanese machine-gun they had captured the previous day, were firing into their retreating enemies as the latter crossed the Bulolo River below.

Meanwhile, from the other side, Scott's men had launched a series of spirited attacks on their opponents' strong positions. Lieutenant Fry's[3] platoon headed their break-through during the afternoon and, as the evening advanced, cleared the vicinity of the road down towards the creek. Scott, holding the remainder of his company west and north of the road, was, however, violently set upon as night was coming and soon twelve more of his men were down just when it seemed that the day's fighting was ended. Rowan's company then joined them and together Scott and Rowan settled for the night while Fry's men joined Bennett.

The morning of the 9th showed many Japanese still in visible retreat along the track to Wandumi harassed by fire from the field gunners and from the infantry's machine-guns. Scott's vengeful men cleaned out the Japanese headquarters areas with mortars and grenades and set about a detached pocket of stubborn Japanese with such grim efficiency that they killed 25 or 30 without loss to themselves. Then, with Rowan's men,

---

[2] Capt C. E. Scott, VX3386; 2/5 Bn. Textile worker; of Brighton, Vic; b. St Kilda, Vic, 25 Jan 1915.
[3] Capt G. McK. Fry, VX50348; 2/5 Bn. Insurance clerk; of Ivanhoe, Vic; b. Ivanhoe, 3 Jan 1916.

they spent the afternoon mopping up smaller confused remnants. In the last of the day Bennett's company and one of Rowan's platoons ranged through to Kaisenik. So the night found the Japanese positions completely reduced, the survivors in full retreat through the hills, dead, wounded and much abandoned equipment scattered in the terrible disorder of defeat. Moten's headquarters estimated that the 2/5th Battalion men killed 150 Japanese that day and the Crystal Creek area came to be called the "slaughterhouse", from 250 to 300 Japanese having been killed there.

On that same day Moten re-defined the action to be taken by his troops. The 2/5th Battalion was to clean up as far as Kaisenik then settle one company there, one at Crystal Creek and return the other two to Wau to rest. Emphasis was now to pass to the 2/3rd Independent Company which was to send one platoon at once to a position 1,000 yards west of Wandumi. On the 10th this platoon was to advance through Wandumi and subsequently make its way along the Jap Track to the vicinity of House Copper. A second platoon was to take a carrier line along the Buisaval Track as far as the Summit and, having sent the carriers forward with supplies to MacAdie's main camp at Skindewai, base itself on the Summit and patrol all the tracks between the Buisaval and Jap Tracks. Warfe was to take the rest of the company to the Black Cat area and, based there, send out his third platoon to join at House Copper with the one which had advanced through Wandumi. On the 11th one of these platoons was to go forward to link with MacAdie's men at Waipali. As soon as Warfe was settled at the Black Cat the 2/6th Battalion men were to return to Wau with the exception of Gullett's company which would remain under Warfe's command until Warfe knew the ground.

The 2/3rd Independent Company were thus faced with a strenuous task. They had, however, been having a fairly uneventful time since they had cleared the Japanese from the copse by the night of the 4th. On the two following days they mopped up the isolated opposition that remained in the vicinity and then concentrated mainly on patrolling and securing the various crossings of the Bulolo River. After Warfe got his orders from Moten on the 9th he was back with his company at 2.30 p.m. and had Lewin and his platoon on the march by 3.15 to take up the position 1,000 yards west of Wandumi. At 9 a.m. on the 10th Captain Hancock[4] started out for the Summit with his platoon and, half an hour later, Warfe, his headquarters and Captain Meares'[5] platoon took the track to the Black Cat and reached the Gap about 4 p.m.

He found on arrival there that the 2/6th Battalion elements had been having a busy time since the 5th when they had decided to cut the new path to a point east of the Jap Track Junction. When his patrols reported no contact and no Japanese movement round this junction on the 6th Wood asked Moten to postpone the artillery and air program he had planned to precede the proposed 2/6th attack on the 7th. Wood wanted

---
[4] Maj R. N. Hancock, MC, VX58990. 2/3 Indep Coy (OC 1943-44); "Z" Special Unit. University student; of Melbourne; b. Colac, Vic, 25 Jul 1919.
[5] Capt W. A. Meares, VX22404; 2/3 Indep Coy. Grazier; of Forbes, NSW; b. Strathfield, NSW, 5 Sep 1908.

to comb the area more thoroughly. Moten agreed. So Gullett's and Laver's companies spent the 7th scouring the tracks towards House Copper, down to the Jap Track Junction and below the junction towards Wandumi for some hundreds of yards. They saw no Japanese although they passed through the area of the previous fighting and found it littered with the debris of battle, marked by Japanese graves and Japanese and Australian dead. Wood then proposed to move down the Wandumi Track the following day and attack those of his enemies he might find there. Before he could do so, however, he was ordered to hold his force at the Gap until the situation in the Crystal Creek area, where by that time the 2/5th Battalion was deeply committed, had resolved itself. This he did—except for patrols and ambushes. Six Japanese were waylaid and killed and patrols reported that about 100 of their enemies were dispersed some 600 yards south of the junction. Wood then proposed to have Gullett attack these on the 9th.

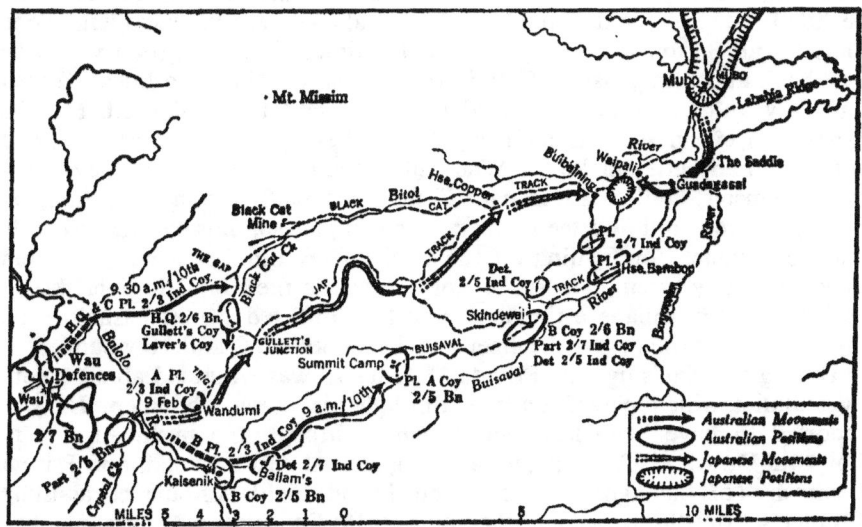

Nightfall, 9th February

On the morning of that day Gullett headed a watchful advance through the junction towards Wandumi. Wood, Hay and the artillery observation officer (Captain Sutton[6]) followed him. Several messages came from Moten telling of the movement of strong Japanese parties up the track from Wandumi (fugitives from the 2/5th Battalion), air attacks and preparations for more air attacks on these parties. About the middle of the morning Gullett, Laver supporting him from the rear and a platoon holding at the junction, began to meet opposition. He pushed on through it for about 400 yards with Laver combing the track behind him. About 12.30,

---

[6] Maj F. M. B. Sutton, NX162. 2/1 Fd Regt; LHQ 1944-45. Accountant; of Cremorne, NSW; b. Glebe Point, NSW, 31 Jul 1915.

however, some 200 Japanese sallied against him from Wandumi and he could not sustain the weight of their attack. He sent Laver back and then began to fall back himself in a well-controlled movement, having lost Lieutenant Park and one man killed, four wounded, and inflicted an estimated twenty to thirty casualties on his attackers. Then he arrived back at the point forward of the junction where Wood had established a temporary headquarters and was waiting with Hay, Sutton and a small party. He sent about half his company back to hold the junction and, with the rest, joined Wood. Chanting and shouting, the Japanese were closing with slow but strong purpose. As they reached an open stretch of the track they were met by withering fire at 30 yards' range from the concealed Australians and at least 20 fell. The main strength, however, moved methodically round both flanks under cover of light machine-gun and rifle fire. About ten Japanese closed tightly on the left but the Australians killed them with grenades. Some twenty moved boldly down the track but most of them were shot. Pressure on the right flank could not be lifted, however, and a number of Australians were hit including Wood himself and Sutton. Knowing that, by this time, his main group would be well back and firmly based, Wood ordered his men into the bush. Gullett and Hay and six soldiers covered them out and then followed. But the Japanese were in such strength that Wood then considered that the group with him had better make for Wau rather than the Gap. This they did—Wood himself, Gullett, Lieutenant Kemp,[7] the badly wounded Sutton, six wounded men and fourteen others. The Japanese, however, apparently had no stomach for fighting off the track. They did not leave it nor did they make any attempt to strike north towards the Gap. So a brisk day ended, the Australians estimating they had inflicted 50-80 casualties on the Japanese at the cost of 1 officer and 3 men killed, 2 and 10 wounded.

During this day's fighting Private McGuigan[8] was wounded about 1 p.m. by a bullet which passed entirely through his upper abdomen. He was reported to have been last seen crawling through the bush. At 5 p.m. Corporal Dowd[9] of Captain Quinn's[1] Regimental Aid Post staff and Private Lemmer[2] (of the light section of the 2/2nd Field Ambulance assisting Quinn) set out through the darkening bush to find him, with two infantrymen as escorts. They searched well below the Jap Track Junction and, disregarding the danger from the many Japanese in that much fought-over area, called McGuigan's name again and again through the gloom. They found him at 7 p.m. and carried him then in the darkness for over an hour, on a blanket slung between two rifles. The night and the mountains temporarily defeated them and they camped forward of the junction and far

---

[7] Capt D. G. Kemp, VX6711; 2/6 Bn. Transport driver; of Warrnambool, Vic; b. Ballarat, Vic, 14 May 1919.

[8] Pte J. J. McGuigan, VX14175; 2/6 Bn. Labourer; of East Brunswick, Vic; b. Brunswick, 12 Dec 1905. Died 14 Jan 1947.

[9] Cpl H. P. Dowd, VX4408; 2/6 Bn. Labourer; of Bayswater, Vic; b. London, 29 May 1916.

[1] Capt W. M. J. Quinn, NX112075; RMO 2/6 Bn. Medical practitioner; of Burrumbuttock, NSW; b. Burrumbuttock, 20 May 1916.

[2] Pte H. H. Lemmer, VX54310. 2/2 Fd Amb; 6 Div Pro Coy. Rubber worker; of West Footscray, Vic; b. Footscray, 1 Nov 1917.

from the nearest Australian positions. With the following dawn they carried the wounded man for another three hours before native bearers met and relieved them.

This incident was typical of the difficulties of medical work in the mountains round Wau. Quinn would send two medical orderlies with soldiers going into action—or would go himself. Wounded men would be brought back to a central point where they would be given first aid. Native bearers would then carry them to the aid post (normally at the Gap). After treatment there they would be carried to the Bulolo River where an ambulance would be waiting. Quinn wrote:

> It would have been impossible to carry on without the native bearers and they cannot be praised too highly.

Apart from battle casualties he found that diarrhoea, bush mites and sheer exhaustion caused most trouble.

Although the main 2/6th Battalion group had made ready on the 10th to move back to Wau as soon as Warfe had taken over, Moten ordered them that evening to remain at the Black Cat until the general situation cleared. Warfe and his men then came under command of Major Norris[3] who had taken over when Wood was wounded. They had no news from Lewin who should have been pushing up the track from Wandumi that day in the key movement. On the 11th the Australian patrols quested along the tracks without major incident. At nightfall news of Lewin came. He reported that, moving forward the previous day, his men had killed eighteen Japanese stragglers but then clashed sharply with Japanese positions near the Wandumi Trig. By nightfall he had lost two men killed and three wounded, his wireless was damaged and the operator was dead, his ammunition was running low. He therefore fell back on Wau to replenish his supply, arrived there at 2 p.m. on the 11th and he and his men started back towards Wandumi two hours later. On the 12th they struggled to make their way to the track junction but reported, late in the day, that time, distance and exhaustion were preventing them from attacking the Japanese concentration near the track junction before dark. Next day Captain Meares led his platoon (less one section) towards House Copper while Lieutenant Cameron[4] waited in ambush with a 2/6th Battalion group to back Lewin as he approached the track junctions and Warfe, a mixed group of commandos and infantrymen with him, ranged the track. This day, however, also passed without Lewin's men getting through. Cameron successfully ambushed a large enemy party though his men were then hard pressed in their turn by a strong encircling movement, lost three wounded and were forced back. Warfe was also engaged, estimated that his men killed some twenty of their opponents and then, with night coming on, the Australians left Cameron at Gullett's Junction with the main forward strength. On the 14th Norris, Warfe and Hay were

---

[3] Lt-Col G. M. Norris, VX290; 2/6 Bn. Departmental manager; of Kew, Vic; b. Upper Hawthorn, Vic, 31 Jan 1909. Killed in aircraft accident 7 Oct 1944.
[4] Lt L. G. Cameron, VX17341; 2/6 Bn. Grazier; of Rockton, via Bombala, NSW; b. Melbourne, 9 Feb 1915.

out along the Jap Track. In the early afternoon Norris set two platoons at a Japanese machine-gun position. They captured this, then took two other machine-guns, and finally pushed on towards Wandumi, having killed, they thought, at least twenty Japanese for the loss of three wounded. In the late afternoon they met Lewin who reported that his men had also killed some twenty Japanese that day—in the area between Wandumi and the track junction, which was now clear of Japanese.

Early on the 15th the 2/6th Battalion men (except those from the Carrier Platoon) were ordered to report back to Wau. By this time the battalion had lost 4 officers and 48 men of the total losses of 30 and 319 suffered by Kanga Force since its creation. Norris led his men out on the same day, leaving the Black Cat task to the 2/3rd Independent Company. Moten was now in a position to carry out the deployment he had planned when the Japanese attack on Wau had mounted in the second half of January. Colonel Starr was therefore told to assume command of all troops along the track from Crystal Creek to Mubo as from midnight on 14th February. Forward of Crystal Creek he would have two of his own companies and the 2/7th Independent Company. His main tasks were to prevent any penetration from the Mubo area into the Wau Valley, and vigorously to patrol the area to gather information of the country and the opposing forces. The 2/6th Battalion was to become responsible for the Bulolo-Markham River area, to prevent penetration into the Bulolo Valley, to scout for information of the enemy and the country, to act offensively against Japanese patrols moving south of the Markham River. Because of the supply difficulties not more than two companies were to be placed forward of Sunshine without express permission.

So mid-February found the 2/5th Battalion at Crystal Creek and, with the 2/7th Independent Company, forward to the Guadagasal area (with their most active attention concentrated temporarily on developments in the Buibaining area); the 2/6th Battalion (less Dexter's company which was already down the Bulolo) concentrating at Wau preparatory to taking over the Bulolo task; the 2/7th Battalion settling to road work under the supervision of the 2/8th Field Company, patrolling widely in the Wandumi area and training; the 2/3rd Independent Company operating from the Black Cat. One battery (complete with 8 guns) of the 2/1st Field Regiment had been deployed at Wau from the 9th when the last sub-section had arrived, the second troop having begun to arrive on the 4th. It was the gunners' intention at this time to try to push two of their guns forward as far as Skindewai from which point they estimated they could shell the Japanese positions at Mubo at extreme range. They thought to experiment first with one gun to try to balance its value to the attacking infantry against the very considerable problem of maintaining it at Skindewai.

The Australians were also at this time trying to extend their anti-aircraft cover. They had had two troops of the 156th Light Anti-Aircraft Battery at Wau since 1st February and, on the 9th, sited an additional gun at Bulolo. On the engineer side, as usual, a most formidable and many-sided task was being attacked. The bulk of the 2/8th Field Company was at work on maintenance and developmental tasks in and around Wau, bridging the Bulolo and the smaller streams which made movement difficult, and developing the road from Wau to Crystal Creek and thence to the Summit. The 2/16th Field Company had moved to Bulolo itself on the 8th and was preparing there the air transport landing strip.

Operationally, it was clear that a new phase was now well under way. With the final reduction of the Crystal Creek positions by the 2/5th Battalion on the 9th the destruction of the Japanese in the Wau Valley was complete. Then began the period of the Japanese withdrawal. And in this period the scene of the greatest Australian activity was the Black Cat area and eastward. In the days following the departure of the main 2/6th Battalion group Warfe had the greater part of Captain Meares' and Lieutenant Lewin's platoons feeling their way towards House Copper by way of both the Jap and the Black Cat Tracks. There were bellicose Japanese bands also at large along those trails and ambushes by both sides and small but spirited encounters marked them. From the third platoon, which had the task of patrolling between the Summit and the Jap Track, two sections (Lieutenant Menzies[5] and Sergeant Brewer's[6]) arrived at the Gap on the 15th and Warfe then ordered them to move east along the Jap Track and follow to the Summit any branch track they might find which would lead them there. On the morning of the 18th Warfe himself, with 15 men, set out along the Jap Track towards House Copper and for some days afterwards was out of touch with his company and hotly engaged at times in fleeting encounters. By the morning of the 23rd the company was considerably extended between Gullett's Junction and House Copper. Hancock's platoon (less Menzies' and Brewer's sections who, unable to find any alternate way back to the Summit, were being used to advantage in the areas of the most forward Australian activity) had moved from the Summit to Gullett's Junction; Lieutenant Winterflood[7] (in command of Lewin's platoon since the 19th) was, with one of Meares' sections, astride the Jap Track about half-way between Gullett's Junction and the junction of the Black Cat and Jap Tracks (now known as Menzies' Junction); Meares, with the rest of his platoon and some of Hancock's men, were at Menzies' Junction; Warfe and his party were in the vicinity of House Copper.

By this time it was clear that the main Japanese force was concentrated in a heavily timbered valley bordered by the Bitoi River on the north and between Waipali and Buibaining and known to the Australians as the Pisser Valley. On the 20th Warfe's patrols near Menzies' Junction had reported one party alone of an estimated strength of some 500 moving past the junction into this valley and the Australians thought then that there were

---

[5] Capt J. R. Menzies, WX11074. 2/3 Indep Coy; 2/3 Cdo Sqn. Bank clerk; of Subiaco, WA; b. Perth, WA, 11 Jul 1920.
[6] Lt F. N. T. Brewer, MM, NX3461. 2/1 Fd Regt; 2/3 Indep Coy; 2/3 Bn. Mechanic; of Bondi, NSW; b. Edendale, NZ, 19 Oct 1917.
[7] Capt J. S. Winterflood, MC, QX19168. 2/3 Indep Coy; 2/3 Cdo Sqn. Student; of Kelvin Grove, Qld; b. Sydney, 10 Jan 1920.

possibly 1,500 Japanese in the valley. Although the Australian patrols and two or more strafing runs by aircraft each day along the tracks harassed the Japanese withdrawal it remained strong and ordered, and reports indicated a controlled movement daily from the Pisser Valley towards Mubo.

On the 23rd Captain Tancred, who was commanding in Warfe's absence, was ordered to destroy the Japanese remaining on the Jap Track, establish a secure base at Menzies' Junction, maintain standing patrols in the House Copper area, organise supplies and communications for a probable forward move on the 26th. These orders were amplified next day, when Tancred was told that, on the 26th, the company was to support an attack from the Australian right flank by the 2/5th Battalion and the 2/7th Independent Company.

Since Starr's assumption of command there the Australians, feeling that supply difficulties were hampering them, had concentrated on reconnaissance to determine the Japanese dispositions, movements and strengths. By the 18th, however, they were preparing to attack, but then the reports from Warfe's men of the flow towards the Pisser Valley caused Moten to stay their hands. On the 20th he determined to have Warfe's men hold firm at Menzies' Junction, to soften the Japanese by some days' intensive air strafing of their positions from House Copper to Waipali and then to have Starr attack from the south. On the 23rd, in view of reports of Japanese withdrawals towards Mubo, he asked Starr if he could clean up the Buibaining staging areas on the 24th. Starr replied that he could launch a heavy raid, but the movement of his main forces for that purpose would jeopardise the safety of the track. Finally it was decided that he would attack on the 26th. Warfe's men would support him by seizing the junction of the Black Cat Track and the branch track to Buibaining. In the event, however, there was virtually no opposition. On the morning of the 26th the air force topped their activity over the preceding days by lashing the Pisser area until 11.35 when heavy mists closed them off. In the wake of the air attacks and mortar fire the attackers moved into the valley but the bulk of the Japanese were gone. By nightfall Starr's men were in complete command of the valley with the main part of Warfe's company at the junction of the Buibaining and Black Cat Tracks. There were many well camouflaged huts in the Pisser area, some partially built, and about 50 Japanese dead were counted—most of them obviously victims of the aeroplanes.

During the next two days the Australian patrols ranged as far forward as the Guadagasal Ridge. They found no Japanese. So, by the end of February, it was clear that another phase of the operations round Wau had ended. The Japanese had withdrawn completely to Mubo from which they had prepared and launched their attack on Wau over a month before.

The struggle in the South-West Pacific had continued to draw fresh Japanese forces into New Guinea and the islands to the north of Australia. In the third quarter of 1942 the *2nd* and *38th Divisions* had been sent to Rabaul and the *48th* to Timor. In December the *6th* had arrived in Rabaul and the *5th* in Ambon. The *XVIII Army* on the New Guinea mainland in February included the *51st Division* round Lae and the *20th* and *41st* on the Wewak-Madang coast. Thus from the Solomons in the east to Timor in the west were deployed eight divisions, plus other smaller formations. It had required only 11 divisions to carry out the Japanese offensive of December 1941-May 1942. Counting the four divisions in Burma and one in Sumatra, the equivalent of 14 were now defending the southern and western frontiers of the Greater East Asia Co-prosperity Sphere.

The attack on Wau had been launched with fresh troops brought in specially for that purpose. These were men of the *51st Division*, veterans of the Shanghai fighting, who had been garrisoning French Indo-China and been brought down to Rabaul when the Japanese were trying to build up their forces in the South-West Pacific in December and January. It was the first echelon of this division that General Adachi landed at Lae on 7th January as his initial step in building up the Lae-Salamaua garrisons. This first echelon consisted of the *102nd Infantry Regiment Group* (Major-General Teru Okabe). In addition to the *102nd Regiment* (Colonel Maruoka), Okabe had the *II Battalion, 14th Field Artillery Regiment, 3rd Company 51st Engineer Regiment, 3rd Company 51st Transport Regiment,* anti-aircraft, mortar, signals, medical and labour detachments and *144th Regiment* reinforcements. The convoy carrying this force was the one to which Blamey had referred in his letter to Herring on 8th January. Although Maruoka's *III Battalion* was weakened by losses sustained in the Allied air attacks Okabe's plans were not seriously jeopardised as a result. Quickly he moved the bulk of his force in small craft across the bay to Salamaua where he assembled them to a strength of almost 4,000. The total Lae-Salamaua garrison then numbered probably about 6,500. On the 19th-20th Okabe cast off a force of about 460 men towards the Mambare with orders to destroy the Allied observation units in the vicinity of Morobe, assist the evacuation of the Buna-Gona coast survivors and establish land-sea communications along the coast from Salamaua to the Mambare.

Meanwhile the *2nd Maizuru S.N.L.F.* were sharp set by the Australian commandos at Mubo as Okabe's men began moving into that area. By the time the Australians fell back they had inflicted about 116 casualties on the marines. This decided Maruoka (who had been given the task of taking Wau) on a new stroke. Feeling that the Australians were in a position seriously to harass his movement along the main Buisaval Track he determined to advance by way of the long forgotten track which the Australians later came to call the Jap Track. But although this move surprised the Australians it brought disadvantages to the Japanese. They had not been able to reconnoitre the country forward of Guadagasal, and had no maps. They miscalculated the time it would take them to mount their attack, and so had not laid down supply dumps but moved with each soldier carrying only limited supplies on his back. Nor could they get their artillery forward along the new track. So, with 2,500-3,000 men moving on Wau, Maruoka needed a quick decision. But this was forbidden him: first, by all the difficulties attendant upon the cutting of the new track; next by the quality of the troops opposed to him; and lastly by the ability of his opponents to apply their air power at the critical moments to augment a garrison which he had underestimated from the beginning, thinking it numbered only about two companies.

Maruoka's plan was to use both the *I* and *II Battalions* (commanded respectively by Major Shimomura and Lieut-Colonel Seki) in a simultaneous attack on Wau. (The truncated *III Battalion* was probably used in part as a reserve at Mubo and in part for the Morobe-Mambare River task.) When the attacking force had cleared Wandumi it would divide, with Seki's battalion forming the right flank and following the Bulolo north to attack Wau from the north-east, and Shimomura advancing by way of the main Kaisenik-Wau road. Maruoka would establish his own headquarters at Crystal Creek. But this plan did not work smoothly. Seki's battalion, leading the advance, met Sherlock's company near Wandumi. Sherlock not only delayed them at a most critical time but inflicted at least 75 casualties on them. Seki himself was among the dead. Then, when the battalion moved forward to their allotted position north-east of Wau, they fell into considerable confusion, partly as a result of air attacks, partly because the units lost touch with one another, partly because of the vigour with which the Australians met them. At the same time Shimomura's battalion had been roughly handled and, although some elements of the *II Battalion* joined them soon after the opening round, the initiative had already been wrenched from them. By the time the Japanese began their withdrawal they not only had been mauled in battle but were in a bad way through lack of food. Hunger, effective harassing artillery fire, strafing aircraft and Australian ambushes, made their retreat a painful ordeal. By the night of the 13th-14th the Australians asserted that they had actually counted 753 Japanese dead and, by the time Maruoka was firm again at Mubo, it is likely that he had lost possibly about 1,200 men killed in battle and numbers more from starvation.

One aspect of both the Japanese methods and their straits was illustrated by a 17th Brigade war diary entry for 12th February:

> Among recent PW's brought in was a Chinese boy of 14, weighing 60 pounds, who had been brutally treated. He had been used by the Japs to carry packs as big as himself across the mountains. When captured and put in the compound he met his father, who was also a prisoner, for the first time since leaving Canton.

Though General Mackay knew that his men had inflicted a painful reverse on the Japanese he was nevertheless convinced that the latter were not yet giving up their hopes of capturing Wau and the Bulolo Valley and that there was stern fighting still to come. On 3rd February he wrote to Blamey that the army forces then in New Guinea were not sufficient to guarantee the performance of the roles allotted to him. Although the 4th and 15th Infantry Brigades were expected, and their arrival would improve the situation, the margin of safety would still be too small. He noted that the Wau-Bulolo Valley must be held as an advanced base for future operations but that its control by the Japanese was most important to their plans for holding Lae and Salamaua, in which area he estimated there was then a minimum of 7,500 Japanese while the indications were that these would be reinforced overland from Madang or by small craft moving down the coast. He wrote that a division of two brigades with supporting arms was required for the defence of the valley. On 11th February he underlined his warning about the likely Japanese movements by writing that he had persistent reports of Japanese patrols moving down the Ramu and Wampit Valleys with Wau as their objective. After his arrival at Wau on a visit that day he stressed this again to Blamey on the 13th and forecast his plans.

> Enemy defeats Guadalcanal and Papua and his anxiety for Lae make another attack on Wau a possibility. Persistent reports from Angau and native agents that enemy is constantly moving troops overland from Madang via Nadzab to Lae with object attacking Wau most probably via Nadzab, Wampit Valley, Bulwa. Estimate enemy strength Lae-Salamaua 8,000, Madang 5,000, Wewak 9,000, with another division arriving. Consider it prudent to forestall enemy by increasing garrison Wau especially as air transport not available last three days owing to weather. Next flying day intend to put in reinforcements to bring Independent Companies up to strength and battalions 17 Brigade to approximately 600 each. After further supplies propose send 39 Battalion in about a week and if situation develops Allen with Advance HQ 11 Division, HQ 30 Brigade and 49 Battalion.[8]

At this time his infantry strengths in the whole of Papua and New Guinea numbered 11,433 Australians and 8,396 Americans, a total of 19,829. At Port Moresby there was the 11th Division with the 14th and 30th Brigades, 2/6th Independent Company, 2/1st Pioneer Battalion, detachments from the forward Australian units, American elements; in the Milne Bay area (in which was included Wanigela, Porlock Harbour and Goodenough Island) there was the 5th Division with the 7th and 29th Brigades; in the Buna-Gona area there were 5,908 infantrymen of the 41st American Division and some 667 of the 18th Brigade; in the Wau-Bulolo area there were 2,982 infantrymen.

In reply to Mackay's message of the 13th Blamey signalled a general concurrence. He said that the 4th Brigade would move from Brisbane to Milne Bay on the 16th and 18th thus releasing the 7th Brigade for return to Port Moresby with a view to its employment at Wau if necessary (they were operationally experienced, and the 4th Brigade still unseasoned); the 15th Brigade would embark for Port Moresby when the 4th Brigade's move was completed. Blamey also suggested that Mackay could have the headquarters of the 3rd Division for use at Wau. Mackay agreed.

---

[8] Maj-Gen Allen was in temporary command of the 6th Division from November to February and of the 11th Division for 16 days in February, after which he was appointed to the command in the Northern Territory.

On this basis New Guinea Force issued an Operation Instruction on the 19th to provide for the future defence of the Bulolo Valley. It accepted that

> as our maintenance is at present entirely dependent on air transport the airfields at Wau and Bulolo, and the road joining them, must be retained. The airfield at Bulwa will be required for future use.

It provided for an increase in the strength of the Wau garrison to constitute it as a two-brigade division (the 3rd) but, since the additional brigade would not be available before 21st March, the 39th Battalion would be flown to Wau to provide a reserve in the meantime. It anticipated another Japanese advance on Wau by way of Nadzab-Bulwa or Mubo or both. It forecast that

> by actively threatening the approaches to Salamaua we should be able to conceal our intention in regard to Lae. In view of the strength of enemy positions at Lae we will require to use artillery and if practicable I tanks. To keep the artillery supplied with sufficient ammunition and to move the guns and tanks a road will be required. Steps will be taken to reconnoitre a route for a road, a bridge over the Markham and to study the best line of approach for I tanks on the north of the Markham River.

The instruction defined a policy of active, offensive patrolling to keep in touch with the Japanese at all times and to prevent them from moving without the Australians' knowledge; of controlling no-man's land; of preparing defences round the airfields and along the approaches to the valley; of developing roads to make quick movement possible. Thirty days' reserve supplies were to be built up.

At this time one of the most ambitious engineering projects ever undertaken by the Australian army was developing. Since the beginning of the New Guinea operations General Blamey's far-seeing military brain had been aware of the need for an overland supply route across New Guinea from south to north, first to assist in meeting the threat of the Japanese movement down the north-east coast, and then to supply the forces in the Bulolo and Markham Valleys, and then to facilitate the operations for the recapture of Lae and Salamaua which he was planning well before the end of 1942. The Bulldog-Wau route offered the most feasible chance to meet this need.

By November 1942, reports from surveyors, Lieutenants Fox and Ecclestone, recommended that the most practicable way of driving a road through the difficult country between Bulldog and Kudjeru was along the course of the Eloa River. Blamey accepted this and, in early December, directed that a jeep track be put through from Bulldog to Wau. The project was placed under the direction of Captain Maynes[9] of the 2/1st Field Company with Fox responsible for route location and construction. The Japanese threat to Wau in January emphasised the urgency of the task. On the 12th Blamey wrote to Herring:

---

[9] Maj J. W. Maynes, MM, NX8734. 2/1 Fd Coy; OC 24, 2/8 Fd Coys. Carpenter; of Richmond River, NSW; b. Kangaroo Valley, NSW, 7 Nov 1909.

In relation to Wau, plans are in hand for the rapid development of the road from Bulldog to Wau. Lieut-Colonel Reinhold[1] (Chief Engineer, 11th Division) has proceeded there to take charge. Extra field companies have been allocated and will shortly be available. . . . I hope Reinhold will be able to push the road through in about four months as a track road. We will probably find difficulties in mounting a big offensive against Lae in a much shorter time than that, but Reinhold is enthusiastic and I would be glad if you would encourage him to push on with all speed as far as you can.

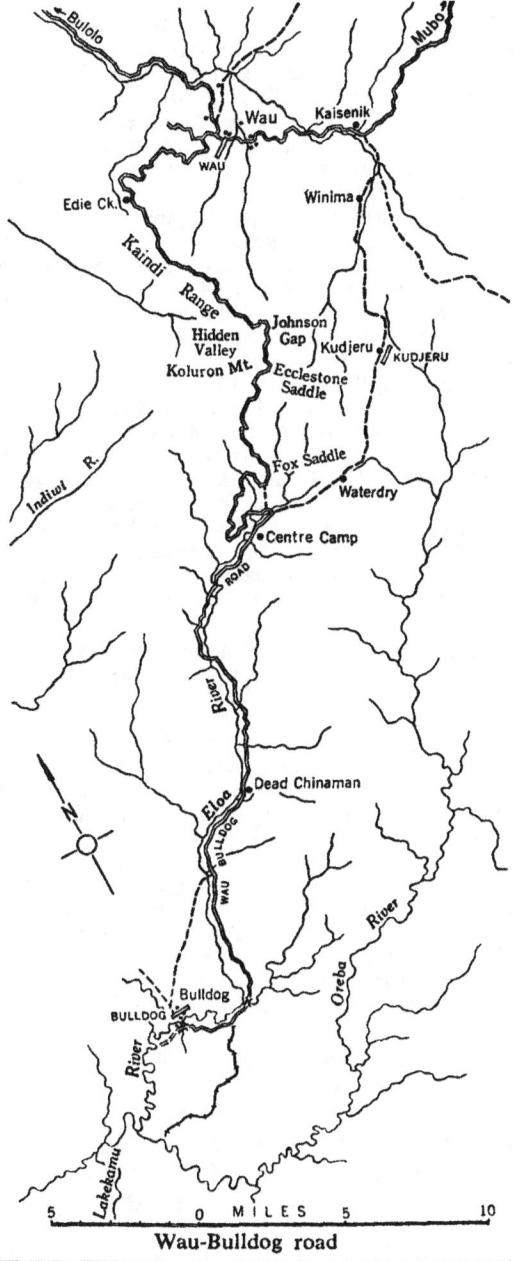

Wau-Bulldog road

Reinhold (with Maynes) was already pushing hard and fast into the wild country between Bulldog and Wau, following the carrier pad that ran by way of Centre Camp, Waterdry and Kudjeru. His examination of this route suggested to him that, particularly between Centre Camp and Kudjeru, it tended to fight the natural trend of the country. He felt that construction on that line would be long and difficult. Study of the topography of the country indicated to him that a more feasible route might be north-northeast from Centre Camp by way of the Koluron Mountains to Edie Creek. He therefore arrived at Edie Creek, on the 25th, to study the possible route from that end. He followed a waterrace, built before the war

[1] Lt-Col W. J. Reinhold, OBE, MC, QX34507. (1914-18: 90 Fd Coy RE.) Comd RAE Northern Comd, Milne Force Engrs; i/c Bulldog Road Construction 1943-44; Comd 14 CRE. Consulting engineer; of Clayfield, Qld; b. Clayfield, 6 Nov 1889.

by a miner named Schrater, south to Hidden Valley where, on the 28th, Warrant-Officer Johnson[2] of Angau and Ecclestone joined him:

> On the 29th January (wrote Reinhold afterwards) whilst the battle for Wau was reaching its climax in the valley below, the little party . . . pushed out into the uninhabited and unknown Koluron region.
>
> There were 16 New Guinea boys of Johnson's, six Papuan boys of the C.R.E., and four New Guinea boys of Ecclestone's. There was no mapping information available. The general intention was to strike for a saddle east of Mount Koluron, which was known to Johnson, and was afterwards called Johnson Gap. The saddle is approximately 8,000 feet high.
>
> The idea then was to follow the range S.S.W. from Johnson Gap along the eastern flank of the Koluron Mountains, directly to Bulldog. Ecclestone Saddle lies a little more than three miles S.S.W. of Johnson Gap, but the existence of this saddle was unknown to the party until a high spur between it and Johnson Gap had been crossed. Between the two saddles lies the basin that forms part of the headwaters of the Bulolo River. It is steep country, but it was deemed and proved suitable for road construction.
>
> In traversing the country a direct line was taken west of south and obstacles were crossed and not avoided. Ecclestone Saddle, with a height above sea level of about 9,500 feet, is the key to the whole of the route. This point was reached on the 5th February and, in the distance, could be seen the Eloa Valley and a saddle, later known as Fox Saddle, an obvious control point.
>
> The prospects were so promising and time so short that Ecclestone was instructed to arrange the survey of the route from Edie Creek to the saddle that was to bear his name. On the 6th February he and his natives returned to Kaindi for this purpose, and the remainder pushed on into the basin that forms part of the headwaters of the Eloa. The divide had been crossed.[3]

Reinhold and Johnson reached Bulldog on 11th February still convinced that they were on the right track. Reinhold wrote:

> It is almost certain that the country between Ecclestone and Fox Saddles had not been traversed previously by white men, and it was avoided by the Kukukukus, the nomadic race of pigmy cannibals that are found more to the south and south-west. During the journey the natives showed remarkable courage and endurance and, at times, carried heavy loads down cliffs ranging to 1,000 feet in height. The canyon of the Eloa is awe inspiring, about 50 feet in width at the bottom, with towering cliffs on either side and waterfalls jutting out on to the stream. It is a barrier that has to be seen to be believed. The stream was waded and steep detours were made up the precipitous sides to provide portage around waterfalls and rapids.
>
> The natives never let up. The trip was a triumph for the ability of Keith Johnson and his knowledge of natives, and for the dependability of the natives themselves. . . . The C.R.E. reported to New Guinea Force at Port Moresby and the Koluron route was recommended and approved for construction.[4]

Difficult supplementary reconnaissances followed Reinhold's initial one. Although they were most arduous and threw up fresh problems they confirmed the general feasibility of the route which had been selected and the construction work was driven ahead at a searing pace. The work which Maynes had begun at the Bulldog end on 1st January with a platoon of the 14th Field Company continued, the problem of de-snagging the Lake-

---

[2] Capt C. K. Johnson, VX73687. Angau; "M" Special Unit. Industrial chemist; of Lae, TNG; b. Grafton, NSW, 26 Dec 1904.
[3] W. J. Reinhold, *The Bulldog-Wau Road* (1946), p. 9.
[4] Reinhold, p. 10.

kamu below Bulldog was attacked, clearing gangs of natives under Angau supervision got to work between Bulldog and Fox Camp, the 9th Field Company became responsible for construction between Bulldog and Ecclestone Saddle and began work on 25th February; at the other end Johnson set 500 natives clearing the route from Edie Creek to Ecclestone Saddle and, from about 27th February, the 2/16th Field Company became the construction authority for all roadwork in that sector.

In its final form the road was to cover 58 miles from Bulldog to Edie Creek (68 miles to Wau). Its highest point would be 9,847 feet (between Ecclestone Saddle and Johnson Gap). Difficulties attendant upon its construction would range from those of a purely technical nature (e.g. the nature of soils, the bogging of mechanical equipment, great landslides, reduced efficiency to compressors and motors at high altitudes) to problems of supply, accommodation, maintenance and retention of tools, native labour. In respect of the second last Reinhold wrote:

> Loss of tools and pilfering were common. Stores, coming into Bulldog, had been opened and pilfered before their arrival. The Kukukuku tribes along the Eloa are born thieves, and they got away with much equipment. Axes and knives particularly attracted them (and, later, explosives) though they were partial to anything metallic or edible. One party came proudly back to the track on one occasion decorated with detonators through their noses.

The native labour problem was always urgent as large numbers of natives were required for clearing and for carrying. Typical of the recurring difficulties was the situation that developed in respect of 1,000 Mount Hagen natives during these early stages of work on the road. These 1,000 were actually assembled on the aerodrome at Mount Hagen to be flown to Wau. But lack of fighter cover for the transport planes led to the abandonment of the move with the result that the road construction was seriously jeopardised at a critical time.

The importance of the development of this road was emphasised by a severe check to the operations out of Wau which developed in the first half of March through the inability of the air forces to maintain supplies to the extent required for a continuation of offensive forward moves. On the 9th General Whitehead wrote to General Mackay:

> With two squadrons of 18 operating carrier planes available for movements to the Wau area, weather conditions have been such that only 14.1 loads per day have been carried into the area. Had twice as many aeroplanes been available the average carry would not have been proportionately larger because of the brief periods when operations into the Wau-Bulolo Valley have been possible. During the next six weeks (until approximately April 15th) there should be a slight increase in convective activity in the Wau area and over the ranges. This means that cumulus clouds will build up earlier in the day with moderate to heavy showers on the slopes of the ranges after 12 noon. On the best operating days there will not be more than four or five hours when operations into Wau are possible. It is probable that one or two hours will be the normal period when operations can be carried out. Ballam's dropping point will be even more difficult to supply. Skindewai will be closed most of the time since between Summit Station and Guadagasal Saddle the mountains are usually covered with mist during this season of year. . . . Operations into the Saddle and into Mubo would be more difficult than into Skindewai.

Whitehead was concerned, too, about the strain of providing fighter cover for air transports into Wau. In the final analysis he was forced to recommend that all available troop carriers should be used to build up a reserve of supplies for the force then in the Wau-Bulolo area; that no more troops should be moved forward of Ballam's than could be supplied by ground; that no more troops should be moved to Wau until reserves were built up; that planning for offensive action against Mubo or Salamaua should be based upon the realisation that supply would have to be maintained by sea.

Despite this small local check, however, the larger picture was a bright one for the Allies. They had just struck a heavy blow at Japanese plans for reinforcing the Lae-Salamaua garrisons. On the night 28th February-1st March a convoy of 16 vessels (8 destroyers, 7 transports and the special service vessel *Nojima*) put out from Rabaul to Lae carrying, mainly, the second echelon of the *51st Division*. The Allied commanders were well aware by this time of the general tenor of the Japanese plans for the reinforcement of the New Guinea mainland and, indeed, by deductions from the increase in shipping in Rabaul harbour and other Intelligence sources, had some little time before forecast the departure of a large convoy about this date. They had laid careful plans for interception by their air forces. The weather initially aided the Japanese and, though scouting aircraft picked them up on the 1st, no attack could be pressed home until next day. Then, towards the middle of the morning of 2nd March, a shadowing aircraft sent back news of the convoy's position off Cape Gloucester and bombers swarmed to the attack over the north coast of New Britain. Although no accurate estimate of the damage could be made then, by nightfall it was clear that an effective blow had been struck at the ships. There were reports of ships "burning and exploding", "smoking and burning amidships", "seen to explode", "in a sinking condition". Through the night an Australian Catalina shadowed the fleet. On the morning of the 3rd torpedo-carrying Beauforts of the R.A.A.F. headed new attacks off the Huon Peninsula. About 10 a.m. the major planned attacks began.

. . . 13 Beaufighters [R.A.A.F.], each armed with four cannons in the nose and six machine-guns in the wings, "went into the target with flights in line astern". Flying at 500 feet when they came within the reach of anti-aircraft fire, they "then lost height rapidly and using rated power attacked in line abreast at a speed of 220 knots". Thirteen B-17's had come into position above to drop their bombs just as the Beaufighters began their sweep. Thirteen B-25's followed the Beaufighters in for a standard bombing attack from medium altitude. And then came twelve of the 90th's [Squadron] B-25 C1's in probably the most successful attack of all. Coming down to 500 feet above the now widely dispersed and rapidly manoeuvring vessels, the new strafers broke formation as each pilot sought his own targets. The forward-firing .50's beat down opposing AA, and 500-pound bombs struck ship after ship. Out of the thirty-seven bombs dropped, seventeen were claimed as direct hits.[5]

More missions sallied out from Moresby during the afternoon but, although they had some successes, bad weather over the mountains lessened the planned force of the strikes. Still, the close of the day found

---

[5] W. F. Craven and J. L. Cate, *The Army Air Forces in World War II*, Vol IV (1950), pp. 143-4.

the work done. There remained only the cleaning up by the PT boats which swept out from their base at Tufi that night; by strafing aircraft in succeeding days which gunned from the surface of the sea survivors of the main battle; by the island garrisons in the Trobriands and on Goodenough who hunted down and killed men cast up by the sea.

In this Battle of the Bismarck Sea 12 vessels were lost and only 4 destroyers survived. The Japanese lost about 3,000 men, but about 5,800 men, including the crews of the 4 destroyers, were saved. But, extensive and brilliant as the Allied victory was, its real significance lay in the lesson of air power which it pointed and the virtual denial to the Japanese thereafter of any hope of swiftly building up their bases in the Lae-Salamaua area by sea.

At this time the Australians in the mountains which surrounded Salamaua and Lae were hoping to be able to increase their pressure on the Japanese. On 2nd March Brigadier Moten reiterated the instructions he had already given to his forward troops: that they were to keep close to every movement the Japanese made, with the 2/7th Independent Company carrying out the most forward reconnaissance and the 2/5th Battalion backing them, building defensive positions in the forward areas as secure bases for future offensive operations and preparing additional camping facilities between the Summit and Skindewai. The 2/3rd Independent Company was withdrawn from the Black Cat to press in on the Salamaua area along the line of the Francisco River. The road from Wau to the Summit was being pushed ahead urgently by two companies of the 2/5th Battalion, the major part of the 2/7th Battalion and the 2/8th Field Company. Wau itself was developing rapidly as a base with a special staff to run it as such.

At this same time Mackay relayed to Moten an expression of Blamey's hopes for a venture against Salamaua:

> I would be glad if you would give consideration to the question of inflicting a severe blow upon the enemy in the Salamaua area . . . since it may have far-reaching results if successful. On the other hand with the force at your disposal, should you find your initial stages unsuccessful and come up against conditions and arrangements for defence as they were in the Gona-Buna area you should not allow your force to become involved in operations amounting to siege conditions as existed in the area referred to.

Moten thereupon planned an "indirect attack" on Mubo by the 2/5th Battalion, the 2/7th Independent Company and a section of the 1st Australian Mountain Battery which was struggling forward up the track from Wau. They were to occupy strategic high ground round Mubo, by-pass Mubo itself and the Mat Mat area, and by offensive operations along the Japanese lines of communication from Mubo to Komiatum make the main Mubo position untenable as the defenders' supplies became exhausted. At the same time the 2/3rd Independent Company were to establish supply bases along the tracks which ran east from Bulwa by way of Missim and prepare to act against the Japanese supply line from Bobdubi to Komiatum. The main advance would not begin before the 12th.

These preparations proceeded quietly enough for some days. But there were the inevitable patrol clashes in the mountains and, on the 9th, 26 Japanese bombers escorted by 12-20 fighters raided Wau. They damaged installations, killed 3 and wounded 10 and spread delayed-action bombs which exploded at intervals during the day. This isolated venture was no more than an inconvenience, however. It was the preoccupation of the Allied air with the larger scene and its consequent inability to further his immediate plans which worried Moten. As an aftermath of Whitehead's recommendations regarding the necessity to curtail land operations out of Wau, Moten decided to hold a general line Guadagasal-Waipali and destroy the Japanese in the Saddle-Vickers Ridge area. Mackay told him he might proceed with his plan provided he did not prejudice his main task of holding the Bulolo Valley, maintained control of the Waipali-Guadagasal area, and did not push his operations beyond the safe limit of maintenance. By the 15th, however, it seemed clear that the Japanese were not disposed vigorously to dispute an edging forward and that day found the Australian forward elements on Lababia Ridge on the right and on Mat Mat Hill on the left. Except for patrol encounters there was no action for the rest of the month. The Australians consolidated and the 31st found them close to the Japanese Mubo positions with one of MacAdie's platoons firm on Lababia Ridge, his headquarters and a second platoon with a section of machine-guns on Mat Mat Hill, the 2/5th Battalion (temporarily commanded by Major Goble[6] since the 24th when Starr relinquished command), less two companies, deployed from the Saddle to Buibaining, two mountain guns and a section of machine-guns in the Saddle, MacAdie's third platoon at Skindewai and two companies of the 2/5th Battalion working on the road between Ballam's and Crystal Creek.

The situation was similarly quiet in the other forward areas. Plans for aggressive action by Warfe's commandos round Salamaua had been modified temporarily. These men had been at work reconnoitring the country and the tracks between Bulwa and the Salamaua-Komiatum region but, in the second half of the month, their main strength was withdrawn to the Bulwa area because of supply difficulties. One platoon was left at Missim to continue the forward reconnaissance and operate observation posts with a view to later occupation of the area by one infantry battalion and an Independent Company. The Independent Company deployment complemented that of the 2/6th Battalion. Colonel Wood (now recovered from his wound and back with his battalion) had this so arranged that, while his main strength was in the Bulolo-Bulwa area, Dexter's company was still forward at Wampit covering the Markham. One platoon of the 2/5th Independent Company (the company had been resting for some weeks at Edie Creek and training under experienced 17th Brigade officers and N.C.O's) had recently joined Wood as the forerunner of the rest of the company and was at Sunshine.

---

[6] Lt-Col N. L. Goble, ED, VX111. 2/5 Bn; CO 5 Bn 1943-44, 47 Bn 1944-45. Grocer; of Abbotsford, Vic; b. Carlton, Vic, 27 Mar 1907.

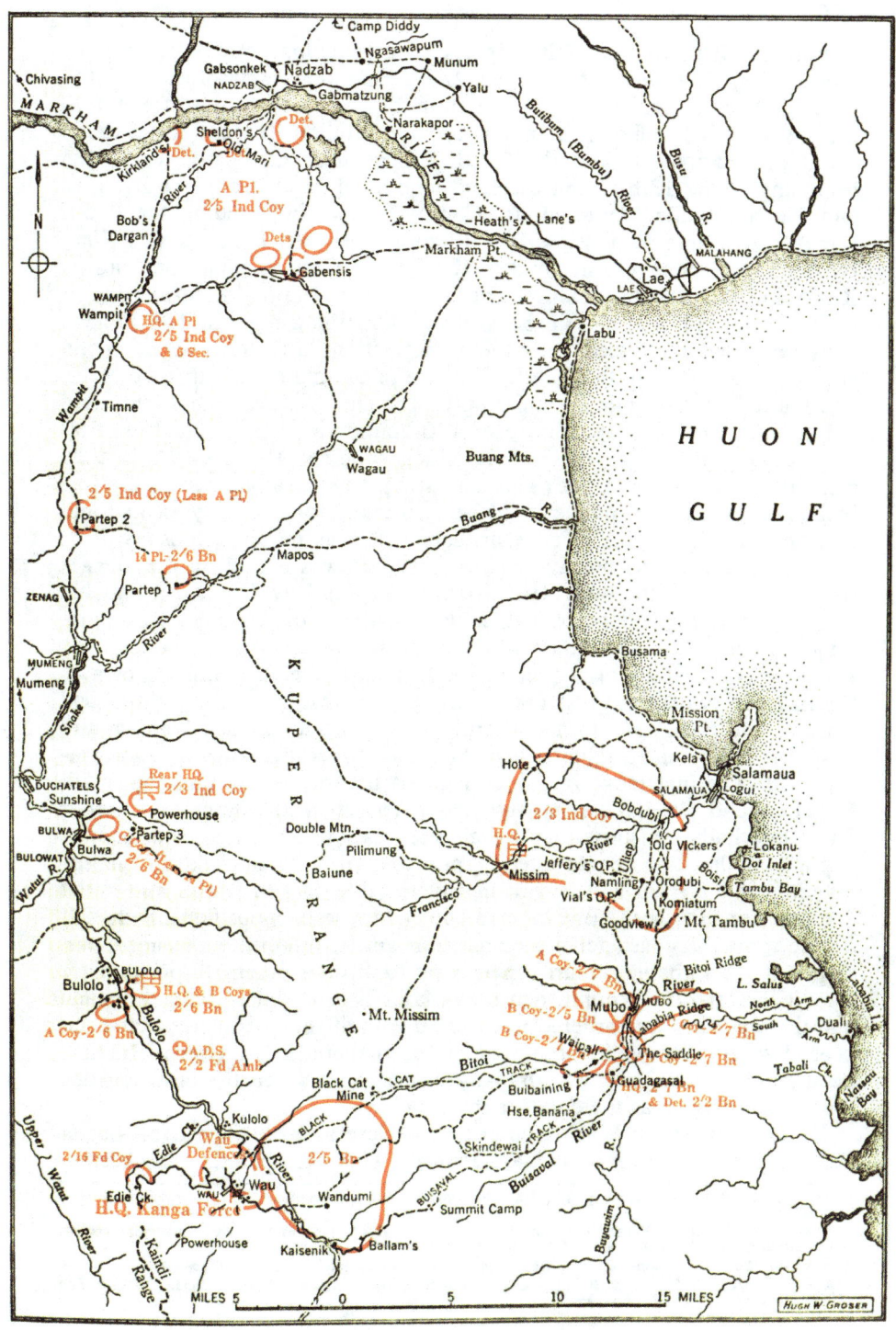

Australian dispositions, 17th April

With April there were faint ripples of quickening activity among the Australians. In front of Mubo the 2/7th Battalion (reinforcements and old members returning to the battalion having brought its strength to more than 700) relieved both the 2/5th Battalion (except for Captain Bradley's[7] company), and the 2/7th Independent Company. From the beginning of the 13th Guinn assumed command of all troops at Ballam's and forward while Lieut-Colonel Conroy,[8] now commanding the 2/5th Battalion, became responsible for all troops between Ballam's and Wau. By the 17th Guinn was firmly settled with Pringle's company on Vickers Ridge and the Lababia feature, one company in the Saddle area, one in the Mat Mat Hill and one in the Waipali-Buibaining regions. The Vickers guns remained integrated with these dispositions and the two mountain guns were still sited in the Saddle. The use of the mountain guns, however, was limited by the ammunition supply problem. On the 10th Moten had pointed out that the expenditure of 140 rounds a week would keep 150 natives constantly engaged in replenishing supplies. Reserves were to be maintained at 200 rounds per gun, harassing fire and area shoots were forbidden. A total of 50 rounds could be earmarked for definitely located and specified targets but the priority artillery task was purely defensive.

Guinn planned two positive moves. The first was a raid on the villages from the mouth of the Bitoi River south to Nassau Bay. There, on Lababia Island and at the village of Duali, just north of the Bitoi mouth, long-range patrols and native talk had indicated the presence of Japanese. The second was an attack on a precipitous heavily-timbered feature known as Green Hill,[9] which was just north-north-east of Mubo in the right-angled bend of the Bitoi as it turned sharply away east-south-east. The capture of Green Hill would facilitate later Australian operations against Observation Hill. The first move had been mooted before the relief of the 2/5th Battalion and Bradley's company had been left with Guinn to carry it out. They had been busy about their preparations for some time and, at 6 p.m. on the 20th, began their approach march to the coast from the junction of the Bitoi and Buyawim Rivers (due east of Mubo and about 7 miles from the sea). But they ran into Japanese opposition about half a mile from the coast, fell into confusion and withdrew to the north-east slopes of the Lababia feature where they took up a defensive position for the night 21st-22nd. Guinn then sent Major Nelson out to take command and the company was ordered not to return until they had completed their coastal task. Meanwhile preparations for the attack on Green Hill had been going ahead, Pringle's company having been given the task, and the 25th April was set as the date for the attack.

During this period Warfe's commandos were also on the move—out of Salamaua. On the 30th Lieutenant Jeffery,[1] who was operating an observa-

---

[7] Capt H. A. Bradley, VX3364; 2/5 Bn. Salesman; of Camberwell, Vic; b. Malvern, Vic, 8 Jan 1917.
[8] Lt-Col T. M. Conroy, SX8886. 2/43 Bn; CO 2/32 Bn 1941-42, 2/5 Bn 1943-44. Industrial chemist; of Melbourne; b. Port Adelaide, SA, 31 Jul 1906.
[9] So known because, among all the greenness on Vickers Ridge, it appeared greenest.
[1] Lt S. G. Jeffery, WX2100; 2/3 Indep Coy. Stockman; of Cottesloe, WA; b. Perth, WA, 7 Feb 1912. Died of wounds 20 Aug 1943.

tion post close to the point where Flying Officer Vial had established himself in the early days of the Japanese occupation (although Jeffery had not yet been able to locate the actual site of Vial's post), was told to reconnoitre the Komiatum area in preparation for a platoon raid on what was thought to be the village. The following days saw much activity along the tracks as the commandos reconnoitred widely, built up their base at the Baiune Power House and established staging camps along the track to Missim, increased their forward strength and battled against the problems of supply and communications. Lieutenant Whittaker of Angau was with them acting as their link with the natives.

Early on the morning of the 11th the platoon detailed for the attack set out from Missim for Base 3 (the most forward base and not far in rear of Jeffery's Observation Post). On the 12th Warfe himself left Missim for Base 3 and, his blood hot at the prospect of the coming encounter, signalled Moten for permission "to bash Bobdubi at the same time as Komiatum". Moten replied that he was not to "bash" Bobdubi but, after raiding Komiatum, if possible was to move south on to the rear of the Mubo defences. But when, on the evening of the 14th, the raiders broke into the village they had marked as Komiatum, it was only to find that there were no Japanese there. The natives said that the village was called Namling and they (the Komiatum natives) had built it after the Japanese had occupied the original Komiatum which was some 2,000 yards to the south-east, consisted of only two remaining huts and was occupied by about 80 Japanese. Warfe thereupon ordered an attack on the old village. By the early afternoon of the 17th, however, the raiders reported another failure—they had not been able to cut their way through the bush to Komiatum. Warfe then ordered Lieutenant Stephens'[2] section to ration at Base 3 and proceed thence via Namling against Komiatum.

Now activity and expectancy mounted higher among the Independent Company men as it became known that they were to attempt a number of heavy strokes against the Japanese. Whittaker arranged for all natives from Bobdubi, Namling and Logui to move back behind Missim—an ambitious plan which demanded much energy and skilful organisation. On the 21st Moten warned Warfe to make firm his base at Missim, advance his plans to move against the Japanese supply lines, on completion of Stephens' raid get all his men away from the vicinity of the Komiatum Track which strafing aircraft would then sweep. The soldiers reacted with even more vigorous excitement to this promise, and news of success by Stephens was a good omen. He had moved his men to the track near Komiatum on the night 19th-20th and then lay in ambush. But no Japanese walked into the trap. On the night of the 21st-22nd the Australians again lay hidden in the still, dark bush. Five or six Japanese passed through but they let these go, hoping for a bigger bag. They got it shortly before 9 p.m. A line of some 60 Japanese approached. The commandos held their fire until the leading enemy soldier was only about

---

[2] Capt K. H. R. Stephens, NX76246. 2/3 Indep Coy; 2/8 Cdo Sqn. Shop manager; of Potts Point, NSW; b. Melbourne, 27 Jun 1918.

4 feet from the muzzle of the Bren. Then all their weapons blazed. Many Japanese fell. Later native reports suggested that 20 were killed and about 15 wounded. The Australians suffered no casualties. Stephens then led his men back to Base 3.

Next day Moten signalled Warfe that he was to begin his offensive on the 24th, was to harass any movements down the track towards Mubo so that the 2/7th Battalion attack projected for the 25th would not be disturbed. Warfe then planned to strike simultaneously with "B" and "C" Platoons at the Mubo Track and Bobdubi respectively. And that was the position on the morning of the 23rd April.

This period had been uneventful for the 2/6th Battalion. (On the 14th the old hands recalled that this was the anniversary of the battalion's embarkation for the Middle East three years before. Of the officers and men who set sail that day only 116 were still with the battalion.) The only major change in dispositions was the relief of Dexter's company at Wampit by a platoon of the 2/5th Independent Company. The 2/5th's headquarters and the other two platoons had settled at Partep No. 2 where Captain Gullett drove them hard in training and, as the month progressed, reported well of their progress. On the 21st the leading elements of the 24th Battalion arrived at Bulolo and prepared to relieve the forward troops at Wampit. As more 24th Battalion men came in they would relieve the balance of the 2/5th Independent Company and allow these tired men to return to Australia for a rest after almost a year of continuous service in the forward areas—a notable achievement.

At 8 a.m. on 23rd April the headquarters of the 3rd Division opened at Bulolo and Major-General Savige assumed command of all Allied forces in the Wau-Lae-Markham area. At the same time Kanga Force was dissolved. Thus there passed from the Order of Battle a name which spanned the whole of the most critical year of war in New Guinea. Originally it was linked with the desperate attempt to strike back at the Japanese in the islands by the only form of Allied ground activity which could then be implemented—guerilla warfare in the mountains. At that time, too, it referred to a very small group of men who, alone in the whole of the South-West Pacific Area, except for those in Timor, were actually facing the Japanese invaders on the ground. From those humble and brave beginnings Kanga Force, as its year drew to a close, identified itself with the adaptation of air power in its most dramatic form to the needs of the army in the field.

While the fighting had been taking place round Wau and forward from Wau the Allied position on the flanks had been strengthening—though not without challenge from the Japanese.

On 12th January Major-General Milford had arrived at Milne Bay with the advance elements of his 5th Division and, by April, had a strong and balanced force of fresh troops including the 4th and 29th Brigades. Sporadic but annoying air raids reminded them, however, that the Japanese were aware of their existence. These might have served also to remind

Milford that the work he was putting in on Goodenough Island had point. Soon after his arrival at Milne Bay he was ordered to carry out an elaborate and well-planned deception scheme to suggest that a brigade group was located on Goodenough (where the actual strength was merely a battalion group). By the end of March the achievement of this plan was completed and an air operational base was under construction on the island to provide for one fighter strip (suitable also for air transports) and one heavy bomber strip. Two radar stations were installed and additional stations were being built at Kiriwina and Woodlark Islands.

Simultaneously some emphasis was moving from Port Moresby (which had its 100th air raid on 23rd January) to the other side of the range. Dobodura was being developed as a major air base and this demanded that the development of Oro Bay as a beach-head keep pace. Wharves were built there, tracks were developed to permit the ferrying to Dobodura by jeeps and native carriers of seaborne supplies. At the same time transport planes rained men and materials down on the airstrips. Since February Dobodura had been used as an advanced staging base for fighter aircraft which would fly in from Port Moresby in the morning and return there at night. By April, however, this extension of fighter range had been made permanent by the actual location at Dobodura of three squadrons.

That these preparations were not passing unnoticed by the Japanese was demonstrated by a series of heavy air raids against the growing installations. The 9th March raid on Wau was the forerunner of a phase of most vigorous Japanese air activity. On the 11th an equally heavy raid on Dobodura caused some casualties and destroyed 3 aircraft on the ground (though Allied fighters claimed 9 of the raiders for the loss of one of their own number). Heavy and effective raids on Oro Bay and Porlock Harbour followed closely. On the 28th about 40 bombers with a strong fighter escort attacked Oro Bay again. Though the interceptors claimed 13 raiders for the loss of 1 fighter, one of the new wharves was shattered, two small ships were sunk and a number of men were killed. On 11th April 45 raiders and 50 defending fighters joined in a furious mêlée over Oro Bay. Though the latter claimed 17 victims they could not prevent devastating hits on a 2,000-ton merchantman, a corvette and a small supply ship in the bay. An even heavier blow was struck at Port Moresby next day (in its 106th raid). Four aircraft were destroyed on the ground, 15 damaged, runways were cratered, a fuel dump at Kila took fire and men were burned to death and killed by the exploding bombs.

During these first months of 1943 there had been movement up the mainland coast. The Papuan Infantry Battalion had been operating detachments from Ioma since before the Japanese first landed in Papua and, farther south, it will be remembered, had made the first contact with the Japanese invaders in July of 1942. After they had played their part in the early fighting round Kokoda they then regrouped round their Ioma base. There they performed a valuable role both in reconnaissance and as killers of Japanese. By early January, however, the battalion was reduced to 10 Australian officers and N.C.O's and 140 native soldiers. Their communications were primitive, their supply difficult and chancy. As 1943 went on it was clear that, reduced as they were, they could be used only as snipers, guides and scouts. So useful were they in this role, however, that, though they were scheduled for relief, this was to be so staged that they would still be in the field by the middle of the year.

After the Sanananda operations came to an end in late January the 41st U.S. Division became responsible for the defence of the Oro Bay-Gona area and took the P.I.B. under their command. Small parties of the Americans then thrust up the coast, leisurely mopping up scattered Japanese with the help of the Papuans. By 22nd February all Japanese had been cleared from the Kumusi to Cape Ward Hunt though parties were still at large from the Mambare north. But after the passage of another month there was evidence that the garrison of the straggler-collecting post which the Japanese had been manning near Morobe was being withdrawn by barge and the 41st Division was ordered to capture and hold Morobe. The twofold purpose of this was to enable a supply staging point to be established to facilitate coastwise supply and relieve the Wau supply line if Salamaua were taken, and to provide a base from which PT boats might operate against the submarine and barge supply lines which had developed within the Huon Gulf. In the event, however, the occupation of Morobe posed no difficulty. At the end of March P.I.B. patrols reported the area clear of Japanese and by early April a combat team of the 162nd Regiment was in possession.

Thus, by April 1943, the Allies firmly held open all the main lines of convergence on the Japanese bases at Salamaua and Lae: up the coast from Morobe; through the mountains between Wau and Salamaua; along the river system between the Bulolo Valley and the Markham.

This month marked also the end of the first year of the formal existence of the South-West Pacific Area, which had begun with the Japanese at the peak of their success and confidence and with corresponding despondency in Australia—a despondency shared in full measure by General MacArthur after his arrival there, the memory of a great defeat dogging him. Then came the forward move by the Allies to fight the war in New Guinea, not because MacArthur at once inspired this on his arrival (as he was later to claim) but because the Coral Sea and Midway battles, and the development of airfields and air power, made possible the achievement of conditions which were fundamental to such a move.

It was a year in which Australians alone in the South-West Pacific Area faced the Japanese on land until November 1942; in which those Australians of the A.I.F. whom Mr Churchill would fruitlessly have diverted to Burma drove the Japanese back across the Papuan mountains and from Milne Bay; in which Australians in Papua (and Americans in the Solomon Islands) first checked the great Japanese southward advance; in which it became clear that the Japanese were outstandingly brave and tenacious soldiers—but were doomed to ultimate defeat.

For Australia generally the year, begun in gloom and preceded by the first blows of war ever to fall on the soil of Australia itself, saw the dark threat of isolation and actual invasion disappear. But it saw also the end of an epoch with Australia's realisation that her strategic destiny lay far outside that of Great Britain, the motherland, and with America, and that her future was dependent upon events in Asia. Perhaps Mr Curtin alone expressed this in words, but the country at large expressed it in its complete acceptance of the revolution which General MacArthur's assumption of overall military command in Australia represented.

For the Australian Army the year brought bitter lessons as well as great triumphs. The ignorance of New Guinea which prevailed in army circles until the year was well under way resulted in losses of life which could have been avoided, in wasted effort and tactical reverses; the divided army system which placed the militia and the A.I.F. in the field side by side affected the spirit of sections of the army and prevented the achievement of uniform standards of efficiency and a common outlook; the lack of training and discipline in some militia units resulted in unnecessary deaths and inefficiency in battle. On the other hand was an amazingly quick and thorough adaptation to the demands of tropical and bush warfare by individuals and units whose previous experience had been in no way related to this type of operation—an adaptation which was perhaps most marked by the use of air power in association with the Australian Army in completely new ways and on a completely new scale; on the part of staffs who quickly became outstandingly expert in new and involved procedures; on the part of the individual soldier; and by the emergence of superb leadership at all levels throughout the army, by officers (often from the humblest peace-time walks of life) of whom many had been proved in battle under varied circumstances and had forced their way to leadership by their own merit as fighting men.

At the very peak of this leadership development was General Blamey himself. His greatness was demonstrated almost daily by a knowledge unparalleled in Australia of how an army should be formed and put to work; by his exercise of the vital field command at the same time as he kept within his grasp a vastly detailed control of the Australian Army as a whole; by his sagacity and strength in meeting the rapidly changing demands of a difficult political situation; by his ability speedily to encompass the requirements of the new war and plan far ahead of the events of the day as he controlled them; by his generally unappreciated humanity.

APPENDIX 1

AFTER ALOLA

THIS appendix briefly describes the experiences of several groups of Australians who were cut off in the Owen Stanleys in late August and early September 1942.

In Chapter 6 it was described how Colonel Key and other parties of the 2/14th were cut off during the withdrawal from the Alola area on 30th August.

One of these included Captain Buckler and some of his company. When the wounded Sergeant Gwillim reported in the darkness that he was not able to clear the track Captain Buckler decided to follow the line of Eora Creek along the lower ground. At 8 p.m. he and his men plunged into the dark bush. They carried two men on stretchers, three wounded were walking and Corporal Metson, shot through the ankle, was crawling. Metson refused to be borne on a stretcher. "It will take eight of you chaps to carry that thing," he said. "Throw it away; I'll get along somehow." Nor would he be carried on another man's back. He bandaged his hands and his knees and crawled on over the mountains, through the mud and the rain.

Early the next morning the party overtook Privates Rockliffe,[1] Boys, Adam[2] and Blair[3] who had carried through the night on a stretcher a wounded sergeant from the 39th Battalion. Lying in the bush they found, a little later, Private Mayne,[4] who had been carried on Lieutenant Greenwood's back to a place of temporary safety and had then crawled away into the bush and hidden himself there so that he would not burden his comrades.

For four days Captain Buckler led his men along Eora Creek cut off by the advancing Japanese from the track above. In those few days he moved only as far as he could have moved in a few hours on the track. On the 4th he gave the following orders to Lieutenant Treacy:

> I want you to leave tomorrow with two men; travel to Myola to contact the unit, obtain medical supplies, food and native carriers, and return here with them. If the unit is not at Myola push on till you find it.
> This party will remain here for four days after your departure and search for native foods. If at the end of that time you do not return, I shall leave two men here for a further two days, and the rest will make for the coast, after moving north to the Kokoda Valley. . . .

Treacy left next morning with Privates Rockliffe and Avent.[5] During the following days they passed through many Japanese bivouac areas,

---

[1] Pte F. O. Rockliffe, TX5322. 2/14 Bn; 3 Ordnance Port Detachment. Farm labourer; of Sassafras, Tas; b. Devonport, Tas, 11 Oct 1914.

[2] Pte R. R. Adam, VX51385; 2/14 Bn. Assurance clerk; of Ivanhoe, Vic; b. Melbourne, 2 Jul 1913.

[3] Pte L. A. Blair, TX5204; 2/14 Bn. Truck driver; of Burnie, Tas; b. Latrobe, Tas, 18 Jan 1919.

[4] Pte A. Mayne, VX68537; 2/14 Bn. Storeman and packer; of Newport, Vic; b. Corindhap, Vic, 19 Jul 1905. Killed in action 4 Oct 1942.

[5] Pte W. A. Avent, NX17137; 2/14 Bn. Railway employee; of Ararat, Vic; b. Ballarat, Vic, 15 Jan 1914.

sometimes just avoiding death or capture, sometimes lying hidden as they watched their enemies moving in numbers near them, sometimes killing Japanese who seemed isolated from large groups. They were living on rice which they took as a result of these killings. They were desperate men who killed both as a duty and for food. Often they ate dry rice as they walked although it was generally mouldy. On the 10th they suddenly encountered a party of eight Japanese face to face. The constant wet had affected all their weapons except Treacy's pistol. With it the officer killed three of the enemy soldiers, but Rockliffe was shot through the leg.

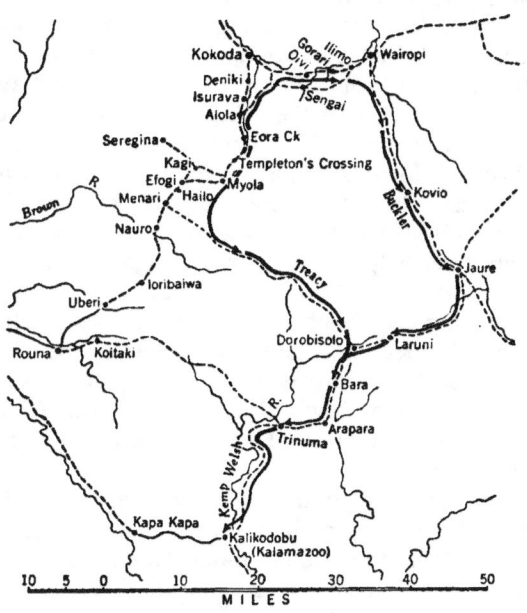

The track was too dangerous for them now so they left it, probably between Templeton's Crossing and Myola, and plunged into the wild country to the east. They were worried about Buckler and the rest but could do no more than they were doing. They shot a pig and its flesh sustained them for many days. On the 21st they met a patrol from the 2/6th Independent Company and were given food and help. They arrived at Dorobisolo next day, rode with the stream down the Kemp Welsh River, and so rejoined their battalion on 2nd October.

Buckler's party, meanwhile, had waited for five days before retracing their steps towards Sengai half-way between Kokoda and Wairopi. It was easier travelling in that direction, warmer, more cultivated with more native food, and the fugitives thought that other Australians were operating in the area. They lived mostly on the boiled tops of sweet potato plants and water. Cold and pain racked the wounded. In the cold nights they tried vainly to sleep in the dank bush wearing soaked clothes. Corporal Metson was still crawling, half-starved but unbeaten. After ten days of this they reached Sengai.

The natives there welcomed and fed them, sheltered them, and advised them about the country which lay ahead. His people would care for the wounded, the native chief said, if Buckler wished. There was much rough country still to be traversed.

In the fighting at Isurava Private Fletcher,[6] a medical orderly, had

---

[6] Pte T. J. Fletcher, MM, VX43033; 2/14 Bn. Farm hand; of Wareek, Vic; b. Mount Egerton, Vic, 2 Aug 1901. Killed in action 4 Oct 1942.

shown himself to be a brave and devoted soldier. During the days and nights since the 30th August he had nursed the wounded and sick with great care although he was weak himself and, like the rest, always hungry. Now he volunteered to stay at Sengai and look after the seven men whom it was decided to leave there for the present. On 21st September their friends paraded before Fletcher's little group and the order "Present Arms" was given. It was at once a salute and, had they but known it, a final farewell for later the Japanese came and killed these helpless men—the chivalrous Fletcher, young Metson who for nearly three weeks had crawled through the bush, Mayne who had crawled away to die rather than burden his comrades, and the others who had endured so much.

But this was hidden from Buckler and Butler and their 37 men as they dropped down to Wairopi, then headed upstream along the swiftly flowing Kumusi. Buckler himself pushed on ahead at a swifter pace than the main body could manage, his idea being to bring out news of his party and fly in help to Fletcher at Sengai. He met American troops on the 28th and Lieutenant Nichols[7] of the 2/6th Independent Company on the following day. Nichols' men at once sent help to Butler and his party who then climbed the main Owen Stanley Range and reached Dorobisolo on 6th October. Only two more days of walking lay ahead of them before they dropped down the Kemp Welsh River by raft to the American camp at Kalamazoo. But, with safety at last in sight, Private King[8] died at Dorobisolo.

It was strange that the wild circle of their wanderings should have brought Butler's main party and Treacy and his two men to the same point of exit from the Papuan mountains within such a short time of one another, after they had set out in opposite directions.

After Colonel Key and his battalion headquarters group were swept off the track in the vicinity of Isurava Rest House on the 30th August, they split into smaller parties which were to try to make their way up the line of the creek to Alola or to the 2/16th Battalion positions on the right flank.

With the colonel were Captain Hall, Corporal Lang,[9] Lance-Corporal Jones,[1] Privates Scott,[2] McGillivray,[3] O'Sullivan,[4] Greenwood,[5] Etty,[6] and

---

[7] Lt W. H. E. Nichols, VX29741; 2/6 Indep Coy. Manager; of Elwood, Vic; b. Balaclava, Vic, 18 Feb 1918. Killed in action 28 Oct 1942.

[8] Pte A. H. King, VX15532; 2/14 Bn. Labourer; of Fitzroy, Vic; b. Carlton, Vic, 17 May 1919. Died of wounds 9 Oct 1942.

[9] L-Sgt E. K. Lang, VX36518; 2/14 Bn. Plan printer; of Hawthorn, Vic; b. Williamstown, Vic, 26 Jan 1920.

[1] L-Cpl F. L. Jones, VX20209; 2/14 Bn. Clerk; of Cheltenham, Vic; b. London, 2 Dec 1912. Missing presumed dead 22 Sep 1942.

[2] Pte L. R. Scott, VX43061. 2/14 Bn; 7 Div Sigs. Sorter; of Yarraville, Vic; b. Portland, Vic, 6 Jul 1917.

[3] Pte C. M. McGillivray, VX36181; 2/14 Bn. Apprentice window dresser; of Melbourne; b. Oakleigh, Vic, 29 Dec 1920. Missing presumed dead 1 Oct 1942.

[4] Pte J. P. O'Sullivan, VX19170; 2/14 Bn. Pump hand, boot trade; of Northcote, Vic; b. Clifton Hill, Vic, 18 Feb 1918. Missing presumed dead 2 Sep 1942.

[5] Sig W. M. Greenwood, VX36347; 2/14 Bn. Railway porter; of Maryborough, Vic; b. Maryborough, 26 Mar 1919. Missing presumed dead 2 Sep 1942.

[6] Pte G. R. Etty, NG162. NGVR; 2/14 Bn. Bank clerk; of Armadale, Vic; b. Brisbane, 21 Jun 1914. Missing presumed dead 2 Sep 1942.

Veale.[7] This group was ambushed about 3rd September and further divided with Lang, Scott, Jones and McGillivray forming one separate party.

These four men then attempted to make their way back alone to the main Australian forces. Jones and McGillivray, finally overcome with exhaustion, hunger and exposure, died, but the other two went on, daily growing weaker. On the twentieth day after the ambush, wasted by their struggle, they were as desperate as starving wolves. They saw a Japanese walking down the track carrying two packets of Australian biscuits. Scott bailed him up with his pistol. The Japanese saw the weakness of the gaunt figure and tried to cut him down with a machete. Scott warded the blow with a shrunken arm while Lang, with all the feeble strength he could muster, hurled a piece of wood at the enemy soldier, giving Scott time for a shot which finished him off. They took the biscuits and staggered on. Eighteen days later a party of Australian engineers picked them up.

Lang said that Key and the five men with him were already suffering from hunger and exposure when he saw them last. But only scraps of their story can be pieced together from that point.

For the 10th September 2nd-Lieutenant Hirano, a platoon commander of the *I Battalion* of the *144th Regiment*, recorded in his diary:

> Captured Lieut-Colonel Key and four others. Though questioned the prisoners stubbornly refused to speak. Tied them securely for the night and decided to send them to the battalion commander tomorrow morning.

Key and his men, in their last extremity, were still giving everything of themselves to their comrades and their duty. For the others the long silence closes there but the pen of the Gona priest, Father Benson, adds a little to the story of Key himself.

It was October or November; Benson was being held prisoner by the Japanese at Buna and, at the time of which he writes, was attending a medical dressing station for treatment.

> . . . During my last visit . . . a tall, gaunt Australian, with the star and crown of a lieut-colonel on his shoulder straps, was brought in. He had a nasty leg wound. He was an emaciated skeleton; evidently he had been alone in the jungle for a very long time. We greeted each other with the raising of a hand. As softly as I could, I said:
> "Benson, missionary."
> But before he could reply Fujioka clouted me over the head and roared:
> "Benson! Speak no!"
> Next day the interpreter came on behalf of the officer and asked if I could lend him any books. I was glad to send him my entire library. This interpreter . . . told me that the lieut-colonel was so weak that he could only drink liquid out of a tin. I asked for his name but the interpreter could not tell me; and soon after I heard he had been taken to Rabaul.[8]

It seems certain that this was Key. He had seen his first duty as a prisoner—not to speak. Just as clearly he must have seen the prisoner's

---

[7] Pte L. R. Veale, VX38589; 2/14 Bn. Signwriter; of Bendigo, Vic; b. Colac, Vic, 21 Dec 1915. Missing presumed dead 2 Sep 1942.
[8] James Benson, *Prisoner's Base and Home Again*, pp. 69-70.

second duty—to escape. It seems likely that he achieved this, continued his struggle to return to his own forces, was wounded and recaptured.

Also in Chapter 6 it was mentioned that Lieutenant McIlroy and 20 men were sent out on 1st September to watch the track along the ridge west of Eora Creek to Kagi and to remain there for three days or until relieved.

McIlroy and his men set out carrying three days' rations. They followed the main track for half an hour, guided by a native, thence swung west. After three more hours' walking they found themselves on a ridge astride a track which led to the village of Seregina. They were misled then by a confusion of faint pads which seemed to fade into bush after a short distance.

For the next four days, making for the main track between Templeton's Crossing and Myola, the patrol struggled through the bush. Most of that time they climbed steadily. Tumbled rocks, valleys and falling water forced detours on them. Since their first night out their clothes and blankets had been soaked. The mountain mists rose out of the valleys in the morning. Rain fell in the afternoons.

On the morning of the 6th they ate the last of their food. That same day they found a track which led generally east. In the afternoon rain they took yams from a native garden. They could hear firing from the left but could see nothing as the mountains blocked their view. As they ate their yams in the evening two soldiers, who had been cut off that day from Lieutenant Bell's patrol of the 2/27th, joined them. The newcomers had tobacco and were the more welcome on that account.

On the 9th the patrol reached the village of Hailo, which they had seen amongst the rising mists on the previous day. The natives, Seventh Day Adventist Mission converts, were kind. They fed the tired and hungry men on yams, taro, bananas, paw paw and sugar cane and gave them a hut in which to sleep. Next day they guided the soldiers along a track which led to Menari.

In the early afternoon Corporal Waller,[9] Privates Bell,[1] Roberts[2] and Smith,[3] having no groundsheets or blankets, moved to reach Menari before the afternoon rains came. As they swung on to the main Efogi-Menari track they were surprised by a Japanese machine-gun post covering the junction. Waller and Bell were killed, it is thought, in trying to move back to warn McIlroy, but Roberts and Smith got through to Ioribaiwa where they rejoined the battalion on the 14th.

Meanwhile McIlroy himself, with one of his sections, had moved to reconnoitre the track junction. The Japanese engaged him and wounded

---

[9] Cpl L. L. Waller, VX16413; 2/14 Bn. Printer; of Bairnsdale, Vic; b. Warragul, Vic, 29 May 1920. Killed in action 10 Sep 1942.

[1] Pte A. Bell, VX44928; 2/14 Bn. Labourer; of Geelong, Vic; b. Geelong, 26 Feb 1913. Missing presumed dead 10 Sep 1942.

[2] Pte A. G. Roberts, VX22830; 2/14 Bn. Farm labourer; of Werribee, Vic; b. Northcote, Vic, 1 Apr 1921.

[3] WO2 L. L. Smith, VX16833; 2/14 Bn. Clerk; of North Balwyn, Vic; b. St Kilda, Vic, 13 May 1918.

one of his men. McIlroy then withdrew but could not regain contact with the rest of his patrol so that he and seven men were left alone. Knowing now of the Japanese strength and their advance along the main track McIlroy avoided it, moving on a parallel course through the bush. He did not get far, however. His men were weak from travelling in the rough country and the native foods did not sustain them. The wounded man was weak and another one of the party injured his leg so that he had to be carried.

On the 16th, therefore, Lance-Corporal Gedye[4] with Privates Brown[5] and Cahill,[6] and Private Matschoss[7] of the 2/27th, were sent ahead. They were to try to reach the Australian positions and send back help. But Gedye's party met trouble. Treacherous natives attacked them on the third day after they left the others, killed Cahill and Matschoss, and dogged Gedye and Brown—the latter with a spear wound in the back. It was not until 3rd October that the two survivors reached safety.

Meanwhile McIlroy, who had kept one man with him to help care for the two casualties, had been forced to remain where he was. Again the natives were kind, digging yams and taro for the Australians and drawing water for them daily. On the 30th, however, the soldier with the injured leg died. His friends buried him in the wild loneliness. Sad but freer, McIlroy then moved off once more with the two remaining members of his own original patrol and two more men of the battalion who had been in the bush since the fighting at Isurava and had recently joined him. A friendly party of mission natives who had been waiting patiently guided them for the next three days.

On the 4th they left the natives and struck out for the Brown River. But the going was still hard. On the 5th the five men shared a small piece of taro and a little fish about four inches long. On the following day they came out on the banks of the river and they followed it down. They were picking green paw paws to cook when a patrol from the 2/6th Independent Company found them.

In hospital McIlroy learned of the fates of various members of his patrol who had become separated from him. Of the main body with which he had lost contact on the 10th September seven had linked with another isolated party under Sergeant Irwin and had arrived spent and worn at Uberi on the 21st September. But there was no word of the four other men who had been with that group.

---

[4] Cpl S. M. Gedye, VX16217; 2/14 Bn. Poultry farmer; of Blackburn, Vic; b. Blackburn, 24 Aug 1917.

[5] Pte D. R. Brown, VX57096; 2/14 Bn. Labourer; of East Devonport, Tas; b. Coburg, Vic, 31 Dec 1913.

[6] Pte W. L. Cahill, VX23326; 2/14 Bn. Linotype operator; of Toowoomba, Qld; b. Richmond, Vic, 31 May 1916. Killed in action 19 Sep 1942.

[7] Pte A. R. Matschoss, SX14602; 2/27 Bn. Labourer; of Waikerie, SA; b. Truro, SA, 18 May 1908. Killed in action 19 Sep 1942.

APPENDIX 2

TIMOR

AFTER resistance by the main part of Sparrow Force had ceased in Dutch Timor on 23rd February 1942, and after men of Major A. Spence's 2/2nd Independent Company had met the Japanese invaders of Portuguese Timor in a series of small but spirited encounters, the leaders of the Independent Company began to reorganise and redeploy their troops in the southern half of Portuguese Timor about the middle of March.[1] Company headquarters was to be established at Atsabe; Captain R. R. Baldwin's "A" Platoon was to be stationed in the Bobonaro area; Captain G. G. Laidlaw's "B" Platoon round Same; Captain G. Boyland's "C" Platoon was to remain deployed in the most northerly positions—in the Hatu-Lia area.

Meanwhile Spence had been down to Lolotoi and had discussed the situation with Brigadier W. C. D. Veale, the Sparrow Force commander who, with a small group of his officers and men, had evaded capture by the Japanese. Veale and Spence agreed that the small bands of Australian and Dutch troops who were still at large in Dutch Timor should be called together at Atambua and thence cross the border and join the Independent Company.

The guerillas, by this time, were suffering badly. They were faced with the task of existing where a complete force had failed to survive. Their last news from Australia had been that Japanese aircraft had raided Darwin heavily on 19th February. Except for scraps from some Dutch radio stations they had since been cut off from news of the rest of the outside world—and when they had fragments of the Dutch broadcasts translated it was only to learn, on 9th March, that the whole of the Netherlands East Indies had surrendered to the Japanese. They were usually hungry. They were wasted with malaria and had little quinine. Their boots were becoming mere remnants of leather about their feet. Despite all this, however, they kept their spirits high.

When Mr David Ross, the Australian Consul at Dili who had been held captive there by the Japanese, was sent to seek out the guerillas with demands for their surrender, he was amazed to find them in such good heart. The senior officers of the company had gathered at Hatu-Lia to meet him on 16th March. He gave to each of them a note saying that any orders for food or other commodities signed by that officer would later be honoured by the British and Australian Governments. He gave them detailed information regarding the defences of Dili and the near-by aerodrome to aid them in raids they were planning. He took back with him to Dili their scornful refusal to surrender.

---

[1] For an account of the operations in Timor up to mid-March 1942 see Lionel Wigmore, *The Japanese Thrust* (1957), Vol IV in this series.

Gradually, aided to some extent by Ross' notes, to a very large extent by the unremitting efforts of Senhor Antonio Policarpe de Sousa Santos, who was in charge of the Fronteira Province, and by their own efforts at organising supplies, their food situation greatly improved and they could look forward to obtaining reasonably adequate supplies from the local residents. Their planning and deployment were made easier because the Portuguese let them use the telephone system which linked the various Portuguese administrative posts. They had large reserves of ammunition which they had built up in the inland areas before the arrival of the Japanese, though sub-machine-gun ammunition was short. Their own vigorous and wide patrolling, information coming to them from native sources, and a constant flow of information through Santos, kept them well aware of the Japanese movements. By the end of March practically all of the remnants of the main force from Dutch Timor (approximately 200) had been safely collected in the south-west corner of the Portuguese territory (though they were mostly unarmed and many were ill and they

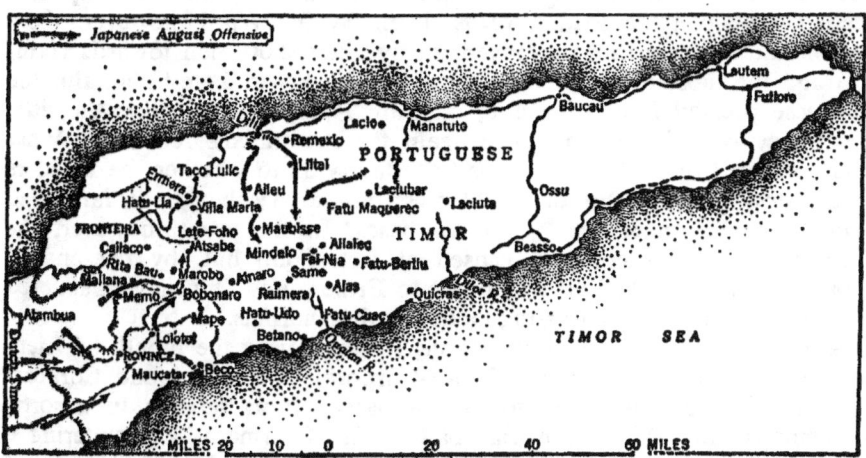

remained under the direct command of Veale who set up his headquarters at Mape); about 40 armed and fit men from this group under Major J. Chisholm, a brave and vigorous officer of the 2/40th Battalion, were watching the frontier from a base at Memo; some 150 Dutch troops were also gathered in the south-west of the colony, spreading into Dutch Timor, and gradually being reorganised there by Colonel N. L. W. van Straaten; ammunition which had been stored at Atambua had been safely got away before the Japanese occupied that area at the beginning of April, and was a useful addition to Spence's reserves.

Early April, therefore, found the forces on Timor in a far better position than they might have hoped for only a few weeks earlier. By that time, however, the Japanese were once more on the move inland. Major B. J. Callinan, Spence's tireless and brave second-in-command, had gone forward to the Hatu-Lia area to relieve Boyland temporarily in command of "C" Platoon. He took with him Lieutenant Turton[2] who commanded the Independent Company's engineer section. They found Lieutenants Burridge[3] and Cole[4] of Boyland's platoon, with their sections, at Hatu-Lia and, while they were there, Lieutenant Cardy[5] (of Laidlaw's platoon), who had been on a wide patrol, came in. Soon Callinan and Turton pushed forward towards Taco-Lulic ordering Burridge and Cole to follow behind them and sending Cardy to sortie against the Japanese from the north of the road which led from Dili. As they approached Taco-Lulic at the end of the day they saw Japanese moving up the road towards them. Next day they watched these from high ground. The day afterwards they narrowly escaped parties searching for them and were themselves frustrated in an attempted ambush. It became clear that the Japanese were interested in moving up the roads which led to Ermera and Hatu-Lia. During the days following, the swift-moving Australians clashed sharply with the advancing Japanese and claimed 30 or 40 killed, without casualties to themselves, before the invaders occupied Ermera. Outflanked, the guerillas then withdrew and later, from Villa Maria, watched the Japanese feeling out along the road towards them. By 9th April, however, these feelers had coalesced into a movement by about 500 men towards Hatu-Lia and the most forward commandos fell back—to Lete-Foho. But the Japanese pressed farther on and, on 13th April, after shelling the little town they occupied it and once again the Australians fell back. What really worried them, however, was uncertainty as to whether the invaders would stop at Lete-Foho, or would press on—to Atsabe or still farther to Ainaro—and menace the Australian bases. In the event, however, the forward movement not only ceased at Lete-Foho but, by the end of April, the Japanese had all withdrawn to Ermera and Dili, having suffered annoying losses to the harassing tactics of the guerillas.

Typical of these tactics were actions fought during the month by Lieutenants Turton and Rose[6] and Lance-Corporal Thompson[7] and Corporal Taylor.[8] On 15th April Turton led a party of his sappers in a sortie to demolish the Dili—Hatu-Lia road north of Ermera. Encountering a party of Japanese at close quarters they claimed to have killed six of them. Soon afterwards two of Turton's men, Thompson and Sapper March,[9] ambushed a party who had been moving along the road and

---

[2] Maj D. K. Turton, WX8440. 2/2 Indep Coy; 2/2 Cdo Sqn. Clerk; of North Fremantle, WA; b. North Fremantle, 13 Jan 1918.

[3] Lt J. C. Burridge, WX8538. 2/2 Indep Coy; 2/2 Cdo Sqn. Clerk; of Claremont, WA; b. Perth, WA, 6 Apr 1918.

[4] Lt R. Cole, WX11076. 2/2 Indep Coy; 2/2 Cdo Sqn. Clerk; of Victoria Park, WA; b. Maylands, WA, 22 Jul 1918.

[5] Lt J. A. Cardy, NX76534. 2/2 Indep Coy; 2/2 Cdo Sqn. Regular soldier; of Auburn, NSW; b. Enfield, Middlesex, England, 3 Mar 1912.

[6] Capt J. A. Rose, NX65630. 2/2 Indep Coy; "Z" Special Unit. Salesman; of Mudgee, NSW; b. Wagga Wagga, NSW, 8 Jul 1920.

[7] L-Cpl L. W. P. Thompson, WX12320. 2/2 Indep Coy; 116 Lt AA Regt. Ice trader; of Perth, WA; b. Bombay, India, 3 Oct 1907.

[8] Lt W. Taylor, WX8527. 2/2 Indep Coy; 2/6 Cdo Sqn. Salesman; of Fremantle, WA; b. Cowdenbeath, Scotland, 1 Jul 1916.

[9] Spr W. E. March, WX12144. 2/2 Indep Coy; 2/2 Cdo Sqn. Printer; of Mt Lawley, WA; b. Perth, WA, 15 Feb 1917.

who alighted from a truck near the Australians. When the two commandos opened fire the driver of the truck made off with his vehicle and left his passengers on the road as targets for the two ambushers who raked them with Bren gun fire and later reported that they thought they had killed 35. On 24th April Taylor and three men, who had been lying in wait for two days, opened up on four trucks which were driving along the road. They wrecked one of these and thought that they left about 30 dead behind them when they disappeared once more into the bush. Next day Rose and four men waylaid a truck load of enemy soldiers near Villa Maria. The approach of a large convoy forced them to take to the bush, however, before they completed their work, though they claimed 12 Japanese dead for their efforts and gave the credit for eight of these to Private Wheatley[1] who was renowned among them for his accurate sniping.

By the end of April not only were the Australians settling to their grim task with practised skill but a marked improvement in their general situation was promised through their opening of a radio link with Darwin. For some time a small group of their signalmen had been at work at Mape attempting (with the generous and skilled help of de Sousa Santos) to build a transmitting set. The most expert and tireless of these was Signalman Loveless,[2] and for some time much of the Australian patrolling was directed towards getting parts for his transmitter. When Captain G. E. Parker, who had been the Sparrow Force signals officer, arrived from Dutch Timor, he was able to advance the work Loveless had so skilfully and patiently developed. On 20th April the weak transmitter which they had contrived was heard in Darwin. However, on the night on which contact was established the batteries failed, and the message had to be continued the following night. The first message had been a simple cipher, using as a keyword the name of an officer. Clues were given in clear as the identity of the officer. That first signal was prefaced by the priorities normally reserved to the Commanders-in-Chief of the Services, but it was felt that something had to be done to attract attention. It was certainly effective as the operator could hear all stations close down and concentrate upon "Winnie the War Winner", as the set had been affectionately named.

The set occupied a room about ten feet square (Callinan wrote later), and there were bits and pieces spread around on benches and joined by wires trailing across the floor. Batteries were charged by a generator taken from an old car and driven by a rope which passed around a small grooved wheel attached to the armature of the generator and around a similar wheel about eighteen inches in diameter. Attached to this latter wheel was another wheel around which a further rope passed on to a wheel about four feet or more in diameter, and to this large wheel were fixed handles by which four natives turned the machine. This was a further example of the work of Sousa Santos, as the whole of this battery charging device had been built under his orders.[3]

---

[1] Lt-Cpl M. L. Wheatley, WX13365. 2/2 Indep Coy; 2/2 Cdo Sqn; AASC 11 Div. Truck driver; of Mt Lawley, WA; b. Kronkup, WA, 28 Oct 1912.
[2] Sig M. L. Loveless, TX4745. 2/2 Indep Coy; LHQ Heavy Wireless Group. Radio mechanic; of Hobart; b. Hobart, 5 Nov 1914.
[3] B. J. Callinan, *Independent Company* (1953), p. 121.

Strangely, this painfully contrived set had been operating for scarcely a week before Lieutenant Garnett[4] handed over a second receiving and transmitting set to the signallers, complete and in good order. This had belonged to Qantas Empire Airways. During a long and difficult patrol Garnett got in touch with some Portuguese "deportados" on the outskirts of Dili. These were men who, because of revolutionary activities, had been banished for varying periods from Portugal itself to the most distant of the Portuguese possessions. Under Garnett's initial prompting they became actively helpful to the Australians and operated with them later in a small and colourful group, usually not more than about six in number, which the Australians called "the International Brigade". Some deportados, led by Pedro Guerre, sneaked the Qantas set out of Dili one night under the noses of the Japanese and passed it over to Garnett who then got it back across practically the whole width of the island to the force headquarters where the signallers used it to supplement the efforts of "Winnie the War Winner".

Meanwhile, back in Australia there had been astonishment and, at first, some doubt when the signals from the forces still fighting on Timor were picked up in the Northern Territory. The doubts, however, were quickly resolved and arrangements were made for the air force to reconnoitre the Dili area on 23rd April and, on picking up visual signals from the ground, to drop batteries and other supplies. In the event, however, the first Hudson aircraft did not get over the Sparrow Force area until 24th April and, unable to pick up any signals, it brought back the batteries and medical stores which it carried. Acting on instructions from Darwin Veale's headquarters then had signal fires burning as aircraft recognition signals round Mape on 26th April. The aeroplanes, however, flying too far to the north, did not pick up the signals, and, once again, could not drop their stores. But the following day the first drop took place: parachute deliveries of 19 packages at 5 p.m. on 27th April, at Beco. More drops took place on 3rd and 8th May. The period of Sparrow Force's isolation was ended.

While these arrangements were being made, however, the future of Sparrow Force was being anxiously considered by the army leaders in Australia. On 28th April Major-General Herring's Northern Territory Force Headquarters reported to Army Headquarters a Sparrow Force signal that, if it were intended to retake Timor from the Japanese (whose main strength—at Dili—Sparrow Force estimated to be 1,500) within one month, the men on the island, reinforced by 300 guerillas, could effectively mop up the Japanese if their own position did not deteriorate badly in the meantime; that, however, if they were not thus reinforced, Sparrow Force could not achieve anything really effective. Next day Herring proposed to inform Sparrow Force that Army Headquarters wished to impress on them that the matter of early relief presented many difficulties; that air assistance would be limited to dropping essential sup-

---

[4] Capt H. J. Garnett, QX21917. 2/2 Indep Coy; Signals Corps 1943-45. Clerk; of Dutton Park, Qld; b. Brisbane, 2 Nov 1919.

plies but that this assistance would not be on any regular schedule; that it was vitally important that the men on Timor should maintain an offensive spirit and continue their guerilla activities and should keep up a flow of information with a view to the later use of Timor as a base for extending guerilla activities to other islands in the vicinity; that there was no possibility of evacuation in the immediate future. On 3rd May Land Force Headquarters told Herring that they had no present intention to reinforce Sparrow Force but intended to maintain them.

By that time the general Sparrow Force plan was to attack Dili from the east and so draw off Japanese troops in that direction while other Australians harassed the Japanese west of Dili.

> The essence of this latter policy was for a body of troops to harass the enemy and, when attacked, to divide and move off in opposite directions at right angles to the line of the Japanese advance. This then gave the Japanese two alternatives, either to pursue our troops and so split their own force, or to push on and ignore our troops. Should they push on, or not continue the pursuit of our troops, then we would come back on their rear and flanks. Ground of itself was not important; the main object was to kill, and our best method of killing was by sharp harassing actions.[5]

Accordingly, by the end of April, an extensive Australian re-deployment had been almost completed. Laidlaw's platoon was carrying out a wide and difficult movement to establish themselves at Remexio, fairly close in to Dili; Boyland's platoon was settling in the Maubisse area; a new platoon ("D"), which had been formed from the Independent Company's sappers and from the fittest of the survivors from Dutch Timor, had been gathered at Mape and given a short intensive course of guerilla training, and, by early May, would be based on Atsabe under the command of Turton, who, though gentle by nature, was already proving himself an outstanding soldier and guerilla engineer; Baldwin's platoon (which had been scattered widely to fill gaps as they developed) was to have the left flank positions in the general area of Cailaco.

Thus the Australians were settling themselves in an arc from the outskirts of Dili to Cailaco, well sited to harass the main Japanese forward base which had developed at Ermera and its lines of communication with the main base at Dili. This arc extended over about 60 miles and was manned by a little over 300 fighting troops. South of it, at Ainaro, Captain C. R. Dunkley, the company's medical officer, established his hospital and a rest centre early in May. Previously his hospital had been at Same. To it the sick and wounded had been transported from the section positions under the most difficult conditions—carried on stretchers for long days over bridle paths and tracks which wound through rugged country or, more often, borne on the backs of small but hardy Timor ponies. Ainaro was almost ideal for Dunkley's purposes. It had been an early missionary centre and was the site of the oldest administrative post on the island. It was a rich area, its natives were friendly Christians, it contained some fine buildings and an existing hospital which Dunkley

---

[5] Callinan, *Independent Company*, p. 100.

took over. As their centre developed there the Australians fed to it the men who, for various reasons, had become physically ineffective—not only commandos but survivors from Dutch Timor. After they were treated in hospital and rested they went to training squads under officers and N.C.O's from neighbouring sections. Men who responded to training were sent forward to platoons as reinforcements; others were given additional medical treatment and rest and training; those who seemed unlikely to make good at all were held in the area for possible evacuation.

During May the Australians busied themselves by chopping at the Japanese whenever opportunity offered—and the existence of the Ermera base played nicely into their hands for traffic between Dili and Ermera was constant—demolishing sections of the roads, destroying bridges at key-points. Callinan has recorded:

> One typical raid was carried out by Sergeant James,[6] who with two sappers sat less than one hundred yards from a Japanese post for two days. When he knew the routine of the post well, he decided that the best time to strike was just as the enemy were having breakfast. So the following morning there was a sharp burst of fire and twelve Japanese were killed, the raiders disappearing into the scrub.
>
> It was seldom that a week went past without two or three successful raids being carried out. The individual number of Japanese casualties was small; it might be five or as high as fifteen, but these numbers quickly provided an amazing total, and their effect on Japanese morale was enormous. Japanese soldiers told natives that the Australians were devils who jumped out of the ground, killed some Japanese and then disappeared, whilst their officers complained that though they had been fighting them for months, many had never seen an Australian.
>
> In an attempt to obtain support from the natives, the Japanese placed a price of one hundred pataccas—approximately eight pounds—on the head of each Australian soldier, and one of a thousand pataccas—approximately eighty pounds—on the head of the Australian commander and "Captain Callinan". . . .
>
> As these pin-pricking raids of ours continued, the Japanese came to blame us for everything that happened, and this is the pinnacle of success for a harassing force. It is a state of mind induced by numerous fruitless endeavours to deal with an enemy who seems able to deal a blow anywhere at any time, but who remains elusive.[7]

In May the Australians prepared the boldest single blow they had yet planned against their enemies. On the afternoon of 15th May, from their base at Remexio, Laidlaw led down towards Dili some 20 of his men, under the direct command of Lieutenant T. G. Nisbet. They had blackened themselves with soot and grime. After night came they crept up to the defending wire which fronted them. They planned to kill silently the Japanese sentries whom they expected to find there. It took them some time to discover, however, that there were none. They then passed quietly through the wire and, by way of the deep drains which flanked them, along the silent streets. There were lamps burning in huts and houses which they passed and in these huts they could see Japanese resting or talking. Laidlaw approached a machine-gun position. To a Japanese there he was just a shape bulking in the darkness and the soldier spoke to him. Laidlaw

---

[6] Sgt H. E. James, WX12127. 2/2 Indep Coy; 2/2 Cdo Sqn. Salesman; of Perth, WA; b. Perth, 9 May 1918.
[7] Callinan, *Independent Company*, p. 104.

shot him in the stomach with a .45-inch revolver at three yards' range. As he fell Nisbet and Lance-Sergeant Morgan[8] almost tore him apart with rifle and sub-machine-gun fire. The whole of the attacking party opened up. Their fire poured into the near-by huts, beat against the walls, shot down disorganised defenders who rushed out of the buildings or milled in confusion. After about ten minutes of this mêlée (at 1.15 a.m.) the attackers began to withdraw, fire from Lieutenant Garnett and his men, who had taken up a position on the beach just outside the town for this purpose, covering them and causing more panic and confusion among the garrison. All the Australians got clean away and the Japanese were apparently too disorganised to arrange any immediate pursuit.

On 22nd May, however, a party of them was moving on Remexio. Lance-Sergeant W. E. Tomasetti and Lance-Corporal Kirkwood,[9] with the little "International Brigade", killed 4 or 5 of them about 4 a.m. before they themselves broke into the bush. Warned by the firing Corporal Aitken's[1] men, farther out along the track, lay waiting in an ambush which they sprang about 10 a.m. They said they shot down about 25 Japanese and the rest then fell back. (Among the first Japanese to fall was "the Singapore Tiger"—a Japanese major, ruthless and versed in bush fighting, so reports said, who had been brought down specially from Singapore to deal with the Australians.) Next day, however, a Japanese party about 200 strong moved on Remexio, but the Australians had melted away. On 26th May the Japanese returned to Dili. The Australians then returned to Remexio.

By this time the spirits of the Australians on Timor were very high. They were operating vigorously and efficiently—a picturesque band, tattered, bearded, each man accompanied by one or more loyal natives (creados) to assist and serve him personally. The two air drops in April and additional drops on 3rd, 8th and 23rd May had made good their most urgent needs. On 24th May a Catalina flying-boat brought more stores from Darwin and (since his own personal role had necessarily been a limited one and the information he could bring back to Australia was valuable) it took Brigadier Veale out on its return flight. With him went also the Dutch commander, van Straaten, 3 wounded and 4 sick men. Spence, promoted lieut-colonel, replaced him as the force commander and Callinan was promoted to command the Independent Company. Baldwin became Callinan's second-in-command and Lieutenant Dexter,[2] stocky, strong and laughter-loving, took over "A" Platoon. Early in the evening of 27th May H.M.A.S. *Kuru* (a naval launch with a cargo capacity of 5 or 6 tons) ran in on the first of what was to become a series of regular

---

[8] Lt H. J. Morgan, WX9954. 2/2 Indep Coy; 2/2 Cdo Sqn. Shop assistant; of South Fremantle, WA; b. Northam, WA, 18 Aug 1912.
[9] Sgt R. S. Kirkwood, WX212. 2/2 Indep Coy; 2/2 Cdo Sqn. Bank officer; of Perth, WA; b. Perth, 11 Jan 1917.
[1] Sgt R. A. Aitken, WX10542. 2/2 Indep Coy; HQ 8 Inf Bde; FELO. Schoolteacher; of Belmont, WA; b. Bayswater, WA, 7 Nov 1915.
[2] Maj D. St A. Dexter, VX38890. 2/2 Indep Coy; 2/2 Cdo Sqn; "Z" Special Unit; OC 2/4 Cdo Sqn 1945. Student; of Melbourne; b. St Albans, Eng, 8 Jan 1917.

trips by it and H.M.A.S. *Vigilant* (capable of carrying about 7 tons) from Darwin.

The establishment of this regular and efficient system of supply by sea followed firm decisions taken early in June by Generals MacArthur and Blamey regarding their future operations on Timor. On 3rd June Blamey suggested to MacArthur that two courses of action were open to him: to recapture Timor with an overseas expedition; or to withdraw the bulk of the forces then there. MacArthur replied on the 11th:

> To attack Timor would require at least two brigades, perhaps a division. Success would require that this force be carefully trained in landings on hostile shores, be equipped with suitable ships and landing craft and be strongly supported by air and naval forces. A careful review of our present position indicates that a number of these requisites are lacking. Without them such an expedition has little chance of success and cannot therefore be considered with the means now available.
>
> The withdrawal of the bulk of the present garrison from Timor does not present any great difficulty. Such a plan, no doubt, could be successfully executed. However, the retention of these forces at Timor will greatly facilitate offensive action when the necessary means are at hand. These forces should not be withdrawn under existing circumstances. Rather, it is believed that they should remain and execute their present missions of harassment and sabotage.
>
> The retention of the bulk of these forces at Timor will necessitate a carefully prepared plan of supply and a plan for the withdrawal of the garrison in case the Japanese make a sustained offensive against them.

Accordingly a link between Australia and Timor was firmly and quickly established. A plan was developed through which supplies (to supplement those the guerillas got from the land, off which they lived substantially during the whole of their stay on the island) were to be delivered from Australia on the basis of a monthly schedule of requirements, with all stores marked in Darwin for delivery direct to platoons and headquarters and packed before dispatch in watertight containers in 100-pound pony loads and 40-pound man-loads. This system was to be supplemented by droppings from Hudson aircraft to meet urgent demands at short notice. The development of the sea route meant also that the Hudsons could be used for the most part to attack targets on information supplied by the troops in Timor and such attacks on key Japanese points (particularly Ermera and Dili) became a feature of the operations.

June passed fairly quietly though marked by a series of small but vigorous forays by the men of the improvised "D" Platoon. It was marked also by a reorganisation of the Dutch forces so that they closely covered the south-west border and extended the line of the Australian positions with the result that the combined line, though jagged and not, of course, capable of complete integration, stretched north-east across the whole of Portuguese Timor to the vicinity of Dili.

Meanwhile, on 9th and 11th June, the Australian Government had learnt through the Dominions Office of a proposal by the Portuguese Government that that government should open negotiations for the withdrawal of the Japanese in return for the surrender of the Australian troops to the Portuguese authorities for internment in Portuguese Timor. The

Australian Chiefs of Staff advised that the proposal be rejected and General MacArthur concurred.

Late in June Ross arrived once more in the Australian positions having been sent out by the Japanese with a second surrender demand. He had warned both the Japanese consul and commander that there was no hope that the Australians would fall in with the demand, particularly as they knew that some of their men who had been taken in February had been murdered. The Japanese commander was most indignant at what he considered this reflection upon the behaviour of Japanese soldiers. He was emphatic that neither he nor any soldiers under his command had ever caused the death of prisoners and added that he, personally, had taken the Australian surrender at Ambon. He gave Ross an undertaking, addressed to the Independent Company commander and signed both by himself and the consul, which read:

> In the name of the Imperial Japanese Government, we hereby guarantee that all Australian soldiers under your command, who surrender to the Japanese Force now in Portuguese Timor, will receive proper treatment as prisoners of war in accordance with International Law.

He also asked Ross to give his compliments to the Australian commander and tell him how much he admired the way in which the Australians had fought and kept on fighting. He added, however, that he thought that they should come into Dili and fight it out to the last man. If they would not do this he would take his men into the hills and fight it out there. Ross said that there were not sufficient Japanese in Timor to round up the Australians. The colonel agreed and admitted that, from his reading about the Boer War, and from his own experiences in Manchuria, he believed that it required about ten regular soldiers to kill each guerilla. He then added "I will get what is required".

When Ross arrived at Spence's headquarters at Mape the Australians gave the Japanese offer scant consideration, and, since Ross had not promised to return to Dili, he remained with them and later was sent out to Australia, where on 16th July, he described the situation on Timor to the Advisory War Council.

As July advanced, however, there were disturbing signs that the Japanese commander's threat was no idle one. Rumours, and reports from the Dili observation post, came to the hills of the arrival of fresh troops at Dili and accretions to the Japanese forces in Dutch Timor. The invaders withdrew to Dili from their forward positions at Ermera and, though the Australian patrols pressed closely in on Dili itself and busied themselves demolishing and blocking roads and destroying key-points, they found the Japanese strangely passive, as though they were gathering and containing themselves for a major effort. There were disturbing and increasing indications also that some natives were becoming not only unfriendly but actively threatening to the Australians.

On 9th August the Japanese methodically bombed Beco and Mape. Next day the bombers were over Mape again and also attacked Bobonaro, where Callinan had his headquarters, and the near-by Marobo, thus ushering in a series of raids on the villages which the Australians had been using as their key-points. It quickly became clear that the Japanese were launched on a widespread and well-organised move to envelop and destroy the Australians and the Dutch. The pattern which subsequently emerged was that perhaps 1,500 to 2,000 Japanese were on the move; that one column was striking south from Manatuto; two struck out from Dili itself, one south-east then south by way of Remexio, one due south through Aileu; another crossed the border at Memo and drove at Bobonaro through Maliana; attacks from Dutch Timor developed against the Dutch positions in the south-west round Maucatar; a party landed at Beco (but in a rather disorganised state after effective attacks on their convoy by 18 Hudsons).

The bombings drove Spence and his headquarters out of Mape and they lost touch temporarily with the main forces. The Portuguese telephone system of which the Australians had been making full use was disrupted and Callinan moved a few miles out of Bobonaro and set up a wireless control through which he was able to keep in close touch with his platoons.

In the most northerly sector Laidlaw, learning of the Japanese approach, left Remexio and, the following day, before an advance of 500 or 600 Japanese, withdrew towards Liltai. His men harassed the Japanese in a series of well-planned encounters as the Japanese felt their way towards Liltai. They hit them hard when the attackers entered Liltai on the night of the 13th and then later swung away to the east to gnaw at their flanks and rear as they went on from Liltai. The Australian platoon lost one man killed. They were fortunate, however, to escape so lightly from the Liltai area as they were almost taken by surprise there by the convergence with the column they had been engaging of the one which had moved unexpectedly from Manatuto. Corporal Loud,[3] in the most forward position, skilfully extracted his sub-section and left the converging Japanese forces hotly engaging one another over the space he had left.

Boyland, meanwhile, from his positions north of Aileu, had been harassing the force which had come south from Dili. But he was pushed beyond Aileu and then fell back on Maubisse. As the Japanese advanced he was then driven farther south again.

Perhaps the most difficult fighting, however, developed in the western sector where Dexter had his platoon based on Rita Bau, and Turton was based on Atsabe farther to the east. As the Japanese advanced, Dexter, fighting hard and manoeuvring skilfully, found his movements hampered by natives (mostly from Dutch Timor) whom the Japanese were using to screen their advance. These natives moved among the bewildered local villagers and completed the demoralisation which the bombings had begun, the locals reasoning that surely this time the end had come for the Australians and no sensible man would side with the losers. Dexter's men fell back towards Bobonaro. Just outside the town one of his sections was

---

[3] Sgt E. Loud, WX9489. 2/2 Indep Coy; 2/2 Cdo Sqn. Timber worker; of Pemberton, WA; b. Yorkrakine, WA, 20 Jun 1916.

almost surrounded and there Private Waller[4] (one of the company's three sets of brothers) was killed. At Bobonaro the column which had come from Memo and the party which had landed at Beco came together on the morning of 13th August and Dexter then joined forces with Turton to fight from a narrow saddle through which the road from Bobonaro passed to Atsabe. On the 14th Dexter himself remained in ambush at the saddle, where he was later joined by Sergeant Hodgson[5] and some other men of Turton's platoon so that the total ambush numbers became 28, while the rest of the group fell back to Atsabe. After a sharp clash Dexter led his ambushers also back to Atsabe.

Meanwhile Callinan himself and his company headquarters had found themselves almost cut off by the Japanese advance through Bobonaro. They therefore struck into the high mountains to the north-east and, after two very cold and hungry days, swung down into Ainaro. There Callinan learned that Dexter and Turton had been forced beyond Atsabe, that Boyland had been pushed back beyond Maubisse and that there was nothing now in front of the Japanese moving down from Liltai. As he set about reorganising his company he knew that he was in a desperate position. The men were very tired and had had little food since the fighting began; small though his transport requirements were they were difficult to satisfy; he had little petrol left for use in his battery chargers and only a few serviceable batteries. At this stage he sent urgent messages off to Australia for money "to coax food and transport from the natives, and for batteries to maintain our vital communications. The same day the gallant Hudsons of R.A.A.F. were over us dropping the vital supplies. This magnificently prompt and effective help cheered us and the three short bursts from the planes' guns as they passed over our headquarters on their way back to Australia was a salute we returned in our hearts."

As the Australian commander, with the Japanese closing in, prepared orders for issue on the 19th for an Australian attack which he hoped desperately might stave off the necessity for breaking away into the largely unknown and difficult country to the east, the end came. On the night of the 18th-19th the Japanese shot a green flare high into the darkness above Same. The Australians felt that this was to signal the final movement towards their destruction or dispersal. But their wary patrols could find no evidence the next day of advancing enemies and then, incredulously, discovered that their attackers were withdrawing. They hurried after them, harassing their rear and flanks.

Though this withdrawal meant at least a temporary relief for the Australians from pressure by the Japanese, troubles with the natives threatened to become increasingly acute. These took the form in late August and during September largely of clashes between Portuguese and the natives

---

[4] Pte D. C. Waller, WX13501; 2/2 Indep Coy. Farmer; of Wyalkatchem, WA; b. Stansbury, SA, 2 May 1921. Killed in action 12 Aug 1942.

[5] Sgt E. Hodgson, VX57492. 2/2 Indep Coy; 2/2 Cdo Sqn. Electric shovel driver; of Nyora, Vic; b. Cranbourne, Vic, 17 Jun 1914.
Hodgson, later becoming separated from the rest, was attacked by natives who stunned him with rocks and later handed him over to the Japanese. These having beaten him, released him after a short while to carry surrender demands back to his fellows.

and between rival bands of natives. In the latter part of August the Maubisse natives rebelled against the Portuguese authority and killed the Portuguese administrator in that area. Detachments of Portuguese police and soldiers at once took to the hills to quell the disorders, having first been assured that the Australians would in no way interfere in these matters of local administration. On 27th August a native band some 200 strong, armed with knives, spears and bows and arrows, set out from Ainaro for Maubisse to join in the hunt for the rebels. Seeing this the Australians felt that they were witnessing merely the opening scenes of large-scale disorders which could not fail to react on their own situation. September made this clearer. The Japanese were obviously fomenting the disorders. How long, therefore, the Australians could hold aloof and regard the troubles as purely domestic was a subject for interesting speculation.

The private local war, Portuguese versus native, still goes on its bloodthirsty way and provides some humour for sub-units here and there (wrote the war diarist of the Independent Company on 3rd September). One of our patrols near Mape, out hunting the Jap, encountered a Portuguese patrol out hunting some natives; they exchanged compliments and went their various ways. Coy HQ witnessed the spectacle of about 3,000 natives, all in war dress and armed to the teeth, also complete with drums and Portuguese flags, returning from the hunt with many of them nonchalantly swinging heads of the unfortunate in battle.

During September there was much Japanese movement inland and along the north coast. The Australians learned that a complete fresh division had relieved the original Japanese garrison of Timor about the beginning of the month.[6] There were reports also that the new regime was imposing much more rigid security precautions in and around the capital. On 12th September Portuguese reported to the guerillas that a strong force of Japanese and Dutch Timor natives were moving from Dutch Timor across to Dili—on the route through Hatu-Lia and Ermera. It seemed that they might have the triple purpose of reconnoitring the roads, reinforcing Dili and fomenting the native disorders. Dexter and Turton sent men to keep a close check on the movements of this band. Turton said that the natives of the areas through which this force was passing seemed to be greatly impressed by its strength. Between 10th and 20th September Japanese troops landed at Manatuto and, though some returned soon to Dili, some pressed farther out along the north coast. At the same time a strong sortie was being launched to the south from Dili. On 21st September a party of about 400 Japanese, many natives accompanying them, entered Aileu, and next day reached Maubisse. Boyland's opinion that they would continue on from there was confirmed on the 23rd when about 150 moved out towards Ainaro, and were smartly engaged by Lieutenant Burridge's section, who thought that they killed or wounded about 30, without loss

---

[6] This was the *48th Division*, which had taken part in the campaign in the Philippines in December 1941-January 1942 and then joined the *XVI Army* for the invasion of Java. It comprised the *1st* and *2nd Formosan* and *47th Infantry Regiments*. The *47th Regiment* arrived in Timor on 24th August; the division was not, however, concentrated in Timor until 9th November.
The *228th Regiment* (a battalion of which had been continuously employed in Portuguese Timor, since the invasion, in operations against the Australians) left Timor for Rabaul on 5th September. Evidently the puzzling end to the Japanese August attack was caused by their need to prepare for departure.

to themselves. Burridge reported that two other parties were following the one which he had engaged, all three parties totalling about 350. In the early afternoon of the 24th Dexter (who had been telephoned from Maubisse by the local Japanese commander that he was coming to destroy Dexter and his men), Turton and their men, from cleverly arranged ambushes, shot many of the invaders and the fight did not flicker out finally until evening. Next day, however, the Japanese occupied Ainaro, with Turton's and Dexter's platoons watching and waiting for a chance to harass them from positions about the town and Boyland's men waiting farther back towards Maubisse to worry them if they retraced their steps.

Meanwhile the Australian strength on Timor had been augmented. On 12th August General Blamey's headquarters in Brisbane had told Major-General Stevens, then commanding the Northern Territory Force and under whose command Sparrow Force had been placed as from 30th July, that they were considering sending a small force to Timor to relieve the pressure on the troops already there and clear the Japanese from the Australian area. They envisaged a maximum strength for this force of some 500. Stevens replied that the minimum Japanese strength for operations against the guerillas in Timor was certainly four if not five battalions; that he believed that the sending of two more Australian companies to the island would lead to useless sacrifice; that, if any more troops were to be sent, they should be of brigade strength to guarantee a successful outcome; he had not the forces available in the Northern Territory to make such a move. Finally, however, it was decided that the 2/4th Independent Company should go.

This company had been formed under the command of Major Walker[7] at the beginning of 1942 round a core of officers and N.C.O's who had been recruited and, in some measure, trained for Independent Companies in 1941, had been diverted to other duties when the decision to discontinue the training of Independent Companies was taken, and had been recalled when this decision was reversed. Walker took his company to the Northern Territory in March 1942, where they were based on Katherine, and set them to work watching and patrolling the lines of approach into the Territory along the Roper, Victoria and Daly Rivers. They were relieved in August by the 2/6th Cavalry Regiment and the North Australia Observer Unit and attached to the 19th Brigade for administration and training. On 9th September, General Stevens told Walker to take his company to Timor, establish observation posts over Dili, obtain information regarding the Japanese and harass these soldiers at every opportunity; but to be wary until he and his men had got to know the country and the natives. Walker then left with an advanced party from Darwin on 12th September and was busy with Callinan getting the local picture when the main body of his company embarked at Darwin on 22nd September in the destroyer *Voyager*. The ship began to unload off Betano in the late afternoon of the 23rd. Then she went aground. The

---

[7] Lt-Col E. McD. Walker, VX53941. OC 2/4 Indep Coy; CRE 6 and 1 CRE (Works) 1945. Civil engineer; of East Malvern, Vic; b. Bairnsdale, Vic, 4 May 1907.

disembarkation went ahead but the falling tide left the ship fast on the sea-bed. Next morning a Japanese reconnaissance aeroplane found her there and hurried back to Dili with the news. A little later three more aircraft appeared. Seamen manned the anti-aircraft guns on the stranded vessel and engaged the Japanese. They thought they destroyed a bomber. Then the ship was attacked repeatedly though the seamen engaged the

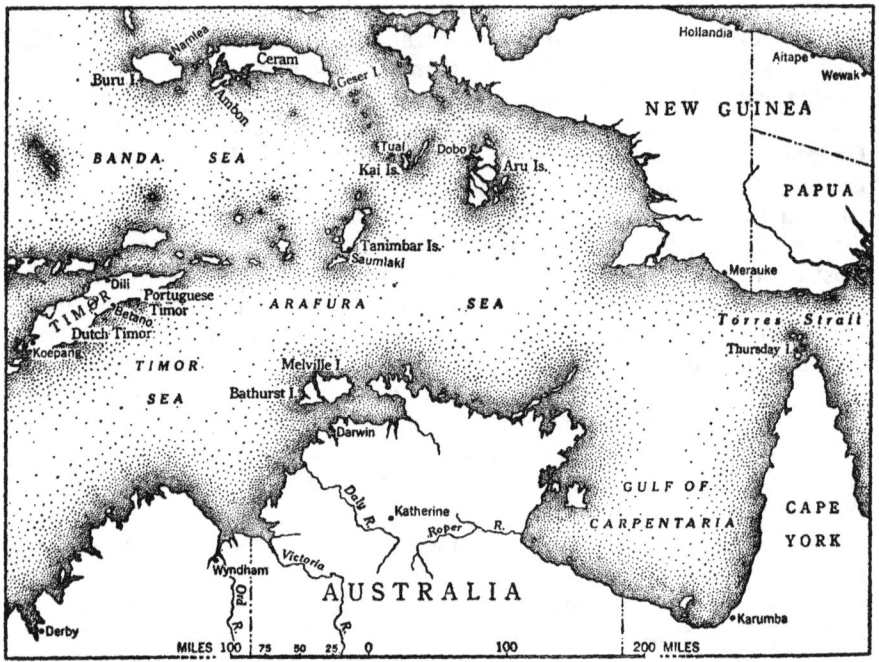

attackers and most of the bombs went wide. As the day advanced the captain ordered that the *Voyager* be destroyed. Her crew set off a series of explosions and then lit fires to complete her destruction. They themselves were picked up soon afterwards by the corvettes *Warrnambool* and *Kalgoorlie*.

Walker's men, however, had not waited to see the final acts of this drama played out but had hurried inland to join the forward troops of the other company. For experience of the country and of active guerilla operations they were then attached to these veterans (whom General Stevens did not consider it practicable to withdraw for some time). Meanwhile Dexter's and Turton's platoons had been watching the Japanese in Ainaro, Boyland's had been waiting for a chance to strike between Ainaro and Maubisse, and Laidlaw's men were in their old area east of Dili. But, on the 27th, Dexter's patrols entered Ainaro to find that the Japanese had eluded them temporarily by swinging away north-west to Atsabe.

On the 27th[8] also some 2,000 Japanese moved south from Dili to Aileu. The next day strong forces, screened by native scouts, continued on to Maubisse, with the Australians making ready to harass them at the first suitable opportunity. This, it seemed, was an expected Japanese movement of strong forces to the area where the *Voyager* had been stranded, the Japanese knowing that fresh Australians had landed, but not in what strength. When the Japanese vanguard left Maubisse on the 29th, Boyland's platoon, and Captain Thompson's[9] of the 2/4th, fought them from a series of ambush positions and believed that they killed about 50 (losing themselves one of the 2/4th men). But these Japanese were determined fighters, coolly proceeded to outflank the ambushers, and forced them to fall back to positions south of Same. After that the Australians lost touch with their enemies and, after a few days had passed with guerilla patrols trying to locate the main Japanese party, it became clear that the Japanese had got through to Betano and were then on their way back to their northern bases. They settled in Aileu with outposts at Maubisse. About this time too it was known that the Japanese were developing the eastern end of the island, moving troops and stores along the north coast road east of Manatuto, building airstrips at Fuiloro (east of Baucau).

Closely watching, and at times harassing, these developments to the east was a 2/2nd Independent Company group under Lieutenant C. D. Doig, known as "H" Detachment. Early in August eight men and Doig, already proved an active young leader, had set out to watch the main road which crossed the island from Baucau in the north to Beasso on the south coast, map and patrol the area, and to send food and horses back to the main body. They had done well. They had become very familiar with the eastern country, had established good relations with the natives, and had kept horses and supplies of food and other useful items flowing back Cooperating with them was a Dutch detachment which had followed them and had taken up positions at Ossu in the centre of the island to hold that section of the road as long as possible against any Japanese southward movement.

With Doig and the Dutch group thus forming their extreme right the Australians, in early October, set about reorganising their positions. Left of Doig, in the main right-flank positions—in the Laclubar area, north-east of Maubisse—were Laidlaw's platoon, and Captain O'Connor's[1] of the 2/4th, watching the north coast road and Dili; Boyland's platoon was south-west of these, east of Maubisse round Mindelo; Dexter was at Same; Turton was between Same and Ainaro, overlooking Maubisse from the south-west; Thompson was at Ainaro with his 2/4th platoon; Lieutenant Murphy's[2] "A" Platoon of the 2/4th was based on the Lete-Foho

---

[8] On this same day Japanese aircraft carried out their thirty-eighth raid on Darwin.
[9] Capt C. A. Thompson, VX60729. 2/4 Indep Coy; 2/4 Cdo Sqn. Clerk; of Black Rock, Vic; b. Yackandandah, Vic, 7 Sep 1916.
[1] Maj E. D. O'Connor, NX70116. 2/4 Indep Coy; 2/4 Cdo Sqn; OC 2/8 Cdo Sqn. Grazier; of Bethungra, NSW; b. Sydney, 27 Apr 1912.
[2] Capt C. D. Murphy, VX62662; 2/4 Indep Coy, 2/4 Cdo Sqn. Civil engineer; of Toorak, Vic; b. Portland, Vic, 10 Sep 1912.

area and, from an observation post west of Dili, covering the sea approaches to Dili from the direction by which most of the Japanese shipping was routed in.

October saw vigorous action against Japanese parties, particularly by O'Connor's fresh troops who chopped hard at Japanese moving east of Dili. Corporal Haire[3] of the 2/2nd Independent Company, who opened coolly on an enemy party moving from Laclo towards Dili on the 28th, estimated that his men shot down about 25 of them, and turned the Japanese back on their tracks. A section of newcomers under Lieutenant Dower,[4] manning an observation post overlooking Dili from the east, were bombed from the air and beaten at from the ground after the Japanese located them, but, learning quickly the lessons the old hands had to teach them, dourly reoccupied their old positions as soon as the pressure eased. Nevertheless the month was chiefly remarkable for Japanese-fomented disorders among the native population, and the necessity for meeting this ever-worsening situation limited the action which the Australians could take against the Japanese themselves.

The Japanese exploited the natives skilfully. Parties of 50 or 60 natives would press against the Australians, usually urged on by a few Japanese in the rear. Almost daily Australian groups would report conflict with such bands resulting in the shooting of 10, 20 or 30 natives and possibly one or two Japanese. But the invaders were now not only concerned with stirring up the natives against the Australians; they were aiming also to destroy completely the Portuguese control.[5] In Aileu they incited attacks on the residence of the District Officer at the beginning of October and, in these, ten Portuguese, including a woman, were killed. In November the District Officer at Manatuto and his secretary were similarly killed and, soon afterwards, the Portuguese official at Fuiloro was murdered. Meanwhile, however, the Japanese had evolved a "neutral zone" idea and ordered all Portuguese to assemble in a specified area west of Dili by 15th November. After that date, they said, all Portuguese within that area would be protected by the Japanese; those outside would be treated as active helpers of the Australians. This proposal inevitably represented a crisis to many of the Portuguese. In the second half of October Callinan (accompanied by Private McCabe[6] who was fluent in Portuguese and the principal native language and was a brave and skilful scout) moved across from his headquarters at Ailalec to Hatu-Lia to meet a gathering of 12 or 15 Portuguese men and discuss the position. The Portuguese said that they wanted the government in Lisbon to know the plight of

---

[3] Lt J. T. Haire, WX10744; 2/2 Indep Coy. Intelligence Corps. Schoolteacher; of Denmark, WA; b. Kalgoorlie, WA, 1 Nov 1907.

[4] Lt A. R. Dower, VX52086. 2/4 Indep Coy; 2/4 Cdo Sqn. Journalist and time and motion study observer; of Brighton, Vic; b. Melbourne, 31 Jan 1916.

[5] Between May and the end of October at least 26 Portuguese (including one woman and three priests) are known to have been killed.

[6] Capt P. P. McCabe, NX73234. 2/2 Indep Coy; OC 57 Sqn Air Liaison Sec 1944-45. Sheep station manager; of Dalby, Qld; b. Brisbane, 11 Jun 1917.

the colony; that they wanted protection for their women[7] and children and arms with which to protect themselves; that, if their women and children could be moved to a safe place, they themselves would fight with the Australians. Callinan said that the only way to ensure the safety of the women and children would be to remove them to Australia but that, though he would explain their position to Australia, it would be most difficult to arrange this; that he would like the officials to remain at their posts and do all they could to maintain order among the natives. He said also that he had already asked Australia for certain arms to issue to the Portuguese and was hopeful that these would arrive soon; he would then issue them to the officials and order the Australian patrols to work in conjunction with them. After further discussion he then set out on his return journey.

When he arrived at Ainaro he found a willing fight going on—near-by villages burning, hostile natives from Maubisse being driven back up the valley by Australian fire, natives loyal to the Australians armed with bows and arrows and spears yelling wildly as they tried to get close enough to the raiders to use their primitive weapons. He found there also a message from Australia ordering him to suspend all offers to arm either Portuguese or natives pending further instructions. On 1st November, however, the arming of local inhabitants for guerilla operations against the Japanese was approved.

By this time it was becoming clear that the men of the 2/2nd Company were almost at the limit of their endurance. They had been in action for nine months under conditions of great mental and physical hardship; their food had never represented a balanced and sustaining diet; malaria had wasted them; dysentery was chronic and widespread; they had suffered some 26 casualties since the Japanese invasion began. On 10th November Spence signalled Northern Territory Force Headquarters that one Independent Company was sufficient to carry out the tasks which had been allotted on Timor; one company was all that could adequately be maintained; the 2/2nd urgently needed relief. On 24th November Land Headquarters approved the relief of the company and the evacuation at the same time of 150 Portuguese.

During November, however, the general situation had improved in one respect at least—Allied bombing attacks on Dili and other key-points became more widespread and effective after the arrival at Darwin for a brief period of American Marauder bombers, and, a little later, Australian Beaufighters, to supplement the few gallant Hudsons on which the men on Timor had been so dependent for air support. On 3rd November the guerilias watched four Marauders cross the island to attack Dili. The men at the combined company headquarters found that one of their wireless sets was netted in on the same frequency as that being used by the American airmen. As the aircraft turned to make for Darwin the

---

[7] There were about 500 Portuguese women and children on the island at this time of whom about 100 were of unmixed European blood. Probably about 300 of them wanted to go to Australia. ("Most Secret" report by Major B. J. Callinan to C.O. Sparrow Force, November 1942—Blamey papers.)

listeners on the ground heard one of the pilots report "Port prop hit by flak!" He began to lag and his leader urged him "Come on, Hitchcock, make formation". Then the soldiers heard him report that there were Zeros on his tail and they saw three fighters close on him from different angles. The other three bombers came roaring down to help him. Then friends and foes alike, still fighting, disappeared into the skies to the south. That night the worried soldiers sent off a message to Darwin asking about Hitchcock. They had no reply. Next morning the Americans were over again. Laidlaw broke into their conversation asking "Did Hitchcock make it?" They were too busy to reply to him but that night a message came through from the American commander at Darwin:

Thanks Diggers, Hitchcock made it. Stop. Crash-landed Bathurst Island.

Of this incident Callinan wrote later:

These brief and personal contacts with the outside world affected us strangely and deeply; we had become accustomed to being engrossed in our own pressing problems and troubles, and to being self-dependent, so that when we experienced a close personal relationship with others, emotions were aroused which had been long suppressed. Hitchcock and his fight were discussed up and down our line, and we were bitterly disappointed when a few days later Darwin told us that the . . . bombers had been withdrawn suddenly to meet an emergency on the east coast of Australia.[8]

Soon after, however, the soldiers learned that a squadron of Beaufighters had arrived at Darwin, and, heavily armed, would be crossing to Timor on strafing missions. They proved most effective especially against Japanese vehicles moving along the roads in the eastern end of the island.

As from 11th November Callinan took over command of the whole of Sparrow Force, with Baldwin, unfailingly loyal and efficient, as his staff captain, and soon afterwards Spence returned to Australia. Laidlaw succeeded to the 2/2nd Independent Company. By this time it was known that the Japanese were working hard to develop the eastern end of the island where they were building airstrips and laying down supply dumps; in the centre Maubisse festered as the main centre of hostility to the Australians; along the south coast the Japanese were slowly moving eastward and were beginning to consolidate in the Hatu-Udo area.

On 27th November Callinan was ordered to prepare for evacuation about 190 Dutch troops who had been fighting with the Australians since the Japanese invasion (a fresh though much smaller Dutch detachment from Australia was to relieve them), 150 Portuguese who were seeking refuge in Australia, and the 2/2nd Independent Company. The Dutch and Portuguese were to go out first. Callinan felt that their embarkation from the island would present comparatively few problems as he would have the 2/2nd available to protect the beach-head. The embarkation of the latter would be more difficult, however, as he could not draw the 2/4th in sufficiently to cover them as they moved.

---

[8] Callinan, *Independent Company*, p. 192.

The arrangement was that *Kuru* and two corvettes *Armidale* and *Castlemaine* would run in to Betano on the night 30th November-1st December, lift the Dutch (leaving the fresh detachment) and the Portuguese and then return to embark the Australians on the night 4th-5th December. With the darkness of 30th November there were signal fires burning on the coast to guide in the promised ships. But only the *Kuru* arrived. The captain told Laidlaw (who was supervising the embarkation) that he did not know where the corvettes were but had intercepted a message from one of them saying that she was being bombed. He waited until the appointed time for departure and then set sail with over 70 Portuguese (chiefly women and children) on board his tiny craft. When daylight came Japanese aircraft attacked his ship heavily. The ship survived, however, and met the two corvettes, which had been delayed by determined attacks from the air and the reported presence of Japanese cruisers off the south coast so that they had arrived late off Betano and, finding no signal fires there, had put out to sea again. The *Kuru* transferred her refugees to the *Castlemaine*. That ship then set course for Darwin while the *Kuru* and *Armidale* (the latter carrying the Dutch replacement troops) turned back for Timor. But Japanese aircraft prevented their landfall and sank the *Armidale*. Callinan and his men, however, knew nothing of this loss until they were instructed from Darwin that the later phases of the evacuation would be delayed. This meant that they had hastily to rearrange their plans for covering the embarkation: Murphy's platoon was to become responsible for the Mindelo area; Thompson's was to cover the Same-Ainaro region; O'Connor's men were to remain east of Dili and continue their observations there, centred on Fatu Maquerec.

The Dutch destroyer *Tjerk Hiddes* was to lift the first flight of the 2/2nd Independent Company ("D" Platoon, Lieutenant Doig now commanding, and the hospital patients) on the night 11th-12th December, together with the Dutch troops and some Portuguese. On the 10th Doig handed over to Thompson and concentrated his men at Same preparatory to moving down to Betano. On the morning of the 10th, however, Japanese suddenly sortied against his rearguard and a pack train (escorted by three soldiers) carrying rifles and supplies to a small group of Thompson's men who were organising, training and arming friendly natives in the Ainaro area. The pack train party fought their way out but had to abandon the rifles and supplies. Of the rearguard Sapper Moule[9] was killed and Sapper Sagar[1] wounded. Doig, however, managed to get the rest of his platoon (except for Sapper Dennis,[2] who, though he could have made good his own escape, stayed to help Sagar) through to the embarkation point. Callinan had hastily changed this point to the mouth of the Qualan River —about five hours' walk from Same—because the Japanese in Same were

---

[9] Spr L. C. Moule, QX15240; 2/11 Fd Coy. Farm labourer; of Sarina, Qld; b. Herberton, Qld, 30 Sep 1919. Killed in action 10 Dec 1942.

[1] Spr D. A. Sagar, QX16071; 2/11 Fd Coy. Rural worker; of Beaudesert, Qld; b. Adelaide, 31 Mar 1914.

[2] Spr M. Dennis, QX9246. 2/11 Fd Coy; 3 Maintenance Platoon. Station hand; of Newstead, Qld; b. London, 11 Jun 1912.

uncomfortably close to Betano. The embarkation went smoothly and before dawn the first flight was on its way back to Australia.

Laidlaw then had his own old platoon (now commanded by Nisbet) deployed east of Alas and disposed his two remaining platoons to observe and cover the outlets from Same. The second and last phase of the evacuation was set for the night 15th-16th December. On the 15th, however, the Japanese moved out of Same to Alas where they arrived about 11 a.m. They then struck down towards Betano round which (and Fatu-Cuac just to the north-east) the remainder of the 2/2nd (except for Nisbet's platoon) were then centred. This move suited Laidlaw quite well as he could slip his party eastward to the Qualan River when night came, sufficiently far ahead of the Japanese to complete their embarkation unhindered. The invaders, however, were not confident. As they approached Fatu-Cuac where Laidlaw had his own headquarters, Laidlaw and his men fired into them and then went off ahead of them. The Japanese entered Fatu-Cuac but then turned and set off back to Same again. The departing Australians, and 24 Portuguese, were thus able to board the *Tjerk Hiddes* unhindered and, before midnight, were on their way home.

Alone of the original Sparrow Force Callinan and Baldwin remained on Timor. They had their headquarters with Walker at Ailalec. They felt the absence of their old comrades deeply. Callinan gathered about him the creados who had served these men so faithfully. Most of them came from areas which the Japanese had now occupied and so could not return home. Each carried a note from his former master which Callinan read.

> In many cases it did not require the surat [note] to tell me that Mau Bessi, Antonio, Bera Dasi, or whatever his name, was "a good boong—treat him well, he deserves it". Their feats of loyalty and courage were well known. This one had stayed with his wounded master whilst Japanese were searching surrounding villages, and moved him out just before the Japanese came to that village. This one had taken a message through the Japanese lines to a section cut off by a rapid enemy move. This one had been captured by the Japanese but had refused to give information of our moves, and had escaped by biting his way through his ropes when they were not watching. This one, while carrying mail and secret messages, had run into a Japanese patrol; he had quickly thrown the bag into the bushes and gone on unarmed to meet the Japanese, and by sheer effrontery had talked his way out of trouble. He had then made a detour back to where he had thrown the bag, which he recovered and delivered.[3]

After the departure of the 2/2nd Independent Company the wide sweeps of the Japanese caused Callinan and Walker to reconsider their position. Soon after the affray at Same Japanese attacks forced some of Murphy's troops out of their positions on the Maubisse-Same road and the invaders' movements seemed likely to cut Thompson's platoon off from the main force. About the same time attacks were jeopardising O'Connor's positions farther to the north. Walker then defined a basic area which he considered it necessary for his men to hold if they were to survive and continue fighting as a force, though, if this were lost, he thought they might continue the fight as small groups and individuals farther to the

---

[3] Callinan, *Independent Company*, pp. 202-3.

east. This area was generally that within an arc sweeping northwards from Alas, through Fai Nia, to Laclubar and thence east to Lacluta. Accordingly Thompson's platoon (less the Ainaro detachment which was completely pocketed by Japanese and hostile natives) was based on Alas; Murphy's was based on Fai Nia; O'Connor's men were based on Fatu Maquerec (with one section still manning the observation post which looked into Dili from a point north-east of Remexio).

The Japanese and hostile natives were quickly becoming more active, however, and their activities more widespread. Scarcely a day passed that the wide-ranging Australian patrols were not skirmishing with them. Callinan told Australia that arming the natives who seemed to be friendly was a danger which might ultimately destroy the guerillas themselves but was nevertheless the only course which offered them a chance of retaining their vital areas. He redoubled his efforts therefore to organise and train native auxiliaries. But the Australian position worsened quickly. Japanese pressure from the west was driving natives eastward from burnt and plundered areas; Japanese, and pro-Japanese natives, followed, burning, looting, wrecking and setting up a cumulative strain on the food resources in the east; O'Connor's men were forced out of their observation area east of Dili; unrest grew to such an extent that natives would not move outside their own local areas and this, in turn, stopped the interchange of native information which had always been the Australians' great source of Intelligence; soon the guerillas had virtually no information of any value to send back to Australia. In addition to their other worries Callinan and Baldwin found more and more of their time being taken up with native administration. The conditions of anarchy which had developed left the natives in the Australian area with no central authority, so they turned to the Australian leaders for directions and for the settlement of their disputes.

Meanwhile the army leaders in Australia had become increasingly concerned with the position of Lancer Force (the new code name given to the troops on Timor in November), which they could well interpret from the detailed reports they were receiving. They had no immediate intention of attempting to retake Timor although, late in December, at the request of the Advisory War Council, the Australian Chiefs of Staff had prepared a study of the strategical importance of Timor in relation to Australian defence and an estimate of the forces that would be required to capture and hold the island. They believed that there then were approximately 12,000 Japanese troops on Timor, disposed more or less equally between the Dutch and Portuguese areas; that its capture and retention would involve the use of strong naval and air forces and three divisions with additional non-divisional troops. They stated, however, that they could not make any recommendations to the War Council regarding the advisability or otherwise of embarking upon any operations concerning the capture of Timor, because neither information regarding the enemy forces likely to be available for concentration against the Allies, nor information regarding the Allied resources likely to be available for use, was held by them; and because they considered that General MacArthur's advice was essential before the Australian Government could consider the matter further.

Blamey was incensed that the Advisory War Council should have followed the matter as far as they did without consulting MacArthur—so incensed that, on a copy of the terms of reference which they had given the Chiefs of Staff, he wrote:

> Many years of training have produced in me a dislike for profanity in writing. This alone prevents me from giving my complete opinion on this imbecility.

This followed a fruitless request he had made in a letter from New Guinea to the Secretary of the Defence Department on 19th December, when he first learned of the Advisory War Council's proposals, that the Prime Minister should approach MacArthur before he allowed the matter to proceed any further. In that letter he wrote also:

> As a matter of simple fact an operation against Timor is in the immediate future completely out of the question. We are involved in a campaign in this region against the Jap which will absorb all our resources, both Australian and American, for many months to come. The Jap does not intend to be driven out of these areas. He has recently elevated this command into that of an Army Group and divided the Guadalcanal and New Guinea areas into two separate Army Commands. He intends to hold on to the Buna area and reinforce it if possible. I hope we will capture it by the extermination of his force, but he has already shown signs of establishing himself on a further line extending from northern New Guinea to Rabaul.
>
> I have no hesitation in saying that the preparation of a scheme for the capture of Timor, is, at the present juncture, a pure waste of time. Firstly, because we cannot disengage ourselves from the present area of operations, and secondly, we cannot spare resources to open up another.[4]

It was not merely the precarious position of the little force on Timor, therefore, but also the lack of any sufficiently important purpose in holding the positions there, which led to a decision on 3rd January 1943, to bring the 2/4th Independent Company back to Australia.[5] Warning of this proposal was sent to Callinan next day. But he was then asked also if a small party (perhaps ten) could be left behind to collect and send information. He advised against this but volunteered to remain himself and organise native resistance (though he suggested that such a course would only be of value if some attack in force from Australia were contemplated for the near future). On the night of the 5th-6th January he was ordered to concentrate his force for evacuation on the night 9th-10th, at an embarkation point to be nominated by him. Since the Japanese had long since occupied Betano and were moving slowly east along the coast from that point, and were also closing in westward, there was little

---

[4] Blamey Papers.

[5] On 25th January 1943 the following observations by General MacArthur on the strategical importance of Timor were read to the Advisory War Council:

"1. General MacArthur said that he viewed the increase in Japanese strength in Timor as purely defensive to secure themselves against any attack from Australia and to suppress continuation of the successful commando tactics which had been pursued by the Australian and Dutch forces.

2. The Commander-in-Chief added that he definitely did not possess the resources to retake Timor. Furthermore, the Japanese have control of the seas in this region, and General MacArthur could not land by air from Australia and keep supplied by air, the force that would be necessary for the recapture of this island.

3. Any plans for the taking of Timor were a long distance project."

choice in respect of this embarkation point. Callinan nominated Quicras, though about the only point in its favour was that it was almost equi-distant between the Japanese eastern and western south coast positions.

The Australians had little time in which to plan their movement and gather in their widely-flung parties. There was no one to cover their movement so they would be extremely vulnerable as they began to move in and gather at Quicras. They therefore not only took elaborate precautions against any premature news of their proposed departure leaking out but also set in train clever deception measures. Everything went smoothly except that there was no word from the detachment at Ainaro. As his plans matured Callinan had time to ponder the wider implications of the departure of his force. He regretted that all the effort of the long period from February 1942 to January 1943 should now apparently come to nothing. He sent off a message volunteering to remain at the head of a small and desperate band of 15 or 20 men. (Baldwin saw the message go out, and formally asked to be allowed to remain as a member of this band.) But General Stevens replied to Callinan that, though he had sent the offer on to Army Headquarters, he had recommended that it be not accepted. Nevertheless, an instruction came through early in the morning of the 9th that one lieutenant and 20 men would remain. Major Callinan was ordered not to be of the party.

On the morning of the 9th the force (now concentrated except for the Ainaro detachment from whom there was still no word) set out with 50 Portuguese (all they could take of over 100 who had asked to go with them) on the last stage of their journey—over open grass country. It was raining heavily. The rivers between them and Quicras might flood and block them. They had to hurry. Soon after they started a Zero fighter suddenly appeared about 1,000 feet above them. They were afraid it would pick them up but the pilot apparently noticed nothing. The afternoon march led through swamps, often up to a man's chest. The going beneath the surface was slippery with mud and twisted mangrove roots. But by 5 p.m. the whole party was in the bush which fringed the beach. Exactly at midnight recognition lights from the sea answered the signal fires. The surf was heavy. Boats sent inshore from a destroyer—the *Arunta* —were swamped. Time was running out. A few strong swimmers swam out beyond the broken water but reported this manifestly too difficult for most. At last, however, through great efforts, the whole group was ferried on board. The sailors were very kind to them. Most of the soldiers were so tired they slept almost all the way to Darwin.

On the island Lieutenant Flood[6] remained in command of the volunteers of "S" Force—the party which was to continue to observe and report Japanese activities. With him were Corporal Ellwood,[7] Signalmen Wynne[8]

---

[6] Capt H. Flood, VX48323. 2/4 Indep Coy, 2/5 Cdo Sqn; Legal Corps. Law clerk; of Wodonga, Vic; b. Albury, NSW, 28 Nov 1914.
[7] Capt A. J. Ellwood, VX67548. NT Force Sigs; "Z" Special Unit. Clerk; of Merino, Vic; b. Casterton, Vic, 16 Dec 1921.
[8] Capt W. P. Wynne, VX52974. 2/4 Indep Coy; "Z" Special Unit. Student; of Warrandyte, Vic; b. Sydney, 12 Sep 1920.

and Key[9] (both of whom had previously been in the observation posts overlooking Dili), Corporals Hayes[1] and Ritchie,[2] Lance-Corporal Hubbard[3] and Privates Whelan,[4] Duncan,[5] Fitness,[6] Hansen,[7] Jacobson[8] and Phillips.[9] Just after the departure of the *Arunta* Private Miller[1] joined them. He had been cut off from one of O'Connor's patrols and had been unable to get through in time to catch the ship.

Flood set up his headquarters at Fatu-Berliu. The Japanese had not yet penetrated that area, the natives were friendly and food was plentiful. Soon after their arrival there Flood's party was joined by Corporal Wilkins,[2] Signaller Fraser[3] and Private Finch[4]—from Ainaro. They had fought their way out of the Ainaro pocket, but were too late to join the evacuation. Private Howell[5] had also been with them but had been killed on the way out. These brave soldiers were tired and sick but their courage was still high.

Soon, however, Japanese patrols also found Flood's party. As they closed in the Australians engaged them but were quickly outflanked and had to fall back, fighting as they went. The pony carrying much of their wireless equipment bolted and so, when they re-established themselves again, they were out of touch with Darwin. But they improvised another set and by 20th January were once more in communication. The Japanese, however, were determined to get them and that same day two strong parties closed on them. There was a vigorous fight with fire being exchanged from a distance of only about 50 yards. The Japanese hunted the little band all day and dispersed them. The pony carrying the wireless was shot while crossing a stream. The swift water carried it away with the wireless still attached to it. The various little Australian groups then struck south-

---

[9] Lt J. R. Key, VX58449. 2/4 Indep Coy; "Z" Special Unit. Student; of Ivanhoe, Vic; b. Melbourne, 20 May 1922.

[1] Sgt W. F. Hayes, QX23890. 2/4 Indep Coy; 2/4 Cdo Sqn. Bank officer; of Eagle Junction, Qld; b. Boonah, Qld, 11 Jul 1910.

[2] L-Sgt D. T. Ritchie, WX8465; 2/2 Indep Coy. Shop assistant; of South Perth, WA; b. Cannington, WA, 14 Oct 1914.

[3] Cpl H. Hubbard, QX15759. 2/4 Indep Coy; 2/4 Cdo Sqn. Labourer; of Edmonton, Qld; b. London, 4 Feb 1908.

[4] Sgt R. C. B. Whelan, QX24764. 2/4 Indep Coy; 2/4 Cdo Sqn. Stockman; of Charters Towers district and Townsville, Qld; b. Cairns, Qld, 2 May 1920.

[5] Sgt S. J. Duncan, VX65417. 2/4 Indep Coy; 2/4 Cdo Sqn. Audit clerk; of Northcote, Vic; b. Northcote, 13 Oct 1922.

[6] L-Cpl D. H. Fitness, NX57689; 2/4 Indep Coy. Factory hand; of Newtown, NSW; b. Bowraville, NSW, 9 Mar 1922. Died 21 May 1943.

[7] Pte E. P. Hansen, QX11727. 2/4 Indep Coy; 2/4 Cdo Sqn. Sugar cane farmer; of Lethebrook, via Proserpine, Qld; b. Townsville, Qld, 1 Apr 1917.

[8] Pte A. L. Jacobson, QX24795. 2/4 Indep Coy; 2/4 Cdo Sqn. Tin scratcher; of Lutwyche, Qld; b. Brisbane, 1 Dec 1920.

[9] L-Cpl R. O. Phillips, VX70083. 2/4 Indep Coy; 2/4 Cdo Sqn. Shearer; of Willaura, Vic; b. Willaura, 19 Dec 1915.

[1] L-Cpl T. Miller, NX81122. 2/4 Indep Coy; 2/4 Cdo Sqn. Motor driver; of North Manly, NSW; b. Hawick, Scotland, 21 May 1914.

[2] Lt A. F. Wilkins, VX61840. 2/4 Indep Coy; "Z" Special Unit. Clerk; of Toorak, Vic; b. St Kilda, Vic, 26 Sep 1920. Killed in action 17 May 1945.

[3] Cpl G. T. Fraser, QX23351. 2/4 Indep Coy; 2/4 Cdo Sqn. Salesman; of Maryborough, Qld; b. Toowoomba, Qld, 8 Aug 1922.

[4] L-Cpl T. F. Finch, QX23078. 2/4 Indep Coy; 2/4 Cdo Sqn. Stockman; of Malvern, Vic; b. Sea Lake, Vic, 9 Sep 1922.

[5] L-Cpl E. G. Howell, QX22765; 2/4 Indep Coy. Labourer; of Coalstown Lakes via Biggenden, Qld; b. Biggenden, 11 Jun 1922. Killed in action 9 Jan 1943.

east through rain and swamp, out of touch with one another and with Australia. They were in strange country. Food was very scarce. Many of the men became sick. The Japanese hunted them continually with aeroplanes and ground patrols. Gradually, however, the groups began to come together again, as they got news of one another from Portuguese and natives, and began to link with a "Z" Special Unit group which had been operating in the eastern end of the island.

"Z" Special was a small unit of the Australian Army of a highly "secret" nature. It was responsible for special operations of various kinds and special Intelligence tasks, often within enemy occupied territory. About the middle of 1942 two officers of this unit (one of them Captain Broadhurst,[6] formerly of the Malayan Police) had arrived in Portuguese Timor to plan operations at the eastern end of the island. They had gone first to de Sousa Santos for information, advice and letters of introduction. Soon afterwards they returned to Darwin on the *Kuru* and, in September, Broadhurst and a small party were landed in the eastern area where they established themselves firmly and began organising the natives there to resist the Japanese.[7] Like Flood's party they were now being vigorously hunted by the Japanese and indeed, on 18th January, had signalled Darwin that their headquarters were surrounded and saying "We are finished", and asked to be taken off. On the 30th they signalled that they had joined up with "7 survivors of Lancer, no wireless". (Their wireless was transmitting but not receiving and thus they had no way of knowing whether or not their messages were getting through.) Hudsons dropped food and wireless sets to them.

On 10th February the combined "Z"-Lancer group were waiting near the mouth of the Dilor River (some 20 miles east of Quicras) with a white cloth hung out as a signal to a submarine, the U.S.S. *Gudgeon,* which was lying off shore. When darkness came the submarine surfaced and exchanged recognition signals with the soldiers. The Americans took the Australians aboard in rubber boats through a heavy surf. They gave them clothes and plenty of good food and their own beds and took them to Fremantle.

Thus the Australian operations on Timor ended in only a few days less than a year from the date on which they had begun. They had no positive strategical value, except that perhaps they diverted a measure of Japanese attention at a critical time and perhaps, in part, led to a build-up of Japanese forces on Timor during 1942 in anticipation of possible Allied attempts to reoccupy the island. They did, however, result in the destruction of some hundreds (at least) of Japanese soldiers at very small cost. But most importantly, possibly, they demonstrated how an apparently

---

[6] Capt D. K. Broadhurst, P242720; "Z" Special Unit. Police officer; b. London, 28 Jun 1910.

[7] A similar but more ambitious attempt to establish Australian and Dutch parties (Plover Force —1 officer and 29 men, 3 and 80, respectively) in the adjacent Aru, Tanimbar and Kai Islands had failed in July. The Australian party left Darwin in the little vessels *Southern Cross* and *Chinampa* on 28th July. Pulling in to the jetty at Saumlaki (Tanimbar) early on the 31st the *Chinampa* was fired on from the shore and the commander of the Australian detachment on board was killed. Both vessels then returned to Darwin taking the whole of the Australian group with them.

lost cause could be revived by brave men and transformed into a fighting cause, and at a time when such a demonstration was of the greatest value to many of their fellow Australians.

Their tactics and the results they achieved (both in relation to the losses they inflicted and the small losses they themselves sustained) can be judged neither by the standards of regular open warfare nor by those of the bush warfare which developed in New Guinea. They were organised and trained for guerilla warfare and the circumstances in which they found themselves permitted them to (indeed demanded that they should) operate as they were organised and trained to do. The country could supply them; there was a friendly population to assist them; there was rugged country to aid them, conceal them, and hinder regular operations against them—but, at the same time, it was not the rain forest country of New Guinea which demanded (even of ambushes) that the attacker and the attacked come to such close quarters that a fierce give and take in fighting was often inevitable; it was bush country of the Australian type which permitted long-range ambushes and a clean getaway. The pattern of warfare developed by the Australians on Timor perhaps more closely paralleled that developed by the Boers than any other (and two of the young Australian leaders at least—Baldwin and Dexter, both scholars as well as soldiers—were students and admirers of the Boers and had closely studied Reitz' *Commando*). The Boers failed finally through exhaustion; because the country could no longer support them; because the friendly population had been swept out of the areas of their operations. When similar circumstances beset the Australians on Timor they had to get out—perhaps most of all because a large section of the local population was either no longer friendly or was actively hostile to them.

APPENDIX 3

BRISBANE, 26TH AND 27TH NOVEMBER 1942

SOME friction is probably inevitable when troops of an Allied contingent and local troops are on leave together, particularly in places where girls and drink abound. Generally American and Australian troops got on very well together, specially in the field, but there were a few regrettable periods when there was a good deal of ill-feeling in one city or another, and clashes occurred. Perhaps the most serious of these took place in Brisbane in November 1942. Because of its gravity it demanded analysis and action at the highest levels and produced a discussion of a recurrent problem that may possess lasting value.

On the night of 26th November there was a clash between American military police and Australian troops outside the American Post Exchange in Brisbane in the course of which an American military policeman fired several shots, wounding nine Australians, one fatally. Next evening between 8 p.m. and midnight four or five groups each of four to six Australian soldiers roamed the streets of Brisbane attacking American military police and, later, attacking other American troops and officers escorting girls. Eleven Americans including four officers were taken to hospitals and about ten were less severely injured. Next day Major-General Berryman, who was at Advanced Land Headquarters in Brisbane, brought into Brisbane more military police from First Army and some men of an Independent Company. General Blamey in New Guinea was informed, and he advised that, if the conditions persisted, focal areas should be picketed by troops brought from the 3rd Division, then at Mooloolah, and a curfew imposed on all troops. There were, of course, very few A.I.F. units in south Queensland at the time; the Australians in Brisbane were almost entirely from base, training and militia units.

There were no disturbances on the 28th.

Berryman discussed the problem with Mr R. J. F. Boyer, then head of the American division of the Department of Information, and Boyer with Colonel Van S. Merle-Smith of American headquarters, and Mr Joseph Harsch, a correspondent of the *Christian Science Monitor,* and it was agreed that efforts should be made to educate the Australian troops "on the question of Australia's present and future relationship with the United States", preferably through the Army Education Service.

The problem was discussed at length in the Advanced L.H.Q. Intelligence Summary of 4th December, when it was decided that factors contributing to the disturbances were (*a*) drunkenness, (*b*) the higher rates of pay and the smarter uniforms of the American Army, (*c*) discrimination in favour of Americans in shops and hotels and by taxi drivers, (*d*) the spectacle of American troops with Australian girls, particularly wives of absent soldiers, and the American custom of caressing girls in public, (*e*) the deliberate stirring up of trouble by certain civilians, (*f*) boasting by some American troops, and their tendency to draw guns or knives in a quarrel, (*g*) the taunting of Australian militiamen by Americans. The summary added that the Americans, used to civil and military police who did not hesitate to display firearms and batons and use them in an emergency, considered the methods of the Australian civil and military police to be namby-pamby.[1]

The report concluded by urging that Australian soldiers should take every step to combat ill-feeling between the two armies. Copies of it were given to MacArthur's headquarters and to Mr Curtin.

Relations between A.I.F. and American formations in New Guinea and Australia at this time were generally remarkably cordial, but the problem of improving those relations continued to exercise Blamey. On 28th January 1943, he wrote to MacArthur proposing new measures. These would include the attachment of selected officers and non-commissioned officers from each force to units of the other, preferably at the rate of one officer per battalion and one N.C.O. per company; the interchange of staff officers (a measure proposed earlier by Blamey but accepted "to a limited degree only" by MacArthur); a concerted but unobtrusive effort by the public relations sections of each army; lectures by good men chosen from each force. Blamey mentioned that interchange of officers and N.C.O's had produced excellent results in 1914-18.[2] He informed Curtin of his proposals.

MacArthur replied on 12th February, politely but definitely rejecting Blamey's proposals.

> I have given very careful consideration to your letter of January 28, 1943 (he wrote), with regard to the means for the development of the most friendly relations between members of the United States Army in Australia and the Australian Military Forces.
>
> I am entirely in accord with your desire to take all practicable steps to develop the most friendly relations between the members of the American and Australian forces. I am inclined to believe, however, that the best results will be obtained by informal means, with each service working through its own channels to control the very small number of unruly individuals who create the difficulties and to counteract any tendency toward discord. I have observed that formal campaigns in such matters sometimes defeat their own purpose by being over-obvious and creating the impression that the situation is more serious than is really the case.
>
> While I am fully in accord with your objective in proposing an extension of the interchange of personnel between the two forces, the situation in the American Forces is such that well qualified officers and non-commissioned officers cannot be spared from their essential duties of leading or training their units. It is felt that, in all probability, such is also the case in the Australian Forces.

---

[1] It is probably a fair generalisation to say that in the United States the display of batons and firearms in the hands of police is an effective way of quelling a riot whereas in Australia it is an effective way of starting one.

[2] In a long interview in *The Sydney Morning Herald* some months earlier the Official War Historian, Dr C. E. W. Bean, had made a similar proposal. In the course of it he said: "Difficulties of cooperation are bound to arise between two armies and air forces whose structures are different and whose men have not the same national outlook. If each army stands apart from the other with only the routine formal interchange of liaison staff officers . . . there will be a tendency for one force to 'sling off' at the other, and cooperation in action will not be as good as it would be if there was the mutual understanding which can be achieved if officers and non-commissioned officers from our Army and Air Force are living, or have lived, with American units, and if Americans have lived with ours." He described instances in which such liaison between Australians and Americans had been successful in France in 1918.

My Public Relations Officer is already cooperating with your Director-General of Public Relations in an effort to promote harmonious relations between the forces. This effort, which must necessarily be unobtrusive, will be continued.

I am of the opinion that an effort to use talks by lecture teams as a means to improve relations may do more harm than good. The reaction of the American soldier to formal talks and lectures is not particularly favorable. He is quick to detect propaganda and inclined to resent it.

In conformity with the foregoing ideas, I suggest that the cooperative efforts of Public Relations officers be continued, but that the other measures suggested be deferred for the present. It is felt at General Headquarters that the recent battle experience of Australian and American forces serving together in New Guinea has practically accomplished the object in view and that further association in combat will undoubtedly eliminate all but minor misunderstandings between the two forces.

Blamey acknowledged this letter without comment and sent a copy to Curtin who also acknowledged it without comment.

Indeed, as mentioned earlier, MacArthur and his staff had made it evident from the outset that they did not wish the two forces to be closely integrated and particularly did not wish to have more than a minimum Australian liaison group at G.H.Q. or in the field. At this stage another factor was probably present: the profound disappointment at the lack of success of the raw American regiments in New Guinea. MacArthur may have seen in Blamey's proposal a suggestion that the Australians could teach the Americans their business.

APPENDIX 4

ABBREVIATIONS

A—*Acting, Assistant.*
AA—*Anti-aircraft.*
AA&QMG—*Assistant Adjutant and Quartermaster-General.*
AAMC—*Australian Army Medical Corps.*
AASC—*Australian Army Service Corps.*
ABDA—*American, British, Dutch, Australian.*
a/d—*Aerodrome.*
Admin—*Administration, administrative.*
ADMS—*Assistant Director Medical Services.*
Adv—*Advanced.*
AEME—*Australian Electrical Mechanical Engineers.*
AF—*Air Force.*
AFA—*Australian Field Artillery.*
AGH—*Australian General Hospital.*
AGT—*Australian General Transport.*
AHQ—*Army Headquarters.*
AIF—*Australian Imperial Force.*
Amb—*Ambulance.*
AMF—*Australian Military Forces.*
AN&MEF—*Australian Naval and Military Expeditionary Force.*
Angau—*Australian New Guinea Administrative Unit.*
Armd—*Armoured.*
Arty—*Artillery.*
Appts—*Appointments.*
ATIS—*Allied Translator and Interpreter Section.*
A-Tk—*Anti-tank.*
AWAS—*Australian Women's Army Service.*

BBCAU—*British Borneo Civil Affairs Unit.*
BCOF—*British Commonwealth Occupation Force.*
Bde—*Brigade.*
BGS—*Brigadier, General Staff.*
BM—*Brigade Major.*
Bn—*Battalion.*
Brig—*Brigadier.*
Bty—*Battery.*

Capt—*Captain.*
Cav—*Cavalry.*
CCS—*Casualty Clearing Station.*

Cdo—*Commando.*
Cdr—*Commander.*
CE—*Chief Engineer.*
C-in-C PAC—*Commander-in-Chief Pacific.*
CO—*Commanding Officer.*
COIC—*Combined Operations Intelligence Centre.*
Comd—*Command, Commander, Commanded.*
Comdt—*Commandant.*
Con—*Convalescent.*
COSC—*Combined Operational Services Command.*
Coy—*Company.*
CRA—*Commander, Royal Artillery (of a division).*
CRE—*Commander, Royal Engineers (of a division).*
CTF—*Commander Task Force.*
Cttee—*Committee.*

D—*Deputy, Director, Directorate.*
DDMS—*Deputy Director of Medical Services.*
DDST—*Deputy Director of Supply and Transport.*
DGMS—*Director-General of Medical Services.*
Div—*Division.*
DMI—*Director of Military Intelligence.*
DMO—*Director of Military Operations.*

Ech—*Echelon.*

Fd—*Field.*
FELO—*Far Eastern Liaison Office.*

Gen—*General.*
GHQ—*General Headquarters.*
GOC—*General Officer Commanding.*
Gp—*Group.*
GSO1—*General Staff Officer, Grade 1.*

Hist—*Historical.*
HQ—*Headquarters.*
Hvy—*Heavy.*
Hyg—*Hygiene.*

i/c—*in command.*
Indep—*Independent.*
Inf—*Infantry.*
IO—*Intelligence Officer.*

ABBREVIATIONS

JW—*Jungle Warfare.*

L-Cpl—*Lance-Corporal.*
LH—*Light Horse.*
LHQ—*Allied Land Forces Headquarters.*
LMG—*Light machine-gun.*
LO—*Liaison Officer.*
L of C—*Lines of Communication.*
Lt—*Lieutenant, light.*

Maj—*Major.*
MD—*Military District.*
ME—*Middle East.*
Med—*Medium.*
MG—*Machine-gun.*
MGGS—*Major-General, General Staff.*
MGO—*Master General of the Ordnance.*
MHR—*Member of the House of Representatives.*
Mil—*Military.*
MLA—*Member of the Legislative Assembly.*
MMG—*Medium machine-gun.*
Movt—*Movement.*
Mtd—*Mounted.*
Mtn—*Mountain.*
NG—*New Guinea.*
NGIB—*New Guinea Infantry Battalion.*
NGVR—*New Guinea Volunteer Rifles.*
NT—*Northern Territory.*

Ops—*Operations.*
OC—*Officer Commanding.*

PA—*Personal Assistant.*
PIB—*Papuan Infantry Battalion.*
PM—*Provost Marshal.*
Pnr—*Pioneer.*
PR—*Public Relations.*
Pro—*Provost.*
PW—*Prisoner of War.*

R—*Royal.*
RAAF—*Royal Australian Air Force.*
RAE—*Royal Australian Engineers.*
RAETC—*Royal Australian Engineers Training Centre.*
RANVR—*Royal Australian Naval Volunteer Reserve.*
RAP—*Regimental Aid Post.*
RAR—*Royal Australian Regiment.*
Regt—*Regiment.*
Rfn—*Rifleman.*
Rft—*Reinforcement.*
RMO—*Regimental Medical Officer.*
RSS&AILA—*Returned Sailors', Soldiers' and Airmen's Imperial League of Australia.*

SEAC—*South-East Asia Command.*
Sec—*Section, Secretary.*
Sgt—*Sergeant.*
Sig—*Signals, Signalman.*
SOPAC—*South Pacific (Command).*
Spr—*Sapper.*
Sqn—*Squadron.*
S-Sgt—*Staff-Sergeant.*
SWPA—*South-West Pacific Area.*

Tk—*Tank.*
Trg—*Training.*
Tpr—*Trooper.*
Tps—*Troops.*

UK—*United Kingdom.*
USASOS—*United States Army Services of Supply.*

VDC—*Volunteer Defence Corps.*

W—*Wing.*
WO1—*Warrant-Officer, Class 1.*

Yeo—*Yeomanry.*

INDEX

ABALU, New Guinea native, 100
ABAU (Map p. 34), 138, 139, 239, 243, 260, 278, 353; airfield construction at, 111
ABBREVIATIONS, 628-9
ABDA COMMAND, 15, 16, 17, 21, 29, 47, 68; Australian representation on, 16; air reinforcement of, 69; Japanese naval superiority in, 79
ABE, Vice-Admiral Hiroaki, 341, 342, 344
ABEL'S FIELD (Sketch p. 353), 354
ABORIGINES, 471
ABRAHAM, Pte A. J., 169, 171
ABUARI (Map p. 216; Sketches pp. 199, 205), 199, 200, 201, 202, 204, 213, 228, 311; action at, 205-6, 209
ABUARI TRACK, 210, 211, 212
ACREMAN, Maj K. A., 172, 177
ADACHI, Lt-Gen Hatazo, 527, 530, 531n, 575; commands *XVIII Army*, 144, 383; reinforces Lae-Salamaua, 530, 544
ADAM, Pte R. R., 592
ADELAIDE (Sketch p. 7), 7, 21, 27, 67, 68, 73, 120, 351
ADELAIDE RIVER (Sketch p. 7), 10, 71
ADMIRALTY ISLANDS (Map p. 37), 39, 40, 63, 86
AFRICA, 29, 157, 159, 193
AHERN, Maj F. J., 200, 204
AHIOMA (Map p. 156; Sketch p. 160), 155, 158, 161, 162, 165, 166, 183
AILALEC (Sketch p. 599), 614, 618
AILEU (Sketch p. 599), 608, 610, 613, 614
AINARO (Sketch p. 599), 600, 603, 609, 610, 611, 612, 613, 615, 617, 619, 621, 622
AIRCRAFT, lack of types suitable for evacuation of wounded from Myola, 317; RAAF shortages of, 336; American strength in Pacific, 190. Types: *Airacobra*, 338; *Beaufighter*, 469, 556, 562, 615, 616; *Beaufort*, 582; *Boston*, 424, 487, 558; *Catalina*, 582, 605; *Dauntless dive-bomber*, 255; *DH-50*, 317; *Douglas*, 268, 316, 396, 565; *Flying Fortress*, 305, 424, 582; *Hudson*, 602, 606, 608, 609, 615, 623; *Kittyhawk*, 338, 378; *Lightning*, 337; *Marauder*, 221, 487, 615; *Mitchell*, 582; *Stinson*, 316, 317; *Wirraway*, 368, 562, 565; shoots down Zero, 368; *Zero*, 352, 354-5, 368, 399, 425, 565, 616, 621
AIR-DROPPING, on Kokoda Track, 229, 308, 311, 312, 314, 315; at Wairopi, 331; effect on ammunition, 301; at Gona, 419
AIR EVACUATION, of wounded, 316-7, 399
AIRFIELDS, in Australia, 10; development in New Guinea, 237, 531-2, 573, 577, 589; developed by Japanese in Timor, 613
AIR POWER, importance in Owen Stanleys, 335; fails to prevent seaborne invasion at Guadalcanal, 336
AIR RAIDS, on Darwin, 69-72, 75-6, 613n; on Broome, Wyndham and Derby, 76-7; on Port Moresby, 39, 43, 65-6, 103, 589; on Wau and Goldfields area, 58-9, 100, 565, 584, 589; on MDS Soputa, 399
AIR SUPPORT, Allied, on Kokoda Track, 227, 297, 304, 322-3, 519; at Buna, 360, 362, 365-6, 368-9, 373, 376, 449, 463; on Sanananda Track, 397, 412; at Gona, 422, 424, 428, 434, 439; at Mambare, 447; in Wau operations, 574, 576
AIR TRANSPORT, 353, 546; New Guinea Force requirements, 261, 262; first movement in New Guinea of ground troops by air, 278; of field guns, 365n, 396; of troops to Wau, 547, 553, 554, 558
AITKEN, Sgt R. A., 605
AKIN, Brig-Gen Spencer B., 28n
ALAMEIN, EL, 118
ALAS (Sketch p. 599), 618, 619
ALASKA, 82
ALBANESE, WO2 R. H., 389, 391
ALBANY (Sketch p. 7), 7
ALEUTIAN ISLANDS (Map p. 19), 83, 112; Japanese landings in, 113
ALFORD, Capt James L., 487
ALICE SPRINGS (Sketch p. 7), 68, 72, 74
ALLAN, L-Cpl R. B., 182
ALLCHIN, Lt-Col E. F., 168n
ALLEN, Maj-Gen A. S. (Plate p. 243), 198, 201, 202, 208, 217, 219, 225, 226, 227, 229, 231, 232, 234, 241, 245, 247, 268, 280, 299, 309; commands 7th

ALLEN, MAJ-GEN A. S.—*continued*
Division, 26, 193; orders that battle be fought out on Imita Ridge, 233; explains delay in recapturing Kokoda, 269, 274, 275, 299, 307-8; General Blamey's signals to, 274, 290; relieves 25th Brigade at Templeton's Crossing, 275; defends rate of progress along Kokoda Track, 290-1; issues orders for advance from Eora Creek, 296; transferred from command, 307, 310; meets General MacArthur, 307; recommended for knighthood, 307n; supply problems of, 308-9; efforts throw open mountain passes, 311; proposed employment at Wau, 577
ALLEN, L-Cpl B. E., 181
ALLEN, Pte J. M., 464
ALLIED AIR FORCES, SWPA, 24, 140, 531; in Australia, 84; attack Japanese reinforcement convoys, 145, 527, 530, 544-5, 582; destroy barges at Goodenough Island, 185; strength in New Guinea, 227, 336, 510; in Buna-Gona operations, 495, 522; support Kanga Force operations, 542, 565. *See also* AMERICAN AIR FORCES; AUSTRALIAN AIR FORCE
ALLIED INTELLIGENCE BUREAU, creation of, 446; at Mambare, 446-7; "Z" Special Unit in Timor, 623
ALLIED LAND FORCES HEADQUARTERS (LHQ), 28, 236, 238, 625; creation of, 24-5; orders reinforcement of Port Moresby, 112n; controls Milne Force, 122; decides against reinforcement of Sparrow Force, 603; approves relief of 2/2 Indep Coy, 615
ALLIED NAVAL FORCES, 24, 527; in Coral Sea battle, 111
ALLIES, THE, 113, 118, 189, 190, 191, 532
ALOLA (Maps pp. 114, 216), 87, 110, 131, 141, 196, 199, 201-4, 207, 208, 210, 269, 274, 276, 285, 289, 291, 296, 308, 311, 314, 429, 594; action at, 209; withdrawal from, 211-12, 592-7; medical arrangements at, 212-13; advance to, 298, 312
AMBASI (Map p. 34), 124, 139
AMBOGA CROSSING (Map p. 370), 384, 418
AMBOGA RIVER (Map p. 370; Sketch p. 385), 384, 438-9, 443-4, 497, 511; operations on, 518-19, 526
AMBON ISLAND, 12, 16, 68, 71, 607; Japanese reinforcement of, 575
AMBUSHES, Australian, on Kokoda Track, 126, 133, 138, 224; Wau area, 557, 562, 569, 571, 576, 587-8; on Timor, 600, 605, 609, 611, 613. *Japanese*, in Markham Valley, 86-7; at Milne Bay, 178; on Kokoda Track, 211, 221, 223
AMERICA, UNITED STATES OF, 10, 20, 22, 38, 113, 120, 225, 248; strength compared to Japan's, 1; reinforcement of Australia, 13, 15, 16, 21, 24; selects Australia as Pacific base, 14; sets up machinery for command and control of Allied forces, 15-16; accepts strategic responsibility for Pacific, 17; strength of defence forces, 32; and Beat Hitler first policy, 188; aids Chinese Army in Burma, 192; strategic relationship with Australia, 591
AMERICAN AIR FORCES, 121, 138-9, 239, 317, 452; in Philippines, 14; strength allotted to SWPA, 23; squadron strength, 32; reinforce New Caledonia, 38; attack Lae and Salamaua, 67, 99; reinforce ABDA Area, 69; at Darwin, 69-70, 71, 73; attack Tulagi Harbour, 80; in Battle of Coral Sea, 81, 255; reinforce Port Moresby, 121; in Midway Island Battle, 113, 255; at Milne Bay, 122; in Guadalcanal operations, 150-1, 154, 256-7, 336-7, 341-2, 343, 529; strength in Australia, 189; distribution of, 190; in Papuan operations, 221, 279, 305, 323, 487; strength in South Pacific; 377; in Wau operations, 558, 565-6, 581; in Battle of Bismarck Sea, 582; in Timor area, 615-16
—GHQ Air Force, 20
—FIFTH AIR FORCE, 261, 266, 565, 581
—1ST MARINE AIRCRAFT WING, 254
—SQUADRONS: No. 90, 582; No. 223, 152; No. 232, 152
AMERICAN ARMY, 14, 29, 31, 33, 335, 350; in Philippines, 1, 24-5, 36, 38; estimates of, 1, 28, 31-3, 119, 450; reinforces Australia, 8, 84; strength in Australia, 20, 24, 112n, 189; expansion of, 32; relations with Australian Army, 33, 174-5, 248,

AMERICAN ARMY—continued
394, 625-7; reinforces New Caledonia, 38; in Darwin area, 69, 73-4; strength in New Guinea, 115n, 227, 234, 239; reinforces Hawaii, 119; at Milne Bay, 122, 155, 159-60, 161, 172-3; distribution of, 190, 338n; on Guadalcanal, 257, 260, 336, 528-9, 590; in New Guinea, 310, 350-1, 361; strength and casualties, 531, 577
—CHIEF OF STAFF, 14
—UNITED STATES ARMY FORCES IN AUSTRALIA, 14, 24, 159
—UNITED STATES ARMY FORCES IN FAR EAST, 16, 18, 38
—UNITED STATES ARMY SERVICES OF SUPPLY, 350-1
—CORPS: I, 33, 371, 374; General Eichelberger assumes command of, 120, 351; XIV, on Guadalcanal, 529
—DIVISIONS, strength and distribution, 32, 189; Americal, 528; at Noumea, 338; on Guadalcanal, 529; 24th, 338n; 25th, 337, 528; in Hawaii, 338n; on Guadalcanal, 529; 27th, 338n; 32nd, 26, 120, 242, 261, 338n, 448, 509, 594; ordered to Australia, 21, arrives, 33, 111; estimates of, 32-3, 351, 450; in Australia, 119; on Rigo-Abau route, 260; air transport requirements, 262; roles allotted, 278, 354; advances on Buna, 345, 356; equipment and weapons, 351; underestimates Japanese at Buna, 352; at Buna, 357, 362, 368, 376, 381, 385-6, 394, 403, 423, 449, 490-1, 493, 495, 510; casualties and strength, 371, 382, 496; condition of, 374, 394; on Sanananda Track, 500, 502-3, 505, 532, casualties, 527; at Tarakena, 517; relief of, 545; 37th, 338n; 40th, 338n; 41st, 26, 338n, 509; ordered to Australia, 15, arrives, 33, 111; estimate of, 32-3; in Australia, 119, 120; compared to 32nd Division, 450; Buna area, 545, 577, 590; 43rd, 338n
—FORCES: Buna, 510-11; Luzon, 34; Urbana, at Buna, 364-7, 370-1, 373, 378-9, 476, 485-6, 488, 490, 496-7, 509; condition of, 369, 380; strength and casualties, 382; Visayan-Mindanao, 36; Warren, at Buna, 362, 364, 366-7, 370, 373-4, 376, 454, 456-7, 461-2, 494, 496-7; condition of, 369; casualties and strength, 382; reinforced by 18th Brigade, 451
—ARTILLERY, divisional war establishment, 33; Anti-aircraft, 111, 121, 278; in Milne Force, 122; at Buna, 381; 101 Coast Arty Bn, 67, 121; 102 Coast Arty Bn, 73; Field Regiments: 129th, 367; 147th, 68-9; 148th, 68-9
—ENGINEERS, 120-1, 157, 352; 43rd Regt, 67, 158, 185; 46th Bn, 121; 96th Bn, 67; 114th Bn, 242, 464-5; 808th Bn, 69; 576th Coy, 67
—INFANTRY REGIMENTS AND BRIGADES: 1st Montana Volunteer, 509n; 84th Bde, 18; 126th Regt, 243; arrives Port Moresby, 239, 242; role allotted, 262; advances on Buna, 278-9, 351-4; at Buna, 357, 380, 487, 493, 495; placed under command 7th Division, 358; in Sanananda area, 388, 394, 397-8, 401, 404, 408, 411, 413, 414, 497, 512, casualties, 415; estimate of, 402, 404; relief of, 513; 127th Regt, at Buna, 381-2, 486-8, 490, 511, 512, 522-3, 528, casualties, 527; 128th Regt, at Port Moresby, 242, 244; role allotted, 262; advances on Buna, 278-9, 290, 351-2, 354-5; at Buna, 356, 361-2, 471, 493; 132nd Regt, 529; 162nd Regt, 590; 163rd Regt, estimate of, 509-10; on Sanananda Track, 510-14, 518, 520, 524-5; 164th Regt, on Guadalcanal, 255, 257, 338-9, 528, casualties, 257; 182nd Regt, on Guadalcanal, 338, 528
—INFANTRY BATTALIONS: I/126 Bn, 354-5; at Buna, 357-60, 364, 366-7, 369, 373-4, 376, 378, 463-5, 468, 470-3, 481, 486; on Sanananda Track, 395-6, 398, 401-4, 414, 501; II/126 Bn, 242, 361; on Jaure Track, 279, 352-3; at Buna, 354, 364-5, 371, 375, 378-82, 395, 397-403; III/126 Bn, 354; on Sanananda Track, 395, 397-403; I/127 Bn, at Buna, 486, 490-1, 493; II/127 Bn, at Buna, 486-7, 489, 490, 493; III/127 Bn, at Buna, 381-2, 487-90, 492; I/128 Bn, at Buna, 356, 358-61, 364, 369, 373-4, 376, 378, 454, 459, 463, 465, 468-73, 476-7, 486; II/128 Bn, 487; at Buna, 356, 360-1, 364-6, 371, 375, 378-9, 382, 493-4; III/128 Bn, at Buna, 356, 358-61, 366-7, 374, 376, 378, 454, 463-6, 480-1, 483, 486; I/147 Bn, on Guadalcanal, 338; I/163 Bn, arrives Port Moresby, 512; on Sanananda Track, 513,

AMERICAN ARMY—continued
524-6; II/163 Bn, 512; on Killerton Track, 513, 524-5; III/163 Bn, on Sanananda Track, 524-6; I/164 Bn, 338; II/164 Bn, 339; III/164 Bn, 257; III/182 Bn, 338
—MEDICAL, air raid on clearing station at Soputa, 399
—MILITARY POLICE, 625-6
—WEST POINT MILITARY ACADEMY, 18, 120n
AMERICAN GOVERNMENT, 82
—JOINT CHIEFS OF STAFF, 15, 17, 22, 23, 27, 82, 120-1, 189, 225, 337, 528; issue first directive governing strategy of Pacific war, 119-20; plan Solomon Islands offensive, 147
—WAR DEPARTMENT, 32, 34; decides to send ground troops to Australia, 15; presses for appointment of Australian to combined ground command, 25
AMERICAN NAVY, 16, 83; role in Pacific, 17, 84, 235; attacks Marshall and Gilbert Islands, 67; submarine activities, 76, in Coral Sea Battle, 80-2, 111; carrier strength in Pacific, 82; at Midway, 113; opposes GHQ SWPA plan for attack on Rabaul, 119; in Guadalcanal operations, 149, 151, 153, 154, 254, 337, 590; in Battle of Savo Island, 151-2; strength and losses, 255, 259, 336-7, 340, 344-5; in Battle of Cape Esperance, 255-6; in Battle of Guadalcanal, 341, 344-5; refuses to make ships available for seaborne landing at Buna, 451; PT boat operations, 468-9, 590; in Battle of Bismarck Sea, 583; evacuation of Timor, 623
—FLEETS: Asiatic, 20; Pacific, 190
—MARINE CORPS, 146; at Midway, 113; strength and dispositions, Dec 1941, 147; air squadrons, 119; in Guadalcanal operations, 151, 152, 255, 258-9, 343, casualties, 256
—MARINE CORPS DIVISIONS: 1st, 147, 338n, estimate of, 148, on Guadalcanal, 149, 150, 152, 528; 2nd, 148; on Guadalcanal, 528
—MARINE CORPS REGIMENTS AND BATTALIONS: 2nd Regt, 338; 7th Regt, 254; 8th Regt, 338, 339; 1 Parachute Bn, 150; 1 Raider Bn, 148, 150; 2 Raider Bn, 338, 339, 344; 3 Defence Bn, 148; II/5 Bn, 150; I/7 Bn, 256, 257, 339; II/7 Bn, 338
AMMUNITION, Australian production rates, 30-1; on Kokoda Track, 122, 141, 196, 221, 265, 281, 322; affected by air dropping, 301; at Buna, 364, 368, 375; Wau area, 586
ANDERSON, Lt-Col A. J., 505
ANDERSON, Maj A. J., 180, 181, 182
ANDERSON, L-Cpl F. T., 87, 88
ANDREW, Maj C. S., 246
ANGO (Map p. 370; Sketch p. 357), 358, 360-1, 364, 366, 367, 368, 374, 454, 486
ANGORAM (Map p. 34), 48, 49
Anshun, Australian motor vessel, 183-4
ANSON BAY (Sketch p. 7), 75
ANZAC AREA, 25; proposed extension of, 16
Aoba, Japanese cruiser, 255
AOLA BAY (Sketch p. 149), 338, 339
ARAKAN, 187n
ARAVIA (Map p. 34), 64, 65
ARCHER, Capt G. R. (Plate p. 130), 60, 61, 93, 95
ARCHER, Maj T. E., 231-2, 270-1
AREA COMBINED HEADQUARTERS, 9
Arizona, American battleship, 255
Armidale, Australian corvette, 617
ARMS, carried by troops on Kokoda Track, 265
ARMSTRONG, Lt R. J. H., 292, 293, 328
ARNOLD, Lt-Col A. S. W., 178, 179, 183, 184, 347, 348, 349, 480, 481, 482, 484, 513, 516, 520, 521, 522; commands 2/12th Battalion, 177
Aroetta, ketch, 75
ARTANGO, Louis, 139n
ARTHUR, Col John M., 338, 339
ARTILLERY: American, divisional strength, 33; on Guadalcanal, 338. Australian, strength and production rates, 10, 30-1; Anti-aircraft, manufacture of, 10; at Port Moresby, 45, 65, 67; at Darwin, 70, 72; Anti-tank, strength, 30-1; lacking at Milne Bay, 163; Field, at Buna, 367-8, 369; shortages at Buna, 362, coastwise transport of, 363, effectiveness of, 364, air transport of, 365n; at Sanananda, 397; Mountain, rate of fire, 357
ARU ISLAND (Sketch p. 612), 623n
Arunta, Australian destroyer, 184n, 347, 621, 622
Asahi Shimbun, 304n

INDEX 633

ASHER, WO2 M. H., 407
ASIA, 29; Australia's future in, 591
ASIGARI (Sketch p. 128), 142
ASISI (Map p. 313; Sketch p. 353), 296, 353
ASSAM, 191
Astoria, American cruiser, 80, 152
Atago, Japanese cruiser, 343
ATAMBUA (Sketch p. 599), 598, 599
ATHERTON TABLELANDS PROJECT, 449, 451
ATKINSON, Capt W. J. S., 245, 273, 274, 275, 319
ATKINSON, Maj W. M., 440-1
Atlanta, American cruiser, 340, 341
ATLANTIC OCEAN, strategic responsibilities in, 17; strength of American forces in, 190
ATROCITIES, Japanese, 139n, 176, 178
ATSABE (Sketch p. 599), 598, 600, 603, 608, 609, 612
ATTU (Map p. 19), 113
AUSTEN, MOUNT, 528, 529
AUSTEN, Lt L. E., 139n
AUSTRALIA (Sketch p. 7), 22, 25, 30, 33, 34, 38, 42, 46, 49, 57, 74, 77, 79, 80, 82, 84, 85, 113, 115, 118, 119, 120, 140, 148, 191, 235, 259, 317, 336, 338, 351, 427, 449, 450, 452, 468, 497, 509, 516n, 528, 588, 590, 598, 602, 605, 606, 607, 609, 615, 616, 618, 620; defence plans, 1-13, 112n, 190; airfield construction in, 10, 121; American strength and reinforcement, 13, 14, 15-16, 20, 21, 23, 24, 29; prejudiced against conscription, 31; lacks voice in determination of Allied policy, 16-17, 190; return of AIF to, 21, 509; represented on Pacific War Council, 21; strength of ground forces in, 29; aircraft strength in, 47; seizes German New Guinea 51; Japanese threat to north-western areas, 68, 190; first blows of war on, 71; threatened Japanese invasion of, 83, 113n, 118; seeks British aid, 118; Japanese Intelligence of, 144; numbers in fighting Services, 189; strategic future of, 591
AUSTRALIAN AIR FORCE, 10, 54, 97; enlistments in, 9; ban on enlistment of militiamen, 13; service squadrons allotted to SWPA Command, 27; at Port Moresby, 46, 65, 66; at Salamaua, 54, 55; fighter deficiencies in New Guinea, 58; in Solomons, 63; at Darwin, 69, 71, 73-4, 76; at Broome, 77; in Battle of Coral Sea, 81; at Milne Bay, 122, 161, 163, 166, 183, 185; cooperation with New Guinea Force, 239; strength of, 336; Buna-Gona operations, 434, 469; Wau operations, 556; in Battle of Bismarck Sea, 582; supplies Sparrow Force, 602, 605, 609; in Timor area, 608, 615-16
—CHIEF OF AIR STAFF, 69
—SQUADRONS: *No. 4 Cooperation*, 368; *No. 75*, 67; at Milne Bay, 158, 161, 182, 187; *No. 76*, at Milne Bay, 158, 161, 182, 187
—WOMEN'S AUXILIARY AUSTRALIAN AIR FORCE, formation approved, 4n
AUSTRALIAN ARMY, 10, 32, 86, 240, 350; distribution of AIF, 1, in Middle East, 4, 25; effect of AIF enlistments on militia, 2, 44; number of enlistments to *Dec 1941*, 9, strength in Australia, 12-13, 24, 29, 31n; PMF strength *Aug 1941*, 2; garrison battalions, 2-3, 12; defence plans, 6-8, 112n; equipment of, 10, 30n, 31; strength and dispositions, 11-12, 31n, 509, 577; limitations on operational role of, 23; reorganisation of, 25-7, 140n; not adequately represented on GHQ, SWPA, 28; First AIF, 30; training of, 32-3; relations with American Army, 33, 120, 174-5, 176, 234-5, 248, 394, 625-7; occupies German New Guinea, 40; at Port Moresby, 65-6; at Darwin, 70-3; diversion to Australia sought of returning AIF, 69; AIF used to strengthen militia, 74-5, 115, sought for Milne Bay, 158, for New Guinea, 226; in Ceylon, 77-9; in New Guinea, 86, 115, strength, 234, supply of, 350-1; strength at Milne Bay, 159, 173; wins first land victory over Japanese, 187; General MacArthur's opinion of, 176, 225, 234-5, 246-8; proposed reductions in, 449; casualties in Papua, 531; achievements in New Guinea, 590-1
—ARMY HEADQUARTERS, 3, 5, 8, 9, 140, 238, 602, 621; becomes GHQ (Aust), later redesignated LHQ, 25; authorises formation of NGVR, 46
—CHIEF OF THE GENERAL STAFF, 4, 5, 10, 30, 111, 140n, 174
—MILITARY BOARD, 3; necessity for existence examined, 4; ceases to function, 25
—ARMIES: *First*, 244n, 625; formed, 25, 28; composition of, 26; allotted to SWPA Command,

AUSTRALIAN ARMY—*continued*
27; role, 80; *Second*, formed, 25-6; allotted to SWPA Command, 27
—COMMANDS AND MILITARY DISTRICTS: *Eastern Command*, 8, 13; absorbed by First Army, 25; *Northern Command*, 25; *Southern Command*, 25; *Western Command*, 13, 76; absorbed by III Corps, 25; strengthening of, 27; *7th Military District*, 72, 73; absorbed by Northern Territory Force, 26; staff replaced by 6th Division, 75; *8th Military District*, 42, 57, 59, 62; becomes New Guinea Force, 26
—CORPS: I, 25, 26, 28, 140, 238; effect of arrival on defence plans, 112n; II, 26, 140n; III, created, 25; composition of, 26; allotted to SWPA Command, 27; *Anzac*, 159
—DIVISIONS: number and composition of, 26, 509; *1st Armoured*, 26, 112n; raising of, 10, 452-3; retained as Command Reserve, 26; allotted to Western Command, 27; quality and equipment of, 29; *1st Cavalry*, 7, 13; disposition of, 12; *2nd Cavalry*, 7, 44; role, 12; *1st Infantry*, 7, 26, 160, dispositions, 12; *2nd Infantry*, 7, 26; dispositions, 12; *3rd Infantry*, 7, 13, 26, 44, 577, 625; roles allotted, 12, 578; opens headquarters at Bulolo, 588; *4th Infantry*, 7, 26, 44; roles allotted, 12, 27; *5th Infantry*, composition of, 26; reinforces Milne Bay, 449, 577, 588; *6th Infantry*, 4, 72-3, 77, 159, 193, 229, 482n, 497, 509, 577n; return of, 8; proposed diversion to Burma, 15; diverted to Ceylon, 21; organised as Northern Territory Force, 25-6, 75; allotted to SWPA Command, 27; quality of, 29; contributes officers to militia, 30; headquarters arrives New Guinea, 244; composition of, 244; period of training preparatory to first action, 351n; needs prolonged period for recuperation, 450; *7th Infantry*, 26, 176, 198, 215, 251, 316, 332, 352, 423, 439, 497, 509, 525; return of, 8; proposed diversion to Burma, 15; diverted to Australia, 21, 27; quality of, 29; contributes officers to militia, 30; proposed employment in attack on Rabaul, 119; goes to New Guinea, 140-1, 159, 193; establishes headquarters at Port Moresby, 196, 227; role allotted, 240; composition of, 244; on Kokoda Track, 261, 274, 280, 309, 312, 322; air transport requirements, 262; liaison with New Guinea Force, 275n; in coastal fighting, 354, 385, 449, 510-11; artillery support for, 357; allotted army cooperation aircraft, 368; needs prolonged period for recuperation, 450; strength and losses, 508-9, 527; *8th Infantry*, 68n, 508; *9th Infantry*, 509; retained in Middle East, 21, 118; return of, 449; *10th Infantry*, 26; *11th Infantry*, 577, 579; *1st Motor*, 26; *2nd Motor*, 26
—FORCES: *Chaforce*, 424, 427, 441; role of, 332; at Gona, 418, 419, 447n; 2/14th component, 420, 425, 435, 441; 2/16th component, 420-1, 432, 437-9; 2/27 component, 435, 441; *Goforce*, 505, 509; *Hatforce*, 261, 278; *Home Forces*, 9; GOC appointed, 4-5, 76; strength of, 8; headquarters established, 8, 13; *Honner Force*, 227, 229, 241, 244; *Jawforce*, 241, 251; *Kanga Force*, 100-1, 103, 105, 262, 334, 534, 536, 539, 545-6; formed, 86; allotted role, 89, 100; strength, 90, 558; physical condition, 102, 104; demolishes Wau and goldfields installations, 106-7; supply of, 140, 197, 198, 260; reinforcement of, 538; achievements of, 544; casualties, 572; deleted from Order of Battle, 588; *Lancer Force*, 619, 621, 623; *Mac Force*, 564-5; *Maroubra Force*, 193-4, 196; formed, 114; command changes, 123, 129, 132, 141, 143; supply of, 130, 140, 197; *Melbourne Covering Force*, 12; *Milne Force*, 160, 166, 171, 173, 175, 238, 240; composition of, 121-2; strength, 159; *Newcastle Covering Force*, 13; forms 10th Division, 26; *New Guinea Force*, 32, 101, 104-5, 122, 129, 136-7, 193, 196-8, 202, 229, 237, 238, 242, 260-1, 266-7, 278, 291, 316, 317, 331, 337, 351n, 358, 368, 469n, 534, 536, 538, 547, 557, 563, 578, 580; absorbs 8th Military District headquarters, 26; allotted to SWPA Command, 27; controls Milne Force, 159; supply and communications for, 260; liaison with 7th Division on Kokoda Track, 275n; controls COSC, 350-1; establishes advanced headquarters at Popondetta, 372, 400; liaison with Kanga Force, 544; creates composite carrier group, 241, 244; *Northern Territory Force*, 73, 140n, 307n, 577n, 602, 611, 615;

634 INDEX

AUSTRALIAN ARMY—*continued*
formed, 26; training of, 74-5; *Plover Force*, 623*n*; "*S*" *Force*, 621-3; *Sparrow Force*, 191; operations of, 598-619
—ARMOUR AND CAVALRY: *2nd Armd Bde*, 375*n*; *6 Armd Bde*, 29*n*; *3 Army Tk Bde*, 29*n*. *2/5 Armd Regt*, 29*n*; *2/6 Armd Regt*, 29*n*; transport of tanks to Buna, 363; at Buna, 451, 452-3, 454-5, 455-7, 459-63, 466-7, 468, 469, 470-1, 477-8, 479-80, 481-2, 483-4; planned employment at Sanananda, 511-12; on Sanananda Track, 514, 515-16, 524-5; *2/7 Armd Regt*, 29*n*; *2/8 Armd Regt*, 29*n*; *2/9 Armd Regt*, 29*n*; *2/10 Armd Regt*, 29*n*; *12 Armd Regt*, 29*n*; *13 Armd Regt*, 29*n*; *14 Armd Regt*, 29*n*; *1 Army Tk Bn*, 29*n*; *2 Army Tk Bn*, 29*n*; *3 Army Tk Bn*, 29*n*; *6 Cav Regt*, 33, 76, 375, 453, 611; *7 Cav Regt*, 244, 413, 415; on Sanananda Track, 450, 498, 501-8, 509, 512-14, 518, 525, 532; history of, 497; casualties, 507; *1st Indep Light Horse Troop*, 116-17
—ARTILLERY, divisional strength, 33; detachments withdrawn from Ocean Island and Nauru, 38. Headquarters units: *Anzac Corps*, 13; *RAA 6 Div*, 73; Anti-aircraft, at Port Moresby, 65-6; at Darwin, 70, 72-3; *2/1 AA Regt*, 72; *2/3 Lt AA Bty*, 67; *6 Hvy Bty*, 121; *9 Lt Bty*, 121; *23 Hvy Bty*, 45, 121; *156 Lt Bty*, 565, 572. Anti-tank, 69; *2/1 Regt*, 412; *17 A-Tk Bty*, 86; *101 A-Tk Regt*, 121, 172, 177. Field Regiments: *2/1st*, 244; at Buna, 363, 365, 367, 368, 371, 373, 374, 375, 454, 456, 512; at Sanananda, 396, 400, 401, 404, 499, 502, 511, 513, 524; Gona area, 422, 424, 428, 431, 432, 440; Blackforce detachment, 363, 365*n*, 396, 424, 431; Bullforce detachment, 363, 365, 366; Japanese raid on, 501; at Wau, 555-6, 563, 567, 569, 572; *2/5th*, 244; at Milne Bay, 159, 160, 164, 168-9, 176, 183, 278; at Buna, 354-5, 362, 363*n*, 367-8, 381-2, 454, 456, 474-5, 481, 512; supports Sanananda operations, 524; *2/6th*, 244; *2/14th*, 68*n*; *13th*, 45, 241, 244, 474; *14th*, 241, 244-6. Fixed Defences, 7-8, 10; *Paga Coastal Defence Bty*, 44. *1 Mtn Bty*, 366, at Buna, 356-7, 362, 367, 382, 454, 456, 474, equipment of, 357; Wau area, 583
—ENGINEERS: *2/1 Fd Coy*, 578; *2/4 Fd Coy*, at Buna, 451, 454; *2/5 Fd Coy*, 330; at Wairopi, 331-2; *2/6 Fd Coy*, 240-1; on Kokoda Track, 300, 315, 316; at Wairopi, 332; at Popondetta, 599; *2/8 Fd Coy*, at Wau, 547, 550, 572-3, 583; *2/14 Fd Coy*, 241; on Kokoda Track, 261*n*, 330; *2/16 Fd Coy*, 573; on Bulldog Track, 581; *14 Fd Coy*, 580; *24 Fd Coy*, at Milne Bay, 122, 157, 163; *25 Fd Pk Coy*, 330
—INDEPENDENT COMPANIES, 625, formation and role of, 84-5; war establishment, 85; dispositions of, 85-6; probable value in Owen Stanleys, 332. 1st, 62; role, 39; at Tulagi, 63, 80; on Bougainville, 63-4, 65; on Manus Island, 65; formation and training, 85-6; with Kanga Force, 86-7, 89, 104; 2/2nd, 12, 34, 76, 86; formation and training, 85; in Portuguese Timor, 598-617; physical state of, 615; evacuation of, 616-18; 2/3rd, 86*n*, 583-4, 588; in New Caledonia, 38, 86; formation and training, 85; Kanga Force operations, 556, 558-9, 560-1, 566, 568, 571-4, 583, 586-8; 2/4th, in Northern Territory, 69, 75, 86; formation and training, 85; history of, 611; in Timor, 612-24; 2/5th, 97; arrives Port Moresby, 67, 86; formation of, 85; joins Kanga Force, 86, 89; Kanga Force operations, 90-8, 100-2, 104, 107, 534, 536-7, 540-3, 547, 549, 550, 551-2, 558, 562, 584, 588; supply of, 103; physical condition of, 539; achievements of, 544; performance criticised, 563; 2/6th, 86*n*, 241, 244, 577, 593, 594, 597; formation of, 85; arrives Port Moresby, 105; in Ioribaiwa area, 224, 227, 245; flown to Wanigela, 278; overland advance to Buna, 279, 352, 355; patrol penetrates to Kokoda, 332*n*; at Buna, 359-60, 364, 367, 369, 370, 373, 376, 378; 2/7th, 262; formation of, 85; arrives Wau, 538; Kanga Force operations, 540-3, 546-8, 557-8, 561, 568, 572, 574, 583-4, 586; 2/8th, 85
—INFANTRY: *Brigades*, 121; 3rd, 69, 74; 4th, 576-7, 588; 7th, 26, 157; arrives Milne Bay, 121-2; at Milne Bay, 155, 158, 166, 167, 173, 175, 450, 577; role and dispositions, 160; proposed employment at Buna, 451; 11th, 26; 12th, 26; 14th, 497; reinforces Port Moresby, 111, 112*n*; condition of, 141, 226; at Port Moresby, 227, 241, 406; compo-

AUSTRALIAN ARMY—*continued*
sition, 244; at Sanananda, 510; Gona area, 512, 518-19, 526; 15th, 577; **16th**, 193, 229, 233, 239, 268, 509; in Ceylon, 77-9, 118; embarks Colombo, 119; arrives Australia, 226, length of stay in Australia, 280; proposed reinforcement of New Guinea with, 234; arrives Port Moresby, 244, 280; on Kokoda Track, 262, 269, 274, 280-1; at Templeton's Crossing, 275-6, 281, 285-6; equipment and strength at outset, 281, 309; at Eora Creek, 287-303, casualties at, 306, achievements at, 306-7; advance to Oivi, 311, 312, 314; at Oivi-Gorari, 317, 318, 320-1, 329, 330-1, casualties, 319, to 7 *Nov*, 322; at Wairopi, 332-3, casualties in Battle of Kokoda Track, 334*n*; advances on Sanananda, 355, 358-9, 361, 384-6; on Sanananda Track, 380, 395-9, 401, 403-4, 407, 411, 423, 450, 497, casualties, 394, 407*n*; strength on relief, 406, 413; rehabilitation of, 449; 17th, 509, 576; in Ceylon, 77-9, 118, 280; embarks Colombo, 119; arrives Australia, 226; reinforces Milne Bay, 244; at Milne Bay, 349, 375, 450, 497, 509; reinforces Wau, 543-4, 545; in Wau operations, 550, 558, 577, 584; forms 17th Brigade Carrier Platoon, 375, at Buna, 376, 454; 18th, 112, 375, 451; at Milne Bay, 159, 160, 173, 176-7, 184, 193, 349, 450; forms commando platoons, 177; at Buna, 383, 451-2, 469*n*, 485-6, 495, 497, 509, 532, 577, casualties, 484, 495; Sanananda area, 448, 510, 512, 513, 516, 517, 518, 520, 525, casualties, 522, 527; rehabilitation of, 449; 19th, 74; diverted to Australia, 21; in Northern Territory, 26-7, 74, 244, 509, 611; 20th, 351*n*; 21st, 112, 143, 195, 196*n*, 240-1, 244, 249, 272, 311, 332, 427; reinforces New Guinea, 193; role allotted, 194; on Kokoda Track, 196 198-9, 206, 209, 211-12, 214, 217, 219, 220-2, 224-5, 229, 231, 245, 281, 309-10, 592-7, performance examined, 247-8, casualties, 252-3, 334; at Gona, 397, 442-5, 430-1, 433-5, 437, 439, 445, 448, 450, 497, casualties, 442; rehabilitation of, 449; Sanananda area, 501, 505; relief of, 512, 518; forms Composite Coy, 194, 219, 221-2; forms Carrier Platoon for operations at Wau, 557, 563; 23rd, in Northern Territory, 68-9, 74; 25th, 112, 224-7, 239-41, 248, 260*n*; proposed employment at Milne Bay, 174-5; arrives Port Moresby, 229, 234; at Ioribaiwa, 231, 233; composition of, 244; at Imita Ridge, 245; on Kokoda Track, 254, 262, 269; strength at outset of campaign, 309; at Templeton's Crossing, 274-5, 277, 280-1; strength and casualties to *23 Oct*, 276; at Eora Creek, 296, 303; advances to Kokoda, 311, 314, 315, 317; at Gorari, 320-3, 325, 329, 330-1; at Wairopi, 332-3; casualties in Battle of Kokoda Track, 334*n*; advances on Gona, 355, 384, 386, 399, 418, 419; at Gona, 359, 423-5, 427, 433-4, 448, 450, casualties, 421, strength, 422, on relief, 435; rehabilitation of, 449; forms carrier platoon for operations at Wau, 557, 563; 29th, 26; at Milne Bay, 545, 577, 588; 30th, 130, 226, 434; at Port Moresby, 43-5; officering of, 114-15; role, 241; composition, 244; on Sanananda Track, 404, 407-8, 412, 439, 450, 498, 501, 509, 510, 512, 513, 517, 518; casualties, 415; strength, 497; relief of, 513; proposed employment at Wau, 577

Battalions, 120, average strength on Kokoda Track, 228, 309; personal equipment of infantrymen, 285, 408; shortage of, 413; **2/1st**, 229, 308, 406; at Templeton's Crossing, 275-6, 281, 283, 285-6; strength in Owen Stanleys at outset, 280; at Eora Creek, 287-9, 290-5, 296-8, 299-300, 302-3, 307, casualties, 287, 295, 306*n*; advances to Oivi-Gorari, 311, 312, 314-16, 319-20; at Gorari, 321, 324-8, 329, casualties, 327; casualties in Battle of Kokoda Track, 334*n*; losses from sick and wounded, 335; advances to Sanananda, 384, 386-90, 392; on Sanananda Track, 393, 397-8, 400, 402-3, 407-8, casualties, 393-4, 407*n*; strength, 394; **2/2nd**, 159; at Templeton's Crossing, 275-6, 281-90, casualties, 284, 285; strength in Owen Stanleys at outset, 280; at Eora Creek, 287, 289, 290, 295, 300, 302-3, casualties, 306*n*; advances to Oivi, 311, 312, 314, 315, 317-19; at Oivi, 321-2, 325, 329; crosses Kumusi, 333; casualties in Battle of Kokoda Track, 334*n*; advances on Sanananda, 384-6, 388-9; on Sanananda Track, 392-5, 397, 400, 402, 408-9, 411, casualties, 407*n*; strength, 413; **2/3rd**, at Templeton's Crossing, 276, 285-7; strength in Owen

INDEX

AUSTRALIAN ARMY—continued
Stanleys at outset, 280; at Eora Creek, 288, 289-90, 291, 294-7, 298-9, 301-3, 307, casualties, 298, 302, 303, 306n; advances to Oivi, 311, 312, 314; at Oivi, 315, 318, 319, 321, 325, 329, casualties, 319; casualties in Battle of Kokoda Track, 334n; advances on Sanananda, 384, 386, 388, 389; on Sanananda Track, 392, 393-5, 397-9, 400, 403, 406-7, 499, 500, strength, 402, 413, 497, casualties, 407n; relief of, 408; 2/4th, 74-5; 2/5th, 114; at Buna, 375; arrives Wau, 547-8, 553-4; in Wau area, 550, 555, 557, 563, 566-9, 572-4, 583-4, 586; 2/6th, arrives Wau, 543, 545-6; at Wau, 546-8, 556, 571, 573; at Wandumi, 548-51, 553, 557, 576; on Black Cat Track, 562, 563, 565, 568, 569-71; in Markham area, 584; casualties, 572; number of originals with battalion, 588; 2/7th, 375. 588; arrives Wau, 553-4; at Wau, 551, 554-6, 558-60, 563-5, 566-7, 572, 583; at Mubo, 586; 2/8th, 194; 2/9th, 405n; at Milne Bay, 160, 173, 180-4, 187, 451, casualties, 185; arrives Oro Bay, 452, strength, 454; at Cape Endaiadere, 455-62, casualties, 462, achievements, 485; at Strip Point, 463-4, 465-8, casualties, 466, 468; on Old Strip, 471-2, 477, 479; on Giropa Point, 481, 483; at Simemi Creek, 484; casualties at Buna, 484n; in Sanananda area, 513, 514, 520-4, casualties, 515; 2/10th, at Milne Bay, 160-1, 165-6, 167-70, 171-3, 176, 193; at Wanigela, 237, 261, 278, 346, 451; at Normanby Island, 346; at Buna, 451, 454, 462-3; on Old Strip, 465, 468, 480; Giropa Point, 481, 483; casualties, 484n; in Sanananda area, 514, 519-20, 521, 522, 523-4; 2/11th, 89, 141; 2/12th, 157, 405n; at Milne Bay, 160, 173, 177-80, 182-4, 187, forms Commando Platoon, 180, casualties, 185; on Goodenough Island, 347-9, 451; at Buna, 480, 494, casualties, 484; Sanananda area, 513, 514, 515-16, 520-2, 524-5, casualties, 516; 2/14th, reinforces New Guinea, 193; on Kokoda Track, 195, 199, 249, strength, 194-5, 248, casualties, 252-3, 334n; at Isurava, 200-1, 202-3, 204-8, 213-14, 228, casualties, 208, 211; at Alola, 204, 211, 592-7; withdraws, 212, 217-19, 220-3; at Ioribaiwa, 231-3, 245; Gona area, 418, 419, 424, 425-6, 429, 431, 433-5, 438-9, 442-5, 447, casualties, 427, 430, 447n, strength, 439; 2/14th-2/16th Composite, 224; at Ioribaiwa, 230, 232-3; resumes separate identities, 245; 2/16th, 193, 311; on Kokoda Track, 130, 195-6, 199, 200, 241, 249-52, 332, strength, 248, casualties, 253, 334n; Alola area, 202, 204, 207, 209, 211, 212, 213, 228, 594; on Abuari Track, 205-6, 209-10; at Isurava Rest House, 208; withdraws, 214, 215-17, 218-24; at Ioribaiwa, 230-1, 233, 245; Gona area, 420, 424, 431-2, 434, 441-2, strength, 430, 439, casualties, 433; see also Chaforce; 2/14th-2/16th, 2/16th-2/27th Composite Bns; 2/16th-2/27th Composite, formed, 434; at Gona, 436, 440, 441, 447; 2/21st, 12, 68; 2/22nd, 115, 408n; at Rabaul, 12; at Salamaua, 57; 2/25th, 405n; at Ioribaiwa, 229, 230-3; at Imita, 245-6; advances to Templeton's Crossing, 263-4, 269-72; at Templeton's, 273-6, 281, 285, strength, 276; at Eora Creek, 296; advances to Kokoda, 311, 312, 314; at Gorari, 321-5, casualties, 327-8; advances to Wairopi, 330-1, 333; casualties in Battle of Kokoda Track, 334n; Gona area, 418, 419, 421-2; strength and casualties, 435n; 2/27th, 194, 199, 201-2, 208, 545; on Kokoda Track, 219, 220-3, 248-52, 596-7, casualties, 252, 334; at Gona, 424-5, 427-8, 430, 432-4 440-2, casualties, 429, 431, strength, 439; see also 2/16th-2/27th Composite Bn; 2/28th, 77, 280; 2/31st, 114; at Ioribaiwa, 225, 229, 230, 231, 232, 233, 245; advances to Templeton's Crossing, 264, 269, strength and casualties to 23 Oct, 276; at Eora, 296, 299; advances to Kokoda, 311, 312, 314; at Gorari, 321-2, 323, 324, 325, 328, casualties, 327, 329; casualties in Battle of Kokoda Track, 334n; at Wairopi, 330-1; advances to Gona, 333, 418-19; at Gona, 420-2, 438; strength on relief, 435n; 2/33rd, 333, 405n; at Ioribaiwa, 225, 229-33; at Imita, 245; advances to Templeton's Crossing, 263-4, 268-9; at Templeton's, 270-1, 272-3, 275-6, 281, 285, strength to 23 Oct, 276; at Eora Creek, 296; advances to Kokoda, 311, 312, 314; at Gorari, 321-2, 324-8, casualties, 327; at Wairopi, 331-2; casualties in Battle of Kokoda Track, 334n; advances to Gona, 418-19; at Gona,

AUSTRALIAN ARMY—continued
421-2, 429, 433, strength and casualties on relief, 435n; 2/40th, 12, 68, 599; 3rd, 227, 240, 244, 247, 334; at Ioribaiwa, 224, 229-31; at Imita, 245-6; advances to Templeton's Crossing, 263-4, 268-9, 271; at Templeton's Crossing, 272-6, 281-2, 284-5; advances to Oivi, 311-12, 316; at Oivi, 318, 319, 321, casualties, 319, 323; crosses Kumusi River, 333; casualties in Battle of Kokoda Track, 334n; at Gona, 421-2, 429, 431-3; relief of, 434; 7th, 69, 75; 8th, 69, 75; 9th, 44; at Milne Bay, 121, 160, 163, 173, 178-9, 512; 9th/49th, 44; 19th, 12, 75; 24th, 588; 25th, at Milne Bay, 121, 158, 160, 163-4, 171-3, 179, casualties, 166; 27th, 68; 36th, 227, 241, 244, 248, 497; in Sanananda operations, 413, 415, 498-501, 532, casualties, 501; strength, 512; on Amboga River, 518-19, 526; 39th, 45, 205, 244, 314, 334, 406, 448; arrives Port Moresby, 44, 65; at Port Moresby, 114, 241; officering of, 115; on Kokoda Track, 117, 122-3, 125-7, 592; at Kokoda, 127-9, 131, 133-6, 144-5; average age of members, 130; at Deniki, 130-2, 135, 137-8, 141; at Isurava, 142-3, 194, 198-9, 200-3, 207-10, 212-13, 228; withdraws, 220; casualties in Battle of Kokoda Track, 334; arrives Gona, 405, 434; in Gona area, 435-7, 439, 440-3, 445, 447, 497, casualties, 437, 444, 447n; on Sanananda Track, 501, 505, 512, 520, 527; proposed employment at Wau, 577-8; 43rd, 68; 49th, 45, 227, 244; at Port Moresby, 43-4, 45, 241; relieves 16 Bde, 405-6; on Sanananda Track, 408-11, 434, 497, 499, 500-1, 505-6, 512; relief of, 513; casualties, 527; proposed employment at Wau, 577; 53rd, 221, 226-7, 241-2, 244, 247, 334, 405n, 406; history of, 44-5, 201; in Alola-Isurava area, 141, 194, 199, 200-1, 203-5, 207, 210, 212, 215; calibre of, 202, 208-9, 228; withdrawn from battle, 211, 217; casualties in Battle of Kokoda Track, 334; amalgamated with 55th Bn, 405, 434; transfers members to 39th Bn, 448; 55th, 44, 121, 227, 240, 244, 406; amalgamates with 53rd Bn, 405, 434; 55th/53rd, 44, 512; arrives coastal area, 405-6; on Sanananda Track, 408, 410-11, 413, 434, 497, 499, 501; Gona area, 519; casualties, 500, 527; 61st, at Milne Bay, 121, 158, 160-2, 163-6, 171-3, 176-7, 179; casualties, 166; NGVR, 50, 54-5, 67; raising of, 42, 45-6; at Madang, 48-9; Lae-Salamaua area, 56-7, 59-61, 63, 79, 86, 534; equipment, 56; establishes headquarters on the Watut, 59; in Markham Valley, 61-2, 63, 87-8, 100-1, 536-7; achievements, 88-9; raids Salamaua, 90-3, 95-6; raids Heath's, 96-9; supply shortages, 103; physical condition, 104; at Mubo, 539; Papuan Infantry, 112, 139; role in Papuan fighting, 45, 334, 589-90; on north Papuan coast, 111, 114, 123-5; at Gorari, 126; at Kokoda, 127-8, 133, 137; composition of, 132; at Isurava, 141, 194; act as stretcher bearers, 212, 213, 214; patrol Kumusi River, 331; on Mambare River, 446
—MACHINE-GUN BATTALIONS, 33; 2/4th, 12, 68; 7th, 558; 19th Light Horse MG Regt, 68
—PIONEER BATTALIONS, 33; 2/1st, 240, 247, 261n, 334, 497, 577; at Ioribaiwa, 224, 227, 244; strength at Imita, 245; 2/4th, in Northern Territory, 12, 68n, 75; sets out for Koepang, 69
—AUSTRALIAN NEW GUINEA ADMINISTRATIVE UNIT, 101, 106n, 116, 129n, 131, 138, 158, 264, 346-7, 577; formation of, 43; at Buna, 124; on Kokoda Track, 127-8, 130-32, 141, 215, 223, 252, 265, 267; on Jaure Track, 242, 279; and COSC, 351; Wau-Salamaua area, 540, 587; on Bulldog Track, 580-1
—EDUCATION SERVICE, 625
—MEDICAL UNITS: 2/2 Fd Amb, at Wau, 570; 2/4 Fd Amb, 241; on Kokoda Track, 252, 277, 309, 316; air attack on, 399; 2/5 Fd Amb, 454; 2/6 Fd Amb, 241; on Kokoda Track, 212, 213, 214, 215, 277, 309; at Myola, 316; 14 Fd Amb, on Kokoda Track, 131-2, 213, 215, 277, 399; 2/9 Gen Hosp, 277
—MOVEMENT CONTROL, 351
—NEW GUINEA ADMINISTRATIVE UNIT, 43
—NORTHERN AUSTRALIA OBSERVER UNIT, 75, 611
—OVERSEAS BASE, MIDDLE EAST, 42
—PAPUAN ADMINISTRATIVE UNIT, 43
—PROVOST CORPS, at Port Moresby, 65; at Darwin, 71; at Brisbane, 625-6
—RECORDS: Central Army Records Office, 306n

AUSTRALIAN ARMY—*continued*
—ROYAL MILITARY COLLEGE, DUNTROON, 447, 538
—SCHOOLS: Guerilla Warfare, 85, 538; Jungle Warfare, Ceylon, 79; *No. 7 Trg Centre,* 85
—SERVICE CORPS, on Kokoda Track, 196, 276; forms Pack Transport Unit, 264; Combined Operational Services Command, 351; *1st Independent Light Horse Troop,* 116-7
—VOLUNTEER DEFENCE CORPS: strength and formation of, 2, 3-4; rifle deficiencies, 10; expansion of, 11; at Broome and Wyndham, 77
—WOMEN'S SERVICE, formation of, 2, 4; recruiting of, 11, 13
AUSTRALIAN GOVERNMENT, 8, 39, 45, 82, 620; issues call-up notices, 1-2; agrees to formation of VDC, 3; seeks appointment of American commander in Pacific, 15*n*, 16-17; lacks voice in determination of Allied policy, 16; agrees to retention of 9th Division in Middle East, 21, 118-9; retains right to refuse use of own forces, 23; allots forces to SWPA Command, 27; seeks reinforcement of SWPA, 31; invokes National Security Regulations in Papua and New Guinea, 116; abolishes 10th Division, 140*n*; anxious about Japanese advance in New Guinea, 310; and Timor, 598, 606
—ADVISORY WAR COUNCIL, 234, 240, 310, 607, 620*n*; General Blamey's address to, 236; orders preparation of plan for recapture of Timor, 619-20
—AIR, DEPARTMENT OF, 310
—ARMY, DEPARTMENT OF, 310; Minister for, 8, 25, 76
—CENTRAL WAR ROOM, 9
—CHIEFS OF STAFFS COMMITTEE, 9, 15, 43, 68, 77, 607, 619, 620; appreciations of, 11, 16, 44
—COMBINED OPERATIONS INTELLIGENCE CENTRE, 111
—DEFENCE DEPARTMENT, 620
—INFORMATION, DEPARTMENT OF, 625
—JOINT PLANNING COMMITTEE, 9
—MILITARY MISSION, WASHINGTON, 140*n*
—WAR CABINET, 30*n*, 234, 310; approves 6 months' recruit training system, 2; approves expenditure on uniforms for VDC, 3; authorises formation of AWAS, 4; appoints GOC-in-Chief, Home Forces, 4-5; lacks experience in military affairs, 5; home defence planning, 8-9; restricts distribution of munitions, 10; approves formation of Armoured Division, 10; orders limited militia call-up, 10-11; prevents enlistment of militiamen in AIF or RAAF, 13; approves proposals for Pacific War Council, 16; nominates General MacArthur as Supreme Commander, SWPA, 17-18; orders return of General Blamey to Australia, 25; appoints General Lavarack acting Commander-in-Chief, 25; evacuation of civil population of Territories, 41-2, 68; approves cessation of civil government in Papua, 43; requests retention of American fighters destined for ABDA at Darwin, 69; places Northern Territory under military control, 72
AUSTRALIAN LABOUR PARTY, 8
AUSTRALIAN NAVY, strength *Dec 1941*, 9; allotted to SWPA Command, 27; organisation at Port Moresby, 47, 66; at Darwin, 73, 74; in Coral Sea Battle, 80-2, 111; in Battle of Savo Island, 151-2; in Buna operations, 451-2; aids Sparrow Force, 605-6, 611-12, 617. *See also* COASTWATCHERS
—AUSTRALIAN SQUADRON, 149
—NAVY OFFICE, 39
AUSTRALIAN WAR MEMORIAL, 531*n*
AVENT, Pte W. A., 592
AVERY, Lt A. R., 206
AWALA (Map p. 114; Sketch p. 123), 110, 114, 123-5, 384, 419
AWALAMA DIVIDE (Map p. 114), 260
Ayanami, Japanese destroyer, 343

BAETCKE, Lt-Col Bernd G., 401, 402, 403, 404, 414
BAIRD, Lt A. C., 169, 176
BAIUNE POWER HOUSE (Sketch p. 52), 59, 587
BAIUNE RIVER (Sketch p. 52), 59
BAKER, Lt F. A., 504
BALDWIN, Hanson, W., 32
BALDWIN, Maj R. R., 598, 603, 605, 616, 618, 619, 621, 624
BALL, L-Cpl J. J., 181

BALLAM, Rfn G. E., 58
BALLAM'S (Sketches pp. 52, 549), 52, 546, 548, 550, 554, 561, 581-2, 584, 586
Ballarat, Australian corvette, 451
BALUS, New Guinea native, 88
BAMFORD, Lt-Col A. E., 73*n*
BANDA SEA (Map p. 37), 69
BARCLAY, Lt G. M., 230*n*
BARCLAY, Capt P., 291, 292, 293, 295, 298
BARE KNOLL, 559, 560
BARLOW, Lt E. D., 501
BARNES, WO2 D. S., 124, 128
BARNES, Lt-Col E., 183
BARNES, Maj-Gen Julian F., 24
BARNES, Sgt M. R., 282, 283
BARNET, Cpl E. H. MacD., 454, 457, 460, 469, 470
BARNETT, Maj A., 263, 264
BARNETT, Lt G. W., 560
Barossa, Australian ship, 70
Barry Commission, Report of, 44*n*
BASABUA (Map p. 370; Sketch p. 123), 144, 228, 416, 427, 433, 530
BATAAN PENINSULA (Map p. 37; Sketch p. 35), 16, 20, 35, 36; capture of, 34
BATCHELOR (Sketch p. 7), 69
BATCHELOR, Lt O. H., 506
BATCHELOR'S PERIMETER, 506
BATES, Maj C. D., 48
BATHURST, NSW, 351*n*
BATHURST ISLAND (Sketches pp. 7, 612), 69, 70, 71, 616
BAUCAU (Sketch p. 599), 613
BAUM, Hellmuth, 50-1
BAYLIS, Maj C. F. W., 282, 283, 284, 285
BAYONETS, American employment of, 338, 380; Australian employment of, 327, 401, 430, 550; Japanese employment of, 172, 328, 422
BEAN, C. E. W., 626*n*
BEAR, Lt L. A., 206
BEASSO (Sketch p. 599), 613
BEAT HITLER FIRST POLICY, 188, 190
BEAVER, Lt-Col Chester M. (Plate p. 307), 379, 454, 463, 464, 465, 468, 470, 471
BEAZLEY, Capt E. T., 322, 323, 418, 420, 421
BECKETT, Capt J. S., 230, 231, 272, 273, 274
BECO (Sketch p. 599), 602, 607, 608, 609
BELL, Pte A., 596
BELL, Lt F. D., 220, 221, 596
BELMER, Capt R. S., 360, 364, 373
BENA BENA (Map p. 34), 65, 554*n*
BENGAL, BAY OF (Map p. 37; Sketch p. 78), 79, 84
BENNETT, Maj A. C., 548, 550, 563, 566, 567, 568
BENNETT, Lt-Gen H. Gordon, 3*n*, 25, 27, 508
BENNIE, Lt J. S., 428
BENSON, Capt A. M., 456, 458, 461, 462, 463, 464, 466
BENSON, Rev James, 123, 139, 595
BERRYMAN, Lt-Gen Sir Frank, 469, 510, 511, 516, 517, 533, 565, 625; becomes DCGS, 244*n*
BESSELL-BROWNE, Brig-Gen A. J., 3*n*
BEST, Capt E. W., 431
BETANO (Sketch p. 612), 611, 613, 617, 618, 620
BEWANI MOUNTAINS (Map p. 34), 47
BEWAPI CREEK (Sketch p. 87), 97, 99
BICKS, Maj C. H., 158, 161, 162, 163, 164, 165, 166, 167, 176, 177
BICYCLES, used by Japanese in New Guinea, 124
BIDSTRUP, Capt M. L., 132, 133, 134, 135, 137, 138, 141, 203, 436, 437, 440, 444, 445
BIERWIRTH, Lt-Gen R., 73*n*
BIG WAU CREEK (Sketch p. 556), 554, 555, 558
BIRDUM (Sketch p. 7), 68, 72, 75
BIRRELL, Sgt D., 564
BISMARCK ARCHIPELAGO (Map p. 34), 22
BISMARCK SEA, BATTLE OF, 582-3
BISSET, Capt S. Y., 211, 213, 218, 426, 431, 442
BISSET, Lt T. H., 207, 208
BITMEAD, WO2 H. F., 124, 128, 138, 139
BITOI RIVER (Map p. 585; Sketches pp. 52, 541), 53, 539, 540, 541, 546, 547, 573, 586
BLACK, Capt A. N., 314
BLACK, Lt-Col J. R., 50
BLACK CAT CREEK (Sketch p. 552), 53, 546, 551, 557, 562, 563, 568, 569, 570, 573
BLACK CAT MINE (Map p. 585; Sketch p. 552), 546, 547, 548, 551, 552, 553, 555, 557, 560, 562, 563, 568, 571, 572, 573, 583
BLACK CAT TRACK (Sketch p. 52), 53, 547, 548, 552, 565, 573, 574

INDEX

BLACKWELL, S-Sgt A. R., 315, 317
BLAIN, Lt R. N., 282, 283
BLAINEY, Capt G. C., 373
BLAIR, Pte L. A., 592
BLAKE, Maj-Gen D. V. J., 72
BLAKE'S CAMP (Sketch p. 535), 107, 536
BLAKISTON, Capt C. S., 293, 294, 326
BLAMEY, Capt J. M., 283, 318, 389, 392, 394, 395, 397, 398, 400
BLAMEY, Field Marshal Sir Thomas (Plates pp. 210, 306), 13, 29, 31, 65n, 89, 120n, 122, 183, 187, 198, 226, 244, 245, 247, 259, 262, 275n, 277, 278, 311, 350, 359, 385, 416, 449, 450, 497, 509, 538, 546, 565, 575, 576, 577, 583, 611, 615n, 625; commands Allied Land Forces SWPA, 24; reorganises Australian Army, 25-7, 84, 140n; experience compared to General MacArthur's, 28; plans minor offensive against Lae and Salamaua, 67; reinforcement of New Guinea, 82, 111; employment of Indep Coys, 86; outlines MacArthur's plan for defence of Australia, 112n; orders that Kokoda area be secured, 114; on conduct of Milne Bay operations, 173-4, 186; relations with General MacArthur, 174, 510; seeks additional supply aircraft, 197; visits New Guinea, 234, takes command in, 235-6; relieves General Rowell, 236-40; estimates supply requirements New Guinea Force, 260; his signals to General Allen, 269, 274, 290-1, 299; replaces General Allen, 307; comments on Mr Forde's report, 310; plans offensive against Lae and Salamaua, 310, 578; addresses 21 Bde at Koitaki, 334n; criticises American infantry at Buna, 371; seeks return of 9th Division, 450; orders 18th Brigade to Buna, 451; returns to Australia, 516n; foresees Japanese threat to Wau, 544-5; orders development of Bulldog Road, 578-9; estimate of, 591; on Timor operations, 606, 620; proposes measures for improving relations between Australian and American forces, 626-7
BLEZARD, Lt J. W. W., 562
BLOCH, Capt Edmund C., 493
BLOODY RIDGE, 154, 155
BLOOMFIELD, Cpl C. A., 438, 439
BLUNDELL, Capt P. L., 275
BOAG, Capt T. C., 230, 231, 263, 274, 275
BOASE, Lt-Gen A. J., 77-8
BOATS, see LANDING CRAFT
BOBDUBI (Map p. 585; Sketch p. 52), 105, 583, 587, 588
BOBONARO (Sketch p. 599), 598, 607, 608, 609
BOB'S CAMP (Map p. 585; Sketches pp. 52, 87), 89, 90, 102, 104, 539
BODDINGTON, Lt W. G., 206
BODY, Lt E. M., 294
BOEREM, Col Richard D., 395, 398, 399, 401, 402, 403, 404, 414, 501
BOERS, THE, 56, 84, 624
BOER WAR, 607
BOFU (Map p. 34; Sketch p. 353), 353, 354, 358
BOGADJIM (Map p. 34), 49, 65
BOGIA (Map p. 34), 50
BOICE, Capt William F., 380, 487
BOISI (Sketch p. 52), 106n
BOLAND, Cpl J. W., 138
BOMANA AIRFIELD (Map p. 114), 67
BOND, Maj George, 395, 398, 401
BOOBY TRAPS, *Australian*, 225, 536, 539, 560, 564; *Japanese*, 537, 548
BOOTH, Sgt R. D., 97-8, 536
BOOTLESS INLET (Map p. 114), 117
BOREO (Map p. 370; Sketch p. 537), 358, 375
BORNEO (Map p. 19), 144
BOSGARD, Capt A. K., 389, 392, 394, 395, 397, 400
BOSTOCK, Pte H. C., 200
BOTTCHER, Capt Herman J. F., 378, 379, 380, 491
BOUCHER, Maj M. C. W., 178, 180
BOUGAINVILLE (Map p. 34; Sketches pp. 81, 148), 39, 40, 63, 259; Japanese invasion of, 64; coastwatchers on, 151
BOUGHTON, Cpl C. G., 515-16
BOULTON, WO2 W. S., 182
BOWEN, Capt G. T., 540, 543
BOWEN, Pte L. J., 206
BOWERMAN, Lt W. P., 483
BOYAN, Capt R. H., 50
BOYER, Maj K. M., 397, 398, 400

BOYER, R. J. F., 625
BOYLAND, Capt G., 598, 599, 600, 603, 608, 609, 610, 611, 612, 613
BOYS, L-Sgt F. R., 426, 592
BRADFORD, Capt Byron B., 490-2
BRADLEY, Capt H. A., 586
BRADLEY, Col J. Sladen, 491-2
BRAGG, Lt William W., 493-4
BRAIN, W Cdr L. J., 77
BRANNELLY, L-Sgt T. A. V., 57
BRAY, Tpr A. G., 459, 460
BRENCHLEY, Miss Margery, 139n
BRETT, Lt-Gen George H., 86; commands American forces in Australia, 14, 16-17; his estimate of General MacArthur, 20; commands Allied Air Forces, 24
BREWER, Cpl C. B., 407
BREWER, Lt F. N. T., 573
BREWER, Capt F. P., 117, 127, 129, 133
BRIDGES, Wau-Bulolo area, 59, 538; at Milne Bay, 157; at Wairopi, 331-2; at Entrance Creek, 488
BRIGHT, S-Sgt W. R., 407
BRINKLEY, Capt P. L., 325
BRISBANE (Sketch p. 7), 7, 8, 11, 14, 27, 38, 80, 111, 193, 234, 310, 351, 577, 611; General MacArthur's headquarters established at, 120; clashes between American and Australian troops at, 625
"BRISBANE LINE", 6-8, 27, 112n
BRITAIN, GREAT 10, 24, 76, 190, 191; dispatch of Australian rifles to, 2; allotment of Australian anti-tank guns to, 10; sets up machinery for strategical command and control of Allied forces, 15-16; proclaims protectorate over Papua, 40; Beat Hitler first policy, 188; and reinforcement of Far East, 189; American ground strength in, 190; strategic relationship with Australia, 591
BRITISH ARMY, 1, 31, 73, 85; in Burma, 79, 187n, 191; in South African War, 84; reinforcements for Australia sought, 118
—ARMIES: *Eighth*, 118
—ARMOUR: promised diversion of division to Australia in event of invasion, 24; *7 Armd Bde*, 29, 191
—DIVISIONS: *70th*, 77, 118
—COMMANDO UNITS AND INDEPENDENT COMPANIES: formation of, 85; *No. 11 Commando*, 85
BRITISH GOVERNMENT, seeks retention of 9th Division in Middle East, 21; represented on Pacific War Council 21; promises aid to Australia in event of invasion, 24; agrees to honour orders for supplies to Timor, 598
—AIR MINISTRY, 4
—CHIEFS OF STAFFS, 15, 118
—DOMINIONS OFFICE, 16, 606
—WAR CABINET, Australia represented on, 16
—WAR OFFICE, 4
British Motorist, British ship, 70
BRITISH NAVY, 235; and reinforcement of Pacific Ocean, 189
—EASTERN FLEET, 24, 84, 189, 190; weakness of, 79
—MARINES, ROYAL, 85, 147
BRITISH PHOSPHATE COMMISSION, 39
BRITISH SOLOMON ISLANDS; see SOLOMON ISLANDS
BROADHURST, Capt D. K., 623
BROCK, Capt B., 302, 317, 318
BROCKSOPP, Maj J. E., 167, 168, 169, 170, 346, 347
Bronzewing, Australian lugger, 161, 162-3, 165
BROOME (Sketch p. 7), Japanese air attacks on, 1, 76-7
Broome, Australian corvette, 451
BROWN, Capt C. K., 286, 289, 291
BROWN, Pte D. R., 597
BROWN, WO2 F. J., 559, 560, 561
BROWN, Pte J. A., 426
BROWN, Lt K. R., 184
BROWN, Maj M. J., 167, 169, 469, 470, 471, 473-4
BROWN, Vice-Admiral Wilson, 67
BROWN RIVER (Map p. 114; Sketch p. 593), 108, 227, 241, 242, 597
BRUMMITT, Lt-Col D. W., 215
BRYCE, Capt J. K., 405n, 408, 409, 411
BUANG MOUNTAINS (Map p. 585; Sketch p. 52), 53, 105
BUANG RIVER (Map p. 585; Sketch p. 52), 53, 59
Buchanan, American destroyer, 340
BUCHECKER, Sgt A. V., 203
BUCKLER, Lt-Col S. H., 202, 204, 206, 207, 211, 320n, 592, 593, 594

638 INDEX

BUDDLE, Lt-Col B. H., 331
BUIBAINING (Map p. 585; Sketch p. 549), 546, 547, 548, 551, 561, 562, 572, 573, 574, 584, 586
BUIN (Map p. 34; Sketch p. 148), 64, 336, 339, 529
BUISAVAL RIVER (Map p. 585; Sketches pp. 52, 541), 53, 539
BUISAVAL TRACK (Map p. 585; Sketches pp. 52, 541), 52, 53, 56, 540, 546, 547, 548, 557, 558, 560, 561-2, 568, 575
BUKA ISLAND (Map p. 34; Sketch p. 81), 39, 63, 64
BUKA PASSAGE (Map p. 34), 63, 65; Japanese occupy, 64
BULLDOG (Map p. 34; Sketches pp. 51, 579), 50, 51, 58, 90, 102, 578, 580, 581
BULLDOG TRACK (Sketch p. 579), 62, 103, 106, 107, 534, 544; development of, 536, 579-81
BULOLO (Map p. 34; Sketches pp. 51, 52), 46, 53, 55, 56, 63, 90, 104, 111, 547, 548, 572, 582, 584, 588; Japanese air raids on, 39, 54, 100; demolitions at, 59, 106; airstrip at, 578
BULOLO GOLD DREDGING COMPANY, 53, 59, 60
BULOLO RIVER (Map p. 585; Sketches pp. 51, 579), 52, 53, 55, 59, 538, 551, 557, 558, 563, 566, 567, 568, 571, 573, 576, 580
BULOLO VALLEY, 52, 53, 62, 89, 90, 101, 105, 106, 107, 534, 538, 539, 544, 545, 546, 565, 572, 576, 577, 581, 584, 590; gold production, 41, Japanese threat to, 88, 100; scorching of, 106-7, 534-6; defence plans, 578
BULWA (Map p. 585; Sketch p. 52), 53, 59, 89, 90, 105, 107, 538, 577, 583, 584; demolitions at, 106; airfield at, 578
BUNA (Map p. 370; Sketch p. 123), 45, 108, 110, 111, 114, 124, 125, 139, 143, 158, 184, 185, 187, 194, 228, 233, 242, 243, 260, 262, 290, 305, 314, 321, 332, 346, 351, 352, 355, 386, 394, 397, 401, 403, 413, 417, 420, 424, 448, 449, 450, 509, 510, 511, 512, 513, 514, 516, 527, 528, 530, 531, 532, 534, 535, 545, 546, 575, 583, 595, 620; proposed establishment of Allied base at, 120, forestalled by Japanese landings, 122-3; Japanese strength and reinforcement of, 145, 314, 358, 383, 385, 485; Japanese withdrawal on, 186, 304; Allied advance on, 260, 277, 278-9, 337, 345, 353-4; American operations at, 356-83, 486-96; artillery and tank reinforcement of, 363; Japanese defences at, 370; Allied strength and casualties at, 371, 484, 495-6, 577; capture of, 382; proposed seaborne landings at, 451; 18th Brigade operations at, 454-85; Australian casualties at, 484; Japanese account, 484-5; necessity for final reduction examined, 531-3; see also ENDAIADERE, CAPE; NEW STRIP; OLD STRIP
BUNA AIRFIELDS, 383; see also OLD STRIP; NEW STRIP
BUNA GOVERNMENT GARDENS (Sketch p. 486), 487-8, 490, 493, 509
BUNA GOVERNMENT STATION (Map p. 370; Sketch p. 486), 356, 361, 378-83, 451, 454, 470, 486, 487-90, 492-5, 497; Japanese strength at, 485; Japanese casualties at, 496
BURKE, Lt J. K., 315
BURKE, Pte J. T., 251, 252
BURMA (Map p. 37; Sketch p. 78), 16, 24, 27, 29, 72, 77, 79, 191, 192, 575; British retreat in, 1, 79, 118; proposed diversion of AIF to, 15, 590; morale of army uplifted by Australian victory at Milne Bay, 187n
BURMA ROAD, 191
BURNS, Sgt J. H., 251, 252
BURR, Sgt Elmer J., 489
BURRELL, Lt-Col J. C., 298, 299, 302, 326, 328, 387, 388, 403
BURRIDGE, Lt J. C., 600, 610, 611
BURSTON, Maj-Gen S. R., 237
BUSAMA (Map p. 585; Sketch p. 52), 100, 105, 106, 107, 534
BUTIBUM (Sketch p. 87), 88
BUTLER, Capt C. G. D., 211, 425, 426, 594
BUTLER, L-Cpl N., 410
BUTLER, Maj W. G., 271, 272, 323
BUTTROSE, Brig A. W., 230, 231, 233, 246, 264, 268, 270, 271, 272, 273, 274, 275, 312, 321, 324, 331, 332, 418, 419, 421, 422; commands 2/33 Bn, 229
BUTU (Sketch p. 60), 91, 93, 94, 96
BUYAWIM RIVER (Map p. 585; Sketch p. 52), 53, 586
BYERS, Brig-Gen Clovis E., 371, 372, 383, 451; commands 32nd Division, 382
BYNOE BAY (Sketch p. 7), 75

CADDY, Lt E. R., 428
CAHILL, Pte W. L., 597
CAILACO (Sketch p. 599), 603
CAIRNS (Sketch p. 7), 11, 72, 81
CAIRNS, Capt T. F., 201, 202, 203, 204
CAIRO, 25
CALING, WO2 G. J., 392
CALLAGHAN, Rear-Admiral Daniel J., 340, 341, 342, 345
CALLINAN, Lt-Col B. J., 599, 600, 601, 603n, 604, 608, 609, 611, 614, 615, 617, 618, 619, 620, 621; commands 2/2 Indep Coy, 605, Sparrow Force, 616
CAMBRIDGE, Sgt C. B., 455, 460
CAMERON, Lt-Col A. G., 57, 130, 133, 134, 136-7, 138, 141, 142, 196, 210, 229, 230, 263, 264, 269, 273, 275, 276, 421, 431, 433; commands Maroubra Force, 132, 53 Bn, 209, 3 Bn, 227
CAMERON, Pte A. J., 377
CAMERON, Capt L. A., 550, 567
CAMERON, Lt L. G., 571
CAMERON, Maj R. W. C., 203, 204, 205, 206, 207, 208, 211, 333, 418, 419, 432
CAMERON'S SPRINGS (Sketch p. 160), 161
CAMPBELL, Capt K. C., 163, 164, 166, 176
CAMPBELL, Capt R. P., 205, 212
CAMP DIDDY (Map p. 585; Sketches pp. 52, 87), 59, 62, 87, 88, 89, 97, 99
CANADA, 17; represented on Pacific War Council, 21
CANBERRA (Sketch p. 7), 310
Canberra, Australian cruiser, 151, 152
CANET, Maj-Gen L. G., 119
CANNIBALISM, 271, 523, 526, 527
CANTEENS, at Wau, 104
CANTON (Map p. 37), 576
CAPETOWN, 25
CAPE YORK PENINSULA (Sketch p. 7), 121, 336
CAPP, Lt C., 508
CARDY, Lt J. A., 600
CARLSON, Sgt L. T. W., 446, 447
CARLYON, Lt-Col N. D., 236, 335n
CARO, Lt-Col A. E., 208, 215, 217, 218, 220, 221-22, 223, 224, 430, 431, 434, 435, 436; commands 2/16 Bn, 195
CAROLA HAVEN (Map p. 34), 64
CAROLINE ISLANDS (Map p. 19), 336
CARPENTARIA, GULF OF (Sketch p. 7), 75
CARRIER, Col Edmund J., 354, 355, 358, 359, 360, 364, 367, 369, 373, 374, 376, 378
CARRIERS, BREN, at Buna, 363, 369, 375-6
CARRIERS, NATIVE, 58, 103, 131, 140, 208, 312, 330, 357, 396, 438, 536, 540, 542, 580, 586, 589; in Salamaua raid, 91; desertion by, 100, 104, 107, 217, 248; on Kokoda Track, 115, 117, 127-8, 130, 141, 196-8, 233, 260-2, 264, 274, 290-1, 308-9; recruitment of, 116, 264-5; medical care of, 132; with Japanese forces, 144; as stretcher bearers, 213, 214, 215, 231, 249, 265, 571; on Jaure Track, 279; with Kanga Force, 536, 548, 561
CARSON, Sgt A. L., 289
CARSON, Sgt R. G. (Plate p. 498), 474, 481
"CARSON'S GUN" (Plate p. 498), 474, 475, 481
CARTER, Sgt S. R., 558
CASEY, Brig-Gen Hugh J., 28n, 141, 239
Castlemaine, Australian corvette, 617
CASUALTIES: in first Darwin raid, 71; in Broome raid, 77. *American*: on Corregidor, 36; on Tulagi, 150; on Guadalcanal, 152, 155, 255-6, 257, 339, 528, 529; at Milne Bay, 185; in *South Dakota*, 343; at Buna, 371, 382, 495; at Sanananda, 415, 525, 526, 527; at Tarakena, 527; total in Papua, 531. *Australian*: on Kokoda Track, 244, 263; totals 334-5; *39 Bn*, 129; *53 Bn*, 204; *2/14 Bn*, 205, 208, 211; *2/16 Bn*, 206; *2/27 Bn*, 252; *21 Bde*, 252; *25 Bde*, 274, 276, 230; *2/2 Bn*, 284-5; *2/3 Bn*, 286, 298, 302, 303; *2/1 Bn*, 287, 295; *16 Bde*, 306, 322; treatment and evacuation of, 132, 212-15, 265 276-7, 309, 316-17, 399; at Milne Bay, 185, 189; *61 Bn*, 166; *25 Bn*, 266; *2/10 Bn*, 171; *2/12 Bn*, 178, 184, 185; *2/9 Bn*, 183, 185; at Oivi-Gorari: *16 Bde*, 319; *2/3 Bn* 319; *2/31 Bn*, 322, 323, 327, 329, 330; *3 Bn*, 323; *2/25 Bn*, 323; *25 Bde*, 327; on Goodenough Island, 348, 349; at Buna-Sanananda-Gona, 355, 393-4, 407n, 411, 421, 427, 429, 430, 431, 433, 434, 437, 442, 444, 447, 462, 466, 468, 484, 495, 500, 501, 507, 509, 515, 516, 520, 521, 522, 524, 527; affect planning, 433; at MDS Soputa, 399; totals in Papua, 531; in Kanga Force operations,

INDEX 639

CASUALTIES—continued
557, 570, 572. *Japanese*: at Salamaua, 96; at Heath's, 99; on Guadalcanal, 152, 155, 255, 257, 339, 529; at Milne Bay, 178, 185, 186; on Kokoda Track, 207, 208, 219, 220, 244, 303; at Gorari, 327, 329, 331; on Goodenough Island, 349; in Buna-Gona area, 446, 485, 496, 520, 522, 531; in operations against Kanga Force, 537, 568, 570, 576; in Timor, 604
CATTERNS, Maj B. W. T., 285, 286, 287, 288, 289, 294, 295, 297, 299, 300, 302, 326, 387, 388, 389, 390, 391, 392, 393, 394, 402, 403
CAUCASUS, THE, 191
CAVANAUGH, Lt J. (Plate p. 130), 60, 61, 92, 93
CEBU (Sketch p. 35), 36
CENTRAL AUSTRALIAN RAILWAY, 72
CENTRAL PACIFIC AREA (Map p. 19), 21
CENTRAL RANGE (Map p. 34), 47, 49
CENTRE CAMP (Sketch p. 579), 579
CEYLON (Sketch p. 78), 26, 79, 226, 244, 349; diversion of AIF to, 21; Japanese threat to, 77-9; AIF in, 118, 119, 280
CHAFFEY, Capt W. A., 101
CHAGNON, Lt Louis A., 511, 528
CHALK, Capt J. A., 124, 125
CHALLEN, Lt-Col H. B., 193, 222, 224, 332, 424, 425, 426, 427, 429, 430, 431, 433, 434, 438, 439, 442, 445, 505; commands 2/14 Bn, 223
CHALMERS, Lt-Col F. R., 38-9
CHAMBERLAIN, John, 235n
CHAMBERLIN, Brig-Gen Stephen J., 28n, 176
CHAMPION, Capt F. A., 111, 123
CHAUVEL, General Sir Harry, 3n
CHENHALL, Lt-Col F. N., 277, 309, 316
Chester, American cruiser, 80
CHESWORTH, Tpr G., 504-5
CHIANG KAI-SHEK, Generalissimo, 192
Chicago, American cruiser, 80, 152
CHILTON, Brig F. O., 159
CHINA, 16, 17, 21, 118, 190, 192, 383
Chinampa, motor vessel, 623n
CHINA STRAIT (Map p. 156), 155
CHINESE, THE, 58, 92, 576
CHINESE ARMY, in Burma, 191; strength in India, 192
CHISHOLM, Maj J., 599
Chocolate and Green, 303n, 386n, 406n
Chokai, Japanese cruiser, 152, 342
CHRISTENSEN, Pte J. C., 466
Christian Science Monitor, 625
CHRISTIE, Col Albert F., 36, 38
CHRISTMAS ISLAND, 338
CHURCH, Sgt J. E., 455, 460, 461, 469, 470
CHURCHILL, Rt Hon Sir Winston, 69, 118n, 190; confers with President Roosevelt, 14, 17; urges diversion of Australians to Burma, 15, 590; suggests dispatch of second American division to Australia, 23; refuses to divert British divisions to Australia, 24; holds Australian brigades in Ceylon, 118, 280; on British reinforcement of Far East, 189
CHYNOWETH, Brig-Gen Bradford G., 36, 38
CIDDOR, Lt M. M., 564
CLARK, Corporal, 62
CLARK, Cpl G. K., 218
CLARKE, Lt D. R., 201, 202
CLARKE, Capt D. S. (Plate p. 466), 483, 521
CLARKE, Brig D. W., 85n
CLARKE, Capt E. R., 426
CLARKE, Cpl M. T., 209-10
CLARKSON, Lt-Col Gordon M., 454, 458, 463, 465, 468, 470, 471, 476, 477
CLEMENS, Capt Martin, 152
CLEMENTS, Lt J. G., 206, 223, 426
CLIVAZ, Rev Father, 39
CLONCURRY (Sketch p. 7), 81, 121, 140
CLOTHING, of infantry in Owen Stanleys, 229, 281
CLOWES, Lt-Gen C. A. (Plate p. 147), 30, 173, 175, 176, 179, 180, 183, 184, 185, 239, 363, 369, 375, 418; commands 1 Aust Div, 13, 26; commands Milne Force, 159-160, 161; problems of, 166-7; tactics at Milne Bay, 174, orders attack along north shore, 177, conduct of operations examined, 186-7; ordered to send force to Wanigela, 237
CLOWES, Capt T. M., 231, 232, 270, 271, 272, 324, 419
COASTWATCHERS, 11, 39, 51, 54, 60, 63, 64, 65, 77, 80, 139, 151, 161, 446
COBB, Lt F. P., 559

COBB, Capt H. W. A., 502, 503, 504, 506
COCONUT GROVE (Sketches pp. 370, 486), 361, 371, 379, 380, 382, 487; captured, 383
COEN (Sketch p. 7), 111
COKER, Lt James T., 511
Colac, Australian corvette, 451
COLE, Lt R., 600
COLLINGWOOD BAY (Map p. 34), 161
COLOMBO (Sketch p. 78), 78, 119
COLOUR PATCHES, 68n
COMBINED CHIEFS OF STAFF COMMITTEE, 10, 15, 17, 21, 22; Australia not represented on, 16
COMBINED DEFENCE HEADQUARTERS, 9
COMBINED OPERATIONAL SERVICES COMMAND, role and work in New Guinea, 349-51
COMBINED OPERATIONS INTELLIGENCE CENTRE, 9
COMMANDOS, origins of, 84-5; possible value in Owen Stanleys, 332
COMMUNIQUÉS, of GHQ SWPA, 22, 225-6, 248
CONDON, Sgt J., 184
CONFERENCES, 1937 Imperial, 4
CONNELL, Cpl E. D., 503-4
CONNELL, Maj J. F., 289
CONRAN, Col H. M., 44
CONROY, Lt-Col T. M., 586
CONSCRIPTION, Australian prejudice against, 31; in America, 32
COOK, Cpl F. T., 271n
COOK, Lt-Col F. W., 519, 520, 521, 522
COOKTOWN (Sketch p. 7), 111
COOPER, Lt-Col G. D. T., 208, 220, 221, 222, 223 248, 249, 250, 251, 427, 428, 430, 431, 432
COOTE, Capt F. G., 499
COPEMAN, Maj J., 298
COPP, Maj W. D.; *see* CULLEN, H. D.
COPPOCK, Tpr M. G., 508n
CORAL SEA, THE (Map p. 37; Sketch p. 81), 83, 113, 189, 255; battle of, 83, 89, 111, 112, 120, 590
Cornwall, British cruiser, 78
CORREGIDOR (Sketch p. 35), 20, 34-38, 79; surrenders, 36, 38
COWEY, S-Sgt J. P., 136
COX, Capt D. L., 263, 264, 268
COX, Brig G. S., 291, 292, 320
COX, Lt W. P., 206
COY, Sgt J. W., 426
COYLE, Capt G., 284
CRACE, Admiral Sir John, 80
CRAVEN, W. F., and CATE, J. L., 582n
CRAWFORD, Lt H. W., 133
CRETE, 74, 147, 194, 280, 544
CROMBIE, Capt W. M., 271, 323, 327
CRONK, Capt Jefferson R., 493, 494, 495
CROW, Lt John W., 359
CROWL, P. A., 188n
CRUTCHLEY, Admiral Sir Victor, 149, 151
CRYSTAL CREEK (Sketches pp. 535, 549), 107, 536, 550, 551, 554, 557, 558, 566, 567, 568, 569, 572, 573, 576, 584
CULLEN, Maj H. D., 268, 270
CULLEN, Brig P. A., 276, 281, 285, 287, 289, 290, 291, 292, 294, 295, 296-7, 298, 299, 300, 307, 311, 316, 319, 320, 321, 324, 325, 326, 328, 329, 386, 388, 389, 393; commands 2/1 Bn, 275; estimate of, 290
CUMING, Capt J. C., 427, 428, 430
CUMMINGS, Col C. J., 180, 181, 182, 183, 184, 456, 458, 462, 463, 464, 465, 466, 467
CUNNINGHAM, Rev C. W. J., 300
CURRIE, WO2 J. W., 60, 61, 91, 93, 95
CURTIN, Rt Hon John, 11, 21, 25, 82, 188, 234, 236, 237, 242, 247, 248, 449, 591, 620, 626; expresses Australian preference for American Commander in Pacific, 15n; refuses to allow diversion of Australians to Burma, 15; nominates General MacArthur as Supreme Commander SWPA, 17-18; relations with MacArthur, 23; seeks reinforcement of SWPA, 23-4, 29; informs General Blamey of appointment as C-in-C AMF, 25; allots all combat sections of Australian Defence Forces to SWPA Command, 27; requests diversion of AIF to Australia, 69; on MacArthur's strategy for defence of Australia, 112n; offers 16th and 17th Bdes to garrison Ceylon, 118; requests diversion of British division to Australia, 118; asks Churchill plans for naval force in Pacific, 189; orders Blamey to take command in New Guinea, 235; on Blamey-Rowell controversy, 239-40

CURTIS, Capt O. A., 482, 516, 521
CURTISS, Lt G. E., 453, 455, 456, 460, 461
CYPRUS, 497

DALBY, Capt H., 138, 142, 203, 440, 445
DAL PONTE, Lt-Col Peter L., 413, 414
DALY RIVER (Sketches pp. 7, 612), 68, 75, 611
DAMES, Capt William H., 489, 490, 492, 493, 494, 495
DANIELS, Lt A. N. T., 401
DARU (Map p. 34), 47, 49
DARWIN (Map p. 37; Sketches pp. 7, 612), 8, 10, 11, 17, 27, 44, 73, 77, 80, 112n, 159, 191, 244, 247, 351n, 422, 598, 601, 602, 605, 606, 611, 615, 616, 617, 621, 622, 623; Area Combined Headquarters established at, 9; reinforcement of, 10, 68-9; first air raid on, 69-72, other raids, 75-6, 613n; supply of, 72; strength of forces, training and deployment, 73-5
DARWIN FORTRESS, 74; anti-aircraft defence of, 73n
DAVAO (Map p. 37; Sketch p. 35), 36, 114, 143
DAVIES, Cpl F. G., 377
DAVIES, Capt J. B., 215
DAVIS, Lt A. J., 202-3, 211
DAVIS, Sgt E. J., 506
DAVIS, Sgt R. J., 172
DAVIS, L-Cpl V. C., 430
DAWSON, Lt-Col L. E., 398
DAY, Lt P. R. H., 60
DEAN, Capt A. C., 126, 130, 133, 134, 145
DEFENCE, 1, of Australian east coast area, 6-8
Defence Act, 1-2, 12
DE GRAAF, Col George, 374, 382
DELLACA, Lt N. C., 411
DEMOLITIONS, at Salamaua, 55; at Lae, 57; in Wau-Bulolo Valley, 59, 106-7; at Tulagi, 80; Salamaua raid, 94; at Ongahambo, 125; in Owen Stanleys, 219, 305; on Guadalcanal, 339; on Timor, 607
DENIKI (Maps pp. 114, 313; Sketches pp. 123, 128), 110, 127, 128, 131-4, 136-8, 142, 145, 199-201, 204, 228-9, 312, 314; Australian withdrawal to, 129-30; Japanese attack on, 135
DENNIS, Spr M., 617
D'ENTRECASTEAUX ISLANDS (Map p. 34; Sketch p. 346), 122, 158, 349
DERBY (Sketch p. 7), air attack on, 77
DESERTION, by native soldiers, 125
DE SOUSA SANTOS, Antonio Policarpe, 599, 601, 623
DE VANTIER, Lt R., 182, 458, 461
DEXTER, Maj D. St A., 605, 608, 609, 610, 611, 612, 613, 624
DEXTER, Lt-Col W. R., 545, 546, 547, 572, 584, 588
DICKENSON, Capt H. E., 201, 202, 204, 205, 206, 207, 211
DILI (Sketches pp. 599, 612), 598, 600, 602, 603, 604, 605, 606, 607, 608, 610, 611, 613, 614, 615, 617, 619, 622
DILI AIRFIELD, 597
DILLER, Col LeGrande A., 28n
DILOR RIVER (Sketch p. 599), 623
DJURA CREEK (Sketches pp. 173, 179), 171
DOBBS, Lt-Col J. G. (Plate p. 307), 165, 166, 167, 169, 171, 465, 468, 469, 471, 472, 473, 476, 477, 478, 480, 481, 483, 514; commands 2/10 Bn, 160
DOBERER, Lt F. W., 90, 96, 97, 98, 99
DOBODURA (Map p. 370; Sketches pp. 353, 357), 139, 354, 355, 356, 358, 363, 365, 367, 368, 371, 372, 375, 381, 382, 405, 451, 454, 474, 518; development of, 532, 589
DODD, Lt-Col R. W. P., 245
DOE, Maj-Gen Jens A., 510, 513, 518, 524, 525-6
DOIG, Capt C. D., 613, 617
Don Isidro, Filipino ship, 71
DONNAN, Capt M. G. F., 271
DONNELLY, Capt V. J., 466
DORAN, L-Sgt J., 289
DORAN, WO2 R. N., 558
DOROBISOLO (Map p. 34; Sketch p. 593), 242, 260, 593, 594
Dorsetshire, British cruiser, 78
DOUGHERTY, Maj-Gen I. N., 423, 424, 425, 427, 430, 431, 433, 434, 435, 438, 439, 440, 442, 445, 501, 508; commands 23 Bde, 74; comments on General Blamey's address to 21 Bde, 334n; takes command 21 Bde, 442; allotted role on Sanananda Track, 505
DOUGHERTY, Lt R. H., 425, 427, 438, 439, 442, 444
DOUGHTIE, 2nd-Lt James E., 468
DOUGLAS, Maj C. D., 499, 500

DOWD, Cpl H. P., 570
DOWER, Lt A. R., 614
DOWNES, Pte D. D., 274
DOYLE, W. H., 39
DRAKEFORD, Hon A. S., 310
DRYSDALE, Lt W., 93, 95, 96, 537
DUALI (Map p. 585), 586
DUFFY, Maj D. G., 213
DUFFY, Maj J. W., 550, 551, 557
DULLARD, Lt E. A., 245
DUNBAR, Lt-Col C. C., 230, 231, 246, 269; commands 2/31 Bn, 229
Duncan, American destroyer, 255
DUNCAN, Sgt S. J., 622
DUNCAN, Lt W. J., 217, 218
DUNKLEY, Maj C. R., 603
DUNLOP, Maj J. W., 406
DUNSHEA, Capt C. J. P., 546, 547
DUROPA PLANTATION (Map p. 370; Sketch p. 357), 356, 358, 370, 378, 480, 485
DUTCH ARMY, in Timor, 598, 606, 608, 613; evacuation of, 616, 617
DUTCH GOVERNMENT, represented on ABDACOM, 15; not represented on GHQ SWPA, 28
DUTCH NAVY, 617-18
DWIGHT, Pte G. E., 274
DWYER, Pte J. D., 134

EARL, Rev Father N. J., 134, 143, 203
EAST CAPE PENINSULA (Map p. 156), 175
EATHER, Maj-Gen K. W. (Plate p. 243), 229, 230, 231, 233, 244, 245, 246, 263, 268, 269, 272, 274, 275, 276, 280, 281, 296, 311, 314, 315, 317, 320, 321, 325, 327, 330, 332, 384, 418, 419, 421, 422, 424, 427, 431, 433, 434; assumes command at Ioribaiwa, 227; withdraws to Imita Ridge, 232-3, 247; supply problems of, 264
EBNER, Sgt E. R., 504n
ECCLESTONE, Capt J. W., 58, 578, 580
ECCLESTONE SADDLE (Sketch p. 579), 580, 581
EDGAR, Brig C. R. V., 281, 282, 283, 285, 295, 311, 315, 317, 318, 319, 384, 385, 386, 389, 392, 393, 395; commands 2/2 Bn, 275
EDGELL, Cpl R. G., 437, 443
EDIE CREEK (Map p. 585; Sketches pp. 51, 579), 53, 58, 579, 580-1, 584
EDNEY, Capt W. K., 554, 555, 558, 559
EDSON, Brig-Gen Merritt A., 150
EDWARDS, Pte L., 231
EDWARDS, Col W. M., 57, 59, 87; commands NGVR, 46
EFOGI (Maps pp. 114, 216; Sketch p. 123), 109, 117, 130, 131, 132, 195, 196, 212, 215, 217, 220, 221, 223, 229, 242, 247, 248, 263, 264, 281, 596; 21 Bde withdrawal to, 219
EFOGI NORTH (Map p. 114), 264, 274
EGERTON-WARBURTON, Capt W. A., 432
EGYPT, 13, 112n, 191, 351n, 497
EICHELBERGER, Lt-Gen Robert L. (Plate p. 323), 372n, 374n, 378, 379, 380, 381, 382, 403, 451, 454, 456, 488, 489, 490, 491, 494, 511, 512, 516, 517, 522, 525-6; his estimate of 32 Div, 33; commands I American Corps, 120; arrives Australia, 351; ordered to take command at Buna, 371-2, arrives Buna, 372, 373; relieves American commanders, 374; tactics at Buna, 381; takes command at Buna, 383, 450; concerned at morale of American troops, 492
EILOGO, 244
EISENHOWER, General of the Army Dwight D., 20n; recommends establishment of American base in Australia, 14
Elevala, Australian lugger, 161, 162-3, 165
ELEVALA CREEK (Sketch p. 160), 180
ELLIOTT-SMITH, Lt-Col S., 43, 131n, 194, 196; suggests airfield sites at Milne Bay, 112
ELLIS, Sgt S. J., 440, 445
ELLWOOD, Capt A. J., 621
ELOA RIVER (Sketch p. 579), 578, 580, 581
ELPHINSTONE, Lt C. B., 483
EMBOGO (Map p. 370; Sketch p. 353), 354, 356, 365, 367
EMERY, Rfn J. R., 87, 88
EMERY, Lt R. E., 46, 88, 97, 104, 536
EMSON, Lt R. A., 477, 479, 481
ENDAIADERE, CAPE (Map p. 370; Sketch p. 357), 354, 356, 358, 360, 366, 367, 368, 373, 376, 383, 451, 454,

INDEX 641

ENDAIADERE, CAPE—continued
463, 511, 512, 524, 532; operations at, 455-62; Japanese strength at, 485
ENGLISH CHANNEL, 85
ENLISTMENTS, in Australian Services, 9; in AIF after 8 Dec 1941, 12-13
Enterprise, American aircraft carrier, 67, 113, 153, 257, 340, 341, 342
ENTRANCE CREEK (Map p. 370; Sketches pp. 370, 436), 364, 365, 366, 379, 382, 383, 486, 488, 492, 493
EORA CREEK (Map p. 114; Sketch p. 123), 110, 130, 131, 132, 142, 196, 199-200, 204, 213, 214, 228, 269, 272, 276, 277, 281, 289, 291, 296, 300, 307, 310, 311, 312, 323, 330, 332n, 592, 596; 21 Bde withdrawal to, 211-12, 215-17; medical arrangements at, 212; action at, 287-303; Japanese defences at, 287, 303; Japanese account, 306; tactical discussion of, 306-7; Australian casualties, 306n
EORA CREEK VILLAGE (Map p. 114; Sketch p. 123), 109, 110, 199, 281, 287, 289, 295, 297
EQUIPMENT, 9-10, 336; of Australian militia, 2, 8, 30; of NGVR, 56; of AIF in Ceylon, 78; carried by Inf Bn on Kokoda Track, 265, 280. American, 32-3, on Guadalcanal, 154; of air forces compared to Japanese, 336; of 32 Div, 351, 352. Japanese, captured in Salamaua raid, 96, at K.B. Mission, 165, at Gorari, 327, 328
ERMERA (Sketch p. 599), 600, 603, 604, 606, 607, 610
ESPERANCE, CAPE (Sketch p. 149), 258, 340, 529; naval battle of, 255
ESPIRITU SANTO (Map p. 37), 255, 340, 341, 342; proposed American base at, 120
ESSON, Lt A. W., 49n
ETTY, Pte G. R., 594
EUROPE, 9, 28, 29, 84, 336; strategic responsibility for, 17
Eva, Australian barge, 468
EVANS, Sgt A. A., 478
EVANS, Capt K. A., 426, 429, 442
EVATT, Rt Hon Dr H. V., 23, 29, 188, 189; cables text of MacArthur's and Nimitz's directives, 21-3
EVENSEN, Capt M. G., 133
EXECUTIONS, at Ocean Island and Nauru, 39n; at Buna, 139; of Australian troops, 263; see also MASSACRES

FAI NIA (Sketch p. 599), 619
FAIRBROTHER, Maj D. N., 284, 285, 286, 315, 318, 392, 394, 395, 397
FAISI (Map p. 34), 64, 259
FAR EAST, 4, 14, 25, 79; strategic responsibility for, 17
FARGHER, Col D. B., 196
FARR, WO2 H. J. W., 91
FATU-BERLIU (Sketch p. 599), 622
FATU-CUAC (Sketch p. 599), 618
FATU MAQUEREC (Sketch p. 599), 617, 619
FAULKS, Capt L. G., 503
FEE, Sgt R. C., 478
FELDT, Cdr Eric A., 51, 151n, 446, 447n
FERGUSON, Lt-Col I. B., 282, 283, 284, 285, 315, 317, 318, 394, 397
FERGUSSON, Brig M. A., 375n
FERGUSSON, Lt T. St D. F., 375, 376, 377, 455, 457
FERGUSSON ISLAND (Sketch p. 346), 349
FERNAN, Lt S. W., 405n
FERNANCE, Pte D. J., 286
FEURY, 2nd-Lt Donald W., 487
FIELD, Brig J., 155, 158, 161, 163, 167, 172, 173, 175, 179; commands 7 Bde, 121; task at Milne Bay, 122; problems of, 155-8
FIELDING, Capt G. A., 376
FIJI (Maps pp. 19, 37), 14; proposed Japanese invasion of, 83, 113, plan abandoned, 143; American reinforcement of, 149
FILA (Map p. 313), 311, 312, 314
FINCH, Capt N. D., 540, 542, 543
FINCH, L-Cpl T. F., 622
FINLAY, Maj W. M., 396
FINSCHHAFEN (Map p. 34), 50, 54
FITCH, Admiral A. W., 80
FITCH, Colonel Burdette M., 28n
FITNESS, L-Cpl D. H., 622
FITZPATRICK, Sgt C. H., 430
FLAME-THROWERS, at Milne Bay, 165; at Buna, 380
FLEAY, Lt-Col N. L. (Plate p. 130), 91, 100, 104, 105, 107, 536, 537, 540; commands Kanga Force, 89; role of, 90, 539; orders attack on Heath's, 96, 99;

FLEAY, LT-COL N. L.—continued
seeks reinforcement of Kanga Force, 105; orders scorching of Bulolo Valley, 106, 534-5; NGF redefines instructions to, 538; problems of, 544
FLEMING, Lt-Col E. W., 405n
FLETCHER, Rear-Admiral Frank J., 80, 153; commands American landings on Guadalcanal, 149; requests permission to withdraw carriers from Guadalcanal area, 151
FLETCHER, L-Cpl J. S., 391
FLETCHER, Pte T. J., 593-4
FLIGHT, Lt J. O., 429
FLOOD, Capt H., 621, 623
Florence D., Filipino ship, 71
FLORIDA ISLAND (Sketches pp. 148, 149), 149, 151, 153
FOGG, Lt C. H., 180
FONA (Map p. 34), 161
FOOD, in Owen Stanleys, 195-6, 198, 281, 297, 300, 305, 308-9, 312; in advance to Oivi, 314; at Kokoda, 320-1; at Gorari, 325; at Buna, 369, 374, 382; in advance to Sanananda, 384-5
FORD, Lt-Col R. M., 73n
FORDE, Rt Hon F. M. (Plate p. 306), 25, 307n; recommends defence of whole of populated area of Australia, 8; asks General Blamey to visit New Guinea, 234; visits New Guinea, 310
FORMOSANS, 144, 145
FORRESTAL, Hon James, 342
FORRESTER, Rfn H. W. T., 54n, 55, 106n
FORSTER, Lt C. E. D., 409
FORSTER, Tpr F. F., 470
FORSTER, Capt R. W., 405n, 408, 409, 411
FORT HERTZ, 191
Fox, Maj C. W. G., 58, 578
FOX CAMP (Sketch p. 579), 581
FOX SADDLE (Sketch p. 579), 580
FRANCE, 1, 3, 18
FRANCISCO RIVER (Map p. 585; Sketches pp. 52, 60), 53, 57, 60, 91-3, 95-6, 100, 105, 583
FRASER, Sgt B., 539
FRASER, Cpl G. T., 622
FRASER, Lt Powell A., 511
FREEMAN, Brig N. M., 30
FREMANTLE (Sketch p. 7), 7, 25, 76, 80, 623; Area Combined Headquarters established at, 9
FRENCH, Maj B. J., 142, 143, 203, 440, 443, 447
FRENCH, Cpl J. A., VC, 182
FRENCH ARMY, 29; Australia aid to, 10
FREW, Capt J. McI., 296
FRONTEIRA PROVINCE (Sketch p. 599), 599
FRY, Capt G. McK., 567
FRYDAY, Lt Carl K., 361, 364, 367, 370, 373
Fubuki, Japanese destroyer, 255
FUILORO (Sketch p. 599), 613, 614
FUJIOKA, Japanese soldier, 595
FULLER, Maj-Gen Horace, H., 26, 120n
FULMER, Lt Tally D., 511
FULTON, Capt I. C., 297, 298, 302, 318, 319, 386
Furutaka, Japanese cruiser, 255
FUSES, artillery, 364
FYFE, Pte A. F., 429

GABENSIS (Sketch p. 52), 54
GABMATZUNG (Map p. 585; Sketches pp. 52, 87), 87, 99
GABSONKEK (Map p. 585; Sketch p. 87), 99, 102
GALAIWAU BAY (Sketch p. 346), 347
GALL, Capt J. M., 291, 292, 294, 295, 297, 298, 299, 318, 319, 386, 392, 393, 394
GALLIPOLI, 136, 195, 351n
GAMA RIVER (Map p. 156; Sketches pp. 173, 179), 165, 169, 170, 171, 175, 176, 178, 179
GARAINA (Map p. 34), 106n
GARARA (Map p. 370), 498, 518
GARDNER, Lt V. G., 208, 211, 220
GARLAND, Lt A. G., 127, 128
GARNETT, Capt H. J., 602, 605
GARRISON HILL (Sketch p. 541), 107, 542
GARTNER, Maj P. E., 443, 444-5, 447
GASKELL, Pte W. H., 430
GASMATA (Map p. 34), 544
GATEGOOD, Maj K. A. J., 178, 180, 347, 348, 481, 482
GAVAGA CREEK (Sketch p. 149), 339
GAVUTU ISLAND (Sketch p. 149), 149-50
GEARD, Lt-Col C. J., 524; commands 2/10 Bn, 513-14
GEDYE, Cpl S. M., 597
GEELONG GRAMMAR SCHOOL, 548-9

GEIGER, Lt-Gen Roy S., 254, 256
GELLIBRAND, Maj-Gen Sir John, 3n
GENERAL HEADQUARTERS, SWPA, 148, 159, 238, 239, 243, 352; establishes headquarters at Melbourne, 24; Australian and Dutch Staffs not represented at senior levels, 28-9; authorises construction of airfields at Milne Bay, 112; reinforcement policy in New Guinea examined, 112n; plans amphibious assault on Rabaul, 119; moves to Brisbane, 120; lacks knowledge of New Guinea conditions, 141; reactions to Milne Bay fighting, 174, 186; opinion of Australians, 176, 225; issue of communiqués, 226; establishes advanced echelon at Moresby, 235n; relations with Australian Army, 248, 626-7; plans offensive in Papua, 260
George F. Elliott, American transport, 151
GERKE, Maj J., 209, 210, 215
GERMAN ARMY, 29; British commandos formed for operations against, 84-5; takes offensive in Russia, 118; advances to Caucasus, 181
GERMANY, 2, 147; Allied decision to concentrate against, 190
GERUA (Map p. 370; Sketch p. 357), 358, 360, 361
GHORMLEY, Admiral Robert L., 147, 151, 188; Commander-in-Chief, Pacific, 119; protests at early date fixed for offensive against Santa Cruz Island, 120; estimates Japanese strength Guadalcanal-Tulagi, 148; lack of cooperation with General MacArthur, 259; replaced by Admiral Halsey, 337
GIBSON, Lt-Col A. R. M., 72-3
GILBERT ISLANDS (Map p. 37), 67, 336
GILHOOLEY, Lt G. J. E., 169, 176
GILI GILI (Map p. 156; Sketch p. 160), 155, 158, 160-1, 164-6, 168, 171, 173, 180, 183, 184-5, 349; construction of airfield at, 121
GILL, Capt T. F., 250, 251, 427, 430, 431, 432
GILLELAND, Capt J. R., 410, 411, 499
GILLESPIE, Capt W. K., 405n
GILMORE, Maj J. C. S., 434, 445
GIROPA CREEK (Sketch p. 481), 476, 485
GIROPA POINT (Map p. 370; Sketch p. 481), 356, 383, 463, 470, 476-7, 494, 497, 512; clearing of, 481-5; Japanese casualties at, 496
GIRUA RIVER (Sketches pp. 353, 357), 354, 356, 358, 380, 382-3, 395, 415, 520, 523
GIRUWA (Map p. 370; Sketch p. 518), 304, 498, 510, 511, 522, 527; Americans enter, 523
GLOUCESTER, CAPE, 582
GOBLE, Lt-Col N. L., 584
GOLD, production in Territories, 41
"GOLDEN STAIRS" (Plate p. 242), 194-5
GOLDIE RIVER (Map p. 114), 227, 241, 242, 243
GOLDMAN, Capt M., 289
GOLDSMITH, Capt D. K., 208, 210, 211, 215, 217, 219, 222
GOMARI, New Guinea native, 93
GONA (Map p. 370; Sketches pp. 123, 357), 108, 110, 125, 143, 144, 158, 194, 260, 279, 333, 352, 355, 359, 371, 394, 397, 399, 405, 413, 415, 417, 448, 450, 496-7, 501, 505, 509, 512, 518-19, 527, 530-1, 534-5, 575, 583, 590, 595; Japanese landings at, 105, 122, 123, 139; Japanese reinforcement of, 145, 193; Japanese plan to withdraw to, 304; Australian advance on, 345, 354, 384, 386, 418; operations at, 418-48; casualties at, 434, 435n, 447; Japanese account, 447; necessity for reduction examined, 531-3; Allied strength at, 577
GONA CREEK (Sketch p. 423), 420, 421, 432, 437, 440, 442
GONA MISSION (Map p. 370; Sketch p. 423), 110, 123, 125, 139, 383, 419, 420, 424, 433, 437, 439, 441-5
GOOD, Percy, 64
GOODE, Maj A. L., 63, 80
GOODENOUGH ISLAND (Map p. 34; Sketch p. 346), 158, 161, 185, 260, 334, 346, 480, 531, 577, 583; 2/12 Bn operations on, 347-9; casualties at, 348-9; deception scheme on, 589
GOOD HOPE, CAPE OF, 24, 118
GOODMAN, Lt P., 282, 283
GORARI (Map p. 313; Sketch p. 123), 110, 125, 321, 325, 329, 334, 416; loss of, 126; Australian advance to, 315, 316, 320; orders for capture of, 321; action at, 322-9; Japanese account, 330-1
GORDON, Sgt J., 181, 458
GORONI (Sketch p. 160), 181, 183
GORS, Anthony, 139n
GOSNELL, Capt I., 326

GOTO, Admiral, 255
GOWLAND, Capt R. E., 163, 164, 166
GRAHAM, WO2 A. McA. (Plate p. 130), 539
GRAHAMSLAW, Lt-Col T., 124, 138, 139, 214
GRAY, Sgt J. G., 549, 550
GRAY, Capt Millard G., 491, 492, 494, 495
GRAY, Lt O., 472
GRAY, Tpr W. M., 508n
GRAYDEN, Capt W. L., 222
GREATER EAST ASIA CO-PROSPERITY SPHERE, 83, 575
GREECE, 29, 30, 73, 74, 141, 142, 147, 159, 193, 194, 280, 307n, 402, 544
GREEN HILL (Sketch p. 541), 586
GREENWOOD, Capt J. R., 223, 438, 592
GREENWOOD, Sig W. M., 594
GREGSON, L-Cpl J. K., 101
GRENADES, *sticky*, at Milne Bay, 163, 172, at K.B. Mission, 167, 170, ineffectiveness of, 168; *hand*, 182, destroy flame-thrower at Milne Bay, 165; number carried by Australian Inf Coy, 221; at Gorari, 327; on Sanananda Track, 390; *rifle*, at Haddy's Village, 445. *Japanese*, at Milne Bay, 164; at Eora, 300, 302; at Gorari, 328
GRIFFIN, Capt R. R., 456, 457, 458, 461, 462, 463, 464, 466, 467
GROOTE ISLAND (Sketch p. 7), 75
GROSE, Col John E., 375, 380, 489, 490, 491, 492, 494, 511, 512; commands Warren Force, 374; commands Urbana Force, 488
GRUENNERT, Sgt Kenneth E., 489
GUADAGASAL (Map p. 585; Sketches pp. 52, 535, 541), 53, 88, 104, 536, 539, 546, 561, 572, 574-5, 581, 584
GUADALCANAL (Sketches pp. 148, 149), 147, 185, 188, 279, 304, 333, 336, 337, 341, 342, 343, 344-5, 352, 528, 530, 544, 577, 620; Japanese occupy, 112; develop air bases on, 120; strength on, 148, 529; Americans invade, 149-51; operations on, 152-5, 254-9, 338-9; American strength and reinforcement of, 260, 338, 529; naval battle of, 340-4, 345, 385
GUAM (Map p. 19), 153
Gudgeon, American submarine, 623
GUERILLA WARFARE, origins of, 84-5; Kanga Force, 534, 536; in Timor, 598-624
GUERRE, Pedro, 602
GUINN, Col H. G., 554, 555, 586
GULLETT, Maj H. B. S., 548, 552, 557, 562, 563, 568, 569, 570, 588
GULLETT'S JUNCTION (Sketch p. 569), 563, 571, 573
GULLETT'S TRACK, 563
GUNN, Lt E. D., 462, 463
GWILLIM, Maj J. E., 211, 592

HAAN, Lt, 411
HADDY, Lt A. C., 217, 333, 420, 421, 432, 437, 438-9
HADDY'S VILLAGE (Sketch p. 444), 438-9, 444, 446-7, 505, 518
HAGEN, MOUNT (Map p. 34), 49, 581
HAGENHAMBO (Sketches pp. 123, 385), 124, 384
HAGITA HOUSE (Map p. 156; Sketch p. 179), 160
HAILO (Sketch p. 593), 596
HAIN, WO2 A. D., 407
HAIRE, Lt J. T., 614
HALE, Col J. Tracy Jnr, 356, 362, 366; relieved of command of Warren Force, 374
HALL, Sgt F. J., 565
HALL, Capt T., 211, 594
HALL, Lt W. D., 282, 283
HALL, Brig W. H. (Plate p. 498), 362, 367, 368, 381, 382, 454, 456, 474, 481, 524
HALSEY, Fleet Admiral William F., 67, 338, 339, 341, 529; becomes C-in-C Pacific Fleet, 337
HAMADA, Corporal, 135
HAMILTON, Sgt R. N., 98
HANCOCK, Maj R. N., 568, 573
HANCOX, Tpr F. C. G., 504-5
HANDRAN-SMITH, Capt T. J., 474-5
HANSEN, Pte E. P., 622
HANSON, Brig A. G., 363, 396, 397, 400, 428, 499, 513
HARCOURT, Maj H. G. (Plate p. 307), 279, 359-60, 364, 373, 376
HARDING, Maj-Gen Edwin F., 261, 354, 355, 356, 358, 359, 360, 363, 364, 365, 366, 367, 373, 395; commands 32nd American Div, 120n, 351; underestimates Japanese at Buna, 352; role at Buna, 358; requests return of battalion of 126

INDEX

HARDING, MAJ-GEN EDWIN F.—*continued*
Regt, 361; readjusts command, 362; seeks employment of tanks at Buna, 369; relieved of command, 372, 374
HARDING, Brig-Gen Horace A., 489
HARGER, Capt Horace N., 490, 491, 492
HARIKO (Map p. 370; Sketch p. 357), 354, 356-7, 362-3, 367, 375, 381-2, 452-4, 462, 468-9, 474, 510
HARMER, F. F., 39
HARRINGTON, Sgt S., 473
HARSCH, Joseph, 625
HART, Admiral Thomas C., 20
HARTLEY, Rev F. J., 506-7, 508n
Haruna, Japanese battleship, 114
HARVEY, F-O T. C., 393
HARVIE, Capt T. G. A., 521, 522
HATTORI, Col T., 531n
HATU-LIA (Sketch p. 599), 598-9, 600, 610, 614
HATU-UDO (Sketch p. 599), 616
HAWAII (Map p. 37), 82, 119, 190, 337, 338, 528
HAWKINS, Maj C. J. T., 202
HAY, Lt-Col D. O., 556, 562, 569, 570, 571
HAYASHI, Commander, 185, 186
HAYDON, Capt F. B., 504, 505, 507
HAYES, Maj H. F., 420, 421
HAYES, Sgt W. F., 622
HAYMAN, Miss May, 139
HEAP, Capt D. A., 479-80, 512, 515
HEARMAN, Maj J. M., 219, 432
HEATH, Miss Doris, 144n
HEATH'S PLANTATION (Map p. 585; Sketches pp. 52, 87), 62, 63, 88, 101, 536; Australian raid on, 90, 96-99, 544
HENDERSON, Capt H. K., 499-500
HENDERSON FIELD (Sketch p. 149), 152, 153, 254, 255, 257, 258, 337, 341, 342, 344, 345, 529; American occupation of, 150; aircraft losses on, 256
Hermes, British aircraft carrier, 78
HERON, Capt H. A., 269
HERON, Cpl P. J., 472
HERON, Lt R. A., 180-1
HERRING, Lt-Gen Hon Sir Edmund (Plate p. 450), 80, 247, 261, 275n, 291, 307, 354, 358, 361, 381, 385, 395, 398, 400, 403, 412, 413, 424, 436, 451, 453, 488, 497, 508, 512, 516n, 517, 538, 545, 546, 548, 553, 563, 575, 578, 602, 603; assumes command at Darwin, 72-3; his charter, 74; commands II Corps, 140n; succeeds General Rowell, 238, 268; opens advanced headquarters at Popondetta, 372; appreciates position Buna-Gona area, 510; issues orders for attack on Sanananda, 511
HERWIG, Capt L. C., 400, 413, 499, 500
HETHERINGTON, John, 240n
HEWITT, Sgt L. R., 124
HICKS, Lt D. S., 106, 107
HICKS, Lt G. T., 218, 433
HIDDEN VALLEY (Sketch p. 579), 580
HILL, Maj I. W., 405n
HIMALAYAS, THE, 191
HIRANO, 2nd-Lt, 595
HITCHCOCK, American pilot, 616
HITCHCOCK, Capt E. P., 96
Hiyei, Japanese battleship, 114, 341, 343
Hiyo, Japanese aircraft carrier, 345
HOBART (Sketch p. 7), 3, 7
Hobart, Australian cruiser, 80
HOBSON, Col A. F., 277, 309, 399
HODDINOTT, Capt F. J., 319
HODGE, Capt C. H., 284, 323n
HODGSON, Col C. R., 451, 452, 453, 460
HODGSON, Sgt E., 609
HOGAN, Capt A. B., 212, 213
HOLLAND, Brig A. C. S., 30
HOLLAND, Rev Henry, 139n
HOLLANDIA (Map p. 34), Japanese invasion of, 49n
HOMBROM BLUFF (Map p. 114), 241, 244
HOMMA, Lt-Gen Masaharu, 34, 35, 36
HOMO CREEK (Map p. 156; Sketch p. 173), 162, 170, 171
HONG KONG, 383, 521
HONNER, Lt-Col R., 142n, 143, 199, 200, 201, 202, 203, 204, 207, 208, 210, 215, 217, 220, 227, 229, 434, 435, 436, 439, 440, 441, 442, 443, 444, 447, 505; commands 39 Bn, 141
HOOKE, Tpr P. W., 503
HOOPER, Capt R. C., 181, 183
HOPKINS, Maj-Gen R. N. L., 236, 451

HORANDA (Sketch p. 357), 358
HORDERN, Maj S., 505, 506, 508
HORII, Maj-Gen Tomitaro, 145, 146, 303-4, 305, 331, 415, 416, 446; commands *South Seas Force*, 83, 114, 144, 228; drowns, 330
HORIYE, Major, 228
Hornet, American aircraft carrier, 113, 154, 257
HORN ISLAND (Sketch p. 7), 111
HORSES, used for transport of supplies in New Guinea, 116, 117, 264, 357
HORTIN, Maj S. E. B., 560
HORTON, Lt D. C., 150
HOSIER, Sgt J. O., 179-80
HOUSE BAMBOO (Sketch p. 52), 53
HOUSE BANANA (Sketch p. 541), 543
HOUSE COPPER (Sketch p. 549), 546-9, 551-2, 568, 569, 571, 573-4
Houston, American cruiser, 69
HOWARD, Lt-Col F. J., 226
HOWARD, Capt N. R., 62, 63, 86, 87, 89, 103, 104
HOWE, Lt-Col Merle H., 522
HOWELL, L-Cpl E. G., 622
HUBBARD, Cpl H., 622
HUGGINS, Capt Meredith M., 403, 404, 413, 415
HUGGINS' ROAD-BLOCK (Sketches pp. 502, 506), 402-4, 413-15, 498-9, 501-8, 512, 513, 517-18, 524-5, 527
HUGHES, Lt F. W., 409
HUGHES, Cpl T., 471
HUGHES, Rt Hon W. M., 40
HUMPHREY, Lt-Col R. J., 277, 292
HUNT, L-Cpl J. L., 292
HUNTER, L-Sgt W. M. T., 93, 95, 96
HUNTINGTON, S. P., 20n
HUON GULF (Map p. 34; Sketch p. 52), 61-2, 590
HUON PENINSULA (Map p. 34), 532, 582
HURRELL, Capt A. L., 322, 323, 327, 329, 418
HURRELL, Capt L. T., 418, 419, 438
HUTCHISON, Lt-Col I., 286, 288, 289, 302, 303, 307, 311, 318, 319, 386, 388, 408, 413, 499, 500; commands 2/3 Bn, 301-2
HUTCHISON, Capt I. McL., 204
HYAKUTAKE, Lt-Gen Harukichi, 114, 144, 152, 153, 154, 257, 258, 259, 304, 344, 345, 529; commands *XVII Army*, 83, 113, 143; arrives Rabaul, 145; orders withdrawal from Owen Stanleys, 305; takes over Solomons battle, 383
HYDE, Maj G. R., 178, 179
HYDROGRAPHER'S RANGE (Sketch p. 353), 353
HYNDMAN, Maj C. W., 232

ICHIKI, Col Kiyono, 153
IFOULD, Capt A. H., 465, 468, 469, 473
IGORA STORE (Sketch p. 385), 384
ILIMO (Map p. 313), 316, 320-2, 324-5, 330
ILOLO (Map p. 114; Sketch p. 123), 108, 114, 116, 117, 126-8, 130-1, 141, 193-5, 244, 261n, 277
ILU RIVER (Sketch p. 149), 152-3, 155, 254, 339
IMAMURA, Lt-Gen Hitoshi, 383, 530; orders evacuation of Guadalcanal, 529
IMITA RIDGE (Map p. 114), 233, 108, 233, 254, 261, 264, 268, 311, 435n; 25 Bde withdrawal to, 232-3, 244-5, 247
INDIA (Sketch p. 78), 16, 22, 24, 82, 118, 190, 191; Japanese threat to, 1, 77; Australian aid to, 10; Congress-inspired disturbances in, 191
INDIAN ARMY, 79, 280
—*XV Corps*, 187n
—*5th Division*, 191
INDIAN OCEAN (Map p. 37; Sketch p. 78), 34, 76; Japanese activities in, 79, 189
INDIWI RIVER (Sketch p. 51), 51
INDO-CHINA, 415, 575
INGLEBURN, NSW, 351n
INKPEN, Lt L. G. J., 441
INNES, Capt W. T. D., 268, 270
INONDA (Sketch p. 357), 358
INOUYE, Admiral S., 82
INTELLIGENCE, *Allied*, 80, 385; formation of COIC, 9; of Japanese plans in New Guinea, 68, 111, 114n, 123, 235n; in Battle of Coral Sea, 82; aided by items captured in Salamaua raid, 96; of Midway, 113; of Solomons, 148. *Japanese*, of Australia and islands to north-east, 114; at Milne Bay, 185
"INTERNATIONAL BRIGADE", THE, in Timor, 602, 605
INUS PLANTATION (Map p. 34), 64
IOMA (Map p. 34; Sketch p. 123), 114, 122, 124, 589

INDEX

IORIBAIWA (Map p. 114; Sketches pp. 230, 233, 250), 108, 117, 132, 195, 212, 223, 227, 243, 245, 254, 263-4, 307n, 424, 596; 21 Bde withdrawal to, 224; Australian consolidation and deployment, 225, 227, 229; Australian withdrawal from, 232-3; recapture of, 246; Japanese withdrawal from, 303-5
IRAQ, 1, 191
IRELAND, 21; number of American divisions in, 190
IRONBOTTOM SOUND, 345
IRVIN, Lt O. B., 284
IRVINE, Lt D. L., 137
IRWIN, Lt-Col A. F. A., 482n
IRWIN, Sgt W. H., 220, 597
ISAACHSEN, Lt A., 200, 204
ISAACHSEN, Lt-Col O. C., 498, 500, 519
ISAGAHAMBO (Sketch p. 123), 124, 128
ISELY, J. A., 188n
ISIVITA (Sketch p. 385), 384
ISKOV, Lt R. F., 443-4
ISURAVA (Maps pp. 114, 216; Sketches pp. 123, 128), 110, 130-2, 137, 141, 194, 220, 228-9, 242, 304, 306, 312, 593, 597; Australian withdrawal to, 138; dispositions at, 142-3, 199; action at, 201-3, 204-5, 206-8; medical arrangements at, 212, 213; Japanese account, 228; recapture of, 311; fate of stretcher party at, 320n
ISURAVA REST HOUSE (Sketches pp. 199, 205), 208, 209, 210, 311, 594
Isuzu, Japanese cruiser, 342
ITIKI (Map p. 114), 193, 194, 243, 252
IVEY, Capt C. H. V., 177, 178, 184, 348, 481, 482, 483, 520, 521, 522

JACKSON, Lt G. K., 514-15
JACKSON, W-Cdr L. D., 158
JACOB, Capt K. R., 135, 137, 138, 143, 201, 202
JACOBSEN'S PLANTATION (Sketches pp. 52, 87), 57, 62, 87, 97
JACOBSON, Pte A. L., 622
JALUIT, 336
JAMES, Sgt H. E., 604
JAMES, Brig J. A., 502, 503, 504, 505, 506, 507, 508
JAMES' PERIMETER (Sketch p. 514), 503, 505-8, 512, 513, 517-18, 524-7
JAPAN (Map p. 37), 10, 18, 20, 22, 23, 29, 39, 43, 45, 46, 79, 80, 84, 85, 119, 147, 153, 189, 191, 192, 405, 607; extent of penetration to *Mar 1942*, 1; probable courses of action predicted, 11; seeks air bases in New Guinea, 50-1; captures Rabaul, 55; plans operations against New Guinea, 68, 146; object in bombing Darwin, 71-2; suffers reversals at Coral Sea and Midway, 120; abandons plans to occupy New Caledonia, Samoa and Fiji, 143; invades Timor, 190
—IMPERIAL HEADQUARTERS, 83, 112, 145, 304, 305, 531n
JAPAN, EMPEROR OF, 305
JAPANESE, THE, relations with New Guinea natives, 88, 103, 104
JAPANESE AIR FORCES, 60, 61-2, 87, 96, 99, 122, 381, 385; attack Port Moresby, 1, 65-6, 67; in Philippines, 20, 35; bomb European centres in New Guinea, 47, 54, 57, 58-9, 100, 565, 584, 589; attack Buka, 64; attack Darwin, 69-71, 75-6, 613n; attack Broome and Wyndham, 76; attack Ceylon, 78-9; attack Tulagi, 79; in Battle of Coral Sea, 81; attack Midway Island, 113; cover Gona landings, 145; in Guadalcanal operations, 150, 151, 154, 255, 340, 529, 530; in Milne Bay operations, 158, 161, 165, 589; strength of, 336; in Buna-Gona campaign, 354-5, 367, 368, 440, 473; attack MDS Soputa, 399; in Bismarck Sea battle, 530, 544-5; in Timor, 607-8, 612, 614, 617
—FLEETS: *First Air*, 114; *Eleventh Air*, 145; *First Air Attack Force*, 70
JAPANESE ARMY, 36, 38, 57, 59, 61, 63, 83, 86-8, 100, 132, 133, 135, 142, 187; Lae-Salamaua area, 90-1, 96, 98, 99; attacks Mubo, 106-7; lands Buna-Gona area, 122, 125, strength, 144-6; estimate of, 130; recaptures Kokoda, 136-7; executes prisoners, 139; on Kokoda Track, 143, 188, 199, 208-9, 224-5, 242, 263, 270-1, 281, 286, 299, 303; strength and reinforcement, 193-4, 333-4; on Guadalcanal, 148, 150, 152, 256-7, 338, 528-9; conquers Burma, 191; strength in New Guinea compared to Allied, 234, 150, 152, 256-7, 338, 528-9; conquers Burma, 191; strength in New Guinea compared to Allied, 234, at Ioribaiwa, 244-5, withdraws, 246-7, 303-5; at Oivi-Gorari, 321, 331; strength in SWPA, 336;

JAPANESE ARMY—*continued*
American underestimate of, 352; at Buna, 358-9, 369, 370, 383, 385, 476-7, 480, 484-5, 494, 496, 510, evacuation of, 519; adjusts command in Pacific, 383; on Sanananda Track, 413, 415-16, 498, 501, 526, casualties, 522, 527, strength at, 530-1; in Gona area, 442, 446, 447; strength employed in Papuan operations, 531; quality of, 532-3; in Kanga Force operations, 537, 573-4, 576; reinforces Lae, 544-5; disposition and strength of, 574-5, 577; losses in Bismarck Sea Battle, 583; in Timor, 598, 602, 607-9, 610, 611, 614, 619, 620n, 622
—AREA ARMIES: *Eighth*, 383
—ARMIES: *XIV*, 34; *XVI*, 610n; *XVII*, 83, 113, 143, 152, 257, 258, 344, 383, 529; *XVIII*, 144, 383, composition, 575
—DIVISIONS: *2nd*, 258, 344, 574; *5th*, 113, 575; *6th*, 575; *18th*, 113; *20th*, 575; *38th*, 258, 344, 574; *41st*, 575; *48th*, 575, 610n; *51st*, 530, 575, 576, 582; *56th*, 113
—BRIGADES: *21st Independent Mixed*, 415, 527
—FORCES: *Aoba*, 185; *Ichiki*, 153, 154, 258, 344; *Kawaguchi*, 144, 145, 154, 155, 185, 258, 304, 344; *South Seas*, 83, 114, 144, 145-6, strength of, 146, 228; *Yazawa*, 144, 145, 228, strength on Kokoda Track, 228
—ARTILLERY: in Philippines, 35-6; *14th Field Regt*, 575; *47th Field A.A. Arty*, 144-5; *55th Mountain*, 144-5
—CAVALRY: *55th*, arrives Papua, 145
—ENGINEERS, *15th Indep Eng Regt*, 144, 145, 305, 383, 415; *51st Engr Regt*, 575
—INFANTRY REGIMENTS: *4th*, 154, 185, 258; *16th*, 258; *28th*, 153-4, *see also Ichiki Force*; *29th*, 258; *41st*, 144-5, 228, 304, 415; *47th*, 610n; *102nd*, 530, 575-6; *114th*, 83; *124th*, 144-5, 154-5, 185, 258, *see also Kawaguchi Force*; *144th*, 114, 144-5, 228, 304, 306, 330, 383, 415, 575, 595; *170th*, 415, 416, 444, 446-7, 530; *228th*, 258, 344, 610n; *229th*, 258, 383, 484; *230th*, 258; *1st Formosan*, 610n; *2nd Formosan*, 610n
—MEDICAL: *67th L of C Hospital*, 523
—TRANSPORT: *3rd Coy 51st Transport*, 575
JAPANESE MANDATED ISLANDS, 67
JAPANESE NAVY, 62, 63, 80, 111, 114, 144, 186, 202, 336, 347, 383, 444, 452, 617; occupies Hollandia, 49n; at Lae and Salamaua, 57, 61, 83, 86, 90, 530; invades Solomons, 64, 80; occupies Manus, 65; in Indian Ocean area, 78, 84; in Battle of Coral Sea, 81; carrier strength of, 82; at Midway, 112-13; bombards Gona, 122; in Battle of Savo Island, 151-2; in Battle of Eastern Solomons, 153-4; at Milne Bay, 171, 176-7, strength and losses, 166, 185-6; in Guadalcanal operations, 254-6, 258-9, 336, 339-40, 529; in Battle of Cape Esperance, 255; in Battle of Santa Cruz, 257; reinforces Buna 314; in Naval Battle of Guadalcanal, 340-1, 344-5; in Bismarck Sea Battle, 583
—FLEETS: *Combined Fleet*, 112; *First*, 154; *Second*, 114; *Fourth*, 82; *Eighth*, 145
—SPECIAL NAVAL LANDING FORCES: *3rd Kure*, 83, at Milne Bay, 186; *5th Kure*, at Milne Bay, 185-6; *2nd Maizuru*, at Mubo, 575; *5th Sasebo*, 144-5: at Milne Bay, 185; part marooned on Goodenough Island, 185, 347, 349; at Buna, 383; *5th Yokosuka*, reinforces Guadalcanal, 153; at Milne Bay, 186; at Buna, 383
—LABOUR UNITS: *10th Labour Corps*, 185; *14th Construction Unit*, 145; *15th Pioneer Unit*, 144-5
JAP TRACK (Sketch p. 549), 547, 548, 550-2, 557, 562-3, 568, 572-5
JAP TRACK JUNCTION (Sketch p. 549), 562-3, 568-70
JARRETT, WO2 H. E., 131, 132
Jarvis, American destroyer, 151
JAURE (Map p. 34; Sketch p. 353), 242, 260, 262, 278-9, 351-3
JAURE TRACK (Sketch p. 353), 279, 351
JAVA (Map p. 37), 15, 20, 29n, 72, 114, 383, 610n; fall of, 34
JAVA SEA, NAVAL BATTLE OF, 255
JAWARERE (Map p. 114), 241, 243, 251
JEEPS, at Buna, 368
JEFFERSON, Capt K. M., 231
JEFFERY, Lt S. G., 586-7
JEFFERY'S OBSERVATION POST (Map p. 585), 587
JEFFREY, Maj J. S., 275, 319

INDEX
645

JENTZSCH, Cpl A. E., 60
JENYNS, Maj E. W., 54, 59, 91
JESSE, Lt J. H., 458, 461, 467
JESSER, Maj H. J., 45, 111, 124, 135
JOHNS, Brig-Gen Dwight F., 350
JOHNS, Lt R. D., 221, 429
JOHNSON, Capt C. K., 580, 581
JOHNSON GAP (Sketch p. 579), 580-1
JOHNSTON, Lt K., 294
JOHNSTON, Lt S. B., 207
JOHNSTON, Brig W. W. S., 317
JOMARD PASSAGE (Sketch p. 81), 81
JONES, L-Cpl F. L., 594-5
JONES, Lt-Col J. H., 47, 48, 49
JONES, Lt-Col J. S., 543, 545, 546, 547, 548, 551, 552, 561, 562
JONES, Sgt L. G., 102
JONES, WO2 R. E. A., 438
JONES, Cpl T. R., 470
JORGENSEN, Sgt E. N., 172
JOSEPH, Capt L. H., 406
JOSSELYN, Lt H. E., 150
JUBB, Sgt L. C., 543
JUMBORA (Map p. 370; Sketch p. 385), 384, 418, 419, 423, 425, 518, 519
Juneau, American cruiser, 341
Junyo, Japanese aircraft carrier, 345

KAGI (Maps pp. 114, 216; Sketches pp. 123, 270), 109, 117, 130, 132, 141, 197, 217, 219, 220-1, 263-4, 268-72, 276, 291, 308, 596
KAI ISLAND (Sketch p. 612), 623n
KAILE (Map p. 313; Sketches pp. 123, 128), 141, 199, 200-1, 204, 311, 312
KAINANTU (Map p. 34), 49
KAINDI RANGE (Map p. 585), 580
KAISENIK (Map p. 585; Sketches pp. 51, 535), 50, 52, 106-7, 534-5, 550, 568, 576
KALAMAZOO (Sketch p. 593), 594
KALGOORLIE (Sketch p. 7), 10
Kalgoorlie, Australian corvette, 612
KAMBISI, 332n
KARAWARI RIVER (Map p. 34), 47-8
KAREMA (Map p. 34), 227
Karsik, Dutch ship, 452, 453
KATHERINE (Sketch p. 7), 69, 75, 611
KAVIENG (Map p. 34), 39, 46, 336
KAWAGUCHI, Maj-Gen Kiyotake, 36, 154, 155, 257, 258; commands *124th Infantry Regiment Group*, 144
KAYZER, Rev Father, 39
K. B. MISSION (Map p. 156; Sketch p. 160), 155, 158, 161-3, 166-7, 170-1, 175-80, 182, 184
KEAST, Maj Roger, 401
KELA (Map p. 585; Sketches pp. 52, 93), 91-4, 96; Australian raid on, 95
KELA POINT (Sketches pp. 52, 93), 92-4, 96; Australian raid on, 95
KELLY, Capt H. H., 440
KELSO, Lt-Col P. W. A., 67
Kelton, lugger, 363
KEMP, Capt D. G., 570
KEMP WELSH RIVER (Map p. 34; Sketch p. 593), 242, 593-4
KEMSLEY, Cpl W. J., 388
KENDARI (Map p. 37), 69
KENNEY, General George C., 372
KERR, Capt J. S., 92, 94, 95, 96, 542, 549
KERSLAKE, Sgt K. R., 203
KESSA (Map p. 34), 64
KESSELS, Col O. A. (Plate p. 130), 405, 408, 409, 410, 411, 498, 499, 500
KEY, Lt-Col A. S., 204, 205, 206, 207, 208, 210, 211, 218, 592, 594, 595-6; commands 2/14 Bn, 194
KEY, Lt J. R., 622
KIENZLE, Capt H. T., 116, 117, 118n, 130, 131, 141, 195, 196, 197
KIETA (Map p. 34; Sketch p. 148), 63, 64
KILA AIRFIELD (Map p. 114), 67, 589
KILARBO (Map p. 156; Sketch p. 160), 158, 167, 171-2
KILIA MISSION (Sketch p. 346), 347, 348, 349
KILLERTON (Sketch p. 518), 519, 520
KILLERTON, CAPE (Map p. 370; Sketch p. 518), 394-5, 397-9, 510, 511, 517, 518; 18th Brigade advance on, 519-20
KILLERTON TRACK (Sketches pp. 502, 518), 397-8, 400, 402, 415, 499, 501-2, 513, 517, 518, 520, 524
KIMMOTSU, Maj Hiaichi, 383

KING, Gnr A. G., 355
KING, Pte A. H., 594
KING, Capt C. J. T., 202, 203, 204, 205, 209
KING, Fleet Admiral Ernest J., 82, 119, 188, 189, 337; C-in-C American naval forces, 120, 140
KING, Maj-Gen Edward P., 34
KING, Lt E. W., 164-5
KING, Maj-Gen R., 74
KINGSBURY, Pte B. S., VC, 206
KINKAID, Admiral Thomas C., 257, 259, 337, 340, 341, 342
KINSEY, Lt J. G. (Plate p. 130), 60, 92, 94, 537, 538
Kinugasa, Japanese cruiser, 342
KIRCHENBAUER, Lt Alfred, 487
Kirishima, Japanese battleship, 114, 341, 343
KIRIWINA ISLAND; *see* TROBRIAND ISLANDS
KIRK, Capt C. S., 178, 180, 481, 482
KIRKLAND'S PLANTATION (Sketches pp. 52, 87), 62, 104
KIRKWOOD, Sgt R. S., 605
KISKA (Map p. 19), 113
KLINGNER, Lt L. M., 163, 164, 165
KNEEN, Maj T. P., 67, 86, 89, 90, 91, 96, 97, 98, 99, 103
KNIGHTHOODS, conferment on Australian commanders, 307n
KNODE, Lt Thomas E., 379
KOBARA (Map p. 313), 314, 318, 321
KOBAYASHI, Major, 228
KOEPANG (Sketch p. 7), 69
KOITAKI (Map p. 114), 334n, 335n
KOIWA, Lt-Col, 228
KOKODA (Maps pp. 114, 313; Sketches pp. 123, 128), 105, 109, 110, 114, 116, 117, 121, 122, 123-6, 130, 131, 136-8, 140, 143-4, 154, 187, 193-4, 213, 229, 239, 242-3, 260-3, 268-9, 287, 291, 296, 299, 308, 311, 312, 314-17, 319-22, 324, 332, 352, 357, 399, 424, 434, 589, 593; topography, 108; action at, 127-9, 132-6; Japanese withdrawal from, 136, 140; Japanese account, 145; recapture of, 314; 2/6 Indep Coy patrol to, 332n
KOKODA AIRFIELD (Sketch p. 128), 110, 125, 131, 261-2, 274, 290, 332n; recapture of, 314-15
"KOKODA PASS", 110, 194
KOKODA TRACK (Map p. 114), 117, 141, 193, 235n, 239, 240, 241, 242, 243, 247, 254, 261n, 262, 277, 278, 308, 310, 333, 345, 355, 422, 497; considered impassable for large-scale operations, 115; GHQ proposes blocking by demolition, 141; Japanese reconnaissance of, 144; crossing of, 194-5; supply problems on, 195-9; medical arrangements on, 212-15, 276-7; supply problems, 264-5; Australian casualties during battle of, 334; lessons of campaign, 335; strength of Japanese forces on, 531
KOKODA VALLEY, 592
KOKOPO (Map p. 34), 46
KOKUMBONA (Sketch p. 149), 153, 155, 258, 338-9, 343-4
KOLB, Lt G. L., 430
KOLI POINT (Sketch p. 149), 338, 339, 344
KOLURON MOUNTAINS (Sketch p. 579), 579, 580
KOMIATUM (Map p. 585; Sketches pp. 52, 60), 53, 57, 59, 61, 63, 86, 100, 106, 542-3, 583-4, 587
KOMONDO (Sketches pp. 123, 128), 134
KONDO, Admiral N., 69, 341, 342, 343, 344, 345; commands *Second Fleet*, 114
Kongo, Japanese battleship, 114
KONOMBI CREEK (Sketch p. 518), 511, 522
KOREANS, in Japanese forces, 145, 521
KOTA BHARU (Map p. 78), 10
KOTZ, Pte J. A., 169
KOVIO (Sketch p. 353), 353
KUDJERU (Sketches pp. 51, 579), 50, 51, 58, 62, 89, 106, 534, 536, 538-9, 561, 578-9
KUKUKUKU, THE, 51, 580-1
KUKUM (Sketch p. 149), 152, 254
KULOLO BRIDGE (Map p. 585), 538
KUMUSI RIVER (Maps pp. 34, 313; Sketch p. 123), 110, 125, 139, 242, 260, 262, 296, 311, 321, 329, 335, 353, 355, 383, 384, 399, 406, 416, 418, 436, 444, 446, 448, 505, 519, 530, 590, 594; crossing of, 330-3
Kuri Marau, Australian ship, 381
Kuru, Australian naval launch, 605, 617, 623
KUSUNOSE, Colonel, 228, 304, 306, 330
KUWADA, Lt-Col 228

LABABIA ISLAND (Map p. 585), 586
LABABIA RIDGE (Map p. 585), 584, 586
LABABIA TRACK, 543

LACEY, Lt A. R., 284
LACLO (Sketch p. 599), 614
LACLUBAR (Sketch p. 599), 613, 619
LACLUTA (Sketch p. 599), 619
LADE, Lt N. A., 543, 547, 548, 561, 562
LAE (Maps pp. 34, 585; Sketch p. 52), 50, 53-5, 58-9, 61-3, 79, 86, 88-9, 96-7, 99, 101, 107, 111, 145, 367, 449, 530, 531, 534, 535, 536, 538, 540, 544, 554*n*, 575, 577, 579, 583, 588, 590; Japanese air raids on, 39, 47, 54; NGVR detachment at, 46; invasion of, 57, 83; American carrier raids on, 67; Japanese strength at, 90, 545, 575, 577, 582; its place in Allied strategy, 119; proposed attack on, 310, 578
LAE AIRFIELD (Map p. 585; Sketch p. 87), 59, 83
LAIDLAW, Maj G. G., 598, 600, 603, 604, 608, 612, 613, 616, 617, 618; commands 2/2 Indep Coy, 616
LAKEKAMU RIVER (Map p. 34; Sketches pp. 51, 579), 50, 51, 55, 58, 63, 580-1
LALOKI (Map p. 114), 227, 229; airfield at, 67
LALOKI RIVER (Map p. 114), 227, 240-1
LAMB, Lt J. D., 560, 561
LAMBERT, Lt H., 222
LANDING CRAFT, *Allied*, developments in, 147; shortages of, 363, 369; at Buna, 488, 492; *Japanese*, destroyed at Milne Bay by RAAF, 187; evacuate Japanese from Kumusi area, 519
LANE, Lt A. W., 92
LANE'S PLANTATION (Sketch p. 87), 97, 98
LANG, L-Sgt E. K., 594-5
LANG, Sgt H., 565
LANG, Maj P. S., 103, 107
LANGLEY, Brig G. F., 30
LANGRIDGE, Capt B. D. N., 208, 210, 211, 215, 217, 219, 221, 222
LARUNI (Sketch p. 353), 262
LAS GOURGUES, L-Cpl L., 561
LASHMAR, Miss Lilla F., 139*n*
LATTIMORE, Sgt J., 454-5, 460, 469, 470
LAVARACK, Lt-Gen Sir John, 120*n*; recommends appointment of a Commander-in-Chief Home Forces, 4; appointed A/C-in-C AMF, 25; appointed GOC First Army, 25
LAVER, Maj H. L., 562, 563, 569, 570
LAWSON, Maj R. A., 236
LEAHY'S FARM (Sketch p. 556), 554-5, 559, 560, 563, 566
LEANE, Brig-Gen Sir Raymond, 3*n*
LEANEY, Lt G. L., 294, 295, 297, 298, 299, 320, 321, 324-5, 326, 387, 390, 391
LEANEY'S CORNER (Sketch p. 324), 320-1
LEARY, Vice-Admiral Herbert F., commands Anzac Area, 16; commands Allied Naval Forces SWPA, 24, 27
LEATHER, Rfn F. L. (Plate p. 130), 537
LEDDEN, Sgt J. P., 391
LEE, Lt-Col A. J., 220, 223, 333, 435, 436, 441
LEE, Capt Bevin D., 395, 397, 398
LEE, Capt J. D., 427
LEE, Rear-Admiral Willis A., 341, 342, 343, 345
LEGA (Sketch p. 52), 53
LEGGATT, Cpl R. G. E., 470
LEITCH, Lt J. C., 92, 95, 96, 540, 542
LEMMER, Pte H. H., 570
LESLIE, Maj D. R., 277, 309
LETE-FOHO (Sketch p. 599), 600, 613
LETHBRIDGE, Lt S. D., 168-9
Le Triomphant, French destroyer, 38-9
LEWIN, Capt J. E., 559, 560, 568, 571, 572, 573
LEWIS, Lt John B., 491, 493, 495
Lexington, American aircraft carrier, 67, 80, 81, 82, 255
LIAISON, on Kokoda Track, 275*n*, 308; with Kanga Force, 544
LIBYA, 141, 194, 351*n*
LILIHOA (Sketch p. 160), 165, 183
LILTAI (Sketch p. 599), 608, 609
LIMADI (Sketch p. 160), 184
LIMBONG, MOUNT (Sketch p. 60), 100
LINDSTROM, Lt-Col Harold M., 512, 513, 524, 525, 526
LISBON, 614
LITTLEJOHN, Capt R. A., 103
LITTLER, Sgt W. A., 560-1
LITTLE WAU CREEK (Sketch p. 559), 558
LLOYD, Maj-Gen H. W., 26

LLOYD, Brig J. E. (Plate p. 323), 268, 274, 275, 276, 280, 281, 285, 289, 290, 294, 296, 297, 306, 311, 312, 314, 315, 316, 318, 319, 320, 321, 322, 329, 384, 385, 386, 388, 389, 394, 398, 399, 403, 404; commands 16 Bde, 77; estimate of, 280
LLOYD, Lt P. A., 514-15
LOCKE, WO1 L. C., 377
LOCKE, Maj-Gen W. J. M., 26
LOGAN, Lt-Col E. P., 501, 502, 503
LOGAN, Maj L., 45
LOGAN, Lt L. G., 461
LOGAN Lt R. L., 202, 204
LOGAN, Lt T. T., 482
LOGUI (Map p. 585; Sketches pp. 52, 93), 53, 93, 95, 587
LOKANU (Map p. 585; Sketch p. 60), 105, 106, 534
LOLOTOI (Sketch p. 599), 598
LONDON, 16, 17, 112*n*, 118
LONG, Gavin, 2*n*
LOOKOUT NO. 1 (Sketch p. 60), 57, 59, 60, 61
LOOKOUT NO. 2, Salamaua, 537
LOOTING, at Port Moresby, 65; at Darwin, 71; in Timor, 619
LORD, WO2 F. A., 130, 214
LORENGAU (Map p. 37), 39, 65
LOUD, Sgt E., 608
LOUISIADE ARCHIPELAGO (Map p. 34; Sketch p. 81), 81, 114, 122
LOVELESS, Sig M. L., 601
LOVELL, Lt-Col D. J. H., 410, 411, 499, 500; commands 55/53 Bn, 406
LOWE, Hon Sir Charles, reports on Darwin raid, 71-2
LOWE, Capt H., 543
LUCAS, Sgt N. A., 375, 376, 377
LUDLOW, Lt J. J., 171, 172
LUNGA POINT (Sketch p. 149), 150, 152-3, 256, 338, 340
LUNGA RIVER (Sketch p. 149), 254, 258, 338-9, 344, 528
LUTJENS, 1st-Sgt Paul R., 379
LUZON (Map p. 37; Sketch p. 35), 34
LYNN, Cpl F. R. T., 516
LYON, Maj G. E., 222, 423
LYON, Maj H. M., 57, 62, 87, 89, 90, 96, 97
LYSAGHT, Maj N. H. L., 295, 296, 297, 298, 299, 318, 319, 393, 394, 395, 399, 400
LYTLE, Lt Wilbur C., 395, 396, 397, 398, 400

McADAM, Maj J. B. (Plate p. 130), 56, 59-61, 90, 91, 92, 100, 104
MACADIE, Tpr T. B., 508*n*
MACADIE, Col T. F. B., 540, 542, 543, 546, 547, 548, 558, 561, 568, 584; commands 2/7 Indep Coy, 538
MACARTHUR, General Arthur, 18, 509*n*
MACARTHUR, General of the Army Douglas (Plate p. 306), 30, 33, 140, 146, 197, 238, 241, 259, 262, 335, 352, 359, 372, 394, 403, 446, 490, 532, 591, 607, 619, 620; withdraws forces to Bataan Peninsula, 16; ordered to Australia, 16, 34; appointed Supreme Commander SWPA, 17; arrives Darwin, 17; estimate of, 18-20; relations with General Marshall, 20*n*; his directive, 21-2; relations with Mr Curtin, 23, 118; strength of forces in SWPA, 24, 32-3, 84; establishes GHQ in Melbourne, 24; opposes appointment of Australians to GHQ, 25, 28-9; assumes formal command of Australian Forces, 27; seeks reinforcement of SWPA, 29, 31, 118, 186, 188-9; assumes command of Visayan-Mindanao Force, 36; reinforcement of New Guinea, 82, 235, 242, 590; agrees with General Blamey on limited offensive, 88; authorises construction of airfields in south-east Papua, 111; gains confidence after Midway, 112; warns Blamey of probable Japanese attack on Port Moresby along Kokoda Track, 114; proposes ambitious attack New Britain-New Ireland area, 119; protests at date fixed for offensive in Solomons, 120; plans to halt Japanese advance in New Guinea, 121; and Milne Bay operations, 174, 180, 186; relations with Blamey, 175, 510; criticises Australian troops, 176, 225, 234-5, 240, 247-8; writes own communiqués, 226; directs employment of American troops in Papua, 227; orders Blamey to New Guinea, 237; relations with Admiral Ghormley, 259; plans recapture of Buna-Gona, 260, 337; stresses need for speedy advance to Kokoda, 274, 290; visits New Guinea for first time, 280; criticises Australian progress along Kokoda Track,

INDEX

MACARTHUR, General of the Army Douglas—*cont.* 299; meets General Allen, 307; advises caution in planning future operations, 310; problems of SWPA Command, 336; orders establishment of COSC at Port Moresby, 350; orders General Eichelberger to Buna, 371, 373, 450; on operations in Timor, 606; rejects Blamey's proposals for improving relations between American and Australian forces, 626-7
MCAULIFFE, Sgt W. H., 473
MCBARRON, Sig-Artificer L. J., 87
MCCABE, J. F., 407
MCCABE, Capt P. P., 614
MCCALLUM, Cpl C. R., 207-8, 222
MCCAMMON, Lt-Col H. G., 284*n*, 323*n*
MCCAMPBELL, Lt Robert P., 491-2, 511
MCCARTHY, Maj D., 73*n*
MACCARTHY, WO2 T. E., 184-5, 463
MCCARTNEY, William F., 33*n*
MCCARTY, Lt-Col J., 74-5
MCCLEAN, Maj D. I. H., 126, 127, 133, 445
MCCLOY, Lt J. B., 292, 293, 294, 328, 387, 393
MCCLURE, Lt J., 390
MCCOY, Lt-Col Robert C., 356, 359, 360, 361, 364, 366, 369, 373, 374, 376, 378, 454
MCCREADY, Capt S. P., 467
MCCREARY, Lt-Col M. C., 489
MCCROHON, Lt V. H., 452, 453, 454, 456, 460, 463, 469, 470, 471, 479, 480, 525
MCDONALD, Lt A. J., 559-60
MCDONALD, Capt D. J., 183
MCDONALD, Sgt F. M., 407
MCDONALD, Lt H. E. R., 426
MCDONALD, Maj H. F. G., 399
MACDONALD, Capt N. A. W., 200-1
MCDONALD, Brig W. D., 331, 396
MCDONALD'S KNOLL, 560, 564
MACDOUGAL, Lt B. H., 286, 287, 303, 403, 404
MCDOUGALL, Capt A. F., 472, 478
MACFARLANE, Maj R. H., 563, 566, 567
MCGAVIN, Capt A. S. D. J., 223, 425, 426
MCGEE, Capt G. M., 204, 205, 206, 209, 211, 212, 218, 222, 223, 224
MCGILLIVRAY, Pte C. M., 594-5
MACGRAW, Pte D. J., 200
MACGREGOR, Sgt K. A., 515, 516
MACGREGOR, WO R., 48
MCGREGOR, Cpl R. G., 252
MCGUIGAN, Pte J. J., 570
MCGUINN, Lt-Col L., 302
MCGUINNESS, Maj A. E., 407
MACHINE-GUNS, introduction of sub-machine-guns into British armies, 31; *American*, infantry establishment, 351; *Australian*, quota of production allotted to NEI, 10; monthly production, 30-1; in Owen Stanleys, 281; Owen Gun, 408; Lewis used against Australians at Buna, 472
MCILROY, Lt R. M., 217, 596, 597-8
MCINTOSH, Lt D. B., 564-5
MACINTOSH, Capt W. F., 457, 466, 467
MACKAY, Lt-Gen Sir Iven, 9, 120*n*, 229, 581, 583, 584; appointed GOC-in-Chief Home Forces, 4-5, 13; home defence plans, 6-8; his memorandum on defence of Melbourne-Brisbane region, 8; commands Second Army, 25; responsible for eastern and southern Australia only, 76; commands NGF, 563; praises cooperation of American Air Force, 565; seeks reinforcement of Wau, 576-7
MACKAY, Lt R., 327
MCKENNA, Capt J. B., 124, 138, 139
MCKENZIE, Maj N. B., 543
MACKIE, Capt C. H., 168, 169, 479
MACKIE, Maj J. H., 63-4
MCLAREN, Capt W. W., 131, 212, 214, 215
MACLEAN, Lt R. J., 472, 478
MCLENNAN, Pte W., 169
MCMAHON, WO2 W. T., 432
MCMULLEN, Col K. C., 58
MACNAB, Col Alexander J., 278, 279, 361-2, 363, 364, 366, 454, 455, 462, 463, 464, 466, 480, 483
MCNICOLL, Sir Walter, 42, 54, 58
MACNIDER, Brig-Gen J. Hanford (Plate p. 307), 239, 241, 261, 355, 360; selects route for American crossing of Owen Stanleys, 242; commands Wanigela Force, 278; Warren Force, 362
MCPHERSON, Maj W. J., 407
MADAGASCAR, 191

MADANG (Map p. 34), 48, 65, 540, 554*n*, 575, 577; bombing of, 39, 47; NGVR detachment at, 46; evacuation of, 49; estimated Japanese strength at 577
MADANG DISTRICT, evacuation of, 49-50
MADIGAN, Sgt E. S., 298
MAGA, Sgt-Maj, 117
MAGAREY, Maj J. R., 212, 213, 214, 215, 277
MAGULI RANGE (Map p. 114), 195, 223
MAIDMENT, Pte G., 209-10
MAIL, at Buna, 382; at Sanananda, 393
MALARIA, 382, 406, 421, 437; at Milne Bay, 157-8; on Guadalcanal, 154, 528; on Sanananda Track, 399
MALAYA (Map p. 37), 1, 10, 15, 22, 28, 68, 144, 191, 193, 235; Japanese invasion of, 10; lessons of, applied to training of AIF in Ceylon, 79
MALIANA (Sketch p. 599), 608
MALO, New Guinea native, 100
MALTA, 118, 189
MAMBARE RIVER (Map p. 34; Sketches pp. 123, 128), 128, 416, 446, 468, 511, 530, 575, 576, 590; Japanese beachhead on, 530
MANATUTO (Sketch p. 599), 608, 610, 613, 614
MANILA BAY (Sketch p. 35), 35, 36
MANNING, Capt H. A., 363, 365, 366, 367, 368, 371, 373, 454, 456, 524
MANPOWER, 243
Manunda, Australian hospital ship, at Darwin, 70; at Gili Gili, 183-4
MANUS ISLAND (Maps pp. 34, 37), 39, 65
MAPE (Sketch p. 599), 599, 601-3, 607-8, 610
MAPOS (Map p. 585; Sketch p. 52), 53, 89, 103, 104
MAPS, capture of first Japanese, 135; of Milne Bay, 157, 166; of Buna, 367; of Gona area, 433
MARCH, Spr W. E., 600
MARCHANT, Lt-Col W. S., 152
MARCUS ISLAND (Map p. 37), 67
MAREEBA (Sketch p. 7), 111
MARIANAS ISLANDS (Map p. 37), 336
MARKHAM POINT (Sketches pp. 52, 87), 62
MARKHAM RIVER (Map p. 34; Sketches pp. 52, 87), 50, 54, 62, 63, 86, 89, 97, 99, 100, 101, 104, 539, 572, 578, 584, 588, 590
MARKHAM VALLEY (Map p. 585; Sketches pp. 52, 87), 54, 57, 59, 89, 90, 100, 104, 107, 310, 536, 538, 578; operations in, 86-88, 101-2, 536-7
MAROBO (Sketch p. 599), 608
MARQUAT, Brig-Gen William F., 28*n*
MARR, Capt W. R., 363
MARSH, S-Sgt H. W., 133, 134, 135
MARSHALL, Maj A., 180, 181, 183
MARSHALL, General of the Army George C., 34, 82, 119, 120, 140, 186, 225, 259; approves plans for establishing American base in Australia, 14; relations with General MacArthur, 20*n*; requests MacArthur to include Allied officers in senior appointments on GHQ, SWPA, 28-9; and Beat Hitler first policy, 188-9; considers holding of Guadalcanal vital, 337-8
MARSHALL, Brig-Gen Richard J., 28*n*
MARSHALL ISLANDS (Map p. 37), 67, 336
MARSON, Colonel R. H., 272, 273, 274, 312, 321, 323, 327, 330, 331, 418, 421, 422; commands 2/25 Bn, 263
MARTIN, Maj-Gen Clarence A., 373, 454, 471, 476; commands Warren Force, 374
MARTIN, Pte S. A., 361
MARTLEW, Pte R. G., 252
MARUOKA, Colonel, 575, 576
MARUYAMA, Lt-Gen Masao, 258, 344
MARYBOROUGH (Sketch p. 7), 11
MASON, Lt L. F., 207
MASON, Lt P. E., 64, 151
MASSACRES, 39*n*; see also EXECUTIONS
MATANIKAU RIVER (Sketch p. 149), 154, 254, 256-8, 338-9, 344, 528
MATHESON, Maj H. R., 167, 168, 170, 171, 173, 462, 463, 471, 472, 473, 476, 478, 479, 480, 524
MATLOFF, M. and SNELL, E. M., 14*n*, 119*n*
MAT MAT HILL (Sketch p. 541), 537, 540, 542, 543, 583, 584, 586
MATSCHOSS, Pte A. R., 597
MATTHEWS, Lt-Col G. R., 526; commands 14 Bde, 512
MATTHEWS, Sgt J. M., 222
MATZ, 2nd-Lt Fred W., 489-90, 491

648 INDEX

MAUBISSE (Sketch p. 599), 603, 608, 609, 610, 611, 612, 613, 616, 618
MAUCATAR (Sketch p. 599), 608
Mauna Loa, American ship, 70
MAUND, Rear-Admiral L. E. H., 147*n*
MAWHOOD, Lt-Col J. C., 85
MAY, Capt R. E. G., 477, 481, 482, 512
Maya, Japanese cruiser, 342
MAY RIVER (Map p. 34), 49
MAYBERRY, Lt L. P., 432, 441
MAYNE, Pte A., 592, 594
MAYNE, Sgt R. C., 87
MAYNES, Maj J. W., 578, 579, 580
Meade, American destroyer, 343
MEANI, Sgt F. W., 200, 443
MEARES, Capt W. A., 568, 571, 573
MEDENDORP, Capt Alfred, 353, 401
MEDICAL ARRANGEMENTS, on Kokoda Track, 212-15, 276-7
Meigs, American ship, 70
MELBOURNE (Sketch p. 7), 7, 8, 24, 27, 111, 119, 120, 148, 280; Area Combined Headquarters established at, 9; GHQ SWPA maintained at, 112*n*
MELDRUM, Lt-Col A., 161, 163, 165, 177; commands 61 Bn, 160
MELROSE, R., 55
MELVILLE ISLAND (Sketch p. 7), 68
MEMO (Sketch p. 599), 599, 608-9
MENARI (Map p. 114; Sketch p. 250), 108-9, 195-6, 212, 215, 221, 227, 229, 248-50, 269, 281, 596; Australian withdrawal to, 222-3; Australian casualties at, 263
MENDAROPU (Sketch p. 353), 354
MENZIES, Capt J. R., 573
MENZIES' JUNCTION, 573-4
MERAUKE (Map p. 34), 140; construction of airfields at, 121
MERLE-SMITH, Col Van S., 625
MERRITT, Maj W. G. T., 137, 138, 142, 203
METAPONA RIVER (Sketch p. 149), 338-9
METSON, Cpl J. A., 211, 592, 593, 594
MIDDENDORF, 2nd-Lt Charles A., 489, 490, 491
MIDDLE EAST, 1, 4, 9, 10, 13, 21, 24, 25, 28, 42, 67, 72, 73, 74, 76, 79, 191, 193, 194, 218*n*, 244, 357, 449, 509; strategic responsibility for, 17; British Independent Companies operate in, 85; 9th Division retained in, 118; deterioration of British position in, 189
MIDWAY ISLAND (Map p. 37), 83, 112, 118, 119, 120, 143, 153, 189, 255, 258; naval battle of, 113, 114, 590
MIETHKE, Maj G. R., 167, 168, 169, 170, 171
MIKAWA, Vice-Admiral Gunichi, 114, 342, 343, 344, 345; commands *Eighth Fleet*, 44
MILES, Lt-Col E. S., 171; commands 25 Bn, 160
MILFORD, Maj-Gen E. J., 588-9; commands 5th Division, 26
MILITIA, THE, 4, 32, 73, 112*n*, 114, 591; strength, training and equipment, 1-2, 9-10, 13, 24, 29-32, 44; estimate of system, 9; call-up of, 11; prevented from enlisting in AIF or RAAF, 13; strengthened by infusion of AIF officers, 30, 115; strength in New Guinea, 115*n*; performance at Milne Bay, 187; in Owen Stanleys, 226, 334; attitude to enlistment in AIF, 405; on Sanananda Track, 413, 501, 527, 532; at Gona, 490; General Blamey's increased respect for, 450; casualties in Papua, 501, 527
MILJATIVICH, S-Sgt Milan J., 492-3
MILLER, J., 254*n*, 257*n*, 337*n*, 338*n*, 528*n*
MILLER, Lt-Col J., 327, 328, 329, 333, 418, 419, 421, 435*n*; commands 2/31 Bn, 321
MILLER, Lt-Col Kelsie E., 356, 359, 360, 361, 366, 367, 374, 376, 378
MILLER, Capt L., 233
MILLER, WO1 S. G., 298, 388
MILLER, L-Cpl T., 622
MILLROY, Maj A. J., commands 2/25 Bn, 274
MILNE, Pte W. F., 464
MILNE BAY (Maps pp. 34, 156; Sketches pp. 160, 173), 105, 140, 147, 161, 176, 193, 202, 208, 225-7, 237, 239, 244, 248, 261, 278, 304, 310, 333-4, 336, 346, 349, 354, 362-3, 369, 375, 381, 413, 450-3, 456, 458, 465, 468-9, 477, 482, 497, 509, 512, 531, 534, 544, 545, 548, 588-9, 590; chosen as airfield site, 112, 121; reinforcement of, 121-2, 159; Japanese plan attack on, 144-5, 154-5; development

MILNE BAY—*continued*
of, 157-8; dispositions at, 158, 160-1, 173; operations at, 161-73, 181; reactions at GHQ SWPA, 174-5; Japanese withdraw from, 183, 186; casualties, 185; Japanese account of operations, 185-6; conduct of operations at, 186; importance of victory at, 187-8; garrisoning of, 310, 449, 577
MILNER, Samuel, 28*n*, 29*n*, 120*n*, 352*n*, 359*n*, 369*n*, 371*n*, 373*n*, 491*n*, 494*n*, 510*n*, 512*n*, 522*n*, 523*n*
MINCHIN, Capt L. J., 105, 106*n*, 534
MINDANAO (Map p. 37; Sketch p. 35), 36, 613, 617
MINES, Japanese, on Sanananda Track, 516
Minneapolis, American cruiser, 80
MINOGUE, Lt-Col J. P., 274, 275*n*, 308
MISIMA ISLAND (Sketch p. 81), 81
MISSIM (Map p. 585; Sketch p. 52), 53, 89, 583, 584, 587
MISSIMA (Map p. 313; Sketch p. 123), 141, 199, 200, 201, 202, 215, 228, 311, 312
MISSIONARIES, 50; on Nauru, 39; on Bougainville, 64; in Papua, 123, 125, 139
MISSION RIDGE (Sketch p. 220), 220
MITCHELL, WO2 D. McR., 61
MITCHELL, Cpl Harold L., 380
MITCHELL, Sgt J., 478-9
MIYAMOTO, Major, 228
MOLONEY, Lt B. W., 224
MOLOTOV COCKTAILS, 172
MONCKTON, C. A. W., 110
MOOLOOLAH, Qld., 625
MOORE, Lt G. G., 204, 207
MOORE, Capt R. McC., 317, 318
MORALE, *American*, at Buna, 359, 360, 369, 374, 491, 492, 494. *Australian*, at Darwin, 73-4; of Kanga Force, 99, 103; on Kokoda Track, 132, 142, 202; after Milne Bay, 187; at Eora Creek, 300; on Sanananda Track, 413, 500, 501; on Timor, 605. *Japanese*, at Ioribaiwa, 305; in Timor, 604
MOREY, L-Sgt G. W., 458
MOREY, Pte L. G., 432
MORGAN, Lt-Col H. D., 160
MORGAN, Lt H. J., 605
MORISON, Rear-Admiral S. E., 342*n*, 345*n*
MOROBE (Map p. 34), 47, 49, 55, 93, 106*n*, 575, 576, 590
MORRIS, Maj-Gen B. M. (Plate p. 66), 45, 46, 57, 59, 62, 63, 65, 67, 68, 72, 80, 104, 105, 111, 126, 129, 130, 159, 197; commands New Guinea Force, 26; issues call-up notices, 42-3; handicapped by shortages of aircraft, 103, 140; suggests construction of airfields at Milne Bay, 112; orders reconnaissance of Awala-Ioma area, 114; considers Kokoda Track impassable for large-scale military movements, 115; terminates native labour contracts, 116; orders 39 Bn to Kokoda, 122-3; hands over command to General Rowell, 140
MORRIS, WO1 G. E., 210, 218, 222
MORRISON, Sgt E. J., 126, 127, 128, 129, 437
MORRISON, Lt L. A., 409
MORSHEAD, Lt-Gen Sir Leslie, 25
MORTARS, *American*, infantry battalion establishment, 351; on Sanananda Track, 398, 404, 524; at Buna, 489. *Australian*, strength and monthly production of, 30-1; at Milne Bay, 163, 164, 183; air dropping affects ammunition for, 272, 301; in Owen Stanleys, 281, 283, 298; at Oivi-Gorari, 319-22; at Buna, 374; on Sanananda Track, 404, 499, 519, 520, 523; in Gona area, 430, 440, 445; in Wau-Mubo area, 542, 558, 562, 567. *Japanese*, 550; at Milne Bay, 170; in Owen Stanleys, 203, 296, 297, 298; at Oivi-Gorari, 318, 322, 325
MORTIMORE, Lt H. E., 125, 128, 443, 445
MORTON, Cpl H. A., 504-5
MORTON, Louis, 34*n*, 36*n*, 38*n*
MOSES, Lt-Col C. J. A., 508
MOSS, Maj N. L., 462, 479
MOTEN, Brig M. J., 375, 546, 547, 548, 550, 551, 553, 554, 555, 557, 563, 568, 569, 571, 572, 574, 583, 584, 586, 587, 588; commands Kanga Force, 545
MOTIEAU (Map p. 156; Sketch p. 173), 163, 164, 165
MOTIEAU CREEK (Map p. 156; Sketch p. 173), 164
MOTIEAU POINT (Map p. 156), 176
MOTT, Colonel John W., 369, 370, 371, 373; commands Urbana Force, 366; replaced, 374
MOULE, Spr L. C., 617
MOUNT ISA (Sketch p. 7), 10, 75
MOUNT KAINDI POWER HOUSE (Map p. 585), 538

INDEX

Moy, Maj F. H., 106n
Moyes, Capt G. E., 500
Moy's Post, 106n
Mubo (Map p. 585; Sketches pp. 52, 535, 541), 53, 56, 57, 59, 60, 61, 89, 91, 101, 102, 103, 104, 105, 534, 535, 536, 538, 539, 543, 544, 546, 547, 548, 562, 572, 574, 575, 576, 578, 581, 582, 583, 586, 587, 588; Japanese attack of 21st July, 100; Japanese capture of, 105-7; Australian attack on, 537, 540-3
Mubo Airstrip (Sketch p. 541), 540
Mubo Gorge (Sketch p. 52), 53
Mud Bay (Sketch p. 346), 347, 348, 349
Mueller, Capt C. A., 354, 362, 363, 367
Mugford, American destroyer, 150
Muir, Lt-Col R. A. C., 550-1, 557-8
Mules, used for transport of supplies in New Guinea, 116-17, 561
Mullen, Lt-Col L. M., 3n
Muller Range (Map p. 34), 47
Mullins Harbour (Map p. 34), 111
Mumun (Sketch p. 385), 384
Munitions Production, 10, 30-1
Munum (Sketches pp. 52, 87), 87, 88, 101; burned by Japanese as reprisal, 102
Munum Waters (Sketch p. 87), 97
Murakumo, Japanese destroyer, 255
Murcutt, WO2 W. M., 97
Murphy, Capt C. D., 613, 617, 618, 619
Murphy, Sgt G. B. J., 438
Murphy, Capt J. J., 101
Murray, Lt A. D. B., 391
Murray, Capt A. McL., 481, 482, 483
Murray, Sir Hubert, 42
Murray, Hon H. L., 42-3
Murray, Lt-Col H. W., VC, 30
Murray, Maj-Gen J. J., 13, 26, 30
Murray, Sgt W., 203
Murray-Smith, Sgt S., 98
Musa River (Sketch p. 353), 278-9, 360
Musita Island (Sketches pp. 486, 495), 487-8, 490, 492-3
Myhre, Pte J. F., 209
Myola (Map p. 114; Sketch p. 593), 195-9, 201, 208-12, 214, 215, 217-19, 221, 243, 249, 263-4, 268, 274-7, 281, 285, 291, 307-9, 311, 317, 592-3, 596; discovery and development of, 130-1; evacuation of casualties from, 214-15, 277, 316-17; Australian withdrawal from, 219-20; supply dropping at, 269

Nadi Nadi (Sketch p. 346), 346
Nadzab (Map p. 34; Sketch p. 52), 54, 57, 62, 86, 97, 99, 102, 310, 577, 578; Japanese ambush at, 87
Nagara, Japanese cruiser, 341, 343
Nagumo, Vice-Admiral C., 114
Nalimbiu River (Sketch p. 149), 339
Namatanai (Map p. 34), 39
Namling (Map p. 585), 587
Namudi (Map p. 34; Sketch p. 353), 260
Nankai Maru, Japanese merchantman, 185
Narakapor (Sketches pp. 52, 87), 88, 97, 101
Naro (Sketches pp. 123, 128), 141, 199, 201-3
Naro Ridge (Sketches pp. 123, 128), 142, 209
Nassau Bay (Map p. 585), 586
Nasu, Maj-Gen Yumio, 258
Nathan, Lt G. MacF., 328
National Security Regulations, invoked in Northern Territory, 72, in New Guinea, 116
Natsugumo, Japanese destroyer, 255
Natunga (Sketch p. 353), 353, 358
Nauro (Map p. 114; Sketch p. 250), 108, 117, 130, 132, 195, 212, 223-4, 227, 229, 230, 241, 243, 249-51, 260-1, 263, 268, 277; abandoned by Japanese, 246; recapture of, 262
Nauru (Map p. 37), 38-9
Neal, Lt F. R., 135-6
Neilson, Pte A. J., 206
Nelson, Cape (Map p. 34), 260, 336
Nelson, Capt J. W., 436
Nelson, Maj St E. D., 559, 563, 586
Neosho, American naval tanker, 80, 81, 82
Neptuna, Australian ship, 70
Nereus, schooner, 49
Netherlands East Indies (Map p. 37), 1, 11, 14, 17, 27, 34, 66, 69, 76, 191, 598; Australian aid to, 10; dispatch of AIF to, 12; represented on Pacific War Council, 21

New Britain (Map p. 37; Sketch p. 81), 39, 40, 48, 50, 57, 60, 80, 84, 119, 336, 408n, 415, 544, 582
New Caledonia (Map p. 19), 11, 148, 338, 557; Australian aid to, 10; reinforcement of, 15, 38; planned Japanese invasion of, 83, 113, 143; 2/3 Indep Coy on, 86
Newcastle, NSW (Sketch p. 7), 6, 7, 8, 12, 27
New Guinea (Map p. 34), 1, 5, 7, 15, 16, 26, 29, 34, 38-9, 43, 45, 47, 49, 50-1, 56, 58-9, 63, 65-6, 83, 112n, 122, 128, 131, 140, 144, 146, 173-4, 190, 218n, 225, 234, 239, 244, 247, 251, 257, 260, 280, 290, 299, 307n, 310, 317, 334n, 336-7, 345, 349, 351, 357, 381, 383, 405-6, 419, 446-7, 450-1, 453, 497, 509, 528, 538, 544-6, 574, 578, 582, 588, 590-1 620, 624, 625, 626, 627; Australian Army strength in, 12, 576-7; included in SWPA Command, 22; civil administration of, 40-1, 42, 46, 49, 54, 58; evacuation of civilians, 41-2, 47-50, 54-5, 57-8; raising of NGVR authorised, 46; naval organisation in, 47; "walking times" in, 50n; Allied reinforcement policy, 82, 84, 111, 121, 140-1, 159, 188, 193, 227, 234, 242; Japanese plans and strength in, 83, 113n, 254, 304, 575; first large airlift of troops in, 89; transport of supplies in, 115, 198, 350-1; Allied strength in, 115n, 234, 577; National Security Regulations invoked, 116; its place in Allied strategy, 119-20; GHQ ignorance of conditions in, 141; Japanese lack knowledge of, 144; General Blamey takes command in, 235-6, 240; effect of Guadalcanal on Allied planning in, 259; casualties in, 334, 531; Allied air superiority in, 336; Japanese strength in, 575
New Guinea, Dutch (Map p. 37), 47, 49n
New Guinea, Native Population of, indenture system, 41, 115-16; on Sepik River, 47-9; effect of war on, 49-50, 55; in Baum country, 50-1; cooperation with Allies, 56, 58, 61, 88, 90, 137, 593, 596, 597; and the Japanese, 88, 100, 102, 105, 135, 144, 145, 519; betray missionaries, 139. *See also* Carriers, Native
New Hebrides (Map p. 37), 12, 38, 39, 63, 80, 86, 119, 255
New Ireland (Map p. 34), 39, 119, 336
New Orleans, American cruiser, 80
New South Wales, 3n, 25, 27, 44, 497; Australian Army dispositions in, 12
New Strip (Sketches pp. 370, 455), 356, 359, 360-1, 364, 367, 369, 370, 373-4, 376, 378, 451, 454-6, 458, 461-3, 465, 477, 479, 485
New Zealand, 9, 10, 15, 16, 17, 38, 83, 113n, 147, 338n; represented on Pacific War Council, 21; 1st Marine Division arrives in, 148; defence of, 190
New Zealand Air Force, Royal, 529
New Zealand Government, protests about proposals for sub-division of Pacific, 21
—Chiefs of Staffs, 16
Ngasawapum (Sketches pp. 52, 87), 86-8, 97, 99, 101-2
Niall, Maj H. L. R., 58, 540
Nicholas, Sgt T., 407
Nichols, Lt W. H. E., 594
Nick's Camp (Sketch p. 87), 101-2
Nimitz, Admiral Chester W., 257; appointed Supreme Commander, Pacific Ocean Area, 17; his directive, 21, 22-3
Ninigo Islands (Map p. 34), 65
Nisbet, Brig T. G., 604, 605, 618
Nishimura, Rear-Admiral Shoji, 342
Nix, Maj L. F., 363, 381
Noakes, Lt L. C., 446-7
Noble, Cpl J. W., 549
Noble, WO2 W. A., 222, 224
Noblett, Capt K. E., 87, 88, 101
Nojima, Japanese ship, 582
Normanby Island (Map p. 34; Sketch p. 346), 346
Norris, Maj-Gen Sir Frank Kingsley, 215, 316, 423
Norris, Lt-Col G. M., 571-2
North Africa, 29, 30, 73, 74, 118, 307n, 337, 402, 544
North Australian Railway, 72
North Carolina, American battleship, 154, 254, 255
Northcott, Lt-Gen Sir John, 4, 449, 451, 469; commands II Corps, 26; appointed CGS, 140n
Northern Territory, 4, 7, 26-7, 73-4, 76-7, 86, 244, 509, 602, 611; Australian Army strength in, 12; administration placed under military commander, 72

NORTH PACIFIC AREA (Map p. 19), 21
NORWAY, 147; British commandos in, 85
NOTESTINE, Lt Ronald E., 316
NOUMEA, 338, 340-1, 528
NOYES, Capt W. H., 405n, 408, 409, 411, 499
NUK NUK (Sketch p. 52), 53
Nulli Secundus Log, 323n, 393n, 406n, 407n
NUMA NUMA (Sketch p. 148), 64
NYE, Capt C. C. P., 201, 203, 204, 205, 207, 211, 222

O'Brien, American destroyer, 154
O'BRIEN, WO2 J. F. P., 170
O'BRIEN, Maj-Gen J. W. A., 355n, 369n, 382n
O'BRYEN, Maj T. J. C., 246, 271, 272
OBSERVATION HILL (Sketch p. 541), 540, 542, 586
OCEAN ISLAND (Map p. 37), 38-9
O'CONNELL, Brig K. E., 363, 375
O'CONNOR Maj E. D., 613, 614, 617, 618, 619, 622
ODA, Maj-Gen Kensaku, 416, 446, 447, 527, 530
O'DONNELL, Sgt L., 407
OESTREICHER, Lt R. G., 70
OFFICERS, *American*, lack of First War experience, 32, Marine Corps, 147. *Australian*, militia, 2, 29-30; recalled from Middle East for home army, 13, 405, in 30th Brigade, 115
O'GRADY, Maj O. J., 272, 323
O'HARE, Lt-Col M. P., 356-7, 366, 367, 382, 454, 456, 474
OIVI (Map p. 313; Sketch p. 123), 110, 128, 133, 134, 296, 311, 314-15, 324, 325, 329, 334, 416; action at, 126-7, 317-20, 322-3, 329; Japanese strength at, 321, Japanese account, 330-1; fate of survivors, 416
OIVI TRACK (Map p. 313), 315
OKA, Colonel, 154, 155
OKABE, Maj-Gen Teru, 575
OKADA, Seizo, 304-6
Oklahoma, American battleship, 255
OLDHAM, Maj J. M., 212, 215
OLD MARI (Sketch p. 87), 104
OLD STRIP (Sketch p. 467), 356, 359, 376, 451, 454, 465, 481, 483, 485; operations on, 468, 469-480; Japanese account, 485
O'LOGHLEN, Capt C. M., 93, 95, 96
O'NEILL, Capt J. H., 431, 432, 433
O'NEILL, Lt W., 92, 94, 95, 96, 537, 539
ONGAHAMBO (Sketch p. 123), 125
OPI RIVER (Sketch p. 123), 124
ORO BAY (Map p. 34; Sketch p. 353), 352, 354, 362-3, 375, 381, 452-3, 480, 510, 512, 590; development of, 532, 589
OROKAIVAS, THE, 110, 126n
Orontes, British transport, 78
ORPWOOD, Cpl J. E., 376, 377, 378
OSSU (Sketch p. 599), 613
O'SULLIVAN, Pte J. P., 594
OTIBANDA (Sketch p. 52), 90
Otranto, British transport, 78
OWEN, Lt F., 390
OWEN, Lt-Col W. T. (Plate p. 130), 122, 123, 125, 126, 127, 128, 129; commands 39 Bn, 115
OWEN STANLEY RANGE (Map p. 34; Sketch p. 353), 102, 108, 109, 112n, 114, 121, 138-9, 140-1, 193, 197, 224-5, 234, 235n, 237, 242, 271, 304-6, 307n, 317, 332, 336, 352, 371, 402, 427, 435n, 450, 531, 534, 594; supply problem in, 196-9, 260-2, 264-7; trials of troops cut off in, 592
OWERS, Capt N., 56, 261n
OWERS' CORNER (Map p. 114), 240, 245, 261n, 280, 308
OWERS' CREEK, 261
OXLADE, Lt L. M., 503

PACIFIC OCEAN, 14, 15, 34, 38, 82, 83, 84, 119, 189, 304, 336, 453; Japanese penetration to March 1942, 1; United States' role in, 16; strategic division of (Map p. 19), 17, 21; American carrier strength, 82; importance of Battle of Midway, 113; Allied strategy in, 119-20, 189; American strength and disposition of forces in, 190; Japanese readjustment of command, 383; Allied reinforcement of, 528
PACIFIC OCEAN AREA (Map p. 19), 17, 21, 22
PACIFIC THEATRE (Map p. 19), 21
PACIFIC WAR COUNCIL, 23, 259; established, 16, 21
PALAU ISLANDS (Map p. 37), 144
PALESTINE, 84, 351n, 497
PALMER, Maj A. S., 65
PANAY (Sketch p. 35), 36

PAPUA (Map p. 34), 7, 26, 38-9, 47, 50, 90, 102-3, 108, 110, 114, 116, 127, 140, 144, 157, 188, 192, 227, 234, 241, 279, 351, 448, 450, 451, 496, 527-8, 530, 531-2, 534, 538, 544-5, 577, 589, 590; Australian Army strength in, 12; history and economic development, 40-1; evacuation of women and children, 41-2; civil administration ceases, 42-3; call-up notices issued, 42-3; naval organisation, 47; airfield development, 111; National Security Regulations invoked, 116; Japanese invasion, 122, 144-6; effect of Milne Bay defeat on Japanese plans in, 187; Allied plans, 260; supply organisation, 266-8; strength of Japanese forces and casualties, 531; Allied casualties, 531; necessity for reduction of Buna-Gona beach-head examined, 531-3; Allied strengths and dispositions, 577
PAPUAN CONSTABULARY, ROYAL, 117, 124, 133, 135, 347
PAPUANS, indentured labour system, 115-16; *see also* NEW GUINEA, NATIVE POPULATION; CARRIERS, NATIVE
PARBURY, Lt-Col C. B., 456, 458, 459, 461, 462, 463, 464
PARER, Kevin, 54
PARER, R. J. P., 54
PARK, Lt J. W., 552, 570
PARKER, Lt-Col G. E., 601
PARKER, Cpl R. P., 560
PARKINSON, Sgt J. H., 172
PARKINSON, Miss Mavis, 139
PARR, Pte W., 129
PARRY-OKEDEN, Lt-Col W. N., 468, 513, 514, 520, 523, 524; commands 2/9 Bn, 467
PARTEP 2 (Map p. 585; Sketch p. 52), 104, 588
PATCH, Lt-Gen Alexander M., 38, 338; commands troops on Guadalcanal, 528; commands XIV Corps, 529
PATERSON, Lt D. A., 215
PATERSON, Capt J., 182
PATROLS, 152; *American*, at Buna, 365, 374, 487, on Sanananda Track, 525. *Australian*, in pre-war New Guinea, 40, 51; of Kanga Force, 88, 97, 100, 104-5, 107, 538-9, 546-7, 555-6, 557-8, 563-4, 568, 571-2, 574, 578, 586; of Papuan Infantry Battalion, 111, 124, 590; on Kokoda Track, 133, 136-7, 143, 199, 200, 201, 209, 217, 220, 231, 244-5, 246, 247, 262, 263, 276, 302; at Milne Bay, 162, 165, 171, 176-7, 179-80, 182-3; at Gorari, 325; Buna-Gona area, 360, 376, 398, 400, 412, 419, 425, 427, 438-9, 442, 501, 505-6, 514, 517, 518, 520-2; Amboga River area, 519, 526; in Timor, 607, 609, 613, 615. *Japanese*, 572, 577, Salamaua-Lae area, 61, 63, 86, 87, 96, 100; on Kokoda Track, 200, 230, at Gona, 422
Patterson, American destroyer, 152
PAUL, Lt-Col A. T., 227
PAULEY, Lt A. E., 104, 539
PEARCE, L-Cpl A. W., 103
PEARCE, Lt G. E., 205, 208, 211, 220, 419
PEARL HARBOUR (Map p. 37), 32, 67, 80, 113, 148, 255, 257
PEARLMAN, Tpr H., 506
Peary, American destroyer, 69, 70
PEEK, Maj E. J. F., 181, 182, 183
PELL, Maj Floyd J., 69, 70
PENGLASE, Maj N., 49, 51, 55, 58, 540
PENNEY, Sgt E. M., 251
Pensacola, American cruiser, 14, 69
PENTLAND, Capt W. C., 138, 142, 202, 207
Perkins, American destroyer, 80
PETT, Cpl L. G., 303
PHELPS, Lt R. S., 420, 421
PHILIPPINE AIR FORCE, 20
PHILIPPINE ARMY, 1, 17, 38
PHILIPPINE ISLANDS (Maps pp. 19, 37; Sketch p. 35), 18, 22, 24-5, 28, 31, 71, 72, 84, 145, 147, 185, 336, 509n, 610n; Japanese air attacks on, 14; operations in, 16, 34-8; placed in SWPA Command, 17; American air forces in, 20
PHILLIPS, Capt R. H. D., 55, 62, 97, 98
PHILLIPS, L-Cpl R. O., 622
PIKE, Cpl T. H., 126
PILL-BOXES, on Sanananda Track, 516-17
PINWILL, Lt F. S., 461, 463, 464
PIRIVI (Map p. 313; Sketches pp. 123, 128), 133, 135, 311, 314, 315
PISSER VALLEY, 573-4

INDEX 651

PIXLEY, Capt S. E. A., 405n
PLANT, Maj-Gen E. C. P., 13, 76
PLATER, Capt R. S., 443, 445, 447
POIN CREEK (Map p. 156; Sketches pp. 173, 179), 172, 177
POINER, Lt H. J., 499
POINT CRUZ (Sketch p. 149), 338, 339, 528, 529
POINT KING (Map p. 156), 178
POINT "X" (Sketches pp. 423, 428), 425, 426, 427, 431
POINT "Y" (Sketches pp. 423, 428), 425, 426, 427
POINT "Z" (Sketch p. 428), 427, 429, 430
POLLARD, Lt-Gen R. G., 414, 439, 513, 516, 517, 525
POLLITT, Capt D. W., 292-3
PONGANI (Map p. 34; Sketch p. 353), 262, 278, 279, 290, 352-5, 360, 363; airfield at, 357
PONOON (Sketch p. 230), 230
POPONDETTA (Map p. 370; Sketches pp. 123, 353), 110, 352, 354, 358, 363, 368, 372, 384, 385, 386, 394, 396, 400, 405, 412, 425, 427, 434, 451, 512, 518
POPONDETTA AIRFIELD (Map p. 370), 396, 398, 406; evacuation of casualties from, 399
PORLOCK HARBOUR (Map p. 34; Sketch p. 353), 161, 354, 369, 375, 381, 451-2, 454, 577, 589
PORT AUGUSTA (Sketch p. 7), 10
Porter, American destroyer, 257
PORTER, Maj-Gen S. H. W. C. (Plate p. 130), 143, 196, 199, 229, 231-2, 245, 408, 410, 412, 434, 498, 499, 500; commands 30 Bde, 114-15, Maroubra Force, 141, 143, 224; hands over to Brigadier Eather, 227; on American troops on Sanananda Track, 414-15; appreciates position, 497-8; criticises 36th and 55th/53rd Battalions, 501
PORT KEMBLA (Sketch p. 7), 6, 7, 8, 9, 12
Portland, American cruiser, 80, 341
Portmar, American ship, 70
PORT MORESBY (Maps pp. 34, 114), 11, 17, 27, 40, 42, 44, 45, 47, 50, 55, 57, 59, 60-2, 66, 69, 72, 80, 86, 99, 104-5, 106n, 108, 111, 117, 120, 121, 123, 126, 129, 130, 136-40, 143-6, 175, 183n, 185, 193-4, 196-8, 202, 212, 215, 217, 220, 224-6, 229, 233-4, 237-9, 241-2, 244, 246, 251-2, 268, 278, 287, 299, 304-5, 307, 310, 311, 316, 317, 333-4, 336, 349, 350-1, 359, 363, 371, 373, 374, 375, 381, 399, 405, 413, 422, 424, 425, 427, 435n, 449, 450-2, 462, 468, 474, 486, 497, 509, 511, 512, 516n, 518, 531, 532, 538, 544-7, 553, 558, 577, 580, 582, 589; Japanese air raids on, 1, 39, 43, 65-6, 67, 589; reinforcement of, 10, 140; Australian Army strength at, 12, 45; defence plans, 44, 66, 115, 227, 243-4; aircraft strength and reinforcement of, 46, 67, 103; Japanese plan capture of, 80-1, 82, 113, 114, 143, 145, 152, 154, 187, 254, 257; airfields at, 83; strategical value, 112n, 242; Advanced Echelon GHQ established at, 235n; General Blamey's arrival, 236
PORT PHILLIP (Sketch p. 7), 7
PORT STEPHENS (Sketch p. 7), 12
PORTUGAL, 602, 614; proposes negotiations for withdrawal of Japanese from Portuguese Timor, 606. *See also* TIMOR, PORTUGUESE
PORTUGUESE, THE, in Timor, 599, 609-10, 614-15, 623; evacuation of, 615, 616, 617, 618; numbers on Timor, 615n
PORTUGUESE DEPORTADOS, 602
POTTS, Brig A. W. (Plate p. 211), 193, 200, 204, 207, 208, 212, 213, 214, 215, 219, 220, 221, 222, 223, 225, 226, 227, 228, 229, 309, 406, 422; commands Maroubra Force, 143; ordered to recapture Kokoda, 194; estimate of, 195; supply problems on Kokoda Track, 196, 197, 198-9; on training and discipline of 53 Bn, 201; asks for 2/27 Bn, 201-2; orders recapture of Missima, 202; handicaps of, 209; orders withdrawal to Eora Creek, 210-11; withdraws to Templeton's Crossing, 217; relinquishes command of 21 Bde, 224; handling of battle examined, 247
POWELL, Lt R. E., 326, 328, 329
POWER, Capt K., 270, 271, 419
POWERS, Capt A. M., 500
POWERS, Capt S. W., 500
PRATT, Fletcher, 255n
PREECE, Lt R., 215, 252
PRENTICE, Capt V. D., 458
Preston, American seaplane tender, 70
PRINGLE, Capt F. B., 554, 555, 556, 558, 560, 563, 586
PRIOR, Capt C. J., 298, 387, 388, 389
PRISONERS OF WAR, Japanese, 65, 281, 346, 386, 484, 496, 517, 520, 522, 523; of the Japanese, 576

P.T. BOATS, 468-9, 590; Buna-Gona area, 510; attack Japanese evacuating Kumusi, 519; in Battle of Bismarck Sea, 583
PULFER, Sgt C., 134
PULLAR, Pte W. J., 101
PURSEHOUSE, Capt L., 54
PURTYMAN, Sgt Howard C., 382

QANTAS EMPIRE AIRWAYS, 77, 602
QUALAN RIVER (Sketch p. 599), 617, 618
QUEENSLAND (Sketch p. 7), 3n, 25, 29, 68, 140, 193, 277, 497, 625; defence plans, 8, 112n; Australian Army dispositions in, 11; reinforcement of, 27; training for jungle warfare in, 243; Atherton Tablelands project, 449
QUEZON, President Manuel, 20
QUICRAS (Sketch p. 599), 621, 623
QUIN, Dr B. H., 39
Quincey, American cruiser, 152
QUINN, Col Lawrence A., 353
QUINN, Capt W. M. J., 570-1

RABAUL (Map p. 34), 10, 11, 39, 40, 42, 44-6, 48, 54-5, 57, 60, 63, 66-7, 72, 80-3, 114, 120, 122, 144-5, 185, 243, 258, 305, 336, 339, 344, 349, 383, 415, 416, 447, 519, 527, 529, 530, 544, 582, 595, 610n, 620; fall of, 1; air operations against, 111; place in Japanese planning, 113n; proposed Allied attack on, 119; Japanese reinforcement of, 575
RABI (Map p. 156; Sketch p. 160), 155, 167, 170-2, 179
RADAR, at Guadalcanal, 255, 343; on Kiriwina and Woodlark Islands, 589
RAE, Capt J. I., 132
RAIDS, on Australian field guns, 501
RAILWAYS, in Northern Territory, 72
RAINEY, Capt D. W., 425, 426, 430
Ralph Talbot, American destroyer, 152
RAMSEY, Pte C. R., 251
RAMU RIVER (Map p. 34), 48, 577
RANGOON (Map p. 37), 1
RANKIN, Lt-Col Walter R., 512, 513, 524, 525, 526
RANSOM, Pte L. F., 231
RATIONS, on Kokoda Track, 195-6, 198, carried on the man, 281. *See also* FOOD
RAVENSHOE, 335n
READ, Maj W. J., 64, 65, 151
RECRUITING, of Australian militia, 2; of AIF after *Dec 1941*, 12-13
REDLICH, Rev Vivian F. B., 139n
REEVE, Capt E. R., 566, 567
REHAK, S-Sgt John F., 487
REID, Pte C. W., 180
REID, Maj W. C., 410, 411
REIDY CREEK (Sketch p. 52), 59
REINFORCEMENTS, 243; militia, 14, 114; at Gona, 427; for 6th and 7th Divisions, 450, 512, 556
REINHOLD, Lt-Col W. J., 579, 580, 581
REITZ, Col Deneys, 624
REMEXIO (Sketch p. 599), 603, 604, 605, 608, 619
RETURNED SAILORS', SOLDIERS' AND AIRMEN'S IMPERIAL LEAGUE OF AUSTRALIA, 3
RHODEN, Lt-Col P. E., 195n, 206, 217, 218, 220, 222, 223
RICHARDS, Capt S. R., 407
RICHARDSON, Lt C. H., 273, 274
RICHARDSON, Pte F. L., 291
RICHARDSON, Maj-Gen Robert C., 120
RIDLEY, WO2 D. R., 162, 166, 176
RIDLEY, Capt W. L., 540, 542
RIFLES, *Australian*, sent to UK, 2; deficiencies in, 10; strength and monthly production, 30-1
RIGO (Map p. 34; Sketch p. 353), 139, 242, 260, 278
RITA BAU (Sketch p. 599), 608
RITCHIE, L-Sgt D. T., 622
ROAD CONSTRUCTION, in Australia, 10; in New Guinea, 578-81
ROBERTS, Pte A. G., 596
ROBERTS, Col C. G., 446
ROBERTS, Capt D. J., 183
ROBERTS, Cpl G. K., 283
ROBERTS, Capt P. C. G., 467
ROBERTSON, Lt-Gen Sir Horace, 30; commands 1st Cavalry Division, 13, 1st Division, 26
ROBERTSON, Lt-Col W. T., 372
ROBINSON, Maj A., 241, 251, 431, 432, 433, 441
ROBINSON, Cpl B. C., 564

ROBINSON, Lt H. D., 162, 164, 166, 176, 177
ROBSON, Lt-Col E. M., 329
ROCKHAMPTON (Sketch p. 7), 11, 120, 371
ROCKLIFFE, Pte F. O., 592, 593
ROGERS, Col Gordon B., 373-4
ROMMEL, Field Marshal E., 351*n*
ROOKE, Capt A. N., 554*n*
ROOSEVELT, Franklin D., 14, 15*n*, 21, 23, 34, 36, 189, 190, 259, 342; urges diversion of AIF to Burma, 15; orders General MacArthur to Australia, 16; reaches agreement with Mr Churchill on division of strategic responsibility, 17; suggests MacArthur to Mr Curtin as Supreme Commander, 17; replies to Curtin's request for reinforcement, 189-90; orders reinforcement of Guadalcanal and North Africa, 337
ROPER RIVER (Sketch p. 612). 68, 611
RORONA AIRFIELD (Map p. 34), 67
ROSE, Capt J. A., 600-1
ROSS, Gp Capt D., 598, 599, 607
ROWAN, Maj A. T., 548, 554, 566, 567, 568
ROWELL, Lt-Gen Sir Sydney (Plate p. 147), 173, 174, 198, 225, 227, 233, 234, 236, 241 242, 244, 248, 262, 268, 278, 536; appointed Deputy Chief of the General Staff, 13; commands I Corps, 26; commands forces in New Guinea, 105, 140, 141, 159; on Japanese tactics, 111; defends conduct of Milne Bay operations, 176, 186; praises work of RAAF at Milne Bay, 187; seeks additional supply aircraft, 197; seeks more AIF reinforcements, 226; relieved of command, 236-40; assesses reasons for Japanese success in New Guinea, 242-4; effect of planning by, 247, 311
RUDALL, Lt J. G., 471, 476, 477, 478
RUDD, L-Cpl J. A., 458
RUPERTUS, Brig-Gen William H., 339, 344
RUSES, *Japanese*, at Busama, 105; at Oivi, 127; at Milne Bay, 165, 177-8; at Buna, 476
RUSSELL, Capt D. McR., 559
RUSSELL, Lt G., 48, 49
RUSSELL, Cpl R. C., 445
RUSSELL, Maj W. B., 195*n*, 223, 232*n*, 426; commands 2/14 Bn, 445
RUSSIA, 23, 118
RYAN, Capt B. T., 171, 172
RYAN, Lt W. P., 281-2
Ryujo, Japanese aircraft carrier, 153

SADDLE, THE (Sketch p. 541), 539, 540, 542-3, 584, 586
SAGAR, Spr D. A., 617
SAGE, Pte A. G., 432
ST GEORGE-RYDER, Lt H. W., 329
ST GEORGE'S CHANNEL (Map p. 34), 416
ST JOHN, Lt E. R., 549, 550, 557
SALAMAUA (Map p. 585; Sketches pp. 52, 60, 93), 50, 52, 53, 56, 57, 58, 59, 60, 62, 63, 79, 86, 88, 89, 90, 103, 106*n*, 107, 111, 130, 145, 530, 531, 534-5, 538, 540, 545, 546, 577, 578, 583, 584, 586, 590; Japanese air attacks, 39, 47, 54; NGVR detachment at, 46; evacuation of, 55-6; Japanese invasion, 57, 83; American carrier strike, 67; Japanese strength and reinforcement, 90, 91, 100, 105, 114, 537, 575, 577; Kanga Force raid, 90-6, 544; place in Allied strategy, 119; General Blamey proposes attack on, 310
SALAMAUA AIRFIELD (Sketch p. 93), 83, 91-2, 94-5
SALVATION ARMY, 407, 412
SAMARAI (Map p. 34), 43, 111
SAMBOGA RIVER (Map p. 370), 452
SAME (Sketch p. 599), 598, 603, 609, 613, 617, 618
SAMOA (Maps pp. 19, 37), 148; proposed Japanese invasion, 83, 113; plan abandoned, 143
SAMPSON, Maj V. E., 483
SANANANDA (Map p. 370; Sketches pp. 353, 518), 108, 355, 359, 371, 383, 394, 395 396, 397, 413, 414, 423, 431, 433, 434, 439, 447, 449, 486, 496, 498, 501, 508, 509, 510, 517, 520, 521, 522, 525, 533, 545, 546, 590; Australian advance on, 354, 384, 386; fall of, 526; Japanese losses 527; Japanese account, 530-1; necessity for final reduction examined, 531-3
SANANANDA POINT (Map p. 370; Sketch p. 518), 384, 498, 501, 502, 511, 520
SANANANDA TRACK (Sketches pp. 387, 506), 424, 434, 448, 450, 495, 532; operations on, 384-417,

SANANANDA TRACK—*continued*
497-526; Japanese account, 415-16, 498, 527; Allied strength on, 497; Allied and enemy casualties, 407, 527
SAN CRISTOBAL (Sketches pp. 81, 148), 81, 340
SANDERSON, Capt A. G., 287, 289, 290, 291, 293, 294, 295, 298, 300, 307
SANDERSON, Cpl O. K., 503
SANDERSON, Capt R. W., 167, 168, 465, 469, 471, 472, 473, 475, 476, 477, 478, 479, 480
SANDERSON BAY (Sketch p. 160), 181
SAN DIEGO, 148
SANDISON, Capt C. H., 249, 250
San Francisco, American cruiser, 340, 341
SANGARA MISSION (Sketches pp. 123, 385), 110, 124, 125, 139, 384, 385
San Juan, American cruiser, 257
SANOPA, L-Cpl, 127, 133, 135, 136
SANTA CRUZ ISLANDS (Map p. 37), 119, 120, 257, 259, 341; naval battle of, 257, 337
SANTA ISABEL ISLAND (Sketch p. 148), 153
SAPIA (Sketch p. 353), 354
Saratoga, American aircraft carrier, 153, 154, 255
SARGENT, Lt A. L., 224, 429
SAUMLAKI (Sketch p. 612), 623*n*
SAVIGE, Lt-Gen Sir Stanley, 30; commands 3rd Division, 13, 26; commands forces in Wau-Lae-Markham area, 588
SAVO ISLAND (Sketch p. 149), 255, 340-3; naval battle of, 151; American losses in, 255
SAYERS, Maj H. T., 397
SCHLOITHE, Cpl C. E., 169
SCHLYDER, Lt E. L., 171, 172
SCHMEDJE, Lt-Col T. J. (Plate p. 307), 169, 170
SCHRATER, New Guinea miner, 580
SCHROEDER, Maj Edmund R., 491, 492, 493, 494
SCHWARTZ, Lt Paul M., 379, 487
SCHWIND, Capt L. C. J., 433
SCOTT, Lt A. R., 168
SCOTT, Capt C. E., 567
SCOTT, Capt D. C. J., 181, 182, 183
SCOTT, Pte L. R., 594-5
SCOTT, Rear-Admiral Norman, 255, 258, 340, 341 342
SCOTT, Capt R. J., 523
SCOUT RIDGE, 57
SCOUTS, AUSTRALIAN, Kanga Force, 59-62, 90, 104, 537-8; on Kokoda Track, 200, 283, 286-7, 294, 297, 303, 315; at Gona, 439; on Sanananda Track, 506
SCRUB TYPHUS, 312, 382, 399, 435*n*
SECOMBE, Lt-Gen V. C., 350
SEEKAMP, Lt A. H., 125, 128, 129
SEKI, Lt-Col, 576
SELECTIVE SERVICE BILL, 32
Selective Service Extension Act, 32
Sendai, Japanese cruiser, 343
SENGAI (Map p. 313; Sketch p. 593), 320, 593-4
SEPIK DISTRICT, evacuation of, 47-9
SEPIK RIVER (Map p. 34), 47-8, 100
SEREGINA (Sketch p. 593), 291, 308, 596
SEVEN MILE AIRFIELD (Map p. 114), 65, 67, 114
SEWARD, Capt M. S., 440, 443, 445
SHANGHAI (Map p. 37), 575
SHARP, Maj-Gen William F, 36; decides to capitulate, 38
SHAW, Capt H. F., 405*n*
SHEARWIN, Sgt H. J., 328
SHEDDEN, Sir Frederick, 620
SHELDEN, Lt E. T., 431, 445
SHELDON'S (Map p. 585; Sketch p. 87), 99, 101, 102, 104, 536, 538
SHEPHERD, Lt-Col A. E. T., 97
SHEPPARD, Col A. W., 73*n*
SHERA, Capt J. A. McK., 131, 134, 203, 212, 213
SHERIDAN, Lt CD. M., 538
SHERLOCK, Capt W. H., 546, 547, 548-9, 550, 551, 553, 555, 557, 576
SHERNEY, S-Sgt Paul, 359
SHERWIN, Lt A. B., 429
SHIMOMURA, Major, 576
SHIPPING, *Allied*, 82; diverted to SWPA, 15; losses to June 1942, 118; for return of 16 and 17 Bdes from Ceylon, 118; shortages of, 120, 140, 188, 226; commitments preclude reinforcements for Australia, 190; coordination of operations by COSC in New Guinea, 351; amount available for

INDEX

SHIPPING—continued
  supply line to Buna, 354. *Japanese*, 55, 105, 122, 161, 166, 174, 175, 181, 254; losses at Guadalcanal, 256, 342, 343, 530; at Rabaul, 544, 582; losses in Bismarck Sea Battle, 583
SHIRLEY, Capt John D., 395, 396, 397, 398, 400, 401, 402, 403
Shoho, Japanese aircraft carrier, 81, 82
Shokaku, Japanese aircraft carrier, 81, 82, 153
SHORTLAND ISLANDS (Sketch p. 148), 64, 154, 259, 341, 342, 345
SHUGG, W., 39
SIAI (Sketch p. 123), 139
SIGA (Map p. 313), 311, 314
SILCOCK, Capt H. I., 483
SILK, Capt T. B., 303n, 386n, 406n
SIMEMI (Map p. 370; Sketch p. 357), 356, 358-9, 375
SIMEMI CREEK (Map p. 370; Sketches pp. 455, 481), 356, 359, 454, 456, 462-3, 468, 470, 476-7, 480-1, 483-5, 494
SIMONSON, Capt D. J., 137, 138, 201, 202
SIMPSON, Capt A. M., 289, 291, 298, 299, 302, 325, 326, 328, 329, 387, 390, 391
SIMPSON, Lt-Col C. L., 71
Sims, American destroyer, 82
SIMS, Lt-Col C. A. W., 220, 221, 249, 250, 427, 428, 430, 431
SINCLAIR, F. R., 310
SINGAPORE (Map p. 37), 1, 9, 11, 16, 30, 68, 72, 508, 605
SIVYER, Lt T. R., 457, 458
SIWORI (Map p. 370; Sketch p. 495), 371, 382, 487, 511
SIWORI CREEK (Map p. 370), 511
SKILBECK, Cpl A. J., 437
SKINDEWAI (Map p. 585; Sketches pp. 52, 569), 53, 540, 543, 546, 548, 552, 561-2, 568, 572, 581, 583-4
SKIPPER, Capt J. W., 428
SLIM, Field Marshal Sir William, 187n
SLOT, THE, 342, 529
SMALL CREEK (Sketch p. 428), 425, 427, 429, 435
Smith, American destroyer, 257
SMITH, Captain, 526
SMITH, Capt A., 563
SMITH, Lt A. A., 124, 139
SMITH, Sgt A. T., 136
SMITH, Lt-Col Herbert A., 356, 360, 361, 364, 365, 366, 371, 375, 379, 382, 383, 486
SMITH, Capt H. C., 284
SMITH, Maj Herbert M., 364, 365, 375, 378, 379, 380
SMITH, Lt L. J., 483
SMITH, WO2 L. L., 596
SMITH, Maj P. S., 249
SMITH, Capt R. A., 279
SMITH, Capt S. S., 242
SMITH, Sgt W. R. D., 211
SNAKE RIVER (Map p. 585; Sketch p. 52), 53, 54
SNIPERS, *Australian*, on Kokoda Track, 231; in Timor, 601. *Japanese*, on Kokoda Track, 206, 230, 274, 286, 298; at Oivi-Gorari, 318, 325; at Buna, 361, 376, 377, 459, 463-4, 469, 482; on Sanananda Track, 410; at Gona, 418, 426, 430, 443
SOGERI PLATEAU, 108, 117
SOLOMON ISLANDS (Map p. 19; Sketch p. 148), 1, 12, 22, 39, 79, 81, 175, 188-90, 235, 257, 259, 336, 345, 383, 385, 575, 590; Japanese invasion, 63-5, 80, 120; Japanese planning in, 83; estimated strength in, 148; Allied offensive planned, 119; American landings in, 146-7, affect Japanese plans for attack on Port Moresby, 152; Naval Battle of Eastern Solomons, 153-4
SOLOMON ISLANDS DEFENCE FORCES, 63, 152
SOLTAN, Pte E., 392
SOPUTA (Map p. 370; Sketches pp. 353, 357), 354, 358, 361, 384, 386, 388, 394-5, 397, 399, 405, 414, 422-3, 425, 427, 434, 435n, 497, 502, 512, 518; airfield at, 398
SORENSON, Capt H. N., 133, 135
SOTUTU, Rev Usaia, 64
SOUTH AUSTRALIA, 3n, 35; Australian Army strength in, 12
South Dakota, American battleship, 257, 341, 343
Southern Cross, Australian examination vessel, 623n
SOUTH PACIFIC AREA (Map p. 19), 21, 23, 192; amphibious force formed, 119; strength of American Army in, 190, 338n; American carrier strength in, 259; reinforcement of, 337-8

SOUTH-WEST PACIFIC AREA (Map p. 19), 14, 15, 21, 23, 29, 38, 41, 67, 114, 119, 188, 190, 192, 234, 235, 259, 260, 446, 575, 588; creation of, 17; General MacArthur nominated as Supreme Commander, 18, his directive, 21-2; reinforcement of, 23-4, 82; allotment of Australian forces to, 27; strength of Allied forces in, 29, 84, 188, 190, 336, 338n; strength of Japanese forces in, 113, 574-5; Allied strategy in, 119; diversion of aircraft from, 189; MacArthur predicts disaster in, 225; MacArthur's plans in, 336; achievements of first year, 590
SPENCE, Lt-Col A., 598, 599, 607, 608, 615, 616; commands Sparrow Force, 605
SPENCER, Sgt G. G., 168, 472, 478
SPENDER, Hon Sir Percy, 4-5
SPRING, Maj G. F., 410, 411
SPRY, Brig C. C. F., 315, 414
Stand-To, 142n, 203n
STANNER, Lt-Col W. E. H., 41n, 75
STARR, Lt-Col P. D. S., 547, 548, 554, 555, 563, 566, 572, 574, 584
STEDDY, Lt E. M. C., 177, 180
STEEL, Lt H. W., 245
STEEL, Capt P. J., 163, 164, 171, 172
STEELE, Lt S. D., 172
STEELE, Maj-Gen W. A. B., 26
STEPHENS, Capt K. H. R., 587, 588
STEPHENS, Pte S. A., 439
STEPHENS' HOUSE, 177
STEPHENS' RIDGE (Map p. 156; Sketch p. 179), 177
STEVENS, Maj-Gen Sir Jack, 611, 612, 621; commands 4th Division, 26, NT Force, 140n
STEVENSON, Capt C. M., 125, 127, 129
STEVENSON, Maj-Gen J. R., 281, 285, 289, 290, 291, 295, 297, 298, 299, 301, 307, 413; commands 2/3 Bn, 276; estimate of, 290
STEWARD, Maj H. D., 213
STEWART, Lt-Col H. McB., 548, 551-2, 557, 563
STEWART, Cpl J. A., 295
STILWELL, General Joseph W., 192
STIVERS, Col Charles P., 28n
STOCK, Sister, 55
STODDART, Sgt R. R., 328
STOKES, Capt N. R., 474
STOKES HILL, Darwin, 70
STOUT, Capt E. W., 539
STRANG, Maj M. R., 501, 502-3
STRATEGY, *Allied*, 15-16, 188-9; in Pacific, 14, 119-20; division of responsibility, 17; for defence of Australia, 112n; Beat Hitler first policy, 190; value of Timor in defence of Aust, 620n. *Japanese*, in South and South-West Pacific Areas, 257
STRETCHER-BEARERS, on Kokoda Track, 210, 212-15, 274, 289; Wau area, 560
STRETCHER-BEARERS, NATIVE, on Kokoda Track, 249, 251, 252, 265, 309
STRICKLAND RIVER (Map p. 34), 47
STRIP No. 1 (Sketch p. 173), 165, 184
STRIP No. 2 (Map p. 156), 157
STRIP No. 3 (Map p. 156), 158, 160-1, 167, 170, 173, 175; Japanese attack on, 171-2, 177
STRIP POINT (Map p. 370; Sketches pp. 357, 455), 356, 367, 457, 512
STRUDWICK, Patrol Officer R., 48
Stuart, Australian destroyer, 346-7
STURDEE, Lt-Gen Sir Vernon, 5, 8, 82, 112n; recommended as C-in-C Home Army, 4; estimates forces required to defend Rabaul, Port Moresby, New Caledonia and Darwin, 11; reinforces Port Moresby, 44, 112; appointed Head, Military Mission to Washington, 140n
SUBLET, Lt-Col F. H., 204, 205, 209, 210, 211, 212, 217-18, 222, 225, 311, 332, 441; criticises Australian tactics at Gona, 434-5; commands 2/16-2/27 Composite Bn, 440
SUBMARINES, *American*, 255; strengthen American Navy in South Pacific, 337, 340. *Japanese*, in naval battle of Guadalcanal, 341; used to supply Goodenough Island, 349; used to supply Papua, 447
SUDEST, CAPE (Map p. 370; Sketch p. 353), 352, 354, 357, 452
SUGARLOAF HILL (Sketch p. 52), 61
SUMATRA, 15, 575
SUMIYOSHI, Maj-Gen Tadashi, 258
SUMMIT CAMP (Sketch p. 569), 561, 568, 573, 581, 583
SUNSHINE (Map p. 585; Sketch p. 52), 53, 572, 584; demolitions at, 106

654 INDEX

SUPPLY, Allied, of Darwin, 72; of Kanga Force, 91, 102-3, 104, 544, 546, 561; on Kokoda Track, 115, 117-18, 122, 130-2, 140-1, 195-9, 217, 229, 231, 260-2, 264-5, 290, 291, 308, 316; affects handling of 21 Bde, 247; organisation of, 226-8; medical, 309; for 3-column advance on Buna, 337; achievements of COSC, 349-51; in Buna-Gona area, 354, 362, 375, 381, 382, 419, 449; in Timor, 598-9, 605-6. *Japanese*, on Kokoda Track, 228, 303; Buna-Gona area, 530

SUPPLY DROPPING: on Kokoda Track, 117, 130, 197, 198, 208, 261, 269, 335; organisation and technique, 131, 266-8; affects performance of mortar bombs, 272; Kanga Force, 536, 558; in Timor, 602, 605, 606, 609, 623

SUTER, Pte D. H., 93
SUTHERLAND, Brig R. B., 73n
SUTHERLAND, Lt-Gen Richard K., 33, 174, 197, 227, 352, 371, 372, 374; appointed Chief of Staff to General MacArthur, 28n; on weakness of forces in SWPA, 84; proposes blocking of Kokoda Track by demolitions, 141
SUTHERS, Capt A. G., 178, 184, 348, 482, 483
SUTTON, Maj F. M. E., 569, 570
Suzuya, Japanese cruiser, 342
Swan, Australian sloop, 69
SWAN, Maj R. G., 177-8
SWINTON, Capt C. N., 284-5
SWORD, Lt R. H., 201, 202, 207, 441
SYDNEY (Sketch p. 7), 6, 7, 8, 9, 12, 148
Sydney Morning Herald, The, 5, 66n, 286n, 453n, 626n
SYMINGTON, Maj N. M., 130, 132, 133, 134, 135, 136, 137, 138, 143, 145
SYRIA, 29, 30, 73, 114, 118, 130, 147, 193, 195, 280, 307n, 497, 544, 545

TAAFE, F-O E. J. M., 430
TACO-LULIC (Sketch p. 599), 600
TACTICS, in New Guinea, 241; *American*, 381. *Australian*, at Milne Bay, 187; at Eora Creek, 290, 306-7; at Oivi, 317; on Sanananda Track, 412, 498, 517; at Gona, 434, 442; at Cape Endaiadere, 461; on Timor, 600-1, 624. *Japanese*, 72, 111; on Kokoda Track, 143, 270, 297-8; in Naval Battle of Guadalcanal, 345; at Buna, 359; on Sanananda Track, 503, 516-17
TAIVU POINT (Sketch p. 149), 153
Takao, Japanese cruiser, 343
TALEBA BAY (Sketch p. 346), 347-8
TANAKA, Lt-Col, 304-5
TANAKA, Rear-Admiral Raizo, 342, 343, 344, 345
TANAMBOGO ISLAND (Sketch p. 148), 63, 150
TANCRED, Lt-Col P. L., 559, 574
TANIMBAR ISLAND (Sketch p. 612), 623n
TANKS, Australian manufacture begun, 10; strength in Australia *Apr 1942*, 29n; employment at Buna, 369, 382-3, 462; sea transportation of, 453; at Sanananda, 517; *Types:* General Stuart, 363, 462; specifications, 452. *Japanese*, at Milne Bay, 162, 163, 167-8, 170, 171-2, 175
TANNER, Lt R. R., 282-3
TAPI, New Guinea native, 100
TARAKENA (Map p. 370; Sketch p. 518), 487, 510, 511, 528; American casualties at, 527
TASMANIA, 3n, 8, 25, 157, 509; army strength in, 12
TASSAFARONGA POINT (Sketch p. 149), 256, 343
TAUPOTA (Map p. 156), 158, 185
TAYLOR, WO2 D. R., 375-7
TAYLOR, Lt-Col E., 58
TAYLOR, Maj J. L., 47, 48
TAYLOR, Maj R., 456, 458, 460, 461, 462, 463
TAYLOR, Lt W., 600-1
TEESDALE-SMITH, Lt-Col P. S., 170
TEMPLETON, Capt S. V., 115, 117, 125, 126, 130
TEMPLETON'S CROSSING (Map p. 114; Sketches pp. 123, 593), 109, 131, 196, 212, 214, 215, 217, 218, 219, 249, 263, 277, 296, 311, 593, 596; 21st Brigade withdrawal to, 217-8; Australian advance to, 268-9; action at, 270-6, 281-7, casualties at, 276; Japanese account, 306
TENNANT CREEK (Sketch p. 7), 10
Tenryu, Japanese cruiser, 186, 342
Thetis, New Guinea administration launch, 48
THOMAS, Lt P. C., 563-4
THOMAS, Sgt R. R., 457
THOMAS, Lt V. F., 466, 481, 483
THOMAS, Cpl V. R. G., 426

THOMPSON, Capt C. A., 613, 617, 618, 619
THOMPSON, Pte G. F., 429
THOMPSON, L-Cpl L. W. P., 600
THOMPSON, Maj R. V., 206
THOMSON, W Cdr D. F., 75
THORN, Capt C. R. H., 322, 323, 329, 418, 419, 420
THORN, Capt J. W., 405n, 408, 409, 410, 411
THORNE, Maj E., 323
THORNE, Sgt L. R., 466
THORNTON, A. G.; *see* MAIDMENT, G.
THURGOOD, Capt J. G., 207, 420, 421, 435, 441
THURSDAY ISLAND (Sketch p. 7), 7, 11, 80
THURSTON, J. H., 47, 49
TIMNE (Map p. 585), 545-6
TIMOR (Map p. 37; Sketch p. 612), 12, 16, 34, 68, 72, 76, 82, 86, 190-1, 588, 602, 616, 618; Japanese reinforcement of, 575; Allied plans, 606; relief of Japanese garrison, 610; Japanese strength in, 610n; strategical importance of, 621
TIMOR, DUTCH (Map p. 37), 69, 598-9, 603-4, 608
TIMOR, PORTUGUESE (Sketch p. 599), guerilla operations in, 598-624; native population of, 605, 607, 608, 609, 610, 614, 615, 618, 619
TIMPERLY, Capt A. T., 158, 346
TIPPETTS, Lt C. H., 481, 483
TIPTON, WO1 L. E., 211, 218
Tjerk Hiddes, Dutch destroyer, 617-18
TOBRUK, 66, 118, 280, 351n
TOJO, General Hideki, 113n
TOKYO (Map p. 37), 83, 145, 305, 531n
TOLAND, Lt D. J., 566
TOLMER, Lt A. R., 408, 411
TOMASETTI, L-Sgt W. E., 605
TOMLINSON, Lt C. B., 164-5
TOMLINSON, Col Clarence M., 357, 358, 361, 362, 380, 388, 394, 395, 396, 398, 400, 401, 403, 486, 487
TOMPSON, Lt-Col R. A. J., 330-1
TONGS, Capt B. G. D., 263, 268, 273
TORRES STRAIT (Sketch p. 7), 121
TORRICELLI MOUNTAINS (Map p. 34), 47
TOWNER, Maj E. T., 30
TOWNSEND, Lt-Col G. W. L., 43
TOWNSVILLE (Sketch p. 7), 7, 8, 11, 27, 80, 81, 82, 111, 140; Area Combined Headquarters established at, 9; reinforcement and development of, 112n, 121
TRAINING, 242; *of American Army*, 32-3, 351; *of American Air Forces*, 32-3. *Of Australian Army*, 2, 8, 9, 29-30, 44, 74-5, 112n, 243; compared to American, 32-3; in Ceylon, 79, 280; of Independent Coys, 85, 603, 604; of 14th Brigade, 111; Malayan lessons applied, 193; of 1st Armoured Division, 452-3. *Of Japanese*, 242
TRANSPORT, *pack horse and mule*, in New Guinea, 116, 264, 561. *Water*, in New Guinea, 279, 453. *See also* AIR TRANSPORT; LANDING CRAFT
TREACY, Capt M. A., 207, 211, 332, 425, 429, 592, 593, 594
TREVIVIAN, Maj J. H. (Plate p. 307), 465, 469, 470, 471, 472, 473, 475, 476-7, 480, 519, 520, 523, 524
TRIANGLE, THE (Sketches pp. 370, 486), 361, 364-6, 370-1, 380, 382-3, 485-8, 491-3, 496-7, 509
Trienza, British ship, 38
TRINCOMALEE (Sketch p. 78), 78
TRINICK, Capt J. A. J., 516, 521
TROBRIAND ISLANDS (Map p. 34; Sketch p. 81), 39, 122, 158, 583, 589
True, 20n
TRUK (Map p. 37), 39n, 119, 120, 153, 257-8, 336, 339, 341
TRUSCOTT, Sgt J. H., 431, 442, 444
TRUSCOTT, Sqn Ldr K. W., 182n
TSUKAHARA, Vice-Admiral N., 145
TSUKAMOTO, Lt-Col 144, 330, 415, 527; commands *I/144 Bn*, 228
TSUKIOKA, Cdr, 185
TUAGUBA HILL (Map p. 114), 45
TUAI, New Guinea native, 100
TUCKEY, Capt P. A., 437
TUFI (Map p. 34; Sketch p. 353), 114, 468, 527, 583
TULAGI (Sketches pp. 81, 148), 39, 63, 83, 119, 147, 152, 343; Japanese air attacks on, 79; Japanese occupation of, 80, 112, 148; American invasion of, 149-51
Tulagi, British ship, 70
TULAGI HARBOUR (Sketch p. 148), 63, 80, 149
TUPLING, Petty Officer W. L., 65

INDEX

TURNBULL, Sqn Ldr P. St G. B., 158, 182
TURNER, Rear-Admiral Richmond K., 151, 340, 345; commands Guadalcanal amphibious force, 149
TURNER, Pte R. L., 210
TURTON, Maj D. K., 600, 603, 608, 609, 610, 611, 612, 613
TYE, Maj K. F., 452, 477, 479
TYLER, Sgt G., 457

UBERI (Map p. 114), 108, 117, 130, 194-5, 212, 224, 227, 229, 244-5, 248, 261-2, 264, 276-7, 310, 332, 399, 597
UMPHELBY, Maj D. H., 46, 56, 60, 63, 89, 91, 92, 96, 103; commands raid on Salamaua, 90
UNDERWOOD, L-Cpl D. W., 102
UNSWORTH, Lt G. G., 409
UPCHER, Capt R. R., 322, 323, 327, 418, 419

VALLI, Pte M., 429
Vampire, Australian destroyer, 78
VANDERGRIFT, Lt-Gen Alexander A., 148, 150, 151, 152, 153, 254, 256, 258, 337, 338, 339, 528; commands 1st Marine Division, 147
VAN STRAATEN, Col N. L. W., 599, 605
VARIETA, CAPE, 161
VARNUM, Pte A. J., 392
VASEY, Maj-Gen G. A. (Plate p. 450), 86, 176, 186, 312, 314, 319, 321, 322, 329, 332, 354, 358, 361, 363, 394, 396, 398, 400, 403, 406, 412, 413, 414, 423, 424, 430, 433, 434, 435, 439, 469n, 505, 508, 509, 511, 512, 513, 516, 517, 518, 524, 525, 526; appointed Chief of Staff to General Mackay, 13; his letters to General Rowell, 174-5, 225, 248; on GHQ communiqués, 226; commands 6th Division, 244; commands 7th Division, 307, 310, 311; hoists Australian flag at Kokoda, 315; issues orders for advance on Gona-Sanananda, 384; plans attack on Sanananda Track, 498
VAUGHAN, Sgt R. R., 560
VEALE, Pte L. R., 595
VEALE, Brig W. C. D., 598, 599, 602, 605
VERNON, Capt G. H., 116, 127, 129, 131, 132
VERNON, Rfn R. E., 46, 101
VERTIGAN, Maj D. H., 65
VIAL, F-Lt L. G., 60, 106, 587
VIAL'S POST (Sketch p. 60), 106n
VICKERS RIDGE (Sketch p. 541), 540, 542, 584, 586
VICKERY, Maj I. F., 277, 399
VICKERY, Brig N. A., 512
VICTORIA, 3n, 27, 69; Army dispositions in, 12
VICTORIA CROSS, 30; awarded to Cpl J. A. French, 182, to Pte B. S. Kingsbury, 206
VICTORIA RIVER (Sketch p. 612), 611
Vigilant, Australian patrol ship, 606
VILA (Map p. 37), 39, 63, 80
VILLA MARIA (Sketch p. 599), 600-1
Vincennes, American cruiser, 152
VISAYAN SEA (Sketch p. 35), 36
VITIAZ STRAIT (Map p. 34), 415
VIVIGANI (Sketch p. 346), 349
VONDRACEK, Sgt Francis J., 489
Voyager, Australian destroyer, 611-12, 613

WADE, Capt E. R., 396
WAGA WAGA (Sketch p. 160), 183
WAIGANI (Map p. 156), 157, 160, 173
WAINWRIGHT, Lt-Gen Jonathan M., 20n, 25, 79; takes command in Philippines, 34, 36; surrenders, 38
WAIPALI (Map p. 585; Sketch p. 549), 88, 546, 548, 561, 562, 568, 573, 574, 584, 586
WAIROPI (Map p. 313; Sketch p. 593), 125, 242, 260, 262, 296, 314, 321, 330-1, 353, 401, 593-4; derivation, 110; destruction of bridge at, 304; advance to, 330-1; crossing of Kumusi at, 331-2
WAKEFIELD, Cpl H. C., 207
WAKE ISLAND (Map p. 37), 67, 345
WALDRON, Maj-Gen Albert W., 365, 367, 373, 378, 382; commands 32nd Division, 374
WALKER, Capt B. G. C., 245
WALKER, Brig-Gen Kenneth, 237, 261
WALKER, Lt-Col E. McD., 611, 612, 618
WALKER, Maj E. S., 318, 319, 386, 397, 398
WALKER, Lt I. W., 375, 378
WALKER, Maj K. R., 554, 555, 556, 558, 560
WALLER, Pte D. C., 609
WALLER, Cpl L. L., 596
WALLMAN, Capt D. R., 132, 212, 213, 215
WALSTAB, Colonel J., 45
WALTERS, Sgt A., 458
WALTERS, Cpl L. A., 445
WAMPIT (Map p. 585; Sketch p. 52), 54, 57, 536, 584, 588
WAMPIT RIVER (Map p. 585; Sketch p. 52), 54, 89, 104, 577
WANDUMI (Map p. 585; Sketch p. 549), 547-8, 552-3, 555, 562, 567-9, 570-2, 576; action at, 549-51, 557
WANDUMI TRIG (Sketch p. 549), 548, 552, 563, 571
WANIGELA (Map p. 34; Sketch p. 353), 158, 237, 260-2, 346, 349, 351-2, 362, 381, 577; development of, 237-8, 240; Hatforce flown into, 278; overland advance from, 279, 310; 2/10 Bn move to, 451
WANIMO, 100
WAR BOOK, COMMONWEALTH, 2-3
WARD, L-Cpl C. W., 326
WARD, Lt-Col K. H., 200, 202, 204
WARD HUNT, CAPE (Map p. 34), 110, 590
WARD'S FIELD, 424
WARFE, Lt-Col G. R., 558, 560, 561, 568, 571, 573, 574, 584, 586, 587, 588; commands 2/3 Indep Coy, 556
WARIA RIVER (Map p. 34), 45, 50, 101, 111, 124
WARNE, Lt H. A., 272
WAR OF 1914-1918, 2, 3n, 28, 30, 32, 412, 626
Warrego, Australian sloop, 69
Warrnambool, Australian corvette, 612
WASHINGTON, D.C., 15, 16, 17, 21, 23, 25, 31, 33, 34, 140, 175, 176, 186, 342; Australian Military Mission, 140n
Washington, American battleship, 341, 343
Wasp, American aircraft carrier, 153, 154, 254, 255
WATER, at Eora, 297, 303
WATERDRY (Sketch p. 579), 579
WATSON, Capt R., 540, 542
WATSON, Maj W. T., 123, 124, 125, 126, 127, 130, 213; commands PIB, 45, Maroubra Force, 129
WATTS, Capt R. D., 225
WATUT RIVER (Sketch p. 52), 59
WAU (Map p. 34; Sketches pp. 51, 553), 50, 51-3, 54-6, 61, 86, 90, 103-6, 111, 121, 140, 197, 237, 262, 336, 534, 536, 539, 540, 546-8, 550-2, 566-8, 570-2, 573-4, 577-9, 580, 581-3, 586, 588, 590; NGVR detachment at, 46; evacuation centre for goldfields area, 57; Japanese air attacks on, 58-9, 100, 565, 584, 589; Australian reinforcement of, 89, 538, 543-4, 548, 553, 558, 578; scorching of, 107; Japanese threat to, 544-5; defence of, 554-63; Japanese account, 575-6
WAU AIRFIELD (Sketch p. 556), 539, 553, 563; defence of, 554-7; Japanese air raid on, 565
WAVELL, Field Marshal Rt Hon Earl, 17, 46, 79, 118, 191; commands ABDA Area, 15; requests reinforcement of Timor, 69; orders return of Timor convoy, 69; on weakness of Eastern Fleet, 79; and AIF in Ceylon, 280
WEDAU (Map p. 156), 158
WEEKS, Cpl S., 430
WEHURIA CREEK (Map p. 156; Sketch p. 173), 173
WELLINGTON, New Zealand, 147
WENTLAND, Capt Roy F., 487
WEST, Lt J., 49n
WESTERN AUSTRALIA, 3n, 25, 68, 141, 509; Australian Army strength in, 12; reinforcement of, 27; defence plans, 76-7, 112n; air attacks on, 76-7
WESTERN DESERT, 280, 453
Westmoreland, British transport, 78
WEWAK (Map p. 34), 575; evacuation of, 47-9; estimated Japanese strength at, 577
WHEATLEY, L-Cpl M. L., 601
WHELAN, Sgt R. C. B., 622
WHITE, Lt C. M., 436
WHITE, Lt G. J., 539
WHITE, Lt S. W., 540
WHITEHEAD, Lt-Gen Ennis C., 565, 584; on air maintenance of Kanga Force, 581-2
WHITEHEAD, Capt N. G., 452, 453, 459, 460
WHITLOCK, Colonel Lester J., 28n
WHITTAKER, Capt G. K., 102, 587
WHITTAKER, Lt Paul, 487
WHITTON, Pte W. C., 162
WICKHAM, Lt H. G., 282
WIGMORE, Lionel, 598n
WILD, Sgt J., 548-9
WILES, Lt-Col H. J., 161, 162, 163

WILKINS, Lt A. F., 622
WILKINSON, WO2 J. D., 128, 133, 137
WILKINSON, L-Sgt L. A., 550
WILKINSON, Cpl R. E. G., 440
WILKINSON, Maj R. S., 252
WILLIAMS, Maj D. E., 394, 396*n*
WILLIAMS, Capt E. A., 179
WILLIAMS, Sgt E. F. E., 439
WILLIAMS, Cpl L. T., 251-2
WILLIS, Cpl J. H. A., 217-18
WILLOUGHBY, Maj-Gen Charles A., 28*n*, 235*n* 403, 404, 446
WILSON, Maj F. P., 519-20
WILSON, Lt K. R. E., 171
WILSON, Brig-Gen L. C., 3*n*
WILSON, Maj W. J. R., 502, 504
WILSON'S PROMONTORY, Victoria, 85
WILTON, Sgt C. H., 376, 377, 378
WINIMA (Sketches pp. 52, 535), 106-7, 536
WINKLE, Lt F. J., 332*n*
"WINNIE THE WAR WINNER", 601-2
WINNING, Maj N. I., 92, 95, 96, 103, 105, 107, 534, 537, 539, 540, 541, 542, 547, 548, 551, 552, 555, 558, 562, 563; commands Salamaua raiding force, 91
WINTERFLOOD, Capt J. S., 573
WIRELESS, in Northern Territory, 75; in Owen Stanleys, 291; at Oivi-Gorari, 320; at Buna, 358; at Sanananda, 409; in Timor, 601-2
WIRELESS CAMP (Sketch p. 60), 61
WISE, WO2 L. G., 172
WISE, Maj R. J., 555-6
WISEMAN, Lt H. C., 300, 326, 390
WITHY, Lt-Col C. B., 230, 232, 233, 245, 246; commands 2/25 Bn, 229
WOOD, Brig F. G., 545, 548, 551, 557-8, 562, 563, 568-9, 570, 571, 584
WOODLARK ISLAND (Map p. 34), 589
WOOTTEN, Maj-Gen Sir George (Plate p. 450), 175, 177, 179, 180, 185, 383, 451, 454, 462, 465, 468, 469, 471, 472, 476, 477, 480, 481, 486, 513, 514, 516, 517, 518, 519, 520, 524; estimate of, 159; assumes command of Warren Force, 454; exasperated by American delays on Sanananda Track, 525

WORKMAN, Capt James W., 490-1
WORT, Lt W. F., 123, 124
WOUNDED, on Kokoda Track, evacuation of, 212-15, 308-9
WRIGHT, Maj G. W., 209-10
WUTONG, 49*n*
WYBURN, Lt R. J., 293, 294
WYE POINT (Map p. 370; Sketch p. 518), 520, 523
WYLIE, Lt D. R., 409-10
WYLIE, Lt M. W., 90, 96, 97, 98, 99, 107, 534, 540
WYNDHAM (Sketch p. 7), Japanese air attacks on, 1, 77
WYNNE, Capt W. P., 621
WYNTER, Lt-Gen H. D., 13

YALU (Sketches pp. 52, 87), 62, 88, 101
YAMAGATA, Maj-Gen Tsuyuo, 415, 446, 447, 527, 530
YAMAMOTO, Colonel Hiroshi, 484, 485, 496
YAMAMOTO, Admiral Isoroku, 112
YANO, Commander, 186
YASUDA, Capt Yoshitatsu, 383, 484, 496
YAZAWA, Col Kiyomi, 144, 146, 228, 304, 330, 331, 416, 527-8, 530
YEING, Cpl E., 432
YEOMAN, Lt S. H., 124
YODDA (Sketch p. 123), 117, 136, 332*n*
YODDA VALLEY (Sketches pp. 123, 128), 108-9, 110, 116, 137
YOKOYAMA, Col Yosuke, 144, 145, 415, 416, 447
YORK, CAPE (Sketch p. 7), 509
Yorktown, American aircraft carrier, 67, 80, 81, 82 113, 255
YOSHIWARA, Lt-Gen, 144, 531*n*
YOUNG, Capt N. H., 430

ZANKER, Pte A. F., 251-2
Zealandia, Australian ship, 70
ZEEF, Maj Bert, 398, 399, 400, 401, 402, 403
ZENAG (Map p. 585; Sketch p. 52), 54, 104
ZINSER, Maj Roy F., 382
Zuikaku, Japanese aircraft carrier, 81, 82, 153

www.ingramcontent.com/pod-product-compliance
Lightning Source LLC
Chambersburg PA
CBHW070753300426
44111CB00014B/2389